ENCYCLOPEDIA OF

WORLD POLITICAL SYSTEMS

Volume 1

ENCYCLOPEDIA OF

WORLD POLITICAL SYSTEMS

Volume 1

J DENIS DERBYSHIRE
IAN DERBYSHIRE

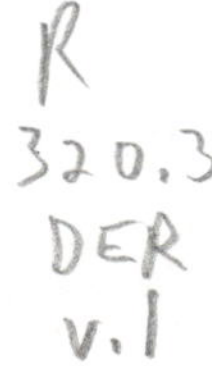

SHARPE REFERENCE
an imprint of M.E. Sharpe. Inc.

SHARPE REFERENCE

Sharpe Reference is an imprint of M.E. Sharpe, INC.

M.E. Sharpe, INC.
80 Business Park Drive
Armonk, NY 10504

Library of Congress Cataloging in Publication Data
Derbyshire, J. Denis.
Encyclopedia of world political systems / J. Denis Derbyshire, Ian Derbyshire.
p. cm.
Includes bibliographic references and index.
Summary: Describes systems of government from throughout the world, relates them to unique social and economic influences, identifies particular features common to all or most, and makes objective comparisons.
ISBN 0-7656-8025-4 (alk. paper)
1. Comparative government. [1. Comparative government.]
I. Derbyshire, Ian. II. Title.
JF51.D465 2000
320.3—dc21
99-34093
CIP

Printed and bound by De Agostini, Novara, Italy

The paper used in this publication meets the minimum requirements of American National Standard for Information Sciences - Permanence of Paper for Printed Library Materials, ANSI Z 39.48.1984.

DA (c) 10 9 8 7 6 5 4 3 2 1

M.E. Sharpe, INC.
Vice President and Publisher: Evelyn M. Fazio
Vice President and Production Director: Carmen P. Chetti
Editorial Coordinator: Aud Thiessen

Helicon Publishing Ltd
Managing Editor: Katie Emblem
Editors: Clare Colinson, Sue Donaldson, Denise Dresner, Francis Gobey, Kate O'Leary, Stephen Pavlovich. Joseph Spooner
Index: Jane Martin
Production: Tony Ballsdon
Design: Terence Caven **Cartography:** Olive Pearson

Contents

Part 2: Political Systems of the World's Nation-states

Part 3: Towards One World

Chapter 8 The Relics of Empire –Colonies, Dependencies and Semi-Sovereign States

Chapter 9 The World Grows Smaller: International Cooperation

Preface

There are 192 sovereign nations in the world today, each with its own unique ethnic and social composition and its own unique history. The interplay of these, and other factors, has created, in turn, a unique system of government.

In this book we describe these systems and try to relate them to the social and economic influences which, over the years, have fashioned them. At the same time, we have identified particular features which are common to all, or most, countries and have classified them in an attempt to make objective comparisons.

In our classification we have sought to distinguish between those nations whose citizens have a completely free choice of which people should control the levers of political power and those where that choice is limited. The first we have called multiparty, or pluralistic, states and the second one-party, or monistic. This is an important distinction but it is not the only criterion for deciding whether or not a political system can be said to be democratic.

When the first edition of this book was written, some six years ago, there were 165 independent, sovereign states. Of these, 83, or just under half, could be classified as truly democratic. By 1995 the number had grown to 145 and remained at this figure in 1999, which was some three-quarters of the total.

As we said in our first study of the international political scene, the accession to power in the Soviet Union of Mikhail Gorbachev, in 1985, had the effect of casting a stone into the apparently static pond of Eastern European politics and we predicted that its ripples would spread to other regions. That prediction has come to pass, within a shorter time than we envisaged, and now one-party, monistic states are very much in a minority in most regions of the world. However, reconstructed communist parties have returned to power in several of the recently democratized states in Eastern Europe, with Lech Wałesa, so instrumental in the downfall of communism, being replaced as Polish president in November 1995 by the communist leader, Alexander Kwasniewski.

In the pages that follow we have tried to provide a better understanding of political institutions and events in the contemporary world and have addressed ourselves not just to academics and professional observers of the political landscape but also to the more general reader who is looking for a serious, but not over-technical, account of global politics.

When we embarked on this task we believed that our approach was new in a number of ways. First, we have considered all the contemporary states and not just the well-known and obvious. Second, we have attempted to identify connections between a country's political system and its historical, social, and economic background. Third, we have looked in some detail at the dynamics of political systems, including the activities of parties and similar groupings, as well as the formal institutions that states have created. Fourth, partly to make the material more manageable, but also to provide a better understanding of geographical and demographic influences, we have adopted a regional approach to our exposition of political systems. Finally, we have looked at examples of how sovereign states, either by choice or necessity, have found it increasingly profitable to co-operate with each other rather than just compete. Six years later, we believe that this approach is still unique and has been justified by recent events.

Although the task has been enjoyable, there have been inevitable frustrations resulting from the almost impossible task of ensuring that the information about each state is still valid in a world where change tends to be the rule rather than the exception.

'To understand others is a certain way of understanding ourselves' might well be the motto for this book. If we have succeeded in this task of creating a better understanding of politics throughout the world we will be well content.

Acknowledgments

We would like to record our appreciation for the encouragement and support we have received from our publishers for their faith in us and our project, and for keeping us to our task and ensuring the accuracy of our work. Having said this, we accept that any consequential errors or omissions are ours. Finally, nearer home, we are particularly grateful to Joyce for her patient encouragement and support.

JDD and IDD
July 1999

Tables

Regional maps

1

The Comparative Approach

CHAPTER 1

Understanding Political Systems

1.1 Political animal

The Greek philosopher, Aristotle (384–322 BC), said that man was by nature a political animal. He argued that it was within man's natural development to live in some sort of ordered society under a system of government. In the times in which he lived the kind of community he saw as natural was the comparatively small city-state of ancient Greece, with thousands, rather than millions, of citizens able to practise direct democracy.

In the world of today there are few communities that resemble those small early communities. The Most Serene Republic of San Marino in Italy is probably the best example. It is the sole city-state which survived after the unification of Italy in the 19th century and has the distinction of being the world's oldest republic, its independence recognized and its protection guaranteed by Italy. Because of its small population, about 25,000, San Marino is able to enjoy a uniquely intimate kind of government.

The majority of countries have considerably larger populations, of course, and their governments are more remote from the average citizen. Nevertheless, Aristotle's belief that mankind achieves natural fulfilment by living in a political community seems to have been borne out by subsequent events, as this account of the political systems of the world will try to show.

1.2 What is a political system?

So that we can better understand the nature of a political system, it will be helpful if we first attempt to define certain words which are frequently used in everyday speech but whose meanings are not always clear.

We use the word 'government' in a variety of ways. In a general sense we use it to mean an orderly way of running a community's affairs and it is possible to distinguish between local government, perhaps regional government, and national government. The absence of government is anarchy, with everyone looking after himself or herself: the law of the jungle. In a more specific sense we speak of 'the government' as a body of people who have power to make us behave in certain ways. Because they are the government they have authority as well as power. In other words, their power is legitimate. We will not concern ourselves for the moment about how this power is achieved. That is something we shall discover as we look at each country more closely.

Another word frequently used in this context is 'state'. Often we see state as synonymous with government, with the two words being interchangeable. To some extent this is quite valid: a government department might also be called a department of state. The word should be used a little more precisely, however. Governments come and go, as we all know, but the state may be said to be permanent, comprising the whole apparatus by which a community is governed: the armed forces, the police, the civil service, the judicial system, and so on. This emphasizes elements included in the classic definition of a state by the German sociologist, Max Weber (1864–1920), most importantly the monopoly of the application of legitimate physical violence within a specific territory and the enforcement of a system of rules.

The word can also be used to describe a country which has an independent, internationally recognized, government, such as the state of Israel or the state of Egypt. What then should we say of the United States of America? Is this another use of the word state? No, the word is applicable to nations or parts of nations. It just happens that the contemporary world consists largely of nation-states and the United States is simply a nation-state comprising 50 subnational states. We will look at the concept of the nation-state more closely a little later.

Within the same broad context we speak of 'politicians'. They are the people who achieve, or hope to achieve, power and, in simple terms, run the government. How do they fit into the scheme of things? Civil servants, members of the armed forces, judges, and similar public servants are the permanent personnel of the state while the politicians provide the temporary element. Politicians are the people who occupy positions of power as long as they have the support of the community, or they may be the people who aspire to power but are temporarily out of office. Exactly how politicians achieve power need not concern us at the moment; this will become evident as our study proceeds. We will see that power is obtained sometimes on the basis of consent, the democratic approach, and sometimes on the basis of force, the autocratic approach.

Both the words government and state are rather static terms but if we add to them the political dimension, provided by politicians and their activities, we have something much more dynamic: a 'political system'.

A political system can probably best be understood in demand-response terms. In the majority of countries politicians are elected to positions of power and authority, the ballot box giving the ordinary citizen an opportunity to make his or her demands known. Politicians will try to anticipate these demands by offering a prospectus of what they will provide if elected – a manifesto of promises – and the elector can then choose between different manifestos . Once a political party has been elected to office it will be judged by its performance and the electorate's response to that performance will again be demonstrated through the ballot box when elections come round again.

A country's political system, then, is more than its institutions and more than the formal processes of government. It includes the dynamic interplay of people's ideas and interests: the whole process of demand and response which politics represents. Even if a government is highly authoritarian, giving little room for the political process to work, there will always be at least an undercurrent of activity which expresses the true aspirations of the people, however subordinated they may be by those with power and authority.

1.3 The advantages of comparing systems

The comparative approach is a particularly advantageous way of arriving at a better understanding of political systems. Not just systems in general, but also a specific one about which you may consider yourself to be very knowledgeable.

First, the comparative approach forces you to stand back and look objectively at a particular system. It should be no surprise that some of the best studies of the American and British systems of government, for instance, have been made by people whose personal experience has been gained in a different political environment.

Second, the comparative approach alerts you to similarities in institutions and processes which make your own system more understandable.

Third, the experience of one country can be used to anticipate the effects of change in the political system of another. For example, a knowledge of the voting system in Ireland, where a form of proportional representation operates, will enable some sort of prediction to be made of the likely impact if it were introduced into the United Kingdom.

Finally, the comparative approach can stimulate interest in the political process and thereby encourage the population's involvement. This is probably the greatest advantage of the approach, achieved through a wider understanding of how countries with different histories, different ethnic compositions, different social problems, and different philosophical backgrounds have tackled the basic problem of creating and sustaining satisfactory institutions and processes of government. It is surely a sad reflection on the state of contemporary democracies that, at best, fewer than 5% of their populations can be classed as being 'regularly' active in a political sense.

1.4 The nation-state

The comparisons of political systems which will be made are based on the concept of the nation-state or sovereign state, defined, following Lane and Ersson, as 'a state that recognizes no higher decision-making power outside itself'. Table 1 lists, in order of formation, those nation-states which will be considered. Although today it is seen as the 'natural' political unit for most areas of the world, the nation-state is a comparatively new concept. The nation-state, or 'stato', in the Weberian sense, characterized by the monopoly of the legitimate use of force within a specified territory and the concentration of power in an impersonal administrative organization, is essentially an early modern and modern phenomenon, a product of the Renaissance and succeeding periods. Prior to this, personalized 'segmentary states' predominated. Here authority was layered and shared between local and central, or imperial, rulers, and clear territorial specification of boundaries was lacking. Nevertheless, in this earlier period substantial, quasi-national political units

Nation-states of the world

Table 1

Country	Region	Year of state formation
China	Asia	2nd century/ 1368/1949
San Marino	N & W Europe	301
Japan	Asia	5th century/1603
France	N & W Europe	741
Denmark	N & W Europe	940/1849
Ethiopia	C & S Africa	11th century
Portugal	N & W Europe	1128
Andorra	N & W Europe	1278
Monaco	N & W Europe	1297
Liechtenstein	N & W Europe	1342
Thailand	Asia	1350
Vatican City State*	N & W Europe	1377/1929
Spain	N & W Europe	1492
Iran	M East & N Africa	1499
Sweden	N & W Europe	1523
Russian Federation	C, E, & S Europe	1547/1917/1991
Netherlands	N & W Europe	1648
Switzerland*	N & W Europe	1648
United Kingdom	N & W Europe	1707
Afghanistan	Asia	1747
Nepal	Asia	1768
United States	N America	1776
Haiti	C America & Caribbean	1804
Paraguay	S America	1811
Argentina	S America	1816
Chile	S America	1818
Costa Rica	C America & Caribbean	1821
Mexico	C America & Caribbean	1821
Brazil	S America	1822
Peru	S America	1824
Bolivia	S America	1825
Uruguay	S America	1825
Greece	C, E, & S Europe	1829
Belgium	N & W Europe	1830
Colombia	S America	1830
Ecuador	S America	1830
El Salvador	C America & Caribbean	1830
Venezuela	S America	1830
Tonga*	Oceania	1831/1970
Honduras	C America & Caribbean	1838
Nicaragua	C America & Caribbean	1838
Guatemala	C America & Caribbean	1839
Dominican Republic	C America & Caribbean	1844
Liberia	C & S Africa	1847
Luxembourg	N & W Europe	1848
New Zealand	Oceania	1853
Italy	N & W Europe	1861
Canada	N America	1867
Germany	N & W Europe	1871/1949/1990
Romania	C, E, & S Europe	1881
Cuba	C America & Caribbean	1899
Australia	Oceania	1901
Panama	C America & Caribbean	1903
Norway	N & W Europe	1905
Bhutan	Asia	1907
Bulgaria	C, E, & S Europe	1908
South Africa	C & S Africa	1910
Albania	C, E, & S Europe	1912
Finland	N & W Europe	1917
Austria	N & W Europe	1918
Estonia	C, E, & S Europe	1918/1991
Hungary	C, E, & S Europe	1918
Poland	C, E, & S Europe	1918
Ukraine	C, E, & S Europe	1918/1991
Yugoslavia	C, E, & S Europe	1918/1992
Lithuania	C, E, & S Europe	1919/1991
Latvia	C, E, & S Europe	1920/1991
Mongolia	Asia	1921
Egypt	M East & N Africa	1922
Turkey	C, E, & S Europe	1923
Iraq	M East & N Africa	1932
Saudi Arabia	M East & N Africa	1932
Ireland, Republic of	N & W Europe	1937
Iceland	N & W Europe	1944
Lebanon	M East & N Africa	1944
Jordan	M East & N Africa	1946
Philippines	Oceania	1946
Syria	M East & N Africa	1946
India	Asia	1947
Pakistan	Asia	1947
Korea, North	Asia	1948
Korea, South	Asia	1948
Myanmar	Asia	1948
Sri Lanka	Asia	1948
Indonesia	Asia	1949
Taiwan*	Asia	1949
Libya	M East & N Africa	1951
Oman	M East & N Africa	1951
Cambodia	Asia	1953
Laos	Asia	1954
Vietnam	Asia	1954
Morocco	M East & N Africa	1956
Sudan	C & S Africa	1956
Tunisia	M East & N Africa	1956
Ghana	C & S Africa	1957
Malaysia	Asia	1957
Guinea	C & S Africa	1958
Israel	M East & N Africa	1958
Benin	C & S Africa	1960
Burkina Faso	C & S Africa	1960
Cameroon	C & S Africa	1960

continues

Nation-states of the world (continued) Table 1

Country	Region	Year of state formation
Central African Republic	C & S Africa	1960
Chad	C & S Africa	1960
Congo, Democratic Republic of	C & S Africa	1960
Congo, Republic of	C & S Africa	1960
Côte d'Ivoire	C & S Africa	1960
Cyprus	C, E, & S Europe	1960
Gabon	C & S Africa	1960
Madagascar	C & S Africa	1960
Mali	C & S Africa	1960
Mauritania	C & S Africa	1960
Niger	C & S Africa	1960
Nigeria	C & S Africa	1960
Senegal	C & S Africa	1960
Somalia	C & S Africa	1960
Togo	C & S Africa	1960
Kuwait	M East & N Africa	1961
Sierra Leone	C & S Africa	1961
Tanzania	C & S Africa	1961
Algeria	M East & N Africa	1962
Burundi	C & S Africa	1962
Jamaica	C America & Caribbean	1962
Rwanda	C & S Africa	1962
Trinidad & Tobago	C America & Caribbean	1962
Uganda	C & S Africa	1962
Samoa (Western)	Oceania	1962
Kenya	C & S Africa	1963
Malawi	C & S Africa	1964
Malta	N & W Europe	1964
Zambia	C & S Africa	1964
Gambia, The	C & S Africa	1965
Maldives	Asia	1965
Singapore	Asia	1965
Barbados	C America & Caribbean	1966
Botswana	C & S Africa	1966
Guyana	S America	1966
Lesotho	C & S Africa	1966
Equatorial Guinea	C & S Africa	1968
Mauritius	C & S Africa	1968
Nauru*	Oceania	1968
Swaziland	C & S Africa	1968
Fiji	Oceania	1970
Bahrain	M East & N Africa	1971
Bangladesh	Asia	1971
Qatar	M East & N Africa	1971
Bahamas	C America & Caribbean	1973
United Arab Emirates	M East & N Africa	1971
Grenada	C America & Caribbean	1974
Guinea-Bissau	C & S Africa	1974
Angola	C & S Africa	1975
Cape Verde	C & S Africa	1975
Comoros	C & S Africa	1975
Mozambique	C & S Africa	1975
Papua New Guinea	Oceania	1975
São Tomé e Príncipe	C & S Africa	1975
Suriname	S America	1975
Seychelles	C & S Africa	1976
Djibouti	C & S Africa	1977
Dominica	C America & Caribbean	1978
Solomon Islands	Oceania	1978
Tuvalu*	Oceania	1978
Kiribati*	Oceania	1979
St Lucia	C America & Caribbean	1979
St Vincent an the Grenadines	C America & Caribbean	1979
Vanuatu	Oceania	1980
Zimbabwe	C & S Africa	1980
Antigua	C America & Caribbean	1981
Belize	C America & Caribbean	1981
St Kitts and Nevis	C America & Caribbean	1983
Brunei	Asia	1984
Micronesia, Federated States of	Oceania	1986
Marshall Islands	Oceania	1990
Namibia	C & S Africa	1990
Yemen	M East & N Africa	1990
Armenia	C, E, & S Europe	1991
Azerbaijan	C, E, & S Europe	1991
Belarus	C, E, & S Europe	1991
Croatia	C, E, & S Europe	1991
Georgia	C, E, & S Europe	1991
Kazakhstan	Asia	1991
Kyrgyzstan	Asia	1991
Moldova	C, E, & S Europe	1991
Slovenia	C, E, & S Europe	1991
Tajikistan	Asia	1991
Turkmenistan	Asia	1991
Uzbekistan	Asia	1991
Bosnia-Herzegovina	C, E, & S Europe	1992
Macedonia	C, E, & S Europe	1992
Czech Republic	C, E, & S Europe	1993
Eritrea	C & S Africa	1993
Slovakia	C, E, & S Europe	1993
Palau (Belau)	Oceania	1994

* Not members of the UN.

The historical and regional pattern of nation-state formation Table 2

	Number of states formed									
Period	Asia	Central America & Caribbean	Central, Eastern, & Southern Europe	Central & Southern Africa	Middle East & North Africa	North America	Northern & Western Europe	Oceania	South America	Total
Pre AD 1000	0	0	0	0	0	0	3	0	0	3
1000–1599	2	0	1	1	1	0	7	0	0	12
1600–1799	3	0	0	0	0	1	3	0	0	7
1800–1899	0	9	2	1	0	1	4	2	10	29
1900–1950	10	1	6	1	6	0	5	2	0	31
1951–1975	7	5	0	40	10	0	2	4	2	70
1976–1999	6	6	15	5	1	0	0	7	0	40
Total	*28*	*21*	*24*	*48*	*18*	*2*	*24*	*15*	*12*	*192*

were established in a number of countries in Europe, Asia, and North Africa and this has been taken as the date of state formation for 11 countries.

As Table 2 shows, no less than 141 of the 192 states which will be examined in Section II of this volume are products of the present century: 98 being post-1959 creations. In the Middle East and Africa only three of the 66 were in existence before 1910, and even in Europe, where a majority of 'old' states might be expected, more than half of them achieved full, independent nationhood after World War I.

Before the 20th century most of the world's inhabitants were, in one way or another, in the thrall of the established Western European powers and if a datum point of, say, 1800 is taken, only 22 of today's 192 states existed in a form that might be readily recognizable now. Between 1800 and 1850 the world witnessed its first significant wave of nation-state formation. Twenty-three states originated during this period, including 18 in Central and Southern America, which had been liberated from Spanish colonial control. The second and, numerically, the most important wave of state-building occurred between 1944 and 1984. During this period, 97, or half of the contemporary world's nation-states, were established. This was made possible by European decolonization in Africa, Asia, the Middle East, the Caribbean, and Oceania. The final, and certainly the most dramatic, wave of state formation occurred between 1990 and 1994. Twenty-five new sovereign states came into existence. The great majority were situated in Central and Eastern Europe and Central Asia, and their formation was the direct result of the dissolution, in 1991, of the formal and 'informal' empire of the Soviet Union and the collapse of the Yugoslav socialist federation. In addition, in Oceania and Western Europe, a number of former 'Trust Territory' colonies and semi-sovereign micro-states have become fully fledged sovereign states since the first edition of this title was published. However, two states have disappeared, as a consequence of the unification of both Germany and Yemen.

Average ages of nation-states (1999) Table 3

Region	Number of states	Average age (years)	Standard deviation
Asia	28	110	170
Central America & Caribbean	21	87	69
Central, Eastern, & Southern Europe	24	56	94
Central & Southern Africa	48	56	132
Middle East & North Africa	18	70	106
North America	2	178	46
Northern & Western Europe	24	442	430
Oceania	15	46	49

Table 3 sets out the average age of states in the

regions of the world. The youngest states, on average half a century old, are to be found in Oceania, Africa, and Central and Eastern Europe. Though formerly known as the 'New World', the states of the Americas are, on average, now more than a century and a half old. However, it is Northern and Western Europe, the birthplace of the Weberian 'modern state', which contains the oldest group of nation-states of the world, with an average antiquity of four centuries.

A nation may be described as a group of people, often from different backgrounds, and sometimes from different races, who have come to live together and have adopted a common identity. The unity of a nation is usually reinforced by a common language and sometimes a common religion. A state is the name given to the whole apparatus of government which a nation creates as the machine for operating its political system.

The nation-state is then enshrined and perpetuated by the adoption of symbols such as a national flag and a national anthem. The human apex of the nation-state is the individual designated as head of state, in the person of a king, queen, or president. Sometimes the head of state is little more than a symbol of national unity, with few or no political powers. Sometimes the roles of head of state and head of government are combined but, in such cases, an attempt is usually made to differentiate between the two roles. In the United States, for example, the office of president generally attracts the respect of most citizens regardless of the personality or political views of the holder.

The nation-state manifests itself in a wide variety of different forms, ranging from the democratic to the highly authoritarian. It is this rich variety which provides the material for what will follow.

1.5 The plan of the book

The first part of the book concentrates on the comparative approach, looking first at the various constitutional forms which can be adopted for political systems and then at the philosophies or ideologies which underlie the constitutional structures. Then executives, heads of state, and heads of government, and assemblies, or parliaments, in different countries are compared. Then, moving on to the more dynamic elements of political systems, voting methods and parties are examined.

The second part is designed to show political systems in action, giving a factual account of the political institutions and processes of each country and an objective summary of how they currently operate. One hundred and ninety-two states are covered. They include the current 185 full members of the United Nations, plus the seven independent states of Kiribati, Nauru, Switzerland, Taiwan, Tonga, Tuvalu, and the Vatican City.

The seven non-UN states have been added because all have full national sovereignties and their presence outside the United Nations organization has no useful bearing on the subject matter of our present examination of political systems. Switzerland, for example, has chosen, on the basis of its long history of neutrality, not to be a UN member and Taiwan was a member, under the title of the Republic of China, from 1945 to 1971, when the People's Republic of China received full international recognition. The South Pacific states of Kiribati, Nauru, and Tuvalu have determined on a neutralist course and have not applied for direct UN representation. However, Tonga applied for membership in 1999. The Vatican City, as a purely theocratic state, has jealously retained its political neutrality.

The states in Table 1 that are not current members of the United Nations are denoted by asterisks. The dates indicate the year of each country's inception as a nation-state. This date will normally be the year of release from colonial control or in which its first constitution was adopted, which may or may not be the one currently in force. In the case of a minority of countries, particularly those with dates prior to the 19th century, the inception of nationhood will predate the adoption of the first constitution or a codified constitution may never have been adopted.

The 192 states have been grouped into nine geographical regions: Asia; Central America and the Caribbean; Central, Eastern, and Southern Europe; Central and Southern Africa; the Middle East and North Africa; North America; Northern and Western Europe; Oceania; and South America. This classification has been chosen in preference to one based purely on philosophical values, such as liberal-democratic, totalitarian, and so on. Such an approach is superficially attractive but fraught with difficulties. It is, inevitably, subjective and can have the effect of distorting the profile of a political system so as to force it into one of the chosen categories. On the other hand there are, apart from convenience, some good reasons for adopting the regional approach.

First, there is an undoubted link, as will be demonstrated, between a country's geography and history and the political system it develops. A look at the continent of America, and its associated islands, will illustrate this point.

The whole of North America was at one time a British colony. The fact that Canada, which retained its connection with Britain, also retained aspects of the British constitution in its political system is understandable. Equally understandable is the recognition that the United States, which broke its link with Britain 200 years ago, chose to develop a different system, which looks more guardedly at the dangers of unfettered executive power and seeks to control and restrain it. The US Constitution, therefore, reflects other influences, such as the political climate in 18th-century France.

The geography and social composition of North America have also had effects on the political systems of both Canada and the United States, resulting in federal structures of government which take into account the size and diversities of both countries.

Moving south down the continent, the fact that much of Central and South America was once part of a Spanish empire whereas the islands of the Caribbean came under British and French influence is, again, reflected in their political systems.

Second, there is a discernible link between a country's ethnic characteristics and the political system it develops and these characteristics tend to be regionalized in many cases. For example, it is not surprising that the majority of Islamic states are to be found in the Middle East, North Africa, and West Asia.

One somewhat artificial region which has been used for classification purposes is Oceania. Where exactly are its boundaries? Indeed, can it be said to exist at all? For the purposes of this book it is regarded as including Australasia and those island territories in the Pacific which do not fit easily into any other of the regional groupings which have been chosen.

The arbitrary nature of the classification is freely admitted and no apologies are offered. Without such an approach much of the material would have been less manageable and, in any event, for the majority of states alternative groupings would not have brought out so clearly the influences of history, geography, and social development.

The third part of the book deals with residual territories in the world which cannot be viewed as fully fledged independent states. Into this category fall the 44 overseas colonies and external dependent territories that still exist in the world of today.

This final part also looks beyond nation-states and their dependencies to regional and global groupings. Here it is recognized that the accelerated improvements in communications of all kinds, and the growing economic interdependence of countries, will, inevitably, cause the world to shrink in political as well as physical terms and, as a result, seems likely to lead to a diminution in absolute levels of national sovereignty.

Recommended reading

Almond, G A, Powell, G B and Mundt, R J *Comparative Politics: A Theoretical Framework*, 2nd edn., Harper Collins, 1996

Anderson, J (ed.) *The Rise of the Modern State*, Humanities Press, 1986

Blondel, J *Comparative Government: An Introduction*, 2nd edn., Prentice Hall-Harvester Wheatsheaf, 1995

Calvert, P *An Introduction to Comparative Politics*, Harvester Wheatsheaf, 1993

Charlton, R *Comparative Government*, Longman, 1986, Chap. 1

Chilcote, R H *Theories of Comparative Politics: The Search for a Paradigm Reconsidered*, Westview Press, 1994

Crick, B *In Defense of Politics*, 2nd edn., Penguin, 1982

Dogan, M and Kazancigil, A.(eds) *Comparing Nations*, Basil Blackwell, 1994

Evans, P B, Rueschemeyer, D and Skocpol, T (eds.) *Bringing the State Back In*, Cambridge University Press, 1985

Hague, R, Harrop, M and Breslin, S *Comparative Government and Politics: An Introduction*, 3rd edn., Macmillan, 1992, Chaps 1–3

Harding, N (ed.) *The State in Socialist Society*, Macmillan, 1984

Hobsbawm, E J *Nations and Nationalism since 1970*, Cambridge University Press, 1990

Kellas, J *The Politics of Nationalism and Ethnicity*, Macmillan, 1991

Keman, H (ed.) *Comparative Politics: New Directions in Theories and Methods*, Free University Press, 1993

King, R *The State in Modern Society: New Directions in Political Sociology*, Macmillan, 1986

Lane, J-E and Ersson, S *Comparative Politics: An Introduction and New Approach*, Polity Press, 1994

Leftwich, A (ed.) *What is Politics?*, Basil Blackwell, 1984

Lukes, S (ed.) *Power*, Basil Blackwell, 1986

Macridis, R C and Burg, S L *Introduction to Comparative Politics: Regimes and Changes*, 2nd edn., Harper Collins, 1991

Roberts, G K *An Introduction to Comparative Politics*, Edward Arnold, 1986, Chap. 1

Smith, A D (ed.) *Ethnicity and Nationalism*

Wiarda, H J (ed.) *New Directions in Comparative Politics*, Westview Press, 1991

CHAPTER 2

Constitutions

2.1 What is a constitution?

A constitution can be regarded in two ways. First, it is a general statement of how a country is governed. For example, the US Constitution could be described as republican, federal, and presidential, whereas that of the United Kingdom would be monarchical, unitary, and parliamentary. For someone familiar with 'constitutional language', but who knew nothing about the political systems of the United States and the United Kingdom, these two statements would say something, but not much.

On the other hand, for someone completely unversed in constitutional and political terminology the two descriptions would do little or nothing to advance a knowledge of the two countries. 'Republican', 'monarchical', 'federal', 'unitary', 'presidential', and 'parliamentary' are all words which are intended to have precise meanings within the context of an exposition of a political system.

In an even more general sense a constitution may be said to be 'liberal' or 'authoritarian', using two contrasting words which can be found in any nontechnical dictionary. These distinctions would probably conjure up a picture of two political systems that a layman would understand. If you had the choice, which would you prefer: liberal or authoritarian? Most people would choose the former, if only because it had a more 'comfortable' sound. But if one constitution was said to be more liberal than another or more authoritarian than another, difficulties would immediately be created.

To use the word constitution in a general sense, therefore, is not particularly helpful. It is rather like saying that France has better weather than Britain. What parts of France and Britain? What times of the year? Is the weather consistent, year in and year out? Obviously, more questions are raised than answered.

In a more specific sense, a constitution is a document or set of documents describing the framework of a political system. It stipulates where power lies within a state, what the institutions of government are, how they are constructed and how they are intended to operate. In doing so, it provides what might be said to be a set of rules for politicians in a particular country to follow: what offices they can hold, how they get to office, what they can do and not do in office, how laws are made, how they are enforced, how disputes between citizens and the state are resolved.

2.2 What is not a constitution?

A constitution falls far short of being an accurate description of a political system. For example, it is unlikely to even mention political parties or any other forms of organized interests. It will say how power is distributed but not how it is used.

There are several possible analogies which could be used to point out differences between a constitution and a political system but the most accurate is probably a theatrical one. A constitution can be said to be the text of a play whereas the political system is its enactment. Often a constitution even falls short of being a complete text and is rather more a plot with a cast of characters. There are two missing elements which are needed if a constitution is to become alive and translated from a written text into a live production.

The first is political activity or the interplay of power. In other words, how a head of government arrives at a position of power, how that power is used, how he/she and his/her supporters try to retain power, and how their opponents try to divest them of it. This is where the activities of parties and interest groups are all important.

The second missing element is what are called constitutional conventions. These are the understandings which politicians accept as being the unwritten rules of how a constitution should work in practice. Conventions bring flexibility and reality into the political process. They allow a constitution to remain firm in its fundamentals but flexible enough to adapt to changing political circumstances.

The use of the word convention is, perhaps, unfortunate because it can have a very different meaning, particularly in the United States where it is the name given to conferences or rallies of political parties. The

Post-1989 constitutions (85) — Table 4

State	Year	Region
Albania	1998	C, E, & S Europe
Andorra	1993	N & W Europe
Angola	1991	C & S Africa
Argentina	1994	S America
Armenia	1995	C, E, & S Europe
Azerbaijan	1995	C, E, & S Europe
Bangladesh	1991	Asia
Belarus	1996	C, E, & S Europe
Belgium	1993	N & W Europe
Benin	1990	C & S Africa
Bosnia-Herzegovina	1995	C, E, & S Europe
Bulgaria	1991	C, E, & S Europe
Burkina Faso	1991	C & S Africa
Burundi	1992	C & S Africa
Cambodia	1993	Asia
Cape Verde	1990	C & S Africa
Central African Republic	1995	C & S Africa
Chad	1996	C & S Africa
Colombia	1991	S America
Comoros	1996*	C & S Africa
Congo, Republic of	1992	C & S Africa
Croatia	1990	C, E, & S Europe
Czech Republic	1992	C, E, & S Europe
Djibouti	1992	C & S Africa
Equatorial Guinea	1991	C & S Africa
Eritrea	1997	C & S Africa
Estonia	1992	C, E, & S Europe
Ethiopia	1994	C & S Africa
Fiji	1990	Oceania
Gabon	1991	C & S Africa
Gambia	1997	C & S Africa
Georgia	1995	C, E, & S Europe
Ghana	1992	C & S Africa
Guinea	1991	C & S Africa
Guinea-Bissau	1991*	C & S Africa
Indonesia	1998	Asia
Kazakhstan	1995	Asia
Kyrgyzstan	1994	Asia
Laos	1991	Asia
Latvia	1993	C, E, & S Europe
Lebanon	1990	M East & N Africa
Lesotho	1993	C & S Africa
Lithuania	1992	C, E, & S Europe
Macedonia	1991	C, E, & S Europe
Madagascar	1992	C & S Africa
Malawi	1994	C & S Africa
Maldives	1998	Asia
Mali	1992	C & S Africa
Mauritania	1991	C & S Africa
Moldova	1994	C, E, & S Europe
Mongolia	1992	Asia
Morocco	1992	M East & N Africa
Mozambique	1990	C & S Africa
Namibia	1990	C & S Africa
Nepal	1990	Asia
Niger	1996*	C & S Africa
Nigeria	1999	C & S Africa
Oman	1996	M East & N Africa
Paraguay	1992	S America
Pelau	1992	Oceania
Peru	1993	S America
Poland	1997	C, E, & S Europe
Romania	1991	C, E, & S Europe
Russian Federation	1993	C, E, & S Europe
Rwanda	1995	C & S Africa
São Tomé e Príncipe	1990	C & S Africa
Saudi Arabia	1992	M East & N Africa
Seychelles	1993	C & S Africa
Sierra Leone	1991	C & S Africa
Slovakia	1992	C, E, & S Europe
Slovenia	1991	C, E, & S Europe
South Africa	1997	C & S Africa
Sudan	1998	C & S Africa
Taiwan	1991	Asia
Tajikistan	1994	Asia
Thailand	1997	Asia
Togo	1992	C & S Africa
Turkmenistan	1992	Asia
Uganda	1995	C & S Africa
Ukraine	1996	C, E, & S Europe
Uzbekistan	1992	Asia
Vietnam	1992	Asia
Yemen	1994	M East & N Africa
Yugoslavia	1992	C, E, & S Europe
Zambia	1991	C & S Africa

* Currently suspended, following military coup

Post-1989 constitutions by region

Region	Number
Northern and Western Europe	2
Central, Eastern, and Southern Europe	21
Middle East and North Africa	5
Central and Southern Africa	36
North America	0
Central America and the Caribbean	0
South America	4
Asia	15
Oceania	2

combined term, constitutional convention, refers, in addition, in the United States to a special meeting of state government representatives, called at the request of two-thirds of state legislatures, to draft new amendments to the constitution. A better approach would be to speak of conventional behaviour, in other words customary practices which politicians adopt because experience has shown that they make the governmental process work more smoothly. This conventional behaviour acts as a lubricant to the political system.

A constitutional convention begins life as an attempt to solve a problem or potential problem. If it is successful then it may be accepted by politicians as an agreed way of approaching a similar problem in the future. If it works successfully on a number of occasions there will be tacit agreement that it has achieved the status of a constitutional convention. It may even be written into a constitution as a formal amendment so that there will be no confusion about whether or not this, procedure should always be followed.

In the United Kingdom there is no legislation which says that the prime minister must be a member of the House of Commons but, although in the second half of the 19th century no fewer than six of the 12 governments were headed by peers, there has been no prime minister sitting in the House of Lords since 1895. A constitutional convention has established this practice. A similar convention ensures that government ministers must be members of one or other of the Houses of Parliament.

To recapitulate, a constitution provides the framework for a political system. It does not give a full, or even accurate, picture of how the system works in practice.

2.3 Written and unwritten constitutions

Most states have a basic, written document that is called its constitution. It may not be the same one that was adopted when the state first came into existence. Even if it is the original, it is likely to have been amended several times since its original adoption.

The world's oldest functioning written constitution is to be found in the micro-state of San Marino, having been first drafted in 1600. The constitutions of Canada (1774) and the United States (1787) are the next oldest (although Canada was British at the time) while a further eight constitutions currently in use, in Western Europe (Belgium, Denmark, Luxembourg, Norway, Sweden, and Switzerland) and South America (Argentina and Bolivia), date back to the 19th century. The remaining states in the world have 20th-century constitutions although in some cases, for example in France and Poland, these have superseded much earlier (late 18th or 19th century) constitutions. Some were adopted, for example those of Austria and Latvia, during the wave of democratic constitutional diffusion that followed the end of World War I. However, most date from the postwar era and, as Table 4 shows, a staggeringly large proportion, 85, corresponding to more than two-fifths of all written constitutions, have been adopted during the current decade, usually replacing an earlier written constitution. As a consequence, many of the world's constitutions are barely half a decade old.

As Table 4 shows, most of these 'fledgling constitutions' have been adopted by states in Africa, where a wave of democratization has swept away many former one-party regimes, and in Central and Eastern Europe and Asia, being related chiefly to the collapse of communism. As a consequence, the average age of constitutions is low in these regions. This is shown in Table 5.

A minority of states do not have such a basic document. Excepting those African states in which the existing constitution has been temporarily suspended, of the 192 states listed in Table 1 only six fall into this category: Bhutan, Israel, New Zealand, San Marino, the United Kingdom, and the Vatican City State. Because of this they are often said to have unwritten constitutions. This is not strictly true.

Although the king of Bhutan would appear to have unlimited powers, with no constitution to restrain him, there are written rules which govern procedures for elections to the Royal Advisory Council and the National Assembly and say how they operate, and the king is expected to ensure they are observed.

Israel has no single document which it calls a constitution, but in 1950 the state parliament voted to adopt one by evolution over an unspecified period of time and since then a number of laws have been passed which are regarded as being part of the constitution. The Jewish Holy Book, the Torah, also remains an ancient source of political authority.

When it became a fully independent state, New Zealand decided to model its political system on that of the United Kingdom even to the extent of not adopting a formal, written constitution. Nevertheless, there are certain pieces of legislation which are seen to have a particular constitutional significance, such as the Acts which determine the eligibility of voters and their representatives and the methods of voting.

San Marino, although lacking a formal constitution, follows a basic set of 'governing principles', framed in 1600; while the Vatican City State follows principles set out in the 1929 Lateran Treaty.

The United Kingdom is usually cited as the classic example of a state without a written constitution but, again, as in the other three countries described above, there are Acts of Parliament which are regarded as being constitutionally important. The most notable probably is the 1689 Bill of Rights which established the legislative supremacy of Parliament and from which the rest of the evolutionary constitution developed. In more recent years the legislation restricting the powers of the House of Lords, the Parliament Acts of 1911 and 1949, and widening the franchise, the Reform Acts of 1832, 1867, 1884, 1918, 1928, 1948, and 1970, must be regarded as being a form of constitutional amendment, as must 1997-98 legislation setting up Welsh and Northern Ireland assemblies and a Scottish parliament.

Thus it is not really accurate to distinguish between written and unwritten constitutions. A better distinction would be between codified and uncodified documents for it is certain that, although it would probably be a long and tortuous process, it would be quite possible to draw up a written, codified constitution for the United Kingdom, and for the other seven countries detailed above, if it was thought useful and necessary.

Average age of state constitutions — Table 5

Average age by world regions as of 1999

Region	Number of written constitutions	Average age
Asia	27	15
Central America & the Caribbean	21	25
Central, Eastern, & Southern Europe	25	9
Central and Southern Africa	39	10
Middle East & North Africa	17	23
North America	2	114
Northern & Western Europe	20	51
Oceania	14	33
South America	12	17

2.4 What a constitution contains

Individual constitutions do, of course, vary but most contain certain basic statements about the institutions which have been created to govern a state and how they are expected to operate. Some constitutions go further and, being framed either at a state's inception or following a major political upheaval resulting in a change of regime, identify the kind of society a political system is trying to create and maintain.

The main thrust of most constitutions is to distinguish between the three basic powers of government: the power to make laws, the legislative function; the power to enforce laws, the executive function; and the power to interpret laws and adjudicate in disputes between the citizen and the state, the judicial function.

The US Constitution, for example, has seven main Articles:

Article 1 defines the legislative powers;
Article 2 deals with the office of president, as the nation's chief executive;
Article 3 sets out the powers of the courts, including the Supreme Court;
Article 4 deals with relations between the individual states;
Article 5 describes how the Constitution can be amended;
Articles 6 and 7 deal mainly with arrangements for transforming a loose federation of states into a full union.

The constitution of the Fifth French Republic has 14 main Titles:

Title 1 deals with the sovereignty of the Republic;
Title 2 sets out the powers and duties of the president;
Title 3 describes the role of the prime minister and the rest of the government;
Title 4 sets out the structure and functions of Parliament;
Title 5 deals with the relationship between Parliament and the government;
Title 7 sets out the composition and role of the Constitutional Council;
Title 8 describes judicial powers;
Title 10 sets out the composition and role of the Economic and Social Council;
Title 14 describes how the constitution can be amended.

The other Titles deal with detailed, specific matters.

Many constitutions begin with a broad statement of the aims which they hope to achieve. The preamble to the US Constitution of 1787 reads:

'We, the people of the United States, in order to form a more perfect Union, establish Justice, insure domestic Tranquillity, provide for the common Defense, promote the general Welfare, and secure the Blessings of Liberty to ourselves and our Posterity, do ordain and establish this Constitution for the United States of America.'

The preamble to the French constitution of 1958 reads:

'The French people hereby solemnly proclaim their attachment to the Rights of Man and the principles of national sovereignty as defined by the Declaration of 1789, reaffirmed and completed by the Preamble to the Constitution of 1946.'

Most states have a Bill of Rights, guaranteeing certain basic individual rights, such as freedom of speech and freedom of assembly, either incorporated in or associated with a codified constitution. It would be possible for any state to adopt such a charter even without a codified constitution, and whether or not to have a Bill of Rights has been a matter of debate for some years within the United Kingdom.

Although the great majority of states have a guarantee of individual rights either built into their constitutions or associated with them, the mere fact of there being such a written guarantee should not be assumed to mean that such rights really exist and are protected. Some of these apparent guarantees are couched in rather limited terms. The Iranian constitution, for example, states that the press is free but adds: 'except in matters that are contrary to public morality or insult religious belief'.

Some constitutions contain explicit guarantees of specific individual rights. That of Honduras, for example, enunciates the right to work but states that daytime work should not exceed eight hours per day and 44 hours per week, while the limits on night work are set at six hours per night and 36 hours per week.

The Egyptian constitution contains a strong statement on human rights and specifically states that 'houses have sanctity' and are protected. The constitutions of Germany and Lebanon also give protection for housing, while El Salvador provides for an attorney-of-the-poor to protect the least advantaged citizens.

The German constitution also asserts the rights of conscientious objectors; the Moldovan constitution establishes 'permanent neutrality' for the country, banning the stationing of foreign troops on Moldovan soil; and that of Japan declares the renunciation 'for ever of war as a means of settling international disputes'. The Croatian constitution, however, contains the caveat that in a state of war some guaranteed rights may be restricted.

The pre-1997 Fijian constitution awarded positive discrimination to ethnic Fijians and Polynesians of Rotuma Island in the allocation of judicial and government posts.

Whether or not individual rights really are guaranteed and protected needs therefore to be determined by rather more objective means than just the reading of such a guarantee in a constitution.

Several constitutions set out the nature and objectives of the state. The pre-1990 constitution of Burkina Faso, for example, described it as a 'revolutionary, democratic, unitary and secular republic'; the 1982 Guinean constitution declared the country to be an 'anti-colonialist and anti-imperialist republic'; while the North Korean constitution describes this socialist state as being in the stage of the 'dictatorship of the proletariat', stresses the importance of national self-reliance, or Juche, and embraces the goal of national reunification, by 'peaceful means'. The constitution of Mongolia proclaims a 'multi-structured economy', taking into account 'universal trends of world economic development and national conditions'.

Clearly the framers of constitutions have often seized the opportunity of putting their personal imprints on documents which they hoped would give clear indications of the paths they wished their countries to follow. The fathers of the US Constitution provided the most significant example of this attempt to define a nation's future.

2.5 Rigidity and flexibility

Sometimes attempts are made to distinguish between what are seen as rigid and flexible constitutions, usually on the basis of how easily a constitution adapts to changing circumstances. If it adapts readily it is said to be flexible and if it does not it is rigid.

Perhaps understandably, an unwritten constitution suggests great flexibility. After all, there is no formal, legalistic procedure for making a change. If the political will is there then a change will take place, probably by introducing a new constitutional convention or usage, or discarding an old one. The assumption that a codified constitution is less flexible than an uncodified one is often misleading. When a usage can be changed or discarded without any technical obstacles it seems reasonable to conclude that the politicians who might make a change will approach a proposal very warily.

If a change has to go through some elaborate, formal procedure, such as in the United States, where an amendment to the Constitution has to be proposed by a two-thirds vote of both houses of Congress and then ratified by the legislatures of three-quarters, or 38, of the 50 states of the Union, it seems reasonable to assume that a lightly or poorly conceived change will get a thorough consideration before it is finally accepted. Thus there have been only 27 amendments to the US Constitution (1789), ten of which, the so-called 'Bill of Rights', were passed in 1791. The most notable proposed change which failed at the second ratification hurdle was the proposed Equal Rights Amendment. This sailed through Congress in 1971–72, but was approved by only 35, or 70%, of the states in the Union. In other states such as Japan and South Korea, constitutional amendments need to be first passed by a two-thirds vote of all members in parliament and then approved in a national referendum, while in Bulgaria they must be carried in the National Assembly by a three-quarters majority at least three times, on different days.

In a nation where such a weighty, formal procedure is absent the onus is placed on proposers of change to be absolutely certain in their own minds that there will no lasting, damaging consequences. Confronted with this responsibility, it is understandable that, in more cases than not, the status quo will be retained and the change cautiously avoided.

This is especially the case in liberal democracies, where constitutional government, government in accordance with formal rules, is most deeply embedded in the public and political psyche. An exception has been France, which has framed 17 constitutions since 1789. Its current Fifth Republic constitution dates back to 1958. It can be amended by the two chambers of parliament meeting together in a special session and the changes attracting 60% support, or by the amendment bill being passed separately by each house of parliament and then approved in a national referendum. Similarly in India, where minor amendments require only the majority support of both chambers of parliament, there have been more than 70 amendments to the constitution since it was first adopted in 1950. This represents almost two amendments a year.

In newer, emergent, or one-party regimes the process of constitution redrafting has been more frequent, with fresh codes being introduced to meet the changed circumstances of the day. The Latin American states, independent since the early 19th century, have been particularly prominent in this respect. Venezuela, for example, has had 26 constitutions, though the present one dates back more than 30 years. The Dominican Republic has had 25; Haiti more than 20; Colombia and Ecuador 17 apiece; El Salvador and Bolivia 16 apiece; Honduras 12; and Brazil 7. Asian and African states subject to frequent military coups are also notable for the number of their constitutions. The most extreme case is Thailand, which has had 16 constitutions since the establishment of a constitutional monarchy. Similarly, in communist regimes new constitutions were regularly framed as a means of giving recognition to the advancing stages of 'socialist development' that had been attained. The Soviet Union had five such documents, in 1918, 1922, 1936, 1977, and 1989, after the Revolution of 1917. Yugoslavia had a similar number after the federal republic was first established in 1945, while Czechoslovakia and Romania each had three.

2.6 Separation or fusion of powers

We have already said that the main area of concern of a codified constitution will be the three main institutions of government: the legislature, the executive, and the judiciary. A comparison of constitutions could attempt to discover whether these institutions are kept separate or are fused.

The best known proponent of the doctrine of the separation of powers was the French philosopher, Baron Montesquieu (1689–1755), who set out the theory in *De l'Esprit des lois* (1748). He argued that by keeping the three institutions separate and balanced the possibility of one of them, and particularly the executive, accruing undue power, and then exploiting it to the detriment of the citizenship, would be avoided.

His views made a considerable impact and were clearly taken into account by the framers of the United States Constitution. As one of them, James Madison (1751–1836), said: 'the accumulation of all powers, legislative, executive and judiciary, in the same hands ... may justly be pronounced the very definition of tyranny'. Oddly enough, Montesquieu cited England as a country enjoying relatively great liberty because the powers of government were distributed between the legislative, executive, and judicial institutions and had the effect of balancing each other. In reality, as will be seen later, a political system based on a parliamentary executive, as in the United Kingdom, creates a fusion, rather than a separation, of the legislative and executive functions.

The concept of a separation or balancing of powers is still a useful test of the degree of freedom from autocratic rule within a political system but, on its own, is an insufficient, and sometimes unreliable, criterion.

2.7 Unitary or federal states

A constitution invariably seeks to clarify the relationship between the government with the responsibility for the whole of a state's territory and that concerned with only part of it; in other words, to draw distinctions between central government and localized government.

Democratic government is believed to have begun in the city-states of ancient Greece, and particularly the city of Athens, which, with a total population of less than 50,000, was able to practise direct and universal participation in government. In fact the very word democracy (*demokratia*), roughly meaning rule (*kratos*) by the people (*demos*), is derived from ancient Greece. In that situation democracy was direct, involving the active and personal participation of all adult 'full citizens' at some time in their lives in government, by accepting office on a rota basis. Citizens' assemblies met around 40 times a year, being attended by around 5,000 people, while morning councils met even more frequently. There are still vestiges of direct democracy in those contemporary states which make use of juries in their judicial systems and more generally, as is noted in Chapter 6, in the increasing resort to regular referenda and 'citizens' initiatives' in a number of West European nations and US states.

Today, of course, there are few, and no major, states small enough to enjoy direct democracy. The unusual, and almost unique, example of the tiny Most Serene Republic of San Marino in Italy has already been noted. Elements of direct democracy also survive in several of the smaller cantons (states) in the Swiss Confederation, with the electorate, numbering, at most, 10,000, meeting in a public place on one day each year to select officials and vote on issues. This tradition of direct Swiss democracy via the annual Landsgemeinde, or sovereign citizens' assembly, is more than seven centuries old, originating in 1294 in the German-speaking canton of Schwyz. These cases are, of course, anachronisms and, although there are suggestions that computerization may, in the future, open up the possibility of a new direct participatory democracy via the Internet, the vast majority of states which claim to be democratic do so on the basis of representative, rather than direct, democracy.

Putting exceptions such as San Marino and the Swiss cantons aside, all modern states find it necessary to have institutions to administer the needs of particular localities as well as the whole population. The larger the area the more obvious the need to cater to local, or regional, as well as national interests. The extent to which power is devolved by the government in the center to the localities, and the nature of the power devolved, indicate whether or not a genuinely federal system is operating.

A nation-state is one which claims sovereignty over the whole of its territory. In other words, everyone within its boundaries is subject to its laws. If a government decides to divide its sovereignty within its boundaries and pass some of it to local bodies, it means the devolution of some of its law-making powers. If the central government retains the right to override these devolved powers at any time, then the state cannot be said to be truly federal.

If a federal system is adopted the respective legislative powers of the governments in the center and the localities must be clearly defined, and the local governments must be protected against the erosion of those powers by central government. This can only be done successfully through the medium of a written, codified constitution. Because circumstances change, there must be provision for this distribution of legislative power to be reviewed. In a truly federal system that review cannot be undertaken arbitrarily by the central government and the process must involve the localities, either by giving them 'blocking' powers with respect to proposed constitutional amendments in their areas of concern or through the adjudicatory medium of an impartial constitutional court.

The supreme example of a genuinely federal system of government is found in the United States Constitution. Section 8 of Article I sets out the powers of the central legislature, Congress, and, by implication, leaves the residue of powers to the state legislatures. Article V prescribes how the Constitution can be amended, such amendments requiring the approval of three-quarters of the state legislatures, and Article III the adjudicatory authority of the Supreme Court.

This form of devolution is effected by prescribing the legislative powers of the center and leaving the residue with the localities. An alternative method is to prescribe the powers of the localities and leave the residue to the center. Virtually all the world's federal systems adopt the former approach although the Canadian constitution comes nearer to the latter, defining precisely the powers of both the federal and state governments.

When executive, rather than legislative, powers are decentralized a state is said to have a unitary constitution. Of the 192 states in Table 1 the great majority are unitary, only 24 having federal structures. As with most other aspects of political systems, history, geography, and culture are the strongest factors behind the choice of a federal system of government. Of particular importance, not surprisingly, is country size, with seven of the eight largest nations in the world, and five of the seven most populous, having federal structures. Moreover, the one exception within this grouping, China, has established five 'autonomous regions', for its non-Han minority border communities, which are of quasi-federal nature. It is for this reason that, despite their small numbers, more than 2 billion people, constituting 38% of the world's population, live in states with federal constitutions, and these 24 states comprise half the world's land area. There are federal states in all nine regions of the world, but the largest number are to be found in the Americas (7), Europe (7), and Africa (5). The broad range of factors that have determined the existence of federal structures in these and the remaining five states are presented in Table 6, together with a brief exposition of the types of federal system in operation.

Table 6 excludes Somalia where, in 1993, an agreement was reached to establish a federal system of government, based on 18 autonomous regions. However, the country has been beset by civil war since the late 1980s. This has prevented the agreement from being made effective. Indeed, one large region, Somaliland in the northwest, has been a self-declared 'independent state' since May 1991. There have been recent proposals to establish a federation in Sri Lanka, while in Madagascar a constitutional amendment to set up a federal system was approved in a March 1998 referendum. South Africa is another possible candidate for a federal system.

As Table 6 suggests, federalism is stronger in some countries than others, the most vigorous being Australia, Canada, Switzerland, and the United States, with India and Germany following closely behind. In Germany a strong federal system was actively sponsored by the occupying powers after the end of World War II because of fears of a resurgence of a powerful and belligerent nationalistic central government. The weakest examples of federal systems are probably the Comoros, where most legislative power is retained by the Federal Assembly, and Austria. The Mexican, Russian, Venezuelan, and Malaysian federal systems are also weak in practice as a result of the *de facto* control exerted over state/regional associates by the federal party leadership and machine.

Federal systems have been established in some states, notably Belgium, Bosnia, Ethiopia, Nigeria, Sudan, and Yugoslavia, to accommodate the political aspirations of regionally based ethnic communities which would otherwise seek secession from the state. In practice, the federal solution has not always proved sufficient to assuage secessionist movements. As a consequence the federal unions of the USSR, greater Yugoslavia, and Czechoslovakia collapsed between 1991 and 1992 and Cameroon abandoned its federal structure in 1972. Meanwhile, Bosnia, Canada, Comoros, St Kitts and Nevis, Ethiopia, India, Mexico, Nigeria, Pakistan, the Russian Federation, Sudan, and Yugoslavia all currently face regionally based secessionist and 'home rule' movements of varying strengths.

Other states which are not strictly federal but have 'highly decentralized' forms of government, are identified in Table 7. During the past two decades there has been a general trend towards political decentralization, entailing the establishment of elected regional governments with enhanced responsibilities and sources of finance. This has been particularly apparent in Western Europe in France, Italy, the United Kingdom (since 1997), and, to the greatest degree, Spain. As a consequence the distinction between 'weak federal' states such as Austria and 'strongly decentralized' states such as Spain is now quite narrow. Indeed, it is noted by Daniel Elazar, who has compiled a handbook of federal and federal-style states, that: 'Nearly 80 per cent of the world's population now live within polities that either are formally federal or that utilize federal arrangements in some way, while only 20 per cent live in polities that can be denominated as outside of any federal arrangements'.

2.8 The distribution of power

Whatever safeguards may be written into a constitution, political realities will ultimately determine the distribution of power between the center and the localities, and the most significant reality is, invariably, a financial one.

Federal states in the contemporary world

Table 6

Chief determinants of federalism and its form*

Argentina (S America) pop. 34.2 m (WR 31) area 2.767 m sq km/1.068 m sq miles (WR 8)
historical, cultural, and geographical
Early history was dominated by a conflict between town and country, particularly the European-style sophistication of Buenos Aires and the rough, basic style of the gaucho. An attempt to impose a unitary system in 1829 failed. There are today 22 provinces, each with its own legislature, governor, and constitution. The five-member Supreme Court adjudges federal–state constitutional conflicts.

Australia (Oceania) pop. 18.4 m (WR 49) area 7.687 m sq km/2.968 m sq miles (WR 6)
geographical and historical
The size of the country and distribution of the population have created distinctive, separate communities. For example, both Darwin, in the north, and Perth, in the west, are more than 3,000 km from the capital, Canberra, whereas the two largest cities, Sydney and Melbourne, are, respectively, less than 300 and 500 km away. Historically, throughout the 19th century the country was divided into six distinct colonies, founded separately, governed separately, and bounded by largely uninhabited land. Not until 1901 did the colonies unite in the Commonwealth of Australia. The six states have their own legislatures and constitutions, with, still today, 60% of the nation's population residing in their capitals. They receive the bulk of their funds from the center, which has authority to levy income tax, in the form of annually negotiated grants. Federal–state conflicts are ruled upon by the seven-member Australian High Court.

Austria (N & W Europe) pop. 8.0 m (WR 85) area 0.084 m sq km/0.032 m sq miles (WR 112)
partly historical and partly artificial
A weak federal system which had operated between the two World Wars was revived, under United States influence, in 1945. There are nine states (Länder), each with its own legislature. The policy-framing powers residing with the state governments are, however, limited to the spheres of regional planning, agriculture, hospitals, and electricity. Federal–state disputes are adjudged by the 14-member Constitutional Court.

Belgium (N & W Europe) pop. 10.1 m (WR 74) area 0.031 m sq km/0.012 m sq miles (WR 136)
cultural and linguistic
The northern people are mainly Flemings, of Teutonic stock, speaking Flemish, while those of the south are chiefly Walloons, of Latin stock, speaking French, while the capital, Brussels, has a mixed, cosmopolitan population. From 1980 northern Flanders and southern Wallonia had regional 'sub-governments', then in 1993 the constitution was amended to create a federation of three, mainly autonomous, regions, Brussels, Flanders, and Wallonia.

Bosnia-Herzegovina (C, E, & S Europe) pop. 3.6 m (WR 120) area 0.051 m sq km/0.020 m sq miles (WR 124)
historical, ethnic, and cultural
The state is one of the remaining pieces of the former multi-ethnic federal Yugoslavia. Following the refusal of the Serbs to accept Muslim-Croat-Serb power-sharing, the Muslim and Croat leaders agreed in 1994 to form a federation of eight cantons, each with a significant degree of local autonomy. A new Muslim-Croat and Serb federation was agreed in 1995.

Brazil (S America) pop. 153.7 m (WR 5) area 8.512 m sq km/3.287 m sq miles (WR 5)
geographical and cultural
The size of the country and distribution of the population favored federalism. The land mass is greater than continental United States, minus Alaska. Each of the 26 states has a single chamber assembly, elected governor, and constitution. In addition, Brasília is a federal district. There is a 16-member Supreme Court to decide on federal–state conflicts. The body is viewed, however, as strongly susceptible to presidential influence. The new constitution, adopted in 1988, enhanced states' powers and their tax-raising capabilities vis-à-vis the federal government, so that half of the federal tax take is now devolved further down the line. This strengthened what was previously a comparatively weak federal system.

Canada (N America) pop. 29.4 m (WR 33) area 9.971 m sq km/3.850 m sq miles (WR 2)
geographical, historical, and cultural
The size of the country and the wide cultural mix created strong regional differences. Historically, the nation was created by the confederation of four British colonies in 1867. Six other former colonies joined the Dominion between 1870 and 1949. The ten resulting provinces have their own assemblies and elected premiers. They can frame their own civil laws and have control of education policy. The nine-member Supreme Court rules on federal–state constitutional disputes.

continues

Federal states in the contemporary world — Table 6

The Comoros (C & S Africa) pop. 0.6 m (WR 155) area 0.002 m sq km/0.0008 m sq miles (WR 167)
geographical and historical
This state is a group of three islands which came together. Each island has its own elected governor and island assembly, with partial administrative and legislative autonomy.

Ethiopia (C & S Africa) pop. 54.9 m (WR 22) area 1.106 m sq km/0.427 m sq miles (WR 26)
historical, cultural, and ethnic
In recognition of the country's ethnic and cultural diversity, in 1952 it became a federation but returned to unitary status in 1962. With the secession of Eritrea, and the acceptance that other regions might seek similar independence, in 1994 the country returned to federalism, based on nine ethnically distinct states, each with a significant degree of autonomy. In making the change, the constitution unusually gave any state the right to secede through a popular referendum.

Germany (N & W Europe) pop. 81.4 m (WR 12) area 0.357 m sq km /0.138 m sq miles(WR 61)
historical and partly artificial
The Weimar Republic, carrying on earlier German Empire traditions, had a weak form of federalism which was destroyed by the Hitler regime. Under United States' influence it was revived in 1945, as a means of providing a check against the possible future abuse of central authority. With unification of the West and East, in 1990, the federal structure was retained. There are 16 states (Länder), each with its own constitution, elected assembly and government headed by a minister-president, and substantial-sized civil service. The states have original powers in education, police, and local government matters and substantial local tax-raising powers, and receive assigned shares of federal revenue accruing from value-added tax (VAT) and income tax. They are responsible for carrying out the administration of federal matters and account for a half of total government spending in the federal republic. Federal–state disputes are policed by an independent 16-member Federal Constitutional Court. In practice, however, German federalism is largely consensual in character, based around the striking of pragmatic committee-room deals between senior federal and state politicians and civil servants. For this reason, the term 'bureaucratic federalism' is frequently employed to describe the German federal system.

India (Asia) pop. 918.6 m (WR 2) area 3.287 m sq km/1.268 m sq miles (WR 7)
geographical, historical, and cultural
The land mass makes it the second largest state in Asia and historically the country was apportioned during the British period into separate provinces, with specified areas of legislative and fiscal autonomy, and princely states, each owing separate allegiance to the Crown. Today there are 25 self-governing states, organized primarily on language lines, and seven 'Union territories'. Each state has its own elected assembly, council of ministers, and chief minister. There is also a figurehead governor appointed by the federal president. The states have primary control over health, agriculture, education, police, and local government. Overall, however, although relatively strong in comparative terms, particularly when non-Congress parties control state assemblies, Indian federalism remains weighted towards the federal government, which has sole control of income tax, the states relying on land and sale taxes and federal grants for their revenue. The government at the center also has the power to impose direct 'President's Rule' in any state during a period of turmoil. A substantially independent 18-member Supreme Court adjudges federal–state constitutional conflicts.

Malaysia (Asia) pop. 20.1 m (WR 46) area 0.330 m sq km/0.127 m sq miles (WR 64)
historical and cultural
The country is a federation of 11 separate states and two British colonies which were brought together into a federation between 1963 and 1965. Each state has its own constitution, elected assembly, led by a chief minister and cabinet, and head of state. The states, however, have only limited original powers in the spheres of land and natural-resource management and are reliant upon the federal government for almost all of their funds. Federal–state constitutional disputes are ruled upon by a traditionally independent Supreme Court. This has, however, been subject to mounting central political pressure, exerted by the prime minister and monarch, during recent years.

Mexico (C America & Caribbean) pop. 93.0 m (WR 11) area 1.958 m sq km 0.756 m sq miles (WR 14)
geographical and partly imitative
The size of the country made a federal system sensible in geographical terms and also the United States' constitution was seen as an attractive model to copy. The 31 states have their own elected Chamber of Deputies, governors, and constitutions. In most states most powers reside with the governor who is pre-selected by the dominant Institutional Revolutionary Party's (PRI) inner-council. For this reason, Mexico remains, in practical terms, a significantly centralized state. For similar reasons, the Supreme Court is subject to effective PRI control.

continues

Federal states in the contemporary world

Table 6

Micronesia, Federated States of (Oceania) pop. 0.104 m (WR 176) area 0.0007 m sq km/0.0003 m sq miles (WR 172)
geographical and historical
The dispersed nature of the state, consisting of hundreds of islands, mostly uninhabited, scattered across the South Pacific, meant a political federation was inevitable. The federation consists of four states, each with its own constitution, providing for a governor and legislature. Each state enjoys considerable freedom under a federal executive president who coordinates and directs policy.

Nigeria (C & S Africa) pop. 108.5 m (WR 10) area 0.924 m sq km/0.357 m sq miles (WR 31)
geographical, historical, and cultural
The recognition of tribal and religious differences, particularly between the north and southeast, which culminated in civil war between 1967 and 1970, has been made in a federal system. Prior to independence, Nigeria was divided, in accordance with the 1946 'Richards constitution', into three semi-autonomous regions. These became four in 1963, 12 in 1967, 19 in 1979, 21 in 1987, and 36 in 1993. There is also the Federal Capital Territory. At present, each state is under the control of a military governor appointed by the central Armed Forces Ruling Council.

Pakistan (Asia) pop. 126.6 m (WR 7) area 0.796 m sq km/0.307 m sq miles (WR 35)
historical and cultural
The absorption of 12 princely states into independent Pakistan in 1948 was achieved by recognizing their earlier history and creating a federal structure of four provinces. These provinces exhibit strong cultural and ethnic distinctions and rivalries. They are administered by centrally appointed governors and local governments drawn from elected provincial assemblies.

Russian Federation (C, E, & S Europe) pop. 148.0 m (WR 6) area 17.075 m sq km/6.593 m sq miles (WR 1)
historical, geographical, and cultural
The federal system was established by the Soviet Union in 1922, allowing national minorities to be recognized while maintaining the unity of the state through the party machine. The Russian Federation now includes 21 republics. Sixteen of them were autonomous republics during the communist period, four were formerly autonomous regions (oblasts), while the last, the Ingushetia republic, was newly created in 1992. The unit called Russia comprises those parts of the Russian Federation that are not included within any of the other 21 republics and, with five-sixths of the Federation's total population, is divided into 68 administrative regions (oblasts and krais) and autonomous territories and districts, which have considerable devolved authority. The republics have, in theory, a free hand in the welfare and social spheres, as well as the right of secession but this freedom is sometimes overridden in practice.

St Kitts (Christopher) and Nevis (C America & Caribbean) pop. 0.041 m (WR 185) area 0.0003 m sq km/0.0001 m sq miles (WR 185)
geographical and historical
The state is a unique union of two islands which are the residue of what was to have been a wider West Indies federation. Nevis Island, with its own elected assembly, prime minister, and cabinet, retains the option to secede.

Sudan (C & S Africa) pop. 28.9 m (WR 34) area 2.506 m sq km/0.016 m sq miles (WR 10)
geographical and cultural
In recognition of the country's geographical and cultural diversity, in 1994 a federation of 26 states was created, each with its own governor, assisted by state ministers, appointed by the federal president. However, with the military still powerful, the durability of this constitutional arrangement must be in doubt.

Switzerland (N & W Europe) pop. 7.0 m (WR 91) area 0.041 m sq km/0.016 m sq miles (WR 131)
historical and cultural
The state is a federation of 26 cantons (including six half-cantons), or political units, dating back to the late 13th century. The cantons also reflect the cultural diversity of a country divided between German-, French-, Italian-, and Romansch-speaking communities and between Catholic majority and Protestant majority areas. Each canton has its own constitution, legislative assembly, and government, with substantial powers in socio-economic spheres such as education, environmental issues, tourism, transport, and police affairs. Cantons also have protected sources of finance and the ability, through the successful use of referenda, to effectively veto federal policies.

United Arab Emirates (M East & N Africa) pop. 2.4 m (WR 134) area 0.084 m sq km/0.032 m sq miles (WR 113)
historical
This is a loose federation of seven sheikhdoms which were under British protection between 1892 and 1971. Each sheikh is an hereditary and absolute ruler in his own emirate.

continues

Federal states in the contemporary world — Table 6

United States (N America) pop. 265.3 m (WR 3) area 9.373 m sq km/3.619 m sq miles (WR 4)
historical and geographical
The federal system resulted from the voluntary coming together of the original 13 British colonies after the War of Independence (1776-83). The state developed by expanding its federal membership and the structure also usefully recognizes the geographical and cultural diversity of the country. Each of the 50 states that presently exist has its own constitution, assembly, elected governor, and supreme court. The federal government has responsibility for defense and foreign affairs and the authority to coordinate 'inter-state concerns'. A liberal interpretation of what the latter phrase might constitute has resulted in a steady expansion in federal government interests. State governments remain, however, influential bodies, framing much of their own civil and criminal law; being substantially involved in health, educational, and welfare affairs; and raising more than three-quarters of their funds from state property sales and, in some cases, local income taxes. Federal–state constitutional disputes are adjudged by the independent nine-member Supreme Court.

Venezuela (S America) pop. 21.2 m (WR 44) area 0.912 m sq km/0.352 m sq miles (WR 32)
historical, cultural, and imitative
The federal system recognizes the historical and cultural differences in the country but also reflects admiration for the US model, the country having been called the United States of Venezuela until 1953. It is divided into 22 states (estados), each with its own elected assembly and executive governor. Since, however, the governor is appointed by the federal president and the states are heavily dependent upon the center for revenue resources, the federal system remains weak in practice. The adjudicatory supreme court is heavily susceptible to political influence.

Yugoslavia (C, E, & S Europe) pop. 10.5 m (WR 67) area 0.102 m sq km/0.039 m sq miles (WR 106)
historical and cultural
Formerly a socialist federation of six republics, following the breakaway of Slovenia, Croatia, Bosnia-Herzegovina, and Macedonia in 1991-92, a new constitution was adopted in 1992 for the 'rump federation' of the republics of Serbia and Montenegro, the federal structure recognizing the historical independence of the different national minorities and religious groupings. The present federal republic consists of the two republics of Montenegro and Serbia and, within Serbia, the autonomous provinces of Vojvodina and Kosovo-Metohija. Each republic and autonomous province has its own elected assembly, although the Kosovo assembly was dissolved in 1990 by the government of the republic of Serbia. Within each republic and province there are locally elected councils. There is a Constitutional Court to adjudge federal–state disputes.

* In brackets are the world rankings (WR) of these states in terms of population and area.

In Australia, for example, the states are dependent on the federal government for about 60% of their revenue, and even in the United States, where the clearest distinction between central and local power is made, the states rely on indirect sales taxes which are much less buoyant and stable than the direct income tax which forms the bulk of federal government revenue.

At the other extreme, in a unitary state such as the United Kingdom local authorities are entirely the creatures of parliament, which is controlled by the party in power, and dependent on central government not only for the bulk of their income but for their very existence. The abolition, in 1986, of a whole tier of local government, the metropolitan county councils, including the Greater London Council (GLC), is evidence of the disproportionate distribution of power in the United Kingdom. However, the creation in 1998 and 1999 of new assemblies in Wales and Northern Ireland, a Scottish parliament, and legislation to restore a London council with, for the first time, an elected mayor, has begun to redress this balance of power.

2.9 The role of the judiciary

Most constitutions speak, directly or indirectly, about the supremacy of law. This is generally seen as the guarantee of personal liberty and the chief protection against the overweening power of the state. Clearly the law of the land is the law enacted, and whether or not the laws which are passed are fair is a matter which the political system, as a dynamic entity, must determine.

However, once a law has been enacted it is the role of the judiciary to ensure that it is fairly enforced, and in practice this means more than just adjudicating in disputes between individuals and groups or between them and the state. It also involves interpreting the law. Since it is virtually impossible to construct a law which is

Unitary states with decentralized features **Table 7**

State	Form of decentralization
Bolivia	9 departments with appointed prefects
Burkina Faso	25 provinces
Burma	14 states and divisions
China	21 provinces, the Hong Kong Special Administrative Region (SAR), and five 'autonomous regions', including Tibet (see Part III)
Denmark	mainland, Faroe Islands and Greenland (see Part III) are administered separately and all are represented in the single chamber Folketing
Dominican Republic	31 provinces
Ecuador	21 provinces
Finland	Åland Islands are a self-governing province
France	22 elected regional councils, influential in the economic planning process, and 96 department councils. Corsica (see Part III) has its own assembly
Georgia	2 autonomous republics: Abkhazia and Adzharia
Haiti	9 departments
Indonesia	24 provinces, a metropolitan district, and two autonomous districts, each with a governor
Israel	since 1993, Palestinians living in the occupied territories of Gaza and the West Bank of the Jordan have enjoyed partial autonomy
Italy	20 regions with elected councils; five enjoy a 'special status'
Kiribati	elected councils on each inhabited island, enjoying considerable autonomy
Moldova	the Gagauz and Dnestr regions have special autonomous status
Netherlands	11 provinces with appointed governors and elected councils
Palau (Belau)	16 states, each with an elected legislature and governor
Papua New Guinea	20 provinces with consultative assemblies
Philippines	12 regions and 75 provinces. Muslim Mindanao is an autonomous region
Poland	16 provinces
Portugal	the Azores and Madeira (see Part III) are autonomous regions, each with an elected regional assembly and an appointed chair
San Marino	9 partially self-governing 'castles'
São Tomé e Príncipe	Príncipe has internal autonomy
Senegal	10 regions with appointed governors and elected assemblies
Solomon Islands	7 provincial assemblies
South Africa	9 regions with elected councils.
Spain	17 regional autonomous communities with elected parliaments and governments. Each has the constitutional right to self-rule
Sri Lanka	8 elected provincial councils
Tanzania	Zanzibar has its own constitution and House of Representatives. The state constitution prescribes that when the president comes from the mainland the vice president must come from Zanzibar, and vice versa. There are 25 regional commissioners
Trinidad and Tobago	Tobago Island has its own House of Assembly, with full self-government since 1987
Tuvalu	each inhabited atoll has its own elected Island Council
Ukraine	the Crimea has been afforded a special status
United Kingdom	Channel Islands and their dependencies (see Part III) have their own assemblies and laws. The Isle of Man (see Part III) has its own lieutenant-governor and legislative council. Northern Ireland has an elected assembly and executive since 1998, and there is a Welsh assembly and Scottish parliament, since elections in 1999
Vanuatu	6 elected regional councils
Zambia	each of the 9 provinces is represented on the president's advisory body, the House of Chiefs

completely unequivocal, the task of judicial interpretation is a continual process and of considerable importance. To have an independent and unbiased judiciary is, therefore, vital if personal liberty is to be protected.

Judges are generally guaranteed their independence in a constitution by a provision which ensures their continuance in office during 'good behaviour'. Although independence and security of tenure usually apply to judges in the higher courts, in lower courts this is not always true. In many US states, for example, members of the state judiciary are elected and may be dismissed by the people who elected them. A notable recent example was the California voters' rejection of Chief Justice Rose Bird in November 1986 for alleged 'liberalism' in her conduct of affairs. This makes judicial office holders responsive to public opinion, but is not always the best prescription for justice. In most one-party states, as well as in many Latin American countries, it is the party which chooses the judges for election by the assembly, another process clearly open to abuse.

In the United Kingdom the judiciary is appointed by the government of the day, and although the Lord Chancellor, as the head of the judiciary, provides advice, to ensure the quality of the appointees and, in theory at least, to avoid political bias, it should not be forgotten that Lord Chancellors are politicians and leading members of the government. The Law Lords, sitting in the House of Lords, serve as a final court of appeal. As witnessed in their decision in 1999 to approve the extradition of Chile's former dictator, General Pinochet, to Spain to face criminal charges, decisions of the Law Lords can have great political significance. In the United States, Supreme Court judges are appointed, subject to Senate approval, which in recent years has by no means been automatic, by the president and, inevitably, subject to some political influence. Nor is it possible to say that any judge, however qualified and experienced, can be completely free from the bias which stems from his or her own social background and political inclinations.

A constitution can, therefore, go some way towards ensuring an independent judiciary but it can never guarantee complete impartiality. In practice most constitutions go little further than setting out the structure of the judicial system, with a few adding something a little more specific. The constitution of the Republic of Algeria states: 'Judges obey only the law. They defend the socialist revolution', and in Cameroon and Gabon the president is given the task of ensuring the independence of the judiciary.

An important role of judges is, of course, to protect the constitution itself and even in a state, such as the United Kingdom, which has no codified constitution, they are required and expected to uphold the rule of law. In federal states, as has been noted, the judiciary's task of upholding the constitution is particularly significant in that they have to interpret as well as enforce, so as to preserve the intended balance between the center and the localities. In quasi-federal Spain there is a Constitutional Court with this specific task, as there is in Italy and, though the body is somewhat less influential, in France also. The similar top level judicial bodies which exist in fully federal states are set out in Table 6.

State or established religions Table 8

Islam *(25)*
Afghanistan, Algeria, Bahrain, Bangladesh, Brunei, The Comoros, Egypt, Iran, Iraq, Jordan, Kuwait, Malaysia, The Maldives, Mauritania, Mauritius, Morocco, Oman, Pakistan, Qatar, Saudi Arabia, Somalia, Sudan, Tunisia, United Arab Emirates, Yemen

Roman Catholicism *(12)*
Argentina*, Colombia*, Costa Rica, Dominican Republic, Haiti, Malta, Panama*, Paraguay**, Peru**, Seychelles*, Vatican City State, Venezuela*

Evangelical Lutheran/Protestant Church *(6)*
Denmark, England & Scotland, Iceland, Norway, Sweden, Tuvalu

Greek Orthodox Church *(1)*
Greece

Judaism *(1)*
Israel

Buddhism *(4)*
Bhutan, Cambodia, Sri Lanka, Thailand

Hinduism *(1)*
Nepal

Pancasila *(1)****
Indonesia

* Quasi-state religion.
** Roman Catholicism is the official religion, although the constitution guarantees religious freedom.
*** A national secular–state ideology, stressing unity and social justice, which is a compulsory belief for all social organizations.

2.10 Religion and the state

Some states have adopted a particular belief as the national religion and enshrined this in their constitutions. Table 8 sets out the current established or state religions. In all, 51 states fall into this category, almost half of which have Islam as the state religion. Fourteen of the states where Islam is established as the state religion are situated in the Middle East and North Africa, six in Asia, and five in Central and Southern Africa. Roman Catholicism is the second most widely officially established religion, with a strong regional bias towards Central and South America.

2.11 Unusual constitutional features

Some constitutions contain unusual or unique provisions, most of them being products of the country's history, geography, or social structure.

The Mexican constitution, reflecting the country's history of exploitation by the wealthy and powerful, places restrictions on the activities of the Church, large landowners, and foreign organizations. Following a record of unequal educational opportunities, the constitution also stresses the importance attached to state education. In similar vein, the 1992 constitution of Paraguay provides for agrarian reform in its Chapter 6, but also guarantees the autonomy of the army.

Because of the small size of the country, the constitution of Nauru permits the president, who combines the roles of head of state and head of government, to take on additional ministerial portfolios himself in a cabinet of only five or six.

To ensure a balance between the religious communities, the Lebanese constitution prescribes that if the president is a Christian the prime minister must be a Muslim, and vice versa.

The constitution of South Africa specifies that parties which secure at least 5% of the national vote are entitled to a proportionate number of ministerial portfolios, while the constitution of Mongolia specifically permits the imposition of forced labor.

The different geographical bases required of the president and vice president by the Tanzanian constitution have already been mentioned.

Finally, the newest Brazilian constitution, whose 245 articles and 70 clauses took 19 months to be scrutinized and approved by the federal Congress, contains the most detailed statement of specific social and economic rights currently in force in a noncommunist regime. These include a prescribed 44 hours for the working week and stipulated rights to five days of paternity leave and extended maternity leave.

In terms of length, currently two of the world's longest constitutions are those of India (1950), which contains 397 articles and nine schedules, and Colombia (1991), which has 380 articles.

2.12 How important are constitutions?

Are constitutions merely statements of a grand design and, as such, removed from the realities of the political process? In the final analysis surely naked, military power must prevail? The answers to these questions, based on recent experience, must be yes and no.

In liberal democratic countries with long established codified constitutions, such as the United States, there can be no doubt about their supreme significance. The content and importance of the American Constitution are made clear to every school child and the newest immigrants will cherish the freedoms it proclaims. Specific provisions are frequently quoted in contemporary life. Both Rear Admiral John Poindexter and Lieutenant-Colonel Oliver North pleaded the Fifth Amendment, the right to remain silent in a criminal case, when required to testify at the 1986 'Irangate' hearings. With the Watergate and Monica Lewinsky affairs, all Americans must be aware of the impeachment powers contained in Articles I-II of the Constitution.

Even in a country such as the United Kingdom, with an uncodified constitution, constitutional controversies arise over such matters as the powers of the House of Lords, devolution, parliamentary sovereignty vis-à-vis the European Union, electoral reform, and the possibility of introducing a Bill of Rights.

Admittedly, given the necessary political will and military might, any constitution can be suspended or annulled, and at the present time there are about ten which fall into this category. Nevertheless, the aura of legitimacy which, accurately or not, a constitution brings is almost universally sought, even by clearly despotic regimes.

Recommended reading

Bogdanor, V (ed.) *Constitutions in Democratic Politics*, Gower, 1988

Burgess, M (ed.) *Federalism and Federation in Western Europe*, Croom Helm, 1985

Burgess, M and Gagnon, A-G *Comparative Federalism and Federation: Competing Traditions and Future Directions*, Harvester Wheatsheaf, 1993

Dunn, J (ed.) *Democracy: The Unfinished Journey, 508 BC to AD 1993*, Oxford University Press, 1992

Elazar, D J (ed.) *Federal Systems of the World: A Handbook of Federal, Confederal and Autonomy Arrangements*, 2nd edn., Longman, 1994

Finer, S E, Bogdanor, V, and Rudden, B *Comparing Constitutions*, Clarendon Press, 1995

Finley, M I *Politics in the Ancient World*, Cambridge University Press, 1994

Griffith, J *The Politics of the Judiciary*, 5th edn., Fontana, 1997

Hesse, J J and Wright, V (eds.) *Federalizing Europe? The Costs, Benefits and Pre-Conditions of Federal Political Systems*, Oxford University Press, 1996

Hicks, U K *Federalism: Failure and Success, A Comparative Study*, Macmillan, 1978

Hodder-Williams, R *The Politics of the US Supreme Court*, Allen & Unwin, 1980

Lane, J E *Constitutions and Political Theory*, Manchester University Press, 1996

Mueller, D C *Constitutional Democracy*, Oxford University Press, 1996

Norton, A *International Handbook of Local and Regional Government: A Comparative Analysis of Advanced Democracies*, Edward Elgar, 1994

Simons, B W (ed.) *The Constitutions of the Communist World*, Sijthoff & Noordhoff, 1980

CHAPTER 3

The Ideological Bases

3.1 The nature of ideology

We are now entering the treacherous world of ideologies where we are as likely to be misled as informed. Nevertheless, it is an area which must be explored if we are to make distinctions between political systems looking not just at their institutional bases but, much more deeply, at the cultures and attitudes which have shaped them.

It is not particularly important to the ordinary citizen that there is a two-chamber assembly or that the head of state is a king or a president. But whether the economy is planned from the center or left to market forces, or whether there is a choice of political parties to support or only one, is important to the individual citizen.

Identifying the ideology on which a political system is based, or influenced by, will help us penetrate the façade of institutions and slogans, but we must first clarify what we mean by ideology.

It is generally recognized that the political system of the Soviet Union had its theoretical beginning in the writings of Karl Marx (1818–83) and Friedrich Engels (1820–95), subsequently developed and adapted by Vladimir Ilyich Lenin (1870–1924), and that the current regime in Iran is motivated by the religion of Islam, through its Shi'ite branch, but what about the system in the United Kingdom? Is it not too evolutionary and pragmatic to have any substantial theoretical or philosophical basis?

It depends on how we construe ideology. 'Ideology' is a much abused and overused word. In recent years it has, more often than not, been associated with zealots and fanatics. The spread of international terrorism has built up a picture of ruthless groups imbued with a single-mindedness which rejects customary morality so as to advance the aims of some particular ideology. An ideology has too often come to mean blind faith and irrationality. This is too narrrow an interpretation, and indeed a distortion, of the word.

The definition which will be used for our purposes is one which might be found in any good, general dictionary. An ideology is a body of ideas which reflects the beliefs and values of a nation and its political system. Such a definition is wide enough to encompass a variety of political cultures, from the mature, rational attitudes to be found in many states in what we call the West, to the more inspirational, and often emotive, ideas found in countries with less experienced political systems.

Ideologies can be individually or socially inspired. More often than not they are both. Politicians are essentially doers rather than thinkers, even though some of them would have the public believe they are both. They adopt and use philosophies as a platform for political action.

But why and how does a philosophy eventually become so much a part of the beliefs and values of a country that it can be said to be the ideology on which its political system is based? Initially, it usually results from a revolution of one kind or another and then proceeds through a process of what might be called evolutionary absorption.

For example, the '*ancien régime*' of 17th- and 18th-century France was ended abruptly by the Revolution of 1789. Opposition to the profligacy and inequity of the absolute monarchy, allied to the democratic message of the 'Enlightenment' philosophers and writers such as Jean-Jacques Rousseau (1712–78), brought about the dramatic change. Then, over a much longer period, the forces which had initially impelled the revolution were modified and absorbed into the French psyche so as to become the ideology which now underlies its political system.

Other writers, such as John Stuart Mill (1806–73) in England, expanded and amended Rousseau's concept of liberal democracy into a more practical idea of representative government, while in other countries French and British experience was adapted to suit differing social and political needs. Thus, liberal democracy became the ideology of a wide family of nations.

The inequities of the Tsarist regime in Russia also ended abruptly in the Revolution of 1917, with, again, practical discontent allying itself with theoretical justification through the writings of Marx and Engels and the 'praxis' of Lenin. The communist ideology of the

Soviet Union was, over the years, adopted and modified by another, mixed family of nations. Then, in the later 1980s, the inequities and inefficiency of the Soviet style of communism, with its emphasis on the command economy and the repression of individual thought, became apparent and produced another revolution, not entirely bloodless, but less violent than many might have anticipated.

In attempting to identify different ideologies and relate them to individual nation-states we realize that the choices are necessarily somewhat arbitrary and, indeed, a purist might well argue that each nation has its own unique ideology and that any classification is misleading. We reject this argument because we believe that, if accepted, the very notion of comparative politics would be questionable and a study such as this would have to be abandoned. Thus, accepting the arbitrary nature of the choice, an eightfold grouping is offered, in the belief that any classification is preferable to none at all. At the same time, some of the deficiencies in the process should be noted.

The first is that the ideology associated with particular countries is, inevitably, a 'broad brush' description of something more subtle and complicated than the simple 'label' would suggest. The second defect is that a static situation has been assumed. This may be acceptable as far as long-established states, with stable political systems, are concerned, but less so for newer states whose systems are still in flux. Where such conditions are believed to exist an appropriate caveat will be added, with several countries, notably Afghanistan, Bosnia-Herzegovina, Liberia, and Somalia, currently in transition.

With the foregoing reservations, the following ideologies will be identified and used:

1. Liberal democracy;
2. Emergent democracy;
3. Communism;
4. Nationalistic socialism;
5. Authoritarian nationalism;
6. Military authoritarianism;
7. Islamic nationalism;
8. Absolutism.

A possible ninth new ideology, that of political Populism, began also to emerge during the 1990s. It is characterized by an emphasis on charismatic individual leadership, rather than politics based around party machines; skilful use of the television media; direct appeals to the populace via frequent referenda; anti-establishment rhetoric; mobilization on ethnic or nationalist lines; and, in the economic and social spheres, the offering of 'simple solutions to complicated problems'. Populism's roots lie in the Midwest-based People's Party, formed by agrarian interests, which was a force in US politics during the 1890s. A century later, its standard bearers have included: the maverick billionaire H Ross Perot, who contested the US presidential elections of 1992 and 1996 as an independent; the Reform Party in Canada; the media tycoon Silvio Berlusconi, who briefly became prime minister in Italy in 1994; the ultra-nationalist xenophobe Vladimir Zhirinovsky, whose Liberal Democrats attracted nearly a quarter of the national vote in Russia's December 1993 parliamentary elections; Alexander Lukashenko, who was elected President of Belarus in July 1994; and Hugo Chavez, who was elected president of Venezuela in December 1998. Populism has begun to put down roots most firmly in those states recently freed from communist monism which are finding the transition to a competitive market economy and multiparty liberal democracy particularly painful and difficult. However, it is currently not sufficiently established as an ideological base to merit inclusion in this volume as a ninth category.

3.2 Liberal democracy

Liberal democracy is a product of two concepts: the right to representative government and the right to enjoy individual freedom. The term 'liberal' is derived from the first concept and 'democracy' from the second. The tests for a political system claiming to be based on this philosophy would, therefore, seem to be the extent to which the government truly represents the mass of the people and the extent to which individuals' rights are protected.

In practice the essential features of a liberal democratic system can be identified as:

1. Representative institutions based on majority rule, through free elections and a choice of political parties;
2. Limitations on the power of government, implying a pluralistic society in which the state is not all-embracing and exists alongside other, sometimes competing, interests;
3. Accountability of the government to the electorate;
4. Freedom of expression and assembly, and personal freedom, guaranteed by an independent judiciary;
5. A skilled and impartial permanent public service

Regional distribution of political regimes — Table 9

Regime	Asia	Central America & Caribbean	Central, Eastern, & Southern Europe	Central & Southern Africa	Middle East & North Africa	North America	Northern & Western Europe	Oceania	South America	Total
Lib-dem	5	17	3	2	2	2	21	13	9	74
Em-dem	10	3	19	30	4	0	1	1	3	71
Communist	4	1	0	0	0	0	0	0	0	5
Nat-soc	0	0	0	4	4	0	0	0	0	8
Auth-nat	5	0	3	4	0	0	0	0	0	12
Military	1	0	0	7	0	0	0	0	0	8
Islam-nat	1	0	0	0	1	0	0	0	0	2
Absolutist	2	0	0	1	7	0	1	1	0	12
Total	*28*	*21*	*25*	*48*	*18*	*2*	*23*	*15*	*12*	*192*

Combined area, population, and GDP (*c.* 1995)

Regime	Area (million sq km)	Population (millions)	GDP (US $'000 m)	Area (% share of world total)	Population (% share of world total)	GDP (% share of world total)
Lib-dem	57.0	2,405	23,855	42.9	42.7	86.2
Em-dem	45.2	1,479	2,303	34.0	26.3	8.3
Communist	10.4	1,327	940	7.8	23.5	3.4
Nat-soc	3.6	73	102	2.7	1.3	0.4
Auth-nat	4.4	99	85	3.3	1.8	0.3
Military	7.5	142	50	5.6	2.5	0.2
Islam-nat	2.3	78	85	1.7	1.4	0.3
Absolutist	2.6	33	240	2.0	0.5	0.9
Total	*133.0*	*5,636*	*27,660*	*100.0*	*100.0*	*100.0*

Lib-dem — Liberal democratic
Em-dem — Emergent democratic
Nat-soc — Nationalistic socialist
Auth-nat — Authoritarian nationalist
Islam-nat — Islamic nationalist
GDP — Gross domestic product

responsible to the government of the day and, through it, to the electorate.

Of the 192 states under examination 74 have been identified as having political systems founded on liberal democracy and they are listed in Table 11. They embrace 2.4 billion people, a figure which corresponds to 43% of the world's total population. The oldest and most stable liberal democracies are to be found in Northern and Western Europe, but by no means all, or even a majority, because, although its roots are European, it is an ideology which has been successfully exported to all parts of the world. Thus, there are 28

Socio-economic characteristics of political regimes (country averages *c.* 1991–95) Table 10

Regime	Per capita GDP (US$)*	Level of urbanization (%)**	Labor force in agriculture (%)**	Adult literacy rate (%)**	Human rights rating (%)**	Government defense spending (% of GDP)*
Lib-dem	9,916	62	21	88	80	1.9
Em-dem	1,557	44	46	66	61	3.5
Communist	708	40	50	87	25	8.4
Nat-soc	1,402	54	42	54	45	5.3
Auth-nat	858	43	41	78	47	3.5
Military	352	26	69	48	25	4.0
Islam-nat	1,085	39	50	39	25	6.3
Absolutist	7,347	59	28	66	44	7.2

* *c.* 1995.

** *c.* 1992.

Lib-dem	Liberal democratic
Em-dem	Emergent democratic
Nat-soc	Nationalistic socialist
Auth-nat	Authoritarian nationalist
Islam-nat	Islamic nationalist
GDP	Gross domestic product

liberal democracies in the Americas and 13 in Oceania. There is, however, a tendency, which is apparent from the national income data provided in Table 11, for this type of political system to flourish best in high-income, 'First World', states. Thus, liberal democracies, are found in 26 of the world's 'Top 30' countries in terms of per-capita incomes, but in only two of the 'Bottom 50'. Similarly, while 18 of the 20 most urbanized states in the world are liberal democracies, none of the top 30 states in terms of the proportion of the labor force employed in agriculture fall into this category. The 74 states with liberal democracies account for a staggering 86% of world GDP and, as Table 10 shows, have high levels of literacy and urbanization and low proportionate levels of government defense expenditure.

In compiling this list of liberal democratic states, the following seven markers have been looked for:

1. Evidence of constitutional government;
2. Evidence of free elections for assemblies and executives;
3. The active presence of more than one political party;
4. Evidence of checks and balances between the three elements of government: executive, legislative, and judicial;
5. Evidence of an independent judiciary;
6. Evidence of the protection of personal liberties through constitutional or other legal guarantees;
7. Evidence of stability in liberal democratic government.

Our test of stability is necessarily arbitrary. We have included those states where liberal democratic systems have been in place for more than 12 years, that is since before 1987. This 'stability' provides the opportunity for the new democratic system to be tested through at least three electoral cycles.

The states that are included in Table 11 include the seven markers listed above to varying degrees. An indicator of this is the 'Human Rights Rating', compiled by Charles Humana, which is displayed in Table 11. It is a composite measure which embraces various aspects of political and social liberties as of 1991. As a useful rule-of-thumb, a 'Human Rights Rating' of 70% or more is indicative of a political system that displays all seven features noted above. States with ratings below this tend to fail most commonly in markers 3 and 4, being characterized by effective dominance of the political

Liberal democractic systems (74) Table 11

Region/country	Year established	Per capita GDP (US$)*	Per capita GDP (world ranking)*	Human rights rating (%)**	Human rights rating (world ranking)**
Asia (5)					
India	1947	350	161	54	69
Japan	1946	39,720	4	82	33
Malaysia	1957	3,900	55	61	59
Singapore	1965	23,480	16	60	60
Sri Lanka	1948	710	135	47	82
Central America & Caribbean (17)					
Antigua	1981	6,970	45	N/A	N/A
Bahamas	1973	11,620	36	N/A	N/A
Barbados	1966	6,705	47	N/A	N/A
Belize	1981	2,700	76	N/A	N/A
Costa Rica	1948	2,900	71	90	21
Dominica	1978	3,060	66	N/A	N/A
Dominican Republic	1966	1,470	98	38	N/A
El Salvador	1983	1,610	94	53	72
Grenada	1984	2,970	68	N/A	N/A
Guatemala	1985	1,380	100	62	57
Honduras	1982	620	142	65	53
Jamaica	1962	1,525	95	72	43
Mexico	1917	3,275	62	64	56
St Kitts and Nevis	1983	5,170	50	N/A	N/A
St Lucia	1979	3,775	58	N/A	N/A
St Vincent	1979	2,280	80	N/A	N/A
Trinidad and Tobago	1962	3,860	56	84	29
Central, Eastern, & Southern Europe (3)					
Cyprus	1960	11,720	35	N/A	N/A
Greece	1974	9,640	39	87	26
Turkey	1982	2,770	74	44	85
Central & Southern Africa (2)					
Botswana	1966	3,035	67	79	37
Mauritius	1968	3,340	61	N/A	N/A
Middle East & North Africa (2)					
Egypt	1971	770	131	50	75
Israel	1958	16,320	27	76	39
North America (2)					
Canada	1867	19,600	20	94	15
United States	1776	26,800	9	90	21
Northern & Western Europe (21)					
Austria	1945	26,900	8	95	14
Belgium	1945	24,900	12	96	12
Denmark	1945	29,700	6	98	4
Finland	1917	20,650	18	99	1
France	1946	25,100	10	94	15
Germany	1949	27,600	7	98	4
Iceland	1944	24,500	13	N/A	N/A

continues

Liberal democractic systems (74) (continued) **Table 11**

Region/country	Year established	Per capita GDP (US$)*	Per capita GDP (world ranking)*	Human rights rating (%)**	Human rights rating (world ranking)**
Ireland	1937	14,600	29	94	15
Italy	1946	19,030	21	90	21
Liechtenstein	1921	46,200	1	N/A	N/A
Luxembourg	1944	40,870	3	N/A	N/A
Malta	1974	7,900	43	N/A	N/A
Monaco	1911	22,000	17	99	1
Netherlands	1945	23,940	14	98	4
Norway	1945	31,140	5	97	9
Portugal	1976	9,840	37	92	19
San Marino	1600	18,670	24	N/A	N/A
Spain	1978	13,480	32	87	26
Sweden	1809	23,900	15	98	4
Switzerland	1874	40,900	2	96	12
United Kingdom	1689	19,650	19	93	18
Oceania (13)					
Australia	1901	18,720	23	91	20
Kiribati	1979	920	121	N/A	N/A
Marshall Islands	1979	1,630	92	N/A	N/A
Micronesia	1979	2,067	86	N/A	N/A
Nauru	1968	16,000	28	N/A	N/A
New Zealand	1853	14,340	30	98	4
Palau	1981	1,765	89	N/A	N/A
Papua New Guinea	1975	1,220	106	70	47
Philippines	1986	1,050	116	72	43
Samoa (Western)	1962	1,120	113	N/A	N/A
Solomon Islands	1978	920	121	N/A	N/A
Tuvalu	1978	780	129	N/A	N/A
Vanuatu	1980	1,210	108	N/A	N/A
South America (9)					
Argentina	1983	8,150	42	84	28
Bolivia	1982	815	128	71	45
Brazil	1985	3,770	59	69	49
Colombia	1957	2,035	87	60	60
Ecuador	1979	1,425	99	83	30
Guyana	1966	600	143	N/A	N/A
Peru	1980	2,380	79	54	69
Uruguay	1985	5,200	49	90	21
Venezuela	1961	3,090	65	75	40

* *c.* 1995.

** *c.* 1991.

system by one ruling party, although opposition parties are officially allowed to function.

Two such classic examples are Mexico and Singapore, which, respectively, had 'Human Rights Ratings' of just 64% and 60% in 1991. In both these states, effective opposition movements are particularly weak, being hampered by alleged pro-government ballot-rigging in the first and by increasing direct harassment in the second. Despite this, however, in comparative terms, the degree of liberal freedom which is tolerated in these two countries remains tolerably high. Moreover, the longevity and stability of the PRI and PAP party regimes in place make alternative classification in the emergent democracy category inappropriate. A more accurate descriptive term for these two countries would, however, be 'restricted' or 'partial' liberal democracies. In Malaysia, where the UMNO has been in power since independence and also controls the legislatures of all but one of the federation's 13 states, the term liberal democracy is also somewhat 'restricted'. Similarly dominance by one party is a prominent feature of the political system of Egypt.

Table 12 sets out the average ages of liberal democratic regimes by regions of the world. This has been computed by calculating, for each state, how many years its liberal democratic regime had been functioning without interruption up to 1999 and then producing regional means. It shows North America, with two well entrenched liberal democratic political systems in Canada and the United States, to have the highest overall regional average, at 177 years, followed by Northern and Western Europe, at 91 years. Within Northern and Western Europe there are states such as San Marino and the United Kingdom with liberal democratic regimes which are even older than those of North America. However, the period of Nazi German occupation of France, the Benelux countries, and parts of Scandinavia, has meant that in many states in this region there has been uninterrupted liberal democracy for only half a century.

The world regions with the youngest liberal democracies are revealed to be Central, Eastern, and Southern Europe, South America, Central America and the Caribbean, and Africa. Many of the liberal democracies in these regions remain very much 'on trial'. In Central and South America, such has been the periodicity of lurches between liberty and military coercion in Argentina, Bolivia, Brazil, Ecuador, El Salvador, Guatemala, Honduras, Peru, and Uruguay that the term 'Latin Americanization' has been coined by political scientists. Indeed, as recently as May 1993 an attempt was made by President Jorge Serrano in Guatemala to revert to type and establish dictatorial rule. However, on this occasion, military support was not forthcoming and Serrano was deposed. In Peru, President Fujimori has ruled in alliance with the military since 1992.

The average ages, in 1999, of other regime types were: absolutist, 97 years; communist, 44 years; nationalistic socialist, 23 years; authoritarian nationalist, 11 years; Islamic nationalist, 13 years; military authoritarian, 7 years; and emergent democratic, 8 years.

Average age of liberal democratic regimes (in 1999) — **Table 12**

Region	Average age (years)
North America	178
Central & Southern Africa	32
Northern & Western Europe	92
Central America & the Caribbean	28
Asia	46
South America	24
Oceania	38
Central, Eastern, & Southern Europe	27
Middle East & North Africa	35
World average	56

3.3 Emergent democracy

The states identified as emergent democracies bear many of the characteristics of liberal democracies except evidence of stability in their political systems, the majority having experienced at least one nondemocratic coup or change of government at some time or other during the past decade. Some have enjoyed stable liberal democratic government for extensive periods only to revert to militaristic or other autocratic rule. Others, for example Indonesia and Nigeria, have emerged from a prolonged spell of autocracy in relatively recent years and it is still too early to judge how permanent the new regime will be. The criterion for inclusion as an emergent democracy is having a democratic system in place since 1987.

One of the most firmly established emergent democracies is that of South Korea, which is now over a decade old and exhibits improving human rights ratings. Also qualitatively high are the liberal democracies of the Central European states of the Czech Republic, Estonia, Hungary, Latvia, Lithuania, Poland, and Slovenia, drawing upon democratic traditions that had been frozen during half a century of communist control. Several of these states are candidates for entry into the European Union within the foreseeable future.

By contrast, the roots of democratic and civil freedoms have barely been planted in more recently emergent regimes, notably those in parts of Central and Eastern Europe and sub-Saharan Africa. In Central, Eastern, and Southern Europe, there are several states, notably Albania, Georgia, Macedonia, and Yugoslavia,

Emergent democratic systems (71) **Table 13**

Region/country	Year established	Per capita GDP (US$)*	Per capita GDP (world ranking)*	Human rights rating (%)**	Human rights rating (world ranking)**
Asia (10)					
Bangladesh	1990	240	175	59	63
Cambodia	1998	260	168	33	90
Indonesia	1999	990	119	34	89
Korea, South	1988	9,755	38	59	63
Kyrgyzstan	1991	690	137	N/A	N/A
Mongolia	1990	325	164	N/A	N/A
Nepal	1991	205	180	69	49
Pakistan	1988	475	148	42	86
Taiwan	1991	12,600	34	N/A	N/A
Thailand	1992	2,630	77	62	57
Central America & Caribbean (3)					
Haiti	1994	250	172	N/A	N/A
Nicaragua	1990	380	155	75	40
Panama	1989	2,750	75	81	35
Central, Eastern, & Southern Europe (19)					
Albania	1991	730	133	N/A	N/A
Bosnia-Herzegovina	1990	1,160	110	N/A	N/A
Bulgaria	1990	1,225	105	83	30
Croatia	1990	3,820	57	N/A	N/A
Czech Republic	1989	4,500	52	97	9
Estonia	1990	2,900	71	N/A	N/A
Georgia	1992	835	126	N/A	N/A
Hungary	1989	4,010	54	97	9
Latvia	1990	2,260	82	N/A	N/A
Lithuania	1990	2,265	81	N/A	N/A
Macedonia	1990	845	125	N/A	N/A
Moldova	1990	910	123	N/A	N/A
Poland	1989	2,790	73	83	30
Romania	1989	1,475	97	82	33
Russia	1990	2,240	83	54	69
Slovakia	1990	2,965	69	N/A	N/A
Slovenia	1990	8,410	40	N/A	N/A
Ukraine	1990	1,190	109	N/A	N/A
Yugoslavia	1990	1,520	96	55	68
Central & Southern Africa (30)					
Angola	1994	415	150	27	97
Benin	1991	380	155	90	21
Burkina Faso	1991	245	173	N/A	N/A
Cameroon	1991	670	139	56	66
Cape Verde	1991	875	124	N/A	N/A
Central African Republic	1995	350	161	N/A	N/A
Chad	1993	185	181	N/A	N/A
Côte d'Ivoire	1990	675	138	75	40
Ethiopia	1993	105	191	13	106
Gabon	1990	2,930	70	N/A	N/A
Gambia	1997	330	163	N/A	N/A
Ghana	1992	385	154	53	72

continues

Emergent democratic systems (71) (continued) Table 13

Region/country	Year established	Per capita GDP (US$)*	Per capita GDP (world ranking)*	Human rights rating (%)**	Human rights rating (world ranking)**
Guinea	1993	555	146	N/A	N/A
Kenya	1997	260	168	46	83
Lesotho	1993	765	132	N/A	N/A
Liberia	1997	670	139	N/A	N/A
Madagascar	1992	225	177	N/A	N/A
Malawi	1994	175	183	33	90
Mali	1992	230	176	N/A	N/A
Mauritania	1991	475	148	N/A	N/A
Mozambique	1994	85	192	53	72
Namibia	1990	2,070	85	N/A	N/A
Nigeria	1999	265	167	49	77
São Tomé	1990	360	159	N/A	N/A
Seychelles	1991	6,625	48	N/A	N/A
Sierra Leone	1998	175	183	67	51
South Africa	1993	3,240	63	50	75
Tanzania	1995	165	186	41	87
Togo	1993	325	164	48	80
Zambia	1991	395	153	57	65
Middle East & North Africa (4)					
Algeria	1995	1,630	92	66	52
Lebanon	1990	3,660	60	N/A	N/A
Morocco	1992	1,100	114	56	66
Yemen	1994	260	168	49	77
Northern & Western Europe (1)					
Andorra	1993	18,750	22	99	1
Oceania (1)					
Fiji	1990	2,440	78	N/A	N/A
South America (3)					
Chile	1990	430	53	80	36
Paraguay	1993	1,735	90	70	47
Suriname	1991	3,110	64	N/A	N/A

* c. 1995.

** c. 1991.

which currently stand midway between the emergent democratic and authoritarian nationalist categories, while Bosnia-Herzegovina has been in an anarchic condition, crippled by ethnic divisions. In Africa, which was dominated when the first edition of this title was published by one-party nationalistic socialist and authoritarian nationalist regimes, there has been a wave of apparent democratization from the early 1990s. Encouraged by changes in Central and Eastern Europe and by the prompting by Western donors of economic aid, the formation of opposition parties has been tolerated in the states shown in Table 13 and multiparty elections have been held. However, in some of the states, for example Cameroon, Gabon, and Mauritania, there have still been charges of election-rigging and intimidation of opposition candidates in what could be viewed as 'façade elections'. Changes of government have occurred in Benin, Cape Verde, Mali, São Tomé, South Africa, and Zambia. However, in some countries there is still a close identification of the ruling party with the state, and the real test of multiparty democracy will come when this ruling party is defeated at the polls and expected to relinquish power.

Several African, Asian, Middle Eastern, and South European states, notably Algeria, Angola, Cambodia, Georgia, Lebanon, Mozambique, and Yemen, still face the problem of continuing insurgencies by rebel groups and ethnic fragmentation is acute in some countries. For this reason, the armed forces, in these and several Asian and American states, remain influential background watchdog arbiters who might be tempted to reassert direct control in the near future if the democratization process moves ahead in a direction which sharply conflicts with their own interests. Indeed, there have been recent attempted coups in Cambodia, Cape Verde, Chad, Paraguay, and São Tomé, while in Lebanon the Syrian army is the dominant force. At present many states in Central and Southern Africa are situated, most accurately, at various positions on a continuum between the emergent democratic and the nationalistic socialist and authoritarian nationalist ideological categories. However, the existence of multiparty politics, despite its fragile, nascent form, has resulted in the tentative inclusion of these states in this ideological category.

Despite these clear variations in degrees of 'democratization', all the states categorized as emergent democracies might usefully be described as liberal democracies on trial, and the 71 so identified are listed in Table 13. The dates of origin of the current regimes are also shown. The states included embrace nearly 1.5 billion people, or 26% of the world's population. Thirty-one are middle-high income states, situated predominantly in Central and Eastern Europe and Southeast Asia. However, the overall share of emergent democracies in world GDP is only 8% and, as Table 10 shows, the average per-capita income in emergent democracies was only $1,557 in 1995.

3.4 Communism

As an ideology communism stems from the writings of Marx and Engels, which were subsequently taken up by Vladimir Ilyich Lenin and his associates, and adapted to meet the needs of early 20th-century Russia. According to Marx, communism is an ideal which is eventually reached when all private property and class distinctions have been abolished and the state has become redundant and 'withered away'. In these terms, the nations which are commonly referred to as communist can hardly be said to be 'without states'. Indeed, they possess some of the most elaborate structures of state institutions in the world.

Nor were the origins of the Soviet Union, which used to be the 'model' for all communist systems, congruent with the classic texts of Marx and Engels. According to these, anticapitalist revolutions should have first taken place in Western Europe, the most developed region of the world, where the industrial proletariat (working class) were expected to rise up in revolt against mounting exploitation by the bourgeoisie (industrial/business middle class). This would then have led on to an intermediate 'socialist' phase in which the state remained in place, serving as the instrument of the working classes in a 'revolutionary dictatorship', and in which inequalities continued to be tolerated, with each producer being paid according to work done. Later, as affluence increased, a final, 'higher' phase of full communism would be achieved, no longer requiring the apparatus of government for its sustenance, in which all labor divisions would be ended and each worker would be able to receive 'according to his needs'.

In reality, however, revolution occurred first in underdeveloped Russia, in October 1917. This revolution was, moreover, far from a spontaneous uprising of industrial workers. Instead, it was a wartime 'coup', stimulated and led by Lenin, a member of the white-collar intelligentsia, with most of its 'revolutionary troops' drawn from peasant stock. Theoretical justification for this was provided by Lenin's theory of 'Imperialism: The Highest Stage of Capitalism'. This envisaged the 'vanguard' position of disciplined communist parties who would foment revolution with the aim to destroy the links which bound together the global capitalist system and thus precipite a final revolutionary cataclysm in the advanced West. This subsequent revolution failed to take place, however, leaving the Soviet Union to protect and 'build socialism' alone during the interwar period. Only after the end of World War II did significant new communist regimes become established. As in the Soviet case, however, they were to be found in the backward 'Second and Third Worlds' of Eastern Europe and Asia, having been imposed either by military force, where, as a consequence, they suffered from a lack of popular legitimacy, or following guerrilla-based, anticolonial liberation struggles.

Today, the followers of Marx and Lenin reluctantly agree that the ideal of communism has not been reached and that the intermediate condition of socialism

Communist systems (5) — Table 14

Region/country	Year established	Per capita GDP (US$)*	Per capita GDP (world ranking)*	Human rights rating (%)**	Human rights rating (world ranking)**
Asia (4)					
China	1949	730	133	21	101
Korea, North	1948	835	126	20	N/A
Laos	1975	370	158	N/A	N/A
Vietnam	1945***/1976****	245	173	20	97
Central America & Caribbean (1)					
Cuba	1959	1,230	104	30	93

* *c.* 1995.
** *c.* 1991.
*** North.
**** South.

remained a truer description of the Soviet system and those of its imitators. In no country did the state 'wither away'. Instead, the communist party remained firmly in charge, dominating state institutions, having assumed its prescribed role as the 'vanguard of the proletariat', so as to protect socialist society before the advent of true communism. The accession of Mikhail Gorbachev to the leadership of the Communist Party in the Soviet Union in 1985 resulted in the effective abandonment of striving for achievement of the theoretical ideal of communism. Instead, through his '*perestroika*' (economic restructuring), '*glasnost*' (openness), and '*demokratsiya*' (democratization) initiatives, an attempt was made to build an economically successful and democratically accountable 'socialist democracy', very much on the lines of Western social democracy. This attempt failed, with the unbottled ethnic and nationalist tensions within the Soviet Union and its satellites, and the tremendous economic hardship caused by the transition from a planned to a capitalist economy, resulting in the collapse of the Soviet bloc between 1989 and 1991.

In Asia, legitimate, purportedly communist regimes have survived in China, North Korea, and Indo-China and, in the Caribbean, Castro's Cuba also remains a defiant outpost. However, these states, which have been distinguished by the charismatic leadership of their 'liberation leaders' and a powerful role for the armed forces, have all followed 'paths to socialism' which have diverged significantly from the Soviet model. In China, in particular, since 1978, under the leadership of first Deng Xiaoping and then Jiang Zemin, there has been emphasis on market-centerd economic reform, while tight political controls have been maintained in almost an authoritarian nationalist manner. During recent years the market has also been embraced in Laos, Vietnam, and Cuba.

The five states which still can be described as 'communist', since one-party control is maintained by a party which subscribes to the ideology of communism, in Marxist terms, are set out in Table 14. They account for a disproportionate share of the world's population, 24%, but only a fraction, 3.4%, of its GDP. Human rights ratings in all five states are abysmally low, but levels of government defense expenditure are exceptionally high, ranging from 2.8% in Cuba to a crippling 25.2% in North Korea. Literacy rates are high.

Four distinguishing features characterize such communist states:

1. Marxism-Leninism (in the case of China, Maoism-Dengism) has been adopted as the official ideology, source of legitimacy, and vocabulary of political affairs;
2. The bulk of economic activity is under state ownership and subject to administrative (central) planning;
3. One party, the Communist Party, dominates the political scene and is tightly controlled from above in accordance with the Leninist precept of 'democratic centralism';
4. The influence of the Communist Party, constitutionally ascribed a 'leading role' in the nation's

> affairs, is all-pervasive, controlling state organs, trade unions, the media, the judiciary, and industrial and agricultural enterprises through both supervision and direct membership.

Communist parties, able to attract a significant share of the national vote and even win shares in power, operate with success in several emergent democratic states in Central and Eastern Europe. However, they accept the tenets of multiparty liberal democracy. This is not the case with restyled former communist parties and their leaders who continue to control the states of Azerbaijan, Kazakhstan, Tajikistan, Turkmenistan, and Uzbekistan in the former Soviet-controlled regions of the Caucasus and Central Asia. Communism has been officially abandoned in these states, so they have been categorized in this volume as authoritarian nationalist states. However, a 'return to type' may occur in future years in several of them.

3.5 Nationalistic socialism

Countries which have been placed in this category display many of the attributes of a communist state but in a less developed and structured form. A key feature is the existence of one political party of avowed socialist orientation, but whose role, in practice, has been more that of a promoter of nationalism and an opponent of imperialism than of a 'guardian of the proletariat' and radical transformer of the country's economic structure. Private farming and petty manufacturing have, for example, remained predominant in these states.

In many countries subscribing to nationalistic socialism the presence of a 'charismatic leader' has been a distinctive characteristic. Muammar al-Kadhafi of Libya, Robert Mugabe of Zimbabwe, Issaias Afwerki of Eritrea, Saddam Hussein of Iraq, and Hafez al-Assad of Syria are obvious examples, the former two having established their reputations as a guerrilla or political leader during their nations' independence struggles. In addition, a significant number of the states included in Table 15, Eritrea, Iraq, Libya, and Syria being the most prominent examples, have been involved, in recent years, in militarized border disputes with their neighbors. This has served to enhance the nationalist standing and inclination of their leaderships and has also resulted in the states being burdened by high levels of defense spending, equivalent to as much as 15% of GDP in Iraq.

The eight states identified as having nationalistic socialist regimes and set out in Table 15 embrace 73 million people, or just over 1% of the world's total population. They are concentrated in the Middle East and Africa. Indeed, it has been seriously argued that in Africa, with many societies divided vertically along tribal, regional, ethnic, and religious lines, rather than

Nationalistic socialist systems (8) — **Table 15**

Region/country	Year established	Per capita GDP (US$)*	Per capita GDP (world ranking)*	Human rights rating (%)**	Human rights rating (world ranking)**
Central & Southern Africa (4)					
Congo, Republic of	1997	710	135	N/A	N/A
Eritrea	1993	170	185	N/A	N/A
Senegal	1960	630	141	71	45
Zimbabwe	1980	565	145	65	53
Middle East & North Africa (4)					
Iraq	1970	1,150	111	17	104
Libya	1977	6,715	46	24	99
Syria	1971	1,140	112	30	93
Tunisia	1963	1,870	88	60	60

* *c.* 1995.

** *c.* 1991.

horizontally by social class, multiparty democracy can be a recipe for chaos and that one-party regimes are able to bring greater stability.

In terms of civil rights restrictions, the overall ratings recorded by most nationalistic socialist regimes are disappointingly low. Three regimes, however, those of Senegal, Tunisia, and Zimbabwe, despite the monism of their political structures, stand out as significantly more 'liberal', exceeding the rating registered by several emergent democratic nations. In all three states multiparty political systems have been recently restored. However, such is the long-standing *de facto* dominance exerted by the ruling party in each state, that it has been sensible to include these regimes in the nationalistic socialist category in preference to that of emergent democracy.

3.6 Authoritarian nationalism

In its starkest form nationalism is a belief that people of the same racial stock are so unique that only they have the right to be regarded as members of a nation. This extreme kind of nationalism is so intolerant of other races and creeds that, at best, they are disenfranchised and, at worst, eliminated. Nazi Germany exhibited this attitude in its most brutal form and until quite recently the formerly white-dominated regime in South Africa pursued its own version of the 'final solution' through the operation of the system of apartheid.

Fortunately, although atrocities of 'ethnic cleansing' have been committed during the 1990s in Bosnia-Herzegovina, Serbia and Rwanda, extreme examples of this kind are rare. Most present-day exponents of nationalism use it as a device to claim the loyalty and obedience of members of the public. Even liberal democratic states are guilty of nationalistic tendencies, though they may disguise the fact under the banner of patriotism. The national flag and the national anthem are manifestations of nationalism under the guise of patriotism and even sport has succumbed to its temptations.

A state which subscribes to the ideology of authoritarian nationalism displays the following three features:

Authoritarian nationalist systems (12) — **Table 16**

Region/country	Year established	Per capita GDP (US$)*	Per capita GDP (world ranking)*	Human rights rating (%)**	Human rights rating (world ranking)**
Asia (5)					
Kazakhstan	1991	1,300	102	N/A	N/A
Maldives	1968	980	120	N/A	N/A
Tajikistan	1991	360	159	N/A	N/A
Turkmenistan	1991	1,080	115	N/A	N/A
Uzbekistan	1991	1,040	117	N/A	N/A
Central, Eastern, & Southern Europe (3)					
Armenia	1990	775	130	N/A	N/A
Azerbaijan	1993	480	147	N/A	N/A
Belarus	1994	2,080	84	N/A	N/A
Central & Southern Africa (4)					
Djibouti	1981	995	118	N/A	N/A
Equatorial Guinea	1991	400	152	N/A	N/A
Rwanda	1994	150	188	48	80
Uganda	1986	225	177	46	83

* *c.* 1995.

** *c.* 1991.

1. Restrictions on the activities of all political parties, or a limitation to one which gives undivided and uncritical support to the state;
2. An authoritarian charismatic personal or collective executive;
3. Either the absence of an assembly to balance the power of the executive, or the presence of an assembly which is essentially the servant of the executive.

For many states adherence to authoritarian nationalism will be a stage in the progression of independence from the rule of a colonial power to emergent democracy and, eventually, to a full, pluralistic democracy. Given a much longer time span, it is conceivable that all states will eventually abandon nationalistic tendencies and move towards regional, and even global, groupings. These developments are examined in Section III.

The 12 countries identified as proponents of authoritarian nationalism are listed in Table 16. Within this grouping it must be stressed, however, that there exist considerable differences between both the policy outlooks and the degree of illiberalism of the regimes in power. For example, those in former Soviet-controlled Central Asia and the Caucasus region are, as noted, successors to powerful state-dominated communist regimes, while that in Indonesia is a military-backed regime which has successfully pursued a program of capitalistic economic modernization. Those in Africa are found in states where tribal-based ethnic divisions are especially acute, leading to a recent civil war in Rwanda.

Despite these clear variations, two elements remain common to all 12 states:

1. The existence of *de facto* one-party dominance;
2. Policy orientations which fall short of being fully socialist.

The second characteristic serves to distinguish these states from those included in the nationalistic socialist category above, thus making their inclusion in this group defensible.

The 12 states identified embrace 99 million people, or nearly 2% of the global population. There is an even division between locations in Central and Southern Africa and Asia. The longest standing authoritarian nationalist regime has been established for more than two decades in the Maldives, with the recent signing of a peace accord in Tajikistan with the Islamic opposition, there were signs that this state might follow the example of Indonesia, in 1999, and become an emergent democracy.

3.7 Military authoritarianism

Military authoritarianism is a form of authoritarian nationalism whereby military leaders take it upon themselves to impose a government on the people, claiming, invariably, that it is for the public good. History is littered with examples of regimes when 'men of action' have felt it necessary to use their military strength to overthrow and replace civilian administrations. In some cases the transition is short-lived, in others military rule has become a quasi-permanent feature.

The characteristics of a state accepting authoritarian nationalism will be found also in this category with, of course, a military regime always in control. Sometimes a state based on military authoritarianism will try to disguise itself by using a civilian administration as a façade, fronting the military power behind. Panama, during the 1980s, provided an example of this. The military remain influential in a number of emergent democratic, nationalistic socialist and authoritarian nationalist states, notably Algeria, Angola, Bosnia, Chile, Ghana, Guinea, Indonesia, Iraq, Mozambique, Pakistan, Paraguay, Rwanda, São Tomé, and Thailand, as well as in 'liberal democratic' Peru.

In Ghana the charismatic Flight-Lieutenant Jerry Rawlings, who twice seized power as a populist military leader in 1978 and 1981, succeeded in effecting the transition from military ruler to popularly elected president in a multiparty, emergent democratic state in 1992. In Indonesia, T N J Suharto, who assumed power in a coup in 1965, remained president from 1967 to 1998, being re-elected at regular five-yearly intervals. The 'presidential path' was also pursued, with varying success, by General Alfredo Stroessner in Paraguay (1954–89), General Zia ul-Haq in Pakistan (1977–88), and Lieutenant-General Hossain Mohammad Ershad in Bangladesh (1982–90). In most other cases military leaders, aware of their lack of legitimacy, have sought to 'return to barracks' and hand over power to civilian leaders once the circumstances that precipitated a coup have been resolved. However, after a country's armed forces have entered the political arena once, they appear to be less inhibited from re-entering again to 'correct' the political process. This has certainly been the experience of Pakistan, Thailand, and the states included in Table 17.

The eight states subscribing to military authoritarianism and listed in Table 17 embrace 142 million people, or 3% of the global total. Four-fifths are located in

Military authoritarian systems (8) — Table 17

Region/country	Year established	Per capita GDP (US$)*	Per capita GDP (world ranking)*	Human rights rating (%)**	Human rights rating (world ranking)**
Asia (1)					
Myanmar	1988	580	144	17	104
Central & Southern Africa (7)					
Burundi	1996	160	187	N/A	N/A
Comoros	1999	380	155	N/A	N/A
Congo, Democratic Republic of	1997	125	190	40	88
Guinea-Bissau	1999	255	171	N/A	N/A
Niger	1999	225	177	N/A	N/A
Somalia	1969	310	166	N/A	N/A
Sudan	1989	415	150	18	103

* *c.* 1995.
** *c.* 1991.

Central and Southern Africa and the states are located in the world's bottom quartile in terms of per-capita GDP. Literacy rates and urbanization levels are also low, as Table 10 reveals, with a high proportion of the labor force still engaged in agricultural activities. There are no military regimes currently in Europe, Oceania, and the Americas and in recent decades only two military states have been established in Europe and Oceania: in Greece between 1967 and 1973 and in Fiji between 1987 and 1990. Periods of military junta rule have, however, been common in Central and South America during the course of this century.

The average age of the world's seven current military regimes is less than seven years. This reflects the necessarily transient character of this illegitimate regime type. The longest entrenched military-based regime is in Somalia, dating back to 1969, although it has a presidential façade. However, in Myanmar the military first effectively came to power in 1962. In Sudan the military regime adheres to Muslim fundamentalist principles and has waged campaigns against the Christian and animist population in the country's south.

3.8 Islamic nationalism

As Table 18 shows, there are two countries with Islamic nationalist political regimes, Afghanistan and Iran. In these states the political process is completely dominated by fundamentalist Islam, a religious ideology that fulfils a political function similar to that performed by Marxism-Leninism in a communist regime. Sharia (Islamic law) is enforced, Islamic spiritual leaders (ayatollahs and mullahs) provide strategic guidance, and the policies of the (Islamic) political parties are framed in accordance with the Koran and Sharia, with religious scholars occupying prominent positions. In Iran, an Islamic state was established in 1979 after a popular revolution, inspired by the exiled Ayatollah Khomeini, succeeded in overthrowing the Western-backed Muhammad Reza Shah Pahlavi. The background to this revolution was the disenchantment of young people, especially students, with the widening gap between rich and poor that had been created by the Shah's economic modernization drive, and their desire to recreate a Golden Age of Islam through a return to traditional Islamic values. In Afghanistan, Islam was established by force after a 13-year guerrilla war by the mujaheddin ('holy warriors') against a Russian-backed communist regime. Nationalism in both states is thus intimately linked with defense of Islamic faith against 'corrupting' outside religions and ideologies, specifically Western materialism and atheistic communism. There have also been attempts to extend the jihad (Islamic holy war) and export fundamentalist Islam to neighboring states, notably Iraq and Tajikistan.

Islamic nationalist systems (2) **Table 18**

Region/country	Year established	Per capita GDP (US$)*	Per capita GDP (world ranking)*	Human rights rating (%)**	Human rights rating (world ranking)**
Asia (1)					
Afghanistan	1992	150	188	28	96
Middle East & North Africa (1)					
Iran	1979	1,380	100	22	100

* *c.* 1995.
** *c.* 1991.

The combined population of the two states with Islamic nationalist regimes is 78 million and, as Table 10 shows, human rights ratings and literacy and urbanization levels are comparatively low. Since 1989 and the death of Ayatollah Khomeini, the Islamic revolution in Iran has entered a less militant phase. The country's economy was greatly weakened by a 1980–88 war with neighboring Iraq. This persuaded Hoshemi Rafsanjani, the president from 1989 to 1997, to rule pragmatically. His successor Professor Khatami has accelerated the process of liberalisation. In Afghanistan, after toppling the socialist regime of Najibullah Ahmadzai in 1992, the mujaheddin became riven by regional and ideological-based factional rivalries. As a consequence, the civil war continued, and in 1996 the mujaheddin were themselves overthrown by the Islamic extremist Talibaan.

In 23 other countries in the world Islam is similarly the state religion (see Table 8). Although Sharia law is followed by many of these states, the party political processes have not yet been so thoroughly permeated by the ideology of Islam as to merit application of the classification 'Islamic nationalist'. However, in Sudan, under the military's patronage, fundamentalist Islam has grown greatly in influence during recent years and Islamic militants were involved in 1998 in virtual civil wars in Algeria and Kashmir (India.)

3.9 Absolutism

Absolutism is an ideology which can be traced back to *The Leviathan,* written by Thomas Hobbes (1588–1679) soon after the mid-17th-century English Civil War (1642–52), in support of the English monarchy as the guarantor of stability and order. The ideology had even earlier roots in the medieval European doctrine of 'The Divine Right of Kings'. It argues that no limits whatsoever should be placed on the activities of a legitimate government, which will usually be in the form of an absolute monarch. Legitimacy is often claimed through the accident of birth, although it is convenient to forget that at some stage in history that legitimacy must have been acquired by force.

For a nation in an early stage of economic and social development, or one threatened by external forces, absolutism is an attractive ideology to accept, offering a guarantee of stability and order. For some countries it may only represent a stage in their development, to be superseded by a republican form of government or by a constitutional monarchy. For others it has become a permanent condition.

The characteristics of a state based on absolutism are:

1. The absence of any constitutional form of government, or a popular assembly or judiciary to counter executive power;
2. The denial of the right to form political parties or other forms of organized interests;
3. Governing systems based on clientism (support derived from patronage) or neo-patrimonialism (rule based on inheritance).

The 12 states adhering to absolutism, or a 'traditional regime', are listed in Table 19 and comprise an assortment of monarchies (Bhutan, Jordan, Saudi Arabia, Swaziland, and Tonga), sultanates (Brunei and Oman), and sheikhdoms and emirates (Bahrain, Kuwait, Qatar, and the United Arab Emirates), in addition to the papacy of Rome. In Bhutan there has been growing popular pressure for democratization and the monarchies in Jordan and Tonga, although absolute in the final analysis, do have vestiges of constitutional checks and balances. One other state, Morocco, is also characterized by monarchical rule, but within a more fully developed and party-based constitutional structure. For this reason it has been assigned, instead, to the emergent democracy category. Nepal was also an absolute state until widespread prodemocracy demonstrations in 1990 resulted in the establishment of a constitutional monarchy on the parliamentary executive model.

The 12 absolutist regimes included in Table 19 embrace a population of 33 million, corresponding to less than 1% of the world total. Seven are located in the Middle East, in which region it constitutes the predominant political type. It should also be noted that seven of these absolutist states, including five in the Middle East, are, as a consequence of their mineral oil wealth, among the world's 'Top 50' nations in terms of per-capita national income. This has meant that, although Bhutan and Swaziland are low-income states, the average per-capita income for absolutist states was $7,347 in *c.* 1995. As Table 10 shows, urbanization rates are also quite high, while levels of government defense spending are very high. Significantly, all the absolute states, except Swaziland, have an established religion.

3.10 The changing balance of ideologies

In 1989, when the first edition of this title was written, slightly more than half, 83 out of 164, of the nation-states of the world had regimes which could be classified as either liberal democratic or emergent democratic. Nearly a quarter, or 37 states, had effectively one-party socialist regimes, categorized either as communist or nationalistic socialist. This state type was

Absolutist systems (12) — **Table 19**

Region/country	Year established	Per capita GDP (US$)*	Per capita GDP (world ranking)*	Human rights rating (%)**	Human rights rating (world ranking)**
Asia (2)					
Bhutan	1907	180	18	N/A	N/A
Brunei	1984	13,030	33	N/A	N/A
Central & Southern Africa (1)					
Swaziland	1968	1,270	103	N/A	N/A
Middle East & North Africa (7)					
Bahrain	1971	8,240	41	N/A	N/A
Jordan	1952	1,220	106	65	53
Kuwait	1961	18,360	25	33	90
Oman	1951	5,090	51	49	77
Qatar	1971	13,800	31	N/A	N/A
Saudi Arabia	1932	7,650	44	29	95
United Arab Emirates	1971	17,900	26	N/A	N/A
Northern & Western Europe (1)					
Vatican City State	1377	25,000	11	N/A	N/A
Oceania (1)					
Tonga	1875	1,700	91	N/A	N/A

* *c.* 1995.

** *c.* 1991.

Number of world political regimes by type in 1989, 1995, and 1998 Table 20

Year	Liberal democratic	Emergent democratic	Communist	Nationalistic socialist	Authoritarian nationalist	Military	Islamic nationalist	Absolutist
1989	50	33	16	21	16	16	0	12
1995	73	72	5	8	13	7	2	12
1999	74	71	5	8	12	8	8	12
Change	*+24*	*+38*	*-11*	*-13*	*-4*	*-8*	*+2*	–

particularly common in Central and Eastern Europe and Africa. The remaining sovereign states in the world had predominantly rightwing authoritarian nationalist, military, and absolutist regimes.

Six years on, when the next edition was produced, as Table 20 demonstrates, the world political map had been radically transformed. With the collapse of the Soviet Union's communist empire and the adoption of multiparty democracy in much of Africa, the number of states with liberal democratic and emergent democratic political systems had increased to 145, equivalent to three-quarters of the world's total. Pluralist democracy predominated in Europe and the Americas, in particular, but had also put down new roots in Asia and Africa. In 1995, only 13 of the world's 192 states had avowedly socialist regimes of a communist or nationalistic socialist type but, while the number of military regimes had also fallen sharply, there were still 25 absolutist and authoritarian nationalist states.

In 1998, the position remained broadly similar to three years earlier. One more state, the Philippines, had moved from emergent democratic to liberal democratic, while the former authoritarian nationalist or military regimes of Gambia, Indonesia, Liberia, Nigeria, and Sierra Leone had become emergent democratic. There had also been some relapses away from emergent democracy, in the cases of Belarus, the Republic of Congo, Djibouti, Equatorial Guinea, Guinea-Bissau, Niger, Comoros, and Tunisia, and into the military category for the Democratic Republic of Congo and Burundi. However, with Algeria, Kenya, and Tanzania making tentative moves into the emergent democratic category, there was overall maintenance of the democratic position between 1995 and 1998.

The onward march of pluralist liberal democracy, allied to a capitalist mixed economy, has been presented by some writers, notably Francis Fukuyama, as an inexorable process. Communism, criticized now as a 'grand oversimplification', and socialism are viewed as failed experiments, while the increasing competitive pressures of the global economy and popular demands for individual liberties are seen as key elements which will force a convergence in political types.

However, the annual reports of human-rights monitoring bodies such as Amnesty International and Freedom House show that, in the mid-1990s, in more than 60 countries prisoners of conscience were held, political killings sanctioned, and people detained without charge or trial. Clearly many states are far from being pluralist entities and are guided by different ideological impulses. In addition, history shows that waves of democratization have been followed later by periods of reversion. Nationalism, mobilizing citizens on ethnic lines, remains a potent political force despite the continued development of regional political groupings. Populism, as noted earlier, is also emerging as a new ideology, while the limitations of free-market capitalism, which produces 'losers' as well as 'winners', mean that democratic socialism, with its recognition of, and compensation for, natural individual inequalities, will remain a relevant and popular political ideology.

Recommended reading

Beetham, D (ed.) *Defining and Measuring Democracy*, Sage, 1994

Bouandel, Y *Human Rights and Comparative Politics*, Dartmouth, 1997

Brzezinski, Z *The Grand Failure: The Birth and Death of Communism in the Twentieth Century*, Macdonald, 1989

Cammack, P, Pool, D, and Tordoff, W *Third World Politics: A Comparative Introduction*, 2nd edn., Macmillan, 1993, Chap. 2

Clapham, C *Third World Politics: An Introduction*, Croom Helm, 1985, Chap. 3

Decalo, S *Coups and Army Rule in Africa*, Yale University Press, 1986

Deutsch, K W, Dominguez, J I, and Heclo, H *Comparative Government: Politics of Industrialized and Developing Nations*, Houghton Mifflin, 1981

Dunleavy, P and O'Leary, B *Theories of the State: The Politics of Liberal Democracy*, Macmillan, 1987

Eatwell, R and Wright, A *Contemporary Political Ideologies*, Pinter, 1993

Ferdinand, P *Communist Regimes in Comparative Perspective*, Harvester Wheatsheaf, 1991

Finer, S E *Comparative Government: An Introduction to the Study of Politics*, Penguin, 1970

Finer, S E *The Man on Horseback: The Role of the Military in Politics*, 2nd edn., Penguin, 1976

Fukuyama, F *The End of History and the Last Man*, Penguin, 1992

Furtak, R *The Political Systems of the Socialist States: An Introduction to Marxist-Leninist Regimes*, Harvester Press, 1986

Ghayasuddin, M (ed.) *The Impact of Nationalism on the Muslim World*, The Open Press, 1986

Harrop, H (ed.) *Power and Policy in Liberal Democracies*, Cambridge University Press, 1992

Hiro, D *Islamic Fundamentalism*, Paladin, 1988

Huntington, S P *The Third Wave: Democratization in the Late Twentieth Century*, University of Oklahoma Press, 1991

Kamrava, M *Politics and Society in the Third World*, Routledge, 1993

Lijphart, A and Waisman, C H (eds.) *Institutional Design in New Democracies: Eastern Europe and Latin America*, Westview, 1996

Macridis, R C and Hulliung, M *Comparative Political Ideologies, Movements and Regimes*, 6th edn., Harper Collins, 1996

Szporluk, R *Communism and Nationalism: Karl Marx versus Friedrich List*, Oxford University Press, 1988

Wesson, R (ed.) *Democracy: A Worldwide Survey*, Praeger, 1987

White, S, Garner, J, and Schopflin, G *Communist Political Systems: An Introduction*, 2nd edn., Macmillan, 1987, Chaps 1 and 2

Whitehead, L (ed.) *The International Dimensions of Democratization in Europe and the Americas*, Oxford University Press, 1996

CHAPTER 4

Executives

4.1 Political executives

It is usual to make a distinction between the political executive and the nonpolitical, or permanent, executive. The latter is the salaried civil service which normally remains in office to work for whichever politicians happen to be in power. They, in turn, constitute the political executive and, as such, provide the leadership for both the political system and the state.

The modern political executive can be personal or collective and is found in a variety of forms including president, prime minister, and party chairman or secretary-general. Whatever the contemporary form and title, each is a direct descendant of the personal autocrat or absolute monarch, at one time universal.

States with more than one operating political party have been identified as liberal democracies or emergent democracies. With only a few exceptions, their executives are either presidents or prime ministers. We shall refer to them, respectively, as presidential or parliamentary executives. In the exceptions, a dual executive, usually of a president and a prime minister, operates.

One-party states have been subdivided into communist, nationalistic socialist, authoritarian nationalist, and military authoritarian. In these cases the most common form of executive is, again, presidential, although in those we have identified as communist the executive assumes a distinctive form, partly collective and partly personal, as, at the apex of power, the state and party machines merge.

Finally, there are the few surviving absolutist states, where political parties have no role to play, and the executives are individuals exercising virtually unbridled power in very much the same way as the original precursors of what we now call democratic governments.

Table 21 shows the current distribution of political executives in the 192 states under consideration.

4.2 The parliamentary executive

This is the second most common form of political executive in the world today, 56 states having adopted it, embracing over a third of the global population. Thirty-one of them are constitutional monarchies and 25 republics. It is sometimes referred to as the 'Westminster model' because it originated, and is found in its clearest form, in the United Kingdom. It is not coincidental that of the 56 nations with parliamentary political executives, 29, including the United Kingdom, were formerly part of the British Empire and are now independent members of the Commonwealth. It is useful, therefore, to examine the UK system, even though the executives of other countries have been adapted from the original example to suit particular needs. All parliamentary executives are found in multiparty liberal (44) or emergent democracies (12), with 18 of the total being in Northern and Western Europe, 11 in the Caribbean region and eight in Oceania. Almost half, 46%, are located in island states This executive type is found mainly in smaller states, although India, the world's second most populous nation, has a parliamentary executive (Table 21). Thus two-thirds of the states with parliamentary executives have populations below 10 million and areas less than 100,000 square kilometres. The full list, showing geographical distributions, is given in Table 22.

The parliamentary executive displays three essential features:

1. The role of head of state is separate from that of head of government and is distant from party politics, serving mainly as the patriotic and ceremonial focus of the nation. The head of state can be a president, as in Germany or India, or a monarch, as in the Netherlands or the United Kingdom. In the majority of Commonwealth countries with parliamentary executives, the head of state is still the British monarch, represented by a resident governor general.
2. The executive is drawn from the assembly and directly responsible to it, and its security of tenure is dependent on the support of the assembly, or parliament. In other words, a 'no-confidence' vote in parliament can bring down the government, resulting in a change of executive or a general elec-

tion. It is in such circumstances that the nonpolitical head of state may become temporarily involved in politics by either inviting the leader of a party in opposition to form a new government, or by dissolving parliament and initiating elections.

A particular characteristic of the 'Westminster model' is that it is, historically, based on the concept of a two-party system. The House of Commons, for example, is physically constructed to accommodate two opposing parties, the govern-

World distribution of executive systems — Table 21

By region

Region	Parliamentary	Limited presidential	Dual	Communist	Unlimited presidential	Military	Absolute	Total
Asia	8	5	2	4	6	1	2	28
Central America & Caribbean	11	8	1	1	0	0	0	21
Central, Eastern, & Southern Europe	6	8	8	0	3	0	0	25
Central & Southern Africa	3	28	1	0	8	7	1	48
Middle East & North Africa	1	3	2	0	5	0	7	18
North America	1	1	0	0	0	0	0	2
Northern & Western Europe	18	1	3	0	0	0	1	23
Oceania	8	6	0	0	0	0	1	15
South America	0	12	0	0	0	0	0	12
Total	*56*	*72*	*17*	*5*	*22*	*8*	*12*	*192*

By population and land area (c. 1995)

Executive type	Number of states	Area (thousand sq km)	Area (% of world)	Population (millions)	Population (% of world)
Parliamentary	56	29,034	21.8	1,914	34.0
Limited presidential	72	69,315	52.1	1,743	31.0
Dual	17	3,813	2.9	228	4.0
Communist	5	10,349	7.8	1,327	23.5
Unlimited presidential	22	12,253	7.8	249	4.4
Military	8	7,497	5.6	142	2.5
Absolute	12	2,644	2.0	33	0.6
Sub-total	192	133,021	100.0	5,636	100.0
Colonies & dependent territories*	41	2,387	–	10	–
Total	*233*	*135,408*	–	*5,646*	–

By state population (c. 1995)

State population size (million)	Parliamentary	Limited presidential	Dual	Communist	Unlimited presidential	Military	Absolute	Total
< 0.1	9	5	0	0	0	0	2	16
0.1 to < 1	12	6	0	0	3	1	4	26
1 to < 10	16	30	10	1	10	4	5	76
10 to < 20	5	12	3	1	6	0	1	28
20 to < 50	4	10	3	1	2	3	0	23
50 to < 100	6	4	1	1	1	0	0	13
100 to < 200	3	4	0	0	0	0	0	7
200 to < 500	0	1	0	0	0	0	0	1
500 to 1,250	1	0	0	1	0	0	0	2
Total	*56*	*72*	*17*	*5*	*22*	*8*	*12*	*192*

continues

World distribution of executive systems (continued) Table 21

By state area

State area (thousand sq km)	Parliamentary	Limited presidential	Dual	Communist	Unlimited presidential	Military	Absolute	Total
< 1	14	7	0	0	1	0	3	25
1 to < 10	4	2	0	0	0	1	1	8
10 to < 100	16	14	10	0	5	2	6	53
100 to < 500	14	20	5	4	12	0	1	56
500 to < 1,000	4	14	1	0	1	2	0	22
1,000 to < 5,000	2	12	1	0	3	3	1	22
5,000 to < 10,000	2	2	0	1	0	0	0	5
10,000 to 20,000	0	1	0	0	0	0	0	1
Total	*56*	*72*	*17*	*5*	*22*	*8*	*12*	*192*

* Excludes Corsica, Western Sahara, and Tibet, whose area and population are included in the totals for France, Morocco, and China, within the dual and communist executive categories.

ment party sitting on benches to the right of the chairperson of the House, or speaker, and the opposition party to the left. Also, the leader of the opposition is acknowledged formally in legislation, provided with a suitable office, and paid a salary out of public funds. This practice is followed in several Commonwealth states, most notably Australia and New Zealand, but is not an essential feature of a parliamentary executive. Indeed, the majority of European states, including Germany, Austria, Belgium, Denmark, Ireland, Italy, the Netherlands, and Norway, have a wide range of parties, and governments are frequently, and in some cases invariably, formed by coalitions of these parties. The term, 'consensus democracy', or consociationalism, has been coined to describe this political model. Conversely, in a number of Asian states with parliamentary executive systems, for example, Malaysia, Singapore and, until recently, India and Japan, effective one-party electoral dominance has been the norm, although opposition parties do operate.

3. The leader of the party, or coalition of parties, commanding the support of parliament is called upon by the head of state, monarch or president, to become prime minister and form a government. The prime minister then chooses a cabinet, drawn from parliament, and they, with other noncabinet ministers, form the government. In Israel, since 1996, the prime minister has been directly elected by popular vote, creating elements of the presidential model.

The fact that the parliamentary executive is drawn from and responsible to the assembly makes it, in theory at least, particularly accountable. In reality much depends upon the state of the parties in parliament. A British prime minister, for example, enjoying a clear parliamentary majority, usually has greater executive power and discretion than a US president, subject to the checks and balances of a constitution which gives significant power and authority to an independent congress. In countries where coalition governments are the norm prime ministerial authority is invariably weaker, with power diffused among ministers drawn from a variety of parties. Special arrangements have been devised in a number of such cases, however, to buttress the chief executive's authority. The most notable example is Germany in which, under the terms of the Basic Law (constitution) of 1949, members of the assembly can only force the replacement of the chancellor (prime minister) through a 'constructive vote of no confidence', by which a majority of members vote positively in favor of a proposed successor.

Four of the newly democratized states of former Soviet-controlled Central and Eastern Europe, Bulgaria, Hungary, Latvia, and Slovakia, now have vigorously functioning parliamentary executives. A further eight, Albania, the Czech Republic, Estonia, Lithuania, Macedonia, Poland, Romania, and Slovenia, have executives which have been categorized as 'dual', but are substantially parliamentary in nature. The remaining 15 states in this region and in ex-Soviet Central Asia have presidential executives, both limited (8) and unlimited (7).

States with parliamentary executives (56) Table 22

Region/country	Republic (R) or monarchy (M)	Member of Commonwealth	Year established	Year current head of state came to power	Year current prime minister came to power
Asia (8)					
Bangladesh	R	Y	1991	1996	1996
India	R	Y	1947	1997	1998
Japan	M	N	1946	1989	1998
Malaysia	M	Y	1957	1999	1981
Nepal	M	N	1991	1972	1998
Pakistan	R	Y	1988	1997	1997
Singapore	R	Y	1965	1993	1990
Thailand	M	N	1992	1946	1997
Central America & Caribbean (11)					
Antigua	M	Y	1981	1981	1993
Bahamas	M	Y	1973	1973	1992
Barbados	M	Y	1966	1966	1994
Belize	M	Y	1981	1981	1998
Dominica	R	Y	1978	1998	1995
Grenada	M	Y	1974	1974	1995
Jamaica	M	Y	1962	1962	1992
St Kitts and Nevis	M	Y	1983	1983	1995
St Lucia	M	Y	1979	1979	1997
St Vincent and the Grenadines	M	Y	1979	1979	1984
Trinidad and Tobago	R	Y	1962	1987	1995
Central, Eastern, & Southern Europe (6)					
Bulgaria	R	N	1990	1997	1997
Greece	R	N	1974	1995	1996
Hungary	R	N	1989	1990	1998
Latvia	R	N	1990	1999	1999
Slovakia	R	N	1990	1999	1998
Turkey	R	N	1982	1993	1999
Central & Southern Africa (3)					
Ethiopia	R	N	1994	1995	1995
Lesotho	M	Y	1993	1996	1998
Mauritius	R	Y	1968	1992	1995
Middle East & North Africa (1)					
Israel	R	N	1948	1993	1999
North America (1)					
Canada	M	Y	1867	1952	1993
Northern & Western Europe (18)					
Andorra	M	N	1993	1995	1994
Austria	R	N	1918	1992	1997
Belgium	M	N	1831	1993	1999
Denmark	M	N	1849	1972	1993
Germany	R	N	1949	1999	1998
Iceland	R	N	1944	1996	1991
Ireland	R	N	1937	1997	1997
Italy	R	N	1948	1999	1998

continues

States with parliamentary executives (56) (continued) Table 22

Region/country	Republic (R) or monarchy (M)	Member of Commonwealth	Year established	Year current head of state came to power	Year current prime minister came to power
Liechtenstein	M	N	1921	1984	1993
Luxembourg	M	N	1868	1964	1995
Malta	R	Y	1974	1999	1998
Monaco	M	N	1911	1949	1997
Netherlands	M	N	1814	1980	1994
Norway	M	N	1814	1991	1997
San Marino	R	N	1600	rotating	rotating
Spain	M	N	1978	1975	1996
Sweden	M	N	1809	1973	1996
United Kingdom	M	Y	1689	1952	1997
Oceania (8)					
Australia	M	Y	1901	1952	1996
Fiji	R	Y	1987	1994	1999
New Zealand	M	Y	1853	1952	1997
Papua New Guinea	M	Y	1975	1975	1999
Samoa	R	Y	1962	1962	1998
Solomon Islands	M	Y	1978	1978	1997
Tuvalu	M	Y	1978	1978	1999
Vanuatu	R	Y	1980	1999	1998

An analysis of the data in Table 22 reveals that 44, or 79%, of the heads of the parliamentary executives in the world, either prime ministers or chancellors, had, in 1999, been in office for fewer than five years. This reflects the effective functioning of multiparty politics in these liberal and emergent democracies. However, six prime ministers and chancellors had been in power for more than seven years, securing re-election several times. These included Mahathir bin Mohamad in Malaysia (1981), James Mitchell in St Vincent and the Grenadines (1984), and Goh Chok Tong in Singapore (1990).

4.3 The limited presidential executive

The limited presidency is the most common form of political executive in the world today, 77 states having adopted it, embracing 31% of the global population, and half the world's land area. It should be noted, however, that 46 of the countries listed in Table 23 are emergent democracies which have only very recently adopted this type of executive, having moved from unlimited presidential, military, or communist executive systems. Their ability to sustain this form of democratic government must, therefore, be viewed with caution. Nevertheless, it is significant that it has been the presidential, rather than the parliamentary, which has been the most popular executive type adopted by newly democratized states. This is shown by the fact that between 1988 and 1999 the number of states with parliamentary executives advanced by more than a quarter, from 43 to 56, while the number with limited presidential executives more than doubled, from 35 to 72. One region which has provided an exception to this trend has been South Asia where, since 1988, Pakistan and, later, Bangladesh moved from presidential to parliamentary executives, with Sri Lanka promising to follow suit.

Derived from the Latin *praesidens*, the term president has a classical meaning of one who superintends, rules, or directs. In the modern world it is used to signify the head of state in a republic. It includes the ceremonial, and often indirectly elected, heads of state of the 25 republics which have parliamentary executives; the autocratic executive heads of state of nationalistic socialist and authoritarian nationalist regimes, who are designated here as 'unlimited presidents'; and the popularly elected, usually directly, although sometimes indirectly, heads of state and government in liberal and emergent democracies, referred to here as 'limited presidents'.

The clearest, though also the most extreme, example of the limited presidential model is provided by the United States and, although there are practical differences between individual systems, many of the features found in the United States are replicated elsewhere. Like parliamentary executives, all limited presidential executives occur in multiparty liberal (26) or emergent democracies (46). The full list, with geographical distributions, is given in Table 23.

A general point which emerges from this table is the predilection for this system of executive in the mainland countries of the Americas. Of the 21 states in this broad region, only two, Belize and Canada, have differing executive systems. Both of these former British colonies have parliamentary executives. For the remaining states of the region, which secured independence from the early 19th century onwards, the influence of United States' political and constitutional conventions and republican ideals is clear. In addition, limited presidential systems are particularly common in the larger states of the world. This is shown by an analysis of the data in Table 21. Two-thirds of states with limited presidential executives have areas in excess of 100,000 square kilometres and 43% have populations greater than 10 million.

As already noted, the limited presidential executive form of government has been a popular model to be adopted in recent years by newly emergent or re-established democracies in the Americas, Oceania, and Asia, the most prominent recently being Argentina, Brazil, the Philippines, South Korea, and Taiwan, as well as in Africa and Central and Eastern Europe. One factor influencing its adoption by such states is its attractive image as a modern form of government for democratic republics. In contrast, as noted above, parliamentary systems are found most commonly in older states, often where there is a hereditary, ceremonial head of state. Another important factor is the perceived need, in newly emergent democracies, for the head of state to act as a strong and charismatic unifying force, exemplified, for example, by Corazon Aquino in the Philippines between 1986 and 1992, Lech Wałęsa in Poland 1990–95, and Nelson Mandela in South Africa since 1994. As a consequence, these states have opted for a directly elected presidential executive, enjoying a clear national mandate, in preference to an indirectly elected parliamentary executive.

There are four key features present in a limited presidential executive:

1. Presidents are elected for a fixed term to perform the dual role of head of state and head of government. As head of state they occupy a mainly ceremonial position and are the focus of popular patriotism. As head of government they lead the executive branch of government, and are usually head of the armed forces and the state civil service. Also, as head of government, they are in charge of foreign affairs and are the main initiator of legislation.
2. Presidents' tenure are secure unless they commit a grave unconstitutional act. The US president, for example, cannot be removed by Congress except by impeachment.
3. Presidents govern with an advisory cabinet of non-elected departmental secretaries, whom they choose and appoint and who are fully responsible to them.
4. Presidential powers are limited by the need for the approval of the assembly for certain executive actions. Under the US Constitution, for example, congress has sole legislative powers and the president's veto of acts of Congress can be overridden by a two-thirds vote. Although presidents are expected to provide national leadership, their ability to do so is constrained by their ability to carry congress with them. The US Senate, in particular, has strong counterbalancing powers whereby presidents can only make key federal appointments, judicial and cabinet, with Senate approval. Foreign treaties require a two-thirds majority of the Senate before coming into effect.

It is this balanced relationship between the president of the United States and Congress, as well as the clear statement of their respective roles written into the Constitution, which make the presidency, although powerful, a limited form of executive and it is these features which are found in the other 72 states whose political executives fall into this category. The degrees of emphasis differ, however, as do the arrangements for the election of presidents, the restrictions on their length and terms of office, and the presence or absence of a separately elected prime minister, in the legislature.

In Botswana, Guyana, the Marshall Islands, Micronesia, Nauru, South Africa, Suriname, and Switzerland, for example, the presidential executive operates in many ways like a parliamentary one, being chosen by the legislature. In Switzerland the presidency is collective or collegial, comprising all seven members

States with limited presidential executives (72) — Table 23

Region/country	Year established	Year current head of state came to power
Asia (5)		
Indonesia	1999	1998
Korea, South	1987	1998
Kyrgyzstan	1990	1990
Mongolia	1990	1997
Taiwan	1987	1988
Central America & Caribbean (8)		
Costa Rica	1821	1998
Dominican Republic	1962	1996
El Salvador	1982	1999
Guatemala	1975	1996
Honduras	1982	1998
Mexico	1917	1994
Nicaragua	1979	1997
Panama	1989	1999
Central, Eastern, & Southern Europe (8)		
Bosnia-Herzegovina	1990	1990
Croatia	1990	1990
Cyprus	1960	1993
Georgia	1992	1992
Moldova	1990	1997
Russia	1990	1990
Ukraine	1990	1994
Yugoslavia	1990	1997
Central & Southern Africa (28)		
Angola	1991	1979
Benin	1990	1996
Botswana	1966	1998
Burkina Faso	1991	1987
Cameroon	1991	1982
Cape Verde	1992	1991
Central African Republic	1995	1993
Côte d'Ivoire	1990	1993
Gabon	1991	1967
Gambia	1997	1994
Ghana	1992	1981
Guinea	1991	1984
Kenya	1997	1978
Liberia	1997	1997
Madagascar	1992	1993
Malawi	1994	1994
Mali	1992	1992
Mauritania	1991	1984
Mozambique	1990	1986
Namibia	1990	1990
Nigeria	1999	1999
São Tomé	1990	1991
Seychelles	1991	1977
Sierra Leone	1998	1998
South Africa	1993	1999
Tanzania	1995	1995
Togo	1993	1967
Zambia	1991	1991
Middle East & North Africa (3)		
Algeria	1995	1999
Egypt	1971	1981
Yemen	1990	1990
North America (1)		
United States	1776	1993
Northern & Western Europe (1)		
Switzerland	1874	1999
Oceania (6)		
Kiribati	1979	1994
Marshall Islands	1979	1997
Micronesia, Federated States of	1979	1999
Nauru	1968	1999
Palau	1981	1992
Philippines	1987	1998
South America (12)		
Argentina	1983	1989
Bolivia	1982	1997
Brazil	1985	1995
Chile	1990	1994
Colombia	1978	1998
Ecuador	1979	1998
Guyana	1966	1997
Paraguay	1989	1999
Peru	1978	1990
Suriname	1988	1996
Uruguay	1985	1995
Venezuela	1961	1999

of the Federal Council (Bundesrat), one of whom is selected annually to assume the formal title of President of the Swiss Confederation (Bundespräsident).

In general, it would be true to say that few states with limited presidential executives approach the high degree of dispersal of power that exists in the United States. Arguably, those in South America and the Philippines come closest. As a consequence, the effective authority of most of the presidents included in Table 23 significantly exceeds that of the US chief executive. In a number of emergent democracies, the most prominent examples being Egypt, Guyana, Mexico, and a number of African states, true competition from opposition parties remains limited, further enhancing presidential authority. There are also some states, notably Angola, Chile, Ghana, Indonesia, Mozambique, Peru, and Taiwan, where the military remains an influential force. In such cases, the presidential system can be viewed as only partially limited.

An analysis of Table 23 reveals that 34, or 47%, of the heads of limited presidential executives had, in 1999, been in office for fewer than five years. Fourteen, or 19%, had been in power for at least a decade and two, the presidents of Gabon and Togo, had been in office since the mid-1960s. However, the latter had originally been presidents in one-party states which had only recently become multiparty. In liberal democratic states in 1998, only one president, that of Egypt, had been in power for more than nine years. The imposition of term limits, preventing a president from serving more than a stipulated number of, often consecutive, terms, has been an important factor in restricting presidential tenures in many other liberal and emergent democratic states. In seven states, Colombia, Costa Rica, Guatemala, South Korea, Paraguay, the Philippines, and Switzerland, presidents are restricted to one term in office. In 25 states, which include Argentina, Brazil, Cameroon, Georgia, Moldova, Nicaragua, Peru, Russia, Ukraine, the United States, and Venezuela, the limit is set at two terms. In four states, Angola, Mozambique, Namibia, and the Seychelles, there is a three-term limit. In contrast, in parliamentary executive systems no formal term limits are imposed, although in Japan they have been operated informally for much of the postwar period by the ruling Liberal Democratic Party, which has regularly changed its leader biennially.

Finally, in some states with a limited presidential executive a relatively high minimum age limit is set for candidates, in an effort to ensure that politicians of experience and judgement are elected. In the United States for example, a minimum age of 35 years is stipulated, five years higher than that required for a senator. A similar minimum age has been set in Brazil and Poland, while in the Philippines and Mongolia the respective minimum ages are 40 and 45 years.

4.4 The dual executive

The dual executive is found in four liberal and 13 emergent democracies, the most notable example being France. There are significant differences between the 17 cases, however, and, although the French system is usually cited as the model, it should not be assumed that the others contain all, or even most, of the French features. In Albania, Chad, the Czech Republic, Estonia, Finland, France, Haiti, Lebanon, Lithuania, Macedonia, Poland, Portugal, Romania, Slovenia, and Sri Lanka the executive consists of a working partnership between the president and the prime minister, while in Cambodia and Morocco the partnership is between the monarch and the prime minister. In Haiti, until recently, the military also retained significant influence. The full list is given in Table 24.

Although not really a 'model' of the other systems, a description of how the dual executive operates in France will be helpful to an understanding of the variations which are found in other countries.

The constitution for the French Fifth Republic was framed in the short time span of three months, during the summer of 1958, while the new administration of Charles de Gaulle was settling into office. Conscious of the recent history of instability in French governments, its authors tried to combine elements of the United States and British constitutions, while, at the same time, seeking to strengthen the executive and encourage greater party discipline and stability. To these ends, provision was made for a two-headed executive of a president, to be elected by an electoral college for a seven-year term, and a prime minister, chosen by the president but responsible to the National Assembly.

Under the terms of the constitution the president has considerable powers, including, as well as the appointment of the prime minister, control of the armed forces, the right to preside over cabinet and Defense Council meetings, the right to dissolve the Assembly once a year, and powers to negotiate treaties, countersign legislation approved by the Assembly, and appoint ambassadors.

Nevertheless, the constitution made provision (Articles 20 and 21) for the prime minister and Council of Ministers to wield ultimate power while the president was expected to remain aloof from day-to-day government and act as a mediator and conciliator, who

States with dual executives (17) **Table 24**

Country/region	Year established	Year current head of state came to power	Year current prime minister came to power
Asia (2)			
Cambodia	1991	1991	1985
Sri Lanka	1978	1994	1994
Central America & Caribbean (1)			
Haiti	1987	1996	1999
Central, Eastern, & Southern Europe (8)			
Albania	1997	1997	1998
Czech Republic	1989	1989	1998
Estonia	1990	1992	1999
Lithuania	1990	1998	1999
Macedonia	1992	1991	1998
Poland	1997	1995	1997
Romania	1992	1996	1998
Slovenia	1990	1990	1992
Central & Southern Africa (1)			
Chad	1996	1990	1997
Middle East & North Africa (2)			
Lebanon	1926	1998	1998
Morocco	1992	1999	1998
Northern & Western Europe (3)			
Finland	1917	1994	1995
France	1958	1995	1997
Portugal	1976	1996	1995

ensured that the different factions, in whatever coalition was formed on the basis of Assembly support, worked successfully together.

The respective roles of president and prime minister were altered when, in October 1962, President de Gaulle forced through, by referendum, a change in the constitution making the president directly elected by the people. This gave him a justifiable claim of popular support and he and his immediate successors used this to dominate policy-making so that the prime minister became, in effect, the political servant of the president, who governed in the style of the US presidency, but without the Congressional checks and balances which limit it.

As long as the French president was able to appoint a prime minister amenable to his directions and acceptable to the National Assembly, the unbalanced twin executive worked. In 1986, however, following Assembly elections which swept to power the opposition conservative coalition, President Mitterrand was forced to appoint a prime minister, Jacques Chirac, whose political stance was well to the right of his. An experiment of 'cohabitation' thus began, in which the prime minister assumed the upper hand. This lasted, at times uneasily, until the presidential and Assembly elections of April–June 1988, which were won by President Mitterrand and his Socialist Party. This restored the status quo until there was a further period of 'cohabitation' between 1993 and 1995, with Edouard Balladur as prime minister, and since 1997, this time between a Gaullist president, Jacques Chirac, and a socialist-party prime minister, Lionel Jospin. The periods of 'cohabitation' proved that the constitution was sufficiently flexible to allow a president and prime minister from different parts of the political spectrum to work together, if need be, for an interim period, with reasonable success.

The dual executive in Lebanon closely resembles that of France but the relationship between the president and prime minister is as much conditioned by religious as political factors. With the object of maintaining religious harmony, the president is always, by tradition, a Christian and the prime minister a Muslim. The president is elected for a six-year, nonrenewable, term by the National Assembly.

In Finland, the dual executive is also very similar to that of France, with the president, who is popularly elected for a renewable six-year term, having responsibility for foreign affairs, the dissolution of the Eduskunta (parliament), the formation and dismissal of governments, and the appointment of senior civil servants. The president also has substantial veto powers over legislation passed by the Eduskunta and more limited decree powers. The multiparty, coalition nature of Finnish politics has served to enhance the effective role of the president, as, until 1991, did the sensitivity and importance of foreign relations with Finland's neighbor, the Soviet Union. This was particularly the case 1956–81 when Urho Kekkonen, of the Center Party of Finland (KP), was president and used the office to ensure the continuance in power of center-left parliamentary coalitions, and to promote a foreign policy of 'active neutrality', despite a dwindling in electoral support. In recent years, however, there have been proposals to significantly reduce presidential powers in the legislative and executive spheres.

The Portuguese variant of the dual executive has been evolving since the adoption of a new constitution in 1976. To effect a smooth transition to civilian government after a long period of dictatorship and military rule, the role of the president was cast as a 'watchdog' for the army, to ensure that its interests were not neglected by a civilian prime minister. The relationship between the two parts of the executive depended as much on personalities as on constitutional rules. The revised constitution of 1982 reduced the powers of the presidency and four years later the first civilian for 60 years was elected to that office. Political power is now weighted towards the prime minister but he does not yet head a genuine parliamentary executive.

The Sri Lankan constitution of 1978 is based loosely on the French model and provides for a directly elected president and a prime minister, drawn from the assembly, who is appointed by the president and acts as his or her 'parliamentary manager'. The president has considerably more powers than the prime minister and can hold several portfolios. Sri Lanka thus represents a weak form of dual executive, compared with the French version, yet falls short of being a full presidential executive, as in the United States. In 1994 Chandrika Bandaranaike Kumaratunga was popularly elected president and appointed her mother, Sirimavo Bandaranaike, prime minister, creating a unique family 'dual executive'. It is intended to re-establish a parliamentary form of executive in Sri Lanka.

In Morocco the executive partnership is between the monarch and the prime minister but, until the constitutional reforms of 1992, it was a very one-sided affair, with the king holding a near monopoly of power.

In newly democratized Cambodia, the dual executive also takes the form of power-sharing between a monarch and a prime minister. Father and son, King Norodom Sihanouk and Prince Norodom Ranariddh, occupied these respective positions between 1993 and 1997, although the latter shared power with a 'dual prime minister', the ex-communist leader Hun Sen.

In the four states of the Czech Republic, Estonia, Lithuania, and Slovenia in Central Europe,the executive types are substantially parliamentary, but the directly elected presidents currently retain sufficient authority for the designation 'dual executive' to be applied. In the Czech Republic the position of president is now chiefly ceremonial, but the current incumbent, Vaclav Havel, as leader of the freedom struggle, retains charismatic and moral authority. In the five states of Albania, Chad, Macedonia, Poland, and Romania, political authority has moved gradually away from the president towards the prime minister, over recent years.

A limit of two terms has been set for the presidents of ten states with dual executives: Albania, Chad, the Czech Republic, Estonia, Lithuania, Poland, Portugal, Romania, Slovenia, and Sri Lanka. In Estonia and Lithuania candidates for the presidency must be at least 40 years old.

The dual executives of the 17 states shown in Table 24 demonstrate the variety of ways in which a constitution can be adapted to suit the circumstances of a particular political environment at a particular time.

4.5 The communist executive

Until recently the Soviet Union provided the 'classic' example of a communist political executive, with its interlocking web of party and state personnel and interests, culminating in a concentration of power at the apex of the political system. Now, however, the Soviet Union has been dissolved and emergent democratic Russia has a limited presidential form of political executive. It is in socialist China where the dominant

States with communist executives (5) — Table 25

Country/region	Year established	Year current head of state came to power	Year current prime minister came to power
Asia (4)			
China	1949	1993	1998
Korea, North	1948	1994	1997
Laos	1975	1998	1998
Vietnam	1945	1997	1997
Central America & Caribbean (1)			
Cuba	1959	1959	1959

model of the communist political executive is today best located.

In a communist system it is the party which determines policy objectives and it is the state apparatus which implements them. Whereas in a liberal democratic country, such as the United States, the constitution determines the distribution and exercise of power, in a communist country the constitution is subservient to the needs of the state, as interpreted by the party. In fact, constitutions are fairly frequently changed to meet party requirements.

In a communist state there is a directly or indirectly elected National Assembly, Supreme Soviet ('soviet' means elected council), or People's Congress, which is, constitutionally, but not in reality, the supreme body of state power. In China the National People's Congress comprises nearly 3,000 members, but meets only briefly for several weeks each year, devolving its powers to a smaller, approximately 134-member permanent Standing Committee, and electing from its membership a Council of Ministers (COM) or state council, as the equivalent of a formal government. The COM, with around 40 members, is headed by a chairman who is the equivalent of a prime minister. There is also a state president, who is elected by the legislature.

The state machinery of the COM, its chairman, and the state president are the external, constitutional, manifestations of political power, but the real power in a communist state lies within the Communist Party, which ensures its hold on policy-making through its membership of the state institutions and the policy of 'nomenklatura'. This means that key posts throughout society and government, including positions in the legislature, are reserved for persons of 'sound' judgement who have been vetted and approved by the party's apparatus.

In China it is in the approximately 340-member Central Committee of the Communist Party where true authority can first be perceived and it is in the Politburo, a 12–25-member cabinet body which is 'elected' by the Central Committee and meets weekly, and the smaller Secretariat, its administrative and policy-formulating wing, where ultimate power lies. Leading members of these bodies, at the apex of the party, also hold key positions, including those of prime minister and state president. Indeed, it is usual for the general-secretary of the Party, who is the country's effective political leader, to take a major state position as a formal insignia of office. Thus the Chinese Communist Party's general-secretary, Jiang Zemin, is also state president. However, his real power derives from his position as head of the Party.

In China, where the People's Liberation Army (PLA) played a key role in the 'liberation struggle' during the 1940s and which crushed a popular prodemocracy movement in 1989, the armed forces retain significant behind-the-scenes political influence. They are also influential in Vietnam, North Korea, and Cuba.

The distribution of states with communist, or, as they should more correctly be termed, socialist, executives and their date of establishent are set out in Table 25. They are found exclusively in Asia and the Caribbean. In Cuba, a personalized, plebiscitarian form of leadership prevails, with Fidel Castro, the leader of the 'communist revolution' providing charismatic leadership. In North Korea, a 'socialist dynasty' is in place, with the 'Great Leader' Kim Jong Il succeeding his father, Kim Il Sung, the self-designated 'Sun of Mankind', on the latter's death in 1994. In both China and Vietnam significant parts of the economy have been opened to market forces and private initiative. Still, however, in all cases, control of the state, including large parts of the economy, through the party, is the dominant, and clearly recognizable, characteristic. It is this, more than anything else, that distinguishes communist from other one-party states. Despite the small number (5) of states falling into this executive category, they embrace, in total, nearly a quarter of the world's population.

4.6 The unlimited presidential executive

The term 'unlimited' is used to describe the executive presidency in one-party, noncommunist states, but in politics, of course, nothing is really unlimited. Even the seemingly all-powerful military dictator can be, and is at times, overthrown. Nevertheless, the 22 states which have been classified as nationalistic socialist, authoritarian nationalist, and Islamic nationalist, have considerably fewer limitations on their political executives than those in their liberal and emergent democratic counterparts. These states comprise a twelfth of the world's population.

As in communist systems, the party is the ultimate source of power but, unlike some communist states, a strong, and sometimes charismatic, leader often predominates and the objectives of the party, even in socialist states, are subordinated to national interests. Most of the countries with this type of executive have comparatively short histories of release from rule by a colonial power and have felt the need to assert their independence. Many, also, have tribal, ethnic, or regional differences which require strong leadership if all social groups are to cohere into a single state. More than half of the countries with unlimited presidential executives are to be found located in Africa and the adjoining Middle East.

Despite this regional concentration, these states display considerable variations in their political systems and it is something of a distortion to group them together in this way. Some have, for example, histories of instability and their current leaders have reached the top through a bloody or bloodless military coup. This has been the experience of Azerbaijan, the Republic of Congo, Iraq, Libya, and Syria, for example. Some, such as Afghanistan, Eritrea, Iraq, Rwanda, and Tajikistan, have been racked by recent wars and border insurgency. In contrast, other states, such as Kazakhstan, the Maldives, and Senegal, have strong records of political stability.

States with unlimited presidential executives (22) — Table 26

Region/country	Year established	Year current head of state came to power
Asia (6)		
Afghanistan	1992	1996
Kazakhstan	1990	1990
Maldives	1968	1978
Tajikistan	1991	1992
Turkmenistan	1990	1990
Uzbekistan	1990	1990
Central, Eastern, & Southern Europe (3)		
Armenia	1990	1998
Azerbaijan	1993	1993
Belarus	1994	1994
Central & Southern Africa (8)		
Congo, Republic of	1997	1997
Djibouti	1977	1999
Equatorial Guinea	1979	1979
Eritrea	1993	1993
Rwanda	1978	1994
Senegal	1963	1981
Uganda	1986	1986
Zimbabwe	1980	1980
Middle East & North Africa (5)		
Iran	1979	1997
Iraq	1970	1979
Libya	1969	1969
Syria	1971	1971
Tunisia	1987	1987

Nevertheless, their political executives have certain features in common, including a much greater authoritarianism than is found in liberal and emergent democratic states. This results mainly from the absence of competition and choice, which an effectively functioning multiparty political system clearly provides. They have no opposition party 'waiting in the wings' to take over should the electorate express a wish for a change. Many unlimited executive states do now formally tolerate opposition groupings but elections are so heavily stacked in the governing party's favor, through its control of the media and state sector resources, and through resort to electoral chicanery, that there is little or no possibility of its being defeated.

The importance of the political leader in such states cannot be overstressed. Some have been in office for much longer periods than their counterparts in liberal democratic states could ever hope for. This longevity is illustrated in Table 26. The average tenure of an unlimited president was, in 1999, 11 years. Seven, or 32%, had been in office for 15 years or more, with several having become virtual legends. Muammar al-Kadhafi has dominated politics in Libya since 1969, and Hafez al-Assad in Syria since 1971. Meanwhile, in the former Soviet states of Central Asia, powerful new personality cults have been established in Turkmenistan and Uzbekistan, suggesting that Presidents Niyazov, the officially styled 'leader of the Turkmen', and Karimov intend to remain in power for a considerable period. However, a limit of two or three presidential terms is officially in place in Armenia, Senegal, Tanzania, and Uzbekistan.

In Iran, on the other hand, the focus of leadership in recent years has tended to shift from one individual to another, as different factions have wrestled for power. Until his death in 1989, the religious leader Ayatollah Khomeini, a revered, charismatic figure, seemed to have the strongest voice, but, at times, the pragmatic Speaker of the Assembly, Hojatoleslam Ali Akbar Rafsanjani, was more influential. He served as president between 1989 and 1997. He was replaced by Sayed Muhammed Khatami who has who has further shifted power away from the country's 'spiritual leader', Ayatolla Sayed Ali Khameini. In Afghanistan political conditions have been anarchic since the overthrow of the former Soviet-installed administration and, before the coming to power of the fundamentalist Talibaan in 1996, the real political controllers appeared to be regionally-based warlords and Islamic mujaheddin forces.

To people accustomed to life in liberal democratic political systems the concept of one-party government and strong personal leadership may seem repressive and undemocratic. It would be unwise, however, to make such a sweeping judgement. A country's political system is, inevitably, the product of its history, culture, and resource base, and the majority of the states with unlimited presidential executives are still on a 'learning curve' in their political development. Indeed some systems are so volatile that there are fundamental changes currently taking place or likely to become evident in the foreseeable future. In other cases, particularly across Africa, the system of one-party monopoly is still firmly embedded in some states, drawing its sustenance from older tribal political traditions, with their inclusive decision-making processes, and from the argument that open democracy, with its costly campaigns and interparty quarrels, is an indulgence that cannot yet be afforded.

4.7 The military executive

Of the eight states listed in Table 27 as having military executives, six are in Central and Southern Africa and one is in Asia. Many share a common feature, a long record of military conflicts and coups. For good or ill, in each case the army has established order, though often at the expense of the loss of civil liberties.

Some countries have seen the pendulum swing from civilian to military rule with bewildering frequency. Burkina Faso, for example, has experienced no less than six coups in 30 years and Thailand 17 since its absolute monarchy was abolished in 1932. In Latin America, unusually without a military executive in 1999, and Central and Southern Africa as a whole, three-quarters of the 68 states have endured at least one military coup since 1960.

Some have suffered long periods of genuinely despotic rule. Jean-Bedel Bokassa, of the Central

States with military executives (8) Table 27

Region/country	Year first established	Most recent coup	Year current head of state came to power
Asia (1)			
Myanmar	1962	1988	1992
Central & Southern Africa (7)			
Burundi	1996	1996	1996
Comoros	1975	1999	1999
Congo, Democratic Republic of	1997	1997	1997
Guinea-Bissau	1999	1999	1999
Niger	1974	1999	1999
Somalia	1969	1991	1991
Sudan	1969	1989	1989

African Republic, who was in power between 1965 and 1979, almost brought his nation to economic ruin through his personal excesses, which included an elaborate ceremony to crown him emperor. The Duvalier family ruled Haiti between 1957 and 1986 like gang bosses with their own private armies. In Burundi, in Central Africa, military rule has been ruthlessly used to sustain tribal despotism, in particular the economic and political pre-eminence of the minority Tutsis over the majority Hutu community.

In contrast, some military rulers have brought great political stability. General Alfredo Stroessner of Paraguay enjoyed absolute power, without any real challenge, for 35 years, from 1954 to 1989, by dealing swiftly and harshly with dissidents and astutely allowing potential rivals to share in the spoils of office, while in Indonesia the later civilian ruler, Suharto, remained at the helm from 1967 to 1998, promoting economic development.

The policies pursued by some military regimes, most especially those in South America, have been strongly reactionary and conservative, designed to protect the interests of narrow business elites and stifle popular social movements. Others, often drawing their leaders and in-service support from the middle officer ranks, have pursued radical economic and social policies. These reformist regimes, usually having been prompted to seize power because of the corrupt excesses of preceding civilian administrations, have also tended to follow puritanical governing styles. The most notable contemporary examples are the populist regimes of Flight-Lieutenant Jerry Rawlings in Ghana and Captains Thomas Sankara (1983–87) and Blaise Compaore (1987-) in Burkina Faso. Both Rawlings and Compaore are elected civilian presidents.

The identification of the six military states has been comparatively straightforward but, inevitably, a little arbitrary. In at least a further 30 states classified under other categories the military remains an influential background political force. These include 20 countries identified as limited presidential executives: Algeria, Angola, Burkina Faso, Chile, Egypt, Gambia, Ghana, Guatemala, Guinea, Indonesia, South Korea, Liberia, Mozambique, Nigeria, Paraguay, Peru, Sierra Leone, Suriname, Taiwan, and Yemen. Ethiopia, Fiji, Lesotho, Pakistan, and Thailand, which have been classified as parliamentary executives, and the dual executives of Cambodia and Lebanon, are other examples of states with a military presence in the background. The armed forces are also influential in the remaining communist states of Asia and the Caribbean, and in the unlimited presidential executives of Afghanistan, Azerbaijan, Republic of Congo, Equatorial Guinea, Indonesia, Iraq, Libya, Rwanda, and Syria.

Table 27 gives the dates when the military came to power in the six states classified as full military executives. In Burundi and the Democratic Republic of Congo the military takeovers were particularly recent, arising out of broader civil wars. The other four states had been dominated by the military even more strongly for several decades, although there had been brief periods of civilian rule, until the most recent coups.

4.8 The absolute executive

With the exception of the Vatican City State, all the states listed in Table 28 as having absolute executives are monarchies of one kind or another. Bahrain, Brunei, Jordan, Kuwait, Oman, Qatar, and Saudi Arabia are all Arab monarchies, sultanates, sheikhdoms, or emirates and the United Arab Emirates is a federation of no less than seven emirates. Bhutan, Swaziland, and Tonga are hereditary monarchies.

Another factor that all the states except the Vatican City State have in common is a history of association with Britain, through either a treaty of protection or trade, or both. In nine of them political parties do not operate at all. In Swaziland there is one party subservient to the ruling regime. Only in Jordan, where the ban imposed on political parties in 1976 was lifted in 1991, have multiparty elections recently been held.

Unlike the military states, the absolute executives have not been imposed following a coup. They have usually been part of the social and political lives of the respective communities for many years, surviving during the colonial period as largely autonomous entities, and the rule, though autocratic, has usually been paternalistic. As such, they could alternatively be designated 'traditional executives'.

The Kingdom of Jordan shows clear evidence of constitutionality, with a written constitutional code and two-chamber assembly, but true democracy has had a fluctuating existence, political activity being banned in 1963, restored in 1971, rebanned in 1976, and restored in 1991. Despite the holding of multiparty elections in 1993, Jordan has not democratized to the extent of Nepal, which had an absolutist system until 1990, and ultimate power remains with the king. In Bhutan, in July 1998, the king gave up his right to nominate the

States with absolute executives (12) — Table 28

Region/country	Year first established	Year current head of state came to power	Written constitution
Asia (2)			
Bhutan	1907	1972	N
Brunei	1984	1968	Y
Central & Southern Africa (1)			
Swaziland	1968	1986	Y
Middle East & North Africa (7)			
Bahrain	1971	1999	Y
Jordan	1946	1999	Y
Kuwait	1961	1977	Y
Oman	1951	1970	Y
Qatar	1971	1995	Y
Saudi Arabia	1932	1982	Y
United Arab Emirates	1971	1971	Y
Northern & Western Europe (1)			
Vatican City State	1377	1978	N
Oceania (1)			
Tonga	1875	1965	Y

cabinet and gave the legislature the power to dismiss him by a two-thirds vote. If these measures prove effective, Bhutan will become a dual executive.

The one universal, and most certain, characteristic of an absolutist regime is that of government by personal, or, in the case of Saudi Arabia, family decree, rather than by collective discussion and agreement, and it is this which merits the description of absolute executive. Seven of the absolutist states are oil-rich and enjoy high per-capita incomes. As a consequence, as Table 10 above shows, the absolutist states enjoyed average per-capita incomes, in 1995, in the region of $7,347 and high levels of urbanization. A trade-off between political liberty and economic affluence of citizens is evident in states such as Brunei, Kuwait, Oman, Qatar, Saudi Arabia, and the United Arab Emirates.

Recommended reading

Baynham, R (ed.) *Military Power in Black Politics*, Croom Helm, 1986

Blondel, J *The Organization of Governments: A Comparative Analysis of Government Structures*, Sage Publications, 1982

Carter, S and McCauley, M (eds.) *Leadership and Succession in the Soviet Union, Eastern Europe and China*, Macmillan, 1986

Clapham, C and Philip, G (eds.) *The Political Dilemmas of Military Rule*, Croom Helm, 1985

Elsie, R *Political Leadership in Liberal Democracies*, Macmillan, 1998

Jackson, R and Rosberg, C *Personal Rule in Black Africa: Prince, Autocrat, Prophet, Tyrant*, University of California Press, 1982

James, S *British Cabinet Government*, Routledge, 1991

Kellerman, B *The Political Presidency: Practice of Leadership*, Oxford University Press, 1984

King, A (ed.) *Both Ends of the Avenue: The Presidency, the Executive Branch and Congress in the 1980s*, American Enterprise Institute, 1983

King, A (ed.) *The British Prime Minister*, 2nd edn., Macmillan, 1985

Laver, M and Shepsle, K A (eds.) *Cabinet Ministers and Parliamentary Government*, Cambridge University Press, 1994

Lijphart, A (ed.) *Parliamentary versus Presidential Government*, Oxford University Press, 1992

Lowenhardt, J *The Soviet Politburo*, Canongate, 1982

Neustadt, R E *Presidential Power and the Modern Presidents: The Politics of Leadership from Roosevelt to Reagan*, Free Press, 1990

O'Brien, P and Cammack, P (eds.) *Generals in Retreat: The Crisis of Military Rule in Latin America*, Manchester University Press, 1985

Paterson, W E and Southern, D *Governing Germany*, Basil Blackwell, 1991

Rose, R and Suleiman, E (eds.) *Presidents and Prime Ministers*, American Enterprise Institute, 1980

Shugart, M S and Carey, J M *Presidents and Assemblies: Constitutional Design and Electoral Dynamics*, Cambridge University Press, 1992

Smith, G B *Soviet Politics: Continuity and Contradiction*, Macmillan, 1988, Chap. 5

Weller, P *First Among Equals: Prime Ministers in Westminster Systems*, Allen & Unwin, 1985

Wright, V *The Government and Politics of France*, 3rd edn., Routledge, 1992

CHAPTER 5

Legislature, Assemblies, and Congresses

5.1 The nature of legislatures

Although in formal, constitutional terms the three branches of government are described as the executive, the judiciary, and the legislature, the term 'assembly' has been deliberately preferred for the third arm because the role of the vast majority of legislatures in the world today is deliberative and policy-influencing, rather than law-making. Indeed the old term 'parliament', or '*parlement*', which is still used in some political systems and is associated with the French verb *parler*, to talk, best identifies the chamber as an 'arena' for debate.

Assemblies do, of course, play a major role in the law-making process but they now mostly legitimize policies presented to them by the executive, rather than initiate them themselves. In doing so, they usually also have a modifying, revising function, based on the concept that assembly members are more likely to have an understanding of what is practical and acceptable to the electorate than politicians in government who, inevitably, become insulated in their positions of power from the real world outside.

Popularly elected assemblies have always epitomized democracy and it is not surprising, therefore, that even the most autocratic rulers have sought to make their regimes 'respectable' by establishing a façade of democratization through puppet assemblies.

The 19th century was the 'golden age' of assemblies as independent law-making bodies, or, as the American political scientist Nelson Polsby has termed them, 'transformative legislatures'. The classic example was the Parliament in London where individual members had a genuine role to play before they were to become overwhelmed by the tyranny of the party system and the burgeoning, and increasingly specialist, scope of legislative affairs. Since that time the balance of power has shifted inexorably towards the executive until we are left with but a few shining examples of assemblies which can, and do, wield real political power. The most notable 'transformative legislature' today is undoubtedly the US Congress. Its position is buttressed by the clear separation of powers that is provided for by the US Constitution, the weakness of party discipline, the powerful standing committee structure, and by the large private offices and staff support with which individual members of the House of Representatives and Senate are provided. It is closely followed by the Riksdag of Sweden, with the States-General in the Netherlands, the Parlamento, comprising the Camera dei Deputati and Senato, in Italy, and the Legislative Assembly in Costa Rica also being influential bodies. Assemblies elsewhere are mostly pale shadows of these and can be categorized as 'arena legislatures', being 'settings for the interplay of significant political forces' as executive actions are debated and scrutinized.

Despite the relative decline in importance of assemblies, they still operate in the vast majority of states and are found within a wide range of ideologies and work alongside all types of political executive. Table 29 gives the basic facts about them, showing that at the present time only seven of the 192 states under consideration do not have active assemblies as a normal feature of their political structures. These nations, Bahrain, Brunei, Oman, Qatar, Saudi Arabia, the United Arab Emirates, and the Vatican City State, are all absolutist states and, with the exception of Bahrain between 1973 and 1975, have never had popularly elected assemblies. However, in each of them there are appointed consultative councils which provide advice to the political executive. In addition, Qatar has an elected central municipal council. In a number of other states, specifically those, with military regimes or which are experiencing civil war, the assemblies described in Table 29 are, in most cases, currently in abeyance. For example, in Myanmar the 485-member Constituent Assembly, which was popularly elected in May 1990 and is dominated by opponents of the military regime, has not

Assemblies of the world

Table 29

Region/country	Name of lower house	Number of lower house members	Lower house term (years)	Lower house electoral system
Asia				
Afghanistan	–	N/A	N/A	N/A
Bangladesh	Parliament (Jatiya Sangsad)	330	5	simple plurality
Bhutan	National Assembly	150	3	mixed-elected/appointed
Brunei	–	N/A	N/A	N/A
Cambodia	National Assembly	122	5	simple plurality
China	National People's Congress	2,979	5	indirect
India	Lok Sabha	545	5	simple plurality
Indonesia	House of Representatives	500	5	proportional representation-party list
Japan	House of Representatives	500	4	proportional representation-additional member system
Kazakhstan	Majlis	67	4	second ballot
Korea, North	Supreme People's Assembly	687	5	simple plurality
Korea, South	National Assembly	299	4	proportional representation-additional member system
Kyrgyzstan	Legislative Assembly	38	5	second ballot
Laos	National Assembly	99	5	simple plurality
Malaysia	House of Representatives	192	5	simple plurality
Maldives	Majlis	50	5	mixed-elected/appointed
Mongolia	People's Great Hural	76	4	second ballot
Myanmar	Constituent Assembly (suspended)	485	transitional	simple plurality
Nepal	House of Representatives	205	5	simple plurality
Pakistan	National Assembly	217	5	simple plurality
Singapore	Parliament	83	5	simple plurality
Sri Lanka	National State Assembly	225	6	proportional representation-party list
Taiwan	Legislative Yuan	225	3	proportional representation-additional member system
Tajikistan	Supreme Assembly	181	4	second ballot
Thailand	House of Representatives	400	4	proportional representation-additional member system
Turkmenistan	Majlis	50	5	second ballot
Uzbekistan	Supreme Assembly	250	5	second ballot
Vietnam	National Assembly	450	5	second ballot
Central America & Caribbean				
Antigua	House of Representatives	17	5	simple plurality
Bahamas	House of Assembly	40	5	simple plurality
Barbados	House of Assembly	28	5	simple plurality
Belize	House of Representatives	29	5	simple plurality
Costa Rica	Assembly	57	4	proportional representation-party list
Cuba	National Assembly	601	5	second ballot
Dominica	Assembly	30	5	mixed-elected/appointed
Dominican Republic	Chamber of Deputies	149	4	proportional representation-party list
El Salvador	National Assembly	84	3	proportional representation-additional member system
Grenada	House of Representatives	15	5	simple plurality
Guatemala	National Congress	80	5	proportional representation-additional member system

continues

Assemblies of the world (continued) Table 29

Region/country	Name of lower house	Number of lower house members	Lower house term (years)	Lower house electoral system
Haiti	Chamber of Deputies	83	5	second ballot
Honduras	National Assembly	128	4	proportional representation-party list
Jamaica	House of Representatives	60	5	simple plurality
Mexico	Chamber of Deputies	500	3	proportional representation-additional member system
Nicaragua	National Assembly	93	5	proportional representation-party list
Panama	Legislative Assembly	71	5	simple plurality
St Kitts and Nevis	National Assembly	14	5	simple plurality
St Lucia	House of Assembly	17	5	simple plurality
St Vincent	House of Assembly	21	5	simple plurality
Trinidad and Tobago	House of Representatives	36	5	simple plurality
Central, Eastern, & Southern Europe				
Albania	People's Assembly	155	4	proportional representation-additional member system
Armenia	National Assembly	131	4	proportional representation-additional member system
Azerbaijan	National Assembly	125	4	proportional representation-additional member system
Belarus	House of Representatives	110	4	second ballot
Bosnia-Herzegovina	House of Representatives	42	transitional	proportional representation-party list
Bulgaria	National Assembly (Duma)	240	5	proportional representation-party list
Croatia	Chamber of Representatives	127	4	proportional representation-party list
Cyprus	House of Representatives	80	5	simple plurality
Czech Republic	Chamber of Deputies	200	4	proportional representation-party list
Estonia	Parliament	101	4	proportional representation-party list
Georgia	Parliament	235	4	proportional representation-additional member system
Greece	Parliament	300	4	proportional representation-party list
Hungary	National Assembly	386	4	proportional representation-additional member system
Latvia	Parliament (Saeima)	100	4	proportional representation-party list
Lithuania	Parliament (Seimas)	141	4	proportional representation-additional member system
Macedonia	National Assembly	120–140	4	second ballot
Moldova	Parliament	104	4	proportional representation-party list
Poland	Sejm	460	4	proportional representation-party list
Romania	Chamber of Deputies	343	4	proportional representation-party list
Russia	State Duma	450	4	proportional representation-additional member system
Slovakia	National Council	150	4	proportional representation-party list
Slovenia	National Assembly	90	4	proportional representation-additional member system
Turkey	National Assembly	550	5	proportional representation-party list
Ukraine	Supreme Council	450	4	proportional representation-additional member system
Yugoslavia	Chamber of Citizens	138	4	proportional representation-additional member system

continues

Assemblies of the world (continued) **Table 29**

Region/country	Name of lower house	Number of lower house members	Lower house term (years)	Lower house electoral system
Central & Southern Africa				
Angola	National Assembly	220	4	proportional representation-party list
Benin	National Assembly	83	4	proportional representation-party list
Botswana	National Assembly	47	5	simple plurality
Burkina Faso	Assembly of People's Deputies	111	5	proportional representation-party list
Burundi	National Assembly	81	5	proportional representation-party list
Cameroon	National Assembly	180	5	proportional representation-party list
Cape Verde	National Assembly	72	5	simple plurality
Central African Republic	National Assembly	109	5	second ballot
Chad	National Assembly	125	4	second ballot
Comoros	Federal Assembly	43	4	second ballot
Congo, Democratic Republic of	(suspended)	–	–	–
Congo, Republic of	National Transitional Council	75	transitional	appointed
Côte d'Ivoire	National Assembly	175	5	second ballot
Djibouti	Chamber of Deputies	65	5	simple plurality
Equatorial Guinea	House of Representatives	80	5	proportional representation-party list
Eritrea	Transitional National Assembly	150	transitional	mixed-elected/appointed
Ethiopia	Council of People's Representatives	548	5	simple plurality
Gabon	National Assembly	120	5	mixed-elected/appointed
Gambia	National Assembly	49	5	mixed-elected/appointed
Ghana	Parliament	200	4	simple plurality
Guinea	National Assembly	114	4	proportional representation-additional member system
Guinea-Bissau	National People's Assembly	100	4	proportional representation-limited vote
Kenya	National Assembly	224	5	mixed-elected/appointed
Lesotho	National Assembly	80	5	simple plurality
Liberia	House of Representatives	64	6	simple plurality
Madagascar	National Assembly	150	4	simple plurality
Malawi	National Assembly	192	5	proportional representation-single transferable vote
Mali	National Assembly	160	5	second ballot
Mauritania	National Assembly	79	5	second ballot
Mauritius	National Assembly	66	5	proportional representation-limited vote
Mozambique	Assembly of the Republic	250	5	proportional representation-party list
Namibia	National Assembly	78	5	mixed-elected/appointed
Niger	National Assembly	83	5	simple plurality
Nigeria	House of Representatives	360	4	simple plurality
Rwanda	Transitional National Assembly	70	transitional	appointed
São Tomé	National Assembly	55	4	proportional representation-party list
Senegal	National Assembly	140	5	proportional representation-additional member system
Seychelles	National Assembly	34	5	proportional representation-additional member system
Sierra Leone	House of Representatives	80	5	mixed-elected/appointed
Somalia	(suspended)	–	–	–
South Africa	National Assembly	400	5	proportional representation-party list

continues

Assemblies of the world (continued) — Table 29

Region/country	Name of lower house	Number of lower house members	Lower house term (years)	Lower house electoral system
Sudan	National Assembly	400	4	mixed-elected/indirect
Swaziland	House of Assembly	65	4	mixed-elected/appointed
Tanzania	National Assembly	275	5	mixed-elected/appointed
Togo	National Assembly	81	5	second ballot
Uganda	National Parliament	276	5	mixed-elected/indirect
Zambia	National Assembly	150	5	simple plurality
Zimbabwe	House of Assembly	150	6	mixed-elected/appointed
Middle East & North Africa				
Algeria	National People's Assembly	380	5	proportional representation-party list
Bahrain	**	N/A	N/A	N/A
Egypt	People's Assembly	454	5	mixed-elected/appointed
Iran	Majlis ash-Shura	270	4	proportional representation-party list
Iraq	National Assembly (Majlis)	250	4	proportional representation-party list
Israel	Knesset	120	4	proportional representation-party list
Jordan	House of Representatives	80	4	simple plurality
Kuwait	National Assembly	50	4	simple plurality
Lebanon	National Assembly	128	6	proportional representation-party list
Libya	General People's Congress	1,112	1	indirect
Morocco	House of Representatives	325	5	proportional representation-party list
Oman	**	N/A	N/A	N/A
Qatar	**	N/A	N/A	N/A
Saudi Arabia	**	N/A	N/A	N/A
Syria	People's Assembly (Majlis)	250	4	simple plurality
Tunisia	National Assembly	163	5	proportional representation /additional member system
United Arab Emirates	**	N/A	N/A	N/A
Yemen	House of Representatives	301	4	simple plurality
North America				
Canada	House of Commons	301	5	simple plurality
United States	House of Representatives	435	2	simple plurality
Northern & Western Europe				
Andorra	General Council	28	4	proportional representation-additional member system
Austria	Nationalrat	183	4	proportional representation-party list
Belgium	Chamber of Representatives	150	4	proportional representation-party list
Denmark	Folketing	179	4	proportional representation-party list
Finland	Eduskunta	200	4	proportional representation-party list
France	National Assembly	577	5	second ballot
Germany	Bundestag	669	4	proportional representation-additional member system
Iceland	Althing	63	4	proportional representation-party list
Ireland	Dáil	166	5	proportional representation-single transferable vote
Italy	Chamber of Deputies	630	5	proportional representation-additional member system
Liechtenstein	Landtag	25	4	proportional representation-limited vote

continues

Assemblies of the world (continued) Table 29

Region/country	Name of lower house	Number of lower house members	Lower house term (years)	Lower house electoral system
Luxembourg	Chamber of Deputies	60	5	proportional representation-party list
Malta	House of Representatives	65	5	proportional representation-single transferable vote
Monaco	National Council	18	5	second ballot
Netherlands	Second Chamber	150	4	proportional representation-party list
Norway	Odelsting	124	4	proportional representation-party list
Portugal	Assembly	230	4	proportional representation-party list
San Marino	Council	60	5	proportional representation-limited vote
Spain	Congress of Deputies	350	4	proportional representation-party list
Sweden	Riksdag	349	3	proportional representation-party list
Switzerland	Nationalrat	200	4	proportional representation-party list
United Kingdom	House of Commons	659	5	simple plurality
Vatican City State	**	N/A	N/A	N/A
Oceania				
Australia	House of Representatives	148	3	alternative vote
Fiji Islands	House of Representatives	71	5	second ballot
Kiribati	Maneaba	41	4	second ballot
Marshall Islands	Nitijela	33	4	simple plurality
Micronesia	Congress of the FSM	14	4/2	simple plurality
Nauru	Parliament	18	3	simple plurality
New Zealand	House of Representatives	120	3	proportional representation-additional member system
Palau	House of Delegates	16	4	simple plurality
Papua New Guinea	Parliament	109	5	simple plurality
Philippines	House of Representatives	254	3	simple plurality
Samoa	Assembly	49	5	simple plurality
Solomon Islands	Parliament	50	4	simple plurality
Tonga	Legislative Assembly	30	3	mixed-elected/appointed
Tuvalu	Parliament	12	4	simple plurality
Vanuatu	Parliament	52	4	proportional representation-party list
South America				
Argentina	Chamber of Deputies	257	4	simple plurality
Bolivia	Chamber of Deputies	130	4	simple plurality
Brazil	Chamber of Deputies	513	4	proportional representation-party list
Chile	Chamber of Deputies	120	4	simple plurality
Colombia	House of Representatives	163	4	simple plurality
Ecuador	Chamber of Representatives	125	4	proportional representation-party list
Guyana	National Assembly	65	5	proportional representation-party list
Paraguay	Chamber of Deputies	80	5	proportional representation-party list
Peru	National Congress	120	5	proportional representation-party list
Suriname	National Assembly	51	5	simple plurality
Uruguay	Chamber of Deputies	99	5	proportional representation-party list
Venezuela	Chamber of Deputies	189	5	proportional representation-party list

(– = not applicable, N/A = not available.)

**Appointed consultative councils exist.

been allowed to convene. Instead, its place has been taken by an appointed State Law and Order Restoration Council.

The contemporary scene, therefore, reveals little diminution in the number of assemblies. However, there has been a deterioration in their power and influence, particularly vis-à-vis the political executive. Undoubtedly, the major reason for this decline is the increase in party strength and discipline. Another important factor has been the increasing volume of government business. This has persuaded the executive, anxious to curtail the length of debate and analysis and prevent the tabling of numerous amendments, to impose 'guillotine' and 'block vote' motions in states such as France and the United Kingdom.

The political systems with parliamentary executives, drawn from and responsible to their assemblies, have, in many cases, seen the virtual disappearance of the independent politician and the rise of strong, highly disciplined, parties, demanding unfailing allegiance from their members and consistent support in the voting lobbies. The UK Parliament, and particularly the House of Commons, provides clear evidence of this trend, which in Britain has been reinforced by the simple plurality electoral system. This method of voting, almost presupposing the existence of a two-party regime, meant that the arrival of a significant third party in 1981 guaranteed parliamentary domination by whichever party gained 40% or more of the popular vote. In the UK elections of 1979, 1983, 1987, and 1992, for example, the Conservatives' share of the national vote was, respectively, 43.9%, 42.4%, 42.3%, and 41.9%. Similar trends have been noted in the case of the Australian House of Representatives. Here the alternative vote majoritarian system is in force.

In one-party states, assemblies have, traditionally, always been more subservient, providing a comforting democratic gloss of legitimacy to policy decisions taken behind the closed doors of party caucuses. In communist states, the sheer size of 'parliamentary' bodies such as the National People's Congress (*c.* 3,000 members) in China, and the fact that they meet in plenary session for, at most, only 10–14 days a year have been significant factors behind such impotence. The most important reason for their relative powerlessness, however, has been the rigid control over agenda and placements exerted by the party leadership above, buttressed by the principle of 'democratic centralism'. Similar tight leadership control is exerted in noncommunist, one-party states.

The political systems where assemblies still retain a degree of robustness are those with limited presidential executives, those where party structures are weak or absent, and the parliamentary executive states with voting systems which encourage a multiplicity of parties and 'consociational' politics.

In a limited presidential executive state, the constitution places clear restraints on the powers of the executive and protects the assembly in its counterbalancing role. This is evident in its purest and most extreme form in the United States, where it is enhanced by the notorious weakness of party structures, with more than half of the votes taken in Congress being bipartisan, in which a majority from both the two dominant parties vote together on an issue. It is also the case, though to lesser degrees, in Brazil, Colombia, Costa Rica, the Dominican Republic, the Philippines, and Venezuela. These are all countries where efforts have been made to copy the 'US model'.

In parliamentary states with electoral systems which stimulate party multiplicity, coalition executives are the norm and accountability to the assembly becomes a reality. Several Northern and Western European countries fall into this category, most notably Italy, which has had more than 50 governments since World War II. Others include Belgium, Denmark, and the Netherlands.

In the region we have called Oceania, the political system of Papua New Guinea, where more than six minor political parties effectively function, is an even more notable example of assembly atomization, with votes of no confidence being frequently registered against incumbent administrations, as members shift fluidly in and out of coalition groups. To redress this problem, the constitution has been recently amended to prevent no-confidence votes being held during the first 18 months of a government's life. In Micronesia, Nauru, Palau, and Tuvalu the absence of formal parties enhances the authority and bargaining power of individual legislators.

5.2 Legislative functions

Whatever degree of strength or weakness they display, what are the functions of contemporary legislative?

First, they have the obvious task of legitimizing policies, in other words turning political decisions into law. Although, at worst, this may mean little more than 'rubber stamping' the actions of the executive, it is a basic function of an assembly and the foundation of what states which claim to be democratic call the 'rule of law'.

Second, they are required to act as the people's representatives and, as such, carry their views to the executives. This is what representative democracy is supposed to be about, but if it is to be effective then the assembly must be able to influence the executive. This brings us back to the question of an assembly's strength.

Third, they are expected to be a 'talking shop': the national debating arena. This is the role for which assemblies in liberal and emergent democracies are best equipped and which they generally best perform. In one-party states it is the party, through whatever closed institutions it devises, which predominantly fulfils this function. However, in one-party states which may be going through a transitional period, as is the case in several contemporary communist regimes, or are torn by internal factions, as, for example, in contemporary Iran, assembly debates can be surprisingly lively and relatively open.

Fourth, in liberal and emergent democracies, assemblies perform the vital 'reactive' role of supervising and scrutinizing the actions of the political executive and bureaucracy, calling attention to abuses of authority and inefficiencies, and suggesting improvements to legislative packages presented to them. This may be done by the regular questioning of government leaders and ministers by opposition deputies, as in the British 'Question Time' model, or by the work of standing and ad hoc scrutiny and investigative committees.

5.3 Comparing legislatures or assemblies

Table 29 provides a variety of data with which to compare assemblies in different states but if it is to be used effectively some criteria need to be established.

For example, is it important that some assemblies are unicameral, with one chamber, and others, bicameral, with two? Why, in two-chamber assemblies, are the 'upper' chambers usually less powerful than the 'lower'? Is it important that membership of some chambers is on the basis of election and others by appointment? Does the duration of the term of office of assembly members have any real significance?

Before these questions can be answered sensibly they must be qualified in some way.

The relationship between assemblies and political executives is arguably the most important basis of comparison because if democratic, rather than autocratic, government is to be achieved then there must be some limits on executive power and in most political systems the only representative body likely to be able to impose such limits is a popular assembly.

As the bases for objective comparisons, we will, therefore, look at single and two-chamber assemblies, and, where there are two, the relationships between them; the membership of assemblies and the criteria for membership; and the relationships between assemblies and executives.

5.4 One chamber or two?

First, the question of one or two chambers. There is a clear link between federalism and two-chamber assemblies. Of the 24 functioning federal states listed in Table 6 above, 19, or 79%, have two-chamber assemblies, compared with only 53 of the 168 unitary states, or just over 31%. In the majority of cases the reason for the link will be obvious and this is illustrated in Table 30. In this table the generic term 'second chamber' or 'upper house' has, for convenience, been used, but this can be slightly misleading. As we will see later, the so-called 'upper house' is often the weaker of the two and in the Netherlands what is listed in Table 30 as the 'second chamber' is in fact known as the 'first chamber' of the bicameral States-General.

It is interesting to observe that one state, Norway, ostensibly has a single-chamber assembly, the Storting, but, after the general election, this divides into two. A quarter of the 165-member Storting becomes an upper house, the Lagting, and the remaining three-quarters the lower house, the Odelsting. Legislation must start in the Odelsting and then be passed by the Lagting. If there is a conflict of view between the two Houses they can consider legislation jointly, as a combined Storting, and approve it by a two-thirds majority. A similar division operated in Iceland until 1991, when a unicameral parliament, the Althing, was established.

A regional pattern is also evident in the distribution of second chambers. They are most commonly found in the Americas, where, influenced by the US and, in the Caribbean, UK constitutional models, 21, or 60%, of the states in the region have bicameral legislatures. In Central, Eastern, Northern, Southern, and Western Europe two-chamber parliaments are also relatively

Second chambers or upper houses

Table 30

Region/country	Federal (F) or unitary (U)	Name of upper chamber	Members	Relative term (years)	Relative powers to lower house	Basis of representation	Upper house electoral system
Asia (9)							
Cambodia	U	Senate	61	–/5	<	national	appointed
India	F	Council of States	245	6/5	<	regional	indirect
Japan	U	House of Councillors	252	6/4	<	national & local	direct-proportional representation/limited vote
Kazakhstan	U	Senate	47	4/4	–	regional	mixed-elected/appointed
Kyrgyzstan	U	People's Assembly	67	5/5	<	national	direct-second ballot
Malaysia	F	Senate	70	6/5	<	mixed	mixed-elected/appointed
Nepal	U	National Council	60	6/5	<	national & local	mixed-indirect/appointed
Pakistan	F	Senate	87	6/5	<	regional	indirect
Thailand	U	Senate	200	6/4	=	national	direct-simple plurality
Central America & Caribbean (11)							
Antigua	U	Senate	17	5/5	<	national	appointed
Bahamas	U	Senate	16	5/5	<	national	appointed
Barbados	U	Senate	21	5/5	<	national	appointed
Belize	U	Senate	8	5/5	<	national	appointed
Dominican Republic	U	Senate	30	4/4	=	regional	direct-second ballot
Grenada	U	Senate	13	5/5	<	national	appointed
Haiti	U	Senate	27	5/5	<	national	direct-second ballot
Jamaica	U	Senate	21	5/5	<	national	appointed
Mexico	F	Senate	64	6/3	=	regional	direct-additional member system
St Lucia	U	Senate	11	5/5	<	national	appointed
Trinidad and Tobago	U	Senate	31	5/5	<	national	appointed
Central, Eastern, & Southern Europe (9)							
Belarus	U	Council of the Republic	64	4/4	>	regional	mixed-indirect/appointed
Bosnia-Herzegovina	F	House of Peoples	15	transitional	<	regional	indirect
Croatia	U	Chamber of Counties	68	4/4	<	regional & local	mixed-elected/appointed
Czech Republic	U	Senate	81	6/4	<	national	direct-second ballot
Poland	U	Senate	100	4/4	<	regional	direct-proportional representation
Romania	U	Senate	143	4/4	<	national	direct-proportional representation
Russia	F	Federation Council	178	4/4	<	regional	indirect

continues

Second chambers or upper houses (continued) **Table 30**

Region/country	Federal (F) or unitary (U)	Name of upper chamber	Members	Relative term (years)	Relative powers to lower house	Basis of representation	Upper house electoral system
Slovenia	U	National Council	40	5/4	<	national	mixed-elected/ indirect
Yugoslavia	F	Chamber of the Republics	40	4/4	=	regional	indirect
Central & Southern Africa (15)							
Botswana	U	House of Chiefs	15	- /5	<	regional	mixed-indirect/appointed
Burkina Faso	U	Chamber of Representatives	178	3/5	<	national	appointed
Central African Republic	U	Economic & Regional Council	–	5/5	<	regional	mixed-indirect/ appointed
Ethiopia	F	Council of the Federation	117	5/5	<	regional	indirect
Gabon	U	Senate	91	6/5	<	local	indirect
Lesotho	U	Senate	33	-/5	<	national	hereditary/ appointed
Liberia	U	Senate	26	9/6	=	national	direct-simple plurality
Madagascar	U	Senate	–	4/4	<	national	mixed-indirect/ and local appointed
Mauritania	U	Senate	56	6/5	<	local	indirect
Namibia	U	National Council	26	6/5	<	local	indirect
Nigeria	F	Senate	109	4/4	>	regional	direct-simple plurality
Senegal	U	Senate	60	varies/5	<	mixed	indirect/appointed
South Africa	U	Senate	90	5/5	<	regional	indirect
Swaziland	U	Senate	30	4/4	=	mixed	mixed-elected/ indirect
Zambia	U	House of Chiefs	27	-/5	<	regional	appointed
Middle East & North Africa (3)							
Algeria	U	Council of the Nation	144	6/5	<	regional	mixed-indirect/appointed
Jordan	U	Senate	40	8/4	=	national	appointed
Morocco	U	Chamber of Councillors	270	9/6	<	regional	indirect
North America (2)							
Canada	F	Senate	104	life*/5	<	regional	appointed
United States	F	Senate	100	6/2	>	regional	direct-simple plurality
Northern & Western Europe (11)							
Austria	F	Bundesrat	64	varies/4	<	regional	indirect
Belgium	F	Senate	71	4/4	=	mixed	mixed-elected/ appointed
France	U	Senate	321	9/5	<	mixed	indirect
Germany	F	Bundesrat	69	**/4	<	regional	indirect

continues

Second chambers or upper houses (continued) — Table 30

Region/country	Federal (F) or unitary (U)	Name of upper chamber	Members	Relative term (years)	Relative powers to lower house	Basis of representation	Upper house electoral system
Ireland	U	Seanad	60	5/5	<	national	mixed-elected/ appointed
Italy	U	Senate	315	5/5	=	regional	indirect
Netherlands	U	First Chamber	75	6/4	<	regional	indirect
Norway	U	Lagting	41	4/4	=	national	indirect
Spain	U	Senate	252	4/4	<	mixed	mixed-elected/ indirect
Switzerland	F	Standerat	46	4/4	=	local	indirect
United Kingdom	U	House of Lords	1,220	life/5	<	national	hereditary/ appointed
Oceania (4)							
Australia	F	Senate	76	6/3	<	regional	direct-proportional representation/ single transferable vote
Fiji	U	Senate	34	5/5	<	mixed	mixed-indirect/ appointed
Palau	U	Senate	14	4/4	=	regional	direct-simple plurality
Philippines	U	Senate	24	6/3	>	national	direct-simple plurality
South America (8)							
Argentina	F	Senate	72	6/4	<	regional	indirect
Bolivia	U	Senate	27	4/4	=	regional	direct-simple plurality
Brazil	F	Senate	81	8/4	=	regional	direct-simple plurality
Chile	U	Senate	47	8/4	=	regional	mixed-elected/ appointed
Colombia	U	Senate	102	4/4	=	national	direct-simple plurality
Paraguay	U	Senate	45	5/5	<	regional	direct-proportional representation
Uruguay	U	Senate	31	5/5	=	national	direct-proportional representation
Venezuela	F	Senate	49	5/5	=	regional	mixed-elected/ appointed

(– = not applicable, > = more power in the upper house, < = less power in the upper house.)

* Retire at age 75.

** Depends on terms of state governments.

common, featuring in 20, or 42%, of the region's states. In contrast, although 16 states established a second chamber during the last decade, they are rare in Africa and the Middle East, being found in only 16, or 24%, of the states. In Asia 32% of states have bicameral legislatures and in Oceania 27%.

Overall, the number of countries with bicameral parliaments has advanced from 50 to 72 since the first edition of this title appeared in 1990. Three states, Afghanistan, Peru, and Zimbabwe, have reverted to unicameral structures, while 25 countries have moved in the other direction, establishing a second chamber.

These are Algeria, Belarus, Bosnia-Herzegovina, Botswana, Burkina Faso, Cambodia, the Central African Republic, Croatia, Ethiopia, Gabon, Haiti, Kazakhstan, Kyrgyzstan, Lesotho, Madagascar, Mauritania, Morocco, Namibia, Nepal, Nigeria, Romania, Senegal, Slovenia, South Africa, and Zambia. It was also planned to establish a second chamber in Malawi and Tajikistan, in 1999.

In making an initial comparison between countries with one- or two-chamber assemblies, Table 30 is relevant, indicating whether the state is unitary or federal, whether members are elected or appointed on a national or regional basis, and whether or not a representative or appointee is required to reside in the constituency he or she represents.

Of the 19 federal states with bicameral assemblies, 17, or 89%, have second chambers which are representative in a regionally or locally biased manner, whereas only 19 out of 53, or 36%, unitary states have similar regionally or locally representative bases. Twenty-six unitary states, or 49%, have national representative bases. There are ten states where the representation is part-national and part-regional and two federal and eight unitary states fall into this category.

This pattern illustrates one of the chief reasons for having a second chamber: to help resolve regional differences in countries which are geographically large and/or socially and culturally diverse. Regional interests, which might object to a centralized government and dominance by large state or metropolitan interests, are to some extent pacified by the knowledge that they are formally represented at the center by a 'local' politician. Indeed, in a number of countries, such as Australia, Germany, Nigeria, and the United States, a feature of the second chamber is the way in which smaller states within the federal system are deliberately over-represented to reduce the threat of 'tyranny by the majority'. In the United States for example, where each state, regardless of size or population, has two senators, theoretically a coalition of senators from the Union's 26 smallest states, comprising less than a sixth of the country's population, could secure a majority to block legislation. Similarly in Australia, New South Wales, with a population of 6 million, sends the same number of senators, 12, to the senate as tiny Tasmania, with a population of less than half a million.

Incidentally, it is interesting to note that, whereas the majority of countries recognize regional aspirations through second chamber representation, Uruguay seeks to achieve this in a reverse way, by having national representation in the second chamber and regional representation in the first.

A minority of constitutions carry this regional representation a stage further by requiring politicians to reside in the region they represent. Argentina, Canada, and the United States have adopted this rule.

The relationship between first and second chambers in terms of political power and authority is another interesting basis of comparison. It is not easy to make clear distinctions and, inevitably, a certain amount of subjectivity will creep in. Table 30 attempts this comparison, using criteria such as the ability to veto legislation, the respective controls of financial legislation, and the extent to which a chamber has powers to interrogate the executive and curb its powers. On the basis of such criteria, it will be seen, in Table 30, that the majority of second chambers are weaker, or enjoy parity, with first chambers, and only four, the United States, Nigeria, and Philippines' Senates, and Belarus's Council of the Republic, it can be argued, are stronger.

Typically, lower houses have primacy in finance matters, while upper chambers have only limited delaying powers. This is certainly the case in the United Kingdom, where the House of Lords has the authority to amend legislation and delay nonfinancial bills by one year, but may not examine, let alone reject, financial bills or, as accepted by the 'Salisbury doctrine', (a convention associated with the Marquess of Salisbury), measures which appeared in a successful party's election manifesto. In Austria, the Netherlands, Spain, and Thailand all bills must commence their passage in the lower house. In Poland, the Senate has the power of veto in specified areas, but this can be overridden by a two-thirds vote in the lower chamber, the Sejm. In Germany, all legislation relating to *Länder* (states) responsibilities require the approval of the Bundesrat upper house and constitutional amendments require two-thirds majorities in both chambers. On other matters, the Bundesrat may suggest amendments to legislation approved by the Bundestag, the lower chamber, send disputed items to a joint Bundestag-Bundesrat 'conciliation committee', and can block items of which it disapproves, but only temporarily, until a countervailing 50% or 66% Bundestag vote is passed. In other states, such as France, India, and Malaysia, where the Senate's delaying powers are restricted to just one month for money bills and one year for other bills, there are similar constitutional provisions to ensure primacy for the lower chamber.

This imbalance in influence is understandable. It is

attributable to the greater popular legitimacy that is enjoyed by lower chambers, which are usually directly elected, and for comparatively short terms, whereas many upper chambers are either elected indirectly or are appointed. In addition, in parliamentary regimes, it is in the lower chamber that the executive, the prime minister and cabinet, sit, and from which they are predominantly drawn.

The exceptions to this are, significantly, to be found in limited presidential states. In the United States, the lower chamber, the biennially elected House of Representatives, also has primacy in financial matters; all revenue raising and general appropriation bills originate there. However, the upper-chamber Senate, whose members serve six-year terms, has effective veto power over lower-house measures and has additional competence in three areas. Its approval is required for key federal judicial, diplomatic, and presidential cabinet appointments; it ratifies foreign treaties; and it acts as the jury when a president is impeached. For these reasons, it can be viewed as the most powerful chamber of Congress. In the Philippines, as in the United States, the approval of both chambers is required for the passage of legislation, with special joint 'conference sessions' being convened to iron out differences when they arise. Similarly, the Senate has special authority over foreign affairs, two-thirds approval from it being required for the ratification of all treaties and agreements.

5.5 Membership and designation of legislatures

Table 29 above shows that, in the vast majority of states, assembly membership is on the basis of election. It would be surprising if it were otherwise since the main purpose of having an assembly is to ensure, or at least suggest, that the ordinary person has an opportunity to be represented by a politician who has been freely chosen. How this is done and whether or not it is done successfully will be examined in the next chapter.

There are a few first chambers or single chambers where a combination of election and appointment is used. In the vast majority of such cases the nonelected members are executive appointees, giving a president or monarch the opportunity of placing his or her own people. Occasionally appointments are made to try to ensure a particular distribution of membership. In Tanzania, for example, a complicated mixture of election and appointment makes provision for regional, female, and party representation as well as presidential nominees. Similarly, in Bangladesh a set quota of National Assembly seats, 30, are reserved for women appointees. In Pakistan, ten National Assembly seats are reserved for Christians, Hindus, Parsis, and other minorities. In India, two Lok Sabha seats are allocated for the Anglo-Indian community and in Romania 15 Chamber of Deputies' seats are set aside for representatives of national minorities. In Singapore the Group Representation Constituency (GRC) rules ensure that at least 15 members of Parliament are of non-Chinese racial origin and in Zimbabwe, ten House of Assembly seats are filled by traditional chiefs. In Venezuela, former state presidents automatically become life members of the Senate.

In the majority of one-party states assembly representatives, whether elected or appointed, are initially selected by the party. In communist systems there is an interweaving of party and state membership, with the party nominees, because of their greater experience and 'professionalism', dominating proceedings. The non-party deputies are selected as exemplary representatives of the full cross section of society by sex, age, ethnic, and occupational groups. They serve their constituents as mandated delegates on a part-time basis, being given only minor 'out-of-pocket' expenses for the five to ten days spent each year at the national assembly.

Of the 72 states with second chambers, members are directly elected in 20, indirectly elected in 19, wholly appointed or placed by hereditary right in 15, and part-elected and part-appointed in 18. Appointed or hereditary second chambers are typically found in countries in the Caribbean and Commonwealth, influenced by the model of the British House of Lords, although in Canada there is compulsory retirement at the age of 75. In some of the small states, with a parliamentary executive fashioned on the British 'Westminster model' (see 4.2), the mixture of election and appointment is constructed so as to reflect the political balance in the first chamber. In Antigua, the Bahamas, Barbados, Belize, Grenada, St Lucia, and Trinidad and Tobago, for example, the prime minister and the official leader of the opposition are entitled to nominate members.

In states with political systems modelled on the United States, most notably those in Latin America, but also the new states of Central and Eastern Europe, direct popular election of the second chamber predominates.

In Northern and Western Europe and South Asia, by contrast, members of second chambers are predominantly elected indirectly, in the majority of cases by regional assemblies. Austria, Belgium, France, Germany, India, Ireland, the Netherlands, Pakistan, and Yugoslavia all provide examples of indirectly elected second chambers. In Germany, the composition of the upper chamber, the Bundesrat, is unusual in that its members are not only appointed by the members of the 16 *Länder* (states), but are themselves members of their own state governments, delegations being made or renewed after each state election. As a consequence, state governments are able to participate directly in the federal parliamentary process. In India the Rajya Sabha is elected by members of state legislative assemblies, using the single transferable vote. In Malaysia a two-term limit is applied to upper-house deputies.

In several African, Central American, and Asian states there are specific literacy requirements for candidates for legislatures. This is the case in Botswana, Cameroon, Costa Rica, Gambia, Kenya, Malawi, the Philippines, and Singapore. The most popular term of membership for first or single chambers is five years, closely followed by four years. The shorter term is found most commonly in Europe and Oceania, where liberal and emergent democratic regimes predominate, while five-year terms are common in Africa and Central America and the Caribbean. The complete analysis is given in Table 31.

Assembly: terms of membership Table 31

Term (years)	First or single chamber: number in world	First or single chamber: % of world	Second chamber: number in world	Second chamber: % of world
1	1	1	0	0
2	2	1	0	0
3	10	5	1	1
4	74	40	18	25
5	86	46	20	28
6	4	2	17	24
7	0	0	0	0
8	0	0	3	4
9	0	0	3	4
life	0	0	2*	3
varies	0	0	4	6
transitional/ suspended	8	5	4	6
Total	185	100	72	100

* With a retirement age of 75 in Canada.

The popularity of a five-year term is understandable. A newly elected government, with a policy package it wished to implement, would probably spend at least the first two years framing the necessary legislation and ensuring its passage through the legislative machine. If a proposal was thought to be beneficial in the long term, but unpopular in a short time span, then a reasonable period would be needed for the public to appreciate its benefits. That would be the government's view. On the other hand, immediately popular proposals might be innately flawed and these defects might only reveal themselves over time. A five-year term of office would give the electorate time to assess a government's performance before it submitted itself again for election. That would be the opposition's view.

Politicians in states with lower chambers with lshort terms of two or three years, such as the United States, Australia, New Zealand, and Sweden, have expressed reservations from time to time about the shortness of the term and some of the practical consequences. Short-term assemblies tend to make governments cautious in their policy proposals, fearing a loss of public support with insufficient time to prove that short-term unpopularity can be replaced by long-term satisfaction.

It should be remembered, however, that assemblies in states with parliamentary executives rarely run their full terms. They may end because the government loses assembly support or, as frequently happens, it, or a coalition partner, seeks a dissolution at what it considers to be the most propitious time to ensure electoral success.

In states with limited presidential executives, assembly terms are, invariably, of a fixed duration. This is of potential value to opposition parties, removing the incumbent administration's control over the election timetable and thus subjecting all members equally to the whims of random external forces. It also serves, however, to institutionalize electioneering, sometimes to an unhealthy degree. This is most clearly seen in the case of the US House of Representatives, whose members, facing biennial elections, find themselves condemned to a nonstop cycle of campaigning and fundraising. Fixed-term assemblies are also the norm in two Scandinavian countries with parliamentary executives, Norway and Sweden, and also in Switzerland. In Germany, the term is not formally fixed, but early dissolution for opportunistic reasons is resisted by the Federal Constitutional Court.

As Table 31 shows, the terms of second chambers are invariably longer than those of lower houses, and are only shorter in one country, Burkina Faso. The most common term for the upper house is, again, five years, but in 17 states it is six years and in six states it is either eight or nine years.

Second chambers with terms of six years or more often stagger those of individual members, with half or a third submitting themselves for election at a time. This serves to 'keep fresh' the accountability of the assembly, but can create problems for a new administration assuming office following a sudden election swing in the lower chamber. The states falling into this staggered category are:

Nine-year term with a third retiring every three years: Argentina, France, and Morocco;

Eight-year term with a third and two-thirds retiring alternately every four years: Brazil;

Eight-year term with half retiring every four years: Jordan;

Six-year term with half retiring every three years: Algeria, Japan, the Netherlands, and the Philippines;

Six-year term with a third retiring every two years: United States, India, and Pakistan;

Four-year term with half retiring every two years: Kazakhstan.

Additionally, constitutions invariably specify qualifications for candidates in assembly elections, including a minimum age. Most states with two-chamber assemblies stipulate a more mature entry age for members of the upper chamber. In Romania and Venezuela, for example, the minimum ages are 21 years for the Chamber of Deputies and 30 years for the Senate. In Argentina, India, Japan, Pakistan, the United States, and Uruguay, they are 25 years for the lower house and 30 years for the upper chamber. In the Philippines and Thailand, the figures are 25 years for the House of Representatives and 35 years for the Senate. In Brazil, the ages are 21 for the Chamber of Deputies and 35 for the Senate; in France, 23 years for the National Assembly and 35 years for the Senate; and in Italy, 25 years for the Camera dei Deputati and 40 years for the Senato.

This requirement of greater maturity, frequently combined with a longer term of office than in the first chamber, tends to add to the authority of second chamber members, who have often already had sufficiently long political careers to qualify them for the description of 'elder statesmen'.

Finally, influenced by the US model, by far the most popular name adopted for the upper chamber has been the Senate. It is used in 48, or 67%, of the states with second chambers. For lower chambers, there is a wider variety of nomenclature. The most popular designation is National Assembly, used in 55, or 30%, of states with lower chambers. A further 31 states have lower houses described variously as the People's Assembly, House of Assembly, Legislative Assembly, Majlis, or, simply, the Assembly. In 30 states, including the United States, the lower chamber is called the House (or Chamber) of Representatives; in 17 states, including ten in Central and South America, the Chamber of Deputies; and in 13 states, many of which are in the Commonwealth, the name which has been adopted is Parliament. It should

Size distribution of contemporary world assemblies — Table 32

Membership	Lower chambers	Upper chambers	Lower chambers (%)	Upper chambers (%)
10 or below	0	1	0	1
11–50	31	30	17	42
51–100	43	23	23	32
101–200	53	9	29	12
201–300	20	4	11	6
301–400	13	2	7	3
401–500	10	0	5	0
501–750	10	0	5	0
751–1,000	0	0	0	0
1,001–3,000	2	1	1	1
N/A	3	2	2	3
Total	*185*	*72*	*100*	*100*

Population per lower house member (*c.* 1995) Table 33

Country	Region	Population (thousands) per lower house member
Over 200,000 (14 states)		
India	Asia	1,685.4
United States	N America	609.9
Pakistan	Asia	583.5
China	Asia	407.9
Indonesia	Asia	384.4
Bangladesh	Asia	364.8
Russia	C, E, & S Europe	328.8
Nigeria	C & S Africa	301.3
Brazil	S America	299.7
Philippines	Oceania	263.9
Kazakhstan	Asia	254.1
Japan	Asia	249.9
Iran	Middle East & N Africa	219.5
Colombia	S America	211.8
Between 100,000 and 200,000 (26 states)		
Peru	S America	192.4
Mexico	C America & Caribbean	186.0
Vietnam	Asia	161.1
Thailand	Asia	151.8
Korea, South	Asia	149.2
Argentina	S America	133.0
Kenya	C & S Africa	130.8
Egypt	Middle East & N Africa	129.9
Guatemala	C America & Caribbean	129.0
Australia	Oceania	124.5
Germany	N & W Europe	121.7
Kyrgyzstan	Asia	121.1
Chile	S America	116.6
Ukraine	C, E, & S Europe	115.8
Spain	N & W Europe	112.8
Venezuela	S America	112.0
Turkey	C, E, & S Europe	111.2
Rwanda	C & S Africa	110.7
Niger	C & S Africa	106.6
Tanzania	C & S Africa	104.9
Malaysia	Asia	104.7
Nepal	Asia	104.2
Netherlands	N & W Europe	103.3
South Africa	C & S Africa	101.1
Ethiopia	C & S Africa	100.3
France	N & W Europe	100.1
Between 50,000 and 100,000 (47 states)		
Canada	N America	97.2
Madagascar	C & S Africa	95.4
Taiwan	Asia	95.3
Myanmar	Asia	93.9
Belarus	C, E, & S Europe	93.3
Italy	N & W Europe	90.8
Ecuador	S America	89.9
Burkina Faso	C & S Africa	89.1
United Kingdom	N & W Europe	88.9
Ghana	C & S Africa	87.2
Cambodia	Asia	86.9
Bosnia-Herzegovina	C, E, & S Europe	85.7
Haiti	C America & Caribbean	84.8
Uzbekistan	Asia	84.8
Poland	C, E, & S Europe	84.0
Morocco	Middle East & N Africa	81.8
Iraq	Middle East & N Africa	79.7
Sri Lanka	Asia	79.6
Côte d'Ivoire	C & S Africa	78.3
Yugoslavia	C, E, & S Europe	76.2
Turkmenistan	Asia	76.2
Burundi	C & S Africa	75.7
Uganda	C & S Africa	74.7
Zimbabwe	C & S Africa	74.3
Sudan	C & S Africa	72.4
Algeria	Middle East & N Africa	71.9
Cameroon	C & S Africa	71.5
Belgium	N & W Europe	67.2
El Salvador	C America & Caribbean	67.2
Romania	C, E, & S Europe	66.2
Mozambique	C & S Africa	66.0
Jordan	Middle East & N Africa	65.0
Benin	C & S Africa	64.9
Zambia	C & S Africa	61.3
Azerbaijan	C, E, & S Europe	60.4
Paraguay	S America	58.8
Senegal	C & S Africa	57.9
Guinea	C & S Africa	57.0
Bolivia	S America	55.7
Syria	Middle East & N Africa	55.4
Sierra Leone	C & S Africa	55.0
Costa Rica	C America & Caribbean	53.9
Tunisia	Middle East & N Africa	53.6
Malawi	C & S Africa	53.5
Yemen	Middle East & N Africa	52.5
Dominican Republic	C America & Caribbean	52.1
Czech Republic	C, E, & S Europe	51.7
Between 10,000 and 50,000 (59 states)		
Chad	C & S Africa	49.7
Togo	C & S Africa	48.5
Angola	C & S Africa	48.5
Malawi	C & S Africa	49.3
Nicaragua	C America & Caribbean	47.3
Laos	Asia	46.5
Honduras	C America & Caribbean	45.1

continues

Population per lower house member (*c.* 1995) (continued) **Table 33**

Country	Region	Population (thousands) per lower house member
Israel	Middle East & N Africa	44.9
Austria	N & W Europe	44.0
Portugal	N & W Europe	42.7
Moldova	C, E, & S Europe	42.3
Liberia	C & S Africa	42.2
Jamaica	C America & Caribbean	41.7
Singapore	Asia	41.0
Panama	C America & Caribbean	37.1
Papua New Guinea	Oceania	36.7
Slovakia	C, E, & S Europe	35.6
Croatia	C, E, & S Europe	35.5
Bulgaria	C, E, & S Europe	35.4
Norway	N & W Europe	35.2
Switzerland	N & W Europe	35.0
Trinidad and Tobago	C America & Caribbean	34.9
Greece	C, E, & S Europe	34.8
Korea, North	Asia	34.2
Uruguay	S America	32.0
Kuwait	Middle East & N Africa	31.5
Mongolia	Asia	31.1
Botswana	C & S Africa	30.7
Tajikistan	Asia	30.5
New Zealand	Oceania	30.4
Central African Republic	C & S Africa	29.7
Denmark	N & W Europe	29.3
Mauritania	C & S Africa	28.0
Armenia	C, E, & S Europe	27.1
Hungary	C, E, & S Europe	26.6
Lithuania	C, E, & S Europe	26.3
Finland	N & W Europe	25.5
Latvia	C, E, & S Europe	25.3
Sweden	N & W Europe	25.2
Lesotho	C & S Africa	25.0
Georgia	C, E, & S Europe	23.0
Eritrea	C & S Africa	22.9
Lebanon	Middle East & N Africa	22.8
Gambia	C & S Africa	22.1
Albania	C, E, & S Europe	22.0
Ireland	N & W Europe	21.8
Slovenia	C, E, & S Europe	21.6
Namibia	C & S Africa	19.2
Cuba	C America & Caribbean	18.2
Mauritius	C & S Africa	17.3
Macedonia	C, E, & S Europe	16.5
Comoros	C & S Africa	14.7
Estonia	C, E, & S Europe	14.5
Swaziland	C & S Africa	12.8
Guyana	S America	12.7
Fiji	Oceania	11.0
Bhutan	Asia	10.8
Gabon	C & S Africa	10.7
Guinea-Bissau	C & S Africa	10.5
Less than 10,000 (35 states)		
Barbados	C America & Caribbean	9.3
Cyprus	C, E, & S Europe	9.2
Djibouti	C & S Africa	8.7
St Lucia	C American & Caribbean	8.3
Suriname	S America	8.2
Micronesia, Federated States of	Oceania	7.4
Solomon Islands	Oceania	7.3
Belize	C America & Caribbean	7.3
Bahamas	C America & Caribbean	7.1
Luxembourg	N & W Europe	6.9
Grenada	C America & Caribbean	6.1
Cape Verde	C & S Africa	5.8
Malta	N & W Europe	5.8
St Vincent and the Grenadines	C America & Caribbean	5.3
Maldives	Asia	5.1
Equatorial Guinea	C & S Africa	4.9
Libya	Middle East & N Africa	4.4
Iceland	N & W Europe	4.3
Antigua	C America & Caribbean	3.8
Samoa	Oceania	3.3
Tonga	Oceania	3.3
Vanuatu	Oceania	3.2
St Kitts and Nevis	C America & Caribbean	2.9
Dominica	C America & Caribbean	2.4
Andorra	N & W Europe	2.3
São Tomé	C & S Africa	2.3
Seychelles	C & S Africa	2.2
Kiribati	Oceania	1.9
Monaco	N & W Europe	1.7
Marshalls	Oceania	1.6
Liechtenstein	N & W Europe	1.2
Palau	Oceania	1.1
Tuvalu	Oceania	0.8
Nauru	Oceania	0.6
San Marino	N & W Europe	0.4

be noted, however, that in the United Kingdom the term Parliament encompasses the monarch, the House of Commons and the House of Lords, and not just the lower chamber.

5.6 Legislature size

In Table 32 the size distribution of contemporary world assemblies, lower and upper chambers, is set out and in Table 33 the general population per lower-house member has been calculated for each state with an assembly.

From Table 32 it emerges that 69% of the world's lower chambers have memberships of 200 or less, with the median size being around 140. In addition, it is apparent that upper houses of bicameral legislatures are almost uniformly smaller than their lower-house counterparts, being, on average, half the size. As a consequence, 75% of upper chambers have memberships of 100 or less, the median figure being around 60.

From Table 33 it emerges, not surprisingly, that a state's population size is the principal determinant both of the membership size of its assembly and of the resultant member:population ratio. Thus, the larger, in demographic terms, the state, the larger, on average, the size of its assembly and, notwithstanding this, the higher its member:population ratio. For this reason, India, the second most populous country in the world, appears at the bottom of the Table 33 ratio listings, with each of its deputies representing 1.7 million people, followed by the United States, the world's fourth most populous state. Conversely, tiny, usually island, states, such as Nauru, Tuvalu, Belau, the Marshall Islands, and Kiribati, are to be found clustering at the head of the listings, having small assemblies, with memberships substantially fewer than 50, yet, despite this, still registering unusually low member:population ratios, with each deputy representing fewer than 2,000 people. In contrast, in the economically developed and densely peopled states of Northern and Western Europe assembly members typically represent between 20,000 and 120,000 people.

There are two notable exceptions to this general, regular pattern.

First, communist or nationalistic socialist states usually have assemblies far larger than equivalent sized liberal or emergent democracies, or one-party, nonsocialist states. As a natural corollary, their resulting member:population ratios are lower than might be expected. China, with its 2,979-member National People's Congress; Libya, with its 1,112-member General People's Congress; and North Korea, with its 687-member Supreme People's Assembly are the most prominent examples. The rationale behind the election of these 'jumbo-assemblies' would, in theory, appear to be a desire to broaden the participation base. In practice, however, as has been noted earlier, these assemblies meet in plenary session for less than two weeks a year. They delegate their authority to smaller standing committees and general secretariats, which variously comprise between 40 to 160 members, a figure substantially below the membership average for the permanent assemblies in liberal or emergent democracies.

In two other countries, Indonesia and Taiwan, large quasi-legislatures are found, with respective memberships of 700 and 334, and with powers to amend their constitutions and (in Taiwan until 1996) to appoint the state presidents. These are, however, only ad hoc bodies, meeting at five- and six-year intervals, unless specially summoned. In the interim periods, they delegate effective authority to smaller, regular, national assemblies below them. For this reason, they have not been treated as full assemblies in this chapter, being excluded from the listings in Table 29 and from the calculations made for Table 33. A smaller supervisory 'super legislature', twice the size of the regular 50-member legislature, also exists in Turkmenistan, being convened to debate important political and economic issues.

The second, and more specific, anomaly which emerges when Tables 32 and 33 are studied, in conjunction with Tables 29 and 30, is found in the United Kingdom. The United Kingdom has, after Germany, the second largest lower house, with 659 members, of all the world's liberal democracies and, for this reason, has a comparatively low member:population ratio for its total population size. Furthermore, it is the only country in the world having an upper chamber with a larger membership than its lower. This results from the anachronistic combination of hereditary succession and government appointment that is still used to fill the House of Lords, as well as the fact that in earlier years it was the pre-eminent chamber. Today, the House of Lords comprises roughly 750 hereditary peers and 470 life peers, including the law lords and the 'lords spiritual', and 1,038 members have voting rights. However, in practice its active membership is less than 400. Indeed, 300 hereditary peers have never even visited the chamber to take the oath of membership.

5.7 Legislative–executive relationships

There are three possible bases on which to examine the assembly-executive relationship. First, the extent to which an assembly can initiate legislation. Second, the extent to which an assembly can influence policy-making. Third, the extent of an assembly's ability to criticize the executive, block its policies, and even dismiss it.

The vast majority of contemporary assemblies are not significant initiators of legislation. They are, as has already been said, mainly amenders and approvers. For this reason they have frequently been categorized as 'reactive' chambers. There are, however, some notable exceptions which stand out as examples of 'active' legislatures. Nonadversarial Sweden, where assembly members are mainly grouped in constituency, rather than party, blocks, is one. So, to an even greater extent, is the United States.

In Sweden private members' proposals (*motioner*) are ten times as numerous in the Riksdag as government bills (*propositioner*), although the bulk of the former are amendments or party alternatives to government bills, designed to spark off new discussion and inquiries.

In the US Congress thousands of bills and resolutions are introduced each year by senators and representatives, several hundred of which ultimately become law. Even here, however, the key legislative measures are those proposed in January by the president in his annual 'State of the Union' address to both chambers and which are subsequently adopted by party supporters within Congress under the promptings of the White House liaison staff.

The ability of assemblies to influence policy-making is also slight, Sweden, again, being somewhat unusual in this respect. An assembly in a state with a parliamentary executive is, in theory, in a strong position to make policy since the executive is drawn from it and responsible to it. In practice, however, an assembly member who has joined the executive to a great extent loses his or her allegiance to the assembly and becomes, psychologically but not physically, separate from it. The obvious example is the distinction between a front-bench (government), member of the UK House of Commons and a back-bencher (a member of parliament who is not a member of the government).

So we are left with the third base on which to examine the legislative-executive relationship: the ability to criticize, block policies and, *in extremis*, to dismiss an executive.

Most assemblies in parliamentary executive systems have built-in mechanisms for regular questioning of ministers. The UK House of Commons has an hour set aside for this four days a week, and each Wednesday afternoon, 30 minutes are set aside for questions specifically addressed to the prime minister. Although probably the most popular event of the parliamentary week in Britain, as far as the media and public are concerned, there is little evidence that Question Time in the House of Commons is anything more than an opportunity for rival parties to score points against each other. In Germany and Finland 'interpellation', or questioning,[seems more successful, the oral questioning of a minister often being accompanied by a snap vote.

Most assemblies in limited presidential and parliamentary executive systems have strong committee structures, partly to expedite the legislative process and partly to oversee the actions of the executive. The US Congress undoubtedly has the strongest committees of any contemporary assembly in the world. The power and authority of these committees, well provisioned with research staff and armed with extensive rights to subpoena staff from the executive, have been dramatically highlighted in recent years through the wide publicity given to the Watergate, Irangate, Whitewater, and Monicagate hearings. The fact that sessions of the congressional committees can receive nationwide television coverage has increased public awareness and enhanced their influence.

By comparison, assembly committees in other states seem weak. In the United Kingdom, as the result of the composition of the House of Commons and the disciplined party system, standing committees which consider government legislation are government-dominated, introducing only minor amendments to bills presented. Even weaker are the investigative select committees which were introduced into the chamber in 1979 to 'shadow' the work of government departments. Although producing informative reports, with the exception of the longer established Public Accounts Committee, their impact as parliamentary watchdogs has not been great. Their counterparts in Canada and France have been only marginally more successful.

Stronger committee systems operate in Germany, Italy, and Japan, all three having constitutions partly modelled on that of the United States. These committees are primarily concerned with legislation but, from time to time, ad hoc investigative committees have been influential. In Japan, in 1976, an assembly committee vigorously investigated the Lockheed bribes scandal, its work eventually resulting in the arrest and trial of the former prime minister, Tanaka. More recently in Germany, where the Bundestag is obliged to set up an investigation committee upon the motion of one-quarter of its members, a committee successfully probed the

'Flick scandal', which was concerned with illegal party financing.

In one-party states, assemblies are inevitably subservient to the party, and hence the executive, although functional 'Specialized Committees' operate in such bodies as China's National People's Congress to discuss and draft bills and resolutions.

In states with parliamentary executives, the ultimate sanction of assembly members is to dismiss the executive, the prime minister and government, through voting against it in a no-confidence motion. This has occurred frequently in postwar Italy and, as noted above, in Papua New Guinea. In other parliamentary states the government's defeat is difficult to achieve as a result of special constitutional rules. Thus in Germany, as noted in Chapter 4, there is the requirement for a 'constructive vote of no-confidence', in which deputies vote for an agreed successor. In France a 'no-confidence' vote can only be carried against the government if it attracts the support of more than half of the National Assembly's total membership and not just a majority of those voting. If such a motion fails, Assembly members are barred from calling another such motion during the same parliamentary session. In limited presidential executives, the ability to remove the executive is even more restricted, being limited to the protracted process of impeachment or, as in the cases of Venezuela in 1993, Brazil in 1992, and the United States in 1974, the threat of impeachment. However, in September 1996 President Zafy of Madagascar was removed by the impeachment process and, in the United States, impeachment proceedings were initiated against President Clinton in 1998. He was impeached by the House but was tried and aquitted by the Senate in 1999.

Thus, on balance, it must be said that, with some rare exceptions, contemporary assemblies have shown little sign of keeping up with, let alone overtaking, the increasing power and authority of executives of all types.

5.8 The representation of interests

The representation of interests is one activity that assemblies usually do well, especially in liberal democratic and emergent democratic states. This representation falls into three broad categories: constituency representation, party representation, and specific group representation.

Constituency representation is a traditional function of all assemblies. In the US Congress it has been developed to a high degree and is reinforced by the residential factor in both the House of Representatives and the Senate. Some members of Congress have devoted virtually their entire political careers to the economic advancement of the constituencies they represent, knowing that this is the surest route to re-election. As a consequence, until the November 1994 'anti-incumbent' Congressional elections, 'return rates' were as high as 90% for representatives and 75% for senators. This has led to calls for the imposition of 'term limits' on congress members, as are imposed in several US state legislatures. In the Philippines, they are set at two consecutive terms for Senators and three for members of the House of Representatives.

Similar, but less well-developed, examples of strong constituency representation can be found in assemblies in other parts of the world, including Kenya, the Philippines, South Korea, France, and the United Kingdom. In the British House of Commons, for example, it is not unknown for a member to ignore a major policy line of his or her party in order to support his or her constituency. Some UK Labor Party Members of Parliament have in recent years been confronted with 'dilemmas of conscience' in trying to follow a non-nuclear power policy when their constituents have been dependent on nuclear generation for their livelihoods.

Party representation has been the fastest growing activity in most assemblies in recent years. Until the election of the anti-corruption candidate, Martin Bell, in June 1997, there had been no independent MPs in the UK House of Commons since the 1960s, and there is now only a minority of assemblies that accommodate them. The Maldives, the Marshall Islands, Micronesia, Monaco, Nauru, Palau, and Tuvalu seem to be the few contemporary states where assembly elections are contested exclusively by politicians standing as independents. However, in some of the recently liberated and democratizing states of the former Soviet Union, for example Kyrgyzstan, Ukraine, and Uzbekistan, where party structures are currently weak, the majority of candidates and deputies are independents, as is also the case in Swaziland.

The representation of group interests is another growing activity of assembly members, particularly in liberal democratic countries. In the UK House of Commons many Labor members are sponsored by trade unions and some Conservatives are paid by a variety of interests to present their points of view. In an effort to bring this activity into the open, the House of Commons has produced a Register of MPs' Interests and members are requested to register their interests as well as declare them during the course of debates. The recommendations of the Nolan Committee in 1995 led to a further tightening of these rules. In the United States, with the growing influence of Political Action Committees, which provide a quarter of the funds used in contesting congressional elections, the influence of single-issue ideological interest groups is substantially stronger.

Recommended reading

Adonis, A *Parliament Today*, Manchester University Press, 1990

Arter, D *The Nordic Parliaments: A Comparative Analysis*, Hurst, 1984

Bailey, C J *The US Congress*, Basil Blackwell, 1989

Beamish, D R and Shell, D (eds.) *The House of Lords at Work*, Oxford University Press, 1993

Blondel, J *Comparative Legislatures*, Prentice-Hall, 1973

Copeland, G W and Patterson, S C *Parliaments in the Modern World: Changing Institutions*, University of Michigan Press, 1994

Damgaard, E (ed.) *Parliamentary Change in the Nordic Countries*, Scandinavian University Press, 1992

Drewry, G *The New Select Committees: A Study of the 1979 Reforms*, 2nd edn., Oxford University Press, 1989

Goodwin, Jr, G 'The New Congress' in P J Davies and F A Waldstein (eds.) *Political Issues in America Today*, Manchester University Press, 1987 (pp. 27–40)

Inter-Parliamentary Union, *Parliaments of the World: A Reference Companion*, 2nd edn., Gower, 1986 (2 vols.)

Judge, D (ed.) *The Politics of Parliamentary Reform*, Heinemann, 1983

Kim, C *et al. The Legislative Connection: The Politics of Representation in Kenya, Korea and Turkey*, Duke University Press, 1984

Laundy, P *Parliaments in the Modern World*, Gower, 1989

Mann, T E and Ornstein, N J (eds.) *The New Congress*, American Enterprise Institute, 1981

Mezey, M L *Comparative Legislatures*, Duke University Press, 1979

Nelson, D and White, S (eds.) *Communist Legislatures in Comparative Perspective*, Macmillan, 1982

Norton, P (ed.) *Parliament in the 1980s*, Basil Blackwell, 1985

Norton, P (ed.) *Parliaments in Western Europe*, Frank Cass, 1990

Norton, P (ed.) *Legislatures*, Oxford University Press, 1990

Olson, D M *Democratic Legislative Institutions: A Comparative View*, M E Sharpe, 1994

Sundquist, J L *The Decline and Resurgence of Congress*, The Brookings Institution, 1981

CHAPTER 6

Elections and Voters

6.1 The importance of elections

The majority of contemporary states claim to be democratic and seek to prove their democratic credentials under the banner of representation. The right to vote is almost the only universal right in the world today. Of the 192 states we are examining only six, Brunei, Oman, Qatar, Saudi Arabia, the United Arab Emirates, and the Vatican City State, do not have, and never have had, any institutions which can, even in the loosest sense, be described as popularly representative. A further ten states, comprising Afghanistan, Bahrain, and those states with military executives, have 'suspended' legislatures and thus no currently functioning electoral systems, while three states – China, Libya, and Rwanda – have indirectly elected or appointed legislatures. Among the other 173 there are wide differences in kinds and degrees of representation.

The first, and obvious, difference is between multiparty and one-party political systems. It is reasonable to assume that an election in a multiparty state means a choice of policies as well as representatives, whereas in a one-party system a representative may be changed but the basic policy thrust, as derived from the party, remains the same.

Why then do one-party states bother to go through the charade of elections? First, most of them, indeed probably all of them, would claim that the elections were not a charade. They might well argue that the reality of choice is no greater in a multiparty system than in their own. They might, with some justification, select one of the world's oldest democracies, the United Kingdom, and point out that no government in the postwar period has been elected by a clear majority of the people voting. They might also compare turnouts of less than 75% in general elections in the United Kingdom and little more than 50% in US presidential elections with turnouts well in excess of 90% in most communist, one-party states.

The politician in a liberal democratic state, while conceding these points, would probably argue that, nonetheless, a choice between parties was a substantially greater choice even though, through ignorance or apathy, some people failed to exercise it. He or she would say that the opportunity of voting for a complete change of policy, and even philosophy, was a vital element in a democratic political system and that without it genuine choice was limited.

Leaving aside such arguments, it is clear that in one-party states the voter knows that whatever decision he or she takes in the polling booth the party in power will not change, so the earlier question must be repeated: why are elections held?

The main reason is to demonstrate popular support for the regime. The important work of selecting the candidate has already been done, within the party machine. The election just legitimizes the 'behind-the-scenes' decisions. In some one-party states the question asked is simply 'Yes or No?'. There is only one candidate and therefore choice is given only in a negative form. In other states a choice of candidate may be given. The former communist states of East Germany, Hungary, Poland, Romania, and Yugoslavia offered candidate choice for some years and the practice was later adopted in the Soviet Union, before its demise. In the contemporary communist states of China, Laos, and Vietnam there is candidate choice. In one-party, noncommunist states candidate choice is fairly common.

Although in one-party states the election would appear to make the candidate choice legitimate, the practice is invariably unnecessary on constitutional or practical grounds. The party decision, once taken, is inviolate. The size of the turnout in each constituency will, however, be of interest to party officials because it will indicate the degree of activity, or apathy, in different areas. It will enable them to gauge the work being done by individual candidates and provide public 'feedback' on sensitive issues, allowing them to take steps to improve local morale and efficiency and, if pressed, introduce measures to deal with grass-roots grievances. This is particularly relevant in communist states.

In noncommunist, one-party, and dominant-party states elections may be important on more personal grounds. In some countries, where candidates are fighting each other within the one party, success will often depend on which politician, in the eyes of the voter, offers the best deal. In Kenya, for example, where the Kenyan African National Union (KANU) is the dominant party, there is usually a large (40–50%) turnover of parliamentary representatives as the record of one politician is judged unsatisfactory in terms of what he or she has 'delivered' by way of state money for some local development, and so is replaced by another who appears to offer more. This is a variant of what is described in congressional elections in the United States as 'pork barrel' politics: the ability to 'bring home the bacon'.

In multiparty political systems elections are much more significant. Not only do they provide the nonpolitically active public, who invariably comprise more than 95% of the population in most liberal-democratic societies, with an opportunity to participate in the political process, but they actually determine who will wield power. This is why in liberal and emergent democracies so much attention is paid to voting qualifications and voting methods.

6.2 Voting qualifications

The great majority of constitutions refer to voting on the basis of universal adult suffrage which, in simple terms, means the right of all adults to cast their vote. For some countries this is a comparatively recently acquired right. In Samoa, for example, until 1990 the franchise was restricted to the holders of *matai* titles, that is to elected clan chiefs. Furthermore, it is a right which varies in detail from state to state.

The age of majority varies and, although 18 is the most common, being the rule in two-thirds of states, in Mongolia it is set as high as 25 years. In more than 20 states the age of voting majority is 21 years. These comprise predominantly a mixture of African, Asian, and South American states, including Gambia, the Ivory Coast, Malaysia, and Singapore, but also European states such as Spain and Turkey. In another ten states, including Austria, Japan, South Korea, Switzerland, and Tunisia, the minimum voting age has been set at either 19 or 20 years. In contrast, in Guinea-Bissau and, in presidential elections in Iran, it is as low as 15, while in Brazil, Cuba, and Nicaragua it is set at 16 years, and in Indonesia, North Korea, and Sudan at the age of 17.

In some Latin American states, Bolivia and Colombia being two examples, the franchise is extended to married persons at an earlier age, 18, than to those who are single, 21, while in Italy the voting age is set at 18 years for the lower house of parliament, but at 25 years for the Senate. Under some constitutions, as in Tonga, literacy is also a necessary qualification, whereas in countries such as India, Honduras, and Madagascar, where the level of literacy is low, there is often provision for people to vote on the basis of party symbols rather than names. In Papua New Guinea, illiterate voters are allowed to cast 'whispering votes' to electoral officers.

Women were the last group in most countries to acquire the right to vote. In New Zealand they were given the franchise as early as 1893, long before it was a fully independent state. In a further 15 states, situated in Europe, North America, and Oceania, the franchise was extended to women between 1900 and 1920. These are: Australia, Austria, Canada, Czechoslovakia, Denmark, Finland, Germany, Iceland, Luxembourg, the Netherlands, Norway, Poland, Russia (the Soviet Union), Sweden, and the United States. In another 20 states, in Africa, the Americas, Asia, and Europe, women were granted the vote between 1921 and 1945. These are: Brazil, Cuba, the Dominican Republic, Ecuador, France, Hungary, Indonesia, Ireland, Italy, Jamaica, Japan, Mongolia, Myanmar, the Philippines, South Africa, Sri Lanka, Thailand, Turkey, the United Kingdom, and Uruguay. In the remaining nations of the world, the female franchise is a postwar phenomenon. It was acquired in Switzerland as late as 1971, in Jordan in 1982, in Liechtenstein in 1984, and in Qatar in 1999, while in Kuwait the franchise remains restricted to adult males who are required, in addition, to fulfil strict residency requirements. However, in May 1999 the emir (ruler) decreed that women would be allowed to stand and to vote from 2003.

Until 1994, South Africa remained the one country in the world where a significant proportion of the population were excluded from electoral participation on racial-ethnic grounds. Between 1909 and 1936, a portion of the black and colored community of Cape Province did enjoy the right to vote. Thereafter, however, the introduction of a series of new laws served to effectively eliminate black suffrage. This was formally acknowledged in 1959, the official date of complete disenfranchisement for blacks. In 1984 voting rights were restored to coloreds, other than Black and Indian people, who comprise 9% of the population, and Indians, who constitute another 3%, for elections to their own assemblies. However, the black community, who comprise more than 75% of the country's total population, were, until 1994, excluded from a political process which was effectively controlled by the 13% white minority.

However, ethnic exclusion persists in several of the newly democratized states of Central and Eastern Europe, where recent citizenship and electoral laws have been framed in such a way as to exclude certain minorities. For example, in Estonia, the voting qualification for the elections of 1992 was restricted to Estonians, or their descendants, who had been citizens of the country between 1918 and 1940. This disenfranchised 38% of the population, predominantly ethnic Russian immigrants. In neighboring Latvia, many Russian speakers were similarly disenfranchised by the 1992 citizenship law.

6.3 Voting systems

Elections are usually held to choose either executives or assemblies, or both. In multiparty states where the executive, usually the president, is separate from, and usually limited by, the assembly, the two elections are quite separate, except in the minority of states where the President is chosen by the assembly. The elections may take place at the same time but there are two distinct sets of choices. In parliamentary systems where the executive is drawn from and responsible to the assembly, the assembly determines which party will form the executive and thus only assembly elections are necessary. In one-party states the executive is usually chosen by the party and then 'legitimized' either by the assembly or through a separate election.

The election of political executives is generally a fairly straightforward process and Table 34 sets out the methods employed in the countries of the world. However, considerable ingenuity has been shown by some multiparty states in devising methods of electing assemblies to try to ensure as close a correlation as possible between the number of votes cast for a particular party and the number of seats that party wins.

6.3.1 Simple plurality (SP)

The most frequently used voting system is the simplest and easiest to understand, the simple plurality (SP), or winner-takes-all 'first-past-the-post' (FPTP), method. Under this system the candidate who wins the most votes is elected, regardless of the candidate's share of the overall vote. It is used for assembly elections in around a third of the word's states which hold elections, including the world's two largest liberal democracies, the United States and India, as well as in the United Kingdom and most of the former British colonies which, after independence, retained a political system modelled on that in force in the United Kingdom, the 'Westminster model'.

This voting system does not, however, make any pretence of trying to equate the number of seats won with the number of votes cast. Consequently, in countries with two major parties, such as the United Kingdom, third or fourth parties tend to win disproportionately fewer seats than votes. This is clearly demonstrated in Table 35. On two occasions, the party which won the largest number of UK votes actually won fewer seats than the second party. This happened in the cases of the Labor Party in 1951 and the Conservative Party in February 1974. At the April 1992 UK general election it took around 42,000 votes to elect each Conservative and Labor Member of Parliament (MP), but 210,000 votes for each Scottish National Party MP and 300,000 votes for each Social and Liberal Democrat MP.

In countries where numerous minor parties, usually regionally or occupationally based, but only one significant national party operate, the larger grouping is usually able consistently to hold power, despite capturing a relatively low share of the total vote. This has been apparent in India, where the Congress Party has been the predominant force. It has been in power for all but five years since independence was achieved in 1947, despite never having secured more than 49% of the national vote. In countries where there are strong, localized, ethnic concentrations, such as Northern Ireland and parts of Scotland and Wales, the SP system can, however, on occasions be of potential advantage to smaller parties. In the Philippines, where SP is used for presidential elections, as well as assembly contests, a consequence in May 1992, when seven candidates contested the presidency, was that Fidel Ramos was elected on the basis of only a 23.6% share of the popular vote, and thus had a weak national mandate. Similarly, in Panama, Ernesto Perez was elected president in May 1994 with barely a third of the national vote.

Simple plurality is used by a significant proportion, 28%, of emergent democratic states. However, 11 of these 20 states are situated in sub-Saharan Africa and have particularly weakly developed pluralist political systems. In contrast, many of the recently democratized states of Central and Eastern Europe, whose prospects for future transition into the liberal democratic regime category appear more promising, have chosen to employ proportional or absolute majority electoral systems. This is because they view these systems as more modern and likely to produce assemblies more repre-

Electoral systems — Table 34

Region/country	Form of political executive choice	Upper house electoral system	Lower house electoral system
Asia			
Afghanistan	party	N/A	N/A
Bangladesh	assembly	N/A	simple plurality
Bhutan	hereditary	N/A	mixed-elected/appointed
Brunei	hereditary	N/A	N/A
Cambodia	college & assembly	appointed	simple plurality
China	party	N/A	indirect
India	assembly	indirect	simple plurality
Indonesia	college	N/A	proportional representation-party list
Japan	assembly	direct-proportional representation/limited vote	proportional representation-additional member system
Kazakhstan	direct	mixed-elected/appointed	second ballot
Korea, North	party	N/A	simple plurality
Korea, South	direct	N/A	proportional representation-additional member system
Kyrgyzstan	direct	direct-second ballot	second ballot
Laos	party	N/A	simple plurality
Malaysia	assembly	mixed-elected/appointed	simple plurality
Maldives	direct	N/A	mixed-elected/appointed
Mongolia	direct	N/A	second ballot
Myanmar	military	N/A	simple plurality
Nepal	assembly	mixed-indirect/appointed	simple plurality
Pakistan	assembly	indirect	simple plurality
Singapore	assembly	N/A	simple plurality
Sri Lanka	direct & assembly	N/A	proportional representation-party list
Taiwan	direct	N/A	proportional representation-additional member system
Tajikistan	direct	N/A	second ballot
Thailand	assembly	direct-simple plurality	proportional representation-additional member system
Turkmenistan	direct	N/A	second ballot
Uzbekistan	direct	N/A	second ballot
Vietnam	party	N/A	second ballot
Central America & Caribbean			
Antigua	assembly	appointed	simple plurality
Bahamas	assembly	appointed	simple plurality
Barbados	assembly	appointed	simple plurality
Belize	assembly	appointed	simple plurality
Costa Rica	direct	N/A	proportional representation-party list
Cuba	party	N/A	second ballot
Dominica	assembly	N/A	mixed-elected/appointed
Dominican Republic	direct	direct-second ballot	proportional representation-party list
El Salvador	direct	N/A	proportional representation-additional member system
Grenada	assembly	appointed	simple plurality
Guatemala	direct	N/A	proportional representation-additional member system
Haiti	direct & assembly	direct-second ballot	second ballot
Honduras	direct	N/A	proportional representation-party list
Jamaica	assembly	appointed	simple plurality

continues

Electoral systems (continued) Table 34

Region/country	Form of political executive choice	Upper house electoral system	Lower house electoral system
Mexico	direct	direct-additional member system	proportional representation-additional member system
Nicaragua	direct	N/A	proportional representation-party list
Panama	direct	N/A	simple plurality
St Kitts and Nevis	assembly	N/A	simple plurality
St Lucia	assembly	appointed	simple plurality
St Vincent and the Grenadines	assembly	N/A	simple plurality
Trinidad and Tobago	assembly	appointed	simple plurality
Central, Eastern, & Southern Europe			
Albania	college & assembly	N/A	proportional representation-additional member system
Armenia	direct	N/A	proportional representation-additional member system
Azerbaijan	direct	N/A	proportional representation-additional member system
Belarus	direct	mixed-indirect/appointed	second ballot
Bosnia-Herzegovina	direct	indirect	proportional representation-party list
Bulgaria	assembly	N/A	proportional representation-party list
Croatia	direct	mixed-elected/appointed	proportional representation-party list
Cyprus	direct	N/A	simple plurality
Czech Republic	college & assembly	direct-second ballot	proportional representation-party list
Estonia	college & assembly	N/A	proportional representation-party list
Georgia	direct	N/A	proportional representation-additional member system
Greece	assembly	N/A	proportional representation-party list
Hungary	assembly	N/A	proportional representation-additional member system
Latvia	assembly	N/A	proportional representation-party list
Lithuania	direct & assembly	N/A	proportional representation-additional member system
Macedonia	direct & assembly	N/A	second ballot
Moldova	direct	N/A	proportional representation-party list
Poland	direct & assembly	direct-proportional representation	proportional representation-party list
Romania	direct & assembly	direct-proportional representation	proportional representation-party list
Russia	direct	indirect	proportional representation-additional member system
Slovakia	assembly	N/A	proportional representation-party list
Slovenia	direct & assembly	mixed-elected/indirect	proportional representation-additional member system
Turkey	assembly	N/A	proportional representation-party list
Ukraine	direct	N/A	proportional representation-additional member system
Yugoslavia	college	indirect	proportional representation-additional member system

continues

Electoral systems (continued) — Table 34

Region/country	Form of political executive choice	Upper house electoral system	Lower house electoral system
Central & Southern Africa			
Angola	direct	N/A	proportional representation-party list
Benin	direct	N/A	proportional representation-party list
Botswana	assembly	mixed-indirect/appointed	simple plurality
Burkina Faso	direct	appointed	proportional representation-party list
Burundi	military	N/A	proportional representation-party list
Cameroon	direct	N/A	proportional representation-party list
Cape Verde	direct	N/A	simple plurality
Central African Republic	direct	mixed-indirect/appointed	second ballot
Chad	direct & assembly	N/A	second ballot
Comoros	direct	N/A	second ballot
Congo, Democratic Republic of	military	appointed	simple plurality
Congo, Republic of	transitional	N/A	appointed
Côte d'Ivoire	direct	N/A	second ballot
Djibouti	direct	N/A	simple plurality
Equatorial Guinea	direct	N/A	proportional representation-party list
Eritrea	direct	N/A	mixed-elected/appointed
Ethiopia	assembly	indirect	simple plurality
Gabon	direct	indirect	mixed-elected/appointed
Gambia	direct	N/A	mixed-elected/appointed
Ghana	direct	N/A	simple plurality
Guinea	direct	N/A	proportional representation-additional member system
Guinea-Bissau	direct	N/A	proportional representation-limited vote
Kenya	direct	N/A	mixed-elected/appointed
Lesotho	assembly	hereditary/appointed	simple plurality
Liberia	direct	direct-simple plurality	simple plurality
Madagascar	direct	mixed-indirect/appointed	simple plurality
Malawi	direct	N/A	proportional representation-single transferable vote
Mali	direct	N/A	second ballot
Mauritania	direct	indirect	second ballot
Mauritius	assembly	N/A	proportional representation-limited vote
Mozambique	direct	N/A	proportional representation-party list
Namibia	direct	indirect	mixed-elected/appointed
Niger	direct	N/A	simple plurality
Nigeria	direct	direct-simple plurality	simple plurality
Rwanda	direct	N/A	appointed
São Tomé	direct	N/A	proportional representation-party list
Senegal	direct	mixed-indirect appointed	proportional representation-additional member system
Seychelles	direct	N/A	proportional representation-additional member system
Sierra Leone	direct	N/A	mixed-elected/hereditary
Somalia	military	N/A	N/A
South Africa	assembly	indirect	proportional representation-party list
Sudan	military	N/A	mixed-elected/indirect
Swaziland	hereditary	mixed-elected/indirect	mixed-elected/appointed
Tanzania	direct	N/A	mixed-elected/appointed

continues

Electoral systems (continued) Table 34

Region/country	Form of political executive choice	Upper house electoral system	Lower house electoral system
Togo	direct	N/A	second ballot
Uganda	direct	N/A	mixed-elected/indirect
Zambia	direct	N/A	simple plurality
Zimbabwe	assembly	N/A	mixed-elected/appointed
Middle East & North Africa			
Algeria	direct	mixed-indirect/appointed	proportional representation-party list
Bahrain	hereditary	N/A	N/A
Egypt	direct	N/A	mixed-elected/appointed
Iran	direct	N/A	second ballot
Iraq	party	N/A	proportional representation-party list
Israel	assembly	N/A	proportional representation-party list
Jordan	hereditary	appointed	simple plurality
Kuwait	hereditary	N/A	simple plurality
Lebanon	assembly	N/A	proportional representation-party list
Libya	college	N/A	indirect
Morocco	hereditary & assembly	indirect	proportional representation-party list
Oman	hereditary	N/A	N/A
Qatar	hereditary	N/A	N/A
Saudi Arabia	hereditary	N/A	N/A
Syria	direct	N/A	simple plurality
Tunisia	direct	N/A	proportional representation-additional member system
United Arab Emirates	hereditary	N/A	N/A
Yemen	direct	N/A	simple plurality
North America			
Canada	assembly	appointed	simple plurality
United States	direct	direct-simple plurality	simple plurality
Northern & Western Europe			
Andorra	assembly	N/A	proportional representation-additional member system
Austria	assembly	indirect	proportional representation-party list
Belgium	assembly	mixed-elected/appointed	proportional representation-party list
Denmark	assembly	N/A	proportional representation-party list
Finland	direct & assembly	N/A	proportional representation-party list
France	direct & assembly	indirect	second ballot
Germany	assembly	indirect	proportional representation-additional member system
Iceland	assembly	N/A	proportional representation-party list
Ireland	assembly	mixed-elected/appointed	proportional representation-single transferable vote
Italy	assembly	indirect	proportional representation-additional member system
Liechtenstein	assembly	N/A	proportional representation-limited vote
Luxembourg	assembly	N/A	proportional representation-party list
Malta	assembly	N/A	proportional representation-single transferable vote
Monaco	assembly	N/A	second ballot

continues

Electoral systems (continued) Table 34

Region/country	Form of political executive choice	Upper house electoral system	Lower house electoral system
Netherlands	assembly	indirect	proportional representation-party list
Norway	assembly	indirect	proportional representation-party list
Portugal	direct & assembly	N/A	proportional representation-party list
San Marino	assembly	N/A	proportional representation-limited vote
Spain	assembly	mixed-elected/indirect	proportional representation-party list
Sweden	assembly	N/A	proportional representation-party list
Switzerland	assembly	indirect	proportional representation-party list
United Kingdom	assembly	hereditary/appointed	simple plurality
Vatican City State	college	N/A	N/A
Oceania			
Australia	assembly	direct-proportional representation/single transferable vote	alternative vote
Fiji Islands	assembly	mixed-indirect/appointed	second ballot
Kiribati	direct	N/A	second ballot
Marshall Islands	assembly	N/A	simple plurality
Micronesia	assembly	N/A	simple plurality
Nauru	assembly	N/A	simple plurality
New Zealand	assembly	N/A	proportional representation-additional member system
Palau	direct	direct-simple plurality	simple plurality
Papua New Guinea	assembly	N/A	simple plurality
Philippines	direct	direct-simple plurality	simple plurality
Samoa	assembly	N/A	simple plurality
Solomon Islands	assembly	N/A	simple plurality
Tonga	hereditary	N/A	mixed-elected/appointed
Tuvalu	assembly	N/A	simple plurality
Vanuatu	assembly	N/A	proportional representation-party list
South America			
Argentina	direct	indirect	simple plurality
Bolivia	direct	direct-simple plurality	simple plurality
Brazil	direct	direct-simple plurality	proportional representation-party list
Chile	direct	mixed-elected/appointed	simple plurality
Colombia	direct	direct-simple plurality	simple plurality
Ecuador	direct	N/A	proportional representation-party list
Guyana	assembly	N/A	proportional representation-party list
Paraguay	direct	direct-proportional representation	proportional representation-party list
Peru	direct	N/A	proportional representation-party list
Suriname	assembly	N/A	simple plurality
Uruguay	direct	direct-proportional representation	proportional representation-party list
Venezuela	direct	mixed-elected/appointed	proportional representation-party list

sentative of voters' wishes. There are statistical grounds for this belief. For 25 states in the developed world, comprising countries in Northern and Western Europe, North America, Oceania, and Japan, 'indexes of proportionality' have been calculated on the basis of the degree to which a party's share of the national vote is reflected by its representation in the legislature. For the four states with the SP system this index, at the most recent elections, was 87%, ranging from 79% in the United Kingdom to 94% in the United States, where only two significant parties operate. For the 18 states with proportional systems, the index averaged 94%,

Parties' share of House of Commons in UK general elections, 1945–97 — Table 35

By vote

General election year	Conservative share (%)	Labor share (%)	Lib/Alliance* share (%)	Total votes (million)	Voter turnout (%)
1945	40	48	9	24.1	73
1950	43	46	9	28.8	84
1951	48	49	2	28.6	82
1955	50	46	3	26.8	77
1959	49	44	6	27.9	79
1964	43	44	11	27.7	77
1966	42	48	8	27.3	76
1970	46	43	7	28.3	72
1974 Feb	38	37	19	31.3	78
1974 Oct	36	39	18	29.2	73
1979	44	37	14	31.2	76
1983	42	28	25	30.7	73
1987	42	31	23	32.6	75
1992	42	34	18	33.6	78
1997	31	43	17	31.6	71

By seats

General election year	Conservative share (%)	Labor share (%)	Lib/Alliance* share (%)	Total seats (number)	Voter turnout (%)
1945	33	61	2	640	73
1950	48	50	1	625	84
1951	51	47	1	625	82
1955	55	44	1	630	77
1959	58	41	1	630	79
1964	48	50	1	630	77
1966	40	58	2	630	76
1970	52	46	1	630	72
1974 Feb	47	47	2	635	78
1974 Oct	44	50	2	635	73
1979	53	42	2	635	76
1983	61	32	4	650	73
1987	59	35	3	650	75
1992	52	42	3	651	78
1997	25	63	7	659	71

Source: Derbyshire J D and Derbyshire I D *Politics in Britain: From Callaghan to Thatcher*, W & R Chambers, 1990, Table 4, p. 6 (updated).

* The Alliance fought its first general election in 1983.

ranging from 87% in Spain to 100% in Malta.

In New Zealand, despite a classic two-party system, the SP voting method has now been abandoned on the grounds of its unfairness towards minority parties and communities, notably indigenous Maoris. In a referendum held in September 1992 voters approved its replacement, from 1996, by a mixed-member proportional system on the German model, with five seats set aside specifically for the Maori community. This new system encouraged a proliferation of parties and the formation of a coalition government, after the October 1996 general election resulted in a 'hung parliament, when no single party achieved parliamentary majority. In Italy, where postwar politics have been characterized by the chronic instability and weakness of party governments, a party list-based system of proportional representation (PR) was replaced in 1994 by a predominantly SP-based system, with single-member constituencies. The attractions of SP were both its perceived ability, on the UK model, to produce strong party executive government on the basis of a relatively low share of the national vote and also the direct link its single-member constituency gives between voters and assembly members or deputies. In the Czech Republic, there are plans to adopt the simple plurality system.

The alternatives to the SP system fall into two broad categories, the absolute majority (see 6.3.2 and 6.3.3) and the proportional systems (see 6.3.4 to 6.3.7). Within each of these two groups there are variations, sometimes in detail and sometimes in substance.

6.3.2 The alternative vote (AV)

The alternative vote (AV) is not theoretically a form of proportional representation (PR) in that it cannot guarantee a close relationship between votes and seats and, indeed, can sometimes produce surprising results. It does, however, go some way towards making the voting system fairer and is relatively simple and easy to understand.

It uses single-member constituencies, the voter choosing a candidate by marking '1' against a preferred choice on the ballot paper. If desired, the elector can also mark '2' against a second choice and so on, but this is not compulsory. First preference votes are then counted and any one candidate who collects more than 50% of all the votes cast is automatically elected. If no candidate achieves more than 50% the candidate with the least number of first-choice votes is eliminated and the second preferences of those who made this candidate their first choice are distributed among the other candidates. This process continues until one candidate emerges with 50+%.

The main objection to AV is that it tends to help compromise candidates and its results can sometimes be quite unpredictable, with the successful candidate being someone whom very few people positively want. At present, only Australia employs this voting system. It was first introduced in 1919 and applies to its lower chamber, the House of Representatives. It has had little perceptible impact on the party system, which remains firmly set in a two-three party structure and the index of proportionality, at 87%, shows little difference from that registered in states with SP systems. However, in the 1998 general election it worked to ensure that the extremist One Nation party, which secured 8% of the vote, won no seats.

6.3.3 The second ballot (SB)

The second ballot (SB) is similar in some respects to AV. A simple majority election is held and if no one gets more than 50% of the total vote, the candidate with the least votes is eliminated and a second election is held, usually within the next week to ten days. The rules concerning who can participate in the 'run-off' contest vary considerably. In France, where the system is used for National Assembly elections, candidates who have received support from at least 12.5% of the registered electorate are entitled to compete in the following week's second ballot. The candidate who achieves a plurality in this second contest is the one who is elected. For French presidential elections, only the top two candidates go forward to the 'run-off' ballot. This is designed to ensure that a president is elected with a majority of the national vote and thus a clear popular mandate. However, in the May 1995 French presidential election, for the first time ever, a president was elected with only a plurality of the vote, Jacques Chirac attracting 49.5% of the second ballot votes cast, with 6% of ballot papers left blank.

In terms of achieving better proportionality, the SB system generally fares worse than AV and even SP, with an 'index of proportionality' of only 81% in recent French National Assembly elections. In addition, it is more costly to operate. The reason for its adoption by the framers of France's Fifth Republic constitution was their concern to encourage the emergence of more streamlined and disciplined party groupings, following the '*immobilisme*' of the Fourth Republic, whose assem-

World election systems: summary table — Table 36

Direct voting systems for lower chambers

All States

Voting system	Number of states	As % of total states
Simple plurality	63	36
Party list proportional representation	55	31
Second ballot	25	14
Additional member proportional representation	25	14
Single transferable vote	3	2
Limited vote	4	2
Alternative vote	1	1
Total	*176*	*100*

Liberal-democratic and emergent-democratic states

Voting system	Liberal democratic (no. of states)	Liberal democratic (% of states)	Emergent democratic (no. of states)	Emergent democratic (% of states)
Simple plurality	31	42	20	28
Party list proportional representation	26	35	25	35
Second ballot	4	5	11	16
Additional member proportional representation	7	9	14	20
Single transferable vote	2	3	1	1
Limited vote	3	4	0	0
Alternative vote	1	1	0	0
Total	*74*	*100*	*71*	*100*

bly had contained representatives from more than a dozen competing parties, elected by the party list system of proportional representation (PR). This has certainly occurred to a substantial extent, with parties of the right of center and left of center frequently entering into coalition or agreed 'stand-down' pacts for second ballot contests, in which the party(ies) securing fewest votes agreed not to contest the next round, with the first ballot being used as an effective intracoalition primary contest.

Twenty-five countries currently use the SB system for their lower chamber elections, including 15 liberal democratic and emergent democratic states. SB is also used by several other states, including Belarus, Bulgaria, Cyprus, Ecuador, El Salvador, Guatemala, Peru, and Ukraine for presidential contests, by Albania, Armenia, Azerbaijan, Georgia, Hungary, and Lithuania as part of an additional member (AM) system (see 6.3.5), and for governorship contests in some southern states of the United States. In Peru the system is unusual since the minimum proportion of the vote required for a first-round candidate to win on a plurality basis is 36%. If this is not achieved, there is a second ballot.

In several democratizing former communist states in Central and Eastern Europe, including Belarus, Macedonia, and Ukraine, the SB system has been used in conjunction with the requirement that voter turnout must be at least 50%. If this is not achieved there is provision for an unlimited number of repeat elections. Thus in Ukraine in 1994 there were five rounds of voting in the parliamentary elections, after which 45 seats in the 450-member Supreme Council still remained unfilled. In Belarus, the first two rounds of voting in the parliamentary elections in May 1995 resulted in only 119 deputies being returned. This left the 260-member Supreme Council inquorate and further elections had to be held in the autumn of 1995.

Compared with the SP system, both the SB and AV systems have had a tendency to promote tactical alliances between minor parties or major and minor parties, improving their chances of success.

Majority voting systems (6.3.2 and 6.3.3) are concerned principally with returning effective governments, usually of a single party, even though they do not always achieve this. In contrast, proportional electoral systems (6.3.4 to 6.3.7) place their chief priority on the principle of representation, seeking to effect the return of assemblies which, in party, social, gender, and ethnic composition, closely mirror the profile and wishes of the electorate. Four principal variants of proportional representation are currently to be found in operation, as detailed below.

6.3.4 The party list (PL)

Party list (PL) systems are, potentially, the most truly representative form of proportional representation (PR), being designed to return members reflecting the broadest possible spectrum of public opinion. To achieve this, unlike absolute majority systems, they are, of necessity, based on large multimember constituencies of, usually, regional but sometimes, as in the cases of Israel and the Netherlands, a national character.

The first stage in the complicated operation of the PL system is the production of lists of candidates by each of the political parties fighting the election. Each list shows names in descending order of preference, as chosen by the party. In many cases, an elector merely votes for the party of his or her choice and seats are then allocated to each party according to the total proportion of votes received. Thus a party winning 30% of the votes would be entitled to 30% of the seats and enough names would be taken from the party's list to fill those seats.

Like the AV, the PL system cannot always guarantee full proportional representation. In general, however, it has been calculated that it results in a correspondence between parties' shares of the national vote and assembly seats of around 94%. This 'index of proportionality' is more than seven points higher than that recorded for plurality and majoritarian SP, AV, and SB systems.

In some versions of the list system, such as the inflexible 'closed list', used in Israel and Spain, the voter is given no choice of candidate and simply votes for the party. This can make an election very impersonal and has been criticized for transferring too much influence to party machines. Other versions, however, allow voters to indicate a preference for an individual as well as a party. Varying examples of these are the 'flexible list' system, used in Belgium, the 'open list' system of Finland, and, the most liberal of all, the 'free list', or *panachage* ('mix-in') system of Luxembourg and Switzerland, which allows voters to choose specific individuals from across the lists.

List systems can be 'doctored' by stipulating a 'cut-off' point of percentage votes to be won below which very small parties get no representation at all. If this is not done then virtually any party, whatever its size, will have a chance of winning at least one seat and an assembly could be peppered with representatives of diverse background. The nature and size of the 'cut-off' threshold can vary considerably. In Denmark it is as low as 2% of the vote; in Bulgaria, Moldova, Romania, and Sweden, 4%; in the Czech Republic, Estonia, Germany, Hungary, Latvia, and Slovakia, 5%; and in Sri Lanka, 12.5%. In Poland, where, following its release from communism, firm party structures are only slowly being established, no cut-off threshold was applied to the 1991 general election. As a consequence, 29 parties secured representation in the Sejm, with the highest share of the national vote attracted by a single party being only 12%, and a period of weak, shifting coalition governments ensued. The electoral law was thus changed for the 1993 parliamentary elections, with a 5% national threshold applied to individual parties and 8% to alliances. The new electoral arrangements ensured that only six parties and alliances secured representation, yet still the most popular party could only attract 20% of the vote. However, with the 1997 elections 80% of the seats were won by the two leading election alliances. In Bulgaria, Moldova, and Estonia the 4% thresholds in force proved effective in excluding, respectively, 50, 30, and 15 minor parties from parliament in the recent 1993 and 1994 general elections.

Currently, 55 states employ list systems. Twenty-six are liberal democracies, 25 are emergent democracies, and four, Burundi, Equatorial Guinea, Iraq, and Zimbabwe, have authoritarian military regimes; 24 are situated in Europe and 11 in Latin America (see Table 42 in Section II). To allocate the seats a variety of electoral quotas and apportionment systems are used. These include: the 'highest average' system, d'Hondt version, used in Belgium, the Netherlands, Portugal, and Spain; the more complex 'highest average' system, Saint-Lague version, used in Denmark, which is more favorable to minor parties; and the Hagenbach-

Bischoff quota, used in Greece, in which the number of votes is divided by the number of seats plus one.

On the whole, list systems have tended to favor the development of multiparty coalition politics. In the Netherlands, for example, where the purest possible form of list system is to be found, no 'cut-off' limits being imposed, a dozen or so parties frequently secure representation in the 'second chamber', although the three principal parties, the Labor Party (PvdA), the Christian Democratic Appeal (CDA), and the People's Party for Freedom and Democracy (VVD), invariably capture around 80–85% of the total vote and assembly seats. Included in the ranks of the minor parties are Calvinist and Evangelical religious groupings, as well as peace, communist, and ecological organizations.

In Switzerland, Belgium, Finland, Denmark, Sweden, and Iceland, where almost similarly liberal 'cut-off' restrictions are in operation, in recent lower chamber elections 12, 9, 9, 8, 7, and 5 parties respectively won seats. However, the consociational character of politics in these states has meant that the consequent coalition administrations have governed with a measure of stability and success.

The absence of a suitable cut-off point for elections to the Knesset in Israel has recently resulted in 'hung' assemblies, in which ten parties have secured assembly representation. As a consequence, minor parties have been given a disproportionately larger influence over the composition of the government than their voting strengths would normally merit. However, in Portugal and Spain, despite list systems being in place, the assemblies have been dominated by a few major parties, with left-of-center governments continually in power from the early 1980s (until 1996 in the case of Spain).

In some countries, tighter 'cut-off' variants of the list system have been used so as to favor the larger parties. The most prominent example is Turkey, where parties need 10% of the national vote to secure entry to parliament and 25% or 33% respectively of the vote in three- or four-member constituencies. In addition, bonus seats are given to the party achieving the most votes. This 'up-loaded' system is designed partly to exclude small religious extremist parties from the National Assembly but also as a means of discouraging a coalition government. It had the consequence, in the November 1987 general election, of giving the incumbent Motherland Party (ANAP) 65% of Grand National Assembly (GNA) seats with only a 36% share of the popular vote.

In less democratic countries, even cruder forms of 'up-loading' are to be found. In Paraguay, for example, before truly multiparty politics were tolerated in 1993, congressional elections were fought on single national party lists, and the party which received most votes was automatically awarded two-thirds of the assembly seats. This approach can be termed a form of 'disproportionate representation'. It is also seen in the British colony of Gibraltar, where the leading party is restricted to a one-seat majority, whatever its share of the vote.

An important consequence of the operation of PL systems is the effect on female representation. A clear feature of its working in Northern and Western Europe has been to promote the return of substantially higher proportions of female members than has been the case in elections based on majoritarian systems, operating in similar socio-cultural conditions. Thus, at the present time, in the assemblies of the Scandinavian countries where a PL system is used, women comprise around a third of their memberships: the highest proportion, at 40%, is Sweden. This is comparable to the level of female parliamentary representation in communist Cuba and higher than that, 21%, in communist China. In Iceland an all-female political party, the Women's Alliance Movement, has held seats in the Althing since 1983. Elsewhere in continental Europe the proportionate figure for female assembly representation is around 15–20%, while in South Africa, where the party list system is used, it is 24%. In comparison, in the SP and SB legislatures of France, the United Kingdom, and United States the figure stands at barely 10%, while in Japan, India, and many South American legislatures the proportion is below 10%.

Another useful aspect of list systems is that there is no necessity for by-elections when members retire or depart. Candidates ranking next on the party's previous list are automatically drafted in to fill vacancies as they arise. There are some exceptions to this, however, Greece being one.

By-elections are also avoided in France, where the SB operates, since all candidates must fight with a running-mate (*suppléant*) who will take their place if they resign to assume ministerial office, retire, or die in office.

6.3.5 The additional member (AM)

The additional member (AM) system makes use of party lists but also allows the elector to vote for a candidate, two votes being cast, one for the candidate and one for the party. Half the assembly is then elected on an SP basis, or, as in Albania, Georgia, and Hungary, via the SB system, and the other half, using the party lists, is chosen so that the membership of the chamber accurately reflects the national vote. The party lists, therefore, are used to correct any unfairness in the SP system.

The main advantage of the additional member system, also known as the mixed member system, is that it uses single-member constituencies and so keeps the link between the candidate and the elector. At the same time, however, a high level of 'proportionality', comparable with the 'best' list systems, is achieved.

The AM system in its purest form is used in elections to Germany's Bundestag. Here lists operate at the state (*Land*) level, but to qualify for assembly representation on the second list ballot (*Zweitstimme*) parties need to secure either at least 5% of the national vote or win three single-member constituency seats. If a party wins more constituency (*Erstimme*) seats than it appears 'entitled' to on a statewide percentage basis, it is allowed to retain these excess, or *Überhangmandate*, seats and the size of the Bundestag is increased accordingly. The 1998 general election resulted in 13 'excess seats'.

Forms of AM systems operate in 24 other states, six of which are liberal democratic and 14 are emergent democratic, including eight of the recently democratized states of Central and Eastern Europe. The exceptions are Senegal, where the system was introduced in 1973 with the assistance of German political consultants, Tunisia, Armenia, and Azerbaijan. In most countries with AM systems the system is not fully proportional. Instead, single-member constituencies predominate, but there is a leavening of proportionality via the supplementary national list. In Georgia 64% of the assembly is filled on a proportional basis; in Senegal 58%; in Japan and Mexico, 40%; in the Seychelles, a third of the National Assembly; in Albania, 29% of the People's Assembly; in Italy, a quarter of the Chamber of Deputies; and in Armenia, Azerbaijan, and South Korea, only a fifth of the National Assembly; in Guatemala, 15% of the Congress; and in Tunisia only 12% of the National Assembly. The Upper Chamber of the Japanese Diet has also been elected by a variant of the AM system since 1982, with 40% of its seats filled by national level PR. The AM system proportional representation also was used for elections to the Welsh Assembly and Scottish Parliament in 1999.

In Russia, the 450-member State Duma is elected on the basis of a pure AM system, 225 seats being drawn from national party lists, with a 5% cut-off threshold imposed for qualification. However, it has been argued that, in a fledgling democracy where party organizations and identities are underdeveloped, the system of national lists accords disproportionate influence to extremist parties. Thus, in December 1993 Vladimir Zhirinovsky's populist-xenophobic Liberal Democratic Party of Russia (LDPR) won only 11 constituency seats directly but, with 23% of national support, qualified for 59 party list seats. As a consequence, President Yeltsin recommended increasing the proportion of Duma members who are directly elected from single-member constituencies, and are thus believed to be more accountable to the electorate, to two-thirds in future elections.

6.3.6 The single transferable vote (STV)

The single transferable vote (STV) is, in many respects, theoretically the best method of ensuring proportional representation, eliminating the problem of wasted votes that is inherent in majoritarian systems. Indeed, it is the electoral system favored by the UK Electoral Reform Society. It uses multimember constituencies which may be large but which can be small enough to elect three representatives. All the candidates are listed on the ballot form, usually in alphabetical order, and the elector states an order of preference, from 1 downwards. All the votes cast are counted and the 'electoral quota' is calculated, in other words, the minimum number of votes needed to be elected.

The calculation would work as follows (droop formula)

$$\frac{\text{(total number of votes)}}{\text{(number of seats + 1)}} + 1 = \text{electoral quota}$$

Thus, in a three-member constituency with a total of 120,000 votes cast, the quota would be:

$$\frac{(120{,}000)}{(3+1)} + 1 = 30{,}001$$

and any candidate with 30,001 or more first-preference votes would automatically be elected.

For example, there might be 12 candidates for the three seats and only one who obtained more than the 30,000 quota, in fact 31,001, or 1,000 more than was needed. All the second preferences of voters who made the top candidate their first choice would be counted and their percentage distribution among the other candidates calculated. The 1,000 'surplus' votes would then be redistributed on this percentage basis. If this redistribution brought another candidate up to the 30,001 quota he or she would be elected and the process would continue until all three seats were filled. If all the surplus second-preference votes were used up and there were still seats to be filled, then the bottom candidates would be progressively eliminated, with their second preferences redistributed among the other candidates on a proportionate basis.

The STV requires multimember constituencies, but they are often smaller than those used in some varieties of the party list system. The STV is also usually more 'personalized' than the list system, theoretically giving electors the power to choose not only between parties but also between different candidates standing for the same party. Despite this, high degrees of proportionality, in terms of the correlation between parties' shares of the national vote and assembly seats, ranging from 95% to 100%, have been achieved.

Described as the 'Anglo-Saxon version of PR', the STV is currently used for lower chamber elections in Ireland (since 1922), Malta (since 1921), and Malawi. In Malta, moreover, a party which secures over 50% of the vote is guaranteed a majority of assembly seats, by allocation of extra seats (if necessary). STV is also used for elections to Australia's and Ireland's Senate, and to the lower House of the Assembly in the state of Tasmania (since 1907), as well as for Sri Lankan presidential elections, local government elections in Northern Ireland, and by state assemblies in India when choosing members for the federal upper house, the Rajya Sabha.

6.3.7 The limited vote (LV)

The final PR variant, the limited vote (LV), is currently used in six states, in Guinea-Bissau (although a military regime assumed power in 1999), Liechtenstein, Mauritius, and San Marino, for lower chamber elections, and in Japan and Spain, for upper house contests. In Japan it is used to fill 152 of the House of Councillors' 252 seats. It was formerly employed in Spain and Portugal in the 19th and early 20th centuries, and in 13 UK parliament constituencies between 1868 and 1880. Under this system, multimember constituencies are used, each returning three to five members, but electors are allowed only one, nontransferable, vote. The three to five candidates winning most votes in each constituency are then subsequently returned on a simple plurality basis.

The use of multimember constituencies means that minor parties, through restricting themselves to one candidate per constituency, can win seats on relatively low shares, about 15–30%, depending on the size of the constituency, of the total vote. In this respect, the LV system, which is really only 'semi-proportional', differs significantly from the SP, with its single-member constituencies. The LV system, while being of some assistance to minor parties, has been criticized for encouraging faction-based and increasingly corrupt 'money politics' in Japan, where it was also used for lower assembly elections up to 1994. The critics argued that it led to backroom deals between the leaders of the main factions of the dominant Liberal Democratic Party (LDP) so as to ensure that the party captured all three to five seats in the multimember constituencies. Consequently, under the terms of the electoral reform act of December 1994, Japan has now adopted an AM system.

6.4 Election turnouts

The size of the election turnout provides some information about popular participation in the political process but it can also be misleading.

Turnouts in the United Kingdom parliamentary general elections of 1979, 1983, 1987, 1992, and 1997 were 76.2%, 72.7%, 75.4%, 77.7%, and 71.6% respectively. These figures compare favorably with those for UK local government elections and for elections to the European Parliament, which have averaged around 35%. German Bundestag election turnouts varied between 78–91% between 1976 and 1994, showing a generally declining tendency. In France, National Assembly election turnouts have invariably ranged between 65–83% during the last two decades, while presidential election figures have averaged around 80%. In the Scandinavian and North European countries of Denmark, Iceland, the Netherlands, Norway, and Sweden, parliamentary election turnouts of between 80–90% are the norm.

In general, then, in the liberal democracies of Northern and Western Europe, turnouts for elections to national assemblies currently cluster within a range of 70–90%. Only Switzerland diverges, with general election turnouts averaging 50% or lower. Elsewhere in the developed world, recent general election turnouts have ranged between 67–86% in Japan, South Korea, and New Zealand. In all the countries for which turnout figures have been quoted voting is not compulsory. The state, however, shoulders the burden of responsibility for registering electors and compiling the electoral roll in advance of polling day.

In contrast, in the United States the burden of registration falls upon individual citizens, with parties being employed as a private backup mobilizing force. At present, however, fewer than 70% of the US population of voting age are registered, including only 40% of Hispanics and 50% of those in the lowest socio-economic category. For this reason, US national election turnouts are, by comparative standards, unusually low, standing at barely 53% of the adult population, though 80% of those registered, for presidential elections between 1980 and 1996, and at around 40% for midterm congressional and governorship elections.

Low electoral participation is also, not surprisingly, a feature of many of the world's poorer liberal and emergent democracies. In India, Nepal, Pakistan, and Botswana, for example, turnouts have averaged between 40–60% for recent assembly elections. In Mexico, the figures have been around 50% for presidential and Chamber of Deputies elections, and in Colombia and Equatorial Guinea, below 40% for assembly elections.

There are, however, some notable exceptions. In Sri Lanka and the Bahamas, for example, parliamentary election turnouts have sometimes exceeded 85%, although they have fallen to around 60% now in Sri Lanka. In South Africa turnout was 89% in the June 1999 general election. In Gambia, Honduras, Morocco, and Vanuatu recent turnouts have been around 80%; in Costa Rica, Dominica, and Surinam, 75%; in Barbados and Malaysia, 70%; and in Papua New Guinea, despite the remoteness of many polling stations, above 65%. In Lebanon, the archaic requirement that electors must cast their ballot in their ancestral villages or towns serves to depress turnouts to a level of 50–55%. In Cambodia, the turnout reached 90% in the May 1993 UN-supervised general election, held after two decades of civil war.

In communist states, turnouts for elections at all levels are invariably high, usually exceeding 95% and sometimes getting as near to a 100% response as is physically feasible. In the Laos National Assembly elections of December 1992, for example, 99.3% of eligible voters participated, according to official figures, while turnout was recorded at 99.9% for North Korea's Supreme People's Assembly elections of July 1998. This does not, however, necessarily denote great popular enthusiam for the party or the electoral process. For such ritualized contests, the local party machine usually puts considerable effort into securing high turnouts, with up to a quarter of the adult population, party members, local state and work council representatives, and 'reputable citizens', being brought into action as campaign workers. Special transport is set up for the housebound and ballot boxes are posted at every workplace and housing complex, as well as being carried out to those living in remote areas.

Faced with this huge mobilization and publicity drive, the average citizen who is not a party member may well feel that for the small cost of casting a vote there may be some potential advantage in openly showing support for the official candidate. Only rarely, as was the case in the Polish local elections of 1984, do citizens 'rebel' and stay at home. On this occasion, the official turnout slumped to 75%, although government opponents suggested the true figure was closer to 60%.

High electoral turnouts are also invariably the case in one-party nationalistic socialist and authoritarian nationalist regimes. In Indonesia, for example, turnouts are put at over 90%. However, in Syria they have been as low as 45%.

In former communist states which remain under autocratic leadership, for example Azerbaijan, Turkmenistan, and Uzbekistan, turnouts in excess of 90% have been recorded for recent national elections and referenda. In many other democratizing excommunist states, for example Bulgaria, Hungary, Latvia, Macedonia, Mongolia, Slovakia, Slovenia, and Ukraine, recent general and presidential election turnouts have ranged between 70–95%. This suggests a transfer of civic responsibility between regime types. However, in Russia, where election turnouts of 99.9% were the norm during the communist era, only 55% of the electorate participated in the December 1993 Federal Assembly elections according to official returns, while unofficial observers claimed that turnout may actually have been as low as 46%.

In 30 countries voting is compulsory. Half of these states are situated in Latin America, including Argentina, Brazil, where election days are also public holidays, the Dominican Republic, and Peru, but seven are also in Europe and Oceania, including Australia, Belgium, Fiji, Greece, Italy, Luxembourg, and Turkey. This compulsion may be real, in the sense of running the risk of being fined for not voting, but in most cases the offenders are rarely, if ever, prosecuted. Some constitutions, including those in most of the communist states, specify that voting is a 'civic' or 'socialist duty' but stop short of compulsion. In addition, in some South American states, the 'constitutional duty' is relaxed for more elderly citizens, who may find it difficult to travel to the ballot booths. Thus in Brazil, voting is optional for those aged 16–17 years, 70 and over, and for illiterates. In Paraguay it is compulsory up to the age of 60 and in Peru up to the age of 70. In a further variant, in New Zealand and Senegal voter registration is compulsory but the actual voting is not.

Whether or not the requirement is enforced, there is evidence that turnouts in countries which formally make voting compulsory are generally perceptibly higher than in those which do not. Turnouts of 85–95% are, for example, the norm in Australia, Belgium, and Italy, and for the latter two states these participation levels are also maintained in European Parliament elections. However, lower turnouts of 80%, and sometimes substantially less, have been recorded in the Dominican Republic, Greece, and Peru, while blank and null ballots are quite common in Brazil. In contrast, in Malta, where voting is not compulsory, general election turnouts of 95% or more are the norm.

6.5 Election-rigging: methods and extent

One hundred and seventy-six countries are shown in Table 36 above as currently holding regular national assembly elections. However, a significant proportion of these polls are either uncompetitive, involving no candidate or party choice, or of a 'façade' nature, involving outward shows of open debate and candidate pluralism but with outcomes that are ultimately rigged by the incumbent regime.

To be truly free and democratic, election contests need to satisfy seven basic criteria:

1. Voting rights: all adults, regardless of race or religion, should enjoy the right to vote;
2. Voting practices: the ballot should be cast freely and secretly, without intimidation or subsequent redress;
3. Election timetable: elections should be held regularly, within prescribed time limits and in accordance with constitutional rules;
4. Candidacy rules: all sections of the community should be free to put forward candidates, form political parties, and openly campaign;
5. Campaign period: the campaign period should be of sufficient length to enable all parties and candidates to get their messages across. There should be reasonable equity in media access and coverage. Voter bribery by candidates and parties should be disallowed and maximum limits placed on campaign spending;
6. Election supervision: the campaign and vote counting should be supervised by an impartial administration, with an independent body available to adjudicate in electoral disputes;
7. Power transfer: all parties and candidates should accept the adjudged results, handing over power to the successful party or parties within a prescribed timetable.

At present, these conditions are approached only by the 145 countries which we have designated in Chapter 3 as liberal democracies or emergent democracies. Communist and other one-party states fall short of the important plurality of condition 4 above, while authoritarian regimes, which allow semblances of candidature pluralism, invariably breach conditions 2, 5, and 6. Even many liberal and emergent democracies, totalling up to half, fall substantially short of meeting these conditions and can thus be viewed as holding only partially democratic elections.

This is true of the four liberal democratic states of Mexico, Singapore, Egypt, and Malaysia, which hold what have been termed 'dominant-party elections'. In these contests, restrictions are placed on the free operation of opposition parties and the holding of public rallies, media coverage is slanted slavishly in the ruling party's favor, and state resources are employed to intimidate and sometimes effectively bribe voters.

In Mexico, the ruling Institutional Revolutionary Party (PRI), which has monopolized power at both federal and state levels for almost six decades since its inception in 1929, has succeeded in winning elections by building up an extensive rural and urban corporate client network. In return for pledging electoral support, the party has ensured a steady flow of contracts, pay rises, and assured employment to its local political bosses (*caciques*). In recent years, however, as economic modernization has progressively weakened the links binding together this system of traditionalist patronage, the PRI has been forced to resort to cruder ballot-rigging as a means of ensuring its continued electoral dominance. For example, in the 1986 Chihuahua governorship election, with the help of the government-appointed Federal Election Commission, it set about falsifying the electoral rolls in areas of PRI strength and restricting polling station access elsewhere. The actual count was also rigged by impersonations and the crude stuffing of ballot boxes. In the July 1988 presidential and congressional elections, faced with a strong challenge by Cuauhtemoc Cardenas of the National Democratic Front (FDN), these practices continued. As counting got underway, the Electoral Commission's computer mysteriously broke down. It was a week later before official returns were published, giving the PRI's presidential candidate 50.7% of the national vote. Condition 7 of a fully democratic electoral system had clearly been breached. There were claims of fraudulent practices again in 1994 in a number of state election contests, notably in the southern state of Chiapas, where Zapatista rebels were based, and nearby Tabasco, and in 1995 it was finally agreed by the government that impartial observers should re-examine these results.

In Singapore, the dominant People's Action Party (PAP) has so far avoided such crude methods of ballot-rigging. Instead, it has maintained its electoral dominance by infringing democratic election requirements 2 and 5. First, both prior and during election campaigns, opposition candidates have been mercilessly hounded by the state, falling prey, for example, to trumped-up fraud and tax evasion charges. Second, and more generally, the electorate has been intimidated by fears that any votes cast against the government party might be traced, with adverse employment and financial consequences. By these means, and aided, it must be noted, by successful management of the economy, the PAP has invariably been able to secure well over 70% of the popular vote in parliamentary elections. In elections the PAP, with 65% of the national vote, captured 81 of the 83 assembly seats.

In Egypt, the National Democratic Party (NDP) has been the dominant force for nearly two decades and its restrictive actions prompted most of the opposition parties to boycott the general election of December 1990, when the NDP attracted 80% of the national vote.

In Malaysia, the United Malays National Organization (UMNO) has been in power continuously since independence, as part of a 14-party National Front coalition. The Front's dominance, attracting 63% of the vote and a record assembly majority at the most recent April 1995 general election, can be ascribed, as in Singapore, partly to its success in promoting rapid economic development, but also partly because of the ability of the National Front to act as a 'catch-all' force, with wings orientated to a range of ethnic communities. However, the party coalition also enjoys strong backing from the state machine, media coverage being biased in its favor and public rallies being outlawed.

For both Mexico and Singapore the striking feature of the past decade has been the marked and steady decline in dominant party support, even on the manipulated official returns. It remains an open question, however, whether official totals, particularly in Mexico where the psychological 50% mark is being rapidly approached, will be permitted to fall much further in future contests and whether a peaceful change of party regime will be accepted.

Ten other countries which have been classified in Chapter 3 as liberal democracies have only partially democratic elections. These comprise chiefly the majority of the mainland states of Central and South America, where election contests have been marred by civil violence and where the military still remains a lingering background influence. In addition, in Samoa, vote buying, both with cash and goods, and impersonation have been past features of electoral contests. Indeed, in the February 1982 elections the Human Rights Protection Party (HRPP) led by Prime Minister Va'ai Kolone, was removed from office by the Supreme Court on these grounds.

The remaining liberal democracies, numbering more than 60 and situated chiefly in Northern and Western Europe, the Caribbean, North America, and Oceania, substantially meet all seven of the 'free-election' criteria. In addition, the majority of them have experienced electorally induced changes of government at some stage or other during the past two decades: a useful, though by no means essential, indicator of election fairness. These states can be said to hold basically democratic elections. Within these states, however, there are gradations of openness, related to variations in election campaign regulations, violating condition 5, in such areas as media access and spending ceilings.

To these 60-odd liberal democracies which conduct substantially democratic elections can be added, from the evidence of recent polls, 22 rapidly progressing emergent democracies situated in Central and Eastern Europe (Bulgaria, Croatia, the Czech Republic, Estonia, Hungary, Latvia, Lithuania, Moldova, Poland, Romania, Russia, Slovakia, Slovenia, and Ukraine), Asia (South Korea, Kyrgyzstan, Nepal, Pakistan, Taiwan, and Thailand), Africa (South Africa), and Western Europe (Andorra).

In South Africa, in April 1994, democratic use of the ballot, in the country's first ever all-race elections, brought about peacefully one of the most dramatic transfers of power and changes of regime in recent history. This *uhuru* (liberation) election has been accepted as having been 'substantially free and fair', although there were localized cases of intimidation and ballot-box fraud. However, the final result was politically clear-cut. The African National Congress (ANC), orientated towards the black majority community, attracted 63% of the vote. This was just short of the two-thirds majority that would have enabled it to write a permanent constitution by itself. However, the old ruling National Party and the Zulu-orientated Inkatha, by securing 20.4% and 10.5% of the vote respectively, received sufficient support to qualify for four and two cabinet seats. This raised suspicions that there may have been some fine-tuning adjustment, the product of behind-closed-doors bargaining by party chiefs, to ensure a politically satisfactory result.

In the remaining 49 emergent democracies, election contests continue to be marred by combinations of vote-counting frauds, dominant-party candidate list-rigging, and bribery, as well as voter intimidation by both government and opposition groups. In Cameroon, for example, multiparty and supposedly democratic elections were held in May 1998, but there were reports of intimidation, violent clashes between rival supporters (claiming five lives), and on polling day many registered voters were without polling cards. Similar accusations of ballot-rigging attached themselves to the multiparty elections in Burkina Faso and Mauritania in 1992, in Malawi in 1997, and the presidential election in Togo in 1993.

A recent prominent example of electoral fraud was the Bangladesh Jatiya Sangsad election of March 1988, which was boycotted by the opposition. It was reported that one villager, Shawkat Ali, from near Dhaka, complained, typically, 'I went to cast my vote, but found that someone else had already done it'.

Vote buying has also been a conspicuous feature of recent elections in Thailand, although contests have become progressively fairer. In the July 1988 assembly elections, despite the imposition of official spending limits of 350,000 baht (US$15,000) per candidate, well over 3 billion baht (US$120 million) were distributed to voters by the 3,606 candidates standing. In the poor northeast, 100 baht (US$4.5) packages were openly on offer for each vote pledged, plus 10,000 baht bounties for entire villages which successfully elected candidates. Altogether, it has been estimated that this election resulted in an expenditure expansion equivalent to 0.5% of Thailand's GDP. In the 1995 election parties concentrated on the more efficient practice of 'buying' amenable MPs once they had been elected, with the going rate for a deputy who was willing to switch parties being estimated at 10 million baht (US$400,000).

Physical violence and intimidation, both during the campaign and on election day, have been a recurrent feature of contests in South and Central America and also in the Philippines. There, 905 were killed during the 1971 local elections. The death toll in the May 1995 congressional elections, put at 80, was thus a significant improvement. In the Congo, a month-long curfew had to be imposed in 1993, after violent unrest had followed disputed legislative elections. Meanwhile, in areas of ethnic unrest, such as the Kosovo and Sandzak regions of Serbia, Chechnya, and Tatarstan in Russia, and Karachi in Pakistan, poll boycotts have been successfully organized at recent elections by opponents of the regime.

Of the 82 liberal and emergent democracies which, on the broadest count, can be viewed as holding substantially democratic elections 27% are in Northern and Western Europe; 21% in Central, Eastern, and Southern Europe; 14% in Oceania; 12% in the Caribbean; and 11% in Asia. Of the remaining 94 countries holding regular assembly elections, five are communist states. Here, election contests are subject to rigid 'democratic-centralist' control. A further 20, situated chiefly in Africa, the Middle East, and Asia, are nationalistic socialist or authoritarian nationalist states, in which opposition activity is either outlawed or strictly controlled. This leaves 69 countries, 36% of the world total, in which elections are at present, to varying degrees, of a 'façade' nature. In these states, despite outward semblances of candidacy pluralism, the results are effectively rigged to the incumbent regime's advantage. Control of the media, the electoral commission, and the vote-counting process are the principal means of achieving this, following the cynical maxim, 'He who counts, elects'.

Also of importance is the imposition of severe constraints, and frequently outright bans, by the ruling regime on the candidature and campaign activity of opposition members. All such features were prominent in the February 1988 presidential and assembly elections in Paraguay, which returned General Alfredo Stroessner and his ruling Colorado Party with a 90% share of the vote, the remaining 10% being apportioned between legalized opposition candidates. A turnout of 93% was officially claimed, but the opposition-formed Committee for Free Elections estimated the true figure to be below 50% in many areas. The stuffing of ballot boxes and the impersonation of dead electors were practices which were frequently alleged. Not surprisingly, such loaded contests are often succeeded by frustrated eruptions of opposition, leading to street violence, and in 1989 General Stroessner was deposed in a coup and by 1993 a multiparty emergent democracy had been established.

In Senegal, where the prepared result for the February 1988 presidential election was announced almost as soon as voting stopped, riots erupted in the streets of Dakar and Thies, prompting the government to arrest opposition leaders and declare a state of emergency which lasted for two months. In the Philippines, in February 1986, stronger and better coordinated public opposition to flagrant ballot-rigging succeeded in bringing down the regime of Ferdinand Marcos. In Myanmar, the sweeping opposition victory in the May 1990 assembly elections was simply ignored by the military regime, while in Cambodia the opposition boycotted the legislature in protest against what they viewed as ballot-rigging in July 1998 polls.

Condition 3 of the basic democratic election criteria, adherence to the election timetable prescribed by the constitution, has been breached in Guyana, North Korea, and the Central African Republic (CAR) during recent years. In Guyana, elections were due to be held in December 1991, but were postponed until October 1992. In the CAR, President Kolingba suspended the second round of presidential elections in 1992 and 1993 after he had failed to finish in the leading position in the first round. Condition 7, acceptance of the verdict of the ballot box, was breached in 1990 by Myanmar's military junta, in September 1992 by the opposition leader in Angola, Dr Jonas Savimbi, and, in June 1993, by Nigeria's military leadership.

6.6 Direct democracy: the growing use of referenda

While regular elections are held to choose legislatures and political executives, more direct legitimizing appeals to the electorate are made, in both democracies and authoritarian regimes, in the form of referenda and citizens' initiatives. Indeed, during recent decades resort to such direct appeals has been increasing, particularly in Western democracies. This has been a consequence of the weakening of voter identification with and allegiance to political parties and the increasing popularity of issue voting and citizens' lobbies. In short, there has been some shift from representative, or 'delegated', democracy towards direct democracy.

A crucial distinction exists between a referendum and an initiative. The former, which is much more common, is a ballot held at the government or parliament's request. It concerns a proposed change in the constitutional framework or policy or a significant and contentious measure which has already been passed by the legislature, but on which electors are now called to pass judgement. It is thus essentially a legitimatizing device, although, on occasions, such plebiscites may also be called by populist executives as a means of using the 'popular will' to overcome the opposition of other elected political forces, usually in the legislature. An initiative is, in contrast, a bottom-up grass-roots device. It is an arrangement, permitted in a limited number of states, by which an individual or group may draft a proposed law or constitutional amendment. Subject to the proposition attracting a certain stipulated measure of initial backing, it is then referred directly to the electorate for approval or rejection.

The citizen's initiative is the ultimate 'populist' instrument of direct democracy. However, its use is very limited in the contemporary world since it is believed that voters are too malleable and short-sighted to be trusted to take sensible decisions. In practice, it is restricted to Switzerland, Liechtenstein, US states, Italy, and the Slovak Republic, although in the UK it is advocated as a policy proposal by the opposition Liberal Democratic Party.

In Switzerland, which is characterized by strong ethnic and religious divisions but where politics are consociational, the first direct vote of citizens on policy occurred in 1294, in the canton of Schwyz, and the first nationwide referendum was held in 1802. Today, proposals for constitutional change (initiatives) must go to a binding national vote (within a two-year period) if at least 100,000 sign a petition, and federal laws, decrees, and long-term treaties must be voted on if at least 50,000 people (corresponding to 0.7% of the population) demand a referendum. During recent decades, between four and five initiatives have been submitted per year. More than a third of parliamentary measures considered in this way by voters in Switzerland are rejected. However, between 1971 and 1997 only five of 68 initiatives have been adopted and turnout has fallen from a peak of 80% in 1947 to only 42% today.

Consequently, there are proposals to make initiatives harder to call, by raising the signature requirements to 150,000.

Within the United States, the constitutions of 23 states permit the calling of initiatives and more than 1,750 statutory and constitutional initiatives have been proposed at state level this century. Forty per cent of these have been approved. Six western states, Oregon, California, North Dakota, Colorado, Arizona, and Washington, have been responsible for nearly two-thirds of the initiatives, some of which, notably the tax-cutting Proposition 13 in California in 1978, have had far-reaching national impacts.

In Italy, voters can trigger a referendum either on a constitutional law, which has not been passed by both houses of parliament with a two-thirds majority, or to veto any nonfinancial law passed by the legislature if at least 500,000 (0.9% of the population) sign a petition. For the result of the referendum to be binding, turnout must exceed 50%.

In the Slovak Republic, a national referendum must be held if at least 350,000 citizens (7% of the population) sign a petition, but again, for the result to be valid, turnout must exceed 50% of the electorate.

Unlike the initiative, the national referendum is a common constitutional device which, at some stage this century, has been used by almost every nation-state in the world. Prominent exceptions have been Argentina, the Federal Republic of Germany, India, Indonesia, Israel, Japan, Mexico, the Netherlands, and the United States. As Table 37 shows, resort to referenda has increased during recent decades and more than 500 have been held worldwide during the postwar era. Switzerland, with 279 referenda between 1941 and 1993, has been responsible for the largest number, followed by Liechtenstein (more than 50), Italy (29), Australia (24), Egypt (19), Ireland (17), Denmark (13), France (12), the Philippines (11), New Zealand (9), and Uruguay (9).

There are two broad purposes for which referenda are held: to sanction a significant change in a country's constitutional arrangements and to approve a fundamental change in policy.

Constitutional-related referenda have been by far the most common, particularly in those states, the majority, where the calling of referenda has been infrequent. Eight categories of constitutional referenda can be identified.

1. Changes in the status of a state: a referendum may be held to approve independence or unification. This occurred in Slovenia in December 1990; the three Baltic states of Estonia, Latvia, and Lithuania in February – March 1991; Armenia and Georgia in March 1991; North and South Yemen and Croatia in May 1991; Macedonia in September 1991; Turkmenistan in October 1991; Azerbaijan, Uzbekistan, and Ukraine in December 1991; Bosnia-Herzegovina in March 1992; Eritrea in April 1993; and Belau in November 1993. It may also result, however, in a vote to reject independence, as occurred in the British colony of Bermuda in August 1995 and in the Canadian province of Québec in 1980 and 1995, or to oppose unification with an adjoining state, as happened in Moldova in March 1994. In Nevis Island, there was a majority in favor of independence from St Kitts in August 1998, but the 'Yes' vote fell below the constitutionally required two-thirds majority. However, German unification, in 1990, and the 'velvet divorce' of the Czech and Slovak republics, in 1992–93, took place without national plebiscites, the approval of preceding parliamentary elections deemed sufficient.
2. Alterations in a state's internal structure: a referen-

Nationwide referenda held in the world 1941–93* — Table 37

Period	Switzerland	Rest of Europe	Africa & Near East	Asia	North & South America	Australia & New Zealand	Total
1941–60	53	21	9	6	6	16	111
1961–80	117	32	54	18	12	21	254
1981–93	109	52	29	6	16	6	218
Total	*279*	*105*	*92*	*30*	*34*	*43*	*583*

*Source: Butler D & Ranney A (Eds.) *Referendums Around the World*, Macmillan 1994, Table 1-1, p. 5.

dum may be held to approve the shift from a unitary to a federal structure, as occurred in Belgium in 1993, or to reject or approve, as occurred in Scotland and Wales in 1979 and 1997 and in Northern Ireland in 1998, the devolution of greater power to constituent regions. In the USSR, an all-Union referendum was held in March 1991 on the preservation of the Soviet Union. This resulted in a large, 75%, 'Yes' vote, but concurrent votes for independence were held in several constituent republics and within nine months the Union had been dissolved.

3. Membership of a regional or international grouping: a referendum has commonly been held by countries prior to entry into the European Union, on continuance of membership (as occurred in the United Kingdom in June 1975), and on fundamental developments in the organization of the Union, notably the 1991 Maastricht Treaty. In the case of Denmark, a referendum held in June 1992 resulted in initial rejection, by 51%, of the Maastricht Treaty, but a year later, in May 1993, there was approval by a 57% majority. In Norway, voters have rejected twice, in 1972 and 1994, proposed membership of the European Community/Union. In Spain, a referendum was held in March 1986 to approve continued membership of the NATO defense organization.
4. Approval or rejection of a new constitution: this has been the most common reason for the holding of referenda. It is a requirement in a number of states and explains why, with so many constitutions recently being framed (see Chapter 2), there has been an upsurge in resort to referenda. Examples of referenda held to approve constitutions include Algeria in 1989, Ghana in 1992, Andorra, Peru, and Russia in 1993, and Armenia and Kazakhstan in 1995. In Albania, in November 1994, voters rejected a government-framed new constitution, and in July 1997 voted against restoring the monarchy.
5. Approval of a fundamental change of regime: in recent years referenda have been used for this purpose in Africa, to replace one-party systems with multiparty democracies, such as Zambia in 1990, Mauritania and Sierra Leone in 1991, Congo in 1992, and Malawi in 1993. There was also a whites-only referendum in South Africa, in March 1992, to establish constitutional equality for all races.
6. Approval of a change in executive type or powers: in Bangladesh, in September 1991, the public approved, by national plebiscite, reversion from a limited presidential to a parliamentary system, while in Brazil, in April 1993, retention of the limited presidential system was supported. In Russia, in December 1993, and in Belarus, in May 1995, a strengthening of presidential powers was approved by national referendum.
7. Approval of a change in the electoral system: in New Zealand, in November 1993, voters backed, in a national referendum, a change from the first-past-the-post system to proportional representation. In Italy, in 1993–94, voters chose to repeal the system of proportional representation, and also to end the state financing of political parties.
8. Approval of an extension of the executive's term: in the authoritarian-nationalist states of Kazakhstan, Turkmenistan, and Uzbekistan in Central Asia referenda were held in 1994–95 to confirm the continuance in office, for periods of between five and eight years, of the executive presidents. They have also been held at regular intervals in Egypt, most recently in October 1993. Taking the place of formal election contests, they have provided a veneer of legitimacy. However, turnouts and approval rates have been so unbelievably high, officially put at 99.3% and 99.6% respectively in Uzbekistan in March 1995, that they cannot be viewed as truly democratic.

The holding of referenda on policy issues has been most typical in states such as Switzerland, Italy, Ireland, Denmark, and Uruguay, where the device is most deeply entrenched. Policy referenda have also been promised in France by Jacques Chirac, who became president in May 1995. In Ireland, such referenda have focused on contentious social issues, notably divorce, adoption, and abortion. In Italy, the range of issues has been considerably wider, embracing nuclear and environmental laws, the decriminalization of drugs, wage indexing, the abolition of specific government ministries, and, in June 1995, trade union and media control issues. In Uruguay, recent referenda have been held on the indexation of pensions, which was approved, and privatization, which was rejected. In England, in a local referendum held in Fenruary 1999 in the city of Milton Keynes, voters approved raising local taxes to support the local authority's spending plans, rather than cut services. Voting was by post and telephone.

The experience of referenda has shown that, in general, turnouts have been significantly lower than in assembly or presidential elections. The differential has been as much as 30% in New Zealand and Austria, and between 10–20% in Denmark, the United Kingdom, Ireland, Switzerland, Italy, and Sweden. This suggests an element of 'democratic exhaustion' or apathy. Indeed, in Guatemala turnout dipped to as low as 16% for a referendum in 1994 which was called by the president on proposals to decentralize government spending and bring forward assembly elections. In France, the November 1988 referendum held on the somewhat tangential issue of a new statute for the overseas colony of New Caledonia resulted in a turnout of only 37%, less than half the norm for a French plebiscite.

An analysis of referenda results shows that normally decisions are quite clear cut. There have been relatively few 'Yes' votes in the range of 49–51% and the verdicts of most referenda have been uncontroversial and, on balance, conservative. For example, 36 out of 42 proposals by referendum to change the Australian constitution have been rejected, devolution was not approved in the United Kingdom in 1979 and secession from the Canadian federation was rejected by Québec in 1995. A notable exception was Italy during 1993–94. Here voters, sickened by the Tangentopoli ('kickback city') political corruption scandal, approved a draft of radical referenda proposals to change the electoral system and constitutional framework. In 1997–98, in the United Kingdom, the 'New Labor' government of Tony Blair used the momentum and goodwill of its recent landslide election victory to secure acceptance of four constitutional referenda to establish assemblies and parliaments in Wales, Scotland, and Northern Ireland and an elected London mayor.

Recommended reading

Bogdanor, V *What is Proportional Representation? A Guide to the Issues*, Martin Robertson, 1984

Bogdanor, V and Butler, D (eds.) *Democracy and Elections: Electoral Systems and their Consequences*, Cambridge University Press, 1983

Butler, D and Kavanagh, D *The British General Election of 1997*, Macmillan, 1997

Butler, D and Ranney, A (eds.) *Referendums Around the World: The Growing Use of Direct Democracy*, Macmillan, 1994

Butler, D and Ranney, A (eds.) *Electioneering: A Comparative Study of Continuity and Change*, Clarendon Press, 1992

Franklin, M, Mackie, T T, and Valen, H *Electoral Change*, Cambridge University Press, 1992

Furtak, R K (ed.) *Elections in Socialist States*, Harvester Wheatsheaf, 1990

Harrop, M and Miller, W *Elections and Voters: A Comparative Introduction*, Macmillan, 1987

Interparliamentary Union *Electoral Systems: A Worldwide Comparative Study*, Interparliamentary Union, 1993

Katz, R S *Democracy and Elections*, Oxford University Press, 1997

Le Duc, L, Niemi, R G, and Norris, P (eds.) *Comparing Democracies: Elections and Voting in Global Perspective*, Sage, 1996

Lijphart, A *Electoral Systems and Party Systems: A Study of Twenty-seven Democracies*, Oxford University Press, 1994

Mackie, T T and Rose, R (eds.) *International Almanac of Electoral History*, 3rd edn., Macmillan, 1991

Pierce, R *Choosing the Chief: Presidential Elections in France and the United States*, University of Michigan Press, 1995

Reeve, A and Ware, A *Electoral Systems: A Comparative and Theoretical Introduction*, Routledge, 1992

Reynolds, A (ed.) *Election '94 South Africa*, James Currey, 1994

Sartori, G *Comparative Constitutional Engineering: An Inquiry into Structures, Incentives and Outcomes*, Macmillan, 1994

Suski, M *Bringing in the People: A Comparison of Constitutional Forms and Practices of the Referendum*, Nijhoff, 1993

Weiner, M and Ozbudun, E (eds.) *Competitive Elections in Developing Countries*, Duke University Press, 1987

CHAPTER 7

Political Parties

7.1 The mobilization of sectional interests

Everyone has an interest in something, even if it amounts to little more than pure self-interest or self-preservation. Millions of people are regular television watchers and if someone sought to deprive them of this pleasure it is certain that they would immediately be up in arms. Some people attach great value to personal privacy and will resist any intrusion, particularly by a public body. Others are more concerned about what they see as the rights of others. Often they feel a duty to protect the seemingly defenseless, especially in the animal kingdom.

Whereas interests are shared by thousands, or even millions, of people, only a relative few will take the trouble to mobilize them into a source of influence and power. These are the organizers of interests: the active members of 'interest groups'.

An interest group is, therefore, an association of people who come together, or are brought together, to represent, promote, and defend a particular interest or set of interests. There are numerous examples to choose from.

Some are chiefly promotional, seeking to bring attention to the needs of particular people, such as unmarried mothers or the disabled. Others are mainly defensive, such as the environmental groups, anxious to protect natural conditions and phenomena. All are representational in one way or another but some, such as the labor unions and professional organizations, are particularly strong in this respect.

A distinction can be made between groups which are concerned with limited, specific interests and those which aim to promote and defend a much wider cross section. These wider interest groups are often referred to as 'cause groups'. They fight for a particular cause, irrespective of whether or not the people they seek to help have direct contact with them, or even know of their existence. They are usually impelled by higher motives than self-interest and could well be called conscience groups.

Cause groups usually ignore national boundaries and can be found throughout the world. Greenpeace, Amnesty International, and Oxfam, are all well-known examples.

7.2 Pressure groups

Sometimes interest groups are referred to as 'pressure groups' as if the two terms are synonymous. This is not strictly the case.

A pressure group is a group representing an interest which seeks to achieve its aims by putting pressure on government. It will use a wide range of tactics to try to influence public opinion but it knows that ultimately the pressure must be on the government in whichever country it operates.

International cause groups will usually exert pressure on governments indirectly, knowing that they are unlikely to gain direct access to national seats of power. They make their case to the public at large, utilizing the mass media, hoping that popular opinion in each country will apply the necessary pressure to produce action.

7.3 Monism, pluralism, and corporatism

A monistic state may be said to be one in which interest group activity is frowned upon, discouraged, or even banned. This contrasts with a pluralistic state where independently organized groups freely operate and act as intermediaries between the public and the government.

Communist regimes and most other one-party states are essentially monistic, mainly because they find it difficult to 'manage' an organization which is outside the established political system. Because it is outside, its actions are unpredictable and unpredictability is seen as a threat to the settled order of things. A good example of this is the protracted opposition, between 1980 and 1989, of the Polish communist government to the independent labor union, Solidarity.

Churches in one-party states produce similar problems. The activities of religious organizations extend beyond national interests, as defined by the ruling regime, and, again, tend to produce unpredictable behaviour. There are, however, states where a religion has been absorbed into the political system so as to become not only acceptable but the main driving force. Iran provides a striking example of this kind of theocratic state.

Some secular one-party states have accepted that interest activity cannot be ignored but can be managed if absorbed into the political system. Thus the pressures, which in a pluralistic system express themselves in a wide variety of outlets, are channelled into the state machine. As the state institutions are invariably controlled by party activists, interests become easily controllable too.

In stark contrast, pressure groups flourish in pluralistic systems, even though the most liberally inclined governments may find them an inconvenience. The United States is an example of a country where interest groups are particularly powerful. Over the years their activities have become increasingly evident and their methods more sophisticated so that members of Congress, state governments, and even the president, ignore them at their peril.

In some parts of the world the pluralistic state has become the corporate state in which a limited number of powerful interest groups, industrial, financial, and labor, dominate the political scene, the government choosing, or being forced, to negotiate with them before making a major policy decision.

In Austria, for example, political decisions are often arrived at, with the government's blessing, following discussions between strong chambers of commerce and labor unions. Once agreement between these powerful bodies has been reached the government takes over the task of legitimizing and implementing what has been agreed.

The so-called 'social contract' in the United Kingdom in the mid-1970s, between the Labor governments of Harold Wilson and James Callaghan and the Trades Union Congress, whereby the unions accepted a policy of wage restraint in return for the government's promise to follow an agreed social welfare plan, was another strong example of corporatism in a liberal democratic state.

It can be argued that pluralism extends and enhances democracy, because it encourages people who would not normally involve themselves in politics to contribute to the policy-making process. Corporatism, on the other hand, can be said to be antidemocratic in that it increases the power of those sections of the community who organize themselves in the pursuit of self-interest.

Furthermore, corporatism is often associated with the fascist regimes of the 1930s when, in Italy in particular, the government incorporated interest groups representing capital and labor into the state machinery.

The dividing line between thriving pluralism and corporatism is not always easy to discern and sometimes, as in the United Kingdom in the 1970s, an essentially pluralistic state may become temporarily corporatist and then, with a change of government, revert. There is evidence of corporatism in some Central and South American countries. Here powerful groups representing capital and labor wield enormous power and influence, and both the church and the military are involved in major policy decisions. Indeed, those states where the military has seized executive power may be said to have taken corporatism to its ultimate limits.

In economically undeveloped areas of the world it is probably misleading to discuss interest group activity in the form of monism, pluralism, or corporatism. Here groups are considerably less well organized and less sophisticated and sometimes represent little more than an updating and extension of old tribal allegiances.

7.4 Pressure groups and political parties

A 'political party' can best be described as an association of people who hold similar views about what should be a community's social and economic priorities and come together to establish these priorities by gaining control of the machinery of government. It is this wish to govern which distinguishes a party from an interest group, but there are other important differences.

First, an interest group is concerned with a clearly defined range of interests whereas a political party is prepared to take on board a virtually unlimited number. Second, each interest group tends to play a distinctive and individualistic role, while the agenda of one political party may be similar to that of another, the differences between them being based on alternative

Principal political parties of the world (1999) — Table 38

Region/ country	Number of parties regularly operating	Number of parties with more than 10% of assembly seats	Leading parties	Orientation
Asia				
Afghanistan	25	–	electoral process is currently in abeyance	–
Bangladesh	22	2	Bangladesh National Party*	right of center
			Awami League*	center left
Bhutan	–	–	no parties permitted	–
Brunei	–	–	no parties permitted	–
Cambodia	40	3	FUNCINPEC*	right-of-center nationalist
			Cambodian People's Party*	reform communist
			Khmer Nation Party	centrist
China	9	1	Chinese Communist Party*	communist
India	43	3	Congress Party*	centrist
			Bharatiya Janata Party*	Hindu nationalist
			United Front	center left
Indonesia	48	4	Indonesian Democratic Party*	centrist
			Golkar**	right of center
			United Development Party	Islamic
			National Awakening Party	Islamic
Japan	15**	3	Liberal Democratic Party*	right of center
			Democratic Party of Japan	center left
			Shinshinto	centrist
Kazakhstan	16	1	People's Unity Party*	moderate nationalist
Korea, North	3	1	Korean Workers' Party*	communist
Korea, South	6	3	New Korea Party*	right of center
			National Congress for New Politics*	center left
			United Liberal Democrats	center right
Kyrgyzstan	22	–	independents dominate the assembly	–
Laos	1	1	Lao People's Revolutionary Party*	communist
Malaysia	42	1***	UMNO/National Front*	center right
Maldives	–	–	no political parties operate	–
Mongolia	12	3	Mongolian National Democratic Party*	center right
			Mongolian Social Democratic Party	left of center
			Mongolian People's Revolutionary Party*	reform communist
Myanmar	9	1	National League for Democracy*	centrist
Nepal	16	2	United Nepal Communist Party*	reform communist
			Nepali Congress Party*	left of center
Pakistan	35	1	Pakistan Muslim League-Nawaz*	right of center
Singapore	25	1	People's Action Party*	right of center
Sri Lanka	30	2	Sri Lanka Freedom Party*	left of center
			United National Party*	right of center
Taiwan	11†	3	Kuomintang*	rightwing nationalist
			Democratic Progressive Party*	centrist
			New Party	rightwing nationalist
Tajikistan	7	1	Communist Party of Tajikistan*	reform communist
Thailand	22	3	Democratic Party*	centrist
			New Aspiration Party*	centrist
			Chart Pattana	right of center
Turkmenistan	3	1	Democratic Party of Turkmenistan*	reform communist

continues

Principal political parties of the world (1999) (continued) Table 38

Region/ country	Number of parties regularly operating	Number of parties with more than 10% of assembly seats	Leading parties	Orientation
Uzbekistan	9	1	People's Democratic Party*	reform communist
Vietnam	1	1	Communist Party of Vietnam*	communist
Central America & Caribbean				
Antigua and Barbuda	7	2	United Progressive Party (UPP)*	centrist
			Antigua Labor Party (ALP)*	center left
Bahamas	4	2	Free National Movement (FNM)*	center left
			Progressive Liberal Party (PLP)	centrist
Barbados	5	1	Barbados Labor Party (BLP)*	left of center
Belize	3	2	People's United Party (PUP)*	left of center
			United Democratic Party (UDP)*	right of center
Costa Rica	28	2	National Liberation Party (PLN)*	left of center
			Christian Social Unity Party (PUSC)*	Christian centrist
Cuba	1	1	Cuban Communist Party (PCC)*	communist
Dominica	4	3	Dominican United Workers' Party (DUWP)*	left of center
			Dominica Freedom Party (DFP)	centrist
			Labor Party of Dominica (LDP)	left of center
Dominican Republic	25	3	Dominican Revolutionary Party (PRD)*	left of center
			Social Christian Revolutionary Party (PRSC)	independent socialist
			Dominican Liberation Party (PLD)*	nationalist
El Salvador	23	4	Christian Democratic Party (PDC)	left of center
			Nationalist Republican Alliance (ARENA)*	right wing
			Farabundo Marti National Liberation Front (FMLN)*	left wing
			National Conciliation Party (PCN)	right wing
Grenada	8	1	New National Party (NNP)*	centrist
Guatemala	36	3	Guatemalan Christian Democratic Party (PDCG)	Christian center-left
			Guatemalan Republican Front (FRG)*	right wing
			National Advancement Party (PAN)*	right of center
			Center Party (UCN)	centrist
Haiti	20	1	Lavalas Political Platform (PPL)*	centrist
Honduras	11	2	Liberal Party of Honduras (PLH)*	center right
			National Party of Honduras (PNH)*	traditional rightwing
Jamaica	4	2	People's National Party (PNP)*	left of center
			Jamaica Labor Party (JLP)	moderate centrist
Mexico	10	3	Institutional Revolutionary Party (PRI)*	centrist/corporatist
			National Action Party (PAN)*	center right
			Democratic Revolutionary Party (PRD)*	center left
Nicaragua	25	2	Liberal Alliance (AL)*	right of center
			Sandinista National Liberation Front (FSLN)*	left wing
Panama	21	2	Democratic Revolutionary Party (PRD)*	center right
			Arnulfista Party (PA)	left of center
St Kitts and Nevis	8	2	St Kitts-Nevis Labor Party*	left of center
			Concerned Citizens' Movement (CCM)	centrist
Saint Lucia	3	1	St Lucia Labor Party (SLP)*	left of center
St Vincent and the Grenadines	3	2	New Democratic Party (NDP)*	right of center
			Unity Labor Party (ULP)*	left of center
Trinidad and Tobago	9	2	United National Congress (UNC)*	left of center
			People's National Movement (PNM)*	centrist

continues

Principal political parties of the world (1999) (continued) Table 38

Region/ country	Number of parties regularly operating	Number of parties with more than 10% of assembly seats	Leading parties	Orientation
Central, Eastern, & Southern Europe				
Albania	34	2	Democratic Party	centrist
			Socialist Party of Albania*	left of center
Armenia	16	1	Republican Party	center left
Azerbaijan	31	1	New Azerbaijan*	left of center
Belarus	35	1	Peasants' Party	left of center
Bosnia-Herzegovina	42	3	Party of Democratic Action*	Muslim nationalist
			Serbian Democratic Party	Serbian nationalist
			Croatian Christian Democratic	Croat Union nationalist
Bulgaria	62	2	Bulgarian Socialist Party*	reform communist
			Union of Democratic Forces*	right of center
Croatia	24	1	Christian Democratic Union*	rightwing nationalist
Cyprus	8	3	Democratic Rally (DISY)*	centrist
			Democratic Rally (DIKO)	federalist, center left
			Progressive Party of the Working People (AKEL) *	left wing
Czech Republic	16	4	Czech Social Democratic Party*	center left
			Christian Democratic Union	center right
			Civic Democratic Party*	right of center
			Communist Party	reform communist
Estonia	21	4	Moderates' Party	center left
			Fatherland Union	rightwing
			Estonian Reform Party	right of center
			Center Party*	moderate nationalist
Georgia	52	3	National Democratic Party of Georgia	center right
			All-Georgian Union of Revival	nationalist
			Citizens' Union of Georgia (CUG)*	centrist
Greece	16	2	Pan-Hellenic Socialist Movement (PASOK)*	nationalist socialist
			New Democracy*	center right
Hungary	50	2	Hungarian Socialist Party*	reform socialist
			Alliance of Young Democrats	center right
Latvia	40	5	Latvian Way*	center right
			People's Party*	center right
			Latvian National and Conservative Party	far right
			Harmony for Latvia	left of center
			Latvian Social Democratic Union	center right
Lithuania	32	2	Conservative Party*	rightwing nationalist
			Christian Democratic Party	center right
Macedonia	18	3	Social Democratic Alliance*	reform communist
			Internal Macedonian Revolutionary Organization/ Democratic Alternative*	nationalist/rightwing
			Party for Democratic Prosperity/National Democratic Party*	ethnic Albanian
Moldova	30	4	Communist Party*	socialist
			Democratic Convention*	right wing
			Movement for a Democratic and Prosperous Moldova*	center right
			Moldovan Party of Democratic Forces	centrist
Poland	60	3	Solidarity Election Alliance*	center right
			Freedom Union	centrist

continues

Principal political parties of the world (1999) (continued) **Table 38**

Region/ country	Number of parties regularly operating	Number of parties with more than 10% of assembly seats	Leading parties	Orientation
			Democratic Left Alliance*	reform socialist
Romania	90	3	Social Democracy Party*	center left
			Democratic Convention*	center right
			Social Democratic Union	center left
Russia	45††	4	Yabloko	center right
			Liberal Democratic Party	rightwing nationalist
			Our Home is Russia	centrist
			Communist Party*	communist
Slovakia	20	4	Movement for a Democratic Slovakia*	center-left nationalist
			Party of the Democratic Left	reform communist
			Hungarian Coalition	Hungarian orientated
			Slovak Democratic Coalition*	center right
Slovenia	16	5	Liberal Democrats*	centrist
			Christian Democrats	right of center
			Social Democrats	left of center
			Social Democratic Party	center left
			Slovenian People's Party*	right of center
Turkey	15	5	Motherland Party	nationalist Islamic right-of-center
			Virtue Party (FP)*	Islamic
			Democratic Left (DP)*	left of center
			Nationalist Action*	far right
			True Path Party	center right
Ukraine	38	1	Ukrainian Communist Party*	reform communist
Yugoslavia	38	4	Serbian Socialist Party*	reform communist
			Serbian Radical Party*	far-right nationalist
			Montenegrin Social Democratic Party	reform communist
			Serbian Renewal Movement	rightwing nationalist
Central and Southern Africa				
Angola	45	2	Popular Movement for the Liberation of Angola Angola-Workers' Party (MLPA-PT)*	Marxist-Leninist
			Union for the Total Independence of Angola (UNITA)*	nationalist conservative
Benin	88	4	Party for Democratic Renewal (PRD)	left of center
			Benin Renaissance Party (PRB)*	centrist
			Action Front for Renewal and Development (FARD)	left of center
			Social Democratic Party (PSO)	centre left
Botswana	12	2	Botswana Democratic Party (BDP)*	center right
			Botswana National Front (BNF)*	left of center
Burkina Faso	46	1	Congress for Democracy and Progress (CPD)*	left wing
Burundi	9	2	Union for National Progress (UPRONA)*	African socialist
			Front for Burundian Democracy (Frodebu)*	left of center
Cameroon	133	2	Social Democratic Front (SDF)*	center left
			Cameroon People's Democratic Movement (RDPC)*	left-of-center nationalist
Cape Verde	5	2	African Party for the Independence of Cape Verde (PAICV)	African nationalist socialist
			Movement for Democracy (MPD)*	centrist
Central African	20	2	Central African People's Labor Party (MLPC)*	left of center

continues

Principal political parties of the world (1999) (continued) — Table 38

Region/ country	Number of parties regularly operating	Number of parties with more than 10% of assembly seats	Leading parties	Orientation
Republic			Central African Democratic Rally (RDC)	right of center
Chad	60	3	Union for Democratic Renewal (URD)*	center left
			National Union for Development and Renewal (UNDR)	center left
			Patriotic Salvation Movement (MPS)*	centrist
Comoros	20	1	National Rally for Development (RND)*	right of center
Congo, Dem. Republic of	9‡‡	1	Alliance of Democratic Forces for the Liberation of Congo-Zaire (AFDL)	African socialist
Congo, Republic of	28	3	Pan-African Union for Social Democracy (UPADS)*	left of center
			Congolese Movement for Democracy and Integral Development (MCDDI)*	center right
			Congolese Labor Party (PCT)	leftwing
Côte d'Ivoire	90	1	Democratic Party of the Côte d'Ivoire (PDCI)*	nationalist-enterprise
Djbouti	4	2	People's Progress Party (RPP)*	authoritarian nationalist
			Front for the Restoration of Unity and Democracy (FRUD)	ethnic-based
Equatorial Guinea	22	1	Democratic Party of Equatorial Guinea (PDGE)*	authoritarian nationalist
Eritrea	6	1	People's Front for Democracy and Justice (PFDJ)*	left of center
Ethiopia	20	1	Ethiopian People's Revolutionary Democratic Front (EPRDF)*	left of center
Gabon	28	1	Gabonese Democratic Party (PDG)*	authoritarian nationalist
Gambia	7	2	Alliance for Patriotic Reorientation and Construction (APRC)*	left of center
			United Democratic Party (UDP)	centrist
Ghana	9	2	National Democratic Congress (NDC)*	centrist
			New Patriotic Party (NPP)*	left of center
Guinea	42	2	Party of Unity and Progress (PUP)*	centrist authoritarian
			Rally of the Guinean People (RPG)	centrist
Guinea-Bissau	14	3	African Party for the Independence of Portuguese Guinea and Cape Verde (PAIGC)*	socialist
			Guinea-Bissau Resistance Party-Bafata Movement (RGB-MB)	centrist
			Party for Social Renovation (PRS)	left of center
Kenya	17	2	Kenya African National Union (KANU)*	centrist nationalist
			Democratic Party (DP)	centrist
Lesotho	14	1	Lesotho Congress for Democracy (LCD)*	left of center
Liberia	14	2	Unity Party (UP)*	left of center
			National Patriotic Party (NPP)*	left of center
Madagascar	100	2	Association for Madagascar's Renaissance (AREMA)*	nationalist socialist
			Leader-Fanilo	left of center
Malawi	14	3	Malawi Congress Party (MCP)*	right wing
			United Democratic Front (UDF)*	center left
			Alliance for Democracy (AFORD)	centrist
Mali	63	1	Alliance for Democracy in Mali (ADEMA)*	center left
Mauritania	21	1	Democratic and Social Republican Party (PRDS)*	left of center
Mauritius	14	2	Mauritian Militant Movement (MMM)*	left wing
			Mauritius Labor Party (MLP)*	center left

continues

Principal political parties of the world (1999) (continued) **Table 38**

Region/ country	Number of parties regularly operating	Number of parties with more than 10% of assembly seats	Leading parties	Orientation
Mozambique	21	2	National Front for the Liberation of Mozambique (Frelimo)*	left of center-free market
			Mozambique National Resistance (MNR-Renamo)*	right of center
Namibia	15	2	South-West African People's Organization (SWAPO)*	left of center
			Democratic Turnhalle Alliance (DTA)*	center right
Niger	20	1	National Union of Independents for the Revival of Democracy (UNIRD)*	authoritarian
Nigeria	30	3	People's Democratic Party (PDP)*	centrist
			All Peoples' Party (APP)*	right of center
			Alliance for Democracy (AFD)	left of center
Rwanda	15	4	Republican Democratic Party (MDR)*	Hutu left of center
			Liberal Party (LP)	Hutu centrist
			Social Democratic Party (PSD)	Hutu socialist
			Rwanda Patriotic Front (FPR)	Tutsi party
São Tomé	6	3	Movement for the Liberation of São Tomé e Príncipe (MLSTP-PSD)*	nationalist socialist
			Democratic Convergence Party-Reflection Group (PCD-GR)*	left of center
			Independent Democratic Action (ADI)*	centrist
Senegal	30	2	Senegalese Socialist Party (PS)*	left of center
			Senegalese Democratic Party (PDS)	centrist
Seychelles	9	1	Seychelles People's Progressive Front (SPPF)*	socialist
Sierra Leone	15	3	Sierra Leone People's Party (SLPP)*	left of center
			United People Party (UNPP)*	left of center
			People's Democratic Party (PDP)	left of center
Somalia	17	–	–	–
South Africa	42	3	African National Congress of South Africa (ANC)*	left of center
			National Party of South Africa (NP)*	right of center
			Inkatha Freedom Party (IFP)	centrist
Sudan	16	1	National Islamic Front (NIF)*	Islamic nationalist
Swaziland	6	–	independents	–
Tanzania	15	1	Revolutionary Party of Tanzania (CCM)*	African socialist
Togo	60	1	Rally of the Togolese People (RPT)*	nationalist socialist
Uganda	20	1	National Resistance Movement (NRM)*	center left authoritarian
Zambia	17	2	Movement for Multiparty Democracy (MMD)*	center left
Zimbabwe	19	1	Zimbabwe African National Union-Patriotic Front (ZANU-PF)*	African socialist
Middle East and North Africa				
Algeria	39	3	Democratic Rally (RND)*	centrist
			Social Movement for Peace (MSP)*	moderate Islamic
			National Liberation Front (FLN)*	socialist-Islamic
Bahrain	–	–	no parties	–
Egypt	16	1	National Democratic Party (NDP)*	center left
Iran	15	–	no formal parties represented	–
Iraq	1	1	Arab Ba'ath Socialist Party*	nationalist socialist
Israel	32	2	Israel Labor Party *	left of center
			Likud (Consolidation Party)*	right of center

continues

Principal political parties of the world (1998) (continued) — Table 38

Region/ country	Number of parties regularly operating	Number of parties with more than 10% of assembly seats	Leading parties	Orientation
Jordan	15	–	independents dominate	–
Kuwait	–	–	no parties	–
Lebanon	30	3	Phalangist Party*	Maronite Christian radical nationalist
			Amal	Shia Muslim
			Hizbollah	Islamic fundamentalist
Libya	1	1	Arab Socialist Union (ASU)*	left wing
Morocco	20	4	Constitutional Union (UC)	right wing
			National Rally of Independents (RNI)	royalist
			Popular Movement (MP)	centrist
			Socialist Union of Popular Forces (USFP)	progressive socialist
Oman	–	–	no parties	–
Qatar	–	–	no parties	–
Saudi Arabia	–	–	no parties	–
Syria	6	1	Arab Ba'ath Socialist Party*	Arab socialist
Tunisia	11	1	Constitutional Democratic Rally (RDC)*	nationalist socialist
United Arab Emirates	–	–	no parties	–
Yemen	30	2	General People's Congress (GPC)*	left of center
			Yemen Reform Group (Al-Islah)	right of center Islamist
North America				
Canada	17	3	Liberal Party of Canada*	center left
			Bloc Quebecois	separatist
			Reform Party	rightwing populist
United States	19	2	Republican Party*	right of center
			Democratic Party*	centrist
Northern and Western Europe				
Andorra	6	2	National Democratic Grouping (AND)*	centrist
			Liberal Union (UL)*	center right
Austria	17	3	Socialist Party of Austria (SPÖ)*	left of center
			Austrian People's Party (ÖVP)*	centrist
			Freedom Party of Austria (FPÖ)*	moderate rightwing
Belgium	2	5	Christian People's Party (CVP)	Christian center left, Dutch-speaking
			Socialist Party (SP)	left of center, Dutch-speaking
			Flemish Liberals and Democrats (VLD)	left of center, French-speaking
			Socialist Party (PS)	left of center, French-speaking
			Liberal Reform Party (PRL)	centrist, French-speaking
Denmark	22	2	Social Democratic Party (SD)*	left of center
			Liberal Party (V)*	center left
Finland	18	4	Finnish Social Democratic Party (SSDP)*	left of center
			Finnish Center Party (Kesk)*	centrist
			National Coalition Party (Kok)*	right of center
			Left-Wing Alliance (VL)	left of center

continues

Principal political parties of the world (1999) (continued) **Table 38**

Region/ country	Number of parties regularly operating	Number of parties with more than 10% of assembly seats	Leading parties	Orientation
France	55	3	Rally for the Republic*	right of center
			Union for French Democracy*	center right
			Socialist Party	left of center
Germany	23	2	Christian Democratic Union*	center right
			Social Democratic Party*	center left
Iceland	7	3	Independence Party (IP)*	right of center
			Progressive Party (PP)	radical socialist
			United Left*	left of center
Ireland	14	3	Fianna Fáil (FF)*	center right
			Fine Gael (FG)*	center left
			Labor Party	left of center
			Progressive Democrats (PD)	radical center left
Italy	31	2	Freedom Alliance*	right of center
			Olive Tree Alliance*	left of center
Liechtentstein	3	2	Patriotic Union (VU)*	right of center
			Progressive Citizens' Party (FBP)*	right of center
Luxembourg	7	3	Christian Social Party (PCS)*	Christian left of center
			Luxembourg Socialist Workers' Party (POSL)*	moderate socialist
			Democratic Party (PD)*	center left
Malta	5	2	Malta Labor Party (MLP)*	left of center
			Nationalist Party (PN)*	Christian centrist
Monaco	–	–	no formal parties	–
Netherlands	21	3	Christian Democratic Appeal (CDA)	Christian right of center
			Labor Party (PvdA)*	left of center
			People's Party for Freedom and Democracy (VVD)*	centrist
Norway	14	4	Norwegian Labor Party (DNA)*	left of center
			Conservative Party	progressive right-of-center
			Christian People's Party (KrF)	center left
			Progress Party (FrP)	right wing
Portugal	19	2	Social Democratic Party (PSD)*	center right
			Socialist Party (PS)*	center left
San Marino	7	4	Christian Democratic Party (PDCS)*	Christian centrist
			Socialist Party (PS)*	left of center
			Progressive Democratic Party (PDP)	moderate leftwing
			Popular Alliance of San Marino Democrats (APDS)	centrist
Spain	56	2	Spanish Socialist Workers' Party (PSOE)*	left of center
			Popular Party (PP)*	right of center
Sweden	15	4	Swedish Social Democratic Labor Party (SAP)*	center left
			Christian Democrats (KdS)	center right
			Moderate Party (M)*	right of center
			Left Party (Vp)	left of center
Switzerland	26	4	Christian Democratic People's Party of Switzerland (CVP-PDC)	Christian centrist
			Radical Democratic Party of Switzerland (FDP-PRD)*	radical center-left
			Swiss Social Democratic Party (SP-PS)*	center left
			Swiss People's Party (SVP-UDC)	centrist
United Kingdom	55	2	Conservative and Unionist Party*	right of center
			Labor Party*	center left

Principal political parties of the world (1999) (continued) Table 38

Region/ country	Number of parties regularly operating	Number of parties with more than 10% of assembly seats	Leading parties	Orientation
Australia	78	3	Australian Labor Party*	center left
			Liberal Party	center right
			National Party	centrist non-metropolitan
Fiji	15	3	Fijian Political Party	Melanesian right-of-center
			Fijian Association Party*	centrist
			Fijian Labor Party*	Indian left of center
Kiribati	2	2	Maneaban Te Mauri*	center right
			National Progressive Party	center left
Marshall Islands	–	–	no formal political parties	–
Micronesia	–	–	no political parties	–
Nauru	–	–	no political parties	–
New Zealand	15	4	Labor Party*	center left
			National Party*	center right
			New Zealand First Party	centrist
			Alliance Party	left of center
Palau	–	–	no political parties	–
Papua New Guinea	16	2	Pangu Pati*	nationalist
			People's Progress Party	right of center
Philippines	24	2	Liberal Party*	centrist
			Laban (LAMMP)*	center right
Samoa	5	2	Human Rights Protection Party*	centrist
			Samoan National Development Party*	center right
Solomon Islands	7	2	Group for National Unity*	nationalist
			Alliance for Change*	centrist
Tonga	1	1	People's Party*	centrist
Tuvalu	–	–	no political parties	–
Vanuatu	17	4	Union of Moderate Parties*	center right
			Vanuaaku Parti*	left of center
			National United Party*	center right
			Melanesian Progressive Party	center left
South America				
Argentina	35	3	Radical Civic Union Party (UCR)*	centrist
			Justicalist Party (PJ)*	right wing
			Front for a Country in Solidarity (Frepaso)*	center left
Bolivia	27	5	National Revolutionary Movement (MNR)*	centrist nationalist
			Nationalist Democratic Action Party (ADN)*	rightwing nationalist
			Movement of the Revolutionary Left (MIR)	leftwing nationalist
			Solidarity and Civic Union (UCS)	populist, free enterprise
			Conscience of the Fatherland (Condepa)	populist
Brazil	20	5	Social Democratic Party (PSDB)	left of center
			Party of the Brazilian Democratic Movement (PMDB)	center left
			Brazilian Progressive Party (PPB)	center right
			Liberal Front Party (PFL)*	center right
			Workers' Party (PT)	left of center
Chile	30	4	Christian Democratic Party (PDC)*	centrist
			Independent Democratic Union (UDI)	right wing

continues

Principal political parties of the world (1999) (continued) **Table 38**

Region/ country	Number of parties regularly operating	Number of parties with more than 10% of assembly seats	Leading parties	Orientation
			Party of National Renewal (RN)	right wing
			Independent Democratic Union (UDI)	right wing
Colombia	20	2	Liberal Party (PL)*	centrist
			Conservative Party (PSC)*	right of center
Ecuador	18	4	Popular Democracy (DP)*	center right
			Social Christian Party (PSC)*	Christian socialist
			Ecuadorean Roldosist Party (PRE)*	center left populist
			Democratic Left (ID)	left of center
Guyana	14	2	People's National Congress (PNC)*	centrist
			People's Progressive Party (PPP)*	left wing
Paraguay	13	3	National Republican Association-Colorado Party (ANR-PC)*	right of center
			Authentic Radical Liberal Party (PLRA)*	centrist
			National Encounter (EU)	right wing
Peru	30	3	Cambio 90*	centrist
			New Majority (NM)*	centrist
			Union for Peru (UPP)	centrist
Suriname	15	2	New Front (NF)*	left of center
			National Democratic Party (NDP)*	left wing
Uruguay	26	3	Colorado Party (PC)*	progressive center-left
			National (Blanco) Party (PN)*	traditional right-of-center
			Progressive Encounter (EP)*	left wing
Venezuela	20	4	Democratic Action (AD)*	center left
			Christian Social Party (COPEI)	Christian center-right
			Project Venezuela	centralist
			Fifth Republic Movement (MVR)*	populist

* Parties with >20% of assembly seats after the most recent elections.
** More than 10,000 political parties are registered in Japan.
*** The National Front is a coalition of 14 parties, dominated by UMNO.
† More than 80 parties are registered in Taiwan.
†† More than 250 parties are registered in Russia.
‡‡ Over 130 parties exist in the Democratic Republic of Congo.

Sources: Day, A J, German, R, and Campbell, J (eds.) *Political Parties of the World*, 4th edn., Cartermill 1996; *Europa Yearbook 1998*, Europa Publications, 1998.

solutions to the same problems. The third difference has already been identified. An interest group aims to influence the government while a party is, or wants to be, the government.

Occasionally an interest group will step over the dividing line and become a party itself. Small political parties with narrowly defined aims, making them little removed from interest groups, have been organized in several countries. Some have been short-lived, some have survived for considerable periods with minimal memberships and funds, and a few have achieved enough popular support to make them formidable political organizations.

In Denmark there is the Single Tax Party (Denmark's Retsforbund) advocating the theories of the 19th-century US economist Henry George (1839–97). Even on such a narrow base it has managed from time to time to win seats in the Folketing. The conservative, antibureaucracy Finnish Rural Party represents the interests of the lower middle class, including small farmers and small enterprises in Finland, and with a membership of about 25,000 has won assembly seats but not a position in government. In several recently democratized states in Central and Eastern Europe farmer-orientated agrarian parties have also had success in recent assembly elections, notably the Polish Peasant Party, which provided the country's prime minister between 1993 and 1995, the Latvian Peasant's Union, which has provided the country's president since 1993, the Agrarian Party and Bulgarian National Agrarian Union in Bulgaria, the Agrarian Party in the Czech Republic, and the Independent Smallholders' Party in Hungary. In France Génération Ecologie and Les Verts (The Greens) speak for ecological and environmental interests, and the National Restoration (estd. 1947) and New Royalist Action parties, although attracting little support, aim for the return of the monarchy. In the Federal Republic of Germany the Five Per Cent Block was established in the mid-1970s, with a membership of barely a hundred, as a political movement to oppose the 5% clause which denies parliamentary representation to parties failing to gain 5% of the national vote. In contrast, Die Grünen (the Greens), with a large and growing membership, has emerged from among a number of ecology parties to become a significant political force. In the September 1998 general election it captured 6.7% of the national vote and 47 Bundestag seats. With representation in most state assemblies and partners in coalition governments in several, it has now effectively supplanted the Free Democrats as Germany's third main party and from October 1998 became partners in a federal coalition government with the Social Democratic Party.

Women's interests are being increasingly represented throughout the world by parties which have grown from nonpolitical groups. In Belgium, for example, there is the Unified Feminist Party, in Iceland the Women's Alliance (estd. 1983), and in Germany the German Women's Movement. In Norway and the Czech Republic, the Pensioners' Party, and in Germany, Die Grauen (the Greys), have also contested recent elections, representing the interests of older citizens. Parties based on specific religious aims are also found. In Israel the National Religious Party advocates the unity of the Jewish people in faith in Israel and throughout the world, and the Netherlands Roman Catholic Party presses for adherence to Catholic principles on subjects such as abortion, euthanasia, and sexuality.

Whereas interest groups, in one form or another, have existed since the beginnings of civilized life, political parties are relatively new, being products of the 18th century onwards. Their predecessors were cliques and factions, based usually on personal or family power. The modern party displays three essential features: a permanent structure and organization; an authority to represent people, whether or not they are members of the party, based on open elections; and, of course, an intention to form a government or participate in government.

Table 38 lists the leading parties in the contemporary world and their political orientations. The number of active parties in each state, as shown in column 2, is something of an approximation in some cases because the emergence and disappearance of minor groupings is often a notable feature of some political systems.

7.5 Parties in liberal and emergent democracies

It is possible to distinguish six different bases of party formation and support in the states we have defined as liberal or emergent democracies. They are: social class, economic status, religion, regional differences, ethnicity, and philosophical leanings. All parties are based on at least one of these factors, some on most, or all.

The United Kingdom provides a clear example of class-based parties, although the divisions are not as stark in contemporary society as they were earlier in the century. The creation of the Labor Party, known originally as the Labor Representation Committee, in 1900, to represent the working classes, provided a striking contrast to the Conservative Party, which sought to protect and promote the interests of the middle and upper classes. Before the advent of the Labor Party Britain's two-party political system had been based on a division between the Conservatives, representing landed interests, and the Liberals, representing urban industrialists.

Class-based parties are not as marked in most other countries. The Labor Party of Australia and the New Zealand Labor Party, although similar in origin to their counterpart in the United Kingdom, reflect the greater social openness in those two countries.

Ironically, communist parties in liberal democratic states have tended to be homes for leftwing, middle class intellectuals rather than for the proletariat, and have seldom won sufficient popular support to control the levers of political power. This has been increasingly true of the two most significant of such bodies in Western Europe, the Italian Communist Party (PCI) and French Communist Party (PCF). In 1991, the PCI, formed originally in 1921, split into two new parties, the social-democratic Democratic Party of the Left (PDS) and the traditionalist Communist Re-establishment Party (PRC).

Economic status has largely replaced, or is replacing, class as an indicator of social position in most liberal democracies. In Italy, for example, class divisions are not clearly defined and economic status is becoming a dominant feature of party support. In the Federal Republic of Germany the postwar rise of a non-unionized working class and a new middle class provide further evidence of the importance of economic, rather than social, factors as a basis for party allegiance.

Religion still provides a widely occurring foundation for political parties in contemporary liberal and emergent democracies. Parties in Italy, Austria, Germany, France, and most other Western European states display this characteristic to varying degrees, having their roots in sides taken during earlier secular – clerical battles. In the United Kingdom economic disparities in Northern Ireland have been underlined by religious divisions.

Regional differences are, arguably, the most common foundation for party support. In the United States, for example, clearly distinguishable parties might well disappear if they were not supported on regional bases. In the Netherlands and Belgium regional variations, accentuated by linguistic differences, have multiplied the party groupings. In Belgium each of the four principal parties, Christian Democrat, Socialist, Liberal, and Green, is currently divided into autonomous, and often antagonistic, Flemish and French wings. In the United Kingdom, nationalist parties operate in Scotland and Wales, and regional parties in Northern Ireland, while support for the two main parties, the Conservatives and Labor, also varies greatly regionally. In Italy, the Lombard League/Northern League, based in northern Italy, has established itself as an influential force with substantial national bargaining power, as have the Catalonia-based Democratic Convergence in Spain, and southern-based Telugu Desam and AIADMK in India.

Ethnic-based parties are a feature of a number of the recently democratized states of Central and Eastern Europe. They include: in Albania, the Greek Albanian-orientated Human Rights Union (EAD); in Bosnia-Herzegovina, the Serb-orientated Serbian Renaissance Movement (SPO) and Croat-orientated Croatian Christian Democratic Union (HDZ); in Bulgaria, the minority Turkish community-orientated Movement for Rights and Freedoms (MRF); in Croatia, the Serb-orientated Serbian National Party (SNS); in the Czech Republic, the Moravian and Silesian communities-orientated Movement for Autonomous Democracy of Moravia and Silesia (MADMS); in Estonia, the ethnic Russian-orientated Our Home is Estonia party; in Macedonia, the ethnic Albanian-orientated Party for Democratic Prosperity (PDP); in Moldova, the Gagauz community-orientated Gagauz People's Movement; in Romania, the ethnic Hungarian-orientated Hungarian Democratic Union of Romania (HDUR); in the Slovak Republic, the ethnic Hungarian-orientated Hungarian Coalition; and in Yugoslavia, the ethnic Hungarian and Albanian-orientated Democratic Community of Vojvodina Hungarians (DZVM) and the Democratic Party of Albanians (DPA).

Philosophy has not provided a reliable basis for mass party support in liberal democratic states in recent years. Indeed, surveys suggest that the great majority of contemporary electors not only care little for social and political theory but have no clear understanding of the philosophical stance of the parties for which they vote. The 'thinking elector' is certainly in a minority throughout the world and the chances of representation by a party which accurately mirrors the views of this kind of voter are very much determined by the vagaries of the electoral system, as we shall see later in this chapter. The new 'postindustrial' ecological parties, which have made notable progress in Northern and Western European states during recent decades, as a result of proportional representation, are examples of this process. They contrast significantly with the eclectic 'catch-all' nature of most major liberal democratic parties.

The internal discipline of parties varies greatly within liberal and emergent democratic states. The parties of the United Kingdom, where a vigorous 'whipping' system is in place to ensure that Members of Parliament vote according to the 'party line', and Germany are particularly cohesive and disciplined. In Japan, in contrast, control within parties is effectively devolved to the leaders of patronage and personality-based factions. In the United States, congressmen and senators operate in the main as 'freelancers', voting according to personal convictions and constituency interests.

7.6 Parties in communist states

The all-pervading influence of the party provides the sharpest contrast between communist one-party and multiparty states. It is the ultimate source of power and permeates all aspects of the political system and the state institutions.

In contrast to parties in most Western democracies, membership of the party in communist states is an elitist privilege. Whereas parties in liberal democracies actively compete with each other to increase their memberships, communist parties are highly cautious and selective about the people who are eventually admitted into full membership. In China, for example, aspirants are initially inducted into the Young Pioneers, a body for children between the ages of 7 and 14 which operates in schools, and then into the party's 'youth' wing for 15–25-year-olds, the Chinese Communist Youth League. Years later, when old enough for consideration for full-party membership, they must be nominated by two full party workers. Then, if accepted, they are required to serve a probationary period, under the title of 'candidate member', and which includes dutiful study of the teachings of Marx, Lenin, Mao Zedong, and Deng Xiaoping.

Despite these hurdles to be surmounted, party membership, with its associated economic and social advantages, is highly sought after in communist states. For this reason, party membership as a proportion of the total population is invariably at a higher level in communist than liberal democratic states, as Table 39 shows.

Parties in communist states have clear ideological bases. Indeed, one of the main purposes, if not the main purpose, of the party is to preserve and project the ideology. This is done by the presence of party representatives throughout the political and social systems, including the media and workplaces.

This all-pervasiveness must be clearly recognized if the political systems of communist states are to be properly understood. Using China as the salient example, it can be seen that any position of reasonable seniority within the state must be 'confirmed' by the party; the more important the post the higher the echelon of approval. The most senior posts of all are closely controlled by the secretariat of the Central Committee of the party. From its earliest days the Chinese Communist Party (CCP) set out to be an elite 'vanguard' organization, comprising the country's 'best citizens', and, although the membership net has been cast more widely since the 1950s, almost tripling between 1961 and 1992, it has never deviated from that original aim. The stress on loyal adherence to the official line has meant that there have been periodic 'purges' of 'disloyal' elements.

Political party membership as a proportion of state populations in communist and liberal democratic states (*c.* 1990) — Table 39

Communist states

State	Ruling party membership (in millions)	Percentage of total population
N Korea	3.000	14.6
Cuba	0.524	5.1
China	44.000	4.2
Vietnam	1.75	2.8
Laos	0.042	1.0

Liberal democratic states*

State	Combined party membership (in millions)	Percentage of total population
Austria	1.300	17.2
Norway	0.500	12.0
Barbados	0.025	9.9
Italy	4.500	7.9
Belgium	0.700	7.1
Belize	0.010	6.0
Denmark	0.300	5.9
Switzerland	0.370	5.7
Ireland	0.150	4.2
Japan	4.350	3.6
Germany (FRG)	2.030	3.3
United Kingdom	1.800	3.2
France	1.700	3.1
Netherlands	0.400	2.8
Australia	0.420	2.7
Sri Lanka	0.200	1.3

* This is a selective sample as accurate data are lacking for other liberal democratic states.

Other communist states, and some nationalistic socialist states, have similarly developed and promoted the party as the custodian of the nation's political future and the 'vanguard of the proletariat'. As Table 39 above reveals, however, there are significant variations in membership 'densities' between the 'mass party' of North Korea and the elitist cadres of Vietnam and Laos.

7.7 The party in noncommunist, one-party states

Most contemporary noncommunist, one-party states are found in what has become fashionable to describe as the 'Third World', even though this description can be a little ambiguous.

In these states the party, in addition to acting as a

Voting and party systems in liberal democracies Table 40

States with majoritarian voting systems		States with some form of party system proportional representation	
Countries	Type of system	Countries	Type of system
Antigua and Barbuda (simple plurality)	two-party	Austria (party list)	multiparty
Argentina (simple plurality)	two-party	Belgium (party list)	multiparty
Australia (alternative vote)	two-party	Brazil (party list)	multiparty
Bahamas (simple plurality)	two-party	Costa Rica (party list)	two-party
Barbados (simple plurality)	two-party	Denmark (party list)	multiparty
Belize (simple plurality)	two-party	Dominican Republic (party list)	multiparty
Bolivia (simple plurality)	multiparty	Ecuador (party list)	multiparty
Botswana (simple plurality)	two-party	El Salvador (additional member system)	multiparty
Canada (simple plurality)	multiparty	Finland (party list)	multiparty
Colombia (simple plurality)	multiparty	Germany (additional member system)	multiparty
Cyprus (simple plurality)	multiparty	Greece (party list)	multiparty
Dominica (simple plurality)	multiparty	Guatemala (additional member system)	multiparty
Egypt (second ballot)	dominant party	Guyana (party list)	two-party
France (second ballot)	two-party*	Honduras (party list)	two-party
Grenada (simple plurality)	multiparty	Iceland (party list)	multiparty
India (simple plurality)	multiparty	Ireland (single transferable vote)	multiparty
Jamaica (simple plurality)	two-party	Israel (party list)	multiparty
Kiribati (second ballot)	two-party	Italy (additional member system)	multiparty
Malaysia (simple plurality)	dominant party	Japan (additional member system)	multiparty
Marshall Islands (simple plurality)	no parties	Liechtenstein (limited vote)	multiparty
Micronesia (simple plurality)	no parties	Luxembourg (party list)	multiparty
Monaco (second ballot)	no parties	Malta (single transferable vote)	two-party
Nauru (simple plurality)	no parties	Mauritius (limited vote)	multiparty
Palau (simple plurality)	no parties	Mexico (additional member system)	dominant party
Papua New Guinea (simple plurality)	multiparty	Netherlands (party list)	multiparty
Philippines (simple plurality)	multiparty	New Zealand (additional member system)	multiparty
St Kitts and Nevis (simple plurality)	multiparty	Norway (party list)	multiparty
St Lucia (simple plurality)	two-party	Peru (party list)	multiparty
St Vincent and the Grenadines (simple plurality)	two-party	Portugal (party list)	multiparty
Samoa (simple plurality)	two-party	San Marino (limited vote)	multiparty
Singapore (simple plurality)	dominant party	Spain (party list)	multiparty
Solomon Islands (simple plurality)	multiparty	Sri Lanka (party list)	two-party
Trinidad and Tobago (simple plurality)	multiparty	Sweden (party list)	multiparty
Tuvalu (simple plurality)	no parties	Switzerland (party list)	multiparty
United Kingdom (simple plurality)	two-party	Turkey (party list)	multiparty
United States of America (simple plurality)	two-party	Uruguay (party list)	multiparty
		Vanuatu (party list)	multiparty
		Venezuela (party list)	multiparty

* Two-party blocs.

political recruitment, socialization, and resource distribution agency, usually performs two main functions: the promotion of nationalism and patriotism, and the maintenance of a certain stable economic and social order. Support for nationalism invariably receives a high priority, the dominant parties usually being those which had spearheaded the independence movement, and the economic and social order is that which is determined by the ruling elite within the party.

Additionally, the noncommunist single party often tends to support and sustain the strong, charismatic leader. Most of the black African states display this characteristic, although it should be noted that the dominance of a strong leader is not always confined to one-party states. The constitution of the French Fifth Republic was originally designed with Charles de Gaulle in mind and the party which supported him not only made his continuance in office its main aim but assumed his name as the popular description of the political movement. Other states, particularly in South America, have spawned strong, autocratic leaders within a highly factionalized, multiparty system.

Compared with parties in liberal and emergent democracies and communist states, those in noncommunist one-party countries are, with notable exceptions in black Africa, such as in Zimbabwe, relatively weak organizations and very much the instruments of those nations' political leaders. Some countries, although in theory one-party states, might better be regarded as having no parties at all. The reason for the comparative docility of party politics in these states stems mainly from history and social organization. Modern political parties are not a 'natural' development in most so-called Third World states and many years may elapse before the economic and social environments can sustain a 'sophisticated' multiparty system. Social organization, sometimes based on tribal loyalties or strong regional differences, has also favored allegiance to the strong, personal leader rather than the 'anonymous' party.

7.8 Parties in militaristic and absolutist states

In states controlled by the military or absolute rulers political parties either do not exist or, if they do, are puppets of the ruling elite and façades for what is little more than autocratic, personal government.

Absolutist states such as those in the Arab world have never experienced what might be described as popular political activity, with representative institutions. Most of the countries which are contemporaneously under the sway of military rulers have, in contrast, previously enjoyed some form of democratic government so that their present condition may be a temporary aberration. There is evidence that military rulers find it difficult to sustain their leadership for protracted periods without creating a single party and building it into the framework of the state or reverting to a multiparty political system.

In Bangladesh, the Jana Dal (People's Party) was formed in 1983 by Lieutenant-General Hossain Mohammad Ershad to support his presidential candidature. Now known as the Jatiya (National) Front, the party has subsequently established itself as a civilian force. In Indonesia, the Joint Secretariat of Functional Groups (Golkar Party), which had been created in 1964 as a loose alliance of anticommunist sectional interest groups, was transformed into a civilian ruling front for the military when, in 1968, it was brought under government control by General Suharto. Similarly, in Ghana, Flight-Lieutenant Jerry Rawlings formed the National Democratic Congress (NDC) in 1992 to successfully support his campaign for the presidency and the NDC also won an overwhelming majority in legislative elections held in December 1992.

7.9 Political parties and electoral systems

Is there a direct connection between a country's electoral system and the structure, and numbers of its political parties? Writers tend to be ambivalent, suggesting a 'chicken and egg' situation. Some argue that the kinds of parties in a particular country simply reflect its social and economic structure while others attribute much greater influence to the methods of voting available to electors. What is the evidence?

Of the 74 countries identified in Table 11 as liberal democracies, 36 employ majority voting systems of an alternative vote, simple plurality, or second ballot type. The remaining 38 have some variety of proportional representation. An analysis of the respective party systems reveals the pattern set out in Table 40.

Of the 36 liberal democratic countries with majority voting methods, 15, 42%, have effectively a two-party system operating, three, 8%, have a 'dominant-party system', in which one party usually dominates electoral contests, and six, 17%, have a system in which parties as such do not operate, candidates fighting for assembly seats as independents. Only 12, 33%, majority voting countries have political systems of a multiparty nature, with three or more parties regularly exchanging or sharing power. Conversely, of the 38 liberal democratic states employing some kind of proportional representation 32, 84%, have multiparty systems and only six, 13%, have effectively two parties operating. In the remaining country a 'dominant-party system' is in force. Although the evidence is not conclusive, a link between electoral systems and party systems seems more than a possibility.

The classic examples of two-party competition, in which minor parties are virtually nonexistent, are to be found in the small island states of the Caribbean and Oceania. In these regions eight, 53%, of the 15 liberal democratic systems where political parties are found, operate in this way. The smallness of their populations, which in the majority of cases average between 100,000–300,000, and of their assemblies, varying typically between 12 and 50 elected members, are important explanatory factors. The personalized style of politics and party formation in these regions has had the effect of creating polarization, as have their simple plurality voting systems.

The textbook example of a two-party system is, however, the United Kingdom. Here the simple plurality voting system has played, arguably, a paramount role in fostering polarization. The two major parties, Conservative and Labor, have shared power exclusively for more than 60 years because the electoral system has made it extremely difficult for third or fourth parties to secure enough parliamentary seats to break the monopoly. The advent of a strong challenge from 1981 onwards, first in the form of the Liberal–SDP Alliance and then the Liberal Democrats, on the center left of the political spectrum, benefited the center-right Conservatives, giving them clear majorities in three successive general elections, until 1997. However, since coming to power in 1997 the 'New Labor' government has introduced proportional representation for elections of the new Scottish parliament and Welsh assembly, and for elections to the European Parliament. A reform of the voting system for Westminster is also contemplated which, if implemented, is likely to lead to coalition politics, with Labour and the Liberal Democrats forming a natural centre-left alliance. The United States has an even more pronounced two party system than the United Kingdom, although a third party, Ross Perot's, Reform Party, did win its first state governorship in the elections of November 1998. The two main parties, the Democrats and Republicans, are broad 'catch all' parties which lack strong national organization structures. However, the single plurality voting system has clearly worked to make it difficult for third and fourth parties to become established.

Canada is only a partial exception to the rule of simple plurality voting producing a two-party system because, although the seats in the House of Commons have been shared in recent years by three parties, for most of the present century the Liberals and Progressive Conservatives have dominated Canadian politics. Similarly, in France, a majority electoral state which currently has a multiparty system, the assembly is invariably dominated by two principal party groupings, with minor 'half parties' holding a much smaller number of seats, though sometimes the balance of power. Only in one majority state, Papua New Guinea, does a full-blown multiparty system operate.

The tendency for majority voting systems to foster restricted party systems thus appears to be strong. In the cases of Canada, the United States, and the United Kingdom the size, social complexity, and regional differentiation of the countries almost guarantee that if proportional voting systems were in place a multiplicity of party groupings would emerge, although a core of three or four major parties would still be likely to predominate. In the case of France, firm evidence exists from the Fourth Republic period and, briefly, from the National Assembly election of 1986, when party list systems were in operation, that the second ballot majority method has served to restrict party development. In New Zealand, the shift from first-past-the-post to a proportional additional member system in 1996 resulted in the election of an increased number of Maori and women MPs, but also to fragmentation of the party system, with the balance of power being held by the populist New Zealand First Party.

The evidence presented in Table 40 also shows, however, that proportional voting systems do not always result in a multiplicity of parties vying for, or sharing, power. The fact that small parties are not disadvantaged by the voting system will not necessarily guarantee them better access to government, as the experiences of Costa Rica, Guyana, Honduras, and Malta reveal. Historical and social factors can sometimes result in domination by two parties, however open the political system might be. In many other states with proportional representation systems, although a multiplicity of parties may have assembly representation, it is usual for three or four major parties to hold a majority of seats.

7.10 Parties and the legal environment

The majority of one-party states have the party's monopoly enshrined within the constitution. In some ostensibly multiparty states legal controls will sometimes favor the dominant government party, making life for opposition groups difficult. Singapore provides evidence of this. In genuine multiparty states the legal environment can range from positive encouragement at one extreme to minimum restraints on fraudulent practices at the other.

Austria provides probably the clearest example of positive support for political parties, the Party Law stating: '... the existence and diversity of political parties is an essential component of the democratic order of the Republic of Austria.' Here the state gives generous financial support. Each party with at least five members in the National Council receives a lump sum and then additional finance is provided on the basis of the number of votes won in the previous federal election. Parties which do not win seats but obtain at least 1% of the popular vote are not overlooked, receiving pro rata support according to votes obtained.

Similarly in Germany, under the law of July 1967, which operates at both the federal and state levels, parties are described as a 'constitutionally necessary element of a free democratic order', with state subsidies of DM5 (US$3) per eligible voter being provided to all political parties which secure 0.5% or more of the popular poll in federal elections, with additional subsidies being granted to parties with more than 2% of the vote. By the mid-1990s, Germany's larger parties secured more than a third of their total funding from the state and smaller parties more than half, while state, federal, and Euro-election campaign spending exceeded 1 billion Deutschmarks per election cycle.

Several other states give finance to help cover election and other party expenses in varying degrees. They include Brazil, Colombia, Costa Rica, Denmark, Ecuador, France (from 1988), Hungary, Israel, Italy (to 1994), Japan, the Netherlands, Norway, Portugal, Spain, Sweden, Turkey, Venezuela, and the United States (for presidential elections only). The amount of the grant usually depends on the size of the vote obtained at the last election, but in Denmark on the size of the party. As a quid pro quo, upper spending limit restrictions are often imposed on election contests. In many countries free time is made available to parties on the state radio and television networks. In the United Kingdom, although there are no state funds for elections, the official opposition party, once elected, is given finance, its leader and a limited number of its parliamentary managers receiving state salaries. In 1998 the Neill Committee on Standards in Public Life recommended a £20 million spending limit be placed on party spending in future UK general elections: in 1997 the Labor Party spent £26 million and the Conservative Party £28 million.

Many states require parties to register and sometimes the conditions of registration can be severe, making it difficult for small or new parties to obtain a foothold on the political ladder. Argentina, Brazil, India (where strict regulations were introduced in 1985 to discourage inter-election changes of deputy allegiance, known as 'floor-crossing'), Malaysia, Mexico, the Philippines, Thailand, and Venezuela are among the countries requiring evidence of popular support as a condition of registration. In Indonesia the number of parties permitted to operate was restricted to three from 1975 to 1998.

At the other extreme, there are states where control is at a very minimum. They include Belgium, where one party fought an election under the banner of 'Snow White and the Seven Dwarfs'; Poland, where the Polish Beer Lovers' Party secured parliamentary representation in October 1991, with 3.3% of the national vote, before becoming split between 'Small Beer' and 'Large Beer' factions; Bolivia, whose elections are generally subject to widespread fraud; Honduras; New Zealand; Sri Lanka; Switzerland; and the United Kingdom, where 'oddball parties', such as The Monster Raving Loony Party, are allowed to contest elections provided they are prepared to sacrifice a deposit of £500 if their vote count falls below 5%. In Japan, where more than 10,000 parties are registered, the July 1995 upper house elections were contested by a drivers' party, campaigning for the abolition of car taxes and regulations, a gay rights' party, and a UFO party, which believes that Japan should prepare to receive aliens coming to Earth.

Recommended reading

Bell, D S and Shaw, E (eds.) *Conflict and Cohesion in Western European Social Democratic Parties*, Pinter, 1994

Coggins, J and Lewis, D S (eds.) *Political Parties of the Americas and the Caribbean*, Longman, 1992

Daalder, H and Mair, P (eds.) *Western European Party Systems*, Sage Publications, 1983

Day, A J, German, R, and Campbell, J (eds.) *Political Parties of the World*, 4th edn., Cartermill, 1996

East, R (ed.) *Communist and Marxist Parties of the World*, 2nd edn., Longman, 1990

East, R and Joseph, T (eds.) *Political Parties of Africa and the Middle East*, Longman, 1993

Graham, B D *Representative and Party Politics: A Comparative Perspective*, Basil Blackwell, 1993

Ingle, S *British Party Politics*, Basil Blackwell, 1989

Laver, M and Schofield, N *Multiparty Government: The Politics of Coalition in Europe*, Oxford University Press, 1991

Mair, P and Smith, G (eds.) *Understanding Party System Change in Western Europe*, Cass, 1990

McDonald, R and Ruhl, J M *Party Politics and Elections in Latin America*, Westview Press, 1989

Sagar, D J and Lewis, D S (eds.) *Political Parties of Asia and the Pacific*, Longman, 1992

Sartori, G *Parties and Party Systems*, Cambridge University Press, 1976

Seldon, A (ed.) *The Conservative Party in the Twentieth Century*, Oxford University Press, 1993

Solomon, S G (ed.) *Pluralism in the Soviet Union*, Macmillan, 1983

Szajkowski, B (ed.) *Political Parties of Eastern Europe, Russia and the Successor States*, Longman, 1994

Thomas, A and Paterson, W (eds.) *The Future of Social Democracy*, Oxford University Press, 1986

Von Beyme, K *Political Parties in Western Democracies*, Gower, 1985

Ware, A *Political Parties and Party Systems*, Oxford University Press, 1996

Wattenberg, M P *The Decline of American Political Parties, 1952–1980*, Harvard University Press, 1984

Wilson, G K *Interest Groups*, Basil Blackwell, 1990

2

Political Systems of the World's Nation-States

INTRODUCTION

Having considered the various ingredients of a political system and suggested bases for comparing one with another, it is now time to look at the circumstances of individual states as they are found in the world today. In the ensuing pages 192 independent nations will be examined and, for comparative purposes, they will be grouped into nine regions: Asia; Central America and the Caribbean; Central, Eastern, and Southern Europe; Central and Southern Africa; Middle East and North Africa, North America; Northern and Western Europe; Oceania; and South America.

Much of the information in Tables 1 to 40 has been extracted from a world database. It has been summarized for each country within a region and additional data have been included to produce a social, economic, and political profile for each state. This profile is set out in Section II at the start of each country entry. Summaries of this information, showing how particular features of political systems are distributed globally, on a regional basis, are given in Tables 2, 9, and 21, and in Tables 41 to 49.

Even though a sovereign nation comes into existence at a particular point in time, it is not created in a vacuum, or some sterile laboratory. It is essentially the product of history and so the political development of each country is also outlined, with particular emphasis on the period since World War II, or since independence was achieved if this happened later.

General note

In the references to income type in Table 48 and elsewhere in this volume, the designation 'High Income' indicates a per-capita national income in c. 1995 in

Regional distribution of states by political structure and number of assembly chambers — **Table 41**

Region	Political structure		Number of assembly chambers			State total
	Unitary	Federal	None	One	Two	
Asia	25	3	2	18	8	28
Central America & Caribbean	19	2	–	10	11	21
Central, Eastern, & Southern Europe	22	3	–	16	9	25
Central & Southern Africa	43	5*	3	32	13	48
Middle East & North Africa	17	1	5	10	3	18
North America	–	2	–	–	2	2
Northern & Western Europe	19	4	1	11	11	23
Oceania	13	2	–	11	4	15
South America	9	3	–	4	8	12
Total	*167*	*25*	*11*	*112*	*69*	*192*

* Includes the federal system in Somalia, which is non-functioning due to civil war.

excess of US$7,000, 'Middle Income' between US$1,000 and 7,000, and 'Low Income' less than US$1,000. The quality of the per-capita income data is good for the more developed nations and those states characterized by political and economic stability. However, unfortunately for many Third World nations, for countries gripped by the scourges of civil war, currency depreciation, or hyperinflation, and for the recently democratized states of Central and Eastern Europe, which have undergone a transition from a command economy to a market economy, the per-capita income figures are less reliable. Widely differing estimates are provided for a number of states by such sources as the United Nations, the *Economist, Keesings, Europa,* and *Whitaker's Almanack*, influenced by the basis of their construction. The best available compromise figures have been used, but it should be noted that there is a general tendency for such monetary-based estimates to understate the

Regional distribution of states by voting systems used for lower house elections **Table 42**

Region	None	A & indirect	E/A mixed	SP	AV	SB	PR-PL	PR-AMS	STV	LV	State total
Asia	2	1	2	10	–	7	2	4	–	–	28
Central America & Caribbean	–	–	1	11	–	2	4	3	–	–	21
Central, Eastern, & Southern Europe	–	–	–	1	–	2	12	10	–	–	25
Central & Southern Africa	–	1	11	10	–	7	9	3	1	2	44*
Middle East & North Africa	5	1	1	4	–	1	5	1	–	–	18
North America	–	–	–	2	–	–	–	–	–	–	2
Northern & Western Europe	1	–	–	1	–	2	12	3	2	2	23
Oceania	–	–	1	10	1	1	1	1	–	–	15
South America	–	–	–	5	–	–	7	–	–	–	12
Total	*8*	*3*	*16*	*54*	*1*	*22*	*52*	*25*	*3*	*4*	*188*

* The voting system is in a transitional state in four countries.

(A = appointed, LV = limited vote, SP = simple plurality, AMS = additional member system, PL = party list, STV = single transferable vote, AV = alternative vote, PR = proportional representation, E = elected, SB = second ballot.)

Social and economic data for soverign states by regions of the world (*c.* 1995) **Table 43**

	Area		Population		Population density	
Region	In sq km /sq mi (in millions)	As % of world total	(In millions)	As % of world total	Per sq km	In relation to world mean*
Asia	25.067/9.673	18.8	3,119.8	55.3	124	295
Central America & Caribbean	2.699/1.042	2.0	155.6	2.8	56	133
Central, Eastern, & Southern Europe	20.367/7.864	15.3	433.2	7.7	21	50
Central & Southern Africa	24.296/9.381	18.3	582.7	10.4	24	57
Middle East & North Africa	11.193/4.322	8.4	273.4	4.8	24	57
North America	19.343/7.468	14.5	294.5	5.2	15	36
Northern & Western Europe	3.572/1.379	2.7	373.2	6.6	104	248
Oceania	8.781/3.390	6.6	95.0	1.7	11	26
South America	17.703/6.835	13.3	308.3	5.5	17	40
*World total***	*133.021/51.401*	*100.0*	*5,635.7*	*100.0*	*42*	*100*

* World mean = 100.

** Excluding colonies and dependencies.

'real' per-capita incomes in Third World states, which will appear higher if based on 'Purchasing-Power Parity'. A comparison with per-capita income figures displayed in the first edition of this volume shows that between c. 1985 and 1995 regional incomes advanced by 189% in Asia, 145% in South America and Northern and Western Europe, 37% in Central America and the Caribbean, 89% in Oceania, and 62% in North America. However, regional incomes increased by just 14% in Central and Southern Africa, and declined by 39% in Central and Eastern Europe and by 12% in the Middle East and North Africa.

Regional distribution of states by area (sq km) Table 44

Region	Size of state: sq km Less than 1,000	1,000–10,000	10,000–>100,000	>100,000–500,000	>500,000–1,000,000	Over 1,000,000	State total
Asia	2	1	4	12	4	5	28
Central America & Caribbean	7	1	8	4	–	1	21
Central, Eastern, & Southern Europe	–	1	15	6	2	1	25
Central & Southern Africa	2	3	10	14	10	9	48
Middle East & North Africa	1	–	6	5	2	4	18
North America	–	–	–	–	–	2	2
Northern & Western Europe	6	1	7	7	2	–	23
Oceania	7	1	3	3	–	1	15
South America	–	–	–	5	2	5	12
Total	*25*	*8*	*53*	*56*	*22*	*28*	*192*

Regional distribution of states by population size (*c.* 1996) Table 45

Region	State population size Less than 0.5 million	0.5–1 m	>1–10 m	>10–20 m	>20–50 m	>50–100 m	Over 100 m	State total
Asia	2	–	7	4	7	2	6	28
Central America & Caribbean	9	–	9	2	–	1	–	21
Central, Eastern, & Southern Europe	–	1	14	5	2	2	1	25
Central & Southern Africa	4	3	25	8	6	1	1	48
Middle East & North Africa	–	2	8	4	2	2	–	18
North America	–	–	–	–	1	–	1	2
Northern & Western Europe	8	–	8	2	1	4	–	23
Oceania	10	1	2	1	–	1	–	15
South America	1	1	3	2	4	–	1	12
Total	*34*	*8*	*76*	*28*	*23*	*13*	*10*	*192*

Regional distribution of states by population density (*c.* 1996) — Table 46

Region	State population density: per sq km						
	10 and below	11–50	51–100	101–250	251–500	Over 500	State total
Asia	3	6	4	7	4	4	28
Central America & Caribbean	1	4	5	6	4	1	21
Central, Eastern, & Southern Europe	1	3	13	8	–	–	25
Central & Southern Africa	10	21	9	5	2	1	48
Middle East & North Africa	3	6	6	–	2	1	18
North America	1	1	–	–	–	–	2
Northern & Western Europe	1	3	3	10	3	3	23
Oceania	2	5	2	3	3	–	15
South America	3	9	–	–	–	–	12
Total	*25*	*58*	*42*	*39*	*18*	*10*	*192*

Regional distribution of states by urbanization and adult literacy levels (*c.* 1996) — Table 47

Region	Urbanization levels* (as % of total population)			Adult literacy levels** (as % of adult population)			
	40% and under	41–70%	Over 70%	40% and under	41–70%	71–90%	Over 90%
Asia	18	6	3	5	1	11	11
Central America & Caribbean	3	15	3	1	5	6	9
Central, Eastern, & Southern Europe	2	19	4	–	–	3	22
Central & Southern Africa	35	12	1	22	20	5	–
Middle East & North Africa	2	7	9	2	12	3	1
North America	–	–	2	–	–	–	2
Northern & Western Europe	1	5	17	–	–	2	21
Oceania	8	1	2	–	3	2	9
South America	1	4	7	–	2	6	4
Total	*70*	*69*	*48*	*30*	*43*	*38*	*79*

* Data are unavailable for four states in Oceania and one in Asia.

** Data are unavailable for one state in Oceania and one in Central and Southern Africa.

Regional distribution of states by shares of world GDP and income type (*c.* 1996) Table 48

Region	GDP ($1,000 m)	Share of world total (%)	Average per capita GDP ($)	State distribution by income type			
				High	Middle	Low	State total
Asia	7,618	27.5	2,440	5	5	18	28
Central America & Caribbean	392	1.4	2,520	1	17	3	21
Central, Eastern, & Southern Europe	1,040	3.8	2,400	3	16	6	25
Central & Southern Africa	297	1.1	510	–	7	41	48
Middle East & North Africa	629	2.3	2,290	6	10	2	18
North America	7,674	27.7	26,050	2	–	–	2
Northern & Western Europe	8,384	30.3	22,465	23	–	–	23
Oceania	470	1.7	4,950	3	9	3	15
South America	1,156	4.2	3,750	1	9	2	12
Total	*27,660*	*100.0*	*4,910*	*44*	*73*	*75*	*192*

Regional distribution of states by human rights rating (*c.* 1996) Table 49

Region	N/A	30% and below	31–50%	51–70%	71–90%	Over 90%	State total
Asia	11	5	4	7	1	–	28
Central America & Caribbean	10	1	–	4	6	–	21
Central, Eastern, & Southern Europe	16	–	1	2	4	2	25
Central & Southern Africa	26	3	9	6	4	–	48
Middle East & North Africa	4	5	4	4	1	–	18
North America	–	–	–	–	–	2	2
Northern & Western Europe	6	–	–	–	2	15	23
Oceania	11	–	–	1	1	2	15
South America	2	–	–	4	6	–	12
Total	*86*	*14*	*18*	*28*	*25*	*21*	*192*

Asia

The region of Asia, covering almost a fifth of the world's surface, is the largest global block in both real and demographic terms, incorporating more than half the world's population and six of its ten most populous nations. Within the region there are 28 states. Twenty-one are found on the main continent, occupying the southeastern, sub-Turkestan and sub-Siberian portion of the vast Euro-Asian land mass. The remaining seven are either offshore archipelagos or islands.

The region constitutes the world's most thickly peopled area, boasting an average population density three times the world norm. It is also the world's fourth poorest in terms of per-capita GDP, with a regional income, at $2,240 in *c.* 1995, half the global average. Indeed, 11 of the region's 28 countries occupy the bottom quarter of world states in terms of national incomes per capita. A further nine are located in the third quarter, while only five, mineral-rich Brunei, the city-state entrepôt of Singapore, industrialized Japan, and the fast industrializing 'little dragons', South Korea and Taiwan, are to be found in the first quarter of high-income nations.

The explanation for this poverty is the continued dominance of rural activities, the agricultural sector still providing employment for more than half the national labor force in 11 of the region's states, including six of its ten most populous. Prior to World War II, only one state, Japan, was substantially industrialized. Since the war it has grown to become the world's economic power house, contributing more than a sixth of global GDP. Within the Asian region, its dominance is even more marked and, enjoying the fourth highest per-capita GDP in the world, accounts for two-thirds of the region's GDP, but only 4% of its population. Japan is also the leading source of foreign direct investment capital. China and India, in contrast, while accounting for 68% of Asia's population can claim barely a sixth of its GDP.

During recent decades, three other Asian countries, South Korea, Singapore, and Taiwan, have industrialized rapidly, in an export-led manner, gaining the acronym NICs, or 'newly industrializing countries'. South Korea, the most successful of these 'little dragons', is now one of the world's ten largest trading nations and joined the OECD in 1997. Three other states, Indonesia, Malaysia, and Thailand, have followed at a quickening pace. The demographic giant, China, has also enjoyed an economic awakening since the early 1980s, as, more recently, have Vietnam, Laos, Cambodia, and Myanmar, following their embrace of the market. This made the Pacific part of the Asian region the world's most dynamic area during much of the 1990s.

The successful growth of these NICs has resulted from a unique blend of free-market economics and selective state support. The industriousness, and high educational levels of the work forces in these countries, combined with the inbred sense of frugality of the general population, have also provided ideal conditions. These traits are underpinned by ancient Confucianist value systems, which have helped to sustain paternalistic, authoritarian political systems, characterized by strict state censorship, enforced conformity, and, in several states, the military retaining a background political role. However, as affluence has spread, there have been growing signs of internal pressure for greater political pluralism.

Since July 1997, and the forced devaluation of the Thailand baht, these NIC 'Tigers' have each, with the exception of Singapore and Taiwan, experienced currency crises and have been forced to devalue and seek assistance from the IMF. This followed over-investment in prestige projects and the property market, and problems of corruption, caused by the close association of business and political interests. The 'bubble' of miracle growth burst five years earlier in Japan, where growth was sluggish throughout much of the 1990s. During 1998, as Thailand, South Korea, and Indonesia followed IMF instructions to retrench, the 'Tiger' economies contracted by more than 3%, spreading recession across the region, as migrant laborers were repatriated and investment dried up. This 'Asian contagion' spread to the rest of the world economy, precipitating financial crises in Russia and South America during 1998. Within Asia, it led to the overthrow of the autocratic Suharto regime in Indonesia and to increased repression in Malaysia.

Further to the west, in the Indian Ocean region, industrial growth has been less impressive. Here, popular literacy and educational levels have traditionally been lower; literacy rates of 35% or lower being recorded for contemporary Afghanistan, Bangladesh, Bhutan, Nepal, and Pakistan. Islamic and Hindu cultural traditions have also proved to be less conducive than Confucianism to the growth process. Since the 1970s, however, with the spread of new 'green revolution' seeds and production technology, notable, peasant-based, agricultural advances have been seen in a number of the states, most notably in the Punjab regions of India and Pakistan. These have enabled the rapidly expanding populations of these countries, currently increasing at an annual rate of between 2% and 3%, to be fed without a fall in general living standards.

The Asian region is, historically and culturally, one of the richest in the world. It has served as the cradle for such ancient and impressive civilizations as the Harappan or Indus Valley, from *c.* 2500 to *c.* 1600 BC, the Xia, from *c.* 2220 to *c.* 1700 BC, the Shang, from *c.* 1500 to *c.* 1066 BC, the Zhou, from 1122 to 249 BC, the Mauryan, from 321 to 184 BC, the Han, from 206 BC to AD 220, the Gupta, from *c.* 300 to 500 AD, the Tang, from 618 to 907 AD, the Khmer, from the 6th to the 15th centuries, and the Ming, from 1368 to 1644. For this reason, an unusually high number, amounting to five, or 18%, of the region's contemporary states date their founding to periods prior to the 19th century. This figure is based on territorial affinity. At least five other countries, Cambodia, India, the Koreas, and Vietnam, which were the sites of ancient or medieval kingdoms of national proportions, might also be included in this category if a looser definition were to be used.

The two dominant civilizations in the region have been the Indian and Chinese, each having originated distinctive religious and moral-philosophical systems which were later diffused throughout Asia by their followers.

The five most important religions or moral systems which are indigenous to the Asian region and have retained their importance are Hinduism, Buddhism, Confucianism, Daoism, and Shintoism. The first two originated in India, the second two in China, and the fifth in Japan. Their distribution across the region is clearly defined today. Hinduism, which is a nonproselytizing faith, is predominant only in India and Nepal, although it is a minority religion in neighboring Bangladesh, Bhutan, and Sri Lanka. Shintoism, which is a unique, national religion, is, similarly, restricted to Japan. In contrast, Buddhism, although it originated in India around 500 BC, and gained popularity during the Mauryan era, has been widely diffused across Asia. Today, it constitutes the dominant faith in Bhutan, Cambodia, Laos, Mongolia, Myanmar, and Sri Lanka. Mixed with Confucianism and Daoism, it also predominates in China, North Korea, South Korea, Singapore, Thailand, and Vietnam, and is an important minority faith in Brunei and Malaysia. It is the state religion in four countries in the region.

To these indigenous religions there were added, from early medieval times, the outside faiths of Islam and Christianity. Islam was spread by land to Afghanistan and Pakistan in West Asia and to Kazakhstan, Kyrgyzstan, Tajikistan, Turkmenistan, and Uzbekistan in Central Asia, although it was suppressed during the Soviet period, and by sea, further east to Bangladesh, Brunei, Indonesia, Malaysia, and the Maldives. Christianity, however, made only a tangential impact on the region. Today, therefore, even in its areas of highest support, such as South Korea, where a quarter of the population are Christians, Indonesia, 10%, and Malaysia, 7%, it remains a minority religion. In contrast, Islam, which was a proselytizing faith in a number of important medieval and early modern kingdoms and is a state religion in six contemporary nations, has had a marked regional impact. Not only is it today the predominant religion in the 12 countries noted above, but more than two-thirds of the world's Muslim population now reside within the Asian region. Indonesia, with 160 million, Bangladesh, 125 million, Pakistan, 116 million, and India, 100 million, possess the four largest national Islamic communities in the world. In Afghanistan, a radical Islamic theocentric state has held sway since 1996, while in Pakistan and Indonesia, Islamic fundamentalists have increasing support.

With the exception of the Muslim incursions during the medieval period noted above, Asia, although open to trading contacts, remained substantially free from external territorial conquest and colonization until the later 16th century, when the Dutch established settlements in some coastal areas of Indonesia. This served to reinforce the cultural distinctiveness of the region. Thereafter, however, particularly following the British conquest of the Indian subcontinent, European influence spread rapidly.

The height of the colonization process in Asia was attained in the late 19th and early 20th centuries, when four zones of imperial control were established: a 'Russian zone' in Central Asia, in the northwest; a 'British zone' in the southwest; a more tightly controlled 'French zone' in the central region; and a smaller, though intensively colonized, 'Japanese zone' to the east.

The Russian zone was carved out between the 1840s and 1870s and was directly connected, by land, to the empire's Muscovy core. It began as a military occupation designed to stabilize a disturbed frontier region, but developed into a full colonization, involving the immigration of ethnic Russian settlers. It was to continue under Soviet rule, the expansion culminating in the invasion of Afghanistan in 1979, before the Soviet empire collapsed in 1991. The British zone extended from Pakistan to Malaysia and was characterized by a substantial measure of 'indirect rule'. The French zone was mainly in Indo-China, and that of the Japanese in Formosa, now Taiwan, and Korea, although it was later extended, briefly, between 1942 and 1945, to incorporate much of East Asia.

Compared with the equivalent process in Africa, the European colonization of Asia began at an early date but also, with the exception of Russian/Soviet-controlled Central Asia, ended sooner. The Japanese colonial empire was dismembered in 1945, much of the British between 1947 and 1957, and the French in 1954. The strength of indigenous nationalist resistance was an important factor behind this early decolonization. It was also important in explaining the failure of the European powers to impose direct control over China and Japan. Five other, more peripheral countries, Afghanistan, Bhutan, Mongolia, Nepal, and Thailand, also escaped direct colonization.

Despite its relative brevity, the experience of colonial rule has left a perceptible, though varied, political imprint on the states of the Asian region. Additional, and in many respects more important, political conditioning factors have been economic structures and conditions and ethnic patterns and rivalries.

The influence of economic factors is most clearly seen in the four states of Cambodia, China, Laos, and Vietnam. In these countries rural overpopulation and distress provided the material conditions which made possible, and successful, the peasant revolutions of the later 1940s, the 1950s, and the 1960s, particularly as they were linked to anticolonial nationalism and communist ideology.

Ethnic rivalries have also been potent political forces, with many of the states experiencing conflict on their frontiers, where ethnic, often tribal, minority communities predominate, all deeply opposed to the imposition of cultural and political hegemony by the majority community. In Indonesia, Myanmar, and Thailand, such minority-versus-majority hostility has sustained persistent peasant guerrilla insurgencies in border zones and has been used to justify a key, unifying political role for the military. In India, similar secessionist movements abound in the northeastern hill zone and in Kashmir, while in the economically successful, Sikh-dominated, Punjab and in culturally resilient Tibet different autonomy movements are found. More generalized, regionally based, ethnic rivalries are also prevalent in contemporary Afghanistan, Pakistan, Tajikistan, and other parts of ex-Soviet Central Asia, impacting adversely on party politics, while in Malaysia, Nepal, and Sri Lanka tensions between the indigenous majority and immigrant minority communities have heightened during recent years.

As a result of these ethnic rivalries, as well as the con-

Asia: social, economic, and political data

Country	Area (sq km/ sq miles)	*c.* 1995 Population (million)	*c.* 1995 Pop. density per sq km/sq mile	*c.* 1992 Adult literacy rate (%)	World ranking	Income type	*c.* 1991 Human rights rating (%)
Afghanistan	652,225/251,825	18.879	29/75	29	175	low	28
Bangladesh	143,998/55,598	120.400	836/2166	35	168	low	59
Bhutan	46,500/17,954	1.614	35/90	18	186	low	N/A
Brunei	5,765/2,226	0.305	53/137	87	89	high	N/A
Cambodia	181,035/69,898	10.600	59/152	86	92	low	33
China	9,571,300/3,695,498	1,215.153	127/329	76	111	low	21
India	3,287,263/1,269,219	918.570	279/724	50	149	low	54
Indonesia	1,904,569/735,358	192.217	101/261	82	99	low	34
Japan	371,815/143,559	124.961	336/870	100	1	high	82
Kazakhstan	2,717,300/1,049,155	17.027	6/16	97	44	middle	N/A
Korea, North	120,538/46,540	23.483	195/505	90	80	low	20
Korea, South	98,222/37,924	44.606	454/1176	96	52	high	59
Kyrgyzstan	198,500/76,641	4.600	23/60	97	44	low	N/A
Laos	236,800/91,429	4.605	19/50	84	97	low	N/A
Malaysia	329,758/127,320	20.103	61/158	78	110	middle	61
Maldives	298/115	0.256	859/2226	98	34	low	N/A
Mongolia	1,565,000/604,250	2.363	2/4	93	70	low	N/A
Myanmar	676,552/261,218	45.555	67/174	81	102	low	17
Nepal	141,181/54,510	21.360	151/392	26	181	low	69
Pakistan	796,095/307,374	126.610	159/412	35	169	low	42
Singapore	623/241	3.400	5,457/14108	91	77	high	60
Sri Lanka	64,453/24,885	17.900	278/719	88	84	low	47
Taiwan	36,000/13,890	21.450	596/1544	93	70	high	N/A
Tajikistan	143,100/55,251	5.513	39/100	97	44	low	N/A
Thailand	513,115/198,115	60.700	118/306	93	70	middle	62
Turkmenistan	488,100/188,456	3.809	8/20	98	34	middle	N/A
Uzbekistan	447,400/172,742	21.207	47/123	85	94	middle	N/A
Vietnam	329,566/127,246	72.511	220/570	88	84	low	27
Total/average/ range	*25,067,071/9,678,446*	*3,119.756*	*124/322*	*18–00*	–	–	*17–82*

* Though dominated by one party.

(A = appointed, AMS = additional member system, E = elected, F = federal, I = indirect, PL = party list, PR = proportional representation, SB = second ballot, SP = simple plurality, U = unitary, Lib-dem = liberal democratic, Em-dem = emergent democratic, Auth-nat = authoritarian nationalist, Islam-nat = Islamic nationalist, Unlim-pres = unlimited presidential, Lim-pres = limited presidential.)

tinuing or simmering state conflicts in Afghanistan, Cambodia, the Koreas, Laos, Myanmar, Sri Lanka, Tajikistan, and Vietnam, contemporary levels of military mobilization and defense expenditure are relatively high in Asia. More than half of the countries in the region appear among the upper half of world states in ratios of soldiers per 1,000 inhabitants, with four, North Korea, Singapore, Taiwan, and Mongolia, in the top ten. Consequently, defense spending as a proportion of GDP is high in all four countries, accounting for a quarter of GDP in North Korea, as well as in Myanmar, Afghanistan, Laos, Brunei, Pakistan, China, Sri Lanka, Malaysia, Taiwan, Cambodia, Tajikistan, and Vietnam, ranging between 4% and 9% of GDP. Indeed, it was estimated that in 1991 the countries of Asia annually spent $85 billion on defense, equivalent to a quarter of such global spending, excluding the United States and USSR. In 1982 the equivalent share was just 15%. Three of the region's states, China, India, and Pakistan are declared nuclear powers, while North Korea has sought to develop a nuclear capability.

The range of political and executive types of the states in the region is unusually broad, all categories, with the exception of nationalistic socialist, being rep-

Table 50

World ranking	Date of state formation	State structure	State type	Executive type	Number of assembly chambers	Party structure	Lower house electoral system
96	1747	U	Islam-Nat	Unlim-pres	none	multi	N/A
63	1971	U	Em-dem	Parliamentary	1	multi	SP
–	1907	U	Absolutist	Absolutist	1	none	mixed-E/A
–	1984	U	Absolutist	Absolutist	none	none	N/A
90	1953	U	Em-dem	Dual	2	multi	SP
101	2nd C/1949	U	Communist	Communist	1	one	I
69	1947	F	Lib-dem	Parliamentary	2	multi	SP
89	1949	U	Em-dem	Lim-pres	1	multi*	PR-PL
33	5th C	U	Lib-dem	Parliamentary	2	multi	PR-AMS
–	1991	U	Auth-nat	Lim-pres	2	multi	SB
102	1948	U	Communist	Communist	1	one	SP
63	1948	U	Em-dem	Lim-pres	1	multi	PR-AMS
–	1991	U	Em-dem	Lim-pres	2	multi	SB
–	1954	U	Communist	Communist	1	one	SP
59	1957	F	Lib-dem	Parliamentary	2	multi*	SP
–	1965	U	Auth-nat	Unlim-pres	1	none	mixed-E/A
–	1921	U	Em-dem	Lim-pres	1	multi	SB
104	1948	U	Military	Military	1	multi	SP
49	1768	U	Em-dem	Parliamentary	2	multi	SP
86	1947	F	Em-dem	Parliamentary	2	multi	SP
60	1965	U	Lib-dem	Parliamentary	1	multi*	SP
82	1948	U	Lib-dem	Dual	1	multi	PR-PL
–	1949	U	Em-dem	Lim-pres	1	multi*	PR-AMS
–	1991	U	Auth-nat	Unlim-pres	1	multi	SB
57	1350	U	Em-dem	Parliamentary	2	multi	PR-AMS
–	1991	U	Auth-nat	Unlim-pres	1	one	SB
–	1991	U	Auth-nat	Unlim-pres	1	one	SB
97	1954	U	Communist	Communist	1	one	SB
–	–	–	–	–	–	–	–

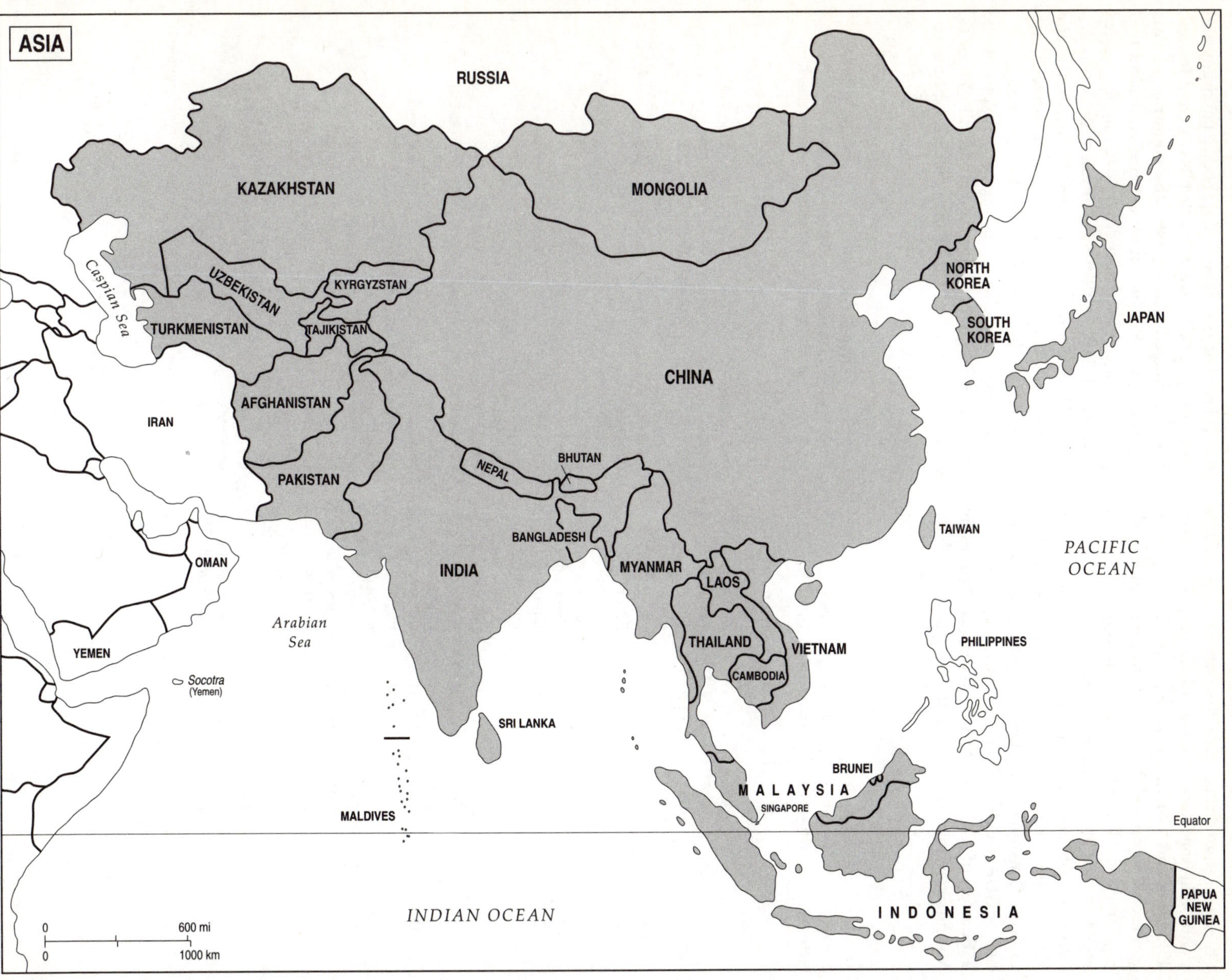
ASIA
RUSSIA
KAZAKHSTAN
MONGOLIA
Caspian Sea
UZBEKISTAN
KYRGYZSTAN
TURKMENISTAN
TAJIKISTAN
NORTH KOREA
SOUTH KOREA
JAPAN
CHINA
AFGHANISTAN
IRAN
NEPAL
BHUTAN
PAKISTAN
TAIWAN
BANGLADESH
PACIFIC OCEAN
OMAN
INDIA
MYANMAR
LAOS
Arabian Sea
THAILAND
VIETNAM
PHILIPPINES
YEMEN
CAMBODIA
Socotra (Yemen)
SRI LANKA
BRUNEI
MALAYSIA
SINGAPORE
MALDIVES
Equator
INDIAN OCEAN
INDONESIA
PAPUA NEW GUINEA
0
600 mi
0
1000 km

resented, as shown in Table 50. This reflects, at least in part, Asia's diversity in historical experiences and varieties of economies and religions. Fourteen, or half, of the countries fall into the categories of either liberal or emergent democracies, while a further four have communist systems. The liberal democracies are predominantly parliamentary in character and are to be found among either the high- or middle-income states, or among parts of what was once British India, where they had been accustomed to democratic structures for at least a century. It is perhaps significant that the emergent democracies are to be found, predominantly, among either NICs or the other remaining parts of British India. By contrast, all the four communist states are low-income countries, being among the 16 poorest states in the region.

Since 1990 the number of states in Asia with multi – party systems has grown significantly and this trend seems likely to continue. However, in several states which are apparently pluralist, notably, Malaysia, Singapore, Taiwan, and several of the ex-Soviet Central Asian states, *de facto* one-party dominance exists. In terms of voting systems, the simple plurality type predominates, although the majoritarian second ballot system is also quite common. Finally, only three of the region's states, India, Pakistan, and Malaysia, have federal structures. This number is surprisingly small, the absence of federalism being especially notable in the cases of Afghanistan, China, Indonesia, Myanmar, and Sri Lanka.

Recommended reading

Andrews, J *Pocket Asia*, 4th edn., Economist Books, 1998

Baxter, C, Malik, Y K, Kennedy, C H, and Oberst, R C (eds.) *Government and Politics in South Asia*, 2nd edn., Boulder, 1993

Curtis, G L *The Japanese Way of Politics*, Columbia University Press, 1988

Derbyshire, I *Politics in China: From Mao towards the Post-Deng Era*, W & R Chambers, 1990

Diamond, L, Linz, J, and Lipset, S M (eds.) *Democracy in Developing Countries*, Vol. 3: *Asia*, Boulder, 1988

Hardgrave, R L and Kochanek, S A *India: Government and Politics in a Developing Nation*, 5th edn., Harcourt Brace Jovanovich, 1993

Hiro, D *Between Marx and Muhammad: The Changing Face of Central Asia*, Harper Collins, 1994

Wang, J C *Comparative Asian Politics*, Prentice Hall, 1994

Watts, D *The Times Guide to Japan*, Time Books, 1993

Wilson, D *China the Big Tiger: A Nation Awakes*, Little Brown, 1996

AFGHANISTAN

Islamic Emirate of Afghanistan
Di Afghanistan Islami Dawlat

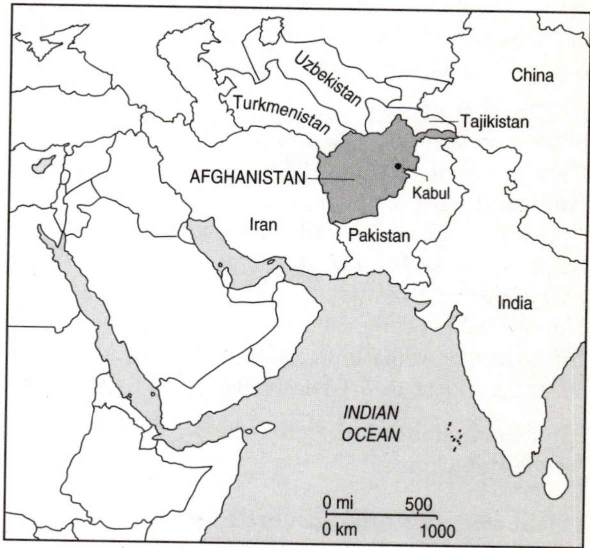

Capital: Kabul

Social and economic data

Area: 652,225 sq km/251,825 sq miles
Population: 18,879,000*
Pop. density per sq km/sq mi: 29*/75
Urban population: 19%**
Literacy rate: 29%**
GDP: $2,800 million*; per-capita GDP: $150*
Government defense spending (% of GDP): 8.7%***
Currency: afghani
Economy type: low income
Labor force in agriculture: 63%**

* 1995
** 1992
*** 1985

Head of state and government

Chair of Interim Council, Mullah Mohammad Rabbani, since 1996
Paramount leader: 'Leader of the faithful', Mohammad Omar, since 1996

Ethnic composition

Pathans, or Pushtuns, comprise the largest ethnic group, 54% of the total population, followed by the northern concentrated Tajiks, 27%, and the Uzbeks, 8%, and Hazaras, 7%. Pushtu and Dari, or Persian, constitute the official languages, spoken by 52% and 30% of the population respectively.

Religions

Eighty-five per cent of the population adheres to Islam of the Sunni sect and 14% to the Shia. Effectively, Islam is the state religion.

Political features

State type: Islamic nationalist
Date of state formation: 1747
Political structure: unitary
Executive: military/unlimited presidential
Assembly: two-chamber*
Party structure: multiparty
Human rights rating: 28%
International affiliations: AsDB, CP, ECO, ESCAP, G-77, IAEA, IBRD, IMF, IsDB, LORCS, NAM, OIC, UN

* In theory, though currently there is a single-chamber 'Leadership Council'.

Local and regional government

The country is divided into 31 provinces (*wilayat*), each of which is, in theory, administered by an appointed governor.

Political system

Since September 1996, when the Talibaan ('seekers of religious knowledge') extremist Islamic militia seized control in Kabul, an appointed interim Council of Ministers has ruled much of Afghanistan. It comprised around 30 members in 1998. The Sharia (Islamic law) is fully in force. However, the internationally recognized government of Afghanistan, including by the UN and United States, is that of the Mujaheddin ('Islamic holy warriors'), who seized power in April 1992 on the downfall of the Najibullah regime and still control parts of the north. The Mujaheddin administration was through a 51-member Leadership Council (Shura), headed from December 1992 by state president Burhanuddin Rabbani. The president was elected by a Constituent Assembly for a two-year term, but this was subsequently extended. He was assisted by a prime minister and a 16-member Mujaheddin coalition cabinet. There was also a broader 1,336-member Shura-e Ahl-e Hal-a-Aqad (Liberation Council), part elected and part appointed.

Previously, under its November 1987 constitution, Afghanistan had a presidential political system. At its apex stood the Loya Jirga (Grand National Assembly), an ad hoc body which comprised members of an elected Meli Shura (National Assembly), the Council of Ministers, the Supreme Court, and the Council of the Constitution. Its task was to elect an executive state president, who, serving a seven-year term, appointed a prime minister and was empowered to approve the laws and resolutions of the Meli Shura. The latter was a two-chamber body, consisting of a 234-member lower house, the Council of Representatives (Wolosi Jirga), and a 192-member upper house, the Senate (Sena), two-thirds of whose members were elected and one-third appointed by the president, for three-year terms. This 'limited presidential' system was suspended following the Soviet troop withdrawal in February 1989 when a new emergency regime was established.

Political parties

In the wake of the April 1978 communist coup, Afghanistan became a one-party state, dominated and controlled by the People's Democratic Party of Afghanistan (Jamiyat-e Demokrati Khalq-e Afghanistan: PDPA). Organized on Leninist 'democratic centralist' lines, the PDPA was governed from above by a 15–20-member Politburo and operated more broadly under the guise of the National Fatherland Front. Single party rule was ended in July and November 1987 by the passage of new constitutional laws which permitted the formation of additional political parties.

Currently, the key political forces are the various Mujaheddin groupings, which developed in opposition to the former communist regime, and the Talibaan. The most important mujaheddin groups are the Sunni fundamentalist, Pashtun-orientated, anti-Western Hesb-i Islami (Islamic Party), whose two factions are led by the 'hardline' former prime minister, Gulbuddin Hekmatyar (b. 1949), and Maulavi Younis Khalis; the more restrained, Sunni fundamentalist, Tajik-controlled Jamiat-i Islami (Islamic Society: estd. 1970), led by Professor Burhanuddin Rabbani; the Movement for Islamic Revolution (Harakat-i-Inqilab-i-Islami), led by Muhammad Nabi Muhammadi; the traditionalist National Islamic Front (Mahaz-i-Melli-i-Islami), led by Pir Sayyed Ahmed Gailani; the Saudi Arabian-backed

Islamic Unity (Ittehad-i-Islami), led by Professor Abd Ar-Rasul Sayef and Ahmad Shah; and the moderate Afghan National Liberation Front (Jebha-i-Najat-i-Melli), led by Professor Imam Sibghatullah Mojaddedi. Unity between the groupings is notoriously strained, although a loose, seven-party alliance has been in force since 1985 and an anti-Talibaan United Islamic Front for the Salvation of Afghanistan (UIFSA) since 1996 and chaired by Rabbani. The Talibaan, now the leading force in Afghanistan, originated in 1994 as a 25,000 strong militia of young Pathan graduates from fundamentalist Islamic schools established by Afghan refugees in Pakistan. They sought to bring an end to the internecine quarrels of the Mujaheddin and create a united Islamic state. The Talibaan are predominantly Sunni Muslim Pushtuns from southern Afghanistan and have their headquarters at Kandahar. It has been alleged that they received military aid from the Pakistan Inter-Services Intelligence (PSA).

The most important Shia Mujaheddin factions are the pro-Rabbani Islamic Movement of Afghanistan (Harakat-i-Islami Afghanistan) and the pro-Iranian and Hekmatyar-allied Islamic Unity Party of Afghanistan (Hesb-i-Wahdat-i-Afghan-istan), led until his murder in 1995 by Abdul Ali Mazari. The Uzbek warlord, General Abdul Rashid Dostam, leads the National Islamic Movement.

The formerly dominant, communist PDPA has been known since June 1990 as the Homeland Party (Hesb-i-Watan). It was founded, illegally, in 1965 by Nur Mohammad Taraki. Two years later, because of disputes over strategy, it split into two wings, the rural-based, Pushtu-speaking Khalq (Masses or People's) group, led by Taraki, and the urban-based, Dari-speaking Parcham (Banner or Flag) group, led by Babrak Karmal. After the overthrow of the monarchy, in 1973, factional differences widened when the Parcham group accepted Soviet Union orders to cooperate with the new Daud Khan regime, as part of a more moderate coalition strategy, while the Khalq wing rejected them, preferring a policy of radical class struggle. Unity, under Khalq leadership, was restored in July 1977, but rivalries swiftly re-emerged and intensified in 1979 following the ousting of Taraki as party leader and president of the republic. From December 1979 and the Soviet Union's installation of Babrak Karmal as PDPA leader, the Parcham group came to dominate the party.

Political leaders since 1970

1933–73 King Zahir Shah, 1973–78 General Daud Khan, 1978–79 Nur Mohammad Taraki (PDPA: Khalq)*, 1979 Hafizullah Amin (PDPA: Khalq)*, 1979–86 Babrak Karmal (PDPA: Parcham)*, 1986–92 Dr Najibullah Ahmadzai (PDPA: Parcham)*, 1992 Sibghatullah Mojaddedi (National Liberation Front), 1992–96 Burhanuddin Rabbani (Jamiat-i Islami), 1996– Mullah Mohammad Rabbani (Talibaan)

* Communist Party leaders.

Latest elections

Elections to the National Assembly were last held in April 1988 and were contested by candidates put forward under the umbrella of the PDPA-run National Front of Afghanistan, which included within its ranks representatives from the communist-leaning political parties noted above, as well as from the armed forces, peasants' cooperatives, the Council of Afghan Women, and the Central Council of Nomads. Only 184 Council of Representatives seats were actually contested, the remainder being reserved so as to tempt moderate Mujaheddin elements to join the political process at a later date. Fifty-one Senate seats were subject to election, with a further 45 senators being appointed by the president. Some 1.55 million voters were said to have participated, the majority of members returned being non-PDPA members.

The last presidential election was on 30 December 1992, when the Constituent Assembly (formerly the National Assembly) elected Burhanuddin Rabbani as state president. This decision was re-ratified by an accord signed by nine Mujaheddin factions on 7 March 1993.

Political history

Under the leadership of Ahmed Shah Durrani (1724–73), Afghanistan became an independent emirate in 1747 and, although defeated by Britain in the 'Afghan wars' of 1838–42 and 1878–80 and subjected to a partial loss of autonomy, after the third Anglo-Afghan war of 1919 Afghanistan was re-established, in 1922, as a fully independent, neutral monarchy. Mohammad Nadir Shah (1880–1933), who played a prominent role in the 1919 Afghan war, became king in 1929, with British diplomatic support, but was assassinated in 1933 after his modernizing reforms had alienated the influential Muslim clergy.

During the 1950s, Lieutenant General Sardar Mohammad Daud Khan, the cousin of King Mohammed Zahir Shah (b. 1914), who had ruled between 1933 and 1973, became prime minister and introduced a major program of social and economic modernization, drawing economic aid from the Soviet Union. Opposition to the authoritarian nature of

Daud's rule, however, forced his resignation, in 1963, and a new constitution was adopted. Under it the king became a constitutional monarch and political parties were outlawed.

Following a serious famine in 1972, the monarchy was overthrown in a military coup, on 17 July 1973, and King Zahir Shah fled to exile in Rome. A republic was declared, with Lieutenant General Daud Khan back at the head of the government. He received Soviet backing for this coup, but, once in power, tried to shift towards a more moderate policy program, building up broader national support among minority tribes, and reducing Afghanistan's dependence on Russia. He began to develop close ties with the nonaligned, Middle East oil states, where large numbers of Afghans were then employed.

A new presidential constitution was adopted in 1977, but the government was undermined by fundamentalist Muslim insurgents, funded by Libya, Iran, and Pakistan. On 27 April 1978, President Daud was assassinated in a military coup, known, from its date, as the 'Saur Revolution', and Nur Mohammad Taraki, the imprisoned leader of the radical Khalq (Masses) faction of the banned Communist People's Democratic Party of Afghanistan (PDPA), took charge, as president of a Revolutionary Council. A new one-party regime was established, a Treaty of Friendship and Mutual Defense signed with the Soviet Union, in 1978, and major social and land reforms were introduced.

These radical policy initiatives, which were designed to mobilize the landless poor and weaken support for traditional social and economic structures and leaders, were opposed, however, by conservative Muslims. Thousands of refugees fled to Iran and Pakistan and there was a major uprising in the Herat region. The internal situation deteriorated rapidly and, following an intra-PDPA power struggle, Taraki was ousted and murdered, in September 1979. He was replaced, as president of the Revolutionary Council, by the prime minister, and foreign minister, Hafizullah Amin.

Internal unrest continued, however, and the Soviet Union was persuaded to organize a further coup, in December 1979. Hafizullah Amin was executed and Babrak Karmal (1929–96), the exiled leader of the more gradualist Parcham (Banner) faction of the PDPA, installed in power, with the backing of 40,000 Soviet troops who invaded the country the day after Christmas.

The 'Soviet invasion' of December 1979 was condemned by many United Nations members and resulted in the American Carter administration implementing a program of economic and diplomatic sanctions against the Soviet Union, bringing about a serious deterioration in East – West relations. Despite these Western actions, however, Soviet forces remained in Afghanistan, with Red Army troop numbers increasing to more than 120,000 in 1985, as Muslim guerrilla resistance, by the Mujaheddin, or 'holy warriors', continued. The guerrillas were now being aided indirectly by the United States, China, and Pakistan. A war of attrition developed, with the Soviets launching regular land and air offensives, but failing to gain full control of many rural areas. Faced with mounting troop casualties, which already exceeded 9,000, and a debilitating drain on economic resources, the new reformist Soviet administration of Mikhail Gorbachev, in 1986, began to take steps to seek a compromise settlement. In May 1986 Babrak Karmal was replaced as PDPA leader by the Pushtun former KHAD secret police chief, Dr Najibullah Ahmadzai (1947–96), and a number of noncommunist politicians were introduced into the new government. Greater toleration of the practices of Islam was also seen and in October 1986, 8,000 Soviet troops were withdrawn, as an initial goodwill gesture. This withdrawal was followed, in January 1987, by an announcement from the Afghan government that there would be a unilateral six-month ceasefire, to allow discussions to take place about the formation of a possible 'coalition government of national unity', which would remain friendly towards the Soviet Union.

However, the Afghan guerrillas, who were divided along tribal and ideological lines into seven groupings, rejected this initiative, determined to effect a full Soviet withdrawal and a replacement of the communist government.

Additional unilateral extensions of the ceasefire by the Afghan government were made in July and November 1987, with, in the latter month, the ratification of a new multiparty constitution, to further the 'national reconciliation' initiative. In Geneva progress was also made in UN-sponsored talks between Afghan and Pakistan representatives about resolving the 'Afghan crisis'. This was followed in February 1988 by an announcement from the Soviet leader, Mikhail Gorbachev, of a phased nine-month plan for Soviet troop withdrawals, beginning in May 1988 and ending in February 1989.

This pull-out started, as planned, in May 1988, being preceded, in April, by the signing in Geneva of an agreement between the Afghan and Pakistan governments which provided for noninterference in each other's internal affairs and the voluntary return of refugees. The United States and Soviet Union were to guarantee the accord. This agreement promised to bring to an end a decade of direct Soviet interference in the internal affairs of Afghanistan, an involvement which had served to ignite a bitter civil war, resulting, according to official Soviet sources, in the loss of 15,000 Red Army troops and 70,000 Afghan security forces personnel, as well as, according to Western estimates, the lives of more than 1 million Afghans and the uprooting, as refugees, of a further 5 million.

After the Soviet troop withdrawal took place, on 15 February 1989, a 'state of emergency' was imposed by the Najibullah regime, with a new Supreme Council for the Defense of the Homeland (SCDH) being established and in June 1990 the PDPA was renamed the Homeland Party. In February 1989 the Mujaheddin met in Peshawar, Pakistan, and elected an Afghan Interim Government (AIG) in exile, with a prominent moderate, Professor Sibghatullah Mojaddedi, as its president, and a Wahabi fundamentalist, Abd Ar-Rasul Sayef, as prime minister. However, the AIG did not receive international recognition.

Between 1990 and 1992 the civil war intensified, with the Mujaheddin establishing control over 90% of the Afghan countryside. However, the Najibullah regime retained charge of the key cities and garrisons, except Khost, near the Pakistan border, which fell to the Mujaheddin in April 1991. In May 1991 the Najibullah government accepted a comprehensive peace plan brokered by the UN's secretary-general, Javier Pérez de Cuéllar (b. 1920). This provided for an immediate ceasefire, the formation of a broad-based interim government, and a multiparty general election to be held after two years. The plan was rejected by the AIG's prime minister and by Gulbuddin Hekmatyar, leader of the fundamentalist Hesb-i Islami, who refused to countenance including representatives from the Najibullah regime in a transitional government.

From January 1992, Pakistan, the United States, and the Soviet Union halted all supplies of weapons to the contending parties. This contributed to the eventual collapse of the Najibullah regime in April 1992, following the defection of government troops to the Mujaheddin troops of the Tajik commander, Ahmad Shah Masoud. Kabul was captured by the Mujaheddin and Najibullah placed under UN protection, pending trial by an Islamic court. Sibghatullah Mojaddedi formally took over as interim head of state for a two-month period, being replaced by Burhanuddin Rabbani (b. 1943) in June 1992, with Masoud as defense minister. By August 1992 more than 1 million Afghan refugees had returned to their homes. However, the new administration failed to restore order in Kabul and surrounding areas as a new ethnic and sect-based civil war broke out between contending Mujaheddin factions. The chief conflict was between Hekmatyar, with his support base in the traditionally dominant Pathan south and a 12,000-strong army, and the northern (Tajik)-based government of Rabbani and Masoud, backed by the 70,000-strong Uzbek militia commanded by General Abdul Rashid Dostam, whose defection and subsequent alliance with Massoud had been crucial in bringing down the Najibullah regime. There was also conflict between pro-Iranian Shia and Saudi Arabian-backed Sunni Muslim groups.

Following heavy fighting between Hekmatyar's Hesbi-i Islami and Rabbani's Jamiat-i Islami, claiming several thousand lives, a temporary ceasefire was agreed in March 1993 and a peace accord in May 1993, with Hekmatyar being appointed prime minister. During the remainder of 1993, Rabbani, based in Kabul, and Hekmatyar, in Charasiab, 25 kilometres to the south, engaged in a power struggle. This soon descended, from January 1994, into another wave of bloody civil war, with Hekmatyar securing military support from General Abdul Rashid Dostam. This fighting claimed at least 3,000 more lives, caused tremendous damage to an already ravaged economy, and led to the flight of a further 1 million refugees to camps in Pakistan. Hekmatyar was officially replaced as prime minister by Arsala Rahmani in November 1994 and was forced to flee his Charasiab headquarters in January 1995, after being surprisingly defeated by the forces of the predominantly Pathan Talibaan (Islamic theology students) army, which, allegedly with indirect Pakistani and US support, had launched an offensive seeking to disarm all the warring Mujaheddin groups, eradicate the booming drugs trade, and establish a united and patriarchal Islamic state. The popular Talibaan were repulsed from Kabul in March 1995 by Rabbani government forces, but in September 1995 Herat, the country's second city, fell to the student army, who now pounded Kabul with rocket attacks. The Rabbani regime received backing from India, Russia, Tajikistan, and Iran and in May 1996 concluded a peace agreement with Hekmatyar, who returned to Kabul to become prime minister, defense, and finance minister once again. However, in September 1996 the Talibaan, under the leadership of Mullah

Mohammad Omar, a 32-year-old veteran Mujaheddin who had lost an eye in battle, captured Jalalabad, in the east, and then stormed Kabul, forcing Rabbani and his troops to flee. Najibullah, the former communist leader, who had been under UN protection since 1992, was captured, shot and his corpse hung for public display. A six-member interim council, composed of clerics and headed by Mohammad Rabbani, was formed to rule the country and strict Islamic law was imposed. Women were now forbidden to go to work or to be educated beyond the age of ten; the wearing of beards was made compulsory for men; television, non-religious music, gambling, and alcohol were banned; and public stonings and amputations enforced as methods of punishment.

By mid-October 1996 the Talibaan had conquered all but six of Afghanistan's 31 provinces to control three-quarters of the country. In these areas, they disarmed local tribespeople, bringing greater order and stability. The non-Talibaan areas lay in the (largely non-Pathan) north and northeast, which were controlled by the forces of the ousted Burhanuddin Rabbani and Masoud, based in the Panjshir valley, and General Dostam, who formed a 'Northern Alliance', called the United Islamic Front for the Salvation of Afghanistan (UIFSA). In November 1996 UN-sponsored peace talks between the two sides began in Islamabad, Pakistan, but little progress was made. The Talibaan continued to enjoy military success until mid-1997 when they became overstretched and suffered heavy casualties at Mazar-i-Sharif, a large town in the northwest with a population of 1.8 million. Masoud then launched an offensive which reached to within 20 kilometres/12 miles of Kabul.

In May 1997 Pakistan, Saudi Arabia, and the United Arab Emirates became the first countries to formally recognize the Talibaan as the legitimate government of Afghanistan and in October 1997 a new official national name, 'The Islamic Emirate of Afghanistan', was adopted. In the same month, General Dostam, who had triumphed in a power struggle within his own fiefdom, assumed military leadership of the UIFSA, with Burhanuddin Rabbani as chairman. Earthquakes in February and May 1998 caused serious damage in northern Afghanistan, killing 10,000 and leaving half a million homeless. This prompted both sides, under US prompting, to agree in April 1998 to a ceasefire and peace talks. However, the ceasefire failed to hold and in August 1998, by capturing four towns in the north, including Mazar-i-Sharif, the Talibaan extended its grip. In August 1998, the US launched Cruise missile strikes against the Afghan base of Osama bin Laden, an exiled Saudi suspected of involvement in the bombing of American embassies in Kenya and Tanzania. This reflected growing concern in the West, and in the neighboring states of Central Asia, that Afghanistan had become a dangerous, destabilizing new center for the export of fundamentalist Islamic revolution. Since the Soviet troop withdrawal, more than 30,000 Afghans have died in the continuing civil war, and 750,000 have fled the Kabul area, chiefly to refugee camps near Jalalabad. In June 1995 agreement was reached with Iran for the gradual repatriation of 0.9 million of the 1.6 million Afghan refugees still in Iran.

In March 1999 exploratory peace talks between representatives of the Talibaan and of the UIFSA opposition alliance were held in Ashgabat, in Turkmenistan. Both sides agreed in principle to the future establishment of a broad-based government with a shared executive, legislature and judiciary. This was seen as an important step forward. However, no ceasefire was agreed and fighting continued.

BANGLADESH

People's Republic of Bangladesh
Gana Praja Tantri Bangla Desh

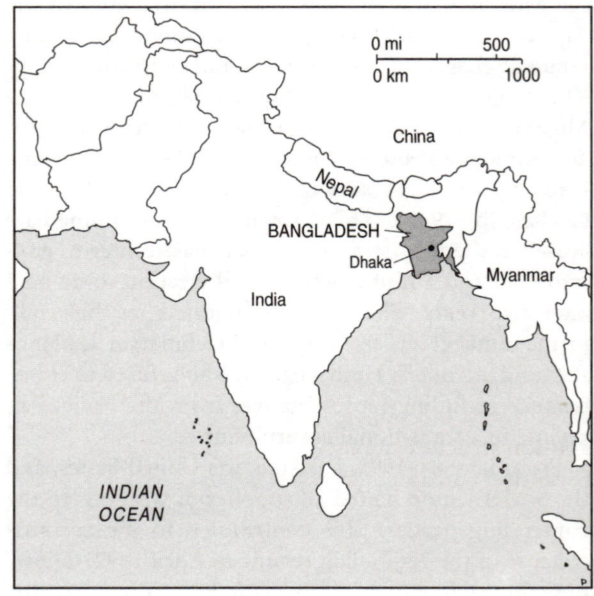

Capital: Dhaka (known before 1984 as Dacca)

Social and economic data

Area: 143,998 sq km/55,598 sq miles
Population: 120,400,000*

Pop. density per sq km/sq mi: 836*/2,166
Urban population: 18%**
Literacy rate: 35%**
GDP: $28,600 million*; per-capita GDP: $240*
Government defense spending (% of GDP): 1.8%**
Currency: taka
Economy type: low income
Labor force in agriculture: 64%**
Unemployment rate: 19.7%
* 1995.
** 1992.

Head of state

President Shehabuddin Ahmed, since 1996

Head of government

Prime Minister Sheikha Hasina Wazed, since 1996

Ethnic composition

Ninety-eight per cent of the population is of Bengali ethnic stock, half a million are Bihari, and around 1 million belong to 'tribal' communities. In the Chittagong Hill Tracts a Chakma separatist organization, the Shanti Bahini (Peace Force) was active until 1998, when it signed a peace agreement and disarmed. Its insurgency led to many Chakmas fleeing to India during the early 1980s. More than 50,000 returned in 1994. Bengali is the official language, with English also being widely spoken.

Religions

Eighty-seven per cent of the population is Muslim, adhering predominantly to the Sunni sect, though influenced by local Hindu practices, and 12% is Hindu. Following a 1977 amendment to the 1972 constitution, Islam was made a 'guiding principle' of the political system. In 1988, with the passage of the Constitution Eighth Amendment Bill, it was declared the official state religion.

Political features

State type: emergent democratic
Date of state formation: 1971
Political structure: unitary
Executive: parliamentary
Assembly: one-chamber
Party structure: multiparty
Human rights rating: 59%
International affiliations: AsDB, CW, CP, ESCAP, G-77, IAEA, IBRD, ICFTU, IMF, IsDB, LORCS, NAM, OIC, SAARC, UN, WTO

Local and regional government

The country is divided into four divisions (Chittagong, Dhaka, Khulna, and Rajshahi) and 64 districts, with elected local councils. At the base of the local government hierarchy there are more than 4,400 rural councils (*parishads*), each serving a population of roughly 20,000. These councils are popularly elected in a fiercely contested manner, more than 150 people losing their lives during the February 1988 contests. Since 1998 the Chittagong Hills Tract has had its own regional council.

Political system

Under the terms of the constitutional amendment of September 1991, the 1972 parliamentary constitution has been restored. There is a single-chamber assembly, or parliament (Jatiya Sangsad), which is composed of 300 members, directly elected for five-year terms from single-member constituencies and an additional 30 female members appointed by the assembly itself. From this body, a prime minister and cabinet are drawn. The prime minister may also hold other ministerial portfolios, such as defense and establishment. The Jatiya Sangsad elects, for a five-year term, a president to serve as a ceremonial head of state.

Political parties

The present ruling party is the Awami League (AL), led by Sheikha Hasina Wazed, the daughter of Sheikh Mujibur Rahman. It was originally formed in 1949 and currently claims a membership of around 1 million, boasting the best national organizational structure of any political party in Bangladesh. It is pro-Indian in international outlook and campaigns for a secular, moderately socialist, mixed-economy state. In August 1993 dissidents within the AL broke away to form the Gano, or People's, Forum, led by Kamal Hossain.

The principal parliamentary opposition party is the Bangladesh National Party (BNP: Bangladesh Jatiyatabadi Dal), led by Begum Khaleda Zia, the widow of Major General Ziaur Rahman. It was formed in 1978 by a merger of parties, including the Nationalist Democratic Party, which supported Major General Ziaur Rahman. The party is a right-of-center grouping which has traditionally been anti-Indian and pro-Islamic in policy outlook.

The third major force in parliament is the Jatiya Dal (JD: National Party). It was originally formed as a civilian political vehicle for Lieutenant General Ershad, the then president, in November 1983, under the designation Jana Dal (People's Party). The party is nationalist in outlook and committed to Islamic ideals. It supported the AL government from June 1996 until March 1998. Mohammad Ershad, was released from prison in January

1997, but was expelled from the party in April 1999 as a result of his seeking to ally the JD with the BNP. Eshad continued to lead a rival JD, while Mizanur Rahman Chowdhury, the prime minister between 1986 and 1988, led the party's other wing.

Around 20 other minor parties are currently active. The four most important are the Islamic fundamentalist, Jamaat-e-Islami Bangladesh, which was established in 1941; the formerly Moscow-linked Bangladesh Communist Party (BCP), which was formed in 1948 and which split, during 1993, into Marxist and reformist wings, and which joined the new eight-party Left Democratic Front in 1994; the National Democratic Alliance, a right-wing, ten-party coalition formed in 1993 by Khandakar Mushtaq Ahmed, who briefly held power in 1975; and the pro-Beijing, National Awami Party-Bhashani (NAP), which dates from 1957. Factionalism, leading to frequent party splits and realignments, is endemic in Bangladeshi politics.

Political leaders since 1970

1971–75 Sheikh Mujibur Rahman (Awami League), 1975 Khandakar Mushtaq Ahmed (Awami League), 1975–76 Abu Sadat Mohammad Sayem (independent), 1976–80 Major General Ziaur Rahman (military/BNP), 1980–82 Abdus Sattar (BNP), 1982–90 Lieutenant General Hossain Mohammad Ershad (military/Jatiya Front), 1990–91 Shehabuddin Ahmed (independent), 1991–96 Begum Khaleda Zia (BNP), 1996– Justice Habibur Rahman (independent), 1996– Sheikha Hasina Wazed (Awami League)

Latest elections

In the most recent Jatiya Sangsad elections, which were held on 12 June 1996, the AL captured 146 seats of the 300 elective seats. The BNP won 116 seats, the JD 32 seats, and the Jamaat-e-Islami Bangladesh, two seats. Turnout exceeded 60%. In September 1996, following by-elections and its allocation of 27 of the 30 nominated seats for women, the AL achieved a parliamentary majority, holding 176 of the 330 seats.

Political history

Contemporary Bangladesh, a vast, low-lying, deltaic plain where the great Ganges, Brahmaputra, and Meghna rivers unite to flow into the Bay of Bengal, formerly consisted of the jute-growing East Bengal province and Sylhet district of Assam in British India. Being predominantly Muslim, it was formed into the eastern province of Pakistan when India was partitioned in August 1947. It differed substantially in culture, language, and geography from the western provinces of Pakistan, 1,000 kilometres/600 miles away, and with a larger population, resented the political and military dominance exerted by West Pakistan during the 1950s and 1960s.

An independence movement developed after 1954, under the leadership of the Awami League (AL), headed by Sheikh Mujibur Rahman (1920–75). This gained strength because of the indifference shown by West Pakistan in 1970, when severe cyclones caused the deaths of half a million people in floods in East Pakistan.

In the first general elections held in Pakistan in December 1970 the AL gained an overwhelming victory in the East and an overall majority in the all-Pakistan National Assembly. Talks on redrafting the constitution broke down, leading to East Pakistan's declaration of secession and the establishment of a Bangladesh ('Bengal Nation') government in exile, in Calcutta, in April 1971. Civil war ensued, resulting in the flight of 10 million East Pakistani refugees to India. There was an administrative breakdown in East Pakistan and an outbreak of famine and cholera. On 16 December 1971 the West Pakistani troops in East Pakistan surrendered to the Bangladesh forces, who had been, briefly, helped by Indian troops. A republic of Bangladesh was proclaimed and it had gained broad international recognition by 1972.

Sheikh Mujibur Rahman became the nation's first prime minister, under a secular, parliamentary constitution, which was adopted in November 1972. He proceeded to introduce a socialist economic program of nationalization, but became increasingly intolerant of opposition. He established an emergency, one-party, presidential system of government in January 1975.

On 15 August 1975 Sheikh Mujibur Rahman, his wife, and close relatives were assassinated in a military coup. Power was held for three months by Khandakar Mushtaq Ahmed of the Awami League, before a further military coup in November 1975 established as president and chief martial law administrator the nonpolitical chief justice, Abu Sadat Mohammad Sayem.

Two years later, in November 1976, the army chief of staff, Major General Ziaur Rahman (1935–81), became chief martial law administrator, before assuming the presidency, in April 1977. He adopted an Islamic constitution, which was approved in a May 1977 national referendum. In June 1978 he achieved victory by a 4:1 majority in a direct presidential election and released political prisoners and relaxed press censorship in readiness for parliamentary elections in February 1979.

Major General Zia's newly formed Bangladeshi

Nationalist Party (BNP) won a parliamentary majority and, with a civilian government installed, martial law and the state of emergency were lifted between April and November 1979. The new administration was rapidly undermined, however, by charges of corruption and by a guerrilla secessionist movement in the Chittagong Hill's Tract in 1980. On 30 May 1981 Major General Zia was assassinated during an attempted coup, forcing Vice President Justice Abdus Sattar to assume power as an interim leader.

With internal disorder increasing, the civilian administration of Sattar was overthrown, on 24 March 1982, in a coup led by army chief of staff, Lieutenant General Hossain Mohammad Ershad (b. 1930). Martial law was reimposed and political activities banned. Under Lieutenant General Ershad, because of the adoption of more market-orientated policies and the introduction of a major 'food for work' rural program, economic conditions improved. Agitation for a return to democratic government gained strength, however, from September 1983, when a broad opposition party coalition, the Movement for the Restoration of Democracy (MRD), was formed.

Lieutenant General Ershad promised to hold presidential and parliamentary elections in 1984, but these were cancelled after an opposition threat of a boycott and campaign of civil disobedience if martial law was not first lifted. In January 1986 the ban on political activities was removed and parliamentary elections were held in May 1986. The AL agreed to participate, but the BNP, together with many other opposition parties, boycotted the poll.

After an election campaign marked by violence, widespread abstentions, and claims of ballot-rigging, and the rerunning of 37 constituency contests, Lieutenant General Ershad and his Jatiya Dal (JD) party gained a two-thirds majority, giving him the constitutional right to pass a law granting retrospective immunity for any otherwise illegal acts.

In October 1986 Ershad, who had formally stepped down as army chief of staff in August and had been elected chairman of the JD a month later, was re-elected president in a direct election, and in November 1986 martial law was lifted and the 1972 constitution restored. Both the AL and BNP had boycotted the presidential contest.

During 1987, opposition groups stepped up their campaign against the Ershad government, calling for the president's resignation and the holding of new free elections. A wave of violent strikes and demonstrations was launched by trade unions and students. The administration's attempt to pass a law which would enable army representatives to participate in district councils heightened the political temperature during the summer and autumn months, just at a time when the country was devastated by the worst floods for 40 years, which claimed at least 1,500 lives.

With the economy rapidly deteriorating and faced by a threat of a general strike, President Ershad proclaimed a state of emergency, on 27 November 1987, and banned all antigovernment protests for 120 days. Political activity and civil rights were suspended and the opposition leaders Sheikha Hasina Wazed (AL) and Begum Khalida Zia (BNP) were placed under temporary house arrest. General urban curfews were also imposed. A month later, with the threat of the mass resignation of the AL's 73 members, parliament was dissolved and new elections were called for March 1988.

The elections were again boycotted by the AL and BNP and, again, there was evidence of flagrant ballot-rigging. In these conditions, the JD gained a sweeping victory, with only a minority of the electorate voting. The president put together a new cabinet, with Moudud Ahmed as prime minister, lifted the state of emergency in April 1988, and intimated that in the forthcoming parliamentary session a bill would be introduced to establish Islam as the state religion. This eighth amendment was duly passed by the Jatiya Sangsad in June 1988.

Extra-parliamentary opposition to the Ershad regime remained strong, however, and to compound the government's difficulties, the country received its heaviest monsoon downpour for 70 years in September 1988. The resulting floods left 30 million homeless, claimed thousands of lives and caused huge infrastructural damage. Ershad was eventually forced to resign on 4 December 1990 after two months of mass popular protests in Dhaka and other cities. He was subsequently charged with and later, in 1992 and 1993, found guilty of corruption and sentenced to imprisonment. Shehabuddin Ahmed, the country's chief justice, took over as interim president. Immediately, the state of emergency was lifted and the Special Powers Act, which had allowed the government to detain persons without trial and summarily close down newspapers, was annulled.

In free, multiparty elections held in February 1991, the BNP, helped by a high turnout of women and young adults in towns, emerged as the dominant force. It captured 140 of the 300 elective seats, while the AL polled less strongly than had been anticipated. Begum Khaleda Zia (b. 1945) duly became the nation's first female prime minister in March 1991. At first she headed a coalition government, with initial support from the Jamaat-e-Islami, until the BNP achieved a narrow absolute majority of seats after by-elections held in September 1991. The Zia administration introduced an outward-looking and deregulationary 'new industrial policy', with the aim of boosting private enterprise, in part via privatization, and encouraging foreign investment, and in September 1991 reversion to a parliamentary system of government was approved by a national referendum. A month later, the Jatiya Sangsad elected its speaker and the BNP nominee, Abdur Rahman Biswas, to become the new ceremonial state president.

In April 1991 the nation was rocked by its worst ever cyclone, which killed an estimated 139,000 people, rendered up to 10 million homeless, and resulted in economic losses of $3 billion. Throughout the period between 1992 and 1995 the Zia administration faced sporadic, and sometimes violent, national strikes (hartals) and political protests. Orchestrated by opposition forces, who demanded the resignation of Zia and the calling of fresh elections, they intensified from May 1994, when the opposition claimed that the BNP had resorted to fraud in recent by-elections. An opposition boycott of parliament was effected, despite the Dhaka High Court declaring this act to be unconstitutional, and general strikes were held in Dhaka and other main towns in March 1995. The opposition boycotted a general election held in February 1996, in which turnout fell to around 10% and the BNP won nearly all the seats. Zia tried to continue as prime minister, but, with continuing political strikes and street protests paralysing Dacca and under pressure from the army, she finally resigned in March 1996. A neutral caretaker government was formed, headed by an Oxford-educated retired chief justice, Muhammad Habibur Rahman, and a new general election was held in June 1996. This was largely peaceful, free and fair, although the campaign was marred by an unsuccessful attempted military coup on 20 May 1996. The election was won by the AL, which formed its first government in 21 years. Sheikha Hasina Wazed became prime minister and pledged to continue with a free-market economic strategy, including privatization, but also to clamp down on terrorism and promote local government and media deregulation. The AL 'national consensus government', which enjoyed support from the JD until March 1998, was initially a minority administration until it achieved a majority in September 1996. As with the preceding government, the AL were faced, from November 1996 by an on-off opposition boycott of parliament. This was provoked partly by the government's launching of an investigation into the 1975 assassination of Sheikh Mujibur Rahman, which they viewed as a politically motivated inquiry. The opposition also sponsored street rallies against the government's economic and foreign policies. In July 1996, Shehabuddin Ahmed was elected unopposed as state president. In August 1998 corruption charges were filed against former prime minister, Begum Khaleda Zia. In foreign affairs, Bangladesh has remained a member of the Commonwealth since 1972 and, although heavily dependent on foreign economic aid, has pursued a broad policy of nonalignment. Its relations with India deteriorated after 1975, as a result of disputes over the sharing of Ganges water and the annual influx of 200,000 Bangladeshi refugees to Assam and West Bengal, which has prompted India to threaten to construct a barbed wire frontier fence. However, they were improved in December 1996 by the signing with India of a 30-year agreement on the equal sharing of water from the River Ganges.

BHUTAN

Kingdom of Bhutan
Druk Yul (Realm of the Dragon)

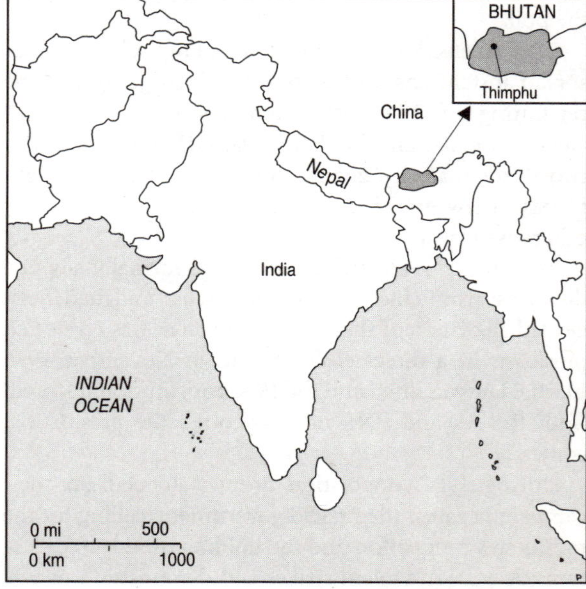

Capital: Thimphu

Social and economic data
Area: 46,500 sq km/17,954 sq miles
Population: 1,614,000**
Pop. density per sq km/sq mi: 35**/90
Urban population: 5%***
Literacy rate: 18%***
GDP: $295 million**; per-capita GDP: $180**
Government defense spending (% of GDP): N/A
Currency: ngultrum
Economy type: low income
Labor force in agriculture: 90%***
** 1995.
*** 1992.
* This is a UN estimate. The Bhutanese government claims the 'official overall population' to be as little as 600,000–850,000 million.

Head of state
King Jigme Singye Wangchuk, since 1972

Head of government
Lyonpo Jigme Thimley, since 1998

Ethnic composition
Fifty-four per cent of the population is of Bhotia ethnic stock, residing principally in the east and north; 32% are descendants of Tibetan immigrants; while a substantial Nepali minority lives in the south, being prohibited from moving into the Bhotia-dominated north. Dzongkha, which is very similar to Tibetan, is the official language and is spoken by 70% of the population. Nepali is the main language for 30% of the population.

Religions
The principal, and state, religion is Mahayana Buddhism, or Lamaism, which was introduced during the 8th century AD. Seventy per cent of the population adheres to it. Twenty-five per cent of the population is Hindu, principally the ethnic Nepalese of the southern districts. The country's 4,000 Buddhist monks play an influential role in national and local political affairs, with their head abbot, the Je Khempo, occupying a prominent position in the Royal Advisory Council.

Political features
State type: absolutist
Date of state formation: 1907
Political structure: unitary
Executive: absolute
Assembly: one-chamber
Party structure: no parties permitted
Human rights rating: N/A
International affiliations: AsDB, CP, ESCAP, G-77, IBRD, IMF, NAM, SAARC, UN

Local and regional government
The country is divided into 20 districts (*dzongkhags*), each headed by an administrative and law and order officer (*dzongda*), and a judicial officer (*thrimpon*), both appointed by the Royal Civil Service Commission, which was established in 1982. Seven districts are further subdivided into subdistricts (*dungkhags*), with 'village blocks' (*gewog*) below. Village-level elections are held every three years, with each family being granted one vote.

Political system
Bhutan is governed by a hereditary executive monarch and lacks a formal constitution. Since 1953, the king, who is called Druk Gyalpo (Dragon King), or 'precious ruler', has worked with an elected legislature, the National Assembly (Tshogdu) and, since 1965, with a partially elected Royal Advisory Council (RAC: Lodoi Tsokde), with which he shares power. Written rules govern the methods of electing members of the Royal Advisory Council and Tshogdu and define their duties and powers, thus giving the political system elements of a constitutional monarchy.

The National Assembly convenes for several months each year to enact laws and serve as a debating forum. It currently comprises 150 members, 105 elected by 'direct popular consensus' in villages, ten representing regional monastic bodies, and the remaining 35 being officials, ministers, and members of the RAC. Its decisions are reached by consensus. Every three years, the Tshogdu is required to pass a vote of confidence in the king by a two-thirds majority. Since July 1998, the National Assembly has had the power to dismiss the monarch through a two-thirds vote, and replace him with another member of the royal family. Also, its bills cannot be vetoed by the king.

The Royal Advisory Council, as its name suggests, has the primary function of providing political advice to the monarch. It also supervises all administrative matters, serving essentially as the *de facto* standing committee of the Tshogdu. It consists of nine members: a chairperson nominated by the king, two Buddhist monks, and six 'people's representatives'. These representatives are endorsed by village assemblies, *dzongdas*, and the National Assembly. Members serve for renewable five-year terms. Today the RAC is the originator of most legislation.

Executive administration is the responsibility of a

Council of Ministers (COM: Lhengye Shungtsog). It was headed by the king until July 1998, when the foreign minister (Lyonpo Jigme Yoser Thinley) became chairperson. It includes prominent additional members of the royal family. Like the RAC, this body is responsible to the Tshogdu. In practice, however, the king remains the dominant political force.

Political parties

There are no legal political parties within Bhutan. However, illegal parties, mainly ethnic Nepali, include the Bhutan People's Party, formed in 1990 as a successor to the People's Forum for Human Rights (estd. 1989), the United Liberation People's Front (estd. 1990), and the Bhutan National Democratic Party (estd. 1992), and the Druk National Congress (estd. 1992).

Political leaders since 1970

1952–72 King Jigme Dorji Wangchuk, 1972– King Jigme Singye Wangchuk

Latest elections

The Tshogdu's directly elected representatives serve three-year terms in individual constituencies at varying dates, depending on the expiry of their terms.

Political history

Formerly ruled by Tibet during the 16th century and China from 1720, Bhutan was invaded by Britain in 1865, and a trade agreement was signed, under which an annual subsidy was paid to Bhutan in 'return for its good behaviour'. The country was thus never formally subjected to direct colonial rule. In December 1907 Bhutan's first hereditary monarch was installed and three years later, under the Anglo-Bhutanese (Punakha) Treaty, foreign relations were placed under the control of the British Government of India.

Soon after India achieved independence in 1947, an Indo-Bhutan Treaty of Perpetual Peace and Friendship was signed, in August 1949, under which Bhutan agreed to seek Indian advice on foreign relations but not necessarily to accept it. Although no formal defense treaty was signed, India has made it clear that it would regard an attack on Bhutan as an act of agression against itself. India also returned to Bhutan, in 1949, territory that had been annexed by British India in 1865.

In 1952 King Jigme Dorji Wangchuk was installed and in the following year a National Assembly was established. In 1959, after the annexation of Tibet by communist China, Bhutan gave asylum to some 4,000 Tibetan refugees, but in June 1979, concerned with their alleged subversive activities, the Tshogdu gave the refugees until the end of the year to take up Bhutanese citizenship or return to Tibet. Most took up citizenship and the rest were accepted by India.

During the reign of King Jigme Dorji Wangchuk, between 1952 and 1972, a series of progressive social, economic, and political reforms was gradually introduced, in an effort to modernize what remained a backward, traditionalist nation. These reforms included the abolition of slavery, in 1958, and the caste system; the emancipation of women; the establishment of a secular school system; and the introduction of an extensive program of land reform and long-term economic planning. In the political sphere, as part of a democratization process, the king appointed his first cabinet, in May 1968, and in the same year renounced his right of veto and gave the Tshogdu the authority to select and remove the monarch.

The king died in July 1972 and was succeeded by his young, Western-educated, son, Jigme Singye Wangchuk. The new king, while maintaining close links with India, which had provided much of the finance for the country's post-1961 five-year economic plans, proceeded to pursue a somewhat more independent and outward-looking course in external relations than his father had done. Bhutan joined the Non-Aligned Movement in 1973, entered into border negotiations with China, and became a founder member of the South Asian Association for Regional Cooperation (SAARC) organization. In May 1985 it increased its political involvement in the region by hosting the first meeting of SAARC foreign ministers. In the economic sphere, a program of privatization got underway from 1992.

Since 1988 Bhutan's Buddhist Dzongkha/Drukpa ethnic minority, headed by the king, has sought to impose its language, religious customs, and national dress on the majority community, which, though divided, is predominantly Hindu-Nepali, particularly in the south where there are many recent immigrants. The Nepalese language and customs have been suppressed and hundreds of thousands of non-Bhutanese have been allegedly deported as part of an 'ethnic cleansing' process which has led to the establishment of large refugee camps in eastern Nepal. Influenced also by the democratization movement in Nepal, interethnic tensions have increased greatly. Political parties have been formed illegally by the Nepalese and in September 1990 several hundred people were reportedly killed during security crackdowns against prodemocracy demonstrations. In November 1993 Tek Nath Rizal, founder of the banned Bhutan People's Party, was sentenced to life imprisonment for 'antinational activities'. In April 1997 Kinley Dorji, leader of the Druk National Congress, was arrested in India and his extradition sought, on charges of 'acts against the state'. In July 1998 the king introduced important reforms to reduce his powers, through enabling the legislature to dismiss him through a two-thirds no-confidence vote, and giving up his right to nominate and chair the cabinet. In August 1998 Lyonpo Jigme Thimley became prime minister.

BRUNEI

Sultanate of Brunei (State of Brunei Darussalam)
Negara Brunei Darussalam

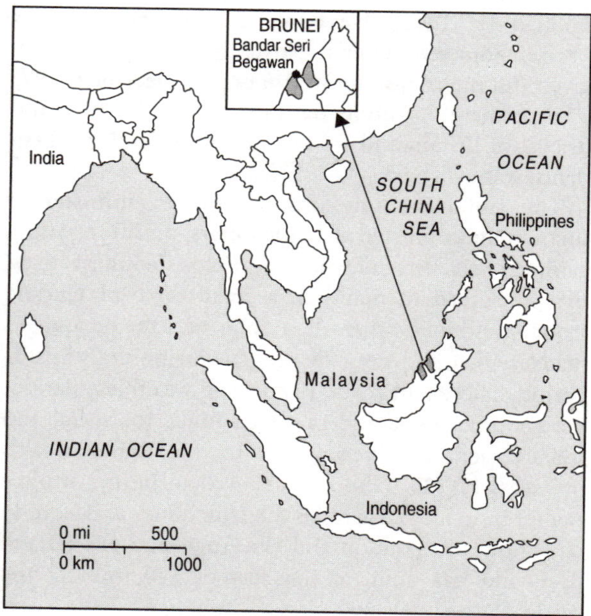

Capital: Bandar Seri Begawan (formerly Brunei town)

Social and economic data

Area: 5,765 sq km/2,226 sq miles
Population: 305,000*
Pop. density per sq km/sq mi: 53/137*
Urban population: 58%**
Literacy rate: 87%**
GDP: $3,975 million*; per-capita GDP: $13,000*
Government defense spending (% of GDP): 6%*
Currency: Brunei dollar
Economy type: high income
Labor force in agriculture: 2%
* 1995.
** 1992.

Head of state and head of government

Sultan Sir Muda Hassanal Bolkiah Mu'izzaddin Waddaulah, since 1968

Ethnic composition

Sixty-eight per cent of the population are indigenous Malays, predominating in government service and agriculture, and more than 20% are Chinese, predominating in the commercial sphere. Malay is the principal and official language, but Chinese, chiefly the Hokkien dialect, is spoken by a quarter of the population and English is also widely spoken. Foreign workers, mainly from Malaysia and the Philippines, comprise two-fifths of the labor force.

Religions

Sixty-six per cent of the population, mainly the ethnic Malays, adhere to Islam, of the Sunni sect. Ten per cent of the people, chiefly Eurasians, are Christians and 14%, largely ethnic Chinese, are Buddhists. Islam is the official state religion, and the sultan is its national head.

Political features

State type: absolutist
Date of state formation: 1984
Political structure: unitary
Executive: absolute
Assembly: none
Party structure: no parties (effectively)
Human rights rating: N/A
International affiliations: APEC, ASEAN, CW, ESCAP, G-77, IsDB, NAM, OIC, UN, WTO

Local and regional government

The state is divided into four administrative districts: Brunei-Muara, Tutong, Belait, and Temburong. Each is governed by a district officer (malay) responsible to the prime minister (sultan) and home affairs minister. There are also four municipalities.

Political system

The September 1959 constitution gives supreme executive authority to the sultan, advised by four Constitutional Councils: the Religious Council, the Privy Council, the Council of Cabinet Ministers, and the Council of Succession. The Council of Cabinet Ministers (CCM) is the most important and has around 11 members. The sultan heads it, acting as both prime minister and minister of defense and finance. Since 1962 he has ruled by decree. His brother, Prince Mohamed Bolkiah, serves as foreign affairs minister. The most important of the sultan's advisers is the internal affairs minister, Pehin Dato Haji Isa, who functions, in many respects, as a chief minister (*mentri besar*).

Political parties

Two political parties were formed in 1985–86: the Brunei National Democratic Party (BNDP: Partai Kebang-Saan Demokratik Brunei), an Islamic and liberal nationalist grouping; and the Brunei National Solidarity Party (BNSP: Partai Perpaduan Kebang-Saan Brunei), a multi-ethnic splinter group, formed by ex-BNDP members. However, in 1988 both the BNDP and BNUP were dissolved by government order. In 1995 the BNSP was given permission to reconvene, under the leadership of the former BNDP leader, Abdul Latif Chuchu.

The opposition Brunei People's Party (BPP: Parti Ra'ayat Brunei) operates in exile. The party was formed in 1959 and won all elective seats to the Legislative Council in 1962, before staging a revolt against the government. As a result, it was banned, in December 1962.

Political leaders since 1970

1968– Sultan Sir Muda Hassanal Bolkiah Mu'izzaddin Waddaulah

Latest elections

There have been no elections since March 1965. Prior to this, a tiered system of indirect elections from district councils to a 21-member Legislative Council, ten of whom were elected, was in operation.

Political history

Brunei was an independent Islamic monarchy from the 15th century, ruling North Borneo, a region which includes contemporary Sabah and Sarawak states which today form part of Malaysia, between the 16th and 19th centuries. However, during the mid-19th century its authority waned, and it lost control of Sarawak in 1841, before eventually becoming a British protectorate in 1888. Under an agreement of 1906, a British resident was appointed as adviser to the sultan, turning the country into a British dependency.

During World War II, Brunei was occupied by the Japanese, from December 1941, but reverted to its former status after Japan's capitulation in September 1945. In 1950, after the death of his father, Sir Muda Omar Ali Saiffuddin Saadul Khairi Waddien, popularly known as Sir Omar, became the new, 28th, sultan. His authority was increased in September 1959 when a written constitution was promulgated making Britain responsible for the country's defense and external affairs, but returning substantial control over internal affairs to the sultan.

In December 1962 a proposal that Brunei should join the Federation of Malaysia (FOM), which was established in 1963, was opposed by a widespread revolution, organized by the Brunei People's Party (BPP), linked to the North Borneo Liberation Army. The revolt, after more than a week of fighting, was put down with the help of British forces from Singapore. A state of emergency was imposed, the BPP was banned, and the sultan began to rule by decree. In 1963 the idea of joining the FOM was abandoned.

In October 1967 the sultan, Sir Omar, refusing to accede to British demands for more representative government, abdicated in favor of his son, Hassanal Bolkiah (b. 1946). He remained, however, as chief adviser. Four years later, in November 1971, Brunei was given full internal self-government. In December 1975 a UN General Assembly resolution called for the withdrawal of Britain and on 1 January 1984 full independence was achieved.

The sultan became prime minister, minister of finance, and minister of home affairs, presiding over a cabinet of six, three of whom were close blood relatives. Britain agreed to maintain a small force of Gurkha troops, paid for by the sultan, to protect the oil and gas fields, which had been developed during the postwar period. These had made Brunei the wealthiest nation, per capita, in Asia and provided funds for social and welfare spending. The sultan, with an estimated wealth in excess of $25 billion, is believed to be the world's richest individual. He owns the Dorchester and Beverly Hills hotels in London and Los Angeles, a private airfleet, and has built, at the cost of $40 million, the world's largest palace.

The 1975 UN resolution had also called for political liberalization, including the return of political exiles and the holding of a general election. Progress in this direction has, however, been slow. In May 1985 the royal family cautiously allowed the formation of a political party, the Brunei National Democratic Party (BNDP), dominated by loyal businessmen. However, ethnic Chinese and government employees, who constitute 40% of the work force, were forbidden to join. A second grouping, the Brunei National Solidarity Party (BNSP), which included ethnic Chinese, was tolerated in February 1986.

Since the death of Sir Omar in September 1986 the pace of political and economic modernization has accelerated. In particular, in the new government, which was formed in October 1986, key portfolios were given to nonroyal commoners and aristocrats. However, severe restrictions are still imposed on the operation of 'radical' opposition groupings, with the BNDP and BNSP being banned in 1988. In 1995 the BNSP was allowed to reconvene and in July 1996 Zaini Ahmed, a prominent political dissident detained since 1962, was released. A conservative, nationalist socio-economic policy has been pursued in recent years, in which preferential treatment has been given to native Malays (*bumiputras*, or 'sons of the soil') in the commercial sphere, at the expense of traditional Chinese, many of whom have emigrated since 1984. Also, an Islamic state is in the process of being constructed, with Melayu Islam Beraja (Malay Islam Monarchy) being promoted as the state ideology. In February 1997 the sultan's youngest brother, Prince Jefri, whose extravagant projects and investments had reportedly cost the state more than $5 billion, was removed as finance minister. Later, in July 1998, he was also dismissed as head of the Brunei Investment Agency. In August 1998, Prince Billah, the sultan's 24-year-old, Oxford-educated eldest son, was formally invested as crown prince, or heir to the throne.

In its external relations since independence, Brunei has maintained close links with Western nations, particularly the United States and Britain, but has also joined ASEAN, and has begun to cultivate warm relations with neighboring Singapore and Malaysia. In 1992 it joined the Non-Aligned Movement. In the economic sphere, there have been attempts at diversification, away from overdependence on oil, the aim being to establish Brunei as a new center for international finance, banking, and tourism. Much of the interior of the country still remains, however, underdeveloped: 70% of it is covered by dense tropical jungle.

CAMBODIA (KAMPUCHEA)

The State of Cambodia (SOC)
Roat Kampuchea

Capital: Phnom Penh

Social and economic data

Area: 181,035 sq km/69,898 sq miles
Population: 10,600,000*

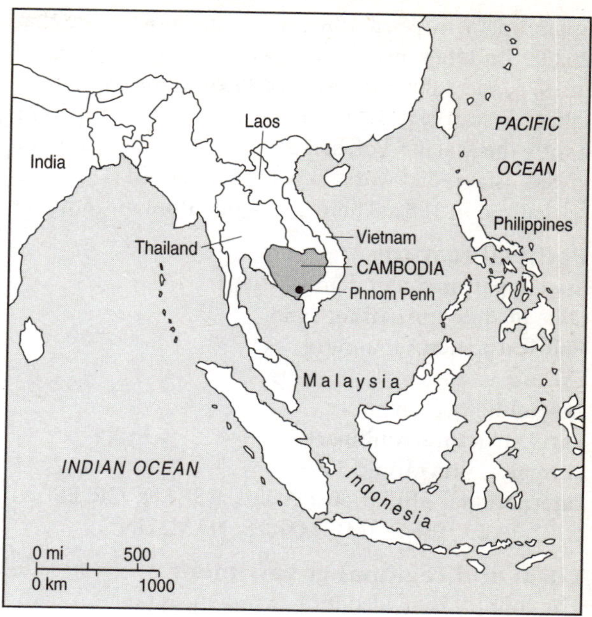

Pop. density per sq km/sq mi: 59*/152
Urban population: 12%**
Literacy rate: 86%**
GDP: $2,720 million*; per-capita GDP: $260*
Government defense spending (% of GDP): 4.7%*
Currency: riel
Economy type: low income
Labor force in agriculture: 68%**
* 1995.
** 1992.

Head of state

King Norodom Sihanouk, since 1991*

* Became king in 1993.

Head of government

Prime Minister Hun Sen since 1985*

* Shared authority with co-premier Prince Norodom Ranariddh 1993–97.

Ethnic composition

Khmers constitute 91% of the population, Vietnamese 4%, and Chinese 3%. The official language is Khmer, but French is also widely spoken.

Religions

The traditional religion is Theravada Buddhism, adhered to by 90% of the population. All religious activity was banned in 1975, but Buddhism was reinstated as the national religion following a constitutional amendment in April 1989. There are now more than 20,000 Buddhist priests (*bonzes*), the same number as in 1975, and 2,800 monasteries. Prior to the communist takeover in 1975, 1.4% of the population, predominantly the Malayo-Polynesian-speaking Cham, also followed Islam. Its worship was banned in 1975, but relegalized in 1989. There are 14,000 Roman Catholics.

Political features

State type: emergent democratic
Date of state formation: 1953
Political structure: unitary
Executive: dual
Assembly: two-chamber
Party structure: multiparty
Human rights rating: 33%
International affiliations: AsDB, ASEAN, CP, ESCAP, G-77, IAEA, IBRD, IMF, LORCS, NAM, UN

Local and regional government

The country is divided into 21 provinces (*khet*), 122 districts (*srok*), 1,325 subdistricts (*khum*), and 9,386 villages (*phum*), in addition to two municipalities (*krung*), Phnom Penh and Kompong Som, which are themselves subdivided into wards (*sangkat*) and groups (*krom*).

Political system

Under the terms of the constitution of September 1993, Cambodia has a pluralistic, liberal-democratic political system based around a limited monarchy. The monarch, Prince Norodom Sihanouk, was elected in September 1993 by a seven-member Throne Council, comprising the two co-chairs of the Provisional National Government of Cambodia (PNGC), three members of the Constituent Assembly, and two Buddhist monks. He acts in consultation with ministers and senior civil servants and is said to 'reign but not rule'. He may only declare a state of emergency with the approval of the prime minister and cabinet. However, so great is the stature and moral authority of the current monarch that the executive system is best described as dual.

The legislature, the National Assembly, comprises 122 members, who are directly elected for five-year terms. From the dominant party or coalition in the Assembly is drawn a prime minister and cabinet, designated the Royal Government of Cambodia (RGC). Control of the 22-member cabinet was shared between 1993 and 1997 by two co-premiers, drawn from the monarchist FUNCINPEC and excommunist CPP.

In March 1999 an upper chamber was created, the Senate, comprising 61 members appointed by the monarch.

Political parties

There are five main political parties in Cambodia: the 'Sihanoukists', the Buddhist Liberal Democratic Party (BLDP), the Cambodian People's Party (CPP), the Khmer Rouge, and the Khmer Nation Party (KNP).

'Sihanoukists', supporters of King Norodom Sihanouk, are organized in the United National Front for an Independent, Neutral, Peaceful and Cooperative Cambodia (FUNCINPEC), a right-of-center nationalist force which originated as the military wing of Sihanouk's National Army of Independent Cambodia (ANS). The party enjoys particularly strong peasant support. The ANS transformed itself into a political party to contest the 1993 general election, with Prince Norodom Ranariddh, the son of the king, being elected its president in February 1992.

The BLDP was established in 1992 to contest the 1993 elections by Son Sann, a former prime minister, as a successor to the Khmer People's National Liberation Front (KPNLF), which was formed in France in 1979. It is a republican, anticommunist and elite-orientated party. Led since 1995 by Ieng Muli, it was a member of the ruling coalition government between 1993 and 1998, having won ten seats in the May 1993 general election.

The CPP, formerly known as the Kampuchean People's Revolutionary Party (KPRP), dominated Cambodian affairs between 1979 and 1991 and has used its control over the bureaucracy and military to subsequently remain in power. As the KPRP, it was formed in January 1979 by 66 exiled Kampuchean communists, at an ad hoc congress called under Vietnamese auspices to 'reorganize the party'. Half of them were ex-Khmer Viet Minh and half ex-Khmer Rouge. The KPRP's roots go back to 1951 when a Cambodian wing broke away from the existing Communist Party of Indo-China, which had been established in 1930 by Ho Chi Minh, to form the Khmer (Cambodian) People's Revolutionary Party. This soon divided into two factions: a pro-Vietnamese grouping, the Khmers Vietminh, which favored collaboration with the Cambodian head of state, Prince Norodom Sihanouk; and an anti-Sihanouk grouping, led by the Paris-trained Marxist, Pol Pot (Saloth Sar; 1926–98).

The second faction became dominant in 1960 and proceeded to rename the party the Communist Party of Kampuchea (CPK) and pursue a new pro-Chinese and anti-Soviet course. Organizing itself among the peasantry, Pol Pot's CPK, popularly known as the Khmer

Rouge, engaged in a guerrilla struggle against, first, the Sihanouk and then the Lon Nol, governments during the later 1960s and early 1970s. As a result, it emerged as the governing force in Cambodia between 1975 and 1979. Its ruthless policies, however, alienated some people in the party's ranks, resulting in the defection of a number of leading figures, including Heng Samrin (b. 1934) and Hun Sen (b. 1950), who formed the new pro-Vietnamese and pro-Soviet KPRP. The designation KPRP was officially adopted in 1981, superseding the title CPK.

The current CPP, though still organized on hierarchical 'democratic centralist' lines, is a reform-socialist body. At an extraordinary Congress held in Phnom Penh in 1991, it formally abandoned its Marxist-Leninist ideology and endorsed multiparty democracy, a free-market economy and the protection of human rights, and upheld Buddhism as the state religion. Chea Sim replaced Heng Samrin as party chairperson, Heng becoming 'honorary president', while the moderate prime minister, Hun Sen, was elected vice chairperson. The Khmer Rouge, known as the Cambodian National Unity Party (CNUP), is the successor to Pol Pot's CPK, which was dissolved in 1981. The new group was led by Khieu Samphan, and, since 1997, Ta Mok. In 1996, the Democratic National United Movement (DNUM) was formed by Ieng Sary as a breakaway from the Khmer Rouge. The KNP was formed in November 1995 by Sam Rainsy, a pro-democracy and anti-corruption campaigner who was formerly a member of FUNCINPEC and a finance minister. The Hun Sen government has repeatedly harassed the party and viewed it as illegal before the 1998 general election, which it fought as the Sam Rainsy Party (SRP).

Political leaders since 1970

1970–75 Lieutenant General Lon Nol, 1975–76 Prince Sihanouk, 1976–79 Pol Pot (Khmer Rouge)*, 1979–81 Pen Sovann (CPK)*, 1981–91 Heng Samrin (KPRP)*, 1991– Prince Norodom Sihanouk (FUNCINPEC)**, 1991– Hun Sen (CPP)***, 1993–97 Prince Norodom Ranariddh (FUNCINPEC)***

* Communist Party leader.

** Executive head of state.

*** Prime minister.

Latest elections

The most recent National Assembly elections, held on 26 July 1998, produced a disputed outcome. The ex-communist CPP claimed a narrow victory, securing 64 of the 122 seats, based on a 41% share of the vote, but polling poorly in its leader, Hun Sen's, home province of Kandal. The royalist FUNCINPEC, with 32% of the vote, won 43 seats and the SRP 15 seats and 14% of the vote. The election was contested by 36 other parties, few of which attracted much support. The two main opposition parties demanded recounts, claiming that the election had not been free and fair. However, despite pervasive intimidation, media bias, and restrictions on campaigning, more than 500 international observers, chiefly from the European Union and UN, were satisfied and there were fewer killings, totalling 21, than in the 1993 election. Turnout was around 90%.

Political history

1. Beginnings to the Khmer Rouge

Cambodia originally constituted part of the Kingdom of Fou-Nan, before being conquered by the Khmers during the 6th century. It became the heartland for the sophisticated and extensive Khmer Empire between the 6th–15th centuries, whose capital was established at Angkor in northwest Cambodia. The region subsequently came within the jurisdiction of neighboring Siam (Thailand) and Champa (Vietnam), but still retained a measure of independence. In 1863 it became a French protectorate but its traditional political and social structures were left largely intact.

From 1887 it formed part of the French Indo-China Union, but during World War II it was occupied by Japan. France regained control of what was then known as the Kingdom of Cambodia, and promulgated a constitution which established a modern parliamentary system. However, in the face of a rural-based guerrilla independence movement that was growing in strength, the country was granted semi-autonomy within the French Union in November 1949, and full independence in November 1953.

Prince Norodom Sihanouk (b. 1922), who had been elected king in 1941, abdicated in favor of his parents in March 1955 and became prime minister, as leader of the Popular Socialist Community mass movement, which swept to power, winning all available seats in the parliamentary elections of 1955, 1958, 1962, and 1966. In June 1960, following the death of his father, Sihanouk was elected head of state.

During the Vietnam War (1954–75), Sihanouk, although critical of the United States' military involvement in Indo-China, sought to maintain Cambodia's neutrality from the surrounding struggle. This became increasingly difficult during the later 1960s. Domestically the Sihanouk regime had to face a mounting communist insurgency, led by the Khmer Rouge.

With the economy deteriorating, Sihanouk was overthrown in March 1970, while absent abroad, in a bloodless right-wing coup, led by the pro-American prime minister, Lieutenant General, later Marshal, Lon Nol. Sihanouk continued to serve as prime minister, between 1971 and 1972, before becoming president of what was termed, from October 1970, the new Khmer Republic. The political system had been reconstituted on presidential executive lines, following the promulgation, in April 1972, of a constitution modelled on that of France's Fifth (Gaullist) Republic. Lon Nol's regime was opposed, however, by the exiled Prince Sihanouk, now head of the exiled, Beijing-based, Royal Government of National Union of Cambodia (GRUNC), and by the communist Khmer Rouge, backed by North Vietnam and China. The two joined together to form the National United Front of Cambodia (FUNC).

A bitter civil war developed and, despite receiving substantial military aid from the United States during its early stages, the Lon Nol government lost control of rural and then urban areas and was toppled in April 1975. The country was renamed Kampuchea and Prince Sihanouk was appointed head of state.

The Khmer Rouge proceeded to ruthlessly introduce an extreme Maoist communist program, involving the abolition of money and markets, the forced removal of urban groups into the countryside, and agricultural collectivization, at a breakneck speed. This resulted in the death of 1–3 million people from famine, disease, and maltreatment. 'Reactionary' political opponents were also summarily executed. A new constitution was promulgated in January 1976, which renamed the state 'Democratic Kampuchea', removed Prince Sihanouk from power, appointed Khieu Samphan, the former deputy prime minister, as president and placed the CPK, led by its notorious guerrilla leader, Pol Pot, in effective political control.

The new Khmer Rouge regime severed all Western contacts and developed close 'clientist' links with China. As a consequence, it fell out with its former sponsors, Vietnam and the Soviet Union, prompting Vietnam to launch raids into the country during 1977–78, culminating in a full-scale invasion in December 1978. The Vietnamese successfully overthrew Pol Pot, who enjoyed little popular support, in January 1979, and put into power a pro-Vietnamese puppet government, led by Heng Samrin, a commander of the Khmer Rouge fourth division until 1978. He was now head of the Kampuchean National United Front for National Salvation (KNUFNS), which had been newly constituted in December 1978, and was later renamed KUFNCD, in 1981. It was an amalgam of anti-Pol Pot Kampuchean communists. A new People's Republic of Kampuchea was proclaimed.

Initially, Heng Samrin ruled as president of an emergency People's Revolutionary Council, sharing effective power with the CPK (later KPRP) general secretary, Pen Sovann, an ex-Khmer Viet Minh who had lived in Vietnam between 1954 and 1979. In December 1981, however, Sovann, who was viewed by Vietnam as too gradualist in his approach, pro-Soviet in his outlook, and autocratic in his governing style, was stripped of all his party and state post and Heng became the new KPRP leader and controlling personality. During the same year a constitution was framed and a National Assembly elected, in an effort to legitimize the regime.

During its first year in power the Heng government was faced with fierce guerrilla resistance by Pol Pot forces based in jungle hideouts in the west of the country, near the border with Thailand, resulting in the flight of more than 300,000 Cambodians to border refugee camps in Thailand. This resistance movement broadened in June 1982, with the formation, in Kuala Lumpur, in Malaysia, of a broad anti-Vietnamese coalition and Democratic Kampuchea government in exile. This comprised Prince Sihanouk, then living in North Korea, as president, Khieu Samphan, the political leader of the Khmer Rouge, as vice president and Sonn Sann, an ex-premier and contemporary leader of the noncommunist KPNLF, as prime minister. The coalition received sympathetic support from the countries of ASEAN, Indonesia, Malaysia, the Philippines, Singapore, and Thailand, as well as from China, and was officially recognized by both the United States and United Nations as the legitimate government of the country. Militarily, however, the coalition was weak. Its 60,000 troops, 60% of whom were members of the Khmer Rouge, were outnumbered by the 170,000 Vietnamese supporting the Heng Samrin government, and its base camps were repeatedly overrun during the annual dry season December/April offensives. The cumulative cost to Vietnam was more than 30,000 of its soldiers' lives.

The Heng Samrin administration at first pursued a relatively liberal policy program, dismantling the Khmer Rouge-established commune structure and adopting a relaxed attitude towards the Buddhist religion, in an effort to secure popular support. Soon, however, these policies were reversed, communes were re-established and a 'Vietnamization' of the country was launched, with more than 500,000 Vietnamese emigrating to southeastern Kampuchea. From 1985, however, following the installation as prime minister of Hun Sen, and under pressure from the reformist new administration of Mikhail Gorbachev in the Soviet Union, a more flexible and pragmatic, mixed economy, policy approach was pursued and indigenous Khmers were inducted into the regime and a Khmer cultural revival encouraged.

Hopes of a political settlement to the 'Cambodian issue' also began to improve from 1985, helped by the formal retirement of the reviled Pol Pot as Khmer Rouge military leader in August 1985, although he remained an influential background figure, and by the beginning of a phased withdrawal of Vietnamese troops. The reconciliation process moved a step further in December 1987 and January 1988, when Hun Sen and Prince Norodom Sihanouk met for a series of talks near Paris. These events were followed, in June 1988, by the withdrawal of 50,000, or half, of the remaining Vietnamese troops within Cambodia, including the high command. The remainder were pulled out in September 1989. Two years of tortuous negotiations followed between the Cambodian government and the resistance coalition. Major concessions were proffered by the Heng Samrin regime, including a promise to liberalize the economy, re-establish Buddhism as the state religion, and alter the country's official designation from the PRK to the ideologically neutral State of Cambodia (SOC).

2. Peace in Paris to the present

A breakthrough was eventually achieved on 23 October 1991, when the country's four warring factions, and 18 interested countries, signed a peace agreement in Paris to end the 13-year-old civil war. Under its terms, at a cost of US $2 billion, a 22,000-strong civilian and military UN Transitional Authority in Cambodia (UNTAC) was established to administer the country in conjunction with an all-party Supreme National Council (SNC) until a new legislature was elected in 1993. The UNTAC's task was to enforce a ceasefire, oversee the demobilization of 70% of each contending faction's armed forces, maintain law and order, run the main ministries, and organize free and fair elections. Meanwhile, the SNC represented the country externally, occupying Cambodia's UN seat, and concentrated on reviving the moribund economy and organizing the resettlement of 200,000 internally displaced citizens and 380,000 Cambodians living in border refugee camps. The latter was completed by March 1993.

Prince Norodom Sihanouk returned to Phnom Penh on 23 November 1991 and resumed residence in his renovated former royal palace as the SOC's legitimate head of state. He worked alongside Hun Sen, who remained as prime minister. The Khmer Rouge also returned, but its leader, Khieu Samphan, was forced to swiftly fly back to Thailand, after being attacked by a lynching mob. In January 1992 hundreds of political prisoners were released and freedom of speech and party formation was restored. In March 1993 the head of UNTAC, the Japanese diplomat, Yasushi Akashi, took up the reins in Phnom Penh. His role was to oversee the implementation of the Paris peace agreement and the transition to democracy.

During 1992 there was mounting concern over ceasefire violations and, in particular, the Khmer Rouge refusal to disarm in accordance with the UN plan. Nevertheless, national elections to a new Constituent Assembly were successfully held in May 1993, resulting in a narrow victory for Prince Norodom Sihanouk's FUNCINPEC, which, with 42% of the vote, won 58 of its 120 seats; Hun Sen's Cambodian People's Party (CPP) won 51 seats and 37% of the vote.

In July 1993 a Provisional National Government of Cambodia (PNGC) was formed, which was a coalition embracing the four parties which had secured the election of deputies in the general election. At its heart was an alliance between FUNCINPEC and the excommunist CPP, with Prince Norodom Sihanouk's son, Prince Norodom Ranariddh, being appointed first prime minister, and the outgoing premier, Hun Sen, second prime minister. The Constituent Assembly promulgated a new liberal-democratic pluralistic constitution in September 1993, which provided for a limited monarchy sharing power with parliament. The Constituent Assembly became automatically transformed into a National Assembly with full legislative powers and a Throne Council elected Norodom Sihanouk as king in October 1993. In the same month, the PNGC was renamed the Royal Government of Cambodia (RGC). During 1994 the RGC foiled an attempted coup by Norodom Chakrapong, a son of King Norodom Sihanouk, and General Sin Song, both members of the CPP, and launched offensives against the Khmer Rouge, who controlled parts of the countryside in the west and north, adjoining Thailand. The Khmer Rouge, now officially outlawed, responded by announcing, in July 1994, the formation of a 'provisional government of national union and national salvation' based in the northern province of Prey Vihear. However, the Khmer Rouge had been reduced to a hard core of between 5,000 and 10,000 troops, after an estimated 7,000 of its fighters, responding to a government amnesty, had surrendered during 1994. The continuing civil war, combined with a serious failure of the rice crop in 1994, caused hardship in rural areas, despite annual GDP growth averaging 5% between 1993 and 1995 and significant foreign aid inflows being received. During 1995 there was Western concern that the FUNCINPEC regime was becoming increasingly authoritarian. This was evidenced by attempts to curb opposition voices in the press, with a Press Law being passed in July 1995, and by the expulsion from parliament and FUNCINPEC, in June 1995, of Sam Rainsy, finance minister until October 1994, who had accused leading members of the government of corruption. Rainsy subsequently formed the Khmer Nation Party (KNP), in November 1995, but it was swiftly banned. In October 1995 Prince Norodom Sirivudh, a half-brother of King Sihanouk and a former foreign minister and general-secretary of FUNCINPEC, who was critical of cooperation with the CPP, was expelled from the National Assembly and subsequently exiled, on charges of allegedly plotting against the government. During 1996–97 the Khmer Rouge began to fracture, heightening tensions within the CPP-FUNCINPEC coalition, as each party attempted to attract defecting troops to strengthen their position. An initial split occurred in August 1996 when the Khmer's deputy leader, Ieng Sary, and two divisions, controlling the strongholds of Pailin and Malai, brokered peace with the Cambodian government, on condition that they were allowed to retain control over their localities, were granted amnesties, and were allowed to form a new political organization, the Democratic National United Movement (DNUM). By February 1997, following the assassination, in November 1996, of Hun Sen's brother-in-law, Kov Samuth, tensions between the CPP and FUNCINPEC had become so strained that localized fighting was reported between their forces in the northwest. Relations worsened when, from April 1997, Hun Sen began to persuade a number of FUNCINPEC deputies to defect to the CPP, thus reducing FUNCINPEC's slim Assembly majority. Prince Ranariddh responded, in June 1997, by brokering an agreement with the Khmer Rouge's 'moderate' leader, Khieu Samphan, in which a political alliance would be formed and the Khmer's more notorious military leaders would go into exile in return for immunity from prosecution. However, Khieu's actions provoked a bloody power-struggle within the Khmer Rouge, which led to the killing of the Khmer's former security chief, Son Sen, on the orders of Pol Pot, and then the latter's capture by the brutal general, Ta Mok. After a 'show trial' on 24 July 1997 at Anlong Veng, the Khmer's jungle headquarters in the northwest, Pol Pot was sentenced to life imprisonment for 'destroying national reconciliation' and he subsequently died in custody, in April 1998. Meanwhile, Ta Mok, in alliance with Khieu Samphan, signed a deal, on 4 July 1997, to end the guerrilla struggle and rejoin the political system. This was the trigger for second prime minister Hun Sen, with firm control over the army and state bureaucracy, to launch, on 5–6 July 1997, a decisive coup. With Prince Ranariddh absent in Thailand, FUNCINPEC's troops were attacked and routed in Phnom Penh, at the cost of more than 40 lives. Foreign minister, Ung Huot, was installed as first prime minister, but real power resided with Hun Sen. This putsch was denounced by the ailing King Sihanouk, who was in Beijing undergoing medical treatment, and by the international community; leading to the freezing of aid and a decision by ASEAN to postpone indefinitely Cambodia's admission to the grouping, which had been planned for later in the month. Meanwhile, the exiled Prince Ranariddh pledged to start a new guerrilla war, in alliance with the Khmer Rouge. However, he was to receive little firm international help and, with 140,000-troops under his control, Hun Sen soon secured a succession of victories against the much smaller resistance movement, based in west and northwestern Cambodia, in a renewed conflict which led to the flight of more than 75,000 refugees to Thailand. Despite these military successes, Hun Sen was anxious to win back international legitimacy and – with the economy deteriorating – financial aid. Thus, in February 1998, he accepted a Japanese-brokered peace plan. It comprised the trial in absentia of Ranariddh on charges of smuggling arms and colluding with Khmer Rouge, followed, after his sentencing, by his pardoning by the king, enabling Ranariddh to return and participate in a new general election. In addition, FUNCINPEC agreed to cut all ties with the Khmer Rouge and begin an immediate ceasefire with government forces. Following this agreement, the government's military offensive intensified against the Khmer Rouge, which, with fewer than 2,000 troops under Ta Mok's leadership, had been thoroughly marginalized. However, while a general election was held, as planned, in July 1998, it failed to produce either a decisive or an accepted outcome. Instead, official figures showed a narrow victory for the CPP, but this was fiercely disputed by FUNCINPEC and Sam Rainsy's KNP, who claimed that there had been ballot-rigging and vote buying. During August 1998 large street protests were held by the opposition's supporters, demanding a recount, and a new government could not be formed. Under the terms of the constitution, a fresh government needed backing from two-thirds of the Assembly, but FUNCINPEC and the KNP refused to enter into a new coalition.

In November 1998 the four-month long political deadlock was resolved when a new coalition government was formed, with Hun Sen (CPP) as sole prime minister and Prince Norodom Ranariddh (Funcinpec) as president of the National Assembly. Chea Sim, the CPP's chairman and the former chairman of the National Assembly, was made chairman of a new upper house, the Senate, whose members were appointed by King Norodom Sihanouk. FUNCINPEC agreed to reintegrate its troops into the government army and in December 1998, Cambodia was allowed to re-occupy its UN seat, which had been vacant for more than a year.

In March 1999 Ta Mok, the last remaining senior Khmer Rouge leader at large, was arrested. It was planned that he, along with other Khmer Rouge figures, would stand trial before a 'truth and reconciliation commission', on the South African model, and would face charges of genocide.The new Senate was created in March 1999 and in May 1999 Cambodia was admitted into ASEAN.

CHINA

People's Republic of China
Zhonghua Renmin Gonghe Guo

Capital: Beijing (Peking)

Social and economic data

Area: 9,571,300 sq km*/3,695,498 sq miles
Population: 1,215,153,000** ***
Pop. density per sq km/sq mi: 127/329***
Urban population: 28%****
Literacy rate: 76%****
GDP: $887,200 million** ***; per-capita GDP: $730** ***
Government defense spending (% of GDP): 5.7%***
Currency: yuan or renminbi (people's currency)
Economy type: low income
Labor force in agriculture: 60%****
Unemployment rate: 2.8%***

* Two-thirds mountain or desert, with only 15% of the country's area being arable.
** Includes Hong Kong.
*** 1995.
**** 1992.

Head of state

President Jiang Zemin, since 1993

Head of government

Prime Minister Zhu Rongji, since 1998

Ethnic composition

Ninety-four per cent of the population are Han Chinese, the remainder being Zhuang, Uygur, Hui (Muslims), Yi, Tibetan, Miao, Manchu, Mongol, Buyi, or Korean. There are numerous lesser nationalities, in 55 groups, numbering around 70 million. The national minorities mainly reside in border regions. The principal language is Northern Chinese (Mandarin), with local dialects spoken in the south and southeast, notably Cantonese and Wu. The Tibetans, Uygurs, Mongols, and other minorities have their own languages.

Religions

Confucianism and Daoism (Taoism), practised by around 20% of the population, and Buddhism, by 15%, are the principal traditional religions, with Muslim, 20 million, and Christian, 10 million, minorities. The Uygur (Wei Wuer) and Hui peoples are the main followers of Islam, which was introduced into China in AD 651. Since 1990 armed Muslim separatists have been active in Xinjiang Uygur autonomous region. The Christians, evenly divided between Roman Catholics and Protestants, chiefly live on the coast.

Political features

State type: communist
Date of state formation: 2nd century BC (1949*)

Political structure: unitary
Executive: communist
Assembly: one-chamber
Party structure: one-party
Human rights rating: 21%
International affiliations: AfDB, APEC, AsDB, ESCAP, IAEA, IBRD, IMF, IWC, LORCS, NAM (observer), UN Security Council (permanent member)

* Present boundaries and communist regime.

Local and regional government

Below the 22 provinces (*sheng*), there are three municipalities, Beijing, Shanghai, and Tianjin, and five autonomous regions, Xizang (Tibet), Nei Monggol (Inner Mongolia), Xinjiang Uygur, Ningxia Hui, and Guangxi Zhuang. Within these are 286 municipalities, 552 rural districts, under city administration, and 2,080 rural counties (*xian*). Local People's Congresses and People's Governments operate at the township and county levels. Multiple, CCP-approved, candidacies were the norm in recent elections. Members are elected directly for three-year terms at the county level and below, and indirectly, by council members, for five-year terms to congresses above. Additionally, since July 1997, Hong Kong has formed a sovereign part of China, with the status of a Special Administrative Region.

Political system

Under its current constitution, the fourth since 1949, which was adopted in December 1982 and amended in 1993, superseding earlier 1954, 1975, and 1978 documents, China, despite its size, is a unitary state. The nation is divided, for administrative purposes, into 22 provinces, five autonomous regions, including Tibet (Xizang), and four municipalities, Beijing, Shanghai, Chongqing, and Tianjin. Each enjoys policy-making discretion in a number of defined areas, exercised by elected Local People's Congresses and Governments.

Ultimate authority resides, however, in a single-chamber assembly, the National People's Congress (NPC: Quanghuo Renmin Diabiao Dahui). The NPC is composed of 2,979 members, indirectly elected every five years through a tiered system of Local People's Congresses. At their lower levels, members of Local People's Congresses are directly elected through universal adult suffrage in constituency contests which involve a measure of competition.

The NPC, which is described in the 1982 constitution as the 'highest organ of state power', meets in full session once a year, for two weeks, electing a permanent, 134-member Standing Committee to assume its functions between sittings. This Standing Committee is dominated by an inner body comprising a chairperson, Li Peng since 1998, and 19 vice chairpersons. Meeting in session twice per month, the Standing Committee directs the work of the NPC's six functional 'Specialized Committees': finance and economic affairs; nationalities; education, science, culture and public health; foreign affairs; legal affairs; and overseas Chinese affairs. It also drafts bills and resolutions. It operates as a 'substitute parliament', interpreting the constitution and current laws, issuing decrees, overseeing the work of lower level governments, and appointing and dismissing ministers and officials.

In addition, for a five-year term, the NPC elects a state president and vice president, a State Central Military Commission, to supervise the work of the army, and leading members of the judiciary. The functions of the state president, who must be at least 45 years of age and who is restricted to two terms in office, are primarily ceremonial.

Executive administration is carried out by a State Council or national cabinet of approximately 40 members, which is headed by a prime minister and which includes vice premiers, departmental ministers, state councillors, and the auditor-general, secretary-general, and governor of the Bank of China. The State Council is 'appointed' by and accountable to the NPC and its Standing Committee. It has the task of directing and overseeing the work of government departments, commissions and local bodies, enacting administrative regulations, drawing up and implementing the economic plan and annual budget, and submitting drafts to the NPC's Standing Committee. A ten-member inner cabinet, consisting of the prime minister, four vice premiers and five state councillors, meets regularly to decide on day-to-day matters. Membership of this body is limited to two five-year terms.

The directing force in the People's Republic of China is, however, the Chinese Communist Party (CCP), headed by its general secretary, Jiang Zemin. The CCP is controlled by a governing Politburo of some 22 members, which has a seven-member inner Standing Committee, comprising the state president, prime minister, a vice premier, chairperson of the NPC Standing Committee, two members of the CCP secretariat, and chairperson of the CPPCC.

During recent years there has been both increased democratization and decentralization in the governmental process. The members of the new NPC's Standing Committee, for example, were elected in a purportedly competitive manner, in March 1988. Votes registered against candidates were recorded for the first time, and NPC deputies were allowed to play a more prominent and independent role in policy discussions. Since 1993 voting in the NPC has been secret. Additionally, an effort has been made to more clearly demarcate party and state spheres of responsibility, with the day-to-day interference of local party committees over state decision-taking being substantially reduced.

Also, as part of a revivified, broad front, policy formulating process, the Chinese People's Political Consultative Conference (CPPCC) has been reactivated since 1978. The CPPCC is a broadly based appointed body which originally operated between 1949 and 1954. Chaired since 1993 by CCP Politburo member Li Ruihuan, it includes intellectuals, overseas Chinese, and 'democratic party' representatives. It now convenes concurrently with the NPC so as to provide an additional advisory voice.

Despite these substantive structural changes, ultimate power in the Chinese polity continues to reside at the uppermost level of the factionalized CCP. The party machine continues to vet nominations in state election contests and control state appointments, according to the 'nomenklatura' principle.

Political parties

The ruling Chinese Communist Party (CCP: Zhongguo Gongchan Dang) was founded in July 1921 at the French concession of Shanghai by a group of intellectuals, led by Chen Duxiu, who was its leader between 1921 and 1927, and Li Lisan, leader from 1927 to 1930. They had been strongly influenced by the 1917 Russian Revolution and by the theoretical writings of Marx, Engels, and Lenin. Soon afterwards, in June 1922, a separate overseas branch, the Young Communist Party (YCP), was formed in Paris by a group of Chinese students, including Zhou Enlai and Deng Xiaoping, who had been sent abroad on a 'work and study' scheme.

The Shanghai-based CCP worked closely with the Moscow-based Communist International (Comintern), seeking to foment urban worker revolutions in the country's seaboard cities during the early 1920s. These proved, however, to be unsuccessful. The party, following Comintern orders, also allied itself closely, during the mid-1920s, with the larger and more popular nationalist (Kuomintang: KMT) movement, led successively by Dr Sun Yat-sen and General Chiang Kai-shek. They were duped, however, by the anticommunist Chiang, in April 1927, when the CCP's Shanghai cell was brutally purged, and its few surviving members were forced underground.

Following the failure of the urban revolution approach, the party's rural wing, led by the charismatic self-taught Marxist, Mao Zedong, gained the ascendancy. Mao, who had been a founder member of the CCP in Shanghai, in 1921, began to construct a unique Third World brand of communism, based on an alliance with the peasantry and the use of antigovernment guerrilla tactics. He established a rural soviet, or 'workers' republic', in Jiangxi province during the late 1920s and early 1930s, and assumed leadership of the 0.3 million-member CCP, with the support of Zhou Enlai's pragmatic 'Paris wing', at the Zunyi conference of May 1935. All this happened in the midst of the 'Long March' of 1934–35. The Maoist brand of rural-based revolution was further refined during the party's period at Yanan, from 1936, and eventually proved successful in overcoming Chiang Kai-shek's KMT forces, in 1948–49.

In the new People's Republic of China, politics after 1949 were to be characterized by periodic struggles between the different personality- and policy-based factions that had been apparent within the CCP since the later 1920s. At the head of the party's 'orthodox', pro-Soviet, faction stood Liu Shaoqi, gaining the ascendancy during the early 1950s and between 1962 and 1965, and pursuing an urban-industrial-orientated and incentives-based development strategy. In stark opposition stood Mao Zedong, predominant between 1957 and 1961 and between 1966 and 1973. He sought to establish a unique 'Sinified' model of socialism, based on parallel progress in both the rural and urban spheres, the maintenance of close and regular contact between party members and the general population, which he called the 'mass line', and on ideological, as well as economic, transformation.

Finally, and in some respects intermediate between the 'right' and 'left' factions, stood the eclectic Paris 'work-study' wing, led initially by the adroit Zhou Enlai, and subsequently by the more innovative and risk-taking Deng Xiaoping. This wing, apart from a break between 1976 and 1978, has generally dominated policy-making in the People's Republic since 1973, seeking to build a new 'socialism with Chinese characteristics', in which market mechanisms are given a prominent role.

The present CCP is organized, parallel to the state government hierachy, on pyramidal lines, based on a hierarchy of elected congresses and committees which function from the village and factory, or 'basic', level upwards and follow orders from above, in accordance with the tenets of Leninist 'democratic centralism'. A 2,048-member National Party Congress,with five-year terms, the most recent (15th) being held in September 1997, elects a Central Committee of approximately 344 members.

This Committee, 193 of whose members have full voting powers, meets at least once a year and 'elects' a smaller Politburo of some 22 members and a seven-member Secretariat. The two bodies exercise ultimate day-to-day control over the party and frame longer-term state and party policy goals.

The Politburo convenes weekly and is the single most significant political body in China. It is dominated by an inner Standing Committee, headed by the CCP's general secretary. Following rule changes, which were adopted at the 13th National Party Congress in October – November 1987, the Standing Committee has formally been given power to nominate the members of the Secretariat. More generally, in recent years competitive inner party democracy and discussion have been encouraged, particularly at the lower levels.

Other senior CCP bodies include the Central Military Commission (CMC), which, headed by Jiang Zemin, maintains party control over the armed forces.

In 1997 membership of the CCP stood at 58 million, a figure which corresponded to 4.8% of the total population. This constituted an advance of 107% on the 1973 total of 28 million and of 241% on the 1961 figure of 17 million. Throughout this period, however, there have been recurrent purges of both 'ultra-Maoist' and 'ultra-rightist' elements.

Over the past few years the stress of the Deng and Jiang administrations has been on the recruitment of well qualified and educated technocrats, able to manage effectively at the local level, as more and more governmental responsibilities are decentralized. However, despite this recruitment bias, fewer than 5% of party members can currently boast a higher education, while more than 50% are illiterate or have been educated only to primary school level.

Closely linked to the CCP is the Young Communist League (YCL), a youth wing for citizens aged between 15 and 25. This has a membership of 56 million. Eight minor 'democratic parties' are now allowed to operate. They include the China Association for Promoting Democracy, which was established in 1945, the China Democratic League, dating from 1941, the China Democratic National Construction Association, which was formed in 1945, the China Zhi Gong Dang, founded in 1925, the Chinese Peasants' and Workers' Democratic Party, which was established in 1947, the Kuomintang Revolutionary Committee, dating from 1948, the Jiu San (3rd September) Society, which originated in 1946, and the Taiwan Democratic Self-Government League, which dates from 1947. Orientated primarily towards bourgeois and intelligentsia groups, these bodies work in alliance with the CCP and are accorded representation in the NPC and on its Standing Committee.

Political leaders since 1970*

1949–76 Mao Zedong (CCP), 1976–81 Hua Guofeng (CCP), 1981–87 Hu Yaobang (CCP), 1987–89 Zhao Ziyang (CCP), 1989– Jiang Zemin (CCP), [1978–97 Deng Xiaoping (CCP)]**

* Communist Party leaders.
** Paramount national leader.

Latest elections

The most recent elections to the (ninth) NPC were held in January – March 1998, taking the form, as usual, of indirect elections by provincial, municipal, and autonomous region level People's Congress and PLA units. There was an element of competition in some constituencies, with more candidates standing than the number of seats available.

Political history

1. Beginnings to 1971

Chinese civilization is believed to date from the Xia dynasty era, 2200–1700 BC, during which period a relatively sophisticated bronze age state, utilizing irrigation and the written word, was established, in the Shaanxi-Henan region of central China. During the Zhou (Chou) dynasty, 1122–249 BC, the great philosophers Confucius (551–479 BC) and Lao Zi (6th century BC) lived. Lao Zi was the founder of Taoism and formulated a distinctive, new cultural-ethical system. Later, during the Qin, 221–207 BC, and Han, 206 BC–220 AD, dynasties, the country's warring states were finally unified and brought under central direction. Buddhism was introduced from India in AD 67 and flourished during the Sui and Tang dynasties, between the 6th and 8th centuries AD.

A Confucianist-educated 'mandarin' bureaucracy was placed in charge of state affairs, with its members, from the Tang dynasty, 618–907 AD, onwards, being recruited through a competitive and open system of public examinations. This scholar gentry elite, in conjunction with a 'divine' emperor and powerful regional potentates, provided a stable political framework within which impressive technical and economic advances were achieved. Thus, during the Song, 960–1279, Ming, 1368–1644, and, early Manchu Qing, 1644–1911, dynasties, China became established at the forefront of world civilization.

During the early Qing era, Chinese sovereignty was extended over the three northeastern provinces of Heilongjiang, Jilin, and Liaoning, commonly designated together as Manchuria, as well as the western provinces of Xinjiang, Xizang (Tibet), Qinghai, and Nei Monggol (Inner Mongolia). This represented the apogee of the Imperial system. Thereafter, during the later Qing period, mounting economic difficulties, resulting from overpopulation, technological stagnation, and the growing seaboard intrusion of the expansionary European powers and Japan, began to dissever the fragile bonds which had held together the Manchu polity.

In the wake of China's ignominious defeat at the hands of Japan in 1895 and the territorial concessions which were thereafter granted to foreign powers, popular nationalist sentiment grew, culminating in the antiforeigner Boxer Rebellion of 1900. A decade later, in 1911–12, regional gentry and Western-trained New Model Army leaders combined to overthrow the infant Manchu emperor Pu-Yi (1906–67), in a 'Republican Revolution'. A parliamentary regime, headed by the Western-educated, Cantonese 'Christian socialist', Dr Sun Yat-Sen (1866–1925), was, at first, established. This was replaced, in 1912, by the presidentialist rule of the northern-based military commander, Yuan Shikai (1859–1916). However, following Yuan's death in 1916, the new republican political system began to be torn apart, and power was increasingly devolved to regional military commanders. Eventually, internal civil war broke out between militarists and Dr Sun's Republicans (Nationalist Party: KMT), with the newly formed Chinese Communist Party (CCP) joining the fray in tactical alliance with the KMT. There began a destructive decade, which became known as the 'Warlord Period', 1916–26.

In northern and central China order was restored in 1928 by the Japanese-trained KMT leader, General Chiang Kai-shek (1887–1975), who had moved decisively both against his erstwhile CCP allies, in the Shanghai putsch of April 1927, and against the warlords of central and northern China, in the 'northern expedition' of 1926–28.

Chiang Kai-shek proceeded to establish a rightist, quasi-fascist, regime, founded on a close alliance with landlord, business, and industrialist elite groups, the propagation of populist nationalism, the building-up of a modern, substantial, German-trained army, and new infrastructural, predominantly railway, investment. The nationalist regime faced, however, internal guerrilla opposition from the remnant forces of the CCP, now led by the Hunanese 'middle peasant', Mao Zedong (Mao Tse-tung; 1893–1976). Mao's forces moved north along a 6,000-mile zigzag course from Jiangxi province to isolated Shaanxi, in the 'Long March' of 1934–35, to establish a firm rural base at Yanan.

In addition, Chiang's regime faced the external threat of Japan, which forcibly annexed Manchuria (Dongbei) in September 1931, before attacking Beijing and invading northern China in 1937. To meet this challenge, a KMT – CCP truce was eventually declared and an anti-Japanese pact signed. However, the Chinese forces were rapidly overwhelmed by the Japanese, the KMT being forced into refuge in the remote western province of Sichuan, while the CCP retired to rural fastnesses in the north and center of the country, from where they harassed the urban-based Japanese in classic guerrilla fashion.

During the war years the CCP established themselves as popular 'freedom fighters' against a brutal Japanese regime, building up substantial support by their just treatment of the local population and the implementation of populist land reform programs in the areas ('soviets') under their charge. By the early 1940s much of the hinterland of north central China was effectively controlled by the CCP. This left the communists in a strong position when the Japanese finally withdrew, in August 1945.

A civil war between Chiang Kai-shek's US-backed KMT forces and the CCP's Red Army (People's Liberation Army: PLA) ensued between 1946 and 1949. Using mobile tactics, the PLA, led by Zhu De (Chu Teh; 1886–1976), emerged triumphant, cutting Chiang's supply lines before decisively defeating his 550,000-strong army at the battle of Huai-Hai, in December 1948. Chiang Kai-shek and his nationalist supporters thereafter retreated to the island province of Taiwan, establishing a KMT regime which they claimed to still be the legitimate government of all China. In reality, however, *de facto* power on the mainland passed to the communists, where a new People's Republic of China (PRC) was proclaimed by Mao Zedong in Beijing on 1 October 1949.

The early years of the new CCP regime were, following more than a decade of constant warfare, consumed with the task of economic and political reconstruction. A centralized Soviet-style constitution was adopted, in September 1954; leading 'commanding-height' industries were nationalized; a system of central planning on a five-year basis was instituted, from 1953; a program of moderate, anti-gentry land reform was introduced; and a major party recruitment drive was launched. This increased CCP membership from 4.5 million to 10.8 million between 1949 and 1956.

The general tone of the early 'post-liberation' years was one of consensual, 'united-front' cooperation, with small-scale private enterprise being tolerated and the cooperation of white collar intelligentsia and technocrat groups sought. Less tolerance was, however, shown towards the traditionally pro-KMT landed elite. In addition to being dispossessed of their holdings, members of this group were, between 1949 and 1953, publicly tried and forced to repent for past misdeeds. Two to four million of those who refused were publicly executed.

During its first decade in power, the CCP administration maintained close links with the Soviet Union, which provided the country with substantial economic and technical aid. A compelling factor behind this close relationship was the active hostility which the infant CCP regime faced from the United States. Thus, during the Korean War of 1950–53, the PLA clashed with American forces, fighting under the United Nations' flag, to defend the neighboring North Korean communist regime. As a result, in 1954, the United States effected a Mutual Security Treaty with the Taiwan-based KMT, recognizing it as the legitimate government of China.

Reflecting these close Soviet ties, the CCP leadership, in its first five-year plan of 1953–57, embarked on a heavy industrialization, and material incentives-based, development strategy, which was substantially modelled on the USSR's Stalinist prototype. Concern grew, however, with the widening of social, regional, and sectoral income and growth differentials which resulted from the implementation of this plan. In 1958, under the charismatic leadership of state president and CCP chairman, Mao Zedong, China suddenly shifted course, instituting a radical new policy program, which Mao called the 'Great Leap Forward'.

Founded on the slogan, 'walking on two legs', this new program sought to achieve rapid and simultaneous growth in both food and manufacturing output, by the collectivization of land and the formation of large new, self-sufficient, agricultural and industrial communes. As well as functioning as cooperative production units, these communes were designed to act as residential units for political and ideological indoctrination, the aim being to remould attitudes and create a new breed of 'complete communists'. This new generation would serve as the progenitors of a new, classless and egalitarian 'true communist' society.

In practice, despite its lofty goals, the 'Great Leap' experiment proved to be over-ambitious and was impossible to coordinate. It was, moreover, strongly opposed by ordinary peasants who were used to more individualistic forms of farming and living. Many cultivators resisted the collectivization drive or only half-heartedly cooperated. As a consequence, with floods and famine ravaging the country, the distribution system falling into chaos and supply bottlenecks developing, more than 20 million died between 1959 and 1962. Output, both in the agricultural and industrial sectors, following an initial surge, dipped sharply during these years.

The 'Great Leap' departure also had serious repercussions for China's external relations, serving as the last straw which prompted the Soviet Union's increasingly estranged new Khrushchev leadership to formally break off relations. The Soviet Union had been subject to mounting criticisms from Mao for its 'hegemonistic' and 'revisionist' policy approach and the severing of diplomatic ties was accompanied by the withdrawal of technical advisers in August 1960.

The failure of the 'Great Leap' experiment served to reduce the influence of Mao between 1962 and 1965. Instead, a successful 'recovery program' was instituted, under the leadership of the CCP first vice chairperson, and new state president, the Moscow-trained Liu Shaoqi (1900–70). This involved the reintroduction of private farming plots and markets, a reduction in the size of communes, and a restoration of income differentials and material incentives. Mao soon struck back, however, against what he termed a return to the 'capitalist road', and against the recrudescence of a new, bureaucratic governing elite, by launching the 'Great Proletarian Cultural Revolution' (GPCR) between 1966 and 1969.

The GPCR was a broad-front 'rectification campaign' directed against 'rightist' elements in the CCP, with the aim of re-establishing the supremacy of ideology (Maoism) over economics, or 'putting politics in command', of re-emphasizing egalitarian communist virtues and of bringing to the fore a new, and more radical, leadership generation. During the campaign, Mao, supported by the PLA chief, Lin Biao (1908–71), and the Shanghai-based 'Gang of Four', encouraged student

(Red Guard) demonstrations against incumbent party and government leaders. The 'Gang of Four' was a grouping comprising Mao's wife, Jiang Qing (1914–91), the radical intellectuals, Zhang Chunqiao and Yao Wenyuan, and the former millworker, Wang Hongwen. The chief targets were Liu Shaoqi, who was dismissed in October 1968 and died in prison in 1969, Deng Xiaoping (1904–97), head of the CCP Secretariat, and Peng Zhen (1902–97), mayor of Beijing. Each of them was forced out of office and publicly disgraced. The campaign grew anarchic, however, during 1967, necessitating direct intervention by the PLA and the dispersal of the Red Guards into the countryside to 'learn from the peasants'.

Traditional government institutions fell into abeyance during the Cultural Revolution and new 'Three-Part Revolutionary Committees', comprising Maoist party officials, trade unionists, and PLA commanders, took over the administration. By 1970, however, Mao, concerned with the mounting public disorder, sided with the long-serving and pragmatic prime minister, Zhou Enlai (Chou En-lai; 1898–1976), leader of the centrist faction within the CPC, and gradually set about restoring order and reconstructing a balanced party-state system. A number of 'ultra-leftists' were ousted during August 1970, and in September 1971 the PLA commander and defense minister, Lin Biao, died en route to Outer Mongolia, after a failed coup attempt.

2. 1972 to the present

During 1972–73 a rehabilitation of purged cadres, including Deng Xiaoping and finance minister, Li Xiannian, commenced, while, overseas, a new policy of détente towards the United States was launched. This reconstruction movement was climaxed by the summoning of the National People's Congress (NPC) for the first time in 11 years, in January 1975, to ratify a new state constitution and approve a new, long-term economic strategy, termed the 'Four Modernizations'. This strategy, involving agriculture, industry, defense, and science and technology, aimed at bringing China on a par with the West by the year 2000.

The reconstruction process was temporarily halted in 1976 when, following the deaths of Zhou Enlai and Mao Zedong, in January and September respectively, a violent succession struggle between the leftist 'Gang of Four', led by Jiang Qing, and moderate 'rightists', grouped around Vice Premier Deng Xiaoping, was unleashed. Deng was forced into hiding by the 'Gang'. However, it was Mao's 'center-left' protégé, Hua Guofeng (b. 1920), who was appointed CCP Chairman in September 1976, having already been selected as prime minister in January 1976.

Hua, in a pre-emptive move, proceeded to arrest the 'Gang', in October 1976, on charges of treason, and held power as a stop-gap leader between 1976 and 1978, implementing Zhou Enlai's 'Four Modernizations' program. His authority was progressively challenged, however, by Deng Xiaoping, who was restored to office in March 1977, following wall-poster campaigns in Beijing. By December 1978, after further popular campaigns, Deng, who enjoyed substantial support among the state bureaucracy and military hierarchy, had gained effective control of the government, establishing a majority in the Politburo.

State and judicial bodies began to meet regularly again, the late Liu Shaoqi was rehabilitated as a party hero and major economic reforms were introduced. These involved the dismantling of the commune system and the introduction of direct farm incentives under a new 'responsibility system', as well as the encouragement of foreign investment in coastal enclave 'Special Economic Zones'.

By June 1981 Deng's paramountcy was assured by the installation of his protégés Hu Yaobang, as CCP chairman, later general secretary, and Zhao Ziyang (b. 1918) as prime minister, in June 1981 and September 1980 respectively. The 'Gang of Four' were sentenced to life imprisonment, Yao Wenyuan receiving 20 years, in January 1981, following a dramatic 'show trial'. A year later, in September 1982, Hua Guofeng was ousted from the Politburo, together with a number of senior colleagues, and in December 1982 a definitive new state constitution was adopted by the NPC. This restored the post of state president, which had been abolished in January 1975, to which office Li Xiannian was elected. The military was placed under firmer party control and a new code of civil rights was introduced.

The new 'Deng administration' took the form of a collective leadership, with Hu Yaobang (1915–89) assuming control of party affairs, Zhao Ziyang overseeing state administration, and Deng Xiaoping, a CCP vice chairman and chairman of the State Central Military Committee (SCMC) and the CCP's Central Military Commission (CMC), the 'power behind the throne', concentrating on the formulation of the longer-term strategy, and maintaining a close eye on the PLA.

The triumvirate proceeded to pursue a three-pronged policy program. The first aim was to streamline the party and state bureaucracies and promote to power new, younger, and better educated technocrats. Second, they sought to curb the influence of the PLA through the retirement of senior commanders and a reduction in manpower numbers from 4.2 million to 3 million. The triumvirate's third priority was for economic modernization, based on the extension of market incentives, 'market socialism', and local autonomy, through the introduction of a new 'open-door' policy to encourage foreign trade and investment.

By 1986 the policies had succeeded in effecting the replacement of half the CCP's provincial-level officers. The new economic reforms met with immediate success in the rural sector, agricultural output more than doubling between 1978 and 1985. They had adverse side effects, however, widening regional and social income differentials and fuelling a wave of 'mass consumerism', thus creating serious balance of payments and inflationary problems. These problems were exacerbated in 1984 when price reform in the urban industrial sector began to be implemented. In the political sphere, the new, pro-Western 'open-door' strategy and liberalization program served to generate, predominantly intelligentsia, demands for fuller internal democratization. These calls culminated in a wave of major student demonstrations which swept across the country in December 1986. As a consequence of his failure to act promptly to check the disturbances, party chief Hu Yaobang was forced to resign in January 1987.

The departure of Hu, Deng Xiaoping's closest associate, appeared to imperil the future of the post-1978 Dengist reform (*gai-ge*) program, as more conservative forces, grouped around the senior figures of the Shanghai-born Politburo member Chen Yun (1905–95) and NPC Standing Committee chairman, Peng Zhen, sought to halt the pace of change and re-establish firm central party control. As part of this strategy, a campaign against what was termed 'bourgeois liberalization', or Western ideas, was launched by the CCP's conservative wing, during the spring of 1987. The more traditional Maoist virtues of frugality and self-reliance were stressed. However, the Dengist 'reform wing' of the CCP held its corner, Zhao Ziyang being temporarily elevated to the positions of both party general secretary and prime minister.

At the CCP's 13th National Congress, held in October 1987, a 'work report' presented by Zhao that described the PRC as still in the 'initial stages of socialism', and thus requiring pragmatic resort to capitalist methods, was accepted. This document stressed the need for continuing reform, including price reform, though at a somewhat more cautious pace; an extension of the 'open-door' strategy; and an enhanced separation between the party and state machines. At the Congress, and during its immediate aftermath, personnel changes were also effected which served to shift the balance on the CCP's Central Committee (CC) and Politburo significantly towards the 'reform faction'. A clutch of young new technocrats and successful mayors were inducted into the Politburo, replacing 'old guard' oppositionist figures, including Chen Yun and Peng Zhen. Deng Xiaoping also retired from both the Politburo and CC, but retained his position as head of the CMC.

However, in November 1987, shortly after the Congress, Li Peng (b. 1928), the Moscow-trained adopted son of Zhou Enlai, replaced Zhao Ziyang as acting prime minister and was formally confirmed in the position when the 7th NPC met for its inaugural session in March 1988. Viewed as a conservative, centralist reformer, this move suggested that the Dengist reform wing had not triumphed completely and that factional and strategy differences still remained at senior party levels. As 1988 progressed economic problems, emanating from the price deregulation strategy, mounted, with supply bottlenecks developing, as a consumer buying spree gained pace, particularly in the booming coastal provinces. The inflation rate rocketed to between 20–30%. This forced a sharp application of the brakes on economic reform, following an emergency CC session held in September, and the introduction of an austerity budget by Li Peng in March 1989.

A month later, following the death of the revered Hu Yaobang, students in Beijing took to the streets in prodemocracy demonstrations. These disturbances spread to provincial cities and gained in strength during May 1989, at the time of the visit to Beijing of the reformist Russian Soviet leader, Mikhail Gorbachev. The government effectively ceded control of the capital for a week to the students, buttressed by workers, as an intense CCP power struggle developed between conservatives, led by the unpopular Li Peng, and 'liberals', aligned to Zhao Ziyang. Li Peng, supported by Deng Xiaoping, gained the immediate upper hand and martial law was proclaimed and troops despatched to subdue the students. The PLA's officers refused, however, to use force against the demonstrators, creating a stalemate situation. However, at the beginning of June 1989, with the protest movement beginning to lose momentum, 27th Army troops, loyal to President Yang Shangkun (1906–98), were sent into Tiananmen Square, in the center of Beijing, to reclaim the capital, brutally shooting dead more than 1,300 unarmed protesters. This action put the hardline Li-Deng-Yang triumvirate in immediate control of the Chinese polity. A month later, Zhao Ziyang was ousted as CCP leader and replaced by the Shanghai party chief, Jiang Zemin (b. 1926). A crackdown against dissidents was launched, thousands being arrested. Martial law continued to be imposed in Beijing until January 1990 and throughout 1990–92 prodemocracy activists were brought to trial and given severe prison sentences.

Deng Xiaoping retired from his last official post in 1990. However, he continued to remain the nation's paramount leader, controlling the direction of change. From 1992, Deng sought again to promote a new phase of economic reform and improved relations with the West. This formed part of an Indonesian-influenced strategy of combining 'market socialism' with political authoritarianism. This Deng sought to underpin through personnel changes at the CCP's 14th Congress, held in October 1992. Elderly 'old guard' conservatives, including President Yang Shangkun, Defense Minister Qin Jiwei, and the economics and organization specialists Yao Yilin (1917–94) and Song Ping, were persuaded to retire from the Politburo. They were supplanted by a clutch of younger, provincial leaders and economic reformers, in their 50s and 60s, notably Zhu Rongji (b. 1928), the former mayor of Shanghai, and Hu Jintao (b. 1942), former party chief in Guizhou province and Tibet. In addition, nearly half the members of the CCP's Central Committee were replaced.

The Chinese economy, after stalling during 1989–90, picked up strongly again from 1991 in response to the continuing, liberalizing reforms. Annual growth averaged, to 1995, officially 12%, although Western specialists have suggested the rate was closer to 8%. During the period since 1980, GDP had quadrupled. However, there were adverse concomitant developments, notably double-digit inflation, a sharp widening in social and regional inequalities in wealth, particularly between the booming coastal regions and the more deprived interior, and the increasing level of urban crime and CCP corruption. In December 1994 and April 1995, Yao Yilin and Chen Yun, two important 'old guard' leaders died and by the summer of 1995 there was increasing concern over the health of Deng Xiaoping. Now in his 90s, and virtually blind and deaf and unable to stand or walk unaided, Deng's influence as 'paramount leader' was nearing an end. This was highlighted by the arrest, on corruption charges, of a number of Deng associates in 1995. Deng's protégé, the CCP leader Jiang Zemin, who also became state president in March 1993, began to build up a power-base within the PLA and brought into the CCP Politburo a 'Shanghai clique' of firm supporters. Consequently, on the death of Deng, in February 1997, there was a smooth succession. In July 1997 Hong Kong returned to Chinese sovereignty and rule, as a Special Administrative Region, and President Jiang declared that China's aim was now for Taiwan to 'rejoin the mainland' under similar terms. Two months, later, at the CCP's 15th Congress, Jiang's commanding, at the head of a new 'collective leadership', was underlined. A clutch of Deng-era leaders were retired and, more surprisingly, Qiao Shi (b. 1924), the chair of the NPC who was viewed as a potential leadership rival to Jiang, was removed from the Central Committee and Politburo. Zhu Rongji, the deputy prime minister, moved to third place in the CCP Politburo. He was a committed economic reformer and also a political liberal, who had defused pro-democracy demonstrations in Shanghai in 1989 without resort to force and was the only member of the party's senior leadership to have been persecuted during the Deng-led 'anti-rightist' campaign of the late 1950s. Before the Congress, Jiang launched a drive against corruption within the party and state apparatus. This led to the expulsion from the party of Chen Xitong, a former leader in Beijing: one of 121,000 to be expelled from the CCP since October 1992. Chen was later (in July 1998) sentenced to 16-years' imprisonment for corruption. In his keynote speech, Jiang pledged continued support for Dengist market-centerd economic reform and declared that, over a three – year period, 370,000 state-owned enterprises would be restructured in preparation for the privatization of many, and the 3-million strong armed forces would be reduced by half a million and be modernized, with the development of well-trained rapid-reaction forces and a high-tech navy.

At the opening session of the new (ninth) NPC in March 1998, Li Peng, as obliged by the constitution, stepped down as prime minister. He became chair of the NPC Standing Committee, replacing Qiao Shi, although 200 of the NPC's 2,979 delegates voted against his nomination. The reformist Zhu Rongji took over as prime minister, while the 'youthful' Hu Jintao, viewed as Jiang's protégé, was elected vice president. The NPC approved proposals comprehensive for a overhaul of the state bureaucracy, entailing scrapping or merging 15 of the government's 40 ministries and departments, creating four new 'super ministries', and the sacking of half of the country's 8 million bureaucrats. The economy continued to grow by more than 8% per annum during 1997, but there was concern at the rising level of urban unemployment, which had reached 4% by September 1997, as well as at crime and labor unrest.

Control over dissent remained tight. In December 1998 Xu Wenli, a renowned dissident, was sentenced to 13 years' imprisonment, after attempting to set up China's first opposition political party, the China Democracy Party. In March 1999 Wang Lixiong, one of the country's best known writers, was arrested, while in July 1999 the Falun Gong, a 70-million member mystical meditation sect formed in 1992, was banned as a threat to political order, following large protests by its devotees in Beijing in April 1999.

In foreign affairs, China's 1960 rift with Khrushchev's Soviet Union over policy differences became irrevocable in 1962 when Russia sided with India during a brief Sino-Indian border war. Relations with the Soviet Union deteriorated further in 1969 after border clashes in the disputed Ussuri river region. China pursued instead a nonaligned, 'Three Worlds', strategy, projecting itself as the spokesperson for Third World nations, although it achieved a nuclear capability by 1964.

During the early 1970s, concerned with Soviet expansionism, a rapprochement with the United States was effected, bringing China's entry into the United Nations, at Taiwan's expense, in 1971, and culminating in the establishment of full Sino-American diplomatic relations in January 1979. Relations with the West remained warm during the 1980s, under the Deng administration, with economic contacts broadening and solutions to the Hong Kong and Macau sovereignty questions being agreed with Britain and Portugal, on the basis of a pragmatic, 'one nation, two systems' formula.

From the mid-1980s, with the coming to power of the reformist leadership of Mikhail Gorbachev in the Soviet Union, Sino-Soviet relations thawed. Helped by progress over the divisive regional problems of Afghanistan and Cambodia and by border demarcation agreements, a heads-of-government-party summit between the two countries eventually took place in May 1989 and in May 1991 Jiang Zemin made the first visit by a CCP leader to Moscow since 1957. An agreement demarcating the eastern section of the Sino-Soviet border was signed. After the collapse of communism in the Soviet Union in the autumn of 1991, China maintained amicable relations with the new Russian republic and, after a peace agreement for Cambodia was signed in Paris in October 1991, its relations with Vietnam were fully normalized in November 1991. In November 1997 an agreement was signed with Russia, marking out the eastern sector of the Chinese border. China's relations with the West received a sharp setback as a result of the government's barbaric actions in June 1989. The United States imposed an embargo on sales of military equipment and scaled back its government contacts. The European Union and Japan also imposed sanctions during 1989–91. With the Chinese vote on the UN Security Council being courted during the 1990–91 'Gulf crisis', relations with the 'developed nations' gradually improved, with visits being paid to China during late 1991 by senior leaders from the United States, United Kingdom, and Japan. Sino-US relations cooled again from 1993, with the accession to power of the Clinton administration in the United States but, helped by the release to the United States, on 'medical parole', of the prominent pro-democracy dissidents, Wei Jingsheng and Wang Dan, during 1997–98 relations were rebuilt. The United States Congress accorded China 'most favored nation' trading status from the mid-1990s, assisting Chinese exports, and in October 1997 President Jiang visited the USA in what was the first Chinese – American summit since 1985.

In November 1998 Jiang Zemin made the first visit by a Chinese head of state to Japan, which expressed its 'deep remorse' for atrocities committed in China during the 1930s and 1940s. However, anti-foreigner sentiment resurfaced in China from May 1999, following NATO's accidental missile strike on the Chinese embassy in Belgrade, killing three Chinese, during the NATO military operation in Yugoslavia.

HONG KONG

Special Administrative Region of China

Capital: Hong Kong

Location

Asia. Hong Kong lies off the south coast of China, 145 km/90 miles southeast of Guangzhou or Canton, and comprises the island of Hong Kong, Stonecutter's Island, the Kowloon Peninsula, and the New Territories, which are part of the Chinese mainland.

Social and economic data

Area: 1,071 sq km/414 sq miles
Population: 6,311,000*
Pop. density per sq km/sq mi: 5,893/15,244*

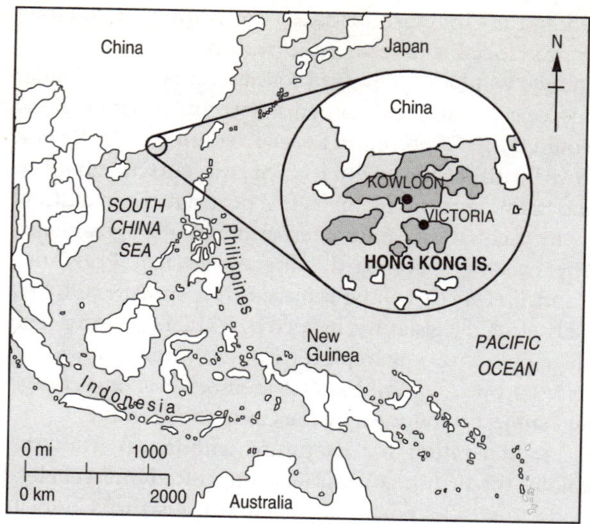

Literacy rate: 90%

Economy type: high income (*c.* $23,000 per capita in 1995)

Currency: Hong Kong dollar

* 1996.

Ethnic composition

Fifty-seven per cent of the population are Hong Kong Chinese and 40% are refugees from the Chinese mainland. English and Cantonese are the official languages.

Religions

The population is predominantly Buddhist, mixed with Confucianism and Daoism, with a 9% Christian minority.

Local government

Hong Kong is divided into the three regions of Hong Kong Island, Kowloon, and New Territories, with 18 districts below, each having its own advisory local board or committee. The first fully democratic local board elections were held in September 1994.

Head of government

Chief Executive Tung Chee-Hwa, since 1997

Political system

Since re-unification with China in July 1997, Hong Kong has been a Special Administrative Region (SAR) of the People's Republic of China, administered by a chief executive, who is accountable to the State Council of China. The chief executive, who must be a Chinese citizen of at least 40 years of age, was selected in December 1996 by a 400-member Selection Committee and serves a five-year term. There is a restriction of two consecutive terms. The chief executive appoints, and chairs, a 15-member Executive Council, which comprises three *ex-officio* members and 11 non-official members. The chief executive also appoints judges and leading officials; makes laws, with the legislature's approval; can veto legislation (but can be overruled by a two-thirds majority); and may dissolve the legislature once in a term. The chief executive does not have any military authority.

During 1997–98 there was a 60-member Provisional Legislative Council (PLC), which was appointed by the December 1996 Selection Committee. It was replaced, in May 1998, by a new 60-member Legislative Council, which comprises 20 directly elected members, through a system of proportional representation, and 40 indirectly elected deputies: ten by an 800-member Election Committee and 30 representatives of 'functional constituencies', selected by professional and business bodies. Under the terms of the SAR's constitution, the Basic Law, the number of directly elected seats in the Legislative Council is to be gradually increased and there is provision for a decision to be taken, in 2007, over whether to move to a wholly directly elected body. The next Legislative Council elections will be held in 2000. In December 1997, 36 Hong Kong delegates were indirectly elected to the Chinese National People's Congress.

Prior to re-unification, Hong Kong was administered by a crown-appointed governor who presided over an unelected Executive Council, or cabinet and chaired a 60-member Legislative Council (Legco). Voting was limited traditionally to 200,000–300,000 professional and skilled people, but from 1995, with the minimum voting age reduced from 21 to 18 years, the number of registered electors was 2.45 million.

Political parties

Political parties developed in Hong Kong during the 1990s as the political system was democratized. The most notable of recent parties has been the pro-reform Democratic Party (DP), led by Martin Lee, and its allies, which was the largest single group in the Legco with 28 seats after the September 1995 elections; the Citizens' Party (CP; estd. 1997), led by Christine Loh; and The Frontier (estd. 1996), led by Emily Lau. The four leading pro-China parties are the pro-business Liberal Party (LP), the Liberal Democratic Foundation (LDF), the Hong Kong Progressive Alliance (HKPA), and the Democratic Alliance for the Betterment of Hong Kong

(DAB), which includes communist members. The Chinese Communist Party and Kuomintang (Chinese Nationalist Party; Taiwan-based) also have organizations in Hong Kong.

Latest elections

The most recent Legislative Council elections were held on 24 May 1998 and resulted in prodemocracy candidates capturing 14 of the 20 directly-elected seats, including nine for the DP, three for Frontier, and one for the CP. The pro-Beijing DAB won five of these seats and independents the other two. Turnout, at 53%, was 17% up on the last elections in 1995. The DP secured a further four seats from the 40 other Legislative Council seats which were indirectly elected, while 18 of the other 36 indirectly deputies were 'independents' and 18 belonged to pro-Beijing parties, including 9 to the LP, four to DAB, and five to HKPA. This meant that prodemocracy parties controlled only 28% of the Council's total seats.

Political history

Hong Kong Island was occupied by Britain in 1841 and ceded by the Chinese government under the terms of the 1842 Treaty of Nanking. The Kowloon Peninsula and Stonecutter's Island were acquired under the Peking (Beijing) Convention of 1860 and the New Territories secured on a 99-year lease signed in June 1898. The colony, which developed into a major center for Sino-British trade during the late 19th and early 20th centuries, was occupied by Japanese forces between December 1941 and August 1945. The restored British administration promised, after 1946, to introduce a greater degree of self-government. These plans were shelved, however, after the 1949 communist revolution in mainland China.

During the 1950s almost 1 million Chinese, predominantly Cantonese, refugees fled to Hong Kong. This immigration continued during the 1960s and 1970s, raising the colony's population from 1 million in 1946 to 5 million in 1980 and forcing the imposition of strict border controls. Hong Kong's economy expanded rapidly during the corresponding period, the colony developing into one of the major commercial, financial, and industrial centers in Asia.

As the date for the termination of the New Territories' lease approached, negotiations on Hong Kong's future were opened between the British and Chinese governments during the early 1980s. These culminated in a unique agreement signed in Beijing, in December 1984, by which the British government agreed to transfer full sovereignty of the islands and New Territories to China in July 1997 in return for a Chinese assurance that Hong Kong's social and economic freedoms and capitalist lifestyle would be preserved for at least 50 years. Under this 'one country, two systems' agreement, Hong Kong would, in 1997, become a Special Administrative Region (SAR) within China, with its own laws, currency, budget, and tax system and retain its free port status and authority to negotiate separate international trade agreements. The existing, only partly directly elected, Legislative Council (Legco) will be replaced by a similar, still partially elected legislature, headed by a chief executive. The chief executive will replace the governor and will be selected by an appointed 600-member electoral college and subject to removal by the Chinese government.

In preparation for its future withdrawal from the colony, the British government introduced indirect elections, to select a portion of the new Legislative Council, in 1984 and direct elections for seats on lower-tier local councils, in 1985. A Sino-British joint liaison group was also established to monitor the functioning of the new agreement and a 58-member Basic Law Drafting Committee, which included 23 representatives from Hong Kong, was formed in Beijing, in June 1985, to draft a new constitution. The first draft of this Basic Law was published in April 1988 and a 176-member Basic Law Consultative Committee established to collect public comments on its provisions. Events in mainland China in June 1989 raised considerable doubts among the population about the value of the People's Republic's 'one country, two systems' assurances, and increased pressure on the British authorities to accelerate the pre-1997 internal democratization process. In 1992 the former UK Conservative Party chairperson, Chris Patten (b. 1944), was appointed governor. He swiftly put forward proposals for enhanced democratization. This raised objections from Beijing, claiming that the 1984 agreement was being breached. In June 1994 the Legco approved a political reform which substantially widened the franchise and the elective element within the Legco and other councils. However, the Chinese government made it clear that it rejected these reforms and that the Legco and other councils would be disbanded upon China's resumption of sovereignty in July 1997 and that a new, initially appointed, Special Administrative Region Legislative Council would be established. In 1994–95 democratic elections were held to the District Boards, Urban, Regional, and Legislative Councils, with the prodemocracy Democratic Party (DP) polling strongly. In July 1995 Governor Patten survived a no-confidence motion tabled in the Legco by DP deputies. In the

September 1995 Legco elections pro-Beijing parties fared badly, with the DP and its allies capturing most seats.

In December 1996, Tung Chee-Hwa, a Shanghai-born shipping magnate who had studied in Britain and the USA before running, with Chinese financial help, a large ocean fleet out of Taiwan and Hong Kong, was elected by a 400-member Chinese-established Selection Committee to become the first chief executive of the SAR in July 1997. In January 1997 Tung announced that the new Executive Council (cabinet) would comprise a mixture of business and political figures with strong links with mainland China. In February 1997 China's parliament voted to greatly dilute the territory's bill of rights and freedoms of association and assembly after reunification. The reversion to Chinese rule, on 1 July 1997, passed smoothly and amid lavish ceremony and brought an immediate 20% augmentation in the GDP and economic weight of the People' Republic. A 4,800-strong garrison of Chinese People's Liberation Army (PLA) troops was established in the SAR to defend Chinese interests. However, in other respects there was little evident change, as the terms of the 1984 'one country, two systems' agreement were adhered to.

Chief Executive Tung announced, in October 1997, that his government planned to spend $11 billion over a five-year period on improving infrastructure and housing, to make the latter more affordable. In the same month, the Hong Kong stockmarket fell by 30% in seven days and the Hong Kong dollar, which is pegged to the US dollar, came under concerted attack from international currency speculators, as the SAR was affected by a broader financial crisis sweeping across Southeast Asia. The Hong Kong monetary authority, with Chinese backing, intervened to defend the currency, raising interest rates. However, there were failures in the financial sector and further falls in the stock market during the first half of 1998, the Hong Kong economy contracted by 4% (the first short-term decline since 1985), and unemployment reached a 15-year high. Consequently, the approval rating of chief executive Tung fell and in elections held to the Legislative Council, in May 1998, prodemocracy candidates performed strongly.

INDIA

Republic of India
Bharat Janarajya

Capital: New Delhi

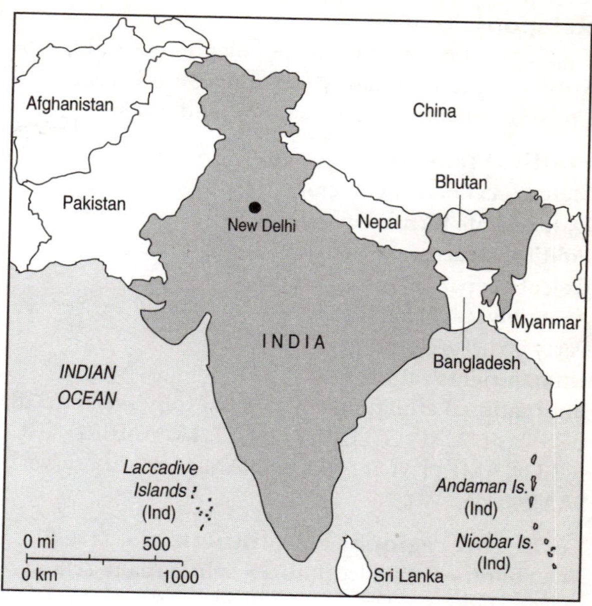

Social and economic data

Area: 3,287,263 sq km/1,269,219 sq miles
Population: 918,570,000*
Pop. density per sq km/sq mi: 279/724*
Urban population: 26%**
Literacy rate: 50%**
GDP: $319,700 million*; per-capita GDP: $350*
Government defense spending (% of GDP): 2.5%*
Currency: Indian rupee
Economy type: low income
Labor force in agriculture: 63%**
* 1995.
** 1992.

Head of state

President Kocheril Raman Narayanan, since 1997

Head of government

Prime Minister Atal Behari Vajpayee, since 1998

Ethnic composition

Seventy-two per cent of the population is of Indo-Aryan ethnic stock, 25%, predominantly in the south, Dravidian, and 3% Mongoloid. The official language is Hindi, spoken by 30% of the population, concentrated in northern and central India, with English used as an associate official language. There are also 17 recognized regional languages and more than 1,500 local dialects. Eight per cent of the population speak Bengali, 8% Telugu, 8% Marathi, 7% Tamil, 5% Urdu, and 5% Gujarati.

Religions

Eighty-three per cent of the population is Hindu, 11% Muslim, predominantly of the Sunni sect, 2% Christian, chiefly Roman Catholic, and 2% Sikh.

Political features

State type: liberal democratic
Date of state formation: 1947
Political structure: federal
Executive: parliamentary
Assembly: two-chamber
Party structure: multiparty
Human rights rating: 54%
International affiliations: AfDB, AG (observer), AsDB, CP, CW, ESCAP, G-15, G-24, G-77, IAEA, IBRD, ICC, ICFTU, IMF, IWC, LORCS, NAM, OAS (observer), SAARC, UN, WTO

Local and regional government

The country is divided into 25 substantially self-governing states, six Union Territories, and one National Capital Territory (Delhi) (see political system). Below them are divisions, districts, municipalities, development blocks, and villages. Districts are administered by appointed 'district collectors', while corporations and councils (*panchayats*) operate at the urban and subdistrict rural level, although elections have been infrequent. Jharkhand, a traditional tribal hill region in southern Bihar, was granted autonomy in October 1994 after a long campaign for self-determination which was led by the Jharkhand Mukti Morcha (Jharkhand People's Party). It was announced, in August 1998, that three new states, Uttaranchal, Vananchal, and Chattisgarh, were to be formed out of parts of Uttar Pradesh, Bihar, and Madhya Pradesh.

Political system

India is a federal republic whose January 1950 constitution, with 397 articles and nine schedules, making it one of the longest in the world, contains elements from both the American and British systems of government. It comprises 25 self-governing states, as shown in Table 51, each of which is administered by a figurehead governor appointed by the federal president, for a five-year term, on the advice of the prime minister.

Each state has a Legislative Assembly, or Vidhan Sabha, of between 32 and 425 members, popularly elected for a five-year term. Five of the larger states, Bihar, Jammu and Kashmir, Karnataka, Maharashtra, and Uttar Pradesh (UP), have a second, smaller, legislative chamber called a Legislative Council or Vidhan Parishad. An executive Council of Ministers, headed by a chief minister, drawn from the Legislative Assembly, and responsible to it, is appointed on the basis of Assembly support.

The states have primary control over education, health, police, and local government, and work in consultation with the center in the economic sphere. In times of crisis, central rule, or 'President's rule', can be temporarily imposed.

There are, in addition, seven Union (and National Capital) Territories: the Andaman and Nicobar Islands; Chandigarh; Dadra and Nagar Haveli; Daman and Diu; Delhi; Lakshadweep, and Pondicherry. Each is governed by a lieutenant governor or administrator appointed by the federal president. Delhi and Pondicherry also have elected assemblies, or councils.

The federal government has sole responsibility in the fields of citizenship, defense, external trade, and foreign affairs, grouped under 97 headings in the constitution, and plays a key role in economic affairs. This, combined with its monopoly control over such 'growth taxes' as income tax, corporation tax, and customs and excise, the states relying on land and sales taxes and federal grants for their revenue, has served to weight the Indian federal system in the center's favor compared, for example, with the US federal model.

The titular, executive head of the federal or 'Union' government is the president, who is elected for a five-year term by a large electoral college composed of members from both the federal and the state assemblies and, since 1992, the Delhi and Pondicherry Union Territories. Real, *de facto* executive power is, however, wielded by a prime minister and a 20–25-member Cabinet, termed the Council of Ministers, drawn from the majority party or coalition within the federal parliament.

The prime minister is served by his or her own influential advisors and often reserves for himself, or herself, a number of important ministerial portfolios. For example, Prime Minister Narasimha Rao was also minister of defense, electronics, industry, ocean development, science and technology, Jammu and Kashmir affairs, atomic energy, and space research.

The federal assembly is a two-chamber body, comprising a dominant, 545-member, lower house, the House of the People (Lok Sabha), which has final authority over financial matters and 543 of whose members are directly elected for a five-year term from single-member constituencies, by universal adult suffrage. Since 1989 the minimum voting age has been 18.

There is also a 245-member upper house, the

The states of India — Table 51

State	Area (sq km/sq miles)	Population (million) 1991	Capital	Ruling party * (May 1998)
Andhra Pradesh	275,068/106,204	66.508	Hyderabad	Telugu Desam (Naidu)
Arunachal Pradesh	83,743/32,333	0.865	Itanagar	Congress (I)
Assam	78,438/30,285	22.414	Dispur	Asam Gana Parishad
Bihar	173,877/67,134	86.374	Patna	Rashtriya Janata Dal
Goa	3,702/1,429	1.170	Panaji/Panjim	Maharashtrawadi Gomantak Party (MGP)
Gujarat	196,024/75,485	41.310	Gandhinagar	Bharatiya Janata Party (BJP)
Haryana	44,212/17,070	16.464	Chandigarh	Haryana Vikas Party
Himachal Pradesh	55,673/21,495	5.171	Simla	Congress (I)
Jammu & Kashmir	222,236/85,806	7.719	Srinagar	Jammu & Kashmir National Conference
Karnataka	191,791/74,051	44.977	Bangalore	Janata Dal
Kerala	38,863/15,005	29.099	Trivandrum/ Thiruvananthapuram	Communist Party of India (Marxist)
Madhya Pradesh	443,446/171,215	66.181	Bhopal	Congress (I)
Maharashtra	307,690/118,800	78.937	Bombay/Mumbai	Shiv Sena
Manipur	22,327/8.620	1.837	Imphal	Congress (I)
Meghalaya	22,429/8,660	1.775	Shillong	Congress (I)
Mizoram	21,081/8,139	0.690	Aizawl	Congress (I)
Nagaland	16,579/6,401	1.210	Kohima	Congress (I)
Orissa	155,707/60,119	31.660	Bhubaneswar	Congress (I)
Punjab	50,362/19,445	20.281	Chandigarh	Shiromani Akali Dal
Rajasthan	342,239/132,139	44.006	Jaipur	Bharatiya Janata Party (BJP)
Sikkim	7,096/2,740	0.406	Gangtok	Sikkim Democratic Front (SDF)
Tamil Nadu	130,058/50,216	55.859	Chennai (Madras)	Dravida Munnetra Kazhagam (DMK)
Tripura	10,486/4,049	2.757	Agartala	Communist Party of Incia (Marxist)
Uttar Pradesh	294,411/113,673	139.112	Lucknow	Bharatiya Janata Party (BJP)
West Bengal	88,752/34,267	68.078	Calcutta	Communist Party of India (Marxist)

* The party which provided the chief minister.

Council of States (Rajya Sabha), 237 of whose members are indirectly elected, a third at a time for six-year terms, by state assemblies, on a regional quota basis. The remaining two seats in the Lok Sabha are reserved for Anglo-Indians, nominated by the president, while eight representatives of the Rajya Sabha are also reserved for presidential nominees.

To become law, bills require the approval of both chambers of the assembly, before formally receiving presidential assent. Ordinary amendments to the constitution require the approval of a two-thirds majority of the members of each house present and voting, and a simple majority of the total membership, to be followed by the president's assent. However, amendments which affect the distribution of powers between the center and states, the representation of states in parliament, and the workings of the adjudicatory Supreme Court and High Courts require ratification by at least half the state legislatures as well, to become law. Since 1950, more than 70 amendments have been adopted.

Political parties

The dominant national political party, which has held power for all but eight years since independence – from 1977 to 1979, 1989 to 1991, and since 1996 – has been the Congress Party. Under British rule it functioned as a 'catch-all' umbrella organization for the nationalist movement, being originally formed by A O Hume (1829–1912) in 1885, under the designation Indian National Congress, as a moderate, port-city-based, intelligentsia pressure group. The movement's support base broadened and its policy outlook grew more radical during the interwar years, under the charismatic leadership of Mahatma Gandhi and the Western-educated Kashmiri Brahmin socialist, Jawaharlal Nehru. After splits, in 1969, 1978, 1981, 1987, and 1995, the main body of the party is today termed the All India Congress Committee and is led by Sonia Gandhi.

The contemporary Congress remains a broad, secular-based, cross-caste and cross-religion coalition, which advocates a moderate center-left policy approach and nonalignment in foreign affairs. It is liberally financed by the major Indian industrial conglomerates.

Its support base has been strongest traditionally in the 'Hindi belt' of northern and central India and in adjoining western India, from which regions it has drawn most of its leaders, and weakest in the Dravidian south. However, recently its support in the Hindi north has waned. The party is a mass organization, claiming a membership of over 10 million, but is controlled from above by a small 20-member 'High Command', the Congress Working Committee.

In 1978 the main body of the party, led by Indira Gandhi, who was later assassinated in 1984, adopted the designation Congress (I), the 'I' standing for Indira.

The other main national-level parties are the Bharatiya Janata Party (BJP: Indian People's Party), the Janata Dal, the Samajwadi Party, the Communist Party of India (CPI), and the Communist Party of India-Marxist (CPI-M).

The BJP was founded in 1980 and is an urban, middle-class and Hindu higher-caste orientated, radical right-wing Hindu grouping led, since 1998, by Kushabhau Thakre, and claiming 10.5 million members. Its roots go further back to the Jana Sangh, founded in 1951 but which later merged with the Janata Party. Initially, the BJP was relatively moderate, but since polling poorly in the 1984 general election it has become a staunchly Hindu-chauvinist force. It has used the Babri Masjid Ramjanmabhumi issue at Ayodhya to mobilize the Hindu community across northern India and has formed governments in 1996 and since 1998. Three even more radical forces on the militant Hindu right are Shiv Sena, led by Balram Thackeray and rooted in western India; the Rashtriya Swayamsevak Sangh (RSS), founded as a paramilitary organization in 1925 by Dr Keshav Hedgewar, and banned in 1948, 1976, and between 1992 and 1993; and the Vishwa Hindu Parishad (VHP), banned between 1992 and 1995, whose purpose is to disseminate the doctrine of Hindu nationalism.

The Janata Dal (People's Party) was formed in October 1988 through the merger of four important centrist and center-left parties: the Janata (estd. 1977), the Lok Dal-B (estd. 1984), the Congress (Socialist; estd. 1984), and the Jan Morcha (People's Front; estd. 1987). It originated as an anti-Congress (I) body, led by the Jan Morcha's founder and leader, V P Singh, but split during 1990, after securing power. There have subsequently been a succession of breakaways. These include the Samajwadi Janata Party (SP; Socialist Party), formed in 1991 and led initially by Chandra Shekhar, but now by the 'middle peasant' leader Mulayam Singh Yadav, and the Rashtriya Janata Dal (RJD; National People's Party), formed in 1997 by Laloo Prasad Yadav. The Janata Dal party, and its offspring, have drawn particularly strong support from Hindu lower castes and, being secular in outlook, have recently drawn away from Congress Muslim support.

The CPI is a 560,000-member pro-Moscow party, which was formed in 1925, and is led by Ardhendu Bhushan Bardhan.

The CPI-M dates from 1964. It has 630,000 members, was formerly pro-Beijing and is orientated towards the landless rural laborer. Its leading member is the reformist West Bengal chief minister, Jyoti Basu, and its general secretary is Harkishan Singh Surjeet.

In addition to these national organizations, there are numerous profederalist regional-level parties, the most important of which are the All-India Anna Dravida Munnetra Kazhagam (AIADMK), the Dravida Munnetra Kazagham (DMK), the Telugu Desam (Telugu Nation), the Jammu and Kashmir National Conference Party (JKNCP), the Shiromani Akali Dal (Akali Religious Party), the Asom Gana Parishad (AGP: Assam People's Council) and the Bahujan Samaj Party (BSP).

The AIADMK was established in 1972, in Tamil Nadu, and is led by Jayalalitha Jayaram, former chief minister of Tamil Nadu and the former mistress of the film star, Marudud Gopalan Ramachandran, who died in January 1988. The DMK (estd. 1949) also operates in Tamil Nadu and, led by Muthuvel Karunanidhi, claims 4 million members.

The Telugu Desam was established in 1982, in Andhra Pradesh, and now has 2.6 million members. It was formed by another former film star, N T Rama Rao (1923–96).

The JKNCP dates from 1931 and, led by Dr Farook Abdullah, has 1 million members.

The Akali Religious Party was formed in 1920, in Punjab. It has 1 million members, and comprises moderate and militant factions.

The AGP was formed in 1985 and is led by Prafulla Kumar Mahanta.

The BSP (Majority Society Party), based in the large north Indian state of Uttar Pradesh (UP), is a populist party orientated towards low-caste and Harijan/Dalit ('untouchable') voters. Led by Kanshi Ram and in alliance with the Samajwadi Party, it secured control of the UP state assembly in the elections of November 1993. In June 1995, the BSP's Mayawati became chief minister of UP. She was the first Dalit ('untouchable') to head a state government, but was forced from office in October 1995.

India's opposition parties have been notoriously fractious, faction-ridden bodies, subject to frequent splits and subsequent reformations in new guises. Personality and policy differences have tended to frustrate the formation of a united opposition to the Congress party, with the notable exception of the successes of 1977, 1989, and 1996.

Political leaders since 1970*

1966–77 Indira Gandhi (Congress), 1977–79 Morarji Desai (Janata), 1979–80 Chaudhury Charan Singh (Lok Dal), 1980–84 Indira Gandhi (Congress: I), 1984–89 Rajiv Gandhi (Congress: I), 1989–90 V P Singh (Janata Dal), 1990–91 Chandra Shekhar (Janata Dal: S), 1991–96 P V Narasimha Rao (Congress: I), 1996 Atal Behari Vajpayee (BJP), 1996–97 H D Deve Gowda (Janata Dal, United Front), 1997–98 Inder Kumar Gujral (United Front), 1998– Atal Behari Vajpayee (BJP)

* Prime ministers.

Latest elections

In the most recent Lok Sabha elections, held, in four phases, between 16 February and 7 March 1998, the BJP captured 179 seats and Congress (I) 141 seats. A further 27 parties secured seats. These included: the BJP-allied AIADMK, 18 seats, Samata Party, 12, Biju Janata Dal, 9, Akali Dal, 8, Trinamool Congress, 7, and Shiv Sena, 6; the Congress (I) allied RJD, 17 seats; and, within the United Front, the CPI-M, 32 seats, SP, 20, Telugu Desam, 12, CPI, 9, DMK, 6, and Janata Dal, 6. Altogether, the BJP and its 12 allied parties won 252 seats, which was 21 seats short of an absolute majority, while Congress (I) and its four allies, 165 seats, and the ten-member outgoing United Front coalition, 97 seats. There was widespread violence and polling irregularities: re-polling being ordered by the electoral commission at 3,934 polling stations.

Political history

1. 321 BC–AD 1984

The Indian subcontinent, with the exception of the Dravidian south, was first unified by the Mauryan regime, 321–184 BC, whose emperor, Asoka (*c.* 273–232 BC), was converted to Buddhism. Later, north central India was reunited by the Gupta dynasty, *c.* AD300–500, during which period Brahmanical Hinduism re-established its dominance. Arab traders and invaders began to spread the Islamic faith in western and northwestern regions from the 7th century, the process deepening with the establishment, over much of northern, central, and western India, of the Delhi Sultanate, 1206–1525, and Mughal Empire, 1525–1780s, by Muslim conquerors from Central Asia. The south, however, which was the site of the Hindu Vijayanagar kingdom during the 14th and 15th centuries and was, later, only partially conquered by the Mughals, remained only tangentially exposed to Muslim influences.

Under British rule, which was established in stages between 1757 and 1856 and was to last until 1947, the subcontinent began, with the spread of railways and the creation of an extensive English-speaking bureaucracy, to be effectively unified for the first time. Nevertheless, during this period of the Raj, or British rule, almost half the land area, mainly the interior, remained free from direct British government. Instead, it was left to the control of 562 semi-independent, though loyal, 'princely states'.

During the later 19th century, Indian national consciousness began to emerge among the intelligentsia community, and was reflected in the creation, in 1885, of the Indian National Congress (INC), which campaigned for greater autonomy and eventual independence. The new nationalist movement grew more extensive and radical during the interwar years, as economic pressures mounted. The progressive self-government concessions made by the Government of India, including the 'dyarchy reforms' of 1919–21, which handed over much of provincial administrative responsibilities to elected assemblies, helping to inculcate a generalized respect for regular electoral processes, failed to satisfy the 'freedom fighters', Mahatma Gandhi (1869–1948) and Jawaharlal Nehru (1889–1964). They led a series of civil disobedience campaigns for which activity they were repeatedly imprisoned.

The Indian subcontinent was eventually granted independence in August 1947 and, as a result of a split in the nationalist movement between the secular INC and the communalist Muslim League, led by Muhammad Ali Jinnah (1876–1948), the country was partitioned along religious lines, with initial bloody consequences. The result was a predominantly Hindu India and a Muslim-dominated Pakistan. Pakistan was, itself, divided into two, widely separated, western (Sind-Punjab-NW Frontier) and eastern (East Bengal) sectors, with the Indian land mass in between.

For more than two years after August 1947, India temporarily remained under the supervision of a governor general appointed by the British monarch, while a new constitution was framed and approved. This was achieved by January 1950, involving, in the process, the integration of former princely states and the restructuring of the old British provinces into new states, with boundaries based on linguistic lines. When the process was completed a fully independent, federal republic was proclaimed.

During its early years, the new republic faced problems in the resettlement of millions of Hindu refugees who had fled from Pakistan at the time of partition, losing, in the process, a similar number of Muslims who had moved out in the opposite direction. This resulted in a number of border skirmishes with its new neighbor over Kashmir.

Domestically, under the leadership of Prime Minister Nehru, limited land reforms and a new socialist economic program were introduced. The program, which involved protectionism, an emphasis on heavy industries and state planning, was initially successful. Meanwhile, the sovereignty of French- and Portuguese-held territories within India, including Chandernagore, Pondicherry, and Goa, was recovered between 1950 and 1961. Resort to force was necessary in the case of Goa.

In its external relations, India remained within the Commonwealth and played a leading role in the formation of the Non-Aligned Movement in 1961. It also, however, became involved in border clashes with communist China, in October 1962.

In May 1964, Prime Minister Nehru died and was briefly succeeded as national leader by his close associate, the Benares-born 'minister without portfolio', Lal Bahadur Shastri (1904–66). The country became entangled in a second border conflict with Pakistan over Kashmir between August and September 1965 before Shastri died, in January 1966.

His successor as INC leader and prime minister was Indira Gandhi (1917–84), the daughter of Jawaharlal Nehru. She adhered to the broad outlines of her father's policy program, but also developed closer links with the Soviet Union, with whom India signed a 15-year economic and military assistance agreement in 1973.

In December 1971, Indian troops invaded East Pakistan in support of the local separatist government. After a 12-day war, they succeeded in defeating Pakistan's forces and oversaw the creation of the new independent, and pro-Indian, state of Bangladesh. This military success, despite contemporary economic difficulties, boosted the national standing of Prime Minister Gandhi. However, her personalized style of control had begun to foment divisions within the ruling INC, precipitating an initial split, in November 1969, in which the Gujarat-born Morarji Desai (1896–1995), a former deputy prime minister and 1966 party leadership challenger, together with a number of fellow senior colleagues, left to form a new Congress (O, or Organization).

Criticism of the prime minister's autocratic methods mounted in June 1975 when, having been found guilty of electoral malpractice during the March 1971 general election by the High Court, in her Allahabad constituency, and having been banned from holding elective office for six years, she imposed a draconian 'State of Emergency', involving the temporary outlawing of opposition parties and the imposition of tight censorship controls. Almost 1,000 of Indira Gandhi's political opponents were imprisoned, under the provisions of the Maintenance of Internal Security Act. Despite her later being cleared of malpractice by the Supreme Court, in November 1975, the 'Emergency' continued for two years, during which time a harsh and unpopular, compulsory birth-control program, by sterilization, was introduced under the supervision of Sanjay Gandhi (1946–80), Indira's youngest son.

The 'State of Emergency' was eventually lifted in March 1977 to allow parliamentary elections to take place. In this contest, the opposition parties, who had united under the umbrella of the newly formed Janata Party, were swept to power with a landslide victory. The new party's leader, Morarji Desai, defeated Indira Gandhi in her home constituency.

The new Janata government, the first non-INC administration since independence, headed by Prime Minister Desai, swiftly introduced constitutional amendments to reverse those pushed through by Indira Gandhi in 1975–76, thus restoring the 'democratic balance'. The Desai coalition was gradually undermined, however, by mounting economic difficulties and internal factional strife. This culminated, in July 1979, in the defection of many Janata members to a new secular party, the Lok Dal, under the leadership of the former health minister, Raj Narain, and home minister, Charan Singh. Desai was eventually toppled as prime minister in July 1979 and a coalition, under the leadership of Charan Singh, assumed power. A month later, however, after only 24 days in office, the Charan Singh government was overthrown.

In the Lok Sabha elections, which followed in January 1980, Indira Gandhi's renamed and revamped Congress (I), promising a firmer and more decisive approach to government after the drift of the Janata years and faced with opposition disarray, was returned to power, gaining a landslide majority.

The new administration proceeded to record success in the economic sphere, helped by the spread of the 'Green Revolution' in the agricultural sector, which resulted in high yields of wheat and rice. It was beset, however, by mounting problems of intercaste violence and regionalist unrest, centerd in Gujarat, where there was caste strife, Muslim-dominated Kashmir, southern India and Assam, where violence was aimed at Bangladeshi immigrants. This resulted in Congress (I)'s loss of control of a string of state assemblies.

The most serious unrest occurred in the prosperous Punjab. Here initial moderate Sikh demands for greater religious recognition and a resolution of water and land disputes with neighboring states, escalated into more extreme calls for the creation of a separate state of 'Khalistan'. In June 1984,Indira Gandhi, concerned with the mounting level of disorder in the province, sent Indian troops into the Golden Temple at Amritsar to dislodge the young Sikh extremist leader, Sant Jarnail Singh Bhindranwale (1947–84), and his armed followers. This 'storming' operation, which caused widespread damage to a revered holy shrine, as well as resulting in the death of Bhindranwale and hundreds of his 'disciples', provoked a Sikh backlash which served to radicalize and spread militancy through the community. Across India, Sikh troop regiments immediately mutinied and, four months later, in October 1984, the prime minister was assassinated by her Sikh bodyguards in the garden of her residence in Delhi. This, in turn, provoked savage Hindu retaliation in Delhi, in November 1984, involving the massacre of 2,000 Sikhs by vigilantes, before the new prime minister, Rajiv Gandhi (1944–91), Indira's eldest son, was able to restore order.

2. 1984–1999

In the new general election which followed, in December 1984, Congress (I), benefiting from a wave of public sympathy, succeeded in securing a record victory, with its highest share, 49%, of the national vote since independence. The new prime minister, Rajiv Gandhi, a former airline pilot who had only reluctantly been persuaded into politics in 1980, following the death of his younger brother, was a popular leader. He was viewed as an upright, managerial 'non-politician', unsullied by the corruptions of the political game. He proceeded to project himself as a forward-looking and healing leader, pledging, under the slogan 'bringing India into the 21st century', to modernize and inject greater market efficiency into the Indian economy and to resolve the Punjab, Assam, Kashmir, and northeastern hill states' regional disputes.

Early deregulationary economic reforms, assaults on bureaucratic 'red tape', support for the launching of Indian space satellites, and the spread of computer technology promised to give substance to these visions, while an early move was made to resolve the Punjab dispute and even greater progress made in Assam, Kashmir, and the hill areas, including Mizoram. Here 25 years of rebellion were ended and it became a new state of the Indian Union.

By 1987, however, Rajiv Gandhi's national standing had been seriously diminished. In the economic sphere, the reformist zeal of 1985–86 had lost its impetus and prospects seemed poor, with the country in the grip of its worst drought of the century. In the external sphere, the Indian army, which had been sent to northern Sri Lanka to 'police' the July 1987 Jayawardene Peace Accord, had become bogged down in a war against its fellow community. Internally, Sikh – Hindu ethnic violence remained a serious problem in Punjab, with communalist Hindu chauvinism gaining in strength in adjoining regions. Politically, Congress (I) support had slumped, the party enduring reverses in state polls, as well as the defection of a number of elder party members who were opposed to the centralization of power within the hands of a tight-knit 'Doon clique' of young Gandhi associates. There were also public disputes between President Giani Zail Singh and the prime minister.

Most serious of all, however, the reputation that had initially been assigned to Rajiv Gandhi as the 'Mr Clean' of Indian politics had been seriously sullied by the uncovering by finance minister V P Singh (b. 1931) of the 'Bofors scandal', involving financial 'kick-backs' received by, it was alleged, government-connected Indian 'front organizations', for facilitating a major arms contract with the Swedish munitions firm.

Although cleared of any personal impropriety in this affair, the 'Bofors scandal' served to undermine popular confidence in the Gandhi administration, while at the same time vaulting on to the national stage V P Singh as a zealous crusader against corruption. Singh, along with other prominent 'dissident' members, was dismissed from Congress (I) in July 1987 and proceeded to form a new 'political forum', the Jan Morcha, in October. Following his election to the Lok Sabha, in a by-election held in his native Allahabad in June 1988, Singh became the focus for an opposition unity drive, culminating in the formation of the new National Front and Janata Dal, in October 1988.

To contest the general election of November 1989, a broad anti-Congress (I) electoral pact was forged, comprising the Janata Dal and the regionally based DMK and Telugu Desam. This ensured that the number of seats captured by Congress (I) fell dramatically from 400 in December 1984 to just 192 and a minority National Front coalition government, headed by V P Singh, was formed after the election. A major objective of this new Singh administration was the lowering of racial tensions. However, as early as January 1990 Muslim separatist violence erupted in Kashmir. This forced the imposition of direct rule and resulted in a deterioration in relations with Pakistan. Interethnic violence similarly reached new heights in Punjab and became so serious in Assam that President's rule had to be imposed in November 1990. However, relations were improved with neighboring Bhutan, Nepal (which had been subjected to a partial border blockade during 1989), and Sri Lanka, where the Indian Peacekeeping Force, sent by Rajiv Gandhi in July 1987, was withdrawn in March 1990.

From the summer of 1990 V P Singh's Janata Dal government was rocked by three developments. First, a decision by the prime minister to advocate implementation of the eight-year-old recommendations of the Mandal Commission on job reservations for disadvantaged castes provoked a bloody caste war in the cities of northern India. Second, from September 1990 there was serious Hindu – Muslim communal conflict, as Hindu militants of the Vishwa Hindu Parishad (VHP: World Hindu Council) pressed for the construction of a temple venerating the warrior-god Rama on the site of a 16th-century Muslim mosque in the north Indian holy city of Ayodhya. Third, Chandra Shekhar, a leading figure within the former Janata Party and a longstanding Singh opponent, established himself as the leader of a rebel faction within the National Front administration.

On 7 November 1990, shortly after troops had fired on Hindu militants in Ayodhya, the Singh government was voted from office and Chandra Shekhar, supported by the Haryana-based 'middle peasant' leader Devi Lal, took over as prime minister. Shekhar's minority administration, which was kept in power by the puppet-master support of Rajiv Gandhi's Congress (I), lasted only 115 days. By shelving the proposals of the Mandal Commission, it lessened intercaste tensions. However, regional and communal strife continued, claiming more than 5,000 lives during 1990, the great majority in Punjab. Meanwhile, the Indian economy, after bumper harvests during 1989–90, suffered from the higher oil prices which resulted from the 1990–91 Gulf conflict.

Shekhar, after falling out with his Congress (I) backers, resigned as premier in March 1991. His small, breakaway Samajwadi Party (SP) party was trounced in the ensuing May – June 1991 general election. This election campaign was the most violent in the history of the Indian Republic, claiming several hundred lives, and was marked by the assassination of Rajiv Gandhi by a bomb strapped to a kamikaze Tamil Tiger female terrorist. Gandhi's Italian-born widow, Sonia, declined entreaties to take over as Congress (I) leader. Instead, the experienced southerner, PTV Narasimha Rao (b. 1921), assumed the helm of Congress (I).

The most notable feature of the May – June 1991 election was the high level of support, a quarter of the national vote, received by the Hindu-chauvinist BJP, which polled particularly strongly in the northern 'Hindi belt'. However, a late sympathy vote surge of support for Congress (I) was sufficient to secure it 227 out of 545 seats and enable Narasimha Rao to form a minority administration. After delayed elections were held in Punjab in February 1992, a Congress (I) majority was achieved. The new Rao government embarked on an ambitious freer market economic program, slashing subsidies, allowing the rupee to float, encouraging foreign investment, and scrapping industrial licensing. It also announced in September 1991 that it would adopt the recommendations of the Mandal Commission. However, in December 1992 the country was rocked by a fresh outbreak of Hindu – Muslim violence, claiming 1,200 lives, after Hindu militants stormed and tore down the Ayodhya mosque. The government reacted by ordering the arrest of the leaders of the BJP and VHP, banning the VHP, and, with the Supreme Court's approval, dismissing the BJP administrations in Uttar Pradesh, Himachal Pradesh, Madhya Pradesh, and Rajasthan, where President's rule was declared.

From 1993, communal violence subsided somewhat. However, bloody insurgencies continued in Kashmir, where 150,000 Indian troops were stationed, and the weekly death toll exceeded 50 people, and in the northeastern hill states of Assam, Nagaland, and Manipur. With the administration of Narasimha Rao facing criticism for favoring the rich rather than the poor with its new economic program, for perceived corruption, and for alienating Muslims over the Ayodhya issue, Congress (I) became increasingly divided and endured crushing defeats in state elections in Karnataka and Andhra Pradesh, the latter being Narasimha Rao's home state, in December 1994. The human resources minister, Arjun Singh, immediately resigned from the government. This established him as a potential challenger to Rao, but the prime minister reacted swiftly by securing Singh's expulsion from Congress (I) in February 1995.

By the spring of 1995, following humiliating defeats in the western Indian states of Maharashtra and Gujarat, where the Hindu-chauvinist Shiv Sena and BJP triumphed, and Bihar, won by a Janata Dal party orientated towards lower-caste voters, the states ruled by Congress (I) accounted for barely a quarter of India's population. Despite strong growth in the economy, Congress (I) seemed unlikely to secure a majority of seats in the 1996 federal election. This became even less likely in May 1995, when a new rift occurred within its ranks after the ousted Arjun Singh and the veteran north Indian politician, N D Tiwari, formed the new breakaway Congress (Tiwari). This claimed the support of 16 Congress (I) members of parliament. In July 1995 a report by the independent Vohra Commission, set up in 1993, disclosed that large areas of northern India were controlled by mafia gangs which enjoyed the patronage of local politicians. In Uttar Pradesh, 180 of the 425 legislators had criminal records and here, and in adjoining Bihar, thugs were routinely engaged to capture polling booths and stuff ballot boxes. The general election, held in April 1996, was fought against the backcloth of corruption scandals, with 65 politicians, drawn from across the political spectrum, being under investigation for taking bribes totalling 650 million rupees ($18 million). The campaign claimed around 25 lives, but was largely peaceful, particularly in Punjab, where the separatists had petered out in 1993. However, the election failed to produce a decisive outcome, with no major party bloc being able to achieve an assembly majority. Somewhat surprisingly, the Hindu nationalist BJP and its allies emerged as the largest single body, despite the BJP's leader, L K Advani, facing corruption charges. It secured only 20% of the national vote, which was 5% down on its 1991 result, but since its support was relatively concentrated in the north and west, it won 160 seats, and its allies, such as Shiv Sena, a further 34 seats. In contrast, Congress (I) won only 136 seats despite attracting, a more evenly spread, 30% of the all-India vote. A party split in the southern state of Tamil Nadu, as a result of its regional alliance with the unpopular Jayaram Jayalalitha leader of the AIADMK, and a loss of support among Muslims and lower caste and 'untouchable' Hindus, some of whom defected to the Bahujan Samaj Party, explained the loss of Congress (I) support. Meanwhile, the National Front-Left Front (NL-LF), a leftwing and regionalist 13-party coalition, which had the Janata Dal and two communist parties at its core, won 179 seats, with 18% of the vote. It drew in considerable Muslim and lower caste Hindu support. After the election, a BJP government, led by the relatively moderate Atal Behari Vajpayee, was formed in May 1996. But, lacking a majority, it collapsed after 13 days. A new center-left NL-LF ('United Front') coalition was formed in June 1996, with H D Deve Gowda, a former Janata Dal chief minister of the southern Indian state of Karnataka, as prime minister. This coalition enjoyed the tacit backing of Congress (I). The new 13-party coalition pledged to continue with economic liberalization, with Palaniappan Chidambaram, a reformist defector from Congress (I), being appointed finance minister. However, while plans were unveiled to cut public spending, reduce taxes, and boost foreign inward investment, a new emphasis was also given to rural development in an effort to ensure that the benefits of economic growth were more widely spread. Meanwhile, Congress (I) changed its leadership and shifted leftwards. In September 1996, having been called to testify in a corruption case, Narasimha Rao stepped down as party president and was replaced by Sitaram Kesri (b. 1918), a veteran member of the newly empowered lower castes in Bihar. In January 1997, Kesri also became the party's parliamentary leader. He was a critic of economic liberalization, believing that, although it had led to an acceleration in the annual GDP growth rate from the traditional level of 4% to more than 6%, it had resulted in Congress (I) acquiring an electorally damaging 'elitist, anti-poor image', He now called for tighter controls over multinational companies. In April 1997, he overthrew the Gowda government, by withholding backing on a no-confidence vote. A new United Front coalition government was formed, in April 1997, comprising similar personnel and led by the former foreign minister, Dr Inder Kumar Gujral (b. 1919), a respected socialist. Two months later, and at a time of increasing caste tensions, Kocheril Raman Narayanan (b. 1921), was selected, by electoral college, to become India's first Dalit ('untouchable') state president. The Gujral government was forced, in September 1997, to perform a partial U-turn on its policy of reducing import tariff levels and, from November 1997, came under pressure from Congress (I) to expel from the ruling coalition the Tamil Nadu-based DMK party, after an investigating commission reported that the DMK had indirectly abetted the Sri Lankan Tamil Tiger guerrillas who had assassinated Rajiv Gandhi in 1991. Congress (I) eventually withdrew its informal backing from the government, leading to Gujral tendering his resignation in December 1997. After attempts to form a stable new coalition government foundered, parliament was dissolved and a general election called for February – March 1998. The campaigning for this election was fierce and bitter. Emerging from six years of seclusion, the Congress (I) campaign was led by Sonia Gandhi, who had formally joined the party in May 1997 and was to replace Kesri as president in March 1998. She had intervened because of her concern at the danger presented to the country by the sectarian and divisive BJP. Sonia Gandhi's intervention revitalized Congress (I), which, following a flood of defections, had seemed on the verge of disintegration. Nevertheless, despite the 'Sonia factor', Congress (I) increased its seat tally by only five, to 141, and was actually defeated in the former constituency of Rajiv Gandhi. Congress (I) finished behind the BJP, which won 179 seats, while the outgoing United Front coalition, with 95 seats, polled particularly badly. Regional parties had the greatest success in an election which was marred by polling irregularities and by unprecedented violence, culminating in the killing of 50 people in the southern city of Coimbatore, in a bomb attack at a BJP rally. In March 1998, Atal Behari Vajpayee became prime minister for the second time, when a fragile BJP-led minority coalition government was formed. The lack of a majority meant that the BJP would be unable to implement its most extreme, pro-Hindu policies, for example abolishing the special autonomy of disputed Kashmir or the building of a Hindu temple on the ruins of the former mosque in Ayodhya. However, it did give an increased emphasis on swadeshi (self-reliance) in its economic policy and, in May 1998, stunned the outside world by implementing what had been a manifesto pledge and carrying out five nuclear tests (the first since 1974), at Pokharan, in Rajasthan. This action was condemned by the international community, leading to the United States immediately halting economic and military aid, and it was soon followed by Pakistan carrying out its own, first ever, nuclear tests. This threatened a nuclear arms race in South Asia and led to a further deterioration in Indo-Pakistan relations, which was reflected in increased cross-border shelling in disputed Kashmir. However, the action was popular, at least in the short term, within India.

In November 1998 economic sanctions were largely lifted, but the BJP polled poorly in state elections. The unstable coalition began to fall apart and in April 1999 the government fell on a no-confidence vote. Sonia Gandhi's Congress Party proved unable to form a minority government and parliament was dissolved, with new elections set for September-October 1999. Vajpayee continued in office as caretaker prime minister and border tensions with Pakistan, over Kashmir, deteriorated. Meanwhile, the Congress Party faced an internal crisis as a result of criticisms, by a faction led by the influential Sharad Pawar, of the party's leadership by an inexperienced, non-Indian. This prompted Sonia Gandhi to briefly tender her resignation, but it was not accepted. Pawar, a former chief minister of Maharashtra, was expelled from the party in May 1999 and set up a new Nationalist Congress Party..

INDONESIA

Republic of Indonesia (ROI)
Republik Indonesia

Capital: Jakarta

Social and economic data
Area: 1,904,569 sq km/735,358 sq miles

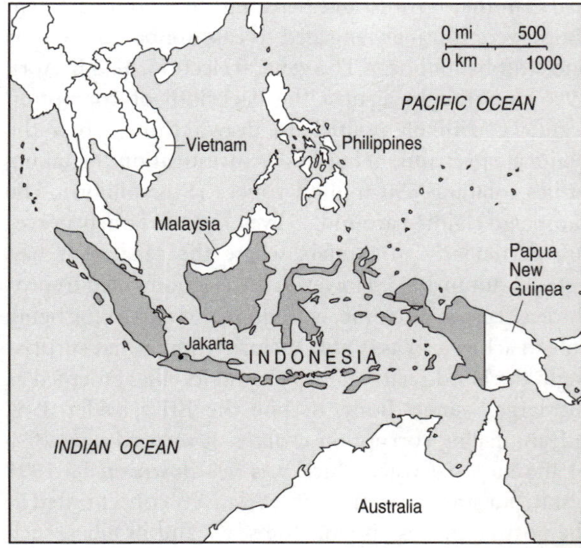

Population: 192,217,000*
Pop. density per sq km/sq mi: 101/261*
Urban population: 30%**
Literacy rate: 82%**
GDP: $190,100 million*; per-capita GDP: $990*
Government defense spending (% of GDP): 1.6%**
Currency: rupiah
Economy type: low income
Labor force in agriculture: 47%**
* 1995.
** 1992.

Head of state and of government

President Bucharuddin Jusuf Habibie, since 1998

Ethnic composition

The country is heterogenous in social composition, comprising more than 300 ethnic groups, the majority of which are of Malay stock. The most important Malay communities are the Javanese, who comprise a third of the population, followed by the Sundanese, 7%, and Madurese, 3%. The Chinese, 2%, constitute the largest non-Malay community, with substantial numbers of Indians, Melanesians, Micronesians, and Arabs, invariably regionally based, also to be found. However, many Chinese left Indonesia in the wake of the May 1998 riots in Jakarta, of which they were the chief victims. The official national language is Bahasa Indonesia, a form of Trade Malay, but 25 local languages, predominantly Javanese, Madurese, and Sundanese, and 250 local dialects, are also spoken.

Religions

Eighty-two per cent of the population is Sunni Muslim and 10% Christian. A third of Christians are Roman Catholics and two-thirds Protestants and other denominations. The Protestant Batak of Sumatra, the Christian Evangelical Minahasan of Sulawesi, the Protestant Moluccans, and the Ibans of Kalimantan constitute the most important Christian communities. Two per cent of the population is Hindu, residing mainly in Bali, and 5% adheres to tribal religions. The country has the largest Muslim community, some 160 million, in the world. The majority of Muslims are, however, nominal, following an amalgam of animistic, Muslim, and Hindu beliefs and rituals. Aceh province in west Sumatra, where Islamic Sharia law is acknowledged, is an exception. During the 1990s, the army has put down a number of separatist rebellions in Aceh. The official state 'religion' is the secular ideology of Pancasila, based on five general principles: a belief in one supreme God; a just and civilized humanity; the unity of Indonesia; democracy, led by the wisdom of deliberations (*musyawarah*) among representatives; and social justice for the whole of the people of Indonesia.

Political features

State type: emergent democratic
Date of state formation: 1949
Political structure: unitary
Executive: limited presidential
Assembly: one-chamber
Party structure: multiparty
Human rights rating: 34%
International affiliations: APEC, AsDB, ASEAN, CP, ESCAP, G-15, G-77, IAEA, IBRD, ICC, ICFTU, IMF, IsDB, LORCS, NAM, OIC, OPEC, UN, WTO

Local and regional government

The country is divided into 27 provinces (*propinsi*), including East Timor, a metropolitan district (Jakarta) and two special autonomous districts (Aceh and Yogyakarta). Each is headed by a centrally appointed governor, two-thirds of whom are drawn from the military. Within the provinces are 246 districts or regencies (*kabupaten*), administered by regents (*bupats*); 54 municipalities (*kota madya*), under the charge of mayors (*walis*); and 3,349 subdistricts (*kecamatan*), headed by a *tjamat*. There is a three-tier system of elected provincial, regency, and village assemblies at local and regional levels.

Political system

Under the constitution of August 1945, which was amended in 1950, 1969, and 1998, the supreme political body in Indonesia is, in theory, the 700-member People's Consultative Assembly (Majlis Permusyawaratan Rakyat: MPR). This consists of 500 members of the House of Representatives and, traditionally, 200 selected representatives from 27 provincial assemblies and 353 functional and political groups. It meets at least once every five years to elect an executive president and vice president and to determine the constitution and the 'broad lines of the policy of the State and Government'. All decisions, in accordance with the tradition of *musyawarah*, are taken unanimously.

The House of Representatives (Dewan Perwakilan Rakyat: DPR) functions as a single-chamber legislature and comprises 462 directly elected members, via proportional representation, and 38 presidential appointees, drawn from the armed forces. It meets at least once a year and elections are held every five years.

All statutes require the House's approval. Individual DPR members may submit draft bills. To become law, however, they need to be ratified by the president, who enjoys veto rights. As in the MPR, legislation is adopted by consensus, rather than voting, the chamber acting as a legitimator of presidential initiatives.

At the head of the executive, and the most powerful political figure in the country, is the president. Presidents are elected by the MPR for a five-year term. They work with an appointed cabinet, exercise, as has already been noted, the right of veto over House of Representatives' bills and appoint governors for each of Indonesia's 27 provinces and special autonomous districts. In May 1998 the president's cabinet had 37 members, the majority of whom were specialist technocrats. Each of these cabinet ministers is responsible only to the president.

The president is assisted by several advisory agencies, including the Supreme Advisory Council (DPA: Dewan Pertimbangan Agung), National Development Council, and the National Security and Political Stabilization Board. During periods of emergency, the president has additional authority to enact ordinances which have the force of law, for up to a year, without parliamentary ratification. Since the May 1998 resignation of President Suharto, the Indonesian political system has been in a state of flux. A revision of repressive legislation has been carried out by Suharto's successor B J Habibie, and fresh, competitive, elections were held in June 1999. The intention has been to reduce the political influence of the military and end the doctrine of '*dwifunnsi*' (dual function) under which the armed forces are responsible for defending the country from both external enemies and internal threats.

Political parties

The dominant political party in Indonesia has been, until 1999, Golkar (Joint Secretariat of Functional Groups: Sekretariat Bersama Golongan Karya), chaired since July 1998 by Akbar Tanjung. The party was formed in 1964 by a group of senior army officers as a means of establishing a loose alliance of sectional interests, farmers, the fishing community, professionals, factory workers, young people, the older generation, and women, so as to counter the growing influence of the Indonesian Communist Party (PKI). This enjoyed national support of around 15% during the 1950s, before being banned in 1966.

Golkar was brought under government control in 1968 and was transformed into the civilian arm of President Suharto's military regime. The party has an extensive national organization, but is tightly controlled from above by an elite, 45-member Central Committee, comprising senior state officials and army officers, all close to the president. It has been described as 'not so much a political party as ... the political arm of the bureaucracy', and is designed to restrict to a minimum the number of assembly seats obtained by other, genuine, political parties. In 1998 Golkar claimed a membership of 35 million. In December 1998 a number of senior former ministers, including General Try Sutrisno, who had been vice-president during 1993-98, set up a breakaway Justice and Unity Party, having become disillusioned with Golkar.

Before the moves to a multiparty system from 1998, there were two permitted 'opposition parties': the Indonesian Democratic Party (PDI: Partai Demokrasi Indonesia), and the United Development Party (PPP: Partai Persatuan Pembangunan).

The PDI was formed in 1973 through the enforced merger of five non-Islamic nationalist and Christian parties. It is heir to the radical and once influential, Sukarno-linked, Indonesian Nationalist Party (PNI). However, it was subsequently deeply penetrated by state intelligence officers and its leader has, traditionally, been effectively appointed by the government.

The PPP was also formed in 1973, by the merger of four Islamic Parties, including the Nahdlatul Ulama and Indonesian Muslims' Party. It is led by Ismael Hassan Metareum, is Islamic in outlook, and enjoys strong support in Aceh province and in east and central Java. However, its four constituent elements remain poorly fused. On non-Muslim issues, the PPP's members generally support government initiatives.

To be officially registered, political parties, until 1999, needed to subscribe to the state philosophy of Pancasila and have a membership which covers more than a quarter of Indonesia. This prevented the formation of narrowly regionalist-based groupings. Between 1975 and 1998, only Golkar, the PDI, and the PPP were permitted to function. Also, the two non-Golkar parties were debarred from organizing below the district level. To compensate for these restrictions, the state provided parties with funds to cover administrative, campaign, and leadership expenses. On the ending of three party dominance, in November 1998, more than 100 parties applied to be registered for the June 1999 parliamentary elections.

The following regionally based separatist groups are in conflict with the government: Front for an Independent East Timor (Frente Revolucionario de

Este Timor Independente: Fretilin, estd. 1974), which seeks independence for East Timor; the Free Papua Movement (Organizasi Papua Merdeka: OPM, estd. 1963), which seeks unification of Irian Jaya with Papua New Guinea; and the Free Aceh Movement (estd. 1990), which campaigns for Aceh's independence. In October 1996 Fretilin's exiled spokesperson, Jose Ramos-Horta, was awarded the Nobel Peace Prize.

Political leaders since 1970

1966–98 T N J Suharto (Golkar), 1998– Bucharuddin Jusuf Habibie (Golkar)

Latest elections

In the most recent DPR elections, which were held on 7 June 1999 and were contested by 48 parties, the DPI, won 34% of the 105 million valid votes counted, Golkar 22%, the Muslim-based National Awakening Party (PKB), led by Abdurrahman Wahid, 13%, the PPP 11%, the National Mandate Party (PAN), led by Amien Rais, 7%, and others, 13%. The vote count, from more than 300,000 polling stations, took more than six weeks to complete and the final seat tallies remained unclear at the end of July 1999, as a result of the complex proportional system of allocation. However, it was expected that the PDI would secure around 154 of the 462 elected DPR seats and Golkar more than 120. Turnout, in these first free elections in 44 years, was exceptionally high, at around 90% of the electorate.

Political history

Indonesia constitutes the largest archipelago nation in the world, comprising 13,667 mountainous and volcanic islands, 6,000 of which are inhabited. They are separated east–west by 5,271 kilometres/3,275 miles and north–south by 2,210 kilometres/1,373 miles. The islands were settled by immigrants from South China between 3000–500 BC, displacing the original Melanesian population. During the early centuries of the Christian era, they came under the influence of Hindu and Buddhist priests and traders, who spread their culture and religion and later, from AD 700 onwards, established substantial Hindu empires. Islam was introduced during the 13th century by Gujarati and Persian traders and had become the chief archipelago religion by the 15th century. Portuguese traders followed, in the early 16th century, and established lucrative spice-trading posts.

The Portuguese commercial monopoly over the 'spice islands' was successfully challenged by the Dutch, in 1595, and the archipelago, now designated the Netherlands Indies, was placed, between 1602 and 1798, under the supreme control of the Dutch East India Company. Initially, during the 17th century, the Dutch had concentrated purely on trade, establishing new trading centers, while leaving internal administration to indigenous Indonesian kingdoms. During the 19th century, however, direct Dutch rule was imposed. The islands were proclaimed a Dutch colony in 1816 and a sugar-based plantation economy was established on Java. In 1922, the Netherlands Indies were designated an integral part of the Netherlands kingdom.

During the 1920s and 1930s the rural economy faced mounting difficulties including, in 1926, a communist-inspired revolt. A nationalist movement developed, under the leadership of the pro-Communist Indonesian Nationalist Party (PNI), which was established in 1926, and headed by the charismatic Achmed Sukarno (1902–70). This was suppressed by the Dutch administration, the PNI's leaders being imprisoned and exiled between 1929 and 1932, but, in March 1942, following the occupation of the islands by Japanese forces, the party was installed in power as an anti-Western puppet government.

When Japan surrendered to the Allies, in August 1945, President Sukarno proclaimed Indonesia's independence from the Netherlands. The Dutch challenged this by launching military expeditions, between 1946 and 1949, before eventually agreeing to transfer sovereignty in December 1949. At the same time, a 'special union' was established between the two countries. This union was abrogated by Indonesia in February 1956.

The new republic was planned as a federation of 16 constituent regions, but was made unitary in August 1950. This naturally resulted in the dominance of Java, provoking revolts in Sumatra and the predominantly Christian South Moluccas. The paramount political figure in the new republic was President Sukarno, who, believing in the concept of 'guided democracy', ruled in an authoritarian manner and pursued an ambitious, expansionist, and nationalist foreign policy. He succeeded in effecting the transfer of Netherlands New Guinea (Irian Jaya) to Indonesia, in May 1963, but failed, after a confrontation with Malaysia, in the cases of Sabah and Sarawak in North Borneo.

In September 1965, amid deteriorating economic conditions, caused by extravagant government overspending and corruption, a coup was attempted against Sukarno by groups connected with the 2.5-million-strong Indonesian Communist Party (PKI). This was firmly put down, with tens of thousands of PKI supporters losing their lives, by army chief of staff, General T N J Suharto (b. 1921). He then proceeded to assume power as emergency ruler in March 1966.

General Suharto ended Indonesia's hostility towards Malaysia over Sabah and Sarawak in August 1966, and formally replaced Sukarno as president in February 1967. He then proceeded to institute what was termed a 'New Order'. This involved the concentration of political power in the hands of a coterie of army and security force (*Kopkamtib*) officers and, mainly American-educated, technocrat planners; the propagation of a new secular state philosophy of Pancasila, stressing unity and social justice; the pursuit of a liberal, free-enterprise and 'open-door' economic policy; the fierce suppression of communist political activity; and the tight control of ordinary party political activity. All opposition groups were fused, by orders, into two, 'neutered' units in 1973.

Aided by income from rising oil exports, significant industrial and agricultural growth was achieved during the 1970s, self-sufficiency in rice production being attained, for example, by the early 1980s. Per-capita GDP rose by 4.8% per year in real terms between 1965 and 1985. In addition, Indonesia's territorial borders were extended by the forcible annexation of the predominantly Catholic former Portuguese colony of East Timor, in 1975–76.

Suharto's authoritarian methods, however, promoted opposition from many quarters. The opposition came from leftwing organizations, radical Muslims, and tribal separatist groups in the outlying islands of Irian Jaya and East Timor. In Irian Jaya there was the Free Papua Movement (OPM) and in East Timor, the Fretilin (Front for an Independent East Timor) and UDI independence fronts.

Following the suppression of an OPM-organized rebellion in Irian Jaya, the Suharto government instituted, in 1986, a 'transmigration program', based on the resettlement there, and on other sparsely peopled 'outer islands', of a projected 65 million Javanese, by the year 2006. This scheme, which began in 1987, encountered strong opposition from indigenous Melanesians, prompting more than 10,000 refugees to emigrate to adjoining Papua New Guinea. In East Timor, meanwhile, it was reported that between 100,000 and 200,000 Timorese, a third to a sixth of the population, died from famine, disease, and continuing internal warfare during the decade immediately following the province's annexation. The United Nations refused to recognize Indonesian sovereignty over East Timor, which continued to be imposed through military force, although travel restrictions were partially eased from 1988.

During the early 1980s economic problems developed as world oil prices fell, oil providing 70% of Indonesia's foreign exchange earnings. The annual GDP growth rate dropped to 3.5% between 1980 and 1985, while the country's population continued to expand at a compound rate of 3.3%. Despite these difficulties, national support for Golkar rose nine points over its 1982 level to 73% in the general election of April 1987. A year later, in March 1988, Suharto was unanimously re-elected, as the sole candidate, for a fifth five-year presidential term.

In April 1991 a 45-member Democracy Forum was launched by leading members of the religious and cultural intelligentsia, including Abdurrchman Wahid, leader of the Nahdlatul Ulama, the country's largest Muslim association, and in August 1991 a Forum for the Purification of People's Sovereignty was set up by General Hartono Resko Dharsono, the country's most prominent dissident, who had been released from prison in September 1990. They aimed to promote more democratic values in a state that remained authoritarian – the latter was shown most clearly in the army's massacre on 12 November 1991 of between 50 and 180 demonstrators during a funeral ceremony in Dili, East Timor, and the subsequent execution of a further 60–80 'subversives'.

Despite a pick-up in the rate of economic growth, averaging 7% per year from 1989, support for Golkar fell to 68% of the national vote in the June 1992 general election. Reacting to this result, the party sought to somewhat reduce its links with the military and tolerate a somewhat greater degree of political openness (*keperbukaan*) and decentralization. Suharto was reelected for a sixth consecutive term as state president in March 1993. In December 1993 the PDI elected as its chair Megawati Sukarnoputri, the daughter of the former president Sukarno. Concerned at the support she drew from moderate Muslims and elements of the military for her more independent and nationalistic policy stance, in June 1996 the government engineered a split in the PDI to install as leader the more 'reliable' Suerjadi. This provoked rioting in Jakarta and the death, on 27 July 1996, of at least three people (Megawati's supporters claimed 54) in clashes with troops. In the following weeks, more than 170 PDI supporters were arrested, along with leaders of the Marxist-influenced People's Democratic Party (PRD), which was subsequently banned (until August 1998). The May 1997 DPR elections produced a landslide Golkar victory, but were marked by increased levels of violence and religious and ethnic tensions. In August 1997, after coming under concerted attack from international currency speculators, the rupiah was forced to float and soon fell by a third. In November 1997 a $43 billion (£26 billion) financial rescue package was agreed with the IMF on condition of restructuring reforms, including closure of 16 overextended banks, including some controlled by relatives of President Suharto, and cuts in government subsidies. The rupiah fell sharply again from January 1998 amid investors' concerns at delays in implementing the IMF austerity package and reports of Suharto's ill health. The unemployment level soared to above 10% and the level of external debt now exceeded annual GDP. In late January 1998, President Suharto agreed new IMF-imposed austerity measures, including a reining in of nepotistic monopolies. However, the consequent rise in fuel and food prices provoked riots in dozens of towns in February 1998, directed chiefly against the economically dominant ethnic Chinese community. Amid this gathering chaos, the 76-year-old Suharto was 're-elected' for a seventh term as president by the MPR in March 1998 and B J Habibie, the minister of research and technology and a long-time favorite of Suharto, became vicepresident. Additionally, the MPR restored to the president emergency powers relinquished in 1993. In March 1998, Suharto appointed a new cabinet, dominated by economic nationalists and cronies, including his daughter, who became welfare minister, and his golfing partner, who became trade and industry minister. From February 1998 anti-government student-led demonstrations against Suharto's re-election broadened into a demand for democratic reforms. They gathered momentum from March 1998, despite government bans, and from May 1998 there were also urban price riots. The security forces responded by firing both rubber bullets and live ammunition and on 12 May, during a peaceful demonstration at Trisakti University, killed six students. This ignited the prodemocracy movement, which coalesced under the leadership of Amien Rais, a university lecturer who headed the 28 million-strong Muhammadiyah Muslim organization. Between 13–15 May 1998 more than 1,188 people were killed in a wave of arson, looting, and rioting and from 18 May large crowds gathered in Jakarta demanding Suharto's resignation. A huge protest of one million people was planned for 20 May in Jakarta's Merdeka (Freedom) Square, to coincide with the country's Day of National Awakening, commemorating the birth of the nationalist movement against Dutch colonial rule. Amid fears of a Tiananmen Square style military crackdown, it was called off at the last moment. However, on the advice of the speaker of parliament and leading generals, Suharto stepped down as president on 21 May 1998, handing over power to his deputy, B J Habibie.

Habibie was viewed as a transitional ruler. He had a reputation for favoring state involvement in industry and had close links with Muslim intellectuals, but lacked a strong power-base. On 22 May 1998 he appointed a new 'reform cabinet', shorn of Suharto cronies, and removed Lt-General Prabowo Subjanto (b. 1951), Suharto's son-in-law, as commander of the Strategic Reserve Command (Kostrad). Habibie promised to revise repressive legislation, review all political detainees, examine the involvement of the military in repressing separatist groups during recent years, relax controls over the press, recognize independent trade unions and hold fresh parliamentary and presidential elections, in June and November, 1999 under revised electoral rules. In July 1998, he offered partial autonomy to East Timor, but ruled out independence. Golkar also moved quickly to distance itself from its association with the unpopular Suharto, removing seven of the former president's relatives from the MPR in July 1998. The new government faced tremendous economic problems, as GDP contracted by more than 10% during 1998, but its commitment to economic reform sufficiently impressed the IMF to persuade it to supply additional funds. By August 1998 more than 40 new political parties had been formed and registered, while Megawati resumed leadership of the PDI. However, opposition to Golkar was fragmented, with Amien Rais heading a new National Mandate Party (PAN) and Abdurahman Wahid the largest Muslim group, Nahdlatul Ulama (NU). During 1998 GDP contracted by more than 15%, causing widespread poverty and social unrest.

A special session of the MPR, held in November 1998, amid continuing student unrest, repealed much of the repressive legislation of the Suharto era, including the restriction to three officially sanctioned political parties. New political parties were now legalised; a two five-year term limit was imposed on future presidents; and the military's quota of seats in the 500-member House of Representatives (DPR) was reduced from 75 to 38.

In January 1999, against a backcloth of worsening ethnic and religious violence across Indonesia, the government agreed to consider the prospect of independence for East Timor. The Timorese guerrilla leader, Jose Xanana Gusmao, was released from prison to house arrest in Jakarta, February 1999. A month later, following talks in New York which involved Portugal and the UN Secretary General, it was agreed that there would be a referendum in East Timor on 30 August 1999, offering voters the choice between 'special autonomy' and independence. Meanwhile, thousands of recent immigrants from other parts of Indonesia began to flee East Timor, as violence escalated. There were also ethnic massacres in west Kalimantan in March 1999, Muslim-Christian riots in Maluku province, in the Spice Islands, and separatist unrest in Aceh province; while the government turned to the IMF and World Bank for fresh loans in an effort to shore up a weakened economy.

A free, multi-party general election – the country's first in 44 years - was held on 7 June 1999 and was contested by 48 political parties. Polling was carried out fairly, according to international observers, and Golkar, with only 22% of the vote, was defeated by the PDI, led by Megawati Sukarnoputri, which won 34% of the vote. However, the PDI was well short of a majority of seats in the DPR and it remained possible that Golkar and Habibie might be able to remain in power and retain the presidency, in the November 1999 MPR election, with the support of other parties.

In its external relations, Indonesia has for a long time pursued a nonaligned foreign policy, hosting the Bandung Conference of Third World nations in 1955 and the tenth summit of the Non-Aligned Movement in August 1992. It has also been a prominent member of ASEAN since its inception in 1967. However, the country's relations, political and economic, with the West have notably improved since the 1980s, although the Netherlands did suspend its foreign aid after the November 1991 Dili massacre. In December 1995 a security agreement was signed with Australia.

JAPAN

Nippon/Nihon ('The Land of the Rising Sun')

Capital: Tokyo

Social and economic data

Area: 371,815 sq km/143,559 sq miles

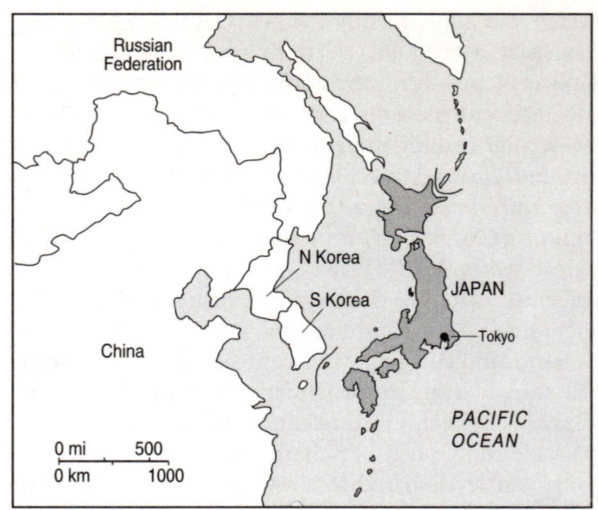

Population: 124,961,000*
Pop. density per sq km/sq mi: 336/870*
Urban population: 77%**
Literacy rate: 100%**
GDP: $4,963,600 million*; per-capita GDP: $39,720*
Government defense spending (% of GDP): 1.1%*
Currency: yen
Economy type: high income
Labor force in agriculture: 6%**
Unemployment rate: 3.2%*
* 1995.
** 1992.

Head of state

Emperor Akihito, since 1989

Head of government

Prime Minister Keizo Obuchi, since 1998

Ethnic composition

More than 99% of the population is of Japanese ethnic stock, with Japanese the official language.

Religions

Around 40% of the population adheres to Shintoism, an indigenous religion embracing the worship of ancestors and nature, 38% adheres to the Buddhist faith, and 4% to a range of Christian denominations. Shintoism and Buddhism are non-exclusive and overlap. Since World War II many new cults have emerged. They are known collectively as the New Religions (Shinko Shukyo), many being Buddhist offshoots.

Political features

State type: liberal democratic
Date of state formation: 5th century

Political structure: unitary
Executive: parliamentary
Assembly: two-chamber
Party structure: multiparty
Human rights rating: 82%
International affiliations: AfDB, AG (observer), APEC, AsDFB, BIS, CP, EBRD, ESCAP, G-5, G-7, G-10, IAEA, IBRD, ICC, ICFTU, IDB, IEA, IMF, IWC, LORCS, NEA, OAS (observer), OECD, UN, WTO

Local and regional government

The country is divided into nine regions, which are further subdivided into 47 prefectures, each of which is administered by an elected governor and has an elected assembly. Below, there are elected city, town, and village chief executives and assemblies. Local bodies are substantially dependent, however, on the central government for funding and policy direction.

Political system

Japan's 99-article, November 1946, constitution was framed by the occupying allied forces, with the intention of creating a consensual, parliamentary form of government and avoiding an overconcentration of executive authority. The head of the state is the emperor, whose functions are purely ceremonial, being described as 'the symbol of the State and of the unity of the people'. Real power is concentrated in the elected assembly and is exercised by a prime minister and cabinet.

The Japanese assembly, the Diet (Kokkai), is a two-chamber body composed of a 252-member upper house, the House of Councillors (Sangiin), and a 500-member lower house, the House of Representatives (Shugiin). The former has 152 representatives, elected from 47 prefectural constituencies on the basis of the 'limited vote' system, and 100 elected nationally by proportional representation. Under the 'limited vote' system electors cast a single vote, the candidates with the highest number of votes in each single-, or multi-member, constituency being returned in rank order. Electors are given an additional, separate, vote for the extra 100 members. To be included in this national ballot, parties must submit a list of at least ten candidates, at least five of whom are existing Diet members, or they must have won at least 4% of the vote at the previous election. Each councillor serves a six-year term, half the chamber being elected every three years.

Members of the House of Representatives used to be elected for a four-year term, subject to dissolution, in large, 3–5 member constituencies, on the basis of the 'limited vote'. However, these were blamed for encouraging 'money politics', and have been replaced, since constitutional changes in 1994, by 300 single-member constituencies. A further 200 deputies in the new 500-member House are now returned by proportional representation on the basis of regional contests. Electors, as in Germany, have two votes: one for a single-member candidate and the other for a proportional representation candidate. In an effort to reduce parties' reliance on business donations, the state financing of political parties has been introduced. The ballot is restricted to those aged 20 years and over.

The House of Representatives is the dominant, and more important, of the two chambers of parliament. It is able to override vetoes on bills imposed by the House of Councillors if a two-thirds majority of those present is obtained. It also has final approved on financial questions. In practice, interhouse disputes, when they arise, are resolved by the convening of a special Joint Conference Committee. In both chambers, legislative business is effected through a system of Standing and Special Committees, with stress placed on achieving a consensus. Also, the opposition is allowed to chair a number of important committees. The legislature convenes at least once a year for a session which must last at least 150 days, but is usually far longer.

To amend the constitution, a two-thirds majority vote of all members of each chamber of the Diet is required, followed by a majority affirmation by the electorate in a special referendum. Despite support for changes among elements within the ruling Liberal Democratic Party (LDP), the 'blocking' strength of the opposition parties has meant that no fundamental amendments to the 1946 'American constitution' have so far been made.

Executive administration is entrusted to a prime minister, chosen by the majority grouping within the Diet, who selects a cabinet of about 20 to 25 members and works from a residence known as the Kantei. All are collectively responsible to the assembly, which can unseat the government by a successful 'no-confidence' motion. Cabinet members oversee the work of both government ministries and agencies and must consist of civilians, according to the rules of the constitution. The majority, including the prime minister, must also be members of the Diet. The cabinet functions in a collective manner based on consensus, with individual ministers working closely with their respective departmental senior bureaucrats, who, in reality, are the crucial policy-framing figures.

The post of prime minister, with its important patronage powers, was, between 1955 and 1993, assigned to the president of the LDP. The frequent changes in personnel occupying the post thus resulted from the desire of party faction leaders to rotate occupancy of this 'plum' position, rather than from substantive 'political' factors. In addition, cabinet posts were also liberally distributed between senior faction members, ministers rarely serving more than two years in a post.

Japan possesses a 15-justice Supreme Court, whose members are appointed by the cabinet, with the exception of the high judge, who is appointed by the emperor, on the nomination of the cabinet. Once appointed, judges serve until the legal retirement age, but are subject to approval in popular referenda taking place every ten years. The Supreme Court enjoys administrative control over lower courts and the power of judicial review. It is able to determine the constitutionality of any law. In practice, however, as a result of the Japanese preference for settling disputes by negotiation and mediation, its use of these powers has been unusually limited.

Political parties

The dominant political party in Japan is the Liberal Democratic Party (LDP: Jiyu-Minshuto). It monopolized power for nearly four decades after its formation, but failed to win House of Representatives' majorities in 1976, 1979, and 1983. In 1993 it was finally ousted from office, but it gained a share of power in 1994 at the heart of an improbable 'grand coalition' which included its traditional opponent, the Social Democratic Party of Japan (SDPJ).

Although tracing its origins back to the first parties established in the 1870s, the LDP was constituted in its present form in November 1955, with the uniting of two conservative parties, the Liberals, led by Taketora Ogata, and the Japan Democratic Party, led by Prime Minister Ichiro Hatoyama. Traditionally, the party has enjoyed strong support in rural areas, these constituencies being currently substantially over-represented in the Diet, in voter–deputy terms, vis-à-vis the growing urban districts. It also enjoys liberal funding from the business community, both small and large, and has developed, during its years in government, close links with the bureaucracy. About a quarter of LDP Diet members are former civil servants, often of senior rank.

Although viewed as 'conservative' in its ideological outlook, the LDP is, in reality, more of a 'catch-all' organization, embracing a broad and shifting variety of domestic and foreign affairs policy ideas which are applied in a pragmatic and corporatist manner. Its uniting principles, however, are a belief in the efficacy of private enterprise, support for the development of a welfare state, and a continuation of Japan's alliance with the United States.

Membership of the LDP was put at 2.7 million in 1994, corresponding to 2.2% of the total population, with its strongest support in the countryside and among the old. However, the party lacks an effective constituency, grass-roots, organization in the West European sense and is notably divided into factions based on personalities, rather than ideology.

In the early 1990s, there were half a dozen important factions, the leading one being the Takeshita faction, which contained more than 100 Diet members. These groupings, which involve the development of personalized patron–client ties between senior leaders and younger aspirants, have operated as a means of promoting the ministerial interests of the former, while advancing the careers of the latter, by step-by-step progression up the political ladder. Based on the Japanese emphasis on the neo-Confucianist principles of duty and obligation and traditional respect for family and personal ties, currently a third of the LDP's Diet members are related to another member by blood or marriage. The existence of factions has served to institutionalize competition within the party. At the local level, factional groupings bargain for acceptance of their members as party candidates in multimember constituencies. However, the ultimate goal of a faction is to secure for its leader the coveted post of LDP president. This is assigned biennially by a majority vote of the party's Diet members. Between 1955 and 1993, and since 1996, this post went with that of prime minister.

Undermined by financial scandals involving faction leaders, notably Takeshita, Kiichi Miyazawa, and Shin Kanemaru, the LDP's hegemony crumbled during the early 1990s and the party splintered in 1993, with the formation of two new parties, Shinseito (Japan Renewal Party) and Shinto Sakigake (New Party Harbinger), by ex-members of the LDP who were committed to reform of Japan's political system. Shinseito included many former members of the LDP faction led by Tsutomu Hata and the ambitious LDP secretary – general, Ichiro Ozawa. Sakigake was led by Masayoshi Takemura. A year earlier, in 1992, another center-right reform party, the Japan New Party (JNP), was set up by Morihiro Hosokawa, a former LDP governor.

More than 10,000 political parties are registered as functioning in Japan. Only five parties other than the LDP and its recent offshoots are, however, significant forces. The second ranking party in the country and leading opposition body is the 115,000-member Social Democratic Party of Japan (SDPJ: Nippon Shakaito), known until 1996 as the Japan Socialist Party (JSP) and led by Takako Doi. The SDPJ traces its roots back to the Socialist Party, which was established in 1925, but was allowed to play only a tangential role in interwar politics. The JSP, itself, was set up in November 1946 and temporarily held power between May 1947 and March 1948. The party subsequently split, in 1951–52, over its response to the US–Japanese Peace Treaty, but reunited in 1955. Formerly, it favored a democratic socialist economic strategy and the establishment of a nonaggressive mutual security system, embracing Japan, China, the United States, and the USSR. However, since April 1990 it has adopted a social democratic policy program and in September 1994 abandoned its traditional pacifist stance. Strongest in urban areas and among unionized workers, it is closely linked to the General Council of Trade Unions of Japan (Sohyo), with a membership of over 4 million. Support for the party has, however, fallen somewhat since the 1960s, when its share of the national vote stood at 27–29%. The party's formation, in 1994, of a 'grand coalition' with its traditional enemy, the LDP, and Sakigake, created unease and divisions within the SDPJ and in March 1996 a number of leftwingers defected to form the New Socialist Party (NSP).

Further to the left stands the Japanese Communist Party (JCP: Nippon Kyosanto), which was founded in 1922, though subsequently banned until 1945, its leaders being imprisoned or exiled. Support for the JCP has increased since the early 1970s, following its assertion of independence from both the Sino and Russian communist ideological camps, its renouncing of a call for violent revolution, and its focusing on economic and social improvement. The JCP is a mass party, with around 370,000 members. It is organized on hierarchical, 'democratic centralist' lines and controlled by a Presidium (Politburo) chaired by Tetsuzo Fuwa.

Occupying center-left ground is the 'humanitarian socialist' Komei (Clean Government Party), which was formed in November 1964 as the political wing of the 8-million-member Soka Gakkai Buddhist sect, Value Creation Society, which was itself established in 1930. It has a membership of 300,000. The party has campaigned for greater honesty in politics and improving the lot of the poor. It draws much of its support from workers, especially female, in small and medium-sized urban industries. The party's religious affiliation has, however, tended to hamper its development. It was known as Komeito until 1994.

In December 1994, in an important political development, a new opposition coalition party was formed, Shinshinto (New Frontier Party). This combined nine parties, including the JNP, Shinseito, the center-left Democratic Socialist Party (DSP: estd. 1960), and defectors from Komeito. Ichiro Ozawa was elected leader of the party in December 1995. It was intended to reverse a trend towards fragmentation of Japanese party politics and establish an effective two-party system, pitting the New Frontier Party against the incumbent LDP, SDPJ, and Sakigake coalition. However, Ozawa's forceful leadership style was disliked and Shinshinto members began to defect to other parties, including the LDP and the Democratic Party of Japan (DPJ), which was formed in 1996 by Naoto Kan, a left-leaning populist. Consequently, Shinshinto was dissolved in December 1997. It was replaced in January 1998 by six new opposition parties, including the Liberal Party (LP), formed by Ichiro Ozawa, with 54 lower-house deputies, and Minseito (Good Governance Party), formed by Morihiro Hosokawa and Tsutomu Hata.

Political leaders since 1970*

1964–72 Eisaku Sato (LDP), 1972–74 Kakuei Tanaka (LDP), 1974–76 Takeo Miki (LDP), 1976–78 Takeo Fukuda (LDP), 1978–80 Masayoshi Ohira (LDP), 1980–82 Zenko Suzuki (LDP), 1982–87 Yasuhiro Nakasone (LDP), 1987–89 Noboru Takeshita (LDP), 1989 Sosuke Uno (LDP), 1989–91 Toshiki Kaifu (LDP), 1991–93 Kiichi Miyazawa (LDP), 1993–94 Morihiro Hosokawa (JNP), 1994 Tsutomu Hata (Shinseito), 1994–96 Tomiichi Murayama (SDPJ), 1996–98 Ryutaro Hashimoto (LDP), 1998– Keizo Obuchi (LDP)

* Prime ministers.

Latest elections

The most recent House of Representatives elections were held on 20 October 1996. The LDP won 239 of the 500 available seats, while Shinshinto won 156 seats and the DPJ 52 seats. The JCP performed surprisingly strongly, winning 26 seats (11 up on its 1993 performance) and finishing ahead of the SDPJ, which won only 15 seats (down 55 on 1993). New Party Sakigake won two seats. The latest elections for half the seats of the 252-member House of Councillors were held on 12 July 1998. The LDP ended up controlling 103 seats (down 15 from its previous totals), while the DPJ controlled 47 (up 9), the JCP 23 (up 9), Komei 22 (down 2), the SDPJ 13 (down 7) and independents 25 (up 11). Turnout, after slumping to a record low of 44% in 1995, rose to 59%, helped by an extension of voting hours and a relaxation of postal-voting restrictions.

Political history

1. Early invasions to the 1986 election

Originally inhabited by Ainu people, Japan was invaded and settled from an early date by Manchu-Koreans and Malayans. In the 5th century AD the country was unified by the Yamato state, and, in the 6th century, Buddhism was introduced from Korea and Confucianist culture from China. During the 7th century a centralized monarchy on Chinese lines was established, but by the 12th century power had devolved to regional potentates, subservient to a absolute military ruler, termed shogun. After a period of decentralization, the Tokugawa family, initially under the leadership of Iyeyasu (1542–1616), reunified the country during the later 16th century, establishing a new capital at Edo, now Tokyo, in central Honshu and creating a bureaucratized and demilitarized quasi-feudal system. From this date, despite self-imposed isolation from the outside world, considerable economic progress was made.

Military pressure from the Western powers, particularly the United States, forced an end to this isolation in the mid-19th century and, fearing colonial invasion, reformist elements within the *samurai* or military caste bureaucracy united with southwestern regional lords (*daimyo*) to overthrow the Tokugawa Shogunate, 1603–1867, and restore executive power to the young emperor Meiji Tenno in 1867. His family, based at Kyoto, had previously been Tokugawa puppets. To buttress imperial authority, Shintoism was established as the state religion, and the emperor was defined as the 'Divine Ruler'. During the next two decades after this 'Meiji Restoration', the feudal system was abolished, *samurai* and *daimyo* lords were pensioned off, the land system was reformed, and a new constitutional system, with an elected assembly and Westernized legal code, was established.

The radical reforms of the early Meiji era constituted a 'revolution from above', carried out by a small clique of nationalistic members of the former Tokugawa bureaucracy, termed the 'Genro', who were to remain the real power wielders, rather than the emperor, until the strengthening of party government during the interwar years. Impelled by a concern to 'catch up' with the West, they oversaw the rapid development of new industries and the build-up of a modern new army and navy. In conflicts in 1894–95 and 1904–05 respectively, China and Russia were defeated, and new colonies were secured, in the form of Formosa, now Taiwan, South Manchuria, Korea, and south Sakhalin. Rapid economic advance was achieved during the World War I and during the 1920s, the 'Taisho era', and there was movement towards democracy and party government, after the electorate had been substantially enlarged by the Reform Acts of 1919 and 1925. The 1925 Act established universal male suffrage for those of 25 years and over.

During the later 1920s, however, with economic conditions deteriorating, army leaders and ultra-nationalists gained the upper hand, launching the nation on an ultimately destructive phase of imperialist expansion. This began with the occupation of Manchuria in 1931, was followed by the invasion of China in 1937, and then war with the United States and Britain, after Japan's pre-emptive attack on the US Pearl Harbor naval base in Hawaii, in December 1941. Initially, during the early stages of the war, Japan successfully took control of much of the Asia-Oceania region, between Burma and the Philippines. By 1944, however, it was in retreat and, on 15 August 1945, following the United States' dropping of atomic bombs on Hiroshima and Nagasaki, Emperor Hirohito (1901–89) was compelled to tender the nation's unconditional surrender. An Allied control commission assumed charge and Japan was placed under military occupation by Allied, chiefly United States, troops, commanded by General Douglas MacArthur (1880–1964). In April 1952 the US–Japanese Peace Treaty came into force and full sovereignty was regained.

As a consequence of Japan's military defeat, Korea was made independent, Manchuria and Formosa were returned to China, and the small, former German, Pacific islands, that had been mandated to Japan after World War I, were now placed by the United Nations under American trusteeship. Japan was subsequently to regain the islands of Ryukyu, in 1972, and Bonin and Volcano, in 1968, from the United States. However, despite frequent appeals, the Northern Territories, which include the islands of the Shikotan and Habomai group, and the southernmost Kurils, which include Kunashiri and Etorofu, are still controlled by the Russian Federation and have not been returned.

During the immediate postwar phase of Allied rule, between August 1945 and April 1952, a sweeping 'democratization campaign' was launched, involving radical land, social, and educational reform and the framing of a new 'Peace constitution', in 1946. Under it, Emperor Hirohito was persuaded to renounce his claims to divinity and become a figurehead constitutional monarch, while the nation, through Article 9, committed itself to a peaceful foreign policy. During the 1950s Japan concentrated on economic reconstruction, retreating towards neutralism in foreign affairs, under the protection of the American umbrella provided by the September 1951 Security Pact.

Postwar Japanese politics were dominated by the new Liberal Democratic Party (LDP), which was formed in 1955 by the merger of existing conservative parties. It was to provide the country with a regular succession of prime ministers. Real decision-making authority, however, became focused on a broader, corporatist grouping of politicians, senior civil servants, and directors of the major *zaibatsu* finance and industrial houses. Through a centralized, guided approach to economic development, which was epitomized by the operations of the influential Ministry for International Trade and Industry (MITI), and by the inspired targeting of, and investment in, promising new transport, consumer-durable, and electronics growth industries, the Japanese economy expanded dramatically during the 1950s and 1960s, with GDP regularly advancing at an annual rate of 10%. During these years, Japan was also rehabilitated within the international community, entering the United Nations in 1958, re-establishing diplomatic relations with Western nations, and, following the lead taken by Nixon in the United States, with communist China, in 1972.

In 1960 and 1968–69 Japan's hitherto tranquil internal politics were rocked by violent demonstrations against alleged American domination, involving the anarchic 'Red Army' terrorist organization. These were followed, in December 1974, by the resignation of Prime Minister Kakuei Tanaka (1918–93), in the wake of a bribery scandal, involving the American Lockheed Corporation. This culminated in Tanaka's arrest and resignation from the LDP, in July 1976, and his later conviction and sentence to four years' imprisonment, in October 1983. This scandal seriously tarnished the image of the LDP and led to the loss of its majority in the House of Representatives in the general election of December 1976. It also resulted in the formation of the New Liberal Club, as a breakaway grouping. The LDP remained in power, however, as the largest single party within the Diet.

During the 1970s and early 1980s, Japanese economic growth continued, though at a reduced annual rate of 4.5%, the country making a major impact on the markets of the United States and Europe, as an exporter of electrical goods, machinery, motor vehicles, and new high-technology items. By 1985 Japan had become the world's largest exporter of manufactured goods, surpassing the United States and (West) Germany. The growth in Japan's trade surplus and, in particular, the concentration of the country's export activity in a few sensitive sectors, served to create resentment overseas, however, as economic recession began to grip Europe and the United States between 1979 and 1982. This led to calls for Japan to open up its internal market to foreign exporters and to assume a greater share of the defense burden for the Asia-Pacific region. Prime ministers Takeo Miki (1974–76), Takeo Fukuda (1976–78), Masayoshi Ohira (1978–80), and Zenko Suzuki (1980–82) firmly resisted these pressures, and the Japanese government, in 1976, imposed a rigid 1% of GNP limit on the level of defense spending permissible.

However, under Prime Minister Yasuhiro Nakasone (b. 1917), who assumed power in November 1982, a review of policy was instituted. Nakasone favored a strengthening of Japan's defense capability, a re-evaluation of attitudes towards the country's past, and the introduction of a more liberal, open-market economic strategy at home. These proposed policy departures proved controversial and could only partially be implemented. However, the forthright Nakasone emerged as a popular national figure and, after becoming, in November 1984, the first prime minister since Eisaku Sato, who had governed between 1964 and 1972, to be re-elected as LDP leader for more than one term, succeeded in securing a landslide victory in the July 1986 general election. In this contest, the LDP, after having experienced its worst ever reverse in the previous national poll of December 1983, achieved its highest level of popular support since 1963 and a record number of seats in the House of Councillors.

Soon after the July 1986 election the by-laws of the LDP were altered so as to allow party presidents a one-year extension beyond the normal limit of two two-year terms each, thus effectively extending Nakasone's tenure as prime minister until November 1987. During his final year in office, Nakasone introduced a sweeping tax reform bill, aimed at restoring 'justice and flexibility' to an archaic system, but was forced, because of Diet opposition, to make major compromises, including the withdrawal of plans to introduce a 5% value-added tax (VAT). Despite this political 'defeat', Nakasone remained sufficiently influential within the LDP, and popular outside, to effectively hand pick his successor as party and national leader. He nominated

LDP secretary general, Noboru Takeshita (b. 1924), after a factional deadlock within the party.

2. Takeshita to economic decline

The new prime minister pledged a continuation of his predecessor's domestic and foreign policies, including improving and extending the country's diplomatic relations, reintroducing a tax reform bill, and making a determined effort to reduce its record $86,690-million balance-of-payments surplus. Takeshita had notable personal success in the area of tax reform, a bill being passed by the House of Representatives in 1988 which lowered income tax and introduced a national sales tax at 3%. This measure proved, however, to be electorally unpopular. More seriously, the new government's popular standing was undermined by the eruption, in July 1988, of the 'Recruit Cosmos scandal'. This involved 'insider' share dealing, indirectly and directly, by senior party figures including Takeshita, Nakasone, and Finance Minister Kiichi Miyazawa (b. 1919). The latter resigned in December 1988, to be followed by Justice Minister Takashi Hasegawa and Deputy Prime Minister Ken Harada in January 1989. Finally, in April 1989, with the government's and the LDP's popularity ratings standing at the unprecedentedly low levels of 4% and 25% respectively, Takeshita announced that he would resign as soon as the annual budget was passed and a successor found. His replacement, in June 1989, was the former foreign minister, Sosuke Uno (1922–98).

After barely 53 days in office, Uno, who was dogged by a geisha sex scandal and whose party endured loss of control of the upper house in the elections of July 1989, announced his intention to step down, in turn, as soon as a successor could be found. This marked an inauspicious start to the new Heisei ('achievement of universal peace') era, which had been proclaimed following the death, in January 1989, of Hirohito (*Showa*) and the accession to the imperial throne of his son, Akihito (b. 1933). In August 1989, Uno's eventual successor as premier was Toshiki Kaifu (b. 1932), a former education minister and a member of the LDP's small, scandal-free Komoto faction. He formed a new cabinet whose members were comparatively young and which, in an attempt to counter the growing appeal to women of the JSP, led by Ms Takako Doi (b. 1929), included two women. The JSP gained 50 seats in the February 1990 Diet election, but the LDP held on to power, capturing 46% of the national vote, down 3% on 1986.

During the Gulf conflict of 1990–91, Japan pledged $13 billion to support the US-led anti-Iraq coalition. Prime Minister Kaifu failed in his attempt to persuade the Diet to approve a bill authorizing the sending there of unarmed, noncombatant military personnel. However, in 1992 a modified Peacekeeping Cooperation Act was passed. Kaifu also failed to secure passage of an electoral reform bill. Though embarrassed from the autumn of 1991 by new securities and crime syndicate (*yakuza*) scandals, the LDP, led by the popular Kaifu, polled strongly in the local elections of April 1991. Nevertheless, Kaifu was replaced in October 1991 as LDP leader and prime minister by the Recruit-implicated ex-finance minister, Kiichi Miyazawa.

The new administration was faced with economic slowdown. Its standing was further damaged by the Sagawa Kyubin financial scandal in which many leading figures within the LDP, including the Takeshita faction 'kingmaker', Shin Kanemaru (1914–98), who was arrested and sent for trial, were implicated. Kanemaru's removal led the powerful Takeshita faction to split into two groups, led by Keizo Obuchi, who had the support of Noboru Takeshita, and by Tsutomu Hata (b. 1936), who was backed by the LDP's secretary general, Ichiro Ozawa (b. 1942). The Hata faction, which was committed to reform of the Japanese political system in an effort to end the scourge of 'money politics', eventually broke with the LDP in June 1993. By voting with the opposition on a no-confidence motion, it brought down the Miyazawa administration and when a general election was called, Hata and Ozawa formed the new Shinseito (Japan Renewal Party) party. Along with Shinto Sakigake (New Party Harbinger), which had been concurrently formed by LDP rebels, and the Japan New Party, set up in 1992 by Morihiro Hosokawa (b. 1938) with the intention of cleansing the political system, and the older centrist and left-of-center Komeito, DSP, and SDPJ, Shinseito succeeded in ousting the LDP from power in the general election of July 1993, as LDP support slumped to just 37% of the national vote and it won only 223 of the 511 contended seats. This was the LDP's first national defeat since its formation in 1955.

The new multiparty coalition government was headed by the popular Morihiro Hosokawa, who was drawn from a distinguished *samurai* (military caste) and was a member of the LDP until 1990, with Tsutomu Hata, serving as foreign minister and deputy prime minister. Its top priorities were to reform the system for electing Diet members and funding political parties and to reflate the economy. A watered-down constitutional reform bill was accepted by both chambers of the Diet in January 1994, providing for replacement of the House of Representative's multimember constituencies by 300 single-member constituencies, with a further 200 deputies to be returned by proportional representation. However, financial scandals, albeit relatively minor, involving Ozawa and Hosokawa, surfaced during 1993–94 and persuaded Hosokawa to resign in April 1994. He was replaced as prime minister by Tsutomu Hata, on 25 April 1994, but immediately the SDPJ left the ruling coalition. This was ascribed to the party's concern that they had been excluded from a new parliamentary group, Kaishin (Innovation), which had been formed by Ozawa and comprised the JNP, Shinseito, the DSP, and recent new defectors from the LDP. Hata thus headed a minority administration and, facing the prospect of defeat on a no-confidence motion, resigned as prime minister on 25 June 1994.

An improbable 'grand coalition' government was formed on 29 June 1994 by the SDPJ, LDP, and Sakigake, with the SDPJ's chairperson, Tomiichi Murayama (b. 1924), serving as prime minister and the LDP's president until September 1995, Yohei Kono (b. 1937), as foreign minister and deputy prime minister. The SDPJ and LDP, erstwhile enemies, were united by a shared opposition to the political aspirations of Ichiro Ozawa and concern at what they viewed as the overly rapid pace of recent economic deregulation and political reform. The coalition created divisions within both the SDPJ and LDP, but also encouraged the opposition to unite in a new coalition party, Shinshinto (New Frontier Party: NFP) in December 1994, one month before a serious earthquake struck the city of Kobe, claiming 6,000 lives and damage estimated at $40 billion. Shinshinto brought together and superseded the JNP, DSP, Komeito, and Shinseito. Led by the popular, former LDP premier, Toshiki Kaifu, and assisted by Ichiro Ozawa, it comprised 214 Diet members and represented a serious future electoral threat to the LDP. The political mood remained uncertain through 1995 as the economy was afflicted by recession, rising levels of unemployment, a falling stockmarket, and decreasing bank reserves, while the public was concerned by the activities of the Aum Shinrikyo religious cult, which was implicated in a terrifying and fatal poison-gas attack in March 1995 on the Tokyo subway. In July 1995 the SDPJ polled poorly in elections to the House of Councillors. Murayama remained as prime minister and in August 1995 made a formal apology for Japanese atrocities during World War II. However, Yohei Kono stood down as the LDP's leader in September 1995 in the face of a challenge from Ryutaro Hashimoto, the populist-conservative international trade and industry minister who became prime minister in January 1996. Wataru Kubo, of the SDPJ, became finance minister. Prime Minister Hashimoto negotiated, in April 1996, an agreement under which the United States would close some military bases, including a large air base on Okinawa island, in the south, but maintain a presence of 47,000 stationed troops. He also dealt with a financial crisis among bankrupt speculative mortgage companies (*jusen*) through a 685 billion-yen bail out package. However, this was unpopular with the public and, despite annual economic growth of 4%, to end three years of recession, Hashimoto's popularity fell to 35% by the spring of 1996. His approval rating recovered somewhat in the summer, while support for Shinshinto, led by Ozawa, dipped to around 10%. However, from September 1996, the LDP faced a new opposition challenge, from the Democratic Party of Japan (DPJ), formed by Yukio Hatoyama, a young reformist who had been a member of the New Party Sakigake, and with Naoto Kan, the popular health and welfare minister. The DPJ, which attracted 52 lower house deputies from Sakigake and the SDPJ, proclaimed that it would campaign for 'real democracy'. A snap general election was held on 20 October 1996, the first under a new system involving 300 first-past-the-post constituency seats and 200 decided by proportional representation and contested in 11 regional blocks. It produced an inconclusive result. The LDP, which was committed to an (unpopular) plan to raise consumption tax from 3% to 5% in April 1997, secured the most seats, 239, but was 12 short of an absolute majority. Shinshinto, which had been backed by the powerful Soka Gakkai Buddhist organization and had promised large tax cuts, secured 156 seats, while the DPJ held on to its existing tally of 52 seats. The chief losers were the LDP's erstwhile coalition partners, the SDPJ, led once again by Takako Doi, and New Party Sakigake. Initially, Hashimoto stayed on as prime minister by forming an informal coalition with the SDJP and Sakigake, but by November 1996 the LDP had attracted sufficient defectors from other parties to achieve an assembly majority. This returned Japan to single-party government for the first time since 1993. The cabinet formed by Hashimoto in November 1996 carefully balanced power on traditional LDP factional lines, with the main posts going to members of the four chief factions: the Keiseikai (Obuchi), Miyazawa, Mitsuzuka, and Nakasone factions. However, the government broke with tradition in its economic policy by deciding to try and promote economic recovery by reducing the budget deficit and overhauling the economic and social system rather than through increased expenditure. In September 1997 Hashimoto, having been re-elected president of the LDP, seemed set to remain prime minister for a further two years and he faced a disintegrating opposition, with Hata and Hosokawa having left Shinshinto, because of opposition to the leadership style of Ichiro Ozawa, along with more than 60 lower house deputies. However, the economy began to re-enter a new downturn, triggered by a slump in the Tokyo stockmarket and, in November 1997, by the collapse of the giant Yamaichi financial house. The government responded, in December 1997, by announcing a $76 billion package of tax cuts and assistance to the financial sector, but this was insufficient, as a financial crisis swept across other parts of Asia during 1997–98. The disbanding of the crumbling and ineffective Shinshinto, in December 1997, led to 44 lower-house deputies re-joining the LDP. However, many others joined the DPJ, which had become an increasingly serious challenger for government. During the first half of 1998, the worsening state of the Japanese economy, with bankruptcies and unemployment (at nearly 4%) reaching record levels and GDP now contracting, along with a succession of financial scandals, led to Hashimoto's public approval rating falling steeply. Despite approving, in March 1998, a record 16,000 billion yen ($124 billion) economic stimulus package, centerd on increased public works spending, by April 1998 Hashimoto, who was blamed for having taxed the country into its worst ever post-war recession, had an approval rating of just 25%. Thus, after the LDP polled disappointingly in elections to the upper house, in July 1998, Hashimoto resigned as LDP president. He was replaced by Keizo Obuchi (b. 1938), who was chosen from among three candidates, and headed the largest LDP faction, the Keiseikai, which was controlled from behind the scenes by Noboru Takeshita. Formerly the foreign minister, Obuchi now became prime minister and he persuaded the veteran Kiichi Miyazawa to become finance minister. The new government pursued a more orthodox Japanese economic program, with renewed emphasis on expansion of public works programs, coupled with anti-recessionary tax cuts. In January 1999 Prime minister Keizo Obuchi (LDP) effectively formed a coalition government with the new Liberal Party (LP), led by Ozawa, which had 47 seats in the lower house. The LP's deputy leader, Takeshi Noda, was brought into the cabinet as home affairs minister. However, the coalition still lacked a majority in the upper house. In April 1999, Shintaro Ishihara, a nationalist writer and ex-LDP politician who was opposed to America's military presence in Japan, was elected governor of Tokyo, defeating the LDP-backed former senior UN official, Yasushi Akashi.

KAZAKHSTAN

Republic of Kazakhstan
Kazak Respublikasy

Capital: Astana (Replaced Almaty (Alma-Ata), situated in the south, as capital in November 1997, and was known as Akmola until June 1998.)

Social and economic data

Area: 2,717,300 sq km/1,049,155 sq miles
Population: 17,027,000*
Pop. density per sq km/sq mi: 6/16*
Urban population: 58%**
Literacy rate: 97%**
GDP: $22,140 million*; per-capita GDP: $1,300*
Government defense spending (% of GDP): 3.0%*
Currency: tenge
Economy type: middle income
Labor force in agriculture: 22%**
Unemployment rate: 1.0%**
* 1995.
** 1992.

Head of state (executive)

President Nursultan Nazarbayev, since 1990

Head of government

Prime Minister Nurlan Balgymbayev, since 1997

Ethnic composition

Forty-five per cent of the population is of Kazakh ethnic stock, 36% ethnic Russians, 6% German, 5% Ukrainian, 2% Uzbek, and 2% Tatar. All nationalities are guaranteed equal status by the constitution, but there have been increasing tensions in eastern Kazakhstan between the Russian-speaking Cossack community and ethnic Kazakhs. Consequently, a forum on inter-ethnic issues, the Assembly of Peoples of Kazakhstan, was formed. In northern Kazakhstan ethnic Russians form a majority of the population and separatist sentiments are growing. The official language, since 1989, has been Kazakh, a member of the Central Turkic language group, but Russian is also used as a language of inter-ethnic communication.

Religions

The Kazakhs, who were converted to Islam in the 19th century, are predominantly Sunni Muslims of the Hanafi school. Since 1985, many new mosques have been opened. The ethnic Russians adhere to the Russian Orthodox Church and there are also significant Protestant, chiefly Baptist, and Roman Catholic communities. The republic is a secular state and religious discrimination is outlawed by the constitution.

Political features

State type: authoritarian nationalist
Date of state formation: 1991
Political structure: unitary
Executive: unlimited presidential
Assembly: two-chamber
Party structure: multiparty
Human rights rating: N/A
International affiliations: CIS, EBRD, ECO, IAEA, IBRD, IMF, NACC, OIC (observer), OSCE, PFP, UN

Local and regional government

There are 14 regions and the capital, each with elected local governments, headed by *akims*, and below there are city and rural districts, towns, and villages with local councils (*masllikhat*).

Political system

Under the terms of the constitution of August 1995, Kazakhstan has a presidential executive system. Supreme executive power is held by a president popularly elected for a seven-year term and who must have a fluent knowledge of Kazakh and be aged over 35. The president, who is head of state and commander in chief, has broad executive powers, can return draft legislation to the legislature 'for further discussion', schedules parliamentary meetings, and addresses an annual message to the nation. The government, which comprised 16 members in March 1998 and is headed by a prime minister, is responsible to the president. Legislative authority is exercised by a two-chamber Parliament (Parlament), comprising a 47-member upper chamber, the Senate, and a 67-seat lower house, the Majlis (Assembly). Seven of the senators are appointed by the president and the remaining 40 are elected in two-seat constituencies by special regional electoral colleges composed of members of local councils. One-half of the Senate is elected every two years, for four year terms. Majlis deputies are directly elected every four years in single-seat constituencies through the second ballot majoritarian electoral system. A seven-member Constitutional Council, appointed for six-year terms partly by the president and by the chairs of the Senate and Majlis, monitors adherence to the constitution. However, its rulings can be vetoed by the president. The constitution guarantees freedom of speech and assembly, and prohibits censorship, although, in practice, restrictions have been imposed by the Nazarbayev regime.

Political parties

The main political parties are the pro-Nazarbayev People's Unity Party (PUP) and Democratic Party (DP). The PUP, formed in 1993, is a centrist body which opposes radical nationalism and promotes social and ethnic harmony. It is led by President Nazarbayev. Opposition forces include the centrist People's Congress of Kazakhstan (NKK; estd. 1991); the nationalist Republican Party (Azat; estd. 1992), led by Kamal Ormantayev; the Kazakhstan Communist Party (KCP), which was suspended in 1991 but allowed to re-register in 1994; the Socialist Party of Kazakhstan (SPK), formed in 1991 to replace the CPK; and the ethnic Slav Lad ('harmony') movement, led by Aleksandra Dokuchayeva. In April 1996 a new opposition movement, Azamat ('Citizen'), was formed by a group of writers, scientists, and public figures, led by Pet Svoik. In January 1998 it united with the SPK and KCP to from a People's Front, to fight for democratic principles and human rights.

Political leaders since 1970

1989– Nursultan Nazarbayev (ex-communist independent)*

* Leader of the Communist Party from 1989 and president from 1990.

Latest elections

The last direct presidential election was held on 10 January, 1999 and was won by the incumbent Nursultan Nazarbayev, who secured 82% of the vote. The closest of his three rivals, Serikbolsyn Abdildin, of the KCP, attracted 12% of the vote. Turnout was 86%. The most recent legislative elections were held in December 1995, to the Senate and Majlis. Forty-three Majlis deputies were returned in the first round of voting on 9 December, with run-off contests held for the other 24 seats on 23 December 1995 and 4 February 1996. Further Senate elections were held in October 1997. In the main Majlis elections of 9 December 1995 turnout was 78%. More than three-quarters of those elected were either independents or members of the pro-president PUP and DUP. Deputies were also elected from the centrist NKK, the communist SPK and KCP, and the Slavic Movement-Lad.

Political history

The Kazakhs are descendants of Mongol and Turkic tribes who settled in the region early in the Christian era. They established their own distinctive tribal confederation, the Kazakh Orda, between the late 15th and early 17th centuries, but then split into large nomadic federations, known as the Large, Middle, and Lesser Hordes, led by Khans (chiefs). The Hordes, militarily threatened by Oirot Mongols from the east, turned to the Russian tsar for protection during the 18th century. Russian control became gradually tighter between 1822 and 1848, with the Khans being deposed, and in the later 19th century many Russian and Ukrainian peasants were resettled in the region. This caused resentment, leading to a fierce rebellion against Russian rule in 1916 in which 150,000 were killed. The Russian Revolution of 1917 led to civil war in Kazakhstan, but in 1920 it joined the USSR as an autonomous republic and became a full union republic in 1936. During the early 1930s more than a million people died in Kazakhstan as a result of starvation and repression associated with the Soviet agricultural collectivization program. During the early 1940s, under the orders of the Soviet dictator Josef Stalin, large numbers of Germans were deported from the Volga region to the republic. Northern Kazakhstan was the site of the Soviet leader Nikita Khrushchev's ambitious 'virgin lands' agricultural extension program during the 1950s, which not only led to overcropping and harvest failures during the early 1960s and drying out of the Aral Sea, but also to a large influx of Russian settlers, who had numbered just 20% of the population in 1926, turning the Kazakhs into a minority in their own republic. Nuclear testing sites established in eastern Kazakhstan, new industries, and the Baikonur space center at Leninsk also drew in Slav settlers.

There were violent nationalist riots in the capital, Almaty, in December 1986 when the long-serving and corrupt Brezhnevite Kazakh Communist Party (KCP) leader, Dinmukahmed Kunayev, was effectively dismissed by the reformist Soviet leader Mikhail Gorbachev and replaced by an ethnic Russian, Gennadi Kolbin. Four people died. In June 1989 Nursultan Nazarbayev (b. 1940), an astute, nationalist-minded, 'reform-communist' who had been the republic's prime minister since 1984, assumed leadership of the KCP and in February 1990 became the republic's president. Nazarbayev embarked on a pragmatic program of cultural and market-centerd economic reform, involving the privatization of the service and housing sectors, and drawing on the advice of outside South Korean and Singaporean economists, and also pressed for greater economic autonomy for the republic, which declared its sovereignty in October 1990.

During the spring of 1991 President Nazarbayev, a member of the Politburo of the Communist Party of the Soviet Union, pressed for the signing of a new USSR Union Treaty 'of sovereign states with equal rights', and 94% of the electorate supported continuation of the Union in the all-USSR referendum of March 1991. Nazarbayev also stood out against the August 1991 anti-Gorbachev attempted coup in Moscow, describing it as 'illegal and unconstitutional' and tendering his resignation from the Communist Party of the Soviet Union and its Politburo. Soon after the coup was thwarted, the KCP was abolished. However, Nazarbayev played a key role in ensuring that the 'uncontrolled disintegration' of the USSR was averted and that non-Slav republics joined the new Commonwealth of Independent States (CIS), which was formed on 21 December 1991 at Almaty.

The independence of Kazakhstan, which was the last of the republics of the USSR to leave the Union, was formally recognized by the United States and other Western nations in January 1992 and it was admitted into the Conference on Security and Cooperation in Europe (CSCE, later the OSCE) in the same month. It became a member of the United Nations in March 1992. Kazakhstan inherited substantial nuclear forces from the USSR, including 1,410 warheads of SS-18 strategic missiles. However, the Nazarbayev administration pledged to gradually remove these, commencing in 1992 with tactical weapons, and to become nuclear-free. The latter pledge was achieved in 1995. In December 1993 the state ratified the START-1 disarmament treaty and Nuclear Non-Proliferation Treaty. In May 1994 Kazakhstan joined NATO's Partnership for Peace program of military cooperation. Kazakhstan was also at the forefront of the formation, in 1994, of a structured economic, social and military union with neighboring Kyrgyzstan and Uzbekistan, entailing coordination of economic, monetary, and labor policies and the free movement of goods, services, capital, and labor among the states.

President Nazarbayev, who secured a popular mandate in December 1991, which was reratified by a referendum held in April 1995, sought to rule in a non-party and non-sectarian based on common consensus manner and to press on with market-centerd and outward-looking economic reforms, while limiting the pace of political change. However, there were indications of creeping authoritarianism by the mid-1990s, with the president ruling by decree and avoiding a direct election in 1996. Mass privatizations commenced in November 1993, with the aim of privatizing a third of the economy by mid-1995, and joint-venture agreements were signed with foreign companies to develop the nation's immense gas, oil, and uranium reserves. However, during the early 1990s the restructuring program led to annual declines in GDP exceeding 10% and a spiralling rate of inflation, causing popular unrest, while the emigration of hundreds of thousands of ethnic Russians and Germans also damaged the economy. The government of Prime Minister Sergei Tereshchenko, after being criticized by President Nazarbayev and by parliamentary deputies for its handling of the economy, resigned in October 1994 and Akezhan Kazhageldin became prime minister. The new administration sought to improve relations with Russia, which still controlled nearly all of the oil pipelines out of Central Asia, by signing an agreement in Moscow in January 1995 which provided for the establishment of joint armed forces by the end of 1995 and a customs union with Russia and Belarus. However, bills to give the Russian language equal status to Kazakh, in an effort to assuage the country's large and important ethnic Russian minority, and to allow the privatization of land, were rejected by parliament. This prompted President Nazarbayev, taking advantage of a Constitutional Court ruling that the recent March 1994 general elections had been technically illegal as a result of a tampering with constituency boundaries, to dissolve parliament in March 1995 and rule by decree until fresh elections were held. A new constitution, approved in a referendum in August 1995, was criticized as reducing democratic freedoms by banning the formation of trade unions in state institutions, preventing dual citizenship, and replacing the Constitutional Court with a Constitutional Council, whose decisions would be subject to presidential veto.

Elections were held to the Parliament in December 1995, but the government faced mounting opposition from trade unions, and within the new Majlis (Assembly), to its socio-economic reforms, particularly pensions' reform, and to wages arrears and energy shortages. In April 1996, a new, intelligentsia-led opposition movement, Azamat ('Citizen') was formed. It led a number of protests and unauthorized demonstrations, resulting in the arrest and brief detention of its leaders, and in January 1998 joined with the KCP to form an anti-government People's Front. During 1997, President Nazarbayev streamlined the government structure, through merging or abolishing many ministries, and in October 1997 Kazhageldin, tarred by allegation of corruption and links to the Soviet KGB in the 1980s, was replaced as prime minister by Nurlan Balgymbayev, head of the Kazakh Oil state petroleum company. A month later, the country's capital was moved, at a cost of $1 billion, from Almaty (Alma-Ata) in the far south to Astana (formerly Akmola) in the north. In 1996 growth in GDP was registered for the first time since independence and continued in 1997 and 1998. The government's privatization program was extended from 1996 to include the energy sector. It was announced, in October 1998, that presidential elections would be held in January 1999, ahead of schedule and the constitution was amended to extend the presidential term from five years to seven and end the restriction of two consecutive terms and the upper age limit of 65 years for candidates.

In January 1999 President Nazarbayev was re-elected by a landslide margin, securing 82 per cent of the vote in the country's first contested presidential poll. However, the OSCE stated that 'the election process fell far short' of international standards, with Nazarbayev enjoying massive media support and his most serious rival, Akezhan Kazhageldin, being barred from standing on a technicality.

In August 1996 an agreement was signed with Kyrgyzstan and Uzbekistan to create a Central Asian single economic market by 1998 and during 1997 and 1998 large deals were signed with Western oil companies for exploration rights and (amounting to $9.5 billion) with China, to construct an oil pipeline to Xinjiang province, in western China. This was an indication of decreasing Russian influence in the ex-Soviet state. It has been estimated, by oil industry experts, that southwest Kazakhstan, around the Caspian sea, may contain oil reserves of up to 200 billion barrels of oil, twice the proven reserves of Kuwait.

NORTH KOREA

Democratic People's Republic of North Korea (DPRK)
Chosun Minchu-chui Inmin Konghwa-guk

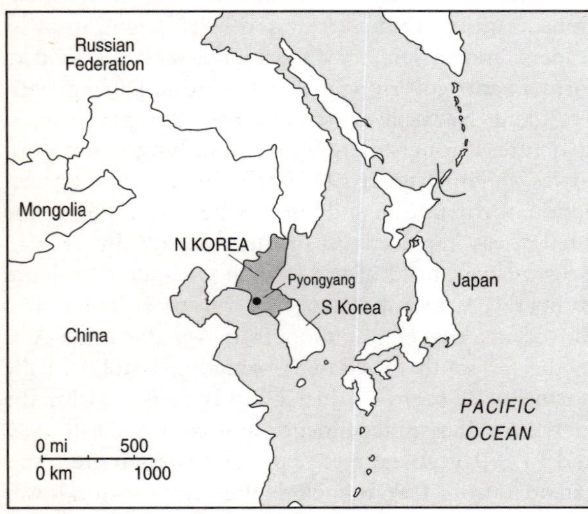

Capital: Pyongyang

Social and economic data

Area: 120,538 sq km/46,540 sq miles
Population: 23,483,000*
Pop. density per sq km/sq mi: 505/195*
Urban population: 59%**
Literacy rate: 90%**
GDP: $19,550 million*; per-capita GDP: $835*
Government defense spending (% of GDP): 25.2%*
Currency: North Korean won
Economy type: low income
Labor force in agriculture: 32%**
* 1995.
** 1992.

Head of state

Chairman of the Central Defense Committee Kim Jong Il, since 1994

Head of government

Prime Minister Hong Sung Nam, since 1997

Ethnic composition

With the exception of a Chinese minority of 50,000, the population is fully Korean. The official language is Korean.

Religions

Buddhism, Confucianism, Chondism, and Daoism are the traditional religions. Today, however, they enjoy apparently little support, their practice having been actively discouraged by a communist regime which sponsors atheism.

Political features

State type: communist
Date of state formation: 1948
Political structure: unitary
Executive: communist
Assembly: one-chamber
Party structure: one-party (E)
Human rights rating: 20%
International affiliations: ESCAP, G-77, IAEA, LORCS, NAM, UN
(E) – Effective

Local and regional government

The country is divided into nine provinces and two cities, below which there are urban districts, regular cities, and more than 150 counties. Each political unit has a Local People's Assembly, elected every four years at the provincial level and every two years below, which convenes once a year and 'elects' a Local People's Committee as its permanent executive organ.

Political system

North Korea's original socialist constitution was adopted in September 1948, being based closely on the 1936 USSR's 'Stalin constitution' model. It was superseded in December 1972 by the current 149-article version, which describes the People's Republic as a 'socialist state' in the stage of the 'dictatorship of the proletariat'. Significant, specifically Korean, departures from the earlier Soviet model are included in the document, most notably the stress that is placed on national self-reliance, called *chuche sasang*, or *juche*, the use of mass mobilization tactics (*chongsalli*), and all-pervasive party control (*te an*). In addition, the document also specifically embraces, in Article 5, the goal of national reunification, by 'peaceful means'.

Under the 1972 constitution, the sole and supreme organ of state power is the Supreme People's Assembly (SPA), or Choe Ko In Min Hoe Ui, a one-chamber body which comprises 687 members elected (unopposed) for five-year terms in single-member constituencies from a list of candidates put forward by the Democratic Front for the Reunification of the Fatherland (DFRF), which dates from 1946. The minimum age for voting is 17 years. The SPA is supposed to convene twice a year for short sessions, lasting several days, in the spring and autumn and 'elects' a 15-member Standing Committee to act for it when it is not sitting. (It failed to convene between 1995 and 1998.) It also elects a 15-member Central People's Committee (CPC), which the constitution describes as the 'supreme leadership organ of state power'. This is headed by the president of the republic.

The CPC determines domestic and foreign policy, can issue decrees, and oversees the work of People's Committees below. It also supervises the day-to-day central executive, in the shape of the State Administrative Council (SAC), a 46-member body comprising 17 departmental ministers, 14 state commission chairpersons and nine vice premiers. The SAC is headed by the prime minister, who is elected by the SPA. Members of the SAC are appointed and dismissed by the CPC.

It is, however, the president of the republic who is the leading figure in the DPRK's presidentialist political system. Elected for renewable five-year terms by the SPA, the president is commander in chief of the armed forces and chairperson of the National Defense Commission. In addition, the president is empowered to issue edicts, preside over SAC meetings and 'guide' the work of the CPC.

The controlling force, and sole permitted political party, in the DPRK is the Communist Party (Korean Workers' Party: KWP). The party leads the broader DFRF mass organization, which includes the minor Korean Social Democratic Party and the Chondoist Chongu Party, and puts forward a single slate of candidates in elections. Its leading members also hold senior state posts.

The overriding and distinctive feature of the DPRK political system has been the extent to which it was dominated between 1948 and 1994 by a charismatic leader, Kim Il Sung (1912–94), who served as both KWP general secretary and state president. Depicted, in a Confucianist manner, as the nation's 'fatherly leader' and 'Sun of Mankind', Kim Il Sung established an extraordinarily pervasive personality cult. A unique 'socialist dynasty' was constructed, with his son, Kim Jong Il, the 'designated heir', taking over as the new 'Great Leader' and effective state leader on his father's death in July 1994. In addition, Kim Il Sung's younger brother, Kim Yong-Ju, re-emerged in December 1993, after 18 years in the political wilderness, to become a member of the KWP's Politburo and a state vice president.

In September 1998 some amendments were made to the 1972 constitution. Curiously, the title of state president was reserved permanently for the deceased Kim Il Sung. This meant that the highest political position was now chairperson of the Central Defense Committee, occupied by Kim Jong Il, overseeing political, economic, and military affairs. However, the country was to be represented for diplomatic purposes by the head of the praesidium of the SPA, enabling the reclusive Kim to continue to avoid contacts with the outside world. The new constitution now allows the introduction of elements of a market economy: allowing farmers greater freedom in the sale of produce and the retention of income; legally guaranteeing inheritance rights; and permitting private companies to own land and machinery, but not buildings.

Political parties

The ruling Korean Workers' Party (KWP: Chosun No-Dong Dang) was established in October 1945, with the title Korean Communist Party (KCP), in the North Korean zone occupied by Soviet forces. It was a coalition of communist-leaning groups who had variously been based in the USSR, China, the 'Yanan faction', and Manchuria and Korea, where they operated underground as anti-Japanese resistance fighters, prior to World War II. In August 1946 the party adopted the designation North Korean Workers' Party (NKWP), when its Chinese-trained wing, termed the New People's Party, merged with the KCP. In June 1949 it assumed its present name when the NKWP merged with the banned South Korean Workers' Party, led by Pak Hon-Yong.

The party was led, until his death in 1994, by the peasant-born Kim Il Sung, who had originally founded the Manchuria-based Korean People's Revolutionary Army in 1932. It enjoyed strong initial Soviet support. By the mid-1950s, following a series of purges of opposing factions, Kim established an unchallenged control over the party machine and, thereafter, proceeded to develop a unique, personalized, and Maoist- and Korean-nationalist influenced policy approach, officially termed 'Kim Il Sungism', which diverged significantly from post-Stalin Soviet communism. Founded on 'mass-line' mobilization methods and based on constant propagandizing, tight secret police control, and blanket censorship, it has moulded the most highly regimented and controlled society in the contemporary world.

The KWP is organized hierarchically on 'democratic centralist' lines, with small, 3–100-member, workplace 'cells' established at its base, district, and county committees higher up, all leading to a supra 2,000-member national Party Congress. The Party Congress, which is formally the supreme party organ, convenes, in theory, every five years, although only three Congresses were, in fact, called between 1961 and 1980. It 'elects' a Central Committee (CC) of about 250 members to assume authority when it is not in session. The CC meets several times a year in full session and, in turn, 'elects' a Politburo, with around nine full and eight non-voting 'alternate members', and a Secretariat, headed by the general secretary, to control party, and state, affairs. The Politburo has been dominated traditionally by an 'inner cabinet', or Presidium, but by the spring of 1995, following the deaths of Kim Il Sung and Oh Jin Woo, Kim Jong Il was left as the sole surviving Presidium member. In October 1997 Kim Jong Il was formally 'elected' general secretary.

Membership of the KWP in 1987 totalled 3 million, which constituted 14.6% of the total population, one of the highest ratios in the communist world. This represented a 50% advance on the 1976 total. In 1997 membership was still put at 3 million.

Two loyal and subservient noncommunist parties are permitted to function under the umbrella of the DFRF and enjoy SPA representation: the Korean Social Democratic Party (KSDP) and the Chondoist Chongu Party (CCP: Ch'ondogyo Yong Friends' Party). The KSDP was established in 1945 and was known, until 1981, as the Korean Democratic Party. The CCP was formed in 1946 and its members adhere to the syncretic, Taoist-Buddhist-Confucian, religious faith.

Political leaders since 1970*

1948–94 Kim Il Sung (KWP), 1994– Kim Jong Il (KWP)

* Communist Party leader.

Latest elections

The most recent SPA 'elections' were held on 26 July 1998, nearly eight years after the previous election. All 687 DFRF candidates were returned. Turnout was put at 99.9%. Each candidate received 100% of the votes cast and 60 of the elected deputies were generals.

Political history

Korea was, according to legend, founded as a state in 2333 BC by the Tangun dynasty. More recent archaeological evidence suggests that the country was invaded and colonized by nomadic tribes from Manchuria and Siberia during the 3rd millennium BC. The descendants of these conquerors established three regional kingdoms, the Koguryo, Shilla, and Paekche at around the time of Christ. Of these, the economically and culturally advanced Buddhist Shilla kingdom, with its capital at Kyongju, was subsequently to emerge as the dominant one, absorbing the others and unifying the peninsula, between 668 and 1000 AD. This Shilla dynasty was succeeded by, first, the Koryu and, then the Chosun, or Yi, dynasty, 1392–1910. During the Yi period, Korea lost its full autonomy, becoming a vassal of China and being subjected to periodic invasions by Mongol and Japanese forces. The country was now also exposed to Confucianism, this philosophy displacing Buddhism as the dominant intellectual force. During the later 19th century, expansionary Japan began to challenge China as the paramount power in the Korean region, before formally annexing the peninsula in 1910, turning it into a colony, administered by a governor general, based at Seoul, now in South Korea.

Under the Japanese, Korea developed rapidly, new heavy industries being established in the coal-rich north and commercialized agriculture being promoted in the south. Japanese rule was, however, bitterly opposed, since the gains from economic growth were largely monopolized by immigrant Japanese nationals, and Korean workers were forcibly conscripted as low paid factory and mine labor. In addition, the new rulers' determined attempt to eradicate Korean culture and enforce the adoption of the Japanese language and customs was deeply resented. Both communist and right-wing nationalist exiled resistance movements thus began to emerge during the interwar period.

Following Japan's surrender in August 1945, at the close of World War II, Korea was divided, at the 38th parallel, into two military occupation zones, with Soviet forces in the North and American in the South. In the northern zone the Soviets installed, in February 1946, a 'North Korean Provisional People's Committee', manned predominantly by Moscow-trained Korean communists, including Kim Il Sung. This held power, introducing a radical program of land reform and nationalization, until the election of a Supreme People's Assembly in 1947. This was based on a 'unity list' of communist-approved candidates. A year later, following the founding of the pro-American 'Republic of Korea', south of the 38th parallel, by the conservative nationalist leader Dr Syngman Rhee (1875–1965), North Korea was formally declared a 'Democratic People's Republic', in September 1948, under the leadership of the Korean Workers' Party (KWP). Soviet Red Army troops initially remained in the country, but finally withdrew, in December 1948.

The two new Korean republics each claimed full jurisdiction over the entire peninsula and, on 25 June 1950, North Korea, seeking immediate unification by force, launched a large-scale invasion of the South, rapidly reaching Seoul. Thus began the three-year-long Korean War, which, following the intervention of the United States, on the side of the South, and China, on the side of the North, ended in stalemate, but claimed the lives of 2 million people.

The 38th parallel border line between North and South was re-established by the armistice agreement of July 1953 and a UN force patrolled a 4,000-metre-wide demilitarized buffer zone (DMZ) which had been created. North Korea, however, never fully accepted this agreement and remained committed to reunification during the succeeding decades. As a result, despite the establishment in 1972 of a North – South coordinating committee to promote peaceful unification, relations with the South have remained tense and hostile. Border incidents have been frequent and in October 1983 four South Korean cabinet ministers were assassinated in Rangoon (Yangon), in Burma (Myanmar), following a bombing incident organized by two North Korean army officers. In addition, a maze of North Korean-dug, secret tank-sized tunnels under the DMZ were uncovered by the UN border command in October 1978.

Domestically, the post-1948 period has seen economic development in a planned socialist manner in the DPRK. During the 1950s, factories and financial institutions were nationalized and agriculture collectivized, with overall priority being given to heavy industries and rural mechanization in investment programs. The growth rate of the North Korean economy has, however, lagged considerably behind that of its more populous southern neighbor, which began to move ahead of the traditionally richer North, in terms of per-capita GDP, during the 1960s. Today, South Koreans are more than five times as affluent as 'Northerners'. The maintenance of substantial armed forces, exceeding 800,000 and consuming a quarter of GDP, has been a factor in checking North Korea's growth. So has the independent, self-reliant policy stance of the KWP leadership, although there has been some relaxation, in a more market-orientated and 'open-door' direction, since the late 1980s.

Politics in North Korea became dominated from the later 1980s by the 'succession question' as Kim Il Sung approached his 80s. After falling out with his brother, Kim Yong-Ju, ten years his junior, in 1975, Kim Il Sung sought to establish his son, Kim Jong Il (b. 1942), as sole heir designate. Kim Jong Il accompanied Kim Il Sung on diplomatic and factory tours, became 'Armed Forces Supreme Commander', presided over key party and state government meetings, and his portrait was placed on public display across the country. However, elements within the Workers' Party and armed forces, concerned at his lack of military experience and rumours of his lavish personal lifestyle, appeared to oppose Kim's succession aims. On the eventual death of Kim Il Sung, in July 1994, Kim Jong Il, known formerly as the 'Dear Leader' was reported by the state media to have been placed 'at the head of the party, administration, and people's armed forces'. He assumed his father's title of 'Great Leader' and the Pyongyang media sought to present a transmigration of political personality from father to son. In February 1995 Oh Jin Woo (1916–95), the defense minister and *de facto* number two in North Korea for more than 20 years, also died. It remained surprising, however, to Western observers that still, by the summer of 1995, Kim Jong Il had not formally been invested as state president and general secretary of the KWP or seen often in public since his father's death. This fed rumours that Kim Jong Il was himself seriously ill. A possible rival existed in his uncle, Kim Yong-Ju, who returned to the KWP Politburo in December 1993. An indication of continuing crisis and confusion was the failure of Supreme People's Assembly (SPA) elections to be held in April 1995 and the legislature to subsequently convene for its normal sessions, until 1998. Prime Minister Kang Song San (b. 1930), a supporter of Chinese-influenced 'open door' economic reforms, was also not seen in public, and from February 1997 his more cautious, and elder, deputy, Hong Sung Nam (b. 1923), took over as acting prime minister. In the same month, Hwang Jang Yop (b. 1924), a reformist member of the secretariat KWP, defected to South Korea. As a result of a combination of disastrous floods and droughts between 1995 and 1997, famine conditions gripped the countryside and made North Korea increasingly dependent on international food aid. During 1997 more than 1 million tons of food aid was sent in, by overseas charities, governments (including China and the USA), and the UN World Food Program. Similar amounts were sent in 1998. A US congressional team calculated that half a million had already died of starvation in each of the previous three years and that a further 2 million were at risk. In July 1997 the official mourning period for Kim Il Sung was officially ended and, three months later, Kim Jong Il was formally acclaimed general secretary of the KCP. The SPA finally convened, in September 1998, following elections in July 1998, and, on the 50th anniversary of the state's founding, adopted changes to the constitution. These reserved permanently the title of president to the deceased Kim Il Sung, and allowed elements of a market economy.

In its external relations, North Korea adopted a determinedly neutral stance in the Sino-Soviet dispute, signing a friendship and mutual assistance treaty with China in July 1961, while at the same time continuing to draw substantial economic and military aid from the Soviet Union, with whom links became closer from the 1970s. Overall stress, however, was placed on nationalistic self-reliance (*juche*), the country remaining largely isolated from external contacts.

From the start of the 1990s, as a result of mounting domestic economic shortages – as GDP progressively declined – and the collapse of communism in Eastern Europe, depriving it of Russian economic aid, North Korea sought to bring to an end its economic isolation. In November 1990, anxious to attract inward investment in Chinese-style 'special economic zones', the first formal contacts were made with Japan, ending four decades of bitter hostility. In September 1990 Prime Minister Yon Hyong Muk made an unprecedented three-day visit to South Korea. This paved the way for North Korea's admission, simultaneously with South Korea's, into the UN in September 1991 and on 13 December 1991 a nonaggression pact was signed by the two states. This provided for the establishment of a military hotline to prevent accidental conflict, the restoration of cross-border communication links, the reunion of divided families, and the liberalization of commerce. In June 1995 North Korea, with its economy in turmoil, agreed to accept 150,000 ton of emergency rice supplies from South Korea.

During recent years there has been great Western concern that North Korea has been embarking on a nuclear weapons development program. In January 1992 North Korea signed a Nuclear Safeguards Agreement, providing for international inspection of its nuclear facilities. In October 1994 the United States and North Korea signed an accord which provided for US economic assistance if North Korea replaced its existing nuclear technology, abandoned its alleged nuclear weapons program, and submitted itself to international nuclear inspection. This was accepted by North Korea, but the West subsequently suspected that the terms were not being kept to and that nuclear weapons development was continuing at secret underground sites. In August 1998 the unexpected test-firing of a newly developed ballistic missile over Japan led to a suspension of Japanese food aid. Meanwhile, naval skirmishes delayed the re-opening of formal talks with South Korea during 1999.

SOUTH KOREA

Republic of Korea (ROK)
Daehan-Minkuk

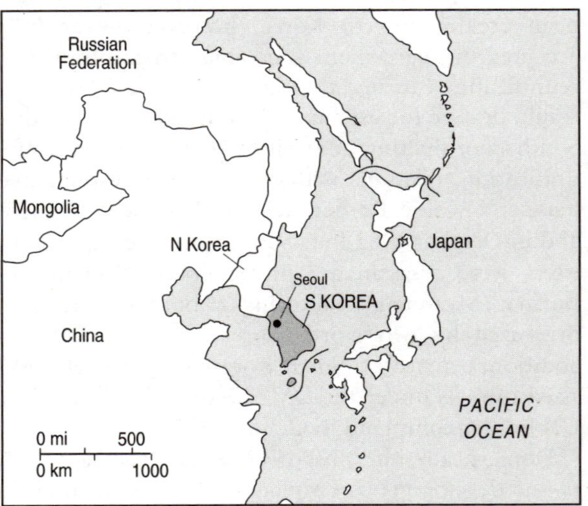

Capital: Seoul

Social and economic data

Area: 98,222 sq km/37,924 sq miles
Population: 44,606,000*
Pop. density per sq km/sq mi: 454/1176*
Urban population: 74%**
Literacy rate: 96%**
GDP: $435,140 million*; per-capita GDP: $9,755*
Government defense spending (% of GDP): 3.4%*

Currency: South Korean won
Economy type: high income
Labor force in agriculture: 16%**
Unemployment rate: 2.0%*
* 1995.
** 1992.

Head of state (executive)

President Kim Dae-Jung, since 1998

Head of government

Prime Minister Kim Jong-Pil, since 1998

Ethnic composition

With the exception of a small Nationalist Chinese minority, the population is almost entirely of Korean ethnic stock. The official language is Korean.

Religions

Mahayana Buddhism, which claims more than 8 million adherents, or 20% of the total population, is the principal religion, along with Christianity, with 8.5 million believers, three-quarters of whom are Protestants, belonging to the Presbyterian Church of Korea, the Korean Methodist Church, and smaller denominations, and a quarter of whom are Roman Catholics. Other important smaller religions are Confucianism, Won Buddhism, and Chundo Kyo, a syncretic religion, combining Shaman, Buddhist, and Christian doctrines, which was developed by nationalists during the later 19th century. Christianity was first introduced during the later 16th century and has been at the forefront of the human rights struggle. Freedom of worship and conscience is guaranteed under the constitution.

Political features

State type: emergent democratic
Date of state formation: 1948
Political structure: unitary
Executive: limited presidential
Assembly: one-chamber
Party structure: multiparty
Human rights rating: 59%
International affiliations: AfDB, APEC, AsDB, CP, EBRD, ESCAP, G-77, IAEA, IBRD, ICC, ICFTU, IMF, IWC, LORCS, OAS (observer), OECD, UN, WTO

Local and regional government

The country comprises nine provinces and six special cities of provincial status: Seoul, Pusan, Taegu, Inchon, Kwangju, and Taejon. Below them, counties, towns, and villages are the administrative units. Under reforms introduced by President Kim Young-Sam, provincial governors, city mayors, and more than 4,650 provincial assembly and local council deputies were elected for the first time from June 1995.

Political system

The current, Sixth Republic, constitution, adopted in February 1988, supersedes the earlier constitutions of 1980 (Fifth Republic), 1972 (Fourth Republic), and 1948 (First – Third Republics). By previous standards, it is a liberal document, guaranteeing the preservation of a 'plural party system'; the fair management of election contests by a nine-member Central Election Management Committee (CEMC); the citizen's right of *habeas corpus* and freedom of speech, press, assembly, and association; and establishing a nine-member Constitutional Court (CC) to police its maintenance. Included within the constitution is the aspiration of the 'peaceful unification of the Korean peninsula ... based on the principles of freedom and democracy'.

Legislative power rests with the 299-member single-chamber National Assembly (*Kuk Hoe*), 253 of whose members are elected for fixed four-year terms, on a first-past-the-post basis, in single-member constituencies. The remaining 46 seats are filled on the basis of proportional representation. Parties require a minimum of 20 seats within the Assembly to be recognized as an official negotiating faction.

The National Assembly convenes annually for a regular session of up to 100 days and also meets in 'extraordinary sessions', at the request of the president or three-quarters of its members. It has the authority to impeach the president and recommend the removal of the prime minister or any other minister; propose changes to the constitution, a two-thirds majority being required, followed by public approval in a referendum; and appoint a third of the members of the CEMC and CC. Approval from the National Assembly is also required for the president's appointment of holders of senior judicial office.

Executive authority lies with the president, who is directly elected for a single, nonrenewable five-year term. Presidents govern with the assistance of an appointed cabinet, called the State Council, of around 20 members and headed by a prime minister. Serving members of the armed forces are debarred from cabinet office. The president is also empowered to appoint a third of the members of the CEMC and CC, as well as the chief justice and justices of the Supreme Court, subject to the National Assembly's assent.

Additionally, presidents may take issues directly to the public through the use of referenda. They may issue vetoes, which can be overridden by the National

Assembly, and assume broad emergency powers, during times of emergency, subject to Assembly agreement. They cannot, however, dissolve the National Assembly. The political structure established by the 1987 Constitution is a mixture of the American and French presidential models, with significant checks built in so as to strengthen the National Assembly in relation to the president. In this respect it differs from the preceding 1972 and 1980 constitutions, and has the danger of engendering instability during periods when party control over the executive and Assembly is split. The new president, since 1998, Kim Dae-Jung, has suggested that the constitution should be amended to increase the authority of the prime minister, to become, by 2001, the real head of government.

Political parties

There are currently two main contending blocs of political parties: the right-of-center Grand National Party (GNP); and the centrist National Congress for New Politics (NCNP), which is currently allied with the right-of-center United Liberal Democrats (ULD). The GNP has its roots in the Democratic Republican Party (DRP), established in February 1963 as a governing party to lend civilian legitimacy to the military regime of Major General Park Chung-Hee. The DRP was superseded, in January 1981, by the Democratic Justice Party (DJP), formed as a 'government party' by the country's newly installed leader, General Chun Doo-Hwan. The DJP was financed by the business community, whose interests it promoted in a corporatist manner. It was also backed by the armed forces. In addition to these important bases, it developed a mass membership of more than 1 million, mainly in the north and east-center of the country, and particularly in rural areas. In February 1990, the ruling DJP merged with the opposition parties, the centrist Reunification Democratic Party (estd. 1987), led by the Presbyterian, Kim Young-Sam, and the rightwing New Democratic Republican Party (estd. 1987), led by former premier and former intelligence agency head Kim Jong-Pil, and was renamed the Democratic Liberal Party (DLP). The DLP served as the ruling party for Kim Young-Sam, when he became president in 1993, but became weakened by internal divisions from 1995. In March 1995, Kim Jong-Pil, who accused the DLP government of being 'too soft' in its relations with North Korea and internal dissidents, broke away to form a new, business-orientated ultra-conservative party, the ULD, which subsumed the New People's Party in May 1995. In December 1995 the DLP was renamed the New Korea Party (NKP) and in November 1997 it changed its name again to the GNP, merging at the same time with a centrist, former opposition party, the Democratic Party (DP). The GNP's chairman, since 1998, has been Lee Han-Tong. The NCNP was formed in September 1995 by Kim Dae-Jung, a veteran leader of the center-left opposition, who had ended his two years' 'retirement' from politics. It immediately attracted 53 legislator defectors from the DP, making it the largest opposition group in the National Assembly. Its forerunner, the DP, was formed in September 1991 through the merger of the Roman Catholic, Kim Dae-Jung's New Democratic Party, itself the heir to the Party for Peace and Democracy (PPD: estd. 1987), with Lee Ki-Taek's smaller Democratic Party. The NCNP draws its support from lower social strata than the GNP, with a strong support bases in the underdeveloped south-western Cholla region and in Seoul, as a result of the immigration of many people from Cholla. The ULD has formed an alliance with the GNP since October 1997, which has continued into government. The other significant national party is the center-right New Party by the People (NPP), which was formed in August 1997 to support the unsuccessful presidential candidacy of Rhee In-Je, who broke away from the GNP after it failed to select him as their presidential candidate.

Political leaders since 1970

1962–79 Major General Park Chung-Hee (DRP), 1979–80 Choi Kyu-Hah (DRP), 1980–88 General Chun Doo-Hwan (DJP), 1988–93 Roh Tae-Woo (DJP/DLP), 1993–98 Kim Young-Sam (DLP), 1998– Kim Dae-Jung (NCNP)

Latest elections

The most recent National Assembly elections, held on 11 April 1996, brought victory for President Kim Young Sam's NKP, which, with 35% of the vote, won 139 of the 299 seats. The opposition NCNP attracted 25% of the vote, but captured only 79 seats, with the party's leader, Kim Dae-Jung, failing to win a seat. The conservative ULD, with 16% of the vote, won 50 seats; the DP, 15 seats; and the remaining seats were won by independents. The election was held at a time of worrying border exercises by North Korean troops and turnout fell to a record low of 64%. Party support was highly regionalized, with the NCNP polling most strongly in Cholla, in the environs of Kwangju, while the NKP did best in Kim Young-Sam's home port of Pusan and in North Kyongsang. The most recent presidential election, held on 18 December 1997, at a time of economic crisis, was narrowly won by Kim Dae-Jung, who attracted 40% of the vote, defeating the GNP's candidate, Lee Hoi-Chang, a former prime minister and supreme court judge, who won 39% of the vote. Rhee In-Je, another conservative, who had broken away from the NKP/GNP, won 19%, while four other candidates shared 2% of the vote. Kim Dae-Jung, in this, his fourth, challenge for the presidency, was backed both by his NCNP and by the conservative ULD. He was also supported by the steel magnate Park Tae-Joon, helping to broaden his support base beyond his power base in the southwest. Turnout was 80.6%.

Political history

1. 1948–1989

The Republic of Korea was formed from the zone south of the 38th parallel of latitude, which had been occupied by American troops after the Japanese surrender in August 1945. The American military government remained in charge of the country until, following national elections, in May 1948, an independent republic was declared three months later. Dr Syngman Rhee (1875–1965), the royal-born and American-educated leader of the rightist Liberal Party, who had been previously exiled, became the nation's first president, under a constitution which was based partially on the United States model.

During its first two years the republic had to deal with a series of problems. They included a massive influx of more than 2 million refugees who had fled from the communist regime in the North and the return of people from forced labor in Japan and Manchuria. It then experienced invasion and bitter warfare during the 1950–53 Korean War.

President Syngman Rhee, whose autocratic and nationalistic regime, known as the 'First Republic', had been accused of corruption and nepotism, resigned in April 1960, following student-led disorder. A new parliamentary style constitution, giving greater powers to the Assembly, was adopted and the opposition Democratic Party (DP) leader, Chang Myon, was appointed prime minister. This parliamentary regime (Second Republic) was characterized, however, by chronic political instability, precipitating a military coup, led by Major General Park Chung-Hee (1917–79), in May 1961. The National Assembly was dissolved, martial law imposed, and a military junta, the 'Supreme Council for National Reconstruction', was initially put into office. During this period, the Korean Central Intelligence Agency (KCIA) was also established, under the direction of Colonel Kim Jong-Pil, a relative of Park, and a government-sponsored party, the Democratic Republican Party (DRP), was created.

This paved the way for a return to 'civilian' rule, under a restored presidential system, with Park Chung-Hee, the DRP's nominee, elected president in December 1963. He had narrowly defeated the opposition New Democratic Party (NDP) candidate, Yun Po-Sun.

President Park proceeded to embark on a major program of export-led industrial development, through a series of five-year plans, and the extension of 'soft loan' financial support to integrated conglomerates (*chaebol*), in a determinedly corporatist manner. Benefiting from the nation's plentiful supply of well educated, industrious and low paid workers, the program proved to be a remarkable success, with more than 9% and 20% per annum rates of GDP and industrial growth being, respectively, attained during the 1960s and 1970s. As a result, South Korea emerged as a major exporter of consumer goods, including textiles, footwear, and electronics, and industrial products, such as steel, ships, and petrochemicals. This 'economic miracle' fundamentally transformed the socio-economic base of what had been a predominantly agrarian economy. A huge urban-industrial sector was now developing through a process of in-migration.

This buoyant economy, with incomes rising for middle and upper-middle urban groups, provided a material basis for the Third Republic regime, enabling Park, aided, the opposition claimed, by ballot-rigging and vote-buying, to narrowly defeat the NDP nominees, Yun Po-Sun and Kim Dae-Jung (b. 1924), in the presidential contests of 1967 and 1971.

Despite the economic growth achieved, opposition to the authoritarian and repressive character of the Park regime, and to the country's growing links with despised Japan, began to mount during the 1970s. In response, martial law was imposed in October 1972 and a new '*yushin*' ('revitalizing') constitution, strengthening the president's powers, was adopted. This was done by a national referendum, in November 1972, which established a Fourth Republic.

Elections to the newly created presidential electoral college, the National Conference for Unification (NCU), and the now 'neutered' National Assembly, then followed, in December 1972. With more bribery and rigging, the DRP won a sweeping majority. The 2,359-member NCU duly ratified Park as president for a new six-year term.

Two years later, in May 1975, a severe clamp-down on political dissent was launched, with the enactment of 'Emergency Measure Number Nine' (EMNN), making it a crime to criticize the yushin system and thus, in practice, the incumbent regime. Thousands of political opponents were jailed or placed under house arrest, including Second Republic president, Yun Po-Sun, and NDP leader, Kim Dae-Jung. The latter was kidnapped by KCIA forces while in a Tokyo hotel.

For the NCU elections of May 1978, which were followed by Park's re-election as president in July, there was a brief political 'thaw'. However, with economic conditions briefly deteriorating, as the republic experienced its first year of negative growth since the war, and with the inflation rate surpassing 30%, worker and student protests erupted during 1979. These disturbances escalated, following the expulsion of NDP leader Kim Young-Sam (b. 1927) from the National Assembly for alleged 'subversive activities'. Then, in October 1979, President Park was assassinated by Kim Jae Gyu, the head of the KCIA, in a coup attempt.

Martial law was briefly imposed before an interim government was set up, under the leadership of the former prime minister, Choi Kyu-Hah. This introduced a number of liberalizing reforms, including the release of opposition leader Kim Dae-Jung, in February 1980, and the rescindment of EMNN. However, with antigovernment demonstrations gaining strength, a new clampdown on dissidents was launched in May 1980, involving the arrest of 30 political leaders, including Kim Dae-Jung, the reimposition of martial law, and the closure of the National Assembly. Riots immediately erupted in Kim's home city of Kwangju. They were forcibly suppressed by paratroopers with the loss of 189 lives according to official sources. Outside observers put the true figure at more than 2,000.

In August 1980, Choi Kyu-Hah resigned as president, to be replaced by the leader of the army and former military intelligence chief, the American-trained Major General Chun Doo-Hwan (b. 1931). After a referendum, a new constitution was adopted in October 1980. It abolished the NCU and restricted the presidency to a single, nonrenewable, seven-year term. Martial law was lifted in January 1981 and, after Chun Doo-Hwan was elected president by a new 5,278-member electoral college, in February 1981, a new Fifth Republic was proclaimed. National Assembly elections followed, in which Chun's newly formed Democratic Justice Party (DJP), secured a substantial majority.

Under President Chun, the pace of economic growth accelerated once more. However, internal and external criticism of the supression of civil liberties continued. A measure of cautious liberalization was to be seen prior to the February 1985 National Assembly elections, involving the release of many political prisoners and the return from exile in the United States, where he had been since 1982, of Kim Dae-Jung. In these elections the New Korea Democratic Party (NKDP), which had recently been formed as a vehicle for the opposition leaders, Kim Young-Sam and Kim Dae-Jung, secured 30% of the direct votes and, when the new Assembly convened, it held 102 of its 276 seats. The DJP held 148 seats, too few to force through fundamental constitutional changes.

Buoyed by their strengthened parliamentary position, the opposition forces launched, outside the Assembly, during 1986 and 1987, a major new campaign for democratic constitutional reform, as the February 1988 date for President Chun's step-down from power approached. The NKDP campaigned for a new system of government, based on direct presidential elections. The DJP countered with a proposal for a new prime ministerial system.

The scale of student unrest escalated in April and June 1987, now drawing support from ordinary workers and the middle classes. Two events triggered off this new spate of dissidence. The first was President Chun's announcement that the reform process would be suspended until after the Olympic Games had been held in Seoul, in September 1988. The second was the nomination of Roh Tae-Woo (b. 1932), a former Korean Military Academy colleague of Chun's, as its presidential candidate for forthcoming indirect elections.

Roh Tae-Woo unexpectedly responded to the growing popular movement against him by submitting a pragmatic, and relatively liberal, eight-point plan of political, constitutional and electoral reform to President Chun. Its key elements included the formation of a new consensual, nonparty, interim cabinet; the establishment of a bipartisan committee to draft a new constitution; the liberalization of labor and censorship laws; and the release from detention, and the restoration of the full political rights, of prominent opposition figures. The 'Roh plan' was accepted and in October 1987 a new constitution was approved in a national referendum. Adopted in February 1988, it provided for a directly elected presidency, serving a nonrenewable five-year term.

In the presidential contest, which was held in December 1987, Roh Tae-Woo, the DJP's nominee, although securing only 36% of the popular vote, emerged victorious, as a result of the candidacy of both Kim Young-Sam and Kim Dae-Jung, respective leaders of the recently formed Reunification Democratic Party (RDP) and Party for Peace and Democracy (PPD), which served to split the opposition's vote. Electoral fraud on the part of the governing party was alleged, but was substantially unproved.

Roh Tae-Woo formally replaced Chun Doo-Hwan as president of the new Sixth Republic in February 1988. However, in the National Assembly elections of April 1988 the opposition regrouped and succeeded in preventing the DJP from securing a majority in the new legislature for the first time since the party's creation. Political conflict calmed during the summer of 1988, as the nation hosted the Olympic Games. However, after the Olympic Games student unrest erupted periodically and calls for reunification of the peninsula grew in strength. After televised investigative work of National Assembly committees uncovered corruption among his close friends and relatives, former President Chun was forced to publicly apologize, in November 1988, on national television for his administration's misdeeds.

2. 1990–1999

In February 1990, when the DJP merged with two opposition parties to form the Democratic Liberal Party (DLP), a stable governing majority was secured. However, in May 1991 more than 250,000 people, mainly students, demonstrated against the government and six attempted suicide after the police had beaten to death a young protester. In the general election of March 1992 the DLP lost its National Assembly majority unexpectedly, but was able, with the support of independent deputies, to hold on to power. The DLP's candidate, the former dissident, Kim Young-Sam, comfortably won the presidential election of December 1992 and succeeded Roh as president in February 1993. The defeated veteran opposition leader, Kim Dae-Jung retired from active politics until August 1995, when he founded a new political party as a vehicle for a further presidential bid in 1997.

Kim Young-Sam, the first South Korean president since 1960 not to have military connections, immediately launched a vigorous anticorruption drive. This claimed many victims in the military and business community and the assets of senior civil servants and politicians were controversially made public. An unpopular decision to open the previously protected rice market to imports, under the terms of a GATT (later WTO) agreement, persuaded Kim to replace his prime minister in December 1993. However, despite a temporary slowdown in GDP growth during 1992–93 from its customary annual rate of 9%, President Kim, with his relatively open governing style, retained a high public approval rating and the level of student protests diminished significantly. From 1994 the Kim administration encouraged greater competition, privatization, and deregulation within the still booming South Korean economy, as part of a 'globalization' (*segyehwa*) initiative. However, in June 1995 the ruling DLP, which had been weakened by a split in its ranks in March 1995, when Kim Jong-Pil left to form the ultra-conservative United Liberal Democratic (ULD) party, polled poorly in the country's first ever local elections. It won only a third of the provincial governorships and city mayorships, with the opposition center-left Democratic Party (DP) and new ULD performing strongly.

During 1996 ex-presidents Chun and Roh were tried and found guilty of treason for their roles in the 1979 coup attempt and 1980 Kwangju massacre and of accepting bribes while in office. Roh publicly admitted that, during his five-year rule, he had secretly amassed 500 billion won (£400 million) in a party slush fund, retaining 170 billion won for personal use after he left office in 1993. After appeal, Chun was sentenced, in December 1996, to life imprisonment and Roh to 17 years, although both were later pardoned in December 1997. A number of military colleagues and business leaders were also found guilty.

To distance itself from Roh, the DLP adopted a new name, the New Korea Party (NKP), in December 1995. It fought the April 1996 National Assembly elections on an anti-corruption platform and, after attracting 12 post-election defectors from the ranks of the DP and independents, managed to retained an Assembly majority. Lee Soo-Sung, who had become prime minister in December 1995, remained in office, but faced a turbulent year. In August 1996 there were violent clashes between riot police and students at Seoul's Yonsei University, where 3,000 students had barricaded themselves in, demanding reunification with North Korea and the withdrawal of American troops. Meanwhile, from December 1996 large-scale street protests and industrial unrest swept across the country, centerd in the car and shipbuilding industries and triggered by a new labor law which ended job security guarantees. In late January 1997, President Kim Young-Sam, whose popularity rating had slumped to 18%, met opposition leaders and agreed to revise the law, which had been a condition of the country's membership of the OECD, which it had entered, as the world's 11th largest economy.

During 1997 the NKP was damaged by corruption scandals centerd around Hanbo, the country's second largest steel company, which collapsed in January 1997 with debts of $6 billion. It was alleged that Hanbo had bribed the government to put pressure on banks to provide it with loans. The home affairs minister resigned; President Kim made a televised official apology; and prime minister Lee stepped down, to be replaced by Koh Kon, the head of Myongju University, who became the country's sixth prime minister in four years. Then, in October 1997, the president's son, Kim Hyun-Chul, was convicted of bribery and tax evasion and sentenced to three years' imprisonment. Meanwhile, the South Korean economy was spiralling rapidly into crisis. This was caused partly by a broader Asian financial crisis, originating in Thailand, but was compounded by the huge (dollar denominated) debts which the country's *chaebol* (conglomerates) had amassed, resulting in the collapse or near collapse of the Hanbo, Sammi, Jinro, and Kia conglomerates. Between October and December 1997, the won and Seoul stockmarket fell by more than 50%, and, with currency reserves exhausted and defaults threatened, a record $57 billion IMF bail-out had to be humiliatingly negotiated in December 1997.

Against this background, a bitter presidential election contest was narrowly won, on 18 December 1997, by the veteran pro-democracy campaigner, Kim Dae-Jung, who had pledged to make the fight against corruption a key chief priority. Kim defeated the Lee Hoi-Chang, the choice of the ruling NKP, which had recently merged with the DP to form a new Grand National Party (GNP), but had won mainly because of a split in the conservative vote, caused by the candidacy of Rhee In-Je, who had broken away from the NKP in August 1997, and the support given to Kim Dae-Jung by Kim Jong-Pil's ULD. Kim Dae-Jung's, accession, in February 1998, represented the first ideologically significant change in government in South Korea since Park's coup in 1961.

In January 1998 citizens donated gold jewellery in a patriotic effort to help pay off the country's $150 billion of foreign debts. However, inflation soared and the unemployment rate increased sharply, as IMF-imposed austerity reforms began to bite and the *chaebol* were restructured. The economy shrank by 6% during 1998 and unemployment rose to more than 10%. President Kim Dae-Jung responded to the economic crisis by introducing new labor laws to allow companies to introduce redundancies, but coupling them with increased provision for retraining and welfare. Reforms were also made to open up South Korea's financial markets to foreigners. He also introduced political reforms: releasing, in March 1998, 2,304 prisoners, including 74 political prisoners; and promising a referendum, before the end of 1999, on plans to introduce a new parliamentary, as opposed to presidential, executive system.

However, the initiatives encountered opposition from workers, who staged a series of anti-austerity and antirestructuring strikes during 1998 and 1999, and from the GNP. Kim Jong-Pil's ratification as prime minister was delayed until August 1998, by which time sufficient GNP members had been persuaded to switch sides to give Kim Dae-Jung's coalition a National Assembly majority.

Externally, the constant threat of invasion from the North has been a key factor in South Korean politics since 1953, helping to justify stern rule. The country has been forced to devote significant resources to modernizing its armed forces, which number 630,000 and annually consume around 5% of GDP, even though they have been supported by more than 35,000 American troops. Both political and economic relations with the United States have remained close since 'liberation' and the United States currently provides a market for 40% of the republic's exports. Anti-American sentiment is, however, strong among opposition groups.

Close political economic links have also been developed with Japan. In recent years, however, as part of what has been termed a reunification directed 'Northern policy', there has been a normalization of diplomatic relations with communist China, in August 1992, and since 1990 relations with North Korea have improved dramatically. Both Koreas were admitted into the United Nations in September 1991 and on 13 December 1991 a nonaggression and confidence-building pact was signed in Seoul. This provided for the restoration of cross-border communications, the reunion of divided families, and the freer movement of people and ideas. On 31 December 1991 both states agreed at Panmujon to ban the testing, deployment, or possession of nuclear weapons. In response, the United States has agreed to withdraw its nuclear weapons from South Korea and reduce its troop strength in the republic. In 1995, South Korea was persuaded by the United States to give North Korea two 'safe' nuclear reactors, to persuade it to abandon its suspected atomic weapons program, and also supplied the North, whose economy was fast deteriorating, with emergency shipments of rice. In September 1996 tensions increased once again, when a North Korean submarine ran aground in South Korean waters. With the accession of President Kim Dae-Jung, in 1998, a new emphasis has been placed on reconciliation with the North, separating political from economic cooperation in what has been termed a 'sunshine policy'. In April 1998 the two Koreas met in their first direct talks since 1994. However, border tensions remained high, with naval skirmishes in 1999 delaying a resumption of talks.

KYRGYZSTAN (KYRGYZIA)

Republic of Kyrgyzstan
Kyrgyzstan Respublikasy

Capital: Bishkek (formerly Frunze)

Social and economic data

Area: 198,500 sq km/76,641 sq miles
Population: 4,600,000*
Pop. density per sq km/sq mi: 23/60*
Urban population: 38%**
Literacy rate: 97%**
GDP: $3,160 million*; per-capita GDP: $690*
Government defense spending (% of GDP): 3.5%**
Currency: som
Economy type: low income
Labor force in agriculture: 47%**
* 1995.
** 1992.

Head of state (executive)

President Askar Akaev, since 1990

Head of government

Prime Minister Amangeldy Muraliyev, since 1999

Ethnic composition

Fifty-seven per cent of the population are of Kyrgyz ethnic stock, 18% Russian, 13% Uzbek, 3% Ukrainian, and 2% German. Kyrgyz, a Turkic language written in the Cyrillic script, is to be fully established as the official language from 2005. However, Russian is to remain the official language in regions predominantly peopled by Russian speakers.

Religions

The principal religion is Islam, with the majority of ethnic Kyrgyz, Uzbeks, and Tajiks being Sunni Muslims of the Hanafi school. Many new mosques have opened since 1991. There is a Russian Orthodox Christian minority.

Political features

State type: emergent democratic
Date of state formation: 1991
Political structure: unitary
Executive: limited presidential
Assembly: two-chamber
Party structure: multiparty
Human rights rating: N/A
International affiliations: CIS, EBRD, ECO, ESCAP, IBRD, IMF, NACC, OIC, OSCE, PFP, UN

Local and regional government

The country is divided into six administrative regions (*oblasts* or *dubans*) and the municipality of Bishkek. There are also elected councils at city and rural district level.

Political system

Since February 1995 the Republic of Kyrgyzstan has had a two-chamber legislature, the Zhogorku Kenesh (Supreme Council), comprising a 70-member house, the lower People's Assembly, and a 35-member upper chamber, the Legislative Assembly. Deputies are elected for five-year terms by the majoritarian system, which provides for a second, and exceptionally a third, ballot 'run-off' race in contests in which there is no clear first round majority. The People's Assembly meets twice yearly to debate issues of regional interest. The Legislative Assembly is a permanent chamber. The state president, who has supreme executive power, has, since 1991, been popularly elected for a five-year term, and must be between the ages of 35 and 65. There is a limit of two consecutive terms and the constitution stipulates that the president must have a fluent command of Kyrgyz. The president, who has decree powers, works with a cabinet of around 20 members and may chair its sessions. This is headed by a prime minister, who acts as the parliamentary manager for the president, who nominates a prime minister for Legislative Assembly approval. There is an eight-member Constitutional Court. The current constitution was approved in May 1993, but was amended substantially in October 1994. Changes to the constitution require approval in a national referendum and in October 1998 voters approved changing the sizes of the upper and lower houses of parliament to 67 and 38 seats respectively.

Political parties

There were 22 registered political parties in 1998. The majority of parties are weak and ill-organized and most parliamentary deputies are independents. The best organized party is the 25,000-member Kyrgyzstan Communist Party (KCP), which was banned in August 1991, but revived in June 1992. It is led by Absamat Masaliyev. Other significant parties are the Kyrgyz nationalist Ata Meken (Motherland, estd. 1992), and Erkin (Free) Kyrgyzstan Democratic Party (estd. 1991), the pro-Akaev Social Democratic Party (estd. 1994), the multiethnic Party of Kyrgyzstan Unity (estd. 1991), the Democratic Movement of Kyrgyzstan (estd. 1990), and the Agrarian Labor Party (estd. 1994).

Political leaders since 1970

1990– Askar Akaev (ex-communist independent)

Latest elections

The most recent legislature elections, the first since independence, were held on 5 and 19 February 1995 for the 35-member Legislative Assembly and the 70-member People's Assembly. Turnout was registered at 61% and 1,000 candidates contested the elections, which were largely free of poll violence. Fourteen People's Assembly and two Legislative Assembly candidates secured the required 50% of the vote majority on the first ballot. More than four-fifths of the candidates and roughly two-thirds of those elected were unaffiliated independents. Turnout was 62%.

In the most recent presidential election, held on 24 December 1995, the incumbent Askar Akaev was re-elected, with 72% of the vote. He defeated two other candidates, including Absamat Masaliyev, leader of the KCP, who attracted 24% of the vote. Turnout was put at 82%.

Political history

Peopled mainly by horse-breeding, mountain-dwelling nomads, the Turkic-speaking descendants of the Mongol invaders who swept across Asia from the 13th century, Kyrgyzstan was annexed by Russia in 1864. It formed part of an independent Turkestan republic between 1917 and 1924, was then an autonomous republic within the USSR and, from 1936, became a full republic within the Soviet Union. Land reforms and agricultural collectivization during the 1920s and 1930s resulted in the settlement of many nomadic Kyrgyz, but also met with strong opposition from local armed groups (*basmachi*).

Long viewed as a bastion of conservatism, in the March 1991 USSR constitutional referendum the republic's voters overwhelmingly endorsed, with 88% in favor, the maintenance of the Union, while its Communist Party (CP) supported the August 1991 anti-Gorbachev attempted coup in Moscow. However, Askar Akaev (b. 1944), a 'reform communist' who had assumed the republic's presidency in November 1990, in the aftermath of Kyrgyz-Uzbek border riots that claimed between 300 and 1,000 lives in the densely settled Fergana Valley, condemned the coup as 'anti-constitutional' and overturned an attempt by local KGB and army chiefs to overthrow his government. On 28 August 1991 he resigned from the Soviet Communist Party and ordered the suspension of the republic's CP and the nationalization of its property. On 31 August 1991 the republic's parliament (Supreme Soviet) voted to declare independence from the USSR. After the Moscow coup was thwarted, Akaev was offered, but declined to accept, the position of USSR vice president by the Soviet leader Mikhail Gorbachev. He was returned, unchallenged, as Kyrgyzstan's president on 12 October 1991 in what was the republic's first ever popular contest.

Kyrgyzstan joined the Commonwealth of Independent States (CIS), which was formed in December 1991, but has also sought to develop close relations with Turkey, with whom it shares linguistic traditions. Its independence was recognized by the United States and other Western states in January 1992. It was admitted into the Conference on Security and Cooperation in Europe (CSCE, later the OSCE) in the same month and into the United Nations in March 1992. Kyrgyzstan soon became described as the 'real center of democracy' within former Soviet Central Asia since its former Communist Party, though revived in June 1992, was substantially destroyed and greatly discredited. During 1991, with nationalism increasing in the new state, more than 100,000 ethnic Russians left the country. This led to fears of a 'brain drain'. The economy, previously heavily reliant on Moscow subsidies, underwent substantial restructuring and price liberalization from 1991. Commercial ties began to be developed with Western capitalist states, but in the short term a decline in GDP was registered, until 1995, and a sharp rise in inflation and levels of crime, these effects being exacerbated by departure from the rouble zone in May 1993 and adoption of its own currency, the som.

During 1993 the Akaev administration became destabilized by allegations of corruption made by conservative communists and nationalists who dominated the 350-member legislature, the Uluk Kenesh, which had been elected during the Soviet era. In December 1993 the prime minister, Tursenbek Chyngyshev, and vice president, Feliks Akulov, were forced to resign, with Apas Jumagulov, a former Communist premier, returning to replace Chyngyshev. However, Akaev, supported by pro-reform deputies, hit back in January and October 1994 by placing before the voters, in two national referenda, a confidence motion and a constitutional reform package, which entailed the replacement of the Uluk Kenesh by a smaller, elected bicameral body. The first plebiscite, on Akaev's reform program, secured a 96% approval rating while the constitutional reform package secured 70% approval. In February 1995 a new, pro-Akaev parliament was elected.

Priorities of the president have been the privatization of land, restoration of Russian as a national language, alongside Kyrgyz, as a means of stemming the continuing exodus of skilled Russians, and preservation of the CIS, which is of great economic value to Kyrgyzstan. Akaev is also keen to ensure that Kyrgyzstan remains a secular state and to prevent the spread of Islamic fundamentalism from such neighboring states as Tajikistan. Meanwhile, close ties have been established with the neighboring states of Kazakhstan and Uzbekistan, with whom Kyrgyzstan forged an economic union in May 1994. This deepened into a social and military union in July 1994 and agreement, in August 1996, to create a Central Asian single economic market by 1998. In February 1995, an Interstate Council, with a rotating annual chair, was formed to devise common policy and to govern the trilateral union. In December 1995 Akaev was re-elected president in a contested election, defeating the KCP's candidate. His powers as president were increased when 94% of voters approved a February 1996 referendum on constitutional changes, and there were concerns during 1996 and 1997 that civil rights were being restricted, with the passage of legislation reducing media freedom and requiring permission to hold rallies. In March 1996 Apas Jumagulov was appointed prime minister, but resigned after two years, at the age of 63, on grounds of age, and was replaced by Kubanychbek Djumaliyev, the head of the presidential administration.

In December 1998 Jumabek Ibraimov, formerly the chairman of the State Property Committee, became prime minister and was given expanded powers to appoint and dismiss ministers and heads of departments. Ibraimov promoted privatisation and led a drive against corruption, but, after an unsuccessful fight against stomach cancer, died in April 1999 and was replaced by Amangeldy Muraliyev, a former finance minister.

The privatization program, which had resulted since 1992 in the transfer of 60% of state industries to the private sector, was suspended in June 1997, pending investigation by a special commission into the allegedly low pricing of some past sales. However, private ownership of land has been permitted since January 1997 and GDP growth has accelerated since 1995, exceeding 10% in 1997. In 1994 Kyrgyzstan joined NATO's Partnership for Peace program of military cooperation. Nevertheless, links with Russia have remained close. In March 1997 it was agreed to extend the period of Russian border control of Kyrgyzstan until the end of 1997 and that Russia and Kyrgystan would jointly guard the unstable border between Tajikistan and Afghanistan.

In July 1998 the Constitutional Court ruled that President Akaev was eligible to run for the presidency again in the 2000 elections, despite the constitution's limit of two terms. In October 1998 voters approved a referendum allowing private ownership of land.

LAOS

The Lao People's Democratic Republic (LPDR)
Saathiaranagroat Prachhathippatay Prachhachhon Lao

Capital: Vientiane (Viengchane)

Social and economic data

Area: 236,800 sq km/91,429 sq miles

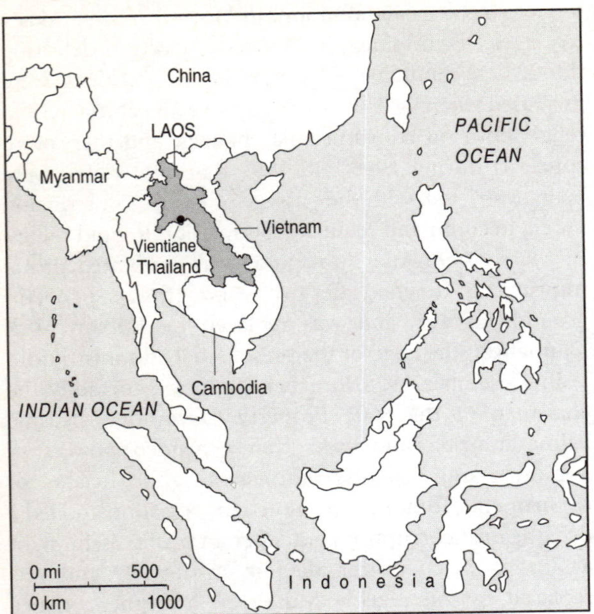

Population: 4,605,000*
Pop. density per sq km/sq mi: 19/50*
Urban population: 20%**
Literacy rate: 84%**
GDP: $1,690 million*; per-capita GDP: $370*
Government defense spending (% of GDP): 4.2%*
Currency: new kip
Economy type: low income
Labor force in agriculture: 70%**
* 1995.
** 1992.

Head of state

President General Khamtay Siphandon, since 1998

Head of government

Prime Minister General Sisavath Keobounphanh, since 1998

Ethnic composition

Sixty per cent of the population is Laotian, predominantly Lao Lum, 35% hill tribes, and 5% Vietnamese and Chinese. Lao is the principal, and official, language, spoken by two-thirds of the population, with French also widely used. The non-Lao tribal ethnic groups, particularly the Meo, have forcibly opposed the new regime's challenges to their traditional way of life. The hill tribes, including the Hmong, resent the political and military dominance of the lowland Laos.

Religions

An estimated 58% of the population adheres to traditional Theravada Buddhism. A secular state was officially established in 1975, but the 1991 constitution respects all lawful activities of followers of Buddhism and other religious faiths. Since 1995, as part of a policy to replace communist ideology with Lao nationalism, Buddhist monks have been encouraged to lead a 'cultural renaissance'. Thirty-five per cent of the people follow tribal, predominantly animist, religions; while, prior to the communist takeover, Roman Catholicism claimed 35,000 adherents.

Political features

State type: communist
Date of state formation: 1954
Political structure: unitary
Executive: communist
Assembly: one-chamber
Party structure: one-party
Human rights rating: N/A
International affiliations: AsDB, ASEAN, CP, ESCAP, G-77, IBRD, IMF, LORCS, NAM, UN, WFTU

Local and regional government

The country is divided into 17 provinces (*khoueng*), administered by People's Revolutionary Committees, which are headed by a governor, appointed by the state president, and controlled by the ruling Lao People's Revolutionary Party (LPRP). In the northern highlands, where non-Lao ethnic groups predominate, a greater measure of self-government is enjoyed. Below the provinces, the units of administration are districts (*muong*), cantons (*tasseng*), and villages (*ban*). At the subprovincial level there are People's Councils and Committees which, in theory, are subject to triennial election.

Political system

The LPDR's first constitution was endorsed in August 1991 by the then existing legislature, the Supreme People's Assembly. This describes the LPDR as a 'people's democratic state' in which the communist party, the Lao People's Revolutionary Party (LPRP), dominates as the leading organ and sole permitted political party. Elected bodies function according to the top-down principle of democratic centralism, but in the economic sphere private enterprise is accepted as part of a market-orientated economy subject to state intervention.

The legislature, the National Assembly, comprises 99 members popularly elected every five years. It meets in ordinary session twice a year and elects as executive head of state a president, who also serves a five-year term, subject to possible removal by the National

Assembly. The president promulgates laws adopted by the National Assembly and, with the Assembly's approval, appoints or dismisses the prime minister and members of the Council of Ministers (COM), or cabinet. The COM comprises an 'inner cabinet' of around 20 ministers or chairpersons of committees and 60 deputy ministers and vice chairpersons. It has the task of framing the economic plan and budget and overseeing the day-to-day work of state ministries, committees, and local bodies. Senior members of the controlling LPRP monopolize key state positions.

Political parties

The ruling Lao People's Revolutionary Party (LPRP: Phak Pasason Pativat Lao) originated as the Lao Independence Front, which was founded in 1951 by Prince Souphanouvong, a member of the royal family, as a breakaway wing from the Communist Party of Indo-China, which was founded in 1930 by the Vietnamese communist, Ho Chi Minh. The movement became known as the Pathet Lao (Lao People's Front) in 1954 and was taken over by the North Vietnamese-backed Kaysone Phomvihane in 1955, although Prince Souphanouvong remained its figurehead leader in negotiations with the incumbent government. Under the designation People's Party of Laos, it played a leading role in the Laotian Patriotic Front during the 1960s, functioning as a guerrilla wing, before adopting its present name in 1972.

The LPRP is organized hierarchically, with a stepped series of local, or branch, district and provincial committees, leading up to an 'elected' national Congress. In the past, the Congress has met irregularly, only two being called between 1955 and 1972. Since 1982, it has been convened at regular five-yearly intervals. The most recent session, the sixth, was in March 1996. The Congress ratifies the party program and 'elects' a Central Committee (CC) to act when it is not sitting. The CC is presently composed of 49 full members.

The CC, in turn, 'elects' a smaller nine-member Politburo and Secretariat, headed by General Khamtay Siphandon. The Politburo, in accordance with the precepts of 'democratic centralism', dominates both party and state machines. A majority of its current members are military figures.

In 1986 membership of the LPRP stood at 44,000, a figure which constituted barely 1% of the total population. This was one of the lowest party:citizen ratios in the communist world, although membership had more than doubled since the late 1970s. Rigorous entry rules are imposed, with the aim of maintaining the LPRP as a disciplined and committed 'vanguard' force. The party dominates the broader Lao Front for National Reconstruction (LFNR), which was established in 1979 as the successor to the Laotian Patriotic Front mass organization. The LFNR includes within its ranks representatives of economic and social 'interest groups' and is designed to mobilize nonparty support for government policy.

A number of illegal political groupings operate from external bases, particularly in hill tribe regions, as armed opposition to the communist regime. These include the Royalist, United Lao Liberation Front, led by Vang Shur, which draws support from among the Hmong (Meo) tribes, and the United Front for the National Liberation of the Lao People.

Political leaders since 1970

1962–75 Prince Souvanna Phouma, 1975–92 Kaysone Phomvihane (LPRP), 1992– General Khamtay Siphandon (LPRP)*

* Communist Party leader.

Latest elections

The most recent elections to the National Assembly were held on 21 December 1997. The 99 seats were contested by 159 candidates approved by the LFNR. Only one (approved) non-partisan candidate won a seat. Turnout was recorded at 99.3% of eligible voters.

Political history

Laos was first occupied by Chinese immigrants during the 4th and 5th centuries AD and adopted Buddhism during the 7th century. Between the 11th–13th centuries it constituted part of the culturally advanced Khmer Empire and became subject to immigration by Lao from Thailand. Not until the 14th century, when the region was united by the legendary King Fa Ngum, was an independent Laos kingdom established.

Initially visited by Europeans in the 17th century, Laos became a French protectorate between 1893 and 1945, and consisted of the three principalities of Luang Prabang, Vientiane, and Champassac. After a brief occupation by the Japanese during World War II, the French re-established control in 1946, despite opposition from the Chinese-supported Lao Issara (Free Laos) nationalist movement. The country was granted semi-autonomy in 1949, when, under the constitutional monarchy of the king of Luang Prabang, Sisavang Vong, it became an Associated State of the French Union. In December 1954, following the Geneva Agreements, Laos secured full independence.

A sporadic civil war subsequently broke out between two factions of former supporters of the Lao Issara. The first was a moderate, royalist-neutralist, group, led by Prince Souvanna Phouma, who served as prime minister on several occasions. It had supported the 1949 French compromise and was the recognized government for the bulk of the country. The second was a more extreme, communist resistance group, the Pathet Lao (Land of the Lao), led by ex-Prince Souphanouvong (1909–95), the half-brother of Prince Souvanna, and Kaysone Phomvihane (1920–92). This was supported by China and the Vietminh, who were in control of much of northeastern Laos.

Following the Vientiane Agreement of 1957, a coalition government was temporarily established. This soon collapsed, however, after the May 1958 National Assembly elections had produced an inconclusive result. In 1960 a third, rightwing, force emerged when General Phoumi Nosavan, backed by the royal army, overthrew Prime Minister Souvanna Phouma and set up a pro-Western government, headed by Prince Boun Gum. A new Geneva Agreement was signed in 1962, establishing a tripartite broad-spectrum government, under the leadership of Prince Souvanna Phouma.

Fighting continued, however, between the Pathet Lao, assisted by North Vietnam, and the neutralists and the right-wing, assisted by the United States. The fighting was exacerbated by the neighboring Vietnam War, until the Vientiane Agreement of 1973 established a ceasefire line, dividing the country northwest to southeast. The communists were given two-thirds of the country, including the Plain of Jars and the Bolovens Plateau, but the Souvanna Phouma government was made responsible for two-thirds of the population.

All foreign forces, North Vietnamese, Thai, and American, were to be withdrawn, and both sides received equal representation in Souvanna Phouma's provisional government of 1974. In 1975, however, the communist Pathet Lao, now renamed the Lao People's Front, following success in Assembly elections, seized full power. King Savang Vatthan, who had succeeded his father in October 1959, abdicated in November and Laos became a 'People's Democratic Republic' under the presidency of Prince Souphanouvong. Prince Souvanna Phouma remained as an 'adviser' to the government, but the real controlling force was now the LPRP leader and prime minister, Kaysone Phomvihane.

The new administration, which inherited a poor, war-ravaged economy, initially attempted to rapidly reorganize the country along socialist lines, nationalizing businesses and industries and collectivizing agriculture. However, faced with mounting food shortages and the flight of more than 250,000 refugees to Thailand, it began to modify this approach in 1979. The private sector was now allowed to continue to operate in a number of spheres and production incentives were introduced, with the stress now being placed on a gradual, step-by-step 'transition to socialism'.

In 1981, the country's first five-year plan came into force. However, in 1985–86, under pressure from the new reformist leadership of Mikhail Gorbachev in the Soviet Union, which supplied the country with considerable economic aid, further 'liberalization' reforms were introduced in the economic sphere, including the adoption of a new 'socialist business accounting system', which freed managers to set prices and wages and required enterprises to make a profit. In the rural sector, more than half the cropped area was privately farmed.

Politically, the country has remained subject to firm LPRP control since 1975. However, since the late 1980s, threatened by the collapse of communism elsewhere in the world, there have been moves, under the new national slogan of 'democracy and prosperity', towards a 'normalization' and liberalization of the political process. Local elections were held in 1988, and national elections followed in March 1989. In August 1991 the communist republic's first constitution was adopted. While confirming the LPRP's 'leading role', it contained no explicit references to socialism and provided for an executive presidency: this position being filled by Kaysone Phomvihane, who replaced Phoumi Vongvichit (1908–94), the acting head of state since 1986. The former vice premier, defense minister, and supreme commander of the Lao People's Army, General Khamtay Siphandon (b. 1923) replaced Phomvihane as prime minister. Five months earlier, in March 1991, at the LPRP's fifth congress, a number of leading 'old guard' revolutionaries, including Souphanouvong and Vongvichit, left the Politburo. In his keynote address, the party's president, Kaysone Phomvihane, called for an acceleration of the pace of restructuring ('New Economic Mechanism'), including the dismantling of collective farms and a full return to private farming, and in April 1991 and June 1993 the IMF, encouraged by the country's market-based reforms, approved major loans.

Following Kaysone Phomvihane's death in November 1992, Nouhak Phoumsavan was elected state president by a special session of the legislature. Strong economic growth, averaging more than 6% per year, was registered during the 1990s, and helped to improve living standards, with foreign investment, principally from Thailand, beginning to increase and some privatization tolerated.

Diplomatically, after 1975 Laos remained closely tied to the Soviet Union, until its demise in 1991, and neighboring communist Vietnam. Initially Vietnam stationed 50,000 troops in the country, as many as the whole Laotian army. However, by 1989 Vietnam's troops had been withdrawn. Relations with neighboring Thailand, which Laos accuses of having 'expansionist' designs, were strained during the 1970s and 1980s, border disputes intermittently breaking out in disputed regions. In addition, Laos accused both Thailand and China of providing assistance to rebel groups which operate in border tracts in the south and north. However, from the early 1980s, for economic reasons, there has been a significant improvement in relations with both countries and with Western states. A security and cooperation agreement was signed with Thailand in July 1991 and an agreement was entered into to provide for the phased repatriation of more than 60,000 Lao refugees who had fled to Thailand during the 1970s and 1980s. (By 1998 fewer than 1,000 Lao refugees remained in Thailand.) In April 1994 an Australian-financed 'Friendship Bridge' was opened, connecting Vientiane to the northern Thai town of Nong Khai, and in November 1994 a draft agreement was signed with Thailand, Cambodia, and Vietnam on developing the Mekong River basin. Diplomatic relations with the United States were upgraded to full ambassadorial level in November 1991 and in May 1995 the United States lifted its 20-year-old aid embargo. In 1996 Japan resumed the provision of official loans. In March 1996, at the LPRP's sixth congress, General Khamtay Siphandon was unanimously re-elected as party leader, but president Nouhak Phoumsavan was removed from the Politburo and moved 'upstairs' to a newly created 'advisory board' to accommodate ageing members of the 'old guard'. Khamphoui Keoboualapha, a leading economic reformist and vice-premier, was also removed from the Politburo. This was interpreted in the West as a sign that the military's grip had been strengthened and that the pace of economic reform would slow. Khamtay Siphandon stepped down as prime minister in February 1998 to replace the 84-year-old Nouhak Phoumsavan as president. The former vice president, General Sisavath Keobounphanh, viewed as a conservative, became prime minister. Formerly only an observer since 1992, Laos became a full member of ASEAN in July 1997. It was affected by the Asian financial crisis of 1997–98, which began in Thailand, with the value of the currency declining sharply and inflation rising.

MALAYSIA

The Federation of Malaysia (FOM)
Persekutuan Tanah Melaysiu

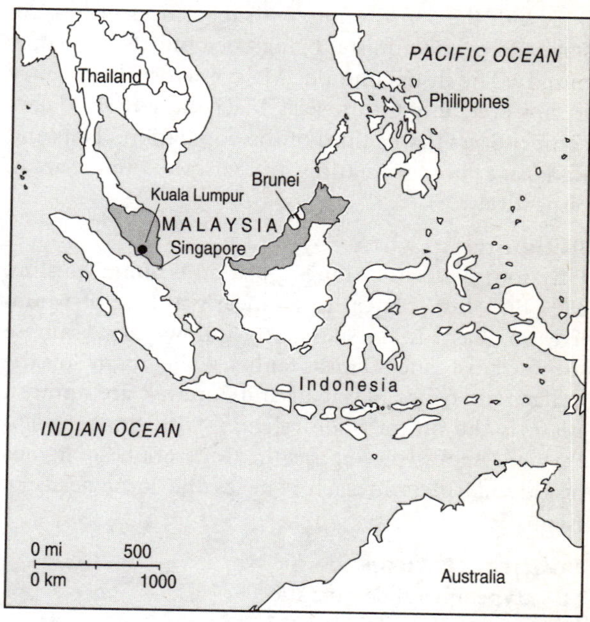

Capital: Kuala Lumpur

Social and economic data

Area: 329,758 sq km/127,320 sq miles
Population: 20,103,000*
Pop. density per sq km/sq mi: 61/158*
Urban population: 45%**
Literacy rate: 78%**
GDP: $78,320 million*; per-capita GDP $3,900*
Government defense spending (% of GDP): 4.5%*
Currency: ringgit or Malaysian dollar
Economy type: middle income
Labor force in agriculture: 26%**
Unemployment rate: 2.8%*
* 1995.
** 1992.

Head of state

Paramount Ruler Salahuddin Abdul Aziz Shah (sultan of Selangor), since 1999

Head of government

Prime Minister Datuk Seri Dr Mahathir bin Mohamad, since 1981

Ethnic composition

Fifty-eight per cent of the population is Malay, four-fifths of whom live in rural areas, 32% is ethnic Chinese, four-fifths of whom are in towns, and 9% is Indian, chiefly Tamil. The official language is Bahasa Malaysia (Malay), but Chinese, Tamil, and English are also spoken. The primacy of ethnic Malays has been built into the constitution, with the offices of head of state and prime minister being open only to this community. The distribution of Malays across the country is, however, uneven. In East Malaysia, ethnic Malays comprise less than a third of the population, Ibans and Kadazans predominating in Sarawak and Sabah, respectively.

Religions

Fifty-four per cent of the population is Sunni Muslim, 19% Buddhist, 7% Christian, nearly a third of whom live in East Malaysia, 12% follow the Chinese Confucianist and Daoist faiths, while many of the indigenous tribes of Sabah and Sarawak are animist. Islam is the official state religion, with the Yang Di-Pertuan Agong serving as the Federation's religious head, and rulers in each state as the local heads of Islam.

Political features

State type: liberal democratic
Date of state formation: 1957
Political structure: federal
Executive: parliamentary
Assembly: two-chamber
Party structure: multiparty*
Human rights rating: 61%
International affiliations: APEC, AsDB, ASEAN, CP, CW, ESCAP, G-15, G-77, IAEA, IBRD, ICFTU, IDB, IMF, LORCS, NAM, OIC, UN, WTO

* Though actually dominated by one party.

Local and regional government

Below the state and federal territory level, the country is divided into 130 administrative districts, headed by a district officer, who is a civil servant. Below these are *mukims* (small districts), administered by *penghulus* (religious leaders). Sabah and Sarawak differ from West Malaysia, being divided into residencies and divisions.

Political system

Malaysia is a federation of 13 states: Johore, Kedah, Kelantan, Malacca, Negri Sembilan, Pahang, Penang, Perak, Perlis, Sabah, Sarawak, Selangor, and Trengganu, plus the capital city, Kuala Lumpur, and the island of Labuan, which are separate Federal Territories. Each state has its own written constitution, head of state (sultan or Yang di-Pertuan Negeri) and elected 14–56-seat Legislative Assembly, led by a chief minister (Menteri Besar) and cabinet, and with powers to legislate on matters outside the federal parliament's sphere.

The federation is headed, under the constitution of 1957, by a constitutional monarch, the Paramount Ruler, Yang di-Pertuan Agong. The monarch is elected, by secret ballot, for five-year terms by and from among the hereditary rulers of nine of the states: Malacca, Penang, Sabah, and Sarawak being the exceptions. For this purpose, a special Conference of Rulers (Majlis Raja) is convened. The Paramount Ruler's powers are similar to those of the British monarch, including discretion in the appointment of the prime minister (Perdana Mentri) and in granting a dissolution of parliament. In normal circumstances, however, the monarch acts on the advice of the elected prime minister and cabinet, who wield effective executive power. The monarch has no powers of veto, but until a constitutional amendment was passed in May 1994, could delay legislation by returning it to parliament for reconsideration.

The federal legislature, or parliament (Parlimen), is a two-chamber body composed of a 70-member upper house, called the Senate (Dewan Negara) and a 192-member House of Representatives (Dewan Rakyat). The Senate comprises 40 members nominated by the monarch, four from the two Federal Territories, and two elected by each of the 13 state Legislative Assemblies. All serve a six-year term. The members of the House of Representatives are elected for five-year terms from single-member constituencies by universal adult suffrage. The constituency system is weighted in favor of Malays in the countryside and against the Chinese in the towns. The House of Representatives is the dominant chamber, the Senate having only delaying powers over bills originating in, and approved by, the lower chamber: one month over money bills and one year over other bills.

The majority party or coalition in the House of Representatives provides the prime minister, who selects an executive council of ministers (Juma'ah Mentri), or cabinet, from within parliament, as the government of the day. The prime minister also holds additional portfolios, such as home affairs and national and rural development. The cabinet is collectively responsible to parliament.

To amend the constitution, a two-thirds vote in the federal parliament is required.

Malaysia's federal system is substantially weighted towards the center, the federal parliament enjoying sole authority to legislate in the fields of external affairs, defense and internal security, justice, except for Islamic law, industry, commerce, finance, education, transportation, and communication. In all other cases, federal legislation takes precedence over state law whenever a conflict arises. In addition, the states enjoy few significant sources of revenue.

It is in the spheres of land and natural resource management and local administration that state authority is greatest. Exceptions are the two East Malaysia (Borneo) states of Sabah and Sarawak. They enjoy a greater measure of autonomy, having been granted special safeguards in matters of land law, local government, finance, official religion, and official language.

Political parties

The principal political party in the Federation of Malaysia is the United Malays National Organization (UMNO), which, headed by Prime Minister Dr Mahathir bin Mohamad, is orientated towards native Malays and dominates a multiparty National Front (NF: Barisan Nasional) coalition, which contests national and state elections. The UMNO was originally formed in May 1946 to 'fight for independence and safeguard the interests of the indigenous people'. Since independence, the party has set as its aim the 'safeguarding of Malay interests', the promotion of national unity, and the pursuit of a 'neutral foreign policy'.

Dissension grew within UMNO during 1987–88, culminating in a High Court ruling in February 1988, which, as a result of irregularities in the party's internal elections of April 1987, declared the UMNO to be an 'unlawful' body. It therefore had to be disbanded, and a New UMNO (UMNO Baru) was immediately founded by Dr Mahathir. By June 1988 this grouping had a membership of 200,000, compared with the old UNMO's 1.4 million. Dissident UMNO members, led by former prime minister, Tunku Abdul Rahman, and former trade and industry minister, Tunku Tan Sri Razaleigh Hamzah, were forced outside and in May 1989 formed an alternative party, Semangat '46 (Spirit of 1946). The latter party returned to the UMNO fold in October 1996, and by 1998 UMNO membership had risen to 2.5 million.

Thirteen other parties are currently also members of the ruling National Front coalition, the majority being communally or regionally based. The most important is the Chinese-orientated Malaysian Chinese Association (MCA), a conservative grouping, formed in 1949, which currently claims a membership of 500,000 and is led by Dr Ling Liong Sik. Another Chinese-orientated party within the NF is the 250,000-strong Gerakan Party (PGRM: Malaysian People's Movement Party), a socialist grouping, formed in 1968, and currently led by Dr Lim Keng Yaik. Orientated towards the Indian community is the 400,000-member Malaysian Indian Congress (MIC), which was established in 1946, and is led by Datuk S Samy Vellu.

Also within the ruling coalition are the People's Progressive Party (PPP; estd. 1955); the Sarawak National Action Party (SNAP; estd. 1961); the Sarawak United People's Party (SUPP; estd. 1959); the United Sabah People's Party (PBRS; estd. 1994); the Parti Bansa Dayak Sarawak (PBDS; estd. 1983); the Parti Pesaka Bumiputra Bersatu (PPBB; estd. 1983); the Sabah-based People's Justice Movement (AKAR, admitted into the NF in July 1991); the Sabah Democratic Party (PDS; estd. 1994); the Sabah Progressive Party (SAPP; estd. 1994); and the Liberal Democratic Party (LDP, admitted into the NF in July 1991).

The principal opposition party in the Federation is the predominantly Chinese, 12,000-member Democratic Action Party (DAP), led by Lim Kit Siang. Formed in 1966, the DAP advocates the establishment of a multiracial society based on the principles of democratic socialism. In August 1998 Lim Guan Eng, leader of the DAP's youth wing, was sentenced to 18 months' imprisonment for publicly criticizing the police. Also important is the Islamic-radical, 300,000-member Pan-Malayan Islamic Party (PAS: Parti Islam Se Malaysia), which was formed in 1951 and advocates the establishment of a fully Islamic society.

The Parti Bersatu Sabah (PBS: Sabah United Party), set up in 1985 by the Roman Catholic ex-chief minister of Sabah state, Datuk Joseph Pairin Kitangan, and a member of the NF until October 1990, is also a member of the opposition, drawing its support from the Christian Kadazan-Dusin people. Smaller, regional parties operate at the state level.

Political leaders since 1970*

1970–76 Tun Abdul Razak (UMNO), 1976–81 Datuk Hussein bin Onn (UMNO), 1981– Datuk Seri Dr Mahathir bin Mohamad (UMNO)

* Prime ministers.

Latest elections

In the most recent House of Representatives elections, which were held on 24–25 April 1995, in tandem with elections to the 13 state legislative assemblies, the ruling National Front coalition captured 162 of the 192 House of Representatives seats and 64% of the vote, a 10% advance on its performance in 1990. Within the National Front, UMNO won 88 seats and the MCA 30 seats. The Chinese DAP, the largest opposition party in the new parliament, retained just nine of the 20 seats it had held before the election and the opposition won no parliamentary seats in seven of the country's 13 states. The fundamentalist PAS held on to control of Kelantan state. However, the other states were won by the National Front, which won 339 of the 394 available state assembly seats. The election campaign was characterized by the state-controlled media adopting a slavishly pro-government line and the opposition being hampered by the banning of public rallies.

Political history

The history of the country is better understood on the basis of a knowledge of its geographical location. The Federation of Malaysia is divided into two broad regions: in the west, Peninsular Malaysia, comprising 11 states and 83% of the total population, and Eastern Malaysia, which includes the states of Sabah and Sarawak, in the north and east of the island of Borneo. The southern and central portion of the island forms part of Indonesia. The small, independent coastal Sultanate of Brunei is encircled by Eastern Malaysia and the two broad regions of Malaysia are separated by 640 kilometres of the South China Sea.

The regions of present-day Malaysia formed part of the Buddhist Sri Vijaya empire between the 9th and 14th centuries, an empire which was eventually overthrown by a Javanese Hindu kingdom. Islam was subsequently introduced and a substantial empire was built up, prior to the Portuguese conquest of Malacca in 1511. Thereafter the area came, successively, under Dutch, 1641–1795, British, 1795–1817, and, again, Dutch, 1818–24, control.

From the mid-1820s, British sovereignty was progressively established over the Malaysia region, and a tin and rubber export-based economy was developed, particularly in the west. Chinese and Indian Tamil laborers were imported to work in the mines and on the plantations. Despite the British presence, local state chiefs were allowed to retain considerable political autonomy. Initially, in 1826, only the states of Singapore, Penang, and Malacca were formally incorporated into the British Colony of the Straits Settlement. But in 1874 British protection was extended to Perak, Selangor, Pahang, and Negri Sembilan. In 1895 they collectively formed the Federated Malay States. Johore came under British protection in 1885. Then, between 1910 and 1930, protection treaties were entered into with Kedah, Perlis, Kelantan, and Trengganu, which, together with Johore, were known as the Unfederated Malay States. Finally, after World War II, and following the extension of British control over Sarawak, in 1948, the protectorates in Borneo and the Malay Peninsula were unified to form, in February 1948, the Federation of Malaysia (FOM) Crown Colony.

Following several years of communist insurrection, the FOM was granted independence, within the Commmonwealth, in August 1957. Six years later, in September 1963, Britain relinquished sovereignty over its crown colonies of Sabah and Sarawak, and a new 14-state FOM was formed. North Borneo had been a British territory since 1881 and administered by the North Borneo Company until 1946. Sarawak was a British territory which had been ruled by the Brooke family since 1841. This new Federation initially included the internally self-governing state of Singapore. However, in August 1965, Singapore, alleging discrimination against its Chinese community, seceded from the FOM.

During its early years, between 1963 and 1966, the existence of the FOM was contested by guerrillas supported by the Sukarno government of Indonesia, while, in 1968, the Philippines disputed the sovereignty of East Malaysia. Tunku (Prince) Abdul Rahman (1903–90) was the country's first prime minister, between 1963 and 1969, governing in a successful, consensual, and multiracial manner at the head of the Alliance Party, which had been established in 1952. Then, in August 1969, serious anti-Chinese race riots erupted in Kuala Lumpur, forcing the formation of an emergency administration. These riots followed a fall in support for the ruling United Malays National Organization (UMNO) in the federal elections and were indicative of a deeper Malay resentment of the economic success and wealth of the Chinese business community.

The disturbances prompted the resignation of Tunku Abdul Rahman in September 1970 and the creation, by his successor as prime minister, Tun Abdul Razak, of a broader ten-party, later 13, National Front governing coalition, to succeed the Alliance Party. The coalition included in its ranks previous opposition parties. In addition, a major 'New Economic Policy' was launched in 1971, with the aim of raising the share of businesses owned by ethnic Malays (*Bumiputras*) from a level of 4% to 30% by 1990. It was also planned to extend the use of pro-Malay 'affirmative action' quota systems for university entrance and company employment. At the same time, greater stress was placed on rural development, in an effort to achieve a better 'economic balance'.

During the 1970s, Malaysia enjoyed healthy rates of economic growth of more than 7%, but the problem of communist guerrilla actions near the Thailand border re-emerged after 1975. Relations with the Chinese community also deteriorated in the later 1970s, as a result of the federal government's initial refusal to accept 'boat people' refugees fleeing from Vietnam. Even more serious was the revival of a fundamentalist Islamic movement in the western and northern provinces.

Dr Mahathir bin Mohamad (b. 1925), formerly the deputy prime minister and trade and industry minister, became the new leader of the UMNO and prime minister in July 1981 and proceeded to pursue a more narrowly Islamic and pro-Malay strategy than his predecessors. In addition, he embarked on an ambitious new industrialization program, seeking to 'look east' and emulate Japan. He secured re-election in April 1982 and August 1986, but, between these dates, began to encounter growing opposition from his Malaysian Chinese Association (MCA) coalition partners. He was also faced with Christian – Muslim ethnic conflict in Sabah and a sudden slowdown in economic growth in 1985, as a result of the fall in world tin, rubber, and palm oil commodity prices. Internal UMNO opposition to Dr Mahathir also began to surface in 1987, when, in April, trade and industry minister, Tunku Razaleigh Hamzah, unsuccessfully, but only by a small margin, challenged for the party's presidency. Two months later, Razaleigh and his closest supporters were dismissed from their cabinet posts.

During the autumn of 1987 racial tensions worsened, Chinese language education and religion emerging as divisive issues. Fearing a renewed outbreak of riots, Prime Minister Mahathir, in October – November, ordered the arrest and detention without trial of 106 politicians, including the DAP leader and deputy leader Lim Kit Siang and Karpal Singh. Among the people arrested were journalists, lawyers, and pressure group leaders. The action was taken under the provisions of the Internal Security Act (ISA). Press censorship regulations were also tightened, and several journals were forced to cease publication. These moves served to heighten intraparty opposition to Mahathir, to the extent that the party's moderate wing, led by Razaleigh and supported by former prime minister, Tunku Abdul Rahman, charged the prime minister with increasing authoritarianism. Eleven dissident members from this wing filed a legal suit, claiming that the party's leadership election of the previous year had been improperly conducted. Their claims were upheld by the High Court, in February 1988, which ruled that delegations taking part in the elections had not been legally registered and that, as a result, the UMNO was 'an unlawful society', and the 1987 elections were null and void.

This created a serious constitutional crisis, putting in doubt the legal status of the incumbent government. However, with the support of the head of state, Tunku Mahmood Iskandar, and with subsequent favorable judicial rulings, Prime Minister Mahathir weathered the storm. Initially, the Razaleigh-Rahman wing of the UMNO attempted to register a new successor party, 'UMNO Malaysia', but the application was rejected by the Registrar of Societies. Dr Mahathir responded by applying to form a 'New UMNO' (UMNO Baru), which excluded dissident members of the old UMNO. This application was accepted by the registrar.

Despite surviving the immediate political crisis of February 1988, Dr Mahathir's public standing was seriously weakened in the short term. The new UMNO Baru was defeated heavily in an opposition-engineered by-election in August 1988. Additional controversy was aroused by the passage of a constitutional amendment, in March 1988, which limited the power of the judiciary to interpret laws and the dismissal, in July 1988, of the lord president of the Supreme Court for alleged 'anti-government bias'. The National Front recovered sufficiently to secure a further clear victory in the October 1990 general election, although its share of parliamentary seats fell from the 84% achieved in August 1986 to just 71%.

In November 1993 finance minister Anwar Ibrahim was elected deputy president of UMNO, thus becoming the obvious heir-apparent to Dr Mahathir. In March 1994 Joseph Pairin Kitangan, chief minister of Sabah since 1985, was forced to resign after being undermined by a conviction for corruption which he had denied. A new UMNO government was formed in the state. This left only one state in the federation, Kelantan, with an opposition administration.

In foreign affairs, Malaysia joined ASEAN in 1967 and originally, during the Tunku Abdul Rahman era, adopted a pro-Western, anticommunist posture. From the 1970s, however, its relations with the communist powers improved, while closer links were also developed with Islamic nations. The country has advocated the creation of a zone of 'peace, freedom and neutrality' in Southeast Asia. In November 1993, concerned at the possibility of United States domination of the region, Malaysia boycotted the inaugural summit of the Asia Pacific Economic Cooperation (APEC) forum.

In the economic sphere, the government has, since the mid-1960s, pursued a system of indicative economic planning, based on the framing of five-year plans. In addition, in 1985, a ten-year Industrial Master Plan (IMP) was introduced, with the aim of fostering long-term development of the manufacturing sector. Joint venture projects have also been entered into with Japanese car manufacturing companies, while special tax and export incentives have been offered by the state's Malaysian Industrial Development Authority, in an effort to attract greater inward investment. These moves, involving a slackening of restrictions on foreign ownership, meant that the 1971 goal of achieving 30% ethnic Malay equity ownership by 1989 had, of necessity, to be revised. In 1986 the Malay share stood at 18%. The 'New Development Policy' (NDP), which was launched in June 1991 to replace the expiring 'New Economic Policy', was consequently less discriminatory against non-Malays. It aimed to achieve an eightfold increase, 7% per annum, in national income by the year 2020, by which date Malaysia, it envisaged, will have become a 'fully developed state'. Between 1986 and 1995 the annual rate of GDP growth averaged 8% and the UMNO increased its parliamentary majority in the general election held in April 1995, securing its biggest victory since independence in 1957. From July 1997 the Malaysian currency and economy was engulfed in a serious Asian financial crisis that had begun in Thailand. After spending US$2 billion trying to defend the linkage to the dollar, the Malaysian central bank allowed the ringgit to float and by January 1998 it had fallen in value by 40%. The stockmarket fell even more sharply and, despite Prime Minister Mahathir's repeated assertions that the economy remained sound, the country, after a decade of spectacular growth, entered a sharp recession: shrinking by 5% in the first half of 1998. Determined to avoid the need to draw on the IMF for financial assistance, it was announced, in December 1997, that a range of government development projects would be shelved. In addition, to encourage Chinese and Indian Malay investment, the bumiputra racial preference quotas were temporarily lifted. Consequently, in March 1998, 17,000 of the 1 million foreign workers in Malaysia (mainly illegal immigrants from Indonesia) were immediately repatriated, with a further 200,000 leaving from August 1998. In June 1998 Mahathir brought back into the cabinet, as economic overlord, Daim Zainuddin a close ally. This reduced the influence of Anwar Ibrahim, the deputy prime minister and finance minister, an ambitious economic conservative who, following the circulation of rumours about his personal life, was suddenly dismissed in September 1998, and expelled from UMNO. After leading a large anti-government demonstration, he was arrested on charges of corruption and sexual misconduct. Currency controls were immediately introduced.

In April 1999 Anwar was found guilty on four charges of corruption and sentenced to six years' imprisonment. Meanwhile, his wife, Wan Azizah Wan Ismail, formed a new political party, the National Justice Party (PKN), which acted as a rallying point for opposition to Mahathir's government.

MALDIVES

The Republic of the Maldives
Dhivehi Raajjeyge Jumhooriyyaa

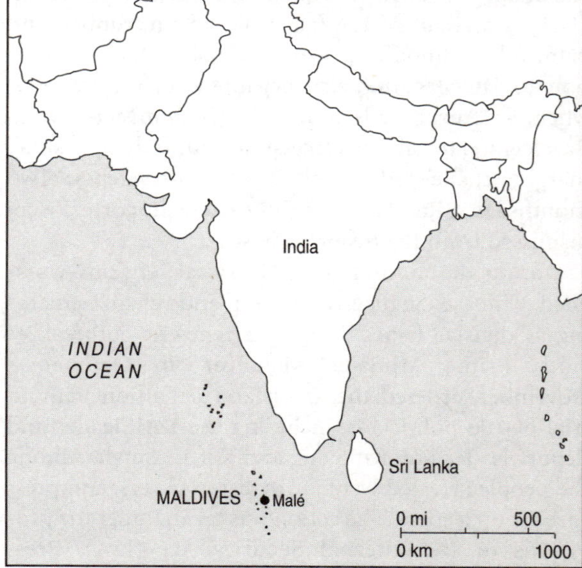

Capital: Malé

Social and economic data

Area: 298 sq km/115 sq miles
Population: 256,000*
Pop. density per sq km/sq mi: 859/2,226*
Urban population: 31%**
Literacy rate: 98%**
GDP: $251 million*; per-capita GDP: $980*
Government defense spending (% of GDP): 0%***
Currency: rufiyaa
Economy type: low income
Labor force in agriculture: 6%**
* 1995.
** 1992.
*** There are no armed forces.

Head of state and head of government

President Maumoon Abdul Gayoom, since 1978

Ethnic composition

The indigenous population comprises four 'ethnic strains': Dravidian, in the northern islands; Arab, in the middle islands; Sinhalese, in the southern islands; and Negro, or Ravare. Dhivehi, or Maldivian, is the official national language derived from languages spoken by ethnic groups. There is also an Indian/Sri Lankan linguistic and religious immigrant minority, including expatriate workers.

Religion

The majority of the population, more than 90%, are Sunni Muslims. Islam is the state religion and Sharia law is enforced.

Political features

State type: authoritarian nationalist
Date of state formation: 1965
Political structure: unitary
Executive: unlimited presidential
Assembly: one-chamber
Party structure: no parties
Human rights rating: N/A
International affiliations: AsDB, CP, CW, CP, ESCAP, G-77, IBRD, IDB, IMF, NAM, OIC, SAARC, UN, WTO

Local and regional government

The country is divided into 21 administrative districts, comprising the capital, which is subject to direct central administration, and the 20 atolls, each of which is governed by an atoll chief (*verin*), appointed by the president. The chief is assisted by an elected committee. Each island is subject to the jurisdiction of a headman (*kateeb*), also appointed by the president.

Political system

The current 156-article constitution was adopted in January 1998 and is an amended version of an earlier 1964 document which was drawn up by the celebrated British constitutional lawyer, Sir Ivor Jennings. It provides for a single-chamber Citizens' Council (Majlis) of 50 members, and an executive president, nominated by the Majlis in a multi-candidate contest and then elected by referendum. They all serve a five-year term. Forty-two of the Majlis' members are elected by universal adult suffrage, two each being returned by the National Capital Island and the 20 constituent atolls, and eight are appointed by the president. The Majlis meets three times a year, acting principally as a debating forum. The president appoints and leads a cabinet, whose members are individually responsible to the Majlis. In April 1998 the cabinet had 19 members and President Gayoom held the key portfolios of defense and national security, and finance and treasury. There are no restrictions on the number of terms a president can serve. There has also been, since July 1985, a 15-member, president-appointed, Special Consultative Council, which advises on economic matters and held discussions, in 1990, on the advantages of promoting greater freedom of speech. Women are precluded from holding political office. The 1998 constitution was framed by a Citizens' Special Majlis, set up in 1980, and introduced greater accountability for ministers, including allowing parliamentary questions.

Political parties

There are no political parties in the Maldives, candidates standing for election on the basis of their 'personal influence' and clan loyalties.

Political leaders since 1970

1968–78 Ibrahim Nasir (independent), 1978– Maumoon Abdul Gayoom (independent)

Latest elections

In the most recent presidential election, or, rather, referendum, held in October 1998, Maumoon Abdul Gayoom was re-elected unopposed for a fifth consecutive term, with 91% of the vote. Turnout was 75%. Non-party elections to the Majlis were last held in December 1994.

Political history

The Maldives comprise 1,196 small coral islands, 203 of which are inhabited, grouped in 20 atolls, situated in the North Indian Ocean, 650 kilometres southwest of

Sri Lanka. The islands lie barely a metre above a rising sea level and the country faces the risk of disappearing beneath the waves if sea levels rise as a consequence of global warming. The original population, which was Dravidian, was displaced during the 9th century by seafaring Arabs, who introduced Islamic practices. During the 16th century, the islands came under Portuguese rule, before becoming a dependency of Ceylon, now Sri Lanka, from the mid-17th century, when Sinhalese and Indian colonies were established. Under the designation 'Maldive Islands', though still remaining a dependency of Ceylon, they were placed under British protection in 1887 and enjoyed a measure of internal self-government under a hereditary sultan.

Between January 1953 and February 1954 a republic was briefly established, before the sultanate, now subject to election, was restored, with Ibrahim Nasir serving as prime minister. In July 1965, with anti-British sentiment rising and reflected in a secessionist rebellion in Suvadivan in 1959–60, the islands were granted full independence outside the Commonwealth, under the new designation 'Maldives'. Three years later, after a referendum, the sultan was deposed and a republic was again established, with the then prime minister, Ibrahim Nasir, elected president. He governed with the aid of a prime minister, Ahmed Zaki, until March 1975, when this post was abolished, after an attempt by Zaki to secure a Majlis no-confidence vote against the president. A fully presidential system was then adopted.

Between 1956 and 1975 Britain had a Royal Air Force staging post on the southern island of Gan and its closure meant a substantial loss of income. The president, nevertheless, refused an offer from the USSR, in October 1977, to lease the former base, saying that he did not want it used for military purposes again, nor leased to a superpower.

In 1978 President Nasir announced that he would not stand for re-election for a third term and the Majlis nominated Maumoon Abdul Gayoom (b. 1937), a former university lecturer in Islamic studies and later a member of Nasir's cabinet, as his successor. He was then elected unopposed in a popular presidential 'referendum', in July 1978, winning 90% of the votes cast. Nasir, meanwhile, left the country for Singapore but was called back to answer charges of embezzling government funds. He denied the charges and attempts to extradite him were unsuccessful. Despite rumours of a plot by groups connected with Nasir to overthrow him, Gayoom was re-elected for a further five years in September 1983, securing 95.6% of the popular vote.

During his period in charge, the country, despite a rapid population growth of over 3% per year, has enjoyed substantial economic progress, with annual GDP growth averaging nearly 10% in the 1980s and 6% thereafter. This has primarily been the result of the promotion of the tourist industry, which generates 20% of current GDP and attracts one-third of a million visitors each year. A further 15% is generated by the fishing industry, in which 20% of the labor force is engaged. The president has also concentrated on the development of poor rural regions and social provision, such as education and health services.

In foreign affairs, while adhering to his predecessor's general policy of nonalignment and close links with the Arab nations of the Middle East, Gayoom brought the Maldives back into the Commonwealth as a full member in June 1985. The country is also a founder member of the South Asian Association for Regional Cooperation (SAARC).

President Gayoom was re-elected in September 1988, but was challenged in November 1988 by an abortive coup led by Abdullah Luthufi, an exiled businessman from the southern atoll of Adu, which had demanded secession during the 1970s. He had recruited a force of around 200 Tamil mercenaries in Sri Lanka. After fierce fighting, which claimed 19 lives, the rebels, who appeared to enjoy the backing of former President Nasir, captured the presidential palace and forced Gayoom into hiding. However, order was restored after the intervention, at Gayoom's request, of 1,600 paratroops sent by India, in fulfilment of its role as a member of SAARC: the Maldives lacked an army of its own. Luthufi and his co-conspirator, Sagar Nasir, were captured and sent for trial and Gayoom re-installed as president. Sixteen of those captured, including Luthufi, were sentenced to life imprisonment in 1989. In 1993 Gayoom faced a leadership challenge from his brother-in-law, Ilyas Ibrahim, the minister of atolls administration, who was forced into exile for 'unconstitutional behaviour' and was sentenced in absentia to 15 years' imprisonment. Ibrahim later returned to the Maldives in 1996 and was kept under house arrest until 1997. Since 1994 President Gayoom has promoted gradual democratization, giving ministers greater autonomy and, with the revised constitution of January 1998, allowing, for the first time, a multi-candidate contest for the Majlis' nomination for the presidency. In November 1996 he established a Supreme Council for Islamic Affairs, to advise the government on matters relating to Islam.

MONGOLIA

State of Mongolia/Mongolian Republic
Mongol Uls

Capital: Ulaanbaatar (Ulan Bator)

Social and economic data

Area: 1,565,000 sq km/604,250 sq miles
Population: 2,363,000*
Pop. density per sq km/sq mi: 2/4*
Urban population: 49%**
Literacy rate: 93%**
GDP: $770 million*; per-capita GDP $325*
Government defense spending (% of GDP): 2.4*
Currency: tugrik
Economy type: low income
Labor force in agriculture: 30%**
* 1995.
** 1992.

Head of state (executive)

President Natsagiyn Bagabandi, since 1997

Head of government

Prime Minister Nyam-Osoriyn Tuyaa, since 1999

Ethnic composition

Ninety per cent of the population is Mongol, 4% Kazakh, 2% Chinese, and 2% Russian. Khalkha Mongolian is the official language. The Cyrillic (Russian) script will remain in use for official publications until 2001, when it will be replaced by the classical Mongolian script.

Religions

Tibetan Buddhism (Lamaism) has been the traditional religion for the Mongol community. It was suppressed during the communist era, but there has been a revival during recent years. The Kazakhs of western Mongolia are Sunni Muslims by descent.

Political features

State type: emergent democratic
Date of state formation: 1921
Political structure: unitary
Executive: limited presidential
Assembly: one-chamber
Party structure: multiparty
Human rights rating: N/A
International affiliations: AsDB, ESCAP, IAEA, IBRD, IMF, G-77, LORCS, NAM, UN, WFTU

Local and regional government

The country is divided into 21 provinces (*aymags*) and one municipality (*Ulaanbaatar*), with appointed governors (*dzasag darga*) and elected local assemblies.

Political system

Under the new, noncommunist, constitution of February 1992, Mongolia has a 76-member parliament, the People's Great Hural (Assembly). Deputies are elected for four-year terms and parliamentary sessions must be held at least every six months for not less than 65 working days. The voting age is set at 25 years and there are 26 constituencies. Election is by simple majority, provided candidates secure at least 25% of the votes in their constituency. The executive president is elected directly for a four-year term and is also commander in chief of the armed forces. Candidates must be at least 45 years old and be resident (for at least five years) ethnic Mongolians. The president works with a prime minister and a cabinet of some 20 members elected by the parliament and may veto legislation. These vetoes can be overturned by a two-thirds majority vote in the Great Hural. Until 1998 members of the legislature were debarred from serving in the cabinet. There is a Supreme Court. This new democratic constitution permits both private ownership and the imposition of forced labor.

Political parties

The traditionally dominant party in Mongolia has been the Mongolian People's Revolutionary Party (MPRP) which originated as a broad front of radical nationalist forces, inspired by the 1917 Russian Bolshevik revolution, who were opposed to China's attempts to restore its sovereignty over Mongolia in 1919. In 1921 those with communist leanings met in the USSR to form the Mongolian People's Party, which was renamed the MPRP in 1924, constituting the nucleus of the country's new 'Provisional People's Government'. The MPRP was divided between a radical left wing and a conservative, moderate rightwing during the 1920s and 1930s and subject to repeated factional conflicts, until party strongman, Marshal Horloogiyn Choybalsan, established his dominance between 1939 and 1952. Under Choybalsan, the regular party machinery fell into disuse, with only two congresses meeting, as power became personalized. Under his successors, however, a regularized structure was re-established. It is now a reform-socialist body which has been converted to free-market economics. It has 85,000 members. The party is organized hierarchically on 'democratic centralist' lines, with a nine-member Party Leadership Council at its apex.

The principal contending party is the Mongolian National Democratic Party (MNDP), which was formed in October 1992 through the merger of the Mongolian Democratic Union (MDU; estd. 1989), the Mongolian Party of National Progress (MPNP), the Mongolian United Party (MUP), and the Party for Mongolian Renaissance. Led by Tsahiagiyn Elbegdorj, it advocates market economics, a revival of traditional Mongolian culture, and a neutral foreign policy. It has 40,000 members and since 1986 has formed an electorally successful Democratic Alliance (DA) coalition with the left-of-center Mongolian Social Democratic Party (MSDP). The MSDP, formed in 1990, has 28,000 members.

There were nine other functioning parties of significance in 1992, including a Mongolian Green Party (estd. 1990), a member of the DA; a (Buddhist) Believers' Democratic Party (estd. 1990); and the 12,000-member United Heritage (Conservative) Party (UHP; estd. 1993).

Political leaders since 1970*

1958–84 Yumjaagiyn Tsedenbal (MPRP), 1984–90 Jambyn Batmunkh (MPRP), 1990–97 Punsalmaagiyn Ochirbat (MPRP/independent), 1997– Natsagiyn Bagabandi (MPRP)

* Communist Party leaders to 1990, then president.

Latest elections

The most recent People's Great Hural elections were held on 30 June 1996. The Democratic Alliance (DA), with 47% of the vote, won 50 of the 76 seats, including 34 for the MNDP and 13 for the MSDP. The MPRP, with 40% of the vote, captured 25 seats. The other seat was won by the UHP. Turnout was 92%. The most recent presidential election, held on 18 May 1997, was won by Natsagiyn Bagabandi, of the ex-communist MPRP, who defeated the incumbent, Punsalmaagiyn Ochirbat, candidate of the ruling DA coalition. Bagabandi received 61% of the vote, Ochirbat, 30%, and Jambyn Gombojav, of the nationalist UHP, 7%. Turnout was 85%.

Political history

The area, dominated by nomadic tribes, was united by Genghis Khan (*c.* 1162–1227) during the early 13th century, and formed the nucleus of a vast Mongol empire which stretched across Asia, reaching its zenith under Genghis' grandson, Kublai Khan (1214–94). It was then conquered by China during the 17th century, being known as the Chinese province of 'Outer Mongolia' between 1689 and 1911. Following the Chinese 'republican revolution' of 1911, Mongolian nationalists proclaimed the country's independence and, receiving the support of Tsarist Russia, succeeded in gaining semi-autonomy, under the leadership of a traditionalist Buddhist monarchy, in the shape of a 'reincarnated' lama. Chinese sovereignty was asserted again in 1915 and, taking advantage of the turmoil in Russia, formal control was reintroduced in 1919. The new Soviet government came, however, to the support of Mongolian nationalists, helping them to overthrow Chinese rule for the last time in July 1921. Constitutionally, Mongolia continued to remain subject to China's formal sovereignty until January 1946, an October 1945 plebiscite having unanimously favored full independence, but a November 1921 treaty with the Russian Soviet Federal Socialist Republic guaranteed its autonomy.

Initially, the newly independent state was subject to joint control by the monarchy and an MPRP-dominated 'People's Government'. However, on the death of King Javdzandamba Hutagt VIII in June 1924, the monarchy was abolished and a 'People's Republic' proclaimed. In November 1924 a Soviet-style constitution was adopted and a program of 'defeudalization' launched. This involved the expropriation of the previously dominant nobility, the collectivization of agriculture, predominantly herding, and the destruction of Lama Buddhism. An armed uprising by anti-government forces, in 1932, was forcibly suppressed, with Soviet assistance. At least 100,000 people were killed in the purges of this period.

The dominant figure in the new state, following

purges between 1936 and 1939, became the former independence fighter, Marshal Horloogiyn Choybalsan, who combined the offices of MPRP leader and prime minister and ruled in a strict Stalinist manner, with minimal consultation. On his death, in January 1952, the two posts were respectively divided between Dashiyn Damba and Yumjaagiyn Tsedenbal, a Soviet-educated economist, until, in November 1958, Tsedenbal once again combined the positions and emerged as the dominant figure, but governing in a more cautious and consensual manner than his predecessor. A new constitution was adopted in July 1960, in recognition of the 'higher stage' of socialist development which had been attained.

Throughout the interwar period Mongolia remained closely dependent on the Soviet Union militarily, economically, and politically. Its MPRP leaders were all trained in Moscow and by the 1980s 95% of its foreign trade was with the USSR and Eastern Europe. This close interdependence received formal recognition in 1962, when Mongolia joined Comecon, and in January 1966, when a 20-year friendship, cooperation, and mutual assistance pact with the USSR was signed. This served to further sour relations with neighboring communist China which, at this time, was in ideological dispute with the Soviet Union. As a consequence, border incidents between the two countries became frequent during the early 1970s.

Internally, Mongolia remained substantially isolated from the outside world during the 1970s, but experienced considerable economic change as new urban industries developed and settled agriculture spread. Politically, MPRP leader Yumjaagiyn Tsedenbal remained the dominant figure, assuming the post of head of state in May 1972, on the death of the long-serving Jamsrangiyn Sambuu, who had been head of state since 1954. Jambyn Batmunkh took over Tsendbal's post of prime minister. Tsedenbal finally retired, on the grounds of ill-health, in August 1984, and was replaced as party leader and head of state by Jambyn Batmunkh. Dumaagiyn Sodnom, Batmunkh's deputy, became the new prime minister.

Mongolia's political leadership had traditionally been notoriously conservative and loyal to the 'Moscow line'. However, following the accession to power in the Soviet Union of Mikhail Gorbachev in 1985, the country was encouraged to be more innovative and to broaden its outside contacts. A large-scale reorganization of government ministries was launched between 1986 and 1988, as a means of streamlining decision-making and enhancing efficiency. In the diplomatic sphere, the level of cultural exchanges with China significantly increased and ambassadorial relations with the United States were established in January 1987. Also, between 1987 and 1990, the number of Soviet troops stationed within the country was reduced. Finally, a more tolerant attitude was adopted towards traditional social customs and religion. This encouraged a revival in Mongolian nationalism.

Influenced by events in Eastern Europe, an opposition grouping, the Mongolian Democratic Union (MDU), was formed illegally in December 1989 and during 1990 it spearheaded a campaign demanding greater democratization. As a result of this pressure, senior figures within the MPRP, including Batmunkh and Sodnom, were forced to resign in March 1990 and were later charged with corruption. Punsalmaagiyn Ochirbat (b. 1942), formerly the minister of external economic relations, became head of state and the People's Great Hural amended the constitution so as to end the communists' monopoly of power.

In the multiparty elections of July 1990 the remodelled MPRP captured 83% of parliament's seats and Ochirbat was subsequently elected indirectly state president. Members of the opposition Mongolian Democratic Party (MDP), successor to the MDU, were brought into a new administration which embarked on an ambitious program of economic transformation, moving from central planning to a market economy by 1994. Prices were freed, the currency was devalued massively, a new banking system and stock exchange were established, industries and agriculture were privatized, via a Czech-style voucher-conversion scheme, and the country joined the IMF and Asian Development Bank (AsDB). In the short term, the process of transition was painful. GDP fell by 10% during 1991 and by 9% during 1992, as the collapse of the Soviet Union led to the ending of its economic aid and supplies of energy, as well as the full withdrawal of Red Army troops. A seventh of the labor force was idle as the country found it difficult to find new markets for its products.

In the wake of the anticommunist repercussions of the failed August 1991 anti-Gorbachev coup in the USSR, President Ochirbat and other senior state officials resigned formally as members of the MPRP. A new constitution was adopted in February 1992 and in a general election held in June 1992 the MPRP held on to power. Puntsagiyn Jasray, an economist, became prime minister in July 1992 and President Ochirbat, now an independent supported by the MNDP (successor to the MDP) and MSDP, was directly elected state president in June 1993. During 1993 the economy contracted by a further 8%, despite pledges of economic aid from Japan, loans from the IMF, and the signing of a Friendship and Cooperation Treaty with Russia and, in 1994, with China. This provoked popular opposition to the government and in April 1994 there was a brief hunger strike by leading figures in the MNDP and MSDP who accused the administration of corruption and ineffective economic reforms. From the mid-1990s vigorous economic growth, averaging 6% per year began and the inflation rate fell. Nevertheless, the incumbent MPRP was defeated, surprisingly, in the June 1996 elections to the Great Hural (parliament) by a new Democratic Alliance (DA) coalition, which brought together the formerly hostile MNDP and MSDP. The DA had campaigned for accelerated economic liberalization and political reform. In July 1996 Mendsayhany Enhsayhan, of the DA, became prime minister and in August 1996 a defense cooperation agreement was signed with the United States. The new DA administration introduced a radical, free-market economic 'shock therapy' program, with the support of the IMF and World Bank. It included, in April 1997, becoming the first country in the world to abolish all commercial taxes and tariffs. However, it led to unemployment rising to over 15%, widening income differentials, food shortages, increased crime, and anti-government demonstrations.

In May 1997 Natsagiyn Bagabandi, the candidate of the ex-communist MPRP, benefited from the new government's unpopularity by defeating the incumbent Ochirbat, who had stood with the DA's backing, in the presidential election. Bagabandi pledged to increase welfare spending and slow the pace of economic reform, which had created social hardship. The MNDP's young new leader, the 35-year-old Tsakhiagiyn Elbegdorj, a former journalist who had helped topple the communist regime in 1990, became prime minister in April 1998. Within three months this government was toppled, after losing a no-confidence vote, following a banking crisis. Later in December 1998 Janlaviyn Narantsatsralt, a MNDP former mayor of Ulan Bator, became prime minister.

In July 1999 Nyam-Osoriyn Tuyaa replaced him as acting prime minister.

MYANMAR (BURMA)

Union of Myanmar/Burma (UOM)*
Myanmar Naingngandaw

* The designation Burma was officially dropped in May 1989, but is still used by the opposition and by the Western media.

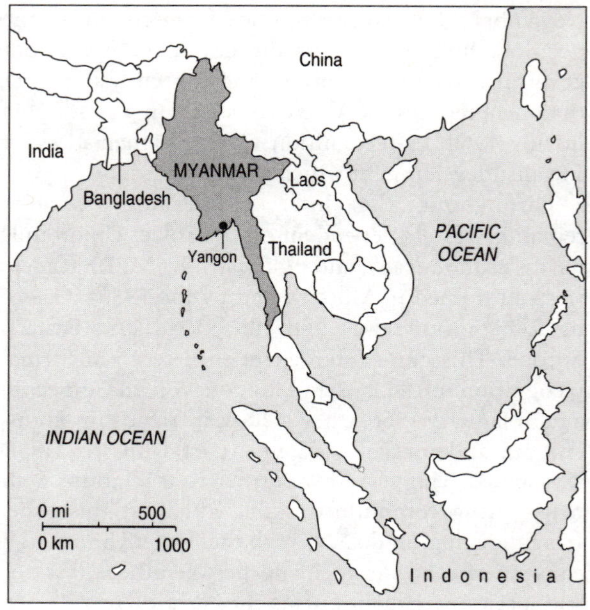

Capital: Yangon (Rangoon)

Social and economic data

Area: 676,552 sq km/261,218 sq miles
Population: 45,555,000*
Pop. density per sq km/sq mi: 67/174*
Urban population: 25%**
Literacy rate: 81%**
GDP: $26,300 million*; per-capita GDP: $580*
Government defense spending (% of GDP): 6.2%*
Currency: kyat
Economy type: low income
Labor force in agriculture: 64%**
* 1995.
** 1992.

Head of state and head of government

General Than Shwe, since 1992

Ethnic composition

Burmans, who predominate in the fertile central river valley and southern coastal and delta regions, constitute the ethnic majority, comprising 72% of the total population. Out of more than a hundred minority communities, the most important are the Karen, 7% of the population, the Shan, 6%, Indians, 6%, Chinese, 3%, Kachin, 2%, and Chin, 2%. The indigenous minority communities, who predominate in mountainous border regions, show considerable hostility towards the culturally and politically dominant Burmans, undermining national unity. It has been alleged that, since 1996, the military government has been relocating Shan civilians, to stop support for the opposition Shan State National Army (estd. 1985), forcing 300,000 to flee their homes. The official language is Burmese, spoken by 80% of the population.

Religions

Eighty-seven per cent of the population is Theravada Buddhist, 5% Christian, 4% Sunni Muslim, 3% animist, and 1% Hindu. Animism and Christianity are concentrated among the ethnic minority communities.

Political features

State type: military authoritarian
Date of state formation: 1948
Political structure: unitary
Executive: military
Assembly: one-chamber
Party structure: multiparty
Human rights rating: 17%
International affiliations: AsDB, ASEAN, CP, ESCAP, G-77, IAEA, IBRD, IMF, LORCS, NAM, UN, WTO

Local and regional government

The country is divided into 14 administrative divisions, including seven states and seven provinces. Below them there are townships, wards, and village-tracts, each, since the 1988 military coup, with their own military-dominated councils.

Political system

Under the constitution of January 1974, Myanmar is a unitary republic. The highest organ of state power is the 485-member People's Assembly (Pyithu Hluttaw), a single-chamber legislature which is elected by universal adult suffrage every four years and convenes twice a year for short sessions. The People's Assembly elects, from among its members, the nation's coordinating executive, the 29-member State Council, which includes a representative from each of Myanmar's 14 states and divisions and is headed by a chairperson who acts as president. The State Council also has authority, delegated by the People's Assembly, to interpret and promulgate legislation. To undertake day-to-day administration, the State Council elects a 16–20 member Council of Ministers, headed by a prime minister, as well as three judicial bodies: the Council of People's Justices, the Council of People's Attorneys, and the Council of People's Inspectors.

The constitution was suspended in September 1988 and all state organs and institutions were abolished and superseded by an army-run 19-member State Law and Order Restoration Council (SLORC) and martial law was proclaimed. The SLORC's chairperson, General Than Shwe, serves as head of state and as prime minister and defense minister. He shares ultimate power with Lieutenant General Khin Nyunt, first secretary of the SLORC and head of the Directorate of Defense Services Intelligence, who is a protégé of Myanmar's former strongman, U Ne Win, who remains influential behind the scenes. The SLORC was renamed the State Peace and Development Council (SPDC) in November 1997. General Shwe also heads a 35-member cabinet of generals and technocrats. From 1993 a 699-member National Convention, comprising representatives of the SLORC and ten opposition parties, including the National League for Democracy, began to meet periodically to discuss the framing of a new constitution. The junta is anxious that any new constitution will guarantee the military a continuing, significant political role, on the model of Indonesia. The National Convention has been in recess since March 1996.

Political parties

Since 1962 the controlling force in the UOM has been the National Unity Party (NUP), known until September 1988 as the Burma Socialist Program Party (BSPP or Lanzin Party). It is closely intertwined with the military. With the passage of the Law to Protect National Solidarity, in March 1964, Myanmar legally became a one-party state. However, following the popular unrest of 1988, opposition parties began to reform.

The BSPP was established in July 1962 as a 'political arm' by the new military regime of General U Ne Win which had recently seized power. The party organized itself on quasi-communist lines, with a hierarchy of ward, village, and district branches at its lower levels and a controlling 280-member Central Committee and 15-member Central Executive Committee (CEC), 'elected' by a supra 1,000-member Congress with a four year term, at its apex. It was assigned a 'leading role' in state affairs, with members of its CEC monopolizing senior executive posts. In 1985 membership of the BSPP was put at 2.3 million, a figure which constituted 6.1% of the total population.

From September 1988, when the multiparty system was relegalized, opposition parties rapidly re-emerged. The most important new party to be formed was the National League for Democracy (NLD), a broad grouping which was the successor to the Democracy and Peace (Interim) League (DPIL). The DPIL had been illegally established in August 1988 by the former prime minister, U Nu, former president, U Mahn Win Maung, the influential former chief of staff and defense minister, General Thura Tin U, and Aung San Suu Kyi, the United Kingdom-based daughter of the assassinated national hero, Aung San. In 1998 the NLD's chair was U Aung Shwe and Suu Kyi was general secretary.

Party formation accelerated from October 1988, so that by March 1989 it was reported that 22 registered political groupings had been recognized by the ruling military government. However, with the coming to power of the SLORC, severe restrictions were placed on effective opposition party activity, and from October 1995 only nine legal political parties remained.

Outside the formal party system, armed ethnic minority insurgent groups have been engaged in guerrilla warfare in border regions against the incumbent BSPP and preceding regimes since independence. The outlawed, 10,000 member, Burmese Communist Party (BCP: White Flag Party) is the most serious insurgent force. Formed in 1946, when the Communist Party, which was established in 1939, split into White and Red Flag factions, it remains an unreconstructed Stalinist body, which enjoyed military backing from China until recent years. It established *de facto* control of parts of northern Myanmar during the 1980s through establishing an alliance with Wa tribespeople. However, the Wa mutinied in 1989 and signed a peace treaty with Myanmar's ruling military junta. This forced the BCP's leaders to flee into exile in China.

Anti-communist groups have operated during recent decades in Karen, in the southeast, Kachin, in the northeast, Shan, in the east, Arakan, in the southwest, Chin, in the west, and Palaung, Mon, Lahu, and Pa-O. They have been organized since 1975 within the 35,000-guerrilla-strong National Democratic Front (NDF). The NDF's goal is to re-establish a federal state based on national self-determination. In 1988 the NDF created the Democratic Alliance of Burma (DAB) to incorporate a further 11 dissident groups, including monks, students, and expatriates. However, since 1991 an increasing number of rebel groups have entered into ceasefire agreements with the ruling SLORC, including the Shan, Palaung, and Pa-O, in 1991, the Kachin, in 1993, and the Mon, in 1995. This has left the Karen isolated as the chief remaining rebel force and the focus of government military offensives.

Political leaders since 1970

1962–88 General U Ne Win (BSPP)*, 1988 Brigadier General Sein Lwin (BSPP)*, 1988 Dr Maung Maung (BSPP)*, 1988–92 General Saw Maung (military), 1992– General Than Shwe (military)

* Ruling party leaders.

Latest elections

The most recent elections to the People's Assembly were held on 27 May 1990, when the opposition National League for Democracy, despite state intimidation, won, surprisingly, 392 of the 485 contested seats. It attracted 60% of the national vote, compared to the NUP's 21%. The NUP won just ten seats, while the Shan Nationalities League for Democracy captured 23, and the Arakan League for Democracy, 11. Ninety-three parties contested the election. The military junta subsequently prevented the Assembly from convening.

Political history

As early as 850 AD, a Burmese state was established, with its capital inland at Pagan. The country was overrun by the Mongols during the later 13th century, but a new Toungoo dynasty was uneasily established in 1486. The nation was reunited by Alaungpaya in 1752, and the port of Rangoon (Yangon) selected as the new capital. Later, however, during the 19th century, with the imperialist intrusion of Britain, this state was gradually dismembered. Following the Anglo-Burmese War of 1824–26, the Arakan coastal strip between Chittagong and Cape Negrais was ceded to British India. Then, in 1852, after defeat in the second Burmese War, Lower Burma, including Rangoon, was annexed by the British. Finally, in 1886, after Thibaw, the last Burmese king, had precipitated a third Burmese War, Upper Burma was conceded.

Britain immediately reunited these annexed portions to form the 'province of Burma', which was governed as part of British India, until constituted as a Crown Colony, with a degree of internal self-government, in 1937. It developed into a major rice, teak, and later oil, exporter, drawing into its coastal urban-commercial centers thousands of immigrant workers from India and China.

During World War II, Myanmar was invaded and occupied by Japan between 1942 and 1945, encouraging the flight of many of the more recent Indian émigrés. The Japanese proceeded to install a government of anti-British nationalists, headed by Ba Maw, and granted the country nominal independence. However, the nationalists, led by Aung San (1914–47) and U Nu (1907–95), both of whom had earlier been imprisoned by the British for their pro-independence activities, later turned against their 'patrons', founding the Anti-Fascist People's Freedom League (AFPFL), which collaborated with the British in their drive against the Japanese occupiers.

The country was liberated by Allied forces, in 1945, and achieved full independence outside the British Commonwealth, under the designation of 'Union of Burma', on 4 January 1948. A parliamentary democracy was established in which the socialist AFPFL, led by Prime Minister U Nu, held power and states were specially created for the Shan, Karen, Kachin, Chin, and Kayah minority peoples, who enjoyed a substantial measure of autonomy as part of a 'limited federal' system. The new republic was weakened, however, by a mounting internal insurgency movement, involving communist guerrillas, Karen tribespeople, and other dissatisfied ethnic group separatists.

In 1958 a split within the AFPFL precipitated a political crisis which persuaded U Nu to 'invite' General U Ne Win (b. 1911), the army Chief of Staff, to form an emergency caretaker government. This administration, which lasted for two years, was the prelude to a full-scale military coup in March 1962 and the abolition of the parliamentary system. General U Ne Win claimed that parliamentary government had proved unworkable in Myanmar and assumed power as head of a Revolutionary Council composed of fellow military officers. He abrogated the 1948 constitution and established a strong, centralized one-party state.

Following a referendum in December 1973, a new presidential-style unitary constitution was adopted in 1974, and the Revolutionary Council was dissolved. The existing military leaders resigned their titles to become civilian rulers, through the vehicle of a specially constituted Burma Socialist Program Party (BSPP).

Ne Win was elected president and re-elected again in 1978, before stepping down to be replaced by another former army chief of staff, General U San Yu (b. 1919), in November 1981. The new post-1962 military-BSPP government adopted an external policy of neutralist isolationism. Domestically, it pursued an unique, self-reliant, Buddhist-influenced and state-dominated socio-economic strategy, termed the 'Burmese Way towards Socialism'. It was founded on strict price control in the agricultural sector, where farming was allowed to remain in private hands, and state enterprises in the commercial-industrial sector. This program, coupled with the continuing internal insurgency, had a debilitating effect on the country's economy, turning Myanmar into one of the poorest, in terms of per-capita GDP, countries in the Asia – Pacific region. This fact was recognized in December 1987 by the UN's grant of 'least developed country' (LDC) status.

Public dissatisfaction with the deteriorating economic situation first became evident in 1974 and 1976 and assumed the form of food shortage riots and student demonstrations. A decade later, in September 1987, new student demonstrations erupted in Yangon after the introduction of precautionary demonetization measures, soon after the domestic trading of rice, which was now in short supply, had been freed from existing restraints. Further, more widespread and better organized, anti-government student and workers' riots followed, in March and June 1988. These were sternly repressed by the armed forces and riot police, at the cost of several hundred lives.

Concerned about the mounting political and economic chaos, an extraordinary BSPP Congress was convened in July 1988 to review the situation. At this meeting, Ne Win, San Yu, and Maung Maung Kha resigned from their respective positions as party leader, state president, and prime minister respectively, and were replaced by Brigadier-General Sein Lwin, who became both president and BSPP chairperson, and Thura U Tun Tin, who assumed the position of prime minister. A series of liberalizing economic reforms was also ratified.

This failed, however, to calm the situation. Instead, in late July and early August 1988, unrest escalated, with more than 100,000 people taking part in demonstrations demanding the removal as president of the reviled Sein Lwin, a 'hardliner' with a long history of dissident repression, and the installation of a new, democratically elected government. Strikes and demonstrations spread to northern urban centers and attracted the support of Buddhist monks and mutinous navy and air force personnel.

With government control of the country rapidly disintegrating, monks and demonstrators began to take charge of several city administrations. Following the killing of 3,000 unarmed demonstrators by riot police on 12 August 1988, and after only 17 days in office, Sein Lwin resigned as BSPP leader and president. A week later he was replaced in both posts by a civilian, the Western-educated former attorney-general, Dr Maung Maung. Despite the apparent 'reformist' credentials of the new national leader, strikes and demonstrations continued, mainly because of the new president's close links with Ne Win, who continued to remain a decisive 'behind-the-scenes' figure.

Caving in to popular pressure, at a new, hastily convened, emergency BSPP Congress on 10 September 1988, the leadership finally approved the holding of a free multiparty general election 'within three months'. A week later, however, with internal disorder continuing, the armed forces, led by former defense minister General Saw Maung, assumed power, in an effort to stabilize the situation. All state institutions were declared abolished and power was transferred to a 19-member military State Law and Order Restoration Council (SLORC), headed by Saw Maung. A night curfew was imposed and all gatherings of more than four people outlawed.

The new military regime, after initially killing hundreds of demonstrators in Yangon, legalized the formation of political parties. However, opposition leaders, notably Aung San Suu Kyi (b. 1945; the daughter of the late Aung San), U Nu, and Tin U, were debarred from standing in the People's Assembly elections which were held in May 1990. To the SLORC's surprise, this general election resulted in a landslide victory for the opposition National League for Democracy (NLD), which won 60% of the popular vote compared to the humiliating 21% secured by the pro-military BSPP, which had been renamed the National Unity Party (NUP). However, the ruling junta refused to accept the people's verdict and did not permit the new People's Assembly to convene. In December 1990 a 'parallel government', headed by Dr Sein Win (a cousin of Suu Kyi), was formed in the eastern city of Manerplaw, in territory controlled by the insurgent Democratic Alliance of Burma (DAB), on the border of Thailand. It was supported by Karen ethnic rebel forces, but was denounced by the bulk of the main opposition force, whose leader, Suu Kyi, held under house arrest from July 1989, was, in October 1991, awarded the Nobel Peace Prize for her 'non-violent struggle for democracy and human rights'. The former prime minister, U Nu, who later died in February 1995, was also kept under house arrest until April 1992, and in 1991 his Socialist Party was outlawed.

Throughout the period from 1989 there were reports of serious human rights abuses, including abduction, torture, and murder, by the security forces and the universities remained closed until August 1992. In addition, the ruling junta continued to wage dry season offensives against Karen ethnic insurgents in the east and moved 75,000 troops into the southwestern Arakan state in an attempt to stamp out a Muslim-led pro-independence movement. This prompted the flight of 200,000 Rohingya Muslims to Bangladesh during 1991–92, many of whom were repatriated from 1993. In response, the West imposed sanctions against Myanmar, which, through opium shipments from the northern Shan and Wa state regions, part of the so-called 'Golden Triangle', had become the source for 60% of the world's heroin. However, the states of ASEAN continued to pursue a policy of 'constructive engagement', culminating in Myanmar's admission to ASEAN in July 1996.

In April 1993 General Saw Maung stepped down as junta leader on the grounds of deteriorating mental health, believing himself to be the reincarnation of a Burmese king. He was succeeded at the head of the SLORC and as prime minister by General Than Shwe, the former defense minister and deputy commander in chief. However, real power in the junta was believed to rest with the younger Lieutenant General Khin Nyunt, head of military intelligence, who was the protégé of the still influential, though ailing, Ne Win and had close links with China. In September 1992 martial law was officially lifted, but human rights abuses continued, with an estimated 2,000 political prisoners languishing in jail. The junta, which had earlier signed a peace agreement in 1989 with the powerful Wa tribe, situated in the far northeast, reached a ceasefire agreement with the Kachin Independence Army (KIA) in October 1993, ending 30 years of hostility between the Kachins and the Yangon regime. This formed part of a new conciliatory approach to the nation's pro-autonomy ethnic minorities. Ceasefire agreements were signed with a further 12 minorities between 1993 and 1995. However, the most important rebel group, the Karens, were subjected to a major military drive which succeeded in toppling the DAB regime based at Manerplaw in January 1995, forcing the Karens to flee south and into Thailand. In the economic sphere, the junta has, since 1989, pursued a more liberal economic course than the preceding Ne Win regime. Foreign inward investment and tourism, in particular, have been encouraged, as well as the gas, oil and logging industries, and annual economic growth of 7% was registered from 1992. However, more than half of government spending was devoted to the defense sector. In July 1995 the pro-democracy leader Suu Kyi was released unconditionally from house arrest by the ruling military junta, the SLORC. Nevertheless, in April 1996 Yozo Yokota, the UN 'special rapporteur', reported that torture, arbitrary killing, and forced labor were 'still widespread' in Myanmar. A month later, the military junta detained around 200 democracy activist supporters of Suu Kyi, and 30 were given long prison sentences. The crackdown against the NLD intensified from September 1996 and in December 1996 clashes broke out between riot police and 2,000 university student demonstrators, in what was the biggest show of civil dissent since 1988. Fourteen of the protesters were sentenced to seven years' imprisonment. The United States responded to the junta's continuing human rights abuses by prohibiting new investments, from April 1997. From the summer of 1997 Myanmar became caught up in the Asian financial crisis, which began in Thailand, and the kyat, under attack from international speculators, was more than halved in value.This led to a rise in the annual inflation rate to over 50% and shortages of basic goods. In November 1997 the SLORC was renamed the State Peace and Development Council (SPDC). A number of new, younger regional military commanders were brought into the junta, but the changes were largely cosmetic since the SPDC remained dominated by its four most senior members, led by Than Shwe and Khin Nyunt. Nevertheless, in March 1998 Japan was sufficiently impressed to resume its supply of economic aid, which had been frozen since 1988. However, Suu Kyi continued her protests, including a two-week roadside hunger strike, in her van outside Yangon, during August 1998, which left her with kidney damage. There were also large antigovernment protests in Yangon in September 1998, involving 4,000 students, which were broken up by riot police.

In November 1998 the military junta leader, Lt_Gen Khin Nyunt, became chairman of a newly formed 16-member political affairs committee.

NEPAL

Kingdom of Nepal
Nepal Adhirajya

Capital: Kathmandu

Social and economic data

Area: 141,181 sq km/54,410 sq miles

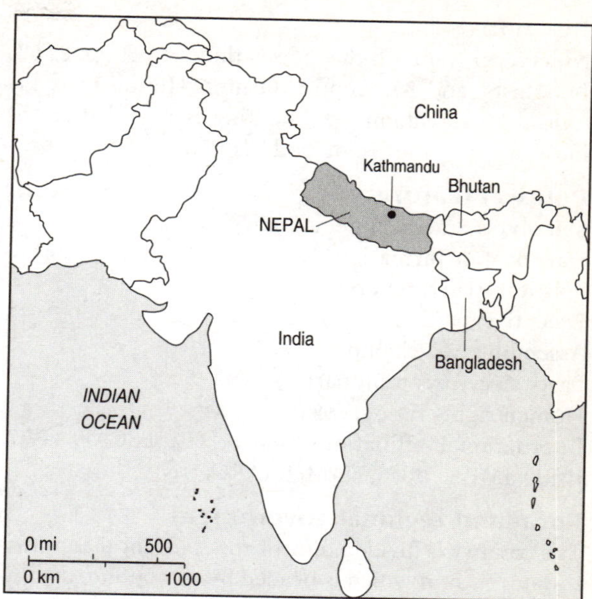

Population: 21,360,000*
Pop. density per sq km/sq mi: 151/392*
Urban population: 12%**
Literacy rate: 26%**
GDP: $4,390 million*; per-capita GDP: $205*
Government defense spending (% of GDP): 1.0%*
Currency: Nepalese rupee
Economy type: low income
Labor force in agriculture: 91%**
* 1995.
** 1992.

Head of state

King Birendra Bir Bikram Shah Dev, since 1972

Head of government

Prime Minister Krishna Prasad Bhattarai, since 1999

Ethnic composition

Eighty per cent of the population is of Indo-Nepalese ethnic stock, which includes the Gurkhas, the Paharis, the Newars, and the Tharus. The remaining 20% is of Tibeto-Nepalese descent, concentrated in the north and east and surviving mainly as subsistence farmers. There is a caste system on the Indian model. Nepali is the official language and is spoken by 58% of the population. Bihari, spoken by 19% of the population, Maithir, by 12%, and Bhojpuri are also important, with English used as the main second language. Since July 1991 nearly 100,000 refugees from Bhutan have arrived in eastern Nepal.

Religions

Ninety per cent of the population are Hindus, 5% Buddhists, and 3% Sunni Muslims. Hinduism is the official state religion and the king is regarded as the incarnation of the Hindu god Vishnu.

Political features

State type: emergent democratic
Date of state formation: 1768
Political structure: unitary
Executive: parliamentary
Assembly: two-chamber
Party structure: multiparty
Human rights rating: 69%
International affiliations: AsDB, CP, ESCAP, G-77, IBRD, IMF, LORCS, NAM, SAARC, UN

Local and regional government

The country is divided into 14 zones for local administration, each of which is headed by an appointed commissioner. Below, there are 75 districts, administered by a district officer. There are 3,524 villages (*gaon*) and 14 towns (*nagar*).

Political system

Under the constitution of November 1990, Nepal is a pluralist, parliamentary democracy headed by a constitutional monarch. It has a two-chamber legislature, comprising a 205-member, directly elected House of Representatives (Pratinidhi Sabha) and a 60-member National Council (Rashtriya Sabha), which consists of ten appointees of the king, 35 members (including three women) elected by the lower house and 15 elected from the country's five development zones by an electoral college. The term for the House is five years and for the National Council, six years. Executive power is vested in the Council of Ministers, which is headed by a prime minister drawn from the House of Representatives' majority party grouping. The prime minister is appointed by the king, but their power, in accordance with the 'Westminster model', derives from their party's support. The cabinet, or council of ministers, comprises around 18 ministers. The constitution explicitly guarantees freedom of expression, press, peaceful assembly, association, and movement. There is a 15-member Supreme Court.

Political parties

Political parties were banned between January 1961 and April 1990, but did function unofficially. There are now two main political parties: the left-of-center Nepali Congress Party (NCP), which dates from 1947 and was led between 1972 and 1994 by Ganesh Man Singh; and the United Nepal Communist Party (UNCP). The latter was formed in January 1991 by the merger of the Marxist-Leninist and Maoist factions of the Communist Party of Nepal (CPN; estd. 1949) and was led by Man Mohan Adhikari until his death in April 1999. It is also known as the Unified Marxist-Leninist Party (UML). In March 1998 a breakaway Communist Party of Nepal-Marxist and Leninist (CPN) was formed, by Bam Dev Gautam. The NCP, which has 50,000 active members, is led by K P Bhattarai. There are three other parties of significance: the rightwing, royalist Rashtriya Prajatantra Party (RPP: National Democratic Party), formed in 1992 and led by Surya Bahadur Thapa; the Nepal Sadbhavana Party (NSP: Nepal Goodwill Party), formed in 1990 to promote the rights of Indian peoples living in the Terai region; and the Nepal Mazdoor Kisan Party (NMKP: Nepal Workers' and Peasants' Party), a Maoist body. In February 1998 a breakaway New Rashtriya Prajatantra Party (NRPP) was formed, under the leadership of Lokendra Bahadur Chand. Political parties must register with the Election Commission to be officially recognized, with at least 5% of candidates presented at elections being female. They should receive at least 3% of the vote in the elections to the House of Representatives.

Political leaders since 1970

1955–72 King Mahendra Bir Bikram Shah, 1972– King Birendra Bir Bikram Shah Dev*, 1991–94 Girija Prasad Koirala (NCP), 1994–95 Man Mohan Adhikari (UNCP), 1995–97 Sher Bahadur Deuba (NCP), 1997 Lokendra Bahadur Chand (RPP), 1997–98 Surya Bahadur Thapa (RPP), 1998–99 Girija Prasad Koirala (NCP), Krishna Prasad Bhattarai (NCP), 1999–

* From 1991 power was shared between the king and the prime minister.

Latest elections

In the most recent House of Representatives elections, held in 36 districts on 3 May 1999 and in another 39 districts on 17 May 1999, the NCP secured a decisive victory. It won 110 seats (compared to 83 in November 1994), based on a 36% share of the vote, the UNCP-UML 68 seats (down 20), with 31% of the vote, the monarchist RPP 11 (down 9), and 10% of the vote, the NSP, 5, the NRPP, 5, the NMKP, 1, and the Sanyunkta Janamorcha Nepal/United People's Front 1. The CPN, despite attracting 6% of the vote, failed to win any seats. Turnout was around 57%, with a total of 30 parties contesting an election which, despite the deaths of at least five people, caused by attacks by Maoist guerrillas, was the most peaceful since the establishment of a multiparty democracy in 1990. The election was held in two phases, with 40,000 police and troops deployed, to ensure order.

Political history

Nepal is a mountainous independent kingdom lying between India and China. Only 14% of the land is cultivated, the remainder being under forest, river bed, or snow. A third of the population live in the southern lowland 'terai' and two-thirds in the central hilly region, predominantly in the Vale of Katmandu. It was formerly an assortment of small principalities, and was unified by the Gurkha King, Prithwi Narayan Shah, in 1768. In 1792 a commercial treaty was signed with Britain and in 1816, after the year-long Anglo-Nepali 'Gurkha War', a British Resident was allowed to reside at Katmandu and the kingdom became a British dependent 'buffer-state'.

During the remainder of the 19th century, Nepal remained an isolated, traditionalist outpost on the border of British India, its main value being the supply of Gurkha troops to the British Indian army. This created a 'remittance economy'. From 1846 effective executive power was wielded by the Rana family, who controlled the office of prime minister, making the monarch a titular figurehead.

In 1923 Britain formally recognized Nepal as a fully independent state. The country was, however, still bound by treaty obligations to the United Kingdom until 1947, the year of India's independence. In 1951 the controlling Rana oligarchy was overthrown in a 'palace revolution', supported by the Nepali Congress Party (NCP), and the monarchy, in the person of King Tribhuvan Bir Bikram Shah, was restored to power. In 1959 King Mahendra Bir Bikram Shah, who had succeeded him in 1955, promulgated the nation's first constitution, creating a two-chamber assembly, with a popularly elected lower house. Following elections, the NCP's pro-Indian socialist leader, Bisweswor Prasad Koirala, became prime minister but soon clashed with the king over policies. King Mahendra dissolved the assembly in December 1960 and put a ban on political parties the following month. In December 1962 he introduced a new constitution providing for a tiered, nonparty system of village councils (*panchayats*), an indirectly elected National Assembly and a prime minister appointed by the monarch.

King Mahendra died in January 1972 and was succeeded by his son, Birendra Bir Bikram Shah Dev (b. 1945), who, faced with mounting agitation for political reform led by B P Koirala, held a referendum on the constitution in May 1980. A majority of 54.8% voted for a royal-backed, 'suitably reformed', *panchayat* system, in preference to a multiparty alternative. As a result, the constitution was amended, in December 1980, to provide for direct, though still nonparty, elections to the National Assembly. The first elections, which were held in May 1981, led to the defeat of a third of the pro-government candidates and returned a more independent-minded National Assembly. In July 1983 the new body proceeded to unseat Prime Minister Surya Bahadur Thapa, through a 'no-confidence' motion, despite his enjoyment of royal support, and put into office Lokendra Bahadur Chand.

Opposition to the banning of political parties increased in 1985, resulting in terrorist bombings in June. As a consequence, a stringent anti-terrorist law was approved by the National Assembly, in August 1985, and more than 1,000 dissidents were arrested. In May 1986 new elections to the National Assembly returned an increased number of members opposed to the nonparty *panchayat* system, and led to the replacement of Prime Minister Chand by Marich Man Singh Shrestha, who had previously been chairman of the Assembly. In an effort to improve the image of the *panchayat* system, the government instituted a stringent anti-corruption drive during 1987. At the same time, however, strict curbs were placed on opposition activity, more than 100 supporters of the banned NCP, including its president, being arrested in the early months of 1988. Tight censorship controls were also imposed.

In the spring of 1990, inspired by events in Eastern Europe, there were mass prodemocracy demonstrations and strikes, coordinated by the NCP-led Movement for the Restoration of Democracy. These were met initially by a strong state response: 150 protesters were shot dead by the police and the NCP's leaders were placed under house arrest. However, after three months, in April 1990, King Birendra bowed to the mounting pressure. He replaced the hardline Shrestha as premier with Lokendra Bahadur Chand and, after talks with opposition leaders, agreed to lift the ban on political parties, abolish the *panchayat* system and renounce his absolute authority. An interim government was installed, headed by the NCP's K P Bhattarai, who had spent 14 years as a political prisoner, and in

September 1990 the king approved a new draft constitution. Promulgated in November 1990, it transferred political power from the monarchy to an elected government. Marking the culmination of a 15-month democratization process, a general election was held on 12 May 1991. The NCP secured a narrow majority of seats in the new House of Representatives and its general secretary, G P Koirala, was appointed prime minister on 26 May 1991.

Within a year, the new government was confronted with large, Communist Party (UNCP)-led, demonstrations in Katmandu and Patan, protesting against the prevailing economic austerity. These escalated into a general strike on 6 April 1992 during which 12 demonstrators were killed when police fired into the crowd. A further 30 people were killed during violent UNCP-organized, anti-government protests which had erupted in June – July 1993 after the death of two communist leaders in a suspicious road accident. Crippled by a power struggle within the NCP, between Koirala, party leader Ganesh Man Singh (1915–97), and party president Krishna Prasad Bhattarai, the government was faced with a series of parliamentary 'no-confidence' motions during 1994. These culminated, on 10 July 1994, in the government's defeat when 36 dissident NCP deputies united with the leftwing opposition. King Birendra dissolved parliament and called fresh elections for November 1994, with Koirala staying on as caretaker prime minister despite UNCP entreaties that a coalition government be formed instead.

The 15 November 1994 general election produced a 'hung parliament', in which the UNCP was the largest single party but was 15 seats short of an overall majority. A minority administration was thus formed by the communists, headed as prime minister by Man Mohan Adhikari (b. 1920), who had spent 17 years in prison for anti-monarchy activities. Adhikari, now a 'reform-communist', pledged that the new administration would encourage the private sector but also seek to help the landless through land reform. However, the new government, after the withdrawal of backing by the NCP in December 1994, found itself with insufficient support to rule effectively and in June 1995, at the request of Prime Minister Adhikari, King Birendra dissolved parliament. New elections were called for November 1995, with Adhikari remaining premier in an interim capacity. The opposition NCP, RPP, and NSP, which together held a small potential one-seat majority in the House of Representatives, filed petitions to the Supreme Court, claiming that the king's actions had been unconstitutional. The Supreme Court ruled in the opposition's favor in August 1995 and in September 1995 Adhikari resigned, after defeat on a no-confidence vote. He was replaced as prime minister by Sher Bahadur Deuba, leader of the NCP, who headed a centrist coalition which included the royalist RPP. Deuba's center-right coalition, weakened by the resignation of seven ministers in December 1996, lost a parliamentary vote of confidence in March 1997. A new coalition government was formed by the rightwing RPP, with its leader Lokendra Bahadur Chand as prime minister (for the fourth time). It included the NSP, and NMKP, but was dominated by the leftwing UNCP. The UNCP were the largest party in parliament and in the May 1997 local elections, which were marred by violence (claiming 30 lives), attracted 52% of the vote. Prime Minister Chand's position became fatally weakened from October 1997 when the RPP's president, Surya Bahadur Thapa, the former prime minister, heading a rival faction, voted against the government on a confidence motion tabled by the NCP. Thapa took over as prime minister and put together a new coalition, incorporating members of the RPP, the NSP, and the NCP. However, it was unstable and, in January 1998, faced with a threatened confidence motion, to be tabled by the UNCP and RPP rebels, Thapa asked King Birendra to dissolve parliament and call a new election. The king was uncertain over what to do and referred the matter to the Supreme Court, who advised against dissolution.

The confidence vote was held in February 1998, and the Thapa government narrowly survived. However, the RPP formerly split, with ten rebels, led by former prime minister Chand, leaving to form a New Rashtriya Prajatantra Party (NRPP). The UNCP also split, in March 1998, following disagreement over a water-sharing pact with India, and, under the leadership of Bam Dev Gautam, formerly deputy prime minister, more than half of its deputies left to form a new Communist Party of Nepal-Marxist and Leninist (CPN). In April 1998, in accordance with the coalition agreement of October 1997, Thapa stepped down as prime minister to be replaced by the NCP leader, G P Koirala. The declared priority of the new minority government was to tackle a serious Maoist insurgency, known as the People's War, which had killed hundreds in western Nepal since its inception in 1996 and which had recently escalated. In August 1998 the government was broadened into a coalition with the CPN.

The CPN withdrew its support in December 1998,

alleging that the NCP had failed to implement coalition agreements, including the withdrawal of Indian forces from western Nepal. A new coalition was formed, by G P Koirala, with the UNCP and the regionalist Nepal Sadbhavana Party (NSP), based on an agreement that there would be a general election in May 1999. This election was won by the NCP, which achieved an absolute majority, thus ending five years of unstable coalition government. The 74-year-old Krishna Prasad Bhattarai, who had previously served as prime minister between 1990 and 1991, now became prime minister, replacing his long time rival, Koirala. The new government expressed its commitment to improving education and employment, and to eradicating poverty.

In its external relations since the war, Nepal has traditionally been closely tied to India, entering into a mutual assistance pact soon after the latter's independence. In recent years, however, Nepal has pursued a more neutral, nonaligned course, seeking to create a 'zone of peace' in southern Asia and to maintain cordial relations with both its neighbors, India and China. In particular, commercial links with China have increased recently. This has been resented by India, who imposed a partial blockade of the country between 1989 and 1990 as a result of a dispute over the renegotiation of expired transit and trade treaties.

Economically and socially, Nepal remains a backward country, rates of literacy continuing to be low, and per-capita living standards depressed by over-rapid population expansion, currently 2.6% per annum, and adverse agricultural conditions. Almost a sixth of current GDP is derived from overseas development aid. However, during the 1990s, following economic liberalization, GDP has grown by more than 5% per annum.

PAKISTAN

Islamic Republic of Pakistan Islami Jamhuria-e-Pakistan

Capital: Islamabad

Social and economic data

Area: 796,095 sq km/307,374 sq miles
Population: 126,610,000*
Pop. density per sq km/sq mi: 159/412*
Urban population: 33%**
Literacy rate: 35%**

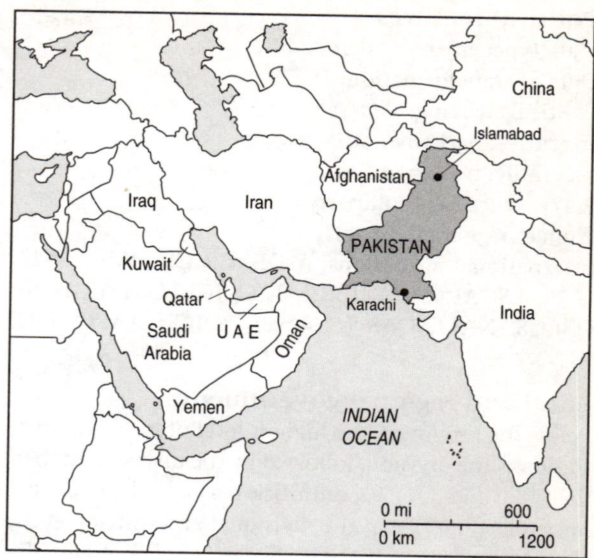

GDP: $60,000 million*; per-capita GDP: $475*
Government defense spending (% of GDP): 6.5%**
Currency: Pakistan rupee
Economy type: low income
Labor force in agriculture: 44%**
Unemployment rate: 4.8%*
* 1995.
** 1992.

Head of state

President Mohammad Rafiq Tarar, since 1997

Head of government

Prime Minister Nawaz Sharif, since 1997

Ethnic composition

Pakistan possesses four principal, regionally based, and antagonistic ethnic communities: Punjabis in the Punjab; Sindhis in Sind; Baluchis in Baluchistan; and, fiercely independent, Pathans (Pushtans) in the North-West Frontier Province. Urdu and English are the official languages. However, 64% of the population speaks Punjabi, 12% Sindhi, 9% Baluchi, 8% Pushtu, and only 20% speaks Urdu, and 2% English.

Religions

Almost 91% of the population is Sunni Muslim and 5% Shia Muslim. Some 1.7% is Hindu and 1.3% is Christian, including 950,000 Roman Catholics, 400,000 adherents to the Protestant Church of Pakistan, and 340,000 to the United Presbyterian Church of Pakistan. Islam is the state religion.

Political features

State type: emergent democratic
Date of state formation: 1947
Political structure: federal
Executive: parliamentary
Assembly: two-chamber
Party structure: multiparty
Human rights rating: 42%
International affiliations: AsDB, CP, CW, ECO, G-24, G-77, ESCAP, IAEA, IBRD, ICC, ICFTU, IMF, IsDB, LORCS, NAM, OAS (observer), OIC, SAARC, UN, WTO

Local and regional government

Below the provinces, the highest level of local administration is the division, followed by the district and then the *tashil* and *taluka*. Commissioners and deputy commissioners operate at the divisional and district levels, alongside elected councils. Since October 1994, the Northern Areas (that part of Kashmir which is controlled by Pakistan, and is known as Azad Kashmir) has had an elected, 24-member council, with legislative, financial, and executive powers.

Political system

Under the restored constitution of April 1973, Pakistan is a federal republic, comprising four provinces: Sind, with a population of 28 million; Punjab, 69 million; North-West Frontier Province, 16 million; and Baluchistan, 6 million. The provinces are administered by centrally appointed governors and local governments drawn from elected Provincial Assemblies and headed by chief ministers. There are also tribal areas, with a total population of 3 million, which are administered directly by the federal government. Responsibility for education, labor, health, industry, social welfare, agriculture, and roads legislation is entrusted to the provinces.

Primary power resides, however, with the central government, which is headed by a president, who is elected for a renewable, five-year term at a sitting of the members of the federal assembly and representatives from the four provincial assemblies. The president must be a Muslim. The presidency was originally a titular post, but following the constitutional amendments of March 1985, the office holder was given powers to dissolve the National Assembly, and appoint and dismiss the prime minister, the cabinet, and provincial governors. The president, therefore, emerged as the dominant political figure. However, following the death, in August 1988, of General Zia, the primacy of this office has diminished and the president is now expected to act on the advice of the prime minister. In April 1997 the constitution was amended to repeal most of the changes of March 1985. In future, the president would act in these areas on the prime minister's advice. Thus the presidency is now chiefly ceremonial.

The federal legislature consists of two chambers: a lower house, called the National Assembly, and an upper chamber, the Senate. The National Assembly has 217 members, comprising 207 directly elected for five-year terms by universal adult suffrage (minimum age 21 years) with ten further seats being reserved for Christians, Hindus, Parsis, and other minorities. The Senate has 87 members, elected, a third at a time, for six-year terms by Provincial Assemblies and tribal areas, in accordance with a quota system. The country's four provincial assemblies each elect 19 senators, the tribal areas, eight, and the Federal Capital Territory of Islamabad has three representatives who are elected by members of the Provincial Assemblies. The federal legislature convenes twice a year, for not less than 130 working days, in sessions which are not more than 120 days apart.

The National Assembly is the more powerful of the two chambers, having sole jurisdiction over financial affairs. The Senate has mainly an advisory role, with the right to send back to the National Assembly, only once, bills of which it disapproves. Joint National Assembly and Senate sittings are convened to iron out differences, by majority vote, on a small number of bills. To become law, bills must be passed by both chambers and must also be approved by the president, who has the power of veto. The presidential veto may, however, be overridden by a simple majority of both chambers.

Day-to-day government is in the hands of a prime minister, drawn from and responsible to the National Assembly, and a cabinet of around 20 members. A prime minister and government can be removed by a no-confidence motion which is supported by two-thirds of the members of the National Assembly and which specifically names a successor. If this is defeated, a further motion cannot be tabled until at least six months later.

Political parties

Political parties have been permitted to operate since December 1985, but under tight registration restrictions, which were not eased until 1988.

The currently dominant party is the Pakistan Muslim League (PML-Nawaz), led by Prime Minister

Nawaz Sharif. The PML traces its roots back to the All-India Muslim League, which was originally founded in 1906, with particularly strong roots in the North Indian province of Uttar Pradesh. Following the death of the PML's leader, Muhammad Ali Jinnah, in 1948, and the assassination, three years later, of its influential prime minister, Liaquat Ali Khan, the party suffered a relative decline. In 1979 it split into two factions, the pro-government Pagara Group, named after the Sind-based religious leader, the Pir of Pagara, and which came to support General Zia ul-Haq, and the anti-Zia Chattha (later renamed the Qasim) Group. This second faction joined the opposition Movement for the Restoration of Democracy (MRD), in 1981. The PML is a conservative party, traditionally viewed as the mouthpiece of large landlords and local 'clan chiefs'. For the November 1988 National Assembly elections, the PML joined with eight other conservative and Muslim parties to form the Islamic Democratic Alliance (IDA). During 1988 the Pagara group of the PML also split into two factions: the Fida Group, led by the former North-West Frontier Province governor, Fida Mohammed Khan; and the Junejo group, allied to the former prime minister Mohammad Khan Junejo, who died in March 1993. In May 1993, Prime Minister Nawaz Sharif broke away from the latter body to form his own, dominant PML-Nawaz grouping.

The chief opposition party is the Pakistan People's Party (PPP), led by Benazir Bhutto. The PPP was formed in 1967, by Zulfiqar Ali Bhutto, a member of a wealthy Sind landowning family, to campaign for democracy, moderate Islamic socialism, a nonaligned foreign policy, and the creation of a federal state. It drew the bulk of its support from student, industrial worker, and peasant ranks and from the provinces of Sind, especially its rural areas, and Punjab. In December 1993 a rift developed within the PPP, when Nusrat Bhutto (b.1934), the mother of Benazir, who had been the party's co-chair since 1986, was ousted after she became estranged from her daughter as a result of declaring political support for her son, Murtaza Bhutto, head of the banned al Zulfiqar organization, who had been arrested on terrorist charges when he returned to Pakistan from abroad in November 1993. In March 1995 Murtaza Bhutto formed a breakaway faction of the PPP which is now known as the PPP (Shaheed Bhutto Group). Numerous other parties function. The four most important are the Pakistan Islamic Front (PIF); the Awami National Party (ANP); the National Democratic Alliance (NDA); and the Muttahida Qaumi Mahaz (MQM: Mohajir National Movement).

The PIF is an alliance of Islamic groups formed in 1993. Its key constituent element is the fundamentalist, rightwing, Jamaat-e-Islami Pakistan (JIP: Islamic Assembly), which was established in 1941 and seeks the establishment of a Sunni Islamic state. It is led by Qazi Hussain Ahmed.

The ANP (People's National Party), founded in 1986 by an amalgamation of socialist groups, is a notable leftwing force, with a strong local base in the North-West Frontier Province.

The NDA was formed in 1992 by six parties and two independent groups, including the Jamhuri Watan Party and the National People's Party (NPP), which was formed in 1986 by the former Chief Minister of Sind, Ghulam Mustafa Jatoi, by breakaway members of the PPP who were critical of Benazir Bhutto's allegedly autocratic leadership style and overly moderate, middle-class orientated, polices, embracing, for example, the 'privatization' of selected state industries and the abandonment of the call for land reform.

The MQM, formed in 1986, is a Sind-based party, led by Altaf Hussain and orientated towards the middle class, Urdu-speaking Mohajir community, who migrated to the province from India at the time of Partition. Since then they have opposed recent ethnic-quota employment restrictions and campaign for recognition of Mohajirs as the country's fifth nationality. Though narrowly based, the MQM has been a rising political force during recent years, scoring heavily in Karachi and Hyderabad in the local and National Assembly elections since 1987 as ethnic tensions and violence have increased. It was known as the Mohajir Qaumi Movement until 1997. Its leader, Altaf Husain, has lived in self-imposed exile in London since mid-1992 and in June 1994 was sentenced in absentia by a Karachi court to 27 years' imprisonment for alleged involvement in the maltreatment of soldiers in Sind in 1991. The dominant Altaf faction of the MQM is opposed by a breakaway Haqiqi faction.

In April 1996 the former national cricket captain, Imran Khan, formed the Justice Movement (Tehrik-i-Insaaf) to fight for social justice and against corruption; but it attracted little support in the 1997 general election.

Party loyalties are weak and fickle in Pakistan and are based predominantly on patronage and regional ties. The major parties are themselves internally divided between provincial and personality-based factions.

Political leaders since 1970*

1969–71 General Agha Muhammad Yahya Khan (military), 1971–78 Zulfiqar Ali Bhutto (PPP), 1978–88 General Mohammad Zia ul-Haq (military), 1988 Ghulam Ishaq Khan (independent), 1988–90 Benazir Bhutto (PPP), 1990 Ghulam Mustafa Jatoi (NPP), 1990–93 Nawaz Sharif (IDA), 1993 Mir Balakh Sher Mazari (independent), 1993 Nawaz Sharif (IDA/PML), 1993 Moeenuddin Ahmad Qureshi (independent), 1993–97 Benazir Bhutto (PPP), 1996 Meraj Khalid (independent), 1997 – Nawaz Sharif (PML-Nawaz)

* A mixture of military leaders, presidents, and prime ministers, reflecting the shifts that have taken place in Pakistan's turbulent political system.

Latest elections

In the most recent National Assembly elections, held on 3 February 1997, the PML-Nawaz secured a landslide victory, winning 134 of the 204 contested seats (up 61 on its October 1993 result). The PPP won only 18 seats (down 68); the Sind-based MQM (Altaf), 12 seats; the ANP, 9 seats; the Jamhuri Watan Party, 2; the Baluchistan National Party, 3; the fundamentalist Sunni Muslim Jamiat-e-Ulema-e-Islam, 2; the NPP, 1; the breakaway PPP (Shaheed Bhutto Group), 1; and independents, 22 seats. In three constituencies polling was delayed until a later date and, overall, turnout fell to around 30%. This reflected disenchantment with the political process. In the last Senate elections, held in March 1997, the PML-Nawaz secured a two-thirds majority in the upper chamber. In the last indirect election of the state president, on 31 December 1997, Mohammad Rafiq Tarar, a former Supreme Court judge and a close ally of Nawaz Sharif, won by a record margin, securing 80% of the votes cast.

Political history

1. Early invasions to the election of Bhutto

The Indus Valley region of contemporary Pakistan supported an advanced, city-based ancient civilization, the Harappan, between 2500 and 1600 BC. The north of the region was later invaded by Aryans from the west, about 2000–1500 BC, and thereafter by successive waves of conquering peoples from Central Asia and beyond, including Muslims from the 10th century AD. These invaders continued on into the North Indian plains, establishing a series of empires with regional capitals in both India and Pakistan. The Mughals, from 1526, constituted the last of these 'conquest empires', prior to the establishment of British sovereignty over the Indian subcontinent. Formal British control was extended over the Punjab and Sind, following wars against local regimes, notably the Sikh 'successor state' in the Punjab, during the 1840s, and over Baluchistan and the North-West Frontier Province in 1896. Subsequent British rule in Pakistan was notable for its substantial investment in major canal irrigation projects in the West Punjab and northern Indus Valley, establishing this tract as a major wheat and cotton exporting area and drawing in settlers from the east. Because of a perceived threat from Russia to the North-West Frontier there was a concentration there of military installations and personnel.

Following the development of a cross-community nationalist movement in the Indian subcontinent, from the mid-1880s, a separate All-India Muslim League was established in 1906 to campaign specifically for Muslim interests. This body was initially dominated by Muslims from north India, before, in 1916, Muhammad Ali Jinnah (1876–1948), a Muslim lawyer educated in Karachi and England, became the League's president. During the interwar period the League veered between campaigning for independence from British rule within a national federation and seeking to establish a separate Muslim state.

In 1933 Choudhary Rahmat Ali invented the name 'Pakistan', or, in Urdu, 'Pure Nation', for a fully independent Muslim territory which would embrace the four provinces of Sind, Baluchistan, Punjab, and the North-West Frontier. Four years later, he called for the inclusion of the Muslim majority areas of Bengal within such a state. Fearing domination by the Hindu majority within India, these ideas were finally adopted by Jinnah in 1940, resulting, in August 1947, in the partitioning of the Indian subcontinent into Hindu and Muslim majority spheres, in accordance with boundaries hastily established by the Radcliffe Commission. More than 7 million Muslims moved into Pakistan from India, while a similar number of Hindus and Sikhs moved in the opposite direction in the days and months preceding and following the Partition. Terrible violence resulted wherever the two refugee courses passed each other.

Independent Pakistan was formally constituted as a Dominion within the British Commonwealth, with the British monarch as head of state. It comprised the five former, and frequently antagonistic, British Indian states of Baluchistan, East Bengal, the North-West Frontier Province, Sind, and West Punjab. It was more broadly divided between an eastern and western section, separated by 1,610 kilometres of Indian territory, and differing substantially in culture, language, and geography. The only thing that united the two sections was religion. The charismatic and respected Jinnah became the country's first governor general (GG) and president of the new Constituent Assembly, but, already gravely ill at the time of independence, he died in September 1948. Khwajah Nazimuddin, Ghulam Mohammad, and Iskander Mirza followed in the post of GG, before a republic was declared, in March 1956, and an 'Islamic' constitution was adopted. This constitution was abrogated in October 1958 and military rule imposed, following a coup by General Mohammad Ayub Khan (1907–74).

The country enjoyed rapid economic growth during the 1960s but mounting regional tension between demographically dominant East Pakistan and West Pakistan, where political and military power was concentrated. Following serious strikes and riots in March 1969, General Ayub Khan stepped down to be replaced by commander in chief, General Agha Muhammad Yahya Khan (1917–80). Pakistan's first elections with universal adult suffrage were subsequently held, in December 1970, the intention being to elect an assembly which would then frame a new constitution. They resulted in the Awami League of Sheikh Mujibur Rahman, which proposed autonomy, gaining a majority of seats in East Pakistan and the Pakistan People's Party (PPP) gaining a majority in the West. East Pakistan declared its independence from the West in March 1971, precipitating a civil war which resulted, following Indian troop intervention on East Pakistan's side in December 1971, in the emergence of the independent republic of Bangladesh.

As a consequence of this defeat, General Yahya Khan resigned and passed power in West Pakistan to the PPP's populist leader, Zulfiqar Ali Bhutto (1928–79). He proceeded to introduce a new federal parliamentary constitution, in April 1973, and a socialist economic program of land reform and nationalization. From the mid-1970s, however, the Sind-based Bhutto faced growing regional opposition, particularly from Baluchistan and from Pathans campaigning for an independent Pakhtoonistan. He was also confronted with deteriorating economic conditions.

Bhutto won a majority in the March 1977 Assembly elections, but was accused of ballot-rigging by the Pakistan National Alliance (PNA) opposition. Riots ensued and, following four months of unrest, the Punjabi Muslim army chief of staff, General Mohammad Zia ul-Haq (1924–88), seized power in a bloodless coup in July 1977. Martial law was imposed and Bhutto was imprisoned for alleged murder. He was hanged in April 1979.

Between 1979 and 1981 Zia imposed severe restrictions on political activity. Economic growth revived, however, helped by a new pro-business strategy, by remittance inflows from workers in the Middle East and by American aid, following the December 1979 Soviet invasion of Afghanistan. This led, additionally, to the influx of more than 3 million refugees, three-quarters of them being housed in the North-West Frontier Province and 20% in Baluchistan.

At home, the general introduced a broad Islamization program, aimed at deepening his support base and appeasing Islamic fundamentalists. This was opposed, however, by middle-class professionals and by the country's Shia minority. In March 1981 nine banned opposition parties, including the PPP, formed the Movement for the Restoration of Democracy (MRD) alliance, campaigning for a return to parliamentary government. The military government responded by arresting several hundred opposition politicians. A renewed democracy campaign was launched in the autumn of 1983, resulting in considerable anti-government violence in Sind province.

From 1982, however, General Zia slowly began enlarging the civilian element in his government and, in December 1984, held a referendum on the Islamization process. He obtained a majority for his proposals but the participation level was low. Nevertheless, the result was taken as legitimizing his continuance as president for a further five-year term.

In February 1985 direct elections were held to the National and Provincial Assemblies, but on a non-party basis. The opposition, as in December 1984, boycotted the poll, and the resultant turnout was only 53%. A new civilian cabinet was, nevertheless, formed and an amended constitution was adopted. In December 1985 martial law and the ban on political parties were lifted, military courts were abolished and military administrators stepped down in favor of civilians. Opposition campaigns for democratization continued, however, with Benazir Bhutto (b. 1953), the Oxford- and Harvard-educated daughter of Zulfiqar Ali Bhutto, returning from self-exile in London, in April 1986, to launch a major autumn campaign for immediate 'open elections'. Riots erupted in Lahore, Karachi, and rural Sind, the tensions being exacerbated by clashes between rival local and immigrant communities. These led to the temporary arrest of the PPP's leaders and the despatch of troops to Sind.

In May 1987, concerned with a downturn in the economy, the slow pace of implementation of the Islamization program, continuing law and order problems and with the growing independence of Prime Minister Mohammad Khan Junejo, President Zia summarily dismissed the Junejo government, dissolved the National Assembly and provincial legislatures and promised fresh elections within 90 days, as required by the constitution. Zia proceeded, in June–July 1988, to put together a new 18-member interim government, but without a prime minister. He also issued a presidential ordinance which decreed that the Sharia, the Islamic legal code, would immediately become the country's supreme law. He then outlined plans for the introduction of a formal presidential system and set 16 November 1988 as the date for new National Assembly elections.

Barely a month later, however, on 17 August 1988, the president was killed in a mysterious military air crash near Bahawalpur, 160 km/100 miles west of the Indian border, in east-central Pakistan. The crash was viewed by many as sabotage, with dissident elements within the Pakistan armed forces, or underground Afghan secret service agents, being variously blamed.

General Zia's death placed the country's political system in confusion, with no obvious successor apparent, within the government or the military forces. Pakistan's senior army commanders had been killed with Zia in the air crash. The elderly senate chairperson, Ghulam Ishaq Khan, took over as interim president, pledging to oversee the holding of the forthcoming national elections.

These were held, as scheduled, in November, and were preceded by intense party jockeying, involving the break-up of the MRD and the formation of a new nine-party conservative Muslim, anti-Bhutto, and anti-PPP, Islamic Democratic Alliance (IDA), by elements from the Muslim League and incumbent Zia loyalists. The PPP, advocating a moderate, centrist policy program and declaring its intention to seek a 'fresh start' and avoid retribution for past actions against its members, succeeded in emerging as the dominant force in the contest. Benazir Bhutto was duly sworn in as prime minister in December 1988.

2. Bhutto's government to 1999

The new government faced many problems, including a deteriorating economy, exacerbated by a population growth of more than 3% per annum, and the difficulties of adjusting to changing circumstances in bordering Afghanistan. More specifically, its majority, which was based partially on a coalition with the Karachi-based Mohajir Qaumi Movement (MQM), remained fragile, while opposition remained strong in the IDA-controlled Punjab, among conservative Muslim religious leaders (mullahs), and among the military. These circumstances constrained the policy choices of the new administration, which pledged itself to continue to follow a free-market economic program, maintain support for the Afghan mujaheddin, and leave untouched the country's substantial military budget.

In November 1989 Bhutto narrowly survived a confidence vote, held a month after the MQM had withdrawn its support. Nine months later, in August 1990, President Ghulam Ishaq Khan controversially dismissed the Bhutto government on accusations of incompetence, and, though subsequently untried, charges of corruption and abuse of power. The National Assembly was also dissolved, with Ghulam Mustafa Jatoi serving as a caretaker prime minister. Bhutto's husband, Asif Ali Zardari, also faced corruption charges, which were to be later dropped during 1993–94. In the ensuing general election, held in October 1990, the IDA, supported by the military, state bureaucracy, and mullahs, swept to victory, winning 105 of the 207 elective seats to the PPP's 45. Mian Mohammad Nawaz Sharif (b. 1949), formerly chief minister of Punjab, became prime minister. The first premier not to be drawn from the country's social elite, he embarked on a free-market economic program, which included privatization and deregulation. Additionally, in May 1991, a Sharia bill, incorporating Islamic laws and designed to create an Islamic welfare state, was enacted and Sharif advocated a reduction in the executive powers of the state president as set out in the Eighth Amendment of 1985. During the summer of 1991 Sharif's reform program became disrupted by labor unrest and terrorist incidents and the prime minister's own position became weakened by the uncovering of a financial corruption scandal which, it was alleged, involved members of his family.

During 1992 an 'Operation Clean-up' anti-crime and anti-terrorism crackdown was launched in Sind, drawing criticism from the MQM for its heavy-handedness. However, with the IDA and PML beginning to fissure and large-scale anti-government demonstrations and marches being organized by Benazir Bhutto and the newly formed opposition National Democratic

Alliance (NDA), Sharif's position became untenable by the spring of 1993. On 18 April 1993, accusing the prime minister of 'maladministration, nepotism, and corruption', President Ghulam Ishaq Khan dismissed Sharif, appointed Mir Balakh Sher Mazari as interim prime minister, dissolved the National Assembly, and called fresh elections. Unexpectedly, the Supreme Court ruled, on 26 May 1993, that President Khan's action was unconstitutional and ordered Sharif to be returned to power. However, within two months, on 18 July 1993, after Sharif had created a crisis in Punjab through imposing federal government rule over the province, both Prime Minister Sharif and President Khan were persuaded to resign from their posts after pressure was exerted by the military.

The former chairperson of the Senate, Wasim Sajjad Jan, and an apolitical former vice president of the World Bank, Moeenuddin Ahmad Qureshi, took over as popular caretaker president and prime minister respectively until the general election of October 1993. This poll returned to power Benazir Bhutto, heading a PPP-led coalition administration which was supported by the Awami National Party and the PML-Junejo. The PPP had won 86 of the 202 contested seats and 38% of the national vote. A month later, the PPP's candidate, Sardar Farooq Ahmad Khan Leghari (b. 1940), formerly the foreign minister, was elected state president, defeating the incumbent Sajjad Jan. During 1994–95 there was escalating ethnic and Shia versus Sunni Muslim sectarian violence in Sind, particularly Karachi, claiming more than 1,500 lives. The turmoil was blamed by the government on MQM extremists who had become urban guerrillas. There was also turmoil in the North-West Frontier Province, where Islamic fundamentalism was growing in strength, and where, in April 1994, a PPP-led administration was controversially installed after a PML-Nawaz-led coalition had been ousted in February 1994. Following an austerity budget, involving $1.2 billion of tax increases, there were strikes and demonstrations in Islamabad and Rawalpindi, during June 1996. Fundamentalist Islamic parties played a key role. The government's popularity was reduced further, in August 1996, when the prime minister's husband, Asif Zardari, was appointed cabinet minister for investments, at a time of mounting concern at government corruption. This had led, in March 1995, to Benazir Bhutto's brother, Murtaza, forming a breakaway PPP faction and embarking upon a campaign to oust his sister. The campaign had attracted little support, but, in September 1996, Murtaza Bhutto was shot dead by police in Karachi. This led to a number of opposition politicians suggesting that the prime minister and Zardari may have helped organize the killing. Popular protest against alleged government corruption grew to such a degree, in late October 1996, following a 40,000-strong opposition march in Lahore, that the capital, Islamabad, was sealed off for three days to prevent a march on parliament by Islamic fundamentalists, led by the Jamaat-e-Islami Pakistan party. A nationwide strike took place and, finally, on 5 November 1996 President Farooq Leghari, accusing the government of incompetence, nepotism, and corruption, dissolved the National Assembly, sacked Benazir Bhutto, (a party colleague took Zardari into 'protective custody'), and called fresh elections for February 1997. The president's specific charges against the Bhutto administration included: eroding confidence in the army, through suggesting that they had been involved in the recent murder of Murtaza Bhutto; undermining the independence of the judiciary, through seeking to pack the higher courts with political appointments; sanctioning the extra-judicial killing of thousands of alleged terrorists in Karachi; and flagrant corruption. He acted at a time of growing economic difficulties, with inflation rising (to 13%), annual GDP growth slowing to 3%, foreign and government debt levels increasing and additional austerity measures being requested by the IMF, and received the army's backing. A former parliamentary speaker, Malik Meraj Khalid, became acting prime minister, and Javed Burki, a vice-president of the World Bank, finance minister. A judicial commission was set up to deal with the endemic problem of corruption in high office and a new law was introduced which disqualified from public office, for five years, politicians charged with corruption and misconduct. The interim government also established, in January 1997, a ten-member Council for Defense and National Security (CDNS) to advise the government on a range of security issues. By including chiefs of staff of the army, navy, and airforce, along with the president, prime minister, and defense, interior and foreign ministers, it gave the military a formal role in the political power structure for the first time since General Zia's death, in 1988.

The February 1997 general election resulted in a crushing defeat for Bhutto's corruption-tarnished PPP and a return to power for Nawaz Sharif, whose right-of-center PML, and allies, won the support of 181 of the National Assembly's 217 deputies. However, turnout was extremely low. In his acceptance speech, Prime Minister

Nawaz Sharif pledged not to seek to 'victimize' his defeated opponents and promised market-centerd economic reforms and improved relations with India. However, although tax and tariff reductions and accelerated privatization were announced, his room for manoeuvre was constrained by IMF-imposed financial restrictions. In April 1997 Sharif used his strong position in both chambers of the federal legislature to reverse 1985 constitutional amendments which had given the president the power to dismiss a government summarily and appoint provincial governors and top military officers. He also introduced measures to stop deputies voting against their party leaders, thus preventing an in-house engineered change of regime. He then, between November and December 1997 became involved in a confrontation with the country's chief justice over the issue of who had the final say over the appointment of Supreme Court judges. After intervention by the army chief of staff, General Jehangir Karamat, the prime minister emerged victorious and both the chief justice, Sajjad Ali Shah, and President Leghari resigned. Rafiq Tarar, a 'liberal Muslim' former Supreme Court judge from Sharif's power-base, Punjab, became the new state president, in December 1997.

Meanwhile, during 1997–98 corruption investigations into the Bhutto and Zardari families continued. They led, in September 1997, to the freezing of four Swiss Bank accounts belonging to Benazir Bhutto and family members, with funds reputedly exceeding $50 million, and, in January 1998, to the government filing 12 corruption charges. The PPP depicted these actions as politically motivated, but, in August 1998, Benazir Bhutto was also indicted on money-laundering charges in Switzerland. Meanwhile, the economy, which was affected by financial turmoil elsewhere in Asia, continued to deteriorate, forcing a 9% currency devaluation in October 1997. Matters became worse from May 1998 when, in response to the recent testing of nuclear weapons by India's new Hindu-nationalist government, Pakistan conducted its first ever nuclear tests. There were six successful underground atomic detonations, in Baluchistan. These were initially popular with the public, heralding the arrival of the first 'Islamic bomb'. However, the United States responded by imposing economic and military sanctions and the IMF suspended its credits. This further damaged the economy, leading to another devaluation of the Pakistan rupee, savage public spending cuts, and, by August 1998, street protests. The increasing public disillusionment with the political class was helping to strengthen the position of Islamic fundamentalists who, although still a clear minority, had growing influence, following the 1980s Islamization reforms, within the army and bureaucracy. In response, Prime Minister Sharif proposed, in September 1998, revising the constitution to introduce full Islamic law, but faced strong opposition within parliament. US economic sanctions were largely lifted in November 1998.

In foreign affairs, Pakistan has experienced strained relations with India throughout the post-independence period, being involved in border wars over Kashmir in 1965 and East Pakistan in 1971. The country left the Commonwealth in 1972, following the acceptance of the new state of Bangladesh, and has been allied with China since the 1950s, mainly because of their shared hostility to India. During the 1980s, with the Soviet Union occupying neighboring Afghanistan, it developed close relations with the United States. It also joined the Non-Aligned Movement in 1979 and improved its ties with the Islamic states of the Middle East and Africa, sending 11,000 troops to Saudi Arabia to guard Islamic shrines during the 1990–91 Gulf conflict. Following the Soviet pull-out from Afghanistan in 1989 and the establishment of a mujaheddin government in Kabul in 1992, the United States' relationship with Pakistan has cooled, and in October 1990, under the terms of the Pressler Amendment, US economic and military aid was suspended after the United States learned that Pakistan was seeking to develop nuclear weapons. This action has fuelled anti-Americanism, which has been drawn upon by Islamic fundamentalist extremist forces. In 1996 Pakistan gave backing to the fundamentalist Talibaan, which seized power in Afghanistan. Tensions with India have also increased since 1989 as a result of the outbreak of a civil and religious war in Kashmir and India's 1998 testing of nuclear weapons. Pakistan rejoined the Commonwealth in October 1989.

SINGAPORE

Republic of Singapore
Republik Singapura

Capital: Singapore City

Social and economic data

Area: 623 sq km/241 sq miles
Population: 3,400,000*
Pop. density per sq km/sq mi: 5,457/14,108*
Urban population: 100%*

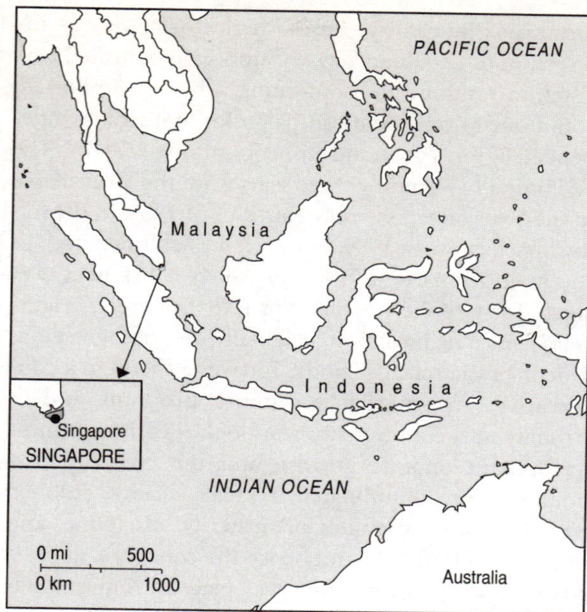

Literacy rate: 91%**
GDP: $79,830 million*; per-capita GDP: $23,480*
Government defense spending (% of GDP): 5.9%*
Currency: Singapore dollar
Economy type: high income
Labor force in agriculture: 0.3%**
Unemployment rate: 2.7%
* 1995.
** 1992.

Head of state

President Ong Teng Cheong, since 1993

Head of government

Prime Minister Goh Chok Tong, since 1990

Ethnic composition

Seventy-seven per cent of the population is of Chinese ethnic stock, predominantly Hokkien, Teochew, and Cantonese, 15% Malay, and 7% Indian, chiefly Tamil, The national language is Malay, but Chinese (Mandarin), Tamil, and English, the language of administration, are also official languages.

Religions

The majority, 54%, of Chinese are Buddhists or Daoists; Malays and Pakistanis are Sunni Muslims, 15% of the population; Indians are Hindus, 4%; and Europeans, Eurasians, and other communities are Christians, 13%. The country is, however, a secular state, with religion, unlike neighboring Malaysia and Indonesia, not a significant aspect of national life.

Political features

State type: liberal democratic*
Date of state formation: 1965**
Political structure: unitary
Executive: parliamentary
Assembly: one-chamber
Party structure: multiparty *
Human rights rating: 60%
International affiliations: AsDB, APEC, ASEAN, CP, CW, ESCAP, IAEA, IBRD, IMF, NAM, UN, WTO
* Though dominated, in practice, by one party.
** As a fully independent state.

Local and regional government

For administrative purposes, Singapore Island is divided into five districts: Singapore City, Katong, Serangoon, Bukit Panjang, and Jurong. There is no elected tier of local government, but 20–50-member Citizens' Consultative Committees have been established in each electoral district, staffed by nominees of the local member of parliament and subject to the approval of the Prime Minister's Office. The task of these Committees is both to serve as a medium through which the government can 'educate' the local people on government policies and to act as a feedback channel, through which popular needs and grievances are made known. They are also employed for the administration of a number of public works programs and to mediate in local ethnic disputes.

Political system

Because of its small size, Singapore has a single-tier system of government. The constitution of December 1965, an amended version of an earlier, June 1959, constitution, has provided for a single-chamber Parliament, whose 83 members are elected for five-year terms by universal adult suffrage from 40 single-member wards, with, since 1988, the remainder being elected from 15 three-to six-member Group Representation Constituencies (GRC) through a simple plurality voting system. At least one member of the 'team' contesting the multimember GRCs must be of non-Chinese racial origin. Voting is compulsory. In addition, since 1990 the government has been able to nominate up to nine (from 1997) politically neutral MPs. These unelected MPs may serve for up to two years and can vote on all legislation except that concerning financial and constitutional matters. There are also up to three 'non-constituency' seats, with restricted voting rights, which are offered to opposition parties. All parliamentary bills, with the exception of defense, public security, and the budget, are subject to the prior scrutiny of a 21-member Presidential Council, which was established in 1967, and is chaired by a chief justice. Its task is to ensure that proposed legislation does not discriminate against any ethnic or religious community.

Executive power is held by a prime minister and a cabinet of around 15 members drawn from the majority party within Parliament. The prime minister is served by an influential Prime Minister's Office, which contains an anti-pollution unit, a corrupt practices investigation bureau, an election department, and a city district secretariat, which liaises with local citizens' consultative committees. First and second deputy prime ministers assist the prime minister in their responsibilities.

The state president was formerly elected indirectly by Parliament and occupied a ceremonial position. The constitutional amendment of January 1991 enhanced the authority of the president, conferring the power of veto of the budget and key cabinet decisions, control over spending of the country's financial reserves, and the right to appoint senior officials. However, new constitutional provisions, adopted in October 1996, reduced these powers by allowing the government to call a referendum if the president vetoes constitutional amendments, and enables parliament (by a two-thirds vote) to overturn presidential appointments. The president is now directly elected for a six-year term, but stringent eligibility rules – restricting candidates to former cabinet members, senior civil servants, or managers of major companies – ensure that the president is drawn from the country's political-economic establishment.

The bulk of decisions in Singapore are taken behind the scenes through consultation between the Prime Minister's Office and an elite of around 300 well educated and loyal technocrats who staff senior posts in the state bureaucracy and in statutory boards and public corporations. They are renowned for their honesty and efficiency. For this reason, the country has been termed an 'administrative state', power being exercised in a paternalistic, though authoritarian, manner.

Although nominally a pluralist 'liberal democracy', the ruling Political Action Party (PAP), led since December 1992 by Prime Minister Goh Chok Tong, tends to dominate the political scene. Since independence, it has tightly controlled all aspects of public and political life, including the mass media, labor unions, defense and police establishments, and educational and social welfare systems.

Political parties

The People's Action Party (PAP) was originally formed in November 1954 by a small group of lawyers, trade unionists, journalists, and intellectuals, under the direction of Lee Kuan Yew, a Cambridge-educated barrister, in response to a mounting, Chinese-supported, communist nonviolent campaign for 'immediate independence for a free and noncommunist Malaya'. The PAP initially won only three seats from the 30 available in the Legislative Assembly elections of 1955. In the following election, in 1959, however, it established itself as the majority party, a position which it has held ever since. In its policy stance, the PAP has veered rightwards since its inception, originally describing itself as a 'democratic socialist' body. Today it adheres to a conservative, free-market economic program and is strongly anti-communist in outlook. Efficiency, uninterrupted economic growth, and the creation of a 'multi-ethnic, multilingual, secular society', imbued with the national values of austerity, discipline, and unity, are the party's, and hence the country's, guiding goals. The PAP has also, however, placed strong emphasis on social welfare, having invested generously in education, public housing, and health and social provision. It has branches in each of the country's electoral constituencies and a membership of around 30,000. It is, however, tightly controlled from above by a 12-member Central Executive Committee, headed by Secretary-General Goh Chok Tong.

There are currently more than 20 registered opposition parties, the majority, however, are 'paper entities', having no real organizational base. The two most important parties are the center-left Workers' Party (WP) and the liberal Singapore People's Party (SPP).

The WP was originally established in 1957 as a socialist grouping which favored greater labor union and civil freedom. It fell into abeyance during the later 1960s before being revived in 1971 by the Sri Lankan-born lawyer, Joshua Benjamin Jeyaretnam, who assumed its leadership and later won a parliamentary by-election in the low-income district of Ansom, in October 1981. He retained this seat at the general election of December 1984. Jeyaretnam was, however, subsequently harassed by the government and forced out of Parliament, in November 1986. In 1988 the WP merged with the Socialist Front (Barisan Socialis). In 1993 Jeyaretnam endeavoured to contest the direct presidential election, but was refused a certificate of eligibility by the official Presidential Election Commission on the grounds that he lacked the requisite 'integrity, good character and reputation'.

The SPP was formed in 1995 as a breakaway from the Singapore Democratic Party (SDP; estd. 1980) and is led by the London-trained barrister, Chiam See Tong, a former SDP leader.

All opposition parties operate in difficult circumstances, their leading members having been subjected to a mixture of crude and subtle harassment by state institutions since the early 1970s. Several have been bankrupted in libel, defamation, and tax fraud suits, bankrupts being debarred from political activities by law.

Political leaders since 1970

1959–90 Lee Kuan Yew (PAP), 1990– Goh Chok Tong (PAP)

Latest elections

In the most recent parliamentary elections, which were held on 2 January 1997, the PAP won 65% of the national vote and 81 of the 83 available seats. The opposition SPP and Workers' Party each won one seat. The PAP won 47 seats unopposed. Three other parties contested the election.

In the country's first direct presidential election, held on 28 August 1993, Ong Teng Cheong, secretary general of the National Trades Union Congress and the former deputy prime minister and chairperson of the PAP, secured 59% of the vote, defeating Chua Kim Yeow, president of the Development Bank of Singapore.

Political history

Singapore Island was leased as a trading post in 1819 from the Sultan of Johore by the British East India Company (EIC), on the advice of Sir Stamford Raffles (1781–1826), at a time when it was a swampy jungle. Seven years later, in 1826, Singapore, Malacca, and Penang were incorporated as the Straits Settlements, remaining under the charge of the EIC. The territory, retaining the designation Straits Settlements, passed to the British Crown in 1858 and formed a Crown Colony between 1867 and 1942. It had a burgeoning deep-water port complex to which Chinese coolies and Indian clerks were drawn. During World War II, the island was a vital British military base. It had been designed to be invulnerable to naval attack, but was invaded by land and occupied by the Japanese between February 1942 and September 1945. Singapore returned to British administration after Japan's surrender, becoming a separate Crown Colony in 1946 and fully self-governing, with Lee Kuan Yew (b. 1923) as prime minister, between 1959 and 1963. It joined the Federation of Malaysia in September 1963, but, following Malay – Chinese race riots in 1964, seceded in August 1965, claiming discrimination against its Chinese citizens. A new independent republic of Singapore was thus formed in September 1965. It remained in the Commonwealth and maintained close commercial and defense ties with neighouring Malaysia.

The new republic's internal political affairs were dominated by Prime Minister Lee Kuan Yew's People's Action Party (PAP), which gained a monopoly of all parliamentary seats in the elections between 1968 and 1980. Under Lee's stewardship, Singapore developed rapidly as a commercial and financial entrepôt and as a center for new export industries, GDP growing at an average annual per-capita rate of more than 8% during the 1960s and 1970s. As a consequence, by the early 1980s it enjoyed the highest per-capita standard of living in Asia outside Japan and the Sultanate of Brunei and had developed an extensive social welfare system. These advances were achieved by a combination of private enterprise, in the trading and financial spheres, and careful state planning and infrastructural support, in the industrial. It was also the result of a willingness on the part of the country's population to accept authoritarian state direction, including the effective control of trade unions, in a benevolent, Confucianist manner.

During the early 1980s, however, as the country endured a brief halt in its growth course, opposition to the Lee regime began to surface, and then grow. In the December 1984 parliamentary elections, the PAP's share of the popular vote fell from 76% to 63% and two opposition parties, the Workers' Party (WP) and Singapore Democratic Party, won national-level seats for the first time.

This partial reverse encouraged Prime Minister Lee to take a progressively firmer line against the expression of dissent by both the media and political activists. As part of this process, in November 1986, J B Jeyaretnam, leader of the WP and a member of parliament, was sentenced to one months' imprisonment and fined S$5,000 for perjury in connection with bankruptcy proceedings. This fine was a sufficient sum, under the terms of the constitution, to deprive him of his parliamentary seat and debar him from standing for election for five years.

Despite these actions, and helped by a once again booming economy, the PAP held its vote share steady at 62% in the September 1988 general election, capturing all but one of the available parliamentary seats. In November 1990 Lee stepped down as prime minister, handing over power to his deputy, Goh Chok Tong (b.

1941). However, he remained as a senior minister within the cabinet, while his Cambridge-educated son, Brigadier-General Lee Hsien Loong (b. 1952), served as deputy prime minister. Having recovered by 1994 from cancer, Lee Jr was clearly being groomed to later succeed Goh Chok Tong as premier. Buoyed by a level of economic growth which had averaged 8% per annum since 1989, support for the PAP remained stable at 61% in the general election of August 1991. It increased further, to 65%, at the January 1997 general election, when the PAP won all but two of the parliamentary seats. The opposition only contested 36 of the 83 seats and it was reported that there were threats of withdrawal of government funding for housing renovation projects in any constituency which returned an opposition candidate. Since the constitution requires that there must be at least three opposition deputies, a third non-constituency seat was granted to the veteran J B Jeyaretnam. Since the late 1980s a privatization program has been followed, reducing the number of state-owned corporations, and there has been some transfer of labor-intensive operations to neighboring Malaysia and Indonesia, where labor costs are lower. Economic growth has slowed sharply since 1997, as a result of the impact of the wider Asian financial crisis, which led to significant falls on the Singapore stock market. GDP growth was halved to below 3% in 1998, but the country's large foreign exchange reserves and high savings rate meant it was better able to ride out this economic storm than neighboring economies. In its external relations, Singapore closely allied itself with the United States between 1965 and 1974. Since the mid-1970s, however, it has pursued a neutralist foreign policy, improving its contacts with communist China and playing an active role as a member of ASEAN. In general, however, diplomatic relations in Singapore are viewed as an extension of trade relations, the overriding goal being to promote exports and attract inward investment and technology flows.

SRI LANKA

Democratic Socialist Republic of Sri Lanka
Prajathanthrika Samajawadi Janarajaya Sri Lanka

Capital: Colombo

Social and economic data

Area: 64,453 sq km/24,885 sq miles
Population: 17,900,000*

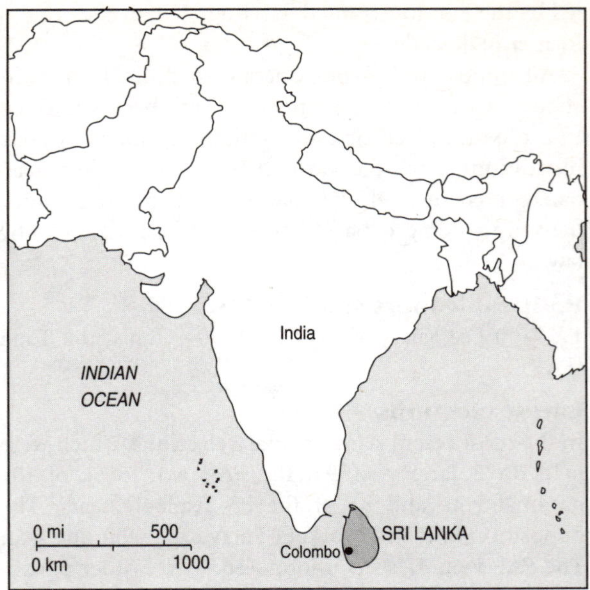

Pop. density per sq km/sq mi: 270/719*
Urban population: 22%**
Literacy rate: 88%**
GDP: $12,620 million*; per-capita GDP: $710*
Government defense spending (% of GDP): 4.9%*
Currency: Sri Lankan rupee
Economy type: low income
Labor force in agriculture: 43%**
Unemployment rate: 12.5%*
* 1995.
** 1992.

Head of state (executive)

President Chandrika Bandaranaike Kumaratunga, since 1994

Head of government

Prime Minister Sirimavo R D Bandaranaike, since 1994

Ethnic composition

Seventy-three per cent of the population is Sinhalese, 19% Tamil, and 7% Moors or Muslims, who are concentrated especially in the east. The Tamil community, which remains poorly integrated, is divided between the long-settled 'Sri Lankan Tamils', 11% of the population, who reside in northern and eastern coastal areas, and the more recent immigrant 'Indian Tamils', 8%, who settled in the Kandyan highlands as tea plantation workers during the 19th and 20th centuries. The latter's descendants were disenfranchised from 1948, but in 1989 voting rights were granted to 320,000 'Indian Tamils'. Sinhala, and, since 1988, Tamil are the official languages.

Religions

Seventy per cent of the population, predominantly Sinhalese, is Buddhist, of the Theravada sect, 15%, mainly Tamil, is Hindu, 8% is Christian, chiefly Roman Catholic, and 7% adheres to Sunni Islam. The 1978 constitution accords Buddhism the foremost place among religions and makes it the state's duty to protect and foster Buddhism. However, freedom of religious choice is also constitutionally guaranteed.

Political features

State type: liberal democratic
Date of state formation: 1948
Political structure: unitary
Executive: dual
Assembly: one-chamber
Party structure: two-party
Human rights rating: 47%
International affiliations: AsDB, CP, CW, ESCAP, G-24, G-77, IAEA, IBRD, ICC, ICFTU, IMF, LORCS, NAM, SAARC, UN, WFTU, WTO

Local and regional government

Following constitutional amendments adopted in 1987–88, a network of eight upper-tier provincial councils, with the northern and eastern provinces merged into one unit, and 68 lower-tier district councils (*pradeshiya sabhas*) has been established.

Political system

Under the constitution of September 1978, Sri Lanka has a presidential form of government based loosely on the French 'dual-executive' model. The head of state and chief executive is the president who is directly elected by universal adult suffrage for a six-year term and is not accountable to the legislature. A two-term limit applies and voting is by the single transferable vote system. The victor is required to secure at least 50% of the national poll and electors are asked to list both first and, transferable, second preferences. The president appoints and dismisses cabinet ministers, including the prime minister, who functions as the president's 'parliamentary manager'. The president is also commander in chief of the armed forces, can hold selected ministerial portfolios, can dissolve parliament 'at will', and may submit to national referendum matters of national importance. Junius Richard Jayawardene, who was president between 1978 and 1988, was particularly influential and, during his last years of office, held six departmental portfolios, including defense, civil security, plan implementation, and higher education. His successor, Ranasinghe Premadasa, combined the posts of president and prime minister. The current incumbent, Chandrika Kumaratunga, although she has pledged to abolish what she views as a 'gravely harmful' executive presidency, holds the finance and defense portfolios.

Parliament, known as the National State Assembly, is a single-chamber body, which has supreme legislative authority and meets once a year for a session of up to four months. Currently it comprises 225 members who are directly elected by a 'modified' system of proportional representation, involving preferential voting, for six-year terms. The country is divided into 22 multi-member constituencies, from which 196 deputies are returned, with the remaining 29 being elected from party lists on the basis of the total national vote of each party. A 12.5% of the vote cut-off level applies for representation. There are no by-elections, with parties being able to appoint successors to deputies who retire or die. A two-thirds parliamentary majority, followed by approval in a national referendum, is required to alter the constitution. A 1983 constitutional amendment inserted a 'no separation' clause, which makes division of Sri Lanka illegal and advocacy of separatism an offence which might lead to a loss of civic rights.

Political parties

Sri Lanka has traditionally been a classic two-party state, power alternating between the center-right United National Party (UNP: Eksath Jathika Pakshaya) and the left-of-center Sri Lanka Freedom Party (SLFP: Sri Lanka Nidahas Pakshaya).

The UNP, whose political roots go back to the inter-war Ceylon National Congress (CNP), was founded in 1946 by the pro-Western liberal-conservative, Don Stephen Senanayake, and, after independence, was the country's first governing party, between 1948 and 1956. Its neglect of the poor, and of Sinhala-Buddhist sensitivities, led to electoral defeat in 1956, persuading the party to adopt a new, democratic-socialist, policy program in 1958. Following an even heavier reversal in 1970, the UNP was remodelled as a mass party by Junius Richard Jayawardene, who was related by marriage to both of the wealthy and influential, upper-caste, Senanayake and Bandaranaike families. The goal of *dharmishta*, or a just and righteous society, was espoused and greater stress placed on rural development, although private enterprise and foreign investment were also encouraged. This strategy enabled the UNP to broaden its support base from its original dependence on the urban and privileged to a much wider electorate. Jayawardene's successor as state president and UNP leader, the lowly born Ranasinghe Premadasa, continued this populist approach. The Democratic United National Front (DUNF), led by Gamini Dissanayake, was formed in 1991 as a breakaway from the UNP by anti-Premadasa deputies. In 1994 Dissanayake returned to the UNP fold, becoming its presidential candidate, before being assassinated in October 1994. In 1998 the UNP was led by Ranil Wickremasinghe, and the DUNF by Srimani Athulathmudali.

The SLFP was founded in 1951 by the Oxford-educated barrister, Solomon W R Bandaranaike, previously a prominent member of both the CNP and the UNP government. He sought to construct a non-Marxist left-of-center alternative to the ruling party. In 1956 Bandaranaike and the SLFP secured power, after heading a Sinhala-Buddhist-orientated united front, directed against the UNP. However, conservative elements defected from the party in 1959, leading to a swing to the left in the policies which were adopted when it was in power, between 1960 and 1964 and, under the leadership of Solomon Bandaranaike's widow, Sirimavo, between 1970 and 1977. During its long period in opposition after 1977, the SLFP machine atrophied and power became centralized within the ranks of the influential Bandaranaike family. The party's policy stance also shifted towards the center. To contest the parliamentary and presidential elections of 1994, a center-left People's Alliance coalition was formed under the SLFP's leadership. In 1998 the SLFP was led by Sirimavo Bandaranaike.

More than two dozen other minor political parties currently operate in Sri Lanka. The most important, which was officially banned in August 1983 as a result of its separatist stance, is the Tamil United Liberation Front (Tamil Vimukthi Peramuna: TULF, estd. 1949), which, with its headquarters in Jaffna, is orientated towards the Tamil community and seeks to establish a separate autonomous Tamil region in the north and east to be known as Eelam. Also banned from 1971–77, after it had staged its first insurrection, and from 1983–88, was the Marxist- and Sinhalese-extremist People's Liberation Front (Janatha Vimukti Peramuna: JVP, estd. 1964), which was greatly weakened by military action against it in 1989–90.

Other significant parties are the Eeelavar Democratic Front (EDF), a Tamil-separatist group; the People's United Front (Mahajana Eksath Peramuna: MEP), a left wing Sinhalese Buddhist body; the Trotskyist Lanka Equal Society Party (Lanka Sama Saamaja Party: LSSP), formed in 1937; the Communist Party of Sri Lanka (CPSL; estd. 1943); the Ceylon Workers' Congress (CWC; estd. 1939), which represents the interests of Indian Tamil tea plantation workers; and the Sri Lanka Muslim Congress (SLMC), led by Mohammed Ashraff, which was founded as an eastern regional grouping in 1980, before becoming a national party in 1986. The LSSP, CPSL, CWC, SLMC, and the DUNF each held a seat in the 30-member SLFP-dominated cabinet of Prime Minister Sirimavo Bandaranaike, from 1994.

Political leaders since 1970

1970–77 Sirimavo Bandaranaike* (SLFP), 1977–88 Junius Richard Jayawardene*/** (UNP), 1989–93 Ranasinghe Premadasa** (UNP), 1993–94 Dingiri Banda Wijetunga** (UNP), 1994– Chandrika Kumaratunga** (SLFP/ People's Alliance)

* Prime minister, in parliamentary system.

** Executive president.

Latest elections

The most recent parliamentary election, held on 16 August 1994, resulted in victory for the People's Alliance, a leftwing coalition led by the SLFP's Chandrika Bandaranaike Kumaratunga. The Alliance won 105 of the contested seats, the ruling UNP 94 seats, the SLMC, 7, the TULF, 5, the Independent Group (Jaffna) (Eelam People's Democratic Party), 9, and the Democratic People's Liberation Front (estd. 1988), 3. Turnout was high, except in the Jaffna region where the Liberation Tigers of Tamil Eelam (LTTE) successfully organized a boycott. During the month-long campaign, 19 people were killed.

In the presidential election, which was held on 9 November 1994, Prime Minister Kumaratunga, representing the SLFP-dominated People's Alliance, secured an overwhelming victory. She captured a record 62% of the national vote, defeating the little known Srima Dissanayake of the UNP, who won 36% of the vote, and four other candidates. Turnout exceeded 60%.

Political history

1. Early invasions to Premadasa's victory

The island of Sri Lanka which was known as Ceylon until 1972, was conquered by Sinhalese invaders from India about 550 BC and became a center for Buddhism from the 3rd century BC. Arab and Portuguese spice traders later introduced Islam and Christianity respectively. Coastal areas, but not the central kingdom of Kandy, became subject to foreign control from 1505 onwards, including Portugal (1505–1658), Holland (1658–1796), and Britain (1796–1802). Finally, in 1802, Ceylon became a British Crown Colony.

Under British rule, 'Sri Lankan Tamils', who had been settled in the northern and eastern regions for centuries, took up English education and progressed rapidly in administrative careers. In addition, new 'Indian Tamils' immigrated to work on the tea and rubber plantations which had been developed in the central highlands region around Kandy. Conflicts between the Sinhalese majority and Tamil minority began to surface during the 1920s, as nationalist politics developed. In 1931, universal adult suffrage was introduced for an elected assembly and executive council, in which power was shared with the British, before, in February 1948, independence was achieved.

Between 1948 and 1972, Sri Lanka remained within the British Commonwealth as a Dominion, with a two-chamber parliamentary system on the 'Westminster model'. This comprised a directly elected House of Representatives, an indirectly elected Senate, and a titular governor general, who was the representative of the Commonwealth monarch. The liberal-conservative United National Party (UNP), led consecutively by Don Stephen Senanayake (1884–1952) and Dudley Senanayake (1911–73), initially held power. In 1956, however, the radical socialist, and more narrowly Sinhalese-nationalist, Sri Lanka Freedom Party (SLFP), led by Solomon Bandaranaike (1899–1959), gained an electoral victory, at the head of the People's United Front (Mahajana Eksath Peramuna: MEP) coalition.

Once in power, it established Sinhalese, rather than English, as the official language to be used for entrance to universities and the civil service. This precipitated Tamil riots in 1958, while the dissatisfaction of the more extremist Sinhalese culminated in the prime minister's assassination, by a Buddhist monk, in September 1959. Solomon Bandaranaike's widow, Sirimavo Bandaranaike (b. 1916), took over as prime minister and proceeded to hold office until 1977, except for UNP interruptions, under Dudley Senanayake, between March and June, 1960, and between 1965 and 1970. She was the world's first female prime minister and implemented a radical economic program of nationalization and land reform; a pro-Sinhalese educational and employment policy; and an independent nonaligned defense policy. In 1972 a new republican constitution was adopted in which the Senate upper chamber was abolished and the new national name Sri Lanka, which is Sinhalese for 'Resplendent Island', was assumed.

During the 1970s economic conditions deteriorated, spawning a serious wave of strikes in 1976, while Tamils complained bitterly of discrimination. For example, from 1956 onwards the Tamils' share of government posts fell dramatically. All this bred a separatist movement which demanded the creation of an independent Tamil state (Eelam) in the north and east. The Tamil United Liberation Front (TULF) coalition was formed in 1976 to campaign for this goal and emerged as the second largest party in parliament in the elections of July 1977. These were fought under the old simple plurality voting system and brought a landslide victory for the UNP, led by Junius Richard Jayawardene (b. 1906).

The new Jayawardene government proceeded to remodel the constitution on French presidential lines in 1978. It discarded simple plurality voting and introduced a new free-enterprise economic program, which, initially, proved to be successful. The government's position was strengthened by the decision of a presidential commission in October 1980 to deprive Sirimavo Bandaranaike of her civil rights for six years, as a result of alleged abuses of power during her period in office. The administration faced mounting unrest, however, in the north and east among Tamil separatist guerrillas, the Liberation Tigers of Tamil Eelam (LTTE), forcing the frequent imposition of a state of emergency.

Initially the UNP profited from a polarization of Sinhalese and Tamil opinion, and Jayawardene was re-elected president in October 1982. Two months later a popular referendum showed 55% in favor of prolonging the life of the UNP-dominated National State Assembly by six years. The referendum turnout was 77%. However, in 1983, the level of terrorist-organized violence escalated, with more than 900 people, mainly Tamils in the Jaffna area, being killed. This adversely affected foreign exchange earnings from the tourist industry and discouraged inward investment. Legislation was introduced to outlaw separatist organizations, including the TULF, in August 1982. All-party talks aimed at solving the Tamil dispute took place, under Indian mediation, in 1984, 1985, and 1986, but broke down as a result of differences over the degrees of autonomy to be conceded. Meanwhile, by 1987 more than 300,000 Tamils, faced with a Sinhalese backlash, had fled from Sri Lanka to India and elsewhere.

By 1987 the LTTE had established almost de facto control of the northern Jaffna region, and the economy was in a debilitated condition. Unemployment stood at

27%, inflation at 15%, and the annual GDP growth rate at 1.5%, compared with 6% between 1977 and 1983. In July of that year a Peace Accord, aimed at solving the 'Tamil issue', was signed by President Jayawardene and the Indian prime minister, Rajiv Gandhi. The plan's provisions included elevating Tamil and English to the status, alongside Sinhala, of official languages; the creation of eight, new, elected provincial councils, with the Tamil-dominated northern and eastern provinces being merged, subject to a referendum in the area; the repatriation of 130,000 Tamil refugees from South India; the disarming of Tamil militants, in return for a general amnesty; and the outlawing of LTTE training on, and supply from, the Indian mainland. Implementation of the Peace Accord in the Jaffna area was to be overseen by a 7,000 strong Indian Peace Keeping Force (IPKF).

This caused a storm of opposition from Sinhalese extremists, viewing the entry of Indian troops as an 'imperialist' invasion. More moderate Sinhalese elements, including the SLFP and several senior UNP government ministers, including Prime Minister Ranasinghe Premadasa (1924–93), strongly criticized the Accord as a 'sell-out' to Tamil interests and protest riots erupted in the Colombo region. An assassination attempt was made on the life of President Jayawardene by the resurfaced Sinhala-chauvinist People's Liberation Front (JVP) in August 1987.

Implementation of the Peace Accord in the Jaffna area by the IPKF met with initial success, but in October 1987 the surrender of arms by the LTTE ceased. The IPKF, which brought in more than 50,000 reinforcements, succeeded in gaining control of Jaffna city, but the LTTE militants, led by the elusive Velupillai Prabhakaran, escaped and established new guerrilla bases in rural areas to the east, inflicting casualty losses of between 600 and 700 on the IPKF. Meanwhile, in the south of the country, JVP terrorist attacks on UNP officials continued, claiming more than 500 lives.

Nevertheless, in April 1988, despite continuing inter-ethnic violence, elections were held for four of the newly created provincial councils, the UNP capturing 57% of the elective seats and control of all the councils. The United Socialist Alliance (USA), a loose grouping of small opposition parties who supported the July 1987 Peace Accord, secured 41% of the seats. The SLFP boycotted the polls. These were followed, in November 1988, by provincial elections in the northern and eastern provinces. The LTTE were unsuccessful in their attempts to force a boycott of an election in which the Tamil, radical, Eeelam People's Revolutionary Front (EPRLF) and Eelam National Democratic Liberation Front (ENDLF) successfully participated, voter attendance being remarkably high.

A month later the presidential election followed. With President Jayawardene unable, under the provisions of the constitution, to seek a further term, Prime Minister Premadasa stood as the UNP candidate and was opposed by Sirimavo Bandaranaike heading a seven-party alliance, which included the Sri Lanka Muslim Congress (SLMC). Opposition to the July 1987 Peace Accord was her principal rallying call. Initially she publicly pledged to abrogate the agreement and demand the withdrawal of the IPKF 'within 24 hours of being elected', but later moderated her stance. Prime Minister Premadasa, in contrast, called only for a 'renegotiation' of the Accord and a phased withdrawal of Indian troops, something that was already underway.

The election campaign was marred by disruptive JVP-induced violence and intimidation, which claimed between 10–20 lives a day and prevented polling in a number of areas. Despite opposition claims of voting 'distortion', Premadasa emerged the victor. A member of the lowly Dhobi, laundrymen's, caste, he became Sri Lanka's first national leader since independence not to be drawn from the influential Goyigama elite. A crucial factor behind Premadasa's electoral victory had been the popular support generated by the program of poverty alleviation and housing improvement that he had implemented during his ten years as prime minister. This program he pledged to continue as president.

2. Lifting of the state of emergency to the continuing civil war

The 'state of emergency' imposed in May 1983 was briefly lifted in January 1989 as campaigning moved underway for National State Assembly elections. Despite the continuation of terrorist disruptive tactics, these elections were successfully held on schedule in February 1989, with the UNP securing a narrow parliamentary majority. The finance minister, Dingiri Banda Wijetunga (b. 1922), was appointed prime minister a month later, retaining his departmental portfolio. Round-table negotiations were held with Tamil Tiger leaders during May, June, and October 1989 and the IPKF was withdrawn in March 1990. However, despite these reconciliatory moves, the 13-month-long Tiger ceasefire broke down in June 1990 and the civil war, with its two fronts in the north and south, resumed. The death toll exceeded 1,000 a month, with around 100 people a week being detained under the emergency laws. The government reacted by renewing its military offensive against the Tigers and the JVP, whose leader, Rohana Wijeweera, died in November 1989 while in army hands.

At the end of August 1991 President Premadasa suspended parliament for a month after an impeachment motion, supported by UNP dissidents led by Lalith Athulathmudali and Gamini Dissanayake, was tabled. It alleged 24 cases of abuse of power, corruption, and illegal family deals, and was prompted by concern that the executive presidential system had resulted in an autocratic over-concentration of power. In December 1991, eight erstwhile UNP deputies, who were expelled from the party and thus parliament, formed the anti-Premadasa Democratic National United Front (DUNF).

Athulathmudali was assassinated in April 1993, apparently by Tamil Tiger terrorists, and a week later, on 1 May 1993, President Premadasa was killed in a bomb explosion in Colombo, with the LTTE again officially blamed. Parliament voted for Prime Minister Wijetunga to take over as president, with Industry Minister Ranil Wickremasinghe being appointed the new premier. Under President Wijetunga the military offensive against the LTTE continued, with some success, but lacking the populist touch of his predecessor, support for the UNP waned in local elections held during 1993–94. Against a backcloth of annual GDP growth of more than 4% since 1991 and of 7% during 1993, President Wijetunga gambled in June 1994 by dissolving parliament and calling early legislative elections to be held in August 1994. These elections were won narrowly by the SLFP-dominated People's Alliance, led by Chandrika Bandaranaike Kumaratunga, the daughter of the SLFP's president, Sirimavo Bandaranaike, and the widow of Vijaya Kumaratunga, a left wing politician who was assassinated in 1988. Kumaratunga became prime minister on 19 August 1994 and formed a coalition government, with a cabinet comprising ministers from the SLFP, DUNF, SLMC, the Lanka Equal Society Party, and two small leftwing parties. She pledged to press for an amendment of the constitution to abolish the executive presidency and return to a parliamentary system of government, create 300,000 new jobs within a year, and start peace talks with the LTTE in an effort to end the ongoing civil war. Three months later, on 9 November 1994, Kumaratunga was herself popularly elected state president, defeating by a landslide margin the UNP's little-known candidate, Srima Dissanayake, who stood in place of her murdered husband, Gamini Dissanayake. She appointed her mother, Sirimavo Bandaranaike, prime minister on 14 November 1994, with the intention that they would later exchange roles once the presidency had been made a purely ceremonial position.

Peace talks were held with the LTTE from October 1994. These resulted in a temporary ceasefire coming into effect in January 1995, which broke down in April 1995. Major differences still existed between the positions of the two sides, so that the negotiation of a permanent political settlement and peace appeared to be still a significant way off. However, in July 1995 the government floated the idea of the creation of a new federal republic, comprising eight substantially autonomous regions, as a possible solution to the impasse. Concurrently, it launched a major military offensive, 'Operation Leap Forward', to drive the Tamil Tigers from the Jaffna peninsula. This met with considerable success, with Jaffna city being recaptured by government forces in December 1995, but it resulted in 500,000 Tamils being made refugees.

In January 1996 the LTTE responded with a suicide bombing in Colombo, which killed 100 and injured 1,400 and in April 1996, the state of emergency, which had formerly been restricted to Colombo and the northeast was extended across all Sri Lanka, to 'preserve public order and maintain essential community services'. The government's military offensive in the Jaffna peninsula continued during the spring of 1996. Areas which had been under LTTE rule for six years were recaptured and many Tigers driven to the Indian mainland. However, in July 1996 the LTTE overran an isolated Sri Lankan army garrison, at Mullaitivu, in the northeast, killing 1,200 government troops. This led to the government, in August 1996, launching a major offensive which resulted, in September 1997, in the capture of the LTTE's new headquarters, at Kilinochchi. Despite the government now controlling Jaffna, fighting continued in its environs throughout 1997–98. The monthly death toll averaged around 300 (chiefly from the LTTE) and the Tigers responded with periodic terrorist bombings in Colombo and, in January, in Kandy, at the Temple of the Tooth, Sri Lanka's most holy Buddhist site. President Kumaratunga continued, meanwhile, to promote her plans for the devolution of powers to regional councils, but these were rejected by the LTTE, Buddhist religious leaders and the UNP. After the Kandy suicide bombing, which had claimed 16 lives, the LTTE, which was still led by Velupillai

Prabhakaran, was formally outlawed by the government. This appeared to rule out the prospect of early peace negotiations. Nevertheless, local elections were held in the north, in January 1998, for the first time in 16 years, producing victories for moderate Tamil groups, notably the Eelam People's Democratic Party, although turnout was only 28%. Further provincial elections had to be postponed when, in August 1998, a month-long state of emergency was imposed.

By 1998 Sri Lanka's civil war had entered its 16th year and there remained no sign of an early end. The war had claimed the lives of 55,000 soldiers and civilians and led to the flight overseas of 520,000 Tamil refugees, chiefly to Europe, North America, and Australia, and the displacement of a further half million people. It had resulted in the armed forces increasing in size tenfold, to 120,000, and defense spending consuming 6% of GDP. Yet, although the conflict's impact had been adverse for the tourist sector, the economy had by now readjusted and had grown by 50% in real terms since 1983 and by 5% per annum between 1990 and 1997. Throughout the 1990s, successive governments have pursued more market-orientated economic policies, including privatization, while remittances, sent back by Sri Lankans working abroad, have been, along with tourism, a valuable source of foreign currency.

Sri Lanka remains a member of the Commonwealth and Non-Aligned Movement and joined the South Asian Association for Regional Cooperation (SAARC) in 1985. Its relations with India, which deteriorated during the early 1980s, as a result of the latter's alleged support for Tamil guerrillas, improved after the accession of Rajiv Gandhi as Indian prime minister in 1984, who was later assassinated, in 1991, by LTTE terrorists.

TAIWAN

The Republic of China (ROC)
Chung-Hua Min-Kuo

Capital: Taipei

Social and economic data

Area: 36,000 sq km/13,900 sq miles
Population: 21,450,000*
Pop. density per sq km/sq mi: 596/1,543*
Urban population: N/A
Literacy rate: 93%**
GDP: $270,000 million*; per-capita GDP: $12,600*

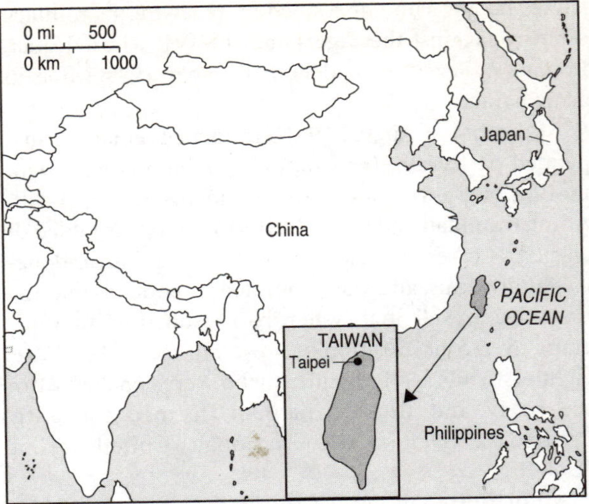

Government defense spending (% of GDP): 5%*
Currency: new Taiwan dollar
Economy type: high income
Labor force in agriculture: 12%**
* 1995.
** 1992.

Head of state

President Lee Teng-hui, since 1988

Head of government

Prime Minister Vincent Siew, since 1997

Ethnic composition

Ninety-eight per cent of the population is Han Chinese and 2% aboriginal by descent. Some 87% are Taiwan-born and 13% 'mainlanders'. The official language is Northern Chinese, Mandarin.

Religions

The predominant religion, with more than 5 million adherents, or a quarter of the total population, is Buddhism of the Mahayana and Theravada schools. There are also 3.3 million, or 16%, adherents to Taoism, 300,000, or 2%, Roman Catholics, 200,000, or 1%, members of the Presbyterian Church in Taiwan, which was established in 1865, and 60,000 followers of Islam. The philosophy of Confucianism also has a wide following.

Political features

State type: emergent democratic
Date of state formation: 1949
Political structure: unitary
Executive: limited presidential
Assembly: one-chamber

Party structure: multiparty
Human rights rating: 50%
International affiliations: APEC, AsDB, BCIE, ICC, ICFTU

Local and regional government

The country has two special municipalities, Taipei and Kaohsiung, which are governed by directly elected mayors. In addition, there are five municipalities, Taichung, Keelung, Tainan, Chiai, and Hsinchu, and 16 counties (*hsien*), each of which has its own elected local governing body. The task of deciding on the provincial budget and administrative policies and of overseeing the work of appointed provincial governors has been delegated to a Provincial Assembly. This works in conjunction with the central government. Quemoy and Matsu are administered by the Fukien (Fujian) Provincial Government.

Political system

Taiwan operates under a constitution adopted in January 1947 by the Republic of China (ROC), but which was substantially amended during 1991–92. It provides for a multilayered, five-power system of government, combining both presidential and parliamentary executive features.

At the apex of the political system is a powerful executive president, who has traditionally been elected indirectly for a six-year term by the National Assembly (Kuo-Min Ta-Hui), a 'super-parliament' which has no legislative functions, but which has the authority to amend the constitution. However, since 1996 the president has been directly elected by the public for a four-year term. The president serves as head of state, commander in chief of the armed forces and has the authority to promulgate laws and appoint members of the Control Yuan. As chief executive, the president works with an appointed, 30–40-member, cabinet, termed the Executive Yuan, which is headed by a prime minister. It is responsible for policy formulation and executive administration.

The government is responsible to a single-chamber working assembly, or parliament, the Legislative Yuan (Li-Fa Yuan). The Legislative Yuan now comprises 225 members, serving three-year terms; 168 are chosen by direct election in multi-member constituencies, while eight are elected by overseas Chinese and eight by aboriginal communities; the remaining 41 are elected on a proportional basis from lists of candidates, in accordance with parties' share of the vote. In 1947 the assembly comprised 933 members, of whom 525 fled from the mainland. The Legislative Yuan holds two sessions a year, of around eight months in duration, and is empowered to hear administrative reports presented by the Executive Yuan and amend government policy. Party blocs with as few as 10% of the seats may introduce legislation.

The overarching National Assembly, which meets infrequently, comprises 334 members who serve four-year terms. They comprise 228 regional representatives, 80 representatives of a national constituency, six mountain and plains aborigines, and 20 presidential appointees from among overseas Chinese. Formerly, the National Assembly was a much larger, supra 1,000-member, body, having comprised deputies who had been originally elected, in 1947, from constituencies in mainland China. These fell under communist Chinese control in 1949, making new elections impossible. The original elected members were thus allowed to retain their seats during the ensuing decades, being termed 'life members', while fresh elections were held only for seats vacated by deceased members. The newcomers, termed 'supplementary members', represented Taiwan-based, 'limited-term' seats and were subject to re-election every six years. In 1947 the National Assembly had 3,330 members and roughly half of these later moved, in 1949, from the mainland to Taiwan. By 1988 natural attrition had reduced the number to around 920, of whom 106 comprised 'supplementary members', representing 'government-controlled, Taiwan-situated, constituencies'.

Three other governmental bodies exist: the 29-member Control Yuan; the Judicial Yuan; and the Examination Yuan. They have, respectively, the tasks of investigating the work of the executive, interpreting the constitution, and overseeing entrance examinations to public offices.

Political parties

The ruling Nationalist Party of China (Chung-kuo Kuo-min-tang or Kuomintang: KMT) was founded in November 1894 as the 'Hsing Chung Hui' by Dr Sun Yat-sen, who played a prominent role in the overthrow of China's Manchu regime in the 'Republican Revolution' of 1911. The party assumed the name Kuomintang (Guomindang) in October 1919 and was led by the Japanese-trained military general Chiang Kai-shek from 1925. Under Chiang's leadership the party, which had been moderately socialist in stance under Dr Sun, veered to the right and established close links with businessmen, gentry landlords, and industrialists. It terminated the tactical anti-warlord alliance which it had maintained with the Chinese Communist

Party (CPC) since the early 1920s, in a violent putsch in Shanghai in April 1927, and Chiang proceeded to establish control over much of China. In October 1928 he set up a new National Government. This Nationalist regime evolved in an authoritarian, quasi-fascist manner, acquiring a large German-trained army, in an effort to expunge Mao Zedong's CPC guerrilla threat. In 1937, however, when the Japanese invaded China, the Nationalists were forced into hiding in the western province of Sichuan. Weakened by this enforced retreat, they proved ill-equipped to take on the strengthened CPC when a civil war for control of China began in 1946, after Japan's departure from the country.

The contemporary Taiwan-based KMT declares as its aim the implementation of the 'three principles of the people'. The first is the liberation of the Chinese mainland from communist control and the establishment of a 'democratic, prosperous and peaceful China', founded on a free-market economy, but with an equitable distribution of wealth. The second is the rejuvenation of the national culture. The third is to 'remain in the camp of democracy'.

Since 1924 the party has been organized on 'democratic centralist' lines similar to those of the Soviet Union's Communist Party. The KMT's supreme organ is the 2,100-delegate National Congress which meets for a week every five years, the most recent meeting being the 14th in August 1992, to ratify leadership decisions and 'elect' a Central Committee to undertake its work when it is not sitting. This Central Committee has around 210 full members and 100 alternate, non-voting, members. The party is dominated by a 31-member Central Standing Committee (CSC), headed by a chairperson, assisted by a general secretary, which controls appointments. Membership of the KMT was estimated at 2.4 million in 1995, constituting 11% of the total population. Substantial numbers are native Taiwanese, securing political and professional advancement from party membership.

The KMT has become increasingly factionalized during recent years. A liberal faction, dominated by native Taiwanese, has coalesced around the figure of State President and Party Chairman Lee Teng-hui. It has been opposed by a conservative 'one China' faction grouped around the former prime minister, Hau Pei-tsun, and comprising predominantly second-generation mainlanders, i.e. those born in Taiwan but of mainlander parents, who emphasized the need for the regime to maintain its claim to be the legitimate government of all China. This rift became formalized in 1993 when 30 conservative legislators resigned from the KMT in May and formed a New Alliance Nationalist Party. Later, in August 1993, six conservative dissidents, led by Jaw Shau-kung, and critical of the pace of recent reform and the leadership style of Lee Teng-hui, also left the KMT to found the Chinese New Party (CNP). This merged with the Chinese Social Democratic Party (CSDP; estd. 1991) in November 1993, retaining the designation CNP, and has 70,000 members. Reflecting the divisions within the KMT, four vice chairperson posts were created at the August 1993 Congress to be filled by faction leaders.

Since 1987 political parties other than the CMT have been permitted and by 1997 83 parties had registered.

The principal opposition party is the Democratic Progressive Party (DPP), which was formed, illegally, in September 1986, to campaign for the lifting of martial law and to contest the December 1986 assembly elections. The DPP is the heir to an earlier, informal, nonparty 'Tangwai' opposition grouping which had operated since the 1970s. Its leader, the veteran dissident Shih Ming-Teh, had spent 25 years in prison on sedition charges. The party advocates the establishment of direct trade, tourist, and postal links with the Chinese mainland and 'self-determination' for Taiwan. In 1999 it had a membership of 50,000, and its chairman was Lin Yi-hsiung. In the December 1986 Legislative Yuan elections, the DPP won more than 20% of the national vote. It then became weakened by internal, moderate-versus-radical, factional rivalries and by the formation of breakaway groups. The most notable of these is the Kungtang, or Labor Party, which adheres to a potentially popular, moderate, nonviolent program of social improvement. The breakaway Green Party and Taiwan Independence Party were also formed in 1996. The DPP adopted an aggressive pro-independence stance at the time of the December 1991 National Assembly elections and polled disappointingly, capturing less than a quarter of the national vote. Subsequently, the party shifted emphasis to issues of social welfare and government corruption, and secured more than 40% of the national vote in the local elections of November 1993, captured the mayorship of Taipei in December 1994, and won 30% of the vote in the March 1996 National Assembly elections. It also attracted 30% of the vote in the December 1998 Legislative Yuan elections, but lost the mayorship of Taipei and after these elections its general-secretary, Chiou I-jen, resigned, to be replaced by You His-kun.

Two other parties date back to the pre-1949 period and still hold a number of seats in the National

Assembly and Legislative Yuan, which they secured in the 1947 elections, and so are effectively tied to the KMT in a 'common front'. They are the Young China Party (YCP), which was formed in 1923, and is a small pro-KMT and pro-unification, anti-communist grouping, and the China Democratic Socialist Party (CDSP) which dates from 1932.

Political leaders since 1970

1949–75 Chiang Kai-shek (KMT), 1975–88 Chiang Ching-kuo (KMT), 1988– Lee Teng-hui (KMT)

Latest elections

The most recent National Assembly elections were held on 23 March 1996. The KMT, based on a 55% vote share, captured 183 of the 334 seats, the DPP, with a 30% vote share, 99 seats, and the CNP, 46 seats and 14% of the vote.

The last Legislative Yuan elections were held on 5 December 1998, when the Kuomintang, with 46% of the vote, won 123 of the 225 seats, the DPP 70 seats and 30% of the vote, the pro-unification CNP 11 seats and 7% of the vote, and other minor parties and independents, 21 seats and 17% of the vote. Voter turnout remained steady at 68%.

The most recent, and first, direct presidential election was held on 23 March 1996 and resulted in victory for the incumbent Lee Teng-hui, of the KMT. He attracted 54% of the votes cast. Peng Ming-min, leader of the pro-independence DPP, finished second with 21% of the vote, while the independent candidates Lin Yang-kang (a former president of the Judicial Yuan who was backed by the CNP) and Chen Li-an (a former president of the Control Yuan, who stood as an 'independent Buddhist') attracted 15% and 10% of the vote respectively. The mainland China government attempted to intimidate Taiwan's voters by holding concurrent large-scale military exercises nearby, including missile tests, which led to the USA stationing two naval convoys near Taiwan.

Political history

1. Early settlings to 1988

Taiwan, which lies 145 kilometres/90 miles off the Chinese mainland, was originally peopled by aborigines of Malayan descent. It was later settled by Chinese from the 6th century AD onwards, first slowly and then, from the 14th century, at a rapid pace. The bulk of these immigrants were drawn from the adjacent mainland provinces of Guangdong and Fujian. Known as Formosa, or 'The Beautiful', the island was briefly occupied, and controlled by, first, the Spanish and Dutch (1624–61) and, then, a Chinese Ming general, Cheng Ch'engkung, during the mid- and later 17th century, before being annexed by China's imperial rulers, the Manchu Qing, in 1683. This encouraged further immigration from the mainland, so that by 1800 a permanent Chinese ethnic majority had been established. Taiwan was subsequently ceded to Japan in 1895, under the terms of the Treaty of Shimonoseki, which concluded the 1895 Sino-Japanese war, and was only regained, by the Nationalist (Kuomintang) regime, after Japan's surrender to the Allies in August 1945.

In December 1949 Taiwan became the refuge for the rightwing Nationalist forces of Generalissimo Chiang Kai-shek (1887–1975), President of the Chinese Republic since 1928, which had been compelled to evacuate the mainland after their defeat at the hands of the Communist troops of Mao Zedong. Chiang and his million or so Nationalist followers, although constituting a minority of only 15%, proceeded, violently, to put down a Taiwanese rebellion in February 1947, and then dominated the island, maintaining an army of 600,000, in the hope of reconquering the mainland over which they still claimed sovereignty. They continued to be recognized as the legitimate government of China, under the designation 'Republic of China' (ROC) by the United States. The ROC leaders themselves viewed Taiwan as just one of their country's constituent 35 provinces. They also occupied China's United Nations General Assembly and Security Council seats until October 1971. Then, following a rapprochement between communist China and the United States, they were finally expelled and their seats taken over by the People's Republic (PRC).

During the Korean War (1950–53), Taiwan was protected by US naval forces, the country signing a mutual defense treaty with the United States in December 1954. Benefiting from this security, Taiwan enjoyed a period of rapid economic growth during the 1950s and 1960s, and emerged as an export-orientated consumer goods producer, acquiring the description of a newly industrializing country (NIC). In the process, Taiwan's socio-economic base was fundamentally moved away from its former dependence on agriculture towards the industrial and service sectors. Thus, while, in 1950, 60% of the island's population had been engaged in agricultural activities and only 18% in industrial, by 1986 the relative shares were 28% and 42%. This transformation was wrought, first, during the 1950s, by the institution of a radical, anti-gentry, 'land-to-the-tiller', land reform program, which dramatically boosted agricultural output. Second, the change in the rural sector was accompanied by the launching of a determined state-guided program of import substitution and export-led industrialization. This was based on a succession of four-year economic plans, beginning in 1953, and substantial infrastructure and human resources investment. Low wages, a disciplined work force, and an expanding American market for the country's wares provided the means and stimulus for this transformation and, in response, the economy proceeded to expand at a 'miracle' rate of more than 8% per annum throughout the 1950s, 1960s, and 1970s. First producing textile goods, then electrical 'consumer durables' and then heavy machinery and petrochemicals, Taiwan is now very much involved in high technology computer production. The country's per-capita income, which had been below that of 'low-income' mainland China in 1949, spectacularly leapfrogged into the higher ranges of the world's middle-income countries. Today, with GDP growth still averaging 7% per year, it is the second wealthiest nation, of substantial size, after Japan, in Asia.

During these 'miracle' years, political change failed to match economic change. Political power was monopolized by the Kuomintang (KMT) and armed forces, led by President Chiang Kai-shek, martial law being imposed and opposition activity outlawed. Constrained by its unification goals, an ossified political system was set up, no elections being held for assembly seats which had originally been secured in mainland constituency elections in 1947. During the 1970s, however, the Taiwanese government was forced to adjust to rapid external changes as the United States' administrations, under Richard Nixon (1969–74), Gerald Ford (1974–77), and Jimmy Carter (1977–81), adopted a new policy of détente towards communist China. This process gathered momentum after the death of Mao Zedong, in September 1976. It culminated in January 1979 in the full normalization of Sino-American relations, the severing of American – Taiwanese diplomatic contacts, and the annulment of America's 1954 Mutual Security Pact. However, the US promised to continue to provide Taiwan with arms 'of a defensive character'. Other Western nations followed suit during the 1970s and early 1980s, leaving, by 1988, only 22 countries with formal diplomatic links.

These far-reaching developments in the diplomatic sphere, coupled with changes within the ageing KMT, and the death of Chiang Kai-shek in April 1975, prompted a gradual review of Taiwanese policies, domestic and external. This reappraisal was set in train by the KMT's pragmatic, new leader, Chiang Ching-kuo (1910–88). He was the son of Chiang Kai-shek and had been prime minister from 1972 to 1978, KMT chairperson from 1975 to 1988, and state president from 1978 to 1988.

The outcome of the review was the adoption of a new program of tentative democratization and 'Taiwanization'. Thus, in December 1972, elections were held for 53 'vacated seats' within the National Assembly and 52 in the Legislative Yuan. There was also an increasingly rapid induction of native Taiwanese into the ruling KMT. Elections for further National Assembly and Legislative Yuan 'supplementary' seats were held in 1975, 1980, and 1983. In these 'contests' the KMT won overwhelming victories over the independent 'Tangwai', 'outside-the-party', candidates. Then, in the December 1986 elections for 80 National Assembly and 73 Legislative Yuan seats, the participation of an opposition party was tolerated. This was the Democratic Progressive Party (DPP), which had recently been illegally established by 135 dissident politicians, led by Chiang Peng-chien. The DPP captured 22% of the popular vote and the KMT, 69%. Finally, in July 1987, martial law was lifted and replaced by a new national security law. Under the terms of this, and related laws, the operation of political parties other than the KMT was at last permitted, but subject to regulation and in conformity with constitutional precepts, most notably the rejection of support for communism and Taiwanese independence. Civilians were freed from the jurisdiction of military courts, press restrictions were lifted, and demonstrations legalized. There was a resultant wave of protest marches by farmers, environmentalists, and regime opponents in 1988.

2. 1988–1999

The process of political liberalization accelerated markedly during 1986 and 1987 as President Chiang Ching-kuo, afflicted by ailing health, sought to both pave the way for a stable succession and secure himself a favorable place in history. Chiang eventually died, in January 1988, and was succeeded, as both state president and KMT chairperson, by Lee Teng-hui (b. 1923), the former mayor of Taipei and the country's vice president since March 1984. Unusually, he was both Taiwanese-born and a devout Christian. The new president was one of a number of 'modernizers' who had been promoted by Chiang Ching-kuo, and formed a 'technocrat' faction within the KMT. Included in this group were KMT General Secretary Lee Huan, and, initially, head of the joint chiefs of staff, the mainland-born Hau Pei-tsun.

President Lee immediately set about accelerating the pace of political reform, as well as instituting a program of economic liberalization, entailing deregulation, privatization, and a greater opening to international economic forces. In February 1988, the KMT's governing CSC approved a plan for drastically restructuring the country's legislature. Its key points were the phasing out, by 1992, through 'voluntary retirement' on substantial pensions, of between 150–200 'life-term' mainland constituency members and the replacing of them with new members representing Taiwanese constituencies. Five months later, at the KMT's 13th National Congress, held between 7 and 13 July, President Lee succeeded in packing the party's new Central Committee with 80% of his own candidates and in removing ten old guard conservative members from the CSC. Several days later, a major cabinet reshuffle in the Executive Yuan was effected, five ministers being replaced, including those in charge of finance and economic affairs. A new clutch of Western-educated, Taiwan-born technocrats was moved in. These changes strengthened significantly the reformist wing within both the party and state machines.

In the December 1989 Legislative Yuan elections the Kuomintang's vote share rose to 59% and the DPP increased its number of seats from 12 to 24. Controversially, however, in October 1991, the DPP, led by Hsu Hsin-liang, introduced a new clause into its charter which advocated Taiwanese independence and called for a plebiscite on the issue, despite the fact that calling for independence remained (until a change in the law in May 1992) a seditious offence. In the subsequent December 1991 National Assembly elections, which were held after the 566 last remaining 'life members' had resigned formally from their legislative posts, the DPP was clearly damaged by this stance. The KMT secured a landslide victory, winning 78% of the 325 seats at stake. This left it in a secure position to push through further liberalizing reform of the constitution.

In 1992 the Sedition and National Security laws were revised so that advocacy of independence and communism were no longer criminal offences, and a number of political prisoners were released. In February 1993 Lien Chan, a committed reformer, replaced the more conservative General Hau Pei-tsun as prime minister. This increased tensions within the KMT between its liberal, predominantly native Taiwanese, and conservative, predominantly second-generation mainlander wings. A formal split occurred in August 1993, at the time of the party's 14th Congress, when the Chinese New Party (CNP) was set up by conservative defectors led by Jaw Shau-kang. Support for the KMT fell below 50%, to 47.5%, for the first time ever in the local elections of November 1993 and in December 1994 Chen Shui-bien of the DPP secured a striking victory in the Taipei mayoral contest. In the latter election, the KMT's candidate finished third, behind both the DPP's Chen Shui-bian and the CNP's leader. The DPP polled strongly in the December 1995 and March 1996 Legislative Yuan and National Assembly elections, attracting around 30% of the vote, while the CNP attracted a further 13%. Nevertheless, the KMT retained majorities in both bodies and in March 1996 Lee Teng-hui secured direct election as state president, winning 54% of the vote. A cabinet re shuffle, in June 1996, brought into the government, as foreign minister, John Chang Hsiao-yen, the grandson of Chiang Kai-shek; and from 1997 the privatization program was accelerated. The broader financial crisis in Asia, during 1997–98, had some impact on the economy, but, protected by foreign exchange reserves of $90 billion (the world's largest), real GDP continued to increase at a rate of around 6% per annum. However, the government came under attack for rising levels of crime and corruption and, in May 1997, narrowly survived a no-confidence motion in the legislature. This persuaded the president, in August 1997, to replace Lien Chan as prime minister with Vincent Siew (Hssiao Wan-chang), as part of a broader cabinet reshuffle. Lien Chan remained as vice-president. Siew's stated aim was to improve relations with China and domestic social order. However, campaigning on a commitment for more open government and downplaying its pro-independence stance, in local elections held in November 1997, for 23 city mayors and district magistrates, the DPP outpolled the KMT for the first time ever, winning 43% of the national vote to 42%. This meant that nearly three-quarters of Taiwan's population would now come under DPP administration. The KMT responded by appointing John Chang (no longer the foreign minister) as its new secretary general and in local elections, held in January 1998, the KMT polled more strongly.

In December 1998 President Lee's ruling KMT increased its majority in parliamentary (Legislative Yuan) and local elections, winning the mayorship of Taipei. The result was seen as showing broad public support for the KMT's promotion of a 'new Taiwanese' identity aimed at ending longstanding ethnic divisions between native Taiwanese and those descended from 'mainlander Chinese'.

In its external relations, the KMT government, despite decreasing international support for its cause since the early 1970s, has continued to claim legitimate sovereignty in mainland China. The United States, under the terms of the March 1979 Taiwan Relations Act, has continued to supply the country with military weapons, for 'defensive purposes', but in steadily diminishing quantities. Meanwhile, since the early 1980s, the new post-Mao leadership in mainland China has launched a succession of initiatives geared towards achieving reunification in a federalist manner. Under these proposals Taiwan would officially become part of China, while retaining considerable autonomy as a 'special administrative region'. As such, it would maintain its own armed forces as well as a capitalist economic system. The model for this scheme, termed 'one country, two systems', has been the formula which has been accepted by Britain and Portugal for the transfer of sovereignty in their dependencies of Hong Kong and Macau during the late 1990s.

Between 1981 and 1987, the Taipei government met these PRC initiatives with its traditional response, the 'three nos': no contact, no negotiation, and no compromise with the mainland regime. During the closing months of the Chiang Ching-kuo administration, however, a significant relaxation of this stance became apparent and human contacts between the two states were allowed to increase. This approach has been continued by President Lee, although military tensions have remained high, exacerbated by a territorial dispute over the oil-rich Spratly Islands.

On 1 May 1991 the president declared an official end to the 42 years of 'civil war' ('Period of Communist Rebellion') between the two Chinas and revoked the 'Temporary Provisions', adopted in 1948, which had blocked major political reform. For the first time, the existence of a Communist Party-led government in Beijing was recognized officially and on 28 April 1991 the first Taiwanese delegation visited Beijing. Nevertheless, in 1994 Taiwan, still fearful of invasion from the mainland, devoted 27% of total budgetary expenditure and 5% of GDP to defense spending and, with armed forces of 485,000, had the 12th largest army in the world. By 1997 the size of the armed forces had been reduced to 376,000, but security had been enhanced by the purchase of Patriot anti-missile air defense systems from the USA. In June 1995 Taiwan offered the United Nations $1 billion if it would agree to restore the membership it lost in 1971. In 1991, under the designation 'Chinese Taipei', Taiwan joined the Asia-Pacific Economic Cooperation (APEC) forum. However, in 1999 it was officially recognized by only 28 states, chiefly from the Third World.

TAJIKISTAN

Republic of Tajikistan
Respubliki Tojikiston/Jumhurii Tojikiston

Capital: Dushanbe

Social and economic data

Area: 143,100 sq km/55,251 sq miles
Population: 5,513,000*
Pop. density per sq km/sq mi: 39/100*
Urban population: 31%**
Literacy rate: 97%**
GDP: $1,980 million*; per-capita GDP: $360*
Government defense spending (% of GDP): 6.9%*
Currency: Tajik rouble
Economy type: low income
Labor force in agriculture: 43%**
* 1995.
** 1992.

Head of state (executive)

President Imamoli Rakhmanov, since 1992

Head of government

Prime Minister Yakhiye Azimov, since 1996

Ethnic composition

Sixty-two per cent of the population is of Tajik ethnic stock, 24% Uzbek, 8% ethnic Russian, 1% Tatar, 1% Kyrgyz, and 1% Ukrainian. The official language, since 1989, has been Tajik, which belongs to the southwest Iranian language group and is similar to Farsi (Persian). Russian has the status of a language of communication between the nationalities.

Religions

Most Tajiks are Sunni Muslims (Hanafi school), as are ethnic Uzbeks. However, Pamirs, concentrated in the province of Gorny-Badakhshan, adhere to the Shia Isma'ili sect. The fabulously wealthy Western-based Prince Karim Aga Khan is their 49th Imam, acting as their spiritual leader and benefactor. There are also Russian Orthodox Church and Jewish minority communities.

Political features

State type: authoritarian nationalist*
Date of state formation: 1991
Political structure: unitary
Executive: unlimited presidential
Assembly: one-chamber
Party structure: multiparty**
Human rights rating: N/A
International affiliations: CIS, EBRD, ECO, EOC, ESCAP, IBRD, IMF, NACC, OIC, OSCE, UN
* In transition to emergent democratic.
** Though effectively dominated by one party.

Local and regional government

There are three administrative regions (oblasts), namely Leninabad (in the north), Khatlon (in the south), and the autonomous region of Gorny-Badakhshan, and the municipality of Dushanbe. Below, there are elected local councils, city and rural districts, towns, and villages.

Political system

Under the terms of the November 1994 constitution, Tajikistan is a secular state with a presidentialist political system. Executive authority is vested in a popularly elected president, who works with 30–35-member cabinet (Council of Ministers) headed by a prime minister (chairperson). The legislature, the Supreme Assembly, comprises 181 members directly elected in accordance with the two-ballot majoritarian system, a second ballot 'run-off' race being held in contests in which there is no clear first-round majority. Exceptionally, third-round repeat elections are required if seats remain unfilled after the second ballot. Presidential and legislature terms are five years. The executive president appoints or dismisses the prime minister and cabinet, subject to the Supreme Assembly's approval, and members of the Constitutional Court and Supreme Court and chairs of regional and local executives. The president also takes the lead in foreign policy and is commander in chief of the armed forces. There is a limit of two consecutive presidential terms. Under the terms of the June 1997 peace agreement with the Islamic-led United Tajik Opposition (UTO) forces, power is to be shared with the UTO, who are to be eventually given 30% of central and regional government posts, and free elections to be held in 1998.

In February 1999 a National Reconciliation Commission (NRC) proposed the establishment, following approval in a future referendum, of a new two chamber legislature, comprising a 91-member lower chamber, Majlis, and a 45-member upper chamber.

Political parties

The strongest and best organized political party in the republic is the 50,000-member Communist Party of Tajikistan (CPT), which supports President Rakhmanov. It works with the 6,000-member People's Democratic Party of Tajikistan (PDPT), which was formed in 1993 and has been led since 1998 by President Rakhmanov. Between 1990 and 1992 three significant anti-communist opposition parties developed: the 16,000-member secular Democratic Party of Tajikistan (DPT; estd. 1990); the 10,000-member Islamic Renaissance Party (IRP), led by Said Abdullah Nuri and Haji Akbar Turajonzonda; and Rastokhez (Rebirth). They secured power briefly in 1992, but were banned by the Supreme Court in June 1993 since they continued to engage in guerrilla war against the CPT-led government. They then came together in the IRP-dominated United Tajik Opposition (UTO), led by Nuri. The DPT split in June 1995 leaving Shodmon Yusuf leading a moderate dominant faction and Jumaboy Niyazov, a former political prisoner, a more extreme faction which opposed any accommodation with the government.

In November 1994 a new opposition force, the Party of Popular Unity and Accord (PPUA), was founded by the former prime minister, Abdumalik Abdullojanov, but it was banned December 1998. In 1996 the DPT was re-legalized and, under the terms of the June 1997 peace agreement, other opposition parties have been legalized.

Political leaders since 1970

1982–85 Rakhmon Nabiyev (CPT)*, 1985–91 Kakhar Makhkamov (CPT)*, 1991 Kadriddin Aslonov (CPT), 1991–92 Rakhmon Nabiyev (CPT), 1992 Akbarsho Iskandrov (independent), 1992– Imamoli Rakhmanov (CPT)

* Communist Party leader.

Latest elections

The most recent legislature elections were held on 26 February and 12 March 1995. Turnout during the first ballot ranged from 60% in the capital Dushanbe to an official 100% in one constituency in the eastern region of Gorny-Badakhshan, and averaged 84%. One hundred and sixty-two seats were filled on the first ballot, with 40% of seats being uncontested, while 19 required a second-ballot run-off contest in March 1995. Two seats remained unfilled after the second round. Opposition parties, complaining of intimidation of their candidates and of widespread violation of the election law, widely boycotted the polls, which resulted in overwhelming victory for candidates from or sympathetic to the CPT and PDPT which supported President Rakhmanov. At least 60 deputies were members of the CPT, five of the PDPT and two of the PPUA.

The latest presidential election was held on 6 November 1994 and resulted in victory for the incumbent Imamoli Rakhmanov, who secured 58% of the popular vote, compared with 35% for his opponent, the ex-prime minister, Abdumalik Abdullojanov. Rakhmanov received particularly strong support from his native region of Khatlon in the south and from the capital, Dushanbe, while his rival polled strongest in his home town of Khodzhent (Leninabad) and the eastern region of Gorny-Badakhshan, which is peopled by ethnic Pamirs who seek independence and support the Lali Badakhshan political movement. Abdullojanov claimed that the contest had been tarnished by vote-rigging. Turnout was 85%.

Political history

The Tajiks are distinguished from their Turkic neighbors by their Iranian language and traditionally sedentary lifestyle. By the 8th century AD they had emerged as a distinct ethnic group and established semi-independent territories under Uzbek tutelage during the medieval period. Northern Tajikistan came under Tsarist Russia rule between 1860 and 1900, while the south was annexed by the Emirate of Bukhara. There was initial resistance, by *basmachi* guerrillas, to the imposition of Soviet control after the 1917 Russian Revolution, but in 1924 the Tajik Autonomous Soviet Socialist Republic was formed and in 1929 it became a full constituent republic of the Soviet Union.

There were repressions of Tajiks during the 1930s Stalinist era of collectivization and in 1978 there was a large anti-Russian riot in which 13,000 participated. With the coming to power in Moscow of the reformist Mikhail Gorbachev in 1985 an anti-corruption drive was launched in the Central Asian republics and there was some relaxation of censorship. Accused of tolerating nepotism and corruption, the leader of the Communist Party of Tajikistan (CPT) since 1982, Rakhmon Nabiyev, was replaced in late 1985 by Kakhar Makhkamov. With greater freedom of expression being now tolerated in this *glasnost* ('openness') era, there was a resurgence in Tajik consciousness during the late 1980s. In 1989 a Rastokhez ('Revival') Popular Front was established and Tajik was declared the state language, with teaching of its traditional Arabic script recommencing in state schools.

However, the outbreak of violent inter-ethnic clashes in Dushanbe in February 1990, after it was rumoured that Armenian refugees were to be settled there, resulted in the CPT regime pursuing a more hardline stance. A state of emergency was maintained throughout 1990 and the nascent opposition parties, Rastokhez, the Democratic Party, and the Islamic Renaissance Party (IRP), were refused official registration.

Makhkamov was indirectly elected, by the parliament (Supreme Soviet), executive president of the republic in November 1990 and the population voted 90% in favor of preserving the USSR in the all-Union constitutional referendum held in March 1991. However, the CPT and Makhkamov supported initially the attempted anti-Gorbachev coup staged by conservative communists in Moscow in August 1991. However, there were prodemocracy demonstrations in Dushanbe, led by the three opposition parties, and, after a vote of no confidence, Makhkamov was forced to resign as president on 31 August 1991. Under acting president Kadriddin Aslonov, a declaration of independence was made on 9 September 1991, and the activities of the CPT, temporarily renamed the Socialist Party of Tajikstan (SPT), were banned on 22 September 1991. However, a day later, at a special session of the CPT-dominated Supreme Soviet, this ban was overturned. Aslonov was replaced as president by Rakhmon Nabiyev, the former Brezhnev-appointed CPT leader, and a three-month state of emergency was imposed.

Following more than a week of popular protest, hunger strikes, and civil disobedience, orchestrated by the opposition Union of Democratic Forces, Nabiyev agreed to resuspend the SPT, lift the state of emergency, legalize the opposition parties, step down as president, and hold direct elections on 24 November 1991. Opposed by six other candidates, including the liberal-minded film producer Davlat Khudonazarov, who was backed by Rastokhez and the IRP, Nabiyev comfortably won the election, capturing 57% of the vote to Khudonazarov's 30%. Nabiyev drew strongest support from the industrialized northern region of Khojand and from the rural Kulyab region in the south. However, the opposition, and outside observers, claimed that the balloting had been rigged. The SPT reverted to its former designation, the CPT, in January 1992.

Tajikistan joined the Commonwealth of Independent States (CIS) on its inception in December 1991 and the Conference on Security and Cooperation in Europe (CSCE) in January 1992, but immediate recognition by the United States was denied. This was because there were fears that Nabiyev, a hardline conservative ruling a uranium-rich but cash-poor republic, might be tempted to help such pariahs of the Islamic world as Libya fulfil their nuclear ambitions. US recognition was eventually forthcoming and in March 1992 Tajikistan became a member of the United Nations.

The government pledged to replace the Cyrillic alphabet imposed by Russia in the 1930s with an Arabic alphabet and, as part of the revival of Islamic tradition, new mosques began to be constructed with Iranian and Saudi Arabian finance, raising the total number from 18 in 1989 to more than 2,500 in 1992.

From the spring of 1992 the Nabiyev regime faced increasing opposition from Islamic and democratic groups, based especially in the Kurgan-Tyube region of the far south and the Garm valley, east of Dushanbe. There were also violent anti-Nabiyev demonstrations in the capital, led initially by Pamiris. These grew fiercer from August 1992, eventually forcing Nabiyev to resign on 7 September 1992. With the support of Islamic and democratic groups, the chairperson of the Supreme Soviet, Akbarsho Iskandarov, took over as interim head of state with the task of ending the civil war. However, fighting intensified, with Islamic and democratic groups forming a Popular Democratic Army (PDA) coalition to fight Nabiyev and his allied Tajik People's Front (TPF) Kulyabi militia, which was led by Sangak Safarov. Iskandarov, who controlled effectively only the Dushanbe area, thus resigned as head of state on 10 November 1992 and the office of president was abolished. Power was assumed by the new chairperson of the Supreme Soviet, Imamoli Rakhmanov, a communist collective farm chairperson from the Kulyab region. The new government was sympathetic to Nabiyev and its forces allied with the TPF to restore control over Dushanbe and much of the country, with the exception of the Garm Valley and Gorny-Badakhshan in the east. The six-month-long civil war had claimed more than 20,000 lives and led to 600,000 becoming refugees, with 70,000 fleeing to neighboring Afghanistan. Safarov was killed in March 1993 and Nabiyev died of a heart attack a month later. From March 1993 peacekeeping forces from the CIS were sent to the republic to help ensure that order was maintained and to patrol the border with Afghanistan, where rebel guerrilla groups were now based.

The economy of Tajikistan, already the poorest of the ex-republics of the USSR on independence in 1991, was affected adversely by the break-up of the union and was damaged further by the 1992–93 civil war, which caused economic losses estimated at 300,000 million roubles. The pace of market-centerd economic reform was also particularly slow and GDP declined annually, on average, by 16% between 1990 and 1996 and there was hyperinflation. Blamed for the poor state of the economy, Abdumalik Abdullojanov was dismissed as prime minister in December 1993 and replaced by Abduljalil Samadov. He, in turn, was replaced by Jamshed Karimov in December 1994. The post of president, which had been abolished in 1993, was re-established following a constitutional referendum held in November 1994, and Rakhmanov was popularly elected to the post in the same month, defeating his challenger, Abdullojanov.

Despite holding legislature elections in March 1995, the new president ruled in an authoritarian manner, with tight curbs being maintained on opposition activities in an effort to curb the spread of Islamic fundamentalism. The republic also remained closely allied to Russia, which provided more than half of the state's budget, as well as stationing 25,000 troops there, and to Uzbekistan. Opposition to the regime remained particularly strong in Gorny-Badakhshan. In January 1996 the southwestern towns of Tursan-Zade and Kurgan-Tyube were captured by breakaway commanders of government troops. The commanders, who included Makhmoud Khudoberdiyev, both ethnic Uzbeks, sought the replacement of Kulyabi ministers, including the prime minister. President Rakhmanov acceded to these demands in February 1996, replacing Karimov as prime minister with Yakhyo Azimov, formerly the head of a carpet-manufacturing factory. An ambitious new economic reform program was now launched, including privatization and the encouragement of Western investment to develop the country's large mineral (particularly gold) reserves. Also, with UN assistance, concerted attempts were now made to negotiate a ceasefire in the civil war with the Afghhan mujaheddin-backed Islamic rebel forces. An initial ceasefire agreement, in July 1996, collapsed within weeks; however, a new agreement, signed in December 1996 in Khosdeh, northern Afghanistan, proved more lasting. It involved the establishment of a 26-member National Reconciliation Commission (NRC), headed by an opposition representative and with seats divided equally between the UTO and the government, which would spend 18 months reviewing proposed amendments to the constitution and preparing for free elections, to be held in 1998. The agreement also provided for an exchange of prisoners, a general amnesty, the merging of the government and opposition armed forces, and the repatriation of 900,000 refugees who had been displaced by the five-year-long conflict which had, by now, claimed over 30,000 lives. In April 1997 President Rakhmanov was seriously injured, and two people were killed, when a grenade was thrown at his motorcade in the northern city of Khojand. Those later implicated included the brother of the former prime minister, Abdullojanov. On 27 June 1997 a four-stage General Agreement on Peace and National Accord was formally signed, in Moscow, between the government and Said Abdullah Nuri, the leader of the United Tajik Opposition (UTO) Islamic rebels, to end the civil war. Nuri was duly elected chairperson of the NRC in July 1997 and returned to Tajikistan in September 1997, after five years in exile in Iran, along with around 500 supporters. The peace accord was tested in October 1997, when 14 members of the presidential guard were killed by unidentified assailants, but who were believed to be connected to the rebel military commander, Khudoberdiyev. However, by December 1997 all the remaining 10,000 Tajik refugees had returned from Afghanistan, while agreement was reached between Rakhmanov and Nuri over the allocation of UTO posts in a new government. The UTO was to receive, eventually, 30% of government posts, including one of the key portfolios of defense, security, or interior. To buttress the agreement and help rebuild the country's infrastructure, a UN-sponsored conference of donor countries pledged, in November 1997, the provision of US$60 million in loans, while a 44-member UN military observer mission was based in the country. In February 1998 the first five UTO representatives were appointed to government posts. They included the UTO's deputy leader, Akbar Turajonzonda, who became first deputy prime minister. Additionally, 109 UTO supporters were released from government prisons: an estimated 1,300 remained. By April 1998 around 4,000 opposition fighters had moved their mountain strongholds to UN-monitored camps, in readiness to be integrated into the Tajik army: a further 2,000 remained 'at large'. These hopeful developments took place against the backcloth of an improving economy, with positive real GDP growth (of 2%) being at last recorded in 1997. In April 1998 Tajikistan joined the CIS Customs Union, which already comprised Russia, Belarus, Kazakhstan, and Kyrgyzstan.

THAILAND

Kingdom of Thailand
Prathet Thai or Muang Thai

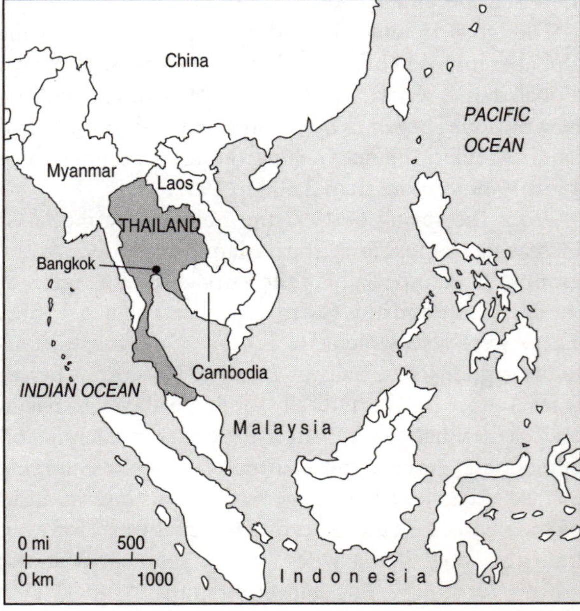

Capital: Bangkok

Social and economic data

Area: 513,115 sq km/198,115 sq miles
Population: 60,700,000*
Pop. density per sq km/sq mi: 118/306*
Urban population: 23%**
Literacy rate: 93%**
GDP: $159,600 million*; per-capita GDP: $2,630*
Government defense spending (% of GDP): 2.5%*
Currency: baht
Economy type: middle income
Labor force in agriculture: 63%**
Unemployment: 1.5%**
* 1995.
** 1992.

Head of state

King Bhumibol Adulyadej (King Rama IX), since 1946

Head of government

Prime Minister Chuan Leekpai, since 1997

Ethnic composition

Seventy-five per cent of the population is of Thai ethnic stock and 14% is ethnic Chinese, one-third of whom reside in Bangkok. Thai Malays constitute the next largest minority, followed by hill tribes. A substantial Kampuchean (Khmer) refugee community also resides in the country in border camps. The official language is Thai, or Siamese, with English being used as a universal second language.

Religions

Ninety-five per cent of the population is Buddhist, 4% is Sunni Muslim, predominantly ethnic Malays based in the south, while 0.5%, or 305,000, are Christians, three-quarters of whom are Catholics. Theravada Buddhism is the state religion.

Political features

State type: emergent democratic
Date of state formation: 1350
Political structure: unitary
Executive: parliamentary*
Assembly: two-chamber
Party structure: multiparty
Human rights rating: 62%
International affiliations: APEC, AsDB, ASEAN, CP, ESCAP, IAEA, IBRD, IMF, NAM, UN, WTO
* With special features: see *Political system*.

Local and regional government

The country is divided into 73 provinces (*changwats*), headed by centrally appointed governors (*phuwaratchakan changwats*). Each province, in turn, is subdivided into 5–10 districts, each administered by a district officer (*nai amphoe*). Some 44,000 villages (*muban*) below are governed by elected chiefs (*phuyaiban*) who are removable by the district officer. The governor and provincial officials are advised by appointed provincial assemblies (*sapha changwats*). The Bangkok-Thonburi connurbation, in which 10% of the nation's population lives, constitutes a separate municipality, governed by an elected mayor and municipal council.

Political system

Under the constitution of October 1997, which superseded earlier documents of 1932, 1946, 1947, 1949, 1952, 1959, 1968, 1971, 1974, 1976, 1977, 1978, and 1991, Thailand is ruled by a hereditary constitutional monarch, working with an elected two-chamber National Assembly. The monarch, who remains a respected and revered figure and retains significant political power, acts as both head of state and head of the armed forces. He appoints a prime minister, on the advice of the National Assembly, selecting the person best able to secure majority support. The monarch is advised by an appointed 16-member Privy Council and has the authority to dissolve the National Assembly and call new elections. In addition, the monarch, acting on the advice of the prime minister, may veto bills, with a two-thirds National Assembly majority being required for this act to be overturned.

The upper house of the National Assembly, the Senate (Wuthisapha), is to comprise, in future, 200 elected members. Previously it comprised 260 independent members, appointed for a six-year term by the prime minister. Traditionally the majority of senators were drawn from the armed forces and the police, giving these institutions an effective 'blocking position' in the Thai political system. Under the terms of a constitutional amendment passed in January 1995, the Senate was reduced to two-thirds the size of the lower house, and senators were not allowed to hold direct or indirect interests in government business concessions.Only 15% of the 260 senators appointed in March 1996 were members of the armed forces.

The lower house, the House of Representatives (Saphaphutan), is to comprise, in future, 400 members elected from single-member constituencies by universal adult suffrage for four-year terms and 100 members elected by proportional representation from party lists. (It formerly comprised 393 members.) The chamber is subject to dissolution within this period. Representatives must be members of a political party and at least 25 years old. The voting age was reduced from 20 to 18 years in the January 1995 constitutional amendment. Voting is compulsory.

The National Assembly debates and approves bills, while the Senate scrutinizes and may veto draft legislation. Joint meetings of the Senate and the House, chaired by the house speaker, are required for the passage of money bills, important legislation, but not, since May 1992, no-confidence motions.

The prime minister (Kayoke Rathamontri) is appointed by the monarch, and a selected 20–30 member cabinet, called the Council of Ministers, constitutes the country's political executive. It is responsible for both policy formulation and day-to-day administration. The prime minister and cabinet ministers may not be serving military officers, government employees, or have an interest in government business concessions. Additionally, since May 1992, there has been a requirement that the prime minister must be drawn from the ranks of elected deputies. The prime minister also heads the National Economic Development Board, the National Security Council, and the National Research Council and is served by a special policy-formulating advisory board, comprising academics and specialists. He enjoys extensive emergency powers, making him the most influential figure in the Thai political system. The strength of his influence has traditionally been closely followed, however, by that of the army leadership. As a consequence of past problems with political corruption, the 1997 constitution has established a new independent Election Commission, to monitor elections, with vote counting being centralized. Additionally, elected officials and their families are now obliged to declare their assets before, and after, taking office; cabinet ministers must resign from the legislature; and citizens can demand an investigation into a politician by the anti-corruption commission, on presentation of a petition with 50,000 signatures. Finally, parliamentary candidates must be educated to degree level.

Political parties

More than 20 political parties currently function. The most important seven are: the Democrat Party (DP: Prachatipat); the New Aspiration Party (NAP); the Palang Dharma Party (PDP); the Thai Nation (Chart Thai) party; Chart Pattana; the Social Action Party (SAP: Kij Sangkhom); and Nam Thai. The two most popular, and best organized, parties are the DP and Thai Nation.

The DP was established in 1946 and is a moderate, liberal grouping. It is the country's oldest legal political party and enjoys strong support in southern provinces. Led by Chuan Leekpai, it spearheaded the 1992 prodemocracy movement. The New Aspiration Party was formed in 1990 and was led until April 1999 by the former supreme military commander and deputy prime minister during 1990, General Chaovalit Yongchaiyut. The Righteous Force PDP (Palang Dharma), an austere anti-corruption Buddhist party, was formed in 1988 by the charismatic Governor of Bangkok (between 1986 and 1996), Major General Chamlong Srimuang. The latter resigned as party leader in May 1995 and the PDP was taken over until March 1996 by the billionaire media tycoon, Thaksin Shinawatra. It was led in 1998 by Chaiwat Sinsawong. Along with Ekkaparb (Solidarity), formed in 1989 through the merger of the Community Action Party, the Prachachon Party, Ruam Thai, and the Progressive Party, these four parties successfully contested the September 1992 general election together as the National Democratic Front and subsequently formed a coalition government which lasted until May 1995.

Thai Nation was formed in 1974. It is a rightwing, cash-rich pro-business party, dominated traditionally by the military. It has a firm popular base in the central and northeastern provinces. Its former leader, ex-premier Chatichai Choonhavan (who died in 1998), formed the breakaway Chart Pattana (National Development) in 1992 and joined the government coalition in December 1994. Thai Nation is led by Banharn Silapa-archa, who was prime minister in 1995–96.

The SAP, which also dates from 1974, is a moderate conservative grouping founded by Kukrit Pramoj (1911–1995), who was prime minister during 1975–76. It was a member of the Democrat-led coalition during 1992–93 and has been in governing coalitions since 1995.

The business-orientated Nam Thai was formed in 1994 by Amnuay Viravan, a former banker and deputy prime minister.

Other parties with recent parliamentary representation are Seritham (Justice Freedom; estd. 1992); Muan Chon (Mass) Party (estd. 1985), led by Police Captain Chalerm Yubamrung; the Thai Citizens' Party (Prachakorn Thai), a far-right, Bangkok-based monarchist body led by Samak Sundaravej, and dating from 1981; and Rassadorn (Citizens' Party; estd. 1981). In May 1998 Muan Chon merged with the NAP. The country's oldest political party, the Communist Party of Thailand (CPT), which dates from 1925, is currently illegal.

Thailand's political parties are loosely constructed, patronage-linked coalitions. Once elected, party members are substantially independent, each enjoying their own firm local base. Changes of party affiliation, in response to inducements, are frequent. In 1995 the going rate for buying an MP, whose loyalty was up for sale and who was willing to switch parties, was said to be 10 million baht ($400,000). Only the Democrat Party, which has more than 80 branches, Thai Nation, and the Social Action Party have extended local party organizations.

Political leaders since 1970*

1963–73 General Thanom Kittikachorn (military), 1973–75 Dr Sanya Dharmasakti Thammasak (independent), 1975 Seni Pramoj (DP), 1975–76 Kukrit Pramoj (SAP), 1976 Seni Pramroj (DP), 1976–77 Thanin Kraivichien (independent), 1977–80 General Kriangsak Chomanan (military), 1980–88 General Prem Tinsulanonda (independent), 1988–91 Major General Chatichai Choonhavan (Thai Nation), 1991–92 Anand Panyarachun (independent), 1992 Narong Wongwan (Samakkhi Tham), 1992 General Suchinda Kraprayoon (military), 1992 Meechai Ruchuphan (independent), 1992 Anand Panyarachun (independent), 1992–95 Chuan Leekpai (DP), 1996–97 Banharn Silpa-archa (Thai Nation), 1996–97 Chavalit Yongchaiyudh (NAP), 1997– Chuan Leekpai (DP)

* Prime minister or military leader.

Latest elections

In the most recent House of Representatives elections, which were held on 17 November 1996, the NAP and DP secured 125 and 123 of the 393 available seats respectively, improving on their 1995 performances. The NAP attracted rural support through 'patronage politics', while the DP polled strongly in Bangkok. Nine other parties secured representation: Chart Pattana won 52 seats; Chart Thai, 39 (down 53); the SAP, 20; Prachakorn Thai, 18; Ekkaparb, 8; the Seritham Party, 4; Muan Chon, 2; the Palang Dharma, 2; and Nam Thai, 1. As usual, the election was marred by alleged extensive ballot-rigging and vote-buying, and by violence.

Political history

Thailand supported a Bronze Age civilization as early as 4000 BC. Control over the country was later contested territorially by Malay, Khmer, Thai, and Mon tribes, before a unified Thai nation, termed Siam, was eventually founded in 1350. In 1826 and 1855 treaties of friendship and trade established Britain as the paramount power in the region and opened Siam to foreign commerce. The country was never formally colonized, however, being established, instead, as a neutral and independent buffer kingdom between British Burma and French Indochina, by the Anglo-French diplomatic agreements of 1896 and 1904.

After World War I, a movement for national renaissance developed, which culminated, in 1932, in a coup against the absolute ruler, King Prajadhipok, and the establishment of a constitutional monarchy and an elected, representative system of government. Political parties developed in the new parliament and the name of Muang Thai, 'Land of the Free', was adopted in 1939. During World War II Thailand was occupied by the Japanese between 1941 and 1945. The Thai government collaborated, although a guerrilla resistance movement also operated. A period of instability followed the Japanese withdrawal and King Ananda Mahidol was assassinated in 1946, before the army seized power in a coup in 1947, led by Field Marshal Pibul Songgram.

The army retained control during the next two decades, ruling through a military junta whose leadership was periodically changed by a series of bloodless coups. Field Marshal Pibul Songgram dominated between 1947 and 1957, Field Marshal Sarit Thanarat between 1957 and 1963, and General Thanom Kittikachorn between 1963 and 1973. The monarch, in the person of King Bhumibol Adulyadej (b. 1927), operated as a figurehead ruler and experiments with elected assemblies were undertaken between 1957 and 1958 and 1968 and 1971. During this era of junta rule, Thailand allied itself with the United States and encountered serious communist guerrilla insurgency along its borders with Laos, Kampuchea, and Malaysia.

Despite achievements in the economic sphere, the junta was overthrown, after violent student riots in October 1973. A democratic constitution was adopted in October 1974, establishing a constitutional monarchy and a National Assembly, to which free elections were held in 1975 and 1976. A series of coalition governments followed, but they lacked stability and, following further student demonstrations, the military assumed power again in 1976–77, annulling the 1974 constitution. Initially, the Army Supreme Commander, General Kriangsak Chomanan, held power between 1977 and 1980 and promulgated a new constitution in December 1978. This strengthened the position of the military and established a mixed civilian – military form of government, under the monarch's direction. However, General Kriangsak was forced to give way to General Prem Tinsulanonda in October 1980. He formally relinquished his army office and headed a series of civilian coalition governments which were formed after the parliamentary elections of April 1983 and July 1986.

Coups, led by junior military officers, were attempted in April 1981 and September 1985, the latter involving General Kriangsak. They were easily crushed, however, by Prime Minister Prem, who governed in a cautious apolitical manner, retaining the confidence of the army leadership, state bureaucracy, business community and monarchy. Under Prem's stewardship, the country achieved a rapid rate of economic growth, of more than 9% per year, and began the process of establishing Thailand as an export-orientated newly industrializing country (NIC). During the spring of 1988, following the introduction of legislation, allegedly at the United States government's behest, to tighten up copyright regulations, divisions began to widen within the ruling four-party coalition. This prompted Prem, who was also concerned that a personal impropriety might be publicized in a forthcoming 'no-confidence' motion, to call, in April, for a dissolution of parliament. This request was acceded to by King Adulyadej.

Following the subsequent general election, in July 1988, a new five-party ruling coalition, consisting of the Thai Nation, Democrat (DP), Social Action (SAP), Rassadorn, and United Democratic parties, was constructed, which, once again, asked Prem to come into parliament and assume its leadership. Prem, however, surprisingly declined this offer on 'personal grounds'. Instead, power passed to the former deputy prime minister, Chatichai Choonhavan, leader of the Thai Nation party.

Chatichai pursued a similar pro-business policy course to his predecessor, but, after criticism of government corruption, was overthrown in February 1991 in a bloodless military coup – the nation's 17th since the abolition of the absolute monarchy in 1932. This coup was led by General Sunthorn Kongsompong, the supreme military commander, and by General Suchinda Kraprayoon, the army chief. Anand Panyarachun (b. 1932) took over as civilian interim prime minister, but his government was subject to the ultimate control of the military junta, which held direct charge of the defense and interior ministry portfolios. The framing of a new constitution, which enshrined the military's *de facto* authority by enabling it to appoint 270 senators, provoked large-scale demonstrations in Bangkok in November 1991. Nevertheless, the constitution was endorsed in December 1991.

In the general election of March 1992 the three leading pro-military parties, the airforce-linked Samakkhi Tham, Thai Nation, and the New Aspiration Party (NAP), secured more than half of the 360 contested seats. Narong Wongwan, leader of Samakkhi Tham, became prime minister, heading a five-party coalition. However, within a month, after the United States had denied him a visa as a result of alleged drug offences, he was replaced by the non-elected General Suchinda. This appointment provoked the largest street protests witnessed in Bangkok for two decades and Major General Chamlong Srimuang, leader of the opposition Palang Dharma (PDP), an austere Buddhist 'moral force' party, commenced a hunger strike. The army response was firm. But, after between 50 and 100 protesters were killed during riots on 17–19 May 1992, King Bhumibol Adulyadej intervened and called for harmony. On 24 May 1992 General Suchinda resigned and fled the country. Two days later, the recently imposed state of emergency was lifted and a package of constitutional reforms was agreed. These included a reduction in the power of the military-appointed Senate and a requirement that, in future, the prime minister should be an elected member of parliament.

The respected Anand Panyarachun returned as interim prime minister, until elections held in September 1992 brought to power a four-party civilian coalition government of so-called 'prodemocracy angels'. The coalition was dominated by the DP, whose leader Chuan Leekpai (b. 1938) became prime minister, and the PDP. The DP had captured 79 seats in the 360-member House of Representatives and the PDP 47 seats, while the main opposition party, Thai Nation, had won just 77 seats. The SAP, with 22 seats, also joined the coalition and General Chaovalit Yongchaiyut, leader of the NAP, which had 51 seats, and a former supreme military commander, became interior minister. The government pledged to eradicate corruption, decentralize administration, liberalize the financial system, reform education, and promote rural development, via redistributing state land to the rural poor.

The governing coalition was weakened in September 1993 when the SAP left. However, the small Seritham (Justice Freedom) party, with eight deputies, joined in the same month and Chart Pattana (National Development), led by Chatichai Choonhavan and which had 60 deputies, in December 1994. The Leekpai government was relatively successful in its policy goals and achieved annual GDP growth of around 8%. However, in May 1995 the coalition was fractured by a withdrawal of support by the PDP, on the grounds of 'political righteousness', after it was revealed that its land reform program, which had resulted in 600,000 poor rural families receiving 4.4 million acres of land, had, in a few cases, benefited wealthy families with connections to the DP. Faced with certain defeat in an impending 'no-confidence' motion, Prime Minister Leekpai dissolved parliament and called a snap general election for 2 July 1995. This was narrowly won by Thai Nation, led by Banharn Silpa-archa, which won 92 of the 391 seats. Silpa-archa subsequently put together a seven-party coalition government. It included support from the PDP, SAP, NAP, Nam Thai, and Prachakorn Thai Party and had as its defense minister Chaovalit Yongchaiyudh and, as deputy prime minister, the media tycoon Thaksin Shinawatra, but excluded the DP. The composition of Silpa-archa's cabinet was criticized for including chiefly professional politicians, some of whom were subject to corruption and vote-buying allegations, rather than technocrats. In March 1996 Silpa-archa became the first elected Thai prime minister (rather than the king) to appoint the Senate's members and he reduced the military's representation from 139 to 39, out of a total of 260 upper house members. The PDP's leader, Major General Chamlong Srimaung, retired from politics in June 1996 after being surprisingly defeated in his bid to be re-elected as governor of Bangkok by Bhichit Rattakul, an independent environmentalist candidate. Two months later, the PDP, the third largest of the seven parties in the ruling coalition, with 23 seats, withdrew from the government after it was alleged that the award of three new bank licences had been decided by bribery. Silpa-archa, left with a wafer-thin majority, resigned as prime minister in September 1996 and a general election – the fourth in four years – was called. Held on 17 November 1996, the election brought to power a new, reshuffled six-party coalition led by retired General Chavalit Yongchaiyudh of the NAP, which finished just ahead of the DP. The new governing coalition, which comprised the NAP, Chart Pattana, the SAP, Prachakorn Thai, Muan Chon, and Seritham and controlled 221 seats, promised to leave control over the management of what had become a faltering economy to appointed technocrats. However, from March 1997 the country faced a severe financial crisis which provoked a political crisis and had broader repercussions across Asia. At its root was overlending by Thailand's financial companies to an overheated local property market, and a halving of GDP growth, to 5% during 1996 (and to -0.4% during 1997). The Thai central bank exhausted its foreign reserves in a failed effort to defend the baht's linkage to the US dollar and loaned US$19 billion (equivalent to 10% of GDP) to the country's 91 finance companies. However, the stockmarket plummeted and on 2 July 1997 the baht was finally allowed to float freely, falling rapidly in value by 20%. An austerity rescue plan was agreed, in August 1997, with the IMF, under which $17 billion in loans were provided, government spending was reduced, taxes raised, privatization accelerated, and 56 financial companies allowed to fail. This austerity program led to a sharp contraction in economic activity, provoking social and political unrest. In August 1997 Chavalit had an audience with the king to discuss the economic crisis and in September 1997 a new constitution, which was drawn up by a committee of experts following months of public consultation, was approved. Designed to limit the influence of money in Thai politics, it included the requirement that all cabinet ministers resign their parliamentary seats and introduced a degree of proportional representation for future elections. However, following anti-government street demonstrations in Bangkok, Prime Minister Chavalit resigned in November 1997. He was replaced by the respected DP leader and former prime minister, Chuan Leekpai, who put together a new eight-party coalition, which comprised: DP, Chart Thai, the SAP, Ekkarparb, Seritham, the PDP, the Thai Party, and part of Prachakorn Thai. This transfer of power was unusual in that it did not involve intervention by the armed forces. The new government, with Tarrin Nimmanhaeminda, a former banker, appointed as finance minister, implemented the IMF austerity package with rigour, with the result that GDP contracted by more than 5% during 1998. There was consequently intermittent social unrest, including a demonstration by farmers in the northeast, in February 1998. However, the government retained a surprising measure of popular support, helped by the announcement of a populist initiative to annually repatriate 500,000 foreign workers (drawn chiefly from neighboring Myanmar) between 1998 and 2000. The first 100,000 of these migrant workers were sent back in April 1998.

Thailand's external relations during the past two decades have been dominated by the civil war in neighboring Cambodia and Laos, which resulted in the flight of more than 500,000 refugees to Thailand after 1975 and provided justification for continued quasi-military rule and the maintenance of martial law. In addition, border concerns encouraged a tightening of Thailand's relations with its ASEAN allies, who became sponsors of the Cambodian Royalist movement, and led to a thawing in relations with communist China.

TURKMENISTAN

Republic of Turkmenistan
Turkmenostan Respublikasy

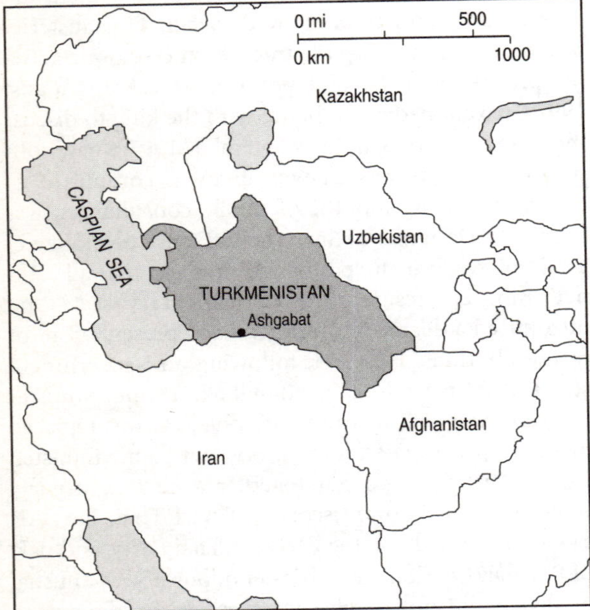

Capital: Ashkhabad (Ashgabat)

Social and economic data

Area: 488,100 sq km/188,456 sq miles
Population: 3,809,000*
Pop. density per sq km/sq mi: 8/20*
Urban population: 45%**
Literacy rate: 98%**
GDP: $4,125 million*; per-capita GDP: $1,080*
Government defense spending (% of GDP): 1.9%*
Currency: manat
Economy type: middle income
Labor force in agriculture: 43%**
* 1995.
** 1992.

Head of state and of government

President Saparmurad Niyazov, since 1990

Ethnic composition

Seventy-two per cent of the population is of Turkmen ethnic stock, 10% ethnic Russian, 9% Uzbek, 3% Kazakh, and 1% Ukrainian. The official language is Turkmen, a member of the Southern Turkic language group. Under the terms of a December 1993 accord signed with Russia, Turkmenistan's 400,000 ethnic Russians have been permitted to hold joint Turkmen and Russian nationality.

Religions

The population is predominantly Sunni Muslim, but the state is secular.

Political features

State type: authoritarian nationalist
Date of state formation: 1991
Political structure: unitary
Executive: unlimited presidential
Assembly: one-chamber
Party structure: one-party*
Human rights rating: N/A
International affiliations: CIS, EBRD, ECO, EOC, ESCAP, IBRD, IMF, NACC, OIC, OSCE, PFP, UN
* Effective.

Local and regional government

There are five regions (*velayats*), with elected councils (*etraps*) operating at the district, town, and village level below.

Political system

Under the constitution of May 1992, Turkmenistan has a strong presidentialist form of government. The president serves as both head of state and head of government (prime minister), with decree powers, and as supreme commander of the armed forces. A personality cult has been developed. Public buildings have been renamed after Niyazov, a public holiday has been established to celebrate his birthday, and large portraits have been erected on major roads and a revolving golden statue in the capital of a president who has been officially styled Turkmenbashi, 'leader of the Turkmen'. The president is directly elected for a five-year term, but in January 1994 President Niyazov's current term was extended, by plebiscite, until 2002. Legislative authority is held by the 50-member Majlis (assembly), popularly elected for a five-year term, and the president works with a Council of Ministers of some 35 members. Parliamentary candidates need to secure more than 50% of the vote, with there being a provision for a second 'run-off' ballot. There is also a People's Council

(Khalk Maslakhaty), which comprises the members of the Majlis and Council of Ministers, plus 50 representatives elected from the regions of Turkmenistan and ten appointed representatives. It is described as the 'supreme representative body' and acts as a supervisory organ and debates important political and economic issues. It is headed by the president.

Political parties

The dominant political party is the 116,000-member Democratic Party of Turkmenistan (DPT), led by President Niyazov. Before 1991 it was known as the Communist Party of Turkmenistan (CPT). It is the only party which is allowed to effectively operate, with opposition figures facing repression. Agzybirlik (Unity) was formed in 1989 as a Turkmen 'popular front' nationalist force. A Peasants' Party was formed in 1993 by some agrarian deputies, but has been denied registration. The opposition Islamic Renaissance Party operates illegally.

Political leaders since 1970

1985– Saparmurad Niyazov (CPT/DPT)*

* Niyazov was leader of the republic's Communist Party and prime minister from 1985 and head of state from 1990.

Latest elections

The most recent Majlis elections were held on 11 December 1994. All candidates were drawn from the ruling DPT or were 'independents' and all but one were elected unopposed. Turnout was officially recorded at 99.8%. People's Council elections were held on 5 April 1998, for 50 seats.

The last presidential election was on 21 June 1992, when the incumbent Saparmurad Niyazov was returned to power, unopposed, with 99.5% of the vote. Niyazov's term in office was extended until 2002 by a national referendum held on 15 January 1994 and carried with the support of 99.9% of voters; only 212 Turkmen voted 'no', officially.

Political history

The principal Turkmen tribes are the Tekkes of Merv and Attok, the Ersaris, the Yomuds, and the Gokluns, all speaking varieties of a Turkic language and descended from the nomadic Oghuz and Mongol tribes who swept across Asia between the 10th and 13th centuries. This isolated region was conquered by Tsarist Russia between 1869 and 1900, with an estimated 150,000 Turkmen being killed in the 1881 battle of Gok Tepe. In 1916 the Turkmen rose up in revolt against Russian rule and an autonomous Transcaspian government was formed after the Russian Revolution of 1917. The Soviet Red Army re-established Russian control in 1919 and it became part of the Turkestan Soviet Socialist Autonomous Republic in 1921, before becoming a constituent republic of the USSR in 1925. Sporadic guerrilla resistance against the Soviet overlords, and their program of agricultural collectivization and secularization, nearly 500 mosques being closed, continued into the 1930s. However, the Russians brought improvements in social, health, and educational facilities, and some economic progress. Much of the republic's land was barren until the Soviet-built Kara Kum Canal brought millions of acres of desert to life, stimulating cotton production, although living standards remained very low.

The nationalist movement was more muted in Turkmenistan than in other former Soviet Central Asian republics. In September 1989 a 'popular front' organization, Agzybirlik, concerned with cultural and environmental issues, was formed illegally by Turkmen intellectuals. In May 1990 Turkmen replaced Russian as the official state language and in August 1990 Turkmenistan's legislature, the Supreme Soviet, declared the republic's 'sovereignty'. However, in the March 1991 USSR constitutional referendum the population voted to maintain the Union, and the attempted anti-Gorbachev coup in Moscow in August 1991 was initially supported by President Niyazov (b. 1940), an old Soviet hand, who had led the republic's Communist Party since 1985. However, in an October 1991 referendum there was an overwhelming 94% vote in favor of independence. It was duly declared.

Turkmenistan joined the Commonwealth of Independent States (CIS) on its inception in December 1991 and was admitted into the Conference on Security and Cooperation in Europe (CSCE, later the OSCE) in January 1992. It became a member of the United Nations in March 1992. Since independence, economic and diplomatic links with neighboring Iran have improved and the new state joined the Economic Cooperation Organization (ECO), founded by Iran, Pakistan, and Turkey in 1975, which aimed to reduce customs tariffs, and eventually form a customs union. In October 1994, along with Turkey, Azerbaijan, Kazakhstan, Kyrgyzstan, and Uzbekistan, it signed the 'Istanbul declaration' pledging to seek deepened economic and cultural cooperation with its 'Turkic brothers'. However, the fundamental principle of Turkmenistan's foreign policy, as enshrined in the constitution, is 'permanent neutrality'.

The Niyazov regime has remained communist-dominated, intolerant of opposition, and increasingly personalized. Indeed, the growing personality cult surrounding the president and the decision to cancel scheduled presidential elections due in 1997 and extend Niyazov's term in office by a plebiscite, duly held in Janury 1994, prompted the foreign minister, Khalyberdy Atayev, to resign in December 1993. Disruptions in inter-republican trade brought about by the dissolution of the USSR in December 1991 affected Turkmenistan less severely than many other republics because of its abundant natural energy resources. Although Turkmenistan is one of the poorest of the former Soviet states, these resources were sufficient to enable the state to provide free electricity and gas to its citizens during 1993. A program of cautious economic reform has been pursued, entailing the successful introduction of a new currency, the manat, in November 1993, gradual price deregulation for nonessential items, and the encouragement of foreign investment in developing the country's huge natural gas and oil reserves. Seven free economic zones, with exemptions from land tax, have been established for the latter purpose. GDP declined by 8% per annum between 1990 and 1996 and there has been no real privatization. However, since 1996 there have been indications of some recovery of outward and increased capital investment, and private land ownership has been allowed since 1997. The new state, with its strict, secular leadership, has avoided the religious conflict and inter-ethnic violence experienced in nearby Tajikistan.

UZBEKISTAN

Republic of Uzbekistan
Ozbekiston Republikasy/Ozbekistan Jumhuriyati

Capital: Tashkent

Social and economic data

Area: 447,400 sq km/172,742 sq miles
Population: 21,207,000*
Pop. density per sq km/sq mi: 47/123*
Urban population: 40%**
Literacy rate: 85%**
GDP: $21,980 million**; per-capita GDP: $1,040*
Government defense spending (% of GDP): 3.6*
Currency: som (sum)
Economy type: middle income
Labor force in agriculture: 40%**

Unemployment rate:: > 0.4%
* 1995.
** 1992.

Head of state (executive)

President Islam Karimov, since 1990

Head of government

Prime Minister Otkir Sultanov, since 1995

Ethnic composition

Seventy-one per cent of the population is of Uzbek ethnic stock, 8% is ethnic Russian, concentrated in the urban centers, 4% Tajik, 3% Kazakh, and 2% Tatar. Uzbek, from the Eastern Turkic language group, is the official language.

Religions

The predominant religion is Islam, mainly from the Sunni sect (Hanafi school). The influence of the Wahhabis and Sufism is well established in the country's south. The ethnic Slav communities are predominantly Orthodox Christians, and there are also 65,000 European Jews and 28,000 Central Asian Jews.

Political features

State type: authoritarian nationalist
Date of state formation: 1991
Political structure: unitary
Executive: unlimited presidential
Assembly: one-chamber
Party structure: one-party (effective)*

Human rights rating: N/A
International affiliations: CIS, EBRD, ECO, IAEA, IBRD, IMF, NACC, NAM, OSCE, PFP, UN
* Opposition activities are restricted.

Local and regional government

There are 12 administrative regions (*oblasts*) and, below, there are city and rural districts and towns and villages with elected councils, and in the regions, governors (*khokims*). There is also one autonomous republic, Karakalpakstan, which has a directly elected president.

Political system

Under the terms of the December 1992 constitution, Uzbekistan is a secular state with a limited presidential political system. Supreme executive authority is held by a state president, who is directly elected for up to two consecutive five-year terms. The current incumbent, Islam Karimov, had his second term approved in March 1995 by a plebiscite.

There is a 250-member legislature, the Oli Majlis (Supreme Assembly), to which deputies are elected for five-year terms by a two-ballot majoritarian system, a second ballot 'run-off' race being held in contests in which there is no clear first-round majority winner. A prime minister and cabinet of around 25 members is drawn from the legislature, but they are subordinate to the president, who, with the approval of the Constitutional Court, may also dissolve the Oli Majlis.

Political parties

The principal political party is the People's Democratic Party of Uzbekistan (PDP), which is the reform-socialist successor to the formerly dominant Uzbekistan Communist Party (UCP). Set up in 1991 and led, until June 1996, by President Karimov, it claims a membership of 1.5 million. Its ally is the Fatherland Progress Party (FP: Watan Taraqioti), which was created in 1992 by the government as a party of business. It has 35,000 members and is supported by Khalq Birliki (People's Unity), formed in May 1995. The main opposition parties are Birlik (Unity Popular Front; estd. 1989), led by Adbdurakhim Pulatov and which claims a membership of 54,000; Erk (Freedom Democratic Party; estd. 1990), which favors a mixed economy; and the Islamic Renaissance Party, which advocates the establishment of an Islamic-based political system. In 1991 all religious political parties were banned and in 1992 Birlik was also outlawed. However, in August 1996 Birlik's leader was allowed to return to Tashkent. In February 1995 a new opposition party, the pro-Islamic Adolat ('Justice') Social Democratic Party of Uzbekistan was formed by Anwar Jurabayev. It claimed to have 6,000 members and the support of 47 recently elected parliamentary deputies and applied for official recognition. A centrist, intelligentsia-led pro-government party, the National Revival Democratic Party, was formed in June 1995. The 1996 law on political parties outlaws additionally ethnic-based parties and requires a minimum membership of 5,000, with wide representation across the country.

Political leaders since 1970

1990– Islam Karimov (UCP/PDP)

Latest elections

The most recent parliamentary elections were held on 25 December 1994 and 8 and 22 January 1995. Only two parties, the PDP and the allied FP, were allowed to participate, with the PDP winning 69 of the 250 Oli Majlis seats, the FP, 14, and nominees of local authorities, 167. It was estimated that 120 of the latter were also PDP members. Turnout was reported at 93.6% and 643 candidates participated, with 205 of the majoritarian races being settled in the first round.

The last presidential election was held on 29 December 1991, when Islam Karimov, then chairperson of the Supreme Soviet (parliament), faced with one opponent, secured 85.9% of the vote. Karimov's tenure as president was extended a further five years, until 2000, in a plebiscite held on 26 March 1995, which secured 99.6% support, with turnout officially recorded at 99.3%.

Political history

The Uzbeks are Turkic-speaking descendants of the Mongol invaders who swept across Asia from the 13th century and mixed with more sedentary Central Asians. During the 18th and 19th centuries the region was politically dominated by the khanates of Samarkhand, Kokand, and Bukhara. From 1865 Turkestan was conquered gradually by Tsarist Russia, with the emir of Bukhara becoming a vassal, and in 1876 Kokand was subjugated. The Tashkent soviet (people's council) gradually extended its authority between 1917 and 1924, with the emir of Bukhara being deposed in 1920. Uzbekistan became a constituent republic of the USSR in 1925, although nationalist guerrilla (*basmachi*) resistance continued for a number of years.

Russia's communist rulers sought to secularize the republic during the 1920s and 1930s. Muslim schools, courts, and mosques were closed and clergy persecuted, while new national symbols and a new literary language were promoted through investment in state education. Skilled ethnic Russian workers also immigrated into urban centers as industries began to be developed. During World War II, in 1944, some 160,000 Meskhetian Turks were forcibly transported to Uzbekistan from their native Georgia under orders from the Soviet dictator, Joseph Stalin.

After the war, Uzbekistan became a major cotton-growing region, producing two-thirds of Soviet output. However, the associated irrigation projects contributed to the desiccation of the adjoining Aral Sea, with grave environmental and health consequences. The Uzbek Communist Party (UCP) leadership, who controlled the republic like a feudal fief, was notorious for the extent of its corruption and for its obedience to Moscow. In return, Uzbekistan received large financial subsidies.

From the late 1980s, as Moscow, under the direction of Mikhail Gorbachev, began to tolerate greater political openness (*glasnost*), there was an upsurge in Islamic consciousness. This provoked violent clashes with Meskhetian, Armenian, and Kyrgyz minority communities, particularly in the Ferghana Valley, which had become a hotbed for Wahabi Islamic militancy. In September 1989 an Uzbek nationalist organization, the Birlik ('Unity') People's Movement, was formed. The UCP, under the leadership of an old Soviet hand, Islam Karimov (b. 1938), responded, in an outflanking nationalist move, by declaring the republic's 'sovereignty' in June 1990 and replacing Russian administrators with Uzbeks. However, the republic's population voted, in the March 1991 all-Union referendum, in favor of preserving the USSR as a 'renewed federation of equal sovereign republics'.

President Karimov did not immediately condemn the August 1991 attempted anti-Gorbachev coup in Moscow. However, once the coup was defeated, the UCP broke its links with the Communist Party of the Soviet Union (CPSU) and on 31 August 1991 the republic declared its independence. Uzbekistan joined the post-Soviet Commonwealth of Independent States (CIS) on its inception in December 1991 and was admitted into the Conference on Security and Cooperation in Europe (CSCE) in January 1992. It became a member of the United Nations in March 1992.

Karimov was directly elected president on 29 December 1991, receiving 86% of the popular vote. At home, he has embarked on a strategy of gradualist, market-centerd economic reform. However, political authoritarianism has been maintained. Communist Party cells have been banned from the armed forces, the police, and civil service and the UCP changed its designation in 1991 to the People's Democratic Party (PDP). Nevertheless, the former UCP apparatus and personnel remained very much in control, with opposition groups harassed and banned, and the media is under state control. In December 1994 – January 1995 elections, from which the opposition was banned from participating, a compliant, pro-Karimov legislature was returned and Karimov's tenure as president was extended in March 1995 for a further five years in a Soviet-style rubber-stamp plebiscite.

In February 1992 Uzbekistan joined the Economic Cooperation Organization (ECO), founded by Iran, Pakistan, and Turkey in 1975, which aimed to reduce customs tariffs and eventually form a customs union. In particular, links with Turkey have been strengthened, with Turkish taught in schools, alongside the Uzbek and English languages and in place of Russian. It also established an economic, military, and social union with neighboring Kazakhstan and Kyrgyzstan in January and July 1994, negotiated a treaty on economic integration and policy coordination with Russia in March 1994, and has encouraged foreign investment in its energy resources and industrial joint ventures. Being largely self-sufficient in energy and foodstuffs, and with large gold resources, Uzbekistan was not so badly affected by the collapse of the USSR as many other Central Asian states. Nevertheless, the pace of economic reform has been slow for reasons of internal stability, after violent student-led food riots erupted in Tashkent in January 1992 following initial price liberalization. The emigration, since independence, of skilled ethnic Russian industrial workers and bureaucrats has also had adverse economic consequences, the inflation rate reached 270% in 1994, food rationing has been in force since 1991, and GDP declined by 35% per annum between 1990 and 1995. Aided by an inflow of funds from Saudi Arabia, a revival of Islamic teaching and studies has been witnessed since independence. However, President Karimov, anxious to avoid the political turmoil caused by ethnic unrest and Islamic fundamentalism in neighboring Tajikistan, has pursued a determinedly secularist stance. In May 1995 he advocated publicly that the five former Soviet Central Asian republics of Kazakhstan, Kyrgyzstan, Tajikistan, Turkmenistan, and Uzbekistan should create a common, unified Turkic republic of 'Turkestan', and in August 1996 an agreement was signed with Kazakhstan and Kyrgyzstan to create a Central Asian single economic market by 1998. In October 1995 a number of opposition groups, including Erk, Birlik, and Adolat, set up a Democratic Opposition Co-ordinating Council in an effort to co-ordinate opposition to the government. However, it was later disbanded, in March 1998. Meanwhile, in December 1995 Abdulkhashim Mulatov was sacked as prime minister, as a result of the country's continuing economic difficulties. He was replaced by Otkir Sultanov. Thereafter, the economy began to pick up, with GDP growth exceeding 5% in 1997. During 1997–98, the government's crackdown against Islamic fundamentalist activity intensified. It was directed, in particular, against the Wahhabi sect, which had been allegedly responsible for an upsurge in violence in eastern Uzbekistan.

VIETNAM

The Socialist Republic of Vietnam (SRV)
Cong Hoa Xa Hoi Chu Nghia Viet Nam

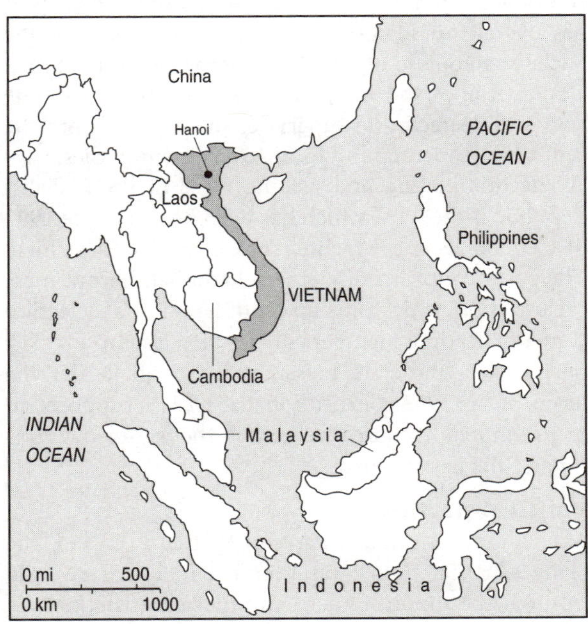

Capital: Hanoi

Social and economic data

Area: 329,566 sq km/127,246 sq miles
Population: 72,510,000*
Pop. density per sq km/sq mi: 220/570*
Urban population: 20%*
Literacy rate: 88%**
GDP: $17,630 million*; per-capita GDP: $245*
Government defense spending (% of GDP): 4.3%*
Currency: dong
Economy type: low income
Labor force in agriculture: 62%**
* 1995.
** 1992.

Head of state

President Tran Duc Luong, since 1997

Head of government

Prime Minister Phan Van Khai, since 1997

Ethnic composition

Eighty-eight per cent of the population is Viet, also known as Kinh, and imbued with a strong sense of national identity; 2% is Chinese, or Hoa, being predominantly based in South Vietnam and engaged in commercial activities; 2% is Khmer; and the remaining 8% belongs to more than 50 minority nationalities, the most important of which are the Hmong, Meo, Muong, Nung, Tay, Thai, and Tho, who live mainly along the border with China, in the North, and are tribal groups. Vietnamese (Quoc-Ngu) is the main and official language.

Religions

The principal religion, followed by 55% of the population, is Buddhism, of the Mahayana, 'Greater Wheel', variety, in the North and the Theravada, 'Lesser Wheel', sect in the South, with the cult of ancestor worship in clan temples being a conspicuous element in it. Confucianism and Daoism are also important related religions. Caodaism, a syncretic, ethical religion, which was developed in the 1920s, claims 5 million adherents, predominantly in the Mekong delta, while Hoa Hoa, a Buddhist-orientated anti-communist sect, founded in 1939, used to have 1.5 million members, chiefly in the western Mekong delta, in South Vietnam. Roman Catholicism claims 6 million followers and Protestant denominations 180,000. Under the constitution complete freedom of worship has been guaranteed. In practice, however, restrictions have been periodically enforced, involving the 're-education' of anti-regime Buddhist and Christian groups.

Political features

State type: communist
Date of state formation: 1954
Political structure: unitary
Executive: communist
Assembly: one-chamber
Party structure: one-party*

Human rights rating: 27%
International affiliations: AsDB, ASEAN, ESCAP, IAEA, IBRD, IMF, NAM, UN
* Effectively.

Local and regional government

The country is divided into 36 provinces, three municipalities, Hanoi, Haiphong and Ho Chi Minh City, and one special zone, Vung Tau-Con Dao, all directly under the control of the central authority. There are also 443 districts and town wards and 9,504 rural communes and street blocks. People's Councils operate and are elected at four-yearly intervals, in multicandidate contests, in the case of the provinces, and every two years at other levels. The People's Councils elect People's Committees as their executive organs, each unit being responsible and accountable to the body immediately above, in accordance with the precept of 'democratic centralism'. Their work is supervised by the Communist Party committee at the same level.

Political system

Vietnam, excluding the American client regime in the South, has had four constitutions since World War II. The first, which was adopted in November 1946, was a moderate, nonsocialist 'united front' document, drawing significantly from both the United States and French systems, and providing for 'the transformation of the country on a democratic basis'. Its replacement, which was adopted in December 1959, was unashamedly socialist, giving pride of place to central planning and collectivization and describing the state as 'a people's democracy, advancing step by step to socialism'. The third constitution, adopted in December 1980, described the country as in a 'period of transition to socialism on the national scale', with the 'socialization of production' yet to fully be attained in the South. It borrowed much from the Soviet Union's 1977 'Brezhnev constitution', explicitly prescribing a 'leading' and 'vanguard' role to the ruling Communist Party of Vietnam (CPV). It was replaced in April 1992 by a new 148-article constitution which, while re-emphasizing the CPV's leading role, also explicitly recognized the rights of citizens to engage in private enterprise, enshrining recent market-centerd economic reforms.

Under the current constitution of 1992, the highest state authority and sole legislative chamber is the National Assembly (Quoc Hoi), a body which is composed of 450 members directly elected every five years by universal adult suffrage in multimember constituencies. Electors choose from a list of candidates selected by the Fatherland Front and its affiliated organization, with an element of choice being theoretically available, there being more candidates than seats. In addition, under the new 1992 election law, independent candidates are permitted. To be elected a candidate must secure 50% of the vote, a second contest being held if this is not achieved.

The National Assembly formally has the authority to decide on 'fundamental questions' of domestic and foreign policy and has the task of adopting the economic plan and state budget. To amend the constitution a two-thirds majority is required. The Assembly also elects from within it a small Standing Committee, to supervise the government, and a president to serve as the formal head of state, as chairperson of the Council on National Defense and Security, and as commander in chief of the armed forces.

Day-to-day government is carried out by a cabinet of around 30 members, headed by a chairperson, or prime minister. It is 'elected' by and responsible to the National Assembly and, in its absence, the president. It has overall jurisdiction over the management of the Socialist Republic of Vietnam's domestic and external affairs; frames the budget, economic plan, and state laws and decrees; and supervises the work of both the central bureaucracy and local government bodies.

The dominating and leading force in the Socialist Republic is the CPV, which has been headed since 1997 by General Secretary Lieutenant General Le Kha Phieu. The party controls the Vietnam Fatherland Front mass organization, which puts up candidates in state election contests. Leading members of the CPV also occupy key positions in the state hierarchy although, under the terms of the 1992 constitution, the CPV is supposed to be prohibited from involvement in the day-to-day running of the government.

Political parties

The ruling Communist Party of Vietnam (CPV: Dang Cong san Viet-Nam) was founded in February 1930 through the union, under Comintern instructions, of three small existing communist groups, the most important of which was the Vietnamese Revolutionary Youth League, which was established in 1925. Initally designated the Indochinese Communist Party (ICP), it was led by the Paris- and Moscow-trained Ho Chi Minh and had an initial membership of 211, backed by 2,000 active collaborators, predominantly drawn from the ranks of the intelligentsia. In June 1941 the party, which now had a formal membership of 2,000 and was supported by 40,000 followers, adopted a new strategy of guerrilla resistance, against Japanese occupation, following the example set by Mao Zedong in China. A 'united front' organization, the Viet Minh, was established for this purpose. By such means the party was swept to power in September 1945, although a further nine years of warfare ensued until its control, in the north, was recognized. In the meantime, following the separation of the Laotian and Cambodian sections, the party adopted a new name, the Lao Dong (Workers') Party, in February 1951, and became purely Vietnam-based. In December 1976, following the successful unification of North and South, the present designation of CPV was adopted.

The CPV is organized hierarchically on 'democratic centralist' lines. At the base there are local party cells (*chi bo*), which are established in factories, cooperatives, villages, wards, and army units, and which have 3–10 members each. Above, there are party organizations, committees 'elected' by congresses, at the district, provincial, and municipal levels, with, at the apex, a national Party Congress, convened every five years. The Party Congress is, theoretically, the supreme authority within the CPV. It meets for a week and has the task of approving the party program and 'electing' a Central Committee (CC) of some 170 members to assume its powers in its absence. The most recent, eighth, Party Congress, was held in June 1996, the previous congresses having been in 1935, 1951, 1960, 1976, 1982, 1986, and 1991. A special mid-term National Conference was held in January 1995. The CC, which meets twice a year, in turn, 'elects' a Politburo of about 19 members, headed by a General Secretary, and a Standing Board (known until 1996 as a Secretariat) of about five members. These function as the real controlling bodies in the party and state structures, with a system of consensual, though factionalized, collective leadership operating. This leadership is of a gerontocratic nature, reflecting the continuing influence of Confucianist political notions.

Membership of the CPV stood, in 1996, at 2.2 million, or 2.9% of the total population, which is a low proportion by comparative communist state standards. Membership surged from a figure of barely 5,000 in 1945 to 760,000 in 1951, before falling during the 1950s, as stricter entry criteria were applied. Thereafter, the total climbed relatively slowly to 1.1 million in 1970 and 1.5 million in 1976. Reliable data on the party's social composition are lacking. However, in general, it appears that the bulk are drawn from peasant and white-collar backgrounds, the proportion who are described as 'blue-collar workers' constituting less than 10% of the total. The party's youth wing, the Ho Chi Minh Communist Youth Union, has 4 million members. There is also an 11 million-member Vietnam Women's Union.

Two other parties, the trader-orientated Democratic Party (Dang Dan Chu), which was formed in 1944, and the intelligentsia-orientated Socialist Party (Dang Xa Hoi), which dates from 1946, are allowed to operate, but not to compete with the CPV. They participate in the Viet-Nam Fatherland Front, a CPV-dominated mass organization, which was established in North Vietnam in 1955 as a mobilizing body and successor to the League for National Union of Vietnam (Lien-Viet), which itself had, in 1946, grown out of the Viet Minh. In January 1977 the Fatherland Front absorbed the South Vietnam-based National Liberation Front and the Alliance of National Democratic and Peace Forces.

Political leaders since 1970

1965–75 Lieutenant General Nguyen Van Thieu*, 1969–75 Le Duan (Lao Dong)**, 1975–86 Le Duan (CPV)***, 1986 Truong Chinh (CPV)***, 1986–91 Nguyen Van Linh (CPV), 1991–97 Do Muoi (CPV)***, 1997– Lieutenant General Le Kha Phieu***

* South Vietnam leader.
** North Vietnam (DRV) leader.
*** Communist Party leaders.

Latest elections

The most recent National Assembly elections were held on 20 July 1997. The 450 seats were contested by 663 candidates. Initially, 112 non-Communist Party members registered as potential candidates, but after screening, only 11 'self-nominated' independents contested the election, of whom three won seats. Less than a third of the outgoing members of the Assembly either sought re-election or were returned.

Political history

The Vietnamese are descended from Mongoloid nomads who settled in the Red River delta region in the north more than 2,000 years ago. The region came under Chinese control from the late 2nd century BC, directly between 111 BC and 938 AD, and indirectly thereafter. In southern Vietnam, the Mekong delta region, however, an independent Indianized kingdom (the Fu-nan), held sway between the 1st and 6th centuries AD. From the mid-10th century Vietnam enjoyed substantial independence, in the 15th century a united, north and south, kingdom being established.This disintegrated during the 17th and 18th centuries, and several small regionally based independent kingdoms took its place, but it was temporarily re-established in the early 19th century by Emperor Nguyen Anh.

The country, which had been exposed to European, initially Portuguese, commercial influence since the 16th century, was conquered by France between 1858 and 1884 and divided into the protectorates of Tonkin (North Vietnam) and Annam (South-central Vietnam) which, together with Laos and Cambodia, which embraced Cochin China, the southernmost tip of Vietnam, formed the French Indochinese Union. The Vietnamese protectorates were unified administratively in 1887, with a single governor generalship being created, thus improving physical north-south links.

During the colonial period, a French expatriate-run plantation economy, based mainly on rubber and rice, was established in southern Vietnam, drawing in press-ganged migrant laborers from the densely populated and heavily taxed north and center. This dislocated existing social patterns and bred an impoverished and embittered peasantry. During World War II, the country was occupied by Japan between 1940 and 1945, although a pro-Vichy French administration remained in place until March 1945. Then the Emperor of Annam, Bao Dai (1913–97), was appointed as a figurehead ruler. In opposition to this regime, the Viet Minh (Independence) League was formed by the Indochinese Communist Party (ICP) leader, Ho Chi Minh (1892–1969). It proceeded to wage a determined rural-based guerrilla war, which, during a period of severe economic difficulties, won considerable popular backing. The Viet Minh established a chain of rural enclaves, or 'base areas', within the Japanese occupied territory, steadily gaining in strength. Finally, in August-September 1945, with famine stalking the country and claiming the lives of 2 million people, and with the Japanese forces in disarray, it successfully mobilized the population in a revolutionary uprising which swept away the Bao Dai puppet regime and established a new Democratic Republic of Vietnam (DRV), with Ho Chi Minh as president, and a communist-dominated government in control.

France refused to recognize the new republic and, re-establishing control in the Saigon area, attempted to reconquer the country in the Indo-China War of 1946–54. The French set up a noncommunist state in the south in 1949, but, after their defeat at Dien Bien Phu, in May 1954, agreed, in the Geneva Accords of July 1954, to a ceasefire and the partitioning of the country along the 17th parallel of latitude. Ho Chi Minh was recognized as state president and Communist Party chairman in the communist-controlled DRV in the North, which had its capital at Hanoi, while Ngo Dinh Diem, the former premier to Bao Dai, headed the pro-Western and anticommunist regime in the South, which was termed the Republic of Vietnam (ROV), and had its capital at Saigon.

The Diem regime, and its repressive military successors, were opposed by former members of the Viet Minh, who became known as the Viet Cong, and then, from December 1960, the National Liberation Front. The two sides became engaged in guerrilla warfare, the National Liberation Front being supplied with military aid by North Vietnam and China, and the Diem regime by the United States. After the Tonkin Gulf incident, in August 1964, when North Vietnamese torpedo boats allegedly attacked two American destroyers, the United States became directly involved militarily in what was to be called the Vietnam War. Meanwhile, Diem had been overthrown, in November 1963, in a coup led by Lieutenant General Nguyen Van Thieu who, from June 1965, emerged as the nation's new 'strongman'.

Between 1964 and 1968 the scale of America's military involvement escalated. Major bombing campaigns were waged in the North and US troop strength was built up to a peak of 545,000. From 1969, however, as a result of mounting casualties and domestic opposition, including, most importantly, opposition from Congress, the United States began to withdraw its forces gradually and to sue for peace. A ceasefire agreement was signed in Paris in January 1973, but was breached by the North Vietnamese, who proceeded to move southwards, surrounding and capturing Saigon, which they renamed Ho Chi Minh City, in April 1975.

A new Socialist Republic of Vietnam was proclaimed in July 1976, and a program to integrate the more affluent, capitalist South was launched. Land reform and collectivization had already been carried out in the North, as had the introduction of a central planning system and the launching of a heavy industrialization drive.

The new republic was to encounter considerable problems. The economy was in ruins, more than 3 million people, including a million guerrillas, having been killed and 4 million maimed during the struggles of the preceding two decades. Fifty-seven per cent of the population had been made homeless, and 70% of the country's industrial capacity had been destroyed by American bombing. Also, the new communist administration faced opposition from the intelligentsia, many of whom were now imprisoned, and from rural groups, who refused to cooperate in the drive to collectivize southern agriculture.

In December 1978 Vietnam was at war again, toppling the pro-Chinese Khmer Rouge government in Kampuchea (Cambodia) led by the brutal Pol Pot, which it alleged was showing expansionist ambitions, and installing a puppet administration led by Heng Samrin. A year later, following accusations of the maltreatment of ethnic Chinese living in Vietnam, China mounted a brief, but largely unsuccessful, punitive invasion of North Vietnam, between 17 February and 16 March 1979. These actions, coupled with the contemporary campaigns against private businesses in the South, induced the flight of an estimated 700,000 Chinese and middle-class Vietnamese from the country in 1978–79. Many of them left by sea and became known, internationally, as the 'boat people'.

In addition, economic and diplomatic relations were severed with China, its former close ally, and Vietnam moved more closely into the Soviet orbit. It was admitted into the Comecon in June 1978 and signed a Treaty of Friendship and Cooperation in November 1978.

Between 1976 and 1985, despite the receipt of substantial economic aid from the Eastern Bloc, planned growth targets were not attained. This forced policy adjustments, involving the extension of material incentives and the decentralization of decision-taking, in 1979 and 1985. In July 1986 the death was announced of Le Duan, the CPV's, and thus the country's, effective leader since September 1969, when Ho Chi Minh died. Then, at the December 1986, sixth CPV Congress, several of the prominent, septuagenarian and octogenarian, 'old guard' leaders retired. They included Prime Minister Pham Van Dong, President Truong Chinh, and senior Politburo member Le Duc Tho, who later died in October 1990.

These significant departures were followed by important policy changes under the direction of the party's pragmatic new leader, Nguyen Van Linh (1914– 98). They were termed 'renovation', or *doi moi* ('new road'), and included permitting the private marketing of agricultural produce and the establishment of private businesses; the scrapping of collective farms and freeing of food prices; and the encouragement of foreign 'inward investment' in joint ventures. The measures were to have most success in the more entrepreneurial and export-orientated South. In general, however, the country faced a severe economic crisis from 1988, with hyperinflation (exceeding 300% pa), rapid population growth (2.1% per annum), the loss of vital economic aid from the disintegrating Soviet Union, famine conditions in rural areas, and rising urban unemployment inducing a further flight of 200,000 'boat people' refugees between 1988 and 1990, principally to Hong Kong.

Liberalization also extended to the political sphere between 1987 and 1988, when more than 10,000 political prisoners, including former high-ranking members of the pre-1976 Republic of Vietnam government, were released from 're-education'. Do Muoi (b. 1917), a supporter of Nguyen Van Linh's policies, took over as CPV general secretary at the party's seventh Congress, held in June 1991. Two months later, Vo Van Kiet (b.1922), a leading advocate of capitalist-style reform, replaced Do Muoi as prime minister. Le Duc Anh (b. 1920), a former defense minister and political conservative, was elected state president in September 1992. The new *doi moi* reforms, which aim to create a 'multisector economy under the capitalist option', began to have a beneficial impact from 1990, being buttressed, in May 1992, by a new constitution which explicitly guaranteed economic freedoms and, in Article 58, the right of citizens to own property. From 1993 to 1996 real annual GDP growth averaged around 8% and inflation 10% and, formerly a rice importer, Vietnam had become one of the world's main rice exporters. In addition, a determined attempt was made to improve Vietnam's external relations, so as to secure greater foreign inward investment and economic aid and reduce the defense burden, which had consumed a crippling third of state expenditure.

At the CPV's eighth Congress, held June–July 1996, the controlling trio of Do Muoi, Le Duc Anh and Vo Van Kiet retained their positions, and all became members of a new five-member Standing Board, within the Politburo. However, from 1997 the economy began to experience difficulties. These were related partly to domestic factors, such as corruption and bureaucratic red tape, and partly to the wider Asian financial crisis. The latter led to a 70% decline in foreign investment in 1997 and devaluations in the dong, in October 1997 and January and August 1998, in an effort to make the country's exports more competitive. Annual GDP growth fell to around 5% and losses by state enterprises increased, draining the budget. Concurrently, in September 1997, Le Duc Anh and Vo Van Kiet, both now in their seventies, retired as state president and prime minister and were replaced by Tran Duc Luong and Phan Van Khai, both in their early sixties. This brought to power a new, and more conservative, leadership. They were joined, in December 1997, by Lieutenant General Le Kha Phieu (b. 1931), viewed as a hard-liner, who replaced as CPV general secretary the pragmatic 80-year-old Do Muoi. The three new leaders entered the CPV Standing Committee in January 1998, replacing the three former leaders.

In June 1988 the staged withdrawal of Vietnam's 140,000 troops stationed in Cambodia commenced. The process, which also included the removal of troops from Laos, was completed in October 1989 and in October 1991 a Cambodian peace agreement was signed. This enabled Vietnam's diplomatic relations with China to be normalized, after a 12-year breach. It also allowed the size of Vietnam's standing army to be reduced by two-thirds between 1989 and 1997, to 490,000. Commercial links also began to be established with ASEAN states, with plans being made for Vietnam to join this organization. The US embargo on trade and investment, imposed in 1975, was eased in April 1992 and finally lifted in February 1994. Rapprochement was furthered in January 1995 when the governments of Vietnam and the United States opened liaison offices in each other's capital cities and in July 1995 full diplomatic relations were re-established. In June 1997 the first visit to the country since the end of the Vietnam War was made by a US secretary of state. Japan resumed its provision of development assistance in November 1992 after a 14-year freeze and IMF loans began to be granted to Vietnam from October 1993. It became a full member of ASEAN in July 1995.

Central America and the Caribbean

The region we have called Central America and the Caribbean contains 21 sovereign states. Eight are on the American mainland and 13 are islands, or island groups, within that part of the Atlantic Ocean usually referred to as the Caribbean Sea, or simply the Caribbean.

This is the smallest of the nine regions in areal size and the second smallest in population. It extends over 2.7 million square kilometres/1 million square miles, or 2% of the world's land area, compared with figures of 15% for North America and 13% for South America. The total population is 155 million, or 2.8% of the world's total, compared with 5.2% in North America and 5.5% in South America. However, with three-quarters of the population contributed by just three states, Mexico, Cuba, and Guatemala, the region includes a substantial number of small states. Indeed, nine have populations of less than half a million, and six have less than 150,000. All of these small countries, or 'micro-states', form part of island groupings in the Caribbean Sea.

In political terms Central America and the Caribbean is a strongly pluralistic region, 20 of the 21 states being liberal or emergent democracies. The one notable exception is Cuba, which has a defiantly communist regime. The historical backgrounds of all the countries have had a marked impact on their present political systems.

The 11 former British colonies, which are now independent members of the Commonwealth, all display the key characteristics of the 'Westminster model', including a two-party system, a parliamentary executive, a simple plurality voting system, and even an officially recognized opposition to the party in power. All, except Belize, are island states.

In contrast, most of the countries which were formerly under Spanish rule, and which are situated on the American mainland, have adopted political systems more in line with that of the United States, with executive presidents whose powers are balanced and limited by elected assemblies.

Haiti and Panama have recently emerged from military-dominated rule, and Panama has adopted the United States' style of limited presidency while Haiti has a dual executive, broadly on the French model. Cuba has a distinctive, populist, communist system, dominated by its charismatic leader, Fidel Castro.

Another interesting difference between the former British and former Spanish colonies is that the Commonwealth group are all post-1945 creations, six of them having been fully independent states only since 1975, whereas the 'Spanish empire' countries are mostly 19th-century creations, the youngest, Panama, having achieved full sovereignty as long ago as 1903.

In many ways the region is one of striking contrasts, with few signs of unity. For example, it is easier to fly from Jamaica to the Dominican Republic via Miami, in other words a round trip of some 1,600 kilometres, than to attempt to travel by the direct route of less than 800 kilometres. Frontier formalities also restrict international movement, with strict passport and customs controls operating even between Commonwealth countries.

The one feature all the Central American and Carribbean states have in common is the fact that they live in the shadow of the northern colossus, the United States. In other words, they are in America's 'back yard'. US interest in the region stems from the Monroe Doctrine of 1823, when the then secretary of state warned off European powers from interfering in what he saw as his country's domestic affairs.

The Spanish–American War of 1898, fought mainly over Cuba, reaffirmed the dominance of the United States and this strategic paternalism was rekindled as recently as 1983, when US forces, without consulting Britain, the British Crown, or the Commonwealth Secretariat, were given orders to invade Grenada. The United States were also instrumental, through their backing of the rightwing Contra army, in securing the removal of the leftwing Sandinista government, at the ballot box, in Nicaragua in 1990. A year earlier, it had intervened directly to depose Panama's military strongman General Manuel Noriega, who was involved in drug trafficking, and in 1994 sent troops to Haiti to help return to power the democratically elected exiled president, Jean-Bertrand Aristide.

In trade and culture, United States influence has grown dramatically in the post-World War II years. For example, 72% of the Dominican Republic's exports are to the United States, and 61% of those of Trinidad and Tobago. Exports from the United States to countries in the region are similarly high. Over 60% of tourists to Caribbean countries come from the United States, compared with less than 10% from Europe, or from Commonwealth countries, such as Canada.

Economically, it is not a rich region by European stan-

Central America and the Caribbean: social, economic, and political data

Country	Area (sq km/ sq miles)	*c.* 1995 Population (million)	*c.* 1995 Pop. density per sq km/ sq mile	*c.* 1992 Adult literacy rate (%)	World ranking	Income type	*c.* 1991 Human rights rating (%)
Antigua and Barbuda	440/170	0.065	148/382	88	84	middle	N/A
Bahamas	13,940/5,382	0.284	20/53	89	82	high	N/A
Barbados	430/166	0.261	607/1572	99	8	middle	N/A
Belize	22,970/8.869	0.211	9/24	91	77	middle	N/A
Costa Rica	51,100/19,730	3.071	60/156	88	84	middle	90
Cuba	110,860/42.803	10.960	99/256	98	34	middle	30
Dominica	750/290	0.072	96/248	94	66	middle	N/A
Dominican Republic	48,072/18,561	7.760	161/418	69	119	middle	78
El Salvador	21,390/8.259	5.641	264/683	67	121	middle	53
Grenada	345/133	0.091	264/684	98	34	middle	N/A
Guatemala	108,890/42,043	10.322	95/246	46	157	middle	62
Haiti	27,750/10,714	7.041	254/657	35	169	low	N/A
Honduras	112,090/43,278	5.770	51/133	57	136	low	65
Jamaica	10,991/4,244	2.500	227/589	96	52	middle	72
Mexico	1,958,201/756,065	93.008	47/123	87	89	middle	64
Nicaragua	127,849/49,363	4.401	34/89	57	136	low	75
Panama	77,080/29,761	2.631	34/88	86	92	middle	81
St Kitts and Nevis	261/101	0.041	157/406	98	34	middle	N/A
St Lucia	620/239	0.141	227/590	82	99	middle	N/A
St Vincent and the Grenadines	390/151	0.111	285/735	96	52	middle	N/A
Trinidad and Tobago	5,130/1,981	1.257	245/635	95	59	middle	84
Total/average/range	*2,699,349/1,042,224*	*155.639*	*58/149*	*35–99*	–	–	*30–90*

(A = appointed, AMS = additional member system, E = elected, F = federal, PL = party list, PR = proportional representation, SP = simple plurality, U = unitary, Lib-dem = liberal democratic, Em-dem = emergent democratic, Lim-pres = limited presidential.)

dards, but, on the other hand, only four of the 21 states, Guatemala, Haiti, Honduras, and Nicaragua, fall into the 'low income' category, and some of them only marginally so, while the Bahamians enjoy a 'high income' status.

Despite the current evidence of disunity, there are encouraging signs that the countries of the Caribbean wish, and intend, to function in a more cohesive fashion. The Caribbean Community and Common Market (CARICOM) was founded in 1973, in Trinidad, as a successor to the Caribbean Free Trade Association. Its declared purpose is to further the integration process which the Association began. Its members include Antigua and Barbuda, the Bahamas, Barbados, Belize, Dominica, Grenada, Guyana, Jamaica, St Kitts and Nevis, St Lucia, St Vincent and the Grenadines, and Trinidad and Tobago, as well as Montserrat, which is still a British possession. In 1994 CARICOM sponsored the formation of the Association of Caribbean States (ACS) trade grouping. On the mainland, some of the Central American states have developed closer ties with their Hispanic neighbors in the south.

It makes good sense for the Caribbean countries, with their small populations and vulnerable economies and frontiers, to work more closely together, but the proximity of the United States cannot be ignored. The Organization of American States (OAS), which includes 19 of the Central American and Caribbean countries, as well as ten of the 11 South American states, has its headquarters in Washington, DC, and is very much an instrument of US foreign policy. However, the North American Free Trade Agreement (NAFTA) between the United States, Canada, and Mexico is perhaps a sign of greater US willingness to be a partner, rather than a dominant neighbor.

Table 52

World ranking	Date of state formation	State structure	State type	Executive type	Number of assembly chambers	Party structure	Lower house electoral system
–	1981	U	Lib-dem	Parliamentary	2	two	SP
–	1973	U	Lib-dem	Parliamentary	2	two	SP
–	1966	U	Lib-dem	Parliamentary	2	two	SP
–	1981	U	Lib-dem	Parliamentary	2	two	SP
21	1821	U	Lib-dem	Lim-pres	1	two	PR-PL
93	1899	U	Communist	Communist	1	one	SB
–	1978	U	Lib-dem	Parliamentary	1	multi	mixed-E/A
38	1844	U	Lib-dem	Lim-pres	2	multi	PR-PL
72	1830	U	Lib-dem	Lim-pres	1	multi	PR-AMS
–	1974	U	Lib-dem	Parliamentary	2	multi	SP
57	1839	U	Lib-dem	Lim-pres	1	multi	PR-AMS
–	1804	U	Em-dem	Dual	2	multi	SB
53	1838	U	Lib-dem	Lim-pres	1	two	PR-PL
43	1962	U	Lib-dem	Parliamentary	2	two	SP
56	1821	F	Lib-dem	Lim-Pres	2	multi	PR-AMS
40	1838	U	Em-dem	Lim-pres	1	two	PR-PL
35	1903	U	Em-dem	Lim-pres	1	multi	SP
–	1983	F	Lib-dem	Parliamentary	1	multi	SP
–	1979	U	Lib-dem	Parliamentary	2	two	SP
–	1979	U	Lib-dem	Parliamentary	1	two	SP
29	1962	U	Lib-dem	Parliamentary	2	multi	SP
–	–	–	–	–	–	–	–

Recommended reading

Booth, J and Seligson, M *Elections and Democracy in Central America*, University of North Carolina Press, 1989

Leiken, R (ed.) *Central America*, Pergamon, 1984

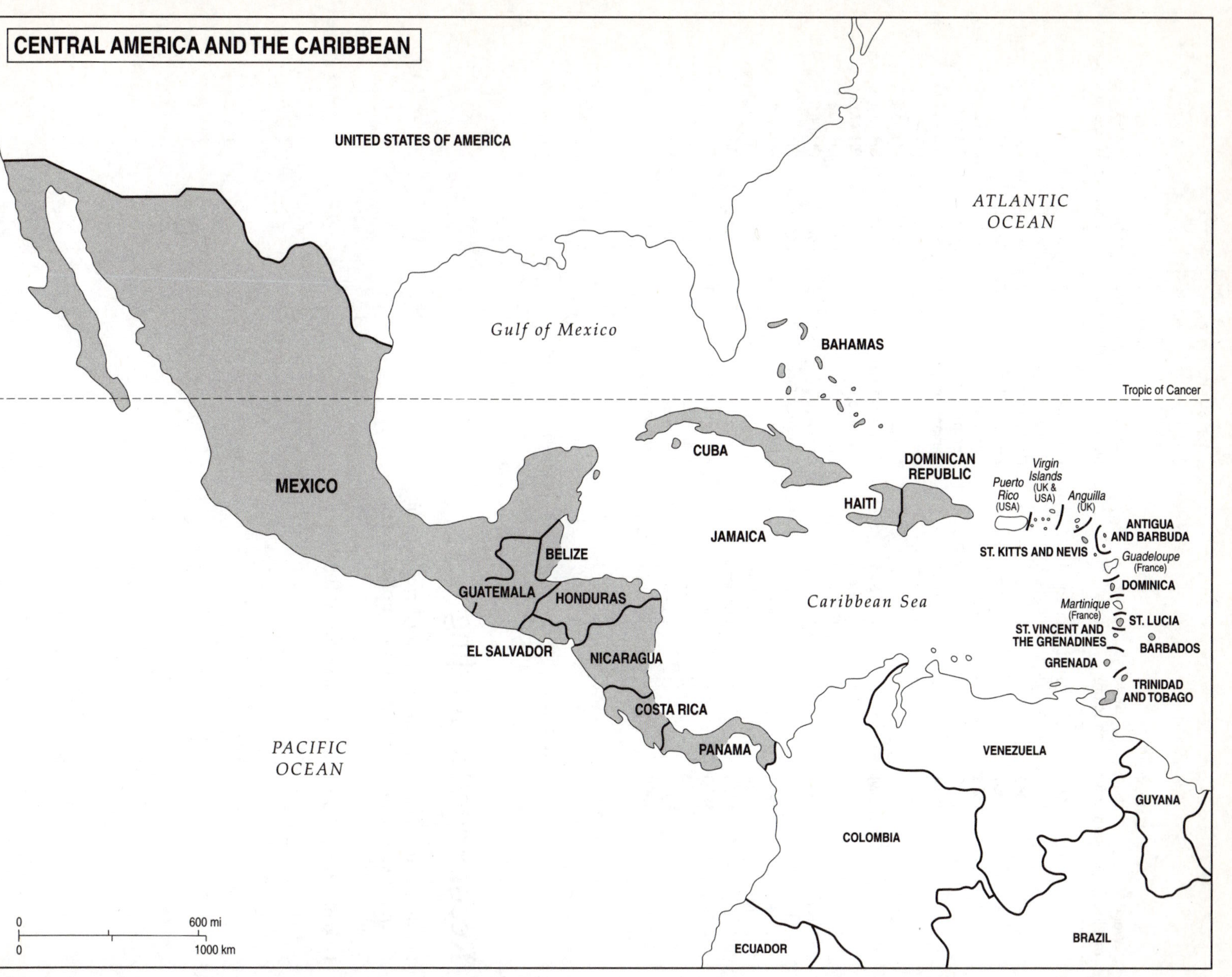
CENTRAL AMERICA AND THE CARIBBEAN
UNITED STATES OF AMERICA
ATLANTIC OCEAN
Gulf of Mexico
BAHAMAS
Tropic of Cancer
MEXICO
CUBA
DOMINICAN REPUBLIC
Puerto Rico (USA)
Virgin Islands (UK & USA)
Anguilla (UK)
HAITI
JAMAICA
ANTIGUA AND BARBUDA
ST. KITTS AND NEVIS
Guadeloupe (France)
BELIZE
DOMINICA
GUATEMALA
HONDURAS
Caribbean Sea
Martinique (France)
ST. LUCIA
ST. VINCENT AND THE GRENADINES
EL SALVADOR
BARBADOS
NICARAGUA
GRENADA
TRINIDAD AND TOBAGO
COSTA RICA
PACIFIC OCEAN
PANAMA
VENEZUELA
GUYANA
COLOMBIA
0
600 mi
0
1000 km
ECUADOR
BRAZIL

ANTIGUA AND BARBUDA

State of Antigua and Barbuda

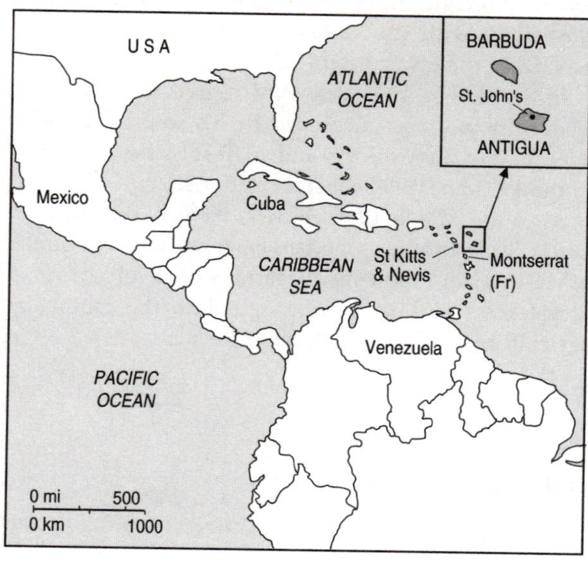

Capital: St John's

Social and economic data

Area: 440 sq km/170 sq miles
Population: 65,000*
Pop. density per sq km/sq mi: 148/382*
Urban population: 47%**
Literacy rate: 88%**
GDP: $453 million*; per-capita GDP: $6,970*
Government defense spending (% of GDP): 0.8%*
Currency: Eastern Caribbean dollar
Economy type: middle income
Labor force in agriculture: N/A
* 1995.
** 1992.

Head of state

Queen Elizabeth II, represented by Governor General Sir James Carlisle since 1993

Head of government

Prime Minister Lester Bird, since 1993

Ethnic composition

The population is almost entirely of African descent.

Religions

Christianity is the dominant religion, the majority of the population, about 60,000, being Anglican.

Political features

State type: liberal democratic
Date of state formation: 1981
Political structure: unitary
Executive: parliamentary
Assembly: two-chamber
Party structure: two-party
Human rights rating: N/A
International affiliations: ACP, ACS, CARICOM, CW, IBRD, IMF, IWC, NAM (observer), OAS, OECS, UN, WTO

Local and regional government

The two islands of Antigua and Barbuda, which are about 50 kilometres apart, are divided into seven parishes for administrative purposes. Barbuda, the smaller of the two islands (161 sq km/62 sq miles), has a considerable degree of internal autonomy.

Political system

Antigua and Barbuda constitute an independent sovereign nation within the Commonwealth, retaining the British monarch as head of state. The constitution dates from independence, in 1981. The governor general represents Queen Elizabeth of the United Kingdom and is appointed on the advice of the Antiguan prime minister in office at the time of the appointment.

The executive is parliamentary and operates in a similar fashion to that in the United Kingdom, the prime minister being chosen, normally after a general election, by the governor general as the person most likely to have the support of the assembly. Once appointed, the prime minister chooses the cabinet and all are responsible to the assembly. The leader of the party with the second largest seat holding in the House of Representatives is automatically the official leader of the opposition.

The assembly, or parliament, consists of two chambers, the 17-member Senate and the 17-member House of Representatives. Senators are appointed for a five-year term by the governor general, 11 on the advice of the prime minister, four on the advice of the leader of the opposition, one at their own discretion, and one on the advice of the Barbuda Council, representing the island of Barbuda. Members of the House of Representatives are elected by universal adult suffrage, through a simple plurality voting system, for a similar term.

Political parties

There are some seven active political parties, the three most significant being the Antigua Labor Partry (ALP), the United Progressive Party (UPP), and the Barbuda People's Movement (BPM).

The ALP was formed in 1968 and has a moderate, center-left orientation.

The UPP before 1992 was called the United National Democratic Party (UNDP), which was itself the result of a merger between two smaller parties, the United People's Movement (UPM), founded in 1982, and the National Democratic Party (NDP), which had been established only the year before. The UPP has a centrist orientation.

The BPM is a left-of-center separatist grouping based in Barbuda.

Political leaders since 1970

1981–93 Vere C Bird (ALP), 1993– Lester Bird (ALP)

Latest elections

In the March 1999 general election Lester Bird and the ALP had another victory, winning 12 of the 17 seats in the House of Representatives. The UPP won four seats and the BPM, one. The ALP secured 53% of the vote and the UPP 44%.

Political history

Antigua was visited by Christopher Columbus (1451–1506) in 1493 and colonized by the British in the 17th century. The neighboring island of Barbuda was annexed in 1860. Between 1860 and 1959 it was administered by Britain within a federal system known as the Leeward Islands and in 1967 given the status of associated state and full internal independence, with Britain retaining responsibility for defense and foreign affairs. What had been the Legislative Council became the House of Representatives, the post of administrator was restyled governor and the chief minister became premier.

The ALP had held power since 1946 and in the first general election as an associated state. In 1971, its main opposition, the Progressive Labor Movement (PLM), won a decisive victory, its leader, George Walter, replacing Vere Bird (b. 1910), leader of the ALP, as premier. The PLM fought the next election, in 1976, on a call for early independence whereas the ALP urged caution until a firm economic foundation had been laid. The electorate preferred the more gradualist approach and the ALP won.

Two years later, in 1978, the government declared itself satisfied that the country was now ready for full independence but opposition from the inhabitants of the island of Barbuda delayed the start of constitutional talks. The territory eventually became independent, as the State of Antigua and Barbuda, on 1 November 1981.

Since independence the ALP government has followed a foreign policy of nonalignment, but retained close links with the United States, whom it actively assisted in the invasion of Grenada in 1983.

In September 1993 Vere Bird retired from the ALP leadership and was succeeded by his son, Lester, who later led the party to fifth and sixth successive victories in the 1994 and 1999 general elections.

After the March 1999 election victory, Vera Bird Jr, Lester Bird's brother, who had been barred from public office in 1990 following allegations of involvement in illegal arms dealing, was brought into the cabinet as agriculture, lands, and fisheries minister.

BAHAMAS

The Commonwealth of the Bahamas

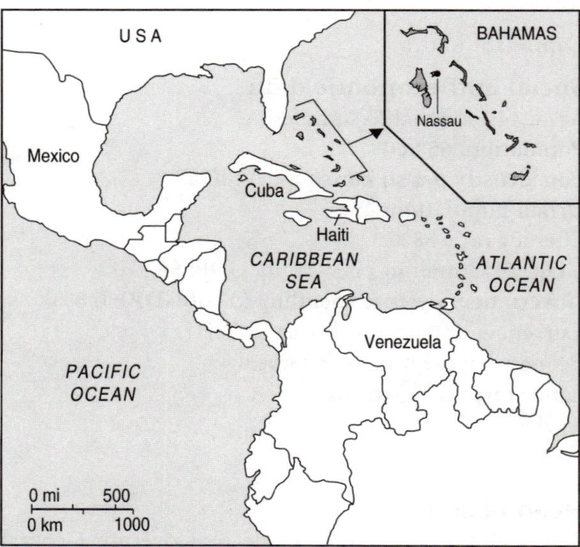

Capital: Nassau (on New Providence)

Social and economic data

Area: 13,940 sq km/5,382 sq miles
Population: 284,000*
Pop. density per sq km/sq mi: 20/53*
Urban population: 75%**
Literacy rate: 89%**
GDP: $3,300 million*; per-capita GDP: $11,620*
Government defense spending (% of GDP): 0.6%*
Currency: Bahamian dollar

Economy type: high income
Labor force in agriculture: 5%**
Unemployment rate: 13.3%*
* 1995.
** 1992.

Head of state
Queen Elizabeth II, represented by Governor General Orville Turnquest since 1994

Head of government
Prime Minister Hubert Ingraham, since 1992

Ethnic composition
About 85% of the population is black, of African origin, and 15% of European ancestry, mostly British, American, and Canadian.

Religions
Most people are Christian. There are about 50,000 Baptists, 40,000 Roman Catholics, 38,000 Anglicans, 12,000 Methodists, and 10,000 Seventh Day Adventists.

Political features
State type: liberal democratic
Date of state formation: 1973
Political structure: unitary
Executive: parliamentary
Assembly: two-chamber
Party structure: two-party
Human rights rating: N/A
International affiliations: ACP, ACS, CARICOM, CDB, CW, IBRD, IMF, NAM, OAS, UN

Local and regional government
Local administration is based on 18 natural island groupings. The islands of New Providence, where the national capital is located, and Grand Bahama have elected councils. The other 16 have district commissioners appointed by the central government.

Political system
Bahamas is an independent sovereign nation within the Commonwealth, accepting the British monarch as head of state and an appointed, resident governor general as her representative. The constitution, which came into effect at independence in 1973, provides for a two-chamber assembly consisting of a Senate and House of Assembly. The governor general appoints a prime minister and cabinet drawn from and responsible to the assembly. The leader of the second largest party in the House of Assembly is the official leader of the opposition.

The Senate has 16 members appointed by the governor general, nine on the advice of the prime minister, four on the advice of the leader of the opposition, and three after consultation with the prime minister. The House of Assembly has 40 members, elected by universal adult suffrage through a simple plurality voting system. The assembly has a maximum life of five years and is subject to dissolution within that period.

Political parties
There are four active political parties, but a two-party system operates through two major groupings: the Progressive Liberal Party (PLP) and the Free National Movement (FNM).

The PLP is a centrist party and was founded in 1953. It was in power from independence, in 1973 to 1992. The FNM was formed in 1972 by a coming together of the United Bahamian Party (UBP) and PLP dissidents. Its orientation is center-left.

Political leaders since 1970
1968–92 Sir Lynden Oscar Pindling (PLP), 1992– Hubert Ingraham (FNM)

Latest elections
In the March 1997 general election the FNM had a landslide victory, winning 34 of the House of Assembly seats. The PLP won the other six seats.

Political history
The islands were first visited in 1492 by Christopher Columbus (1451–1506), when inhabited by Arawak Indians. The Bahamas became a British colony in 1783 and were given internal self-government in 1964. The first elections for a National Assembly on a full adult voting register were held in 1967. The PLP, drawing its support mainly from voters of African origin, won the same number of seats as the European-dominated UBP and Sir Lynden Pindling (b. 1930), the PLP leader, by drawing support from outside his own party, became prime minister. In the 1968 elections the PLP scored a resounding victory and this success was repeated in 1972, enabling Pindling to lead his country into full independence, within the Commonwealth, in 1973. A tourist-based economy was subsequently developed, with, today, 70% of GDP contributed by this activity. Ninety percent of the visitors are from the United States.

With the opposition parties in some disarray, Pindling increased his majority in 1977 but by 1982 the FNM had regrouped and become more convincing opponents. Despite this, and despite allegations of government complicity in drug trafficking, the PLP was again successful at the 1982 general election and Pindling's leadership was unanimously endorsed at a party convention in 1984. The 1987 general election, fought again against a background of alleged drug trafficking, was similarly won by the PLP, but with a reduced majority.

The August 1992 general election saw a massive swing towards the FNM and its leader, Hubert Ingraham, ended Pindling's 25 years of power. He won a second term in March 1997.

BARBADOS

Capital: Bridgetown

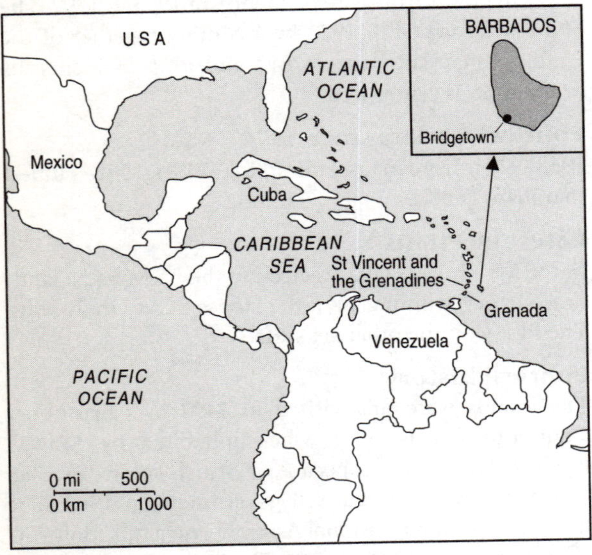

Social and economic data

Area: 430 sq km/166 sq miles
Population: 261,000 million*
Pop. density per sq km/sq mi: 607/1,572*
Urban population: 46%**
Literacy rate: 99%**
GDP: 1,750 million*; per-capita GDP: $6,705*
Government defense spending (% of GDP): 0.7%*
Currency: Barbados dollar
Economy type: middle income
Labor force in agriculture: 8%**
Unemployment rate: 19.7%
* 1995.
** 1992.

Head of state

Queen Elizabeth II, represented by Governor General Sir Christopher Husbands since 1996

Head of government

Prime Minister Owen Arthur, since 1994

Ethnic composition

About 80% of the population is of African descent, about 16% of mixed race, and about 4% of European origin, mostly British. English is the official language.

Religions

There are about 150,000 Anglicans, about 24,000 Roman Catholics, and significant numbers of other Christian faiths.

Political features

State type: liberal democratic
Date of state formation: 1966
Political structure: unitary
Executive: parliamentary
Assembly: two-chamber
Party structure: two-party
Human rights rating: N/A
International affiliations: ACP, ACS, CARICOM, CW, IBRD, IMF, NAM, OAS, SELA, UN, WTO

Local and regional government

Elected local government bodies were abolished in 1969 and replaced by 11 parishes, each administered by the central government.

Political system

The country is a constitutional monarchy, with a resident governor general representing the United Kingdom monarch. The constitution dates from independence in 1966 and provides for a system of parliamentary government on the British model, with a prime minister and cabinet drawn from and responsible to the assembly.

This consists of two chambers, the Senate and the House of Assembly. The Senate has 21 members appointed by the governor general, 12 on the advice of the prime minister, two on the advice of the leader of the opposition, and the rest on the basis of wider consultations. The House of Assembly has 28 members elected by universal adult suffrage, through a simple plurality voting system. The assembly has a maximum life of five years and is subject to dissolution within this period.

The governor general appoints the prime minister on the basis of likely support in the House of Assembly. He or she also appoints the leader of the party with the second largest number of seats in the House as the official leader of the opposition.

Political parties
There are five active political parties, the most significant being the Barbados Labor Party (BLP), the Democratic Labor Party (DLP), and the National Democratic Party (NDP). The BLP was founded in 1938 and has a moderate, left-of-center, social-democratic orientation. The DLP was formed in 1955, mainly from BLP dissidents, and has a roughly similar political stance. The NDP was formed in 1989 after a split from the DLP.

Political leaders since 1970
1966–76 Errol Barrow (DLP), 1976–85 'Tom' Adams (BLP), 1985–86 Bernard St John (BLP), 1986–87 Errol Barrow (DLP), 1987–94 Erskine Lloyd Sandiford (DLP), 1994– Owen Arthur (BLP)

Latest elections
In the January 1999 general election the ruling BLP increased its share of the vote by 17% (over September 1994) to 65% to secure a landslide victory, winning 26 House of Assembly seats. The other two seats were won by the DLP, with 35% of the vote.

Political history
Barbados became a British colony in 1627 and remained so, being famous for its sugar production, until it achieved full independence, within the Commonwealth, in November 1966. After riots in the country in 1937, moves towards a more independent political system began in the 1950s. Universal adult suffrage was introduced in 1951, with the BLP winning the first general election. Ministerial government was established in 1954 and the BLP leader, Sir Grantley Adams (1898–1971), became the first prime minister. In 1955 the DLP was formed by party activists disenchanted with the BLP. Six years later full internal self-government was achieved and in the general election in December 1961 the DLP was victorious under its leader, Errol Barrow (1920–87). When Barbados attained full independence in 1966 Barrow became the new nation's first prime minister.

The DLP was re-elected in 1971 but in the 1976 general election the BLP, led now by Sir Grantley Adams' son 'Tom', ended Barrow's 15 years of power. Both parties were committed to maintaining a free enterprise system, with tourism and alignment with the United States being encouraged. However, the DLP government established diplomatic relations with Cuba in 1972 and the BLP administration supported the US invasion of Grenada in 1983. In 1981 the BLP was re-elected but Adams died suddenly in 1985 and was succeeded by his deputy, Bernard St John, a former BLP leader. In the 1986 general election the DLP, led by Barrow, was returned to power, winning 24 of the 27 seats in the House of Assembly. Errol Barrow died in 1987 and was succeeded by Erskine Lloyd Sandiford (b. 1937).

Dame Nita Barrow, sister of Errol Barrow, became governor general in 1990 and in the following year the DLP was re-elected, but with a reduced majority. In June 1994 Sandiford lost a confidence vote and sought a dissolution of the assembly. He was replaced as DLP leader by David Thompson. In the September 1994 elections the BLP, under Owen Arthur, had a resounding victory, winning 19 of the 28 seats.

Following five years of unbroken economic growth, the BLP was re-elected for a second term, in the January 1999 general election, with an increased majority.

BELIZE

Capital: Belmopan

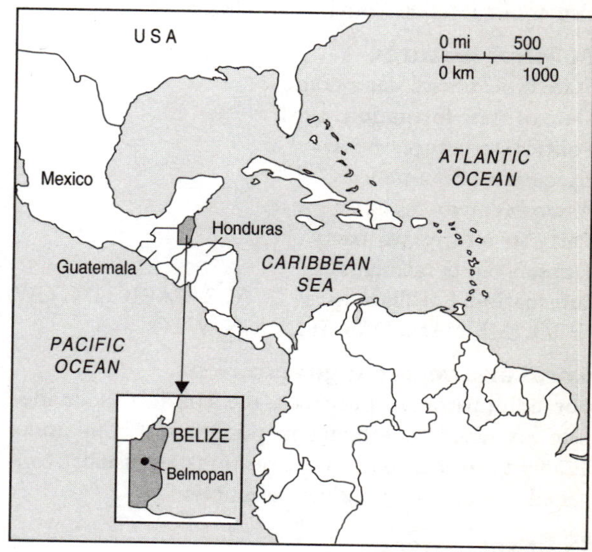

Social and economic data
Area: 22,970 sq km/8,869 sq miles
Population: 211,000*
Pop. density per sq km/sq mi: 9/24**
Urban population: 51%**
Literacy rate: 91%**
GDP: $570 million*; per-capita GDP: $2,700*
Government defense spending (% of GDP): 2.6%*

Currency: Belizean dollar
Economy type: middle income
Labor force in agriculture: 30%*
Unemployment rate: 11.1%
* 1995.
** 1992.

Head of state

Queen Elizabeth II, represented by Governor General Dr Norbert Colville Young since 1993

Head of government

Prime Minister Said Musa, since 1998

Ethnic composition

There is a wide mix of races, comprising Creoles, mestizos, Caribs, East Indians, and Europeans, including Spanish, British, and Canadian Mennonites. The 1991 census showed that the Spanish-speaking population, boosted by economic immigrants, outnumbered the native black Creoles for the first time.

Religions

Christianity is the chief religion, about 64% of the population being Anglicans and Methodists. There are also about 100,000 Roman Catholics.

Political features

State type: liberal democratic
Date of state formation: 1981
Political structure: unitary
Executive: parliamentary
Assembly: two-chamber
Party structure: two-party
Human rights rating: N/A
International affiliations: ACP, ACS, CARICOM, CW, IBRD, IMF, NAM, OAS, SELA, UN, WTO

Local and regional government

For administrative purposes, the country is divided into six districts, ranging in population from under 12,000 to over 50,000. Local elections are usually contested as strongly as national elections.

Political system

Belize is a constitutional monarchy, with a resident governor general representing the United Kingdom monarch. The constitution dates from independence in September 1981 and provides for parliamentary government on the British model, with a prime minister and cabinet drawn from the assembly and responsible to it.

The two-chamber National Assembly consists of the Senate and the House of Representatives. The Senate has eight members appointed by the governor general for a five-year term, five on the advice of the prime minister, two on the advice of the leader of the opposition, and one after wider consultations. The House of Representatives has 29 members elected by universal adult suffrage, through a simple plurality voting system. The governor general appoints the prime minister on the basis of majority support in the House of Representatives and the leader of the party with the next largest number of seats as the official leader of the opposition.

Political parties

The three active political parties are the People's United Party (PUP), the United Democratic Party (UDP), and the National Alliance for Belizean Rights (NABR).

The PUP was founded in 1950 by a small group, believing strongly in the need for national independence and social justice, who called themselves the People's Committee. The group soon split up but one of the founders, George Price, remained to create the PUP. Its orientation is left-of-center.

The UDP was formed in 1974 by the merger of three groups, the People's Development Movement, the Liberal Party, and the National Independence Party. It is moderately conservative and is held together more by its opposition to the PUP than by a coherent ideology. The NABR was formed in 1992 by UDP members opposed to a compromise solution to a territorial dispute with Guatemala.

Political leaders since 1970

1965–84 George Price (PUP), 1984–89 Manuel Esquivel (UDP), 1989–93 George Price (PUP), 1993–98 Manuel Esquivel (UDP), 1998– Said Musa (PUP)

Latest elections

In the August 1998 general election the PUP, with 59% of the vote, won 26 seats, while the UDP, with 39% of the vote, won three seats.

Political history

In ancient times Belize was one of the sites of the Mayan Indian civilization. Colonized as early as the 17th century, British Honduras, as it was then called, was not recognized as a British colony until 1862. A 1954 constitution provided for partial internal self-government, with Britain retaining responsibility for defense, external affairs, and internal security. The first general election under the new constitution was won by the PUP, led by George Price (b. 1919). PUP won all the subsequent elections until 1984. In 1964 full internal self-government was granted and Price became prime minister, working with a two-chamber assembly. In 1970 the nation's capital was moved from Belize City to the new town of Belmopan and in 1973 the whole country became known as Belize. Between the 1950s and 1980s the economy relied heavily on sugar exports, but has subsequently diversified into citrus exports and tourism.

The frontier with Guatemala had long been a source of dispute and in 1975 British troops were sent to defend it. Two years later negotiations with Guatemala began but no final conclusion was reached. In 1980 the United Nations called for full independence for Belize but a constitutional conference, which was called in 1981, broke up because of a dispute over Guatemala's demand for territory rather than just access to the Caribbean. Eventually, in September 1981, full independence was achieved and George Price became the first prime minister of the new nation. Britain agreed to leave troops to protect the frontier and to assist in the training of Belizean forces.

In 1984 PUP's 30 years of uninterrupted rule ended and the new prime minister was the UDP leader, Manuel Esquivel, but in 1989 PUP returned with a working majority. Four years later Esquivel unexpectedly returned to power, the UDP winning 16 of the House of Representatives' seats.

In 1984 Britain reaffirmed its undertaking to protect Belize's frontier and, despite renewed talks with Guatemala in 1985, no permanent solution to the dispute between the two countries was found until 1991, when diplomatic relations between the two countries were restored after Guatemala at last recognized Belize's sovereignty. By the end of 1993 Britain felt the situation sufficiently secure to announce that it would no longer have responsibility for the country's defense.

The August 1998 general election was won by the PUP, under the leadership of Said Musa, who became prime minister.

COSTA RICA

Republic of Costa Rica
República de Costa Rica

Capital: San José

Social and economic data

Area: 51,100 sq km/19,730 sq miles
Population: 3,071,000*
Pop. density per sq km/sq mi: 60/156*

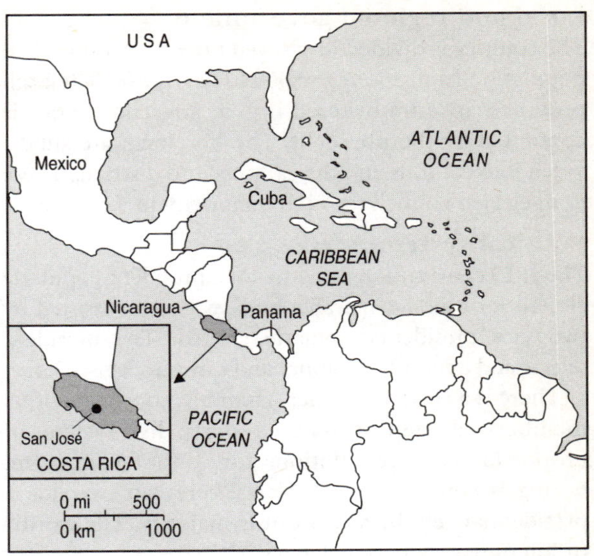

Urban population: 48%**
Literacy rate: 88% **
GDP: $8,900 million*; per-capita GDP: $2,900*
Government defense spending (% of GDP): 0.3%*
Currency: colon
Economy type: middle income
Labor force in agriculture: 25%**
Unemployment rate: 5.2%*
* 1995.
** 1992.

Head of state and head of government

President Miguel Angel Rodríguez, since 1998

Ethnic composition

About 97% of the population is of European descent, mostly Spanish, and about 2% is of African origin.

Religions

Roman Catholicism is the official religion and about 90% of the population practises that faith, although all beliefs are tolerated.

Political features

State type: liberal democratic
Date of state formation: 1821
Political structure: unitary
Executive: limited presidential
Assembly: one-chamber
Party structure: two-party
Human rights rating: 90%
International affiliations: ACS, AG (observer), ALADI (observer), BCIE, CACM, IAEA, IBRD, IMF, IWC, NAM (observer), OAS, SELA, UN, WTO

Local and regional government

The country is divided into seven provinces, ranging in population from about 150,000 to nearly 900,000. Each province is administered by a governor who is appointed by the president. The provinces are subdivided into cantons and the cantons into districts. There is an elected council for each major city in a canton.

Political system

The 1949 constitution provides for a president popularly elected for a non-renewable four-year term, assisted by two vice presidents similarly elected. The president selects and appoints a cabinet and can veto legislation.

There is a single-chamber Assembly, consisting of 57 members, elected through a party list system of proportional representation, for a four-year term. Voting is compulsory. The legislature can override a presidential veto by a two-thirds majority. The constitution outlaws a national army.

Political parties

Out of more than 20 political parties, two have dominated the political scene for many years. They are the National Liberation Party (PLN) and what is now called the Christian Socialist Unity Party (PUSC).

The PLN began to form in 1948 and was officially founded in 1951. It is a left-of-center, social democratic party, affiliated to the Socialist International.

In its present form, the PUSC is a development from the Unity Party which was formed in 1978 as a coalition of four parties to oppose the PLN. It became the United Coalition (CU) and then, with other similarly orientated centrist groupings, the PUSC, in 1984.

Political leaders since 1970

1970–74 José Figueres Ferrer (PLN), 1974–78 Daniel Oduber Quiros (PLN), 1978–82 Rodrigo Carazo (CU), 1982–86 Luis Alberto Monge Alvárez (PLN), 1986–90 Oscar Arias Sánchez (PLN), 1990–94 Rafael Angel Calderon (PUSC), 1994–98 José Maria Figueres (PLN), 1998– Miguel Angel Rodríguez (PUSC)

Latest elections

In the February 1998 presidential elections Miguel Angel Rodríguez (PUSC) won a narrow victory over his PLN opponent, Jose Miguel Corrales, securing 47% of the vote to 44%. Turnout, at 71%, was at a postwar low.

In the simultaneous assembly elections the PUSC won 27 seats, the PLN 23, and independents 7.

Political history

Costa Rica, formerly inhabited by Guaymi Indians, was first colonized by Spain in the early 16th century and became an independent nation, within the Central American Federation, in 1821. It seceded from the Federation in 1838. European immigrants were attracted to the country to run and work small farms. Apart from a period of military dictatorship between 1870 and 1882, and a brief civil war in 1948 because of a disputed presidential election, it has been one of the most democratically governed states in Latin America.

Present-day Costa Rica dates from the civil war of 1948 when the army, under José Figueres, restored order and adopted a new constitution. Figueres abolished the army, relying on the civil guard for the country's future defense, and then surrendered power to a civilian government. He soon returned, however, to become president the following year. He cofounded the PLN, nationalized the banks, and introduced a comprehensive social security system. He was reelected in 1953.

There followed 16 years of mostly conservative rule, when some of the PLN policies were reversed. Then, in 1974, Daniel Oduber won the presidency for the PLN. He returned to socialist policies, extending the welfare state and establishing friendly relations with communist states. Communist and left-wing political parties were legalized.

In 1978 Rodrigo Carazo, leader of the conservative Unity Coalition (CU), became president. His presidency was marked by a disastrous collapse of the economy and allegations of involvement in illegal arms trafficking between Cuba and El Salvador.

The conservative administration was ended in 1982 when Luis Alberto Monge Alvárez, a former trade union official and cofounder, with Figueres, of the PLN, won a convincing victory in the presidential election. To reverse the damage done by the Carazo government, he introduced a 100-day emergency economic program. He also maintained a policy of strict neutrality.

His government came under increasing pressure from the United States to abandon its neutral stance and condemn the left-wing Sandinista regime in Nicaragua. It was also urged to re-establish a national army. The pressures were resisted and in 1983 Monge reaffirmed his country's neutrality. However, relations with Nicaragua deteriorated after border clashes between Sandinista forces and the Costa Rica civil guard, so that, in 1985, Monge reluctantly agreed to create an anti-guerrilla guard, trained by the United States.

This increased doubts about Costa Rica's declared policy of neutrality but in 1986 the United Kingdom university-educated Oscar Arias Sánchez (b. 1940), leader of the PLN, won the presidential election on a neutralist platform, defeating the pro-US candidate, Rafael Angel Calderon. This contributed to the start of direct talks between the Nicaraguan government and the Contra rebels the following year.

A deteriorating economy produced public disenchantment, and in 1990 the PLN lost both the presidential and assembly elections, but, with economic growth resuming, it returned in February 1994 and José Maria Figueres, the 39-year-old son of the former president, José Figueres Ferrer, assumed power. In February 1998 the PUSC returned to power, Miguel Angel Rodríguez (the defeated candidate in 1994) being elected president, but without an overall majority in the Assembly. Rodríguez, who was sworn in as president in May 1998, vowed to encourage foreign inward investment, promote privatization, fight inflation, and achieve annual GDP growth of 6%.

CUBA

The Republic of Cuba
La República de Cuba

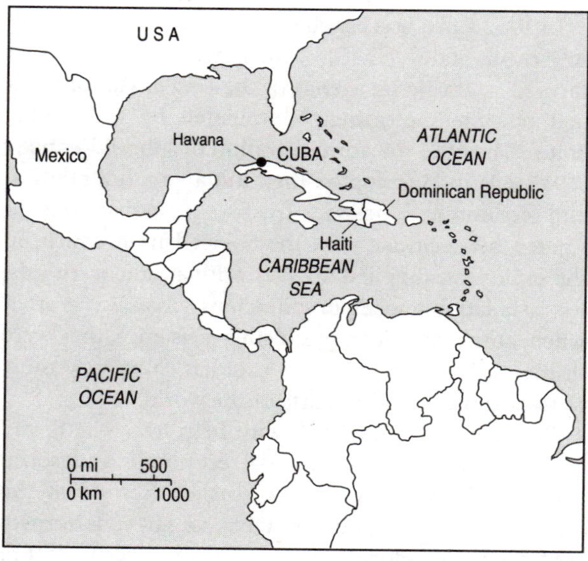

Capital: Havana

Social and economic data

Area: 110,860 sq km/42,803 sq miles
Population: 10,960,000*
Pop. density per sq km/sq mi: 99/256*
Urban population: 75%**
Literacy rate: 98%**
GDP: $13,500 million*; per-capita GDP: $1,230*
Government defense spending (% of GDP): 2.8%*
Currency: Cuban peso
Economy type: middle income
Labor force in agriculture: 25%**
* 1995.
** 1992.

Head of state and head of government

Dr Fidel Castro Ruz, since 1976

Ethnic composition

The majority of the population is of mixed Spanish and African or Spanish and Indian origin. About a third are European and a tenth African.

Religions

All religions are permitted and there is no established church. Around 40% of the population is Roman Catholic.

Political features

State type: communist
Date of state formation: 1899
Political structure: unitary
Executive: communist
Assembly: one-chamber
Party structure: one-party
Human rights rating: 30%
International affiliations: ACS, ALADI, IAEA, NAM, OAS (suspended 1962), SELA, UN, WTO

Local and regional government

The country is divided into 14 provinces varying in population from just under 60,000 to nearly 2 million. Within the provinces are 169 municipalities, each with an elected assembly, which, in turn, elects an executive committee.

Political system

The 1976 constitution, amended in 1992, created a socialist state with the National Assembly of People's Power as its supreme organ. It consists of 601 deputies directly elected (since 1993) by universal adult suffrage, through a majoritarian voting system, for a five-year term. The National Assembly, which holds twice-yearly sessions, elects 31 of its members to form the Council of State. It also elects the head of state who is president of the Council, head of government, and first secretary and chairperson of the Political Bureau of the only authorized party, the Communist Party of Cuba (PCC). Fidel

Castro thus occupies all the key positions within the state and the party, where ultimate political power lies. His brother, Raúl Castro, is defense minister and first vice president. The minimum voting age is 16 years and minimum age for assembly deputies, 18 years.

Political parties

The origins of the PCC date back to 1925 when a socialist party was formed by a group of leftwing activists. In 1943 it became known as the People's Socialist Party (PSP). When Castro seized power in 1959 some of the old guard of the PSP found his methods and ideological leanings too anarchic for their comfort and were reluctant to give him their full support. Meanwhile Castro was leading his own movement and in 1961 the misgivings within the PSP were sufficiently allayed to allow it to merge, in 1961, with Castro's movement and other socialist groups, into the Integrated Revolutionary Organization (ORI). Two years later this became the United Party of the Socialist Revolution (PURS) and finally, in 1965, the Communist Party of Cuba (PCC).

It is a Marxist-Leninist party organized on top-down, Leninist 'democratic centralist' lines, with a 150-member Central Committee, a 24-member Political Bureau, Secretariat, and five Commissions. It had around 700,000 members in 1995.

Political leaders since 1970

1959– Fidel Castro Ruz (PCC)

Latest elections

The second direct elections to the National Assembly were held in January 1998. All the 601 candidates elected were PCC nominees, and all obtained the necessary 50% of the vote. Turnout was 98.4%.

Political history

After being under Spanish rule from the 16th century, Cuba was ceded to the United States in 1898, at the end of the Spanish—American War. This followed anti-colonial uprisings between 1868 and 1878 and 1895 and 1898. It became independent in 1902 but the United States retained its naval bases and a right to intervene in internal affairs until 1934. In 1933 an army sergeant, Fulgencio Batista (1901–73) seized and held on to power until 1944, when he retired. In 1952, however, he seized power again in a bloodless coup and began another period of rule which many of his fellow countrypeople found oppressive.

In the following year a young lawyer and son of a sugar planter, Dr Fidel Castro Ruz (b. 1927), tried to overthrow him but was defeated. He went into exile to prepare for another coup, returning in 1956 but was again unsuccessful. He fled to the hills, with Argentine-born Dr Ernesto ('Che') Guevara (1928–67) and ten other fighters, to form a guerrilla force to fight the increasingly corrupt Batista regime.

In 1959 Castro's forces were finally successful and Batista was deposed, to great popular acclaim, and forced into exile in the Dominican Republic. The 1940 constitution was immediately suspended and replaced by a 'Fundamental Law', with all power vested in a Council of Ministers led by Castro as prime minister and his brother, Raúl, as his deputy. Che Guevara, who had assisted in the overthrow of Batista, was, reputedly, made Castro's 'number three'.

The following year all US businesses in Cuba were appropriated without compensation, provoking the United States into breaking off diplomatic relations. In 1961 it went further, sponsoring, in April, a full-scale but abortive invasion, the 'Bay of Pigs' episode. In December of the same year Castro announced that Cuba was now a communist state and would follow a Marxist-Leninist program of economic development, entailing radical land reform, the nationalization of industries, and investment in education and health-care.

In 1962 Cuba was expelled from the Organization of American States (OAS), which had originally been formed as a regional agency of the United Nations, but had become increasingly dominated by the United States. The 1961–63 administration of John F Kennedy (1917–63) in Washington then initiated a full political and economic blockade. Castro's response was to tighten his relations with the Soviet Union which, in the same year, supplied missiles, with atomic warheads, for installation on Cuban soil. A tense crisis was averted when, at the American president's insistence, they were dismantled. In 1965 Che Guevara left Cuba, ostensibly to fight causes in other parts of the world.

Between 1965 and 1972, with help from the Soviet Union, Cuba made substantial economic and social progress. However, many Cubans, concerned at the restrictions in their political rights, sought exile abroad, particularly in Florida. In 1972 Cuba became a full member of the Council for Mutual Economic Assistance (CMEA), a Moscow-based organization linking communist states. Cuba was to export sugar to the communist states and receive in return foodstuffs, machinery, and oil, and by the 1980s 85% of its trade was with CMEA members. In 1976 a referendum approved a new socialist constitution and Fidel Castro and his brother were elected president and vice president. The following five years saw Cuba playing an increasingly assertive role in world affairs, particularly in Africa, usually to the disquiet of the United States.

In 1981, after being re-elected for another term, Castro offered to discuss foreign policy with the US administration but the offer was not accepted. Castro's support for Argentina, against Britain, during the 1982 Falklands conflict, cooled relations with the United States but improved them with other Latin American countries. The US invasion of Grenada in 1983 lowered the diplomatic temperature again. From the mid-1980s, as the Soviet Union, under the reformist leadership of Mikhail Gorbachev, abandoned the 'Brezhnev doctrine' of suppporting Third World revolutions, Cuba adopted a more conciliatory posture in its international relations, including those with the United States. In 1988 it signed a peace treaty with South Africa, providing for the withdrawal of Cuban forces from Angola. As a further indication of Cuba's return to the fold of international politics, in September 1988 it established formal relations with the European Community.

Despite the demise of the Soviet Union in 1991 and the almost universal abandonment of communism, Castro maintained his commitment to the ideology. However, by the early 1990s there were signs of some liberalizing of his regime, with the holding of direct municipal and national elections for the first time in 1992–93 and moves towards a more market-orientated economy. This was forced by a worsening economic crisis, as the country, faced with the collapse of the CMEA, tried to find new markets and sources of foreign exchange. GDP fell by 75% between 1989 and 1994 and there were serious fuel shortages and food rationing, encouraging the flight of thousands more Cubans to Florida. A US embargo on trade with Cuba remained in force, but the prospects of Cuba rejoining the OAS and joining CARICOM began to improve as a result of its political and economic reforms. In September 1995 Cuba's parliament passed a law permitting foreign ownership in nearly all parts of the economy. In January 1998 Pope John Paul II paid an unprecedented visit and in the following month Castro was confirmed as president for a further five-year term. By April 1998, full diplomatic relations had been re-established with all other Caribbean countries – and in November 1998 Cuba became a full member of the ALADI regional grouping. In January 1999 there was a further slight relaxation of US restrictions on contacts with Cuba, including the introduction of a direct postal service and increased charter passenger flights to the US.

DOMINICA

Commonwealth of Dominica

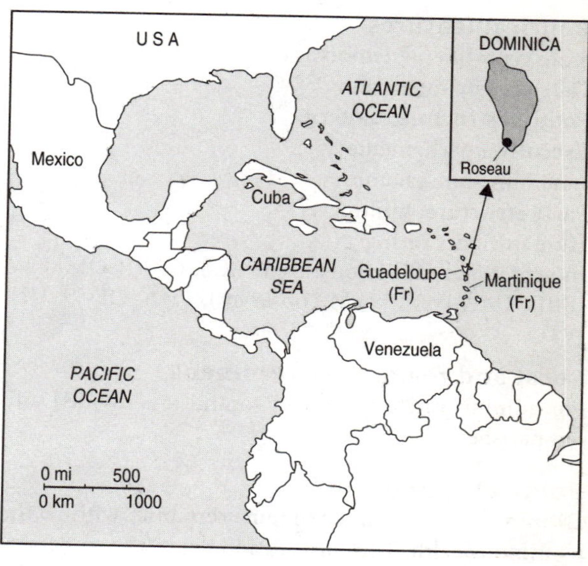

Capital: Roseau

Social and economic data

Area: 750 sq km/290 sq miles
Population: 72,000 *
Pop. density per sq km/sq mi: 96/248*
Urban population: 57%**
Literacy rate: 94% **
GDP: $220 million*; per-capita GDP: $3,060*
Government defense spending (% of GDP): 0%***
Currency: East Caribbean dollar
Economy type: middle income
Labor force in agriculture: 31%**

* 1995.
** 1992.
*** The Defense Force was disbanded in the 1980s after its involvement in attempted coups against the DFP administration.

Head of state

President Vernon Shaw, since 1998

Head of government

Prime Minister Edison James, since 1995

Ethnic composition

Most of the inhabitants are descended from African slaves who were brought to the island as plantation laborers in the 17th and 18th centuries. A small number of the original people of Dominica, the Arawaks, remain.

Religions

The vast majority of the population is Christian, about 80% Roman Catholic.

Political features

State type: liberal democratic
Date of state formation: 1978
Political structure: unitary
Executive: parliamentary
Assembly: one-chamber
Party structure: multiparty
Human rights rating: N/A
International affiliations: ACP, ACS, CARICOM, CW, IBRD, IMF, IWC, NAM (observer), OAS, OECS, UN, WTO

Local and regional government

For administrative purposes Dominica is divided into ten parishes.

Political system

Dominica is an independent republic within the Commonwealth. The constitution dates from independence, in 1978, and is broadly modelled on the parliamentary system of the United Kingdom. It provides for a single-chamber, 30-member, House of Assembly. Twenty-one are representatives, elected by universal adult suffrage, through a simple plurality voting system, and nine are senators appointed by the president, who is head of state. Five of the senators are appointed on the advice of the prime minister, who is head of government, and four on the advice of the official leader of the opposition, who is the leader of the party with the second largest number of Assembly seats. The Assembly has a life of five years.

The president is elected by the Assembly for a five-year term, renewable once only, and appoints the prime minister on the basis of support in the Assembly. The prime minister chooses the cabinet and all are collectively responsible to the Assembly.

Political parties

There are three main political parties, the Dominica Freedom Party (DFP), the Labor Party of Dominica (LPD), and the Dominica United Workers' Party (DUWP).

The DFP was founded in 1970 as a center-right party, drawing its leaders from the wealthier sections of the community but also receiving support from the poorer, rural sector.

The LPD was founded in 1985 as an alliance of three parties, the Dominica Labor Party (DLP), the Dominica Liberation Movement (DLM), and the United Dominica Labor Party (UDLP). The DLP dates from 1961, when it was formed to represent the labor movement. The alliance has a left-of-center orientation.

The DUWP was formed in 1988 and also has a left-of-center orientation.

Political leaders since 1970

1961–74 Edward Le Blanc (DLP), 1974–80 Patrick John (DLP), 1980–95 Dame Mary Eugenia Charles (DFP), 1995– Edison James (DUWP)

Latest elections

In the June 1995 general election the DUWP won 11 of the 21 elected Assembly seats and the DFP and LPD, 5 each. The DFP surprisingly attracted most votes, 36%, against 34% for the DUWP and 30% for the DLP.

Political history

A British colonial possession since the 18th century, Dominica was part of the Leeward Islands federation until 1939. In 1940 it was transferred to the Windward Islands and remained attached to that group until 1960, when it was given a separate, semi-independent, status, with a chief minister and a Legislative Council. In 1961 the leader of the Dominica Labor Party (DLP), Edward Le Blanc, became chief minister and, after 13 years in office, retired, to be succeeded by Patrick John (b. 1937). The DLP held office until full independence was achieved in 1978 and its leader, John, became the first prime minister under a new constitution.

Opposition to John's increasingly authoritarian style of government soon developed and in the 1980 elections the DFP won a convincing victory on a free-enterprise policy program. Its leader, Eugenia Charles (b. 1919), a London-trained barrister, became the Caribbean's first woman prime minister, John losing his seat in the Assembly. In 1981 John was thought to be implicated in a plot to overthrow Charles' government and a state of emergency was imposed. The following year he was tried and acquitted. He was retried in 1985, found guilty, and given a 12-year prison sentence.

A regrouping of left-of-center parties resulted in the Labor Party of Dominica (LPD) becoming the main opposition to the DFP, but in the 1985 elections it was unable to prevent Eugenia Charles being re-elected. Under her leadership, Dominica developed strong links with France and the United States and in 1983 contributed a small contingent to the US-backed invasion of Grenada. In 1990 there were provisional moves to integrate with St Lucia, St Vincent, and Grenada into a Windward Islands federation.

In April 1994 the government declared a state of emergency, following industrial protests about its economic policies, but eventually the storm was weathered. After losing the 1995 general election to the DUWP, led by Edison James, Dame Eugenia Charles announced her retirement from politics.

DOMINICAN REPUBLIC

República Dominicana

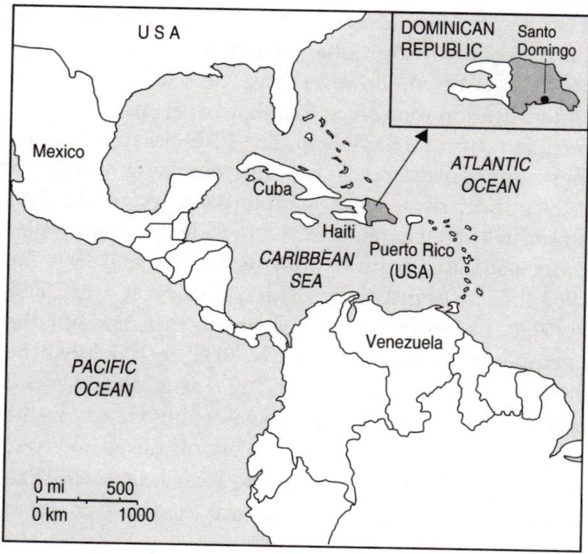

Capital: Santo Domingo

Social and economic data

Area: 48,072 sq km/18,561 sq miles
Population: 7,760,000*
Pop. density per sq km/sq mi: 161/418*
Urban population: 62%**
GDP: $11,390 million*; per-capita GDP: $1,470*
Government defense spending (% of GDP): 1.3%*
Currency: Dominian Republic peso
Economy type: middle income
Labor force in agriculture: 46%**

* 1995.
** 1992.

Head of state and head of government

President Leoned Fernández, since 1996

Ethnic composition

About 73% of the population are mulattos, of mixed European and African parentage, about 16% European, and 11% African.

Religions

Roman Catholicism is the established religion and about 90% of the population adheres to it, although there is complete freedom for other beliefs.

Political features

State type: liberal democratic
Date of state formation: 1844
Political structure: unitary
Executive: limited presidential
Assembly: two-chamber
Party structure: multiparty
Human rights rating: 78%
International affiliations: ACP, ACS, ALADI (observer), CARICOM (observer), G-11, IAEA, IBRD, IMF, NAM (guest), OAS, SELA, UN, WTO

Local and regional government

The country is divided into 30 provinces and the National District. Each province has a governor, appointed by the president. The provinces are subdivided into 115 municipalities, each with a mayor and an elected council.

Political system

Although not a federal state, the Dominican Republic has a highly devolved system of regional and local government. The 1966 constitution provides for a president, popularly elected for a four-year term by the second ballot majoritarian system, and a two-chamber Congress, of Senate and Chamber of Deputies, elected for a similar term. Elections to the Senate are by a simple plurality voting system and to the Chamber by means of a party list system of proportional representation. The Senate has 30 members and the Chamber of Deputies has 149. The president is head of government as well as head of state and chooses their own cabinet. Voting is compulsory.

Political parties

There are more than 20 active political parties, the three most significant being the Dominican Revolutionary Party (PRD), the Christian Social Reform Party (PRSC), and the Dominican Liberation Party (PLD).

The PRD was founded in Havana in 1939 by a group of anti-government exiles. It became active in the

Dominican Republic after the death of the dictator, Rafael Trujillo. It is a moderate left-of-center party and has about 400,000 members.

The PRSC was formed in 1961, after Trujillo's assassination, by the merger of several Christian, socialist, and other democratic groups. It has an independent, center-right orientation.

The PLD was formed in 1973 by Juan Bosch, who had originally founded the PRD and then abandoned it. It has a strongly nationalist, left wing orientation.

Political leaders since 1970

1966–78 Joaquín Balaguer Ricardo (PRSC), 1978–82 Silvestre Antonio Guzmán (PRD), 1982–86 Jorge Blanco (PRD), 1986–96 Joaquín Balaguer Ricardo (PRSC), 1996– Leoned Fernández (PLD)

Latest elections

The PLD candidate, Leoned Fernández, won the run-off presidential election in June 1996. He defeated José Francisco Péna of the PRD, securing 51% of the vote. In the May 1998 assembly elections the PRD secured a majority in both the Senate and Chamber of Deputies. It won 83 Chamber of Deputies and 24 Senate seats, against 49 and 4 for the PLD, and 17 and 2 for the PRSC. Turnout reached a record low of 52%. Twelve people were killed during the election campaign.

Political history

Originally inhabited by Carib and Arawak Indians, the island, then known as Hispaniola (which included Haiti), was visited by Christopher Columbus (1451–1506) in 1492 and the Spanish established in 1496, at Santo Domingo, the first European settlement in the Western hemisphere. The western third of the island, comprising Haiti, was ceded by Spain to France in 1697 and from 1795 Santo Domingo also came briefly under French rule. Between 1803 and 1821 several native republics held sway and then in 1844, after two decades of rule by Haiti, the Dominican Republic was formally established. The country was later temporarily occupied by US military forces, between 1916 and 1924. In 1930 the elected democratic government of Horacio Vázquez was overthrown in a military coup and General Rafael Trujillo Molina (1891–1961) began a long and ruthless personal dictatorship until he was assassinated in 1961.

In the following year the country's first free elections were won by Dr Juan Bosch (b. 1909), founder and leader of the leftwing party, PRD. Bosch himself had been in exile for more than 30 years. He attempted to institute agrarian and labor reforms, but within a year he too was overthrown by the military who set up their own three-person ruling junta. An attempt to re-establish Bosch in 1965 was defeated, with the help of US troops, and in 1966 Joaquín Balaguer Ricardo (b. 1907), a protégé of Trujillo, and leader of the PRSC, won the presidency. A new, more democratically orientated, constitution was adopted and Balaguer, despite his links with Trujillo, proved to be a popular leader, being re-elected in 1970 and 1974.

The 1978 election was won by the PRD candidate, Silvestre Antonio Guzmán, and the PRD was again successful in the 1982 election when Jorge Blanco, the party's leftwing nominee, became president-designate. However the sitting president, Guzmán, committed suicide before he had finished his full term, after allegations of fraud by his family. An interim president was, therefore, chosen before the start of Blanco's term in August.

Despite his leftwing credentials, Blanco steered a restrained course in foreign policy, maintaining good relations with the United States and avoiding too close an association with Cuba. The state of the economy began to worsen, however, and in 1985 the Blanco administration was forced to adopt harsh austerity measures in return for IMF help. The PRD became increasingly unpopular and it was not suprising when the PRSC, under the veteran Joaquín Balaguer, returned to power in 1986. He retained the presidency, despite allegations of fraud by his opponents, in 1990 and 1994. By 1993 the rate of inflation, which had stood at over 100% in 1990, had been brought down to just 3%, but the unemployment level was nearly 30%. In July 1996 the presidency was won by the PLD candidate, Leoned Fernández, but the PRD won a sweeping victory in the May 1998 assembly elections. This promised to make governing difficult for President Fernández, who had relied on PRSC assembly support for the passage of reform measures.

EL SALVADOR

The Republic of El Salvador
La República de El Salvador

Capital: San Salvador

Social and economic data

Area: 21,390 sq km/8,259 sq miles
Population: 5,641,000*
Pop. density per sq km/sq mi: 264/683*
Urban population: 45%**
Literacy rate: 67%**

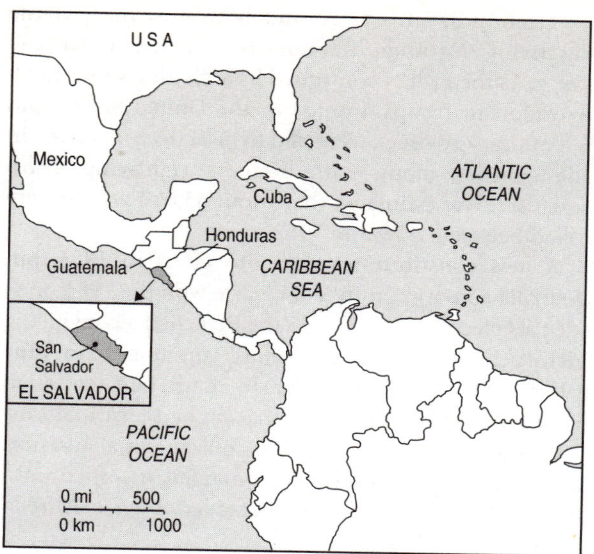

GDP: \$9,060 million*; per-capita GDP: \$1,610*
Government defense spending (% of GDP): 1.8%*
Currency: Salvadorean colon
Economy type: middle income
Labor force in agriculture: 40%**
Unemployment rate: 7.7%*
* 1995.
** 1992.

Head of state and head of government

President Francisco Guillermo Flores Pérez, since 1994

Ethnic composition

El Salvador has a largely homogeneous population. About 92% of the people are mestizos, 6% Indians, and 2% of European origin.

Religions

Roman Catholicism is the dominant religion, about 80% of the population following that faith. There are also about 200,000 Protestants.

Political features

State type: liberal democratic
Date of state formation: 1830
Political structure: unitary
Executive: limited presidential
Assembly: one-chamber
Party structure: multiparty
Human rights rating: 53%
International affiliations: ACS, ALADI (observer), BCIE, CACM, IAEA, IBRD, IMF, NAM (observer), OAS, SELA, UN, WTO

Local and regional government

The country is divided into 14 departments, ranging in population from about 140,000 to nearly 700,000. Each department is administered by a centrally appointed official. Within the departments there are municipalities, with elected mayors.

Political system

The 1983 constitution, amended in 1985, provides for a single-chamber Legislative, or National, Assembly of 84 members, elected for a three-year term. Sixty-four members are elected in multi-member constituencies and 20 by proportional representation. The president is popularly elected for a five-year term. The president is assisted by a vice president and a Council of Ministers (cabinet), whom he or she appoints. Presidential vetoes can be overridden by a two-thirds Assembly majority.

Political parties

Of the more than 20 active political parties, the most significant are the Christian Democrats (PDC), the National Republican Alliance (ARENA), the Farabundo Martí National Liberation Front (FMLN), and the National Conciliation Party (PCN).

The 150,000-member PDC was formed in 1960. It is strongly anti-imperialist and favors Latin American integration.

ARENA was founded in 1981. It has a strong rightwing orientation and is led by President Calderón Sol. The FMLN was a guerrilla group. It translated itself into a political party in 1992. It has a leftwing orientation but is reform-minded.

The PCN is another rightwing grouping which fought the 1985 elections on a joint platform with ARENA. It dates from 1961.

Political leaders since 1970

1967–72 Fidel Sánchez Hernández (PCN-military), 1972–77 Arturo Armando Molina (PCN-military), 1977–79 Carlos Humberto Romeros Mena (PCN-military), 1979–80 military junta, 1980–82 José Napoleón Duarte (PDC-military), 1982–84 Alvro Magana Borga (independent-military), 1984–89 José Napoleón Duarte (PDC), 1989–94 Alfredo Cristiani Burkard (ARENA), 1994–99 Armando Caldrón Sol (ARENA), 1999– Francisco Guillermo Flores (ARENA)

Latest elections

The March 1999 presidential election was won outright in the first round by the ARENA candidate, Francisco Flores, who attracted 52% of the vote, defeating Facundo Guardado of the FMLN, who secured 29% of the vote, and five other candidates. Turnout was below 40%.

El Salvador latest election results

Party	Seats
ARENA	28
FMLN	27
PCN	11
PDC	7
Others	11

Political history

El Salvador became a Spanish colony in 1523 and achieved independence, within the Federation of Central American States, in 1821. This federation dissolved in 1838 and it became a fully sovereign state. Since then there has been a history of frequent coups and political violence. In the 1930s a peasant uprising, led by Agustín Farabundo Martí, was put down with, reputedly, some 30,000 lives lost, and there were three more military takeovers in 1944, 1948, and 1960. Wide income differentials, with wealth and power concentrated in the hands of a relatively few families, has exacerbated social tensions.

Following another coup, in 1961, the conservative Party of National Conciliation (PCN) was established, winning all the seats in the National Assembly. The PCN stayed in power, with reports of widespread violations of human rights, until challenged, in 1979, by a socialist guerrilla movement, the Farabundo Martí National Liberation Front (FMLN). A civilian-military junta deposed the president and promised to introduce a democratic system of government with free elections. Elections were postponed, however, as the violence continued. In 1980 the Archbishop of San Salvador, Oscar Romero (1917–80), who was a well-known champion of human rights and had been nominated for the Nobel Peace Prize, was shot dead in his cathedral. The murder of three American nuns and a social worker prompted US president Jimmy Carter to suspend economic and military aid.

In December 1980 José Napoleón Duarte (1925–90), founder of the Christian Democratic Party (PDC) in 1960 and leader of the left-of-center coalition, was sworn in as president. The US administration of Ronald Reagan gave him its backing, as an anticommunist, and encouraged him to call elections in 1982. The left wing parties refused to enter the contest, which was held amid great violence, at least 40 people being killed on election day. It was eventually won by the extreme rightwing National Republican Alliance (ARENA) party. As the FMLN continued its activities, some 1,600 Salvadorean troops, trained in the United States, and US military advisers, were said to be actively involved in the conflict, along with extreme rightwing death squads. It was estimated that about 35,000 people were killed between 1979 and 1982.

A new constitution came into effect in 1983, but guerrilla activity continued. Duarte won the 1984 presidential election and in 1985 the PDC had a convincing victory in the Assembly. It was announced, in June 1988, that President Duarte had had tests in Washington that confirmed that he had terminal cancer. Despite this condition, and consequential absences for treatment, the president remained in office until June 1989, when he was succeeded by Dr Alfredo Cristiani, from ARENA.

Later that year the FMLN agreed to talk with the new president and a peace agreement was signed in December 1991, bringing to an end the 12-year-long civil war. Having transformed itself into a political party, FMLN presented a strong challenge to ARENA in the 1994 elections. These elections brought to an end a two-year-long UN Observer Mission, that had monitored the transition. FMLN finished one seat behind ARENA in its total number of seats won in the 1997 Assembly elections. Rising crime levels and widening income differentials explained ARENA's loss of support.

However, ARENA's Francisco Flores secured an easy victory in the March 1999 presidential election and succeeded Calderon Sol as president in June 1999.

GRENADA

The State of Grenada

Capital: St George's

Social and economic data

Area: 13,321 sq miles
Population: 91,000*
Pop. density per sq km/sq mi: 7*
Urban population: 63%**
Literacy rate: 98% **
GDP: $270 million*; per-capita GDP: $2,970*
Government defense spending (% of GDP): N/A
Currency: East Caribbean dollar
Economy type: middle income

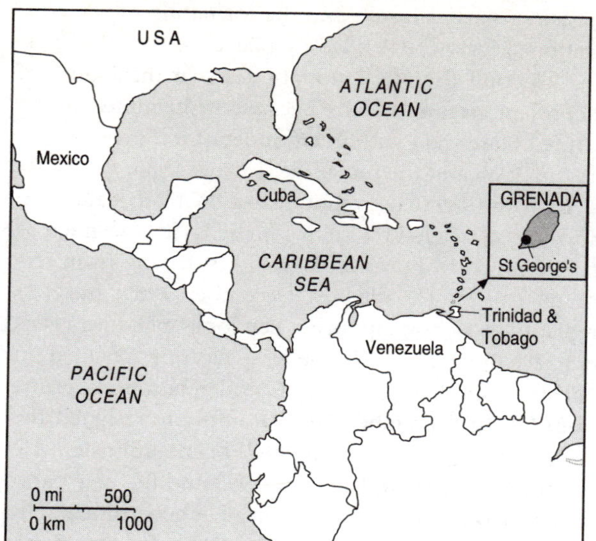

Labor force in agriculture: 25%**

* 1995.

** 1992.

Head of state
Queen Elizabeth II, represented by Governor General Sir Daniel Williams since 1996

Head of government
Prime Minister Keith Mitchell, since 1995

Ethnic composition
The majority of the population is of black African descent.

Religions
The great majority of people, 82%, are Roman Catholics.

Political features
State type: liberal democratic
Date of state formation: 1974
Political structure: unitary
Executive: parliamentary
Assembly: two-chamber
Party structure: multiparty
Human rights rating: N/A
International affiliations: ACP, ACS, CARICOM, CW, IBRD, IMF, IWC, NAM, OAS, OECS, SELA, UN, WTO

Local and regional government
The country is divided into six parishes, each administered by an appointed district commissioner. The capital of St George's is administered by the central government.

Political system
The constitution, which dates from full independence in 1974, has created a system modelled on that of the United Kingdom, with a resident governor general, representing the British monarch, as the formal head of state and a prime minister and cabinet drawn from and collectively responsible to parliament.

Parliament consists of two chambers, a 15-member House of Representatives, elected by universal adult suffrage, through a simple plurality voting system, and a Senate of 13, appointed by the governor general, seven on the advice of the prime minister, three on the advice of the leader of the opposition, and three after wider consultation. The official opposition is the party with the second largest number of seats in the House. The normal parliamentary term is five years.

Political parties
There are eight political parties, the main ones being the National Democratic Congress (NDC), the Grenada United Labor Party (GULP), and the National Party (TNP).

The NDC was formed following the US invasion in 1983. It has a centrist orientation. The TNP emerged from a coalition of centrist parties which came together as the New National Party (NNP) in 1984. GULP dates from 1950 and is Grenada's oldest party. Its orientation is nationalist. Formerly left-of-center, it has shifted increasingly rightwards.

Political leaders since 1970
1967–79 Sir Eric Gairy (GULP), 1979–1983 Maurice Bishop (NJM), 1983 Hudson Austin (military), 1983–84 interim council, 1984–89 Herbert Blaize (NNP), 1989–91 Ben Jones (TNP), 1991–95 Nicholas Braithwaite (NDC), 1995 George Brizan (NDC), 1995– Keith Mitchell (NNP)

Latest elections
In the January 1999 general election the NNP, led by prime minister Mitchell, achieved a landslide victory, winning 62% of the vote (up 29% on June 1995) and all 15 House of Representatives' seats (up 7). The NDC attracted 25% of the vote (down 8%) and no seats (down 5) and the GULP 12% and no seats (down 2). Turnout was 57%.

Political history
Grenada was visited by Christopher Columbus (1451–1506) in the 15th century but not colonized until about 200 years later. French settlers came from Martinique and ousted the local Caribs. Then, after being ceded to Britain in 1783, retaken by France and ceded to Britain again, it became a British colony in

1887. In 1958 it joined the Federation of the West Indies, until its dissolution in 1962, and then was granted internal self-government in 1967. It achieved full independence within the Commonwealth in 1974.

The early political life of the nation was dominated by two figures, Eric Gairy (1922–97), a trade union leader who founded the Grenada United Labor Party (GULP) in 1950, and Herbert Blaize (1918–89), of the Grenada National Party (GNP). On independence, in 1974, Gairy was elected prime minister. He was knighted in 1977 but his rule was regarded as increasingly autocratic and corrupt and in 1979 he was replaced, in a bloodless coup, by the leader of the leftwing party, the New Jewel Movement (NJM), Maurice Bishop.

Bishop suspended the 1974 constitution, established a People's Revolutionary Government (PRG), and announced the formation of a People's Consultative Assembly to draft a new constitution. He promised a nonaligned foreign policy but became increasingly convinced that the United States was involved in a plot to destabilize his administration. This was strenuously denied. Relations with Britain and the United States deteriorated, while Grenada's links with Cuba and the Soviet Union grew stronger. In 1983 Bishop tried to improve relations with the United States and announced the appointment of a commission to draft a new constitution. This conciliatory attitude was opposed by the more leftwing members of his regime, resulting in a military coup, during which Bishop and three of his colleagues were executed.

A Revolutionary Military Council (RMC), led by General Hudson Austin, took control. In response to the outcry caused by the executions, Austin promised a return to civilian rule as soon as possible but on 25 October 1983 about 1,900 US troops, accompanied by 300 from Jamaica and Barbados, invaded the island. It was not clear whether the invasion was in response to a request from the governor general or on the initiative of the Organization of Eastern Caribbean States (OECS). In any event, concerned that Grenada might become a Cuban base, the United States readily agreed to take part. Neither Britain nor other members of the Commonwealth appeared to have been consulted. The RMC forces were defeated and Austin and his colleagues arrested.

In November 1983 the governor general appointed a nonpolitical interim council and then the 1974 constitution was reinstated. Several political parties which had gone into hiding re-emerged. After considerable manoeuvring, an informal coalition of center and left-of-center parties resulted in the formation of the New National Party (NNP), led by Blaize. In the 1984 general election the NNP won 14 seats in the House of Representatives and Blaize became prime minister. The United States had withdrawn most of its forces by the end of 1983 and the remainder by July 1985.

Early in 1989 Blaize relinquished the NNP leadership and was succeeded by Keith Mitchell. He continued as prime minister, however, although suffering from terminal cancer. He died in December 1989 and was replaced by a close supporter, Ben Jones, pending a general election. The 1991 general election resulted in Nicholas Braithwaite, the NDC leader, becoming prime minister. In September 1994 Braithwaite resigned the NDC leadership but remained prime minister. He resigned that post in February 1995 and the new party leader, George Brizan, became head of government. His tenure was short-lived as the NNP, led by Keith Mitchell, won the June 1995 general election. He inherited an economy with a low inflation rate, of only 5%, but with an unemployment level of nearly 25%.

In a January 1999 general election, Mitchell's NNP secured a crushing victory, winning all the seats in the House of Representatives to become the first party to secure two successive terms in office since the restoration of democracy in 1984. The election had been triggered by the NNP's loss of its overall majority in the legislature in November 1998 after foreign affairs minister Raphael Fletcher had left the government and switched parties to the GULP.

GUATEMALA

Republic of Guatemala
República de Guatemala

Capital: Guatemala City

Social and economic data

Area: 108,890 sq km/42,043 sq miles
Population: 10,322,000*
Pop. density per sq km/sq mi: 195/246*
Urban population: 40%**
Literacy rate: 46%**
GDP: $14,255 million*; per-capita GDP: $1,380*
Government defense spending (% of GDP): 1.4%*
Currency: quetzal
Economy type: middle income
Labor force in agriculture: 54%**

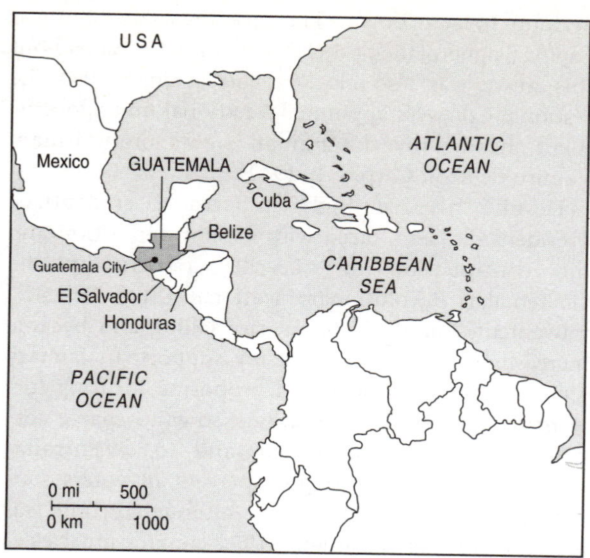

* 1995.
** 1992.

Head of state and head of government

President Alvaro Arzú Irigoyen, since 1996

Ethnic composition

The population consists mainly of two ethnic groups, Indians and ladinos. The word ladino is used to describe all non-Indians, including Europeans, black Africans, and mestizos. The Indians are descendants of the highland Mayas.

Religions

The great majority of the people are Christians, mostly Roman Catholics, 65%, with a largely Evangelical Protestant, 34%, minority.

Political features

State type: liberal democratic
Date of state formation: 1839
Political structure: unitary
Executive: limited presidential
Assembly: one-chamber
Party structure: multiparty
Human rights rating: 62%
International affiliations: ACS, ALADI (observer), BCIE, CACM, G-24, IAEA, IBRD, IMF, NAM, OAS, SELA, UN, WTO

Local and regional government

The country is divided into 22 departments, including Guatemala City, ranging in population from about 100,000 to 1.75 million, each administered by a governor appointed by the president.

Political system

The 1986 constitution provides for a single-chamber National Congress of 80 members, 64 of whom are directly elected in departmental congressional districts and 16 on a national basis, by proportional representation. They serve a five-year term by the second ballot majoritarian system. The president is also directly elected for a similar term. He or she appoints a cabinet and is assisted by a vice president. Presidents are not eligible for re-election.

Political parties

Of the many political parties, the most significant are the Guatemalan Christian Democratic Party (PDCG), the Union of the National Center (UCN), the Movement of National Liberation (MLN), the Democratic Institutional Party (PID), the Guatemalan Republican Front (FRG), the National Advancement Party (PAN), and the Social Democratic Party (PSD).

The PDCG was founded in 1968. It is a Christian, center-left party. The UCN is a centralist party formed in 1984. The PR was originally founded in 1944 and reformed in 1957. It has a radical orientation. The MLN is an extreme right-wing party which dates from 1960. The PID is a moderate conservative party which was formed in 1965. The FRG, PAN, and PSD in 1990 formed a right-of-center coalition.

Political leaders since 1970

1970–74 Carlos Araña Osorio (MLN-military), 1974–78 Kjell Laugerud Garcia (MLN-military), 1978–82 Fernando Romeo Lucas Garcia (MLN-military, 1982–83 Efrain Ríos Montt (military), 1983–86 Oscar Humberto Mejía Victores (military), 1986–91 Mario Vinicio Cerezo Arevalo (PDCG), 1991–93 Jorge Serrano Elias (MAS), 1993–96 Ramiro de León Carpio (independent), 1996– Alvaro Arzú Irigoyen (PAN)

Latest elections

In January 1996 the PAN candidate Alvaro Arzú Irigoyen defeated his FRG opponent, Alfonso Portillo, and assumed the presidency. He secured 51% of the run-off round vote, after 19 candidates had contested the first round in November 1995.

In the November 1995 congressional elections, PAN won 43 of the 80 elective seats, the FRG 21, and the PDCG, PSD, and UCN, fighting as a National Alliance (AN), won 9.

Political history

Guatemala was a site for the ancient Mayan Indian civilization. It later became a Spanish colony in 1524, but obtained its independence successively from Spain in 1821, then Mexico, and, in 1827, from the Federation of Central American States. A republic was finally established in 1839. It was then ruled by a succession of dictators until the presidency of Juan José Arevalo, in 1944, and his successor, Colonel Jacobo Arbenz Guzmán (1913–71). Their socialist administrations both followed programs of reform, which included the expropriation of large estates and the redistribution of the land to landless peasants, but Arbenz's nationalization of the plantations of the United Fruit Company, in 1954, so alarmed the United States government that it sponsored a coup, led by Colonel Carlos Castillo Armas, who then assumed the presidency.

He was assassinated in 1963 and the army continued to rule until 1966. There was a brief return to constitutional government until the military returned, in 1970. The next ten years saw a spate of political violence, in which it was estimated that more than 50,000 people died. In the 1982 presidential election the government candidate won but his opponents complained that the election had been rigged and, before he could take office, there was a coup by a group of young rightwing officers who installed General Ríos Montt (b. 1926) as head of a three-person junta. He soon dissolved the junta, assumed the presidency, and embarked upon a policy of fighting corruption and ending violence. The antigovernment guerrilla movement was, however, growing, being fuelled by the suppression of the left. It was countered by repressive measures by Montt, so that by the beginning of 1983 opposition to him was widespread. After several unsuccessful attempts to remove him, a coup, led by General Mejía Victores, was successful.

Mejía Victores declared an amnesty for the guerrillas, the ending of press censorship, and the preparation of a new constitution. This was adopted in 1985 and in the elections which followed the Guatemalan Christian Democratic Party (PDCG) won a majority in the Congress as well as the presidency, Mario Vinicio Cerezo Arevalo (b. 1942) becoming its first civilian president for 20 years.

After the 1991 elections the new president, Jorge Serrano Elias, took a firm line against military dissidents. He also, surprisingly, restored diplomatic relations with Belize, whose territory had been claimed by Guatemala. In May 1993, citing student and industrial unrest as his reason, President Serrano, with some army support, attempted to impose an authoritarian regime on the country. In a rare display of unity, trade union, civic, and some army groups opposed the move, forcing Serrano to step down. The vice president, Gustavo Espina Salguero, then proclaimed himself president but this move was also blocked and in June 1993 the National Congress appointed a national unity government, headed by the human rights ombudsman, Ramiro de León Carpio (b. 1942).

Despite his seemingly impeccable credentials, President de León, faced with violent opposition and the continuation of guerrilla activity by the Guatemalan Revolutionary National Unity (URNG) movement, found his popularity falling and became increasingly dependent on army support. In January 1994 a referendum was held proposing to bring forward the congressional elections, so as to enable corrupt deputies to be ousted, and to decentralize government spending. Eighty percent of voters supported this presidential initiative, although turnout was a paltry 16%. In the August 1994 congressional elections, rightwing parties won a majority of seats and there were fears of a return to the autocratic governments the country had experienced in previous years. At the same time, the UN-sponsored peace talks with the URNG had made only slow and hesitant progress, but a final agreement was reached in December 1996 to end the 36-year conflict. Assembly and presidential elections, held in November 1995 and January 1996, were won by the rightwing PAN. Meanwhile, by May 1997 the URNG's guerrillas had demobilized and the URNG became registered as a political party.

The country was badly affected, in October 1998, by 'Hurricane Mitch', with claimed 253 lives and affected one million people, or a tenth of the population.

In March 1999 the report of the independent 'Truth Commission', which had been set up under the 1996 peace accords to investigate the 36-year-long civil war in which 200,000 people had died, blamed the army for more than 90% of the crimes committed and left-wing guerrillas for only 3% of the atrocities. It described the military's policy at the height of the war as one of 'genocide', directed against the indigenous Mayan population, and noted the role of the US military and CIA in helping to train and finance the army. In March 1999, during a visit to Guatemala, US president Bill Clinton expressed regret for America's past role.

In May 1999 voters rejected, by a two to one margin in a national referendum, proposals by Congress to change the constitution to limit the military's role and to give recognition to the rights of the majority indigenous population. Barely a fifth of the population registered a vote.

HAITI

The Republic of Haiti
La République d'Haïti

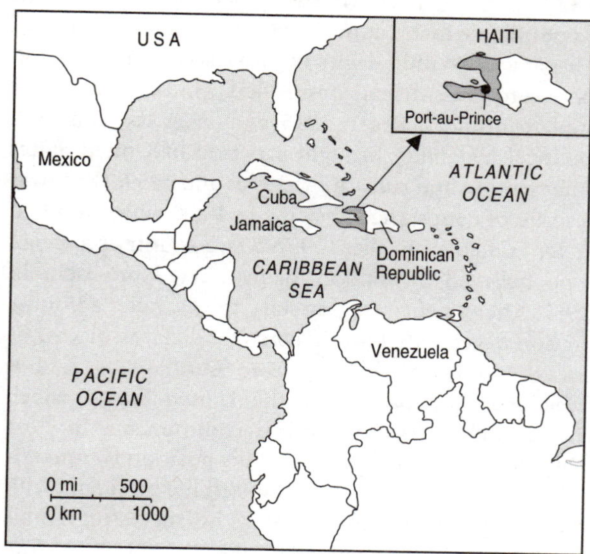

Capital: Port-au-Prince

Social and economic data

Area: 27,750 sq km/10,714sq miles
Population: 7,041,000*
Pop. density per sq km/sq mi: 254/657*
Urban population: 30%**
Literacy rate: 35%**
GDP: $1,780 million*; per-capita GDP: $250*
Government defense spending (% of GDP): 2.1%*
Currency: gourde
Economy type: low income
Labor force in agriculture: 50%**
* 1995.
** 1992.

Head of state (executive)

President René Préval, since 1996

Head of government

Prime Minister Jacques Edward Alexis, since 1998

Ethnic composition

About 90% of the population is of black African descent, the remainder being mulattos or Europeans. French and Creole are official languages.

Religions

About 80% of the population follows Roman Catholicism, which is the official religion. Voodoo is also a folk religion and has been given official status under the 1987 constitution.

Political features

State type: emergent democratic
Date of state formation: 1804
Political structure: unitary
Executive: dual
Assembly: two-chamber
Party structure: multiparty
Human rights rating: N/A
International affiliations: ACP, ACS, CARICOM (observer), IAEA, IBRD, IMF, OAS, SELA, UN, WTO

Local and regional government

The country is divided into nine departments, which are further subdivided into arrondissements and then communes. Departments are administered by appointed prefects and each commune has an elected mayor.

Political system

The constitution of 1950 was revised in 1957, 1964, 1971, 1983, and 1985 and then replaced with a new version in 1987. Between 1957 and 1986 the Duvalier family, father and then son, ruled Haiti with absolute power, maintaining their positions with the help of a private army. Although the constitution provided for an elected National Assembly, it had become a façade for the Duvaliers' own dictatorships.

In 1986 Henri Namphrey led a military coup and established a Governing Council, with himself as head, and the future of democratic government in Haiti was again under test. Although a new constitution was introduced in 1987, providing for the sharing of executive power between a president, prime minister, and two Houses of Congress, together with an independent judiciary, the congressional elections held in November 1987 and January 1988 were viewed by outside observers as largely fraudulent and the military was seen as retaining considerable power behind the façade of the civilian government.

The civilian government which was restored at the beginning of 1988 was overthrown later in the year by the military, again casting doubt over Haiti's democratic future, despite the new regime's promises to establish 'an irreversible democracy'. The 1990 election of a truly civilian government again raised hopes, but these were dashed a year later when military intervention was resumed.

The 1987 constitution provides for a two-chamber assembly consisting of a Senate of 27 members and a Chamber of Deputies, or National Assembly, of 83 members, elected by universal adult suffrage through a two-ballot majoritarian voting system, for a five-year term. There is also provision for a 'dual executive', with power being shared between a president, popularly elected for a five-year term, and a prime minister, appointed by the president on the basis of assembly support. A president may not serve consecutive terms. The prime minister chooses a cabinet in consultation with the president.

Political parties

Of around 20 active political parties, the most significant are the Lavalas Political Platform (PPL), the Lavalas Family Party (LFP), the Front for Change and Democracy (FNCD), and the National Committee of the Congress of Democratic Movements (KONAKOM). The LFP is a centrist pro-Aristide grouping which broke away from the PPL in 1996. The PPL party alliance includes the centrist Organization of People in Struggle (OPL; estd. 1991) and the centrist Movement of the Organization of the Land (MPO; estd. 1946).

The FNCD was formed in 1990 as a loose coalition of peasants, trade unionists, and intellectuals with a left-of-center orientation. KONAKOM is a center-left body formed in 1987.

The ANDP was formed to fight the 1990 election. Its orientation is also left-of-center.

Political leaders since 1970

1964–71 François Duvalier (National Unity Party), 1971–86 Jean-Claude Duvalier (PNP), 1986–88 Lieutenant General Henri Namphrey (military), 1988 Leslie Manigat (civilian), 1988–90 General Prosper Avril (military), 1990–91 Jean-Bertrand Aristide (FNCD), 1991–94 General Raoul Cedras (military), 1994–96 Jean-Bertrand Aristide (FNCD), 1996– René Préval (FNCD)

Latest elections

The December 1995 presidential election was won by an Aristide nominee, René Préval, who secured 88% of the vote. In the June and September 1995 assembly elections the PPL won 17 of the 18 contested Senate seats and 68 of the 83 seats in the lower chamber. The FNCD won two seats and KONAKOM, one. The results of partial assembly elections in April 1997 were disputed and a second round was postponed indefinitely.

Political history

First visited by Christopher Columbus (1451–1506) in 1492, Spain ceded Haiti, which comprised the western part of the island of Hispaniola, to France in 1697. Haiti became an independent state in 1804, after an uprising against French colonial rule led by the former slave, Toussaint l'Ouverture (1746–1803). Between 1822 and 1844 Haiti also ruled the Dominican Republic, which comprised the eastern half of Hispaniola. Within Haiti there was constant friction between the African-descended Haitians and the mulattos, and between 1915 and 1924 the country's political instability brought a period of United States intervention and rule. In the 1940s and 1950s there was a series of coups, the last being in 1956, which resulted in Dr François Duvalier (1907–71), a country physician who believed in voodoo, being elected president in 1957. After an encouraging start, the Duvalier administration degenerated into a personal dictatorship, ruthlessly maintained by a private militia, the Tonton Macoutes, and backed by the United States, which viewed him as a prop against communism. In 1964 Duvalier, 'Papa Doc', cemented his position by amending the constitution to make himself life president, with the power to nominate his son as his successor. On his death in 1971 Jean-Claude Duvalier (b. 1951) therefore came to the presidency at the age of 19 and soon acquired the name of 'Baby Doc'. Although the young Duvalier repeatedly promised a return to democratic politics, there was little real change and popular opposition to the regime mounted.

In 1985 Duvalier announced a further reform of the constitution, including the legalization of political parties, but this was not enough to prevent his overthrow in 1986. He went into exile in the south of France. The task of establishing democratic government fell to the new regime led by Lieutenant General Henri Namphrey. In 1987 a new constitution was adopted, providing for democratic government and an independent judiciary, but congressional elections in 1987 and 1988 were deemed largely fraudulent by outside observers. Leslie Manigat was elected president but was ousted in a military coup, led by General Prosper Avril, eight months later. Avril installed a largely civilian government, but a few months later handed over power again to the military.

After a period of turbulence and uncertainty, presidential and congressional elections were held at the end of 1990, resulting in the election of a leftwing peasant Catholic priest, Jean-Bertrand Aristide (b. 1953), who immediately tried to end army corruption and return to genuine civilian rule. He was ousted by the army, led by General Raoul Cedras and police chief

Colonel Michel François, in September 1991, and forced into exile. A provisional government, backed by the military, was installed, despite wide international criticism, and a reign of terror was instituted by the secret police.

While Aristide was exiled in the United States, three years of economic pressure, through United Nations-backed trade sanctions and eventually a naval blockade, and the illegal flight of thousands of Haitians to the United States, so weakened the Haitian economy that in September 1994 the former US president, Jimmy Carter, was able to broker an agreement with the Cedras regime, allowing US troops to enter the country without opposition and restore President Aristide.

In October 1994 Cedras stood down, having been granted an amnesty, and Aristide returned as the legitimate president. He appointed a former businessman, Smarck Michel, as prime minister and said that he was renouncing the priesthood so that he could concentrate on his political duties.

In February 1996, in the first peaceful handover since independence, René Préval succeeded Aristide. In June 1997 the prime minister, Rosny Smarth, resigned, following criticism of his austerity program, and a long political crisis ensued. Aristide, who had broken with Préval and had ambitions to contest the presidency in 2000, was a particularly strong critic of the austerity measures. René Préval's nominees as prime minister were repeatedly rejected by the Senate, and the political instability meant that much needed foreign loans were not received. Finally, President Préval reached an agreement with Gérard Pierre-Charles, leader of the opposition Organization of People in Struggle (OPL), which enabled him to nominate education minister Jacques Alexis as prime minister.

However, it was 18 months before, eventually, in December 1998 Congress formally approved the appointment of Alexis. In March 1999 the government reached an accord with a number of opposition parties, including KONAKOM, which, through the promise of early legislative elections, was designed to bring a greater measure of political stability.

HONDURAS

The Republic of Honduras
La República de Honduras

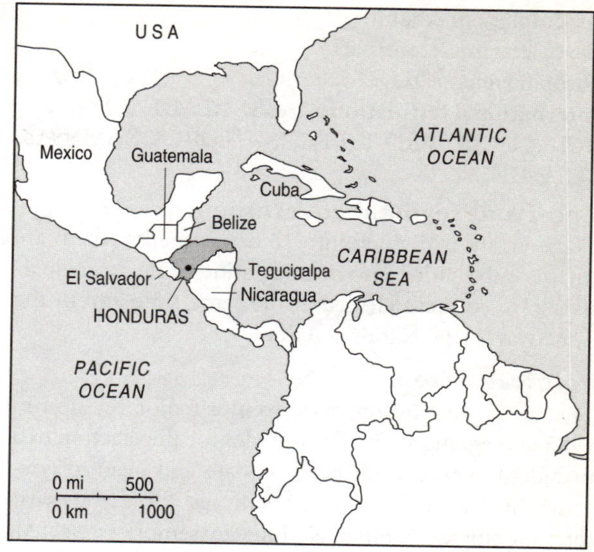

Capital: Tegucigalpa

Social and economic data

Area: 112,090 sq km/43,278 sq miles
Population: 5,770,000*
Pop. density per sq km/sq mi: 51/133*
Urban population: 45%**
Literacy rate: 57%**
GDP: $3,570 million*; per-capita GDP: $620*
Government defense spending (% of GDP): 1.3%*
Currency: lempira
Economy type: low income
Labor force in agriculture: 65%**
Unemployment rate: 3.2%*
* 1995.
** 1992.

Head of state and head of government

President Carlos Roberto Flores Facussé, since 1997

Ethnic composition

About 90% of the population is of mixed Indian and Spanish descent and known as ladinos, or mestizos. There are also Salvadorean, Guatemalan, American, and European minorities.

Religions

Almost 85% of the population is Roman Catholic and 15% belongs to Protestant Evangelical churches.

Political features

State type: liberal democratic
Date of state formation: 1838
Political structure: unitary
Executive: limited presidential

Assembly: one-chamber
Party structure: two-party
Human rights rating: 65%
International affiliations: ACS, ALADI (observer), BCIE, CACM, IBRD, ICFTU, IMF, LORCS, NAM, OAS, SELA, UN, WTO

Local and regional government

The country is divided into 18 departments which are further subdivided into municipalities. The municipalities have councils elected at the same time and in the same way as the National Assembly.

Political system

The 1982 constitution underwent a major revision in 1985 and again in 1995. It provides for the election of a president, who is both head of state and head of government, by universal adult suffrage for a four-year term. A single-chamber National Assembly is elected, through a party list system of proportional representation, for a similar term. The size of the Assembly may be amended in the light of population changes. It currently has 128 members. The president may not serve two terms in succession.

Political parties

There are some 11 political parties and a number of organized guerrilla groups. The two most significant parties are the Liberal Party of Honduras (PLH) and the National Party of Honduras (PNH).

The PLH appeared in its present form in 1980 but its origins go back to the 1890s. It has a number of internal factions which sometimes oppose the leadership. It has a center-right orientation.

The PNH was formed in 1902, and underwent a major reorganization in 1916. It is a traditional rightwing party and, like the PLH, it too has its own internal factions.

Political leaders since 1970

1965–71 General Oswaldo López Arellano (PLH), 1971–72 Ramón Ernesto Cruz Ucles (PNH), 1972–74 General Oswaldo López Arellano (PLH), 1974–78 General Juan Melgar Castro (military), 1978–81 General Policarpo Paz Garcia (military), 1981–84 Roberto Suazo Córdova (PLH), 1984–86 General Walter López Reyes (military), 1986–90 José Simeón Azeona del Hoyo (PLH), 1990–94 Rafael Leonardo Callejas (PNH), 1994–98 Carlos Roberto Reina Idiaquez (PLH), 1998– Carlos Roberto Flores (PLH)

Latest elections

In the November 1997 presidential election the PLH candidate, Carlos Roberto Flores, defeated his PNH opponent, Alba Nora Gúnera de Melgar, securing 53% of the vote against 43%. There were three other candidates. Flores was sworn in as president in January 1998.

The PLH also won a majority in the November 1997 National Assembly elections, capturing 67 seats to the PNH's 55. It secured 50% of the vote, against 42%. Turnout was 82%.

Political history

Formerly a site of the ancient Mayan civilization, Honduras became a Spanish possession from the early 16th century. It broke away in 1821 to form a federation of Central American States with El Salvador, and achieved full independence in 1838 when this federation dissolved. There was political instability and wars with neighboring states throughout much of the 19th and early 20th centuries and US involvement was significant, with the United Fruit Company controlling much of the country's crucial banana production. In 1925 there was a brief civil war and from 1939 to 1949 a dictatorship was established by the leader of the National Party (PNH). Then the government constantly changed hands in a series of military coups, with General Oswaldo López Arellano holding power for much of the period between 1963 and 1974.

In 1980 civilian rule returned, but the army retained control of security and was able to veto cabinet appointments. Although the 1981 general election was won by the Liberal Party (PLH) and its leader, Dr Roberto Suazo, became president, real power was still in the hands of General Gustavo Alvárez, the commander in chief of the army, who, in 1982, managed to secure an amendment to the constitution which reduced government control over the armed forces. General Alvárez was virtually in charge of foreign policy, working closely with the United States and agreeing, in 1983, to the establishment of naval and air bases in Honduras. The American CIA was also active in providing assistance to Nicaraguan counter-revolutionaries based in Honduras.

In 1984 Alvárez was ousted by a group of junior officers and Honduras' close relationship with the United States came under review. In the same year divisions arose within the PLH over selection procedures for the party's presidential candidates and two years later the electoral law was changed. In the elections of 1986 Suazo was not eligible to stand for the presidency and the main PLH candidate was José Azeona. Although the PNH nominee won most votes, the revised constitution made Azeona the eventual winner.

In 1989 the PNH, led by Rafael Callejas, won both the presidential and assembly elections but in November 1993 the situation was reversed and the PLH returned to power, with Carlos Reina as president. Under Reina, the economy began to improve, with economic growth of 5% during 1993 and inflation in single figures. However, the unemployment rate exceeded 40%. In November 1997 the PLH was successful in both the presidential and assembly elections with Carlos Flores being sworn in as president in January 1998. In May 1998 a new program was introduced to stimulate the economy.

In October 1998 Honduras was devastated by 'Hurricane Mitch', which caused damage and losses of $4 billion (equivalent to the country's annual GDP), claimed 6,500 lives, and affected two million people. In February 1999 President Flores assumed the position of commander-in-chief of the armed forces, on the retirement of General Mario Hung Pacheco. This brought to an end a long period in which the military had enjoyed great autonomy, with its leaders acting at times as a parallel government.

JAMAICA

Capital: Kingston

Social and economic data

Area: 10,991 sq km/4,244 sq miles 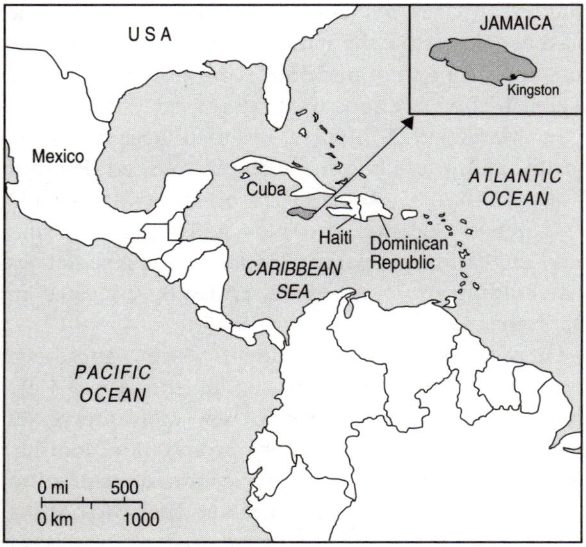
Population: 2,500,000[*]
Pop. density per sq km/sq mi: 227/589[*]
Urban population: 54%[**]
Literacy rate: 96%[**]
GDP: $3,810 million[*]; per-capita GDP: $1,525[*]
Government defense spending (% of GDP): 0.6%[*]
Currency: Jamaican dollar
Economy type: middle income
Labor force in agriculture: 25%[**]
Unemployment rate: 15.9%[**]

[*] 1995.
[**] 1992.

Head of state

Queen Elizabeth II, represented by Governor General Sir Howard Cooke since 1992

Head of government

Prime Minister Percival J Patterson, since 1992

Ethnic composition

Nearly 80% of the population is of African descent and about 15% of mixed African-European origins. There are also Chinese, Indian, and European minorities.

Religions

The great majority of people are Christians, the largest number being Anglicans. There is also a large Rastafarian community.

Political features

State type: liberal democratic
Date of state formation: 1962
Political structure: unitary
Executive: parliamentary
Assembly: two-chamber
Party structure: two-party
Human rights rating: 72%
International affiliations: ACP, ACS, CARICOM, IAEA, IBRD, IMF, NAM, OAS, SELA, UN, WTO

Local and regional government

For administrative purposes, the country is divided into 14 parishes, each with an elected council.

Political system

The constitution came into force on independence in 1962. It follows closely the unwritten British model, with a resident constitutional head of state, in the shape of the governor general, representing the British monarch, who appoints a prime minister and cabinet, collectively responsible to the assembly. This consists of two chambers, an appointed 21-member Senate and a 60-member elected House of Representatives. Thirteen of the senators are appointed on the advice of the prime minister and eight on the advice of the leader of the opposition. Members of the House are elected by universal adult suffrage, through a simple plurality voting system, for a five-year term. It is subject to dissolution within that period.

Political parties

There are four active political parties, the two which have been the main adversaries in the political contest since independence being the Jamaica Labor Party (JLP) and the People's National Party (PNP).

The JLP was founded by Sir Alexander Bustamente in 1943 as the political wing of the Bustama Industrial Trade Union. It has a moderate, centrist orientation, and supports free enterprise in a mixed economy and cooperation with the United States.

The PNP was formed in 1938 by Norman Manley. It has a left-of-center social-democratic orientation and believes in the pursuit of socialist principles within a self-sufficient, national framework, although this stance has been moderated in recent years. In October 1995 a new centrist party, the National Democratic Movement (NDM), was formed by Bruce Golding, a former chairperson of the JLP.

Political leaders since 1970

1967–72 Hugh Shearer (JLP), 1972–80 Michael Manley (PNP), 1980–89 Edward P G Seaga (JLP), 1989–92 Michael Manley (PNP), 1992– Percival J Patterson (PNP)

Latest elections

In the December 1997 general election the PNP won another landslide victory, securing 50 of the House of Representatives' 60 seats and 56% of the vote, and Percival Patterson continued as prime minister. The JLP, with 39% of the vote, won ten seats.

Political history

Visited by Christopher Columbus (1451–1506) in 1494, Jamaica was initially ruled by Spain from the early 16th century, with many of the indigenous Arawak Indians dying as a result of exposure to new diseases brought from the 'Old World'. Jamaica was a British colony from 1655. During the 1930s depression and social and economic problems led to rioting and a developing political awareness. The country was granted internal self-government in 1959 and then full independence within the Commonwealth in 1962. The two leading political figures in the early days of independence were Sir Alexander Bustamente (1884–1977), the Spanish-raised adopted son of an Irish planter, and Norman Manley (1893–1969), a skilled barrister who became prime minister in 1955. Bustamente's Jamaica Labor Party (JLP) won the 1962 election and was again successful in 1967 under Bustamente's successor, Hugh Shearer. Then the PNP, under Norman Manley's son Michael (b. 1923), came into office in 1972.

Michael Manley was a strong advocate of social reform and economic independence from the developed world. Despite high unemployment, his party was returned to power in 1976 with an increased majority but by 1980 the economic position had worsened and, rejecting the conditions attached to an IMF loan, Manley sought support for his policies of economic self-reliance.

The 1980 general election campaign was extremely violent, despite calls by Manley and the leader of the JLP, Edward Seaga (b. 1930), for moderation. The outcome was a surprisingly decisive victory for the JLP. It won 51 of the 60 seats in the House of Representatives. Seaga thus received a mandate for a return to a renewal of links with the United States and an emphasis on free enterprise. He severed diplomatic links with Cuba in 1981.

In 1983 Seaga called an early snap election, with the opposition claiming they had been given insufficient time to nominate their candidates. On this occasion the JLP won all 60 seats. There were violent demonstrations when the new parliament was inaugurated and the PNP said it would continue its opposition outside the parliamentary arena.

In the February 1989 general election Michael Manley's PNP won a landslide victory, after which he hastened to assure the nation and the world that he intended to pursue moderate economic policies and establish good relations with the United States.

In March 1992 Manley resigned because of ill health and the PNP immediately elected Percival Patterson (b. 1935) as his successor. In the March 1993 snap general election Patterson had a personal success, increasing his party's House of Representatives seat holding by seven, to 52, and was re-elected in December 1997.

During 1998-99 the budget deficit increased significantly. However, efforts, in the April 1999 budget, to finance it through new consumer taxes provoked three days of violent protests and looting, bringing Kingston to a virtual closure. Troops had to be called out to assist the police and the scope of the tax increases was subsequently reduced.

MEXICO

United States of Mexico
Estados Unidos Mexicanos

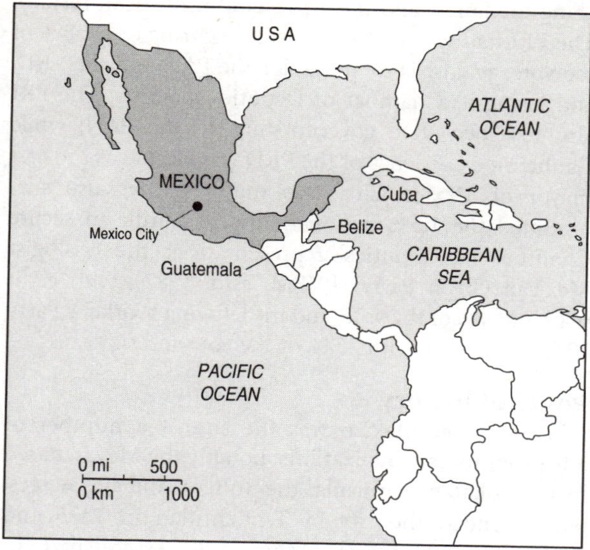

Capital: Mexico City

Social and economic data

Area: 1,958,201 sq km/745,065 miles
Population: 93,008,000*
Pop. density per sq km/sq mi: 47/123*
Urban population: 74%**
Literacy rate: 87%**
GDP: $304,600 million*; per-capita GDP: $3,275*
Government defense spending (% of GDP): 0.9%*
Currency: Mexican peso
Economy type: middle income
Labor force in agriculture: 23%**
Unemployment rate: 4.7%*
* 1995.
** 1992.

Head of state and head of government

President Ernesto Zedillo Ponce de León, since 1994

Ethnic composition

About 60% of the population are mestizos, of Spanish-American and American-Indian parentage, about 30% are Indians, and the rest are mainly of European origin.

Religions

About 92% of the population is Roman Catholic. There is also a 5% Protestant Evangelical minority. Roman Catholicism was the established religion until 1857 and is still under a measure of state control.

Political features

State type: liberal democratic
Date of state formation: 1821
Political structure: federal
Executive: limited presidential
Assembly: two-chamber
Party structure: multiparty*
Human rights rating: 64%
International affiliations: AVS, AG (observer), ALADI, APEC, BCIE, CARICOM (observer), G-3, G-15, G-24, IAEA, IBRD, IMF, IWC, NAFTA, NAM (observer), OECD, RG, SELA, UN, WTO

* Though dominated by one party.

Local and regional government

Mexico is a federal republic of 31 states and a federal district, based on Mexico City. It displays several of the features of the United States federal system, with each state having its own constitution, governor, and single-chamber assembly, termed the Chamber of Deputies, directly elected for six-year and three-year terms respectively. In broad terms, the powers of the federal government are set out in the federal constitution and the residue resides with the states. Within the states there are over 2,000 municipalities, each with an elected council.

Political system

The constitution dates from 1917, following the 1910 revolution which proclaimed a drastic change in land ownership, new labor legislation, and a reduction in the powers of the Roman Catholic Church. Since then it has been amended several times, most recently in 1993, but its essential provisions remain. It provides for a president, who is both head of state and head of government, and a two-chamber National Congress of Senate and Chamber of Deputies, broadly based on the United States model. The Senate has a six-year term and the deputies serve for three years. The president is directly elected for a six-year term and chooses the cabinet.

The Senate has 128 members, each state and the Federal District being represented by four senators. Three of these are elected by majority election and the fourth by proportional representation.

The Chamber has 500 members, 300 representing single-member constituencies, being elected by a majority vote, and 200 elected by proportional representation, from party lists. The voting system is intended to give due weight to the minority parties, with the majority party in the Chamber being limited to no more than 315 seats. Voting is compulsory.

Political parties

There are around ten active parties, but to remain officially registered a party must secure at least 1.5% of the national vote in two consecutive federal elections. The most significant parties are the Institutional Revolutionary Party (PRI), the National Action Party (PAN), and the Party of the Democratic Revolution (PRD).

The PRI was formed in 1929 as the natural successor to the parties of the revolutionary period of Mexico's history and then called the National Revolutionary Party. It was redesignated as the Mexican Revolutionary Party in 1938. It is a broad-based party which has been a dominant force in Mexican politics for many years. It has a moderate, corporatist orientation.

The PAN was formed in 1939. Its orientation is moderate, Christian, center-right reformist. Its leader is Carlos Castillo Peraza.

The PRD was formed in 1988 as an opposition force to the PRI. It has a centrist reformist orientation.

Traditionally, the opposition PAN and PRD have been granted a number of congressional seats and the occasional state governorship by the dominant PRI in exchange for keeping their attacks on the regime within bounds. In this way, a unique multiparty dictatorship has survived for nearly 70 years. However, in recent years the increasingly confident PAN has begun to eschew such deals and now presses for outright power.

Political leaders since 1970

1970–76 Luis Echeverria Alvárez (PRI), 1976–82 José Lopéz Portillo (PRI), 1982–88 Miguel de la Madrid Hurtado (PRI), 1988–94 Carlos Salinas de Gortari (PRI), 1994– Ernesto Zedillo Ponce de León (PRI)

Latest elections

In the August 1994 presidential election the PRI candidate, Ernesto Zedillo, won with 48.8% of the vote, his nearest rival, the PAN candidate, Diego Fernández, securing 25.9%. This was the lowest ever victory margin for the PRI since its formation in 1929.

The results of the July 1997 congressional elections were as follows:

Mexico latest election results

Party	Senate seats	Chamber of Deputies seats
PRI	12	239
PAN	9	122
PRD	8	125
Other parties	3*	14

* The other three senators for each state were set to be elected in 2000.

Turnout was 70% and the elections were viewed as being the fairest and most peaceful in Mexican history. The PRI had its worst-ever result, securing only 38% of the vote, against 26% apiece for the PAN and the PRD, and losing its Chamber of Deputies majority. The PRI also lost two state governorships to the PAN, while Cauhtémoc Cárdenas of the PRD was elected as the first mayor of Mexico City. Two minor parties also surmounted the 1.5% national support hurdle to secure Chamber of Deputies' representation: the ecologist Mexican Green Party (PVEM; estd. 1987), with eight seats and 4% of the vote, and the leftwing Worker's Party (PT; estd. 1991), with 2.5% of the vote and six seats.

Political history

In early times Mexico was the site of a number of advanced Indian civilizations, notably the Mayas, based in the Yukatan peninsula, the Toltecs, and the Aztecs, who founded the city of Tenochtitlán in 1325 and under Montezuma II (1466–1520) established an extensive empire. This was overthrown by Spanish conquistador invaders, led by Hernando Cortés (1485–1547), between 1519 and 1521. Centuries of economic exploitation and harsh repression by the Spanish colonial authorities created a vigorous movement for independence. This was eventually achieved in 1821, following a guerrilla war led by Vicente Guerrero. Mexico's early history as an independent nation was marked by civil and foreign wars, notably with the United States between 1846 and 1848, which resulted in the loss of Mexican territories north of the Rio Grande, including Texas, New Mexico, and California. Under Porfirio Diaz (1830–1915), who was president between 1877–80 and 1884–1911, there was considerable economic modernization and growth, with railroads being developed with American finance, but there was political repression and a lack of social reform. This provoked his overthrow in 1911 by the reformist Francisco Madero (1873–1913) and the populist revolution of the same year, led by Emiliano Zapata (1879–1919). Zapata sought to reclaim land taken by the Spanish from indigenous Mexicans, but was driven into retreat in 1915 and assassinated in 1919. In 1917 Mexico adopted a new constitution, designed to establish a permanent form of democratic government. With several amendments, that constitution has lasted until the present day. A program of social reform was also launched.

The broadly based Institutional Revolutionary Party (PRI) has dominated Mexican politics since the 1920s, pursuing largely moderate and, traditionally, left-of-center policies. During the 1930s much of the economy was nationalized and large estates were divided. Its popularity was damaged from the 1970s by the country's poor economic performance and rising international debts. However, despite criticisms from vested interest groups, such as the trade unions and the Church, the PRI scored a clear win over all other parties in the 1985 elections, with no serious challenger in evidence. Soon afterwards the government's problems were exacerbated by a massive earthquake in Mexico City, which caused thousands of deaths and made hundreds of thousands of people homeless.

Mexico has been strongly influenced by its proximity to the United States. Its constitution, for example, reflects many aspects of that of its more powerful neighbor. At times, however, the Mexican government has been strongly critical of US policy in Central America and, as a member, with Colombia, Panama, and Venezuela, of the Contadora Group, has argued strongly for the withdrawal of all foreign advisers from the region.

With the price of oil, a vital export earner, falling sharply, the economic situation worsened so much in the 1980s that the Mexican government, after prolonged negotiations, felt obliged, in 1986, to sign an agreement with the IMF. This provided loans sufficient to keep the country solvent for several years. The agreement was extended in 1992. Two years later the Free Trade Agreement between the United States and Canada was expanded to include Mexico and retitled the North American Free Trade Agreement (NAFTA).

In the 1988 presidential election the PRI candidate, Carlos Salinas de Gortari (b. 1948), won by a small margin amid claims of election frauds. The PRI also increased its majority in the 1988 assembly elections. President Salinas then embarked on an ambitious program of market-centerd economic reform, encouraging inward investment with considerable success.

In 1989 the first non-PRI state governor was elected, when the National Action Party (PAN) won in Baja California state. In November 1993 the PRI chose Luis Donaldo Colosio as its candidate for the 1994 presidential elections. However, the country was thrown into turmoil when, in March 1994, Colosio was assassinated while attending a political rally in Baja California. Ernesto Zedillo (b. 1952) was chosen as Colosio's replacement. Meanwhile, Indian groups, led by the mysterious figure of Commandante Marcos, had rebelled in January 1994 in the southern state of Chiapas, operating under the banner of the Zapatista National Liberation Army (EZLN), demanding political reform and land distribution. They took control of part of the territory, declaring it independent. A peace agreement was reached in December 1994 but the situation continued to be unsettled.

The PRI enjoyed successes in the August 1994 presidential and congressional elections, Zedillo taking the supreme office and the party securing a majority, though much reduced, in both chambers. However, the opposition claimed that there had been electoral fraud in a number of regions, notably Chiapas, where the PRI controversially secured the state governorship. Instability of the political system was again in focus when, in September 1994, the PRI secretary general, José Francisco Ruiz, was killed in Mexico City. Rául Solinas, the brother of Carlos Salinar, was later imprisoned (in 1999), with a 50 year sentence for his role as architecht of this murder. In December 1994 Zedillo was sworn in as president, but within weeks he was faced by a grave currency crisis, with foreign investors, concerned at continuing political instability and Mexico's high level of indebtedness, seeking to sell their clearly overvalued peso holdings. Sharp devaluations in the peso became necessary and support was received from the new Clinton administration in the United States. This helped stabilize the situation, but inflation rose sharply during 1995 and there was a sudden contraction in GDP and deep spending cuts. New privatizations of the ports, railroads, and airways were also announced. In August 1995 the PRI's president, Maria de los Angeles Moreno, resigned after a string of bad election results, which saw the PRI lose the governorships of several more states to the opposition PAN, and in 1997 for the first time it lost control of the Chamber of Deputies.

Despite continuing violence in 1998 the government reactivated talks with the Zapatista rebels and said it would introduce legislation to ensure indigenous rights.

However, relations between the government and the EZLN remained uneasy and were exacerbated in March 1999 when the EZLN organized and held an unofficial nation-wide referendum on Indian rights, which secured the participation of three million people. In preparation for presidential elections, due in 2000, both the PRI and PAN announced that their candidate would be chosen via a primary election, in November 1999: previously the PRI's candidate had been hand-picked by the incumbent president.

NICARAGUA

Republic of Nicaragua
República de Nicaragua

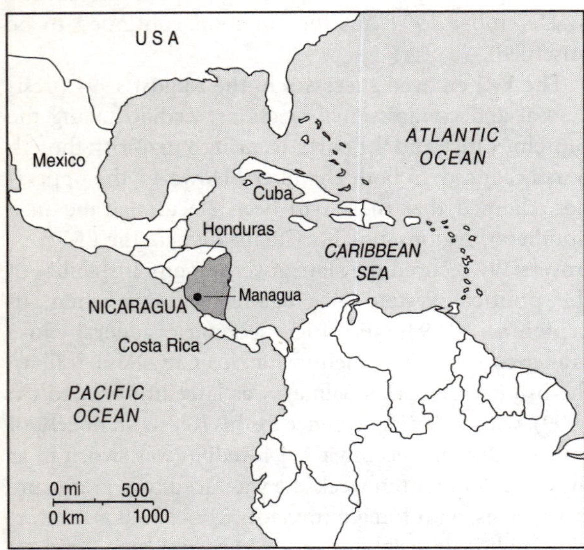

Capital: Managua

Social and economic data

Area: 120,254 sq km/46,430 sq miles
Population: 4,401,000*
Pop. density per sq km/sq mi: 34/95*
Urban population: 61%**
Literacy rate: 57%**
GDP: $1,660 million*; per-capita GDP $380*
Government defense spending (% of GDP): 1.8%*
Currency: gold cordoba
Economy type: low income
Labor force in agriculture: 46%**
Unemployment rate: 14.0%*
* 1995.
** 1992.

Head of state and head of government

President Arnoldo Alemán Lacayo, since 1997

Ethnic composition

Over 70% of the population is of mixed Indian, Spanish, and African origin. About 9% is of African descent and 5% Indian.

Religions

All religions are tolerated. About 90% of the population is Roman Catholic and there is a strong following of the Protestant Moravian Church, particularly along the Atlantic coast.

Political features

State type: emergent democratic
Date of state formation: 1838
Political structure: unitary
Executive: limited presidential
Assembly: one-chamber
Party structure: two-party
Human rights rating: 75%
International affiliations: ACS, ALADI (observer), BCIE, CACM, IAEA, IBRD, IMF, NAM, OAS, SELA, UN, WTO

Local and regional government

The country is divided into 16 departments, ranging in population from about 30,000 to over 800,000. Below the department level are municipalities, with elected councils, but limited powers.

Political system

The 1986 constitution, amended in November 1994, provides for a president, who is head of state and head of government, with veto powers, and a 90-member single-chamber National Assembly. The president is elected by universal suffrage for a five-year non-renewable term, and is assisted by a vice president, elected in the same way, and an appointed cabinet. The National Assembly, comprising 70 regional and 20 national seats, is also elected by universal suffrage, through a party list system of proportional representation, for a six-year term. Supplementary non-elected seats in the National Assembly are awarded to unsuccessful candidates in the presidential election who secured as many votes as deputies elected for regional seats.

Political parties

There are around 25 active political parties. The main two groups are the Sandinista National Liberation Front (FSLN) and the Liberal Alliance (AL).

The FSLN was founded in 1960 to pursue a guerrilla struggle against the ruling Somoza regime. Between 1979 and 1990 it was the principal government party. It is a Marxist-Leninist grouping, but is divided between moderate reformist and hardline wings. Its leader is the hardline Daniel Ortega. The AL has a right-of-center orientation. It is an electoral alliance of six parties, formed in 1996, and which includes the Liberal Constitutionalist Party (PLC; estd. 1968).

Political leaders since 1970

1967–79 Anastasio Somoza Debayle (military), 1979–85 junta (FSLN), 1985–90 Daniel Ortega

Saavedra (FSLN), 1990–96 Violeta Barrios de Chamorro (UNO), 1997– Arnoldo Alemán Lacayo (PLC)

Latest elections

In the October 1996 presidential election the FSLN candidate, Daniel Ortega, was defeated by the Liberal Alliance candidate, Arnoldo Alemán Lacayo, who secured 51% of the vote against 38%. Three of the defeated candidates secured sufficient support to be allocated a 'supplementary seat' in the National Assembly, increasing its size to 93 seats.

In the simultaneous Assembly elections the Liberal Alliance won 44 seats but not an overall majority.

Political history

Nicaragua, formerly inhabited by Indian tribes, was conquered by Spain in 1552. It achieved independence from Spanish rule in 1821 and was briefly united with Mexico and then with the United Provinces of Central America, before becoming fully independent in 1838. In 1912, as the political situation deteriorated, at the Nicaraguan government's request, the United States established military bases in the country but their presence was opposed by a guerrilla group, led by Augusto César Sandino. The United States withdrew its forces in 1933 but not before it had established and trained a National Guard, commanded by a trusted nominee, General Anastasio Somoza Garcia (1896–1956).

Sandino was assassinated in 1934, reputedly on Somoza's orders, but some of his followers continued their guerrilla activity on a small scale. The Somoza family began a near-dictatorial rule which was to last for over 40 years. During this time they developed wide business interests and amassed a huge personal fortune, while political opponents were exiled. General Somoza was elected president in 1936 and stayed in office until his assassination in 1956 when he was succeeded by his son, Luis Somoza Debayle (1922–67). In 1960 the leftwing Sandinista National Liberation Front (FSLN), named after the former guerrilla leader, was formed with the object of overthrowing the Somozas by revolution. This was not to happen, however, for some 17 years. Luis Somoza was followed as president in 1967 by his brother, Anastasio Somoza Debayle (1925–80), who was to head an even more notorious and oppressive regime. In July 1979, after considerable violence and loss of life, Somoza was ousted and fled the country. He was later assassinated in Paraguay in 1980, by the 'hit team' directed by the new Sandinista government's secret police.

The FSLN established a provisional Junta of National Reconstruction led by Daniel Ortega Saavedra (b. 1945), who had earlier spent seven years in prison for his involvement in urban guerrilla activities; published a statute guaranteeing civil rights; and appointed a Council of State, prior to an elected National Assembly and, later, a new constitution.

Nicaragua's relations with the United States deteriorated rapidly with the election of the conservative Republican Ronald Reagan as US president in November 1980. He froze the package of economic assistance arranged by his Democrat predecessor, Jimmy Carter, alleging that the Sandinista government was supporting attempts to overthrow the administration in El Salvador. In March 1982 the Nicaraguan government declared a state of emergency in the wake of attacks on bridges and petroleum installations. The Reagan administration embarked on a policy of destabilizing the Sandinista government by actively supporting the counter-revolutionary forces (the 'Contras'), with bases in Honduras, and by covert CIA operations to undermine the economy. In February 1985 President Reagan denounced Ortega's regime, saying that his objective was to 'remove it in the sense of its present structure'.

A Central American Peace Agreement, instigated by President Oscar Arias Sánchez of Costa Rica, was signed in Guatemala by leaders of Nicaragua, El Salvador, Guatemala, Honduras, and Costa Rica in August 1987, but it failed to halt the fighting. In January 1988, however, President Ortega instituted direct talks with the rebels and the US Congress refused to vote additional military aid to them. In October 1988 President Reagan announced that he would be seeking no more aid for the Contras.

In February 1989 the presidents of Guatemala, El Salvador, Honduras, and Costa Rica agreed to disarm the Contra rebels and Ortega undertook to hold new elections in February 1990 and to restore civil rights to everyone. These elections resulted in wins for the broad-based right-of-center National Opposition Union (UNO) coalition at both presidential and Assembly levels, Violeta Barrios de Chamorro becoming president. However, the defection to the FSLN of ten UNO deputies after the election left the president without a clear Assembly majority. In addition, President Chamorro inherited an economy which was in ruins after more than a decade of civil war, with an estimated 60% of the population unemployed.

In February 1994, after months of negotiations, a

final peace accord was signed with the residue of the rebels, known as Recontras, who had hitherto stayed aloof from negotiations.

In November 1994 the constitution was amended, reducing the presidential term from six to five years, and barring consecutive terms of office. Also, in a bid to destroy nepotism, the constitution now barred relatives of serving presidents from standing for election. The October 1996 presidential and assembly elections were won by the right-of-center Liberal Alliance.

In October 1998 Nicaragua was devastated by 'Hurricane Mitch', which caused damage and losses of $1.5 billion, claimed 2,500 lives, and affected 760,000 people.

PANAMA

The Republic of Panama
La República de Panamá

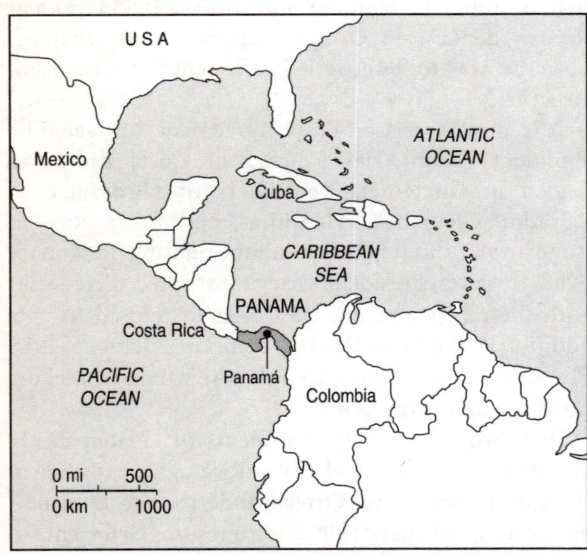

Capital: Panama City

Social and economic data

Area: 77,080 sq km/29,761 sq miles
Population: 2,631,000*
Pop. density per sq km/sq mi: 34/88*
Urban population: 54%**
Literacy rate: 86%**
GDP: $7,235 million*; per-capita GDP: $2,750*
Government defense spending (% of GDP): 1.3%*
Currency: balboa
Economy type: middle income
Labor force in agriculture: 25%**
Unemployment rate 13.7%*
* 1995.
** 1992.

Head of state and head of government

President Mireya Elisa Moscoso de Gruber, since 1999

Ethnic composition

About 70% of the population are mestizos, of Spanish-American and American-Indian parentage, and are called Panamenos. About 14% are West Indian, 10% white American or European, and 6% Indian.

Religions

Eighty-five per cent of the population is Roman Catholic and Roman Catholicism is a quasi-state religion. There are also Evangelical Protestant and Jewish minorities.

Political features

State type: emergent democratic
Date of state formation: 1903
Political structure: unitary
Executive: limited presidential
Assembly: one-chamber
Party structure: multiparty
Human rights rating: 81%
International affiliations: AG (associate), ALADI (observer), IAEA, IBRD, IMF, IWC, NAM, OAS, SELA, UN

Local and regional government

The country is divided into nine provinces and three autonomous Indian reservations. Each province has a governor, appointed by the president. The provinces are further subdivided into districts, each with its own mayor.

Political system

The constitution underwent a major revision in April 1983, following a referendum. This has resulted in a new, single-chamber Legislative Assembly of 71 members, elected by universal adult suffrage, through a simple plurality voting system, for a five-year term. The president is elected in the same way for a similar period of office. He or she is assisted by two elected vice presidents and an appointed cabinet. Voting is compulsory but the armed forces are banned from participating in elections.

Political parties

There are more than 20 political parties, ten of them

functioning in three main blocs. However, to retain official status, a party must have won at least 5% of the vote in the most recent legislature elections. There are six such parties. The most significant individual parties are the Democratic Revolutionary Party (PRD), the Arnulfista Party (PA), the Authentic Liberal Party (PLA), the National Liberal Republican Movement (MOLIRENA), and the Papa Egoró Movement (MPE). The PRD was founded in 1979 by supporters of General Torrijos and the army, headed by General Antonio Noriega. It now has a center-right orientation and a membership of 160,000.

The PA was formed in 1990. It has a left-of-center orientation and a membership of 110,000. The PLA was an ally of the PA in the 1994 elections and has a similar orientation. MOLIRENA was formed in 1982. It has a right-of-center orientation. The MPE was founded in 1991 and has a moderate, center-left orientation. It is led by Rubén Blades.

Political leaders since 1970

1968–78 General Omar Torrijos Herrera (military), 1978–82 Aristedes Royo Sánchez (effective military), 1982–84 Ricardo de la Espriella (effective military), 1984–85 Nicolás Ardito Barletta (effective military), 1985–88 Eric Arturo Delvalle (effective military), 1988–89 Manuel Solis Palma (effective military), 1989–94 Guillermo Endara Galimany (ADOC), 1994–99 Ernesto Pérez Balladares (PRD), 1999– Mireya Elisa Moscoso de Gruber (PA)

Latest elections

In the May 1999 elections there were three main electoral blocs: the Union for Panama (UP), led by the PA and including MOLIRENA; the New Nation (NN), led by the PRD and including the MPE; and Opposition Action (OA). The NN coalition achieved a clear majority in the Legislative Assembly elections, winning 46 of the 71 seats, including 33 for the PRD and six for the MPE, while the UP won 17, including 11 for the PA and six for MOLIRENA, and the OA three seats. The PLA, standing alone, won three seats.

The PA candidate, Mireya Moscoso secured victory in the presidential election, attracting 45% of the vote and defeating Martin Torrijos Espino, the son of the late military strongman, General Omar Torrijos Herrera, who led the PRD and won 38% of the vote. Alberto Vallarino of OA finished third, with 18% of the vote. Turnout was 77%.

Political history

Established as a Spanish colony early in the 16th century, Panama became part of Spanish New Granada (Columbia) in 1821 and, with the help of the United States, achieved full independence in 1903. The US support was a form of self-interest because, at the same time, it bought the rights to build the Panama Canal, connecting the Atlantic and Pacific Oceans. This was eventually opened in 1914. Under the original 1903 treaty the United States was given control of a ten-mile wide strip of territory, known as the Canal Zone, in perpetuity. At the same time, Panama was guaranteed US protection and an annuity. In 1939 Panama's protectorate status was ended by mutual agreement, and in 1974 the two countries agreed to negotiate an eventual complete transfer of the canal to Panama, despite opposition from the US Congress.

In 1977 two treaties were signed by Panama's president, General Omar Torrijos Herrera, and the US president, Jimmy Carter. One transferred the canal and the other guaranteed its subsequent neutrality. A referendum in Panama approved the change but the US Senate demanded amendments to the effect that, after the complete transfer of all facilities in 1999, only Panamanian forces would be stationed in the zone, and that the United States would have the right to use force to keep the canal open if it became obstructed. On this revised basis, the two treaties were finally approved.

The 1980s saw a deterioration in the state of Panama's economy, with opposition to the austerity measures which the government introduced to try to halt the decline. In the 1984 elections, after a very close result, Dr Nicolás Ardito Barletta, the Democratic Revolutionary Party (PRD) candidate, was declared the winner, but in 1985 he resigned amid speculation that he had been forced to by the commander of the National Guard, General Manuel Noriega (b. 1940). Relations between Panama and the United States deteriorated with the departure of President Barletta, the US administration of President Ronald Reagan announcing a cut in its financial aid. Barletta was succeeded by Eric Arturo Delvalle, who immediately set about seeking a national consensus on economic policy. US criticism continued, Noriega being accused of drug trafficking. In February 1988 President Delvalle attempted to dismiss Noriega as head of the armed forces and was immediately voted out of office by the National Assembly and replaced by the former education minister, Manuel Solis Palma. Delvalle's downfall was seen as further evidence of the power and influence of General Noriega, who had become the country's *de facto* ruler. US support for the former president was also seen as a reason for his demise. The US government's immediate reaction was to increase its forces in the Canal Zone, as a show of military strength, and to put economic pressure on Panama by freezing its assets in the United States.

With mounting unrest in the country, a group of Panamanian officers, led by police chief Leonidas Macias, attempted a coup but this was quickly foiled by troops loyal to Noriega. The US administration then attempted to negotiate the general's departure by offering to drop federal charges against him for drug trafficking, but the attempted deal had the effect of discrediting the Reagan administration and strengthening support for Noriega.

In May 1989 the elections for the Legislative Assembly were clearly fraudulent and were eventually declared invalid. The United States put more pressure on Noriega to resign and strengthened its Canal Zone garrison. Then, in December 1989, US troops were ordered to enter the country by force to arrest him. The mission was code-named 'Operation Just Cause'. After seeking refuge in the Vatican embassy, Noriega eventually gave himself up and was taken to Florida for trial, and in 1992 was found guilty of drugs offences. He was given a 40-year prison sentence. In October 1993 he was also convicted of murder in Panamanian courts. but in March 1999 a US judge reduced his existing sentence by 10 years. The US authorities installed Guillermo Endara as president in December 1989. He was said to have won the earlier invalid election and now embarked on an economic reform program, including privatization.

The influence of the military in Panama was progressively reduced and in December 1991 the Assembly formally dissolved the army. However, a referendum held in November 1992 rejected a reform package, which would have outlawed the creation of a standing army. The position was eventually clarified in August 1994, when the Legislative Assembly overwhelmingly approved a constitutional amendment abolishing the army 'in order to avoid a return to military rule'.

In May 1994, in the first completely free elections in the nation's history, the Revolutionary Democratic Party (PRD) won the presidency, in the person of Ernesto Pérez (b. 1946), and most seats in the Legislative Assembly. Pérez, a US-educated millionaire businessman, formed a minority PRD government.

On 8 January 1998 the last US troops pulled out of Quarry Heights, the nerve center of the US's Southern Command. In an August 1998 referendum, voters rejected a proposed change in the constitution which would have allowed president Peréz to run for a second term. This was seen as partly a verdict on the president's radical program of free-market economic reforms, which had sharply increased the level of unemployment.

The May 1999 presidential election was won by Mireya Moscoso, of the AD, who had been runner up to Perez in 1994. Moscoso was the widow of three times president Arnulfo Arias and took over from Perez, to become the country's first female president, in September 1999. Facing an opposition-dominated Legislative Assembly, after concurrent elections, she announced her intention to convene a constituent assembly to reform the constitution.

ST KITTS (CHRISTOPHER) AND NEVIS

St Kitts and Nevis

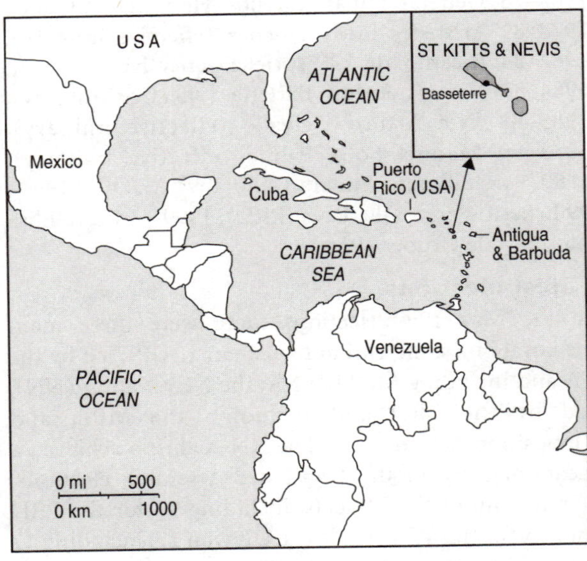

Capital: Basseterre

Social and economic data

Area: 261 sq km/101 sq miles
Population: 41,000*
Pop. density per sq km/sq mi: 157/406*
Urban population: 41%**
Literacy rate: 98%**
GDP: $212 million*; per- capita GDP: $5,170*
Government defense spending (% of GDP): N/A
Currency: East Caribbean dollar

Economy type: middle income
Labor force in agriculture: N/A
* 1995.
** 1992.

Head of state

Queen Elizabeth II, represented by Governor General Sir Cuthbert Montraville Sebastian since 1996

Head of government

Prime Minister Denzil Douglas, since 1995

Ethnic composition

The population is almost entirely of African descent.

Religions

The majority of the population belongs to the Anglican, 36%, and Methodist, 32%, Protestant churches, with a Roman Catholic, 11%, minority.

Political features

State type: liberal democratic
Date of state formation: 1983
Political structure: federal
Executive: parliamentary
Assembly: one-chamber
Party structure: multiparty
Human rights rating: N/A
International affiliations: ACP, ACS, CARICOM, CW, IBRD, IMF, IWC, OAS, OECS, UN, WTO

Local and regional government

Despite the smallness of the land area and population, a limited federal system operates. Nevis Island has its own Assembly, of five elected and three nominated members, a prime minister and cabinet, and a deputy governor general representing the British monarch. Nevis has the constitutional right to secede from the union with St Kitts, subject to approval in a referendum. St Kitts is run directly by the federal government. The two islands are divided into parishes, for administrative purposes, St Kitts having nine and Nevis five.

Political system

The islands of Saint Christopher, often called St Kitts, and Nevis are a federation constituting an independent state within the Commonwealth. Although the total population is only about 41,000, it has, in effect, a federal constitution which dates from independence in 1983 and provides for a parliamentary system for the two islands, on the lines of that of the United Kingdom. The governor general is the formal head of state, representing the British monarch.

There is a single-chamber National Assembly of 14 members. Eleven representatives are popularly elected for five years by universal adult suffrage, through a simple plurality voting system, comprising eight from St Kitts and three from Nevis Island. Three senators are appointed by the governor general: two on the advice of the prime minister and one on the advice of the leader of the opposition. The governor general also appoints the prime minister and cabinet who are drawn from and responsible to the Assembly. As in the United Kingdom, the leader of the second largest party in the Assembly is the official leader of the opposition.

Political parties

There are currently eight active political parties, the four most significant being the People's Action Movement (PAM), the Nevis Reformation Party (NRP), the Saint Kitts-Nevis Labor Party (SKLP), and the Concerned Citizens' Movement (CCM). The PAM was formed in 1965. It has a center-right orientation. The NRP was created in 1970 as the focus of a movement to secure the separation of Nevis from St Kitts. It has a centrist orientation.

The SKLP is the country's oldest political organization, dating back to the Workers' League of 1932. It is a moderate, left-of-center party.

The CCM is a recently formed centrist party, based in Nevis and led by Vance Amory, the island's premier. It advocates independence.

Political leaders since 1970

1967–78 Robert Bradshaw (SKLP), 1978–79 Paul Southwell (SKLP), 1979–80 Lee L Moore (SKLP), 1980–95 Kennedy Alphonse Simmonds (PAM-NRP coalition), 1995– Denzil Douglas (SKLP)

Latest elections

In the July 1995 general election the SKLP won 7 National Assembly seats, the CCM, 2, the PAM, 1, and the NRP, 1.

Political history

St Kitts (known locally as Liamuiga), visited by Christopher Columbus (1451–1506) in 1493, was the first British colony in the West Indies, dating back to 1623, and Nevis was settled very soon afterwards. Anguilla (see *Chapter 8*) was joined to the two islands in 1816 and between 1871 and 1956 they were administered as part of the Leeward Islands Federation. Sugar cane planting became the mainstay of the economy. After World War I a campaign began for the islands' independence. The Labor Party (SKLP) was formed in 1932 as the vanguard of the independence movement.

Saint Kitts-Nevis-Anguilla joined the West Indies Federation in 1956 and remained in membership until its dissolution in 1962. There was an abortive attempt to form a smaller East Caribbean Federation and then the three islands became Associated States, with internal self-government, within the Commonwealth, in 1967.

Robert Bradshaw, leader of the SKLP, became the first prime minister and was re-elected in 1971 and 1975. In 1970 the Nevis Reformation Party (NRP) was formed, calling for separation for Nevis, and the following year Anguilla, disagreeing with the government in St Kitts, chose to return to being a British dependency. Bradshaw died in 1978 and was succeeded by his deputy, Paul Southwell, but he, too, died the following year to be replaced by Lee L Moore.

The 1980 general election produced a 'hung' Assembly and, although the SKLP won more than 50% of the popular vote, a PAM-NRP coalition government was formed, with the People's Action Movement (PAM) founder and leader, Dr Kennedy A Simmonds (b. 1936), as prime minister. Full independence was scheduled for 1983 and the SKLP argued there should be a general election before then but this was rejected by the government, in the face of sometimes violent opposition.

On 1 September 1983 St Kitts and Nevis became a fully independent federal state, within the Commonwealth, with an opportunity for Nevis to secede, under certain conditions, being written into the constitution. In the 1984 general election the PAM-NRP coalition was decisively returned to office.

The 1993 general election produced an inconclusive result and a minor political crisis, as Simmonds tried to construct a new government. Because of demonstrations outside government offices, the governor general declared a one-day state of emergency but, eventually, a PAM-NRP administration was agreed, with Simmonds continuing as prime minister. A snap election in July 1995 resulted in a win for the SKLP and its leader, Denzil Douglas, became prime minister.

The islands' proximity to Colombia has placed them within direct line of the 'cocaine route' and in 1995 the growth of drug trafficking became apparent, with retaliations by drug dealers as the police tried to stamp out the menace.

In October 1998 the Nevis Island assembly voted to secede from St Kitts, since it believed that the island's interests were neglected within the federation. Nevis had a population of 10,000 and contributed 40% of the federation's total tax revenue. However, a subsequent referendum, held in August 1998, produced a 'yes' vote of 62% for independence, which was below the required two-thirds majority. Meanwhile, a federal constitution commission recommended creating a more genuinely federal system of government, headed by an elected president within a republic.

ST LUCIA

Capital: Castries

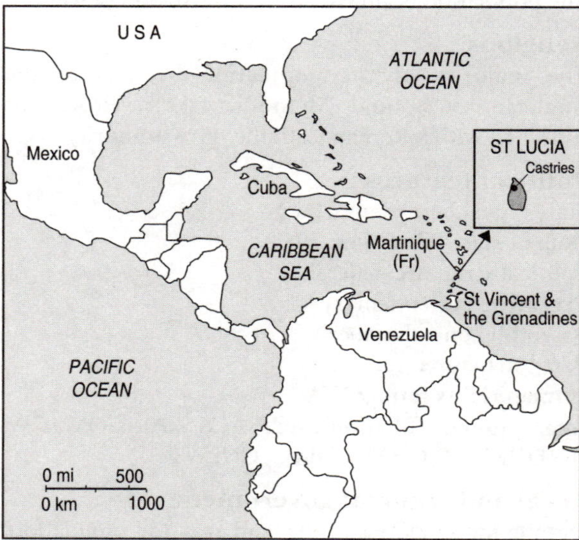

Social and economic data

Area: 620 sq km/239 sq miles
Population: 141,000*
Pop. density per sq km/sq mi: 227/590*
Urban population: 47%**
Literacy rate: 82%**
GDP: $532 million*; per-capita GDP $3,775*
Government defense spending (% of GDP): N/A**
Currency: East Caribbean dollar
Economy type: middle income
Labor force in agriculture: N/A
* 1995.
** 1992.

Head of state

Queen Elizabeth II, represented by Governor General Perlette Louisy since 1997

Head of government

Prime Minister Kenny Anthony, since 1997

Ethnic composition

The great majority of the population is of African descent.

Religions

Eighty per cent of the population is Roman Catholic. The rest belongs mainly to the Anglican or other Protestant churches.

Political features

State type: liberal democratic
Date of state formation: 1979
Political structure: unitary
Executive: parliamentary
Assembly: two-chamber
Party structure: two-party
Human rights rating: N/A
International affiliations: ACP, ACS, CARICOM, CW, IBRD, IMF, IWC, NAM, OAS, OECS, UN, WTO

Local and regional government

The country is divided into 16 parishes, each representing a town or village. They have partly elected and partly appointed councils.

Political system

The constitution dates from independence in 1979. It provides for a constitutional monarchy with a parliamentary system based broadly on that of the United Kingdom. There is a two-chamber parliament, comprising a Senate, of 11 appointed members, and a House of Assembly, of 17 members, elected from single-member constituencies by universal adult suffrage, through a simple plurality system of voting. Members of the Senate are appointed by the governor general, six on the advice of the prime minister, three on the advice of the leader of the opposition, and two after wider consultation. Parliament has a life of five years but is subject to dissolution within that period. The governor general appoints a prime minister and cabinet on the basis of House of Assembly support. They are all drawn from and responsible to it. The leader of the party with the second highest number of seats in the House is the official leader of the opposition.

Political parties

There are three active political parties, the United Workers' Party (UWP), the St Lucia Labor Party (SLP), and the Progressive Labor Party (PLP).

The UWP was founded in 1961 by John Compton as a rightwing breakaway from the SLP, which itself developed from the Workers' Union in the late 1940s. The PLP was formed in 1981 by SLP dissidents. The PLP and SLP have moderate, left-of-center orientations.

Political leaders since 1970

1964–79 John Compton (UWP), 1979–81 Allan Louisy (SLP), 1981–82 Winston Cenac (SLP), 1982–96 John Compton (UWP), 1996–97 Vaughan Lewis (UWP), 1997– Kenny Anthony (SLP)

Latest elections

In the May 1997 general election the SLP inflicted a major defeat on the governing UWP. It secured 61% of the vote and 16 seats to the UWP's one seat with 37% of the vote.

Political history

St Lucia was ceded to Britain by France at the Treaty of Paris of 1814 and remained a British colony within the Windward Islands federal system until 1960. The federal system was ended and, in 1967, it acquired internal self-government as a West Indies Associated State. The founder and leader of the United Workers' Party (UWP), John Compton (b. 1926), a UK-trained barrister, became prime minister with the St Lucia Labor Party (SLP) forming the opposition. In 1975 the Associated States agreed to seek independence separately and, in February 1979, after prolonged negotiations, St Lucia achieved full independence within the Commonwealth, with Compton as prime minister.

Later that year the SLP returned to power under its leader, Allan Louisy, but a split developed within the party and in 1981 Louisy was forced to resign, being replaced by the attorney general, Winston Cenac. Soon afterwards George Odlum, who had been Louisy's deputy, left, with two other SLP members, to form a new party, the Progressive Labor Party (PLP). For the next year the Cenac government had to fight off calls for a change of government which culminated in a general strike. Cenac eventually resigned and in the general election held in May 1982 the UWP won a decisive victory enabling John Compton to return as prime minister. The UWP retained its control of the House of Assembly in the 1987 and 1992 elections. In April 1996 John Compton announced his retirement and was succeeded as UWP leader and prime minister by Vaughan Lewis, but in the May 1997 general election the UWP suffered a heavy defeat and the SLP leader, Kenny Anthony, formed a government.

Banana production remains crucial to the country's economy, providing 40% of export earnings, and a fall in prices in 1993 resulted in unrest and strikes by farmers and agricultural workers. Unemployment is high, but tourism is being developed. In

1991 exploratory moves were made towards a Windward Islands Federation, with Dominica, Grenada and St Vincent, but little progress was subsequently evident.

ST VINCENT AND THE GRENADINES

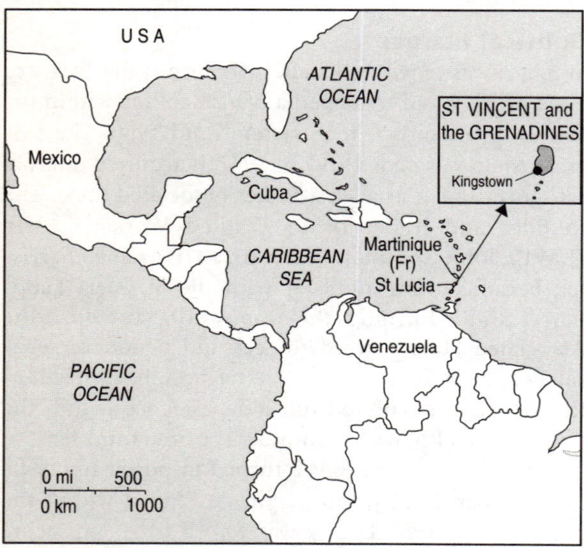

Capital: Kingstown

Social and economic data

Area: 390 sq km/151 sq miles
Population: 111,000*
Pop. density per sq km/sq mi: 285/735*
Urban population: 25%**
Literacy rate: 96%**
GDP: $253 million*; per-capita GDP: $2,280*
Government defense spending (% of GDP): N/A
Currency: Caribbean dollar
Economy type: middle income
Labor force in agriculture: 50%**
* 1995.
** 1992.

Head of state

Queen Elizabeth II, represented by Governor General Sir David Jack since 1989

Head of government

Prime Minister Sir James F Mitchell, since 1984

Ethnic composition

Most of the original, indigenous Caribs have disappeared and the population is now largely of African origin.

Religions

The great majority of people are Christian: Anglicans, 42%, Methodists, 21%, or Roman Catholics, 12%.

Political features

State type: liberal democratic
Date of state formation: 1979
Political structure: unitary
Executive: parliamentary
Assembly: one-chamber
Party structure: two-party
Human rights rating: N/A
International affiliations: ACP, ACS, CARICOM, CW, IBRD, IMF, IWC, OAS, OECS, UN, WTO

Local and regional government

For administrative purposes, the country is divided into five parishes, with 13 divisions within them.

Political system

The constitution dates from independence in 1979. It provides for a constitutional monarchy with a parliamentary system of government based in several respects on that of the United Kingdom, a resident governor general representing the British monarch. There is a single-chamber House of Assembly, with 21 members. Of these, 15 representatives are directly elected by universal adult suffrage, through a simple plurality voting system, four senators are appointed by the governor general on the advice of the prime minister, and two senators are appointed on the advice of the leader of the opposition. The Assembly has a life of five years but is subject to dissolution within that time. The governor general appoints a prime minister and cabinet who are drawn from and responsible to the Assembly. The leader of the party with the second largest number of seats in the Assembly is the official leader of the opposition.

Political parties

There are some three active political parties, the two most significant being the New Democratic Party (NDP) and the Unity Labor Party (ULP).

The NDP was formed in 1975 by James Mitchell, a former member of the St Vincent Labor Party (SVLP) and prime minister. It has a right-of-center orientation.

The ULP was formed in 1994 by a merger of the SVLP and the Movement for National Unity (MNU). It has a moderate center-left orientation.

Political leaders since 1970

1967–72 Milton Cato (SVLP), 1972–74 James Mitchell (PPP), 1974–79 Milton Cato (SVLP-PPP coalition), 1979–84 Milton Cato (SVLP), 1984– James Mitchell (NDP)

Latest elections

In the June 1998 general election the NDP, with 54% of the vote, won eight Assembly seats (down four) and James Mitchell continued as prime minister. The remaining seven seats were won by a center-left alliance, led by the ULP, who secured 46% of the vote.

Political history

The island of St Vincent was visited by Christopher Columbus (1451–1506) in 1498 on St Vincent's day. Possession was disputed by France and Britain during the 17th and 18th centuries, but in 1783, under the terms of the Treaty of Versailles, the island, along with the Grenadines, a chain of 32 tiny islands and cays, was finally ceded to Britain. The colony was part of the West Indies Federation until it was dissolved in 1962. The islands then acquired internal self-government in 1969 as an Associated State, within the Commonwealth. They achieved full independence, still within the Commonwealth, as St Vincent and the Grenadines, in October 1979.

Until the 1980s two political parties dominated politics in the islands, the St Vincent Labor Party (SVLP) and the People's Political Party (PPP). Milton Cato, SVLP leader, was prime minister at independence but his leadership was challenged in 1981 when a decline in the economy and his attempts to introduce new industrial relations legislation resulted in a general strike. Cato survived mainly because of divisions in the opposition parties and in 1984, hoping to take advantage of these divisions, he called an early general election. The New Democratic Party (NDP), which had been formed by an SVLP defector and former prime minister, James Mitchell (b. 1931), won a surprising victory, which was confirmed in 1989, when the NDP won all 15 elective seats.

In September 1991 provisional moves were made to integrate with Dominica, Grenada, and St Lucia into a Windward Islands Federation and, after being re-elected in February 1994, Prime Minister Mitchell said he would still pursue the proposal. He secured a fourth successive term, but with a reduced majority, in June 1998.

Banana production and tourism are the staples of the islands' economies.

TRINIDAD AND TOBAGO

The Republic of Trinidad and Tobago

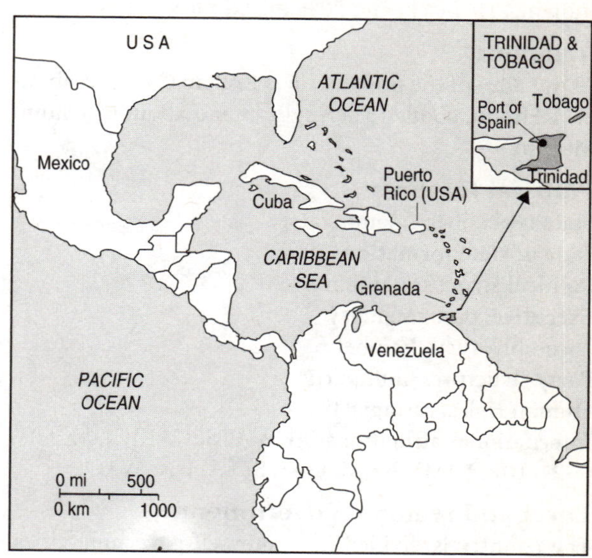

Capital: Port of Spain

Social and economic data

Area: 5,130 sq km/1,981 sq miles
Population: 1,257,000*
Pop. density per sq km/sq mi: 245/635*
Urban population: 66%**
Literacy rate: 95%**
GDP: $4,850 million*; per-capita GDP: $3,860*
Government defense spending (% of GDP): 1.3*
Currency: Trinidad and Tobago dollar
Economy type: middle income
Labor force in agriculture: 12%**
Unemployment rate: 17.2%*
* 1995.
** 1992.

Head of state

President Arthur N R Robinson, since 1997

Head of government

Prime Minister Baseo Panday, since 1995

Ethnic composition

There are two main ethnic groups, one comprising Africans, who were originally brought in as slaves to work on the sugar plantations, and the other East Indians, who came to the country as indentured laborers from India after the abolition of slavery in the

1830s. There are also minorities of Europeans, Afro-Europeans, and Chinese. The original Carib population has largely disappeared. Today the country is 40% Indian, 40% black, and 20% mixed race.

Religions

About 34% of the population is Roman Catholic, about 25% Hindu, about 15% Anglican and about 6% Sunni Muslim.

Political features

State type: liberal democratic
Date of state formation: 1962
Political structure: unitary
Executive: parliamentary
Assembly: two-chamber
Party structure: multiparty
Human rights rating: 84%
International affiliations: ACP, ACS, CARICOM, CW, G-24, IBRD, IMF, NAM, OAS, SELA, UN, WTO

Local and regional government

The country is divided into four self-governing cities, six counties, and the semi-autonomous island of Tobago. The local government system displays some of the features of the unreformed system of the United Kingdom, with elected councillors and aldermen being politically responsible for the provision of local services.

Political system

Trinidad and Tobago is an independent republic within the Commonwealth. The 1976 constitution provides for a president, who is a constitutional head of state, and a two-chamber assembly, consisting of a Senate of 31 members and a House of Representatives of 36 members. The president appoints the prime minister and cabinet who are collectively responsible to the House of Representatives. The leader of the party with the second largest number of seats in the House is the official leader of the opposition. The president also appoints the 31 senators, 16 on the advice of the prime minister, six on the advice of the leader of the opposition, and nine after wider consultation. The 36 members of the House of Representatives are elected by universal adult suffrage, through a simple plurality voting system. The assembly has a life of five years. The president is elected by an electoral college drawn from the Senate and the House.

Tobago island was given its own House of Assembly in 1980. It has 15 members, 12 popularly elected and three chosen by the majority party. It achieved full internal self-government in 1987.

Political parties

There are some four major political parties. They are the National Alliance for Reconstruction (NAR), the People's National Movement (PNM), the United National Congress (UNC), and the Movement for Social Transformation (Motion).

The NAR was formed in 1984 as a coalition of moderate, leftwing parties. It became a united, separate party in 1986. It has a nationalistic, left-of-center orientation.

The PNM was founded in 1956 by Eric Williams, a well-known Caribbean historian. It had its origins in the Teachers' Economic and Cultural Association. The PNM has a nationalistic, moderate centrist stance. It seeks to appeal to all races, but its chief constituency is black.

Until the 1991 general election the NAR and the PNM had dominated the country's politics. This domination was challenged by the formation of the UNC, led by Basdeo Panday, and Motion. The UNC was formed by NAR dissidents in 1989 and draws its support from the Indian community. Motion was formed in the same year. Both have left-of-center orientations.

Political leaders since 1970

1959–81 Eric Williams (PNM), 1981–86 George Chambers (PNM), 1986–91 Arthur Robinson (NAR), 1991–95 Patrick Manning (PNM), 1995– Baseo Panday (UNC)

Latest elections

In the November 1995 general election the PNM won 17 seats, with 48% of the vote, and the UNC also 17, with a 46% vote share. The NAR won the remaining two seats in Tobago. The February 1997 presidential election was won by Arthur Robinson (NAR).

Political history

Trinidad was colonized by Spain in the 16th century and ceded to Britain, under the Treaty of Amiens, in 1802. Tobago had been colonized by Dutch, English, and French settlers and became a British colony, in the Windward Islands group, in 1814. The two islands became a joint British Crown Colony in 1899 and, after World War II, movement towards self-government, and eventual independence, began.

The country's first political party, the People's National Movement (PNM), was formed by Dr Eric Williams, a renowned historian, in 1956, and when the colony was granted internal self-government in 1959 he became the first chief minister. Between 1958 and 1961 it was a member of the Federation of the West Indies but withdrew and achieved full independence, within the Commonwealth, in 1967, Williams becoming the first prime minister. His moderate policies provoked an army mutiny and Black Power revolt in 1970.

A new constitution was adopted in 1976 and made the country a republic. The former governor general, Ellis Clarke, became the first president and Williams continued as prime minister. He died in March 1981 without having nominated a successor and the president appointed George Chambers for an interim period until the PNM formally adopted him as leader, in May 1981. In the general election of that year the PNM marginally increased its majority, while the leader of a moderate left wing party grouping, the Trinidad and Tobago National Alliance, Arthur 'Ray' Robinson (b. 1926), a former deputy leader of the PNM, was leader of the opposition.

In the next few years the National Alliance was reorganized into a more credible party, as the National Alliance for Reconstruction (NAR), and in the 1986 general election it swept the PNM from power and Arthur Robinson, a UK-trained barrister, became prime minister. By 1988 the fall in world oil prices had had an adverse effect on the economy, resulting in strains within the NAR and the government. In July 1990 an attempted coup by 120 Islamic fundamentalists, who held parliamentarians and ministers hostage, shooting Prime Minister Robinson in the legs, was foiled after a six-day siege. Disenchantment with Robinson led to an astonishing defeat for his party in the December 1991 general election, its seat holding dropping from 33 to two. Patrick Manning, leader of the triumphant PNM, became the new prime minister.

In August 1995 the speaker of the House of Representatives, Occah Seapaul, was placed temporarily under house arrest for refusing to resign after allegedly bringing her position into disrepute after trying unsuccessfully to sue a former business partner for defrauding her. A state of emergency was briefly imposed. The opposition parties described the speaker's detention as madness.

A general election, held in November 1995, produced a dead heat between the PNM and the predominantly Indian UNC. A UNC-led government led by Baseo Panday and supported by the Tobago-based NAR was formed. Arthur Robinson was elected president in February 1997 following the retirement of Noor Mohammad Hassanali, amid claims by opposition parties that Robinson had been too active in politics to be a fair-minded president.

Central, Eastern, and Southern Europe

Before 1991 it was sensible to view Central and Eastern Europe as a politically homogenous block. There were nine states, Albania, Bulgaria, Czechoslovakia, East Germany, Hungary, Poland, Romania, the Soviet Union, and Yugoslavia, each having a communist political system. However, between 1989–91 communism collapsed; the federations of Czechoslovakia, Russia, and Yugoslavia splintered into 22 separate sovereign states; East Germany was reunited with the Federal Republic of Germany; and emergent democratic regimes were widely established across the region. Thus for this second edition, Eastern Europe, essentially a political construct, has been replaced by a more coherent geographical entity, Central, Eastern, and Southern Europe. This new region embraces the postcommunist successor states of Central and Eastern Europe as well as the three Southern European states, Cyprus, Greece, and Turkey, but excludes the five countries of 'Turkestan' (Kazakhstan, Kyrgyzstan, Tajikistan, Turkmenistan, and Uzbekistan), which were formerly part of the Soviet Union but are rightly part of Asia.

The 25 states of Central, Eastern, and Southern Europe, including Russia, the world's largest country, cover 20 million square kilometres. This is equivalent to almost a sixth of the world's land area. However, with a combined population of 433 million, the region accounts for only 8% of the global population, and its GDP of $1,040 billion is 4% of the world's total. Per-capita GDP in the region averaged $2,400 in *c.* 1995. Two-thirds of the states have middle incomes, six low incomes, and only three, Cyprus, Greece, and Slovenia, high incomes.

Politically, the region comprises 19 emergent democracies, three authoritarian nationalist regimes, and three liberal democracies: Cyprus, Greece, which is a member of the European Union and NATO, and Turkey, which is also a member of NATO. However, as noted in Chapter 3, at least six of the region's emergent democracies (Albania, Georgia, Macedonia, Moldova, Romania, and Yugoslavia) are still very much in an embryonic state and possess a number of authoritarian nationalist features, while democracy in Bosnia-Herzegovina was nonfunctioning until 1996 as a result of the ongoing civil war. The republican form of government is uniform across the region and only three states have federal structures: Bosnia-Herzegovina, Russia, and Yugoslavia. In eight of the region's states the limited presidential executive type is found, with the parliamentary executive in a quarter, the dual executive in eight, and the unlimited presidential in three. All of the countries have multiparty systems. However, in many of the states party structures are weakly developed and, consequently, government coalitions fragile and unstable. For example, 29 minor parties secured representation in Poland's parliament in October 1991 and in 1993 between 5–7 parties held seats in the parliaments of Bulgaria, the Czech and Slovak republics, Hungary, and Romania. This is because these states are currently situated in only the first or second phase, that of 'basic democracy' and constitution-building, of the three-phase transition from communist totalitarianism to a mixed economy-based political pluralism that has been posited by Zbigniew Brzezinski. Entry into the crucial third phase, one characterized by a full legal and entrepreneurial culture and the existence of a stable party system, may take anything between 10–20 years. In 22 states in the region, the electoral system is based on proportional representation. Elsewhere, the second ballot majoritarian system is employed in two states and the single plurality in one.

Socio-economically, Central, Eastern, and Southern Europe is a middle income, or 'Second World', region. However, the pattern of income distribution and spending differs significantly from that found in a similar middle-income region, Latin America, with the state, as a result of the legacy of communism, playing a much greater role in economic and social life. For example, in 1992 social spending on welfare, education, and health accounted for 25% of GDP in Central and Eastern Europe compared to just 10% in Latin America. In addition, government defense spending exceeded 3% of GDP in 18 of the region's states, compared to just three states in South America, and was between 7–11% in Russia, Cyprus Ukraine, and Yugoslavia.

Since 1989 the nations of Central and Eastern Europe have abandoned central planning and embraced the market to differing degrees and with varying measures of success. One consequence of this 'transition to capitalism' was a severe contraction in regional and national GDPs, by at least 20%, between 1989–94. In addition, rates of inflation and unemployment increased sharply as uncompetitive, state-subsidized enterprises were left to compete in an 'open economy' and as prices were freed. In some states, notably Poland, Ukraine, Russia, Belarus, Georgia, and Yugoslavia, hyperinflation was experienced during the

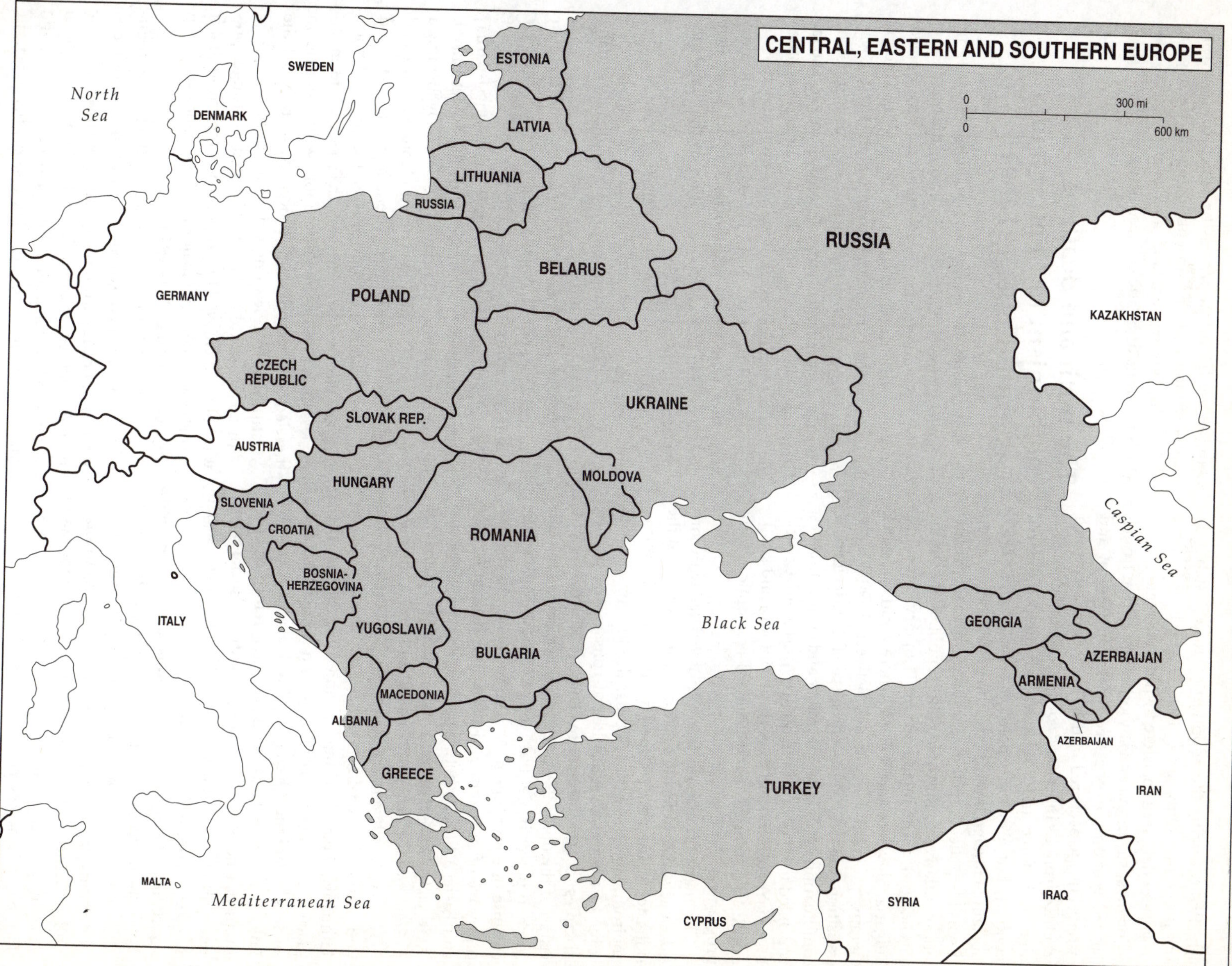

CENTRAL, EASTERN AND SOUTHERN EUROPE
0
300 mi
0
600 km
North Sea
SWEDEN
DENMARK
ESTONIA
LATVIA
LITHUANIA
RUSSIA
RUSSIA
BELARUS
GERMANY
POLAND
KAZAKHSTAN
CZECH REPUBLIC
UKRAINE
SLOVAK REP.
AUSTRIA
HUNGARY
MOLDOVA
Caspian Sea
SLOVENIA
CROATIA
ROMANIA
BOSNIA-HERZEGOVINA
ITALY
Black Sea
GEORGIA
YUGOSLAVIA
BULGARIA
AZERBAIJAN
ARMENIA
MACEDONIA
ALBANIA
AZERBAIJAN
GREECE
TURKEY
IRAN
MALTA
Mediterranean Sea
SYRIA
IRAQ
CYPRUS

early 1990s, forcing the adoption of austere stabilization programs. Only since 1995 has a broad-based growth in GDP been registered within the region.

The most successful and smoothest transition from a planned economy to the free market in Central and Eastern Europe occurred in the Czech Republic, which benefited from its inheritance of a skilled and well-educated work force and a relatively advanced industrial economy, but also from political stability after 1989, substantial foreign inward investment and the adoption of sensible policies, including a successful mass privatization initiative. In the three Baltic republics of Estonia, Latvia, and Lithuania, and in Hungary, Slovenia, Bulgaria, Slovakia, and Poland, where a radical 'shock therapy' program was pursued between 1990–93, the transition was also relatively successful. Elsewhere, a combination of political instability and ethnic disputes, which led to civil wars in Armenia, Azerbaijan, Croatia, Bosnia, Yugoslavia, and in parts of Moldova and southern Russia, stymied market-centerd economic reform programs.

The 'market transition' has been associated with considerable social suffering for those who have lacked the skills to adjust and prosper in the new competitive environment. This led to popular disillusionment with some of the more radical liberal-conservative parties, disciples of the Reaganite–Thatcherite 'new right' vision of the unbridled free market, which had initially come to power in Central Europe in 1989–90 after the collapse of communism. As a consequence, in the second wave of postcommunist elections held in Central and Eastern Europe between 1992–95, voters rejected 'new right' conservative parties such as Isamaa in Estonia and the internally divided and politically inexperienced, intelligentsia-led center-right Popular Front and nationalist coalitions that had held power in Lithuania, Poland, Hungary, and Bulgaria. In their place, they returned to office either maverick populists, such as Vladimir Meciar in Slovakia and Alexander Lukashenko in Belarus, or experienced reformed communists, who pledged to maintain a strong 'social safety net' within the framework of a German-style 'social market economy'. Elsewhere in the region, in Azerbaijan, Georgia, Romania, Russia, Ukraine, and Yugoslavia, excommunists had never really left power. Clearly then, outside Cyprus, Greece, and Turkey, the communist legacy remains strong, continuing to shape and influence political developments. To understand current political dynamics in Central and Eastern Europe, it is necessary to go beyond the present and examine the historical process by which communism became established and so entrenched in the region during the postwar era and also analyse the forces which led to its dramatic collapse between 1989–91.

The birth and death of communism in Central and Eastern Europe: 1917–91

The first communist regime was established in 1917 in the Soviet Union (USSR) when, following the March and October revolutions, the Tsarist autocracy was toppled and a new socialist republic, under the 'guiding hand' of the Communist Party of the Soviet Union (CPSU), was created. This embraced the current sovereign states of Armenia, Azerbaijan, Belarus, Estonia, Georgia, Latvia, Lithuania, Moldova, Russia, and Ukraine. The other communist political executives in Central and Eastern Europe dated from the end of World War II. In most cases, they were set up with Soviet support soon after their liberation from Nazi occupation, as the Red Army advanced westwards in 1944.

The actual method by which these communist systems were established and the degree of popular support which they initially enjoyed varied substantially from country to country.

In the cases of Poland, the newly created German Democratic Republic (GDR), and Romania, the new system was arbitrarily imposed by fiat.

In Bulgaria and Hungary, more subtle quasi-parliamentary means were pursued, with the Soviet-linked, indigenous communist parties (CPs) initially forming a 'Popular Front' coalition with moderate socialist and radical-centrist groupings. Then, between 1947 and 1949, by establishing control over the media, police, and state electoral commissions, the CPs, despite enjoying less than 15% of popular support, won majorities in the elected assemblies and proceeded to remodel the constitutions in a new one-party direction.

In Czechoslovakia the CP inherited a stronger prewar base and enjoyed broad popular support, so that it was able to secure the majority of the national vote in the free election of May 1946.

Finally, in Albania and Yugoslavia, the new communist regimes, which assumed control in 1944–45, differed significantly from those to the northwest, having been established, without direct Red Army aid, by local guerrilla resistance leaders, Enver Hoxha in Albania and Marshal Tito in Yugoslavia. Because of their 'Partisan' anti-Nazi activities, they initially enjoyed popular support.

By 1949, all the states of contemporary Central and Eastern Europe had communist systems firmly in place. They were initially structured, with the notable exception of Tito's Yugoslavia, in close conformity with the 'Stalinist model' then prevailing in the USSR. This involved tight, hierarchical party control over all aspects of political, social, and cultural life; the promotion of leadership 'personality cults'; the terroristic use of secret police to suppress internal political opposition and dissent; and, in the economic sphere, agrarian collectivization, bureaucratic central planning, and concentration on heavy industrialization.

However, with the maverick exception of Hoxha's Albania, which broke with the USSR in 1961 in opposition to Khrushchev's denunciation of the Stalin era, 'Stalinization' was never fully completed in the Central European satellites. Bulgaria came closest. Elsewhere, internal opposition, pressing for more liberal and inclusive political structures, periodically surfaced in the form of workers' revolts and intelligentsia campaigns, forcing prudent changes of course. In the cases of East Berlin in 1953, Hungary in 1956, and Prague in 1968, Soviet or Warsaw Pact troops had to be employed to restore CP control. In Poland, in December 1981, martial law was imposed by the country's own military forces as a means of suppressing a serious internal challenge to the incumbent Polish United Workers' Party regime.

In Central and Eastern Europe the postwar era was thus characterized, on the one hand, by broad stability and on the other, by periodic challenges to the authority of the ruling CPs. The stability was achieved by tight links with their dominant eastern neighbor, the USSR, through the economic, military, and political structures of Comecon, the Warsaw Treaty Organization, and the Comintern. Only the Balkan states of Albania and Yugoslavia remained aloof from these. The recurrent periods of opposition forced policy adjustments and partial departures from the Soviet model in both the political and economic spheres. The socio-cultural heterogeneity of this region, coupled with a history of subjection to autocratic, external rule, economic backwardness, and nascent democratization during the interwar decades, were crucial factors helping to explain these conflicting trends. They resulted in the creation of a unique 'political culture'.

With the exception of the Muscovy (RSFSR) heartland of what was the Soviet Union, which formed the core for the successive Kiev-based (10th–12th centuries), Moscow-based (1462–1709), and St Petersburg (Leningrad)-based (1709–1917) Russian empires, state creation came late to Central and Eastern Europe. Albania, Armenia, Bulgaria, Czechoslovakia, Georgia, Hungary, Lithuania, Macedonia, Poland, Romania, Ukraine, and Yugoslavia (Serbia) had formed the cores of ancient and medieval kingdoms, but none had emerged as a substantially coherent nation-state until the late 19th and early 20th centuries. The majority were formed only at the close of World War I.

Before this, and because of their strategically important position between Asia and Northwestern Europe, they found themselves at various times under the authority of either the Turkish, Austrian, German, or Russian empires. As a consequence, Central and Eastern Europe was exposed to a variety of influences, religious, legal, scriptural, and institutional.

Although differing in detail, all the empires had a common autocratic-bureaucratic character. This served to rule out autonomous political evolution in a liberal-democratic direction. Similarly, it checked the growth of national cultural traditions, fostering, instead, localized, subregional identities. These legacies are still apparent today. They generated, on the one hand, deferential and subservient attitudes to those in positions of authority and, on the other hand, regional divisions which have tended to undermine the cohesion of national movements, pro- or anti government.

In the economic sphere, the centuries of control by alien empires resulted in 'peripheral' Central and Eastern Europe's relative underdevelopment compared with that of adjoining Western Europe. This arose partly from resource deficiencies, but, more significantly, from the retention of outmoded socio-economic structures, most notably serfdom, more than a century after they had been discarded in the West. Industrial development was consequently retarded and began only fitfully at the close of the 19th century, with the state playing a directing role and large capital-intensive factories becoming the norm. This tended to restrict the growth of urban working-class communities and a powerful middle class. Only in eastern Germany and in parts of Czechoslovakia, Slovenia, and West Poland did a more rounded development occur.

During the interwar years, there were significant changes in the East European political and socio-economic scene as new states came into existence and tentative experiments were made with new liberal-democratic constitutional forms. The exception, of course, was the USSR where, under Stalin's lead, attention was focused on establishing 'socialism in one country', by a radical restructuring of the nation's economic and political system.

Elsewhere, the 1919 Treaty of Versailles had established new parliamentary structures, supported by broad franchises and generous proportional representation electoral systems. Unfortunately, the new states were, in many respects, arbitrary territorial constructions, below the foundations of which lay the seeds of internal religious and ethnic conflicts. These differences worked themselves through into the political systems, resulting in a multiplicity of parties achieving assembly representation and creating chronic governmental instability.

Reacting against this, the conservative-nationalist parties who gained the upper hand over centrist-liberal groups during the mid- and later 1920s, proceeded, in all the Central and East European states, with the notable exception of Czechoslovakia, to abrogate parliamentary forms of government and establish new monarchic or presidential autocracies of a quasi-fascist kind.

The resulting regimes, such as those of King Boris in Bulgaria (1934–43), Admiral Horthy in Hungary (1920–44), King Karol in Romania (1930–40), King Zog in Albania (1928–39), Ullmanis in Latvia (1934–39), Voldemaras and Smetona in Lithuania (1926–29 and 1929–40), Marshals Piłsudski and Smigly-Rydz in Poland (1926–35 and 1935–39), and King Alexander and Regent Paul in Yugoslavia (1929–34 and 1934–39) continued to hold power until the outbreak of World War II. During this period the socialist and communist parties, which had drawn between 10–20% of the national vote during the early

Central, Eastern, and Southern Europe: social, economic, and political data

Country	Area (sq km/sq miles)	*c.* 1995 Population (million)	*c.* 1995 Pop. density per sq km/sq miles	*c.* 1992 Adult literacy rate (%)	World ranking	Income type	c. 1991 Human rights rating (%)
Albania	27,393/10,576	3.414	125/323	75	112	low	N/A
Armenia	29,800/11,506	3.548	119/308	99	8	low	N/A
Azerbaijan	86,600/33,436	7.553	87/225	97	44	low	N/A
Belarus	207,600/80,155	10.265	49/128	98	34	middle	N/A
Bosnia-Herzegovina	51,129/19,741	3.600	70/182	93	70	middle	N/A
Bulgaria	110,994/42,855	8.500	77/198	95	59	middle	83
Croatia	56,538/21,829	4.504	80/206	97	44	middle	N/A
Cyprus	9,250/3,571	0.734	79/206	91	77	high	N/A
Czech Republic	78,864/30,450	10.333	131/339	99	8	middle	97
Estonia	45,100/17,413	1.464	32/84	99	8	middle	N/A
Georgia	69,700/26,911	5.400	77/201	99	8	low	N/A
Greece	131,944/50,944	10.426	79/205	93	70	high	87
Hungary	93,033/35,920	10.260	110/286	97	44	middle	97
Latvia	64,589/24,938	2.529	39/101	99	8	middle	N/A
Lithuania	65,200/25,174	3.710	57/147	98	34	middle	N/A
Macedonia	25,713/9,928	2.142	83/216	89	82	low	N/A
Moldova	33,700/13,012	4.400	131/338	96	52	low	N/A
Poland	312,683/120,728	38.643	124/230	99	8	middle	83
Romania	237,500/91,699	22.700	96/248	97	44	middle	82
Russia	17,075,400/6,592,846	147.980	9/22	99	8	middle	54
Slovakia	49,035/18,933	5.347	109/282	99	8	middle	N/A
Slovenia	20,251/7,819	1.942	96/248	99	8	high	N/A
Turkey	779,450/300,947	61.183	78/203	81	102	middle	44
Ukraine	603,700/233,090	52.100	86/224	98	34	middle	N/A
Yugoslavia	102,173/39,449	10.515	103/267	93	70	middle	55
Total/average/range	*20,367,339/7,863,870*	*433.192*	*21/55*	*75–99*	–	–	*44–97*

AMS = additional member system, PL = party list, PR = proportional representation, SB = second ballot, SP = simple plurality, Lib-dem = liberal democratic, Em-dem = emergent democratic, Auth-nat = authoritarian nationalist, Unlim-pres = unlimited presidential, Lim-pres = limited presidential, Trans = transitional.)

1920s, were proscribed and forced underground.

The interwar years were, therefore, with the notable exception of economically advanced and socially differentiated Czechoslovakia, a period of abortive democratization. Despite its initial failure, this democratic experiment was to have a long-term impact on the 'political culture' of the region, tending to undermine traditional attitudes of political subservience and shifting popular political expectations in a more pluralist direction than in what was the Soviet Union.

During the early postwar period the economic performance of Central and Eastern Europe was creditable, GDP advancing at an average annual rate of 4.5% between 1950 and 1979. As part of this growth process, there was fundamental structural transformation, with a major rural to urban industrial shift occurring, and the proportion of the population engaged in agriculture fell from 45% in 1960 to 25% in 1985. However, from the later 1970s, as the economies of Central and Eastern Europe 'matured', growth rates slumped. Between 1980 and 1985 regional GDP advanced by only 2% per annum, while in strife-torn and debt-encumbered Poland and Yugoslavia negative growth was recorded.

During this same period, the nations of the Warsaw Pact were faced with an economically crippling 'Cold War' arms race with the West, driven both by innovative new technologies and by the anticommunist rhetoric of the American president, Ronald Reagan (1981–88). This concatenation of developments persuaded Mikhail Gorbachev, who became leader of the CPSU in March 1985, to sanction a radical three-pronged new course for communism in the Soviet Union and its 'satellites'. The centerpiece of the

Table 53

World ranking	Date of state formation	State structure	State type	Executive type	Number of assembly chambers	Party structure	Lower house electoral system
–	1912	U	Em-dem	Dual	1	multi	PR-AMS
–	1991	U	Auth-nat	Unlim-pres	1	multi	PR-AMS
–	1991	U	Auth-nat	Unlim-pres	1	multi	PR-AMS
–	1991	U	Auth-nat	Unlim-pres	2	multi	SB
–	1992	F	Em-dem	Lim-pres	2	multi	PR-PL
30	1908	U	Em-dem	Parliamentary	1	multi	PR-PL
–	1991	U	Em-dem	Lim-pres	2	multi	PR-PL
–	1960	U	Lib-dem	Lim-pres	1	multi	SP
9	1993	U	Em-dem	Dual	2	multi	PR-PL
–	1918/1991	U	Em-dem	Dual	1	multi	PR-PL
–	1991	U	Em-dem	Lim-pres	1	multi	PR-AMS
26	1829	U	Lib-dem	Parliamentary	1	multi	PR-PL
9	1918	U	Em-dem	Parliamentary	1	multi	PR-AMS
–	1920/1991	U	Em-dem	Parliamentary	1	multi	PR-PL
–	1919/1991	U	Em-dem	Dual	1	multi	PR-AMS
–	1992	U	Em-dem	Dual	1	multi	SB
–	1991	U	Em-dem	Lim-pres	1	multi	PR-PL
30	1918	U	Em-dem	Dual	2	multi	PR-PL
33	1881	U	Em-dem	Dual	2	multi	PR-PL
69	1547/1917/1991	F	Em-dem	Lim-pres	2	multi	PR-AMS
–	1993	U	Em-dem	Parliamentary	1	multi	PR-PL
–	1991	U	Em-dem	Dual	2	multi	PR-AMS
85	1923	U	Lib-dem	Parliamentary	1	multi	PR-PL
–	1918/1991	U	Em-dem	Lim-pres	1	multi	PR-AMS
68	1918/1992	F	Em-dem	Lim-pres	2	multi	PR-AMS
–	–	–	–	–	–	–	–

Gorbachev program was encouragement of market-centerd and decentralized economic reforms under the slogan '*perestroika*' (economic restructuring) in an effort to inject new life into the region's stagnating economies. This was coupled, second, with détente and military retrenchment overseas, evidenced by the withdrawal of Soviet troops from Afghanistan in 1989, as the existing 'Brezhnev doctrine' of expansionist support for all left-leaning regimes was replaced with a new 'Sinatra doctrine' which accepted that the governments and peoples of USSR 'satellite states' should be allowed to develop in their 'own way'. Third, believing that, for the program of economic reform to be successful, it needed to be accompanied by greater political freedoms, on a 'social democratic' model, Gorbachev encouraged political openness (*glasnost*), tolerance of the expression of religious and ethnic identities, and a measure of democratization and 'socialist pluralism' in the political process.

The 'Gorbachev experiment' was a bold and idealistic attempt to breathe new life into communist systems which had become increasingly sclerotic. However, ultimately it was to prove to be a failure since it failed to deliver the promised economic improvements, with living standards deteriorating across Central and Eastern Europe between 1985–89, and because it ignited dangerously divisive and destabilizing nationalist and ethno-religious separatist elements frozen for half a century by communist regimes that had propagated atheism and 'socialist patriotism'.

One basic indicator of the profound socio-cultural heterogeneity of Central, Eastern, and Southern Europe is the religious affiliations of its peoples. Within the region, four principal faiths are to be found, with regional concentrations of support. Roman Catholicism predominates in the westerly states of Poland, Lithuania, the Czech and Slovak republics, Croatia, Slovenia, Hungary, and the western Ukraine, most of which were at one time under Austrian imperial control. Protestantism is found in the west-central states of eastern Germany, Estonia, Latvia, the Czech Republic, and Hungary. Eastern Orthodoxy, with its Armenian, Georgian, Greek, Macedonian, Serbian, Romanian, Russian, and Ukrainian branches, is practised in the eastern and southern Slav lands of Armenia, Belarus, Bulgaria, Cyprus, Georgia, Greece, Macedonia, Moldova, Romania, Russia, and Yugoslavia. Islam is the predominant religion in Albania, Azerbaijan, northern Cyprus and southern portions of Bulgaria, the USSR, and Yugoslavia.

The most spiritually homogenous states in Central, Eastern, and Southern Europe are Poland, where 95% of the population are baptized as Catholics, and Greece, where 98% are adherents to the Greek Orthodox faith. The most spiritually heterogenous states are Bosnia-Herzegovnia, with its contending Muslim, Serbian Orthodox, and Croatian Catholic communities and Cyprus, with its Greek Orthodox and Muslim divisions which have led to the partitioning of the island.

The distribution of ethnic and national groups closely follows that of religious communities, adding a further dimension to community rivalries. The most culturally diverse state within the region, not surprisingly when account is taken of its size, is Russia, which embraces more than 100 ethnic-language groups. There have also been intense intra-state ethnic rivalries in Czechoslovakia, between Czechs and Slovaks, leading to the country's division in 1993, and in the Transylvania region of Romania, between Magyar Hungarians and Romanians, precipitating an inter-state political crisis in 1988. Even more serious have been the ethnic rivalries in Yugoslavia. These resulted in the ruling communist party becoming factionalized along ethnic–regional lines and ultimately, in 1991, to secession from the federation by Croatia and Slovenia.

In the Soviet Union, which had comprised 15 'sovereign republics', it was the release of long pent-up ethnic tensions and nationalist aspirations by Mikhail Gorbachev's *glasnost* policy which ultimately proved to be corrosive of the entire communist edifice. In the three Baltic republics and in Armenia, Georgia, and the western Ukraine nationalist sentiment was especially powerful and during 1990–91 'sovereignty' and independence declarations were issued by the parliaments of these states. In addition, revenues and resources were held back from the center, crippling the USSR's tightly integrated planned economy, while the Red Army troops became embroiled in policing internal ethnic conflicts, notably in the Baltic, Caucasus, and Central Asian regions. In August 1991 a last-ditch effort was made by communist hardliners to recentralize political and economic authority within the Union, with Gorbachev being ousted. However, this ill-organized putsch lasted just 61 hours and destroyed any lingering popular legitimacy that the CPSU may have held. Gorbachev subsequently returned to power, but his credibility was fatally diminished and within four months the Soviet Union had been dissolved and communism abandoned.

The collapse of communism occurred two years earlier in the 'satellite states' of Central Europe. There the pacesetters for reform were Hungary, where in February 1989 an internally reformed communist party abandoned its constitutionally guaranteed leading role and established a new pluralist political system, and Poland, where in April 1989 a historic accord was reached between the communist party and the Solidarity free trade union, in which the formation of opposition parties was sanctioned and the state's media monopoly lifted. In East Germany, Czechoslovakia, and Bulgaria, intelligentsia-led 'Popular Front' organizations, heirs to earlier human rights bodies such as Charter '77, sprang up between 1988–89 to press for democratization. Large-scale pro-democracy demonstrations were held during 1989–90, exerting sufficient popular pressure to persuade the ruling communist parties to step down from power peacefully and hold multiparty elections. Only in Albania and Romania, where the reviled dictator Nicolae Ceausescu was forced from office and executed in December 1989, was the transition violent. Elsewhere, the collapse of communist regimes occurred with a whimper rather than a bang. The once dominant ruling parties were undermined by their lack of popular legitimacy, their out-of-touch and gerontocratic leadership, their inept economic management, and, perhaps most crucially, by the refusal of the Soviet Union to provide, or threaten to provide, external military support on the models of East Berlin in 1953, Budapest in 1956, and Prague in 1968.

Recommended reading

Ascherson, N '1989 in Eastern Europe: Constitutional Representative Democracy as a "Return to Normality"?', in J Dunn (ed.) *Democracy: The Unfinished Journey 508 BC to AD 1993*, Oxford University Press, 1992, Chap. 2

Garton Ash, T *We the People: Revolution of '89 Witnessed in Warsaw, Budapest, Berlin and Prague*, Granta, 1990

Banac, I (ed.) *Eastern Europe in Revolution*, Cornell University Press, 1992

Berglund, S and Dellenbrant, J A (eds.) *The New Democracies in Eastern Europe: Party Systems and Political Cleavages*, Edward Elgar, 1994

Brzezinski, Z *The Grand Failure: The Birth and Death of Communism in the Twentieth Century*, Macdonald, 1989

Glenny, M *The Rebirth of History: Eastern Europe in the Age of Democracy*, Penguin, 1990

Hawkes, N (ed.) *Tearing down the Curtain: The People's Revolution in Eastern Europe, The Observer*, 1990

Keep, J *Last of the Empires: A History of the Soviet Union 1945–1991*, Oxford University Press, 1996

Lewin, M *The Gorbachev Phenomenon: A Historical Introduction*, Hutchinson Radius, 1989

Roskin, M G *The Rebirth of East Europe*, Prentice Hall, 1991

Sakwa, R *Russian Politics and Society*, 2nd edn., Routledge, 1996

Shopflin, G *Politics in Eastern Europe 1945–1992*, Blackwell, 1993

Sword, K (ed.) *The Times Guide to Eastern Europe: The Changing Face of the Warsaw Pact*, Times Books, 1991

White, S, Batt, J, and Lewis, P G (eds.) *Developments in East European Politics*, Macmillan, 1993

White, S, Pravda, A, and Gitelman, Z (eds.) *Developments in Soviet and Post-Soviet Politics*, 3rd edn., Macmillan, 1996

ALBANIA

Republic of Albania
Republika e Shqipërisë

Capital: Tiranë

Social and economic data

Area: 27,393 sq km/10,576 sq miles
Population: 3,414,000*
Pop. density per sq km/sq mi: 125/323*
Urban population: 36%**
Literacy rate: 75%
GDP: $2,500 million*; per-capita GDP: $730*
Government defense spending (% of GDP): 2.8%*
Currency: lek
Economy type: low income
Labor force in agriculture: 48%**
Unemployment rate: 9.1%**
* 1995.
** 1992.

Head of state (executive)

President Dr Rexhep Mejdani, since 1997

Head of government

Prime Minister Pandeli Majko, since 1998

Ethnic composition

Ninety per cent of the population is of Albanian, non-Slavic, ethnic stock and 8% is ethnic Greek. In recent years relations with Greece have been strained by Greek allegations that the Greek community, concentrated in southern Albania, has been subjected to persecution. The official language is Albanian, with the Gheg dialect being spoken in the north and the Tosk in the south. A sixth of Albanians of working age work abroad, particularly in Greece, with drachma remittances contributing a quarter of GDP.

Religions

Historically, 70% of the population has adhered to Islam, Sunni and Bektashi; 20%, predominantly in the south, to the Eastern Orthodox Church; and between 5–10%, mainly in the north, to Roman Catholicism. Between 1967 and 1990 Albania officially declared itself an 'atheist state', outlawing all forms of religious worship and organization.

Political features

State type: emergent democratic
Date of state formation: 1912
Political structure: dual
Executive: dual
Assembly: one-chamber
Party structure: multiparty
Human rights rating: N/A
International affiliations: COE, EBRD, ECE, IAEA, IBRD, IMF, LORCS, OIC, OSCE, PFP, UN

Local and regional government

Albania is divided into 36 districts (*rreth*), which include 64 municipalities and 309 communes for the purpose of local government, which is by multiparty executive committees.

Political system

An interim constitution was adopted in April 1991, replacing the communist-era constitution of 1976. It describe Albania as a secular, pluralist parliamentary republic, with an economy based on 'diverse systems of ownership', and was amended in April 1992 to increase the powers of the presidency, creating a limited presidential political system. Since the overthrow of the Berisha government in 1997, there have been moves towards a parliamentary executive, although currently, with the president retaining significant executive powers, the system is dual. A new constitution is was approved in a national referendum in November 1998. Subsequent to the 1997 civil war, a contending breakaway state has been formed in the mountainous far north by ex-president, Sali Berisha, and his armed supporters. The political system described below relates to the recognized government, which controls the rest of Albania, including the capital, Tiranë.

Under the constitution there is a single-chamber 155-member People's Assembly (Kuvendi Popullor). One hundred and fifteen deputies are directly elected in individual constituencies by a two-ballot, majority vote system for a four-year term. The remaining 40 seats are allocated on a proportional representation basis, with a 3% national support threshold for representation. The state president, who is also commander in chief of the armed forces, is elected by the Assembly in a secret ballot for a maximum of two consecutive five-year terms. A successful candidate needs to secure a two-thirds majority of the votes cast. The president exercises the duties of the People's Assembly when it is not in session. A prime minister, appointed by the president, and Council of Ministers (COM), or cabinet, of around 20 members approved by the Assembly, has day-to-day charge of the government. Members of the COM may not hold any other state or professional position. Amendments to the constitution may be proposed by the president, the COM or by a quarter of the People's Assembly's deputies and can only be adopted by a two-thirds majority of all deputies.

In April 1997, Leka Zog I (b. 1939), who was proclaimed king in exile in South Africa on his father's death in 1961, returned to Albania. However, in a referendum held in July 1997, 67% voted against restoring the monarchy.

Political parties

There are two principal political parties: the Albanian Democratic Party (Partia Demokratike Shqipërisë: PDS) and the Socialist Party of Albania (Partia Socialiste Shqipërisë: PSS).

The PDS was formed in December 1990 by members of the Tiranë intelligentsia, including Dr Sali Berisha, in order to challenge the country's one-party communist regime. Led by Berisha, it favors political pluralism and market-centerd economic reform. Much of its support is drawn from the country's north. In 1992 some PDS members left to form the small breakaway Democratic Alliance Party (DAP).

The southern-based PSS, known until June 1991 as the Party of Labor of Albania (PLA), is the 'reform-socialist' successor to the former ruling communist party. The PLA was founded, with Yugoslav assistance, in November 1941 by a French-educated schoolteacher, Enver Hoxha, as a small 200-member underground body. It organized itself on Leninist 'democratic centralist' pyramidal lines and between the 1950s and 1980s adhered to the classic Marxist-Leninist-Stalinist doctrines which were being abandoned by those whom the PLA viewed as 'revisionists' elsewhere in the communist world. By 1986 full party membership stood at 128,000, corresponding to 4.2% of the total population. An 'Enverist' rump of the PLA, led by Hysni Milloshi, broke away from the remainder of the party when it was relaunched as the PSS in 1991, but it was outlawed subsequently by a June 1992 People's Assembly law on political organizations (suspended in April 1998). The PSS is now committed to a market economy and democratic socialism. It is led by Dr Rexhep Mejdani and has 110,000 members.

More than 30 other parties currently function. Significant smaller parties include the center-left Social Democratic Party of Albania (PSDS; estd. 1991) and the Albanian Republican Party (PRS; estd. 1991), which held ministerial posts in the PDS-led government of Sali Berisha; and the Human Rights Union (EAD; estd. 1992), which is orientated towards the 400,000 Greek and Macedonian minority communities concentrated in the south and east of the country. The interests of Albania's ethnic Greek community are also promoted illegally by the banned OMONIA ('Concord') organization (estd. 1992). There is also a small monarchist party, the Legality Movement Party (Legalitetit), formed in 1992.

Political leaders since 1970

1944–85 Enver Hoxha (PLA)*, 1985–92 Ramiz Alia (PLA)*, 1992–97 Dr Sali Berisha (PDS)**, 1997– Dr Rexhep Mejdani (PSS)**, 1997–98 Fatos Nano (PSS) ***, 1998– Pandeli Majko (PSS)***

* Communist Party leaders.
** President.
*** Prime minister.

Latest elections

The most recent People's Assembly elections were held on 29 June and 6 July 1997. They resulted in a clear victory for the left-of-center PSS, which attracted 53% (up 27% on March 1992) of the vote, securing 101 of the 155 seats. The incumbent center-right PDS won 26% of the vote (down 36%) and 29 seats. Eight other parties secured representation, but all of these parties attracted less than 3% of the vote. The center-left PSDS and the EAD, each with nearly 3% of the vote, won eight and four seats respectively, while Legalitetit won two seats and the PRS one seat. Campaigning was marred by violence, including bomb explosions in Tiranë, and, despite the presence of a Multinational Protection

Force, there were three election day killings. Nevertheless, OSCE observers declared the poll 'adequate and acceptable'. Turnout was 67%.

Political history

Albania successively formed part of the Byzantine and Ottoman Empires between the 5th century and 1347 and between 1468 and 1912. It achieved independence in November 1912, but was then occupied by Italy between 1914 and 1920. In 1925 a republic was proclaimed, with Prime Minister Ahmed Bey Zogu (1895–1961), a conservative Muslim landlord, as president. Three years later, he was enthroned as King Zog I and was to reign continuously as an absolute monarch until Albania was occupied once again by Italian forces in April 1939. The country remained backward and rural-based, 80% of the population being dependent on agriculture in 1930, with a feudal Islamic landholding structure still surviving.

During World War II a communist-led National Liberation Front (NLF) was established, in 1941, with help from Yugoslav communists. Under the leadership of Enver Hoxha (1908–85), the NLF emerged as the most successful resistance group in the country and in 1944 forced the withdrawal of German forces, who had entered Albania in the previous year. Liberation was thus achieved without Soviet Red Army assistance.

In November 1944 the NLF, now known as the Democratic Front, following the purge of noncommunist elements, assumed power and called elections in December 1945, based on a single list of communist party-sponsored DFA candidates. The new Constituent Assembly proclaimed Albania a republic in January 1946, forcing the deposed King Zog to continue to live in exile. A Soviet-style communist constitution was adopted in March 1946, with the PLA now the sole legal political party.

At first, the new regime was closely allied to Yugoslavia, its armed forces being controlled by Yugoslav advisers and the economic plans of both Balkan states being coordinated. Yugoslavia's expulsion from the Cominform in 1948, following an ideological rift between Stalin and Tito, provided an opportunity for this state of dependency to be severed. Instead, Albania developed close economic links with the Soviet Union between 1949 and 1955, entering Comecon in 1949 and the Warsaw Pact in 1955.

During the late 1950s and early 1960s Soviet – Albanian relations progressively deteriorated as the country's leader, Enver Hoxha, a committed Stalinist, refused to accept Khrushchev's 'revisionist' denunciations of the Stalin era and his rapprochement overtures to Yugoslavia. Following attacks on the Soviet leadership by Hoxha, the USSR terminated its economic aid in June 1961 and broke off diplomatic relations in December 1961. Albania responded by ceasing cooperation within Comecon in 1962 and formally withdrawing in 1968 from the Warsaw Treaty Organization, after the Soviet invasion of Czechoslovakia. Close ties were now developed, instead, with Mao Zedong's communist China.

Inside the country, a strict Stalinist economic and political system was imposed by Hoxha, involving rural collectivization, industrial nationalization, central planning, totalitarian one-party control, the frequent purging of cadres to prevent the emergence of an elitist governing stratum, and the propagation of a 'cult of personality' centerd upon Hoxha himself. A major drive against the Islamic and Christian religions was also launched, in 1967, involving the closure of more than 2,000 mosques and churches, in an effort to create the world's 'first atheist state' and expunge all remaining centrifugal tendencies.

Initially, between 1946 and 1954, Hoxha combined the key posts of PLA leader and state premier but in 1954 he was replaced in the second post by Mehmet Shehu, who remained as COM chairperson until his death in December 1981. Shehu was officially reported to have committed suicide but nonofficial sources suggest he was 'liquidated' after having been involved in a leadership struggle against Hoxha. His replacement was his deputy, Adil Carcani.

The 'Hoxha experiment', with its stress on national self-reliance, the 1976 constitution forbidding the acceptance of foreign credits, and on the minimization of urban – rural and blue- and white-collar income differentials, despite progress in the agricultural and energy spheres, left Albania with the lowest per-capita income in Europe by the time of the leader's death in 1985. Internationally, the country became one of the most isolated in the world, diplomatic relations with communist China having been severed in 1978, following the post-Mao leadership's accommodation with the United States.

Ramiz Alia (b. 1925), the Moscow-trained president of the presidium of the People's Assembly, was elected first secretary of the PLA on Hoxha's death in April 1985. The new regime, although pledging to uphold the independent policy line of its predecessor, began to make policy adjustments in both the foreign and domestic spheres. External contacts broadened and the number of countries with which Albania has diplomatic relations increased from 74 in 1978 to 111 in 1988. This diplomatic 'thaw' was accompanied by a growth in two-way external trade. Internally, political reforms remained limited, but in the economic sphere, new incentives, in the form of wage differentials for skilled tasks, were slowly introduced.

Opposition to the PLA regime began to mount during 1990 around the northwest border town of Shköder and, in early June 1990, unprecedented anti-government street demonstrations erupted in Tiranë. Faced with a government crackdown, thousands of demonstrators sought refuge in foreign embassies and were later allowed to leave the country. In December 1990, amid continuing protests which were threatening an economic collapse, the PLA leadership announced that opposition parties would be allowed to operate and the ban on religious activity would be lifted. In response, the pluralist Democratic Party was formed, under the leadership of Dr Sali Berisha (b. 1945), a cardiologist from Tiranë. In February 1991 a huge bronze statue of Enver Hoxha was toppled in Tiranë by demonstrators and there were riots in several other towns. President Alia responded by replacing his unpopular prime minister, Adil Carcani, with the more reform-minded Fatos Nano and imposing presidential rule. Tanks were also moved into the streets of the capital and, fearing a hardline coup, thousands of Albanians fled by sea to Greece, Yugoslavia, and Italy.

In the spring of 1991 diplomatic relations with the United States and United Kingdom, suspended since 1946, were restored. In multiparty elections held in March – April 1991, the ruling PLA, polling strongly in rural areas, won 169 of the 250 seats in the new People's Assembly, a two-thirds majority sufficient to enable it to effect constitutional changes. The opposition's frustration was vented in anticommunist riots in Shköder, with four people being shot dead by the police, including the local PDS leader.

A new interim constitution was adopted in April 1991, the country being renamed the Republic of Albania and the PLA's leading role rescinded. The People's Assembly elected Ramiz Alia as executive president, replacing the former presidium, and commander in chief of the armed forces. In June 1991 an all-party 'government of national stability' was appointed, with Ylli Bufi, the former food minister, as prime minister and a PDS member as deputy premier. The PLA renamed itself the Socialist Party of Albania (PSS) on 13 June 1991, with Fatos Nano as its chairperson, and in July 1991 a land privatization act restored land to peasants dispossessed under the communist regime.

Unrest, food riots, and anticommunist demonstrations continued during 1991 and, complaining of manipulation, the PDS withdrew from the coalition, forcing Prime Minister Bufi's resignation on 6 December 1991. He was replaced on 18 December 1991 by the former nutrition minister, Vilson Ahmeti, who became Albania's first noncommunist premier, and in January 1992 a number of former communist officials, including Enver Hoxha's widow, Nexhmije Hoxha (b. 1920), were arrested on corruption charges. (Nexhmije Hoxha was subsequently sentenced to 11 years' imprisonment in May 1993, but was later released, in January 1977, and her eldest son, Ilir Hoxha, to one year in jail in June 1995.) In the March 1992 general election, the PDS won a convincing victory, securing 62% of the national vote and 92 of the 140 elective seats, and the new Assembly elected Dr Sali Berisha as state president on 6 April 1992, voting him increased executive powers. On 13 April 1992 Aleksander Meksi, from the PDS, became prime minister, heading a PDS-dominated coalition administration. The former president, Ramiz Alia, was arrested in September 1992 and charged with the misuse of state funds and abuse of power and in July 1993, in what appeared to be a politically motivated move, Fatos Nano was also charged with corruption and subsequently imprisoned. (Alia was later convicted in September 1994, at what amounted to a political 'show trial', and was sentenced to eight years' imprisonment, while the former prime minister, Adil Carcani, received a five-year suspended prison term. However, in July 1995 Alia was released, following an appeal court ruling.)

The new government introduced a program of market-centerd economic reforms, including privatization of land and industries. From 1993 the economy began to recover, with GDP growth of 8% being registered during that year and the monthly inflation rate falling to 1.5%. However, relations with neighboring Greece were strained during 1994–95 by Greek claims that the ethnic Greek community residing in southern Albania were facing discrimination. Despite the economic improvement, popular support for the PDS waned during 1994. This was shown by the failure in November of a PDS-sponsored referendum on a new draft constitution. Despite a turnout of 84%, only 42% backed the proposed changes. President Berisha reacted by increasing the degree of state control over the media, with newspaper distribution in Tiranë being restricted to government-owned kiosks and state bookshops from June 1995.

In September 1995 a 'law against communist genocide' was passed, banning from running in national and local elections until 2002 any person who had been a member of parliament or the Central Commitee or Politburo of the Communist Party before May 1991. This prevented some PSS deputies from standing in the next elections. During 1994 and 1995 real GDP grew by an annual average rate of 9%. This provided the platform for the PDS to secure a crushing victory in the parliamentary elections held in May–June 1996, winning 122 of the 140 elective seats. However, the opposition, led by the PSS, claimed that there had been widespread intimidation of voters by the security forces and electoral malpractice, and thus boycotted the later stages of the contest, reducing turnout to 59%. These charges were supported by OSCE observers, who urged the government to conduct fresh elections. After PSS deputies initiated a hunger strike in protest, President Berisha sanctioned repolling in 17 constituencies. After the election, Aleksander Meksi was re-appointed prime minister. From January 1997 the Berisha administration became faced with a spiralling civil crisis, centerd in the south of the country. It was triggered by the collapse of 'pyramid' financial investment schemes, in which, with promised returns of 50% a month, a half of the population had participated, 'investing' $1 billion. Some sold their homes and land to buy shares, but, inevitably, once the supply of new investors dried up, the schemes collapsed. It was alleged that PDS sponsors had been associated with some of the schemes. Serious anti-government demonstrations and riots broke out first in Tirana, on 19 January 1997, and, President Berisha, promised investors only limited compensation. On 9 February 1997, the violence escalated in the southern port of Vlore, where the headquarters of the PDS was burned down. The police responded by killing three demonstrators. As the populist protest escalated, the opposition, including the PSS and the liberal Democratic Alliance Party (DAP), which had been established in 1996 by PDS dissidents, formed a ten-party Forum for Democracy (FfD). This demanded the government's replacement by a government of non-party technocrats, and the calling of new elections. By early March 1997 several dozen people had been killed and hundreds arrested, and the southern third of the country, where PSS support was strongest and pyramid scheme losses had been the biggest, was under the control of armed rebel 'committees of public salvation', who had established 'free zones', with many members of the government forces having deserted or changed sides. In response, on 2 March 1997 President Berisha dismissed Prime Minister Meksi, and the head of the army, closed down opposition newspapers, and declared a state of emergency, which included a dusk to dawn curfew and a ban on public gatherings. A day later, amid an opposition boycott, the People's Assembly re-elected Berisha, unopposed, for a second five-year term as president. With popular pressure continuing, in mid-March 1997 Berisha appointed an FfD-dominated caretaker Government of National Reconciliation, headed by Bashkim Fino, an American-educated economist and a former PSS mayor of the rebel-held southern town on Gjirokaster, pending new elections. Nevertheless, the rebels and mafioso who now controlled southern Albania refused to cooperate with the new Tiranë government unless Berisha resigned, while pro-Berisha paramilitaries controlled the north. In late March 1997, as unrest continued, more than 15,000 Albanians fled by boat to Italy, with more than 80 drowning en route, and in April 1997 the European Union (EU) agreed to send in a 6,000-strong humanitarian force to distribute food and medicine. This, chiefly Italian, French, and Greek, multinational force was intended to stay for at least three months, while an international team, headed by Franz Vranitzky, a former Austrian chancellor, oversaw fresh elections. The general election, held in June and July 1997 resulted in a resounding victory for the opposition reform-socialist PSS, led by Fatos Nano, the former communist prime minister who had been sentenced to 12 years' imprisonment in 1994 on corruption charges but who was officially pardoned in March 1997 and released from prison (along with Alia). The PSS won nearly two-thirds of the People's Assembly seats, giving them power to change the constitution and reduce presidential power. The PDS was heavily defeated and Berisha resigned as president. A new, broad-based, PSS-led government was formed, including the DAP, the Social Democratic Party of Albania (PSDS), the Human Rights Union (EAD), and the Agrarian Party (AP), with Nano as prime minister and Fino as deputy prime minister. Dr Rexhep Mejdani, of the PSS, was elected by the Assembly to become the new president and the state of emergency was ended. Although Vlore was recaptured and its rebel leaders arrested, civil unrest continued after the election and the withdrawal, in August 1997, of the multinational force. In October

1997 the World Bank and other international donors pledged some $670 million to help rebuild the shattered economy and infrastructure. Meanwhile, in September 1997, the Supreme Court overturned the convictions of all 32 communist-era leaders who had been sentenced to prison for crimes against humanity.

From January 1998 there was a fresh wave of violence and unrest, in the mountainous north, where the opposition PDS had power-bases in Shkodra and Tropoje, Berisha's home town. This was against a background of soaring inflation (exceeding 50% per annum) and unemployment, which exceeded 20%, as GDP contracted by 7% during 1997. Meanwhile, the PDS boycotted parliament, preventing the drafting of a new constitution, and there was spillover from civil war in neighboring, predominantly ethnic Albanian, Kosovo province, in Yugoslavia. Instability continued during 1998 and in September 1998, following the assassination of Berisha's lieutenant, Azem Hajdari, in strange circumstances, the PDS mounted five days of armed street protests in Tirana. Nano responded to this pressure and resigned, being replaced as prime minister by the 30-year-old Pandeli Majko, the PSS general secretary. In May 1992 Albania signed a ten-year trade and cooperation agreement with the EU and in June 1992 became a founding member of the Black Sea Economic Cooperation Group, designed to promote greater economic development and cooperation in the region. It joined the Organization of the Islamic Conference (OIC) in December 1992 and NATO's 'Partnership for Peace' program of military cooperation in April 1994. Albania was admitted into the Council of Europe in July 1995.

A new constitution was overwhelmingly approved in a November 1998 national referendum, although turnout was only 51%. Nano resigned as a leader of the PSS in January 1999, but announced plans to launch a new 'emancipating movement'. During 1999 the economy recovered, with growth of more than 5%.

ARMENIA

Republic of Armenia
Hayastani Hanrapeut'yun

Capital: Yerevan

Social and economic data

Area: 29,800 sq km/11,506 sq miles

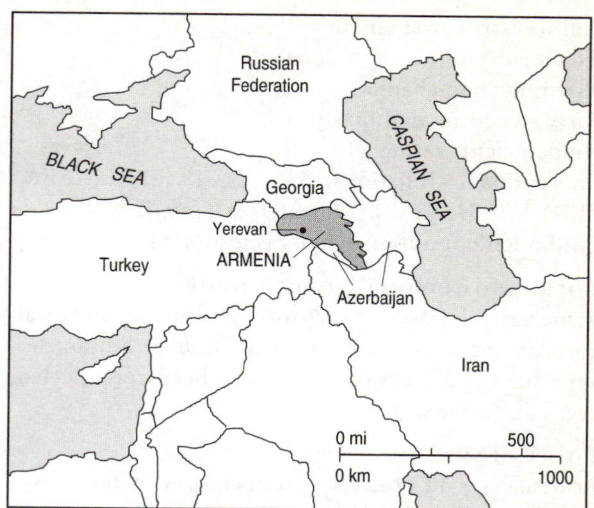

Population: 3,548,000*
Pop. density per sq km/sq mi: 119/308*
Urban population: 68%
Literacy rate: 99%**
GDP: $2,750 million*; per-capita GDP: $775*
Government defense spending (% of GDP): 4.4%*
Currency: dram
Economy type: low income
Labor force in agriculture: 10%**
* 1995.
** 1992.

Head of state (executive)

President Robert Kocharyan, since 1998

Head of government

Prime Minister Vazgen Sarkisyan, since 1999

Ethnic composition

Ninety-one per cent of the population is of Armenian ethnic stock, 5% Azeri, 2% Russian, and 2% Kurd. The official language is Armenian, a distinct Indo-European language.

Religions

The population is predominantly Christian, with the leading denominations being the Armenian Apostolic Church, which has supported the nationalist movement, the Russian Orthodox Church, and Protestant churches. The number of Muslims has declined as a result of the exodus of many Azerbaijanis. Kurds are also adherents of Islam.

Political features

State type: authoritarian nationalist
Date of state formation: 1991

Political structure: unitary
Executive: unlimited presidential
Assembly: one-chamber
Party structure: multiparty*
Human rights rating: N/A
International affiliations: BSECZ, CIS, EBRD, IAEA, IBRD, IMF, NACC, NAM (observer), OSCE, UN
* Although opposition activity is restricted.

Local and regional government

Armenia is divided into 67 districts (*rayons*) for local government, with an additional *rayon* to administer Yerevan. Local mayors and village heads are elected every three years.

Political system

Armenia has an executive presidency, with the president being directly elected for a five-year term since 1991. Under the terms of the July 1995 constitution, there is a 131-member legislature, the National Assembly, to which deputies are elected, for a four-year term. Election is by a German-style additional member system, with voters casting two ballots. One is to elect a deputy for one of the 75 single-member constituencies, by the second ballot majoritarian system. The other is for a party list, with 56 deputies being elected proportionately, allocated to parties winning more than 5% of the national vote.

The president, whose powers were greatly strengthened by the 1995 constitution, is restricted to two consecutive terms and must be at least 35 years old. The president works with a subordinate prime minister and a council of ministers, or cabinet, comprising around 25 members. There is also a nine-member Constitutional Court.

Political parties

The dominant party over recent years has been the conservative-authoritarian Pan-Armenian National Movement (PNM), known before 1995 as the Armenian Pan-national Movement (APM). It was formed in 1989 by Levon Ter-Petrossian as an anticommunist nationalist party. However, in recent years the party has become riven by factions and there have been some defections to the breakaway National Democratic Union (NDU), formed in 1991 by Vazgen Manukyan, and to Azatutyun (Freedom), formed in 1997 by Hrand Bagratian.

Among more than a dozen other significant parties which function, four stand out: the Communist Party of Armenia (CPA); the National Self-Determination Union (NSDU); the Republican Party (RPA) and the Armenian Revolutionary Federation (ARF: Dashnakhsutyun). The CPA, which formerly dominated the republic, was suspended in September 1991, but relegalized in 1992. It has 50,000 members and is led by Sergei Badalian. The NSDU is an extreme-nationalist body, led by Paruyr Ayrykian, which seeks recovery of lands lost to Turkey after World War. The RPA was formed in 1990. The 40,000-member center-left ARF was formed in 1890 and was the ruling party in independent Armenia between 1918–20. It was banned under Soviet rule and, after being accused of involvement in terrorism, was again suspended by presidential decree in December 1994 . This ban was lifted in May 1998. In July 1998 the People's Party of Armenia (PPA) was formed by the former CPA leader, Karel Demirchyan.

Political leaders since 1970

1990–98 Levon Ter-Petrossian (APM/PNM), 1998– Robert Kocharyan (PNM)

Latest elections

The most recent presidential election was held on 16 and 30 March 1998. The victor was the prime minister and acting president, Robert Kocharyan, who won 60% of the vote in the second ballot run-off race with Karel Demirchyan, a former leader of the CPA. In the first round turnout was 64%, with Kocharyan attracting 39% of the vote; Demirchyan, 31%, Vazgen Manukyan, a former prime minister, 12%; Sergei Badalian, leader of the CPA, 11%; and Paruyr Ayrykian, leader of the NSDU, 5%. Monitors from the OSCE reported violations of electoral procedure in 15% of polling stations.

National Assembly elections were last held on 30 May 1999 and resulted in the Unity bloc, based around the RPA and PPA. This bloc secured 41% of the vote and 55 of the 131 Assembly seats, including 23 for the RPA. The CPA finished second, with 12% of the vote and 11 seats, while the Right and Unity Party and ARF 8% of the vote each and the NDU and NSDU 5% and 2% respectively. The PNM attracted only 1% of the vote and won one seat. Independent candidates won 32 seats.

Political history

Formerly an ancient kingdom in an area extending into what is now the Van region of Turkey and part of northwestern Iran, Armenia reached the height of its power under King Tigranes I, 'the Great', between *c.* 95 and 55 BC, becoming the strongest state in the Roman east and controlling an empire that stretched from the Mediterranean to the Caucasus. Afterwards, it was dominated by foreign powers. This bred an intense, defensive national consciousness. Christianity became the official religion in 301 AD and the country fell under the sway of the Byzantine Empire, then the Muslim Turks, from the late 11th century, the Mongols in the 13th century, and the Ottomans from the 16th century.

With the advance of Russia into the Caucasus during the early 19th century, Russia taking east Armenia between 1813 and 1828, there was a revival in Armenian culture and, inspired by the successes of the Greek and Balkan peoples, a struggle for independence. This provoked an Ottoman backlash in west Armenia and growing international concern at Armenian maltreatment: the 'Armenian question'. In 1915 an estimated 1,750,000 Armenians were massacred and deported by the Turks. The territory was conquered by Russia in 1916, but, after the Versailles settlement, briefly became an independent state in 1918. Two years later it was occupied by the Red Army. Along with Azerbaijan and Georgia, it formed part of the Transcaucasian Soviet Socialist Republic, but became a constituent republic of the USSR in 1936 and a showpiece for Stalinist industrial development.

The *glasnost* (openness) initiative launched by Mikhail Gorbachev, who became Russia's communist leader in 1985, reawakened Armenian national identity. In 1988 demands for reunion with neighboring Nagorno-Karabakh (Nagorny Karabakh), an Armenian Orthodox Christian-dominated enclave situated within the predominantly Muslim republic of Azerbaijan, led to riots, strikes, and, ultimately, during 1989–91, to a bloody civil war, necessitating the intervention of Soviet troops. The Armenian Pan-National Movement (APM), which was formed in November 1989 by Levon Ter-Petrossian (b. 1945) and Vazguen Manukyan, and the militant Karabakh Committee were at the fore of this growing nationalist campaign. The campaign included attempts to secure full control over the Azerbaijani-peopled autonomous region of Nakhichevan, situated within Armenia, causing the flight of almost 200,000 Azeris from the republic. This fuelled anticommunist feeling and in the May 1990 elections to the republic's Supreme Soviet (parliament) nationalists, particularly the APM, polled strongly and Ter-Petrossian and Manukyan were chosen as president and prime minister respectively, defeating communist challengers.

On 23 August 1990 a declaration of independence was made, but it was ignored by Moscow and the international community. The republic boycotted the March 1991 USSR referendum on the preservation of the Soviet Union and in April 1991 the property belonging to the Communist Party of Armenia (CPA) was nationalized. Four months later, the CPA dissolved itself.

In a referendum held on 21 September 1991, shortly after the collapse of an attempted anti-Gorbachev coup by communist hardliners in Moscow, 99% of Armenians voted for secession from the USSR, with turnout reaching 94%. Two days later, independence was formally proclaimed by President Ter-Petrossian, but this failed to secure Western recognition. A ceasefire agreement, brokered by the presidents of the Russian Federation and Kazakhstan, was signed by Armenia and Azerbaijan on 24 September 1991. It provided the basis for a negotiated settlement to the Nagorno-Karabakh dispute, including the disarming of local militias, the return of refugees, and the holding of free elections in the enclave. However, the agreement collapsed in November 1991 when the Azerbaijan parliament, dominated by communists-turned-nationalists, voted to annul Nagorno-Karabakh's autonomous status. Red Army troops were gradually withdrawn from the enclave, leaving it vulnerable to Azeri attacks. In response, after a referendum and elections in December 1991, Nagorno-Karabakh's parliament declared its 'independence', precipitating an intensification of the conflict.

On 16 October 1991, in the republic's first direct elections, Ter-Petrossian was overwhelmingly reconfirmed as president, capturing 83% of the national vote. On 21 December 1991 Armenia agreed to join the new confederal Commonwealth of Independent States (CIS), which was formed to supersede the Soviet Union, and in January 1992 was accorded diplomatic recognition by the United States and admitted into the Conference on Security and Cooperation in Europe (CSCE, later the OSCE). It also became a full and independent member of the United Nations.

Since independence most land has been returned to private ownership. However, Armenia's real GDP declined by over 10% per annum between 1985–95. The Nagorno-Karabakh dispute with Azerbaijan, which has claimed more than 18,000 Armenian and 5,000 Azerbaijani lives since 1988 and made over 1 million people refugees, and unrest in western Georgia during 1993 resulted in supply routes being blocked, leading to severe energy and food shortages. There has also been a huge influx of refugees to Yerevan, doubling the city's population, and parts of the country have still not fully recovered from a devastating earthquake in 1988, which claimed 20,000 lives. Nevertheless, taking advantage of the weakness of the Azerbaijani regime, the ethnic Armenians of Nagorno-Karabakh extended the area under their territorial control during 1993–94, being allegedly aided by Armenia, before a ceasefire agreement was signed in May 1994. This left Armenia in effective control of Nagorn-Karabakh.

In February 1993 Hrand Bagratian replaced Khosrov Haroutunian as prime minister. Subsequently, the pace of economic reform began to accelerate, with a new privatization and price liberalization program being launched in March 1995. However, popular support for President Ter-Petrossian and the APM dipped to a low level during 1994–95 and there were demands for fresh elections and large anti-government demonstrations in Yerevan in July and November 1994. The president's response, in December 1994, was to suspend by decree the chief opposition party, the ARF, and close down 11 anti-government newspapers. Parliamentary elections, held in July 1995, resulted in victory for the ruling APM and a constitution, strengthening presidential powers, was concurrently approved in a referendum, by 68% of the electorate. However, the election was tarnished by intimidation of the opposition.

The increasingly autocratic Ter-Petrossian was re-elected president on 22 September 1996, winning 52% of the first round vote to defeat Manukyan, the prime minister between 1990–91 who was now leader of the National Democratic Union (NDU) and was backed by four other opposition parties, and two other challengers. Manukyan, who attracted 42% of the vote, polled particularly strongly in Yerevan, and his supporters launched protest rallies, claiming that there had been ballot-rigging and demanding the president's resignation. OSCE observers concurred that there had been serious electoral irregularities. On 25 September 1996 Manukyan's supporters stormed the National Assembly and the government responded by deploying tanks in Yerevan, temporarily banning rallies and arresting many opposition activists. Although, in November 1996 the Constitutional Court upheld the election result, opposition protests continued into 1997, led by a seven-party alliance, the Union of National Accord, which included the NDU and ARF. Opposition political disquiet was underpinned by broader concerns about the state of the economy and welfare infrastructure. Although, from 1995 economic growth resumed, averaging 6% per annum, and the inflation rate fell from 5,000% in 1994 to below 10% by late 1996, the harsh measures taken had led the unemployment rate rising to 10% and social services deteriorating. In November 1996, Prime Minister Bagratian decided to resign and he was replaced, briefly, by Armen Sarkissian, Armenia's ambassador to the United Kingdom, before, in March 1997, Robert Kocharyan, the president of Nagorno-Karabakh, took over, in what was seen as a move designed to reduce opposition pressure for new elections to be held.

Since the May 1994 ceasefire accord with Azerbaijan, on-going, OSCE-brokered negotiations had failed to find a permanent settlement to the dispute over Nagorno-Karabakh and in April – May 1997 there were renewed border clashes. In September 1997 Arkady Gukasyan, a young hardliner, was elected president of Nagorno-Karabakh. However, President Ter-Petrossian and foreign minister, Alaksandr Arzumanian, anxious to secure a lifting of the border blockades imposed by Turkey, gave support to a new OSCE-proposed step-by-step peace plan. This envisaged Armenian troop withdrawals from areas in Azerbaijan around Nagorno-Karabakh as a preliminary to the commencement of wide-ranging talks on the enclave's future status.

This change in approach, with Ter-Petrossian acknowledging that full independence for the enclave was not realistic, brought to a head divisions within the APM, which was now known as the Pan-Armenian National Movement (PNM). A large faction, grouped around defense minister, Vazgen Sarkisian, and Prime Minister Kocharyan, opposed any concessions. There were defections to Azatutyun, a new political party formed in June 1997 by Hrand Bagratian, and, with intra-party opposition mounting, Ter-Petrossian and Arzumanian unexpectedly resigned in February 1998, leaving Kocharyan as acting president. Presidential elections held in March 1998 were won, on the second ballot, by Kocharyan; although, again, voter intimidation was claimed by the opposition. President Kocharyan declared policy priorities were to secure international acceptance of a right of self-determination for the people of Nagorno-Karabakh, and further economic and political reform. He appointed as prime minister Armen Darbinyan, formerly the finance minister, who was committed to market-centerd economic reform and to further privatization: by 1998 virtually all of the agricultural sector was in private ownership and 60% of enterprises. Kocharyan also lifted the ban on the ARF, in May 1998, and brought two members of the ARF into his cabinet. In the same month, a commission, chaired by Paruyr Ayrykian, was appointed to recommend changes in the constitution to reduce the president's executive powers.

Relations have remained close with Russia since independence and in August 1997 a treaty of 'friendship, cooperation and mutual understanding' was signed. In April 1997 the Armenian National Assembly ratified a treaty allowing Russia to maintain military bases in Armenia for 25 years.

AZERBAIJAN

Republic of Azerbaijan
Azerbayjan Respublikasy

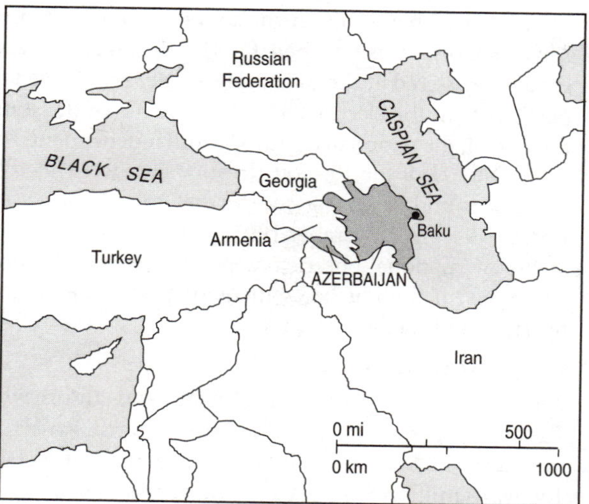

Capital: Baku

Social and economic data

Area: 36,600 sq km/33,436 sq miles
Population: 7,553,000*
Pop. density per sq km/sq mi: 206/226*
Urban population: 53%**
Literacy rate: 97%**
GDP: $3,600 million*; per-capita GDP: $480*
Government defense spending (% of GDP): 5.0%
Currency: manat
Economy type: low income
Labor force in agriculture: 19%**
* 1995.
** 1992.

Head of state (executive)

President Geidar Aliyev, since 1993

Head of government

Prime Minister Artur Rasizade, since 1996

Ethnic composition

Eighty-three per cent of the population is of Azeri ethnic stock, 6% Russian, and 6% Armenian. The official language is Azerbaijani, a member of the South Turkic language group.

Religions

Ethnic Azeris are predominantly Muslim, 70% adhering to the Shi'ite Ithna sect and 30% the Sunni (Hanafi school). There are also sizeable Russian Orthodox and Armenian Apostolic Christian communities.

Political features

State type: authoritarian nationalist
Date of state formation: 1991
Political structure: unitary
Executive: unlimited presidential
Assembly: one-chamber
Party structure: multiparty *
Human rights rating: N/A
International affiliations: BSECZ, CIS, EBRD, ECO, ESCAP, IBRD, IMF, NACC, OIC, OSCE, PFP, UN

* Although opposition activity is restricted.

Local and regional government

There are two autonomous regions within Azerbaijan, Nagorno-Karabakh and Nakhichevan (which is actually situated within Armenia), nine independent cities, and 54 districts, with elected local governments. Nagorno-Karabakh is under the *de facto* control of breakaway ethnic Armenians, with a 133-seat legislature and elected president.

Political system

Under the constitution of November 1995, which was endorsed by 92% of the electorate in a national referendum and replaced the amended Soviet constitution of 1978, Azerbaijan has a presidentialist political system. The executive president is directly elected for a five-year term and serves as head of state and commander in chief of the armed forces, and appoints a council of ministers, or cabinet, comprising around 30 members and headed by a prime minister. The president also oversees a security council, created in 1997. The state is described as a secular state, committed to a market economic system and freedom of entrepreneurial activity.

The legislature is the Milli Majlis (National Assembly), and comprises 125-members elected for five-year terms. Deputies are returned by a mixed

German-style system of voting: 25 seats are filled by proportional representation according to party lists and 100 are returned from single-member constituencies through the second ballot majoritarian system, with a 'run-off' race being held where there is no clear first-round majority. The constituencies include Armenian-held Nagorno-Karabakh and other occupied territories, with refugees casting their votes in other parts of Azerbaijan.

Political parties

The principal political parties are the Popular Front of Azerbaijan (PFA: Khalqu Jibhasi), the New Azerbaijan (Yeni Azerbaijan: YAP), the Communist Party of Azerbaijan (CPA), the Muslim Democratic Party (Musavat), the Party for National Independence (Istikal; estd. 1992), led by Etibar Mamedov, and the Social Democratic Party (estd. 1990).

The PFA is a democratic nationalist body formed in 1989 and is led by former president, Albufaz Elchibey. Since the coming to power of President Aliyev, it has been subject to a crackdown by security forces who have accused it of seeking to destabilize the regime. In May 1995 the PFA's leader, Elchibey, advocated creation of a 'greater Azerbaijan', unifying Azerbaijan with northern Iran.

New Azerbaijan was set up in 1992 to support Geidar Aliyev, a former communist and the current president. It is an authoritarian body.

The CPA, which is led by Ramiz Ahmadov, was suspended in 1991 and briefly renamed the Republican Democratic Party, but was reconstituted in November 1993. It was banned again in September 1995 by the Supreme Court after it was accused of intending to destroy the country's independence.

Musavat promotes Islamic values and the unity of Turkic peoples. Formed in 1911, it functioned until 1920 and was re-established in 1992 by Isa Gambarov and became an ally of the PFA. Its general secretary is Niyazi Ibrahimov.

In March 1995 the Grey Wolves opposition party was banned by President Aliyev. In 1997 the leader of the 50,000-member Islamic Party of Azerbaijan (estd. 1992) was imprisoned on grounds of treason.

Political leaders since 1970

1990–92 Ayaz Mutalibov (CPA/Republican Democratic Party), 1992 Isa Gambarov (PFA/Musavat), 1992–93 Abulfez Elchibey (PFA), 1993– Geidar Aliyev (New Azerbaijan)

Latest elections

The most recent direct presidential election was held in October 1998 and won by Geidar Aliyev, who secured 76% of the vote, with turnout recorded at 67%. The election was dominated, according to outside observers, by biased pro-Aliyev media propaganda. His nearest challenger, Etibar Mamedov, won 11.6% of the vote officially, but he claimed it should have been at least 26% and that there were widespread electoral irregularities. Five opposition parties boycotted the poll. Aliyev's margin of victory meant that he comfortably passed the 66% of the vote hurdle for victory in the first round.

Legislative elections to the Milli Majlis were last held on 12 November 1995. Turnout was 86% and a pro-Aliyev majority was returned. Of 31 political parties and groups registered at the time, only eight were allowed to participate in the election. The YAP won 67 of the seats, the PFA, 4, the nationalist Istikla, 4, and independents, 46 seats. Only 72 of the 100 constituency seats were filled in the first round of voting and further rounds of voting were held on 26 November 1995, and 4 and 18 February 1996. International observers reported 'serious electoral violations', including harassment of party leaders and restriction of media activities.

Political history

Azerbaijan shares a common language and culture with Turkey, but, prior to its conquest by Tsarist Russia in the early 19th century, it was a province of Persia. Today, 15 million Shi'ite Azeris live across the border in Iran. The name Azerbaijan is derived from the independent state first established in the region in the 4th century BC by Atrophates, a vassal of Alexander III (356–323 BC) of Macedon. During the mid-18th century there were independent khanates in the area, but these became Russian protectorates after 1805. During the late 19th century, Baku became the center of an important oil industry.

A member of the Transcaucasian Federation in 1917, it became an independent republic in 1918, with Gyanja (Kirovabad) as the capital, but was occupied by the Red Army in 1920 and was subsequently forcibly secularized. During the 1930s there were peasant uprisings against the Stalinist collectivization of agriculture and a series of violent purges of the Azerbaijani Communist Party (CPA). Despite these purges, the CPA became notorious for the extent of its corruption, being described as a 'state-run mafia'. This persuaded the reformist Mikhail Gorbachev, who became leader of the Soviet Communist Party (CPSU) in 1985, to engineer the dismissal in October 1987 of Geidar Aliyev (b. 1923), who had been the CPA's leader since 1969 and a member of the CPSU's Politburo since 1982.

Taking advantage of the new openness (*glasnost*) encouraged by Gorbachev, there was a growth in Azerbaijani nationalism from the later 1980s. This was spearheaded by the Azerbaijani Popular Front (PFA), which was established in 1989, and was fanned by the dispute with Christian Armenia over Armenian-peopled Nagorno-Karabakh (Nagorny Karabakh) and Azerbaijani-peopled Nakhichevan, two neighboring enclaves, with the status of Azerbaijani autonomous regions, in Azerbaijan and Armenia respectively.

This dispute over control, which reawakened centuries-old enmities, flared up into full-scale military and economic civil war from December 1989, prompting Azerbaijani calls for secession from the Soviet Union. It led, in January 1990, to the despatch of Soviet troops to Baku to restore order and communist authority, and the imposition of a state of emergency. Opportunistically, the CPA, under the leadership of Ayaz Mutalibov, allied itself with the nationalist cause. It rejected compromise in the Nagorno-Karabakh dispute and adopted a new state flag and designation in December 1990. In the September 1990 Supreme Soviet (legislature) elections, the Popular Front, having been on the verge of power before the January 1990 crackdown, was convincingly defeated by the CPA. Azerbaijanis voted overwhelmingly in favor of preserving the Union in the March 1991 USSR constitutional referendum – although the opposition claimed turnout was only 20%, rather than the officially claimed 75% – and the August 1991 anti-Gorbachev coup in Moscow was warmly welcomed by President Mutalibov, who ordered militia and tanks on to the streets of Baku to break up demonstrations. These had been organized by the Popular Front and had been supported by Geidar Aliyev, a former leader of the CPA who was now chairperson of the legislature of Nakhichevan, whose people had voted against the March 1991 USSR referendum proposal.

However, with the failure of the Moscow coup, Mutalibov resigned from the CPA, which was soon disbanded, and on 30 August 1991 independence was declared and the state of emergency, still in force in Baku, was lifted. On 8 September 1991, Mutalibov was directly elected state president as the sole candidate in a contest which was boycotted by the opposition National Democratic/ People's Front and was characterized by fraudulent practices. Mutalibov won 84% of the vote.

On 21 December 1991 Azerbaijan joined the new Commonwealth of Independent States (CIS), which superseded the Soviet Union. Turkey recognized its independence in November 1991, but the United States and other Western nations withheld recognition because of Azerbaijan's poor human rights record and its 'aggressive policy' towards Nagorno-Karabakh. However, in January 1992 it was admitted into the Conference on Security and Cooperation in Europe (CSCE, later the OSCE) and became a member of the United Nations in March 1992. As another measure of its independence, the new state began to form its own independent armed forces. Diplomatic and commercial links with Turkey were established and relations with Shi'ite Iran improved. In February 1992 the republic joined the Economic Cooperation Organization (ECO), founded by Iran, Pakistan, and Turkey in 1975, which aimed to reduce customs tariffs and eventually form a customs union. Also in February 1992 Azerbaijan reverted from the Cyrillic alphabet, imposed by Moscow in 1937, to the Latin alphabet.

In March 1992 President Mutalibov resigned, as a result of mounting nationalist opposition to Azeri deaths, which were approaching 5,000, and defeats in Nagorno-Karabakh, which he had placed under direct presidential rule in January 1992, and was replaced by Yakub Mamedov, the chairperson of the legislature, now known as the National Assembly. An internal power struggle developed and Mutalibov was briefly restored to power in May 1992 by the National Assembly and a state of emergency was declared, However, after the parliament building had been stormed by Popular Front supporters, Mutalibov was ousted again and replaced as interim president by Isa Gambarov, chairperson of the PFA. On 7 June the Popular Front leader, Albufaz Elchibey (b. 1938), was directly elected state president, capturing 59% of the national vote and defeating four rival candidates.

Morale improved in the armed forces with the coming to power of the nationalist Elchibey and a number of military successes were initially recorded between June and October 1992 in the struggle with Armenia over Nagorno-Karabakh. Thereafter, however, Azeri troops suffered a succession of disastrous military defeats which destabilized the Elchibey regime and left Armenian forces in control of a tenth of Azerbaijan's territory. This culminated in the president's overthrow in June 1993 in a military coup led by Colonel Surat

Guseinov, a wealthy wool merchant who had established his own private army in the Gandja area of western Azerbaijan to fight the Armenians in Nagorno-Karabakh. It was rumoured that he was in receipt of Russian military support. Geidar Aliyev, leader of the Nakhichevan autonomous region, became the new head of state, while Guseinov served as prime minister and 'supreme commander'. Elchibey fled to Nakhichevan and a referendum was held on 29 August 1993 in which it was officially claimed that only 2% of Azerbaijanis expressed 'trust' in the ousted president. The PFA, whose leadership and supporters became subjected to a security crackdown, including arrests, disputed the veracity of the poll's reported results. Aliyev was duly elected state president on 10 October 1993, in a contest boycotted by the opposition parties.

The new, and authoritarian, Aliyev regime developed closer ties with Russia, but Turkey, courted by Elchibey, remained a key regional ally. However, militarily Azerbaijan continued to lose ground to Armenia in the dispute over Nagorno-Karabakh, with a fifth of Azerbaijani territory, including the Lachin corridor which links Armenia with the enclave, being controlled by Armenians by the spring of 1994. Hopes of an end to the six-year-old conflict were raised in May 1994 when a ceasefire agreement was reached in Moscow in May 1994. Apart from border skirmishes in April-May 1997, this has largely held. However, a definitive agreement on the enclave's status has remained elusive, with a sixth of Azerbaijan's territory effectively still remaining in Armenian hands.

In October 1994 President Aliyev was faced by a coup attempt allegedly supported by Surat Guseinov, who, as a result, was replaced as prime minister by Fuad Kuliyev. In February 1999 Guseinov was sentenced to life imprisonment for his actions. A further attempted coup, led by the deputy interior minister, Ravshan Javadov, was foiled in March 1995 and the state of emergency imposed in October 1994 was extended. Javadov was killed in the fighting. Another coup plot, hatched by supporters of former president, Mutalibov, was foiled in August 1995 and three months later parliamentary elections were held, from which more than 20 opposition parties were banned from participating.

President Aliyev strengthened his grip on power in June 1996 when two of his most serious exiled political rivals, Mutalibov, the former president, and Rahim Haziev, a military strongman, both wanted in connection with recent coup attempts, were arrested in Moscow. A month later, Fuad Kuliyev, whom Aliyev accused of economic mismanagement, was replaced as prime minister by his deputy, Artur Rasizade. However, in May 1997 the opposition joined forces to form a new coalition, the Democratic Congress, under the leadership of Abulfaz Elchibey, who later returned to Baku, in October 1997, after four years in internal exile. In response, the ruling New Azerbaijan Party and eight other progovernment parties formed, in October 1997, a new progovernment parliamentary bloc, called Democratic Azerbaijan. In May 1999 President Aliyer successfully underwent heart bypass surgery.

Since independence Azerbaijani GDP declined at an average rate of more than 10% per annum until 1995 and inflation spiralled to a peak of 1,700% in 1994 as a result of the disruption of former ties with the ex-Soviet Union and the conflict with Armenia over Nagorno-Karabakh and Nakhichevan, which resulted in the influx of an estimated 900,000 refugees into the republic and a quarter of annual spending being consumed by the military. A market-centerd economic reform program involving price liberalization and privatization is being gradually implemented and joint ventures have been negotiated with Western companies to develop the country's mineral wealth and open new pipeline routes through Georgia and Turkey. The aim is, by 1999, to have transferred 75% of all state-owned property to private control: by 1997 this had been achieved for agriculture. From 1996 positive GDP growth began to be registered and the inflation rate fell to below 20%. Oil extraction commenced from the Caspian Sea in November 1997 and production is expected to climb to a peak of 800,000 barrels a day in 2010. Nevertheless, half of the country's population lived below the poverty line, a quarter had no job and there remained 850,000 refugees.

BELARUS (BYELORUSSIA)

*Republic of Belarus**
Respublika Belarus

* Belarus is the UN's preferred English language transliteration of the republic's name, although Byelarus, Bielarus, and Byelorussia are also widely used.

Capital: Minsk (Mensk)

Social and economic data

Area: 207,600 sq km/80,155 sq miles
Population: 10,265,000*
Pop. density per sq km/sq mi: 49/128*
Urban population: 67%**

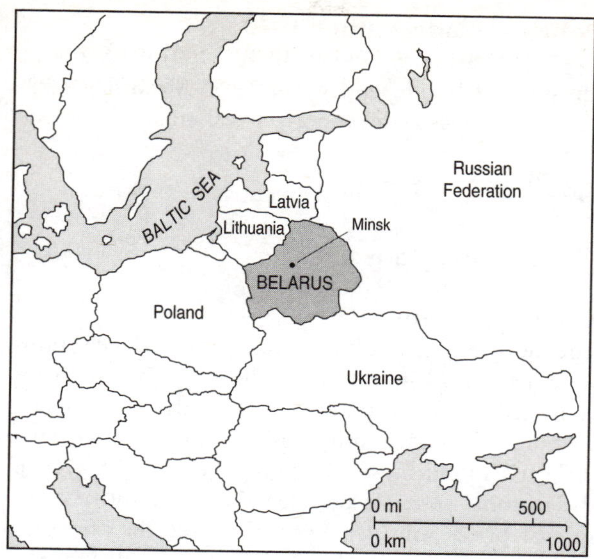

Literacy rate: 98%**
GDP: $21,360 million*; per-capita GDP: $2,080* ***
Government defense spending (% of GDP): 3.3%*
Currency: Belarussian rouble (to be replaced, it is planned, by the Russian rouble)
Economy type: middle income
Labor force in agriculture: 19%**
Unemployment rate: 2.7%*
* 1995.
** 1992.
*** Per-capita GDP has decreased significantly since 1992.

Head of state (executive)

President Alexander Lukashenko*, since 1994

* Also transliterated as Lukashenka.

Head of government

Prime Minister (chairperson of the council of ministers) Syargey Ling, from 1996

Ethnic composition

Seventy-eight per cent of the population is of Belarussian ('eastern Slav') ethnic stock, 13% is ethnic Russian, 4% Polish, 3% Ukrainian, and 1% Jewish. The official language since 1990 has been Belarussian, an eastern Slavonic tongue written in the Cyrillic script, but which is only the main tongue for 4% of the population. Russian, the most widely spoken language in the republic, was made a co-equal 'state' language in 1995, after a referendum held on the issue.

Religions

The population is predominantly Christian, most ethnic Belarussians and Russians belonging to the Eastern Orthodox Church. There are also 2 million Roman Catholics, who include ethnic Poles and Uniates, or 'Greek Catholics', and more than 200 Baptist churches. The small ethnic Tatar community adheres to Islam.

Political features

State type: authoritarian nationalist
Date of state formation: 1991
Political structure: unitary
Executive: unlimited presidential
Assembly: two-chamber
Party structure: multiparty
Human rights rating: N/A
International affiliations: CIS, EBRD, ECE, IBRD, IMF, NACC, OSCE, UN

Local and regional government

For the purposes of local government, Belarus is divided into six regions (*oblasts*) and the capital city of Minsk. Below these there are districts (*rayons*), cities, towns, and villages, with local councils. In October 1994 'primary level' soviets, i.e. village and some town councils, were abolished.

Political system

Under the terms of the constitution of March 1994, as amended in November 1996, Belarus has a strongly presidential political system. The executive president is directly elected for a maximum of two five-year terms. The president serves as head of state and commander of the armed forces, appoints the cabinet and prime minister and may declare a state of emergency, call referenda, and dissolve parliament. Since November 1996, the president has had increased decree powers and has been able to appoint half the members of the 12-member Constitutional Court and 12-member Electoral Commission.

Prior to the November 1996 constitutional changes, there was a one-chamber legislature, the Supreme Council; it comprised up to 260 members, elected directly for four-year terms by a majority system, with a second ballot 'run-off' race being held in contests in which there is no clear first-round majority winner. Turnout had to be at least 50% for an election result to be valid and sufficient deputies, 174 (or two-thirds of 260), had to be returned to form a parliamentary quorum, so that further 'repeat elections' could be held.

Since November 1996 there has been a two-chamber legislature, the National Assembly, comprising a 110-member lower house, the House of Representatives, and a 64-member upper house, the Council of the Republic. Deputies of the House are to directly elected, in future, every four years, but it presently comprises members selected from the Supreme Council by President Lukashenko. The Council of the Republic comprises eight members appointed by the president, and the remainder are representatives of the country's six regions and the capital Minsk, with eight drawn from each and elected indirectly by local councils from lists approved by President Lukashenko. There is an age limit of 21 years for members of the lower house and of 30 years for the upper house. Proposed legislation is considered initially by the House, but is then either approved or rejected by the Council, although, ultimately, the president has the right to abolish acts of the government. The upper house also appoints half the members of the Constitutional Court and Electoral Commission. In October 1997, it flexed its muscles in rejecting proposals by President Lukashenko to further curtail media freedoms.

The day-to-day government comprises a large council of ministers (cabinet), of around 50 ministers and state committee chairs, headed by a chair, or prime minister, appointed by the president and responsible to the National Assembly. National referenda may be called by the president, National Assembly, and on the initiative of at least 450,000 citizens.

Political parties

In 1998 around 35 parties were registered officially. The principal political parties are the Belarus Communist Party (BCP), the Belarus Patriotic Movement (BPM), the Belarussian Popular Front (BPF, or 'Adradzhenye'), the Peasants' (Agrarian) Party (estd. 1990), the Christian Democratic Union of Belarus, and the Socialist Party of Belarus (estd. 1994).

The 15,000-member BCP was suspended in August 1991 after the anti-Gorbachev putsch in Moscow, but was relegalized in June 1992.

The BPF was formed in 1988 as a Christian-democratic nationalist umbrella force and in 1994 claimed a membership of 500,000. It promotes the concept of a 'Baltic – Black Sea community' embracing Belarus, Ukraine, and the Baltic States, advocates Czech-style market-centerd economic reform, and seeks supremacy for the Belarussian language, although 96% of Belarussians speak Russian as their main tongue. It is led by Zenon Poznyak.

The BPM was formed in November 1994 as an authoritarian populist force supporting President Lukashenko.

Political leaders since 1970

1990–94 Vyacheslav Kebich (BCP)*, 1991–94 Stanislav Shushkevich (independent)**, 1994 Mechislav Grib (BCP)**, 1994– Alexander Lukashenko (independent)***

* Prime minister (in a dual executive to 1994).
** Head of state.
*** Executive president.

Latest elections

The most recent, and first direct, presidential elections were held on 23 June and 10 July 1994. Six candidates contested the first round, with Alexander Lukashenko, a young independent pro-Russian populist, dubbed the 'Belarussian Zhirinovsky', topping the poll with 47% of the national vote. He defeated the conservative communist prime minister, Vyacheslav Kebich, who captured 18% of the vote, the moderate nationalist former head of state Stanislav Shushkevich, 10%, Zenon Poznyak, a human-rights campaigner representing the Belarussian Popular Front, 14%, Alexander Dubko (Peasant's Party), 6%, and Vasil Novikau (Communist Party), 5%. Turnout reached 79%. In the second round 'run-off' with Kebich, Lukashenko won an 85% share of the vote. He attracted support from both the young and, by promising to reimpose tighter state controls over the economy, the elderly, offering 'simple solutions to complicated problems'. The election was viewed as free and fair, although the printing of the only independent newspaper, *Svabada* ('Freedom'), was mysteriously halted during the campaign and there were occasions when the electricity was turned off in halls where Lukashenko was speaking.

The first two rounds of the most recent legislature elections were held on 14 and 28 May 1995. Only 18 of the 260 seats were filled in the first round and a further 101 in the second, as a consequence both of voter apathy and limited media coverage, with turnout falling below the required level of 50% for a contest to be valid, and a multiplicity of candidates, which prevented a clear majority winner emerging. Of the 2,348 candidates contesting the first round, 43% were independents, and 432 candidates contested the second round. Twenty-four of the elected deputies were members of the Belarussian Communist Party and 26 from the Peasants' Party, with the remainder being chiefly independents and directors and chairs of state and collective farms. The Supreme Council was inquorate after the first two rounds, but further elections on 29 November and 10 December 1995 filled 79 more seats.

It was replaced in November 1996 by the House of Representatives, comprising members drawn from its ranks.

Political history

Having been subject to centuries of Lithuanian, Polish, Russian, and then Soviet rule, Belarus's claims to a separate national identity are somewhat tenuous. A medieval Belarussian state did develop around the city of Polotsk on the Dvina river, but from the 13th century it became incorporated within the Slavonic Grand Duchy of Lithuania and from 1569 there was union with Poland. Belarussia, or 'White Russia', was brought into the Russian Empire in the late 18th century by Catherine the Great (1729–96). It served as Russia's land bridge to the West and as an important agricultural region. From the later 19th century there was an upsurge in national consciousness and, amid the chaos of the Bolshevik Revolution in Russia, an independent Belarussian National Republic was proclaimed on 25 March 1918. However, it failed to receive international recognition. Instead, in January 1919, a Belarussian Soviet Republic was established, with some loss of territory to Poland. Initially, national culture and language were encouraged until the Soviet leader, Joseph Stalin, launched a 'Russification' drive from 1929, which resulted in more than 100,000 people, predominantly writers and intellectuals, being executed near Minsk between 1937 and 1941. Agriculture was also collectivized despite peasant resistance. Under the terms of the 1939 Nazi–Soviet pact, western and eastern Belarussia were reunified, regaining lands lost to Poland and Lithuania in 1921, but the country then suffered severely under German invasion and occupation between 1941 and 1944. An estimated 1.3 million died, including the bulk of its large Jewish population.

'Russification' continued between the 1960s and mid-1980s, with the teaching of the Belarussian language dwindling, strict state censorship being imposed, and large-scale immigration by ethnic Russians occurring. However, with the coming to power of the new Soviet leader, Mikhail Gorbachev, in 1985 and the launching of the *glasnost* (political openness) initiative, there was an urban-based and intelligentsia-led national cultural revival. Influenced by developments in the neighboring Baltic Republics, a Belarussian Popular Front (BPF: Adradzhenye), demanding greater autonomy, was established in October 1988. In the wake of the April 1986 Chernobyl nuclear reactor disaster in Ukraine, which rendered one-fifth of the republic's agricultural land and one-sixth of its forests unusable and forced the resettlement of several hundred thousand people from southern Belarus, the Belarussian Ecological Union (BEU) was also formed. Despite official and media restrictions, both the Popular Front and the BEU contested the March–April 1990 Belarussian parliamentary (Supreme Soviet) elections under the Democratic Bloc banner and captured more than a quarter of the 310 elective seats, polling strongest in the larger cities of Minsk and Gomel. In response, a Declaration of State Sovereignty was issued in July 1990 and Belarussian was re-established as the republic's official state language from September 1990.

Having been an industrially advanced republic within the Soviet Union, specializing in the assembly of lorries, tractors, motorcycles, and televisions and the production of fertilizers and petrochemicals, a switch to self-management and self-financing of nonstrategic industries began in January 1990. Belarus had a reputation as a cautious and 'compliant' republic within the USSR. In the March 1991 all-Union referendum on the preservation of the USSR, 83% of those participating – turnout was also 83% – supported Gorbachev's proposal to form a 'renewed federation of equal sovereign republics'. However, in April 1991 the republic was rocked by a series of workers' strikes and demonstrations in Minsk and other cities demanding not just higher wages, to counteract recent price rises, but also the removal of the Belarus Communist Party (BCP) government. Four months later, in August 1991, Belarussia's communist head of state, Nikolai Dementei, expressed support for the anti-Gorbachev attempted coup launched in Moscow by communist hardliners. After the coup failed, Dementei resigned and the republic's Supreme Soviet declared Belarussia's independence on 25 August 1991. The BCP was also suspended. On 19 September 1991 the Supreme Soviet voted to adopt the name of Republic of Belarus and elected Stanislav Shushkevich (b. 1934), a university physicist who was the son of a famous Belarussian poet who was silenced in the 1930s and who was an advocate of democratic reform and the swift transition to a market economy, as its chairperson and thus *de facto* state president. Shushkevich played an important role in the creation in December 1991 of a new Commonwealth of Independent States (CIS), the confederal successor to the USSR, with Minsk being chosen as the CIS's initial center.

In January 1992 Belarus was formally recognized as an independent state by the United States and other Western countries and was admitted into the

Conference on Security and Cooperation in Europe (CSCE, later the OSCE). It had been a member of the United Nations since its foundation in 1945.

After independence, Belarus's new administration, with Shushkevich sharing power with Vyacheslav Kebich, a pro-Russian BCP politician and former industrial manager who became prime minister in 1990, was cautious in its implementation of market-centerd economic reform. Privatization and price liberalization were introduced very gradually, the machine-building and chemicals industries were slowly restructured, and the country remained heavily dependent upon Russia for its industrial raw materials. This was explained by the resistance of both Kebich and the Supreme Soviet, which was dominated by communists, to significant economic changes. Indeed, a 75% profits tax was imposed on those private firms which did exist. The new state inherited a substantial arsenal of nuclear weapons from the USSR. These the Shushkevich administration pledged to remove gradually, beginning, in 1992, with tactical nuclear weapons and in February 1993 ratifying the START-1 and Nuclear Non-Proliferation treaties. (The last nuclear warhead was removed to Russia in November 1996.) However, in December 1993 a collective security treaty was signed with the CIS, which substantially subordinated Belarus's military policy to Russia's.

The condition of the Belarus economy deteriorated rapidly between 1992 and 1994, with inflation exceeding 2,000% per annum in the latter year, and industrial production being nearly halved as it adjusted to the loss of key markets in Russia and elsewhere in the ex-Soviet Union. Living standards also fell sharply to near Albanian levels. In January 1991, in an effort to stabilize the economy, the Kebich government entered into negotiations with Russia for the proposed exchange of the republic's *zaichiki* ('little hare') coupons, which were introduced in 1992, for Russian roubles at a 1:1 rate. This promised to enable Belarus to secure access to Russian oil and raw materials at Russia's low domestic prices, but meant the surrender of monetary sovereignty to Moscow. However, the deal was criticized by nationalists and the independent trade unions and remained unratified.

Accused of unproven corruption by a communist-dominated parliamentary commission, the nationalist-minded Stanislav Shushkevich was ousted as head of state in January 1994, following a no-confidence vote, and was replaced by Mechislav Grib, a lawyer and former general of the Soviet Union's interior ministry. Both Shushkevich and, with the backing of the BCP, Prime Minister Kebich contested direct elections to a new position of executive president in June–July 1994, but the surprise winner, by a landslide margin, was Alexander Lukashenko (b. 1955). A 39-year-old former collective farm boss who had risen to become chairperson of the Supreme Soviet's anti-corruption commission, Lukashenko fought the election on an anti-corruption and an earthy populist platform. He pledged a 'job and home for every Belarussian', spot checks on the income sources of the owners of villas in suburban Minsk, price freezes 'to end inflation', large credits to prop up agriculture and industry, and the establishment of a Slav union with Russia. Indeed, Lukashenko boasted that he had been the only Belarussian deputy to vote against the disintegration of the Soviet Union in December 1991.

However, apparently reneging on campaign pledges, in July 1994 President Lukashenko appointed a cabinet, headed by Prime Minister Mikhail Chigir, which was largely supportive of continued market-centerd economic reforms. Milk and bread prices were liberalized in August 1994 and the idea of monetary union with Russia shelved. However, a friendship and cooperation treaty was signed with Russia in February 1995. With new parliamentary elections set for 14 May 1995, President Lukashenko sought to hold a concurrent referendum asking the people to give him more powers over the still deteriorating economy and in the battle against crime, and to amend the constitution so as to enable him to dissolve parliament at will. Nationalist-minded Popular Front deputies in parliament protested against this authoritarian move and the president's pro-Russian policies, and went on hunger strike. President Lukashenko responded by sending in troops to storm the parliament building in April 1995 and dissolve the legislature pending the new elections.

In the 14 May 1995 referendum, voters overwhelmingly approved, by a 4:1 margin, with turnout of 65%, reducing the country's independence vis-à-vis Russia and strengthening President Lukashenko's powers. They agreed to restore Russian as an equal official language with Belarussian, restore the Soviet flag and symbols of Belarus, supported plans for economic integration with Russia (a customs union being established in May 1995), and gave the president his requested dissolution powers. The simultaneous parliamentary elections were marked by voter apathy, with repeat elections being held in December 1995, since less than half the electorate bothered to vote. Indeed, many electors followed the controversial lead of the president who crossed out all the names of candidates in his electoral district, stating that none was worth voting for. Those deputies which were returned were predominantly unreformed communists. The parliament, being inquorate, was unable to sit until after the December 1995 run-off elections.

In April 1996, with the economy continuing to deteriorate, an agreement on 'economic union' was signed with Russia. It involved the formation of a Community of Sovereign Republics (SSR), shared used of 'military infrastructure', the introduction of a common currency from 1998, and a common foreign policy. There were protest marches against the agreement, leading to a ban on demonstrations and, in August 1996, the flight of the nationalist politicians, Zenon Poznyak and Sergei Naumchik, to the United States. Meanwhile, the Constitutional Court and legislature criticized the president's extension of his authority over the security services and media. Lukashenko responded by unveiling plans to call a constitutional referendum on 24 November 1996, in which he would ask voters to extend his term from five to seven years and augment his powers, to enable the president to appoint an upper house (within a new two-chamber National Assembly) and half the members of the Constitutional Court and Electoral Commission, to increase his existing decree powers. The Supreme Council (legislature) reacted with its own proposals to impeach Lukashenko and hold a concurrent referendum to approve a new, non-presidentialist constitution. During October 1996 government riot police clashed with 10,000 anti-Lukashenko demonstrators.

The referendum, containing questions proposed by both Lukashenko and the Supreme Council, was held in November 1996. It brought victory for President Lukashenko, whose constitutional proposals were endorsed by 71% of voters, with an 84% turnout. However, voters rejected the president's proposal to allow free buying and selling of land and the Supreme Council's suggested changes. Prime Minister Chigir, who had disagreed with the referendum, resigned shortly before the vote and was replaced by his deputy, Syargey Ling. Four Constitutional Court judges also resigned in protest, while, in January 1997, the Council of Europe suspended Belarus's 'guest status'.

In late November 1996 a new lower house, the 110-member House of Representatives, was formed by President Lukashenko, from among the 198 members of the existing Supreme Council. However, around 50 members of the Supreme Council broke away to the unofficial alternative, anti-Lukashenko Public Coalition Government. A new upper house was, meanwhile, convened in January 1997. The president continued to press ahead with his plans for a Slavic re-union with Russia and in June 1997, a new Union Treaty and Charter of Union between Russia and Belarus came into force. It created a joint body, the Russian-Belarussian Parliamentary Assembly, which comprised 36 members from the legislatures of each state and would meet twice-yearly, and the union was to be governed by a Supreme Council, chaired in rotation by the presidents of Russia and Belarus. The treaty committed the states to closer integration, including future unification of economic and budgetary policies and the creation of a common legal system and currency.

In November 1997 large rallies were held in Minsk by pro- and anti-Lukashenko forces, and 100 leading figures, drawn from the intelligentsia and arts, signed a prodemocracy manifesto, 'Charter '97', modelled on 'Charter '77', the movement which had spearheaded the drive for democracy in Czechoslovakia. Two months earlier, there was a bomb explosion in Minsk by a self-styled Belarussian Liberation Army.

Following a decade of annual contraction by 10%, the Belarus economy begun to slowly grow in 1996 and the inflation rate fell to around 50%. However, the privatization program was halted, with only a fifth of the agricultural sector in private hands and an even smaller proportion of industries. Slow reform led to the IMF stopping the allocation of financial credits and to a drying up of the already minimal foreign investment, and to a sharp fall in the value of the Belarus rouble during 1997–98.

Shortages of food and consumer goods grew worse during 1999 and the annual inflation rate approached 100%. Meanwhile, the country's 'Alternative Coalition Government' sought to hold alternative presidential elections in May 1999. The former prime minister Mikhail Chigir and the exiled leader of the Popular Front, Zenon Poznyak agreed to stand as candidates. However, in March 1999 Chigir was arrested and charged with abuse of office, while Poznyak, concerned at the lack of proper voting procedures, withdrew his candidacy at a late stage. The unofficial poll, nevertheless, went ahead, on 16 May 1999. There was a turnout of 53%, with Poznyak attracting most support, despite his withdrawal. However, 'irregularities' led to the results being declared invalid.

BOSNIA-HERZEGOVINA

Republic of Bosnia-Herzegovina
Bosnia i Hercegovina

Capital: Sarajevo

Social and economic data

Area: 51,129 sq km/19,741 sq miles
Population: 3,600,000*
Pop. density per sq km/sq mi: 70/182*
Urban population: 36%**
Literacy rate: 93%**
GDP: $4,180 million*; per-capita GDP: $1,160*
Government defense spending (% of GDP): 18.8%*
Currency: Bosnia-Herzegovina dinar
Economy type: middle income
Labor force in agriculture: N/A
* 1995.
** 1992.

Head of state

President Dr Alija Izetbegovic, since 1990

Head of government

Prime Minister Haris Silajdzic and Svetozar Mihajlovic, since 1997 and 1998

Ethnic composition

The republic contains a complex mosaic of ethnically mixed communities. According to the 1994 census, 44% of the population is ethnic Muslim, 31% Serb, 17% Croat, and 6% 'Yugoslav'. Croats are most thickly settled in southwestern Bosnia and western Herzegovina and Serbs in eastern and western Bosnia. The ethnic Muslims are known as 'Bosniaks'. However, the civil war since 1991 has led to large-scale population movements, with hundreds of thousands of, principally, Croats and Muslims fleeing as refugees to neighboring states. The war has also claimed more than 200,000 lives, the greatest proportion being Muslims. The main language is Serbo-Croat, with Muslims and Croats using the Roman alphabet, while Serbs use the Cyrillic script.

Religions

Prewar figures state that 44% of the population adheres to Sunni Islam, 33% to the Serbian Eastern Orthodox Christian faith, and 17%, comprising ethnic Croats, is Roman Catholic. The Muslim community is composed of chiefly Bosnian Muslims, Slavs who converted to Islam during the Ottoman period, but also includes some Albanian and Turkish Muslims.

Political features

State type: emergent democratic
Date of state formation: 1992
Political structure: federal
Executive: limited presidential
Assembly: two-chamber
Party structure: multiparty
Human rights rating: N/A
International affiliations: COE, NAM (guest), OIC (observer), OSCE, UN

Local and regional government

As a result of the continuing civil war, local government institutions have been superseded by effective military rule by locally dominant ethnic militias, although it is envisaged that the new Muslim-Croat Federation of central Bosnia will be divided into eight cantons with a significant degree of autonomy and that municipalities will have their own local administrations.

Political system

The political system of Bosnia-Herzegovina has been in an unsettled condition, as a result of the bitter civil war which raged from 1991 to 1995. In mid-1995 the country was effectively partitioned between two contending states, a Muslim-Croat federation, which controlled central parts of the country, as well as the enclave of Bihac, situated in northwestern Bosnia, and a self-proclaimed Serb republic, Republika Srpska, based at Pale, near Sarajevo, which controlled eastern and much of western Bosnia-Herzegovina.

The internationally recognized government of the republic was headed by the Bosnian Muslim Dr Alija

Izetbegovic, who had been president of the directly elected seven-member Collective State Presidency since November 1990. Izetbegovic held power under the constitution of 1974, as amended between 1989 and 1991. This had provided, in accordance with traditions inherited from the Yugoslav Republic, for rotating leaderships, balanced ethnic representation, and 'ethnic vetoes' on key issues.

In May 1994, following an accord signed in March 1994 by the Croatian government and Bosnia's Muslim and ethnic Croat leaders, a new Muslim-Croat federation was formed, which would operate parallel to existing executive institutions of the Muslim-dominated Republic of Bosnia-Herzegovina and the self-styled 'Croatian Republic of Herzeg-Bosna', which comprised 51% of the area of Bosnia-Herzegovina, controlled by ethnic Croats. The federation, which comprised 51% of the area of Bosnia-Herzegovina, was to be divided into eight Swiss-style cantons, four of which were majority-Muslim, two were Croat, and two (Mostar and Travnik) were multi-ethnic. There was to be a federal government, responsible for defense, foreign policy, and economic affairs, with the offices of president and prime minister rotated annually between Muslims and Croats and a multi-ethnic Cabinet.

The Serb-controlled regions of Bosnia-Herzegovina, Republika Srpska, refused to enter into such a federation and, instead, had their own elected assembly, as well as a president and a prime minister. The November 1995 Dayton Peace Accord provided Bosnia-Herzegovina with a new constitution, the 'General Framework Agreement for Peace in Bosnia and Herzegovina', which was signed in December 1995. It provides for a federal system of government, with a federal executive presidency and a chamber federal Parliamentary Assembly, comprising the House of Peoples and House of Representatives. Two-thirds of the seats in both chambers are allocated to representatives of the Muslim-Croat Federation and one-third to deputies of Republika Srpska, which remain below, with their existing constitutions and political bodies. The federal government has responsibility for foreign affairs, trade, immigration, citizenship and refugee issues, inter-entity transportation, international communications, and monetary policy. The federal state presidency comprises three members: an ethnic Muslim (Bosniak) and a Croat, directly elected from the Muslim-Croat Federation, and a Serb, elected from the Serb Republic. The initial term for each president was two years; thereafter four years. The member receiving the largest number of popular votes chairs the state presidency, and is effective head of state. The presidency is responsible for foreign policy, proposes an annual central budget, and nominates a prime minister. (The other co-presidents each also appoint a co-prime minister.) Any presidency decision which is destructive to the vital interests of the subordinate Muslim Croat Federation or Serb Republic can be vetoed by a two-thirds majority vote in the relevant subordinate assembly.

The federal lower house, the House of Representatives, comprises 42 directly elected members, two-thirds drawn from the Muslim Croat Federation and one-third from the Serb Republic. It confirms in office the prime minister, nominated by the president. The upper house, the House of Peoples, comprises 15 deputies, including five Bosniaks, five Croats and five Serbs selected from among delegates to the House of Representatives of the Muslim-Croat Federation and the National Assembly of the Serb Republic.

The federal prime minister nominates other members of the cabinet, Council of Ministers, for approval by the House of Representatives and there are special guarantees to ensure that at least one-third of ministers are drawn from Republika Srpksa and that deputy ministers are drawn from a different constituent people to their minister. Compliance with the Dayton Accord is overseen by a UN-approved High Representative of the Peace Implementation Council, who is assisted by a team of international administrators, many of whom are Americans, and a UN police force of 1,700. Since December 1997 the High Representative has had increased authority to impose decisions, in areas such as design of a common flag, passport and currency, where no decision can be reached by the Bosniak, Croat, and Serb political leaders. There is also a nine-member Constitutional Court. In December 1997 a streamlined Muslim-Croat Federation was formed, with the abolition of the 'Croatian Republic of Herzeg-Bosnia'. This federation has a 140-member elected assembly, the House of Representatives of the Federation, as well as ten cantonal assemblies. The Republika Srpska has an 83-member National Assembly and a directly elected president, ruling from the capital in Banja Luka, in the west. Under the terms of the Dayton Accord, these 'statelets' are allowed to maintain their own armies and develop 'special parallel relationships' to neighboring states, such as Croatia and Serbia, in Yugoslavia.

Political parties

There are more than 40 political parties in Bosnia-Herzegovina. The main parties are ethnically based.

They comprise the Muslim-orientated Party of Democratic Action (SDA), the ethnic Serb-orientated Serb Democratic Party of Bosnia and Herzegovina (SDP), Serb National Alliance (SNA), Socialist Party of the Bosnian Serb Republic (SPBSR), Serb Radical Party of the Serb Republic (SRS-SR), the Croat-orientated Croatian Christian Democratic Union of Bosnia-Herzegovina (HDZ), and the League of Communists (LC) and Socialist Alliance (SA).

The SDA is the main Muslim nationalist organization in the republic and was founded in 1990 by President Izetbegovic.

The SDP was formed in 1990 by Dr Radovan Karadzic as a Serbian nationalist force. It has also been known as the Serb Renaissance Movement (SPO) and its current leaders include Momcilo Krajisnik who contested unsuccessfully, in September 1998, for the tripartite Bosnian president. It is allied to the SDP in Croatia. The SNA, led by Dr Biljana Plavsic, was formed in 1997 and is a moderate-nationalist party which supports cooperation and full implementation of the November 1995 Dayton Peace Accord. The 40,000-member SPBSR, led by Zivko Radisic, is linked to the Socialist Party of Serbia. The SRS-SR is an extreme nationalist body which is linked to the SRS which operates in Serbia, in Yugoslavia, and is led by Dr Nikola Poplasen, who was elected president of Republika Srpska in September 1998.

The HDZ, which is affiliated to Franjo Tudjman's HDZ in Croatia, is a Croat nationalist party which was formed in 1990 by Mate Boban and is now led by Bozo Rajic.

The LC, and its mass organization ally, the SA, was the former ruling party in the republic until 1990. It adopted the designation Social Democratic Party in 1990, becoming a reform-socialist party. In April 1996 Dr Haris Silajdzic, a moderate former prime minister who supported the creation of a truly multi-ethnic state, formed the integrationist Party of Bosnia and Herzegovina (PBH).

Political leaders since 1970

1990– Dr Alija Izetbegovic (SDA)

Latest elections

The most recent elections were held on 12–13 September 1998 and were overseen by OSCE officials. Detailed restrictions were imposed to prevent candidates from campaigning against the Dayton Accord or from publicly challenging key principles, such as the rights of refugees to return home. More than 30 candidates were later disqualified for violating these rules. The incumbent Bosnian Muslim, Dr Alija Izetbegovic, of the SDA, was overwhelmingly re-elected as chairperson of the federal presidency, attracting 511,000 votes, 87% of the Bosniak total. The Serb seat on the federal tripartite presidency was won by Zivko Radisic, a moderate from the SPBSR, with 360,000 votes, 51% of the those cast in Republika Srpska. He defeated Momcilo Krajisnik of the more extreme SDP. Kresimir Zubak, the moderate Croat member of the federal presidency, lost decisively to the hard-line Ante Jelavic of the HDZ, who won 189,000 votes, 53% of the Bosnian Croat total cast. The concurrent presidential election in Republika Srpska was won by the extreme-nationalist, Nikola Poplasen, of the SRS-SR, who defeated the moderate, Western-backed incumbent, Dr Biljana Plavsic, of the SNA, In the National Assembly elections in the Serb Republic 11 party groups secured representation. The SRS and SDP, in alliance, won 30 of the 83 seats, a coalition led by the SDA 15, an SNA-led grouping 12, the SPBSR 10, and a moderate grouping led by the moderate prime minister, Milorad Dodik, 6 seats. In the Muslim-Croat Federation, 68 of the 140 House of Representatives' seats were won by an SDA-led coalition, 28 by the HDZ, and 19 by the ex-communist Social Democratic Party. This meant that the SDA-led grouping held 17 seats overall in the 42-member all-Bosnia House of Representatives, the HDZ, six, the SRS and SDP alliance six, and the SPBSR, four. Turnout was 79%. However, in Republika Srpska, 17% of the votes cast were declared to be invalid.

Political history

1. Beginnings to 1994

Once the Roman province of Illyria, the area of Bosnia and Herzegovina which forms the southwestern component of the contemporary state enjoyed brief periods of independence in medieval times, before being conquered by the Ottoman Turks in 1463. It remained part of the Ottoman Empire until the late 19th century and many of the Slav inhabitants were converted to Sunni Islam. Following a Bosnian revolt (1875–76) against Turkish rule, it became an Austrian protectorate in 1878, eventually being annexed by the Austrian Habsburgs in 1908, following the Turkish Revolution of that year. It was the assassination in Sarajevo on 28 June 1914 of Archduke Franz Ferdinand (1863–1914), the heir to the Austro-Hungarian Empire, by a Bosnian Serb student, Gavrilo Princip (1895–1918), which precipitated World War I. In 1918, following the collapse of the Habsburg Empire, Bosnia and Herzegovina were incorporated in the new Kingdom of Serbs, Croats, and Slovenes, which became known as Yugoslavia in 1929. After invasion by Nazi Germany in 1941, it was included in the Ustasa puppet state of 'Greater Croatia' until the communist Partisan resistance leader, Marshal Tito (1892–1980), established his provisional government at liberated Jajce in Bosnia in November 1943. Bosnia-Herzegovina was kept undivided because of its ethnic and religious mix of Orthodox Christian Serbs, Roman Catholic Croats, and Muslim Serbo-Croat-speaking Slavs and it became a republic within the Yugoslav Socialist Federal Republic in November 1945.

During the 1960s, in an effort to create a counterpoint to the increasingly hostile Serb and Croat communities, Tito encouraged a strengthening of the position of the Slav Muslims, who were granted a distinct ethnic status in the 1971 census and were given a share in power through a rotating collective presidency, introduced in 1971. However, the republic's communist leadership became notorious for its corruption, racketeering, and authoritarianism and from 1980 there was an upsurge in Islamic nationalism and worsening Muslim–Serb ethnic tension from 1989. Multparty republic assembly elections were held in November – December 1990 and resulted in the defeat of the ruling League of Communists (LC) and the formation of a coalition government by Muslim, Serb, and Croat nationalist parties. This complicated the republic's dealings with Serbia. From the spring of 1991 the Serb-against-Croat civil war in neighboring Croatia spread disorder into Bosnia-Herzegovina, with ethnic Croats establishing barricades to attempt to prevent the predominantly Serb Yugoslav National Army (JNA) from moving through into Croatia. In August 1991, the republic's president, Dr Alija Izetbegovic (b. 1925), a devout Muslim lawyer and former anti-communist political prisoner, expressed concern that Serbia intended to divide up Bosnia-Herzegovina between Serbia and Croatia, with a reduced Muslim buffer state in between, and appealed for support from Turkey and the European Community (EC).

From September 1991 border areas began to fall into Serbian hands and Serbs began to form autonomous enclaves within the republic. In October 1991 the Bosnian parliament proclaimed the republic's 'sovereignty', but this was rejected by ethnic Serbs, who established an alternative assembly and held a referendum in November 1991 on remaining within the rump Yugoslav federation. In response, Muslims and Croats formed an alliance in the republic's parliament and voted, in January 1992, to seek recognition of independence by the EC. A subsequent referendum, held on 29 February – 3 March 1992 at the EC's request, resulted in an overwhelming pro-independence vote. However, this referendum was boycotted by Bosnian Serbs, who were fierce opponents of independence. Independence from Yugoslavia was declared on 3 March 1992. Violent ethnic clashes ensued, with bombings in several Bosnian cities, and on 27 March 1992 Serb leaders proclaimed their own 'Serbian Republic of Bosnia and Herzegovina', stating their desire to remain in Yugoslavia. Despite the worsening situation, the EC and the United States officially recognized the country's independence on 7 April 1992 and in May 1992 Bosnia-Herzegovina was admitted into the United Nations (UN).

In the spring of 1992 Serb militia units, led by Dr Radovan Karadzic (b. 1945), an accomplished psychiatrist and poet, and effectively backed by Serbia, took control of border towns in eastern Bosnia. They also launched attacks on the capital, Sarajevo. As Croats, led by militia leader Mate Boban, who was designated president of the Croatian Community of Herceg-Bosna, and the ill-armed Muslims also struggled to gain disputed territory, a state of emergency was declared. A number of ceasefires were quickly broken. By the end of May 1992 hundreds had been killed and hundreds of thousands had been rendered homeless by the all-out civil war. Bosnian Serbs had established control over an area stretching from the northwest to the southeast, comprising seven-tenths of the country. They expelled or killed Muslims and Croats from these occupied zones as part of an 'ethnic cleansing' process, with the aim of establishing a more homogenous Serb population. They established a network of detention camps where atrocities, including torture, rape, and arbitrary executions, were reportedly perpetrated. Meanwhile, Croats dominated large portions of the western part of the country, comprising a fifth of Bosnia-Herzegovina, aiming to later unite these territories with their home republic so as to form a new 'Greater Croatia'.

The UN called for the withdrawal of the JNA by 19 May 1992 and imposed economic sanctions against Serbia. In June 1992 the UN Security Council voted to deploy UN forces in Bosnia so as to ensure the supply of humanitarian aid and to protect besieged Sarajevo airport. This mandate was extended in August 1992 to allow the UN's 'blue beret' troops, the UN Protection Force in the former Yugoslavia (UNPROFOR), to use force to protect relief supplies and the first UN troops arrived in Bosnia in November 1992. The UN and EC appointed Cyrus Vance, a former US State Department secretary, and Lord David Owen (b. 1938), a former British foreign minister, to act as mediators and reach a political settlement with the Bosnian Serbs, Bosnian Muslims, and Bosnian Croats. A Vance – Owen peace plan, providing for a federal, ethnic-based Bosnia, was accepted in principle in January 1993 by the Croats and Serbs, but Muslim politicians expressed initial reservations. The Muslims later agreed to the plan, but it was rejected by the self-styled Bosnian Serb Assembly in April 1993 and overwhelmingly in a referendum of Bosnian Serbs held on 15–16 May 1993, which involved the simultaneous endorsement of the establishment of a Bosnian Serb state.

By September 1993 it became accepted that the establishment of a federation of ten cantons, with three for each community and Sarajevo shared by all, was no longer feasible, and the UN and EC mediators, Thorvald Stoltenberg, a former foreign minister of Norway who replaced Vance as UN negotiator in April 1993, and Lord Owen entered into discussions in Geneva with the contending parties and drew up new plans to partition the country into three separate states organized on ethnic lines. This was criticized as rewarding ethnic cleansing and military aggression, but was viewed as the only practicable solution. However, the three communities, particularly the Serbs, disagreed on where boundaries should be drawn. As a result interethnic fighting continued, with Croats attacking the Muslim city of Mostar in February 1994 and Serbs bombarding Gorazde, a Muslim enclave in eastern Bosnia, in April – May 1994. By the latter date, the number of UN forces deployed in the country had reached 22,000. Their chief tasks were the 'containment' of fighting, the airlifting of relief food and medical aid into starving, isolated eastern Bosnia, the enforcement of a 'no-fly zone' over Bosnia, and the protection of militarily vulnerable 'UN safe areas', as designated by the UN in May 1993. These included Gorazde, which was defended by NATO air strikes against Serb forces in April 1994, yet, nevertheless, effectively fell to Bosnian Serb forces, Tuzla, Zepa, Bihac, and Srebrenica.

In March 1994 the Bosnian Croats and Muslims, formerly adversaries until a ceasefire was signed in February 1994, agreed, under United States prompting, to sign an accord providing for the establishment of a new Bosnian Muslim-Croat Federation of ethnically delineated cantons, with Sarajevo as its neutral capital (see *Political system*) and the long-term goal of forming a confederation with Croatia. This new Muslim – Croat coalition began to change the military balance in the republic, although the Bosnian army, which included more than 200,000 troops, continued to be deprived of weapons with which to defend itself by an international arms embargo. On 9 June 1994 the UN Special Envoy, Yasushi Akashi, negotiated a temporary ceasefire in the civil war. This was flouted within days. However, in July 1994 the recently formed 'Contact Group', which comprised diplomats from the United States, Russia, Britain, France, and Germany, put together a peace plan. This provided for 51% of the country's territory being accorded to the Bosnian Muslim-Croat Federation, comprising much of central Bosnia and Herzegovina, as well as the eastern enclaves of Zepa, Gorazde, and Srebenica and the western outposts of Bihac and Orasje. The remaining 49% of the land area would be governed by the Bosnian Serbs, with Sarajevo placed under UN administration for several years, Mostar administered by the European Union (EU) and the UN also controlling thin strips of territory to link central Bosnia with its outlying enclaves. The UN and EU threatened to impose strict sanctions if the plan was rejected. The Bosnian Muslim-Croat Federation accepted the proposal. However, the Bosnian Serbs, unwilling to give up 21% of the country, rejected the plan, following a referendum held on 27–28 August 1994. This was despite pressure to accept being imposed by Slobodan Milosevic, the nationalist-minded president of Serbia, whose republic's economy had been damaged gravely by international sanctions which had been imposed in May 1992 as punishment for Serbian support of the Karadzic regime. Serbia responded by imposing an economic blockade on the Bosnian Serbs for all but humanitarian aid from August 1994, while the United States announced, in November 1994, that its forces in the Balkan region would no longer enforce the international arms embargo against Bosnia-Herzegovina, thus making it easier for the Bosnian Muslim-Croat Federation to build up its military strength.

In December 1994 the former US president, Jimmy Carter, negotiated a four-month ceasefire accord, which took effect from 1 January 1995. However, there were fears that a new wave of fighting would break out once the truce expired. The two contending parties, the Bosnian Muslim-Croat Federation and the Bosnian Serbs, had used the period of peace to regroup and rearm. The former, with 150,000 troops and 115 tanks, had agreed a military cooperation pact with Croatia and had become increasingly confident of its military strength and ability. The latter, with 75,000 troops and 400 tanks, while now denied assistance from Serbia, which appeared to be moving towards recognition of the borders of Bosnia-Herzegovina in exchange for a lifting of crippling UN sanctions, had closened their ties with the ethnic Serbs of the 'Republic of Krajina', in neighboring eastern Croatia.

2. 1995–1999

In May 1995 the Bosnian crisis intensified when Bosnian Serbs took 370 UN peacekeepers as hostages against further NATO air strikes and bombarded Muslim civilians in the 'safe area' of Tuzla. The West reacted by sending out a 12,500-troop Rapid Reaction Force to protect the 22,500-strong UNPROFOR. By 17 June 1995, following mediation by Serbia, the release of all the Bosnian Serb-held UN hostages had been secured. Ignoring belated UN air strikes, in July 1995 the Bosnian Serbs captured the UN 'safe areas' of Srebrenica and Zepa, situated in eastern Bosnia-Herzegovina, forcing more than 40,000 Muslim civilians to flee and allegedly murdering at least 4,000 Muslim troops. With the Bosnian Serbs' army chief, General Ratko Mladic, now apparently beyond the control of the civilian leader, Dr Radovan Karadzic, they also attacked the Muslim enclave of Bihac in western Bosnia-Herzegovina and shelled Sarajevo. However, these actions provoked an effective riposte by the Croatian army, which overran the Serb-held 'Republic of Krajina' in August 1995 and launched assaults on Serb positions in western and southern Bosnia-Herzegovina.

The four-year-long conflict had wrecked the already poor economy of Bosnia-Herzegovina. It had claimed around 200,000 lives, injured many more, and rendered nearly half of the population homeless refugees. In July 1995 the US Senate voted to lift the arms embargo on Bosnia, although this was vetoed by President Clinton. Meanwhile, a number of Western countries, disillusioned by the failure of UNPROFOR to prevent the fall of 'safe areas', now advocated the withdrawal of UNPROFOR. However, in September 1995 progress towards a peace deal was made when the Bosnian Serbs agreed 'in principle' to recognize the sovereignty of the Bosnian Muslim-Croat Federation on condition that the separate Bosnian Serb state, 'Respublika Srpska', comprising 49% of the territory, was also internationally recognized.

Under US prompting, the foreign ministers of Bosnia, Croatia, and Serbia met in New York and agreed on the preliminary outlines of a new constitution for post-war Bosnia. This provided for a common parliament and elected presidency. From 12 October 1995 a ceasefire came into force and in November 1995 negotiations between leaders of Bosnia, Croatia, and Serbia began in Dayton, Ohio, USA. In the same month Bosnia and Serbia opened liaison offices in their respective capitals. Full diplomatic relations were later established with Yugoslavia in October 1996.

The Dayton talks produced an historic accord, on 21 November 1995, accepted by the leaders of Bosnia, Croatia, and Serbia. This provided for the country to remain a single multi-ethnic federal state, with free, supervised elections, a rotating presidency, the return of refugees, and the banning from public office of indicted war criminals. The peace plan was policed from January 1996 by a 60,000-strong NATO-led force, replacing the UN mission, and which included 20,000 American and 2,500 Russian troops. The peace accord was formally signed in Paris in December 1995.

In January 1996 Haris Silajdzic, a moderate who strongly supported the concept of a multi-ethnic state, resigned as Bosnia's prime minister and was replaced by Hasan Muratovic. In accordance with the Peace Accord, Sarajevo was reunited in March 1996. In the next month, an international conference of aid donors, including the World Bank and EU, pledged $1.8 billion for the rebuilding of Bosnia. In May 1996 proceedings against alleged war criminals from former Yugoslavia commenced in The Hague and in June 1996 an arms control accord was agreed by all parties to the Dayton agreement. Meanwhile, a $400 million US 'train and equip' program began to be implemented, with the aim of raising the strength of the Muslim-Croat Federation's army. It proved so successful that by 1997 the 45,000-strong Federation army was more than a match for the 30,000-strong Bosnian Serb army.

Dr Radovan Karadzic, who had been earlier indicted in The Hague for alleged war crimes, stepped down as president of Republika Srpska in July 1996, but remained a controlling behind-the-scenes force. A month later, Bosnian-Croat officials agreed to dismantle 'Herzeg-Bosnia' Croat statelet within the Muslim-Croat Federation and merge the functions into the Federation's. Despite many of the Dayton Accord's conditions, notably freedom of association, expression, movement, the press and television, still lacking in what, outside cosmopolitan Sarajevo, were ethnically cleansed territories, in September 1996 OSCE-supervised national elections were held. They passed off peacefully, with two-thirds of the electorate participating. Voting was largely on ethnic lines, with the incumbent President Izetbegovic receiving most votes overall, 730,000, to become the first chairperson of the new three-person presidency. He was to work alongside Momcilo Krajisnik (690,000 votes), a Serb nationalist closely allied with Karadzic, and a pragmatic Croat, Kresimir Zubak (330,000 votes). In the elections to the 42-member federal House of Representatives, the (Muslim) Party of Democratic Action (PDA) won 19 seats, while Karadzic and Krajisnik's Serb Democratic Party (SDP) won nine seats and the Croatian Democratic Union (HDZ), seven seats. Within the Muslim-Croat Federation, the PDA won a majority of assembly seats and control over seven of the ten cantonal assemblies: the other three were won by the HDZ. In Republika Srpska the SDP remained dominant, and its candidate, Biljana Plavsic, was elected president.

In December 1996 a 35,000-strong NATO-led Stabilization Force (S-For), led by US General William Crouch and with a 18-month mandate, replaced the 55,000-member Implementation Force (I-For). It was to work alongside a UN civilian operation and included 8,500 US troops, 5,000 from the UK, and 3,000 German, and 2,500 French troops working in a joint Franco-German force, as well as two Russian battalions and troops from 17 non-NATO countries. In January 1997 Haris Silajdzic returned to power as one of two federal co-prime ministers, working with Boro Bosic, of the SDP. Meanwhile, Carlos Westendorp, a former Spanish foreign minister, took over as the UN-approved High Representative of the Bosnian Peace Implementation Council in June 1997, replacing Carl Bildt. Westendorp declared his priority to be the bringing to justice of those indicted in The Hague for war crimes. Also in June 1997, the Bosnian parliament approved a 'quick start' package to create a central bank, common currency (to be known as the marka), customs union and common external tariffs. This was intended to clear the way for IMF credits and further international aid to help boost economic recovery: with real GDP rising by 50% in 1996 and by 35% in 1997, to reach 60% of its pre war level. However, the unemployment rate exceeded 40%.

Progress in implementing the Dayton Accord's aims of creating a single multinational state remained disappointing. A unified diplomatic service and citizenship had still not been created nor a common design for a new flag agreed. Moreover, only a seventh of the 2 million displaced by the civil war had returned home, and barely a tenth of these had returned to territory controlled by a different ethnic group: fewer than 1,000 displaced Croats or Muslims had returned to the Serb Republic. This was underlined by difficulty in enforcing the results of the September 1997 in towns such as Serb-occupied Srebrenica, where exiled refugees voted to power the Muslim SDA. During 1997–98 there was a power struggle between Serb extremists and moderates in Republika Srpska. In March 1997 an agreement was signed on joint customs with Yugoslavia. However, from June 1997 the statelet's president, Biljana Plavsic, formerly seen as an ardent nationalist ally of Karadzic, became more amenable to closer integration with Bosnia. This was linked to pressure from Slobodan Milosevic, the president of Serbia, who wished to see the lifting of Western economic sanctions on Yugoslavia. Plavsic launched a drive against corruption, directed against the Karadzic clique. She tried to dismiss the interior minister, Dragan Kijac, but failed to receive backing from the republic's assembly and was thrown out of the ruling party. Republika Srpska now became effectively split into two contending parts, a Western-backed, pro-Dayton part, controlled by Plavsic and based around Banka Luka in the west, and an extreme-nationalist area around Pale, in the east, controlled by Karadzic and Krajisnic. Assembly elections in Republika Srpska, in November 1997, resulted in supporters of Karadzic failing to secure a majority of seats and the new party led by Plavsic attracting a fifth of the vote. This enabled, in January 1998, Milorad Dodik, a Western-backed entrepreneur-turned-politician who promoted ethnic tolerance and stated he would acquiesce in the arrest of suspected war criminals, to become prime minister. He led a non-party government of professionals, which also enjoyed the support of 18 Muslim MPs. The EU rewarded this change by providing the Republika with 6 million ECUs ($6.6 million) in aid: aid had previously been frozen because of non-compliance with the Dayton terms. The new government announced that the statelet's capital would be moved from Pale to Banja Luka and that refugees would be welcomed back to their pre-war homes, press freedom encouraged, privatization promoted, and the Serb Orthodox Church separated from the state.

In December 1997 Bosnia's tripartite presidency agreed on a common passport and citizenship law, while Carlos Westendorp was granted more power to impose decisions on the country's leaders. In February

1998 NATO announced that S-For would remain at least until the Bosnian general elections of September 1998. Thereafter, its strength would be reduced to 20,000 troops and the mandate of this new Dissuasion Force (Department-For) would be periodically reviewed. However, the outcome of the September 1998 elections were deeply disappointing for the international community, which had poured $3 million into reconstruction of the country and $2 billion a year into policing it. The elections resulted in Plavsic's replacement as Republika Srpska president by a hardline nationalist, Dr Nikola Poplasen, who advocated the creation of an 'ethnically cleansed' Greater Serbia transcending present boundaries and saw increasing support for Croat extremists. The 'Western protectorate' established over Bosnia seemed set to continue well beyond the millenium.

In March 1999 Westendorp dismissed Poplasen on the grounds of abusing his power by seeking to replace the Serb enclave's prime minsiter, Milorad Dodik. Poplasen refused to accept his removal.

BULGARIA

Republic of Bulgaria
Republika Bulgariya

Capital: Sofia

Social and economic data

Area: 110,994 sq km/42,855 sq miles
Population: 8,500,000*
Pop. density per sq km/sq mi: 80/198*
Urban population: 69%**
Literacy rate: 95%**
GDP: $10,400 million*; per-capita GDP: $1,225*
Government defense spending (% of GDP): 3.3%*
Currency: lev (pegged to German Deutschmark from June 1997)
Economy type: middle income
Labor force in agriculture: 17%**
Unemployment rate: 11.1% *
* 1995.
** 1992.

Head of state

President Petar Stoyanov, since 1997

Head of government

Prime Minister Ivan Kostov, since 1997

Ethnic composition

The Bulgarians, who constitute around 90% of the population, are a Southern Slavic race. Nine per cent of the population are ethnic Turks, who during the later 1980s were subjected to government pressure to adopt Slavic names and to resettle elsewhere. In 1989 an estimated 340,000 fled to Turkey, but 140,000 came back after the 'Bulgarization' program and legal discrimination was abandoned in 1990. The official language is Bulgarian, a Slavonic tongue written in the Cyrillic alphabet.

Religions

Eighty-seven per cent of the religiously active population adheres to the Bulgarian Orthodox faith and 9%, predominantly ethnic Turks, to Islam. In addition, there are 65,000 adherents to the Latin branch of Roman Catholicism and 30,000 to its Bulgarian, Byzantine-Slavrite, branch, 60,000 Protestants, as well as 10,000 followers of the Armenian Orthodox Church. Religious freedom is guaranteed by the 1991 constitution.

Political features

State type: emergent democratic
Date of state formation: 1908
Political structure: unitary
Executive: parliamentary
Assembly: one-chamber
Party structure: multiparty
Human rights rating: 83%

International affiliations: BIS, BSECZ, COE, DC, EBRD, ECE, IAEA, IBRD, ICFTU, IMF, LORCS, NACC, NAM (guest), PFP, OSCE, UN, WEU (associate partner), WFTU

Local and regional government

There are nine regions (*oblasti*), including the capital, each administered by a governor appointed by the Council of Ministers. There are 273 municipalities, with councils, elected every four years, and executive mayors.

Political system

Under its July 1991 constitution, Bulgaria is a parliamentary republic. It has a single-chamber, 240-member parliament, the National Assembly (Narodno Sobraniye), or Duma, which is elected every four years by universal suffrage in multi-seat constituencies, through a system of proportional representation, with a 4% threshold for party representation. The prime minister and cabinet, or Council of Ministers (COM), are drawn from the group able to command a majority in the Assembly. For the government to be overthrown in a no-confidence motion the opposition must secure an absolute majority of the votes, that is, 121. A party needs at least ten deputies to form a recognized group in the assembly. A state president, who is also commander in chief of the armed forces, is popularly elected for a five-year term in a two-round majoritarian election. The president's powers are principally ceremonial, but the office holder has certain emergency powers and may return legislation to the National Assembly for further consideration, but can be overruled. Candidates for the presidency must be at least 40 years old and resident in Bulgaria for at least five years before the election. This residency qualification prevented Simeon II, the pretender to the Bulgarian throne, who had lived in exile since 1946, from contesting the 1992 presidential election. A turnout level of at least 50% is required for a presidential election result to be valid. The separation of powers between the legislature, executive, and judiciary is monitored by a 12-member Constitutional Court. Amendments to the constitution must be carried by a majority of three-quarters of the National Assembly's members in three ballots on three different days. A new constitution may only be adopted by an elected 400-member Grand National Assembly.

Political parties

There are three principal political parties in Bulgaria: the ex-communist Bulgarian Socialist Party (BSP: Bulgarska Sotsialisticheska Partiya); the right-of-center Union of Democratic Forces (UDF: Sayuz na Demokratichni Sili, SDS); and the Turkish community-orientated Movement for Rights and Freedoms (MRF: Dvizhenie za Prava i Svobodi, DPS).

The BSP is the successor to the formerly dominant Bulgarian Communist Party (BKP: Bulgarska Komunisticheska Partiya). It adopted its present name in April 1990 and is led by Georgi Purvanov. Arguably the least 'reform-socialist' of the ex-communist parties of Central Europe, it favors improved links with Russia and the construction of a social safety net to cushion the impact of the transition to a market economy. The BKP was formed in 1919 by a radical faction that split away from the Bulgarian Social Democratic (Workers') Party, which had been established in 1891. From its earliest days, it was closely tied to the Russian communist movement. Banned within Bulgaria in 1923, it was forced underground during much of the interwar period. The party has been organized traditionally on pyramidal, Leninist 'democratic centralist lines', being controlled by a small Politburo. By 1986 the BKP's membership had risen to 932,000, representing 10.4% of the country's total population. Membership of the BSP was put, in 1996, at 320,000.

The UDF was formed in December 1989 as an umbrella alliance of anti-communist forces committed to political pluralism and market-centerd reform. It is led by Ivan Kostov and is an increasingly fractious coalition of 17 parties, embracing economic liberals, environmentalists, independent trade unions, intellectuals, and nationalists. Much of its support is drawn from the urban middle classes. In October 1998 it became a single party.

The 95,000-member MRF, founded in 1990, is orientated towards Bulgaria's rural-based Turkish minority community and is led by the former dissident philosopher, Ahmed Dogan.

More than 60 other political parties function, including the Bulgarian Agricultural People's Union (BAPU), a peasant organization, which was founded as the Agrarian Party in 1899, and was allowed to operate under communist rule as a force subservient to the BKP. In June 1997 the Real Reform Movement (DESIR) was formed by a former prime minister, Reneta Indzhova.

Political leaders since 1970

1954–89 Todor Zhivkov (BKP)*, 1989–90 Petar Mladenov (BKP/BSP)*, 1990–91 Alexander Lilov (BKP/BSP)+, 1990– Zhelyu Zhelev (UDF)**, 1990 Andrei Lukanov (BKP/BSP)***, 1990–91 Dimitur Popov (independent)***, 1991–92 Filip Dimitrov

(UDF)***, 1992–94 Lyuben Berov (MRF)***, 1994–95 Reneta Indzhova (UDF)***, 1995–96 Zhan Videnov (BSP)***, 1997 Nikolai Dobrev (BSP)***, 1997 Stefan Sofiyanksi (UDF)***, 1997– Ivan Kostov (UDF)***

* Communist party leader and state president.
** State president.
*** Prime minister.
+ Communist party leader.

Latest elections

The most recent National Assembly elections were held on 19 April 1997 and resulted in a victory for the right-of-center UDF alliance, which attracted 52% (up 28% on December 1994) of the vote and won 137 of the 240 seats. The Democratic Left alliance, comprising the BSP and allied Alexander Stamboliiski Bulgarian Agricultural People's Union and the Ecoglasnost Political Club (estd. 1989), won 22% of the vote (down 22%) and 58 seats. Assembly representation was also achieved by the MRF-dominated Alliance for National Salvation, which won 8% of the vote and 19 seats, and by Euro-Left (estd. 1997 by former members of the BSP) and by Georgi Ganchev's Bulgarian Business bloc, which, with 5% of the vote each, won 14 and 12 seats respectively. Turnout slumped to 59% (down 16%).

The most recent direct presidential election was on 27 October and 3 November 1996. The first round was contested by 14 candidates, with Petar Stoyanov of the UDF winning 44% of the vote. He defeated Ivan Marazov, the candidate of the BSP-dominated Democratic Left, in the run-off, winning 60% of the vote. Turnout was 61%.

Political history

Settled by the Slavs in the late 6th century, the area covered by contemporary Bulgaria was conquered in the 7th century by Turkish Bulgars who merged with the local population. They adopted Eastern Orthodox Christianity in the later 8th century and established powerful empires in the 10th and 12th centuries. From 1396 Bulgaria formed part of the Ottoman Empire. National liberation revolts occurred during the later 19th century, being aided by the defeat of the Ottomans in 1878 by the Russian tsar, Alexander II, but full independence was not achieved until 1908.

During World War I, Bulgaria allied itself with Germany, and, after its early defeat, lost Aegean coastal lands which it controlled to the Allied forces. The retreating troops mutinied and proclaimed a republic. The uprising was, however, suppressed, with German military aid. After the war, support for the leftwing Social Democratic and Agrarian parties increased and in 1919 an independent Agrarian government was formed under the leadership of Alexander Stamboliiski. It introduced a series of radical measures, including land reform, before being overthrown in a fascist coup in June 1923, in which Stamboliiski was murdered. A further coup in 1934 established a monarchical-fascist dictatorship under the leadership of King Boris III. The country remained backward, with more than 70% of the labor force employed in agriculture.

In 1941 Bulgaria again allied itself with Germany, joining in the occupation of Yugoslavia and declaring war on Britain and the United States. King Boris mysteriously died in 1943, following a visit to Hitler, and was succeeded by his young son, Simeon II. The country was subjected to German occupation, and then invaded by the USSR in September 1944.

The Soviet Union put into power a communist-inclined anti-fascist alliance, the Fatherland Front, under the leadership of General Kimon Georgiyev. Within the Front, the Bulgarian Communist Party (BKP), led by Georgi Dimitrov (1882–1949), who had returned from exile, controlled the key interior and justice ministries and set about purging the bureaucracy and armed forces of opposition elements.

In September 1946, following a referendum, the monarchy was abolished and a new People's Republic proclaimed. In October 1946, elections were held to the Grand National Assembly (Sobranje) on a single Fatherland Front basis, with the Communists gaining 277 of the 465 seats. A new, Soviet-style constitution was then drafted and adopted in December 1947, establishing a single-party state.

The new regime, headed, respectively, by BKP first secretaries Georgi Dimitrov and Vulko Chervenkov, the brother-in-law of Dimitrov, between 1945 and 1949 and between 1950 and 1954, proceeded to nationalize industrial and financial institutions and introduce cooperative farming, central planning, and repressive police control in a Stalinist manner. Political opponents were summarily executed, including the Agrarian Party leader, Nikola Petkov.

The more moderate Todor Zhivkov (1911–98) succeeded Chervenkov as BKP leader in 1954. He pursued a determined industrialization program, creating significant growth in the engineering and electronics sectors during the 1960s. In May 1971 he introduced a new presidential constitution. This enabled him to relinquish the chair of the Council of Ministers (COM), a post he had held since 1962, and become president of the newly formed State Council. Stanko Todorov (1920–96) became chairperson of the COM, holding the post continuously until 1981, when he was replaced by Grisha Filipov.

Under Zhivkov, who enjoyed particularly close relations with the Soviet leader, Leonid Brezhnev, Bulgaria emerged as one of the USSR's most loyal satellites. Only limited political and economic reforms were tolerated at home, industrial growth being based on the formation of large, integrated State Economic Organizations (SEOs). Externally, Bulgaria strictly adhered to Brezhnev's 'Moscow line' during international disputes and became a closely integrated member of Comecon and the Warsaw Treaty Organization. During the 1980s the country faced mounting economic problems and, prompted by Mikhail Gorbachev, who became the new reformist Soviet leader in 1985, a haphazard series of administrative and economic reforms, under the slogan *preustroistvo* ('restructuring'), were introduced and a new generation of leaders promoted to power. The reforms involved greater decentralization in the planning process, based on factory 'management'; greater openness in party affairs; the introduction of market efficiency principles ('the new economic mechanism') to eliminate weak enterprises; the streamlining of the state bureaucracy; and the launching of a series of campaigns against corruption and inefficiency. However, these measures proved insufficient for reformers inside and outside the BKP and, influenced both by public demonstrations and the dramatic changes which were occurring in other Soviet satellites and backed by the army and Soviet leadership, Zhivkov was replaced as BKP leader and state president on 10 November 1989 by the foreign minister, Petar Mladenov (b. 1936). In January 1990 the BKP's 'leading role' in the political system was terminated, enabling opposition parties and independent trade unions to function. In addition, political prisoners were freed and the secret police wing responsible for the surveillance of dissidents was abolished.

In February 1990 as an estimated 200,000 UDF supporters gathered in Sofia to demand an end to BKP rule, Alexander Lilov, a reformer, became BKP leader and Andrei Lukanov was appointed prime minister, replacing Georgi Atanasov, who had been premier since 1986. A special commission was established to investigate allegations of nepotism and fraud by the administration of Todor Zhivkov, who was placed under house arrest. Zhivkov was subsequently tried in September 1992, found guilty and sentenced to seven years' imprisonment, while Atanasov was sentenced to ten years' imprisonment for embezzlement. As part of the new reform drive, private farming was made legal once again and price controls were eased, resulting in shortages of foodstuffs and spiralling inflation. The BKP renamed itself the Bulgarian Socialist Party (BSP) in April 1990 and in a multiparty general election held on 10 and 17 June 1990 captured 47% of the national vote and 211 of the 400 elective seats. The opposition liberal-conservative Union of Democratic Forces (UDF), formed in December 1989, won 36% of the vote and claimed that the contest had been marred by ballot-rigging.

Petar Mladenov resigned the presidency in July 1990 and was succeeded by the UDF's leader, Dr Zhelyu Zhelev (b. 1935), a former philosophy professor. Following mass demonstrations and a general strike, Andrei Lukanov was also replaced as prime minister in December 1990 by the independent Dimitur Popov, who headed a caretaker coalition government. A new constitution was adopted in July 1991, defining the country as a parliamentary republic with a 'democratic, constitutional and welfare state'. By October 1991 prices had increased tenfold and unemployment stood at 300,000. The October 1991 general election, held under the new constitution, resulted in a hung parliament, with the UDF edging out the BSP, capturing 34% of the national vote and 110 of the 240 elective seats, but not securing an overall majority. The BSP secured 33% of the vote and 106 seats. This left the ethnic Turkish community-orientated MRF holding the balance of power with 24 seats, based on an 8% vote share.

A minority UDF government was duly formed, the first noncommunist administration in Bulgaria for 46 years, with Filip Dimitrov, an ex-Green Party lawyer, becoming prime minister. Western aid to the republic began to slowly increase and the United States reduced its import tariffs imposed on Bulgarian goods. Zhelyu Zhelev became Bulgaria's first directly elected president in January 1992, but the new UDF administration soon encountered mounting dissension as the economic situation deteriorated, after a GDP fall of 26% in 1991 led to severe food and fuel shortages and the rationing of basic commodities. There were strikes by miners, public transport workers, civil servants, and teachers in July and September 1992 and in October 1992 the MRF and BSP voted together to bring down the Dimitrov administration. Lyuben Berov (b. 1925), an academic economist and member of the MRF, became the new prime minister in December 1992, heading an MRF and BSP-backed 'government of experts'.

The new administration pressed ahead with gradualist economic reforms, with a program to privatize 500 medium-to-large state enterprises, on the Czech 'mass privatization' voucher model, being approved in August 1993. It also signed a ten-year treaty of friendship and cooperation with Russia in April 1993. However, Berov secured little positive support in a series of seven no-confidence votes which were held during 1994 and in September 1994 the prime minister tendered his resignation. He was replaced in October 1994, in a caretaker capacity, by Reneta Indzhova from the UDF, who was the former head of the Privatization Agency and who became the country's first female prime minister.

The general election, held on 18 December 1994, resulted in a clear victory for the BSP, which captured 44% of the national vote to the divided UDF's 24%, and a parliamentary majority. The BSP profited from growing nostalgia for the communist era, especially among the old, living on fixed incomes, and rural communities who were concerned by the country's economic decline and high rates of inflation (120% during 1994), unemployment (20%), and crime. In addition, unlike other central European states, opposition parties were unable to benefit from a strong nationalist or anti-Russian sentiment. Indeed, Bulgarians shared a common Slavonic and Orthodox Christian heritage with the Russians and had never rebelled during the communist era or required the deployment of Red Army troops.

The Moscow-trained Zhan Videnov, leader of the BSP since December 1991, but still only 35 years old, became the new prime minister in January 1995. He put together a cabinet, which comprised a number of independent technocrats, and pledged to work towards closer relations with Russia and to reduce the pain of market reform through giving more attention to social and welfare issues, in a 'social-market' manner, while continuing with privatization.

However, the BSP administration soon became unpopular as GDP contracted by 11% in 1996. The currency fell sharply in value, large parts of the banking sector became insolvent and, in May 1996, 67 loss-making state companies were shut down in an effort to restore the country's international creditworthiness. There were bread shortages, corruption scandals, rising levels of crime and, in October 1996, the mysterious assassination of Andrei Lukanov, a former prime minister and leader of the BSP's social democratic wing. Amid this turmoil, in November 1996 Petar Stoyanov (b. 1952), a pro-reform divorce lawyer, who had defeated Zhelyu Zhelev in Eastern Europe's first ever US-style primary election to become the UDF candidate, was elected state president. He defeated Ivan Marazov, the BSP minister for culture.

After this electoral setback, Prime Minister Videnov sought a vote of confidence from his BSP colleagues, but the popular foreign minister, Georgi Pirinski, who had been unable to contest the presidential election as he was ruled to be not a Bulgarian citizen by birth, resigned. He claimed that the government no longer had a mandate to remain in office. The UDF, meanwhile, started a campaign of demonstrations and strikes to demand the calling of an early general election to enable a new government to be formed to tackle the economic crisis. On 21 December 1996, at an extraordinary party congress, Videnov unexpectedly resigned as BSP leader and prime minister. He was replaced as party leader by his deputy, Georgi Parvanov, and, in January 1997, as prime minister by the interior minister, Nikolai Dobrev, who formed a government of experts.

These leadership changes intensified the economic and political crisis, with inflation spiralling during 1997 and the lev going into freefall. Faced with the threat of a general strike on 30 January 1997, Dobrev agreed to step aside, allowing an interim government to be formed, headed by Stefan Sofiyanski, the popular UDF mayor of Sofia, pending elections in April. The new government succeeded in bringing the monthly inflation rate down from 243% in February 1997 to 5% in April 1997 and announced Bulgaria's intention to seek full NATO membership. In the April 1997 general election, the reformist UDF secured a clear Assembly majority and a new government was formed, with the UDF's leader, Ivan Kostov, a former finance minister, as prime minister. His administration pledged to attack crime and corruption, accelerate privatization and establish an IMF-imposed currency control board to stabilize the currency (to be pegged to the German Deutschmark) and inflation rate. In return, the IMF agreed to provide US$657million in financial assistance. This enabled the economy to gradually recover, with GDP growth of 4% in 1998. By 1999 four-fifths of state-owned enterprises will have been transferred to the private sector. In 1996 Bulgaria submitted an official application for membership of the European Union and in 1999 it joined the Central European Free Trade Agreement (CEFTA).

CROATIA

Republic of Croatia
Republika Hrvatska

Capital: Zagreb

Social and economic data

Area: 56,538 sq km/21,829 sq miles
Population: 4,504,000*
Pop. density per sq km/sq mi: 80/206*
Urban population: 51%**
Literacy rate: 97%**
GDP: $17,200 million*; per-capita GDP: $3,820*
Government defense spending (% of GDP): 12.6%*
Currency: kuna (formerly the Croatian dinar)
Economy type: middle income
Labor force in agriculture: 14%*
Unemployment rate: 16.8%*
* 1995.
** 1992.

Head of state (executive)

President Dr Franjo Tudjman, since 1990

Head of government

Prime Minister Zlatko Matesa, since 1995

Ethnic composition

In 1991 77% of the republic's population were ethnic Croats, a south Slavic people, 12% ethnic Serbs, and 1% Slovenes. However, the civil war of 1991, subsequent 'ethnic cleansing' (involving the forcible expulsion by one ethnic group of another to create a more homogenous population) in Croat and Serb-dominated areas, and the protracted conflict in neighboring Bosnia have been associated with large-scale population movements. More than 300,000 Croats have been displaced from Serbian enclaves within the republic and there are an estimated 500,000 refugees from Bosnia in the republic. Serbs are most thickly settled in areas bordering Bosnia-Herzegovina, particularly in the Krajina region, between Bosnia and the Adriatic coast, and in Slavonia, in eastern Croatia. However, more than 150,000 fled from Krajina to Bosnia-Herzegovina and Serbia, following the region's recapture by the Croatian army in August 1995. The official language, since 1991, has been Croatian, though Serbian is widely spoken. Both languages are versions of Serbo-Croat, but the Roman Catholic Croats use the Latin script, while the Eastern Orthodox Serbs use the Cyrillic script.

Religions

Most Croats adhere to the Roman Catholic faith, while Serbs are predominantly Serbian Eastern Orthodox Christians. There are small Muslim, Protestant, and Jewish minorities.

Political features

State type: emergent democratic
Date of state formation: 1991
Political structure: unitary
Executive: limited presidential
Assembly: two-chamber
Party structure: multiparty
Human rights rating: N/A
International affiliations: CE, COE, IAEA, IBRD, IMF, NAM (observer), OSCE, UN

Local and regional government

For the purpose of local administration, the republic is divided into 21 counties, 420 municipalities, and 61 towns. Between 1991 and 1995, one-third of the country, divided into four zones adjoining Bosnia-Herzegovina, was ruled by technically illegal ethnic Serb regimes. The largest Serb-controlled enclave was the self-declared 'Republic of Serbian Krajina' (RSK) which had its own Serb-elected parliament, with a president, Milan Martic, and prime minister, Borislav Mikelic. It included smaller Serb enclaves in Slavonia. The UN Confidence Restoration Operation (UNCRO) supervised an uneasy truce in these zones. However, the Croat army retook Western Slavonia in May 1995 and Krajina in August 1995. This left only Eastern Slavonia, adjoining Serbia in the northeast, and with a capital at Vukovar, under the control of Croatian Serbs. It returned to Croatia's control in January 1998. In the formerly Italian-ruled peninsula of Istria, situated along the Adriatic coast in the far northwest of Croatia, there is a growing separatist movement, led by the Istrian Democratic Assembly (IDS).

Political system

Under the terms of the December 1990 constitution Croatia has a mixture of a presidential and parliamentary system. However, such is the charismatic authority of the current incumbent of the office of president, Franjo Tudjman, that at present the form of executive is best characterized as 'limited presidential' rather than 'dual'. The president is directly elected for a five-year term and serves as head of state, representing the country abroad, and supreme commander of the armed forces, appoints and dismisses the prime minister and members of the government, presides over government meetings, calls referenda, calls elections for parliament, and, at times of crisis or war, has decree powers. During the 1991–92 civil war, a war cabinet, the Special Council, was established, which was chaired by the State Council. The parliament, known as the Assembly (Sabor), is a two-chamber body, comprising a 127-member lower house, the Chamber of Representatives (Zastupnicki Dom), and a 68-seat upper house, the Chamber of Counties (Zupanijski Dom). Lower-house deputies are popularly elected for four-year terms: 80 members are elected by proportional representation from national lists; 28 are returned by the first-past-the-post system from single-member constituencies; 12 are chosen by proportional representation to represent Croats living abroad; and there are seven seats for members of ethnic minority communities whose share of the population exceeds 8%. Three upper-chamber representatives are elected from each of the republic's 21 counties and there are an additional five presidential appointees. The Chamber of Representatives is the most influential of the two houses, approving laws, adopting the state budget, and deciding on wars and peace. The upper house can, however, propose legislation and, after a bill is adopted by the lower chamber, return laws for reconsideration. The prime minister and government (cabinet), though appointed by the president, need to be able to command a majority within the Chamber of Representatives. From January 1993 proportional representation replaced first-past-the-post as the electoral system used in the republic. Three lower chamber seats are guaranteed to the country's Serbian minority. A constitutional amendment adopted in November 1997 prohibits the re-establishment of a union of Yugoslav or Balkan states.

Political parties

There are seven significant parties in Croatia: the Christian Democratic Union (HDZ), the Croatian Social Liberal Party (HSLS), the Social Democratic Party (SDP), the Croatian Party of Rights (HSP), the Croatian Peasants' Party (HSS), the Croatian National Party (HNS), and the Serbian National Party (SNS).

The HDZ is a right-of-center Christian democratic nationalist force, led by President Franjo Tudjman, and is the dominant party in Croatia, controlling both houses of parliament. It claims to have 400,000 members. Formed in 1989, it was subject during the early 1990s to divisions between its right and liberal, or left, wings, particularly over the issue of whether or not to pursue an active military policy in Bosnia-Herzegovina. This culminated, in April 1994, in Stipe Mesic and Josip Manolic, respectively chairs of the lower and upper chambers of parliament and leaders of the liberal wing, leaving to form the breakaway Croatian Independent Democrats (HND), claiming the support of 16 deputies. The HND was critical of Tudjman's allegedly 'dictatorial' leadership style and the support given to the Bosnian Croat Army's campaign in southern Bosnia.

The 9,000-member HSLS, a centrist force formed in 1989 and led by Drazen Budisa, is the chief opposition party.

The SDP is the reform-socialist successor to the formerly dominant Croatian League of Socialists, or communist party, later known as the Party of Democratic Renewal (PDR). It adopted its current name in 1991 and has 20,000 members.

The 30,000-member HSP is an ultranationalist rightwing Croat-orientated body, formed in 1990. It has a paramilitary wing, the Croatian Defense Association (HOS), which was involved in fighting in the Croatian civil war and has been linked with anti-Serb incidents. The activities of the HSP are kept under close surveillance and in November 1991, Dobroslav Paraga, the party's then leader, was arrested on charges of terrorism. He was subsequently acquitted in November 1993.

The 40,000-member HSS, led by Zlatko Tomcic, is orientated towards rural interests, notably peasants, and the SNS to the Serbian minority.

There are around 40 other parties, including three

small parties which campaign for regional autonomy: the Istrian Democratic Assembly (IDS), the Dalmatian Action Party (DA), and the Rijeka Democratic Alliance (RDA).

Political leaders since 1970*

1990– Dr Franjo Tudjman (HDZ)

* Executive president.

Latest elections

The most recent elections to the Chamber of Representatives, held in October 1995, were won by the governing HDZ. With 45% of the votes, it won 75 of the 127 seats, falling short of the two-thirds majority which would have enabled the constitution to be amended to increase the president's powers. The HSS-IDS-HNS alliance secured 18% of the vote and 18 seats, the HSLS 12% and 12 seats, the SDP 9% and 10 seats, and the HSP 5% and 4 seats; 290,000 Bosnian Croats voted in the election. Turnout was 69%.

The HDZ also secured a clear majority of seats, 42 out of 63, to the upper house, the Chamber of Counties, in the elections held on 13 April 1997.

The HDZ's leader, Dr Franjo Tudjman, was re-elected in the direct presidential election held on 15 June 1997, attracting 61% of the vote. He defeated Dr Zdravko Tomac, an excommunist from the SDP, who won 21% of the vote, and the poet Vlado Gotovac of the HSLS, who won 18%. Turnout was 55%.

Political history

Part of Pannonia in Roman times, the region was settled by Carpathian Croats in the 7th century. Formed into a kingdom under Tomislav in 924, for eight centuries from 1102 it enjoyed autonomy under the Hungarian crown, except for Slavonia, in the east, which between 1526 and 1699 was held by the Ottoman Turks. In the 19th century, Croatia formed part of the Austro-Hungarian Habsburg Empire. After World War I and the dissolution of the Habsburg Empire in 1918, it became a constituent part of the new kingdom of the Serbs, Croats, and Slovenes, known from 1929 as Yugoslavia. The Roman Catholic Croats resented the domination of this kingdom by Serbs, who were Eastern Orthodox Christians, and a Croat terrorist organization, the Ustasa, became active during the 1930s. This body was responsible for the assassination, in 1934, of King Alexander I of Yugoslavia, who was a Serb and had set up a royal dictatorship in 1929, during a state visit to France. During World War II, after the Germans occupied Yugoslavia, a Nazi puppet state, 'Greater Croatia', was established from April 1941 under the 'Poglavnik' (leader) Ante Pavelic (1889–1959), the Herzegovina-born Ustasa leader. This included most of Bosnia-Herzegovina and parts of Serbia, as well as the modern republic. As many as 500,000 Serbs, 55,000 Jews, and thousands of Romanies (gypsies) were brutally massacred in extermination camps by this Croatian fascist regime, which sought to establish a 'pure' Croat Catholic republic. The Ustasa state met with fierce resistance from the communist Partisans and, after a bitter civil war, was overthrown in 1944.

In November 1945, Croatia became a constituent republic within the communist-dominated Yugoslav Socialist Federal Republic, whose dominant figure, Marshal Tito, was a Croatian who had led the Partisan resistance to the Pavelic regime. Along with neighboring Slovenia, Croatia became one of the richest republics in the federation, with a thriving agricultural sector, substantial manufacturing industries, and a burgeoning tourist industry along the Dalmatian, or Adriatic, coast. Haunted by memories of the Ustasa regime, the federal republic's communist leadership treated with hostility expressions of Croatian nationalism, which they equated with fascism. However, Croats grew increasingly to resent the economic subsidies that the republic paid to poorer members of the federation in the east and south and also the fact that the federation and even the League of Communists of Croatia (LCC), following a purge of its Croat leadership in 1972, were dominated by Serbs. Consequently, from the 1960s there was an upsurge in Croat nationalism. Initially it took the form, in the Maspok ('mass movement'), of a cultural revival, but, from the 1970s, a violent separatist movement began to gain ground, which was not appeased by Tito's construction of a looser federation in 1974.

Nationalist agitation continued through the 1980s and there was mounting industrial unrest from 1987 as spiralling inflation caused a sharp fall in living standards. In an effort to court popularity and concerned at the Serb chauvinism of Slobodan Milosevic, Communist Party chief and president of Serbia from 1986, the LCC, later renamed the Party of Democratic Renewal (PDR), adopted an increasingly anti-Serb line from the mid-1980s. In addition, following Slovenia's lead, it allowed the formation of rival political parties from 1989.

However, in the first multiparty republic elections, which were held in April May 1990, the PDR was comprehensively defeated by the rightwing nationalist Croatian Democratic Union (HDZ). Led by the former Tito Partisan and revisionist historian, the retired

General Dr Franjo Tudjman (b. 1922), who had been imprisoned in 1972 and 1981 for his nationalist activities and who advocated the creation of a 'Greater Croatia', which would include Bosnia-Herzegovina, the HDZ won almost a two-thirds assembly majority. This was based on a 42% share of the republic's vote. Tudjman was duly elected state president by the Sabor (parliament) on 30 May 1990.

As president, Tudjman was initially conciliatory, declaring his government's aim to be simply a demand for greater autonomy. However, in February 1991 the Croatian Assembly, in conjunction with that of neighboring Catholic Slovenia, issued a proclamation calling for secession from Yugoslavia and the establishment of a new confederation which would exclude Serbia and Montenegro. It also ordered the creation of an independent Croatian army.

Concerned at possible maltreatment in a future independent Croatia, in March 1991 Serb militants announced the secession from Croatia of the self-proclaimed 'Serbian Autonomous Region of Krajina', situated in western Croatia between the Adriatic coast and the border with Bosnia-Herzegovina. Centerd on Knin and economically underdeveloped, Krajina contained 250,000 Serbs. The region's full traditional name, 'Vojna Krajina', meant 'military frontier'. In a referendum held on 12 May 1991 there was 90% support in Krajina for it remaining with Serbia and Montenegro, in a residual Yugoslavia. A week later, on 19 May 1991, Croatia's electors voted overwhelmingly, by a 94% margin, for independence within a loose confederation of Yugoslav sovereign states and on 25 June 1991 the Croatian government, in concert with the Slovenian government, issued a unilateral declaration of independence.

From July 1991, despite Croatia agreeing to suspend implementation of its independence declaration for three months, there was an escalating conflict between Croatian government forces and the Serb-dominated Yugoslav army (JNA) and civil war between Serbs and Croats within Croatia. Independent Serbian 'governments' were proclaimed in Krajina and also in Eastern and Western Slavonia. A succession of ceasefires ordered by the Yugoslav federal presidency and European Community (EC) observers passed unobserved and by September 1991 a third of Croatia had fallen under Serb control. The most intense fighting took place around the towns of Osijek and Vukovar in Slavonia, near Croatia's eastern border, as Serbs sought to link together Krajina and Serbia in a new 'Greater Serbia'. Three thousand people, mainly Croats, died in the attempted defense of Vukovar. Croatia's ports were besieged and at least 500,000 people had been made refugees. The fighting lasted longer than in Slovenia since the Serb-dominated Yugoslav federal authorities were unwilling to accept the loss of a republic which contained such a substantial Serb minority.

Rich in oil, Croatia retaliated with an oil-supply blockade on Serbia and announced, in October 1991, that it had formally severed all official relations with Yugoslavia. At the same time, attacks were launched on federal army barracks within the republic. By the end of 1991 the conflict had claimed as many as 10,000 lives. However, on 2 January 1992 a peace plan was successfully brokered in Sarajevo by the United Nations (UN) envoy, Cyrus Vance. This provided for an immediate ceasefire, the full withdrawal of the JNA from Croatia, and the deployment, from February 1992, of 14,000 UN 'blue beret' troops, the UN Protection Force in Yugoslavia (UNPROFOR), later known as the UN Confidence Restoration Operation (UNCRO), in contested Krajina and Eastern and Western Slavonia, while demilitarization was effected and a political settlement worked out. This accord was disregarded by the breakaway Serb leader in Krajina, Milan Babic, but was recognized by the main Croatian and Serbian forces. Under German pressure, the independence of Croatia and Slovenia was recognized by the EC and the United States on 15 January 1992 and in May 1992 Croatia was admitted to the UN.

During 1992 an uneasy truce lasted within Croatia and its four Serb-controlled enclaves. The JNA withdrew from the republic in mid-May 1992 and the Serbs ended their 238-day siege of the port and tourist resort of Dubrovnik on 28 May. However, UNCRO was unsuccessful in its efforts to enforce demilitarization in the Serb enclaves and there was sporadic Croat – Serb fighting in Krajina and Slavonia, as well as reports of forced expulsions of minority communities, part of an 'ethnic cleansing' process. Tensions were strained further by the outbreak of civil war in neighboring Bosnia-Herzegovina, where Bosnian Serbs were the initial aggressors, but where Croats also sought, initially, to establish by force their own independent enclaves. The crisis in Bosnia led to an influx of hundreds of thousands of refugees into Croatia.

Presidential and parliamentary elections held in Croatia in August 1992 resulted in the re-election of President Tudjman and the governing HDZ, whose control over the media had been tightened during 1992. However, the ethnic disputes in Krajina, Slavonia, and Bosnia were fomenting widening divisions between the HDZ's extreme nationalist rightwing, which advocated Croat military action in Bosnia to carve out a new 'Greater Croatia', and its liberal left wing, which favored establishing a defensive military alliance with the Bosnian Muslim government so as to pool resources against the common Serb threat. President Tudjman sided with the latter faction on 1 March 1994 when he signed the Washington agreement with the Bosnian Muslims and Bosnian Croats. This provided for a ceasefire in fighting between Muslims and Croats in Bosnia, the formation of a Muslim-Croat Federation in Bosnia-Herzegovina and included the long-term goal of confederation with Croatia.

The Croatian economy was devastated by the civil war of 1991–92 and the subsequent Croat – Serb tensions. GDP fell by 45% between 1990 and 1992, with the Dalmatian coast tourist industry and foreign investment collapsing; the annual inflation rate rose to more than 500%; wartime physical damage amounted to at least $15 billion; the maintenance of a refugee population of 500,000 was consuming a fifth of the annual budget; while the armed forces, which numbered more than 100,000, were an even greater resource drain. Despite these distractions, the HDZ administration continued to press on with market-centerd economic reforms, including privatization, driven on by the eventual goal of seeking entry into the European Union (EU).

In January 1993 Croat forces violated the 1992 UN peace agreement, launching a military offensive into Serb-held Krajina. This, and an 'Operation Blitz' offensive in May 1995, which resulted in the recapture of Western Slavonia, met with some success. However, still, by mid-1995, Serbs continued to control around 27% of Bosnia. Their position appeared to be effectively safeguarded by UNCRO. In the 'Republic of Serbian Krajina' (RSK), which included Serb-inhabited parts of Slavonia, the Serbs had their own parliament and, in January 1994, elected as president the moderate nationalist, Milan Martic, who replaced the more extreme Milan Babic. In March 1995 President Tudjman agreed reluctantly to sanction an extension of UNCRO's mandate in Croatia, but insisted that the force must be scaled down in size and should concentrate on policing the borders between Croatia and Bosnia and Serbia.

In August 1995, taking advantage of increasing international revulsion at the actions of the Bosnian Serbs, who had launched brutal offensives against Muslim UN 'safe area' enclaves within Bosnia-Herzegovina, including Bihac, adjoining Croatia, a lightning advance into Serbian Krajina was launched in August 1995 by more than 150,000 Croat army troops. Heavily overwhelmed, the 50,000 Serb irregulars defending the self-proclaimed republic were forced to withdraw into western Bosnia-Herzegovina and within 30 hours the Croats had recaptured Knin, capital of the Krajina region. Three UN peacekeepers were killed during the 'Operation Storm' blitzkrieg assault, which was followed by Croat raids into Serb-held areas of adjoining Bosnia-Herzegovina. At least three-quarters of the Serb inhabitants of Krajina, numbering 200,000, fearing reprisals by the Croats, fled east into Bosnia and Serbia, producing a self-imposed form of 'ethnic cleansing'. By September 1995 only the narrow belt of Eastern Slavonia, lying in northeast Croatia along the country's border with Serbia, remained in the hands of Croatian Serbs. There were 1,500 UN peacekeepers in Eastern Slavonia and plans were made to withdraw 7,500 UN troops stationed in Krajina and Western Slavonia. A snap general election, held in October 1995, resulted in a clear victory for Tudjman's HDZ, and a new government was formed, with Zlatko Matesa as prime minister. In November 1995 Serbia agreed to hand back control over Eastern Slavonia to Croatia over a two-year period, with international administration in the interval.

In August 1996 diplomatic relations were restored with Serbian-dominated Yugoslavia and there was mutual recognition of the two states. Two months later, Croatia entered the Council of Europe. From 1995, helped by financial support from the IMF, a stable new currency (the kuna) and a gradual recovery in tourism, there was strong and accelerating economic growth. Real GDP growth averaged 5% per annum between 1995 and 1997 and the inflation rate fell to 4%; although the unemployment rate was 15% in mid-1997. Despite reportedly suffering from stomach cancer, the 75-year-old Tudjman was re-elected president in June 1997, defeating Zdravko Tomac, a former communist from the Social Democratic Party. OSCE observers declared that the contest had been free, 'but not fair' and had been 'fundamentally flawed', as opposition parties had not been permitted campaign coverage in the state-controlled media.

In April 1997 local elections were held in Eastern Slavonia and the Independent Democratic Serbian Party (SDSS), which was led by Dr Vojislav Stanimirovic and was orientated towards the 110,000 Serbs living in the region, polled strongly, gaining control of 11 of the 28 municipalities. Nevertheless, in January 1998 Eastern Slavonia was reintegrated into Croatia and formal sovereignty regained. UN troops were replaced by 100 OSCE monitors, as attention became focused on rebuilding the shattered local economy, where unemployment was 80%.

In March 1999 the government of President Tudjman was charged with being 'authoritarian' in a US State Department report, which also criticised Croatia for its lack of cooperation with the Hague-based UN International 'war crimes' Tribunal for the Former Yugoslavia and failing to integrate 300,000 displaced ethnic Serbs.

CYPRUS

Republic of Cyprus
Kipriakí Dimokratía
(and Turkish Republic of Northern Cyprus
Kibris Cumhuriyeti)

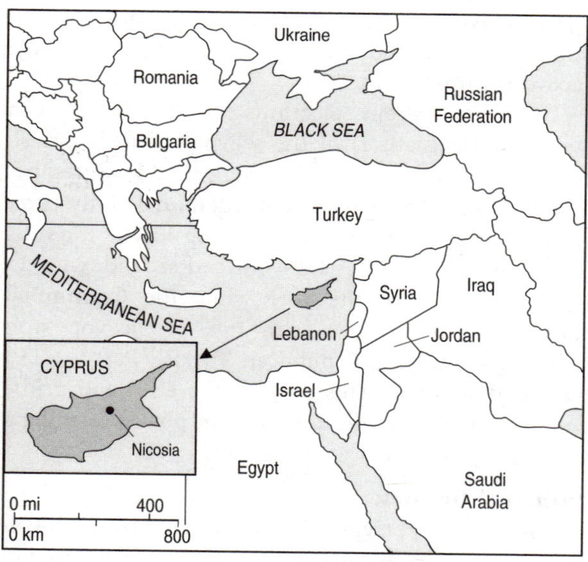

Capital : Nicosia

Social and economic data

Area: 9,250 sq km/3,571 sq miles
Population: 734,000*
Pop. density per sq km/sq mi: 79/206*
Urban population: 54%**
Literacy rate: 91%**
GDP: $8,600 million*; per-capita GDP: $11,720*
Government defense spending (% of GDP): 4.5%*
Currency: Cyprus pound
Economy type: high income
Labor force in agriculture: 17%**
Unemployment rate: 2.6%*
* 1995.
** 1992.

Head of state and head of government

Greek: President Glafkos Clerides, since 1993
(Turkish: Rauf Denktas, since 1976)

Ethnic composition

About 80% of the population have Greek origins and are Greek-speaking, while about 18% have Turkish roots and speak Turkish, living in the northern part of the island, within the self-styled Turkish Republic of Northern Cyprus.

Religions

There are about 444,000 members of the Greek Orthodox Church, mainly in the south, and about 105,000 Muslims, mainly in the north.

Political features

State type: liberal democratic
Date of state formation: 1960
Political structure: unitary
Executive: limited presidential
Assembly: one-chamber
Party structure: multiparty
Human rights rating: N/A
International affiliations: ACP (associate), CE, CSCE, CW, IAEA, IBRD, ICC, ICFTU, IMF, NAM, OIC, UN, WTO

Local and regional government

For administrative purposes, the country is divided into six districts, ranging in population from just over 30,000 to over 230,000.

Political system

The 1960 constitution provided for power-sharing between Greek and Turkish Cypriots, on a basis of numerical parity, but in 1963 the Turks declined to participate and the following year set up a separate community in northern Cyprus, refusing to acknowledge the Greek government in the south. The Greek Cypriot government claims to be the government of all Cyprus and is generally accepted as such, except by the Turkish community. There are, therefore, two republics, each with its own president, council of ministers, assembly, and judicial system. The self-styled 'Turkish Republic of Northern Cyprus' even has its own representatives overseas. Greek Cyprus has a president, elected for five years by universal adult suffrage, through a second ballot voting system, and a single-chamber assembly, the House of Representatives, with 80 members, elected by simple plurality and also for five years. Twenty-four of the seats are reserved for Turkish members but, since they have never been taken up, all the current 56 members are Greek. The president appoints and heads a council of ministers.

Turkish Cyprus adopted a separate constitution, after a referendum in 1985, providing for a president, Council of Ministers, and assembly similar to that in the southern part of the island. This separate government has only received external recognition from Turkey. In 1988 the newly elected president, Georgios Vassilou, pledged himself to construct a national government and to work speedily towards an end to the division of the island. Later that year talks between him and the Turkish Cypriot leader began, under United Nations auspices, but did not come to a successful conclusion. His successor, Glafkos Clerides, continued the search for unity. Meanwhile, Turkey maintains a 30,000-strong expitionary force in the north to counter 10,000 Greek Cypriot national guards.

Political parties

Of seven political parties, the four most significant in the Greek sector are the Democratic Party (DIKO), the Progressive Party of the Working People (AKEL), the Democratic Rally (DISY), and the Socialist Party-National Democratic Union of Cyprus (EDEK).

DIKO was formed in 1976. It has a center-left orientation and believes that the solution to Cyprus's problems lies in a federal strategy, achieved through the good offices of the United Nations.

AKEL was formed in 1941 as the successor to the Communist Party of Cyprus. Although its orientation is socialist, it was not formally aligned with the Soviet bloc. It supported the candidature of Georgios Vassilou for the presidency in 1988, even though he himself stood as an independent.

DISY was formed in 1976. In 1977 it absorbed the Democratic National Party (DEK) into its ranks. It has a centrist orientation and supports the idea of Western nations taking an active part in bringing Cyprus's racial and religious troubles to an end.

EDEK was formed in 1969 as the Socialist Party of Cyprus. It supports the idea of a nonaligned, independent, unitary, and demilitarized Cyprus, with a socialist social and economic structure.

Political leaders since 1970

1960–74 Archbishop Makarios III (EDEK), 1974 Nicos Sampson (military), 1974–77 Archbishop Makarios III (DIKO), 1977–88 Spyros Kyprianou (DIKO), 1988–1993 Georgios Vassilou (independent), 1993– Glafkos Clerides (DISY)

Latest elections

In the May 1996 House of Representatives elections the results were as follows:

Cyprus latest election results

Party	% votes	Seats
DISY	34.48	20
AKEL	33.03	19
DIKO	10.42	10
EDEK	8.12	5
Other parties	13.97	2

In the February 1998 presidential election, Glafkos Clerides was re-elected with 50.8% of the second ballot votes, defeating the independent candidate, George Iacovou. Turnout was 94%.

The most recent elections to the Republican Assembly (legislature) of the self-proclaimed Turkish Republic of Northern Cyprus were held in December 1998 and saw the right-of-centre National Unity Party (UBP) win 24 of the 50 seats, securing 40% of the vote. The Democratic Party (DP) finished second, with 13 seats and 23% of the vote while the Communal Liberation Party (TKP), with 15% of the vote won seven seats and the Republican Turkish Party (CTP) 13% and six seats. This enabled the UBP and prime minister Dervis Eroglu to remain in power, forming a coalition government with the TKP.

Political history

Originally Greek, Cyprus was conquered by the Turks in 1571 and then by the British in 1878, and annexed in 1914. In 1955 a guerrilla war against British rule was started by Greek Cypriots seeking 'Enosis', or unification with Greece. The chief organization in this campaign was the National Organization of Cypriot Combatants (EOKA) and its political and military leaders were the Head of the Greek Orthodox Church in Cyprus, Archbishop Makarios III (1913–77), and General George Grivas (1898–1974). Because of their activities Makarios and other Enosis leaders were deported by the British government in 1956.

After three years of intensive negotiations, Makarios was allowed to return to Cyprus and, with the granting of full independence in 1960, was elected president of the new Greek–Turkish state. As part of the independence agreement, Britain was allowed to retain its military and naval bases on the island.

Relations between the Greek and Turkish political leaders deteriorated and in 1963 the Turks withdrew from power-sharing and fighting broke out between the two communities. The following year a United Nations peacekeeping force was established to keep the two sides apart. After a prolonged period of mutual hostility, relations improved to the extent that talks were resumed, with the Turks arguing for a federal state and the Greeks wanting a unitary one.

In 1971 General Grivas returned to the island and started a guerrilla campaign against the Makarios government, believing that it had failed the Greek community. Three years later Grivas died and Makarios carried out a purge of his supporters, but in 1974 he himself was deposed by Greek officers of the National Guard and Nicos Sampson, who was a political extremist calling again for Enosis, was appointed president. Makarios fled to Britain.

At the request of the Turkish Cypriot leader, who feared the extremism of Sampson, Turkey sent troops to the island, taking control of the northern region and dividing Cyprus along what became known as the 'Attila Line', cutting off about a third of the total territory. Later in 1974 Sampson resigned, the military regime which had appointed him collapsed, and Makarios returned. The Turkish Cypriots had, however, by now established their own *de facto* independent government for what they called the 'Turkish Federated State of Cyprus' (TFSC), with Rauf Denktas (b. 1924) as president.

In 1977 Makarios died and was succeeded by Spyros Kyprianou (b. 1932), who had been president of the House of Representatives. He saw the way forward through international mediation and in 1980 UN-sponsored peace talks between the Greek and Turkish communities were resumed. The Turkish Cypriots offered to hand back about 4% of the territory they controlled and to resettle 40,000 of the 200,000 refugees who had fled to the north, but this failed to satisfy the Greek Cypriots and stalemate was reached. The Turks wanted equal status for the two communities, equal representation in government and firm links with Turkey. The Greeks, on the other hand, favored an alternating presidency, strong central government and representation in the assembly on a proportional basis. Between 1982 and 1985 several attempts by the Greek government, in Athens, and the UN to find a compromise solution failed and the Turkish Republic of Northern Cyprus (TRNC), with Denktas as president, was formally declared, but recognized only by Turkey.

In 1985 a summit meeting between Denktas and Kyprianou failed to reach agreement and the UN secretary general drew up proposals for a bizonal federal Cyprus, with a Greek president and a Turkish vice president but this was not found acceptable. Meanwhile, both Kyprianou and Denktas had been re-elected.

The dispute between the two communities seemed to be insoluble until the election of the independent candidate Georgios Vassilou (b. 1931) to the presidency in 1988. Vassilou seemed likely to be better placed to find a solution because of his lack of involvement in party politics. He immediately set about creating a government of national unity and taking steps to bridge the Greek–Turkish divide. However, despite a series of talks with the Turkish-Cypriot leader, under UN auspices, hopes of reunification remained unfulfilled.

In the 1993 presidential elections the leader of the Democratic Rally (DISY), Glafkos Clerides (b. 1920), narrowly defeated Vassilou. Clerides continued to seek a solution to the island's divisions and in May 1995 talks between representatives of the two communities were resumed. In June 1997 the negotiator of the Dayton Peace Agreement, Richard Holbrooke, was appointed US envoy to Cyprus, but in April 1998 he announced that his mission had failed. Meanwhile, in February 1998 President Clerides was narrowly re-elected, and formed a broadly based 'national unity' government, including members of the DISY, Liberal Party, and rebel members of the Democratic Party (DIKO). In November 1998 the European Union began membership talks with Cyprus.

CZECH REPUBLIC

Ceská Republika

Capital: Prague (Praha)

Social and economic data

Area: 78,864 sq km/30,450 sq miles
Population: 10,333,000*
Pop. density per sq km/sq mi: 131/339*
Urban population: 75%**

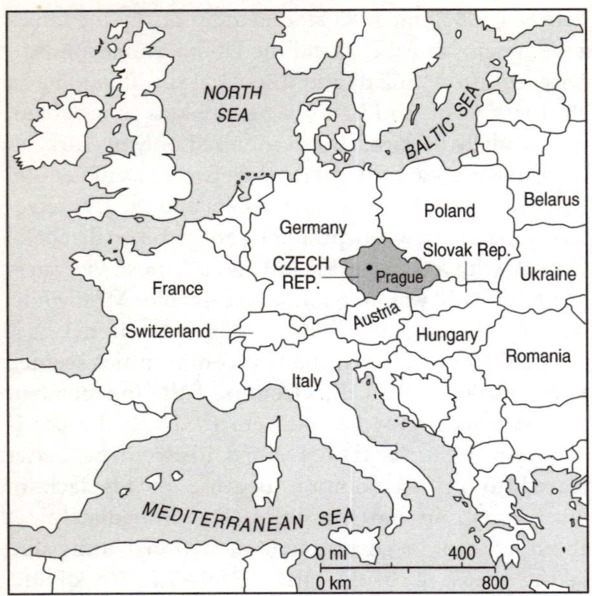

Literacy rate: 99%**
GDP: $46,500 million*; per-capita GDP: $4,500*
Government defense spending (% of GDP): 2.8%*
Currency: koruna
Economy type: middle income
Labor force in agriculture: 9%**
Unemployment rate: 3.4%*
* 1995.
** 1992.

Head of state

President Václav Havel, since 1993*

* President of Czechoslovakia from 1989.

Head of government

Prime Minister Milos Zeman, since 1998

Ethnic composition

The bulk of the population is of Czech ethnic stock, a Western Slav race. There is also a sizeable Slovak minority and small Polish, German, and Hungarian minorities. The official language is Czech, but 4% of the population speaks Slovak.

Religions

Around 40% of the population is Roman Catholic. Significant minorities adhere to the Czech Hussite Church (172,000), the Presbyterian Evangelical Church of Czech Brethren (168,000), and the Eastern Orthodox Church.

Political features

State type: emergent democratic
Date of state formation: 1993*
Political structure: unitary
Executive: dual
Assembly: two-chamber
Party structure: multiparty
Human rights rating: 97%
International affiliations: BIS, CEI, CERN, COE, EBRD, ECE, IAEA, IBRD, ICFTU, IMF, LORCS, NACC, NAM (guest), NATO, OECD, OSCE, PFP, UN, VG, WEU (associate partner), WTO
* Czechoslovakia was formed in 1918.

Local and regional government

The country is to be divided, from 2000, into 14 regions (*kraje*), including the city of Prague, subdivided into municipalities for the purposes of local administration. There are currently 72 administrative districts.

Political system

Under the terms of the December 1992 constitution, which came into force on 1 January 1993 when the federal republic of Czechoslovakia split into two separate Czech and Slovak republics, the Czech Republic has a dual executive political system. Most executive authority is wielded by the prime minister on the parliamentary model. However, the state president, although largely a ceremonial figure, has the power to veto legislation and, in certain circumstances, may dissolve the lower house of parliament. The present incumbent, Václav Havel, wields considerable moral authority, having played a key role in the struggle against communist authoritarianism.

Legislative power resides with a two-chamber parliament, which comprises the 200-member Chamber of Deputies (Poslanecká Snemovna), the lower house, and the 81-member Senate (Senát). The Chamber of Deputies is elected for four years under a system of proportional representation by universal suffrage, the minimum voting age being 18 years. Senators are directly elected in single-member constituencies for six-year terms in a staggered manner, with one-third being subject to election every two years. The Senate was initially expected to be elected in 1993, but delays resulted in the postponement of its first elections until 1996. Its main role is to scrutinize legislation. Both houses meet in a joint session to form an electoral college to elect the state president for a maximum of two consecutive five-year terms. The president appoints and dismisses the prime minister, is supreme commander of the armed forces, represents the state in external affairs, and appoints, with the Senate's consent, the judges of the

15-member Constitutional Court, who serve ten-year terms, and the chair and deputy chairs of the Supreme Court. The prime minister, appointed by the president, appoints a Council of Ministers (COM), or cabinet, of around 20 members that commands a majority in the Chamber of Deputies to assume charge of day-to-day executive government.

Previously, before the Czech Republic became a separate state in January 1993, each of the two national republics had its own constitution, assembly, and government, while the federal republic of Czechoslovakia also had its own two-chamber Federal Assembly. This comprised the directly elected 200-member Chamber of the People, which included 134 deputies from the Czech Republic, and the 150-member Chamber of Nations, with 75 Czech members. Both chambers elected a state president, who appointed a prime minister and government. There were special procedural safeguards to prevent domination by either nationality, for example separate voting by Czech and Slovak deputies when adopting the economic plan and budget, with majorities from both groups needed before they could be passed. The individual republics had special jurisdiction over such matters as culture, education, health, and justice, while the federal administration concentrated on economic, financial, and diplomatic issues.

Political parties

The main political parties in the Czech Republic are the right-of-center Civic Democratic Party (CDP), Civic Democratic Alliance (CDA), and Freedom Union; the center-left Free Democrats-Liberal National Social Party (FD); the Communist Party of Bohemia and Moravia (KSCM); the centrist Agrarian Party, Liberal National Social Party (LNSP, formerly the Czech Socialist Party, or CSP) and Czech Social Democratic Party (CSDP); the Christian Democratic Union-Czech People's Party (CDU-CPP); the Moravian Nationalist Party (MNP); and the far-right Czech Republican Party.

The CDP, CDA, and CM were all formed in 1991 following a split in the Civic Forum (Obcanske forum), which was set up in 1989 as an intelligentsia-led umbrella body to spearhead the 'Velvet Revolution' prodemocracy movement. The 35,000-member CDP, led by Prime Minister Václav Klaus, is a right-of-center anticommunist body, committed to the establishment of a Western-style free-market economy. The Christian Democratic Party merged with it in 1996. The CDA, which was a coalition partner of the CDP 1992–98, is similar in outlook. The Freedom Union was formed in January 1998 by more than 30 deputies who broke away from the CDP, under the leadership of Jan Ruml, the former interior minister. The FD, led by Jiri Dienstbier, is a more liberal left-of-center force supportive of President Havel. It originated as the Civic Movement (CM).

The 300,000-member KSCM, formed in 1991, is the reform-socialist successor to the formerly dominant Communist Party of Czechoslovakia (CPCZ: Komunista Strana Ceskoslovenska). The CPCZ originated in May 1921 as a leftwing breakaway faction from the Czechoslovak Social Democratic Party (estd. 1897). With an initial membership of 350,000, the party was multi-ethnic in character. It was allowed to operate legally throughout the interwar period, capturing more than 10% of the vote, but did not share power in any of the cabinets of that period. Membership declined to less than 100,000 and the party was forced underground when Hitler invaded the country. In 1945, however, the CPCZ received a massive influx of new members and captured 38% of the vote in the free elections of 1946. It later endured major purges during the early 1950s and immediately after the 'Prague Spring' of 1968. As a result, party membership contracted from 1.68 million in 1962 to 1.17 million in 1971. In 1986 it rose again to 1.68 million, representing 10.8% of the total population. Following a split in the KSCM in July 1993, after the traditionalist Miroslav Grebenicek was elected the party's new leader, the breakaway Party of the Democratic Left was formed by the reformist Jiri Svoboda.

The Agrarian Party, formed in 1990 to seek compensation for farmers whose property was confiscated during collectivization, and the CSP, an urban white-collar middle-class orientated party formed in 1948 by elements from the Czechoslovak National Socialist Party (estd. 1897), contested the 1992 Czech National Council elections, along with the Green Party (estd. 1989), under the banner of the 'Liberal Social Union (LSU)'. In June 1993 the CSP, which had been tolerated during the communist era, renamed itself the Liberal National Social Party (LNSP) and left the LSU and a month later the LSU's two remaining members joined with the CSDP (estd. 1878), which was re-established in 1989 after being banned in 1948, and the Christian Social Union (CSU), to form the moderate-left 'Realism Bloc'. The CSDP is led by Milos Zeman.

The CDU-CPP, formed in 1992, is a center-right body, incorporating the Czech People's Party, a Roman

Catholic party founded in 1919 and permitted to function during the communist era. It is led by Josef Lux.

The MNP advocates the establishment of a self-administered Republic of Moravia situated in the east of the Czech Republic. The far-right Republican Party was formed in 1989 and is led by Miroslav Sladek.

Political leaders since 1970*

1969–87 Gustáv Husák (CPCZ)**, 1987–89 Miloš Jakeš (CPCZ)**, 1989 Karl Urbanek (CPCZ)**, 1989– Václav Havel (Civic Forum/independent)***, 1992–97 Václav Klaus (CDP)****, 1997–98 Josef Tosovsky (independent)****, 1998– Milos Zeman (CSDP)****

* Leaders of Czechoslovakia to 1993.
** Communist Party leaders.
*** State president.
**** Prime minister.

Latest elections

The most recent Chamber of Deputies elections were held on 19–20 June 1998 and were narrowly won by the center-left Social Democrats (CSDP), led by Milos Zeman. They won 32% of the vote and 74 of the parliament's 200 seats. The mainstream right won 45% of the vote, but this was divided between three parties: ex-prime minister Vaclav Klaus's Civic Democrats (CDP), which finished second, with 28% of the vote and 63 seats; the center-right Christian Democrats (CDU), 9% and 20 seats; and the economically and socially liberal Freedom Union, 9% and 19 seats. The largely unreformed Communist Party won 24 seats and 11% of the vote. The racist Republican Party, which had won 8% of the vote and 18 seats in the 1996 election, attracted 3.9% of the vote, just below the 5% threshold for parliamentary representation.

After the most recent Senate elections, held in two rounds in November 1998, the CDP held 26 of the 81 seats, the CSDP, 23 seats, the CDU-CPP, 17 seats; the CDA, 11 seats and the KSCM, 4 seats and 2% of the vote. Turnout was 46%.

Political history

1. 1918–1989

An independent state of Czechoslovakia emerged in October 1918 following the dissolution of the Austro-Hungarian Habsburg Empire at the close of World War I. It incorporated the Czech lands of Bohemia and Moravia, which had been under Austrian rule since the 16th century, and Slovakia, which had been ruled by Hungary for nearly 1,000 years. Despite the problems posed in integrating the diverse ethnic groups within the new nation, Czechoslovakia was the only East European state to retain a parliamentary democracy throughout the interwar period. This took the form of a five-party coalition government, dominated by the Agrarian and National Socialist parties, under the leadership of the influential Slovak-born Tomás Masaryk (1850–1937), who was president between 1918 and 1935. It was made possible by the relatively advanced state of the country's economic and social development. In 1930, for example, as few as a third of the population were involved in agricultural activities, while 40% of males were employed in the industrial sector.

During the later 1930s, with the rise to power of the Nazi leader Adolf Hitler in Germany, opposition to the government was fomented by German- and Magyar-speaking irredentists. This provided the pretext for the Munich Agreement of September 1938 between Britain, France, Germany, and Italy under which Czechoslovakia was forced to surrender its Sudeten German districts to Nazi Germany. Six months later, the German army invaded and annexed the remainder of the country. President Eduard Beneš (1884–1948) immediately resigned in opposition to these actions, setting up a government in exile in London.

During World War II, the Czech lands were subjected to direct German occupation, although Slovakia was granted 'independent' status in 1944 and Bohemia-Moravia was governed as a 'protectorate'. Liquidation campaigns were directed against the intelligentsia and in 1942 the inhabitants of Lidice were massacred. The country was liberated in 1945 by Soviet and American troops, including a Soviet-trained native contingent under the direction of General Ludvík Svoboda (1895–1975). A government of national unity was immediately formed, with Beneš as president, but with communists occupying prominent ministries, including the interior, which included the police, and information. Communists also dominated local administration. Two million Sudeten Germans were summarily expelled.

In elections to the 300-member Constituent National Assembly in May 1946, the left, which included communists and social democrats, achieved a narrow majority, enabling the CPCZ leader, Klement Gottwald (1896–1953), to become prime minister. By 1948 the CPCZ was in full control, seizing power in a coup in February 1948 and, under the National Front banner, winning a single-list ballot victory in May 1948, following the framing of a new, Soviet-style constitution. Beneš duly resigned as president in June 1948 and was succeeded by Gottwald.

Czechoslovakia's historic provinces were abolished in 1948, the country being divided, first, into 19 and then, under the new constitution of July 1960, 12 regions. Earlier, in 1945, the nation's leading industries and financial institutions had been taken into state ownership and a program of agricultural collectivization launched.

During the 1950s, under Presidents Gottwald, Antonin Zapotocky, and Antonin Novotný (1904–75), a strict Stalinist regime was maintained, opposition members being purged. Policy adjustments began to be made, however, from the mid-1960s, as a result of mounting pressure from students and intellectuals, particularly among the Slovaks, and from deteriorating economic conditions.

In January 1968 the orthodox CPCZ leader Antonin Novotný was replaced by the reformist Slovak, Alexander Dubcek (1921–92). In March 1968 the war hero, General Svoboda, became president and in April 1968 Oldřich Černik was appointed prime minister. The new regime embarked on a major liberalization program (the 'Socialist Democratic Revolution'), promising the restoration of freedom of assembly, speech, and movement; the imposition of restrictions on the secret police; decentralized economic reform; and the introduction of elements of democratized political pluralism. These proposed changes, despite assurances that Czechoslovakia would remain within the Warsaw Pact and that the CPCZ would retain its leading political role, were viewed with suspicion by the Soviet Union and on 20–21 August 1968, 600,000 Soviet, Bulgarian, East German, Hungarian, and Polish troops invaded Czechoslovakia to restore the orthodox line and eradicate an experiment which had been termed 'socialism with a human face'.

Following the Soviet invasion, a major purge of liberals within the CPCZ was launched, party membership falling by a third, and Dr Gustáv Husák (b. 1913), a Slovak Brezhnevite, replaced Dubcek as CPCZ leader in April 1969, and Lubomír Štrougal, a Czech, was appointed prime minister in January 1970. However, General Svoboda remained as president until May 1975, successfully negotiating the phased withdrawal of Soviet troops. A new federal constitution was adopted in October 1968, satisfying the nationalist aspirations of the country's Slovak minority.

In 1973 an amnesty was extended to some of the 40,000 who had fled Czechoslovakia after the 1968 invasion, signalling a slackening of repression. However, in 1977, following the signature of a human rights manifesto, 'Charter 77', by more than 700 intellectuals and former party officials, in response to the 1975 Helsinki Agreements, a new crackdown commenced. The arrest of dissidents continued in May 1981 during the Polish 'Solidarity' crisis.

Under the leadership of Gustáv Husák, Czechoslovakia emerged during the 1970s and early 1980s as a loyal ally of the Soviet Union. Minor economic reforms were introduced, but ideological orthodoxy and strict party control were maintained in the political sphere. However, after the accession of the reformist Mikhail Gorbachev to the Soviet leadership in 1985, pressure for economic and administrative reform mounted. In December 1987, while remaining president, Husák was replaced as CPCZ leader by Miloš Jakeš (b. 1922), a Czech-born economist. Working with the reformist technocrat Ladislav Adamec, prime minister since October 1988, he began to introduce a reform program (*prestavba*, 'restructuring') on the USSR's *perestroika* model. His approach was cautious, and dissident activity, which became increasingly widespread during 1988–89, was suppressed.

Influenced by events elsewhere in Eastern Europe, a series of, initially student-led, prodemocracy rallies were held in Prague's Wenceslas Square from 17 November 1989. Support for the protest movement rapidly increased after the security forces' brutal suppression of the early rallies, injuring more than 500 people, and by 20 November 1989 there were more than 400,000 demonstrators in Prague and a growing number in Bratislava. An umbrella opposition movement, Civic Forum, was swiftly formed under the leadership of the playwright and Charter 77 activist Václav Havel (b. 1935), which attracted the support of prominent members of the small political parties that were members of the ruling CPCZ-dominated National Front coalition.

With the protest movement continuing to grow, Jakeš resigned as CPCZ leader on 24 November 1989 and was replaced by Karel Urbanek, a South Moravian, and the party's ruling Politburo was purged. Less than a week later, following a brief general strike, the National Assembly voted to amend the constitution to strip the CPCZ of its 'leading role' in the government, and thus of its monopoly on power. Opposition parties, beginning with Civic Forum and its Slovak counterpart, Public Against Violence (PAV), were legalized. On 7 December 1989 Adamec resigned as prime minister and was replaced by Marián Čalfa, who formed a 'Grand Coalition' government in which key posts, including the foreign, financial, and labor ministries, were given to former dissidents. Čalfa resigned from the CPCZ in January 1990, but remained premier.

2. 1989–1999

On 27 December 1989 the rehabilitated Alexander Dubcek, who had addressed mass protest rallies in Prague and Bratislava, in November 1989, was sworn in as chair of the Federal Assembly, and on 29 December 1989 Václav Havel became president of Czechoslovakia. The new reform government immediately extended an amnesty to 22,000 prisoners, ended censorship, secured agreements from the CPCZ that it would voluntarily give up its existing majorities in the federal and republic assemblies and state agencies, and promised multiparty elections for June 1990. These were won by the Civic Forum and PAV, which captured 46% of the federal vote to the CPCZ's 14%, and Marián Čalfa continued at the head of a new Civic Forum-PAV dominated government. The Čalfa administration announced plans for reducing the size of the armed forces, called on the USSR to pull out its 75,000 troops stationed in the country, and applied for membership of the IMF and World Bank. Václav Havel was re-elected president, unopposed, for a further two years by the new Federal Assembly on 5 July 1990.

Some devolution of power was introduced in 1990 to ameliorate friction between the Czech and Slovak republics. A bill of rights was passed in January 1991, and moves were made towards price liberalization and privatization of small businesses. In May 1991 a bill was passed to return property nationalized after 25 February 1948 to its original owners, the first such restitution measure in Eastern Europe. The name 'Czech and Slovak Federative Republic' was adopted in April 1990 and in November 1990 the Slovak Republic declared Slovak the official language of the republic, a move promoted by the Slovak National Party, which had organized pro-autonomy rallies and demonstrations in the republic during the second half of 1990.

During the opening months of 1991, Civic Forum began to split into two distinct factions: a center-right faction under the leadership of finance minister, Václav Klaus (b. 1941), designated the Civic Democratic Party (CDP) in April 1991; and a social-democratic group, the Civic Forum Liberal Club, renamed the Civic Movement in April 1991, led by foreign minister, Jiri Dienstbier and deputy prime minister, Pavel Rychetsky. In March 1991 PAV also split when Slovak premier, Vladimir Meciar, formed a splinter grouping, the Movement for a Democratic Slovakia (MDS), pledged to greater autonomy from Prague. In April 1991 he was dismissed as head of the Slovak government by the presidium of the Slovak National Council (parliament) because of policy differences. Protest rallies were held in the Slovak capital of Bratislava by Meciar supporters. Jan Carnogursky, leader of the Christian Democratic Movement, junior partner in the PAV-led ruling coalition, took over as Slovak premier.

In July 1991, a month after the final withdrawal of Soviet troops from the state, the USSR agreed to pay the equivalent of US $160 million to Czechoslovakia in compensation for damage done to the country since the 1968 USSR invasion. In August 1991, the phased privatization of Czech industry commenced, with 50 of its largest businesses put up for sale on international markets. Friendship treaties were signed with France, Germany, and the Soviet Union in October 1991. In the same month, PAV became a liberal-conservative political party, and was renamed the Civic Democratic Union-Public Action Against Violence, led by Martin Porubjak.

With the major political parties already divided into separate Czech and Slovak groups, it was anticipated that the outcome of the June 1992 general election would determine whether or not the country would break up into separate Czech and Slovak states. In the Czech republic, the right-of-center CDP polled strongly, winning 76 of the 200 seats, with 30% of the vote. A CDP-dominated four-party coalition government, with the Civic Democratic Alliance (CDA), the CDU-CPP, and the Christian Democratic Party, was formed, with Václav Klaus becoming Czech prime minister. In the Slovak republic, the pro-independence MDS, led by Vladimir Meciar, triumphed. Its success was attributed, in part, to its campaign against the federal government's economic reforms, which had led to a rise in the unemployment level to 10% in the more backward Slovak republic, against just 2.5% in the more advanced Czech republic. The MDS also emerged, with 57 seats, as the second largest party group in Czechoslovakia's 300-member Federal Assembly, and used this position to block concurrence on a new federal agreement and further its separatist demands.

Because of its largely bloodless nature, the progressive democratization of Czechoslovakia from 1989 had been called the 'Velvet Revolution'. During 1992–93 the federal republic witnessed an ordered and peaceful 'velvet divorce'. On 17 July 1992 the Slovak National Council (parliament) issued a symbolic declaration of

Slovak sovereignty. Also in July 1992, a transitional federal government was formed, being dominated by members of the CDP and MDS, with Jan Strasky (CDP) as prime minister. Negotiations on the division of federal assets and liabilities, applying a 2:1 ratio to reflect the relative size of the Czech and Slovak populations, and on the mechanics of the separation of the two republics progressed during the remainder of 1992. The 'divorce' proved amicable since Czech leaders saw the advantage of independence for a republic which was more economically developed than Slovakia. In addition, the dissolution occurred against a background of only muted public concern, with opinion polls suggesting that more than 60% of Czechs and Slovaks actually opposed the country's division. However, despite President Havel's repeated calls for a referendum to be held on the issue, the break-up was left to be decided by elected politicians. A new Czech Republic constitution was adopted in December 1992 and came into force on 1 December 1993, when Slovakia achieved independence and a separate Czech Republic was established. A customs union treaty was signed in October 1992 and a treaty of good neighborliness on 17 December 1992 to consummate the 'divorce', and the former president of Czechoslovakia, Václav Havel, was elected president of the new state in January 1993. Václav Klaus remained prime minister and the Czech National Council, elected in June 1992, was redesignated the Chamber of Deputies, being due for re-election in 1996.

In June 1993 the Czech Republic became a member of the Council of Europe (COE) and, while indicating its longer-term goal of joining the European Union (EU), signed a friendship and cooperation treaty with Russia in August 1993.

The center-right Klaus administration concentrated during 1992–95 on implementing market-centerd economic reforms so as to establish a Western-style capitalist economy. Although GDP declined significantly, by as much as a quarter, between 1991–93 and there were associated problems of rising crime and corruption, the Czech reform program was one of the most successful in Central Europe. Service sector-led growth began to be registered from 1994 and inflation was kept down to around 10% per annum. In January 1993 VAT was introduced, and the Prague stock exchange was reopened in April 1993 after more than 50 years' closure. By 1994 the private sector's share of GDP had surpassed 50% and more than 6 million Czechs had participated in the first wave of mass privatizations, carried out via an innovative voucher scheme which transferred effective control to state-owned banks. Encouraged by its political stability, significant Western, especially German, investment was attracted to the new state which entered the OECD in November 1995 and formally applied for European Union membership in January 1996.

Unexpectedly, in the June 1996 general election Klaus' three-party conservative coalition, comprising the free-market CDA, the 'social market' CDU-CPP, and the right-of-center CDP, lost its parliamentary majority. This was despite GDP growth of 5% and unemployment down to 2.8%, with 70% of the economy now in private hands. The coalition, with 44% of the vote, captured 99 of the 200 seats, a reduction of 13, while the left-leaning 'social-ecologist' Social Democrats, led by Milos Zeman, quadrupled its share of the vote to 26% and, with 61 seats, became the second largest party. The Communists, with 10% of the vote, won 22 seats, while the far-right, xenophobic Republicans won 18 seats. Nevertheless, Klaus remained in power – the only conservative leader in Central Europe to win a second term in office after the 1989 collapse of communism. He headed a minority coalition government under the understanding that the Social Democrats would be granted leadership of the parliament and that privatization would be slowed and important concessions would be made on pensions, healthcare, and education.

In the November 1996 Senate elections the ruling coalition polled more strongly, attracting 65% of the vote. Thereafter the coalition began to fracture, the economy sharply deteriorated, and scandals in the banking sector, led, from May 1997, to pressure on the koruna. Despite the Czech National Bank spending US$2 billion in its defense, the koruna had to be devalued. In September 1997 an austerity budget was introduced, projecting annual economic growth of below 1%, and in November 1997 Klaus was accused of misleading parliament over the source of an anonymous large donation to the CDP. This led to the CDA and CDU-CPP withdrawing support, forcing Klaus' resignation.

The CDU's leader, Josef Lux, was unable to form a new coalition government, so, in mid-December, Josef Tosovsky, the former governor of the Czech Central Bank, became caretaker prime minister. In January 1998, despite suffering from lung cancer, President Havel was re-elected, by the legislature, for a second term, which he committed to combating the growth of xenophobic nationalism.

The CDP re-elected Klaus as its leader in December

1997, but was weakened by the defection, in January 1998, of more than 30 deputies to a new party, the Freedom Union, formed by the former interior minister, Jan Ruml. Campaigning on an anti-corruption and 'social market' platform, the center-left Social Democrats, led by Zeman, attracted 32% of the vote in the June 1998 general election, against the mainstream right's 45%. However, Zeman became prime minister, heading a minority coalition government with the Communist Party, who were given seven places in the 19-member cabinet. The coalition was able to survive because of a pact with the CDP, who had come second, with 28% of the vote. Under this pact, the CDP's leader, Vaclav Klaus, became the Chamber of Deputies' speaker, with significant control over the legislative agenda, and it was believed that Zeman and Klaus wished to change the voting system to first-past-the-post, in order to reduce the influence of smaller parties. The new government pledged to continue to press for early EU membership, with negotiations now underway, and agreed to join NATO in March 1999. However, it sought to slow down the pace of privatization and utility price liberalization.

ESTONIA

Republic of Estonia
Eesti Vabariik

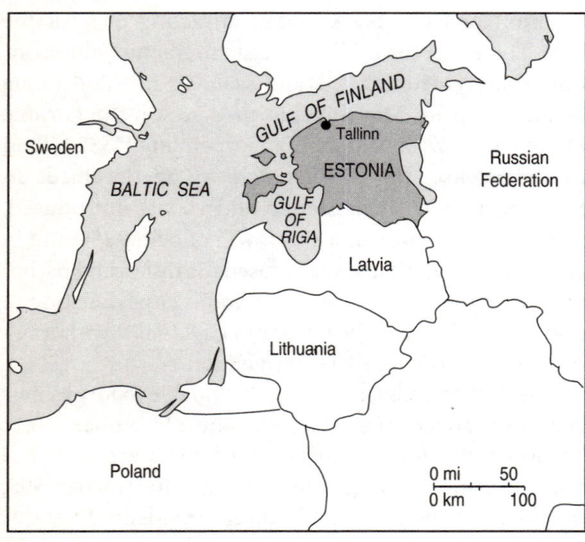

Capital: Tallinn

Social and economic data

Area: 45,100 sq km/17,413 sq miles
Population: 1,464,000*
Pop. density per sq km/sq mi: 32/84*
Urban population: 72%**
Literacy rate: 99%**
GDP: $4,250 million*; per-capita GDP: $2,900*
Government defense spending (% of GDP): 5.3%*
Currency: kroon
Economy type: middle income
Labor force in agriculture: 13%**
Unemployment rate: 8.9%*
* 1995.
** 1992.

Head of state (executive)

President Lennart Meri, since 1992

Head of government

Prime Minister Mart Laar, since 1999

Ethnic composition

Sixty-two per cent of the population are ethnic Estonians, a Finno-Ugric people, 30% Russian, 3% Ukrainian, 2% Belarussian, and 1% Finnish. Estonian, a language closely related to Finnish, has been the republic's official language since 1989, although 85% of ethnic Russians are unable to speak Estonian. However, local government authorities may use the language of the majority of permanent local residents for internal communication. By 1997 more than 100,000 ethnic Russians living in Estonia had chosen to take Russian rather than Estonian citizenship.

Religions

The population is predominantly Christian, with most ethnic Estonians belonging to the Evangelical Lutheran Church and ethnic Russians to the Russian Orthodox Church.

Political features

State type: emergent democratic
Date of state formation: 1918/1991
Political structure: unitary
Executive: dual
Assembly: one-chamber
Party structure: multiparty
Human rights rating: N/A
International affiliations: BC, BIS, CBSS, COE, EBRD, ECE, IAEA, IBRD, ICFTU, IMF, NACC, OSCE, PFP, UN, WEU (associate partner)

Local and regional government

The republic contains 15 counties or districts (*maakond*), which are subdivided into communes (*vald*), and six towns.

Political system

Under the terms of the constitution of July 1992, Estonia has a democratic parliamentary political system, with a strong presidency. The current president, Lennart Meri, was originally directly elected, in September 1992. However, since 1996 the president has been indirectly elected, for a maximum of two consecutive five-year terms, by the parliament (Riigikogu). To be elected, a candidate needs to secure the votes of at least two-thirds (68) of the deputies. If after three rounds of voting this is not achieved, selection is by means of a broader electoral college, including additionally 273 representatives from local government. The president, who must be an Estonian citizen by birth and at least 40 years old, represents Estonia in diplomatic relations, is commander in chief of the armed forces, initiates amendments to the constitution, and nominates the prime minister. The legislature, Riigikogu, comprises 101 members popularly elected for four-year terms on the basis of proportional representation, with a 5% cut-off limit for representation. An executive prime minister, nominated by the president, is drawn from the legislature and works with a Council of Ministers, or cabinet, of some 15 members. The constitution includes the right to healthcare and education.

Political parties

The most important of the more than 20 political parties which function in Estonia are: the liberal Coalition Party; the liberal Estonian Reform Party (ERP); the centrist Center Party (CP); the reform-communist Estonian Democratic Labor Party (formerly the Communist Party of Estonia, or CPE); the Our Home is Estonia alliance of ethnic Russian parties; the rightwing Fatherland Union (Isamaaliit); and the center-left Moderates' Party.

The Coalition Party (estd. 1991), led by Andrus Oovel, is a left-of-center force which favors a German-style 'social market economy' and includes a number of former communists. It is allied to the Rural Union bloc, which includes the Estonian Rural People's Union (ERPU; estd. 1994), which is orientated towards agrarian interests. Led by the former state president, Arnold Rüütel, a Brezhnev-era politician favoring state subsidies for agriculture and preserving collective farms, it is a successor to the early nationalist body, Kindel kogu (Secure Home), which included a number of former communists.

The ERP, formed in November 1994 by Siim Kallas, the former president of the Bank of Estonia, also favors a free-market economic policy, including the scrapping of income tax, but seeks improved relations with Russia and Estonia's ethnic Russian community.

The CP (estd. 1991), led by Edgar Savisaar, is a successor to the Estonian Popular Front (EPF: Rahvarinne), a moderate nationalist umbrella organization formed in 1988. In 1996 seven of the CP parliamentary deputies broke away to form the Development Party.

The CPE was originally formed in 1920 and renamed itself the Estonian Democratic Labor Party in 1992. Along with the Our Home is Estonia alliance and the ESDP, it draws much of its support from ethnic Russians.

The Fatherland Union, was formed in 1995 through the merger of Isamaa (National Fatherland Party) and the Estonian National Independence Party (ENIP). Isamaa (also known as Pro Patria) was a rightwing nationalist party founded in 1992 by Mart Laar, a strong advocate of a free-market economic strategy. It was the ruling party between 1992–94. The ENIP (estd. 1988), a radical nationalist force, originated in 1987 as the Estonian Group for the Publication of the Molotov–Ribbentrop Pact (MRP-AEG).

The Moderates' Party, led by Andres Tarand, was formed in 1996 through the merger of the Estonian Rural Central Party and the Estonian Social Democratic Party.

Political leaders since 1970

Head of state: 1988–92 Arnold Rüütel (Kindel kogu), 1992– Lennart Meri (Isamaa); Prime minister: 1988–90 Indrek Toome (CPE), 1990–92 Edgar Savisaar (EPF), 1992– Tiit Vahi (independent ex-communist), 1992–94 Mart Laar (Isamaa), 1994–95 Andres Tarand (independent/Greens), 1995–97 Tiit Vahi (Coalition Party), 1997–99 Mart Siimaan (Coalition Party) 1999– Mart Laer (Islamaa)

Latest elections

The most recent, and third post-independence, legislature elections were held on 7 March 1999. The Centre Party won the most seats, 28 out of the 101 available, based on a 23% share of the vote, while the Fatherland Union (Isamaa) and the ERP finished joint second, with 16% of the vote and 18 seats apiece. The Moderates' Party, with 15% of the vote, won 17 seats and the Coalition Party and the Country People's Party each won 7% of the vote and seven seats, and the United People's Party 6% and six seats. Turnout was 57%, with 12 parties contesting the election.

The most recent presidential election was held in August–September 1996. The incumbent, Lennart Meri, faced a challenge from Arnold Rüütel of the ERPU and, after three rounds of voting in the Riigikogu on 26–27 August, was unable to secure the two-thirds' majority (68 votes) needed. Consequently, a larger 374-member electoral college was convened on 20 September, including 273 representatives from local government as well as the 101 Riigikogu deputies. Five candidates contested the first round, but none was able to secure the absolute majority of votes. A run-off round was thus held, between Meri and Rüütel, and Meri was re-elected, winning 196 votes to 126.

Political history

Independent states were formed in the area now known as Estonia during the 1st century AD and the Vikings mounted an invasion in the 9th century AD. In the 13th century southern Estonia came under the control of the Teutonic Knights, German crusaders, who converted the inhabitants to Christianity, while Tallinn joined the Hanseatic League, the union of European commercial towns that stretched from London to Novgorod. The Danes, who had taken control of northern Estonia, sold this area to the Teutonic Knights in 1324, but by the 16th century German nobles owned much of the land. In 1561 Sweden took control of the north and also wrested the south from Poland in 1625. The Swedes continued to rule the whole country until control was ceded to Tsarist Russia in 1721. Repressive Russian government and German economic control spurred an Estonian nationalist movement during the late 19th century. It focused initially on cultural themes, but after the turn of the century pro-independence political parties began to be formed.

Estonia was occupied by German troops during World War I. The Russian Red Army forces, who tried to regain power in 1917, after the Russian Revolution, were overthrown by Germany in March 1918, after Estonian nationalists, led by Konstantin Pats, had proclaimed independence on 24 February 1918. Soviet authority was restored in November 1918, but it was overthrown again, by German and British forces, in May 1919 and a democratic republic was established. In January 1921 the major Western powers recognized Estonia's independence. The 1920s saw cultural and economic advances and major land reforms. However, in March 1934, at a time of deep economic depression, the liberal-democratic parliamentary system was overthrown by Konstantin Pats in a quasi-fascist coup. Political parties were banned and an authoritarian presidentialist system was established.

In August 1939, as part of the supplementary protocol to the Molotov–Ribbentrop Pact, Germany and the USSR secretly agreed that Estonia should come under Russian influence and the country was incorporated into the USSR as the Estonian Soviet Socialist Republic in August 1940. Mass deportations of 60,000 Estonians to Siberia followed. In July 1941 Estonia was again occupied by Germany, prompting large-scale emigration to the West, but the USSR regained control in September 1944. The process of 'sovietization' was continued, involving agricultural collectivization, the development of heavy industries, deportations of Estonians, and the immigration of ethnic Russians. There was sporadic resistance from the 'forest brethren' (*metsavennad*) guerrillas until the mid-1950s and, thereafter, dissent focused on cultural issues. In particular, there was great antipathy towards the creeping 'Russification' of a republic which had been 92% ethnic Estonian in 1939.

From 1985, encouraged by the policies of *glasnost* (openness) and *perestroika* (economic restructuring) espoused by the Soviet Union's new leader, Mikhail Gorbachev, nationalist dissent became more vocal. In April 1988 an Estonian Popular Front (EPF) was unofficially formed, advocating the transformation of the USSR into a truly confederal body, and in August 1988 the more radical Estonian National Independence Party (ENIP) began to campaign, via mass rallies, for full independence. The EPF included a number of members of the Communist Party of Estonia (CPE), which began to respond to the changing public mood. On 16 November 1988 the CPE-dominated Supreme Soviet (parliament) adopted a declaration of sovereignty, which included a power of veto over Soviet legislation, and a new constitution which allowed private property and placed land and natural resources under Estonian control. However, the USSR's Supreme Soviet rejected this declaration as unconstitutional. In January 1989 Estonia's parliament also voted to replace Russian with Estonian as the republic's official language and, in November 1989, denounced the 1940 incorporation of the republic into the USSR as a 'forced annexation'.

In February 1990 the Communist Party's monopoly of power was abolished and a multiparty political system became established. In elections held in March 1990, pro-independence candidates won a majority of seats in the Supreme Soviet and a coalition government was formed, with the EPF's leader, Edgar Savisaar, becoming prime minister in April 1990. Arnold Rüütel, an adaptable communist-era politician who had previously been chairperson of the presidium of the Supreme Soviet, and thus effective head of state, remained as head of state. Unofficial elections were also held concurrently, in March 1990, to a rival nationalist parliament, the Congress of Estonia, for which the franchise was limited to those who had been citizens of the pre-1940 Estonian Republic and their descendants.

On 8 May 1990 Estonia's Supreme Soviet issued an effective declaration of independence and the state emblems and name of the pre-1940 Republic of Estonia were restored. However, the Russian president, Mikhail Gorbachev, anulled the declaration as unconstitutional and there were protests and strikes by ethnic Russians in Tallinn. Estonians, concerned at the USSR's attempted military intervention in Latvia and Lithuania in January 1991, boycotted the March 1991 all-Union referendum on the future of the USSR and, instead, held a plebiscite on independence, which, with a turnout of 83%, resulted in 78% voting in favor of independence. By the summer of 1991 the republic had embarked on a program of privatization and the prices of agricultural products had been freed. On 20 August 1991, in the midst of the attempted anti-Gorbachev coup in the USSR, which led to Red Army troops being moved into Tallinn to seize the television transmitter and the republic's main port being blocked by the Soviet navy, Estonia declared its full and immediate independence (it had been in a 'period of transition' since March 1990) and outlawed the Communist Party. On 6 September 1991 this declaration was recognized by Moscow and on 17 September, along with the other Baltic States, Estonia was admitted into the United Nations (UN) and the Conference on Security and Cooperation in Europe (CSCE, later the OSCE).

Prime Minister Edgar Savisaar and his cabinet resigned in January 1992 after failing to alleviate food and energy shortages. Tiit Vahi, the former transport minister, formed a new government which included seven key ministers unchanged from the previous cabinet. A new constitution, which had been framed by a Constitutional Assembly including equal numbers of delegates from the Supreme Soviet and the Congress of Estonia, was approved in a national referendum held in June 1992. Voting in the parliamentary and general elections which followed in September 1992 was restricted, by the new Citizenship Law, to persons who had been citizens of pre-1940 Estonia and their descendants. The elections resulted in victory for the Isamaa conservative-nationalist alliance, which won 29 of the 101 seats in the new Riigikogu. A coalition government was formed with the ENIP and Moderate Group, with Isamaa's Mart Laar (b. 1960), a 32-year-old historian and political disciple of Britain's conservative leader, Margaret Thatcher, becoming prime minister and Lennart Meri (b. 1929), a former foreign minister, president.

The new Laar administration, which included a 28-year-old foreign minister and 29-year-old interior minister, embarked on an ambitious program of market-centerd economic reform, involving large-scale privatization, with 80% of state-owned enterprises being sold by 1995 and the adoption of a 'flat tax' (single rate of income tax).. In the short term, GDP declined during 1992–93, but from 1994 growth in the economy resumed, being aided by substantial foreign investment. The withdrawal of the remaining Soviet troops stationed in Estonia was also successfully negotiated, with the last troops leaving on 29 August 1994, and Estonia entered the Council of Europe in May 1993. Despite these successes, popular support for the abrasive Laar and the Isamaa party slumped to barely 5% by mid-1994. One factor was the controversial law on aliens, passed in July 1993, which defined the 500,000 former Soviet citizens in Estonia as 'foreigners' who would be required to apply for a residency permit or face expulsion. Another was the cutbacks that had been made in social spending. In September 1994 the prime minister was defeated in parliament on a no-confidence motion. This followed revelations that Laar had secretly ordered the sale in October 1992 of 2,000 million Russian roubles to the breakaway Russian republic of Chechnya.

Andres Tarand, the environmental minister who was a member of the Green movement, became caretaker prime minister in October 1994, holding power at the head of a broad-based coalition until elections were held in March 1995. These resulted in a crushing defeat for Isamaa, which attracted less than 8% of the national vote, and victory for the center-left in the form of the Coalition Party and Rural People's Union (ERPU), led respectively by Tiit Vahi and Arnold Rüütel. A new coalition government was formed in April 1995 by Vahi, a former communist-era factory manager, which included members of the Center Party (CP). It was expected to pursue a 'social market' economic program, with a bias to the agricultural sector, and seek to improve relations with Russia and the state's own, and now discriminated against, ethnic Russian minority community. However, the new government remained committed to Estonia's integration into Western and

European institutions, signing a trade and cooperation agreement with the European Union in June 1995. Following a scandal involving the interior minister, Edgar Savisaar, concerning secret recordings of political conversations, the government collapsed in October 1995, but a new centrist Vahi-led coalition with the ERP was formed a month later. It included the ERPU and the liberal Estonian Reform Party (ERP).

Lennart Meri was re-elected president, by an electoral college, in September 1996, overcoming a strong challenge from the ERPU's Arnold Rüütel. However, in November 1996 the ruling coalition fell apart, when six ERP ministers resigned in protest against a local cooperation agreement signed by the Coalition Party and the opposition CP, which broke the ERP's hold on the Tallinn city council. Prime Minister Vahi attempted to remain in office, heading a Coalition Party-ERPU minority government, but it controlled only two-fifths of the legislature's 101 seats. He eventually resigned in late February 1997, after narrowly surviving a no-confidence vote, triggered by opposition allegations of abuse of his office, which he denied. He retired from politics in September 1997. Mart Siimann, the Coalition Party's parliamentary leader, took over as prime minister and, in March 1997, constructed a new minority coalition based around the Coalition Party and ERPU, but with the support of some independents.

By 1998 Estonia had one of the stronger economies in Central Europe and had begun negotiations with the European Commission on full membership of the European Union: it had become an associate member in July 1995. Real GDP growth had averaged 4% per annum since 1995; the annual inflation rate, which had exceeded 1,000% in 1992, was around 11% in 1997; the unemployment rate was 4%; and, since independence, there had been $700 million of foreign inward investment. Meanwhile, relations with the other two ex-Soviet Baltic states, Latvia and Lithuania, have continued to grow closer since independence. A tripartite agreement on free trade and regional security was signed in 1993 and a customs agreement, in June 1996.

In the March 1999 general election Siimaan's Coalition Party lost support and power and a new three-party centre-right coalition government was formed comprising the Fatherland Union, the Moderates' Party and the ERP, with Mart Laar, of the Fatherland Union, returning as prime minister. Laar faced a difficult economic situation, forcing sharp cuts in public spending in 1999.

GEORGIA

Georgia
Sakartvelos

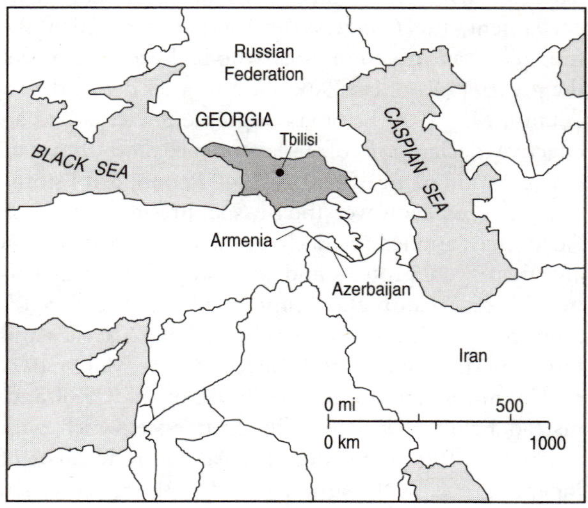

Capital: Tbilisi

Social and economic data

Area: 69,700 sq km/26,911 sq miles
Population: 5,400,000*
Pop. density per sq km/sq mi: 77/201*
Urban population: 56%**
Literacy rate: 99%**
GDP: $4,500 million*; per-capita GDP: $835*
Government defense spending (% of GDP): 3.4%*
Currency: lari
Economy type: low income
Labor force in agriculture: 22%**

* 1995.
** 1994.

Head of state (executive)

President Eduard Shevardnadze, since 1992

Head of government

Minister of state Nikoloz Lekishvili, since 1995

Ethnic composition

Seventy per cent of the population is of Georgian ethnic stock, 8% is Armenian, 7% ethnic Russian, 5% Azeri, 3% Ossetian, 2% Abkhazian, and 2% Greek. Georgian, a non-Indo-European language, is the official language, but in Abkhazia both Georgian and Abkhazian are recognized as state languages.

Religions

Around 80% of the population belongs to the Christian

Georgian Orthodox Church. Islam is professed by Azeris, Abkhazians, Adzharians, and Kurds.

Political features

State type: emergent democratic
Date of state formation: 1991
Political structure: unitary
Executive: limited presidential
Assembly: one-chamber
Party structure: multiparty
Human rights rating: N/A
International affiliations: BSECZ, CE, CIS, IBRD, IMF, OSCE, PFP, UN

Local and regional government

There are two 'autonomous republics', Abkhazia and Adzharia. Abkhazia, situated in the far northwest of the republic, has an area of 3,320 square kilometres and a population of 538,000, with its capital at Sukhumi. It was a republic during the 1920s, but was incorporated into Christian Georgia in 1931 and Georgians were resettled there. By 1990 ethnic Georgians comprised 46% of its population and ethnic Abkhazians, a Turkic-speaking Muslim people who have sought secession, only 18%. Adzharia, situated in the southwest, has an area of 1,158 square kilometres and a population of 382,000, with its capital at Batumi. Its people are ethnic Georgians, but adhere chiefly to Islam, and the autonomous status is the result of a 1921 Soviet–Turkish Friendship Treaty. South Ossetia, situated in the north-center of the republic, with its capital at Tskhinvali, is an 'autonomous region'. Its inhabitants, 66% Ossetian, an East Iranian people, have been traditionally pro-Russian, with North Ossetia forming part of the Russian Federation. The minorities in these territories, which have elected legislatures and chairs (or presidents), seek autonomy and, in the case of the South Ossetians, reunion, within the Russian Federation, with North Ossetia. Below there is a hierarchy of provinces, or regions, rural territories, districts, municipalities, and villages.

Political system

Under the constitution of August 1995, which replaced a November 1992 Decree on State Power, Georgia has a strongly presidentialist political system. The executive president is directly elected for a five-year term, limited to two consecutive terms. The president serves as head of state, and commander in chief of the armed forces, and governs with an advisory government (cabinet) of around 20 ministers, coordinated by a minister of state (no longer known as prime minister), and appointed with the legislature's consent. The president can remove ministers; submits the draft state budget to the parliament; and also heads a National Security Council, which advises on defense and security issues. Candidates for the presidency must be at least 35 years old and have lived in Georgia for at least 15 years.

The legislature is the Georgian Parliament (Sakartvelos Parlamenti), which was previously known as the Supreme Soviet. It comprises 235 members who are elected, for four-year terms, through a mixed system of proportional and direct: 150 deputies are elected by proportional representation from party lists (with a 5% of the vote cut-off limit) and 85 from single-member systems in accordance with the second ballot majoritarian system. Deputies must be at least 25 years old and (along with ministers) may not hold any position in state service or engage in entrepreneurial activities. Deputies can form official factions in the Parliament, but these must comprise at least ten members: there were seven such factions in 1998. It is proposed that, once Georgia's territorial integrity has been restored, with Abkhazia and South Ossetia re-integrated, a new two-chamber legislature, with a regionally based Senate, will be established.

There is also a nine-member Constitutional Court, comprising three judges each appointed (for ten years) by the president, parliament, and Supreme Court.

Political parties

Georgia has an exceptionally fragmented multiparty system, which is riven by clan and regional rivalries. Dozens of parties compete for power, but many have large military components and are based on kinship or loyalty to charismatic leaders.

The most significant of the myriad of parties which operate are: the Citizens' Union of Georgia (CUG); the National Democratic Party of Georgia (NDPG); the Round Table/Free Georgia Bloc; the Georgian Popular Front (GPF); the Georgian Communist Party (GCP); the National Independence Party (NIP); the All-Georgian Union of Revival (AGUR), and the left-of-center Socialist Party of Georgia (estd. 1995).

The 100,000-member CUG is a centrist party formed by head of state, Eduard Shevardnadze, in September 1993.

The NDPG was founded in 1981 by Giorgi Chanturia to campaign for Georgian independence. The party is Christian-democratic in outlook and has been supportive of the Shevardnadze regime. Chanturia was assassinated in December 1994 and the party is now led by Irina Sarishvili-Chanturia.

The Round Table-Free Georgia group was founded by Zviad Gamsakhurdia, a longstanding nationalist dissident, to contest the 28 October and 11 November 1990 Supreme Soviet elections. Its leader died in December 1993.

The GPF was formed in July 1989 as a moderate nationalist, prodemocratization umbrella force.

The GCP, now known as the United Communist Party of Georgia, was the ruling party in Georgia until 1990 and has been a pro-independence nationalist body since 1989. It was banned in August 1991, in the wake of the unsuccessful Soviet coup attempt, but was revived in June 1994 under the leadership of Major General Paneleimon Giorgadze.

The NIP is an extreme nationalist body.

AGUR is a regionalist party, founded in Adzharia in 1992. It has 26,000 members and is led by Aslan Abashidze, the elected chairperson of the Adzharia legislature.

Political leaders since 1970

1990–92 Zviad Gamsakhurdia (Round Table), 1992 Military Council, 1992– Eduard Shevardnadze (independent/CUG)

Latest elections

The most recent legislative elections were held on 5 and 19 November and 3 December 1995 and were contested by over 50 parties. No single party dominated the contest, but the largest number of seats, 107, was won by the pro-Shevardnadze CUG, with 24% of the vote. The center-right opposition NDPG and All-Georgian Union of Revival attracted 8% and 7% support, winning 34 and 31 seats respectively. Eight other parties won between one and four seats each.

In secessionist Abkhazia, the election was boycotted, so the mandate of the 12 deputies elected in 1992 was renewed. Overall, turnout was 64%.

Eduard Shevardnadze was directly elected president on 5 November 1995, with 75% of the vote, defeating Jumber Patiashivili, the former communist chief, and four other candidates. Turnout was 64%.

Political history

Georgia was converted to Christianity in the 4th century AD, when the first Georgian state was established. From the 7th century, with the weakening of the Persian and Byzantium empires, an independent Georgian feudal kingdom was created by the Gagrationi house, tracing its ancestry to King David. The kingdom became especially powerful between the late 11th and early 13th centuries, under David II (1089–1125) and Queen Tamara, who died in 1212, and the Georgian Church became an independent body. Thereafter the country fell under the sway of Persian, Mongol, and Turkish imperial powers, before being annexed by Tsarist Russia in 1801. Tbilisi (Tiflis) developed into an important commercial center under the tsars; however, the Georgian language and church were gradually suppressed.

On 26 May 1918, amid turmoil in the Russian Empire, Georgia reasserted its independence but, denied economic help from the West and with its ports subject to blockade, its rebellion was crushed by the Red Army in February 1921. Between 1922 and 1936 Georgia entered the USSR as part of the Transcaucasian Federation, along with Armenia and Azerbaijan, before becoming a full republic in 1936. There was rapid industrial development between the 1920s and 1950s, but considerable resistance to rural collectivization, and political purges were instituted during the 1930s by Lavrenti Beria (1899–1953), the Transcaucasia party leader, under the orders of the Soviet leader, Joseph Stalin, himself an ethnic Georgian. During World War II, Stalin ordered the deportation of 200,000 Meskhetians from southern Georgia to Central Asia.

During the 1950s and 1960s, Georgia's administration became notorious for its laxity and corruption. A drive against crime and corruption was launched between 1972 and 1985 by Eduard Shevardnadze (b. 1928), leader of the Georgian Communist Party (GCP), and there was accelerated 'Russification'. This provoked a growing nationalist backlash, witnessed in the form of mass demonstrations in Tbilisi in 1978 and 1981, terrorist incidents, and the founding, in 1977, of the Initiative Group for the Defense of Human Rights in Georgia by the university lecturer Zviad Gamsakhurdia (1939–93), the son of a famous Georgian novelist.

With the *glasnost* (political openness) initiative launched by the reformist Mikhail Gorbachev, who became the new Soviet leader in 1985, there was an intensification of the nationalist campaign in the later 1980s, with the separatist National Democratic Party of Georgia (NDPG), established in 1981, becoming increasingly assertive and a Georgian Popular Front (GPF) being formed in July 1989. This fuelled anti-Georgian feeling among the republic's Abkhazian and Ossetian minority communities. The Tiananmen-style massacre in Tbilisi of at least 20 peaceful Georgian pro-independence demonstrators by Soviet troops, firing toxic gas, on the night of 8–9 April 1989 added momentum to the nationalist movement and during

1989–90, with its old-guard leadership purged, the GCP joined the secessionist camp. In November 1989 the republic's Supreme Soviet declared the supremacy of Georgian laws over all-Union laws and in February 1990 the constitution was amended to abolish the GCP's guaranteed monopoly on power.

After the seven-party Round Table-Free Georgia nationalist coalition triumphed in Georgia's 28 October and 11 November 1990 free multiparty Supreme Soviet elections, capturing 64% of the vote and 155 of the 250 seats, Zviad Gamsakhurdia was chosen as state president on 14 November 1990, while Tengiz Sigua, also from the Round Table-Free Georgia group, became prime minister. The GCP, despite also adopting a nationalist stance, won only 64 seats. The new parliament voted, in January 1991, to establish a republican National Guard and end conscription to the Soviet Red Army.

In March 1991 all parts of Georgia, except the pro-Union autonomous territories of Abkhazia and South Ossetia, boycotted the all-Union USSR constitutional referendum. Instead, the republic held a plebiscite on independence on 31 March 1991, which secured 93% approval, with a turnout of 95%. Independence was declared on 9 April 1991 and a campaign of civil disobedience against Soviet interests was launched. On 26 May 1991 Gamsakhurdia became the first republic president in the USSR to be directly elected, winning 87% of the vote and defeating five other candidates. However, voting did not take place in Abkhazia or South Ossetia. President Gamsakhurdia failed to strongly denounce the anti-Gorbachev coup in Moscow in August 1991, prompting the resignation in protest of Prime Minister Tengiz Sigua. However, the GCP was banned in the wake of the failed Moscow coup.

From September 1991 Gamsakhurdia became an increasingly dictatorial president, banning opposition parties, arresting political opponents, and instituting tight press censorship. This led to a growing popular protest movement, fuelled further by government troops firing on the crowds. With disorder mounting, Gamsakhurdia declared a state of emergency on 24 September 1991. He ordered the arrest in October 1991 of most of the leadership of the nationalist NDPG, headed by Giorgi Chanturia. However, the power struggle intensified, as the president's opponents resorted to force to oust him, and from December 1991 Gamsakhurdia had to take refuge in a basement bunker in the shell-shattered Tbilisi parliament building. He fled to Armenia on 6 January 1992 and later to the Chechen republic in southern Russia. Distracted by these events, Georgia failed to join the new Commonwealth of Independent States (CIS), which was established in December 1991 after the USSR had been dissolved. Although the United States withheld diplomatic recognition of Georgia until conditions on human rights and democracy could be met, it officially acknowledged the republic's independent status. In January 1992 Georgia was admitted into the Conference on Security and Cooperation in Europe (CSCE, later the OSCE) and in July 1992 into the United Nations (UN).

The leaders of the anti-Gamsakhurdia rebel troops, Tengiz Kitovani, a former schoolmate of Gamsakhurdia's and a commander of a faction of the Georgian National Guard which broke away to oppose the Gamsakhurdia regime from August 1991, and Dzhaba Ioseliani, a former convict and playwright who was commander of the paramilitary Mkhedrioni ('the Horsemen'), established a Military Council. Tengiz Sigua returned as prime minister, but fresh elections were promised for April 1992. Subsequent rebellion by Gamsakhurdia supporters, 'Zviadists', between January and July 1992, which were especially strong in the fugitive president's home region of western Georgia, was crushed by the Military Council. In February 1992, Chanturia and Temur Zhorzholiani, leader of the Monarchist Party, travelled to Spain to meet the Bagrations, descendants of Georgia's royal family, with the aim of returning with the heir to Tbilisi in preparation for a coronation the following year. However, in March 1992, the republic's former communist leader and former Soviet foreign minister, Eduard Shevardnadze, returned to Georgia and the ruling Military Council transferred its powers to a newly created 50-member, all-party State Council, chaired by Shevardnadze and including Sigua, Kitovani, and Ioseliani.

In July 1992 the autonomous republic of Abkhazia declared its independence, forcing Shevardnadze to deploy the Georgian National Guard as a bloody armed conflict erupted. The situation was calmer elsewhere, notably in the secessionist autonomous region of South Ossetia, where a ceasefire agreement was signed in July 1992, ending two years of fighting which had claimed the lives of more than 1,000 Ossetians and 400 Georgians and had led to thousands fleeing to North Ossetia, in the Russian Federation. This made it possible, in August 1992, for Shevardnadze to lift the state of emergency imposed by Gamsakhurdia. Elections to the Supreme Soviet, held in October 1992, were boycotted in South Ossetia and in parts of Abkhazia and western Georgia and produced an inconclusive outcome. However, Shevardnadze secured popular approval as head of state, winning 95% of the national vote in an uncontested election.

The major problem facing Shevardnadze was the continuing conflict in Abkhazia. In August 1990, following fighting with Georgian government troops which claimed more than 100 lives and led to 50,000 fleeing to southern Russia, Vladislav Ardzinba, leader of the independence campaign and chairperson of the Abkhazian parliament, fled north from the capital, Sukhumi. However, the Abkhazians, receiving support from Russian nationalist volunteer fighters, launched a counter-offensive from October 1992, shelling Georgian troops stationed in Sukhumi. In July 1993, under the terms of a peace deal mediated by the CSCE, some Georgian troops were withdrawn from the autonomous republic. This enabled Abkhazian forces to humiliatingly defeat the Georgian army and capture the Black Sea resort of Sukhumi on 16 September 1993, forcing Shevardnadze temporarily into hiding and 120,000 civilians to flee into western Georgia. In the wake of this debacle, supporters of ousted ex-president, Gamsakhurdia, launched a new rebellion. To save the situation, Shevardnadze was moved to turn, reluctantly, to Russia for military aid to crush the dual insurgencies. The price for this was an agreement, in October 1993, that Georgia would enter the CIS in December 1993, thus ceding significant political and economic sovereignty. In addition, it was agreed that 20,000 Russian troops could remain stationed in four bases in Georgia, including some strategic Black Sea ports, for at least 25 years.

With Russian aid the Gamsakhurdia rebellion was crushed in November 1993 and its leader died in December 1993, apparently committing suicide. In May 1994 a ceasefire agreement was reached with Abkhaz rebels, with considerable autonomy being ceded to the republic and 2,500 Russian peacekeeping troops being deployed in the autonomous republic. This promised to end four years of fighting which, by official estimates, had claimed 30,000 lives and led to the flight of 250,000 Georgian refugees. In November 1994 the Abkhazian parliament issued a sovereignty declaration, but in February 1995 the autonomous republic's nationalist leaders announced that they would shelve their demands for independence in the light of Russia's invasion of the Chechen republic.

The economic damage wrought by the internal conflicts in Abkhazia and South Ossetia and the civil war between pro- and anti-Gamsakhurdia supporters was enormous. During 1991–92 alone, output fell by 60% and during 1993 and 1994 the annual fall in real GDP, averaged 15%. Inflation exceeded 15,000% per annum by 1994, the budget deficit was the equivalent of 60% of GDP, and there were severe fuel and food shortages, with bread rationing being imposed as Abkhazia's productive agricultural land was placed temporarily out of use. There was also a surge in the level of crime and political terrorism, as mafia gangs and paramilitaries increased their influence. In February 1994 the powerful Mkhedrioni irregulars were disbanded and in January the unregistered paramilitary National Liberation Front maintained by former defense minister, Tengiz Kitovani, was disarmed. This formed part of a general demilitarization drive. The Mkhedrioni was later reconstituted as the Rescue Corps, which was itself substantially disarmed in May 1995. A ten-year friendship and cooperation treaty was signed with Russia in February 1994 and economic and commercial agreements seemed to pave the way for Georgia's re-entry into the rouble zone. With the granting of a large IMF loan to the republic in December 1994, the launching of a mass privatization campaign in April 1995, and a reduction in the monthly rate of inflation to below 3% during the first half of 1995, the economic outlook began to improve somewhat. In August 1995 Eduard Shevardnadze survived a car bomb assassination attempt, blamed variously on the paramilitary Mkhedrioni and mafia groups and a former security minister. In November 1998 the leader of the disbanded Mkhedrioni; Pzaba Loseliani, was sentenced to 11 years' imprisonment in connection with this incident: Shevardnadze convincingly won the November 1995 presidential election, while the pro-Shevardnadze Citizens' Union of Georgia (CUG) finished as the largest single party in the concurrent parliamentary elections. In December 1995 Nikoloz Lekishvili, formerly the mayor of Tbilisi, was appointed minister of state, to co-ordinate the new government.

With a new currency, the lari, in place and the establishment of a legal framework to encourage private-sector economic activity, the country entered a phase of strong economic recovery from 1996. Annual real GDP growth averaged 10% in 1996 and 1997; the annual inflation rate fell to 7% in 1997; and, by 1998, almost all small-scale, as well as increasing numbers of medium and larger, enterprises had been transferred to the private sector. Indicative of these changes, in April 1996, along with Armenia and Azerbaijan, President Shevardnadze signed a symbolic co-operation agreement with the European Union.

During 1997–98, the president faced continued opposition from supporters of the former president, Zviad Gamsakhurdia. In March 1997 they formed a new nine-party Front for the Reinstatement of Legitimate Power in Georgia and in February 1998 were implicated in a further unsuccessful assassination attempt on Shevardnadze, which killed three presidential bodyguards. However, the president's greatest challenges continued to be presented by secessionist Abkhazia and South Ossetia, with matters compounded by turmoil in neighboring Chechnya and Dagestan, in Russia. In November 1996, (illegal) elections were held to the breakaway Abkhaz parliament, the People's Assembly, and to the presidency of South Ossetia. Peace talks, brokered by Russia, did begin, in June 1997, with Abkhazia's president, Vladislav Ardzinba, but in May 1998 there was a brief resumption of conflict, leading to the flight of 20,000 ethnic Georgians. Consequently, Russian peacekeeping forces remained in Abkhazia and, since 1993, there has been an UN Observer Mission in Georgia (UNOMIG), to monitor intra-state relations.

During 1999 the refugees who had fled Abkhazia 1992–93 and 1998 were repatriated. Meanwhile, in December 1998, after falling in value by 30% in one week, the Georgian currency, the lari, was allowed to float. In February 1999 Georgia was admitted into the Council of Europe and in May 1999 it appeared that Georgia might not seek to remain a member of CIS.

GREECE

Hellenic Republic
Elliniki Dimokratia

Capital: Athens

Social and economic data

Area: 131,944 sq km/50,944 sq miles
Population: 10,426,000*
Pop. density per sq km/sq mi: 79/205*
Urban population: 64%**
Literacy rate: 93%**
GDP: $100,500 million*; per-capita GDP: $9,640*
Government defense spending (% of GDP): 4.6%*

Currency: drachma
Economy type: high income
Labor force in agriculture: 25%**
Unemployment rate: 10.0%*
* 1995.
** 1994.

Head of state

President Constantine Stephanopoulos, since 1995

Head of government

Prime Minister Costas Simitis, since 1996

Ethnic composition

Over 97% of the population is Greek. The main minorities are Turks, Slavs, and Albanians.

Religions

The Eastern Orthodox Church is the established religion and it has about 9 million adherents, or most of the population. There are also about 47,000 Roman Catholics, 5,000 Protestants, and 5,000 Jews.

Political features

State type: liberal democratic
Date of state formation: 1829
Political structure: unitary
Executive: parliamentary
Assembly: one-chamber
Party structure: multiparty
Human rights rating: 87%
International affiliations: CE, CERN, CSCE, EEA, EU, IAEA, IBRD, IMF, NACC, NAM (guest), NATO, OECD, UN, WEU, WTO

Local and regional government

Although the 1975 constitution prescribes that 'the administration of the States shall be organized on the basis of decentralization', Greece has tended to be a highly centralized state. In 1983 measures were introduced to devolve more power to the ten regions into which the country is divided and the departments into which they, in turn, are subdivided.

Political system

The 1975 constitution provides for a parliamentary system of government, with a president, who is head of state, a prime minister, who is head of government, and a single-chamber Parliament (Vouli). The president is elected by Parliament for a five-year term. The prime minister is appointed on the basis of parliamentary support. Amendments to the constitution in 1986 transferred virtually all executive powers from the president to the prime minister. The president and the cabinet are collectively responsible to Parliament. This has 300 members, all elected by universal adult suffrage, through a party list system of proportional representation, for a four-year term, with a 3% threshold for representation. Bills passed by Parliament must be ratified by the president, whose veto, however, can be overridden by absolute majority of the total number of members of Parliament.

Political parties

There are some 17 political parties, the two most significant being the Panhellenic Socialist Movement (PASOK) and the New Democracy Party (ND).

PASOK was formed in 1974 by the incorporation of the Democratic Defense and the Panhellenic Liberation Movement, two organizations committed to the removal of the military regime which had been dominating Greek politics. Although strongly nationalistic, it favors socialization through international cooperation.

The ND was also formed in 1974. It is a broad-based, center-right party, favoring social reform through a free enterprise system. It is a strong supporter of EU and NATO membership.

Political leaders since 1970

1967–73 Colonel George Papadopoulos (military), 1973–74 Lt-Gen Phaidon Ghizikis (military), 1974–80 Constantine Karamanlis (ND), 1981–89 Andreas Papandreou (PASOK), 1989 Tzannis Tzannetakis (ND-Communist coalition), 1989 Yannis Grivas (caretaker administration), 1989–90 Xenophon Zolotas (caretaker administration), 1990 Yannis Grivas (caretaker administration), 1990–93 Constantine Mitsotakis (ND), 1993–96 Andreas Papandreou (PASOK), 1996– Costas Simitis (PASOK)

Latest elections

The results of the September 1996 general election were as follows:

Greece latest election results

Party	% votes	Seats
PASOK	41.5	162
ND	38.1	108
Other parties	20.4	30

Political history

Historically the birthplace of democracy, Greece became an independent modern nation-state in 1829 and a constitutional monarchy in 1843. Relations with neighboring Turkey were strained for much of the 19th century, resulting in an unsuccessful war in 1897 and a more successful one in 1912–13. Politics were dominated between 1910 and 1935 by Eleutherios Venizelos (1864–1936), who was prime minister for nearly half the period. The monarchy was removed between 1923 and 1935, when King George II (1890–1947) was restored by the army, but was to remain dependent upon the military leader General Ioannis Metaxas (1871–1941). Soon after the outbreak of World War II an attempted invasion by Italy was successfully resisted but a determined onslaught by Germany proved too powerful and occupation followed.

During the German occupation, between 1941 and 1944, a communist-dominated resistance movement armed and trained a guerrilla army and after the war the National Liberation Front, as it was called, attempted to create a socialist state. If the Greek royalist army had not been massively assisted by the United States, this undoubtedly would have happened. As it was, the monarchy, in the shape of King Paul (1901–64), was re-established, and in 1964 he was succeeded by his son, Constantine II (b. 1940).

Dissatisfaction with the performance of the government and conflicts between the king and his ministers resulted in a coup, in 1967, led by Colonel George Papadopoulos (b. 1919). The monarchy was replaced by a new regime, which, despite its democratic pretensions, was little more than a military dictatorship. All political activity was banned and opponents of the government were forced out of public life. In 1973 Greece declared itself a republic and Papadopoulos became president.

A civilian cabinet was appointed but before the year was out another coup brought Lieutenant General Phaidon Ghizikis to the presidency, with Adamantios Androutsopoulus as prime minister. The failure of the government to prevent the Turkish invasion of Cyprus led to its downfall and a former prime minister, Constantine Karamanlis (b. 1907), was recalled from exile to form a new Government of National Salvation. Karamanlis immediately ended martial law, press censorship, and the ban on political parties and in the 1974 general election his New Democracy Party (ND) won a decisive majority in Parliament. A referendum held the same year emphatically rejected the idea of a return of the monarchy and in 1975 a new constitution for a democratic 'Hellenic Republic' was adopted, with Constantine Tsatsos as the new president.

The ND won the 1977 general election with a reduced majority and in 1980 Karamanlis resigned as prime minister and was elected president. The following year Greece became a full member of the European Community, having been an associate since 1962. Meanwhile, the ND found itself faced with a growing challenge from the Panhellenic Socialist Movement (PASOK), which won an absolute majority in Parliament in the 1981 general election. Its leader, Andreas Papandreou (b. 1919), the son of a prominent left-of-center republican politician, became Greece's first socialist prime minister.

PASOK had been elected on a radical socialist platform, which included withdrawal from the European Community, the removal of US military bases, and a sweeping program of domestic reform. Important social changes, such as lowering the voting age to 18, the legalization of civil marriage and divorce, and an overhaul of the universities and the army, were carried out, but, instead of withdrawing from Europe, Papandreou was content to obtain a modification of the terms of entry, and, rather than close US bases, he signed a five-year agreement on defense and economic cooperation. Despite introducing tight austerity measures to deal with growing inflation, PASOK won a comfortable majority in the 1985 elections, and in March 1986 the constitution was amended, limiting the powers of the president in relation to those of the prime minister.

In 1988 relations with Turkey showed a marked improvement. Papandreou met Prime Minister Turgut Özal of Turkey for talks in Switzerland and later Özal paid a visit to Athens, the first by a Turkish prime minister for over 35 years. Later in 1988 the personal life of Prime Minister Papandreou became difficult. It was announced that he and his wife were about to divorce and that he had a heart condition for which he underwent surgery.

In 1989 Papandreou sought a renewal of his mandate but the general election result was inconclusive, resulting in a short-lived coalition between the conservative ND and the Communists, led by Tzannis Tzannetakis. This collapsed and a caretaker government was formed prior to another general election in April 1990.

The ND won half the assembly seats and its leader, Constantine Mitsotakis, was able to form Greece's first single-party government for a decade. The main events during this administration were the election of the former ND leader, Constantine Karamanlis, as president, the signing of an agreement for siting US bases in Greece, the ratification of the Maastricht Treaty on European unity, and the clearing of Andreas Papandreou of corruption charges levelled against him.

In September 1993 Mitsotakis called a general election to renew his mandate but failed, PASOK winning a clear majority and the veteran politician Papandreou returning to office. In March 1995 Constantine Stephanopoulos was elected president by Parliament. PASOK maintained its assembly majority in the September 1996 elections.

In January 1996 Papandreou retired because of ill health and was succeeded by the new PASOK leader, Costas Simitis. Papandreou died five months later. PASOK maintained its assembly majority in the September 1996 elections.

In July 1997 direct talks with Turkey began, with an agreement to settle future disputes peacefully.

HUNGARY

Republic of Hungary
Magyar Köztársaság

Capital: Budapest

Social and economic data

Area: 93,033 sq km/35,920 sq miles
Population: 10,260,000*
Pop. density per sq km/sq mi: 110/286*
Urban population: 66%**
Literacy rate: 97%**
GDP: $41,130 million*; per-capita GDP: $4,010*
Government defense spending (% of GDP): 1.4%*

Currency: forint
Economy type: middle income
Labor force in agriculture: 14%**
Unemployment rate: 10.3%*
* 1995.
** 1992.

Head of state
President Arpád Göncz, since 1990

Head of government
Prime Minister Viktor Orban, since 1998

Ethnic composition
The majority, 93%, of the population is native Hungarian, or Magyar, of non-Slavic stock. There exist, in addition, minorities of about 170,000 Germans, 120,000 Slovaks, 50,000 Croats, and 20,000 Romanians. There is also a large Romany (gypsy) community of around 600,000, which has its own elected governing body to administer the funds disbursed by the central government. Hungarian (Magyar) is the main language.

Religions
About 60% of the population is Roman Catholic. Until the 1960s, this church was subject to state repression, the primate Cardinal Jaggar József Mindszenty being imprisoned and given a life sentence. A quarter of the population is Protestant, the principal denominations being the Presbyterian Reformed Church of Hungary, with 2 million members, and the Lutheran Church of Hungary, with 430,000 adherents. The Jewish community numbers around 90,000 people.

Political features
State type: emergent democratic
Date of state formation: 1918
Political structure: unitary
Executive: parliamentary*
Assembly: one-chamber
Party structure: multiparty
Human rights rating: 97%
International affiliations: BIS, CEFTA, CEI, CERN, COE, DC, EBRD, ECE, HG, IBRD, IMF, LORCS, NACC, NAM (guest), NATO, OAS (observer), OECD, OSCE, UN, VG, WFTU, WTO

* Although the president has some executive powers.

Local and regional government
For local administration, the country is divided into 19 counties (*megyed*) and the capital city, subdivided into 22 districts and local councils, elected every five years.

Political system
Under the terms of the 'transitional constitution', adopted in October 1989, Hungary is a unitary state with a one-chamber 386-member National Assembly (Orszaggyülés). Its members are elected for four-year terms under a mixed system of direct and proportional representation. One hundred and seventy-six are directly elected, on a potential two-ballot majoritarian run-off basis, from single-member constituencies; a maximum of 152 are returned from 20 regional, county and metropolitan multi-member constituencies via lists on a proportional basis (with a 5% cut-off limit being applied to determine representation); and a minimum of 58 are elected indirectly from party-nominated national 'compensation' lists, designed to favor smaller parties able to muster at least 5% of the vote. The National Assembly, which meets at least twice a year, elects the state president, for a maximum of two five-year terms, and a Council of Ministers (COM), or cabinet, of some 15 members headed by a prime minister. The president, who must be at least 35 years old, and is also commander in chief of the armed forces, has the authority to initiate legislation, hold plebiscites, and appoint higher civil servants. National Assembly decisions are only valid if carried by a majority when a quorum of at least half its members is present. Constitutional changes require a two-thirds majority. The 15-member Constitutional Court ensures compliance with the constitution.

Political parties
More than 50 political parties operate in Hungary today, supported by partial state funding. Seven of these are sig-

nificant organizations: the Hungarian Socialist Party (HSP: Magyar Szocialista Párt, or MSzP); the conservative Hungarian Democratic Fórum: MDF); the Christian Democratic People's Party (Kereszténydemokrata Néppárt: KDNP); the Independent Smallholders' Party (Fuggetlen Kizgazda es Pólgari Párt: FKgP); the far-right Hungarian Justice and Life Party; the liberal Alliance of Free Democrats (Szabad Demokratak Szövetsége: SzDSz); and the conservative-liberal Federation of Young Democrats-Hungarian Civic Party (Fiatal Demokraták Szövetsége-Magyar Pólgai Párt: FIDESZ–MPP).

The HSP is the reform-socialist successor to the formerly ruling Hungarian Socialist Workers' Party (HSWP), adopting its current name and changed political stance in October 1989. The 40,000-member HSP is led by Gyula Horn. The former HSWP was itself an offspring of the Hungarian Communist Party (HCP), which was founded in November 1918 and which, in alliance with the Hungarian Social Democratic Party (HSDP), which dated from 1890, briefly established a 133-day 'Soviet Republic' under the leadership of Béla Kun, between March and August 1919. It was proscribed and forced underground by the succeeding Horthy dictatorship, many of its thousand or so members fleeing to Moscow. There, the party was purged and 'Stalinized'. With Soviet military support, it moved into a dominant position in the country from 1945, forcing the left wing of the HSDP to merge and form a new United Workers' Party, in 1948. It was renamed the Hungarian Workers' Party (HWP) in 1949 and the HSWP in 1956, being substantially reconstituted, following the 'national uprising' of that year. Party membership totalled 1.5 million in the immediate post-World War II period, but, after falling to 500,000 in 1962, grew to 880,000 in 1987, representing 8.3% of the total population. Many members left the party between 1987 and 1989. A rump HSWP, known since 1992 as the Hungarian Workers' Party and led by Gyula Thurmer, has continued to function after the party's reconstitution in September 1989. It secured only 4% of the vote in the May 1998 general election and no parliamentary representation.

The MDF was founded in September 1988 by a group of Populist intellectuals as an umbrella body embracing reformist communists, Christian Socialists, and Christian Democrats. Under the leadership of József Antall, who died in December 1993, it developed into a center-right nationalist force. The MDF, led by Sándor Lezsák, has 25,000 members.

The KDNP (estd. 1989) and FKgP (estd. 1988) are, similarly, right-of-center bodies, but the FKgP split during 1992 into two rival factions. The 60,000-member FKgP has advocated the restoration to its original owners of land collectivized after 1947. In June 1993 an extreme nationalist and anti-Semitic faction of the MDF, led by István Csurka, a prominent novelist, and Lajos Horvath, broke away to from the new Hungarian Justice and Life Party (MIEP).

The 35,000-member SzDSz, led now by Gabor Kuncze, was formed by dissident intellectuals in November 1988 as a radically pro-Western and pro-free-market party. Closely related is the 10,000-member FIDESz, which, formed in March 1988, gained a reputation as the most militant of the anticommunist pluralist forces. It originated as a liberal-minded youth party, but in April 1993 lifted its age limit of 35 for members and elected Viktor Orbán, aged 30, as its chairperson. During 1993 opinion polls suggested that the FIDESz was the country's most popular party. However, its performance in the May 1994 general election was disappointing and it adopted the new designation FIDESz-MPP in April 1995. Led by Viktor Orban, it polled particularly strongly in the 1998 general election.

Political leaders since 1970

1956–88 János Kádár (HSWP)*, 1988–89 Károly Grár (HSWP)s*, 1989–90 Rezsö Nyers (HSP)*, 1990–93 Jezsö Nyers (HSP))s**, 1993–94 Peter Boross (MDF)**, 1994–98 Gyula Horn (HSP)**, 1998– Viktor Orban (FIDESz)**

* Communist Party leader.

** Prime minister.

Latest elections

In the most recent National Assembly elections, held on 10 and 24 May 1998, the ex-communist HSP secured the largest share of the national vote, 32% (down 1% on May 1994), but finished as the second largest party, capturing 134 of the 386 seats. Its coalition partner, the liberal Alliance of Free Democrats, slumped to only 8% of the vote (down 12%), winning 24 seats. It was the conservative-liberal Federation of Young Democrats which made the greatest gains, surging to 28% of the vote (up 21%) to capture 148 seats. The MDF, with 3% of the vote (down 9%), lost further support, but still won 17 seats; while the xenophobic Justice and Life Party, with 6% of the vote, won 14 seats, its first ever representation.

Political history

1. 1000–1989

Having previously been subjected to Roman and Germanic rule, a Magyar kingdom was first established in 1000 AD by St Stephen (*c.* 977–1035), who converted the country's inhabitants to Christianity. From the early 14th century the nation again came under foreign control, with the south and center falling to the Turks from the 16th century. They were replaced in the later 17th century by the Austrian Habsburgs. Lajos Kossuth (1802–94) led a Hungarian renaissance during the mid-19th century, with an independent republic being proclaimed and serfdom abolished in 1848–49. This was quickly suppressed by joint Austrian and Russian forces and an Austro-Hungarian empire was re-established within which Hungary enjoyed substantial self-government.

Full independence was finally obtained in 1918, following the dismemberment of the Austro-Hungarian Empire at the close of World War I. A brief 'Soviet Republic' experiment during 1919 was suppressed by Romanian and Czechoslovak troops and a conservative dictatorship was then established, under the leadership of the regent, Admiral Nikolaus Horthy de Nagybánya (1868–1957).

The new regime restricted the franchise to only 27% of the population, paving the way for perpetual dominance by the rightwing Party of Unity, although during the later 1930s the fascist Arrow Cross party emerged as a serious challenger. Only limited advances were achieved in the economic sphere during these years, with still, in 1930, more than half the population remaining dependent upon agricultural activities. In these circumstances, the subsequent 1930s depression had a particularly adverse effect on the country.

On the outbreak of World War II, Admiral Horthy allied Hungary with Germany and the Axis powers, joining Adolf Hitler in the invasion of the Soviet Union in 1941. In March 1944, however, the country was overrun by Soviet forces and the Horthy regime toppled. A provisional five-party coalition government was formed in December 1944, headed by General Miklos. It included the communist agriculture minister, Imre Nagy (1895–1958), who set about distributing land to the peasants as a means of broadening the party's support base. In addition, the Communist Party (HCP) held a majority of seats in the temporary Assembly and was given control of the police forces.

In free elections held in November 1945, the HCP secured 17% of the total votes and 70 of the 409 seats. The Smallholders' Party emerged as the most popular force, capturing a majority of seats, but the HCP, with Soviet support, succeeded in forcing the formation of a coalition with other leftist parties. It then proceeded to introduce a program of nationalization and central economic planning. In February 1946 a republic was inaugurated and from June 1948, when the HCP and HSDP merged to form the HWP, all other political parties were outlawed. This was followed, in August 1949, by the adoption of a new Soviet-style constitution.

Under HWP leader Mátyás Rákosi, a strict Stalinist regime was imposed between 1946 and 1953, involving forced collectivization and the launching of a wave of secret police terror. Liberalization in the economic sphere began tentatively between 1953 and 1955, when Imre Nagy, supported by the Soviet premier, Georgi Malenkov, replaced Rákosi as prime minister. However, Nagy, in turn, was removed in April 1955, after the fall of Malenkov.

In 1956, in the wake of the Soviet leader Nikita Khrushchev's denunciation of Stalin in his February 'secret speech', pressure for democratization mounted. Rákosi stepped down as HWP leader in July and, following student and worker demonstrations in Budapest on 23 October, Nagy was recalled as prime minister and János Kádár (1912–89) was appointed general secretary of the HWP. Nagy proceeded to lift restrictions on the formation of political parties, released the anti-communist primate, József Mindszentry (1892–1975), and announced plans for Hungary to withdraw from the Warsaw Pact and become a neutral power. These changes were, however, opposed by Kádár, who set up a rival government in East Hungary. He then returned to Budapest, with Soviet tanks, and overthrew the Nagy government on 4 November 1956. Two hundred thousand refugees fled to the West during the 1956 'Hungarian National Uprising' and 2,500 citizens were killed.

In the immediate wake of this 'rebellion', the HWP was purged and reconstituted as the HSWP. Several years of repression followed, with 2,000 participants in the uprising, including Nagy, being executed and many others deported to the USSR. During the 1960s, however, Kádár proceeded to introduce pragmatic, liberalizing reforms, including a decentralization of economic planning, styled, in 1968, the 'New Economic Mechanism'. This gave Hungary the reputation of being one of the freest and most market-orientated Eastern European states. It became a member of the IMF and the World Bank in 1982, and enjoyed a considerable improvement in living standards. Greater participation in local affairs was also encouraged as part of this 'self-governing' process. Externally,

Hungary emerged as a loyal member of the Warsaw Pact and Comecon during the 1960s and 1970s.

Hungary's relations with Moscow improved significantly during the post-Brezhnev era, with the *perestroika* (economic restructuring) program adopted by the reformist Mikhail Gorbachev, who became Soviet leader in 1985, being influenced by Hungary's 'market socialism' experiment. Between 1987 and 1988 there were further reforms, including more price deregulation, the creation of a stock market, the introduction of value-added tax (VAT), and the establishment of 'enterprise councils'.

As elsewhere in Eastern and Central Europe, change came quickly to Hungary from 1988. In May 1988, two months after a large prodemocracy march was held in Budapest, Kádár, who had become an obstacle to reform, was replaced as HSWP general secretary by Károly Grár in a new phase of political reform. This aimed to achieve a clearer separation between party and state and to introduce a new system of 'socialist pluralism' in which noncommunist parties would be admitted into a more influential, decision-taking parliament, censorship laws would be relaxed, the HSWP would no longer have a guaranteed leading role in society, and independent trade unions would be allowed to form. Outside momentum was added to this process by the formation of 'reform clubs' by intellectuals and dissidents, under the 'Network of Free Initiatives' umbrella organization. These were superseded, in September 1988, by the Hungarian Democratic Forum (MDF), an umbrella movement for opposition groups, and several dozen other political parties were formed during 1989 and 1990.

In February 1989 the official interpretation of the events of 1956 was also radically revised, it being now seen as a 'popular uprising' rather than a 'counter-revolution', and in June 1989 Imre Nagy was posthumously rehabilitated, cleared of alleged past crimes by the Supreme Court, and reburied in a state funeral attended by 300,000 people. The border with Austria was opened in May 1989, with adverse effects for East Germany's communist regime, as thousands of East Germans escaped to the West via Hungary. Two months later, as the reform momentum continued to build up, Grósz was forced to share power with the more radical trio of Nyers, Pózsgay, and Miklós Németh (prime minister since November 1988), as a four-person ruling praesidium was formed. The HSWP had earlier, in February 1989, agreed to abandon the clause in the constitution guaranteeing the party a leading political role.

2. 1989–1999

In October 1989 a series of significant constitutional changes, the result of round-table talks held with opposition groups through the summer, were approved by the National Assembly. These included the adoption of a new set of electoral rules, the banning of workplace communist party cells, and the change of the country's name from the 'People's Republic' to simply 'Republic'. Also in October 1989 the HSWP changed its name to the Hungarian Socialist Party (HSP), and adopted adopted Pózsgay as its presidential candidate. Grósz, and other conservatives, refused to play an active role in the renovated party, which had become a 'social-democratic' pluralist force. Despite these changes, the HSP's standing was damaged badly by the January 1990 'Danubegate scandal', when it was revealed that the secret police had bugged opposition parties and passed the information obtained to the HSP. The HSP polled disastrously in the March–April 1990 multiparty general election, attracting, in the first round, only 11% of the national vote to the MDF's 25%, the SzDSz's 21%, the Independent Smallholders' 12%, the FIDESz's 9%, and the KDNP's 7%. After the election, a MDF-dominated coalition government was formed in May 1990, embracing the KDNP and Independent Smallholders' Party and independents, and headed by the MDF leader, Dr József Antall (1932–93), a former museum director, who became prime minister. Arpád Göncz (b. 1922), a former dissident playwright, translator, and a member of the SzDSz, who was jailed between 1956 and 1963 for opposing the communist regime, was elected state president by the legislature in August 1990, replacing Mátyás Szuros, who had been acting president since October 1989. The new right-of-center administration declared its aims as withdrawal from the Warsaw Pact, to seek membership of the European Union, and to effect a full transition to a Western-style market economy.

Externally, events moved swiftly during 1990. The Soviet Union was asked, in February 1990, to withdraw its troops and the government announced, in June 1990, that Hungary would no longer participate in Warsaw Pact military exercises. As the Warsaw Pact and Comecon had disbanded by July 1991, the country was able to move towards the West more directly. Hungary joined the Council of Europe (COE), becoming its first Eastern European member, in November 1990 and, on schedule, in June 1991 the last Soviet troops withdrew from the country. In February 1991 Hungary signed the

Visegrad declaration of economic, political, and security cooperation with Poland and Czechoslovakia (which became two separate states from 1 January 1993), while treaties of cooperation were signed with Russia and Ukraine in December 1991. In March 1994 it applied for full membership of the European Union.

Of all the former Soviet satellite states, Hungary experienced the smoothest transition towards a market economy during the early 1990s, although GDP did decline by more than 20% between 1990–93. This was probably because it was the first to adopt a policy of self-management and privatization, even before the downfall of the communist regime in 1989. Although economic problems persisted, including an increase in unemployment to 12% of the work force, Hungary provided a gradualist model for other 'newly freed' East European states to be compared to the 'shock therapy' model of Poland. In January 1991 the forint was devalued by 15% in an effort to boost exports and in June 1991 a Compensation Bill for owners of land and property expropriated under the communist regime was approved by the National Assembly. It was hoped that, by clearing up the uncertainty over ownership, the bill would stimulate the privatization program and inward investment. By the start of 1994, with the economy beginning to grow again, around 40% of the work force were employed by the private sector and nearly half of the 2,000 state enterprises which existed in 1989 had been either sold or liquidated.

Politically, the period between 1992 and 1994 was one of relative stability, but there were growing strains within the MDF-led ruling party. In June 1992 the Independent Smallholders' Party (FKgP) split into two factions, one of which supported the Antall administration, while the other allied itself with the opposition. A year later, in June 1993, a split also occurred in the MDF, with its vice chairperson, Istvan Csurka, leaving to form the extreme nationalist and anti-Semitic Hungarian Justice and Life Party (MIEP). During 1993 the health of Prime Minister Antall, who was suffering from lymph-gland cancer, deteriorated progressively and on his death, in December 1993, the interior minister, Peter Boross (b. 1928), took over as prime minister.

The MDF trailed throughout 1993–94 in the opinion polls behind the HSP and the FIDESz and in the general election of May 1994 was able to secure a mere 12% of the national vote, finishing behind the HSP, which attracted 33% of the vote, and the SzDSz, with 20% popular support. The HSP was in a position to form a majority administration on its own, but chose instead to form a powerful socialist-liberal coalition government with the SzDSz Alliance of Free Democrats and which controlled 72% of the legislature's seats. Gyula Horn (b. 1932), a trained economist who had been a member of the procommunist militia which had fought against democrats in 1956, but was later a reformist foreign minister during the final period of communist rule in 1989–90, became prime minister on 15 July 1994. A member of the leftwing of the HSP, he constructed a 14-member technocratic cabinet, which included three representatives of the SzDSz, and pledged to adopt a less nationalist posture than the preceding MDF administration. In particular, efforts were made to improve relations with neighboring Slovakia, with whom friendship and cooperation treaties were signed in 1996, and with Romania, where large ethnic Hungarian communities resided. In addition, Hungary renounced any claim to territory in Transylvania, while Romania pledged to guarantee the rights of its ethnic Hungarian minority.

The Horn administration became beset by divisions over economic policy, leading to the resignation of its staunchly promarket finance minister, Lászlo Bekesi, in January 1995 and the dismissal, in the same month, of the privatization chief, Ferenc Bartha. However, in March 1995 a radical economic reform package was unveiled by the Horn administration which, in a dramatic policy U-turn, sought to institute major cuts in public spending, including social and welfare programs, so as to reduce the level of indebtedness and to boost exports via devaluing the forint by more than a quarter and increase the pace of privatization. In June 1995 the popular Arpád Göncz was re-elected by Hungary's parliament for a second term as state president, being backed by the SzDSz and HSP.

Despite an export- and foreign-investment led economic recovery from 1995 and securing the highest share, at 32%, of the first round vote Horn's Socialists finished in second place, behind the right-of-center Young Democrats (FIDESz) after the end of the second round of the May 1998 general election. Led by a young, 35-year-old populist, Viktor Orban, FIDESz quadrupled its share of the national vote to 28%, while support for the Socialists' coalition partners, the Free Democrats (SzDSz), was more than halved, to 8%. The SzDSz was damaged by divisions generated by the acrimonious resignation of its leader, Ivan Peto, in April 1997, the high level of unemployment, which exceeded 10%, crime, and pressure on living standards. The election was also characterized by a further fall in support for the MDF, which had formed an electoral pact with the FIDESz, and by the capture of 14 National Assembly seats by the extremist MIEP. A new four-party center-right coalition government was subsequently formed by Viktor Orban, incorporating the FIDESz, the MDF, the Christian Democratic Federation, and the FKgP, but little change was expected in the country's rigorous free-market economic policy.

In March 1996 Hungary became a member of the OECD and in July 1997 was agreed to join the NATO military alliance, in March 1999, along with the Czech Republic and Poland. (Since 1996 it has contributed troops to the international peacekeeping force in Bosnia.) A referendum was subsequently held in Hungary on 16 November 1997 and 85% of participants voted 'Yes' to joining NATO: turnout was 49%. An associate member of the European Union since February 1994, Hungary commenced full EU membership negotiations in 1998.

LATVIA

Republic of Latvia
Latvijas Republika

Capital: Riga

Social and economic data

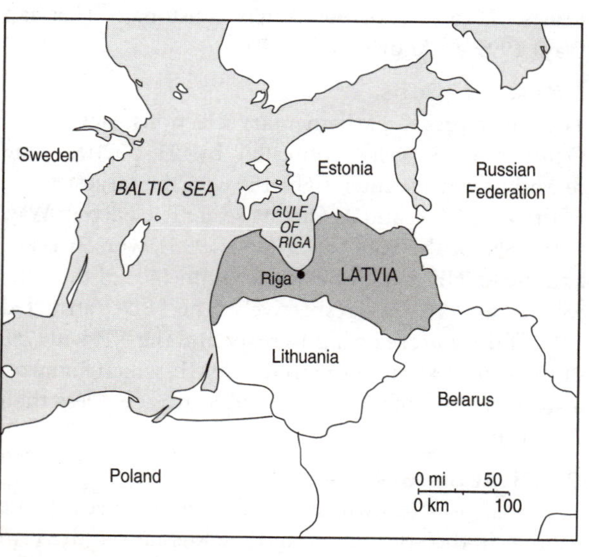

Area: 64,589 sq km/24,938 sq miles
Population: 2,529,000*
Pop. density per sq km/sq mi: 39/101*
Urban population: 72%**
Literacy rate: 99%**
GDP: $5,710 million*; per-capita GDP: $2,260*
Government defense spending (% of GDP): 3.2%*
Currency: lat
Economy type: middle income
Labor force in agriculture: 17%**
Unemployment rate:6.6%*
* 1995.
** 1992.

Head of state

President Vaira Vike-Freiberga, since 1999

Head of government

Prime Minister Andris Skele, since 1999

Ethnic composition

Fifty-three per cent of the population is of Latvian ethnic stock, 34% is ethnic Russian, 4% Belarussian, 3% Ukrainian, 2% Polish, and 1% Lithuanian. The official language, since 1988, has been Latvian, or Lettish, a member of the Baltic group of Indo-European languages which is written in the Latin script. Only a quarter of ethnic Russians are fluent in Latvian, and there have been concerns over their treatment since independence. In June 1998 a new law was passed making it easier for ethnic Russians to acquire Latvian citizenship.

Religions

The predominant religion is Christianity, with most ethnic Latvians belonging to the Lutheran or Roman Catholic churches, and most ethnic Russians are Russian Orthodox or Old Believers. During the period of Soviet rule, until the late 1980s, many churches were closed and the clergy imprisoned.

Political features

State type: emergent democratic
Date of state formation: 1920/1991
Political structure: unitary
Executive: parliamentary
Assembly: one-chamber
Party structure: multiparty
Human rights rating: N/A
International affiliations: BC, BIS, CBSS, COE, EBRD, ECE, IAEA, IBRD, IMF, NACC, OSCE, PFP, UN, WEU (associate partner)

Local and regional government

Latvia is divided into 26 districts, 56 towns, and 37 urban settlements for the purposes of local government.

Political system

Under the constitution of 1922, which was fully restored in July 1993, Latvia is a democratic parliamentary republic. Legislative authority is vested in the 100-seat Saeima (parliament), whose members are elected for four-year terms (three years before December 1997) on the basis of proportional representation, with a 5% cut-off limit being applied to determine representation. Executive power is held by a prime minister, drawn from the majority party or grouping in the Saeima and Cabinet of Ministers, comprising around 12 ministries. The Saeima elects a president to serve as titular head of state, also for four years. The minimum age for members of the Saeima is 18 years, and for the president, 40 years. Draft laws may be presented to the Saeima by the cabinet, the president, committees of the Saeima, a group of at least five members, or, exceptionally, by one-tenth of the electorate. A Constitutional Court was set up in 1996.

Political parties

Latvia, like many other central European post-communist states, has a diffused multi-party system, comprising numerous recently formed and poorly organized bodies.

In 1998 there were 40 registered parties. The most important are: the Latvian Way (Latvijas Cels); the Conservative Union for Fatherland and Freedom (CUFF)/Latvian National and Conservative Party (LNNK); the National Harmony Party (HLRNE); the Latvian Farmers' Union (LZS); the People's Movement for Latvia (PML); the Democratic Party Saimnieks (DPS: The Master); the New Party (NP); the People's Party (PP: Tautas Partija); and the Latvian Social-Democratic Union (LSDU).

The Latvian Way was formed in February 1993 as a right-of-center force which favors development of a market economy, private ownership of land, and Baltic cooperation. The then head of state, Anatolijs Gorbunovs, was a founder member and the party includes a number of ex-communists. It is now led by Andrejs Pantelejevs.

The CUFF was formed in June 1997 through the merger of the nationalist For Fatherland and Freedom (FFF) Party with the Latvian National and Conservative Party (LNNK), a rightwing nationalist force founded in June 1988 by Eduards Berklavs under the designation National Independence Movement of Latvia.

HLRNE is committed to the extension of Latvian citizenship to all ethnic Russians.

The LZS was originally formed in 1917, and was re-established in 1990 to fight for the interests of the agrarian community.

The extreme rightwing nationalist and anti-Russian PML, led by Joahims Zigerists, a German citizen and former LNNK deputy, advocates reduced taxes, greater foreign inward investment, and a tough approach to fighting crime and corruption. It was formed in 1994.

The left wing populist DPS (estd. 1995) is led by Ziedonis Cevers, a former leader of the Young Communists, and is dominated by the former communist *nomenklatura*; it seeks to protect agriculture, with tariffs and the stopping of land privatization.

The formerly dominant party before the elections of June 1993 was the 150,000-member Latvian Popular Front (LPF: Latvijas Tautas Fronte), which was set up in 1988 as a moderate umbrella nationalist organization.

The pro-business NP and PP were formed in 1997 and 1998 by Raimonds Pauls and Andris Skele respectively. The LSDU is a left wing body, formed in 1997 through the merger of the Latvian Social Democratic Workers' Party (estd. 1904) and the Social Democratic Party of Latvia, the name adopted by the reformed Communist Party of Latvia (CPL) in 1989.

Political leaders since 1970

1990–93 Ivars Godmanis (LPF), 1993–94 Valdis Birkavs (Latvian Way), 1994–95 Maris Gailis (Latvian Way), 1995–97 Andris Skele (independent), 1997–98 Guntar Krasts (LNNK) 118–999 Vilvis Kristopans (Latvian Way) 1999– Andris Skele (PP)

Latest elections

The most recent parliamentary elections, held on 3 October 1998, were contested by 21 parties. The recently formed center-right PP won the largest share of the vote, 21%, and 24 Saeima seats. The Latvian Way, with 18% of the vote (up 3% on 1995), won 21 seats, and the LNNK and HLRNE, each with 14% of the vote, won 17 and 16 seats respectively. The LSDU attracted 13% of the vote, securing 14 seats, and the NP, with 7% of the vote, 8 seats. The extremist PML, which had won a surprise 15% of the vote in 1995, attracted less than 2% of the vote.

Political history

The area now known as Latvia was invaded by the Vikings in the 9th century and the Russians in the 10th century. After lengthy resistance, it was taken over by German crusaders, the Teutonic Knights, in the 13th century and governed by them for more than 200 years, with the inhabitants being converted to Christianity. More changes of control followed, by Poland, Lithuania, and Sweden, during the 16th and 17th centuries, before Tsarist Russia took over in 1710. By 1800 all of Latvia had come under Russian control. The Latvian independence movement began to emerge in the early 1900s. During World War I, Latvia was partially occupied by the Germans and on 18 November 1918 proclaimed its independence. This was achieved after Soviet forces were expelled by German, Polish, and Latvian troops between May 1919 and January 1920.

A democratic parliamentary constitution, based on pure proportional representation, was adopted in 1922. The dominant party was the Latvian Farmers' Union, led by Karlis Ulmanis, which introduced successful land reforms. However, there were 18 changes of government from 1922 until May 1934, when, at a time of economic depression, Ulmanis assumed power in a bloodless coup. Ulmanis dissolved the legislature, the Saeima, banned all political parties, and became president in 1936. In August 1939 a secret German – Soviet agreement assigned Latvia to Russian rule and in July 1940 Latvia was incorporated as a constituent republic of the USSR. During World War II, Latvia was again occupied by German forces from July 1941, but the USSR regained control in 1944.

There followed mass deportations of Latvians to Russia and Central Asia, the immigration of ethnic Russians (in 1935 three-quarters of the population had been ethnic Latvian), the development of heavy industries and collective farms, and the establishment of one-party communist rule. Repression of Latvian cultural and literary life was particularly extreme during the 1960s and 1970s as a result of a purge of the Communist Party of Latvia (CPL) instituted by the Soviet leader Nikita Khrushchev, which saw the replacement of Latvian-born members with those born in the USSR, termed *latovichi*.

As in the other Baltic republics, nationalist dissent grew from 1980, influenced by the Polish example and by the *glasnost* (political openness) and *perestroika* (economic restructuring) initiatives launched by Mikhail Gorbachev, who became the new Soviet leader in 1985. An Environmental Protection Club (EPC) was formed in 1986, the pro-independence National Independence Movement of Latvia (LNNK) in June 1988, and the intelligentsia-led Latvian Popular Front (LPF) in October 1988 as an umbrella force, which included many communists and claimed a membership of 250,000, to campaign for political pluralism and autonomy. In September 1988 Latvia's prewar flag was relegalized and official status accorded to the Latvian language. In July 1989, with many members of the CPL having been won over to the nationalist cause, Latvia's parliament, the Supreme Soviet, declared its sovereignty and economic independence from the USSR.

The CPL's constitutional guarantee of a monopoly of power was abolished in January 1990 and in elections held to the Supreme Soviet in March – April 1990 the LPF secured a clear victory, capturing 131 of the 201 contested seats. The LPF's deputy chairperson, Ivars Godmanis, became prime minister and Anatolijs Gorbunovs, from the CPL, became the new head of state. The Supreme Soviet was renamed the Supreme Council and a number of articles of the 1922 constitution were restored as the new parliament announced, in May 1990, that Latvia's incorporation into the USSR in 1940 was illegal and the republic was now commencing a transitional period that would lead to full political and economic independence. At the same time, the CPL split into two separate Moscow-linked and independent wings. An unofficial alternative parliament, the Congress of Latvia, was also established in May 1990 after voting by citizens of the pre-1940 republic and their descendants. This was dominated by the LNNK.

The Soviet leader, Mikhail Gorbachev, anulled Latvia's declaration of independence in May 1991 and during 1991 non-Latvians organized anti-independence strikes and demonstrations. In January 1991, fearing a complete break-up of the Union, Soviet interior ministry (OMON) paratroopers were sent to seize key installations in Riga, killing one civilian. This enabled Alfred Rubiks, leader of the pro-Moscow wing of the CPL to set up the 'Committee of Public Salvation' as a rival government to the legitimate one headed by Godmanis. However, following internal and international protests, the Soviet forces withdrew later in January 1991. Latvia boycotted the March 1991 all-Union referendum on the continuance of the USSR and held, instead, a plebiscite on independence, which received 73.7% support, based on a turnout of 87.6%. On 21 August 1991, in the midst of the failed anti-Gorbachev coup in the USSR, which led to Red Army troops seizing the radio and television station in Riga, the republic declared its full and immediate independence. The CPL was also outlawed and

Rubiks imprisoned (until 1997). This declaration was recognized by the Soviet government and Western nations on 6 September 1991. The new state was admitted to the United Nations (UN) and Conference on Security and Cooperation in Europe (CSCE, later the OSCE), but was to remain in dispute with Russia over the use of 1,640 sq km/630 sq miles of land transferred from Latvia to Russia during the Soviet period.

The LPF administration headed by Godmanis instituted market-centerd economic reforms, with a new national currency, the lat, being introduced to replace the rouble in March 1993 and the service sector, particularly banking, being encouraged. However, in the short term, the republic suffered from disruption of traditional trading relations with the USSR and shortages of fuel and raw materials. As a consequence, GDP declined by 8% in 1991, more than 25% in 1992, and 15% in 1993, while inflation and crime increased sharply. In 1992 a controversial provisional new citizenship law was also introduced which required those who had not been, or were not the descendants of, citizens of the pre-1940 republic to apply for naturalization. The requirements for naturalization included knowledge of the Latvian language and residence of 16 years in Latvia.

The general election, held on 5–6 June 1993, resulted in a complete defeat for the unpopular LPF, which failed to win a seat in the new Saeima, and brought to power a more centrist government coalition, with Valdis Birkavs (b. 1942), from the recently formed Latvian Way, becoming prime minister and Guntis Ulmanis (b. 1939), from the Latvian Farmers' Union (LZS), president. Ethnic Russians had been effectively excluded from voting in this election, with the franchise being restricted to citizens of the interwar Latvian Republic and their descendants. In July 1994 the withdrawal of LZS support led to the resignation of Prime Minister Birkavs and his replacement, in September 1994, by Maris Gailis, also from the Latvian Way. The new coalition government included Birkavs as foreign minister and deputy prime minister. The final withdrawal of Russian troops from Latvia was completed in August 1994, and during 1994–95, although there was a wave of banking failures, the economy began to grow. In June 1995 a trade and cooperation agreement was signed with the European Union (EU), offering the eventual prospect of joining the EU. In June 1996 a customs agreement was entered into with the neighboring Baltic states of Estonia and Lithuania.

The October 1995 general election produced a hung parliament, in which three parties each obtained 15% of the vote, while a further six parties secured over 5% of the vote and thus assembly representation. The Latvian Way saw its vote share halved, to 15%, while two new populist extremist parties attracted an equivalent vote share: the rightwing nationalist People's Movement for Latvia (PML), led by Joahims Zigerists, a German citizen who had been convicted of inciting racial hatred in Germany in 1994; and the leftwing protectionist Democratic Party Saimnieks (DPS: Master in Your Home) party, led by Ziedonis Cevers, a former leader of the Young Communists. In December 1995 a new government was formed, including all Saeima parties except the PML, with, as prime minister, Andris Skele (b. 1958), an entrepreneur with no party affiliation. The former prime minister, Gailis, became deputy prime minister and environment minister, and Valdis Birkavs was foreign minister. In June 1996 the country's pro-Western and reformist president, Guntis Ulmanis, was re-elected by the Saeima for a second term. However, in September – October 1996 the Skele government was weakened by divisions within the DPS. In September 1996 the finance minister, Aivars Kreituss, was expelled from the DPS since it was thought that the balanced budget which he had proposed for 1997 had failed to promote the party's interests. Then, in October 1996, Cevers, the DPS leader, resigned as deputy prime minister, accusing Skele of an 'authoritarian' leadership style. Kreituss also now resigned as finance minister and was replaced by Vasilijs Melniks, who had recently been investigated (but cleared) of an alleged conflict of interest by the Prosecutor's Office. His appointment drew such strong criticism that Skele stood down, in January 1997, for nine days.

In mid-1997 a restructuring of political parties took place, with the merger of the conservative nationalist LNNK and the For Fatherland and Freedom (FFF) party, to form the Conservative Union for Fatherland and Freedom (CUFF). However, some LNNK deputies refused to join the CUFF and formed, instead, the Latvian National Reform Party, under the leadership of Aleksandrs Kirsteins. The Skele government disintegrated in July 1997, following a succession of ministerial resignations which had arisen from investigations by the Prosecutor's Office into compliance with anti-corruption legislation. A new coalition government was formed by Guntar Krasts, formerly the economy minister. It comprised five parties: the DPS; Latvian Way; the CUFF; the Latvian Farmers'

Union (LZS); and the center-right Christian Democratic Union (CDU). In April 1998 the DPS withdrew from the coalition, leaving it as a minority government. The October 1998 general election produced a hung parliament in which the People's Party, recently formed by Andris Skele, was the largest single party. However, in November 1998 Vilis Kristopans, leader of Latvia's Way, became prime minister, forming a three-party minority coalition government which also comprised the LNNK and the New Party (NP), but excluded the PP. Guntars Krasts (LNNK) became deputy prime minister. The new government's declared priorities were to continue with the predecessor's policies of privatization, improved relations with Russia, a balanced budget and legislative harmonization with the EU. However, divisions within the ruling coalition led to Kristopans resigning as prime minister in July 1999, providing an opportunity for the populist Andris Skele to form a new government.

LITHUANIA

Republic of Lithuania
Lietuvos Respublika

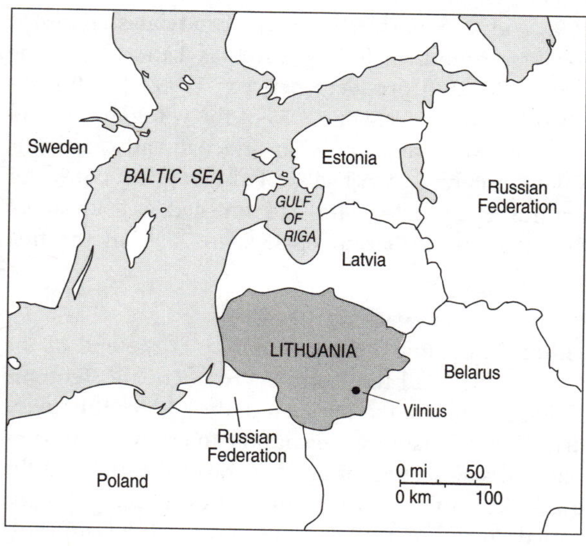

Capital: Vilnius

Social and economic data

Area: 65,200 sq km/25,174 sq miles
Population: 3,710,000*
Pop. density per sq km/sq mi: 57/147*
Urban population: 70%**
Literacy rate: 98%**
GDP: $8,400 million*; per-capita GDP: $2,265*
Government defense spending (% of GDP): 2.4%*
Currency: litas
Economy type: middle income
Labor force in agriculture: 17%**
Unemployment rate: 7.3%*
* 1995.
** 1992.

Head of state

President Valdas Adamkus, since 1998

Head of government

Prime Minister Rolandas Paksar, since 1996

Ethnic composition

Eighty per cent of the population is of Lithuanian ethnic stock, 9% is ethnic Russian, 7% Polish, 2% Belarussian, and 1% Ukrainian. Lithuanian, a Baltic tongue which used the Latin script, replaced Russian as the official language in 1988. Inter-ethnic relations deteriorated immediately after independence, but have since improved. Under the 1989 citizenship laws, all residents, regardless of ethnic origin, may apply for naturalization, and more than 90% of the non-ethnic Lithuanian residents have since been granted citizenship.

Religions

Ethnic Lithuanians are predominantly Roman Catholics and in 1992 three-quarters of the republic's population followed this faith. Ethnic Russians, Belarussians, and Ukrainians largely adhere to the Russian Orthodox Church or are Old Believers.

Political features

State type: emergent democratic
Date of state formation: 1919/1991
Political structure: unitary
Executive: dual
Assembly: one-chamber
Party structure: multiparty
Human rights rating: N/A
International affiliations: BC, BIS, CBSS, COE, EBRD, ECE, IAEA, IBRD, IMF, NACC, OSCE, PFP, UN, WEU (associate partner)

Local and regional government

The republic is divided into ten districts and 56 municipalities, for the purposes of local government.

Political system

Under the terms of the constitution of October 1992,

which is modelled on that of 1938, Lithuania is a democratic-pluralist state, with a predominantly parliamentary form of executive, though the president retains considerable authority in the selection of the prime minister. A proposal to introduce an executive presidency was rejected in a referendum held in May 1992.

Legislative authority is vested in the 141-deputy Seimas, or parliament, which is directly elected, in accordance with a mixed system of majority voting and proportional representation, for a four-year term. Candidates must be aged 25 years or more and the Seimas meets for two regular four-month sessions each year. The state president is directly elected for a maximum of two consecutive five-year terms and must be at least 40 years old. With the approval of the Seimas, the president appoints a prime minister who shares executive power with a 15–20-member Council of Ministers. The president also has an active role in foreign affairs. There is a Constitutional Court and a Supreme Court.

Political parties

Currently more than 30 political parties operate in Lithuania. The five most important are: the Lithuanian Democratic Labor Party (LDLP); the Conservative Party of Lithuania (CPL); the Christian Democratic Party of Lithuania (CDPL); the Lithuanian Social Democratic Party (LSDP); and the Lithuanian Center Union (LCU).

The 9,000-member LDLP was formed in December 1990 as the reform-socialist successor to the Lithuanian Communist Party (LCP), which broke away from the Soviet Communist Party in December 1989 and was outlawed in August 1991. The LDLP is divided between a faction which supports accelerated market-centerd economic reform and an agrarian lobby which opposes land reforms. The party favors improved relations with Russia and other ex-Soviet states.

The 16,000-member CPL, or Homeland Union-Lithuanian Conservatives, was formed in May 1993 to succeed Sajudis (Lithuanian Restructuring Movement), set up in June 1988 to spearhead Lithuania's drive for independence. It is a right-of-center nationalist force, modelled on the British Conservative Party, led by former president, Vytautas Landsbergis. Closely aligned is the center-right 11,000-member CDPL, which was first formed in 1905 and was re-established in February 1989. It is led by Algirdas Saudargas. The left-of-center 1,500-member LSDP originated in 1896 and was also re-established in 1989. The centrist 1,500-member LCU was formed in 1993.

Political leaders since 1970

Head of state: 1988–90 Algirdas Brazauskas (LCP), 1990–93 Vytautas Landsbergis (Sajudis), 1993–98 Algirdas Brazauskas (LDPL), 1998– Valdas Adamkus (independent); Prime minister: 1990–91 Kazimiera Prunskiene (LCP), 1991–92 Gediminas Vagnorius (independent), 1992 Aleksandras Abisala (Sajudis), 1992–93 Bronislovas Lubys (independent), 1993–96 Adolfas Slezevicius (LDLP), 1996 Laurynas Stankevicius (LDLP), 1996–99 Gediminas Vagnorius (CPL) 1999– Rolandar Paksas (CPL)

Latest elections

The most recent legislature elections were held on 20 October and 10 November 1996 and resulted in victory for the right-of-center CPL, which won 70 of the 137 seats filled. (Four seats remained vacant until by-elections in 1997.) The incumbent LDLP won 12 seats (down 61 on November 1992), the CDPL,16, the LCU 13, and the LSDP 12. Eight other parties won a single seat, with the remaining seats being won by independents. Proportional representation was used to fill 70 seats in the first round, while the remaining seats were decided on a simple majority basis, in November. Turnout was 53% (down 22%) in the first round and 40% in the second round.

The last presidential election was on 21 December 1997 and 4 January 1998. Seven candidates contested the first round, including Vytautas Landsbergis, the CPL leader and president between 1990–93, who finished in third place, with 16% of the vote. The run-off race was won narrowly by an independent candidate, Valdas Adamkus, by 50.4% of the vote to 49.6% for Arturas Paulauskas, who had finished well ahead of Adamkus, by a margin of 45% to 28%, in the first round.

Political history

Lithuania became a separate nation at the end of the 12th century and the German crusaders, the Teutonic Knights, who tried to invade it in the 13th century were driven back, enabling the country to extend its territorial limits almost as far as Moscow to the east and the Black Sea to the south. In the 16th century Lithuania joined Poland in a single state, and in 1795 both came under the control of tsarist Russia. Revolts in 1831 and 1863 failed to win independence. A more organized nationalist movement emerged in the 1880s, but self-government was refused by the Russians in 1905.

During World War I, Lithuania was occupied by German troops. After the war, it declared independence on 16 February 1918, but the USSR claimed Lithuania as a Soviet republic. There was an uprising, supported by Germans and Poles, and in 1919 a democratic republic was established. A coup, in December 1926, led by Antanas Smetona, brought back authoritarian rule until, in 1939, it was invaded by Nazi Germany and later handed over, in the secret Molotov–Ribbentrop pact, to the Soviet Union. Following Germany's invasion of the USSR in 1941, Lithuania revolted against Soviet rule and established its own government. However, the Germans soon occupied the country until Soviet rule was restored in 1944. Some 210,000 people, including 165,000 Jews, were killed during the brutal Nazi occupation of 1941–44. As in Estonia and Latvia, there was fierce guerrilla resistance to the imposition of Soviet rule until the early 1950s and the 'sovietization' policies of forcible agricultural collectivization and persecution of the Roman Catholic Church. The Russian authorities reacted by deporting an estimated 570,000 Balts to Siberia during the late 1940s.

An intelligentsia- and Roman Catholic Church-led dissident movement was in place during the 1960s and 1970s, producing illegal *samizdat* publications. This grew in strength during the early and mid-1980s, influenced by the Polish example and encouraged by the policies of *glasnost* (political openness) and *perestroika* (economic restructuring) espoused by Mikhail Gorbachev, who became the new Soviet leader in 1985. In 1987 the Lithuanian Freedom League (LFL) was set up by dissidents recently released from prison and began to organize public demonstrations. In June 1988 a popular front, the Lithuanian Restructuring Movement (Sajudis), was formed to campaign for increased autonomy, and on 17 November 1988 Lithuania's parliament, the Supreme Soviet, recognized Lithuanian as the state language and readopted the flag and other state symbols of the independent interwar republic.

During 1989 the Lithuanian Communist Party (LCP) became increasingly nationalistic in an attempt to win public support and on 18 May 1989 the Supreme Soviet passed a declaration of sovereignty which asserted the supremacy of Lithuanian legislation over all-Union laws. Later in the year, the LCP's monopoly of political power was abolished and a multi-party system was sanctioned, freedom of religious expression was re-established, and, in December 1989, the LCP split in two, with the majority faction formally breaking away from the Communist Party of the Soviet Union (CPSU) and establishing itself as a social-democratic Lithuanian-nationalist body. These moves took place against the background of an increasing level of popular participation in nationalist demonstrations, with more than 1 million people forming a 'human chain' extending from Tallinn in Estonia to Vilnius in Lithuania in August 1989 to protest against the 50th anniversary of the Nazi–Soviet Baltic Pact.

In the parliamentary elections of February – March 1990 Sajudis and its allies won a clear majority of seats, 88 out of 141, and the party's chairperson, Vytautas Landsbergis (b. 1932), a former music professor, was elected the country's new head of state, replacing Algirdas Brazauskas (b. 1932), leader of the LCP since 1988. On 11 March 1990 Landsbergis unilaterally proclaimed the restoration of Lithuania's independence and the Supreme Soviet was renamed the Supreme Council. The Soviet Union responded by imposing an economic blockade on 16 April 1990. By June 1990 Lithuania had exhausted its energy reserves and in July 1990 its Supreme Council was forced to suspend the independence declaration in order to have the blockade lifted. Criticized by militant nationalists as being too conciliatory towards Moscow, Kazimiera Prunskiene, a member of the LCP who had been prime minister since March 1990, resigned on 8 January 1991 and went into exile. She was replaced by Gediminas Vagnorius. This change of prime minister took place at a time of national crisis, with Soviet interior ministry (OMON) paratroops being sent to Vilnius to occupy Communist Party buildings which had been nationalized by the Lithuanian government after President Landsbergis had rescinded the suspension of the declaration of independence. On 13–14 January 1991, 13 civilians were killed when the OMON black beret troops seized the radio and television center in Vilnius, but, faced with internal and international condemnation, the Soviet forces began to withdraw in late January 1991. The Soviet action increased support for independence among ethnic Lithuanians who, on 9 February 1991, gave 90% approval to the re-establishment of an independent Lithuania in a referendum in which turnout reached 84%.

In the wake of the failed anti-Gorbachev coup in the Soviet Union in August 1991, Lithuania's declaration of independence was formally recognized by the Soviet government and Western nations on 6 September 1991. The new state became a full member of the United Nations (UN) and was admitted into the Conference on Security and Cooperation in Europe (CSCE, later the OSCE). In July 1992, having been criticized by opposition deputies for his authoritarian governing style, Vagnorius resigned as prime minister and was replaced by Aleksandras Abisala, a close ally of President Landsbergis. However, Sajudis endured a crushing defeat in elections to the new legislature, the Seimas, which were held in October–November 1992. The party was accused of mismanaging economic reform, comprising price liberalization and privatization, which had resulted in GDP declining by 13% during 1991 and 76% of families being officially reported as living in poverty in 1992. The ex-communist LDLP, now a social-democratic force supportive of a market economy, secured a parliamentary majority, with 73 of the 141 seats, and its leader, Vytautas Brazauskas, became the new head of state and Bronislovas Lubys (b. 1938), prime minister. The new government was a coalition which included six members of the previous administration, but no members of Sajudis, which preferred to remain in opposition.

On 14 February 1993 Brazauskas was directly elected state president, with 60% of the national vote, convincingly defeating Stasys Lozoraitis, a Lithuanian émigré, and then announced his formal resignation from the LDLP. In March 1993 Adolfas Slezevicius became the new prime minister and on 31 August 1993 Russia removed the last of its remaining troops stationed in Lithuania. During 1993 the Lithuanian economy remained in severe recession, GDP decreasing by 30%, and the governing party was itself divided over the optimal pace of economic reform. A free trade agreement was entered into in September 1993 with the other Baltic States, Estonia and Latvia, and relations were improved with neighboring Poland, with whom a Friendship and Cooperation Treaty was signed in April 1994, despite the continuing campaign of Lithuania's Polish minority community for Polish to be recognized as one of the republic's official languages. In June 1995 a trade and cooperation agreement was signed with the European Union (EU), while, in the same year, an accord on 'most favored nation' status in bilateral trade with Russia came into effect.

From 1994 the government's economic stabilization program began to have an impact, with annual GDP growth averaging 3%, while the inflation rate, which was 1,000% in 1991, fell rapidly to 9% in 1997, and by 1996 85% of state assets had been transferred to the private sector. However, with unemployment at 8%, bank failures and corruption scandals, this did not translate into popularity for the LDLP. In February 1996 Slezevicius was removed as prime minister by presidential decree, after it was revealed that he (and the interior minister) had withdrawn funds from a large commercial bank only two days before its operations were suspended. Laurynas Stankevicius, hitherto the minister of administrative reforms and municipal affairs, took over as prime minister and Ceslovas Jursenas as leader of the LDLP.

In the October – November 1996 general election, support for the LDLP slumped and the Conservative (Homeland) Party of Lithuania (CPL), which was a successor to Sajudis and was led by Vytautas Landsbergis, returned to power with a narrow overall assembly majority. After the election, Landsbergis became chairperson of the Seimas while a right-of-center coalition government was put together. It was led by Gediminas Vagnorius, a reform-minded economist, and dominated by the CPL, but also included the center-right Christian Democratic Party of Lithuania (CDPL) and the centrist Lithuanian Center Union (LCU). This new government accelerated the pace of market-centerd economic reform and the drive for entry into NATO and the EU. Russia strongly opposed Lithuania's ambitions to enter NATO. Nevertheless, in October 1997 a state border delimitation treaty was signed with Russia during what was the first visit to Russia by a Baltic head of state since the disintegration of the Soviet Union. Then, in January 1998, a Charter of Partnership was signed in Washington DC with the two other Baltic states and the USA, providing for closer political and economic ties between the four states. However, in December 1997 the EU announced that Lithuania would not be in the first group of Central European states who would be invited to start accession talks in 1998.

The presidential elections of December 1997 and January 1998, which were not contested by the incumbent Brazauskas, were won, suprisingly, by an independent candidate, Valdas Adamkus (b. 1926), who narrowly defeated Arturas Paulauskas, a young former deputy prosecutor-general, who was supported by the Lithuanian Liberal Union. Adamkus, after spending his early life fighting the Nazi and Soviet occupations of Lithuania, had emigrated to the USA in 1944 and then risen to become head of the US Environmental Protection Agency (EPA), before returning to his homeland on retirement. He was expected to seek to improve Lithuania's links with the USA and Western Europe, while continuing rapprochement with Russia.

In May 1999, after losing the confidence of President Adamkus, prime minister Vagnorius resigned and he was replaced by Rolandas Paskas, the CPL mayor of Vilnius. Paskas pledged to continue his predecessor's tight fiscal policies and further liberalise the economy.

MACEDONIA

Republic of Macedona (official internal name)
Republika Makedonija
The Former Yugoslav Republic of Macedonia (FYRM, international name)

Capital: Skopje

Social and economic data

Area: 25,713 sq km/9,925 sq miles
Population: 2,142,000*
Pop. density per sq km/sq mi: 83/216*
Urban population: 54%**
Literacy rate: 89%**
GDP: $1,810 million*; per-capita GDP: $845*
Government defense spending (% of GDP): 7.8%*
Currency: Macedonian denar
Economy type: low income
Labor force in agriculture: 16.5%*
Unemployment rate: 35.6%*

*1995
**1992

Ethnic composition

Sixty-six per cent of the population is, according to 1991 and 1994 official censuses, of Macedonian ethnic stock, 22% is ethnic Albanian, 5% Turkish, 3% Romanian, 2% Serb, and 2% Muslim, comprising Macedonian Slavs who converted to Islam during the Ottoman era and known as Pomaks. This ethnic breakdown is disputed by Macedonia's ethnic Albanian population, who, concentrated in the west of the republic, claim that they form 40% of the population and seek autonomy. It is also contested by ethnic Serbs, who claim that they number 250,000 and seek constitutional recognition as a distinct ethnic group. Macedonian, a Slavic language closely related to Bulgarian, is the official language, but minority languages, such as Albanian, are used at the local level.

Religions

Macedonia is a predominantly Christian state. More than 60% of the population adheres to the autocephalous (independent) Macedonian Orthodox Church, but there is a large Sunni Islam minority, comprising around 25% of the population and including mainly ethnic Albanians.

Political features

State type: emergent democratic
Date of state formation: 1992
Political structure: unitary
Executive: dual
Assembly: one-chamber
Party structure: multiparty
Human rights rating: N/A
International affiliations: COE, IAEA, IBRD, IMF, OSCE (observer), PFP, UN

Local and regional government

The basis unit of local government has, traditionally, been the local commune or township. Following legislation approved in September 1996, Macedonia has been divided into 123 elected municipalities for local government.

Head of state (executive)

President Kiro Gligorov, since 1991

Head of government

Prime Minister Ljubco Georiewski, since 1998

Political leaders since 1970

1991– Kiro Gligorov (SDSM)*, 1992–98 Branko Crvenovski (SDSM)** 1998– Ljubco Georiewski (VMRO-DPMN)

*President
**Prime minister

Political system

The November 1991 democratic-pluralist constitution

describes the state as one based on citizenship rather than ethnicity. It provides for a 120-member single-chamber National Assembly (Sobranje), elected by universal adult suffrage for a four-year term, with provision for its size to be increased to 140 members. Elections are on a majority basis, with a second round 'run-off' contest being held in the 85 single seat constituencies where no candidate wins at least 50% of the vote in the first round. The 35 members are elected by proportional respresentation. The president, who is head of state and of the armed forces, is directly elected for a five-year term. He or she appoints the prime minister as head of government. Other ministers in the 15-20 member cabinet of ministers, or government, are elected by the National Assembly. The prime minister and other ministers cannot concurrently be members of the Assembly. There is a Constitutional Court.

Political parties

Around 20 parties currently operate in Macedonia. The main parties are the Alliance of Macedonia (SM) bloc; the Party for Democratic Prosperity of Albanians in Macedonia (PDPSM); the Internal Macedonian Revolutionary Organization–Democratic Party for Macedonian National Unity (VMRO–DPMNE) and the Democratic Alternative (DA).

The SM is an alliance of three parties, the excommunist Social Democratic Alliance of Macedonia (SDSM), which is led by Prime Minister Branko Crvenovski and President Kiro Gligorov, the centrist Liberal Party (LP); and the leftwing Socialist Party of Macedonia (SPM; estd. 1990). The reform-socialist SDSM was known until 1991 as the League of Communists of Macedonia–Party for Democratic Reform, which, formed in 1943, had been the ruling party in the republic during the communist era. In 1994 the LP merged with the Democratic Party (estd. 1992), to form a new Liberal-Democratic Party (LP), under the leadership, until 1999, of Petar Gosev. In February 1996 the LP was removed from the SDSM-led coalition government.

The PDPSM, formed in 1990, is a predominantly Albanian and Muslim party which, although splitting into two rival factions (moderate and radical) in February 1994, has participated in the SM-led governing coalition, led by Abdurahman Aliti. It seeks to improve conditions for the Albanian minority in Macedonia.

The VMRO–DPMNE and DN are the two main right of center parties. The VMRO–DPMNE is the most staunchly nationalist force in the country. It originated in 1893 as an opponent of the partition of Macedonia and a supporter of the idea of forming a Southern Slav federation of Macedonians, Bulgarians, and Serbs. Refounded in June 1990, it secured the largest number of parliamentary seats in the November–December 1990 general election. However, in the October–November 1992 Sobranje elections it failed to win any seats. It claimed that the results were rigged, but its pro-Bulgarian stance was believed to have lost its support. The DA is a pro-business party, founded by Vasil Tupurkouski.

Latest elections

The most recent parliamentary elections, held on 18 October and 1 November 1998, resulted in the defeat of the ruling SDSM to a right-wing coalition, comprising the VMRO-DPMNE and the DA. The SDSM, with 25% of the vote (down 23% on 1994) won 27 of the 120 National Assembly seats, while the VMRO-DPMNE and DA, with 38% of the vote, won 62 seats. The PDPSM and National Democratic Party (NDP), running together, attracted 19% of the vote to win 25 seats and the LP and SPM won four seats and two seats respectively.

The last presidential election was held on 16 October 1994 and was won by the incumbent Kiro Gligorov, an excommunist backed by the SM, who attracted 69% of the vote, defeating Ljubro Georgievski, a theatre director and leader of the VMRO–DPMNE, with 19% of the vote, while 12% of votes cast were spoilt or invalid. Turnout was 76%, but the election was tainted by allegations of ballot-rigging which led the State Electoral Commission to order a repeat poll in ten constituencies.

Political history

Macedonia was an ancient country of southeast Europe between Illyria, Thrace, and the Aegean Sea, becoming a significant kingdom under Alexander the Great (356–323 BC), who conquered Greece, Egypt, and the Persian Empire. In 148 BC it became a province of the Roman Empire. Macedonia was settled by Slavs in the 6th century, but then suffered a series of conquests, by Bulgars in the 7th century, by Byzantium in 1014, by Serbia in the 14th century, and by the Islamic Ottoman Empire in 1371. Following the First Balkan War of 1912, Macedonia was partitioned, with its Greek-speaking areas being assigned to Greece and the remainder divided between Bulgaria and, the area that constitutes the present republic, Serbia. During World War I, Bulgaria temporarily occupied the region. After the war, Serbian Macedonia became part of the new federal kingdom of Yugoslavia, but, with Serbian being imposed as the official language, demands for greater autonomy continued to be made. During World War II, Macedonia was again occupied by Bulgaria between 1941 and 1944. A separate Macedonian republic was formed in 1945 when Yugoslavia, now under communist control, was reorganized on Soviet federal lines by Marshal Tito. During the postwar period, Macedonia, predominantly agricultural, remained the least developed part of Yugoslavia, but it received effective subsidies from the other richer republics. The Macedonian language and cultural identity was encouraged as a means of countering any lingering pro-Bulgarian sentiment. The republic's Albanian Muslim community also grew progressively, and tension resurfaced between ethnic Macedonians and the Serb-dominated federal government.

After the death of the Yugoslav president, Tito, in 1980, it became increasingly apparent that the federal structure would not hold. Internal pressures and the monumental changes that occurred in the Soviet bloc countries following the advent to the leadership of the USSR of the reformist Mikhail Gorbachev in 1985 stimulated nationalist fervour based on ethnic and religious differences and growing fears of Serb-nationalist expansionism. In 1988, influenced by developments in the neighboring Albanian-dominated autonomous province of Kosovo, in Serbia, there were large nationalist demonstrations by ethnic Albanian students in western Macedonia. In mid-1989 the ruling League of Communists of Macedonia (LCM) agreed to relinquish its dominant role. This paved the way for multiparty elections to the republic's parliament in November–December 1990 in which nationalist parties, notably the Internal Macedonian Revolutionary Organization–Democratic Party for Macedonian National Unity (VMRO–DPMNE), polled strongly. However, the overall result of this contest was inconclusive and an all-party coalition 'Government of Experts', though dominated by the VMRO–DPMNE, was formed in March 1991, with the independent Nikola Kljusev as prime minister. Indirect presidential elections held on 27 January 1991 resulted in Kiro Gligorov (b. 1918), a pragmatic former communist, being chosen by the parliament as the new head of state. The secession of Croatia and Slovenia from the Yugoslav socialist federation in June 1991 gave impetus to Macedonia's drive for full autonomy, and the Macedonian government, formerly supportive of the continuance of the Yugoslav federation but now concerned that a reduced 'rump Yugoslavia' would be dominated by Serbia, held a referendum on independence on 8 September 1991. This poll was boycotted by the republic's substantial ethnic Albanian and Serb minorities, but received overwhelming support from the majority ethnic Macedonian community.

Sovereignty was declared by the Macedonian parliament in September 1991 and independence in January 1992. Swift recognition was accorded by neighboring Bulgaria and also by Turkey, but not by Serbia or by Greece, the latter being concerned that it might imply a territorial claim on its own northern province of Macedonia. In an unofficial referendum, also held in January 1992, Macedonia's Albanian community voted by a 99.9% margin for autonomy, as the 'Republic of Ilirida', with many harbouring the desire to unite with neighboring Albania and Kosovo province in Yugoslavia to form an enlarged 'greater Albania' ruled from Tiranë. Serbia effectively acceded to Macedonia's independence in March 1992 by sanctioning the full withdrawal of federal Yugoslav troops from the republic and in April 1992 the new Yugoslav constitution referred only to the republics of Serbia and Montenegro. Macedonia was eventually admitted into the United Nations (UN) on 8 April 1993 under the designation 'The Former Yugoslav Republic of Macedonia' (FYRM), and a 700-strong multinational UN force was stationed in the republic to help ensure its integrity. In December 1993 it was recognized by the states of the European Union (EU) and in February 1994 by Russia and the United States. However, Greece continued to campaign for the designation 'Skopje' to be used instead and remained concerned that Macedonia's November 1991 constitution contained a reference to speaking for 'all Macedonians' and that its flag carries the Vergina Star of the Macedonian dynasty of Alexander the Great. As a consequence, in February 1994, with a new Papandreou government in power, Greece suspended diplomatic ties and imposed a trade embargo on Macedonia, excepting only foodstuffs and medical supplies. Although alternative trading routes were provided by Bulgaria and Albania, this action caused severe damage to the Macedonian economy which was already crippled by the disruption of trade with Serbia, against whom international sanctions were in force. GDP halved between 1989–94 and inflation exceeding 30% a month by 1994, and the unemployment level was more than 30% from 1993.

In October 1991 the VMRO–DPMNE withdrew from the coalition 'Government of Experts', complaining that it was being excluded from the decision-making process, and in July 1992 Branko Crvenovski became prime minister, heading a new administration dominated by the excommunist Social Democratic Alliance of Macedonia (SDSM), which he led. The administration sought to gradually introduce market-centerd economic reforms and improve relations with neighboring countries. The Crvenovski administration included ministers from the ethnic Albanian-orientated Party of Democratic Prosperity (PDPSM), although two of its senior figures, Husein Haskaj, the deputy defense minister, and Mithad Emini, were arrested in November 1993 and later convicted, in June 1994, for plotting to organize an Albanian-funded 'All-Albanian Army' in the Albanian peopled region of Testovo, situated in northwest Macedonia. Crvenovski continued as prime minister and Gligorov as president after parliamentary and presidential elections, held in October–November 1994, saw the SDSM and its allies gaining a clear victory over the nationalist VMRO–DPMNE, although there were allegations of poll irregularities. As energy shortages worsened, a state of emergency was declared in December 1994.

In September 1995 Greece finally officially recognized Macedonia and restored diplomatic relations after Macedonia agreed to redesign its flag and change two articles of its constitution to remove any suggestion of possible claims on the Greek province of Macedonia. The issue of a permanent name for the country remained unresolved; however, regular trade with Greece, and Serbia (after the November 1995 Dayton Peace Accord on Bosnia), resumed in late 1995, and by 1997 more than 75 countries had recognized Macedonia, with two-thirds using its constitutional name, the 'Republic of Macedonia'. Between September and November 1995 Macedonia was admitted into the Council of Europe, the OSCE, and NATO's 'Partnership for Peace' program, while in July 1995 a 20-year mutual cooperation and security accord was signed with Turkey. In January 1996 full diplomatic relations were established with the EU and in September 1996 bilateral agreements were signed with Yugoslavia, providing for formal mutual recognition as sovereign states and the possibility of forming a free-trade zone linking the two states, in 1999.

In October 1995 President Gligorov was seriously injured in a car bomb assassination attempt in Skopje, which was blamed on nationalist extremists. Stojan Andov, the president of the Sobranje (assembly), and a member of the business-orientated Liberal Party (LP), took over temporarily as acting president, before Gligorov resumed his duties in January 1996. A month later, Prime Minister Crvenkovski expelled the LP from the coalition government, which now comprised three parties, the SDSM, the PDPSM and the Socialist Party of Macedonia (SPM). In April 1996 the opposition VMRO-DPMNE and Democratic Party (DP) collected 200,000 signatures on a petition calling for a referendum for there to be early elections as a result of the government's loss of public support. However, although the constitution provided for the holding of referenda at the request of at least 150,000 citizens, the Sobranje ruled that a referendum on this issue was unconstitutional. During 1997–98 there was increasing political instability, with a campaign by ethnic Albanians that an Albanian-language university established at Tetovo in 1994 be legitimized, and with civil conflict in neighboring Albania and Kosovo, in Yugoslavia. This persuaded the UN Security Council to maintain the strength of the UN Preventative Deployment Force in Macedonia (UNPREDEP) at its current level of 1,100 troops. The government also came under attack for the rising level of organized crime and corruption, and for the collapse of 'pyramid' savings schemes, which resulted in at least 30,000 people losing US$60 million and led, in May 1997, to large anti-government protest rallies in Skopje, organized by the opposition VMRO-DPMNE. From 1997 the country experienced modest economic growth and the annual inflation rate was down to 3%. However, the unemployment level remained stuck at 30% and the pace of privatization remained slow, while regional instability deterred foreign inward investment and forced a devaluation of the currency in mid-1997. The nationalist VMRO-DPMNE polled strongly in new legislative elections, held in October 1998.

In November 1998 the ruling SDSM lost power, after a general election, to a right-wing coalition, comprising the nationalist VMRO-DPMNE and the pro-business Democratic Alternative (DA), with the VMRO-DPMNE leader, Ljubco Georgievski, as prime minister. The radical, ethnic Albanian National Democratic Party (NDP), led by Arben Xhaferi, also joined the governing coalition. The new prime minister pledged to fight against corruption and to promote private enterprise and inward foreign investment. However, during early 1999 the government had to cope with the mounting crisis over ethnic Albanian-peopled Kosovo, in neighbouring Yugoslavia. In December 1998 a 1,700-strong and French-led NATO 'extraction force' was deployed in Macedonia to assist civilian monitors operating in Kosovo. However, in March 1999 the six-year long mission of UNPREDEP was ended, after China used its UN veto to punish Macedonia for having recently extended diplomatic recognition to Taiwan.

MOLDOVA

Republic of Moldova
Republica Moldoveneasca

Capital: Chisinau (formerly Kishinev)

Social and economic data

Area: 33,700 sq km/13,012 sq miles
Population: 4,400,000*
Pop. density per sq km/sq mi: 131/338*
Urban population: 48%**
Literacy rate: 96%**
GDP: $4,000 million*; per-capita GDP: $910*
Government defense spending (% of GDP): 3.7%*
Currency: leu
Economy type: low income
Labor force in agriculture: 32%**
Unemployment rate: 1.0%*
* 1995.
** 1992.

Head of state (executive)

President Petru Lucinschi, since 1997

Head of government

Prime Minister Ion Sturza, since 1999

Ethnic composition

Sixty-five per cent of the population is of Moldovan (Romanian) ethnic stock, 14% Ukrainian, 13% ethnic Russian, 4% Gagauzi, 2% Bulgarian, and 2% Jewish. Romanian (Moldovan), a Romance language written in the Latin script, has been the official language since 1989. Russian and Turkish, spoken by the Gagauz, are minority languages.

Religions

The population is predominantly Christian, adhering principally to the Russian Eastern Orthodox Church. Despite their Turkish origins, the Gagauz also adhere to Orthodox Christianity. There is a small Jewish minority.

Political features

State type: emergent democratic
Date of state formation: 1991
Political structure: unitary
Executive: limited presidential
Assembly: one-chamber
Party structure: multiparty
Human rights rating: N/A
International affiliations: BSECZ, CIS, COE, IBRD, IMF, NACC, OSCE, PFP, UN

Local and regional government

The country comprises 40 districts and ten cities for the purposes of local government. The Gagauz minority, concentrated around Komrat in southwestern Moldova, concerned at growing nationalism among the country's Romanian majority, have attempted to establish a separate 'Republic of Gagauzia' since 1990. Their leader currently has a seat in the Moldova cabinet. Ethnic Russians, who dominate the region east of the Dnestr (Dnestrsa) river in the far east of the country, have also sought to establish their own separate 'Dnestr Soviet Republic', with its capital at Tiraspol. Both the Gagauz and the Dnestr regions have been granted special autonomous status by the August 1994 constitution.

Political system

Under the terms of the August 1994 constitution, Moldova is a 'presidential, parliamentary republic'. The constitution seeks to enshrine political pluralism and free ethnic and linguistic expression. It also bars the stationing of foreign troops on Moldovan soil, establishing 'permanent neutrality' for the state, and grants special autonomous status to the Gagauz and Dnestr regions. The country has had an executive presidency since 1991, with decree powers granted in 1993 and the authority to appoint and dismiss cabinet ministers. The state president is directly elected, for a four-year term, through the second ballot majoritarian system, and appoints a prime minister and cabinet, or Council of Ministers, of around 20 members. The president is allowed to participate in parliamentary proceedings and presides over government meetings. The president is commander in chief of the armed forces, must be at least 35 years old, and is restricted to two consecutive terms. The legislature, the Moldovan Parliament (Parlamentul), has 104 members who are directly elected by proportional representation for four-year terms. The parliament holds two ordinary sessions a year and has the authority to remove the president, by a two-thirds majority vote, if a criminal or constitutional offence has been committed. This removal is subject to confirmation by the Supreme Court, for a criminal offence, or a national referendum, for a constitutional offence. There is a six-member Constitutional Court and revision of the constitution may be initiated by the president, the government, one-third of parliamentary deputies, or a petition signed by at least 200,000 citizens drawn from at least half the country's districts and municipalities.

Political parties

There are around 30 political parties in Moldova, including the Dnestr and Gagauz regions. Fifteen parties contested the March 1998 parliamentary elections and four parties and alliances secured significant levels of representation: the Moldovan Communist Party (MCP); the Democratic Convention of Moldova (DCM); the Movement for a Democratic and Prosperous Moldova (MDPM); and the Moldovan Party of Democratic Forces (MPDF).

The MCP was banned in August 1991, but was allowed to re-register in late 1994. It is led by Vladimir Voronin. It is more traditionalist than the Socialist Party (SP), which was formed as a reform-communist successor to the MCP. Both the MCP and SP favor closer ties with Russia.

The DCM is an alliance of rightwing parties which was formed in June 1997 to contest the 1998 elections. Its most important constituent party is the centrist Party of Revival and Accord of Moldova (PRAM), which was formed in August 1995 by the then president, Mircea Snegur, and 11 breakaway deputies from the then ruling center-left nationalist Agrarian Democratic Party (ADP). The ADP was formed in 1991 by moderates from the MCP and the nationalist Moldovan Popular Front (MPF: estd. 1989). The other key element is the center-right Christian Democratic Popular Front (CDPF), which was formed in 1992 from the MPF.

The centrist MDPM was formed in February 1997 to support President Lucinschi and favors market-centerd economic reform but also closer ties with Russia.

The MPDF, formed in 1995 and led by Valeriu Matei, is also centrist and it includes the Congress of Intellectuals, which was formed in 1993 by former MPF members and which favors union with Romania. In the breakaway Dnestr Republic the dominant party is the socialist Union of Patriotic Forces. Another party of some significance is the Gagauz Halky (Gagauz People's Movement), which represents the 150,000-strong Gagauz minority community and advocates Gagauz separatism.

Political leaders since 1970*

1990–97 Mircea Snegur (ex-communist independent/PRAM), 1997– Petru Lucinschi (communist independent/MDPM)

* President.

Latest elections

The most recent parliamentary elections were held on 22 March 1998 and produced a hung parliament, with four parties and alliances each securing between 9% and 30% of the vote and winning all but three of the 104 Parlamentul seats. The MCP won 30% of the vote and 40 seats, the DCM 19% and 26 seats, the MDPM 18% and 24 seats and the MDPF 9% and 11 seats. The remaining 11 parties which contested the election, including the ADP which had secured 43% of the vote and won 86 seats in February 1994, and the PS, failed to achieve the minimum of 4% of the national vote needed to secure representation. Three independents, out of 67 independent candidates, were elected. Turnout was 67%, although, as in the previous election, the poll was boycotted in the separatist Dnestr region.

The last presidential election was held on 17 November and 1 December 1996 and resulted in defeat, on the second ballot, for the incumbent Mircea Snegur. Nine candidates contested the first ballot, with the most popular five being: Snegur, with 39% of the vote; Petru Lucinschi, the ADP-backed chairperson of the Parlamentul, 28%; Vladimir Voronin, leader of the MCP, 10%; Andrei Sangheli, the prime minister, 9%; and Valeriu Matei, leader of the MPDF, 9%. In the run-off second ballot, with turnout climbing to 72%, Lucinschi turned the tables and finished by winning 54% of the vote to 46% for Snegur.

Political history

Formerly a principality in Eastern Europe, occupying an area divided today between the republic of Moldova and modern Romania, the region was independent from the 14th to the 16th century, when it became part of the Ottoman Empire. Its eastern part, Bessarabia, was ruled by Russia between 1812 and 1917, when it declared its independence, but was transferred to Romania in 1918. After Nazi Germany recognized the USSR's interest, in the secret Molotov–Ribbentrop pact of August 1939, Romania was forced to cede Bessarabia in June 1940 and it was joined with part of the Soviet/Ukrainian-controlled Autonomous Moldavian Republic to form the Moldavian Socialist Republic in August 1940. Before and after World War II, the republic was brutally 'sovietized'. The intelligentsia and *kulak* (rich peasant farmer) communities were liquidated or deported to Central Asia, agriculture was collectivized, private enterprises were taken over by the state, and ethnic Russians and Ukrainians were settled in the republic. Previously predominantly agricultural, Moldova witnessed significant urban and industrial growth from the 1950s.

Encouraged by the *glasnost* (political openness) instituted by Mikhail Gorbachev, who became the Soviet Union's new leader in 1985, and the Baltics' independence movement, there was an upsurge in Moldovian nationalism during the late 1980s. This took the form, initially, of a campaign for language reform and for reversion from the Cyrillic to the Latin alphabet. In 1988 a Moldavian Movement in Support of *perestroika* (economic restructuring) was formed and in May 1989, after large demonstrations in Chisinau, the Moldavian Popular Front (MPF) was established. In August 1989 the MPF persuaded the republic's parliament (Supreme Soviet) to make Romanian the state language and reinstate the Latin script. This provoked demonstrations and strikes by the republic's Russian speakers and led the 150,000-strong, Turkish-speaking but Orthodox Christian, Gagauz minority, concentrated in the southwest, to campaign for autonomy.

In November 1989, after MPF radicals had staged a petrol bomb assault on the interior ministry headquarters in Chisinau, the conservative leader of the Moldavian Communist Party (MCP), Semyon Grossu, was dismissed and replaced by the more conciliatory and reformist Petru Lucinschi. In the wake of the Chisinau riots, with inter-ethnic strife worsening, a temporary state of emergency was imposed and a ban placed on public meetings. This restricted campaigning for the February 1990 Supreme Soviet elections. Nevertheless, the MPF polled strongly and, as a result, 40% of the deputies returned were aligned to the MPF and a further 30% were sympathetic to its aims. In April 1990 the new Supreme Soviet elected Mircea Snegur (b. 1940), a reform-nationalist MCP member who was supported by the MPF, as its chairperson and effective head of state, and in May 1990 Mircea Druc, an MPF reform-economist, became prime minister.

After this election and the leadership changes of April–May 1990, the movement towards independence gathered momentum. A 'sovereignty' declaration was made by the Supreme Soviet in June 1990 and a republican guard was established in November 1990. The republic decided to boycott the March 1991 USSR referendum on the preservation of the Union because of concern that it might worsen inter-ethnic tensions. However, 650,000 people, predominantly ethnic Russians, defied the official boycott and voted overwhelmingly for the Union. During the August 1991 attempted anti-Gorbachev coup in Moscow by communist hardliners, which was denounced by President Snegur but supported by the Dnestr and Gagauz regions, there were large prodemocracy demonstrations in Chisinau. After the coup, MCP activity was banned in workplaces and on 27 August 1991 the republic formally declared its independence. Immediate recognition was accorded by Romania. However, the highly industrialized, predominantly ethnic Russian-peopled Dnestr region in the east, centerd around Tiraspol and with a population of 700,000, which had been part of Ukraine until 1940, declared its own independence from Moldova on 2 September 1991 and adopted a separate constitution. The declaration and a subsequent plebiscite on independence, held in December 1991, were rejected by Moldova.

Moldova joined the Commonwealth of Independent States (CIS) on its inception on 21 December 1991, but did not sign its January 1993 charter on closer political and economic integration. It was admitted into the Conference on Security and Cooperation in Europe (CSCE, later the OSCE) in January 1992, and became a member of the United Nations (UN) in March 1992. However, following pro-unification border rallies, the Moldovan and Romanian presidents met in January 1992 to discuss the possibility of union. Snegur, who was directly elected state president in December 1991 in an unopposed contest, favored a gradual approach towards unification with Romania.

In January 1992, as armed conflict in the secessionist Trans-Dnestr escalated, having broken out in December 1991, a state of emergency was imposed by President Snegur. By June 1992 the fighting between the Dnestr region's Slav militia and the Moldovan army had claimed 700 lives and had led to 50,000 refugees fleeing to Ukraine. It was alleged that the Dnestr militia received Russian nationalist support. The conflict was ended in July 1992 by the signing of a Moldovan – Russian peace agreement. This provided for the continued stationing of Russian 14th Army troops in the region to help maintain the peace and grant of 'special status' within Moldova to the area. In effect, the region had broken away from Moldova and, controversially, Lieutenant General Alexander Lebed, the Russian nationalist commander of the 14th Army, was later elected to the Dnestr Supreme Soviet in September 1993. Lebed was later dismissed from the Russian army, by President Yeltsin, in June 1995.

In July 1992 the MPF-dominated government fell as a result of lack of popular support for its policy of seeking reintegration into Romania and the rapidly deteriorating performance of the economy as a transition was sought from a command to a market economy. In 1991 real GDP fell by 12% and during the first half of 1992, as a result of the Trans-Dnestr conflict and a devastating drought, a further 28% decline was registered. Moldova was particularly dependent on Russia for fuel supplies and Ukraine for access to the Black Sea. Andrei Sangheli, the former agriculture minister, took over as prime minister, heading a 'government of national accord' formed in July 1992, whose principal support was drawn from the Agrarian Democratic Party (ADP) and the Conciliation group of ethnic Russian deputies.

The new administration concentrated on attempting to improve the economy, through beginning privatization, initially in the service sector, in October 1993, and introducing a new currency, the leu, in November 1993 to replace the Russian rouble. This program began to have some effect in slowing the decline in GDP and reducing the annual inflation rate from 1,800% in 1993 to 30% in 1995. In addition, from 1993, President Snegur, realizing that pro-Romanian parties were becoming increasingly unpopular, relaxed his earlier policy of seeking closer ties with Romania and concentrated, instead, on improving relations with Russia, seeking full membership of the CIS, which was achieved in April 1994, and strengthening Moldovan statehood. This policy proved electorally popular, with the pro-Russian ADP and Socialist Party (SP) polling strongly in the February 1994 parliamentary elections, attracting 65% of the national vote, while the pro-Romanian Peasants and Intellectuals bloc and Christian Democratic Popular Front (CDPF), the successor to the MPF, won less than 17% support. Underlining this public mood, a national referendum on continued independence from Romania and Russia, which was held on 6 March 1994, won 95% approval, based on a turnout of 75%. In August 1994 Russia agreed to fully withdraw its 14th Army troops, still stationed in the Dnestr region and numbering 15,000, by 1997, although the people of the Dnestr region opposed this decision. Moldova acceded to the Council of Europe in July 1995.

In December 1995 a new two-chamber legislature was elected in the Trans-Dnestr region, although, at the same time, voters in the region overwhelmingly approved illegal referenda on a new 'independence constitution' and for the region to join the CIS (which the CIS rejected). The withdrawal of Russian 14th Army troops proceeded broadly as planned between 1994–97, but in 1998 several thousand still remained, pending a final political settlement. In May 1997 a memorandum of understanding was agreed, normalizing relations 'as part of a single state', but the status of the Dnestr region was still not precisely defined. In contrast, in the special autonomous region of Gagauzia a definitive settlement was agreed, in December 1994. Gagauz was made one of three official languages in the region, along with Moldovan and Russian, and an elected 35-seat regional assembly ('halk toplusu') was established, and an elected 'bashkan' (president) who was given a seat in the Moldovan Council of Ministers. Gheorghe Tabunshchik, of the MPC, was elected 'bashkan' in June 1995.

In June 1995 President Snegur, who had joined the ADP after its electoral victory in February 1994, resigned his membership in protest against the ADP-dominated parliament rejecting a proposal to establish Romanian as the official state language. With the support of 11 defectors from the ADP, in August 1995 he formed the centrist Party of Revival and Accord of Moldova (PRAM). In March 1996 President Snegur attempted to dismiss the defense minister, Pavel Creanga, charging him with 'incompetence', but the move was judged unconstitutional by the Constitutional Court, as he had acted without the prime minister's consent. This persuaded Snegur to base his campaign for re-election as president, in November – December 1996, on the proposal that presidential powers should be increased. However, Snegur was defeated in the run-off round by Petru Lucinschi, the chairperson of Parliament since 1993, ex-leader of the MCP and a former high-ranking member of the Communist Party of the Soviet Union (CPSU), who had received backing from the ADP in this election. Lucinschi advocated closer ties with Russia and the CIS.

On becoming president in January 1997, Lucinschi appointed Ion Ciubuc, an independent economist who was chairperson of the State Auditing Chamber, as prime minister. In June 1997, the center-right PRAM and the CDPF came together to form a new electoral alliance, the Democratic Convention of Moldova (DCM). However, the March 1998 elections produced a surprise in that support for the ADP collapsed while the MCP won the largest share, 30%, of the vote, finishing with 40 of the 104 Parlamentul seats. Nevertheless, lacking an overall majority, the MCP were unable to form a government and Ion Ciubuc remained as prime minister, putting together a Movement for a Democratic and Prosperous Moldova (MDPM), DCM and Moldovan Party of Democratic Forces (MPDF) centrist coalition administration. It pledged to continue with market-centerd reforms, including privatization, which were beginning to bear fruit, with GDP at last beginning to increase, modestly, in 1997.

In February 1999 prime minister Ciubuc, cited unacceptable divisions within the ruling coalition. He was replaced, in March 1999, by Ion Sturza, the former deputy prime minister and economics minister, drawn from the MDPM, who led a coalition comprising the MDPM, MPDF, and PRAM. In May 1999 a non-binding referendum on the issue of strengthening the powers of the president was held. Although 60% supported the proposed changes, turnout, at 56%, was 4% short of the required level for the result to be valid.

POLAND

Republic of Poland
Polska Rzeczpospolita

Capital: Warsaw (Warszawa)

Social and economic data

Area: 312,683 sq km/120,728 sq miles
Population: 38,643,000*
Pop. density per sq km/sq mi: 124/320*
Urban population: 63%**
Literacy rate: 99%**

GDP: $107,830 million*; per-capita GDP: $2,790*
Government defense spending (% of GDP): 2.5%*
Currency: new zloty
Economy type: middle income
Labor force in agriculture: 25%**
Unemployment rate: 13.1%*
* 1995.
** 1992.

Head of state (executive)

President Alexander Kwasniewski, since 1995

Head of government

Prime Minister Jerzy Buzek, since 1997

Ethnic composition

Ninety-eight per cent of the population are ethnic Poles, a Western-Slav race. There are also small ethnic German, Ukrainian, and Belarussian minorities. The rights of the 500,000-strong German minority in Poland to their own culture, language, and religion have been recognized in a treaty of good neighborliness and friendly cooperation with Germany, which also confirms the Oder – Neisse border. The official language is Polish.

Religions

Ninety-five per cent of the population adheres to the Roman Catholic faith; 2%, or 870,000, to the Polish Autocephalous Orthodox Church; and 100,000 to Protestant denominations, mainly the Evangelical Augsburg Church. The Roman Catholic Church is an influential institution with a buoyant membership. It is closely connected with the idea of Polish nationhood and played an important role, particularly during the primacy of Cardinal Stefan Wyszynski, in the campaign for human rights. The Catholic Church was granted full legal status in May 1989.

Political features

State type: emergent democratic
Date of state formation: 1918
Political structure: unitary
Executive: dual
Assembly: one-chamber
Party structure: multiparty
Human rights rating: 83%
International affiliations: CEFTA, CERN, COBSS, COE, IAEA, IBRD, IMF, NACC, NAM (guest), NATO, OECD, OSCE, PFP, UN, VG, WEU (associate partner), WTO

Local and regional government

Before 1999 the country was divided into 49 provinces (*voivodships*) administered by appointed governors and 2,348 elected and autonomous local councils. Since 1999 the number of provinces has been reduced to 16, and a second local government tier of 300 districts (*powiats*) has been created. These local government bodies oversee half of the country's tax revenues.

Political system

Under the new constitution, which came into force in October 1997 and replaced the interim 'small constitution' of December 1992, Poland has a dual – presidential and parliamentary – executive system. Formerly the system was limited presidential, but the 1997 constitution increased the powers of parliament. The executive president is directly elected for a maximum of two consecutive five-year terms in a two-round majority contest. The president, who must be at least 35 years old, has responsibility for military, foreign, and police affairs and has the authority to appoint the prime minister, who commands a majority in the Sejm, call elections to parliament, call referenda, appoint senior public officials, and impose martial law.

There is a two-chamber legislature, the National Assembly (Zgromadzenie Narodowe), comprising a 460-member lower assembly, the Sejm (parliament), and a 100-member upper chamber, the Senate (Senat). Deputies are elected to the Sejm for four-year terms by means of proportional representation in free multiparty contests. Three hundred and ninety-one Sejm deputies are elected from 37 multimember electoral districts and 69 through national party lists. Under the terms of electoral regulations adopted in May 1993, parties (except national minority groups) must gain 5% of the national vote to qualify for seats (with alliances needing at least 8%), and bonus seats, from the national list, are awarded to parties which attract more than 7% support. The Senate is elected also for four years, on a provincial basis, each province returning two senators, except Warsaw and Katowice, which elect three. The minimum ages for membership are 21 years for the Sejm and 30 years for the Senate. The Sejm passes bills, adopts the state budget and economic plan, and appoints an executive council of ministers of around 20 members, headed by a chairperson, or prime minister. The Senate has the power of veto in specified areas, which can be overridden by an absolute majority Sejm vote, in which at least half the deputies participate. The prime minister administers with a cabinet, or council of ministers. The Sejm may remove the council of ministers through passing a 'no confidence' motion which attracts support from at least half the Sejm's members and specifies the name of a candidate for prime minister. The president can be removed by the National Assembly, if an indictment (impeachment) vote is supported by two-thirds of the statutory members. Referenda may be called by the president, the government, parliament, and by a group of at least 100,000 citizens. A Constitutional Tribunal adjudicates in constitutional disputes.

Political parties

Since the collapse of communism, numerous political parties have been formed, but most have been short-lived and able to attract only small shares of the national vote. In the October 1991 general election, for example, 29 parties secured representation in the Sejm, but no single party was able to win more than 12% of the vote. The 1993 general elections, encouraged by changes to the electoral law (see *Political system* above) saw a reduction in the number of parties securing representation to seven, but again no party polled more than 20% of the vote. The 1997 election saw a continuation of this trend, with six parties securing representation and two parties/alliances winning nearly 80% of the seats. Changes in party law have also served to reduce the number of parties. Prior to 1997 parties were not required to file for registration and in 1996 there were around 360 parties operating. They have since been required to register, by presenting a list of 1,000 supporting signatures, and by 1998 there were around 60 registered parties.

Currently, the seven most important parties, which

attracted more than 2% national support in the September 1997 general election, are: the Democratic Left Alliance (Sojusz Lewicy Demokratycznej: SLD); the Polish Peasant Party (PSL); the Freedom Union (UW); the Labor Union (UP); the Solidarity Election Alliance (Akcja Wyborcza Solidarnosc: AWS); the Movement for the Reconstruction of Poland (ROP); and the National Pensioners' Party (KPEiR).

The 60,000-member SLD was formed in 1990, as the Social Democracy Party, to be the reform-socialist successor to the Polish United Workers' Party (Polska Zjednoczona Partia Rabotnicza: PZPR), the dominant party in Poland until 1989. The SLD, led by the young and charismatic Alexander Kwasniewski and Leszek Miller, favors the building of a market economy, but seeks to ensure that its social costs to poorer sections of society are alleviated. It also proposes abolition of the Senate. The preceding PZPR was heir to the Communist Workers' Party of Poland (KPRP) which was founded in 1918 by Marxist wings of the nationalist Polish Socialist Party (PPS), which dated back to 1892 (and was later illegally revived in 1987), and the internationalist Social Democracy of the Kingdom of Lithuania and Poland Party (SDKPiL), which was established as long ago as 1895. The KPRP later changed its name to the Communist Party of Poland (KPP) in 1925, but was forced to operate underground when proscribed by the Piłsudski regime. Because of its close Soviet links, it enjoyed little domestic support, membership standing at barely 10,000, and it was dissolved by Stalin in 1938. Four years later the pro-Moscow Polish Workers' Party (PPR) was established as a successor body. It was divided into two wings, a Moscow-based Stalinist faction, led by Boleslaw Bierut, and a 'native' anti-German resistance wing led by party first secretary, Władysław Gomułka. Gomułka was ousted by Bierut as leader in 1948 and the party was soon afterwards merged with the PPS to form the PZPR. In 1987 membership of the PZPR stood at 2.13 million, or 5.7% of the total population.

The 200,000-member center-left rural sector-orientated PSL, led by Jaroslav Kalinowski, was formed in 1990 to replace the United Peasants' Party (ZSL), which, along with the intelligentsia-orientated Democratic Party (SD; estd. 1939), had been permitted to operate during the communist period under the umbrella of the PZPR-led Patriotic Movement for National Rebirth (PRON) mass organization. The ZSL was established in 1948 as a successor to the earlier peasant nationalist movement, the Polish People's Party.

The 12,500-member UW, led since April 1995 by Leszek Balcerowicz, a former finance minister, was formed in April 1994 by Tadeusz Mazowiecki through the merger of Mazowiecki's Democratic Union (DU) and the Liberal Democratic Congress (KLD; estd. 1988). Both former parties had their roots in the Solidarity free trade union movement, the DU being formed in 1991 as a centrist successor to the Citizens' Movement-Democratic Action (ROAD), formed in 1990. The left wing Labor Union (UP), known formerly as Labor Solidarity, also had its roots in Solidarity, along with the Non-Party Bloc in Support of Reforms (BBWR), a Christian Democratic right-of-center alliance formed in 1993 by Lech Wałęsa and backed by the Catholic Church. Two other parties which had their roots in Solidarity are the center-right Center Alliance (CA; estd. 1990) and the Peasant Alliance (PL), which united in May 1994 with three other rightwing bodies, including the Christian National Union (CNU; estd. 1989), to form the Covenant for Poland 'confederation'.

The AWS was formed in June 1996 by Marian Krzaklewski, leader of the Solidarity trade union, to bring together 36 right-of-center, populist, nationalist, and centrist Christian democratic parties to campaign against the 1997 constitution and to contest the 1998 general election as a bloc. It incorporates such bodies as the CA, CNU and also the rightwing Patriotic Camp (estd. 1996), a grouping which includes the BBWR, ledby Leszek Zielinski, and the 35,000-member Confederation for an Independent Poland (KPN; estd. 1979).

The ROP is a rightwing patriotic party formed by Jan Olszewski, the prime minister between 1991–92, who used to be a member of the CA. It was superseded in 1998 by a new broader grouping, the Patriotic Movement for the Fatherland.

The KPEiR, led by Zenon Zuminski, promotes the interests of older voters.

In October 1997, Lech Wałęsa, the former president, formed a new political party, the right-of-center Christian Democratic Party of the Third Republic.

Political leaders since 1970

1970–80 Edward Gierek (PZPR)*, 1980–81 Stanislaw Kania (PZPR)*, 1981–90 General Wojciech Jaruzelski (PZPR)*, 1990–95 Lech Wałęsa (Solidarity/independent)** 1995– Alexander Kwasniewski (SLD)**, 1997– Jerzy Buzek (AWS)***

* Communist Party leaders.

** Democratic executive president.

*** Prime minister.

Latest elections

The most recent Sejm and Senate elections were held on 21 September 1997 and saw a resurgence in support for the center-right Solidarity movement, in the form of the AWS, and a significant fall in support for the left-of-center agrarian PSL. In the Sejm elections, the AWS alliance of right and center parties attracted 34% of the vote and won 201 of the 460 seats. The liberal UW, with 13% of the vote, won 60 seats. The left-of-center SLD, fighting the election as a Democratic Left Alliance, in conjunction with the All Poland Trade Unions Alliance, finished in second place, with 27% of the vote (up 7% on September 1993) and 164 seats; but its erstwhile ally the PSL slumped to 7% of the vote (down 8%) and 27 seats. Only one other party surmounted the 5% threshold for representation, the rightwing ROP, which, with 5.6% of the vote, secured six seats. The other two Sejm seats were filled by representatives of the German Minority of Lower Silesia party. Voter turnout was 48% (down 4%). In the concurrent Senate elections, the AWS secured a slim majority, 51, of the 100 seats, while the SLD won 28 seats, the UW 8, the ROP 5, the PSL 5, and independents 5.

The last direct presidential elections were held on 5 and 19 November 1995. Lech Wałęsa won 48% in the second round vote, Alexander Kwasniewski, the leader of the reformed communists, 52%. In the first round, Kwasniewski won 35% of the vote, Wałęsa 33%, Jacek Kuron, a former dissident representing the UW, 9%, Jan Olszewski, of the ROP, 7%, and Waldemar Pawlak, of the PSL, 4%. There were 10 other candidates in the first round. Turnout was around 65%.

Political history

1. 1386–1989

During the medieval period, particularly from the 14th century, Poland was an influential Central European power under its own Jagellion dynasty, which ruled between 1386 and 1572. When it was united with Lithuania in 1569, Poland became the largest country in Europe. Defeat in the mid-17th century in a war against Russia, Sweden, and Brandenburg brought about its decline and a century later the country was partitioned between Russia, ruling the east, Prussia, the west, and Austria, the south-center, where a measure of autonomy was granted. There were uprisings in 1830 and 1863 against the repressive Russian regime, leaving behind a legacy of deep antipathy.

At the close of World War I, in November 1918, a fully independent Polish republic was established. Marshal Józef Piłsudski (1867–1935), the founder of the PPS, was elected the country's first president and, taking advantage of upheavals in the Soviet Union, he proceeded to launch an advance into Lithuania and the Ukraine which reached stalemate in 1921. Politically, the immediate post independence years were characterized by instability, with 14 multiparty coalition governments holding power between 1918 and 1926. Marshal Piłsudski then seized complete power in a coup in May 1926 and proceeded to govern in an increasingly autocratic manner until his death in 1935. The country remained backward, only pockets of industrialism existing at Lodsz and in Upper Silesia, with, in 1930, 60% of the total population remaining dependent upon agricultural activities.

A military regime, under the leadership of Smigly-Rydz, remained in power until the German invasion of September 1939. Western Poland was immediately incorporated into the Nazi Reich, while the remainder of the country, except for a brief Soviet occupation of East Poland between 1940 and 1941, was treated as a colony and endured tremendous suffering. A third of the educated elite were liquidated, while, in all, 6 million Poles lost their lives – half of them Jews, slaughtered in concentration camps. By the middle of 1944, parts of eastern Poland had been liberated by Soviet Red Army forces, allied with Polish troops commanded by General Rola-Zymierski, and a communist-dominated multiparty coalition government was set up at Lublin. In March 1945 the remaining German forces were driven out of the country.

The Soviet Union immediately recognized the 'Lublin coalition' as the Provisional Government of all Poland, but this was challenged by the Polish exile government, based in London and backed by the Western Allies. It was headed, as prime minister, by the peasant leader Stanislaw Mikolajcyk (1901–67). Following the Yalta Conference, in February 1945, it was agreed to set up a joint government, but this was dominated by the Lublin coalition and PPR, which secured effective control of the security police and armed forces. Their position was further strengthened when, at the manipulated Sejm elections of January 1947, the Lublin coalition's list of candidates, the 'Democratic Bloc', secured 80% of the votes and 88% of the 444 seats. A month later, a 'People's Republic' was proclaimed, with the PPR predominant, and in October 1947 Mikolajcyk fled to the West.

The new regime was faced with immediate resettlement problems as a result of the drastic 240-kilometre westward shift of the borders of the Polish state engineered at the Potsdam Conference in July 1945. Under the terms of this agreement, Poland's eastern frontier was set at the 1921 Curzon Line, with 180,000 square kilometres in the east, almost half of 'old Poland', being lost to the Soviet Union, while 100,000 square kilometres of former German territories along the line of the Oder and Neisse rivers were added from the west.

A Soviet-style one-party constitution was adopted in July 1952 and a harsh Stalinist form of rule instituted by Boleslaw Bierut, the PZPR leader between 1948 and 1956. This involved rural collectivization and the persecution of Catholic Church opponents, including the arrest, in 1953, of Cardinal Wyszynski (1901–81). During this period, Poland also joined Comecon, in 1949, and the Warsaw Pact, in 1955, and remained under close Soviet supervision, with the USSR's Marshal Konstantin Rokossovsky serving as minister for war between 1949 and 1956.

In June 1956 serious strikes and riots, resulting in 53 deaths, erupted in Poznan in opposition to Soviet exploitation and food shortages. This prompted the reinstatement of the more pragmatic, 'nativist', Władysław Gomułka (1905–82) as PZPR first secretary and the introduction of a series of moderate reforms, involving, most importantly, the reintroduction of private farming (by the mid-1980s 85% of Poland's cropped area was privately tilled), the release of Cardinal Stefan Wyszynski, and toleration of Catholicism.

Sudden food price rises, in December 1970, caused a further outbreak of strikes and rioting in Gdansk, Gdynia, and Szczecin. These demonstrations had to be forcibly suppressed. This led to Gomułka's replacement as PZPR leader by the Silesia party boss and leader of the party's technocratic faction, Edward Gierek (b. 1913), who proceeded to institute a new economic reform program directed towards achieving a rapid rise in living standards and production of consumer goods. The country became heavily indebted, however, to foreign creditors and further strikes and demonstrations took place at Radom and Ursus, in June 1976, on the announcement of a proposal to raise food prices.

Opposition to the Gierek regime, which was accused of gross corruption, mounted in 1979, following a visit paid to his homeland by the recently elected Pope John Paul II (b. 1920), the former Cardinal Wojtyla of Kraków. Strikes commenced in Warsaw in June 1980, following a poor harvest and meat price rises, and rapidly spread across the country. The government attempted initially to appease workers by entering into pay negotiations with unofficial strike committees, but, at the Gdansk shipyards, demands emerged for permission to form free independent trade unions. The government conceded this request and recognized the right to strike, resulting in the formation, in August 1980, in Gdansk, of the Solidarnosc (Solidarity) union, under the leadership of the electrician, Lech Wałęsa (b. 1943).

In September 1980, the ailing Gierek was replaced as PZPR first secretary by Stanislaw Kania, but the unrest continued as the 10-million-member Solidarity campaigned for a five-day working week and a rural Solidarity was established. Meanwhile, inside the PZPR, rank and file pressure began to grow for greater democratization, and a quarter of the party's members actually joined Solidarity. With mounting food shortages and PZPR control slipping, Kania was replaced as PZPR leader by the joint prime minister and defense minister, General Wojciech Jaruzelski (b. 1927), in October 1981.

With Soviet military activities taking place on Poland's borders, martial law was imposed on 13 December 1981. Trade union activity was banned, the leaders of Solidarnosc arrested, a night curfew imposed, and a Military Council of National Salvation established, headed by Jaruzelski. Five months of severe repression ensued, resulting in 15 deaths and 10,000 arrests. The actions of the Polish government were condemned by the United States administration and economic sanctions were imposed.

In June 1982 curfew restrictions were eased, prompting further serious rioting in August. Three months later, Lech Wałęsa was released and in December 1982 martial law was suspended, and then formally lifted in July 1983. Pope John Paul II visited Poland in June 1983 and called for conciliation. The authorities responded in July by dissolving the Military Council and granting an amnesty to political prisoners and activists. This amnesty was broadened in July 1984, with the release of 35,000 prisoners and detainees on the 40th anniversary of the People's Republic, prompting the US government to relax its economic sanctions. The residual sanctions were later fully removed, in February 1987.

The Jaruzelski administration pursued pragmatic reform, including liberalization of the electoral system. The political atmosphere remained tense, however, and was strained by the murder of Father Jerzy Popieluszko (1947–84), a pro-Solidarity priest, by members of the security forces in October 1984, by the continued ban on Solidarity and by a threat, which was eventually withdrawn in February 1986, to try Lech Wałęsa for slandering state electoral officials when disputing the October 1985 Sejm turnout figures. Economic conditions and farm output slowly improved, but Poland's foreign debt remained huge. During 1988 the nation's shipyards, coalmines, ports, and steelworks were paralysed by a wave of Solidarnosc-led strikes for higher wages to offset the effect of recent price rises. With its economic strategy in tatters, the government of Prime Minister Zbigniew Messner resigned, being replaced in December 1988 by a new administration headed by the reformist communist Mieczyslaw Rakowski, and the PZPR's Politburo was infused with a new clutch of technocrats.

After six weeks of PZPR – Solidarity – church negotiations, an historic accord was reached in April 1989 under whose terms Solidarity was relegalized, the formation of opposition political associations was tolerated, legal rights were conferred on the Catholic Church, the state's media monopoly was lifted, and a new 'socialist pluralist' constitution was drafted. In the subsequent National Assembly elections, held in June 1989, Solidarity captured all but one of the Sejm and Senate seats for which they were entitled to contest: 55% of the Sejm's seats had been reserved for contests between candidates from the Patriotic Movement for National Rebirth (PRON), the PZPR broad front organization; 10% for nationalist dignitaries; and the remaining 161 (35%) for non-PRON candidates. Jaruzelski was elected president by parliament in July 1989.

In September 1989 a 'grand coalition' was formed with Tadeusz Mazowiecki (b. 1927), editor of Solidarity's newspaper, as prime minister. Jaruzelski continued as president. The new government, which attracted generous financial aid from Western powers, proceeded to dismantle the command economy and encourage the private sector. A tough austerity program approved by the IMF was also instituted to address the problem of hyperinflation, which ran at 550% in 1989.

2. 1990–1999

In January 1990 the PZPR voted to disband itself and reform as the Social Democracy Party (SLD). In April 1990 the Sejm voted to restore 3 May (the anniversary of the creation of the 1791 constitution) as national day and to cancel the 22 July (anniversary of the 1944 Lublin Manifesto establishing communist rule) as a national holiday. Censorship was also abolished in April 1990. During 1990 real GDP in Poland fell by 12% and unemployment rose to over 1 million. In July 1990 40 members of the 259-strong Solidarity caucus, under the leadership of Zbigniew Bujak and Władysław Frasyniuk, established the Citizens' Movement-Democratic Action Party (ROAD) to provide a credible alternative to the Wałęsa-orientated Solidarity Center Alliance (SCA), which had been established in May 1990.

In the first round of direct presidential elections, held on 25 November 1990, the rupture within Solidarity was exposed as both Prime Minister Mazowiecki and Lech Wałęsa contested for the position. Having run a populist campaign, Wałęsa topped the poll with a 40% vote share and Mazowiecki, defending an unpopular government, finished in third position, with 18% of the vote, behind Stanislaw Tyminski, a previously obscure, rightwing, returned émigré Canadian entrepreneur, who captured 23% of the vote. In the second round, held on 9 December 1990, Wałęsa defeated Tyminski by a large margin.

The defeated Mazowiecki resigned as prime minister in December 1990 and the newly elected Wałęsa stood down from the Solidarity chair and was sworn in as president. He chose for prime minister an economist and former Solidarity activist, Jan Krzysztof Bielecki (b. 1951), and the new government included the IMF-backed finance minister, Leszek Balcerowicz, and other ministers from the outgoing administration. They pledged to consolidate the free market they had introduced, and the first privatization share sales were held in January 1991, with mixed success.

In the short term, the new 'shock therapy' program of radical market-centerd restructuring reform resulted in a continuing sharp decline in living standards – real GDP falling by around 10% in 1991 – and growing public discontent and industrial unrest as unemployment climbed to more than 2 million (11% of the work force) by December 1991. Bielecki offered his resignation in late August 1991, complaining that he no longer enjoyed the support of a Sejm that still contained many communists. Parliament refused to either accept the resignation or approve the government's crucial proposed budget cuts. President Wałęsa urged it to confer emergency powers to enable the government to rule by decree until the general election. However, this plea was rejected, creating an impasse, although Bielecki agreed to stay on as prime minister, pending elections.

The October 1991 general election was Poland's first postcommunist, fully free, multiparty contest. With a generous system of pure proportional representation being operated and party roots being still weak, 29 parties were successful in winning Sejm seats. No dominant party emerged from the voting, with the best performances being recorded by Mazowiecki's Democratic Union (DU), which attracted 12% of the national vote, and the Wałęsa-orientated Center Alliance (CA) and Polish Peasant Party (PSL), which each won 9% of the vote. In the light of this unsettled outcome, President Wałęsa proposed that he should combine the positions of president and prime minister for two years, heading a 'national unity' grand coalition government. However, this failed to gain broad support. An attempt was then made to construct a left-of-center coalition led by Broneslaw Geremek. This foundered, and in December 1991 Wałęsa reluctantly allowed Jan Olszewski, a former Solidarity defense lawyer and a representative of the CA, to set about forming a five-party center-right coalition government. This government pledged to pursue a more gradual approach to market-orientated reform and, in particular, to slow down the privatization program by concentrating instead on helping ailing state industries.

In October 1991 a treaty was signed with the Soviet Union providing for the withdrawal of all Soviet combat troops by 15 November 1992 and the remainder by the end of 1993. This agreement was substantially upheld by the new Russian administration, with the last Russian troops actually leaving Polish soil in September 1994. During 1992 unemployment continued to rise, reaching 2.5 million (14% of the work force) by the year's end, as the demise of the intensive, inefficient state-owned industry of the communist era progressed. However, the 'shock therapy' reform program began to have an effect. The annual rate of inflation was brought down from 684% in early 1990 to 60% in early 1992 and during that year the Polish economy became the first in Eastern Europe to resume growth after the collapse of communism, with the private sector now accounting for more than 50% of economic activity.

Despite these achievements, the Olszewski government remained unpopular and in June 1992 fell after losing a no-confidence motion in the Sejm. In July 1992 Hanna Suchocka, from the DU, became the new, and Poland's first female, prime minister, leading a new seven-party coalition government. The Suchocka coalition was beset by constant internal wranglings and in May 1993, after refusing the strike demands of 600,000 teachers and health-care workers, was itself brought down in a no-confidence motion. However, Suchocka remained as prime minister in a caretaker capacity until new parliamentary elections were held in September 1993. These elections were held under new electoral rules, which, with a 5% threshold having been introduced for gaining seats, were designed to ensure that a smaller number of large parties achieved representation. To general surprise, the Democratic Left Alliance (SLD) and PSL, which were successors to the ruling parties of the communist era, the PZPR and ZSL, returned to power, attracting 36% of the vote between them and capturing 303 of the 460 available Sejm seats. These reform-socialist parties benefited from public dissatisfaction with the social costs of the transition to a market economy, from some concern about a strict abortion law approved in January 1993, and also from the failure of right-of-center parties to construct a broad-based alliance to contest the poll. The center-left DU attracted 11% of the vote, and won 74 seats, while the Non-Party Bloc in Support of Reforms (BBWR), a movement launched by President Wałęsa in June 1993, secured barely 5% of the vote and just 16 seats.

Waldemar Pawlak (b. 1959), a former farm manager who was now leader of the PSL, was appointed prime minister in October 1993, forming a coalition government with the ex-communist SLD which commanded sufficient seats, a two-thirds majority in both houses, to press through an amendment of the constitution. Although a number of the new government's ministers had held power during the communist period, the Pawlak administration pledged to continue to work towards the construction of a market-based economy, while seeking to ensure, through increased welfare spending, that costs were distributed more equitably and suffering was alleviated. In addition, with Andrzej Olechowski, a pro-Wałęsa independent, being appointed foreign minister, the administration reaffirmed Poland's desire to join NATO and, at some future date, the European Union (EU).

Between 1993–95 the economic upturn began to gather pace, with annual GDP growth averaging nearly 5%. However, Prime Minister Pawlak clashed increasingly with President Wałęsa, who accused Pawlak of stalling the process of mass privatization, blocking measures which favored the Catholic Church, and putting more emphasis on rebuilding ties with Russia than improving links with the West. In February 1995, after the pro-West Olechowski had resigned as foreign minister and the prime minister and president had been unable to agree on a suitable defense minister, President Wałęsa presented Pawlak with the ultimatum that he must resign or otherwise face a dissolution of the legislature. Pawlak gave way and resigned, being replaced as premier in March 1995 by Jozef Oleksy, the former Sejm speaker and a former communist who had held a position in the communist cabinet of 1988. Oleksy agreed to appoint Wałęsa nominees to the key cabinet portfolios of defense, foreign affairs, and the interior ministry. The 1994–95 power struggle between the right-of-center Wałęsa, seeking to present himself as the defender of the postcommunist market and social reforms, and the left-of-center SLD-PSL administration helped to boost the popularity rating of the president. Nevertheless, he was defeated in the November 1995 presidential election by Alexander Kwasniewski, leader of the SLD.

In January 1996, Prime Minister Oleksy, who had faced allegations (from which he was later exonerated) that he had been an informer to Russia's secret service since the 1980s, resigned. He was replaced as prime minister, in February 1996, by Wlodzimierz Cimoszewicz (b. 1950), the deputy speaker of the Sejm and deputy leader of the SLD, who headed a new SLD – PSL left-of-center coalition government. During the same month, a referendum on further privatization failed as a result of a lack of public interest, with turnout only 32%. Nevertheless, 3,763 enterprises had already been privatized since 1990, and from February 1997, with the appointment of Professor Marek Belka, an independent economist, as finance minister, the privatization program accelerated. Structural economic reforms also continued, including plans to close the bankrupt Gdansk shipyard. With the largest economy in former-communist Central Europe, Poland was admitted to the Organization for Economic Cooperation and Development (OECD) in July 1996 and, although the unemployment rate remained above 10%, strong economic growth, of more than 5% per annum, continued between 1995–97.

In May 1997 a new constitution, superseding the December 1992 'small constitution', was narrowly approved by 53% of votes in a national referendum. It guaranteed free basic education (to the age of 18) and basic healthcare (as set out in a 1952 charter), increased the powers of parliament at the expense of the president, and committed the country to a 'social market economy', respecting free enterprise and private ownership. It was opposed by the Roman Catholic Church since it failed to outlaw abortion. The recently formed Solidarity Electoral Action (AWS), an alliance of centrist, populist, Roman Catholic, and rightwing parties, led by Marian Krzaklewski, head of the Solidarity trade union, was at the forefront of the campaign against the constitution, leading to turnout falling to 43%.

In the September 1997 general election the AWS alliance, which had campaigned for faster privatization, decentralization, reform of pensions, and early membership of the EU, was swept to power, with 34% of the national vote and 201 of 460 Sejm seats. After the election a coalition government was formed by the AWS and the liberal, pro-business Freedom Union (UW). The new prime minister was Jerzy Buzek (b. 1939) of the AWS, a Protestant chemical-engineering professor and Solidarity organizer in the 1980s; but Marian Krzaklewski, the AWS leader, was expected to exert behind-the-scenes influence while preparing for a presidential bid in 2000. The UW's leader, Leszek Balcerowicz, resumed his position as finance minister, which he had held during 1990–91, while the former prime minister, Hanna Suchocka, of the UW, became the justice minister. The new government pressed ahead with its reform agenda, including its decentralization reforms. However, by the autumn of 1998 its majority had been reduced to 17 seats. This followed defections by populists, nationalists, and hard-line Roman Catholics from the 'broad church' AWS, with some joining the Patriotic Movement for the Fatherland, an embryonic rightwing party formed by the former prime minister, Jan Olszewski. In 1999 it faced a succession of strike, and protests, by miners and farmers who demanded increased state support.

Poland, which had joined NATO's 'Partnership for Peace' program in 1994 and become an associate partner in the Western European Union (WEU) in the same year, was invited, in July 1997, to join NATO, along with Hungary and the Czech Republic, in 1999. Already an associate member of the EU since 1994, it was also among the 'first wave' of Central European states to be invited to start negotiations, in 1998, on becoming a full EU member.

ROMANIA

Rômania

Capital: Bucharest

Social and economic data

Area: 237,500 sq km/91,699 sq miles

Population: 22,700,000*
Pop. density per sq km/sq mi: 96/248*
Urban population: 55%**
Literacy rate: 97%**
GDP: $33,490 million*; per-capita GDP: $1,475*
Government defense spending (% of GDP): 3.1%*
Currency: leu
Economy type: middle income
Labor force in agriculture: 29%**
Unemployment rate: 8.0%*
* 1995.
** 1992.

Head of state
President Emil Constantinescu, since 1996

Head of government
Prime Minister Radu Vasile, since 1998

Ethnic composition
Eighty-nine per cent of the population is ethnic Romanian, a non-Slavic race. There exist within the country substantial Hungarian, German, and Serbian minorities. The Hungarians number 1.6 million and are concentrated in Transylvania, in the northwest, a region which formed part of Hungary prior to 1918 and was traditionally more affluent than neighboring parts of Romania. During the later 1980s, plans by Nicolae Ceausescu to demolish 7,000 villages here and replace them with 500 new agro-industrial complexes, involving the dispersed resettlement of ethnic Hungarians, formed part of a controversial forced assimilation, or 'Romanization', policy, which precipitated a diplomatic crisis between Hungary and Romania in 1988. There was further unrest in Transylvania in March 1990 when violent clashes between ethnic Hungarian and Romanian nationalists led to the exodus of some Hungarians. The official language is Romanian, a Romance language.

Religions
Nearly 80% of the population adheres to the Romanian Orthodox Church, a body which is organized into patriarchates. There are also 1.5 million Roman Catholics, belonging chiefly to the Latin and Romanian, or Byzantine rite, sects. Among Protestant churches, which draw support from the German and Hungarian ethnic communities, the Reformed (Calvinist) Church currently has 700,000 members, while the Pentecostal Church has 250,000 adherents. Islam has 55,000 followers, mostly among the Turkish-Tatar community.

Political features
State type: emergent democratic
Date of state formation: 1881
Political structure: unitary
Executive: dual
Assembly: two-chamber
Party structure: multiparty
Human rights rating: 82%
International affiliations: BSECZ, COE, DC, IAEA, IBRD, IMF, NACC, NAM (guest), OSCE, PFP, UN, WEU (associate partner), WTO

Local and regional government
The country is divided into 41 counties (*judete*), excluding the municipality of Bucharest, for the purpose of local administration, with municipalities below.

Political system
Under the December 1991 constitution, Romania has a dual executive pluralist political system. An executive president is directly elected for a maximum of two four-year terms in a two-round majority contest. The president appoints the prime minister, who in turn appoints a 25–30 member cabinet, or Council of Ministers. Candidates are eligible for election to the presidency if supported by at least 100,000 electors and, once elected, the president may not remain a member of a political party. The legislature comprises two chambers, a 343-member lower house, the Chamber of Deputies (Camera Deputatilor), in which 15 seats are

set aside for representatives of the country's national minorities, and a 143-member upper chamber, the Senate (Senatul). Both are elected for four-year terms by means of proportional representation in multiparty contests, with a 4% cut-off limit for representation. Candidates for the Senate must be at least 30 years old and those for the Chamber, 21 years. Former members of the Securitate (the secret police in the communist era) are ineligible for election. Once elected, a president may not remain a member of any political party.

Political parties

In common with the other post-communist states of Central Europe, Romania has a fluid party system. At the time of the November 1996 general election there were around 90 registered political parties. The results of this election showed that there are currently six important political parties and party groups: the Social Democracy Party of Romania (PSDR); the Romanian National Unity Party (RNUP); the Greater Romania Party (GRP; Romania Mare); the Social Democratic Union (SDU); the Hungarian Democratic Union of Romania (HDUR); and the Democratic Convention of Romania (DCR).

The PSDR was established in July 1993 as a body supportive of President Iliescu through the merger of the Democratic National Salvation Front (DNSF), the Republican Party, and the Romanian Social Democratic Party (RSDP). Its key constituent element, the social-democratic DNSF, was formed in April 1992 by supporters of President Iliescu after a split occurred in the National Salvation Front (NSF), the center-left body which had been formed in December 1989 by Ion Iliescu and Petre Roman to fight for political democracy and the transition to a market economy. The PSDR, which contains many ex-communists and favors only limited reforms, was supported in government between 1994–96 by the RNUP (estd. 1990), a rightwing anti-Hungarian Romanian nationalist body formed by Gheorghe Funar, mayor of the Transylvanian capital, Cluj, and the far-right ultra-nationalist and anti-Semitic Romania Mare, led by Corneliu Vadim Tudor. In June 1997 a number of reformist members of the PSDR split away to form the center-left Alliance for Romania party.

The center-left, promarket SDU was formed in 1996, under the leadership of a former prime minister, Petre Roman, as a coalition of the Democratic Party (DP) and remnants of the RSDP. The DP was known before 1993 as the DP-NSF, and originated as a breakaway from the NSF.

The HDUR, formed in 1990 and led by László Tokes and Bela Marko, campaigns for the grant of 'special status' to ethnic Hungarians in Romania. The mainstream opposition parties have refused to cooperate with the HDUR, viewing it as an extreme nationalist force.

The DCR is an alliance of 15 center-right parties which has operated since 1992. One of its key elements is the Christian Democratic National Peasants' Party (CD-PNC), a tolerant center-right pro-market party. It was formed in 1990 through the merger of the CD and the traditional PNC, which had been first established in 1869, but banned by the communists in 1947. It claims 615,000 members. Two other important constituent parties in the DCR are the pro-free-market National Liberal Party (NLP), which originated in 1869 but was banned in 1947, and the Romanian Ecological Party (REP). In April 1999 Victor Ciorbea broke away from the CD-PNC to form the new Christian Democratic National Alliance (CANCD).

Prior to the December 1989 revolution, the dominant and sole legal political party in Romania was the Romanian Communist Party (PCR). However, it was banned in December 1989, although the Socialist Labor Party (SLP) was formed in 1990 by former members and a new PCR relaunched in 1997. The original PCR was established in May 1921 by a leftwing section of the Social Democratic Workers' Party (SDWP), which was itself originally founded in 1893. The party was proscribed by the Romanian government in 1924 and forced underground, during which period it developed close links with Moscow. It merged with the SDWP in October 1947 to form the Romanian Workers' Party, changing its name to the PCR in July 1965. Membership of the PCR stood at 3.69 million in 1987, or 16.2% of the total population, the highest proportion for any East European communist state. In 1962 membership had been just 0.9 million.

Another party of note which currently lacks parliamentary representation is the Agrarian Democratic Party of Romania (ADPR), a leftwing body which claims 172,000 members and advocates the protection of Romanian villagers' traditional lifestyle.

Political leaders since 1970

1965–89 Nicolae Ceausescu (PCR)*, 1989–96 Ion Iliescu (NSF/independent)**, 1996– Emil Constantinescu (DCR/independent)**, 1992–96 Nicolae Vacaroiu (PSDR)***, 1996–98 Victor Ciorbea (DCR)***, 1998– Radu Vasile (DCR)***

* Communist Party leader.

** Democratic executive president.

*** Prime minister.

Latest elections

The most recent, and second post-communist, multi party parliamentary elections were held on 3 November 1996 and resulted in six party groups (comprising 11 individual parties) securing representation in the Chamber of Deputies and Senate. In the Chamber of Deputies, the most successful party group was the center-right DCR, which attracted 30% of the vote (up 10% on September 1992) and won 122 of the 328 elective seats, including 88 for the CD-PNC, 25 for the NLP and nine for three small ecologist parties. In second place, with 22% of the vote (down 6%) and 91 seats was the authoritarian left PSDR, while in third place, with 13% of the vote and 53 seats, was the center-left Social Democratic Union (SDU) of the DP (43 seats) and RSDP (10 seats). The nationalist HDUR secured 7% of the vote and 25 seats; the xenophobic GRP 5% of the vote and 19 seats; and the extreme-nationalist RNUP, 4% of the vote and 18 seats. In the Senate, the DCR won 53 of the 143 seats; the PSDR, 41; the SDU, 23; the HDUR, 11; the GRP, 8; and the RNUP, 7.

The most recent presidential election was held in two rounds on 3 and 17 November 1996. The first round was contested by 16 candidates. The top five were: the incumbent, Ion Iliescu (PSDR), who won 32% of the vote; Emil Constantinescu (DCR), 28%; Petre Roman (SDU), 21%; Gyorgy Frunda (HDUR); Corneliu Tudor (GRP), 5%; and Gheorghe Funar (RNUP), 3%. The second round run-off was won by Constantinescu, who secured 54% of the valid votes to Iliescu's 46%.

Political history

1. Beginnings to 1989

Romania was the site of the Dacian kingdom, which was occupied by the Romans between 106 and 271 AD, and Christianity was introduced. Later, under the influence of neighboring Byzantium, the people became Orthodox Christians. From medieval times, Romanians lived in the three autonomous kingdoms of Wallachia, Moldavia, and Transylvania, which fiercely resisted the westward expansion of the Ottoman kingdom.

Part of the Ottoman Empire from the 15th century, and then subject to Russian suzerainty, between 1829 and 1856, a Romanian nation-state was initially formed by Prince Alexandru Ioan Curza, between 1859 and 1866, by the union of the principalities of Moldavia and Wallachia. The Great Powers recognized Romania's full independence in 1881, under King Carol I (1839–1914). The country, having fought on the Allied side during World War I, extended its boundaries in 1918, receiving Transylvania and Bukovina from the dismembered Austro-Hungarian Empire, as well as, until 1940, Bessarabia, from Russia. It thus emerged as the largest state in the Balkans.

During the inter war period Romania remained economically backward, with 72% of its population dependent upon agriculture. It enjoyed a brief experiment with representative institutions, until, in 1930, as a means of countering the growing popularity of the Fascist 'Iron Guard' mass movement, King Carol II (1893–1953) abolished the democratic constitution of 1923 and established his own dictatorship.

Early in World War II, the country was forced to surrender Bessarabia, North Transylvania, and South Dobruja to the Soviet Union, Hungary, and Bulgaria respectively, in accordance with the August – September 1940 Vienna Arbitration and Craiova Treaty. Additionally, as a result of German pressure, King Carol II abdicated, handing over power to General Ion Antonescu, who, ruling in the name of Carol's son King Michael (b. 1921), signed the Axis Pact, in November 1940, allying Romania with Nazi Germany. This was followed, in June 1941, by Romania's declaration of war on the Soviet Union. Between 1941–44 the Antonescu regime allowed thousands of Jews to be killed or deported to Nazi concentration camps in Poland.

In August 1944, with the Red Army on Romania's borders, King Michael supported a coalition of left and center parties, including the Romanian Communist Party (PCR), to oust the Antonescu regime. Romania subsequently joined the war against Germany and in the Paris Peace Treaty, of February 1947, recovered Transylvania, but lost South Dobruja to Bulgaria and Bessarabia and North Bukovina to the Soviet Union.

The initial post-liberation government was a broadly based coalition, termed the National Democratic Front (NDF), under the leadership of General Santescu. Then, in March 1945, under Soviet pressure, a communist-dominated administration was set up, nominally headed by the radical peasants' Ploughmans' Front leader, Petru Groza. Parliamentary elections were held in November 1946, in which the NDF stood as the Bloc of Democratic Parties, polling 80% of the votes. In the following year, all the noncommunist parties were dissolved and King Michael I was forced to abdicate. This paved the way for the adoption of a one-party Soviet-style republican constitution in April 1948. (Michael I subsequently lived in exile in Switzerland, before returning to Romania in 1997.)

A program of industrial nationalization and agricultural collectivization was immediately launched by the new regime and there was a rapid purge of opposition leaders, so as to firmly establish the PCR in power. Soviet troops remained in the country, however, until 1958. The dominant political personality between 1945 and 1965 was PCR leader and head of state, Gheorghe Gheorghiu-Dej (1901–65). He took Romania into Comecon in 1949 and the Warsaw Treaty Organization in 1955.

On his death in March 1965, power passed to Nicolae Ceausescu (1918–89), who immediately oversaw the framing of a new constitution, in June 1965, which placed greater emphasis on national autonomy. Under Ceausescu, who was created state president in 1975, Romania adopted a foreign policy line independent of the Soviet Union, condemning the 1968 invasion of Czechoslovakia and refusing to participate directly in Warsaw Pact manoeuvres or to allow Soviet troops to cross its borders. Additionally, Ceausescu called for multilateral nuclear disarmament and the creation of a Balkan nuclear weapons-free zone. He also maintained warm relations with communist China.

At home, the secret police (Securitate) maintained a tight Stalinist rein on dissident activities, while a Ceausescu personality cult was propagated, with several members of the president's extended family, including his wife Elena and his son Nicu, occupying senior state and party positions. Economic difficulties mounted as Ceausescu, pledging himself to repay the country's accumulated foreign debt, embarked on an austerity program. This led to food shortages and widespread power cuts in the winters from 1985 onwards. The army occupied power plants and in 1987 brutally crushed workers' strikes and demonstrations at Brasov.

After a referendum in 1986, military spending was cut by 5%. Ceausescu was re-elected general secretary of the PCR in 1984 and 1989 and state president in 1985. He remained steadfast in his policies, ruling out any question of economic or political reform on the 'Gorbachev model' in the Soviet Union, even calling in the spring of 1989 for Warsaw Pact nations to intervene to prevent the opposition Solidarity movement from assuming power in Poland. The country's relations with neighboring Hungary also reached crisis point during 1988–89 as a result of a Ceausescu's 'systematization plan' to demolish 7,000 villages and replace them with 500 agro-industrial complexes, in the process forcibly resettling and assimilating Transylvania-based ethnic Hungarians.

2. 1989–1998

The unexpected overthrow of the Ceausescu regime occurred dramatically in December 1989, in events which, for some observers, represented a popular uprising, and for others, a coup by members of the old guard. It was sparked off by the government's plans to exile a dissident, ethnic Hungarian Protestant pastor, László Tökes (b. 1952), to a remote village. Ethnic Hungarians and Romanians joined forces in the city of Timisoara to form an anti-Ceausescu protest movement. Hundreds of demonstrators were killed in the state's subsequent crackdown on 17 December 1989. Four days later, an officially sponsored mass rally in Bucharest for President Ceausescu, who had returned from Iran, backfired when the crowd chanted anti-Ceausescu slogans and civilians were shot dead in subsequent violent clashes with the security forces. Disturbances spread swiftly to other parts of the country, prompting Ceausescu to declare a state of emergency. Divisions between the military, who were unwilling to open fire on demonstrators, and the Securitate rapidly emerged and on 22 December 1989 the army chief of staff, General Stefan Gusa, turned against the president and called on his soldiers to 'defend the uprising'. Ceausescu attempted to flee by helicopter, but was caught near Tirgoviste and summarily tried by a military tribunal. He was found guilty of genocide, corruption, and destruction of the Romanian economy, and was executed, along with his wife, on Christmas Day.

Battles between Ceausescu-loyal Securitate members and the army ensued in Bucharest, with several thousand being killed, but the army seized the upper hand. A National Salvation Front (NSF) was established in late December 1989, embracing former dissident intellectuals, reform communists, and military leaders. At its head was Ion Iliescu (b. 1930), a Moscow-trained communist engineer and former propaganda secretary in the PCR, while Petre Roman (b. 1947), an academic without political experience, was appointed prime minister. The Front's council proceeded to relegalize the formation of alternative political parties and draft a new constitution. Faced with grave economic problems, it initiated a ban on the export of foodstuffs, the abandonment of Ceausescu's 'systematization program', the dissolution of the Securitate, the abolition of the PCR's leading role, and the relegalization of small-plot farming (with cooperative farmland being returned to its original owners), and of abortion (all contraception had been banned by Ceausescu).

In April 1990 a new Romanian Intelligence Service, accountable to parliament, was set up to replace the disbanded Securitate. The government legalized the Eastern Orthodox Church and the Vatican re-established diplomatic relations. In May 1990 Ion Iliescu won the country's first free presidential elections since World War II, capturing 85% of the vote, and the NSF secured an overwhelming victory in the concurrent parliamentary elections. However, these victories heightened tension between Romanians and the Hungarian ethnic minority in Transylvania. Moving towards a legal market economy, the government cut subsidies, the leu was devalued, and prices were allowed to float. Industrial exports slumped and strikes and protests increased until the government agreed to postpone its price liberalization program. Refugees continued to leave the country and there were demonstrations against the government during December 1990 and January 1991, especially in Timisoara and Bucharest.

The second stage of price liberalization commenced in April 1991, despite trade union protests against the sharply rising cost of living and level of unemployment (over 1 million). At the same time the leu was devalued by 72% to meet the loan conditions set by the IMF and as a step towards internal convertibility by 1992. In the same month a new treaty on cooperation and good neighborliness was signed with the USSR, which obliged the two states 'not to take part in any type of alliance directed against either of them'.

In August 1991 President Iliescu signed a law to allow for the privatization of all state enterprises except utilities, with adult Romanians being given a 30% stake in state-owned ventures. In November 1991 the leu was made internally convertible. Prices rose 400% during 1991 and hundreds of thousands were on short-time work. GNP fell during 1991 by 12%.

In September 1991 Prime Minister Petre Roman resigned after three days of riots in Bucharest by thousands of striking miners, protesting against soaring prices and a fall in their living standards. Theodor Stolojan, the finance minister and a proponent of accelerated price liberalization, took over as premier, forming a new, cross-party, coalition government in October 1991. He promised to remain politically neutral and vowed not to stand in the 1992 elections.

A national referendum in December 1991 overwhelmingly endorsed a new constitution which guaranteed pluralism, human rights, and a free market. This cleared the path for a general election in 1992. Romania's 2 million-strong Hungarian minority opposed the new constitution on the grounds that it failed to grant special minority or language rights.

The September–October 1992 parliamentary and direct presidential elections resulted in the pro-Iliescu Democratic National Salvation Front (DNSF), which was an offshoot from the NSF, emerging as the largest single party, with 28% of the national vote, and Iliescu being re-elected state president by a convincing margin. After the elections, the DNSF, which became known as the Social Democracy Party of Romania (PSDR) from 1993, formed a coalition government with the Agrarian Democratic Party of Romania (ADPR), with Nicolae Vacaroiu (b. 1943), an economist, as prime minister. The new administration pressed on with economic reform, including privatization, but the pace was slow compared to other Central European states and the economy continued to deteriorate, with the unemployment level exceeding 10%. This provoked student and labor unrest, notably by coalminers, but also including, on 28 January 1994, a general strike by more than a million workers. In March 1994, in an effort to strengthen the position of the minority Vacaroiu administration, which had only narrowly survived a series of no-confidence motions instigated during 1993–94 by the more reformist-minded opposition, two rightwing extreme nationalist parties, Romania Mare and the Romanian National Unity Party (RNUP), were brought into the coalition. However, this action persuaded the ADPR to withdraw and increased the sense of concern among ethnic Hungarians, who had been appeased during 1993 by such concessions as the granting of more Hungarian language teaching and Hungarian street signs, and further strained relations with Hungary. Two RNUP members were brought into the cabinet in August 1994 and in January 1995 a governing pact was signed with the anti-Semitic Romania Mare (GRP) and with the Socialist Labor Party (SLP), the successor to the PCR. These events led to increasing Western concern over the future development of democracy in Romania.

During 1995–96 the economy showed signs of improving, with annual GDP growth averaging 5% and the annual inflation rate falling from a level of 260%, seen in 1993, to below 30% in 1996. Nevertheless, the IMF-approved economic austerity program, which included the elimination of price subsidies for staple goods and services, was unpopular with the public. In local elections, held in June 1996, support for the ruling PSDR slumped, while the Democratic Convention of Romania (DCR), a coalition of 15 center-right parties, made significant advances. Its candidate, Victor Ciorbea (b. 1954), a former trade unionist and a leader of the Christian Democrat-National Peasants' Party (CD-PNC), became mayor of Bucharest, defeating the PSDR-backed former tennis star, Ilie Nastase. Meanwhile, the governing coalition began to fall apart. In October 1995 the GRP and SLP withdrew parliamentary support and in September 1996 the RNUP was thrown out of the ruling coalition, after failing to support a Treaty of Cooperation with Hungary, in which Romania agreed to guarantee rights to its large ethnic Hungarian minority and Hungary renounced any claim to territory in Transylvania.

The reformist DCR, which enjoyed strong support among city dwellers, the young, and the ethnic Hungarian minority, polled strongly in the November 1996 parliamentary elections, attracting 30% of the vote, eight more than the PSDR. The center-left Social Democratic Union (SDU), led by former premier Petre Roman, finished third and agreed to form a coalition government with the DCR and the minority Hungarian Democratic Union of Romania (HDUR). The concurrent presidential election was also won, more surprisingly, by DCR, whose leader Emil Constantinescu, an academic who had once been a member of the PCR, defeated President Iliescu. The DCR's success was attributed to public concern at the corruption of the Iliescu regime, the chaotic condition of the economy and a general feeling that the PSDR had 'hijacked' the popular revolution of 1989. Constantinescu's victory represented the first time in Romanian history when a head of state had been removed by peaceful ballot. The new prime minister, Victor Ciorbea, pledged to accelerate economic reforms, tackle corruption, improve relations with Hungary, and seek early entry into NATO and the European Union (EU), and introduced, in February 1997, a radical 'economic shock therapy' economic reform program. It included accelerated privatization, public spending cuts, a freeing of the currency and a scrapping of price controls. It led, in 1997, to a surge in the annual inflation rate to 160%, a contraction in GDP by 7% and, with falling living standards, labor unrest, but persuaded the IMF and World Bank to approve $1 billion in loans and stand-by credit. Meanwhile, as part of the anti-corruption drive, a quarter of county police chiefs were sacked and investigations were launched into public – private mafias and banking fraud, and the files of the Securitate, from the communist era, were opened.

With the economy deteriorating and the currency falling in value, and against the backcloth of large anti-government rallies in Bucharest and Brasov, in February 1998 the SDU criticized the Ciorbea government for the 'economic chaos' and slow pace of reform and effectively withdrew its support. After the budget was blocked, in March 1998, by the SDU, Ciorbea resigned and was replaced as prime minister by Radu Vasile, the general secretary of the CD-PNC and a vice president of the senate. The SDU re-entered the coalition government, which promised to adopt measures to encourage greater foreign inward investment and accelerate economic restructuring, although 7% contraction in GDP occurred in 1998.

In June 1992 Romania was a founding member of the Black Sea Economic Cooperation Group, which aimed to encourage regional trade and cooperation, and in February 1993 an association agreement was signed with the European Union (EU). It was admitted into the Council of Europe in October 1993 and in May 1994 was granted associate partnership status of the Western European Union (WEU). In April 1997 Romania became the sixth signatory to the Central European Free Trade Agreement (CEFTA), joining the Czech Republic, Slovakia, Slovenia, Poland, and Hungary. However, Romania was told in 1997 that it was not among the 'first wave' of Central and East European states which would be invited, in 1998, to start negotiations on early membership of the EU or NATO.

RUSSIA (ROSSIYA)

*Republic of the Russian Federation**
Rossiyskaya Federativnaya Respublika

* Known until 1991 as the Russian Soviet Federal Socialist Republic (RSFSR).

Capital: Moscow

Social and economic data

Area: 17,075,400 sq km/6,592,846 sq miles
Population: 147,980,000*
Pop. density per sq km/sq mi: 9/22*
Urban population: 74%**
Literacy rate: 99%**
GDP: $331,950 million*; per-capita GDP: $2,240*
Government defense spending (% of GDP): 3.8%***
Currency: rouble
Economy type: middle income
Labor force in agriculture: 13%**

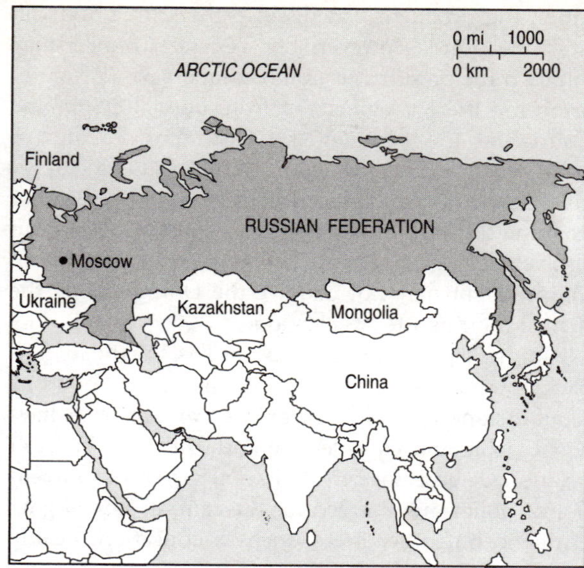

Unemployment rate: 8.3%*

* 1995.

** 1992.

*** 1997.

Head of state

President Boris Yeltsin, since 1990

Head of government

Prime Minister Sergei Steparhin, since 1999

Ethnic composition

The population is predominantly, 83%, of ethnic or 'Great Russian' stock, an eastern Slav race. There are also significant Tatar, 4%, Ukrainian, 3%, Chuvash, 1%, Belarussian, 1%, Bashkir, 1%, and Chechen, 1%, minorities. The official language is Russian, but more than 100 minor languages are also spoken within the federation. The Tatar, Bashkir, and Chechen peoples have campaigned for full autonomy during recent years.

Religions

The Russian Orthodox is the most important church, claiming 40 million adherents, constituting 27% of the total population, with many new churches having been built since the late 1980s. There are also small Roman Catholic, Protestant, Islamic, and Jewish communities. The principal adherents to Islam are Volga Tatars, Chuvash, Bashkirs, and the Chechens, and the Ingush and Ossetians of the northern Caucasus region. Despite large-scale emigration since the 1970s, the Jewish community in the Russian Federation numbers 2 million, being concentrated in the main urban centers.

Political features

State type: emergent democratic
Date of state formation: 1547*/1917**/1991***
Political structure: federal
Executive: limited presidential (moving towards dual)
Assembly: two-chamber
Party structure: multiparty
Human rights rating: N/A
International affiliations: BSECZ, CERN (observer), CIS, COBSS, COE, DC, IAEA, IBRD, IMF, IWC, NACC, OSCE, PFP, UN Security Council (permanent member), G-7 (observer)

* Ivan IV became the first Russian Tsar.

** The communist Union of Soviet Socialist Republics (USSR).

*** The contemporary Russian Federation.

Local and regional government

The Russian Federation includes 21 republics, with a combined population of around 25 million. The populations of the republics range from nearly 4 million in the most populous, Bashkortostan (Bashkiria) and Tatarstan, to under 200,000 in the smallest. Sixteen of these republics were autonomous republics within the RSFSR during the communist period, namely, (capitals in brackets): Bashkortostan (Ufa); Buryatia* (Ulan-Ude); Chechnya (Grozny); Chuvashia (Cheboksary); Daghestan (Makhachkala); Kabardino-Balkaria (Nalchik); Kalmykia (Elista); Karelia* (Petrozavodsk); Komi* (Syktyvkar); Mari-El (Yoshkar-Ola); Mordovia* (Saransk); North Ossetia (Vladikavkaz, formerly Ordzhonikidze); Yakutia*, formerly Sakha (Yakutsk); Tatarstan (Kazan); Tuva (Kizyl); and Udmurtia* (Izhevsk). Four were formerly autonomous regions (*oblasts*), namely, Adygeya*, Gorno-Altai*, Karachevo-Cherkassia, and Khakassia*, while the Ingushetia republic was newly created in June 1992. Ethnic Russians form a majority of the population in only nine of the republics, viz. those marked with an asterisk. The unit called Russia comprises the parts of the Russian Federation that are not included within any of the other 21 republics and, with five-sixths of the Federation's total population, is divided into one autonomous region (*oblast*), 49 administrative regions, six provinces (*krais*), ten autonomous districts (*okrugs*), and the cities of Moscow and St Petersburg, which have considerable devolved authority.

Political system

The Russian Federation's December 1993 constitution provides for a federal republic with a presidentialist executive system, checked by a two-chamber legislature, the Federal Assembly. The constitution also guarantees basic human rights and freedoms, including a right to housing, free healthcare, education, and qualified legal assistance. The president, who is directly elected for a maximum of two four-year terms, serves as head of state and the armed forces and chooses and appoints the prime minister and a Council of Ministers (cabinet) of around 30 members. The president, who is advised by a 'kitchen cabinet' of trusted friends and officials, may issue decrees, veto parliamentary legislation, and sets out the government's political and economic policy in an annual address to the Federal Assembly. The president also appoints and heads a Security Council, which is concerned with defense issues, and proposes the chair of the Central Bank, the prosecutor general, and key members of the judiciary. Furthermore, since January 1994 the security services and the interior, defense, and foreign affairs ministries have been directly subordinate to the presidency. Candidates for the presidency must be nominated by a minimum number of electors: 1 million in 1996, with no more than 7% drawn from any one region or republic.

The bicameral Federal Assembly (Federalnoe Sobranie) consists of a 450-seat lower house, the State Duma (Gosudartsvennaya Duma), and a 178-seat upper chamber, the Federation Council (Sovet Federatsii). The State Duma comprises 225 members directly elected for a four-year term in single-member constituencies on the basis of first-past-the-post, and 225 members drawn from national party lists on the basis of proportional representation, with a 5% qualification threshold being imposed. Electors thus have two votes: one for a local constituency and one for the national list. Duma candidates must be at least 21 years old and, once elected, cannot hold another paid job or government post. The Federation Council comprises two appointed delegates drawn from each of Russia's 89 regions and republics, comprising the head of the executive and of the legislature. The Federal Assembly is relatively weak vis-à-vis the president. While the State Duma may oust a government through a vote of no confidence, for which an absolute majority is required (i.e. 226 Duma votes), it must do so twice within three months before the president is forced to take action. The president can then either form a new government or dissolve the Duma and call fresh elections. Duma approval is needed to ratify the apppointment of a new prime minister and government. However, if the Duma rejects a candidate proposed by the president three times, the president can dissolve the Duma and call fresh elections. However, the Federal Council may impeach the president if both chambers pass a vote in favor and there is agreement from both the Supreme Court and the 19-member Constitutional Court, a body which was established in October 1991 to supervise Russian laws and treaties with foreign states, and to examine territorial disputes. The Federal Council can also veto legislation adopted by the Duma. In addition, the president may not dissolve the Duma during the first 12 months after its election.

Although the 1993 constitution has sought to claw back powers to the center, the Russian Federation's 21 republics and 68 regions, provinces, and districts have equal rights and considerable authority. The areas of taxation, defense, foreign affairs, energy, and socio-economic policy are reserved for the central, federal government, but other areas, such as education, health, social security, culture, and land use are jointly managed with the local governments. The republics have their own constitutions, elected governments, and budgets. They effectively determine the pace and direction of economic and social reforms, having the main control over land ownership and being responsible for 80% of state welfare spending. Indeed, mineral-rich Tatarstan and secessionist Chechnya have become virtually independent states in recent years.

Political parties

Formerly a one-party communist state, Russia has seen the formation of numerous political parties since political pluralism was tolerated from the start of the 1990s, but few have been substantial or lasting. Party ties and loyalties are weak and many politicians are elected as independents, drawing on local support bases, and form opportunistic alliances within parliament. Parties must collect at least 200,000 signatures to be able to contest the parliamentary elections.

At the time of the December 1995 legislature elections there were around 250 registered parties, of which 43 participated in the elections and 23 won seats. However, nine-tenths of the 373 State Duma seats which were not won by independents were won by five separate parties: the Communist Party of the Russian Federation (CPRF); the Liberal Democratic Party of Russia (LDPR); Our Home is Russia (NDR); Yabloko; and the Agrarian Party of Russia (APR). By July 1996 the number of legally registered nationwide political parties had fallen to 86. Russia's parties are arranged ideologically into three broad, and well-balanced, groupings: conservative ex-communist; radical rightwing nationalist and populist; and liberal-centrist or right-of-center promarket and pro-pluralism bodies.

The conservative ex-communist bloc comprises the Communist Party of the Russian Federation (CPRF), which has been led since December 1992 by the Russian nationalist Gennady Zyuganov and was relegalized in October 1993; the allied center-left APR, led by Mikhail Lapshin, which favors the continuance of collective state farming and large state subsidies for the rural sector; the Women of Russia Party, which encourages women's participation in politics; and Power to the People, a left wing nationalist party formed by the former communist prime minister, Nikolai Ryzhkov. In 1996–97 these parties contested regional elections together under the banner of the Patriotic Popular Union of Russia (PPUR).

The CPRF, which favors firmer state control over the economy, is the only slightly reformed heir to the formerly dominant Communist Party of the Soviet Union (CPSU). It claims a membership of 500,000 and prints its own newspaper, *Pravda Rossii* ('Russia's Truth'). The CPSU was founded in 1903, following a split in the Russian Social Democratic Workers' Party (RSDWP), established in 1898 by Georgi Plekhanov (1857–1918), between a majority (Bolshevik) wing led by V I Lenin, which saw the need, in Russian conditions, to organize the party as a tightly disciplined vanguard of professional revolutionaries ready to lead a sudden worker-peasant revolution, and a minority (Menshevik) wing led by Martov, which favored a traditional mass organization and viewed the attainment of socialism as still distant, and needing to be initially preceded by a bourgeois revolution. In 1912, Lenin's Bolsheviks formally set themselves up as a separate group and became the sole permitted party within the Soviet Union when they seized power from the Mensheviks in the revolution of October 1917. The party, which had a membership of 23,600 on the eve of the revolution, subsequently changed its name to the All-Russian Communist Party (Bolsheviks) in 1918, to the All-Union Communist Party (Bolsheviks) in 1925, and to the CPSU in 1952. By 1987 the party had a membership of 19 million and more than 440,000 'workplace cells'. Organized on top-down 'democratic-centralist' principles, the CPSU was controlled by a small, circa 12-member Politburo and Secretariat, which were 'appointed' by a circa 300-member Central Committee which, in turn, was 'appointed' by a quinquennial, circa 5,000-member Party Congress.

The most important extreme-nationalist and rightwing populist party in the Russian Federation is the misleadingly titled Liberal Democratic Party of Russia (LDPR). Led by the xenophobic Vladimir Zhirinovsky and formed in 1990, the LDPR advocates tough measures to crack down on crime and a fancifully expansionist foreign policy with the aim of establishing a 'Greater Russia', incorporating former Soviet states and also parts of Central Europe, the Middle East, and Asia. The LDPR is dominated by Zhirinovsky, who was re-elected as leader for a ten-year term in April 1994 and has absolute power to appoint and dismiss party officials. Another less extreme nationalist party is the People's Republican Party (RPRP), formed in 1997 by Alexander Lebed, a popular ex-general who became governor of mineral-rich Krasnoyarsk in May 1998. It was preceded by the Congress of Russian Communities party, which was formed to fight the 1995 legislature elections. Somewhat more moderate is the Russian All-People's Union, led by Sergei Baburin, which seeks to recreate the former Soviet Union; and the communist-nationalist Great Power (Derzhava) party, led by Aleksandr Rutskoi, a former vice president who has been governor of Kursk since 1996. The latter is described as a 'social patriotic movement' and claims a membership of 1 million people.

A large number of liberal-centrist and pro market-reform parties operate in the Federation, but they currently remain small and quarrelsome. A significant center-right party is Russia's (Democratic) Choice (estd. 1993), which is a bloc of radical reformers led by Yegor Gaidar, the architect of Russia's market-centerd reform program up to 1994. It incorporates Democratic Russia, which was formed in 1990, believes in 'freedom, property, legality' and draws most support from Moscow and St Petersburg. Until December 1994, and the invasion of Chechnya, Russia's Choice supported President Yeltsin.

Another significant centrist grouping, also formed in 1993, is the Yabloko bloc, which is led by the popular pro-reform economist, Grigori Yavlinsky. It favors gradualist, as opposed to radical 'shock therapy', market-centerd reforms.

In 1995–96 three significant new parties were formed. In May 1995, the then prime minister, Viktor Chernomyrdin, became leader of the new NDR party. It originated as a pro-Yeltsin centrist force, which sought to appeal to those who sought 'progress without shocks or revolutions, who are tired of disorder and lies, and who are proud of Russian statehood', and claimed the support of many government ministers and regional leaders, as well as rich industrialists and financiers. In 1996 the center-left Socialist Party of Russia was formed, embracing elements from the Agrarian Party and Agrarian Union and with Ivan Rybkin, a former chair of the State Duma, as its leader. In 1995, Forward Russia was formed by the nationalist-populist reformer Boris Fedorov.

Political leaders since 1970

USSR*: 1964–82 Leonid Brezhnev (CPSU), 1982–84 Yuri Andropov (CPSU), 1984–85 Konstantin Chernenko (CPSU), 1985–91 Mikhail Gorbachev (CPSU); Russian Federation: 1990– Boris Yeltsin (ex-CPSU independent)

* Communist Party leaders.

Latest elections

The most recent State Duma elections were held on 17 December 1995. The Communist Party (CPRF) polled most strongly, attracting 22% of the federal vote and winning 157 seats. The allied Agrarian and Power to the People parties won 5% of the vote and a further 29 seats. Communist support was greatest in the central and southern regions, beyond the Urals. The ultra rightwing LDPR, drawing in high levels of support in military districts, the far east and 'frontier' districts, secured 11% of the vote (half its 1993 result) and 51 seats. The centrist Our Home is Russia party and Yabloko bloc, with 10% and 7% of the vote, won 55 and 45 seats respectively and polled strongest in the cities of Moscow and St Petersburg. The nationalist Congress of Russian Communities and liberal Russia's Democratic Choice each secured only 4% national support, winning five and nine seats respectively. Thirty-seven other parties attracted less than 5% support, thus failing to secure a share of the 225 seats filled proportionately, although 15 minor parties did win seats in single-member constituencies. There were 2,687 candidates for the single-seat constituencies and 77 independents were elected. The latter included Andrei Kozyrev, the foreign minister, who was forced to resign since under the constitution a deputy may not be a minister. Turnout, at 64%, was up on the December 1993 level of 55%.

The most recent, and second, direct presidential elections were held on 16 June and 3 July 1996 and were won in the second ballot run-off by the incumbent Boris Yeltsin, who defeated the CPRF leader, Gennady Zyuganov, and secured 54% of the votes cast to 40%. The first round had been contested by ten candidates, including: the former Soviet president, Mikhail Gorbachev, who attracted a derisory 0.5% of the vote; the LDPR extremist, Vladimir Zhirinovsky, 6%; the free-market liberal leader of Yabloko, Grigori Yavlinsky, 7%; and General Alexander Lebed, the former leader of Russia's 14th Army in the Dnestr region of Moldova, who finished third with 15% of the vote. Yeltsin won 36% of the first-round vote and Zyuganov 32%, with turnout around 70%.

Political history

1. Early settlings to Stalin

The Russian Federation, as it is now called, was the 'Muscovy' heartland of the Soviet Union. It was originally settled by nomadic Slavs, Turks, and Bulgars between the 3rd and 7th centuries before, in the 9th and 10th centuries, Viking chieftains established a Russian dynasty based around the town of Novgorod in the northwest. The center of control moved to Kiev between the 10th and 12th centuries, and this formed the capital of the first Russian Empire. Its peoples were converted to Eastern Orthodox Christianity, which had been introduced by Greek missionaries from Byzantium, or Constantinople.

Mongol-Tatar rule was subsequently imposed over the east and center of the country, during the 13th and 14th centuries, with Belarussia and Ukraine ruled by Poland. It was not until the late 15th century that a new Russian Empire was established by Ivan III, 'the Great' (1440–1505), and the capital became located in what is now Moscow. The empire was considerably extended in scope by Ivan IV, 'the Terrible' (1530–84), who assumed the title tsar in 1547 and resumed control of the northwest, annexed Kazan and Astrakhan and began the colonization of Siberia. Under the subsequent tsars and tsarinas, Peter I, 'the Great' (1672–1725) and Catherine II, 'the Great' (1729–96), the Baltic lands, the Crimea, West Ukraine, and eastern Poland were added, and the capital was moved to St Petersburg in the northwest. Under Tsar Alexander II (1818–81; ruled 1855–81), the borders of the Russian Empire were further extended, being pushed east to the Pacific and south into Central Asia.

Although militarily a 'great power' by the later 19th century, the country remained economically and politically backward compared with its neighbors in Western Europe, from which it remained culturally isolated. Serfdom persisted until 1861 and it was not until 1906, following the abortive revolution of 1905, that the country's first constitution and national representative assembly, the Duma, were established. The Duma was elected on a narrow franchise, with, in 1910, barely 2.4% of the population enjoying the right to vote. It thus did little to temper the despotic character of the tsarist regime.

At the start of the 20th century a state-led crash industrialization program was belatedly launched, but towards the close of World War I, when its armed forces were in retreat and the economy was in ruins, the tsarist autocracy was finally overthrown in the revolution of March 1917 by a combination of disaffected soldiers, workers, peasants, and Russian Social Democratic Workers' Party (RSDWP) activists. Tsar Nicholas II (1868–1918) abdicated and a republic was declared, headed first by Prince Georgi Lvov (1861–1925) and then by the agrarian-populist Socialist Revolutionary Party leader, Aleksandr Kerensky (1881–1970).

This provisional government was soon itself overthrown, in the 'October Revolution' of 1917, by the Bolsheviks, led by the charismatic, white-collar intellectual, Vladimir Ilyich Lenin (1870–1924), who had recently returned from exile in Zurich, and the Ukrainian Jew who had played a directing role in the 1905 revolution, Leon Trotsky (1879–1940). This second 'revolution' was, in fact, a coup, rather than a popular uprising. This is demonstrated by the fact that the Bolsheviks polled only 25% of the votes in the free elections held to the Constituent Assembly in November 1917, compared with the 63% secured by other socialist parties. Lenin, however, ignored the result of this election, swiftly dissolved the Constituent Assembly in January 1918, and established, instead, one-party control through an extensive system of Bolshevik-dominated soviets ('people's councils').

The initial four years of the new Bolshevik regime were consumed with repelling external attacks by the allied powers and Poland, and fighting an internal civil war against a combination of pro-tsarist, 'bourgeois democrat', socialist revolutionary and Menshevik 'White' forces. These struggles were eventually overcome and, in December 1922, the Soviet Union (USSR) was formally established as a federation and a new constitution was adopted in 1923.

The problems of reconstruction meant that, in the economic sphere, a pragmatic mixed-enterprise approach was initially pursued, between 1921 and 1927, under the title of the 'New Economic Policy' (NEP). Peasants were allowed to till their own land and small- and medium-sized private industries operated, while the 'commanding heights' of the economy were brought under state control. This social democratic strategy was gradually abandoned, however, by Lenin's successor as party leader, Joseph Stalin (1879–1953), the son of a poor Georgian cobbler-serf.

Seeking to rapidly transform the nation from an agrarian to a top-ranking industrial power and, in the process, fundamentally rearrange its socio-economic base in a socialist direction, he embarked, from 1927, on a radical program of forced collectivization and heavy industrialization, founded on a system of firm, party-controlled, central planning. The first Five-Year Plan was introduced in 1928.

Stalin's program of 'socialism in one country' was opposed by some of his leading party colleagues, including Trotsky, who favored an internationalist policy of fomenting supportive revolutions abroad. Other opponents were Trotsky's 'leftist' supporter, Lev Kamenev (1883–1936); the moderate pro-NEP 'rightist', Nikolai Bukharin (1888–1938); the 'Old Bolshevik', Grigori Zinoviev (1883–1936); and the Leningrad (St Petersburg) Party leader, Sergei Kirov (1888–1934). Stalin's response was a series of ruthless party purges and 'liquidations' which were launched during the 1920s and 1930s. As a result, party membership fell from 3.5 million in 1933 to 1.9 million in 1938.

In the economic sphere, Stalin's ambitious transformatory program had significant results, Soviet industry recording a growth rate of 16% per annum between 1929 and 1940, its blue-collar work force quadrupling in size and the country's urban population doubling. However, the social and political costs were enormous. Millions of 'rich peasants' (*kulaks*) were executed or sent to labor camps in Siberia, agricultural produce was forcibly marketed, depressing rural per-capita living standards, and the countryside was squeezed to provide investment income for industry. Both the party and state political structures were disfigured, democratic consultation giving way to personalized control, supported by the intrusive and terroristic use of the NKVD secret police, under the direction of Stalin's Georgian crony, Lavrenti Beria (1899–1953).

The Stalin regime, although unpopular with rural groups and with the intelligentsia, did, however, receive support from a number of sections of Soviet society. These included the new post revolution generation of socialist educated 'worker-bureaucrats' who had benefited from the new opportunities for rapid advancement. Support also came from urban workers and the military, the groups which had been the prime beneficiaries of the 'forced industrialization' strategy. In addition, during World War II, Stalin's role as a determined leader (*Vozhd*), successfully standing up to German Nazi aggression in a bitter struggle, termed the 'Great Patriotic War', in which 25 million Russians perished, brought him broad popular nationalist support.

The Red Army's success in repelling Germany's forces in 1943 re-established the country as a 'great power' and at the close of World War II it was able to gain effective dominance over Eastern Europe, setting up a series of satellite socialist governments, as well as securing the direct annexation of Baltic and Polish territories in the northwest and a substantial area in Moldova and West Ukraine in the southwest, which had formerly been controlled by Romania. During the immediate postwar period these gains were consolidated, and indirect support was provided to anti-colonial movements in the Far East. The USSR therefore became established as a globally active 'superpower' and this approach inaugurated a new East – West 'Cold War' era.

2. 1953–1984

On Stalin's death in March 1953 a collective leadership, which included the Communist Party's (CPSU) first (general) secretary, Nikita Khrushchev (1894–1971), the prime minister, Georgi Malenkov (1901–88), the foreign minister, Vyacheslav Molotov (1890–1986), as well as the first deputy prime ministers, Nikolai Bulganin (1895–1975) and Lazar Kaganovich (1893–1991), assumed power. They swiftly combined to remove NKVD chief, Beria, in December 1953, and proceeded to introduce a new legal code which regularized the political system. However, although agreed on the need to reform and 'humanize' the 'Stalin system', strong intra-leadership differences soon emerged over the exact emphasis and direction of new policy approaches. As a consequence, a fierce succession contest developed between 1953 and 1958.

Khrushchev emerged as the victor, succeeding in first ousting the 'anti-party' triumvirate of Malenkov, Molotov, and Kaganovich in June 1957, and then Bulganin, who had succeeded Malenkov as prime minister in 1955, in June 1958. Khrushchev was now able to combine the key posts of prime minister and CPSU first secretary. Once installed in power, Khrushchev introduced a radical new party program, at the 22nd CPSU Congress of October 1961, which envisaged rapid agricultural, industrial, and technological development, to enable the Soviet Union to move ahead of the United States in economic terms by 1980, and for the nation to attain full communism.

To achieve these goals, an ambitious 'virgin lands' cultivation campaign was launched in underdeveloped Kazakhstan, with the aim of swiftly boosting agricultural output. In addition, a program of decentralized industrial management was unveiled, based on the formation of new regional economic councils (*sovnarkhozy*). Material incentives were also introduced in the rural sector.

In the political, social, and diplomatic spheres, Khrush-chev introduced radical new party rule changes, directed towards curbing the authority of entrenched officials (*apparatchiki*); sanctioned a cultural 'thaw'; and enunciated the new principle of 'peaceful co-existence' with the West, as a means of diverting resources away from the defense sector.

These reforms enjoyed initial success and following the explosion of its first hydrogen bomb in 1953 and the launching of a space satellite, the *Sputnik I*, in 1957, the Soviet Union appeared to be emerging for the first time as a serious technological rival to the United States. However, Khrushchev's liberalization policy and his denunciation of the errors and crimes of the 'cult of personality' Stalin era, at the 20th CPSU Congress in February 1956, had serious repercussions among the Soviet Union's East European satellites, encouraging a nationalist revolt in Hungary. A breach in relations with China also resulted and his administrative reforms were fiercely opposed by senior party and state bureaucrats.

After a series of poor harvests in overcropped Kazakhstan, workers' riots in Soviet cities, and the Cuban missile crisis climbdown of 1962, opposition to Khrushchev began to coalesce, and at the Central Committee meeting of October 1964 the party leader was dismissed and forced into retirement.

A new and conservative collective leadership assumed power, centerd around the figures of the former head of state Leonid Brezhnev (1906–82), First Deputy Prime Minister Alexei Kosygin (1904–80), Party Organization Secretary Nikolai Podgorny, and Party Ideology Secretary Mikhail Suslov (1902–82). They immediately abandoned Khrushchev's *sovnarkhozy* and party reforms and reimposed strict censorship in the cultural sphere. Priority was now given to the expansion and modernization of the Soviet armed forces, including the creation of a naval force with a global capability. This, coupled with the Soviet invasion of Czechoslovakia in 1968 to suppress a gathering reform movement, resulted in a renewal of the East – West 'Cold War' between 1964 and 1970.

During the later 1960s and early 1970s, Leonid Brezhnev, by inducting his supporters into the CPSU

Politburo and Secretariat, established himself as the dominant figure within the Soviet polity. He continued to govern, however, in a cautious and consensual manner, bringing into the Politburo, in April 1973, leaders from all the significant centers of power, including the KGB, in the person of Yuri Andropov (1914–84), the army, Marshal Andrei Grechko, and the diplomatic service, Andrei Gromyko (1909–89).

Working with Kosygin, who was prime minister 1964–80, Brezhnev introduced a series of minor economic reforms and gave new priority to agricultural and consumer goods production. In 1977 he oversaw the framing of a new constitution which established a settled new political system in which the limits for dissent were clearly set out and which described the state as in a stage of 'developed socialism' whose future development would rely increasingly on the technocratic use of scientific innovation.

Brezhnev, who became the new state 'president' in May 1977, emerged as an international statesperson during the 1970s, frequently meeting Western leaders during what was a new era of détente. The landmarks of this period were the SALT-1 and SALT-2 Soviet – American arms limitation agreements of 1972 and 1979 and the Helsinki Accord of 1975, which brought Western recognition of the postwar division of Eastern Europe.

During this détente era there was a new cultural 'thaw' which resulted in the emergence of a vocal dissident movement, led by the nuclear physicist Dr Andrei Sakharov (1921–89). The political and military influence of the Soviet Union was also extended into Africa and the 'Horn' with the establishment of new communist-leaning governments in Angola in 1975, Mozambique in 1974, Ethiopia in 1975, and South Yemen in 1978.

The détente era was eventually ended, however, by the Soviet invasion of Afghanistan in December 1979 and the Polish crisis of 1980–81, ushering in a further 'Cold War' era and a period of domestic repression. Sakharov, for example, was arrested and sent into internal exile in 1980.

During its final years the Brezhnev administration, with its leader physically incapacitated by a series of strokes, and his rivals jockeying for position to succeed him, was characterized by policy sclerosis, mounting corruption, and economic stagnation.

On Brezhnev's death in November 1982, Yuri Andropov, a former KGB chief, was elected CPSU chairperson by his Politburo colleagues. He proceeded, energetically, to introduce a series of substantive economic reforms, styled the 'enterprise management' initiative, which were aimed at streamlining and decentralizing the planning system and inculcating greater labor discipline. Andropov also launched a major campaign against corrupt and complacent party and state bureaucrats. These measures had a perceptible impact on the Soviet economy during 1983.

The reform impetus waned, however, when Andropov died in February 1984 and was succeeded by the cautious and elderly Konstantin Chernenko (1911–85), a man who had previously served as Brezhnev's political secretary and closest aide. Chernenko held power as a stopgap leader for 13 months, his sole initiative being a renewed search for détente with the United States which was rejected by the hardline Reagan administration.

3. 1985–1990

On Chernenko's death in March 1985, power was transferred to a new generation led by Mikhail Gorbachev (b. 1931), the protégé of Yuri Andropov and a former agriculture secretary, who, at the age of 54, was the CPSU's youngest leader since Stalin. Although elected on a divided Politburo vote, Gorbachev vigorously took up the reins of reform, sharply criticizing the preceding Brezhnev era. His reform prescription was three-pronged.

First, in the economic sphere, under the slogan of *perestroika*, or 'restructuring', he pressed for greater decentralization in decision-taking. Farmers and factory managers were to be freed from pettifogging bureaucratic interference and there was to be increased emphasis on material incentives, cost accounting, and factory self-financing, as part of a new *khozrachiot* or 'market socialist' system. Second, working with Nikolai Ryzhkov (b. 1929), a former industrial manager, who became prime minister in September 1985, replacing Nikolai Tikhonov (1905–97), he set about radically overhauling the party and state bureaucracies, replacing cautious Brezhnevite placemen with ambitious technocrats. To support these political changes, Gorbachev, under the slogan *glasnost*, or 'openness', encouraged criticism of bureaucratic inefficiencies and opened up a free discussion in the media of existing problems, reform options, and previous party history. Third, he embarked on a détente initiative abroad in the hope of achieving an arms reduction agreement with the United States, which would allow resources to be diverted to the civilian sector. Working with his emollient foreign minister, the Georgian Eduard

Shevardnadze (b. 1928), he made skilful use of the international television media to put the US Reagan administration on the defensive over the issues of space weapons and nuclear testing.

Following summit meetings held in Geneva in November 1985, Reykjavik in October 1986, and Washington in December 1987, Gorbachev signed an Intermediate-Range Nuclear Forces (INF) Treaty with the United States, designed to eliminate medium- and shorter-range nuclear missiles stationed in Europe. As part of this détente process, the USSR also agreed on a phased withdrawal, by February 1989, of all of its 100,000 troops from Afghanistan, ending a ten-year entanglement which had cost the lives of 13,000 Soviet soldiers, and a unilateral 500,000 reduction in the size of its armed forces within two years, including the withdrawal of 50,000 troops and 5,000 tanks from Europe. In effect, Gorbachev had signalled his intention of abandoning the 'Brezhnev doctrine' of ratchet-like Soviet military expansion overseas.

The new Soviet leader consolidated his position at the CPSU's 27th Congress, held in March 1986, by ousting a number of ailing senior Brezhnevites from the controlling Politburo and Secretariat and replacing 40% of the party's Central Committee. However, during 1987–88, as Gorbachev pressed for an acceleration (*uskoreniye*) in the reform process, including adoption of a comprehensive economic revitalization plan, the 'New Economic Mechanism', he began to encounter increasing domestic opposition. This came from both conservatives within the CPSU, grouped around ideology chief Yegor Ligachev (b. 1920), and a smaller group of party radicals, led by Boris Yeltsin (b. 1931), the Moscow party chief until his dismissal in November 1987. Gorbachev faced additional problems, with the eruption of serious nationalist challenges to his administrations in a number of the USSR's 15 Union Republics, notably the three Baltic republics, Kazakhstan and Armenia, Azerbaijan, and Georgia in the region of Transcaucasia, and the continued sluggish performance of the economy. A new opposition group, the Democratic Union, was formed in Moscow in 1988 and there were Russian language demonstrations in Leningrad (St Petersburg), where the tsarist flag was raised.

In an effort to add momentum to the reform process, in June 1988 Gorbachev convened a special 4,991-member All-Union Party Conference, the first since 1941. At this meeting a radical constitutional overhaul was approved. A new 'superlegislature', the 2,250-deputy Congress of the USSR People's Deputies (CUPD), was created, from which a full-time bicameral working parliament, the 542-member Supreme Soviet, was subsequently to be elected, headed by a state president with increased powers. The members of this CUPD were to be chosen in competition with one another and inner-party democracy was to be introduced to the CPSU, replacing top-down 'democratic centralism'. The authority of the local soviets ('people's councils') was enhanced and their structures made more democratic, while, in the economic sphere, it was agreed to reintroduce private leasehold farming, reform the price system, and allow part-time private enterprise in the service and small-scale industry sectors.

The June 1988 reforms constituted the most fundamental reordering of the Soviet policy since the 'Stalinist departure' of 1928, entailing the creation of a new type of 'socialist democracy' (*demokratizatsiya*) and accountability, as well as a new mixed economic system. The CUPD elections of March-April 1989 showed clear opposition to conservative apparatchiks and in May 1989 the new CUPD elected Gorbachev as its chair, and thus as state president. Gorbachev continued to strike against conservative and 'old guard' opponents during 1988–89, demoting Ligachev to the lowly agriculture portfolio. In addition, in 1989, as further evidence of his abandonment of the 'Brezhnev doctrine', the Soviet president sanctioned the establishment of noncommunist and 'reform-communist' governments elsewhere in Eastern Europe. As a consequence, the ruling communist regimes in Poland, Czechoslovakia, East Germany, Bulgaria, Hungary, and Romania were overthrown in a wave of 'people's power' during 1989–90. Responding to these developments, in February 1990, the CPSU Central Committee decided to create a new directly elected state executive presidency on US and French models. In March 1990, the Soviet parliament authorized private ownership of the means of production, which had been forbidden since the 1920s. Further constitutional amendments passed during 1990 supported the right of self-determination, including the secession of republics, and terminated the CPSU's monopoly of power.

The Gorbachev reform program showed signs of running out of control during 1989–90 as a result both of growing nationalist tensions – which in April 1989 and January 1990 had prompted the despatch of troops to the Caucasus region, first to break up demonstrations in Tbilisi, Georgia, and then to attempt to quell a civil war between Armenia and Azerbaijan over the disputed enclave of Nagorno-Karabakh – and mounting popular discontent over the failure of *perestroika* to improve living standards.

In their December 1989 summit meeting in Malta, Gorbachev and the new US president, George Bush, declared an official end to the Cold War. This opened up the prospect of the USSR securing 'most favored nation' trading status with the United States, membership of GATT, and an influx of Western investment. However, throughout 1990 the political and economic situation deteriorated. In pluralist elections held at local and republic levels, anti-communist nationalist and radical deputies polled strongly, particularly in the Baltic republics and in major cities. The new republican governments, including the RSFSR in June 1990, issued declarations of state economic and political sovereignty and, in the case of the Baltics, independence in March – May 1990. These were ignored by Moscow, which, instead, imposed a temporary economic blockade on Lithuania. As the year progressed, a 'war of laws' developed between the center and the republics, who kept back funds, which contributed to a worsening of the federal budget deficit, and the system of central economic planning and resource distribution began to break down. As a consequence, with crime and labor unrest also increasing, the USSR's national income fell by at least 4% during 1990 and was to decline by a further 15% during 1991. Indeed, mounting food shortages led to rationing and an emergency international airlift of food aid during the winter of 1990–91.

The CPSU also began to fracture during 1990 as a result of nationalist challenges within the republics and divisions over the direction and pace of economic and political reform between conservatives, who had grouped themselves in the 'Soyuz' and 'Communists for Russia' factions, liberals, in the 'Communists for Democracy' faction, and radicals, aligned to the 'Democratic Platform'. A split was formalized at the 28th CPSU Congress, held in July 1990, when Boris Yeltsin, who was indirectly elected president of the Russian Republic (RSFSR) in May 1990, and Gavriil Popov and Anatoly Sobchak, respectively the radical mayors of Moscow and (until 1996) St Petersburg, resigned their party membership. Earlier, in the RSFSR, a new Russian Communist Party had also been formed and in September 1990 the Russian Federation's parliament adopted the 'Shatalin Program' of rapid market-centerd economic reforms, although this was soon shelved in the face of public opposition.

4. 1990–1991

In December 1990, concerned at the gathering pace of economic and political disintegration and ethnic strife, President Gorbachev, now immensely unpopular, with his public approval rating in single figures, persuaded the Soviet parliament to vote him increased emergency powers and approve a new federalized political structure. Subsequently, under pressure from the 'Soyuz' group, the military, and the KGB secret service, a clear rightward shift in policy became apparent. This was manifested by the appointment of the conservative Valentin Pavlov as prime minister, Gennady Yanayev as vice president, and the hardline Boris Pugo (1937–91) as interior minister; by the resignation of Foreign Minister Eduard Shevardnadze, who warned that a new dictatorship was impending; by the dispatch in January 1991 of black beret paratroopers to Vilnius and Riga in Lithuania and Latvia to seize political and communications buildings; and by a retightening of press and television censorship. In protest, striking Kuzbas coalminers called, between March and May 1991, for Gorbachev's resignation.

From the spring of 1991, after his March 1991 proposal to preserve the USSR as a 'renewed federation of equal sovereign republics' secured public approval by 76% of participating voters in a Union-wide referendum, which was boycotted by six republics, Gorbachev again attempted to reconstruct a center-left reform alliance with liberals and radicals. In April 1991 a pact aimed at achieving stable relations between the federal and republican governments and with promoting economic reform was signed by the presidents of nine republics: the three Baltic states, Armenia, Georgia, and Moldova were the republics which refused to sign. Two months later, the draft of a new Union Treaty, entailing a much greater devolution of authority and the establishment of a new two-chamber federal legislature and a directly elected executive president, was also approved by nine republics. In July 1991 Gorbachev's standing was further enhanced by the signing, in Moscow, of a Strategic Arms Reduction Treaty (START), to reduce the number of US and Soviet long-range nuclear missiles. At home, however, Boris Yeltsin, who in June 1991 was directly elected president of the giant Russian Federation, pressed for even greater reform and in July 1991 Communist Party cells were banned from operating in factories, farms, and government offices within the Russian Republic. In the same month a Democratic Reform Movement was formed by Shevardnadze, Sobchak, and Popov.

These liberal – radical initiatives raised disquiet among CPSU conservatives and in June 1991 Prime

Minister Pavlov unsuccessfully attempted to persuade the Soviet parliament to vote him extra powers. Two months later, on Monday 19 August 1991, a day before the new Union Treaty was to be signed, an attempted anti-Gorbachev coup was launched by a reactionary alliance of leaders of the CPSU apparatchiki, the military-industrial complex, the KGB, and the armed forces. It was declared in the early hours of the morning that President Gorbachev, who was on holiday in the Crimea, was ill and that Vice President Gennady Yanayev would take over as president, as part of an eight-person emergency committee, which also included Prime Minister Pavlov, Defense Minister Dmitri Yazov, KGB Chief Vladimir Kryuchkov, and Interior Minister Boris Pugo. This committee assumed control over radio and television, banned demonstrations and all but eight newspapers, imposed a curfew, and sent tanks into Moscow. They failed, however, to arrest the Russian president, Boris Yeltsin, who defiantly stood out against the plotters as the head of a democratic 'opposition state' barricaded in the Russian parliament building, the so-called 'White House', where external telephone links remained in operation. Yeltsin called for a general strike and the reinstatement of President Gorbachev. On Wednesday morning, having failed to wrest control of the 'White House' and win either international or Union-wide acknowledgement of the change of regime, and having endured large demonstrations in Moscow, St Petersburg, Kishinev (in Moldova), and Lviv (in Ukraine), the coup disintegrated. The junta's inept leaders were arrested, with the exception of Pugo, who committed suicide, and in the early hours of Thursday 22 August 1991 President Gorbachev, fully reinstated, arrived back in Moscow. There were 15 fatalities during the crisis.

In the wake of this failed attempted coup, established CPSU structures, as well as the Union itself, rapidly disintegrated in the face of a popular backlash which saw such icons of communism as the Felix Dzerzhinsky statue outside the KGB headquarters in Moscow being toppled and the Red Flag being burned and replaced by traditional tsarist symbols. President Gorbachev initially misjudged the changed mood, intimating his continued faith in the popularly discredited CPSU and seeking to keep to a minimum the necessary changes in personnel and institutions. However, forced by pressure exerted by the public and by Boris Yeltsin, whose stature both at home and abroad had been hugely enhanced, a succession of far-reaching reforms were instituted which effectively sounded the death knell of Soviet communism and resulted in the fracturing of the Union.

The new federal cabinet was selected effectively by Yeltsin and was staffed largely with radical democrats from the Russian Republic, with Ivan Silaev, prime minister in the RSFSR since June 1990, becoming federal prime minister. Yeltsin also declared himself to have assumed charge of the armed forces within the Russian Republic and, at a heated session of the Russian parliament, pressurized President Gorbachev into signing a decree suspending the activities of the Russian Communist Party. In addition, a new Russian national guard was established and control assumed over all economic assets in the republic. Recognizing the changed realities, President Gorbachev announced on 24 August 1991 that he was immediately resigning as general secretary of the CPSU and ordered the party's discredited Central Committee to dissolve itself.

The attempted coup of August 1991 speeded up the movement towards dissolution of the Soviet Union. During the coup, when Red Army tanks were sent into their capitals with orders to seize radio and television stations, the Estonian and Latvian parliaments followed the earlier example of Lithuania and declared independence. After the coup the largely conservative-communist controlled republics of Azerbaijan, Belarus, and Uzbekistan, as well as the key republic of Ukraine, also joined the Baltics, Georgia, Moldova, and Armenia in declaring their independence. Their governments acted partly in the hope of shoring up their authority and privileges and partly because they feared Russian domination of the existing USSR and possible future territorial disputes.

At an emergency session of the Congress of People's Deputies held in September 1991, the Union was partially salvaged through the negotiation of a new Union Treaty in which each republic was to be allowed to decide its own terms of association, with much greater power being devolved from the center in what represented a new loose confederation, or 'Union of Sovereign States', though with the armed forces retained under a single military command. Ten republics – the three Baltic states, Georgia, and Moldova being the exceptions – declared a willingness to sign this agreement. The Congress also voted on 5 September 1991 to establish a new system of government in which the CUPD would be abolished and its powers would be assumed by a revamped two-chamber Supreme Soviet, with its upper chamber being chosen by the republics and its decisions ratified by the latter, a

State Council (government), comprising President Gorbachev and the heads of the ten republics, and an Inter-Republican Economic Committee, with equal representation from all 15 republics and chaired by Ivan Silaev. It also acknowledged the rights of republics to secede, opening the way on 6 September 1991 for President Gorbachev to formally recognize, by decree, the independence of the Baltic states.

The possibility of forging a new decentralized union receded as 1991 progressed. Concerned at the accumulation of political and economic authority by Russia, other republics began to seek full independence so as to escape Russian domination, including Armenia, Azerbaijan, Georgia, Moldova, and, crucially, Ukraine, and refused to sign new economic and political agreements. Participation in the new Supreme Soviet and State Council was patchy, their gatherings attracting members from, at most, ten republics. Although a declaration of intent to maintain a 'common economic zone' of inter-republican free trade and to uphold existing factory ties was initialled in October 1991, along with a civic and inter-ethnic accord, the republics proved unable to agree on specific details of a proposed new economic and political union. As a consequence, President Gorbachev occupied the position of a figurehead leader, possessing little real authority, although his position was slightly strengthened by the return of Shevardnadze to head the foreign ministry in November 1991. Instead, the pre-eminent leader in the new USSR, governing significantly from the former office of the CPSU Politburo, was Russia's president, Boris Yeltsin, who now also combined the position of Russian prime minister. In November 1991 the Russian Republic took over control of the Soviet money supply and exchange rate, and began implementing a market-centerd economic reform program. On 14 November 1991 preliminary agreement was reached on the formation of a new 'Union of Sovereign States', but at a subsequent meeting, held on 25 November 1991, the republican delegations which attended refused to initial the treaty.

5. 1991–1995

On 8 December 1991, a week after a referendum on independence was held in Ukraine, the three most powerful republics, Russia, Belarus, and Ukraine, agreed to form a new Commonwealth of Independent States (CIS), a military and economic grouping of sovereign states. This development was denounced by President Gorbachev, but by mid-December the five Central Asian republics of Kazakhstan, Kyrgyzstan, Tajikistan, Turkmenistan, and Uzbekistan had announced that they would also join the CIS. Accepting the inevitable, President Gorbachev agreed on a transfer of power from the centralized USSR government to the CIS. The remaining republics, Armenia, Azerbaijan, and Moldova, with the exception of Georgia, which was distracted by civil war, joined the others in signing agreements on 21 December 1991 to establish the new Commonwealth, or alliance, of Independent States. The formal dissolution of the USSR came on 25 December 1991, when Gorbachev resigned as president, and in the same month the United States and European Community accorded the Russian Federation diplomatic recognition as an independent state.

The new Russian Federation, despite the weakness of its economy, remained a 'great power' and the most significant of the post-Soviet successor states. It inherited much of the former USSR's strategic and diplomatic assets, including a permanent seat on the United Nations Security Council, embassies overseas, and a considerable conventional and nuclear military arsenal. It was admitted into the Helsinki Conference on Security in Europe (CSCE, later the OSCE) in January 1992 and sought to use its membership of the new CIS as a means of maintaining its economic and strategic hegemony in Eastern Europe and Central Asia. Containing almost half the population of the former USSR and around 70% of its agricultural and industrial output, the republic was a vast federation, spanning 11 time zones, stretching 2,000 miles from the Arctic Ocean to China, comprising numerous autonomous republics, regions, and districts and catering for distinct non-Russian ethnic groups, including Tatars, Chechens, Chuvash, Dagestanis, Buryats, Yakuts, Kalmyks, and Chuchi, each with its own parliament and laws. After 1990 many of these autonomous areas made sovereignty or independence declarations, most conspicuously oil-rich and predominantly Muslim Tatarstan, where Russia's largest ethnic minority resided, gas-rich Bashkiria, Siberian Yakutia, and Chechnya-Ingushetia, situated in the southwest. In March 1992, 18 of Russia's 20 republics signed a treaty agreeing to remain within a loose federation: Tatarstan and Chechnya-Ingushetia, which later became two separate republics, dissented. The Russian Federation also faced the threat of territorial claims and border conflicts with neighboring republics, since 25 million ethnic Russians lived outside the federation. Of particular concern was the Russian-dominated Crimea, which formed part of Ukraine.

Russia's immediate concern from 1992, however, was the rapid deterioration in living standards and shortages of food and consumer goods as a result of price liberalization and the restructuring of commerce, the defense sector, and industry, as the republic sought to effect the transition from a planned to a market economy. The government conceded that output would drop by 20% during the first quarter of 1992 and inflation during the year was to exceed 2,000%. This prompted mounting criticism from within parliament, from its speaker, or chairperson, the Russian nationalist Ruslan Khasbulatov (b. 1943), who in January 1992 called for the government's resignation, and from Russia's vice president, Aleksandr Rutskoi, an Afghan war veteran who believed that privatization should have preceded price liberalization. Fears began to mount that Yeltsin might be challenged by a military-backed nationalist coup.

In December 1992 Yegor Gaidar, a committed pro-market economic reformer who was blamed for the dismal state of the economy, was ousted as Russian prime minister by the 1,033-member Congress of Russian People's Deputies, the federation's conservative ex-communist dominated parliament, although Gaidar was to return as an economics minister in September 1993. Viktor Chernomyrdin (b. 1938), a more cautious former communist apparatchik whose former career had been as head of the huge state gas concern, Gazprom, became the new premier and in March 1993 the Congress sought to limit President Yeltsin's powers to rule by decree and cancelled a planned constitutional referendum. Yeltsin struck back by temporarily imposing 'special rule', pending the holding of this referendum. Held on 25 April 1993, the plebiscite gave a clear, 53–59%, vote of confidence to the Yeltsin presidency and its reform program, but apathy was such, turnout being 64%, that the approval level failed to reach the supra 50% absolute majority of the electorate which was required for a constitutional reform to be carried.

President Yeltsin's battle with the obstructive, conservative Russian parliament continued throughout 1993 and on 21 September 1993, faced with its unveiling of proposals to reduce the presidency's powers and derail proposed economic reforms, notably the mass privatization program, Yeltsin summarily dissolved the Congress and the subordinate Supreme Soviet, a bicameral standing body elected from the Congress, and, anxious to bring a rapid end to the political stalemate, called fresh parliamentary elections for 11–12 December 1993. The Congress responded by voting to impeach Yeltsin, arguing that his dissolution of parliament had been unconstitutional, and designated the vice president, Aleksandr Rutskoi, as the new 'acting president'. Supported by speaker Khasbulatov, 'president' Rutskoi took refuge in the parliament building. A two-week siege of parliament ensued, which, claiming at least 145 lives, was broken on 4 October after troops, following the orders of Defense Minister General Pavel Grachev, were sent on 4 October 1993 to arrest the putschists, resulting in the surrender of Rutskoi and Khasbulatov. Later, in February 1994, Rutskoi, Khasbulatov, and others involved in the 'October rebellion' were granted an amnesty and released from detention.

A new Russian parliament was elected on 12 December 1993 and a constitution, based on the French model, which increased the powers of the presidency, was approved narrowly in a concurrent plebiscite. However, the parliament elections failed to resolve the political uncertainty in the country since the outcome was inconclusive. The extreme rightwing nationalist-populist Liberal Democratic Party (LDPR), led by the xenophobic Vladimir Zhirinovsky (b. 1947), captured 23% of the national vote and emerged as the largest single party in the new State Duma (lower house), while the Communist Party of Russia (CPRF) and its Agrarian Party (APR) and Women of Russia allies attracted a further 28% of the vote. A new coalition cabinet was formed in January 1994, which was headed by the centrist Prime Minister Viktor Chernomyrdin and retained the reformist Anatoly Chubais (b. 1955) as minister for privatization and Andrei Kozyrev (b. 1951) as foreign minister, but the two leading radical reformers, the economy and finance ministers, Yegor Gaidar and Boris Fedorov, resigned, being replaced by more centralist 'Soviet-style economists' and members of the Communist-aligned Agrarian Party, as Prime Minister Chernomyrdin declared that the 'period of market romanticism had ended'. The economy had contracted by a further 8% during 1993, the inflation rate remained high, and there was a new scourge of organized crime. However, by 1994, 30% of state-owned enterprises had been privatized and the private sector produced 62% of officially recorded GDP.

During 1994 Russia was hit by a major currency crisis in October, which led to the dismissal of the finance minister and central bank chief. However, overseas, in its 'near abroad', the country's influence increased significantly, as its forces were called upon to help restore order after civil wars erupted in Armenia, Georgia, and Tajikistan in former-Soviet Transcaucasia and Central

Asia, and the CIS became a more effective body. In June 1994 Russia joined NATO's Partnership for Peace (PFP). Internally, an autonomy agreement was reached with Tatarstan in February 1994. However, relations with the mountainous republic of Chechnya, situated in the Caucasus region, which had proclaimed its independence from Russia as early as November 1991, deteriorated greatly. This autonomous republic was the home base of Ruslan Khasbulatov and a center of organized crime. Civil war broke out in the region in September 1994 as opposition forces, supported by Khasbulatov, attempted to overthrow Chechnya's president, General Dzhokar Dudayev, and the Russian army invaded the republic in December 1994 in an effort to reimpose central control, thus setting an example to other secessionist-minded republics. The army met with fierce guerrilla resistance and the fighting, which lasted several months and claimed the lives of 1,800 Russian soldiers and an even greater number of Chechen guerrillas and civilians, led to a third of the Chechen population being made refugees, consumed resources equivalent to more than 1% of Russian GDP, and gravely tarnished the reputation of President Yeltsin. On 30 July 1995 a peace deal, brokered by Prime Minister Chernomyrdin, was signed by the contending parties. It provided for an immediate ceasefire, demilitarization of the republic, enhanced autonomy, and the holding of elections in December 1995.

By the spring of 1995 Yeltsin's public approval rating had fallen to single figures and centrist democratic parties, notably Russia's Choice, led by Yegor Gaidar, withdrew their backing from the Yeltsin regime. This resulted, in June 1995, after 140 people had been killed in the southern Russian town of Budyonnovsk following the mishandling of a Chechen hostage siege, in the Duma passing a motion of no confidence in the government. To prevent defeat in a second no-confidence motion, which would have precipitated the holding of early parliamentary elections, President Yeltsin sacked the interior minister, head of the security service and the deputy prime minister in late June 1995. The president, whose public appearances had become infrequent and erratic, with his health deteriorating, was seen increasingly as having become, like Gorbachev in 1990–91, a prisoner of a conservative military-nationalist grouping. In July 1995 Yeltsin was admitted to hospital suffering from a heart complaint, and in November 1995 Prime Minister Chernomyrdin was given temporary control over security and foreign policy after President Yeltsin was hospitalized following a serious heart attack.

6. 1995–1999

New State Duma elections were held in December 1995 and the CPRF and its APR and Women of Russia allies attracted the largest share, 30%, of the vote to win 180 of the 450 seats. They had benefited from growing nostalgia, especially among the old, poor, and rural communities, for the certainties of the communist past. The extreme nationalist LDPR secured 11% of the vote. The new parliament, which passed a resolution, in March 1996, denouncing the December 1991 Belovezhsk Agreement which had ended the Soviet Union, contained a strong majority against radical market-centerd economic reform. This persuaded President Yeltsin, from January 1996, to tack to the right. He sacked his reformist economy and foreign ministers, Chubais and Kozyrev, replacing them respectively with Vladimir Kadannikov, an old-style Soviet factory boss, and Yevgeny Primakov (b. 1930), formerly head of the Foreign Intelligence Service. In January 1996 the Russian army also took a harder line in Chechnya, where the ceasefire remained on-off.

Nevertheless, despite ill health and a public approval rating in February 1996, of only 8%, President Yeltsin orchestrated a remarkable revival in his fortunes by moving back to the center-ground and presenting himself as the defender of the post-1991 reforms against the threat of a return to communism. In February 1996, he oversaw Russia's admission to the Council of Europe and negotiated with the IMF an agreement to lend $10 billion over a three-year period. With the economy having 'bottomed out', Yeltsin built on returning optimism by pledging $10 billion in special-interest handouts, to students, pensioners, teachers, and soldiers; promised an end to military conscription by 2000 (later put back to 2005); and, in May 1996, negotiated a Chechnya peace deal.

Assisted by a supportive media and financial support provided by a small consortium of business tycoons, Yeltsin secured 36% of the first round vote, in the June 1996 presidential election, finishing ahead of the CPRF leader Gennady Zyuganov. In a surprise third position, with 15% of the vote, came Alexander Lebed (b. 1950), a former Red Army commander in Afghanistan and general in charge of the Russian 14th army in the Dnestr region of Moldova between 1992–95, who had campaigned on an anti-corruption and anti-crime platform. Shortly afterwards, Lebed was appointed as President Yeltsin's national security chief and *de facto* deputy and Pavel Grachev, the unpopular defense chief, was sacked. This enabled Yeltsin to secure a clear victory over

Zyuganov, in the second round run-off in July 1996

The new government, still headed by Prime Minister Chernomyrdin, included a stronger reformist element, with Anatoly Chubais, the architect of the privatization program, as the president's new chief of staff and Vladimir Potanin (b. 1961), a young commercial banker, first deputy prime minister, in charge of the economy. Fighting resumed in Chechnya, but Alexander Lebed secured agreement to a new ceasefire and peace plan on 31 August 1996, with the Chechen's guerrilla commander, Aslan Maskhadov (b. 1951). This provided for: the formation of a transitional government, headed by Maskhadov; the withdrawal of Russian troops by early January 1997; the granting of Chechnya 'special status' within the Russian Federation; the holding of elections in late January 1997; and a referendum on independence in 2002. This proved durable and, in May 1997, a peace treaty was signed, ending a 21-month separatist war which had claimed an estimated 80,000 lives (including 10,000 Russian troops) and displaced 415,000 refugees. The price was the granting of virtual independence to a state which, by 1997 under President Maskhadov's leadership, had proclaimed itself the Islamic Republic of Ichkeria, in which Sharia (Islamic) law was in force.

However, in October 1996 Lebed was dismissed by President Yeltsin after a dispute with the interior minister, Anatoly Kulikov. A month later, Yeltsin, who, it emerged, had suffered heart problems in June 1996 between the presidential election rounds, underwent a seven-hour quintuple heart bypass operation. During the subsequent three-month convalescence period, executive power was shared among a new council which included Chubais, Prime Minister Chernomyrdin, and the speakers of the two houses of parliament. Yeltsin returned to work on 23 December 1996, but was hospitalized again on 8 January 1997, with pneumonia.

Concerned at the continuing economic and social problems caused by tax evasion and wage and pensions arrears, President Yeltsin, in the spring of 1997, gave his backing to greater reform by promoting Chubais to the posts of first deputy prime minister and finance minister and appointing Boris Nemtsov (b. 1959), the reforming governor of Nizhny Novgorod province, as another first deputy prime minister, in charge of restructuring state energy and transport monopolies. In effect, they assumed control of the economy from Prime Minister Chernomyrdin, while Potanin was sacked. Later, in June 1997, the president's younger daughter, Tatyana Dyachenko (b. 1959), an ally of Chubais, was made a presidential adviser. The key priorities of this new administration were to reduce the levels of household subsidies, streamline the tax code, and reduce the armed forces from a strength of 1.7 million to 1.2 million, by 1999. Its reformist intentions impressed the World Bank sufficiently for it to agree, in June 1997, to lend Russia $12 billion over two years. Meanwhile, Prime Minister Chernomyrdin announced that, after nine years of continuous decline, the Russian economy was at last expected to grow in 1997 – albeit by a mere 0.4%.

From the autumn of 1997, the Yeltsin government faced mounting opposition from the State Duma, which opposed its plans to cut household subsidies and allow the sale and purchase of land, 40% of which remained under state ownership. The president averted a threatened Duma vote of no-confidence in Prime Minister Chernomyrdin, in October 1997, by agreeing to hold round table negotiations, involving government, State Duma, and Federation Council representatives. A month later, President Yeltsin sacked, as deputy secretary of the Security Council, Boris Berezovsky, who was one of the most prominent of the country's top tycoons, known as 'the oligarchs', who had established control over key sectors of the economy and benefited from privatization, tax breaks, and contract perks. A media mogul, with a reputed worth of $3 billion, Berezovsky was accused of seeking to use his political position to further his business interests. However, his dismissal destabilized the government. It was followed, in November 1997, by the removal of of Anatoly Chubais, who had controversially received a $90,000 advance for a planned book on privatization. Then, on 23 March 1998, President Yeltsin unexpectedly sacked Chernomyrdin as prime minister and nominated as his replacement the energy minister, Sergei Kiriyenko (b. 1962), a young, former oil-industry executive who had had less than a year's experience of national politics. It was suggested that Yeltsin acted in response to rumours that 'the oligarchs' were plotting to install Chernomyrdin as president before new elections were due in 2000. However, President Yeltsin's nomination of Kiriyenko was opposed by the State Duma and was only ratified on a third and final vote, on 24 April 1998, after Duma deputies had been enticed by the promise of larger *dachas* (country houses) and cars.

Kiriyenko put together a new cabinet which restored most senior ministers to their posts, with the exceptions of Chubais and Chernomyrdin. The reformist

Boris Nemtsov remained as a deputy prime minister. Within weeks the government was faced by a grave financial crisis as international investors lost confidence in the Russian 'crony capitalist' economy, in which 'mafia-style' groups controlled over two-fifths of output. Amid broader uncertainty in the world financial market, there was a 'run' on the recently redenominated 'new rouble' and, although interest rates were tripled to 150%, the rouble was eventually devalued by more than 20% in August 1998 and a moratorium placed on foreign debt repayments. In desperation, President Yeltsin dismissed Kiriyenko and re-nominated Chernomyrdin as prime minister. However, the State Duma rejected twice Chernomyrdin's nomination and, in September 1998, to avert a constitutional crisis, Yeltsin proposed instead Yevgeny Primakov, the foreign minister. This nomination was ratified by the Duma.

The appointment as prime minister of Primakov, a wily but cautious bureaucrat who had served every Soviet and Russian leader since Khrushchev, marked an important U-turn and abandonment of economic reform, with emphasis now turning to the re-establishment of internal order and stability. As foreign minister, Primakov had championed Russian interests and rebuilt ties with neighboring ex-Soviet states. In April 1997 a 'charter of union' was agreed with Belarus, creating a new joint Russian – Belarussian Parliamentary Assembly; in May 1997 a ten-year 'treaty of friendship, cooperation, and partnership' was signed with Ukraine; and, in May 1997, in an agreement on cooperation and mutual relations with NATO, Russia removed its objections to allowing the ex-Soviet states of Central and Eastern Europe from gradually joining NATO, while a NATO – Russia Permanent Joint Council was established to discuss matters of mutual interest. The Primakov government, formed in mid-September 1998, lacked economic and political liberals and included prominent figures from the Soviet era, including Yuri Maslyukov, the last head of the Gosplan state planning agency. This suggested that Russia was heading for a period of renewed protectionism and hyperinflation, and that attempts would be made to re-establish greater central control. However, this would be difficult to achieve, as Russia's regions now operated substantially autonomous economic, and even foreign, policies. It seemed that Boris Yeltsin's political influence was now eroded and that effective authority had shifted decisively back to the CPRF old guard. Within the State Duma there were plans to amend the constitution to reduce the president's powers; while outside, Alexander Lebed, now the governor of Krasnoyarsk, and Yuri Luzhkov, the popular left-leaning mayor of Moscow, were viewed as potential successors as national strongman.

President Yeltsin returned to hospital, in January 1999, for treatment of a stomach ulcer. However, in May 1999 he threw the country's politics into turmoil once more when he sacked the popular Primakov, who had helped stabilise the economic situation and instiuted an anti-corruption campaign, along with a number of Soviet era ministers, including Maslyukov. The 46-year-old interior minister, Sergei Stepashin, was nominated by Yeltsin as the new prime minister and, surprisingly, received Duma backing. Later, Primakov announced plans to contest the next presidential election, and received support from the popular Luzhkov. Meanwhile, during 1999 Russia's relations with the West deteriorated as it found itself at odds with NATO's policy of armed intervention during the Kosovo crisis of the spring.

SLOVAKIA

Slovak Republic
Republika Slovenska

Capital: Bratislava

Social and economic data

Area: 49,035 sq km/18,933 sq miles

Population: 5,347,000*
Pop. density per sq km/sq mi: 109/282*
Urban population: 57%**
Literacy rate: 99%**
GDP: $15,850 million*; per-capita GDP: $2,965*
Government defense spending (% of GDP): 2.8%*
Currency: Slovak koruna
Economy type: middle income
Labor force in agriculture: 12%**
Unemployment rate: 13.1%*
* 1995.
** 1992.

Head of state (ceremonial)

President Rudolf Schuster, since 1999

Head of government

Prime Minister Mikulas Dzurinda, since 1998

Ethnic composition

Eighty-seven per cent of the population is of Slovak ethnic stock and 11% is ethnic Hungarian (Magyar). There are also small Czech (1%), Moravian, Silesian, and Romany (gypsy) communities. Slovak, a member of the western Slavonic group, has been the sole official language since 1996. The large ethnic Hungarian minority, who live in the south of the state, have been demanding greater cultural and educational autonomy and new laws guaranteeing minority rights.

Religions

Sixty per cent of the population is Roman Catholic. The Protestant Slovak Lutheran (Evangelical) Church has 330,000 members, the Reformed Christian Church of Slovakia, 89,000 adherents, and the Orthodox Church, 55,000 members.

Political features

State type: emergent democratic
Date of state formation: 1993*
Political structure: unitary
Executive: parliamentary
Assembly: one-chamber
Party structure: multiparty
Human rights rating: N/A
International affiliations: BIS, CE, CEI, CEFTA, CERN, DC, EBRD, ECE, IAEA, IBRD, ICFTU, IMF, LORCS, NACC, OSCE, PFP, UN, VG, WEU (associate partner), WFTU, WTO

* Czechoslovakia was formed in 1918.

Local and regional government

The republic is divided into eight regions (*kraje*), one of which is the city of Bratislava, and 79 districts (*okresy*) for the purpose of local government.

Political system

Under the terms of the September 1992 constitution, which came into force on 1 January 1993, Slovakia has a parliamentary political system. There is a single-chamber legislature, the National Council of the Slovak Republic, whose 150 members are elected by universal adult suffrage for a four-year term through a system of proportional representation. The state president, until June 1995, as commander in chief of the armed forces, appoints the prime minister, represents the republic internationally, and may declare a referendum and state of emergency. Since 1999 the president has been directly elected for a first year term. Previously election was by top National Council.. A president can be removed from office if the National Council passes a no-confidence resolution with a 60% majority. The prime minister, drawn from the grouping holding at least 60% support from the National Council, is executive head of government and nominates a cabinet of about 15 members. There is provision for a national referendum to be held if a petition is signed by at least 350,000 citizens. For a referendum to be valid, turnout must exceed 50%.

Political parties

Out of around 20 parties which operate in Slovakia, the seven main ones are: the Movement for a Democratic Slovakia (MDS), the Democratic Union of Slovakia (DUS), the Party of the Democratic Left (PDL), the Party of Civic Understanding (SOP), the Christian Democratic Movement (CDM), the Slovak National Party (SNP), and the Hungarian Coalition.

The center-left nationalist-populist MDS was formed in March 1991 by Vladimir Meciar as a breakaway from the moderate Public Against Violence (PAV), which was set up in 1989 as an intelligentsia-led umbrella body to spearhead the prodemocracy movement in Slovakia. The MDS pressed for full autonomy for the Slovak Republic and was instrumental in securing the dissolution of Czechoslovakia and the formation of independent Slovakia in January 1993.

The centrist DUS was formed in February 1994 as a breakaway from the MDS by Jozef Moravcik and merged in April 1994 with the Alliance of Democrats, which had been formed in June 1993 by Milan Knazko, after his dismissal from the Meciar government and the MDS.

The PDL is the reform-socialist successor to the formerly dominant Communist Party of Slovakia. It was formed in 1991 and is led by Peter Weiss. The SOP is a center-left, anti-Meciar group.

The CDM, led by Jan Carnogursky, is a right-of-center force, in favor of rapid transition to a Western-style full market economy, which was formed in 1990. The SNP is a strongly nationalist party set up in 1990 and led now by Jan Slota. It was weakened in February 1994 when its leader, Ludovit Cernak, left to form a new center-right party, the National Democratic Party.

The Hungarian Coalition, led by Bela Bugar, is an electoral alliance of parties orientated towards Slovakia's large ethnic Hungarian minority community. It comprises the Hungarian Civic Party, the Hungarian Christian Democratic Movement, and Egyutteles (Coexistence).

Political leaders since 1970*

1990–91 Vladimir Meciar (PAV), 1991–92 Jan Carnogursky (CDM), 1992–94 Vladimir Meciar (MDS), 1994 Jozef Moravcik (DUS), 1994–98 Vladimir Meciar (MDS), 1998– Mikulas Dzurinda (SDC)

* Prime minister.

Latest elections

The most recent elections to the National Council, on 25–26 September 1998, produced a 'hung parliament' in which no single party held an overall majority. The largest number of seats, 43 out of the 150 available, was won by the MDS, which attracted 27% of the vote (9% down on 1994). The five-party opposition center-right Slovak Democratic Coalition (SDC), which comprised the CDM, DUS, the Social Democratic Party, the Green Party, and the Democratic Party, finished a close second, with 42 seats and 26% of the vote. The reformed-communist PDL and nationalist SNP polled more strongly than in 1994, respectively securing 15% and 9% of the vote and 23 and 14 seats. The Hungarian Coalition, with 9% of the vote, won 15 seats and the center-left Party of Civic Understanding (SOP), with 8% of the vote, won 13 seats. Eleven other political parties contested the election. They attracted 6% of the vote in aggregate, but fell individually below the 5% cut-off threshold for individual party representation and the 10% threshold applied to coalitions of four or more groups. The best performance among these parties was the Slovenia Communist Party, which won 2.8% of the vote. Turnout was 84%, up 8% on 1994.

The country's first direct presidential elections, held on 15 and 29 May 1999, were won in a second round run-off by Rudolf Schuster, the leader of SOP and the candidate of the ruling coalition. A former mayor of Kosice, Schuster attracted 57% of the vote, defeating the former prime minister, Vladimir Meciar, of the MDS, who won 43% of the vote. Turnout was 75%, with four other candidates contesting the first round.

Political history

In the 9th century AD Slovaks and Czechs, both western Slavic peoples, were united under the Great Moravian Empire. But from the 10th century, following the empire's dissolution, Czechs formed an independent kingdom which lasted until the Habsburgs assumed control in the 16th century, while Slovaks came under Hungarian rule and remained under the latter's tutelage until the 20th century. Slovak national revival movements were mounted during the 19th century and in October 1918, following the dismemberment of the Austro-Hungarian Habsburg Empire at the end of World War I, the independent state of Czechoslovakia was formed, reuniting the Slovak and Czech peoples.

Slovaks resented the fact that economic development in interwar Czechoslovakia was concentrated in the Czech lands and that, while Roman Catholics predominated in Slovakia, the central government in Prague was anti-clerical. However, Slovak demands for the establishment of a federal system, in which the Slovak lands would be granted autonomy, were rejected. In October 1938, following the September 1938 Munich Agreement which ceded to Nazi Germany predominantly German-peopled areas of Czechoslovakia, Slovak autonomy was declared by Slovak nationalists. The German dictator, Adolf Hitler, responded by agreeing to the establishment of a separate, pro-Nazi Slovak state in March 1939 under the fascist leadership of Jozef Tiso. Jews, in particular, were persecuted by the Tiso regime, which lasted until April 1945, despite an armed rebellion, the 'Slovak National Uprising', being mounted in August 1944.

During the early 1950s, with a communist state being established in Czechoslovakia (see *Czech Republic, Political history*), Slovak nationalism was forcibly suppressed, with even the Slovak-born Gustáv Husák (b. 1913), who was later to become communist party leader in Czechoslovakia between 1969 and 1987, being imprisoned. However, there was economic development, with heavy industry being introduced into Slovakia. In January 1968, another Slovak-born politician, Alexander Dubcek (1921–92), rose to become leader of the ruling Communist Party of Czechoslovakia (CPCZ) and instituted the 'Prague Spring' political reforms. These met with Soviet disapproval and an invasion by Czechoslovakia's Warsaw

Pact allies in August 1968 and Dubcek's dismissal. Husák, who replaced Dubcek as CPCZ leader, introduced a new federal constitution in 1969, which granted Slovakia its own government and legislature, the Slovak National Council, and greater autonomy in the cultural, educational, and judicial spheres.

Continued repression of the Roman Catholic Church and Slovak nationalists during the 1970s and early 1980s meant that when, in the later 1980s, political openness began to be encouraged by the new Soviet leader, Mikhail Gorbachev, the anti-communist prodemocracy movement was especially strong in Slovakia. In 1989 the Public Against Violence (PAV) umbrella grouping was formed in the republic to spearhead this protest campaign and in November 1989 large mass rallies were held in Bratislava and were addressed by the formerly disgraced Alexander Dubcek.

In the June 1990 Federal Assembly and National Council multiparty elections, which were held after the CPCZ had renounced its monopoly of power and a new post-communist reformist administration, headed by Prime Minister Marian Čalfa and President Václav Havel (b. 1935), had assumed power in Prague, the PAV polled particularly strongly in Slovakia. So did the Slovak National Party (SNP), an extreme nationalist party which, critical of Czech predominance in the political and economic affairs of Czechoslovakia, campaigned for the republic's full independence. Vladimir Meciar (b. 1931), a founding member of the PAV, became Slovak prime minister after the election, heading a PAV-dominated coalition administration. Throughout 1990 the SNP organized pro-autonomy rallies and demonstrations in Slovakia as the political temperature rose. The moderate-nationalist PAV administration attempted to appease this nationalist sentiment by declaring Slovak the official language of the republic in November 1990. Then, in March 1991, Prime Minister Meciar formed a breakaway faction from the PAV, termed the Movement for a Democratic Slovakia (MDS), whose platform was greatly increased autonomy for Slovakia within a much looser federation. In response, the Slovak National Council replaced Meciar as prime minister with Jan Carnogursky, leader of the center-right Christian Democratic Movement (CDM).

The federation's fate was decided by the outcome of the 5–6 June 1992 federal and republic elections, which resulted in Meciar's MDS becoming the second largest party group in the Federal Assembly and the dominant group in the Slovak National Assembly. Meciar became Slovak prime minister again, heading an MDS-dominated, but SNP-supported, administration, and on 17 July 1992 the Slovak National Council voted overwhelmingly to declare Slovak sovereignty. Agreement was reached in the summer of 1992 with the Czech Republic prime minister, Václav Havel, on the arrangements for separation and in September 1992 a new Slovak constitution was adopted by the Slovak National Council.

It was agreed that federal assets and liabilities should, in accordance with relative population strengths, be apportioned 2:1 between the Czech and Slovak republics and property on a territorial basis. In October 1992 a customs union treaty was signed by the two republics, providing for the abolition of trade restrictions between the two states on independence, and in December 1992 a cooperation agreement was signed. On 1 January 1993 all remaining federal structures were dissolved and the new separate Czech and Slovak republics were created. Slovakia was automatically admitted into the UN, CSCE (later the OSCE), IMF, and World Bank, while the Slovak National Council, elected in 1992, remained as the legislature, with Meciar as prime minister. After two rounds of voting by the legislature had not produced a winner with the requisite three-fifths majority support, Michal Kovac (b. 1930), the deputy leader of the MDS and a former banker who had been chair of Czechoslovakia's Federal Assembly from 1992, was elected state president on a third vote on 15 February 1993. On assuming the presidency, in March 1993, he dropped his membership of the MDS and was to emerge as a political rival to Meciar.

The new state was faced with grave economic problems. The attempt to move from a planned economy to a market economy and to find new markets for its increasingly obsolete steel, chemicals, and arms heavy industries had led to a sharp fall in GDP between 1991–93 and an increase in the unemployment level to more than 15% and, with a new national currency being introduced, inflation to 30%. There were also accusations of corruption in the privatization process. Not until 1994 did GDP begin to grow again. Relations with Hungary, a member with Slovakia of the Visegrad Group (VG), which promotes economic integration in Central Europe, were also strained by the issue of the large Hungarian minority resident in Slovakia, who were campaigning for cultural and educational autonomy. However, a Treaty of Friendship and Cooperation was later signed by the two states in March 1995. In addition, the country was less politically stable than the neighboring Czech Republic. The MDS's coalition with the SNP was an uneasy one and between March and November 1993 there were, temporarily, no SNP ministers within the cabinet. There were also splits within the MDS after the foreign minister, Milan Knazko, was dismissed in March 1993 and went on to form the Alliance of Democrats as a liberal, right-of-center party.

Slovakia entered the Council of Europe in June 1993, reflecting the country's increasingly pro-Western orientation. In February 1994 the MDS split again when Deputy Prime Minister Roman Kovac and Foreign Minister Jozef Moravcik (b. 1945) joined a new anti-Meciar party faction, the Alternative of Political Realism (APR), later termed the Democratic Union for Slovakia (DUS), which called for the establishment of 'a government of politically nonaligned experts'. Within days they were dismissed from the MDS and resigned from the cabinet, creating a government crisis. In February 1994 the SNP was also weakened by the defection of its former leader, Ludovit Cernak. Following defeat in a no-confidence vote in the National Council and deteriorating relations with President Kovac, who expressed 'serious reservations about the style and ethics of Meciar's politics', Vladimir Meciar resigned as prime minister on 14 March 1994. Jozef Moravcik, now leader of the DUS, was appointed interim prime minister, pending new elections. He headed a broad-based five-party coalition government including members from the ex-communist Party of the Democratic Left (PDL), the Christian Democratic Movement (CDM), the Alliance of Democrats, which had been formed by Milan Knazko, the DUS, and the conservative National Democratic Party, formed by Cernak. The new government succeeded in halting the rise in unemployment and inflation, as the economy began to grow once more, cut back the budget deficit, and introduced a voucher privatization program on the Czech model. Despite these achievements, the governing coalition was defeated in the general election of September – October 1994, capturing just 29% of the national vote to the populist MDS's 35%, which won 61 of the 150 National Council seats.

On 13 December 1994 Meciar was sworn in again as prime minister, heading an MDS-dominated 'red-brown' coalition government with the ultra-nationalist SNP, the left wing Association of Slovak Workers (ZRS), which was a breakaway of the PDL, and the Farmers' Party of Slovakia (RSS), which had been the MDS's electoral partner. The new populist-nationalist government immediately postponed the planned second wave of mass privatization, based on coupon sales, and pledged to revitalize the arms industry and boost pensions and teachers' salaries.

In May 1995 the National Council passed, with a 53% majority, a vote of no confidence in President Kovac over his alleged failure to control the domestic intelligence service, and Prime Minister Meciar, who resented the independent stance adopted by the president, called for Kovac's resignation. Kovac, enjoying strong popular support, refused to step down, although in June 1995 the National Council stripped the president of his role as head of the armed forces. In September 1995, as part of an alleged campaign of intimidation orchestrated by supporters of Prime Minister Meciar, the son of President Kovac was mysteriously kidnapped and beaten up.

Throughout 1996–97 the prime minister and president remained at loggerheads. In May 1997 President Kovac succeeded, through an opposition-backed petition signed by 400,000 citizens, to force a referendum on the possible introduction of direct presidential elections to be held at the same time as a referendum on NATO membership. But Prime Minister Meciar opposed the idea and ballot papers were printed which omitted the question on presidential elections, leading to such confusion that turnout fell to an invalid level of below 10%. Foreign minister, Pavol Hamzik, an independent, resigned from the government in protest.

Meciar's undemocratic methods and flirtation with racist language led to Slovakia being excluded from the first wave of NATO and European Union (EU) enlargement negotiations, although it did sign an association agreement with the EU in October 1993. The economy grew by around 7% per annum between 1995–97 and inflation fell to 6%; however, unemployment exceeded 13%, in 1998.

Between January and July 1998 the National Council failed to elect a successor to President Kovac, whose term expired in March 1998. A successor needed to obtain three-fifths majority support, but this was not achieved because the MDS deliberately failed to put forward a candidate and abstained in the voting so as to enable Prime Minister Meciar to temporarily assume presidential powers. Meciar controversially used his authority to replace 28 of Slovakia's foreign ambassadors and cancel a new referendum on presidential elections, which was due to be held in April 1998. In

August 1998 the National Council chair, Ivan Gasparovic, took over as acting head of state.

Nevertheless, in the September 1998 general election Meciar's coalition was heavily defeated. The MDS won only 43 of the 150 National Council seats and the ZRS no seats (against 13 in 1994), while the opposition Slovak Democratic Coalition (SDC) alliance won 42 seats. In October 1998 the SDC leader, Mikulas Dzurinda, became prime minister, heading a coalition which comprised the SDC, the PDL, the Hungarian Coalition, and the Party of Civic Understanding. The government pledged to seek to improve inter-ethnic relations and an ethnic Hungarian was appointed as minister for minorities and human rights.

In January 1999, after further unsuccessful attempts by the National Council to elect a new state president, the constitution was amended to provide for direct elections. These were won, in May 1999, by the ruling coalition's candidate, Rudolf Schuster, who defeated Vladimir Meciar, who had re-emerged from a brief political 'retirement' to contest the poll. This victory suggested that, despite its imposition of austerity measures and an economic slowdown, the four-party left-right coalition remained popular.

SLOVENIA

Republic of Slovenia
Republika Slovenija

Capital: Ljubljana

Social and economic data

Area: 20,251 sq km/7,819 sq miles
Population: 1,942,000*
Population density per sq km/sq mi: 96/248*
Urban population: 49%**
Literacy rate: 99%**
GDP: $16,330 million*; per-capita GDP: $8,410*
Government defense spending (% of GDP): 1.5%*
Currency: tolar
Economy type: high income
Labor force in agriculture: 13%**
Unemployment rate: 7.4%*
* 1995.
** 1992.

Head of state

President Milan Kucan, since 1990

Head of government

Prime Minister Dr Janez Drnovsek, since 1992

Ethnic composition

Ninety per cent of the population is of Slovene ethnic stock, 3% is ethnic Croat, and 2% Serb. Slovene, which resembles Serbo-Croat and is written in Roman characters, is the official language, but Hungarian and Italian are also widely used in ethnically mixed areas and 5% of the population speak Serbo-Croat.

Religions

The population is predominantly, more than 90%, Roman Catholic, with minority Serbs adhering to the Serbian Orthodox faith.

Political features

State type: emergent democratic
Date of state formation: 1991
Political structure: unitary
Executive: dual
Assembly: two-chamber
Party structure: multiparty
Human rights rating: N/A
International affiliations: COE, IAEA, IBRD, IMF, NAM (guest), OSCE, PFP, UN, WTO

Local and regional government

There are 148 self-governing municipalities, including 11 urban ones. Municipalities raise their own revenue.

Political system

Under the December 1991 constitution Slovenia has predominantly a parliamentary pluralist political system, but the president retains a degree of moral authority which enables the system to be currently characterized as 'dual executive'. The president is directly elected for a maximum of two five-year terms and has chiefly ceremonial power. The legislature comprises two chambers, the 90-member National Assembly (Drzavni Zbor) and the 40-member National Council (Drzavni Svet). The National Assembly is elected for four years and comprises 38 directly elected deputies, 50 members selected on a proportional basis by an electoral commission from among parties that have secured at least 3% of the national vote and two elected representatives of the Hungarian and Italian minorities. (December 1996 proposals to change the electoral system were defeated in a referendum.) The National Council serves a five-year term and comprises 22 directly elected members and 18 chosen indirectly by an electoral college to 'represent various social, economic, trading, political and local interest groups'. The National Assembly is the most significant chamber and the prime minister, who is formally appointed by the president, must be able to command a majority within it. The National Council performs principally an advisory function, but a new government needs to be approved by the Council and it may propose laws to the Assembly and demand that the latter review its decision on a law before promulgating it.

Political parties

Out of 16 parties operating, the principal ones are the Liberal Democracy of Slovenia (LDS), the Slovenian Christian Democrats (SKD), the Slovenian Nationalist Party (SNS), the Slovenian People's Party (SLS), the Social Democratic Party of Slovenia (SDPS), the Democratic Party of Pensioners of Slovenia (DeSUS), and the United List of Social Democrats (ZLSD).

The LDS, SLS, and DeSUS currently form the governing coalition. The LDS is a centrist force which was formed in 1990 out of the Union of Socialist Youth, a communist youth organization. Led by Prime Minister Dr Janez Drnovsek, it has abandoned its former socialist orientation, and has 18,000 members. In March 1994 it merged with the Democratic Party (DS), the Green Alliance (ZS), and the ex-communist Socialist Party to increase its strength in the National Assembly to 30 seats. The DS originated in 1990 after a split in the Slovenian Democratic Union (estd. 1989), the first party to be formed in opposition to the communists.

The 34,000-member SKD is a right-of-center conservative party, formed in 1989 and led by former premier, Lojze Peterle.

The 4,000-member SNS is a rightwing nationalist body and the 40,000-member SLS is also a conservative force which originated, in 1989, as the Slovenian Farmers' Association.

The DeSUS is orientated towards pensioners and the SDPS is a center-left body formed in 1989, which has 16,000 members.

The ex-communist ZLSD originated as an alliance of four left-of-center parties formed to contest the 1992 parliamentary elections: the Social Democratic Union (estd. 1990), the Workers' Party of Slovenia (estd. 1990), the DeSUS, and the Social Democratic Reform of Slovenia. It became a single party (without DeSUS) in 1993 and has 23,000 members.

Political leaders since 1970

1990– Milan Kucan (PDR/ex-communist independent)*, 1990–92 Lojze Peterle (SKD)**, 1992– Dr Janez Drnovsek (LDS)**

* President.

** Prime minister.

Latest elections

The most recent parliamentary elections, the second since independence, were held on 10 November 1996. Seven parties secured more than 3% of the national vote and thus representation in the National Assembly the center-left LDS, which, with 27% of the vote, won 25 seats; the conservative SLS, 19% of the vote and 19 seats; the center-left SDPS (16%), 16 seats; the right-of-center SKD (10%), 10 seats; the left-of-center ZLSD (9%), 9 seats; the center-left DeSUS (4%), 5 seats; and the rightwing nationalist SNS (3%), 4 seats. The SLS, SDPS, and SKD fought the election as an alliance, 'Slovenian Spring'.

The most recent presidential election, on 23 November 1997, resulted in the re-election of Milan Kucan. Standing as an independent, he won 56% of the vote and defeated seven other candidates, with Dr Janez Podobnik of the SLS, who was president of the National Assembly, finishing second, with 18% of the vote.

Political history

The area corresponding to contemporary Slovenia was settled by the Slovenes in the 6th century and later by the Slavs and Franks, from 788, before coming under Hungarian domination between 907–55. It was absorbed in the Austro-Hungarian Habsburg Empire from 1335, forming part of the Austrian crownlands of Carniola, Styria, and Carinthia. From 1848 the Slovenes began their struggle for national unification and this was largely achieved in December 1918 following the collapse of the Habsburg Empire. The territory was incorporated, along with the Serbs, Croats, and Montenegrins, into the Kingdom of the Serbs, Croats, and Slovenes, which became known as Yugoslavia in 1929. However, a sizeable Slovene community lived under Italian rule in Istria, until borders were rearranged after World War II.

Unlike in neighboring Croatia, there were few Slovenian demands for autonomy during the 1930s. During World War II the region was occupied by Germany and Italy and in 1941 an anti-Nazi Slovene Liberation Front was formed. This became allied with Marshal Tito's communist-led all-Yugoslav Partisan army and with British and American forces. After the war, in November 1945, Slovenia became a constituent republic of the communist Yugoslav Socialist Federal Republic. Benefiting from its Habsburg legacy, it was the most economically advanced and politically liberal republic within the federation, helping to subsidize the poorer southeastern republics.

From the 1980s, however, there was economic decline and, particularly after the death of the federation's leader, Marshal Tito, increasing nationalist unrest. The leadership of the ruling Slovene League of Communists (LCS) responded by pressing for greater autonomy within the federation to enable the republic to pursue a strategy of economic liberalization and political pluralism. In 1989 opposition parties were legalized and a free, multi party election was held in April 1990. Despite renaming themselves the Party of Democratic Reform (PDR) and adopting a social democratic program, the now reformed communists were convincingly defeated by the six-party Democratic Opposition of Slovenia (DEMOS), a nationalist, center-right coalition, which campaigned for independence within a year and attracted a 55% share of the national vote. However, the PDR's reformist leader, Milan Kucan (b. 1941), who was an outspoken opponent of the nationalist-populist president and communist party leader of Serbia, Slobodan Milosevic, was popularly elected state president, renouncing his party membership once installed in office.

After the parliamentary elections, a new DEMOS-dominated government was formed with Lojze Peterle, leader of the right-of-center Slovenian Christian Democrats (SKD), as prime minister. It sought to promote the formation of a new loose Yugoslav confederation. However, this was resisted by an increasingly assertive Serbia. On 2 July 1990 the Slovenian National Assembly declared the sovereignty of the republic, with its laws now taking precedence over federal legislation. Following a referendum on independence, which was held on 23 December 1990 and received 89% support, plans began to be made for secession. An independent army, the Slovenian Territorial Defense Force, was established in the spring of 1991 and on 8 May 1991 it was announced that the secession of both Slovenia and Croatia from the federation would take place on 25 June 1991.

Around 3,000 soldiers from the federal Yugoslav National Army (JNA), which was dominated by Serbians, moved to the Slovenian border on 27 June 1991 and around 70 died during a week of sporadic clashes with the new Slovenian army. The European Community (EC) sought to broker a ceasefire, but could not prevent an aerial bombardment of Ljubljana on 2 July 1991, the first bombardment of a European city since World War II. However, during its short campaign against the new Slovenian forces, the JNA endured a number of reverses, and the federal government agreed later on 2 July 1991 to accept the EC ceasefire terms of a three-month suspension of Slovenia's declaration of independence and the withdrawal of the JNA from the republic. This was successfully implemented as the focus of the Serb-dominated JNA's activity switched to Croatia, with its much larger Serb minority.

On 8 October 1991, after the three-month moratorium on disassociation had expired, Slovenia proclaimed its full independence and introduced its own currency, the tolar. Slovenia's independence was formally recognized by the EC in January 1992 and by the United States in April 1992, and in May 1992 it became a member of both the United Nations (UN) and Conference on Security and Cooperation in Europe (CSCE, later the OSCE). On 23 December 1991 Slovenia adopted a new constitution and on 30 December the ruling DEMOS coalition, which had become undermined by increasing factionalism, dissolved itself. Peterle continued as prime minister until April 1992, when his government was defeated in a no-confidence motion and Dr Janez Drnovsek, leader of the Liberal Democratic Party (LDS) and a former president of Yugoslavia, took over as premier.

The parliamentary and presidential elections of December 1992 resulted in little change, with Kucan being re-elected state president with 64% of the popular vote, although this position had been made largely ceremonial by the new constitution, and Drnovsek continuing as prime minister. His center-left LDS attracted 24% of the vote and he put together a coalition government with the center-right Christian Democrats (SKD), and, until its withdrawal in January 1996, the United List of Social Democrats (ZLSD). Benefiting from its greater ethnic homogeneity and its location adjoining Italy and Austria, Slovenia managed to successfully divorce itself from the tragic events elsewhere in the former Yugoslavia between 1992–95 and, although relations with Croatia and Serbia remained strained, it was able to concentrate on building a competitive market economy and its drive for associate membership of the European Union (EU). This was secured in June 1996 and talks on full membership began in 1998. Between 1989–93 GDP fell by 20% in the republic and unemployment climbed to 14% of the work force. However, from 1994 the economy began to grow again, by around 4% per annum, unemployment decreased to 7% in 1996, the inflation rate was brought down to around 9% per annum, and the exchange rate remained stable.

In the parliamentary elections held in November 1996 Drnovsek's LDS raised its share of the national vote to 27% in a contest which saw support fall for the nationalist Slovenian National Party (SNS) and the ex-communist ZLSD. The LDS had been opposed by a new center-right 'Slovenian Spring' alliance comprising the SKD, the conservative Slovenian People's Party (SLS), and the Social Democratic Party of Slovenia (SDPS), which, together, won 45% of the vote and half of the National Assembly seats. However, in January 1997 one SKD deputy defected to support the LDS, giving the LDS and its smaller left-of-center allies, including the Democratic Party of Pensioners of Slovenia (DeSUS), a slim overall majority. In March 1997, when the SLS switched sides, a stable coalition government was formed, based around three parties, the LDS, DeSUS, and the SLS, with Drnovsek continuing as prime minister.

Economic growth became more sluggish during 1997–98 and the unemployment level moved above 10%. Privatization had scarcely begun for larger enterprises, and in the private sector, in 1998, accounted for barely a half of employment and value added.

Slovenia joined NATO's 'Partnership for Peace' program in 1994, but was unsuccessful in its bid to be included in the first wave of the eastward expansion of NATO. In January 1996 Slovenia became the fifth member of the Central European Free Trade Association, along with the Czech Republic, Hungary, Poland, and Romania, and formally recognized Yugoslavia in November 1995, following the Dayton peace accord on Bosnia. Relations with neighboring Croatia have been largely harmonious since independence.

TURKEY

Republic of Turkey
Türkiye Cumhuriyeti

Capital: Ankara

Social and economic data

Area: 779,450 sq km/300,947 sq miles
Population: 61,183,000*
Pop. density per sq km/sq mi: 78/203*
Urban population: 64%**
Literacy rate: 81%**
GDP: $169,450 million*; per-capita GDP: $2,770*
Government defense spending (% of GDP): 3.6%*
Currency: Turkish lira
Economy type: middle income
Labor force in agriculture: 50%**
Unemployment rate: 6.6%*
* 1995.
** 1994.

Head of state

President Suleiman Demirel, since 1993

Head of government

Prime Minister Bülent Ecevit, since 1997

Ethnic composition

Over 90% of the population can be said to be Turks but only about 5% can claim Turki or Western Mongoloid ancestry. Most people are descended from earlier conquerors of their country, such as the Greeks. The Kurdish community in the southeast fight for separate statehood.

Religions

About 99% of the people are Muslims, mainly of the Sunni sect. Islam was the state religion for a brief period, between 1924 and 1928.

Political features

State type: liberal democratic
Date of state formation: 1923
Political structure: unitary
Executive: parliamentary
Assembly: one-chamber
Party structure: multiparty
Human rights rating: 44%
International affiliations: ACP (associate), CE, CERN, CSCE, ECO, IAEA, IBRD, IMF, NACC, NATO, OECD, OIC, UN, WEU (associate), WTO

Local and regional government

The country is divided into 76 provinces (*il*) and 2,074 municipalities. The provinces have appointed governors and there are elected assemblies at all levels.

Political system

After a military coup in 1980, a National Security Council (NSC) was installed with its president as head of state. In 1982, a new constitution was adopted, and later amended in 1987. It provides for a single-chamber National Assembly of 550 members, elected through a weighted party list system of proportional representation, for a five-year term. Parties must obtain at least 10% of the popular vote before they can win representation in the National Assembly. The executive president is elected by the Assembly for a seven-year term. They then appoint a prime minister to lead the government. The relationship between the president and prime minister is not entirely clear particularly in matters of constitutional authority.

Political parties

Political activities were banned between 1980 and 1983 when new parties were allowed to form. There are now some 15 active groups, the five main ones being the Motherland Party (ANAP), the Republican People's Party (CHP) the True Path Party (DYP, formerly TPP), the Welfare Party (RP/GB), Bülent Eçevit's leftwing Democratic Left Party (DSP), and the Nationalist Action Party (MHP).

The center-left CHP was formed in 1931 by Demal Atatürk and in 1995 merged with the Social Democratic Populist party. ANAP was founded in 1983 by Turgut Özal. It has a nationalist-Islamic right-of-center orientation. The SHP was originally formed in 1985 by a merger of the Populist and Social Democratic parties.

The DYP originates from 1983 when it replaced the old Justice Party. It merged with the Citizen Party in 1986. It has a center-right pro-Western stance.

RP, led by Necmettin Erbakan (b. 1926), was an Islamic fundamentalist body, opposed to membership of NATO and the EU. It was banned in January 1998 and regrouped as the Virtue Party (FP). The MHP is a far right nationalist body, founded by Alparslan Turks.

Political leaders since 1970

1965–71 Süleiman Demirel (JP), 1971–73 'nonparty' leaders (military), 1973–74 Bülent Eçevit (RPP-NSP coalition), 1974–75 transitional coalition, 1975–78 Süleiman Demirel (JP coalition), 1978–79 Bulent Eçevit (RPP coalition), 1979–80 Süleiman Demirel (JP), 1980–83 General Kenan Evren (military), 1983–89 Turgut Özal (ANAP), 1989–91 Yildirim Akbulut (ANAP), 1991 Mesut Yilmaz (ANAP), 1991–93 Süleiman Demirel (DYP), 1993–96 Tansu Ciller (DYP), 1996 Mesut Yilmaz (ANAP), 1996–97 Necmettin Erbakan (RP), 1997–99 Mesut Yilmaz (ANAP) Bülent Ecevit (DSP)

Latest elections

The results of the 18 April 1999 general election were as follows:

Turkey latest election results

Party	% votes	National Assembly seats
DSP	22.1	136
MHP	18.0	129
FP	15.4	111
ANAP	13.2	86
DYP	12.0	85
Others	19.3	3

Political history

During the Middle Ages Turkey's power and influence were legendary and the Ottoman Empire spread into southern Russia, Hungary, Syria, Arabia, Egypt, and Cyprus. Its power began to decline in the 17th century, as the armies of Russia and Austria pushed the Turks back towards the Bosporus. Britain and France, however, saw Turkey's value as a bulwark against Russia's imperialist ambitions and fought the Crimean War (1853–56) to defend its frontiers.

Towards the end of the 19th century the Ottoman Empire began to disintegrate and Turkey was spoken of as 'the sick man of Europe'. The European powers were quick to take advantage of this weakness, France seizing Tunis in 1881, and Britain, Egypt in 1882. The final humiliation came after World War I when Turkey had allied itself with Germany and shared in its defeat. The Treaty of Sèvres finished the Ottoman Empire and the army, led by Kemal Atatürk (1881–1938), removed the sultan in 1922 and proclaimed a republic in 1923.

Atatürk (CHP) ruled with a firm hand until his death in 1938. During this time he secularized and Westernized his nation, emancipated women and turned Turkey into a modern industrial state, substituting national pride for the old Islamic loyalties.

Atatürk was succeeded by Ismet Inonu (1884–1973), who continued his predecessor's work, but in a more pluralist fashion. During World War II Inonu allied himself with Britain and the United States, although he delayed entering the war until near its end, in 1945. He liberalized the political system and was then defeated in Turkey's first free elections, held in 1950, which were won by the Democratic Party (DP), led by Celal Bayar and Adnan Menderes (1899–1961). Bayar became president and Menderes prime minister.

In the post-1945 period Turkey felt itself threatened by the USSR and joined a number of collective defense organizations, including NATO in 1952 and the Baghdad Pact in 1955. This became the Central Treaty Organization (CENTO) in 1959 and was eventually dissolved in 1979. Turkey strengthened Western links and by 1987 was making overtures about possible membership or association with the European Community.

In 1960 the government was overthrown in a military coup and President Bayar was later imprisoned and Menderes executed. A new constitution was adopted in 1961 and civilian rule restored even though the leader of the coup, General Cemal Gürsel, became president. There followed a series of civilian governments, led mainly by Ismet Inonu, now very much an elder statesman, until 1965, when the Justice Party (JP), led by Süleiman Demirel (b. 1924), came to power.

Following strikes and student unrest, the army forced Demirel to resign in 1971 and for the next two years the country came under military rule again. A civilian government was restored in 1973 in the shape of a CHP coalition led by Bulent Eçevit (b. 1925). The following year Turkey sent troops to Cyprus to protect the Turkish-Cypriot community, resulting in the effective partition of the island. Ecevit's government fell when he refused to annex north Cyprus and in 1975 Suleiman Demirel returned at the head of a rightwing coalition.

Elections held in 1977 were inconclusive and Demirel precariously held on to power until 1978 when Ecevit returned, leading another coalition. He was faced with a deteriorating economy and outbreaks of sectional violence and by 1979 had lost his working majority and resigned. Demirel returned in November but the violence continued and in September 1980 the army stepped in and set up a National Security Council (NSC), with Bülent Ulusu as prime minister. Martial law was imposed, political activity suspended, and a harsh regime established.

Law and order were eventually restored but at a high cost in the loss of civil liberties, and, in the face of strong international pressure, work was begun on the draft of a new constitution. In May 1983 political parties were allowed to operate again. The old parties reformed under new names and in November three of them fought the Assembly elections, the conservative Motherland Party (ANAP), the Nationalist Democracy Party (MDP), and the Populist Party (SDHP). ANAP won a narrow, but clear, majority and its leader, Turgut Özal (1927–93), became prime minister.

Following a referendum in September 1987, the political ban on the opposition leaders, Süleiman Demirel and Bülent Eçevit, was removed, and in a relatively free and open general election two months later Prime Minister Turgut Özal and ANAP retained their National Assembly majority. Immediately after the election Bulent Ecevit announced his retirement from active politics and in November 1989 Turgut Özal was elected as Turkey's first civilian president for more than 60 years. In November 1989 Yildirim Akbulut, speaker of the National Assembly and ANAP leader, was appointed prime minister. Two years later he lost the party leadership and President Özal appointed his successor, Mesut Yilmaz, as head of government.

Dissatisfaction with the state of the economy reduced ANAP's popular support and the inconclusive 1991 general election resulted in a coalition government of the DYP and the SHP, with Süleiman Demirel as prime minister.

Internationally, Turkey had supported the US-led coalition in the Gulf War and awaited a reply to its 1989 application for EC membership. Its human-rights record and unresolved dispute with Cyprus were obstacles to full international recognition.

The death of Turgut Özal in April 1993 brought Süleiman Demirel to the presidency and appointed Tansu Ciller (b. 1946), as the country's first female prime minister. In 1995 military actions against Kurds in northern Iraq put a strain on the relationship with Turkey's NATO allies. In December 1995 a customs union deal was agreed with the EU, but the concurrent general election produced a 'hung parliament'.

In March 1996 a deal was struck between ANAP and the DYP, resulting in a center-right coalition government, headed by the ANAP leader, Mesut Yilmaz. Two months later, the DYP withdrew from the coalition, and a new administration was eventually formed, with the RP leader, Necmettin Erbakan, heading it. This was the first government led by an Islamic party since the creation of the secular state of Turkey in 1923.

During 1997 tension increased between the military and the government as the former detected a drift towards radical Islamism. Eventually, in June 1997, Erbakan offered to resign and this offer was accepted by President Suleyman Demirel. After protracted discussions with other parties, Yilmaz was invited to form a new secular government, which was a coalition of the ANAP, DSP, and Democratic Turkey Party (DTP), with the support of independents and the CHP. Relations with Greece steadily improved and in October 1997 the two countries agreed to solve any future disputes peacefully. In January 1998 the Constitutional Court banned the Islamic Welfare Party (RP). Its members immediately regrouped as the Virtue Party (FP).

In November 1998 Yilmaz's minority coalition government, which had been tarnished by corruption allegations, collapsed after losing a legislative vote of confidence. Eventually, in January 1999, the former deputy prime minister, Bulent Ecevit, of the DSP, took over as caretaker prime minister, holding power with the support of Tansu Ciller's DYP, pending new elections in April 1999. A staunch secularist, Ecevit held on to power after these elections, with his party emerging as the largest single party in the Grand National Assembly and the Islamist parties polling poorly. In May 1999 he formed a three-party coalition government, comprising the leftwing DSP, the far right nationalist Nationalist Action Party (MHP), led by Devlet Bahceli, which had polled strongly, and Yilmaz's ANAP. This coalition enjoyed a majority within the Assembly – the first since the December 1995 general election – and was committed to continuance of a tight anti-inflationary economic policy and to opposing any compromise with Kurdish rebels or with Greece in the continuing dispute over Cyprus. In March 1999 Abdullah Ocalan, leader of the separatist Kurdish Workers' Party (PKK) and the country's most wanted man, was finally captured by the Turkish authorities, triggering a wave of bomb attacks in Istanbul. He was subsequently tried and in June 1999 was sentenced to death at an unspecified future date.

UKRAINE

The Ukraine
Ukraina

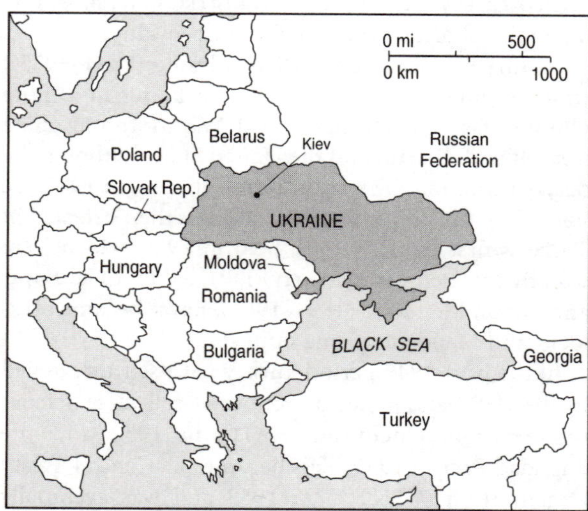

Capital: Kiev (Kiyev)

Social and economic data

Area: 603,700 sq km/233,090 sq miles
Population: 52,100,000*
Pop. density per sq km/sq mi: 86/224*
Urban population: 68%**
Literacy rate: 98%**
GDP: $62,000 million*; per-capita GDP: $1,190*
Government defense spending (% of GDP): 3.0%*
Currency: ihryvna
Economy type: middle income
Labor force in agriculture: 24%**
* 1995.
** 1992.

Head of state (executive)
President Leonid Kuchma, since 1994

Head of government
Prime Minister Valeriy Pustovoytenko, since 1997

Ethnic composition
Seventy-three per cent of the population is of Ukrainian ethnic stock, 22% is ethnic Russian, 1% is Jewish, and 1% Belarussian. Some 1.5 million émigrés live in the United States and 750,000 in Canada. Ethnic Russians are most densely settled in industrialized eastern Ukraine and in Crimea. The official state language is Ukrainian, an Eastern Slavonic language written in the Cyrillic script.

Religions
The population is predominantly Christian, adhering chiefly to the Ukrainian Eastern Orthodox Church. This church originated as the Ukrainian Autocephalous Orthodox Church (UAOC), but split in 1930 when the communist regime incorporated it into the Russian Orthodox Church, as the Ukrainian Orthodox Church (UOC, Moscow Patriarchate). A UAOC continued to operate underground and was revived in 1990. Today it is known as the Ukrainian Orthodox Church (Kievan Patriarchate). Its disputes with the UOC (Moscow Patriarchate) over the right to control Kiev's main cathedral, St Sophia's, led to two deaths in violent clashes in July 1995. The Catholic Church is strong in Western Ukraine and Transcarpathia. Known as the Uniate Church, it was established in 1596 by Orthodox clergy who retained Eastern rites and liturgies while acknowledging the primacy of the Pope. The Uniate Church operated underground in Ukraine between 1946 and 1990 and today claims 5 million adherents. Ethnic Poles adhere to the Latin-rite Catholic Church. There are small Protestant, Jewish, and Muslim communities.

Political features
State type: emergent democratic
Date of state formation: 1918/1991
Political structure: unitary
Executive: limited presidential
Assembly: one-chamber
Party structure: multiparty
Human rights rating: N/A
International affiliations: BSECZ, CIS, COE, DC, IAEA, IBRD, IMF, NACC, OSCE, PFP, UN

Local and regional government
Ukraine comprises 24 provinces (*oblasts*) and one metropolitan area, Kiev. Below there are city and rural districts, towns, and villages, with elected councils. Crimea, situated in the far south of Ukraine, adjoining the Black Sea, is an autonomous republic with special status. It has an area of 25,881 square kilometres/9,995 square miles and a population of 2.55 million, with its capital at Sevastopol. Part of the Russian Federation until 1954, it contains a large ethnic Russian majority, as well as 165,000 Crimean Tatars who were forcibly deported from their homeland in 1944, but have begun to return since 1989. One half of the Crimean Tatars do not have voting rights as they lack Ukrainian citizenship. The autonomous republic has been opposed to Ukraine's independence and, despite Ukraine granting it greater autonomy in April 1992, its parliament declared its sovereignty in May 1994. In December 1994 a new Crimean constitution was approved, which established Ukrainian as the language in Crimea, but with Russian as the official language for correspondence.

Political system
Ukraine's constitution was adopted in June 1996. It replaced the constitution of 1978, which dated back to the communist era, but was substantially modified during the early 1990s to provide for political pluralism and to create a presidency with significant executive authority.

The state president is directly elected for a five-year term, has decree powers, and appoints and dismisses a prime minister and cabinet of ministers, able to command support within parliament. Candidates must be at least 35 years old and be supported by at least 1 million signatures. Presidents are restricted to two consecutive terms and must be at least 35 years old. The legislature, the Supreme Council (Verkhovna Rada), comprises 450 deputies who are popularly elected for four-year terms. Under the election law in force between 1993–97 there was provision for the polling to take place over several rounds, if necessary. A candidate was elected in the first round if able to secure more than 50% of the vote, with turnout also exceeding 50%. Run-off elections were then held between the two leading candidates in constituencies where voting failed to produce a clear majority. However, further rounds of voting were required where turnout fell below 50% in the run-off contests. A succession of repeat elections was needed after the March – April 1994 general election. The election law was consequently changed in September 1997 to one of mixed proportional representation and first-past-the-post. Half of the Supreme Council's 450 seats are elected from single seat constituencies by a simple majority, and the other 225 are apportioned by proportional representation from party lists, for those parties which secure more than 4% of the vote.

The division of executive authority in Ukraine between the president and prime minister was confused before June 1995, when parliament voted the president full control over ministerial appointments and enhanced decree powers.

Under the new 1996 constitution the president can return legislation to the Supreme Council for reconsideration, but if it is re-adopted by a two-thirds' majority the president is obliged to sign it. The president has important decree powers, which were used in December 1996 to make the key ministries of internal affairs, foreign affairs, defense and information directly subordinate. Another presidentialist feature of the constitution is that, while the cabinet of ministers is appointed with the consent of the Supreme Council, its members may not sit in the Supreme Council and must resign when a new president is elected. However, the legislature can remove a president, for reasons of treason or another crime, by an impeachment vote, carried by a three-quarters' majority. Constitutional amendments may be initiated either by the president or by one-third of the Supreme Council and then carried by a two-thirds' Supreme Council majority and approved in a national referendum. There is a National Security Council and an 18-member Constitutional Court.

Political parties

There is no clear governing party in Ukraine and currently a third of the parliament are independents, comprising managers of state-owned factories and collective farms, academics, and private *biznesmeni* (business executives), with no firm party links. A large number, around 40, parties do, however, function. The most important, which attracted more than 4% national support in the March 1998 general election, are the Ukrainian Communist Party (UCP) and its allies, the Peasant's Party of Ukraine (PPU), the Ukrainian Socialist Party (USP), the Progressive Socialist Party (PSP), the moderate-nationalist Rukh, the center-left Social Democratic Party of Ukraine (SDPU), the ecologist Green Party of Ukraine, Hromada, and the People's Democratic Party of Ukraine (PDPU).

The UCP was the dominant and only permitted political party in Ukraine until 1990. It was banned in October 1991, but was relegalized in October 1993 and emerged as the largest single party in parliament in the 1994 and 1998 elections. The UCP, led by Petro Simonenko, and with a membership of 120,000, stands for closer political and economic ties with Russia and a partial return to central planning. Ideologically, it is supported by the 62,000-member PPU (estd. 1992), which seeks to retain the collective farm system and opposes land privatization, and the 90,000-member USP, formed in 1991 as a breakaway from the UCP and led by Oleksandr Moroz. The PSP was formed in 1996 as a breakaway from the USP.

The moderate-nationalist Rukh (People's Movement of Ukraine) emerged in 1988 as the Ukrainian People's Movement for Restructuring, an umbrella 'popular front' body which pressed for political pluralism and independence from the Soviet Union. It became a formal political party in 1993 and claims 62,000 full members and 500,000 associate members. Its leader is Yury Kurtenko. A breakaway faction Rukh, formed in 1991 by Rukh, former leader, Vyocheslav Churnovil, and lead by Hennady Ydovenka, following Chornovil's death in March 1999.

The SDPU, formed in 1990, advocates the creation of a federal Ukraine.

The Green Party was formed in 1990 as the political wing of Green World (estd. 1987). It has 3,000 members. The centrist Hromada is led by Pavlo Lazarenko, the prime minister between 1996–97. Other minor parties of significance include: the nationalist 13,000-member Ukrainian Republican Party (URP), formed in 1990 as a successor to the Ukrainian Helsinki Union (estd. 1988) and closely allied 5,000-member Democratic Party of Ukraine (DPU: estd. 1990), which advocate withdrawal from the Commonwealth of Independent States (CIS); the extreme-nationalist 10,000-member Ukrainian National Assembly (UNA) and 3,000-member Ukrainian Conservative Republican Party (UKRP); the center-right 12,000-member Christian Democratic Party of Ukraine (CDPU); and the centrist Inter-Regional Reform Bloc (IRRB), formed in 1994 to support President Kuchma.

Political leaders since 1970

1973–89 Vladimir Shcherbitsky (UCP)*, 1989–90 Volodymyr Ivashko (UCP)*, 1990–94 Leonid Kravchuk (ex-communist independent)**, 1994– Leonid Kuchma (ex-communist independent)**

* Communist Party leader
** Executive president

Latest elections

The most recent elections to the Supreme Council were

held on 29 March 1998 and were contested by 30 parties and blocs. Eight parties cleared the 4% of the national vote threshold to secure a share of the 225 seats which were allocated from party lists on the basis of proportional representation. The UCP, which attracted 25% of the vote, finished as the largest single party, winning 123 of the 450 seats. The nationalist Rukh finished second, with 9% of the vote and 41 seats, while the left-of-center PPU and USP, which fought the election in alliance, secured 8% of the vote and 29 seats. The other parties which cleared the 4% hurdle were the PDPU (28 seats), Hromada (20 seats), the Green Party (19 seats), the PSP (14 seats), and the SDPU (14 seats). As in the previous election, of March 1994, a large number of independents were elected: 136 of the 225 directly elected seats. Many were either members of the old provincial *nomenklatura* (communist ruling class) or reformist business executives. Turnout was 71%; however, OSCE monitors reported a large number of violations of the election laws, including restrictions on the opposition media during the campaign and incidents of violence and unjustified arrests.

The latest presidential election was held, in two rounds, on 26 June and 10 July 1994. Seven candidates contested the first round in which the incumbent president, Leonid Kravchuk, attracted 37.7% of the vote, while the former prime minister, Leonid Kuchma, captured 31.3%, and the Supreme Council chair, Oleksandr Moroz, 14%. In the run-off race, Kuchma, securing 52% of the vote, unexpectedly defeated Kravchuk, who polled only 45%. Kuchma, backed by the UCP, swept Russified eastern Ukraine and Crimea, while Kravchuk, supported by Ukrainian nationalists, won 90% of the vote in large tracts of western Ukraine. Turnout was 71%.

Political history

1. Beginnings to 1991

'Ukraine' means 'borderland' and Ukrainians belong to the southern branch of Eastern Slavs. Their country formed the heartland of the medieval state of Kievan Rus which emerged in the 9th century. Uniting Ukrainians, Russians (Muscovites), and Belarussians, it became the leading power in eastern Europe, before being destroyed by Mongol invasion in the 13th century. Christianity was adopted from Byzantium in 988 AD and the region came under Catholic Polish rule from the 14th century, with the peasantry being reduced to serfdom. In 1648 there was a revolt against Polish oppression led by Cossacks, composed originally of runaway serfs, and a militarist state was established by *hetman* (elected leader) Bohdan Khmelnytsky (d. 1657). In 1667 East and West Ukraine were partitioned between Muscovy and Poland.

Under the Russian tsar, Peter I, the publication of Ukrainian books was banned in 1720. Later, in 1783, serfdom was introduced into Eastern Ukraine, or 'Little Russia', as it was known. In the late 18th century, Russia also secured control over all of Western Ukraine, except for Galicia in the far west, which was annexed by Austria in 1772. The 19th century witnessed a Ukrainian cultural revival and the establishment of secret nationalist political organizations, especially in Galicia, where Austrian rule was relatively liberal. During the late 19th and early 20th centuries there was rapid economic development and urbanization in the fertile and mineral-rich Russian Ukraine, but under the later tsars suppression of Ukrainian culture and 'Russification' intensified.

In January 1918, after the overthrow of the tsar, an independent Ukrainian People's Republic was proclaimed, allying itself with the Central Powers (Germany and Austria-Hungary), although a Soviet government was established in Kharkov in the east. The Germans installed a conservative *hetman* regime, which was popularly overthrown at the close of World War I. After two years of civil war, Western Ukraine (Galicia-Volhymia) was transferred to Polish rule, while the rest of the country came under Soviet control, becoming a constituent republic of the USSR in December 1922. In the mid-1920s a conciliatory policy of 'Ukrainization' was pursued. However, during the 1930s, under the Soviet leadership of Joseph Stalin, there was a mass purge of intellectuals, *kulaks* (rich farmers), and the destruction of the Ukrainian Autocephalous (Independent) Orthodox Church. During the man-made 'collectivization famine' of 1932–33 at least 7 million peasants died.

Polish-controlled Western Ukraine was occupied by the Red Army from September 1939 until the Nazi German invasion of the USSR in June 1941. This led to mass deportations and exterminations of more than 5 million Ukrainians and Ukrainian Jews. In 1944 Moscow ordered the deportation en masse to Central Asia of Crimean Tatars, who were accused of collaboration. After World War II, Soviet-ruled Ukraine was enlarged to include territories formerly under Polish (Western Ukraine), Czechoslovak (Transcarpathian Ukraine), and Romanian (North Bukovina and part of Bessarabia) control and became a founding member of the United Nations (UN) in 1945.

Western Ukraine remained the site of partisan resistance by the Ukrainian Insurgent Army (UPA) until the early 1950s and, as part of a 'sovietization' campaign, there were mass arrests and deportations to Siberia of 500,000 people and inward migration of ethnic Russians. The Uniate Church was proscribed in 1946 and forcibly merged with the Russian Orthodox Church. After the death of Stalin in 1953, Ukraine was treated in a more conciliatory fashion by Nikita Khrushchev, Soviet leader until 1964, who had been the Ukrainian Communist Party (UCP) leader between 1938 and 1947. In February 1954, to 'celebrate' the 300th anniversary of Slavic 'fraternal union', Crimea was transferred back to Ukraine's jurisdiction and in the 1960s there was a Ukrainian literary revival and growth of the dissident movement.

In 1972–73 a crackdown on dissent was launched and Vladimir Shcherbitsky, a close ally of the Soviet leader Leonid Brezhnev, replaced the more liberal Petro Shelest as UCP leader. However, from the mid-1970s Helsinki Monitoring Groups became active and the Uniate Church continued to operate underground in Western Ukraine. In the wake of the Chernobyl nuclear power plant disaster in April 1986, which claimed thousands of lives from radiation sickness and contaminated much surrounding agricultural land, a popular environmentalist movement, Green World (estd. 1987), emerged in Ukraine.

Emboldened by the *glasnost* (political openness) and *perestroika* (economic restructuring) initiatives launched by Mikhail Gorbachev, who became the Soviet Union's new leader in 1985, nationalist and pro-reform demonstrations increased. At the forefront of this popular movement was the People's Movement of Ukraine for Restructuring (Rukh), which was established in November 1988. In September 1989, following a strike by Donbass coalminers, Shcherbitsky was ousted as UCP leader; in December 1989 the Uniate Church was allowed to reregister; and in the March 1990 republic Supreme Soviet elections, 'reform communist' and Rukh candidates in the Democratic Bloc polled strongly in urban areas and Western Ukraine. In all, the Democratic Bloc won 170 of the 450 Supreme Soviet seats and in July 1990 the new parliament declared the republic's economic and political sovereignty.

Ukrainian nationalist sentiment developed a head of steam from the autumn of 1990. In October 1990 protest marches by 100,000 students in Kiev forced the resignation of Prime Minister Vitaly Masol and in the spring of 1991 striking Donbass coalminers called for the resignation of the Soviet president, Mikhail Gorbachev. The republic participated in the March 1991 all-Union referendum on the future of the USSR, with 70% approving Gorbachev's proposals for a 'renewed federation'. However, in Western Ukraine an additional question on independence received 90% support. In May 1991 the republic's Supreme Soviet agreed to hold a referendum on independence later in the year. Ukraine's president, Leonid Kravchuk (b. 1934), formerly the UCP's pragmatic ideology chief, was slow to condemn the August 1991 attempted anti-Gorbachev coup launched in Moscow by communist hardliners, which had provoked a series of Rukh-led prodemocracy rallies in Lviv (Lvov). However, after the coup's failure, Kravchuk swiftly donned nationalist colors, banning the UCP and declaring the republic's provisional independence on 24 August 1991, pending the referendum. There was a resounding 90% vote in favor of independence in the 1 December 1991 plebiscite and, simultaneously, Kravchuk was popularly elected president. He captured 62% of the vote, defeating the ex-dissident Vyacheslav Chornovil, who, as leader of Rukh and leader of the radical Lviv regional council, attracted a 23% share of the vote, and five other challengers.

2. 1991–1998

Ukraine joined the Commonwealth of Independent States (CIS) on its inception on 21 December 1991, and its independence was swiftly recognized by Canada, home to around 1,000,000 Ukrainians, as well as by Ukraine's central European neighbors, the United States, and the European Union. In January 1992 Ukraine was admitted into the Helsinki Conference on Security and Cooperation in Europe (CSCE, later the OSCE), in 1994 joined NATO's 'Partnership for Peace' program, and in November 1995 was admitted to the Council of Europe.

Ukraine inherited a substantial nuclear arsenal. It was pledged by President Kravchuk that the country would ratify fully the START-1 treaty and become a nuclear-free state by 1994, while establishing an independent 200,000–400,000-strong army. However, Ukrainian nationalists were in favor of retaining some nuclear weapons. A program of market-centerd economic reform and privatization was launched, with some prices being freed in January 1992. Coupons were introduced as a secondary currency to the rouble, pending the creation of an independent currency, the grivna. However, the continued strength of ex-communist apparatchiks in the bureaucracy and parliament served to frustrate successful implementation of the economic program between 1991 and 1994, with prices being reregulated from February 1992. There were also post independence quarrels with Russia over the division of the Red Army and the Black Sea fleet, over which Russia and Ukraine held joint sovereignty, and unsatisfactory relations with the Crimean autonomous republic, which, with its 70% ethnic Russian community, issued an independence declaration of its own in September 1991.

In October 1992 Leonid Kuchma (b. 1938), a former manager of the world's largest missile factory at Dnepropetrovsk, became prime minister and attempted to steer through parliament a program of gradual market reform and closer economic relations with Russia. He assumed power at a time when the Ukrainian economy was rapidly collapsing. GDP declined by 10% in 1991, 15% in 1992, and 20% in 1993, the annual inflation rate shot up to more than 4,000% during 1993 and there was periodic labor unrest. Unable to gain parliamentary support for more radical reforms, Kuchma resigned as premier in September 1993 and President Kravchuk began to take firmer control over government policy, with a more cautious, centrally controlled economic strategy being adopted.

Elections to the Ukrainian parliament in March – April 1994, the first to be held since independence, resulted in the UCP and allied parties continuing as the largest force and in June 1994 the ex-communist Vitaly Masol, who had been premier between 1987–90, became prime minister. In the presidential elections of June – July 1994, the country's division between a nationalist west and a pro-Russian eastern majority was clearly demonstrated. The incumbent president, Kravchuk, backed effectively by the nationalist Rukh, polled strongly in Western Ukraine, winning as much as 94% of the vote in the regions of Lviv, Ternopil, and Ivano-Frankivsk. However, his challenger, the former prime minister, Leonid Kuchma, backed by the UCP and advocating closer ties with Russia, swept Eastern and Central Ukraine, capturing as much as 90% of the vote in Crimea. As a consequence, Kuchma, somewhat surprisingly, was elected the new state president, defeating Kravchuk on the second run-off ballot by a margin of 52% to 45%.

The new Kuchma administration and Supreme Council ratified the Nuclear Non-Proliferation Treaty in November 1994, giving up Ukraine's inherited nuclear arsenal and receiving, in return, pledges of substantial US economic aid. (By June 1996 all Ukraine's nuclear weapons had been transferred to Russia for destruction.) This brought about a significant, and unexpected, improvement in Ukraine's relations with the West. A large $2.5 billion loan was provided to Ukraine by the IMF on the condition that a tough monetary stabilization plan, entailing tight public spending restrictions, price liberalization, and privatization, was adhered to. This brought the annual inflation rate down to 80% by 1996. In March 1995, in an effort to speed up the pace of market-centerd economic change, President Kuchma replaced Vitaly Masol, an anti-reformer, as prime minister with Evhen Marchuk, a former head of the Ukrainian Secret Service, who was nevertheless viewed as a pragmatist. However, the communist-dominated Supreme Council continued to block radical reforms, with the consequence that by 1995 barely 2% of state enterprises had been privatized. In April 1995 parliament sought to oust the pro-reform Marchuk government. However, in June 1995, faced by the threat that Kuchma would hold a national referendum asking Ukrainians whether they 'trust president or parliament', it relented and approved a 'constitutional accord' which gave the president full control over ministerial appointments, without needing to refer to parliament for approval, and enhanced the president's decree powers.

During 1994 the autonomous republic of Crimea became increasingly assertive in its drive for greater autonomy. In January 1994 the pro-Russian Yuri Meshkov was elected the republic's president and, following a March 1994 referendum on autonomy, in May 1994 the Crimean Assembly approved an effective sovereignty declaration. Enjoying a personal mandate in Crimea, President Kuchma and Ukraine's parliament reacted in March 1995 by annulling Crimea's constitution and sacking Meshkov. In April 1995 Kuchma assumed direct control over the Crimean Republic for four months. The Russian government of President Yeltsin acquiesced, insisting that Crimea remained an internal affair for Ukraine. However, a 'treaty of friendship, cooperation, and partnership' was not signed with Russia until May 1997, when Russia became the last of Ukraine's neighbors to recognize its borders. With this treaty, Russia acknowledged Ukrainian sovereignty over the Crimean peninsula, but was given ownership of four-fifths of the Russian Black Sea Fleet and allowed to lease bases at Sevastopol for 20 years at an annual cost of US$100 million. In March 1996 Ukraine rejected membership of a CIS Customs Union, established by four other CIS states.

In May 1996 President Kuchma replaced Prime Minister Marchuk with the more loyal Pavlo Lazarenko (b. 1953), a former collective farm chairperson who had previously been the first deputy prime minister and was viewed as less of an economic reformer. A month later, the country's first post-independence constitution was adopted. It recognized the right to private ownership, abolished the traditional hierarchy of soviets (local people's councils) that had been enshrined in the previous 1978 constitution, and gave increased powers to the president. Prime Minister Lazarenko, who narrowly escaped death in a car bomb attack in July 1996 blamed on 'criminals' opposed to his plans to shut inefficient coalmines, sought to accelerate the pace of market-centerd economic reform. Privatization, which was by now virtually complete for small-scale enterprise, was extended to medium- and large-scale concerns and a new currency, the hyrvna, was introduced in September 1996. In February 1997 new reformist finance and economy ministers were appointed.

The UCP-dominated parliament's obstruction of reforms persuaded Viktor Pynzenyk, a deputy prime minister and leading economic reformer, to resign in March 1997. By 1997 inflation, at 16% per annum, had been brought under control, but GDP continued to decline – by 10% in 1996 and by 4% in 1997 – while wage and pension arrears bred popular unrest and miners' strikes, and rampant corruption discouraged foreign inward investment. In his March 1997 annual 'state of the nation' address to parliament, President Kuchma criticized his prime minister for inefficiency and financial mismanagement and three months later Lazarenko was sacked. He was replaced initially by his deputy, Vasyly Durdynets, and then, in July 1997, by Valeriy Pustovoytenko, a close ally of President Kuchma. Concurrently, the IMF agreed to lend $750 million – increased, in August 1998, to $2.2 billion over three years – to prevent default of $10 billion of foreign debt.

The legislature elections held in March 1998, under a new election law, brought victory for the UCP, which campaigned for voluntary reunification with Russia, and its allies, although a large number of independent technocrats were also elected. Holding more than a quarter of the Supreme Council seats, the UCP seemed set to continue to block reform in what was one of the least progressive of the transitional economies of eastern Europe, leading Kuchma to threaten to resort to decrees.

In March 1999 the leader of the nationalist Rukh, Vyacheslav Chornovil, was killed in a car accident, shortly after forming a breakaway party. Meanwhile, in February 1999 the former prime minister, Pavlo Lazarenko was arrested (in the USA) on charges of largescale embezzlement during his term in office.

YUGOSLAVIA

The Federal Republic of Yugoslavia (FRY), including the republics of Serbia and Montenegro
Federativna Republika Jugoslavija

Capital: Belgrade

Social and economic data

Area: 102,173 sq km/39,449 sq miles
Population: 10,515,000*
Pop. density per sq km/sq mi: 103/267*
Urban population: 50%**
Literacy rate: 93%**
GDP: $16,000 million*; per-capita GDP $1,520*
Government defense spending (% of GDP): 22.1%*
Currency: New Yugoslav dinar
Economy type: middle income
Labor force in agriculture: 26%**
* 1995.
** 1992.

Head of state

President Slobodan Milosevic, since 1997

Head of government

Prime Minister Momir Bulatovic, since 1998

Ethnic composition

According to the 1991 census, 62% of the population of the rump federal republic is ethnic Serb, 17% Albanian, 5% Montenegrin, 3% 'Yugoslav', and 3% Muslim. Serbs predominate in the republic of Serbia, where they form, excluding the autonomous areas of Kosovo and Vojvodina, 85% of the population and in Vojvodina they comprise 55% of the population. Albanians constitute nearly 90% of the population of Kosovo; Montenegrins comprise 69% of the population of the republic of Montenegro; and Muslims predominate in the Sandzak region which straddles the Serbian and Montenegrin borders. Since 1992 an influx of Serb refugees from Bosnia and Kosovo has increased the proportion of Serbs in Serbia, while many ethnic Hungarians have left Vojvodina, and, faced by harassment by Serb militias, an estimated 500,000 Albanians have left Kosovo. Serbo-Croat in its Serbian form, written in Cyrillic script, is the main language, but Albanian is widely spoken in Kosovo.

Religions

Nearly 75% of the population adheres to the Eastern Orthodox faith, belonging to the Serbian Orthodox Church and the Montenegrin Orthodox Church, which was re-established in November 1993, while 19%, chiefly in Kosovo and Montenegro, follows Sunni Islamic beliefs. There is also a small Roman Catholic minority in Vojvodina.

Political features

State type: emergent democratic
Date of state formation: 1918/1992*
Political structure: federal
Executive: limited presidential
Assembly: two-chamber
Party structure: multiparty
Human rights rating: N/A
International affiliations: AG (observer), CERN (observer), G-24, IAEA, NAM, OSCE (suspended), UN (suspended), WTO

* The present 'rump federation' was formed in 1992.

Local and regional government

As the rump of a larger state, the present federal republic consists of the two republics of Montenegro (**Area:** 13,812 sq km/5,333 sq miles; **Population:** 0.65 million) and Serbia (**Area:** 88,361 sq km;/24,116 sq miles **Population:** 9.95 million) and, within Serbia, the autonomous provinces of Vojvodina (**Area:** 21,508 sq km/8,304 sq miles; **Population:** 2.4 million) and Kosovo-Metohija (**Area:** 10,817 sq km/4,176 sq miles; **Population:** 2 million). Each republic and autonomous province has its own elected assembly, although the Kosovo assembly was dissolved in 1990 by the government of the republic of Serbia. Within each republic and province there are locally elected councils.

Political system

Formerly a socialist federation of six republics, following the breakaway of Slovenia, Croatia, Bosnia-Herzegovina, and Macedonia in 1991–92, a new constitution was adopted in April 1992 for the 'rump federation' of the republics of Serbia and Montenegro. This has provided for a two-chamber Federal Assembly (Savezna Skupstina), consisting of a 138-member Chamber of Citizens (Vece Gradjana) and a 40-member Chamber of the Republics (Vece Republika). In the Chamber of Citizens 108 seats are directly elected from the republic of Serbia and 30 from Montenegro. Half of the Serbian seats are elected by single-member constituencies through a majoritarian system of voting and half by a party list system. Six of the Montenegro seats are elected from single-member constituencies and the rest by the party list system. The Chamber of Republics has 20 members selected by each of the two republican parliaments so as to reflect party strengths. The combined assemblies elect an executive federal president who chooses a prime minister to chair a cabinet of around 20 members. The constitution provides that the president and prime minister must be drawn from different republics. There is also a Supreme Defense Council, which comprises the federal president, who commands the army, and prime minister, the presidents of Serbia and Montenegro, and the chief of general staff of the Yugoslav army.

Until 1997, although the Federal Assembly was empowered to declare a state of emergency in a constituent republic without reference to its assembly and the federation was supreme in defense matters, the authority of the federal government was, in general, much less than that of the individual republics of Serbia and Montenegro. However, matters began to change when the Serbian strongman, Slobodan Milosevic, became federal president. Nevertheless, each of the two republics is a substantially autonomous state, with its own legislature and political executive. Serbia has a 250-member National Assembly and a directly elected executive president, while in Montenegro the Assembly comprises 78 members and the president is also directly elected. Under the Serbian constitution of September 1992 the formerly autonomous regions of Vojvodina and Kosovo-Metohija within Serbia no longer have autonomy.

Political parties

The dominant parties in the two constituent republics of Yugoslavia are the Socialist Party of Serbia (SPS) and the Montenegrin Social Democratic Party (SDPCG), which are reform-socialist heirs to the League of Communists of Yugoslavia (SKJ), formerly the ruling party in a wider federation. More than 30 radical nationalist, center-right, leftist and ethnic-orientated parties also operate in each republic, the most important being the Serbian Radical Party (SRS); the Serbian Renewal Movement (SPO); the People's Assembly Party (NSS), formerly known as the Serbian Democratic Movement (DEPOS); the Democratic Party (DS); the Democratic Party of Serbia (DSS); the Democratic Community of Vojvodina Hungarians (DZVM); and the Democratic Party of Albanians/Party of Democratic Action (DPA/PDA).

The SKJ was founded in April 1919 under the title of the Socialist Workers' Party of Yugoslavia (Communist) (SWPY) by a union of socialist organizations based in Serbia, Croatia, Slovenia, and Bosnia. With a membership of 60,000, it changed its name to the Communist Party of Yugoslavia (CPY) in June 1920 and in the Yugoslav Constituent Assembly elections of that year emerged as the third largest grouping, capturing 0.2 million votes and 59 seats. A year later it was banned and forced underground, its membership dwindling to several hundred during the early 1930s. The Croatian-born Josip Broz (Tito) assumed the party's leadership in 1937, and began building up membership. He later developed it into a popular 'Partisan', anti-Nazi, liberation force during World War II, so that it was eventually able to assume power in November 1943. The designation SKJ was adopted in 1952 to symbolize its alignment on a new, non-Soviet-linked, socialist course. Membership of the SKJ in 1987 stood at 2.10 million, corresponding to 9.1% of the total population and in December 1994 Branko Loza became the party's new president.

The authoritarian SPS was formed in 1990 through a merger of the SKJ's Serbian branch, the League of Communists of Serbia, and the Socialist Alliance of the Working People of Serbia. Under the leadership since 1986 of Slobodan Milosevic, a populist demagogue, it has become increasingly identified with Serb nationalism.

The SDPCG was known until 1991 as the League of Communists of Montenegro. It supports the continuation of a Yugoslav federation, but is less nationalist than the SPS. In 1997 the party split into rival factions: a reformist faction led by Milo Djukanovic, who became Montegnegro president in October 1997; and a pro-Milosevic faction, led by Momir Bulatovic, who became federal prime minister in May 1998. Bulatovic's faction is now known as the Socialist People's Party of Montenegro (SPPM).

The SRS is an extreme rightwing Serbian nationalist body, whose paramilitary wing, the Chetnik movement, was implicated in fighting in Croatia and Bosnia during 1991–93. In November 1993 the party's leadership, including Dr Vojislav Seselj, commander of the Chetniks, was arrested on charges of the commission of war crimes in Croatia and Bosnia and in September 1994 Seselj was jailed for four months after being involved in a scuffle in parliament. The SRS abolished its Chetnik paramilitary wing in April 1994, but in January 1995 half of its members left to join a new ultra-rightwing party, the Nikola Pasic Serbian Radical Party (SRS-NP), formed by Jovan Glamocanin.

The SPO is a rightwing Serbian nationalist party, founded in 1990 and led by Vuk Draskovic. During 1992 it advocated the creation of a 'Greater Serbia' encompassing the Serb-occupied Krajina region of Croatia and most of Bosnia-Herzegovina. It fought the 1996 federal parliamentary elections as part of the Zajedno ('Together') opposition alliance, which also included the centrist DS, the moderate nationalist DSS and the liberal Civic Alliance of Serbia (CAS), but withdrew from the alliance in June 1997.

The NSS is a centrist Christian-democratic opposition force, led by Slobodan Rakitic, which was known until January 1995 as the DEPOS bloc. DEPOS was an umbrella opposition grouping which had included the SPO.

The 20,000-member DZVM, formed in 1990, supports the interests of the ethnic Hungarian minority in Vojvodina, and the DPA/PDA, the ethnic Albanian community, along with the pro-independence Democratic Alliance of Kosovo, which is led by Dr Ibrahim Rugova.

Political leaders since 1970*

1944–80 Marshal Tito (SKJ)**, 1992–93 Dobrica Cosic (SPS)***, 1993–97 Zoran Lilic (SPS)***, 1989–97 Slobodan Milosevic (SPS)****, 1990–98 Momir Bulatovic (SDPCG)*****, 1997– Slobodan Milosevic (SPS)***, 1997 Dragan Tomic (SPS)****, 1997– Milan

Milutinovic (SPS)****, 1998– Milo Djukanovic (SDPCG)*****

* There was an annually rotating, republic-based leadership from 1980–92.
** Communist Party leader.
*** Federal president.
**** President of the Serbian republic.
***** President of Montenegro.

Latest elections

The most recent federal elections were held on 3 November 1996 and resulted in the SPS-dominated 'United List' securing 42% of the vote and 64 Chamber of Citizens seats (up 17 on December 1992). The United List also included New Democracy and the Yugoslav United Left, a party led by Slobodan Milosevic's wife, Mirjana Markovic. The opposition Zajedno coalition, comprising the nationalist SPO and DSS and the centrist DS and CAS, attracted 22% of the vote and won 22 seats; the Montenegro-based SDPCG, with 3% of the federal vote, won 20 seats; and the extreme-nationalist SRS, which rejected the Dayton Peace Accord on Bosnia, with 18% of the vote, won 16 seats. Six other parties won between one and eight seats apiece, including the DZVM, three seats, and the Montenegrin-nationalist People's Party of Montenegro (PPM), eight seats. Turnout exceeded 50%, but the election was boycotted by 2 million ethnic Albanians in Kosovo.

The last legislature elections were held in Serbia on 21 September 1997 and saw the SPS-dominated United List secure 36% of the vote and win 110 of the 250 National Assembly seats. The SRS, with 29% of the vote, won 82 seats, and the SPO, with 20% of the vote, 45 seats. Serbia's last presidential elections, held on 7 and 21 December 1997, were won in the second round run-off by Milan Milutinovic of the SPS, who defeated the SRS leader, Dr Vojislav Seselj, by a margin of 61% of the valid votes to 39%. Five other candidates contested the first round, including Vuk Draskovic, leader of the SPO, who finished third with 15% of the votes.

Republican Assembly elections were last held in Montenegro on 31 May 1998 and were won by the 'For a Better Life', an electoral alliance comprising the SDPCG, the PPM, and the Social Democratic Party of Montenegro, which, with 49% of the vote, won 42 of the 78 seats. Momir Bulatovic's SPPM attracted 36% of the vote and won 29 seats. Direct presidential elections were held earlier, on 5 and 19 October 1997, and were won in the second round run-off by Milo Djukanovic of the SDPCG, who secured 50.8% of the vote, against 49.2% for Bulatovic. Six other candidates contested the first round.

Political history

1. The early medieval period to 1991

Formerly under Roman rule, during the early medieval period the republics of what became Yugoslavia in 1918 existed as substantially independent entities. The kingdom of Serbia was the most important, being the nucleus of an extensive Balkan empire during the 14th century. From the late 14th to the mid-15th centuries much of eastern, southern, and central Yugoslavia, Bosnia-Herzegovina, Macedonia, and Serbia, was conquered by Turks and incorporated into the Ottoman Empire. Mountainous Montenegro was an exception and survived as a sovereign principality. During this period northwestern Yugoslavia, consisting of the republics of Croatia and Slovenia, became part of the Austro-Hungarian Habsburg Empire. They were to enjoy, however, a greater measure of political autonomy than the Turk lands.

Uprisings against Turkish rule in the early 19th century won Serbia a similar degree of autonomy, before full independence was achieved in 1878. The new kingdom of Serbia proceeded to enlarge its territory, at the expense of Turkey and Bulgaria, during the Balkan Wars of 1912–13. However, it was not until December 1918, following the collapse of the Austro-Hungarian Empire, that Croatia and Slovenia were 'liberated' from foreign control. A new 'Kingdom of the Serbs, Croats and Slovenes' now came into existence, with the Serbian, Peter Karageorgevich (1844–1921), Peter I, assuming its leadership, as a constitutional monarch, and working with an elected legislative assembly. Montenegro joined the union after its citizens had voted for the deposition of their own ruler, King Nicholas.

Peter I died in August 1921 and was succeeded by his son and regent, Alexander I (1888–1934), who renamed the country Yugoslavia, or 'Nation of the Southern ('Yugo') Slavs'. Faced with opposition from Croatian federalists at home and from the Italians abroad, in January 1929 he established a Serbian-dominated military dictatorship. The country remained backward during this period, with more than three-quarters of the population dependent on agricultural activities.

Alexander I was assassinated in October 1934 in Marseilles by a Macedonian with Croatian dissident links. His young son, Peter II, succeeded him and a regency under the boy's uncle, Paul, was set up and came under increasing influence from Nazi Germany and Italy. The regency was briefly overthrown in a coup by pro-Allied airforce officers in March 1941, precipitating a successful invasion by German troops. Peter II (1923–70; reigned 1934–45) fled to safety in England, while two guerrilla groups began resistance activities. One was the pro-royalist Serbian-based Chetniks, or 'Army of the Fatherland', led by General Draza Mihailovic (1893–1946), and the other the communist Partisans, or 'National Liberation Army', led by Josip Broz, to be later known as Marshal Tito (1892–1980).

The communist Partisans, comprising, towards the end of the war, 800,000 men, gained the upper hand in their struggle with the Axis forces and at liberated Jajce, in Bosnia, Tito established a provisional government, called the 'Executive Committee of National Liberation', in November 1943. Two years later, in November 1945, following the expulsion, with only limited Soviet assistance, of the remaining German forces, a new Yugoslav Federal People's Republic was proclaimed.

Following Constituent Assembly elections, based on a single list of candidates for the communist-dominated People's Front, a new Soviet-style federal constitution was adopted in January 1946 which established the dominance of the Communist Party of Yugoslavia (CPY, known from 1952 as the League of Communists, or SKJ) and during the succeeding years remaining royalist opposition was expunged. Although at first closely linked with the USSR, Tito objected to Soviet 'hegemonism', broke with Stalin in 1948, and proceeded to introduce his own independent brand of communism. This was given shape in the Constitutional Law of January 1953, which established the framework of a more liberal and decentralized system, based on the concept of workers' self-management and supporting the notion of private farming. As a result, by the 1980s 85% of Yugoslavia's cropped area was privately tilled. Having established himself as the clearly dominant force in the Yugoslav polity, Tito also assumed the newly created post of president of the Republic in 1953. This was a position which he was to hold until his death in May 1980.

In foreign affairs, the country, which had been expelled from Cominform in June 1948 and which remained outside the Warsaw Treaty Organization and Comecon, sought to establish for itself an intermediate position between East and West, playing a leading role in the creation of the nonaligned movement in 1961.

Domestically, the nation endured continuing regional discontent, particularly in Croatia, where a violent separatist movement gained ground in the 1960s and early 1970s. To deal with these problems, Tito initially encouraged further decentralization and devolution of power to the constituent republics in amendments to the constitution which were introduced between 1966 and 1968. In addition, a system of collective leadership and a regular rotation of office posts was introduced in July 1971, in an effort to prevent the emergence of regional cliques. Partial corrective recentralization was, however, a feature of the February 1974 constitution.

On Tito's death in May 1980 the position of executive president, which he had been accorded for life under the terms of the 1974 constitution, was effectively abolished and a collective and rotating (between republics) presidential leadership assumed power instead. However, this new collective leadership, lacking a dominant, 'guiding hand' personality at its head, became subject to internal cleavages, resulting in fudged policy paralysis, and confused demarcation lines emerging between differing federal and republican executive bodies.

In these circumstances, there was a recrudescence of regionalist conflict, with a serious popular movement emerging in 1981–82 among the Muslim Albanians of Kosovo autonomous province who, forming four-fifths of the population, campaigned for full republican status. These demonstrations had to be suppressed by the armed forces. In Bosnia-Herzegovina and Croatia, unrest emerged among the Muslim and Catholic communities respectively during the mid-1980s. This regionalist discontent was aggravated by a general decline in living standards after 1980, caused by a mounting level of foreign debt, whose servicing absorbed 10% of GDP, and a spiralling inflation rate, which reached 200% in 1988 and 700% in 1989.

In 1987–88, the federal government, under the leadership of Prime Minister Branko Mikulic (b. 1928), a Bosnian, introduced a radical 'market socialist' package, in an effort to restructure the economy. This involved the freeing of prices and wages from residual controls, the introduction of a federal value-added tax (VAT), and a new bankruptcy law. The private sector was extended further and foreign inward investment, in special free-trade zones, was encouraged. There was also a general switch towards an 'indicative', rather than central, planning system. The short-term consequence of this program was, however, an austerity wage freeze, sparking off a wave of industrial strikes, and a rise in the unemployment level to above 1 million, or 15% of the worforce. Following a wave of strikes and mounting internal disorder, Mikulic was replaced as prime minister in January 1989 by Ante Markovic, a reformist Croatian.

In the political sphere, constitutional amendment proposals were put forward by the federal presidency in 1988, aimed at enhancing the federal government's authority and abolishing the right of veto enjoyed by republican and provincial assemblies. In addition, an emergency 'Extraordinary Party Conference' was convened in May 1988, in an effort to formulate fresh solutions to the economic and political crisis. At this meeting, the system of regional rotation employed for filling the top party post was temporarily abandoned, and the new SKJ leader, Stipe Suvar, was elected in a competitive ballot. The party remained acutely divided, however, between regionally based liberal Slovenian and conservative Serbian wings on the questions of decentralization and democratization.

However, the most significant development from the late 1980s was the emergence of a new prospective national 'strongman' (*vozd*) in the form of the SKJ's Serbian party leader since 1986, Slobodan Milosevic (b. 1941). A populist hardliner, Milosevic lent his support to grassroots campaigns to terminate Kosovo and Vojvodina's autonomous province status and fully integrate the regions within Serbia, Kosovo being seen as the Serbs' historic home. These aims were substantially secured in March 1989 when the Vojvodina and Kosovo assemblies, following Serbian pressure, endorsed earlier changes to the Serbian constitution which served to return control over their defense, state security, foreign relations, justice, and planning to Serbia. These actions immediately triggered a wave of violent ethnic riots in Kosovo which claimed at least 29 lives. In addition, Milosevic was seen to have been behind street protests in Titograd in October 1988 which forced the resignation of the entire state and party leadership of the Montenegro republic and its replacement with pro-Serbian cadres. His 'Serbian nationalist' stance and conservative policy prescriptions were firmly opposed, however, by the rich northwestern republics of Croatia and Slovenia. The growing schism within the ruling SKJ was confirmed in January 1990 when the party's congress had to be abandoned after a walkout by the Slovene delegation.

In late July 1990 the Serbian assembly voted to dissolve the Kosovo assembly and in September 1990 a new multiparty constitution came into force in the Serbian republic, which effectively stripped Kosovo and Vojvodina of their autonomy. In addition, there was a closure of those Kosovo schools in which the Albanian language was used. Kosovo's ethnic Albanian community reacted by calling a general strike on 3 September 1991 and by convening an underground parliament that proclaimed a new, unrecognized constitution for the province. In multiparty elections held in Serbia in December 1990 Milosevic was re-elected president of the republic by a landslide margin and the communists, renamed the Socialist Party of Serbia (SPS), also retained a convincing assembly majority. The communists were also re-elected in Montenegro. However, in Croatia, Slovenia, Bosnia-Herzegovina, and Macedonia, following multiparty elections held between April and November 1990, new noncommunist government coalitions came to power. These called for the establishment of a looser confederation. Prime Minister Markovic was sympathetic to these wishes and formed the Alliance of Reform Forces in July 1990 which advocated the preservation of Yugoslav unity within a pluralist federation. However, Milosevic refused to compromise. Instead, as Croatia and Slovenia pressed for secession from the federation, the Serb minority community in Croatia, activated by memories of wartime persecution by Croatia's Ustasa regime, was encouraged to demand the creation of autonomous regions to be allied within a new 'Greater Serbia'. In March 1991 there were large anti-Milosevic and anti-communist demonstrations in Belgrade by a crowd of 30,000. These spread to Novi Sad in Vojvodina, but were crushed violently by riot police and tanks.

By the spring of 1991, following Croatia and Slovenia's issuing in February 1991 of a joint notice of secession, to become effective in June, Yugoslavia's collective presidency had broken down and federal institutions had become progressively Serbianized. On 15 March 1991 the state president, Borisav Jovic, a Serbian, dramatically resigned, after other members of the collective state presidency refused to support his plan to introduce martial law across the country. There were fears that his departure might presage a military takeover in Yugoslavia.

On 25 June 1991 both Slovenia and Croatia issued unilateral declarations of independence, or 'dissociation', from the Yugoslav federation, though declaring their continued willingness to discuss the formation of a new, much looser Yugoslav confederation. This precipitated, from 27 June 1991, military confrontations between the federal army and republican forces, with more than 100 people being killed in four days of fighting. A European Community (EC) delegation of foreign ministers brokered a ceasefire at the end of June, including a three-month suspension in implementation of Slovenia's declaration of independence and withdrawal of the Yugoslav National Army (JNA) from Slovenia. However, between July and Sept 1991 civil war intensified in ethnically mixed Croatia, between Serbian Chetnik guerrillas and Croats, particularly near its eastern border (especially the towns of Osijek and Vukovar) and in the Krajina region, where 250,000 Serbs lived. Several hundred died in fighting during July 1991 and a similar number in August. It became uncertain who (politicians or the military) now controlled the country at the federal level. Furthermore, the JNA had become factionalized, with many units refusing to heed the call by President Stipe Mesic, a noncommunist Croatian, for a return to barracks.

A new ceasefire was ordered by the federal presidency on 7 August 1991, after the EC – which viewed Serbia as the real aggressor, seeking, via the JNA and rebel Serb militias within Croatia, to carve out a new 'Greater Serbia' – threatened to apply economic sanctions against the republic. However, again it failed to hold and by September 1991 around a third of Croatia was under Serb control and at least 120,000 people had become refugees. Oil-rich Croatia responded by imposing an oil supply blockade on Serbia and attacking federal army barracks within the republic. Later in September 1991, Serbian forces attacked the Croatian port of Dubrovnik, laying siege to the city. This persuaded the EC to impose an economic embargo on the republic in November 1991.

Concerned at Serb expansionist ambitions, the republic of Bosnia-Herzegovina proclaimed its sovereignty in October 1991 and a referendum on independence was held in Macedonia in September 1991. The latter received overwhelming support, although it was boycotted by the Albanian and Serbian minorities. In Kosovo, an unofficial referendum on sovereignty was also held in September 1991 and similarly received overwhelming support. A provisional unofficial government was elected, being accorded immediate recognition by Albania. The Yugoslav federal government effectively collapsed between September and October 1991 as Croat, Slovene, Bosnian, and Macedonian representatives resigned from federal bodies, including the federal presidency. On 3 October 1991 four of the eight members of the collective state presidency, drawn from Serbia, Montenegro, Kosovo, and Vojvodina, voted to take on the powers of the Yugoslav assembly, despite the meeting falling short of the five members required for a quorum. In effect, Serbia was left dominating a 'rump Yugoslavia', comprising two ethnically close republics and two autonomous regions, one of which, Kosovo, was secessionist minded. On 5 December 1991 Stipe Mesic resigned from the federal presidency, declaring that 'Yugoslavia no longer exists'. On 20 December 1991 the federal prime minister, Ante Markovic, also resigned.

2. 1992–1999

In early January 1992 a peace plan was successfully brokered in Sarajevo by UN envoy Cyrus Vance which provided for an immediate ceasefire in Croatia, withdrawal of the Yugoslav army, and the deployment of 10,000 UN troops in contested Krajina and eastern and western Slavonia until a political settlement was worked out. This accord was disregarded by the breakaway Serb leader in Krajina, Milan Babic, but was recognized by the main Croatian and Serbian forces. The independence of Slovenia and Croatia was recognized by the EC and the United States on 15 January 1992 and that of Bosnia-Herzegovina in April 1992. Macedonia also declared its independence in January 1992.

In April 1992 a new federal constitution was adopted for the 'rump Yugoslavia', which guaranteed the right to private ownership. In the May – June 1992 federal elections Dobrica Cosic, a Serb writer, was elected federal president and Milan Panic became prime minister in July 1992. In concurrent elections held illegally in Kosovo, the ethnic Albanian-dominated Democratic Alliance of Kosovo secured a clear victory and proclaimed the foundation of a new 'Republic of Kosovo', with Ibrahim Rugova as president. Meanwhile fighting continued in Bosnia-Herzegovina, where Serb irregulars, driven by the vision of a 'Greater Serbia', seized 70% of the republic's land area, with thousands of non-Serbs being killed or evicted from their homes as part of an abhorrent policy of 'ethnic cleansing'. Concern for ethnic minorities in Serbia, notably in Kosovo where ethnic Albanians were being subjected to harassment by Serb militias led by Zeljko Raznjatovic (known as 'Arkan'), and Serbia's attempted 'carve-up' of the newly independent Bosnian republic prompted the United States to deny recognition of the 'new Yugoslavia' and to call for the country's expulsion from the Conference on Security and Cooperation in Europe (CSCE, later the OSCE) and its removal from its UN seat.

Fresh elections to the republican and federal parliaments, held on 20 December 1992, resulted in the former communist SPS and Montenegrin Social Democratic Party (SDPCG) emerging as the largest single party in each republic, with a plurality of the vote, and Slobodan Milosevic being re-elected as Serbia's president. However, the neofascist Serbian Radical Party (SRS) and the nationalist Democratic Movement of Serbia (DEPOS) also polled strongly, forcing the SPS to share power in a socialist-nationalist coalition government in Serbia. Milosevic's opponent in the Serbian presidential election was the federal prime minister, Milan Panic, who was swiftly ousted on 29 December 1992, following defeat in a no-confidence motion and was replaced, in February 1993, by a Milosevic ally, Radoje Kontic, who headed a SPS and SDPCG federal coalition government. In June 1993 the federal president, Dobrica Cosic, was also removed, at Milosevic's instigation, and replaced by the pro-Milosevic Zoran Lilic (b. 1953) and in new Assembly elections in Serbia in December 1993 the SPS achieved a near majority, winning 123 of the 250 available seats.

Throughout 1992–94 the economies of Serbia and Montenegro were devastated by the impact of international economic sanctions imposed, by the EC from November 1991 and by the UN in May 1992 and April 1993, as a result of the federal republic's continuing indirect support of ethnic Serbs fighting in Bosnia-Herzegovina and the Republic of Krajina, within Croatia, and its refusal to recognize Croatia and Bosnia. Output slumped to barely 30% of the prewar level, nearly half the population were unemployed, hyperinflation, with prices rising in Serbia at the rate of 5% an hour in December 1993, exceeded the levels seen in Germany in the 1920s, and there were severe shortages of fuel, food, and medicine, precipitating a wave of strikes by industrial and transport workers. This economic hardship intensified nationalist feeling in Serbia, but was resented by Montenegrins, whose president, Momir Bulatovic, pursued an increasingly independent line.

During 1994 the Serbian leadership began to give increased emphasis to economic reconstruction. A new currency, known popularly as the 'super dinar', was introduced in January 1994. This, and the formation in February 1994 of a new national unity coalition government in Serbia, headed by a new prime minister, Mirko Marjanovic, a former company manager, and supported by the New Democracy party, formerly a member of the opposition DEPOS bloc, resulted in a sharp reduction in the inflation level. More importantly, President Milosevic came to accept the need for the Serbians of Bosnia to agree to a peace plan devised by the five-nation Contact Group, comprising diplomats from Russia, the United States, France, Germany, and Britain, which would give them control over 49% of Bosnia-Herzegovina. When the Bosnian Serbs' leader, Dr Radovan Karadzic (b. 1945), rejected this proposal, the Yugoslav Federation imposed an economic blockade on the Bosnian Serbs and the Milosevic-controlled Serbian media began to charge the Bosnian Serb leadership with wartime racketeering and corruption. The blockade held during 1994–95 and was rewarded by the UN suspending a number of international sanctions, including the reopening of international flights to Belgrade and the Montenegrin port of Bar. A full suspension of sanctions was promised if Yugoslavia would recognize the existence of Bosnia-Herzegovina and Croatia. In August 1995 President Milosevic rejected appeals by Radovan Karadzic and Milan Martic, the respective leaders of the Bosnian and Krajina Serbs, to provide military aid as the Croatian army launched offensives against the self-proclaimed 'Republic of Serbian Krajina' and the Bosnian Serbs.

In November 1995 Serbia played a key role in the US-brokered Dayton Peace Accord for Bosnia-Herzegovina and finally accepted the separate existence of Croatia and Bosnia. As a consequence, in December 1995 the UN lifted its economic sanctions against Yugoslavia.

Full diplomatic relations were restored with Croatia in August 1996 and opened diplomatic negotiations with Bosnia in October 1996.

The elections held, in November 1996, to the federal Yugoslav parliament were won by Milosevic's SPS and its Montenegrin SDPCG allies, which together won 84 of the 138 Chambers of Citizens seats and 46% of the vote. Concurrent elections to the Republican Assembly in Montenegro were won by the SDPCG. However, there were opposition complaints – substantiated by OSCE observers – of malpractice in the concurrent municipal elections, which had prevented Zajedno from securing control of the assemblies (and mayorships) of 14 of the Serbian republic's largest 18 cities, including Belgrade. This sparked large anti-government protests in Belgrade, involving students, the intelligentsia, and trade unionists, and spearheaded by the SPO. On 15 December 1996 a march in Belgrade was attended by 250,000 people, but from 26 December further marches were banned and a crackdown was launched by the riot police, leading to the deaths of two protesters. Students defied the ban throughout January 1997 until, in February 1997, the Serbian parliament relented and recognized the Zajedno municipal victories.

On 5 July 1997, Slobodan Milosevic, who was barred by the constitution from running for a third term as Serbian president, was elected federal president by the Federal Assembly. The Serbian presidential elections, in September 1997, produced an invalid result, with the SRS leader, Dr Vojislav Seselj, securing a slightly higher share of the vote than his SPS opponent, the former federal president Zoran Lilic, but turnout, at 49%, was below the constitutionally required 50%. In concurrent, Serbian Assembly elections, the SPS finished first, with 36% of the vote, but failed to secure an absolute majority of seats. A fresh Serbian presidential election was held in December 1995, in which the SPS candidate was the foreign minister, Milan Milutinovic, who convincingly defeated Seselj in the run-off round, although OSCE observers described the poll, with turnout, 50.1%, as 'fundamentally flawed'.

Following the lifting of some international sanctions at the end of 1995, the economy grew and the annual inflation rate fell to around 50%. However, with the government pursuing an austere monetary policy, the unemployment rate was as high as 40% in 1997. The backing given by Slobodan Milosevic during 1997–98 to the relatively moderate Bosnian Serb government of Biljana Plavsic and Milorad Dodik was rewarded, in February 1998, by the US granting Yugoslavia permission to open a consulate in New York and start charter flights to the United States. However, Milosevic's actions in Montenegro and Kosovo during 1998 led to further international condemnation of his regime.

In Montenegro, Milosevic fell out with the young, reformist SDPCG prime minister, Milo Djukanovic (b. 1962), who described Milosevic as 'unfit to hold public office'. Djukanovic was elected Montenegro's president in October 1997, narrowly defeating the Milosevic-backed incumbent, Momir Bulatovic, who led an opposing faction of the SDPCG. However, Milosevic supporters challenged the result, with violent street fighting and protest rallies in Podgorica, the Montenegrin capital, during early January. Order was restored when Radoje Kontic, the Yugoslav prime minister, a Montenegrin, brokered a deal for fresh Republican Assembly elections to be held in Montenegro in May 1998, and based on a new system of proportional representation. These elections produced victory for parties allied to Djukanovic.

From November 1997 even more serious challenges to Serbian authority were presented by the ethnic Albanians of the southern province of Kosovo. A recently formed Kosovo Liberation Army (KLA), comprising a core of around 500 guerrillas committed to independence from Serbia and unification with Albania, stunned the Serb authorities with a successful police ambush near the capital, Pristina. In January and February 1998 the KLA extended its activities and grew in strength. In response, after four policemen were allegedly killed, a Serb crackdown was launched, with as many as 80 Albanians being killed, while protesters were tear-gassed. Fearing retribution, many Serbs fled from the province. The West responded by imposing further sanctions against Yugoslavia, including a UN arms embargo. In March 1998 Ibrahim Rugova, a moderate who advocated peaceful struggle and negotiations with Serbia, was re-elected president of the self-declared Kosovo Albanian republic. Although the Serbian authorities declared the elections illegal, it enabled talks to begin with President Milosevic, in May 1998, land the lifting of a Western investment ban. However, in July – August 1998 the situation deteriorated again when, to recapture territory lost to the KLA, including the town of Orahovac, a major Serbian army and police offensive was launched. It met with military success, but at the cost of hundreds of lives and led to a further flood of 200,000 civilian refugees – equivalent to 10% of Kosovo's population. A local ceasefire was agreed in August 1998 in western Kosovo, to allow aid agencies to help the 20,000 civilians trapped there, but failed to hold.

During 1998 the Serbian economy went into freefall again and in late March the dinar was devalued by 45%. Meanwhile, in March 1998, the SPS, lacking an assembly majority, formed a coalition government in Serbia with the extremist SRS, which continued to campaign for the creation of a Greater Serbia, including parts of Bosnia and Croatia. Two months later, President Milosevic sacked Radoje Kontic as Yugoslav prime minister on the grounds that he was insufficiently hostile to Montenegro's reformist president, Milo Djukanovic. He appointed Djukanovic's arch rival, Momir Bulatovic as the new prime minister, although Montenegro refused to recognise the appointment.

From January 1999 the crisis concerning Kosovo became internationalized when General Wesley Clark, NATO's supreme allied commander in Europe, blamed Milosevic for provoking military tension in Kosovo province, where 2,000 international 'verifiers' were now based to monitor an unstable ceasefire. A Western-brokered attempt, in February 1999, to secure a political settlement over Kosovo failed when representatives of the Yugoslav government and KLA secessionist guerrillas met in Rambouillet, France, and failed to reach agreement. With 250,000, or a sixth of Kosovo's population, homeless refugees because of the intensifying civil war, on 24 March 1999 NATO began to launch 'Operation Allied Force', involving large-scale airstrikes, involving satellite-guided cruise missiles and laser-guided bombs, against Serbian military and communications targets. These air raids were designed, according to US President Clinton, to deter further Serb attacks on civilians in Kosovo and damage Serbia's capacity to make war. They were also aimed at forcing Milosevic to accept the Rambouillet plan, which had provided for Kosovo's political autonomy within Serbia, policed by a 30,000-strong NATO-force and with safeguards for the province's Serb minority. However, during March and April 1999 Serb 'ethnic cleansing' continued, leading to a further mass exodus of around 500,000 Kosovo refugees. This served to increase support for extremists within the Kosovar community, culminating, in late April 1999, in the Kosovo Liberation Army (KLA), led by Hashim Thaci, declaring a provisional independent government, and to the sidelining of Ibrahim Rugova, the moderate political leader of the Kosovar community. It also led to growing divisions within Serbia, with Vuk Draskovic, the deputy prime minister being sacked after criticising the Serb leadership.

NATO's bombing campaign in Yugoslavia lasted 11 weeks, but was of only limited effectiveness, hitting only three of 250 Yugoslav tanks in Kosovo. More effective were economic sanctions, which crippled the Yugoslavia economy. Consequently, on 9 June 1999 President Milosevic finally accepted a Russian, American and EU brokered peace deal for Kosovo. This provided for the withdrawal from the province of the Serb army's 45,000 troops, the KLA's demilitarization and the entry of a 20,000-strong NATO peacekeeping force (KFOR), with a separate Russian component, to keep the peace and the UN overseeing the province's civil administration. NATO's takeover of the province proved to be largely peaceful, with more than 400,000 Kosovo refugees (a half of the total) swiftly returning to their homeland during June 1999. However, within Serbia President Milosevic faced mounting opposition to his rule, as demonstrators called for his resignation and the calling of early elections.

Readers' note

Part 2 continues in volume 2 on page 464.